D1871843

CENSUS OF INDIA 1891

Census of India 1871-1951, 9 Sets In 384 Bindings (9788121258876) Rs. 700000

Census of India 1891, 28 Vols. In 49 Bindings (978-81-212-7129-5) Rs. 125000

1. General Report (9788121269834) Rs. 1450
2. General Tables For British Provinces And Feudatory States (9788121269810) Rs. 2710 (Vol. I)
3. General Tables For British Provinces And Feudatory States (9788121269797) Rs. 950 (Vol. II)
4. Assam - Report (9788121269773) Rs. 2390 (Vol. I, V.1)
5. Assam - Tables (9788121269759) Rs. 2210 (Vol. II, V.2)
6. Assam - Provincial Tables (9788121269735) Rs. 1310 (Vol. II, V.3)
7. The Lower Provinces of Bengal and their Feudatories - The Report (9788121269711) Rs. 1660 (Vol. III)
8. The Lower Provinces of Bengal and their feudatories - The Administrative Tables (9788121269698) Rs. 4200 (Vol. IV)
9. The Lower Provinces of Bengal and their feudatories - The Caste Tables (9788121269674) Rs. 2600 (Vol. V, Pt. 1)
10. Lower Provinces of Bengal - The Provincial Tables (9788121269650) Rs. 1980 (Vol. V, Pt. 2)
11. Berar or the Hyderabad Assigned Districts (9788121269636) Rs. 3360 (Vol. VI)
12. Bombay and Its Feudatories - Report (9788121269612) Rs. 4010 (Vol. VII, Pt. 1)
13. Bombay And Its Feudatories - Imperial Tables (9788121269599) Rs. 790 (Vol. VIII, Pt. 2)
14. Imperial Series - Burma Report (9788121269575) Rs. 2320 (Vol. IX-V.1)
15. Imperial Tables - Burma Report (9788121269551) Rs. 3360 (Vol. X-V.2)
16. Provincial Tables Burma Report (9788121269537) Rs. 3510 (Vol. X-V.3)
17. Provincial Tables Burma Report (9788121269513) Rs. 3630 (Vol. X-V.4)
18. The Central Provinces And Feudatories - The Report (9788121269490) Rs. 2290 (Vol. XI, Pt. 1)
19. The Central Provinces And Feudatories - Imperial tables and supplementary returns (9788121268936) Rs. 2010 (Vol. XII)
20. Madras The Report On The Census (9788121269476) Rs. 2870 (Vol. XIII)
21. Madras - Tables I to XVII-C, British Territory (9788121269452) Rs. 3490 (Vol. XIV)
22. Madras - Tables A TO E, British Territory. Tables for feudatory States and A Caste Index (9788121269438) Rs. 2820 (Vol. XV)
23. The North Western Provinces and Outh - Report and Provincial Tables (9788121268912) Rs. 3100 (Vol. XVI, Pt. 1)
24. The North - Western Provinces and Oudh- Imperial Tables (9788121269414) Rs. 2000 (Vol. XVII, Pt. 2)
25. The North - Western Provinces and Oudh- Imperial Caste Tables (9788121269391) Rs. 3020 (Vol. XVIII, Pt. 3)
26. Punjab and Its Feudatories - The Report on the Census (9788121269377) Rs. 2710 (Vol. XIX, Pt. 1)
27. Punjab and Its Feudatories - Imperial Tables and Supplementary Returns for the British Territory (9788121269353) Rs. 1370 (Vol. XX, Pt. 2)
28. Punjab and Its Feudatories - Imperial Tables and Supplementary Returns for the Native States, Together With A Caste Index (9788121269339) Rs. 4910 (Vol. XXI, Pt. 3)
29. Report on The Census of The Districts of Ajmere-Merwara (9788121269056) Rs. 720 (Vol. XXII)
30. His Highness The Nizam's Dominions - Report (9788121269315) Rs. 2240 (Vol. XXIII, Pt. 1)
31. His Highness The Nizam's Dominions - Report (9788121269292) Rs. 2410 (Vol. XXIII, Pt. 2)
32. His Highness The Nizam's Dominions - Imperial And Supplementry Tables and Caste Index (9788121269278) Rs. 3390 (Vol. XXIII, Pt. 3)
33. Baroda - Report (9788121269254) Rs. 3810 (Vol. XXIV, Pt. 1)
34. Baroda - Tables (9788121269230) Rs. 2620 (Vol. XXIV, Pt. 2)
35. Mysore - Report (9788121269216) Rs. 2590 (Vol. XXV, Pt. 1)
36. Mysore - Imperial Tables (9788121269193) Rs. 1600 (Vol. XXV, Pt. 2)
37. Mysore - Tables (9788121269179) Rs. 5320 (Vol. XXV, Pt. 3)
38. Mysore - Supplementary Tables (9788121269155) Rs. 3590 (Vol. XXV, Pt. 4)
39. Mysore- Supplement to the Mysore census report of 1891 being a list of villages in the Mysore province and : comparing the population as per Censuses of 1891, 1881 & 1871 (9788121279024) Rs. 5350 (Vol. XXV, Pt. 5)
40. Rajputana - The Report, Imperial Tables And Supplementary Returns (9788121269131) Rs. 2330 (Vol. XXVI, Pt. 1)
41. Rajputna - The Provincial Tables and Remarks (9788121269117) Rs. 550 (Vol. XXVI, Pt. 2)
42. Central India (9788121269094) Rs. 2000 (Vol. XXVII)
43. Kashmir State - The Report on the census and Imperial and supplementary Tables (9788121269070) Rs. 2290 (Vol. XXVIII)
44. The Census of Calcutta (9788121269032) Rs. 890
45. Report on the census of Cochin (9788121269018) Rs. 790 (Pt. 1)
46. Report on the census of Cochin - The Final Census Tables with Appendices (9788121268998) Rs. 910 (Pt. 2)
47. Report on the Census of Coorg (9788121268974) Rs. 730
48. Report on the census of Travancore -Report (9788121274029) Rs. 4220 (Vol. I)
49. Report on the census of Travancore -Appendix (9788121268950) Rs. 5300 (Vol. II)

Owing to the antiquity and rarity of this book, certain pages are regrettably absent, and readability is compromised due to the blurring of the original text. If you possess any insights regarding the availability of these missing sections, kindly inform us. Your assistance is crucial in ensuring the completion of this significant work for the benefit of future generations.

CENSUS OF INDIA, 1891

BOOK-23: VOLUME XVI

THE NORTH WESTERN PROVINCES
AND
OUTH

PART I.—REPORT AND PROVINCIAL TABLES

D. C. BAILLIE

GYAN

Published by

Gyan Publishing House
5, Ansari Road
Daryaganj, New Delhi-110002
Phone: 011-47034999, 9811692060
E-mail: books@gyanbooks.com

Distribution Network
gyanbooks.com
India, USA, Canada, UK, Australia

© **Publisher**
All rights reserved. No part of this work may be reproduced, stored, adapted, or transmitted in any form or by any means, electronic, mechanical, photocopying, micro-filming, recording or othrwise, or translated in any language, without the prior written permission of the copyright owner and the publisher.

ISBN: 978-81-212-7129-5 (Set) 28 Vols. In 49 Bindings
978-81-212-6891-2 (PB) Book-23, Vol. XVI, Pt. I

First Published, 1893

2nd Impression 2024

Printed at: Gyan Press, Delhi.

The book is sold subject to the condition that it shall not, by way of trade or otherwise, be lent, resold, hired out, or otherwise circulated without the prior publisher's written consent.

CENSUS OF INDIA 1891

CENSUS OF INDIA, 1891.

VOLUME XVI.

THE NORTH-WESTERN PROVINCES

AND

OUDH.

BY

D. C. BAILLIE, I.C.S.,

PROVINCIAL SUPERINTENDENT OF CENSUS OPERATIONS.

PART I.

REPORT AND PROVINCIAL TABLES.

Published by Authority.

ALLAHABAD:

NORTH-WESTERN PROVINCES AND OUDH GOVERNMENT PRESS.

1894.

INDEX TO PART I.

Chapter I.—ADMINISTRATION.

PARA.		PAGE.
1	Earlier census operations in the North-Western Provinces	9
2	The census estimate of 1826	ib.
3	The estimate of 1848	ib.
4	The census of 1853	10
5	Ditto of 1865	13
6	The Oudh census of 1869	14
7	The census of 1872	15
8	Ditto of 1881	16
9	Ditto of 1891. The Agra conference of 1889	17
10	The Provincial Rules for 1891	19
11	The census sub-division of the provinces	ib.
12	The house numbering	ib.
13	Census definition of village	20
14	The definition of town	ib.
15	Definition of house	21
16	The house numbering	23
17	The date prescribed for the completion of house numbering	24
18	The block list	25
19	Census sub-divisions	ib.
20	The circle list	28
21	Census maps	ib.
22	The census staff	29
23	The charge superintendent	30
24	Census supervisons	32
25	Ditto enumerators	34
26	Instruction of census officers	36
27	The instructions to enumerators	37
28	Amendments suggested in census rules	41
29	The use of the Kayathi character	42
30	The characters in which enumerators' records were written	43
31	Drafts of the enumeration record	44
32	The testing of the enumeration record	45
33	The final enumeration	ib.
34	The attitude of the people	46
35	The preliminary abstraction	ib.
36	The Railway census	47
37	The census in cantonments	48
38	Enumeration of travellers	49
39	Ditto in forest and desert tracts	ib.
40	The census in the Himalayas	50
41	Enumeration in Native States, Rampur	51
42	Tehri-Garhwal	52
43	Enumeration by private schedules	ib.
44	The cost of the enumeration	53
45	Reasons for the higher expenditure in 1891	55

Para.		Page.
46	The enumeration forms ...	56
47	The district indents for enumeration forms	57
48	Proposals as to enumeration forms for next census	58
49	The enumeration printing	*ib.*
50	The cost of superintendence	59
51	Abstraction, Tabulation and compilation	*ib.*
52	The change of system in abstraction	60
53	The abstraction work	61
54	Tabulation	62
55	The testing of tabulation registers	64
56	The census office work in districts	*ib.*
57	Cost of census work in districts	67
58	The patwári as an abstractor	69
59	Compilation	*ib.*
60	Cost of census operations	70
61	Printing for abstraction and tabulation	72
62	Abstraction and tabulation at next census	*ib.*

Chapter II.—GENERAL REMARKS ON THE RESULTS OF THE CENSUS OF 1891.

Para.		Page.
63	Brief topographical description of the provinces	74
64	The Tarái	*ib.*
65	The Dúns	75
66	The Himalayan Tract	*ib.*
67	The Plains districts	*ib.*
68	Bundelkhand and Mirzapur	*ib.*
69	The Gangetic plain	76
70	The rainfall	77
71	The climate	78
72	The history of the provinces	*ib.*
73	Epidemic disease	79
74	The irrigation system	*ib.*
75	The cultivated area	82
76	Executive divisions	84
77	The changes in area	85
78	The total population	*ib.*
79	The density of the population	86
80	The proportion of Urban and rural population	89
81	Instances of great density of population of pargana areas	92
82	Towns and villages—the distinction	*ib.*
83	The towns of the provinces	93
84	The important towns	94
85	Size of towns compared with those in other countries	95
86	Density of population in towns	96
87	The density in villages	100
88	Distribution of the population between large and small towns and villages	*ib.*
89	Inhabited sites	103
90	The population per inhabited house	106
91	The house population in towns	*ib.*
92	The areality	107
93	The proximity	108

Chapter III.—THE AGE TABLES.

Para.		Page.
94	The population recorded in each age-period	109
95	Figures showing the exact age of 100,000 persons	*ib.*
96	Corresponding figures in England	111
97	The causes affecting the accuracy of the age returns	*ib.*
98	Methods in which those defects have to be remedied	113
99	The ages of males below ten	115
100	The age-periods for males above ten	117
101	The age-periods for females	118
102	Corrected age tables	123
103	The proportion of the sexes	*ib.*
104	Special circumstances in Garhwál	126
105	Other districts showing an excess of females	130
106	Comparison of proportion of sexes in the European countries	132
107	The low proportion of females in the Agra Division	133
108	Proportion of the sexes in the different religions of the province	*ib.*
109	Proportion of the sexes in the leading groups of castes	134
110	Comparison of the age tables with European countries	*ib.*
111	The average age of the population	139

Chapter IV.—THE MOVEMENT OF POPULATION.

Para.		Page.
112	The vital history of the decade	140
113	The public health during the decade	141
114	Prices during the decade	142
115	The variation of population	143
116	The area of low increase or decrease	144
117	The area of high increase	145
118	Examination of the accuracy of enumeration in different districts	*ib.*
119	Increase in Himalayan districts partly due to better enumeration	146
120	Reasons to believe that the Oudh figures of 1881 were too low	148
121	Low enumeration in 1881 in Bijnor	*ib.*
122	The real increase allowing for differences in enumeration	149
123	The causes of variations	*ib.*
124	The causes of the decrease and slow increase in certain districts and tahsíls, Etawáh ...	150
125	Ditto ditto ditto ditto Etah ...	*ib.*
126	Ditto ditto ditto ditto Mainpuri ...	151
127	Ditto ditto ditto ditto Farukhabad ...	152
128	Ditto ditto ditto ditto Bundelkhand ...	*ib.*
129	Ditto ditto ditto ditto Agra ...	153
130	Ditto ditto ditto ditto The Jumna pargana in the Upper Doab	*ib.*
131	Ditto ditto ditto ditto Rohilkhand ...	*ib.*
132	Ditto ditto ditto ditto The eastern districts	*ib.*
133	The areas of large increase. The Himalayas	154
134	Ditto. The Sub-Himalayan districts	*ib.*
135	Ditto. Oudh...	155
136	Movement of population in earlier intercensal periods	158
137	The effect of variations on the food-supply	159
138	The movement of population in towns	*ib.*
139	Remarks on the movement of town population in certain districts	160
140	ummary of remarks as to movement in towns	164
141	Movement of population in hill stations	*ib.*

Chapter V.—THE VITAL STATISTICS OF THE DECADE.

PARA.		PAGE.
142	The vital statistics as collected by the Sanitary Commissioner	166
143	The comparative accuracy of these statistics	*ib.*
144	Reasons for the variation from census figures in certain districts	167
145	The death-rate as shown by comparison of census figures	168
146	The birth-rate	170

Chapter VI.—THE RELIGIONS OF THE PROVINCE.

PARA.		PAGE.
147	The distribution by religion	171
148	Religions entirely foreign	*ib.*
149	Buddhists	*ib.*
150	Sikhs	172
151	Hinduism	*ib.*
152	Muhammadanism	173
153	The distribution of Muhammadanism	175
154	Local features of Muhammadanism	*ib.*
155	Muhammadan sects, Shias and Sunnis	176
156	Ahl-i-Hadis...	177
157	Increase in Muhammandans	178
158	Reasons for the increase in Mahammadans	182
159	Jainism	*ib.*
160	Connection with Hinduism	183
161	Jain sects	*ib.*
162	Increase in Jains	184
163	Jain castes	*ib.*
164	Christians	*ib.*
165	Europeans and Eurasians	*ib.*
166	British-born and Foreign European Christians	185
167	Native Christians	186
168	Aryas	187
169	The history and principles of Arya Samaj	188
170	The distribution of Arya Samajists in the province	189
171	The future of the Samaj	190
172	The distribution of religions between town and country	191

Chapter VII.—HINDUISM AND ITS SECTS.

PARA.		PAGE.
173	Hinduism	192
174	The origin of modern Hinduism	*ib.*
175	The Division of Hinduism into sects	193
176	The instructions as to record of sects	194
177	The meaning to be attached to the word sect	195
178	The classification of the sect returns	196
179	Non-sectarian and unspecified	*ib.*
180	The beliefs of the ordinary Hindu	*ib.*
181	Monotheistic non-sectarian Hindus...	197
182	Pre-Puranic forms of worship	198
183	The general distinctions between Vaishnavas and Saivas	199
184	Vaishavism...	200
185	Saivism	206
186	Saktism	208

PARA.		PAGE.
187	Miscellaneous divinities of modern Hinduism	210
188	Gods of disease	*ib.*
189	Serpent worship	*ib.*
190	Animism in the Hindu system	212
191	Ghost worship	*ib.*
192	Worship of Muhammadan Saints	216
193	Ancestral and caste gods	218
194	Low caste gods	219
195	Demon gods	221
196	Village, forest and local gods	222
197	Rivers and river gods	223
198	Worshippers of holy places	224
199	Worshippers of deified devotees	*ib.*
200	Miscellaneous Puranic gods	225
201	Sectarian sub-divisions, Saiva	*ib.*
202	Vaishnava, Unitarian and miscellaneous sects	227
203	Sectarian distribution of population	243

Chapter VIII.—THE CIVIL CONDITION OF THE POPULATION.

PARA.		PAGE.
204	Table showing conjugal condition	245
205	Infant marriage	246
206	Widow marriage	249
207	The fecundity of the population	250
208	Local variations in marriage statistics	251
209	Caste variations in marriage statistics	255

Chapter IX.—EDUCATION.

PARA.		PAGE.
210	The tables showing education	256
211	Reasons to believe the return of learners inaccurate	*ib.*
212	The proportion of literate persons in the population	257
213	Education by religion	258
214	Ditto districts	259
215	English education	261
216	The increase in education	*ib.*
217	Education by caste	*ib.*
218	Eurasian education	263

Chapter X.—MOTHER TONGUES.

PARA.		PAGE.
219	The classification of languages	264
220	Languages of the provinces	*ib.*
221	The term Hindustani why used	*ib.*
222	The variations popularly recognised	266
223	The variations of Hindi recognised by travelled natives	*ib.*
224	A possible connection between dialectic variations and the distribution of Bráhmans ...	269
225	The other languages of the provinces	270
226	Languages of other Indian provinces	*ib.*
227	Foreign languages	272

Chapter XI.—THE BIRTH—PLACES OF THE PEOPLE.

PARA.		PAGE.
228	The birth-place figures	274
229	Migration within the district of birth	275
230	Local migration in Kumaun and Garhwál	*ib.*
231	Movement between neighbouring districts	276
232	Movement between distant districts of the province	280
233	Movement to and from other provinces of India	281
234	Movement between the North-Western Provinces and Oudh and foreign countries... ...	285
235	Excess of emigration over immigration	286

Chapter XII.—THE INFIRMITIES OF THE PROVINCE.

PARA.		PAGE.
236	Instructions as to record of infirmities	287
	PART I—INSANES.	
237	The figures for insanity	287
238	Remarks by the Civil Surgeon of Bijnor on Insanity	288
239	Causes of insanity	290
240	Variation in the proportion of insanity in 1881 and 1891	*ib.*
241	Local distribution of insanity	291
242	Comparison of proportion of insanity in the two sexes	*ib.*
243	Insanity in the different religions	292
244	Insanity in different castes	*ib.*
245	Comparison with European countries	293
	PART II—DEAF-MUTES.	
246	The variation in the proportion of deaf-mutism	293
247	Extent of concealment of deaf-mutism	295
248	The local distribution of deaf-mutism	296
249	Comparison with deaf-mutism in European countries	*ib.*
250	Comparative deaf-mutism in the sexes	297
251	Deaf-mutism by religion	*ib.*
252	Ditto caste	298
	PART III—THE BLIND.	
253	Decrease in blindness since last census	298
254	The causes of blindness...	299
255	Small-pox as a cause of blindness	*ib.*
256	Reasons for the decrease in blindness	301
257	The local distribution of blindness	303
258	Proportion of blindness in the sexes	*ib.*
259	Blindness in different religions	*ib.*
260	Ditto castes	304
261	Comparison with foreign countries	305
	PART IV—LEPERS.	
262	The figures for leprosy	305
263	Considerations suggesting a decrease	306
264	Leprosy by locality	*ib.*
265	Leprosy in the sexes	307
266	Leprosy by religion	308
267	Ditto caste	*ib.*
268	Leprosy in other provinces of India	*ib.*

Chapter XIII.—THE CASTES, RACES AND TRIBES OF THE PROVINCES.

PARA.		PAGE.
269	The caste tables	309
270	Classification of castes by traditional occupation	310
271	Distribution of different castes	*ib.*
272	Statement showing variations in castes unreliable	314
273	Remarks on various castes	315
274	Muhammadan castes ill-defined	323

Chapter XIV.—THE OCCUPATIONS OF THE PEOPLE.

PARA.		PAGE.
275	The enumeration of persons dependent on each occupation...	324
276	Tabulation and final occupation tables	325
277	The classification of occupations	326
278	Causes producing inaccuracy in occupation tables	327
279	Additional occupations of agriculturists	328
280	Persons dependent on the service of Government	*ib.*
281	Agricultural population	330
282	Other classes of occupations	332

APPENDICES.

APPENDIX.		
I	Return of Census Agency—Town blocks	2—3
II	Ditto Rural blocks	4—5
III	Ditto All blocks	6—7
IV	Number of enumerators writing each character	8—9
V	Population of the districts of the North-Western Provinces and Oudh, according to both the preliminary and the final returns	10
VI	Number of private schedules issued	11
VII	Expenditure on enumeration in each district together with the incidence of expenditure on population	12
VIII	Census accounts year by year in detail	13—14
IX	Gross and net amounts expended on account of abstraction and tabulation in the districts of the North-Western Provinces and Oudh	15
X	Density of population in the typical towns of the Provinces—Total area	16
XI	Ditto ditto ditto City area	17
XII	Ditto ditto ditto Selected mohallas ...	18
XIII	Average death-rate from different census for 10 years	19
XIV	Percentage of variations of population in the tahsils of the North-Western Provinces and Oudh	20—22
XV	Comparing the 1881 population with that of the present census aged 10 or more ...	23
XVI	Death returns by districts for the years 1881 to 1890	24—27
XVII	Variations in the Urban population	28—29
XVIII	Detailed comparison of the population as calculated from that of 1881 by adding births and deducting deaths	30
XIX	Deaths of children aged from 0—9 amongst the population registered under the infanticide Act	31
XX	Different sects of Muhammadans by districts	32—33
XXI	Return of British-born subjects	34—35
XXII	Return of foreigners of Non-British nationality	36—37
XXIII	Urban population by religion in the districts of the Provinces	38
XXIV	Numbers returned as belonging to each Hindu sect or class of worshippers	39—43
XXV	Summary of Table XI (birth-place)	44—47
XXVI	Population of the preliminary and general censuses in the districts of Kumaun and Garhwál	48
XXVII	Proportion of total insane population and variations since last census	49

APPENDIX.		PAGE.
XXVIII	Percentage of insanes, deaf-mutes, blind persons and lepers for castes numbering above 100,000	50
XXIX	Number of deaf-mutes in 1872, 1881 and 1891 by districts	51
XXX	Classification of castes by traditional occupation	52—65
XXXI	Occupations which are likely to be confused with each other in the census schedules ...	66—68
XXXII	Proportion of population dependent on each class, order and sub-order of occupations and the proportion in towns for each class	69—71
XXXIII	Age distribution of the various classes of occupations	72
XXXIV	Proportion to divisional populations of the population of the classes	73

PROVINCIAL TABLES.

TABLE.		
I	Variations in the population of the tahsils since the previous census	1—13
II	Population of the tahsils distributed according to religion	1—13
III	Number of villages and towns in each tahsil classified by population	1—13
IV	Educational position of each tahsil in the North-Western Provinces and Oudh	1—23
V	Variations in the population of the parganas since the previous census	1—21
VI	Variations in the population of the police circles since the previuos census	1—27
Supplement to VI	Variations in the population of the pattis of the Kumaun Division since the previous census arranged according mortuary circles	28—31
VII	Population of the police circles distributed by religion	1—27
Supplement to VII	Population by religion of the pattis of the Kumaun Division arranged according to mortuary circles	28—35
VIII	Ages of the population of towns with above 10,000 inhabitants	1—9

REPORT

ON THE

CENSUS OF THE N.-W. PROVINCES AND OUDH,

1891.

Chapter I.—ADMINISTRATION.

1. **Earlier Census Operations in the North-Western Provinces.**—On the 26th February 1891, for the fifth time in the History of the North-Western Provinces and for the third time in Oudh, a general enumeration of the population was carried through. The returns prepared and methods employed in each succeeding census have been elaborated from those of that preceding, assistance being derived from the experience of other provinces only in the two last censuses which were conducted simultaneously throughout India. It will therefore be not amiss to preface a short account of the census administration of 1891-92, with a brief sketch of that of earlier years.

2. **The Census estimate of 1826.**—Isolated District Officers throughout the North-Western Provinces had on various occasions before 1848 estimated, and in some instances enumerated, more or less completely, the population of their districts. So early as 1826 a calculation was made of the population of the provinces, excluding the ceded districts on the Narbada and in Berar. It was founded on an actual enumeration of the villages in the provinces and a partial enumeration of the houses. The total population was estimated at 32 millions and the density of population at 484 per square mile.

The contrast afforded by this density to the figures estimated some years later for Bengal, (243 to the square mile,) was believed to afford satisfactory evidence of the unreliable character of the statistics of the North-West. Subsequent enquiries showed, however, that the estimate of population, roughly acquired as it was, was fairly good. A considerable mistake had, however, been made in ascertaining the area.

3. **The estimate of 1848.**—In 1848 a general estimate of the population of the provinces was prepared under the orders of Government for the first time simultaneously in all districts. The instructions directed that an estimate of the average number of persons residing in each house should be prepared by enumeration within a selected average area and that the houses counted throughout the districts.

The methods actually employed varied from district to district. In some districts the population appears to have been enumerated throughout. In the majority the instructions of Government were followed. In other cases the population of a given *area* was enumerated and the population estimated at the same rate, for the total area which was more or less accurately known. Other methods were still rougher and in a later report it is stated the census of the city of Benares for 1848 was "made on the basis of the quantity of salt that was used by the city during a twelve month." The population of the regulation districts including those of the Delhi Division was estimated to be 23 millions and the density 322, a result certainly as much below the truth as that of the previous estimate was above it.

4. **The Census of 1853.**—Reasons to believe the latest estimate unsatisfactory were speedily found, but the attention of public officers had been attracted to the subject, and in some districts a new census was made annually for several years on the 1st of January, whilst in others "a single great effort was made to procure a faithful return of the population." In 1851, the Lieutenant-Governor considered that means were available for the "formation" of a new census and that the measure was likely to cause no alarm or apprehension amongst the people. Instructions were therefore issued for a general census to be taken on the 1st January 1853, the population to be *enumerated throughout.*

A copy of the specimen return for a single village will most briefly indicate the scope and methods of the census so taken.

Returns of persons who on the night of the 31st December 1852 or 5th Poos 1260 fasli, were present in the mauza of Khundauli, pargana Sikandra.

Number of enclosure.	Number of house.	Name of the master of the house or head of the family.	Hindus.				Muhammadans and others not Hindus.				Remarks.
			Agricultural.		Non-agricultural.		Agricultural.		Non-agricultural.		
			Males.	Females.	Males.	Females.	Males.	Females.	Males.	Females.	
1	1	Baldeo Singh ...	3	4	...	...	...	...	...	...	
2	2	Richpal Singh ...	4	2	...	...	...	...	...	...	
...	3	Nihal Singh	2	5	...	...	...	...	...	...	
3	4	Nathoo	...	...	3	3	...	...	...	...	
...	5	Seyrhoo	...	...	5	4	...	...	...	...	
4	6	Khuda Bakhsh ...	...	...	...	...	...	...	3	2	
5	7	Muhammad Khán ...	...	...	...	...	4	1	...	...	
6	8	Pohpal Singh ...	2	3	...	...	...	...	...	...	
		Strangers	3	2	...	...	...	...	...	...	Visitors from another village.
7	9	Kalloo, Bhatiyara ...	...	...	...	...	...	...	3	2	
		Strangers	...	...	...	...	...	...	5	1	Travellers put up for the night.
		Total ...	14	16	8	7	4	1	11	5	66 Total of persons.

It will be observed that the returns show the numbers only of the persons male and female in each house.

Such a return was prepared for each hamlet or mahál in a village, combined into one for the village and afterwards into a general return for the pargana. The agency employed was in agricultural villages the patwári and his relatives, in towns the muhalladárs or in some cases the police. The instructions ordered that the first three columns of the return were to be filled up before the date prescribed for the census and the rest on the day fixed. The figures so ascertained for the districts then and now in the provinces are compared with those for subsequent censuses in a statement given in a later chapter. This census must, considering that it was the first and that all detail of arrangements was left to District Officers, be considered remarkably successful.

The general lines of the system on which the enumeration of 1891 was taken have been founded on the procedure followed in several districts in 1852-53. Mr. DeGruyther's account of his procedure in Farukhabad requires but slight alteration to be a correct outline of the present enumeration procedure.

"The first step was to number the houses. This duty was performed by the village patwári by a certain rule which obliged him to preserve an unbroken series of numbers. The next step was to make a rough census. The number of inmates of each house was ascertained as carefully as possible by enquiry of the head of the family and of his neighbours; strangers were not taken into account, but the actual members of the family only, including such as were temporarily absent, but expected to be at home on the night of the 31st December. In this way the columns four to eleven were filled up *in red ink*. The work was commenced on 10th December 1852, and was required to be completed in ten days. What had thus been accomplished was then tested by the kanúngo or other tahsíli official. It was the duty of the testing officer to visit each village entered in his list and satisfy himself as to the accuracy of the entries. By this means it was ascertained that the houses had been duly numbered; that the returns had so far been prepared with care; and that those who were to take the census on the 1st January clearly understood and were fully qualified for the work. Travellers in inns, saráis and paráos were enumerated between 8 and 9 P. M. on the night preceding the 1st January. The rest of the enumeration was simultaneously carried out throughout the district on the 1st January. The red ink entries leisurely made in columns four to eleven were found very useful when the actual enumeration took place, the result of which was inserted in black ink just below the red."

"The number of strangers or visitors was entered on a separate line in the same column which had been made sufficiently wide for the purpose."

We have in this brief report a complete outline of the scheme subsequently adopted for the provinces. This first census of the population of the North-West Provinces like the earlier enumerations of houses appears to have been received by the people without any special manifestations of alarm. It was taken exactly a century after it had been first proposed to take a census in England and the Bill was rejected unhesitatingly by the House of Commons, where the opponents of the measure could hardly believe "that there was any set of men or indeed any individual of the human species so presumptuous and so abandoned as to make such a proposal." It was taken only half a century after the Commons of England first were able to disabuse themselves of the notion that a census was the most effectual engine of oppression and rapacity ever used against an injured people and likely to be followed by " some public misfortune or epidemical distemper."

Sir Theophilus Metcalfe at Delhi, then in the provinces experimented in regard to the possibility of carrying out a census on the English system of distributing schedules to householders to be filled up by them. Five thousand were distributed in one part of Delhi city, and all returns very correctly filled up. The system has not commended itself for general adoption. It is little suited for the more elaborate schedule now in use, and open to very serious objection on account of the burden necessarily imposed upon the poorer householders in paying for having the schedules written. The returns of the 1853 census showed for the present Meerut, Agra, Robilkhand, Allahabad (excluding the late Jhánsi Division), Benares and Gorakhpur Divisions a total population of 14,989,161 males and 13,087,541 females; 12,923,096 males and 11,188,636 females were Hindus; 2,066,065 males and 1,898,905 females were shown as Muhammadans; and others. 18,204,865 persons were shown as agriculturists, and the rest as non-agriculturists.

The points in the returns which chiefly attracted notice were the great density of population shown in certain districts and parganas, and the disproportion between the numbers of the sexes; 53·9 per cent. of Hindus and 52 per cent. of Muhammadans being shown as males. The density for districts was greatest in Benares with 856 persons per square mile, in Jaunpur with 737, and in Gházipur with 732. In connection with the density it was considered necessary to defend the accuracy of the returns at some length, but as still higher figures are now accepted the arguments employed have ceased to be of practical interest. Regarding the disproportion of the sexes, still to many minds an unsettled question, I may quote *in extenso* the conclusions of the author of the 1853 report, Mr. G. J. Christian, then Secretary to the Board of Revenue and afterwards Commissioner of Sitapur, where he was killed during the mutiny.

" There appears, therefore, to be no reason for questioning the accuracy of the returns on this account. The supposition that the number of females has been intentionally concealed from feelings peculiar to the east is refuted by the reports of the returning officers, who deny that any such disposition was evinced, and still more by the fact that the deficit of females is least among the Muhammadans. The disproportion may be due, among other causes, to the small value attached to female life. A large portion of the Hindus, and it is with them that the preponderance of males is most striking, consider the birth of a daughter almost as a misfortune. Their daughters in infancy and childhood meet with but little care or attention in health or sickness, and the waste of female life at these early periods must be very great. To this must be added the effect of early marriages, and among some of the agricultural Hindus of hardship and labour unsuited to the sex. Infanticide must also influence the number of Hindu females especially if, as there is reason to believe, the deficit of females mainly obtains among children under 12 years of age."

" The returns do not distinguish the castes which are known or suspected to practise female infanticide, but they chiefly belong to the agricultural community, for which the deficit of females is greatest and abound in the districts of Farukhabad, Mainpuri and Etáwah, where the percentage of males is above the average. But it must be left for another census, when the castes and ages of the population shall be recorded to show fully the effect of this custom on the number of female children."

"Among the Muhammadans these causes severally operate either to a less extent or not at all, but for them as for the Hindus allowance must be made for males absent from their homes on service. There are probably not less than half a million of sepoys and camp followers, most of whom belong to these provinces, in the Panjáb, Burma and elsewhere beyond the limits of the census."

"Up-countrymen are also found in great numbers in the Bombay army and in Civil situations throughout the Panjáb and Lower Bengal, while hardly any natives of those parts of India are employed in these provinces."

5. **The Census of 1865.**—It was the intention of the North-West Government in 1853 that this first census should be followed at intervals of ten years by similar operations, but in the succeeding period the mutiny intervened and was succeeded by a destructive famine and pestilence. No steps towards a second census were therefore taken till October 1863 when the Board of Revenue, to which Mr. W. C. Plowden was then Secretary, was instructed to arrange for the census, which was finally taken on the 10th January 1865. In the method of enumeration there was but little change as compared with that in the most efficiently supervised districts in 1853. The preparation of a preliminary record and its correction in red ink in the actual census were now prescribed. As in 1853, the number only of persons in each house was entered. The form of schedule was as follows :—

Number of enclosure.	Number of house.	Name of the master of the house or head of the family.	Caste of the master of the house or head of the family.	Occupation of the master of the house or head of the family.	Males.		Females.		Remarks.
					Adult.	Children.	Adult.	Children.	

In addition to filling up this return the enumerator had to prepare four village abstracts from which pargana abstracts were prepared under the orders of Tahsíldárs and district abstracts in the district office. The final tables were drawn up in the Board's office. The final tables published were of two kinds A. General—B. Detailed.

The general statements were :—

No. I.—Area and population in the Divisions and districts of the North-Western Provinces.

No. II.—Area and population, showing the differences as exhibited in the census of 1865 and of 1853, with the percentages of increase or decrease and the proportion of males to females.

No. III.—Land revenue, area and population.

No. IV.—Population, arranged according to castes.

No. V.—Population, arranged according to occupations.

No. VI.—Number of houses, with the average number of persons to each house, in parganas and in towns with more than 20,000 inhabitants.

No. VII.—Classified statement of towns and villages in the North-Western Provinces.

The detailed statements were similar to the above, but gave the statistics for parganas. A very brief examination of the two more elaborate of these tables is sufficient to convince one of the unsuitableness of the system of enumeration and compilation for returns of any complexity.

In the caste statement, castes universally well known are apparently shown with a fair degree of accuracy, but the less known castes appear very irregularly, one so well known as Ahar appearing only for one district. In regard to occupations, though there was some advance on the former census in distinguishing agriculturists from non-agriculturists, the return was in general very incomplete. The record of the occupation of the head of the family only, prevented all record of those minor occupations which are carried on by the younger members and women of the family, whilst abstraction by means of the enumerators and unsupervised tahsíl officials tended to combine all allied occupations under one general head, even more completely than the bareness of the record itself made necessary. The faults of the 1865 returns made it evident that for the future several improvements in the procedure were necessary. It was clear—

1st.—That the record must be by persons, not by families.

2nd.—That enumerators cannot be depended on to interpret the nature of the entries to be made without more detailed instructions than were likely to reach them verbally from the tahsíl officials.

3rd.—That returns involving more than the addition of the different columns of the schedule cannot be effectively and accurately prepared by the enumerators.

4th.—That the district officials cannot be depended on to furnish properly arranged and classified final lists for castes and occupations, but that the superintendence of an officer specially deputed to census duty was absolutely necessary in order that the returns should be presented in a uniform and well-arranged manner.

The report regarding the 1865 returns was written by Mr. W. C. Plowden. As his more matured conclusions in regard to the figures of later censuses will have to be referred to in connection with the figures for 1891, no further account of the 1865 report appears necessary.

6. **The Oudh Census of 1869.**—The first census of Oudh is the next in the history of these provinces. The Oudh Government had the advantage of the experience acquired in the North-West Census of 1853, and, in regard to the appointment of a special census officer and of a special establishment to tabulate the returns, profited by this experience. Enumeration by persons instead of by families was, however, considered too elaborate for a young province and, in the preliminaries of the census, the procedure in the North-Western Provinces in 1853 was followed without alteration.

It is perhaps not remarkable that the census in Oudh in 1859 created more alarm amongst the persons enumerated than did the earliest of which we have any record in the North-West Provinces. In North-West Provinces censuses we occasionally hear of a supposed connection between the census and taxation, and even with levies for the army or public works; but the idea of a conscription of women for the use of the European army, and such a report as was prevalent in Bara Banki that two maidens from each village were wanted to fan the Queen, owing to the climate of England having become exceedingly hot, are in this part of India peculiar to Oudh or the wildest parts of Bundelkhand. From the border districts it was reported that large numbers of people had crossed into the North-West to avoid being enumerated.

7. **The Census of 1872.**—In 1872 we have for the first time a census on the present system, in which each resident in a house is entered separately by name in the enumerator's schedule. We have now for the first time instructions, slight enough it is true, issued in print to each enumerator, and now for the first time in the North-West Provinces a special officer to compile and comment upon the returns; as the result of these changes, the accuracy and fullness of the information collected and compiled is such that it can be made use of for purposes of comparison with the results of later censuses.

The 1872 schedule was as follows :—

	Number of dwelling-houses in the enclosure.		Males.						Whether able to read and write or not.		Females.						
Number of enclosure.	Built by skilled labour.	Built by unskilled labour.	Name.	Age.	Religion.	Caste or class.	Race or nationality.	Occupation.	Over 12, able to read and write.	Under 12, under instruction.	Number or name.	Relation to head of house.	Age.	Religion.	Caste or class.	Race or nationality.	Remarks.
1	2	3	4	5	6	7	8	9	10	11	12	13	14	15	16	17	18

The general statements compiled from this schedule were as follows :—

I.A.—Area and population.

I.B.—Details of population.

I.C.—Infirmities.

II.A.—Population according to age and sex, classified under (*a*) Hindus, (*b*) Muhammadans, (*c*) Christians and others.

III.A.—Population according to education.

III.B.—Percentages taken from the preceding statement.

IV.—Area, population and revenue.

V.B.—Population classified by nationalities, castes and tribes.

VI.—Occupations of the male population not less than 15 years of age.

VII.—Number of villages and towns in each district, classified according to the number of their inhabitants.

VIII.—Towns containing more than 5,000 inhabitants, classified according to population.

IX.—Details for the above towns.

The report, just over 100 pages, was, leaving out figured statements, comparatively brief. The remainder of the three bulky volumes, in which Mr. Plowden's report was published, consisted of detailed statements showing the figures and percentages of the general statements for each of the parganas and cities of the province.

In compilation three abstracts were prepared by a special staff in district offices for each village.

(1) The main abstract arranging the inhabitants by sex, creed, nationality, caste, and giving also certain information as to the occupations of the people, their ability to read, and statistics of the blind, deaf and dumb, insane, idiots and lepers.

(2) A synopsis of the number of persons, male and female, distinguishing those of 12 years and upwards from children under 12.

(3) A statement of the occupations followed by males not less than 15 years of age. These were so drawn up as to afford checks on the mutual accuracy of the three abstracts; and from these abstracts, drawn up in the several offices, the central office compiled the statements which accompany the report.

These abstracts were compiled in a central office in Dehra Dún into the final statements and tables. The respective merits of this system and of those adopted in 1881 and 1891, will be referred to further on. The figures of 1872 and the conclusions arrived at in Mr. Plowden's report will have to be frequently referred in the course of this report and need not now be further referred to.

8. **The Census of 1881**.—In regard to 1881 it is just now enough to draw attention to the greater completeness of the instructions issued before the census to District and to Census Officers, due largely to the fact that in 1881 a Census Officer was deputed to his work before any steps towards the census were taken in districts, and to give the following list of the tables prepared:—

Table A(a).—The number of families and houses and the residents as permanent and temporary.

Do. 1.—Hindus by conjugal condition and age.

Do. 2.—Muhammadans ditto.

Do. 3.—Persons of other religions ditto.

Do. 4.—Ages of the Hindus.

Do. 5.— Ditto Muhammadans.

Do. 6.— Ditto persons of other religions.

Do. 7.—Conjugal condition.

Do. 8.—Religion.

Do. 9.—Christians by sect and race.

Do. 11.—Hindu castes.

Do. 11(*a*).—Rájputs, Ahirs, Gujars, Tagas, Ahars and Minas by subdivision and age.

Do. 12.—Musalmáns of five tribes, *viz.*, Rájputs, Gujars, Játs, Tagas and Newátis.

Do. 13.—Mother tongue.

Table 14.—Birthplaces within the North-Western Provinces and Oudh.

Do. 14(*a*).—Birthplaces outside the North-Western Provinces and Oudh.

Do. 15.—Occupations of males.

Do. 16.—Occupations of females.

Do. 17.—Instruction.

Do. 18.—Unsound mind.

Do. 19.—Blind.

Do. 20 —Deaf mutes.

Do. 21.—Lepers.

Do. 22.—General village abstract.

In all respects not noted in the following pages the census of 1891 so closely followed the lines of that of 1881, that from the account of the former necessary to the completeness of this report the method of the latter may *mutatis mutandis* be gathered. As in 1881 the census of 1891 was conducted simultaneously throughout India.

9. **The Census of 1891. The Agra Conference of 1889.**—Mr. J. A. Baines, Census Superintendent in Bombay in 1881, was appointed Census Commissioner for India on the 19th August 1889, and shortly after, under his presidentship, a conference of ex-Census Officers was assembled to consult on the measures to be adopted and the tables to be prepared in the census of 1891. The form of the enumeration schedule was the first question considered by the Agra Conference. The headings of the 1881 schedule and of that suggested by the Conference and adopted for the present census are given below :—

A.

ENUMERATION SCHEDULE OF 1881.

(*Size varying in each province.*)

Serial number of each inmate.	Name.	Condition, *i.e.*, whether married, unmarried, widow or widower.	Sex.	Age last birthday.	Religion.	Caste, if Hindu; sect if of other religion.*	Mother tongue.	†‡§ Place of birth.	‖ Occupation of men, also of boys and females who may do work.	Education. 1. Under instruction. 2. Not under instruction, but able to read and write. 3. Not under instruction, and not able to read and write.	Infirmities. 1. Unsound mind. 2. Deaf mutes from birth. 3. Blind. 4. Lepers.
1	2	3	4	5	6	7	8	9	10	11	12

* In this column such details of tribes, clans and sects as the Local Government may direct should be introduced.

† If a European British subject, add "British subject."

‡ If a foreigner, state of what country.

§ If of mixed European and Asiatic parentage, add Eurasian.

‖ Boys at schools, girls, small children and women who perform no regular work should not be shown at all under column 10.

B.

ENUMERATION SCHEDULE PROPOSED FOR 1891.

(*Uniform size prescribed* 20″ × 8½″.)

Serial number and name.	Religion.		Caste or race.								Instruction.		
	Main religion.	Sect of religion.	Main caste, &c.	Subdivision.	Male or female.	Age.	Married, single or widowed.	Parents' tongue.	Birth—district or country.	Occupation or means of subsistence.	Learning, knowing, illiterate.	Foreign language known (if any.	*Note.*—If any be blind, insane, deaf mute, or a leper, enter the infirmity below.
1	2	3	4	5	6	7	8	9	10	11	12	13	14

The value of the alterations made by separating completely the columns for entries as to religion and caste is at once apparent to any one who has had to do with census matters. Even were the only entries required those of the main religion and the main caste, the added columns for sect and sub-caste would be of value to correct mistakes which are invariably made in regard to some religions and some castes.

A very clear and succinct code of instructions to enumerators was drafted by the Conference and afterwards prescribed by the Government of India for general adoption, with only such modification in details as might be considered locally necessary. The methods by which the information obtained in the schedules was to be abstracted into the final tables were outlined, and the forms which the tables were to take were drafted in almost precisely the shape in which they were adopted by the Government of India. The conference recommended and the Government of India adopted an important change in the method of enumeration of occupations. It was decided that record should be made of the occupation which formed the means of subsistence of every individual, whether he was an actual worker or not, instead of, as at last census, of the occupation of actual workers only. The effect of the change as regards both the accuracy and the value of the information acquired will be referred to in the chapter on the occupations of the provinces. Local Governments were consulted as to whether this suggestion should be adopted. The North-Western Provinces Government, whilst believing that the change would be a statistical improvement, considered that for the purpose of a correct record it would be preferable to follow the precedent of 1881 and record in the column of occupation only those persons who are actually engaged in it. The difficulty, which the Local Government considered would be felt by enumerators in carrying out the instructions as drafted, was more specifically stated by a Collector consulted, who pointed out how ludicrous it would be considered by the census staff to have to record the wife and ten children of a head constable as head constables, and the invalid husband of a midwife as also a midwife. The difficulty was a real one. It would have required the most minute superintendence to have got the census staff to regard such entries as proper, but a very useful amendment of the rules, made by the Government of India, made it possible to have the desired record without difficulty. For non-workers it was directed that the word dependent should be added. We should therefore in the above quoted instances have the entries of "dependent on head constable" "dependent on midwife" instead of those objected to. So amended, the rule as to record of occupations worked well, and it gave no trouble in subsequently abstracting the returns to omit the detail as to dependents and workers.

10. **The provincial rules for 1891.**—Provincial census operations started in April 1892, with the revision of the detailed instructions issued in 1881 to District Officers for procedure in enumeration. The proceedings of the Agra Conference and the remarks of selected officers on the census of 1881 afforded some guide as to the emendations necessary. Mr. E. White had, after the conclusion of the 1881 enumeration, called for reports from all districts as to what alterations were considered necessary, and had embodied these recommendations and the result of his own experience in a detailed note for use in the following census; but the fact that all census records of 1881, except the printed report itself, were destroyed by fire in the Secretariat office, deprived me of much information which would, no doubt, have been of value. Mr. White's circulars and a few final reports were, however, procured from District Officers, and the instructions for the census of 1891 issued on the 3rd June 1890.

11. **The Census subdivision of the provinces.**—The first steps, which the District Officers of the province were called on to take in connection with the census, were—the subdivision of their districts into accurately defined areas of suitable size for enumerators' blocks; the grouping of these blocks into circles and charges, each to be under the care of a supervisor or superintendent; and the provision and training of the necessary enumerators, supervisors and charge superintendents. The rules provided that the census subdivisions should be roughly marked out and the superior census staff provided by the 15th July, and that the accurate and final definition of the blocks, circles and charges and the appointment of all Census Officers should be complete by the 1st October.

It was intended that the record of the census subdivisions made in 1881 should be corrected, where recent considerable changes made it necessary, to provide the rough indication required by the 15th July; and in those districts in which any record of the 1881 subdivisions had been preserved this course was followed. There were, however, many districts in which no trace of the 1881 record of census charges could be found, and in these it was necessary to make an entirely fresh arrangement. At both censuses the rules to be observed were that a block should contain on an average about 60 houses or 300 persons; that a circle should consist of about ten blocks; and a charge of all the circles in some well-known territorial division of a district.

12. **The house numbering.**—The accurate definition of the enumerator's block was the part of the preliminary arrangements which called for most

attention and required most labour. It implied the numbering of every house, landing stage, camping ground or other place in which any persons were likely to be found on the census night, and the preparation of a list giving a description of all such places and the numbers allotted to them. One of these lists was prepared for each "mauza," that being the smallest clearly defined and continuous unit of area which can be employed for executive purposes in these provinces. The term mauza has had a variety of English words used as its equivalent. It has been translated as village, township, hamlet and even as parish. Of these words, village has the sanction of general use, and I propose to make use of it in future; but as it would, in general English use, apply more properly to the inhabited site only, a note as to the actual meaning of the term so translated may be added. It is defined by Mr. Vincent Smith as consisting of "a plot or plots of land with definite permanent boundaries and a separate name in the revenue register, usually, though not necessarily, surrounding an inhabited village site." That is to say, it is a defined area traditionally regarded as a mauza. No more logical definition can be given. The use of the word township implies a theory which does not apply to a majority of the villages as now constituted in the North-Western Provinces and Oudh, whilst the word parish is as inapplicable as a word could well be. The revenue definition of mauza was modified in two respects for census purposes.

The mauza.

(*a*) Uninhabited mauzas or villages were excluded for obvious reasons.

(*b*) Within the boundaries of a town village demarcation was ignored. A town is occasionally included within the area of a single village (mauza), but more generally includes part of the area of several villages. For all census purposes the town itself is the important unit, mauza boundaries are important elsewhere because they are the unit for all administrative purposes, and indeed the only absolutely fixed unit which can be employed. Within the town area the usefulness of the mauza boundaries disappears.

13. **Census definition of village.**—The census definition of a village was therefore as follows:—

"A village denotes the area demarcated for revenue purposes as a mauza, provided that where a village or part of a village forms a part of the area of a town, it will be included in such town. The remainder, if any, will be regarded, for census purposes, as the village.

Explanation 1.—A village includes all hamlets situated within the area of the revenue mauza.

Explanation 2.—A mauza will be regarded as a village for census purposes only when it contains a place or places in which persons may probably be found on the census night.

Explanation 3.—"Forest tracts not included within the boundaries of a revenue mauza will be entered as villages, the boundaries being those recognised by the Forest Department."

14. **The definition of town.**—The definition of town given in the rules was—

A town denotes—

(1) Every area within which the Chaukidári Act (XX of 1856) or either of the Municipal Acts (XV of 1873 or XV of 1883) is in force;

(2) Every other continuous group of houses inhabited permanently by not less than 5,000 people.

By the area of a town is meant—

(1) The area demarcated for the purposes of the above Acts.

(2) The area occupied by the group of houses and the land immediately appurtenant thereto.

Explanation. 1—If the houses of several villages form together a continuous group with a population exceeding 5,000, such a group will be a town. But if the houses of a village are divided into distinct groups, no one of which contains more than 5,000 residents, then, though the total population exceeds 5,000, they will not be a town.

Explanation 2.—Where separate groups of houses have been united for the purposes of the above Acts, it must be considered in each case whether the circumstances require the statistics to be separate or combined. In the first case, groups will be considered separate towns, in the latter, one town : as, however, for administrative purposes, these groups are treated as forming one aggregate, unless there is some strong reason for a contrary course, they should be regarded as one town.

This definition differs materially from that adopted at last census. An attempt was then made to specially demarcate towns for census purposes and to ignore the known demarcation already made executively. The result was, as will appear from the remarks on the movement of population in towns, such as to necessitate the adoption of the present definition. The instructions regarding the special demarcation of towns for census purposes were sometimes carried out and were sometimes ignored; when they were carried out the returns obtained were useless for executive purposes, and when the arrangements for the present census were being made, it was found impossible to ascertain to what areas they applied.

15. **Definition of house.**—An important preliminary to the preparation of the lists for each town or mauza was the definition of the word "house." Had it been possible to satisfactorily define the word in a way applicable to the whole of India the definition would have been of some statistical as well as of administrative importance. The resolution of the Agra Conference on the subject was as follows :—

"On discussing the definition of a house for the purpose of the census, it was found that, looking at the extreme variety of dwellings prevalent in India, the only use made of the return in the tables was of insignificant statistical value. For administrative purposes the Conference recommend the definition of 1881, in which the leading feature is the existence of an independent entrance from the common way. Special cases of common occurrence, such as are found in every province, must be met by special mention in the instructions to the agency employed to register and number the buildings. The definition published for the guidance of supervising officers will be "The dwelling place of one or more families with their resident servants, having a separate principal entrance from the common way." For enumeration purposes it will remain, as before, a building having a separate number affixed to it, and, as such, it will appear in the preliminary returns under the heading of occupied or unoccupied respectively."

The definition was thus left to the discretion of Local Governments. That recommended by the Conference was not adopted without consideration by the Local Government. Of the officers consulted only one, Mr. E. J. Kitts, had any alteration of importance to propose. Mr. Kitts suggested as the definition of house "a permanent or temporary dwelling place on a separate site and inhabited by one or more families." Mr. Kitts stated his objections to the Conference definition as follows :—

"My first objection to that definition is that under it the census enumeration becomes not an enumeration of houses, so much as an enumeration of front doors (sadar darwázas). It often happens in towns that an upper story of a house has a separate side door which is "a separate principal entrance upon the public way." In the English census this would be enumerated as a separate tenement, but not as a separate house; in India it is enumerated as a separate house."

"My second objection is that the old definition cannot be made, without violence, to provide for cases such as are noticed on page 140, North-Western Provinces Census Report, Volume I, which caused the return for the Sahâranpur district to be so abnormal. The words "public way" might be further explained as "land over which different families exercised a right of way," but this would make the definition longer than at present. I am aware that the old definition was suggested by an authority for which I have the greatest respect and admiration: but the 1881 census showed that the definition did not work well and uniformly. I would suggest the following :—A house is a permanent or temporary dwelling place upon a separate site and inhabited by one or more families." This definition would in practical working meet the two cases which I have mentioned, and I do not think it would raise any new difficulties."

There can be no doubt that the defects, pointed out by Mr. Kitts in the conference definition are real. His definition however appears to introduce far more serious difficulties. The term a separate site is indefinite in the extreme. An ordinary plan of house for a fairly well-to-do zamíndár is a number of small built huts round a central enclosure; each of these huts is but a separate room of the house; but in so far as the site is concerned they are each just as much on a separate site as is the house of a Chamár family in an enclosure of the type referred to by Mr. Kitts as common in Sahâranpur. The object of the definition was to provide not statistical information regarding houses, but a definite and workable unit for the enumerators' lists. It was clear, I think, that from this point of view the definition by means of the separate public way was both more explicit and simpler than that by means of the separate site, as well as more in accordance with native ideas on the subject. It was however necessary to provide in the definition for the sub-division of the enclosures common in the western districts, each of which have but one separate entrance from the public way, but which may contain the dwelling houses of forty or fifty families, and for which therefore a single number is not a sufficient guide to an enumerator. With this view a proviso was added to the definition which was published in the rules as follows :—

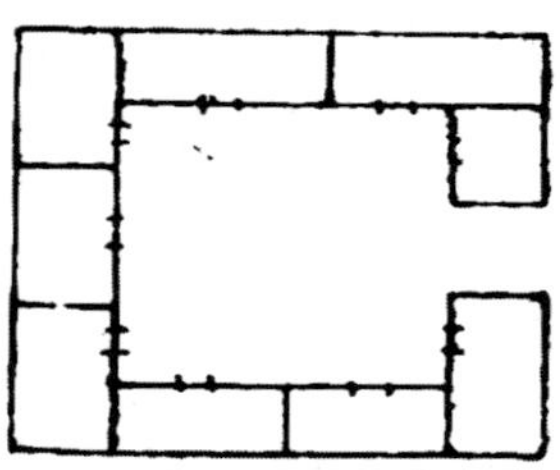

"A house is the dwelling place of one or several families having a separate entrance from the public way."

"*Provided* that where such a dwelling-house consists of an enclosure inhabited by four or more *independent* families, the parts of the enclosure inhabited by each family may be considered separate houses."

"*Explanation.*—For census purposes, a shop or storehouse will not be a house unless some one reside in it. If, however, any person is likely to be found residing in it on the census night, it will be treated as a house."

That the proviso had the effect of breaking up the enclosures which gave so much trouble at last census, the accompanying comparison of the population per house in certain western districts now and at last census shows clearly enough. There has been however no part of the enumeration rules so much criticised or which has given so much trouble as this definition. It was overlooked by the persons who numbered the houses that the proviso referred only to *enclosures* which were the dwelling places of several separate families and in consequence four or five numbers painted on the single door of a single tenement were not infrequently met with. The meaning which it was desired to attach to the italicized word *independent* was overlooked, and a father and his sons living in the ancestral house had their dwelling rooms often designated by separate numbers, because each cooked his food separate from the others. The discretion allowed by the use of the word 'may' is stated to have led to diversity of practice in adjoining quarters of the same town.

District.	No. of persons per house.	
	1881.	1891.
Sahāranpur	11·1	4·94
Bulandshahr	9·8	5·58
Meerut	9·1	5·49
Budaun	8·9	5·69
Muzaffarnagar	7·6	6·89
Bijnor	8·5	5·61
Provincial average ...	6·4	5·703

The provision that only enclosures containing four or more independent families should be divided up is liable to the serious objection that so arbitrary a line of demarcation deprives statistics as to house population of much of the small value that can otherwise be attached to them. It was made in consideration of the instruction to the enumerator directing that each house should occupy a separate page of the enumerator's book, and in order to prevent waste of the forms by dividing all enclosures into separate houses.

The very frequent objections made in district reports to the definition are entirely unaccompanied by any suggestion as to how it should be amended. The proviso is, there can be little doubt, absolutely necessary to provide a guide for enumerators in enclosures. It might at next census be amended by being made compulsory by the substitution of "will" for "may." It would be more statistically correct if for "four or more *independent* families" were written "two or more independent families," thus providing for the subdivision of all enclosures inhabited by families not connected by the ties of close relationship."

16. **The house numbering.**—The house numbering was carried out in municipal towns by an establishment provided by the Municipal Boards, in Act XX towns by the tax Collector or other official agency provided by the District Magistrate, and in villages almost entirely by that mainstay of the census administration, the patwári. In the towns the houses had for the most part been permanently numbered before the census, but there were few instances in which this earlier numbering was found to be so systematic or so complete as to make it of use without almost complete revision. The rules provided that in towns the serial number for houses should run by muhallas or wards, but that where houses had already been numbered by streets or otherwise, the existing numbers should be utilized for census purposes. It was abundantly proved, in my opinion, that numbering by

muhallas was the only plan suitable for ordinary towns in these provinces. In large towns and in the more densely populated and permanently built parts, numbering by streets and lanes is possible, but even in such towns it is impossible in the maze of petty lanes and by-ways, which form the poorer parts. Distribution of enumerators by streets was in most places found to be impossible, and where it was attempted it had often at the last moment to be abandoned in favor of a distribution by muhallas. In several cities in which I inspected the numbering myself, great delay was caused in census work by its being assumed, to start with, that the old numbers could be employed. Mirzapur was completed numbered twice over for this reason, and in Benares work was thrown so far back that the numbering was only completed before the enumeration had to be started by great efforts on the part of the Joint Magistrate, the late Hafiz Altaf Husain, Deputy Collector, and several members of the Municipal Board. Lucknow and Fyzabad may be mentioned as cities in which the house numbering was particularly well and promptly done. In the former it was effected by an entirely separate staff of muharrirs appointed for the purpose and working under the orders of the Municipal Secretary and the City Magistrate. In general the numbering in towns was when completed absolutely exhaustive, and the intelligence and carefulness with which this work was done for the most part by the members of the Municipal Boards deserves mention. The numbers affixed for census purposes were, in so far as I know, every municipal town of the provinces adopted permanently, tin plates with the number painted on them being in general affixed to the houses. In Act XX towns the procedure was not materially different. In the villages the numbers were in general painted in red ochre on the different houses by the patwári. In a few districts more or less permanent wooden tickets were provided by the zamíndárs. All officers who have reported in detail on the house numbering in villages note with confidence on its complete correctness. The patwári, even in those districts in which patwári intelligence is lowest, has, from his thorough local knowledge, no difficulty in carrying through this part of the work in an unexceptionable manner.

17. **The date prescribed for the completion of house numbering.**—The date fixed for the completion of the house numbering was the 1st October. Objection has been taken to this date, on the ground that it implies much of the work being done in the rains, and makes it necessary in many cases to have it redone owing to the numbers being washed out. In the present census heavy rain in September, in the eastern districts, not only washed out the numbers to a great extent, but in not a few cases obliterated even the houses themselves. The majority of officers, however, were of opinion that the date fixed was not too early. The numbering of the houses has to be done before the blocks can be finally decided on and before enumerators can be appointed; and it was clearly better to risk the obliteration of a percentage of the numbers than to delay the rest of the census work. The block list being written up with the first numbering, it gives little trouble to replace the numbers on the houses later on. One or two officers report that *geru* (red ochre) numbers were considered unlucky, and washed out by the people themselves. Geru markings appear not uncommonly to be considered unlucky, but that

this feeling should affect the census numbering was not a general occurrence. In general, when houses were plastered after the numbers had been affixed, the women were most careful to plaster all round but not over the numbers. The care taken of the wooden or metal numbers provided in towns and in some districts in rural tracts also was almost ludicrous. They were far too precious to remain exposed on the houses and were carefully wrapped up in a cloth and put away in the basket which contained the festival dresses of the women, to be proudly produced when a Census Officer came round.

18. **The block list.**—The block list showing the houses and the numbers they bore was to be the enumerator's guide round his block, and it was therefore necessary, that besides actual dwelling houses, all camping grounds, landing stages and other places where any persons were likely to be found on the census night should bear a separate number. Amongst such places a number of shops had to be numbered. The rule as to the numbering of shops has in places been somewhat misunderstood. It is common for householders to sleep in their shops at night by way of safeguard, but it was not intended that such persons should be enumerated at the shop if they had a dwelling house from which they were temporarily absent. To distinguish between persons sleeping in shops and who ought to be enumerated elsewhere and those who had no other place of residence in the neighbourhood and practically lived in the shop, required a considerable amount of correspondence between enumerators. This, however, was found in practice to be inevitable, to avoid either the possibility of the double enumeration or the omission of people sleeping in shops.

The specimen village or ward list printed for the guidance of District Officers was as follows :—

Name of village or ward. *No in circle list.*

Serial number.	Description of house or place.	Name of head of each family or principal resident.	Remarks.
1	2	3	4
	Main abadi.		
29	Dwelling house	(1) Bhagwant, lambardár. (2) Genda, pattidár. (3) Rám Diyal, pattidár.	
30	Chaupal	...	Travellers spend the night here.
31	Police station	Ránjit Singh, head constable ...	Separate block.
32	Dwelling-house	(1) Rám Bakhsh, Kachhi. (2) Mukanda, ditto	
33 &c.	Bungalow with servants' houses ... &c	Mr. John Smith, Indigo Planter ... &c.	Private schedule. &c.
	Chamárán.		
97	Dwelling-house	(1) Sheo Diyal, Chamár. (2) Gurdas, ditto (3) Rup Rám, ditto	
98	Ditto ... ... &c.	Ganga ditto &c.	

19. **Census subdivisions.**—House numbering finished, District Officers were instructed to draw up for each town or tahsíl of their charge a register giving exact details of all census subdivisions as finally fixed, and the names

of the enumerators and supervising Census Officers appointed to take charge of these subdivisions. A specimen of the prescribed form follows :—

Circle list. Charge of Superintendent, tahsil, district.

Serial number of village or muhalla.	Name of village or muhalla.	Serial number of block.	Description of block.	Name of enumerator.	Character written by enumerator.	Forms to be issued to enumerators.					Name of supervisor.	Number of schedule sheets filed by enumerator.	Remarks.
						Books of 12 schedules.	Books of 24 schedules.	Books of 48 schedules.	European schedules.	Household (native) schedules.			
1	2	3	4	5	6	7	8	9	10	11	12	13	14
21	Garbi Abdullah.	1	Main abadi, houses 1 to 53.	Mokand Lál, assistant patwári.	Nágri ...	1	...	1	1	4*	Johari Mal continued.	58	*English.
		2	Chamárán, houses 54 to 63, Agaighát, houses 64 to 71.	Agand Lál, Bania,	Do. ...	...	1	...	...	...	Ditto ...	23	
22	Muhalla Kattra, kasba, Rámpur.	1	Houses 1 to 49, including paráo.	Mata Bakhsh Singh, zamíndári.	Urdu ...	1	...	1	...	1†	Gauhari Mal, Town Bakhshi.	59	†Urdu.
		2	Houses 50 to 102, except sarái No. 92.	Dharm Das, patwári.	Do. ...	...	1	1	...	...	Ditto ...	61	
		3	Houses 104 to 140	Muhammad Husain, mukhtar.	Do. ...	...	...	1	.	...	Ditto ...	45	
		4	Thána No. 103 ...	Jan Muhammad, head constable.	Do. ...	1	...	...	.	...	Ditto ...	12	
		5	Sarái No. 92 ...	Constable Kunwar Singh.	Do. ...	1	...	...	...	...	Ditto ...	7	
23	Muhalla Kaharan, kasba Rámpur.	1	Houses 1 to 30, including temple.	Rám Bakhsh, schoolmaster.	Do. ...	...	...	1	...	2†	Ditto ...	39	

The different subdivisions prescribed have already been mentioned. The following statements show for each of the Commissionerships of the Provinces the average number of houses, the average area and average population of each description of census subdivision.

ABSTRACT No. 1.

Showing the average size of each superintendent's charge.

Divisions.	Average number of houses.	Average area.	Average population.
Meerut	4,986·10	59·61	28,036·00
Agra	7,711·71	96·56	45,407·23
Rohilkhand	7,402·96	88·68	43,444·50
Allahabad	4,011·03	62·55	20,859·13
Benares	6,799·05	80·11	41,298·28
Gorakhpur	9,749·69	85·51	58,685·37
Kumaun	2,481·00	167·59	14,409·35
North-Western Provinces ...	5,844·87	81·89	33,681·67
Lucknow	7,471·40	87·88	42,749·00
Fyzabad	7,714·25	74·70	41,682·65
Oudh	7,603·20	80·72	42,169·44
North-Western Provinces and Oudh ...	6,245·40	81·63	35,615·10

ABSTRACT No. 2.

Showing the average size of each supervisor's circle.

Divisions.	Average number of houses.	Average area.	Average population.
Meerut	482·36	5·77	2712·20
Agra	471·05	5·90	2773·57
Rohilkhand	438·61	5·25	2574·90
Allahabad	483·43	7·54	2514·03
Benares	392·14	4·62	2381·88
Gorakhpur	376·82	3·30	2266·20
Kumaun	300·62	20·27	1742·72
North-Western Provinces	429·09	6·01	2472·70
Lucknow	471·48	5·54	2697·70
Fyzabad	566·15	5·48	3059·10
Oudh	519·34	5·51	2873·60
North-Western Provinces and Oudh	450·82	5·89	2570·85

ABSTRACT No. 3.

Showing the average size of each enumerator's block.

Divisions.	Average number of houses.	Average area.	Average population.
Meerut	51·91	·62	291·88
Agra	45·92	·58	270·40
Rohilkhand	49·73	·60	291·88
Allahabad	47·11	·73	245·02
Benares	42·12	·50	255·85
Gorakhpur	44·00	·89	264·61
Kumaun	26·10	1·76	151·60
North-Western Provinces	45·35	·64	261·36
Lucknow	48·87	·57	279·63
Fyzabad	53·70	·52	290·15
Oudh	51·42	·55	285·18
North-Western Provinces and Oudh	46·89	·61	267·38

It will be observed that except in Kumaun, the circumstances of which are special and will have to be referred to at length further on, there was, as a rule, no great general diversity in the size or importance of the different sub divisions in different parts of the province. A superintendent had ordinarily charge of 6,245 houses, extending over an area of 82 square miles and containing a population of 35,615 persons. A supervisor had to test in detail the enumerator's work in 451 houses over an area of nearly 6 square miles and a population of 2,571 persons. An enumerator had on an average 47 houses, $\frac{2}{3}$ of a square mile of area and 267 persons to enumerate.

These figures are sufficient to show that, as a rule, it was not found necessary to make the charge of a census official unfairly large. The actual average size of the charges was in no Commissionership or district in ex cess of that prescribed by the rules, and which had been ascertained in previous censuses to be perfectly manageable. In one respect, the number of houses and population placed in a single enumerator's block, Rámpur State contrasts with the British districts. The work in a block was there rather more than twice as much as in an average block in the rest of the provinces. The census administration of Rámpur will be referred to further on. It is here enough to note that I do not consider either that it was practicable to make the blocks smaller or that the census results were materially injured by the size of the blocks.

20. **The circle list.**—The circle list showing in detail the houses allotted to each blocks and the grouping of block into charges afforded district officers the means of completely examining in detail the census arrangements made by the tahsíli officials. During my cold weather tour before the census I myself summarily examined these lists in all except four of the districts of the provinces. The objection which I had most frequently to take was that blocks were allowed to run too large, especially in outlying tracts where educated enumerators were not easily obtained. A maximum size of block, both as regards number of houses and population, should in future be insisted on. The maximum will vary considerably with the nature of the block. In a compact town block I consider that 100 houses and 600 persons can be efficiently enumerated by *a selected enumerator*. In the scattered rural blocks of the eastern districts 70 houses and 450 persons are a quite high enough maximum. In jangal tracts with scattered hamlets the largest block should be still smaller. Many District Officers were found to be of opinion that still larger blocks could be easily managed by one enumerator; but in my opinion the risk of bad enumeration is much increased by having blocks of over 100 houses. Even in towns the size of the block has to be regulated with regard to the number of houses which the enumerator can visit on the census night after the hour appointed for starting and before the patience of householders has been exhausted. From nine o'clock to near midnight on the census night householders were waiting for the enumerator ready to give him the information he wanted. After 12 the belated enumerator has to rouse people from their beds, and the chances of his record being incomplete are greatly increased. I do not believe that in any part of the provinces it is necessary, in view of the supply of capable enumerators available, to raise the size of the blocks above the maximum suggested.

21. **Census maps.**—A form of examining the census distribution of work not prescribed in the rules, but adopted in several districts, was the preparation of a map showing for the whole of a tahsíl or district the census blocks, circles, and charges. The most complete census maps I have seen were those prepared in Etáwah by Mr. E. B. Alexander, which showed on a large scale district map not only the accurate boundaries of the rural blocks with the number of houses and population of each, but the course which the enumerator was to take on the census night from one hamlet to

another. Such a map properly prepared affords superior officers a very excellent means of examining the details of the circle list and of making certain that the blocks have been judiciously demarcated. Maps cost from Rs. 10 to Rs. 17 per district. I consider that they should be prescribed at next census.

22. **The Census staff.**—The total number of Census Officers appointed to conduct the enumeration in these provinces is shown in the following statement :—

	Superintendents.	Supervisors.	Enumerators.
Town	276	1,938	19,014
Rural	1,041	16,307	156,408
Total ...	1,317	18,245	175,422

Of all grades there were 194,984 Census Officers employed.

The Act allowed the district authorities to adopt an authoritative tone in calling for assistance in taking the census ; but it is a reason for the greatest satisfaction that the need for the Act was practically *nil* in these provinces. From only one district were any prosecutions reported, and even there the offences were not such as to give any reason to believe that the census could not have been carried out without the assistance of any provisions making service as Census Officers compulsory. The provincial rules directed that the Census Officers should be appointed from amongst persons willing to aid, and of such there were found to be enough without resorting to compulsion. In connection with this subject a remark of the Officiating Collector of Jaunpur may be quoted :—

"Most of those who worked this time gratuitously were encouraged to do so by the hope of some eventual benefit of a tangible nature. It should be the aim of District Officers to justify such hopes as far as possible when responsible work has been well done, and there can be little doubt that it will be done again on the same terms."

The census staff employed was so large even as compared with the very large number of appointments at the disposal of Government officers in the provinces that service even as a very efficient census enumerator cannot be regarded as constituting a strong claim to Government employment ; but, on the other hand, the fact that such assistance was refused or given in a half-hearted way should be, and I have no doubt is, regarded as a strong reason for not giving such employment.

The instructions of Government in regard to the selection and appointment of Census Officers are contained in the following extract from the Manual of Census Rules :—

"The Government of India have laid down the general rule that the agency employed in taking the census must be unpaid. The success with which the last census of the North-Western Provinces and Oudh was taken, almost entirely without paid agency, leaves no doubt that the enumeration now proposed can be carried on in the same manner."

"Except subordinate police officers, and employés of the Irrigation Department, all other Government servants, including those of the Civil Courts, Forest and Opium Departments, will be eligible to perform any work in connection with the census to which they may be appointed by the District Officer."

"A gazetted officer, in general, of the district staff will be placed in general charge of the census arrangements in each tahsíl. He will be assisted in his examination and testing of census arrangements and work by the Tahsíldárs and by gazetted officers of any Department, including the Police and the Forests, Opium, Survey and Settlement, who can conveniently be appointed to work in his tahsíl. All such gazetted officers when on tour should take every opportunity of examining the census work already done and which is being done: and, by inspection and catechizing the specially appointed census staff, see that the instructions of Government have been intelligently grasped and are being correctly carried out. In towns similar assistance may be occasionally rendered by stationary officers during their leisure hours."

"The charge superintendent will be strictly responsible for the whole of the census arrangements within his charge, for the instruction and efficiency of the enumerators and supervisors and for the accuracy of the enumeration; it is therefore essential that he should be a man of known ability and energy. He will ordinarily be appointed from amongst the principal tahsíl and district subordinate officials; but non-officials, and in particular ex-officials known to possess the requisite ability and to be thoroughly reliable, may be appointed. The District Magistrate should himself make certain that all superintendents appointed are of the class prescribed."

"Supervisors and enumerators will be selected from all respectable persons willing to aid. Except Police Officers, all other Government servants, including those of the Civil Courts and Forest and Opium Departments, will be eligible to perform the general work of enumerators and supervisors. In the performance of the duties of supervision considerable clerical ability is required, the discretion of the person appointed has to be largely trusted, and there are fewer means than in the case of enumerators of testing and controlling his actual work. For these reasons it is very desirable that Government servants should, as far as possible, be appointed to the rank of supervisors and superintendents. If non-officials, on whom less influence can be brought, are appointed they must be known to be thoroughly trustworthy. The relations of patwáris and other Government servants, pleaders and mukhtars, applicants for employment, zamíndárs and their agents, village school-masters, &c., will furnish a large supplementary staff of unpaid enumerators, and the cases will be very rare where paid agency must be employed."

"The census of persons present in thána buildings, police lines and saráis in which a record of travellers is ordinarily kept up by the police, will be made by Police Officers. The census of wandering tribes, and also, with the special sanction of the District Superintendent of Police, of people at fairs on the census night, will be made by the police. The census of persons present in the jails, lunatic asylums, hospitals, camps of civil officers on tour and similar buildings and assemblages will be made under the orders of the officers in charge, who will appoint enumerators."

Figures showing in detail for each district the census agency employed and the classes from which it was mainly drawn are given in Appendices I, II and III.

23. **The charge superintendent.**—The duties required from a census charge superintendent were such as to call for his attention throughout the

whole of the six months preceding the census. He was required to superintend and correct the house numbering throughout his charge, to instruct all his supervisors in census work, to test the draft schedules filled up by each and all of his enumerators, and to test and correct largely the enumerators' records when finally prepared. In a town of ordinary size these duties could be performed by a man otherwise employed in his leisure hours, but in a rural charge the duties were so extensive as to occupy the whole or nearly the whole of the charge superintendent's time, especially during the months employed in numbering and in actually preparing the enumeration record. The classes from which charge superintendents were mostly drawn is shown in the following statement :—

	District staff.	Other departments.	Non-officials.	Total.
Town	133	51	92	276
Rural	874	96	71	1,041
Total ...	1,007	147	163	1,317

As might be expected, the superintendents in towns, and particularly in the larger towns, were, in a far larger proportion than in the country, drawn from the non-official classes and from the departments of Government service not subordinate to the District Magistrate; officers in the judicial line, the native Bar and the more intelligent members of Municipal Boards suppied for head-quarter towns a staff of superintendents as intelligent and well-educated as could be desired and whose devotion to the work undertaken by them deserves the highest commendation. A list of such superintendents whose services were specially worthy of notice has been submitted by District Officers for a recognition of their services by Government. Of the persons shown as belonging to the district staff, most were municipal or local fund employés. In the smaller towns the local tax collector was sometimes put in charge of the census. I do not consider that officials of this rank are well suited for the comparatively independent position occupied under the rules by a charge superintendent, and in a few of these small towns only, out of the whole of the provinces has there been any reason to suspect the accuracy of the enumeration. I should recommend that in future every effort should be made to get a suitable non-official superintendent of standing for the position of charge superintendent in small towns away from headquarters. If no suitable non-official should be available, it would be better to have a small town included in the charge of one of the rural superintendents than to trust it to a town tax collector or other official of similar rank.

Rural charge superintendents were, as the figures in the general return of census agency show, in the majority of districts, almost exclusively officials of the district staff. A few District Officers were able to utilize the services of unusually well-instructed and energetic landholders, but in general even where such assistance was available it was considered inadvisable to commit the care of so important a charge to men so little trained in either clerical or executive work. It was in general found possible to allot a small town as the charge of a capable landholder, and these charges, the superintendence of which was a trifle as compared with that of a rural charge, were found to be well looked after and well managed.

The officials appointed to rural charges were in almost all districts supervisor kanúngos and Naib Tahsíldárs. A few District Officers considered it advisable to appoint gazetted officers to be charge superintendents, but I consider that there can be little doubt that the system of reducing the size of charges and appointing officials of a lower grade to them, worked more satisfactorily. The gazetted officer cannot within his extensive jurisdiction personally fulfil all the duties imposed by the rules on superintendents, and it is better that the personal responsibility of each individual Census Officer be fully recognised by his being put in charge of a definite and workable area, than that an officer with an unworkably large area should have to depend on the assistance of official subordinates whose census responsibilities are badly defined and badly recognised. As a whole, the work of the charge—superintendents in the rural tracts of the districts was most efficiently done. The official position of the charge superintendent gave him the authority necessary in dealing with subordinate officers, and even though many of the supervisors who worked under official charge superintendents were men of a rank socially superior to the charge superintendents, I have not heard of a single case in which there was any material friction. For the work done by the kanúngo staff in charge of the rural census, I have nothing but praise to report from any district.

24. **Census supervisors**.—The work to be done by supervisors was in the present rules more clearly defined than at last census, when it was reported from several districts that supervisors had been found more or less useless, all the real work being done by the superintendents. I am not prepared to state that there was not, in the present census also, a tendency on the part of the supervisors to slip out of responsibility by letting the superintendents deal directly with the enumerators. I believe that to a great extent this is unavoidable. Officials of a grade accustomed to supervision can rarely be provided for supervisor's work, and the more energetic a superintendent is the more likely he is to deal directly with the enumerators. The difficulty of efficiently working the supervisors has led to the suggestion that the grade should be abolished and the services of the persons so employed utilized as enumerators. This proposal I regard as a most dangerous one. Very few indeed of the superintendents could possibly be held responsible for supervision of the whole of their enumerators' work, and such supervision is in my opinion absolutely necessary. We have been able in the present census to provide as supervisors a sufficient number of persons able to thoroughly master the system of enumeration. However successful a District Officer may be in providing enumerators of a good class, it is absolutely certain that, of the very large number employed in this rank, a large proportion will be so poorly educated that every column they fill up will require inspection. A superintendent might show them how to enumerate and revise a part of their work, but this would not prevent their repeating the same mistakes in every succeeding entry. A more accurate estimate of the value of the services of the supervisors

was arrived at by those officers who were induced by the difficulty of insisting on the full performance of their duties by supervisors to suggest their payment, both now and in future censuses. In the present census supervisors were paid only in Mainpuri and the hill districts, and that for the special reason that in these districts a large part of the patwári staff was engaged on settlement work. It was however suggested by more than one officer that provision should be made in future for their payment. The Deputy Commissioner of Gonda suggests that for his district fifty paid supervisors should in future be provided for two months at Rs. 20 a month each. This would imply the expenditure of Rs. 2,000 in one district and of about a lakh of rupees in the province, in addition to nearly the whole of the present expenditure. It is so unlikely that the money will be forthcoming that the proposal may be regarded as beyond the range of practical politics. It is however in this direction rather than in that of payment of enumerators that expenditure, if it were possible, would be most useful. I do not however consider that whilst it is clearly recognised by Government that the principal work of the patwári and kanúngo establishment in a census year is to be connected with the census, any such payment is necessary. Patwáris and kanúngos' ordinary work is certainly unavoidably interrupted and injured by census work ; but I do not see that this interruption in any way permanently affects the district work injuriously. I would suggest that, in future censuses, it be arranged with the Department of Land Records that part of the field work be omitted in census years. There could so far as I see be no injury to district administration by the omission of the khasra round for one year in ten and by the preparation for that year of only the siyaha and terij jamabandi.

The classes to which the supervisors chiefly belonged are shown in the following statement :—

	Patwáries.	Other district staff.	Other departments.	Non-officials.	Unspecified.	Total.
Town	126	583	494	735	...	1,938
Rural	7,236	1,514	1,608	5,674	275	16,307
Total ...	7,362	2,097	2,102	6,409	275	18,245

The urban supervisors were to a much greater extent than urban superintendents drawn from the non-official class and from Government servants not under the District Officer. They were drawn from the same classes as the urban superintendents, and in both intelligence and probity were not materially inferior to them. Of the rural supervisors the class I found most efficient and to whose work a great part of the success of the enumeration is due were the patwáris. All of them who were appointed to the rank of supervisors were picked men. Many of them had not only to supervise the work of their enumerators, but often to do nearly the whole of the preliminary work for the enumerators of their own village or group of villages. Of the non-official supervisors probably the most efficient were the employés of large landholders, fairly well trained in clerical work and in general kept closely to their census work by their employers, who were anxious to assist as far as it was possible to do so by proxy.

25. **Census enumerators.**—Census enumerators are classified in the following statement :—

	Patwáris.	Other officials.	Zamíndárs.	Zamíndár's agents.	School-boys.	Other non-officials.	Unspeci-fied.	Total.
Town ...	290	4,215	1,475	642	781	10,871	740	19,014
Rural ...	20,179	4,728	36,304	8,212	2,367	78,726	5,892	156,408
Total ...	20,469	8,943	37,779	8,854	3,148	89,597	6,632	175,422

The provision of this large staff of unpaid workers was the first *great* difficulty to be overcome by the district staff. Since first a general census was taken in these provinces by unpaid agency, there have periodically been prophecies that the difficulty of providing them was owing to the waning influence of the District Officer so greatly on the increase that Government would have to be prepared to pay census enumerators at no distant date. Such prophets have not been absent on the present occasion either, but as a matter of fact there was no district in which it was found impossible to provide as many men as were necessary without paying more than a trifling sum to an inconsiderable number of enumerators and without any resort whatsoever to the provisions of the Census Act by which a person might be compelled to act as a Census Officer. The difficulties to be overcome of course varied greatly from district to district. They were least in the western districts where the standard of education is highest and the difficulties of enumeration least. They were greatest in Bundelkhand and in the Mirzapur and the Himalayan districts where education is most backward and the physical labour of enumeration greatest.

They were however nowhere so considerable as to make the payment of enumerators necessary on other than the most trifling scale. I believe that the fact that we have now obtained the largest number of enumerators ever employed in the provinces with the smallest amount of payment and absolutely no legal compulsion indicates that the difficulty in obtaining enumerators diminishes from census to census instead of increasing, as there is a tendency to believe that it does. The census history of 1890-91 in these provinces proves that unless some change in the attitude of the people of which there is now no indication takes place, Government will not on any future occasion find it necessary to pay the general body of the enumerators. As regards the value of the work done by paid and unpaid enumerators, I fully agree with Misr Banarsi Das, Deputy Collector, who wrote the Farukhabad district report, that payment to such an extent as the financial condition of the country would make possible would be worse than useless; that the unpaid man working with the prospect of attracting the attention and obtaining the patronage of the district staff does better work than an insufficiently paid muharrir would.

Payments were actually made to enumerators and charged to the imperial grant as follows :—

In Muzaffarnagar, Rs. 40 were paid as travelling allowance to men who had to be sent to assist in the census of the swampy tract in pargana Gordhanpur.

In Mainpuri, Rs. 20 were paid to special enumerators employed to enumerate people returning from a fair.

In Etáwah, Rs. 74-4-8 were paid to enumerators, who were sent across the Chambal into the waste trans-Chambal pargana.

In Mirzapur, Rs. 91 were paid to enumerators in the hilly tracts to the south.

In Garhwál, Rs. 6, and in Rae Bareli, Rs. 10 were paid.

In the Kumaun Bhábar Rs. 100 were paid.

In all, the payments to enumerators were Rs. 341-4-8.

To this has to be added Rs. 57-4-3 paid to railway enumerators, making in all Rs. 298-8-11 charged against the imperial grant for remuneration of enumerators. The amount paid at last census was Rs. 3,099-9-1.

Besides this amount certain sums were paid for enumeration by Municipal Boards, who were charged by the Government of India with the conduct and cost of enumeration within the municipal areas. In general, these amounts also, so far as reported to me, were very small; for example, the Agra municipality spent Rs. 12, and that of Cawnpore Rs. 62 for carriage hire. In Lucknow only, the enumeration of which will have to be separately referred to as conducted on a system different from that prescribed by the rules, was a considerable sum paid in remuneration for the work of enumeration.

In towns nearly three-fourths of the enumerators were non-officials. There was in general an ample supply of men in education well above the rural standard. The only difficulty found, and it is referred to in several districts, was in inducing these men to do the preliminary part of the work, which required their appearance in their blocks for some eight or ten mornings or evenings. The legal profession, petition writers, revenue agents, stamp venders, supplied a large proportion of the town enumerators, and in tractability as well as ability, probably the best of them. All difficulties connected with the supply of enumerators appear to have been easily overcome except in Lucknow, where the Municipal Board considered it preferable to employ special muharrirs at a cost of Rs. 1,130-12-0 to number the houses and to write up the census record. Enumerators were employed only for the census night, and were all of them who were not officials paid at the rate of Re. 1-8-0 each for the night's work and the day or two employed in learning their work and getting a knowledge of their blocks. The Lucknow work thus done was excellent, perhaps better in all-over quality, certainly better in handwriting and neatness than that in any other large town. The plan, too, saved the members of the Board and the district officials a lot of trouble in hunting up enumerators in a town in which from its size the work of getting enumerators to attend for ten days would have been particularly burdensome.

The mainstay of the rural enumeration was the inevitable patwári. Twenty-thousand patwáris were shown as enumerators in charge of single blocks, but in reality there were few patwáris who were not employed in assisting the non-official enumerators in charge of other blocks, and many of them had to write the entire record for several blocks. The relatives of patwáris and applicants for patwáris' posts supplied a very large proportion of the non-official enumerators. The other official enumerators were mostly schoolmasters. The only Government servants exempt were the police, whose employment in general census work was considered inexpedient, and the employés of the canal department, who managed at the last moment to obtain a general exemption, thereby to some extent disturbing arrangements already made in Mainpuri and Etáwah. The non-officials most numerous after patwáris' relatives were landholders and their agents and employés. Schoolboys, village mahájans and shopkeepers, Government pensioners, persons on the lookout for Government service were all largely represented.

The date prescribed for the conclusion of appointment of census officers was the 1st October, and none of the districts were materially later in reporting that these arrangements were complete. Changes due to the discovery of the incompetency of persons appointed, to deaths, movements and other causes continued to the very day of the census, and demonstrated the necessity for providing everywhere a small reserve of persons who might be appointed enumerators when it became necessary.

26. **Instruction of Census officers.**—The provisions of the rules as to the instruction of census officers were as follows :—

"The first step in training the agency will be the instruction of the superintendents. District Officers should, by having specimen schedules filled up by them and by examining them on their knowledge of the instructions, thoroughly satisfy themselves of their capacity to instruct the enumerators and supervisors. This testing of the knowledge of the superintendents must in no case be delegated to an officer of a lower standing than a Deputy Collector. The District Officers should insist on having reports from his assistants regarding the qualifications of each superintendent."

"The instruction of enumerators and supervisors will be effected through the superintendents; but it will be necessary for the tahsíldár or other member of the district staff to meet the enumerators and supervisors of each pargana at some convenient place after the superintendent reports them efficient, and to satisfy himself that they thoroughly understand the instructions. Regarding each supervisor, the superintendent will submit through the tahsíldár to the tahsíl officer a separate report as to his efficiency. Instruction to supervisors or enumerators should not be delayed till all are appointed. It should be commenced, especially in the case of supervisors, as soon as each is appointed. No enumerator is to be permitted to make any entries in the books supplied to him until he has made a draft on loose forms for at least ten complete houses and the draft has been tested and approved by the superintendents. In cases where, from the frequency of mistakes in the draft, it appears likely that the schedules as prepared by any enumerator will have many erasures and spoiled pages, the superintendent may direct the enumerator to make a draft for the whole of his block."

"Valuable assistance can be given in the instruction and examination of Census Officers by Gazetted Officers of Departments not directly under the Collector. District Engineers, Opium Officers, Survey and Settlement Officers, all of whom spend much time in the district, can, without much trouble and without any injury to their other work, question and instruct any Census Officers they may meet. A brief report as to the result should be sent to the Tahsíl Officer."

27. **The instructions to enumerators.**—The instructions to enumerators for the province, which contain in brief a summary of the entire work of enumeration, are given below. The outlines of these rules were drafted by the Simla Conference, and the admirably clear and at the same time brief way in which the instructions are expressed is due to them.

1. "**A.—The First Round.**—Beginning from the 15th of January 1891, you will visit every house in your block to which a separate number has been affixed, in the order in which they are entered in the list in your book, and enter in the schedules in that book every person residing in those houses in the manner prescribed below."

2. "You must use black ink, and write very clearly in the character you know best."

3. "You must take a fresh page for each house. If there are more than eight persons in a house, you should continue the entries for that house on the next page, repeating at the top of that page the number of the house in question, with the word 'continued' after it in brackets. You must never begin the entries for a fresh house in the middle of a page, but should leave the unused lines blank."

4. "If the entry for any person in any of the columns of the schedule be the same as that of the person entered on the line above, you must repeat the entry and never write the word 'ditto' or make dots."

5. "If one of the houses on the list be found unoccupied, you should write the word 'empty' after the number of that house on the top of the form."

6. "You are to enter on this visit all persons who ordinarily live and take their meals from the house, even though any of them may be, at the time of your visit, absent for a short time at the bazár, or town, watching crops, fishing, or even for a few days at a wedding or on a pilgrimage, provided they are to be back at the house before the 26th February. After these ordinary residents you should enter the visitors, if any, stopping in the house, but not such as are only there for a day or two, as for a wedding, &c., and will not remain there till the 26th February. In dharamshalas, saráis or temples, you should enter on this occasion only those who usually live there, and not travellers, &c., stopping only a day or a night or so in the building."

7. "Before beginning to make these entries you must read carefully the rules for filling up each column, which are printed (1 to 14), and also the specimen schedule filled up opposite those rules."

8. "Before filling up any of the schedules in the book you should write on loose forms, draft entries for ten houses and submit them to your supervisor for approval. You should not commence making entries in the book until the draft has been approved. Whilst you are filling up these schedules the supervisor will inspect your work, and see if you understand the rules. You should point out to him entries about which you are in doubt, and receive his instructions. You must have completed all the entries in your block by the 1st of February 1891."

9. "**B.—The Second Round.**—At 9 P. M. on the 26th February 1891 you will take this book as already filled in and visit every house in your block in order."

10. "Before you leave to go on your round you must make certain that you yourself will be enumerated as present in the house where you are stopping."

11. "You must summon the chief member of each family residing in the house, and read over to him the entries made for his family in the schedule. You will strike out the entries for persons who are not present, and fill up the form for any person now in the house who was not there when the first visit was made, such as guests, infants newly born, and others."

12. "You are to consider as present all living in or taking their meals from the house, even though any of them may be out fishing or watching in the fields, &c., for the night."

13. "You must enter the letter 'V' for visitor in column 1, after the names of all who have only come to the house for a short time, and do not ordinarily reside there."

14. "If there be no room left on the schedule for the fresh entries above mentioned, you must take a fresh page at the end of the book, and enter on it the house number with the word 'continued' after it, as prescribed in paragraph 3 above."

15. "You must make no alteration whatever in any entry against the name of any person whom you do not strike out because he or she is no longer present. When you so strike out an entry, you must draw the line completely through all the entries relating to that person and not merely through column 1."

16. "You must use red ink only for entries and erasures made on the round on the 26th February."

17. "Whilst going on this round you must visit every house marked 'empty' in your book to see whether any person is now living there."

18. "After visiting as above, all the dwelling-houses, you must go to the dharamshalas, saráis, encampments and landing places, where travellers rest for the night, and enter all particulars in the schedules for the wayfarers, pilgrims, &c., you may find there, and strike out the entries against residents, &c., who are not now present. You should ascertain from the village watchmen if any wandering gang, &c., has come to pitch in your block, and if there be any such you should go and enumerate it as above prescribed for other persons, unless a police office has been deputed from the thána to enumerate them.

19. "If any householder in your block has been given a separate schedule, you should collect it on the morning of the 27th February, and after seeing that the rules have been complied with in filling up the columns, you should stitch or pin it into your book next to the last schedule filled up by you.

20. After your book has been inspected by the supervisor, you will prepare the short abstract printed on the back of the specimen schedule in it, as directed by the supervisor, and when he has certified it to be correct, he will receive it from you and let you go."

21. "According to the Census Act, every person is legally bound to furnish you with such information as is necessary for filling up the schedule; but you are forbidden to ask for any information not required for the purposes of the census, as for instance, the amount of any person's income. Any enumerator detected in extorting money on any pretext connected with the census renders himself liable to punishment under the Census Act or the Penal Code.

C.—Rules for filling up the schedule—

"*Rule* 1, *column* 1 (*serial number and name*).—Enter first the chief resident member of the family, whether male or female, then the other members of the family and their resident servants, if any, and lastly, visitors or temporary residents, after whose name write a (V) in brackets for "visitor." If there be any objection made to giving the name of a female, write the word "female" in this column, adding her relationship to some member of the household."

"If an infant has not yet been named, enter the word 'infant.' The enumerator is not to insist upon any female giving her own or her husband's name. The serial number must not be added till the night of the 25th February."

"*Rule* 2, *column* 2 (*religion*).—Enter here the religion which each person returns, as Hindu, Musalmán, Jain, Christian, Parsi, Sikh, Budhist, Brahmo, Jew. Forest tribes who are not Hindus, Musalmáns, &c., should have the name of their tribe entered in this column, as Bhil, Gond, &c. Low castes, as Chamár, Dom, &c., should be entered by the religion which they themselves return, and no dispute about it is to be raised. Note particularly that Brahmos, Jains and Sikhs will be entered separately from all others who profess themselves Hindus."

Rule 3, *column* 3 (*section of religion*).—Enter the sect of religion followed by each person as they return it, as Vaishnav, Walabacharya, Kabirpanthi, &c., for Hindus, Sunni, Shiah, &c., for Musalmáns, and for Christians enter whether Church of England, Roman Catholic, Presbyterian, Lutheran, Baptist, American Episcopalian, &c. If a Hindu cannot name his sect, the name of the divinity he especially worships should be entered. (The question will be *Ishta devata kaun hai?* or *kis devate se mantar lete ho?* For persons entered in column 2 as Bhils, Gonds, or of other forest tribes, the náme of the *devata* will invariably be entered. If the sect or *devata* cannot be stated, enter "not returned" in this column, but do not leave it blank.

Rule 4, *column* 4 (*caste, &c.*).—Enter the caste of Hindus and Jains, and the tribes of those who have not castes, add the races of Christians, &c.; as Bráhman, Rájput, Bania, Kunbi for Hindus; Pathan, Moghal, &c., for Musalmáns; Eurasian or native Christian for Christians. Do not enter vague terms, such as Hundustani, Marwari, Panjábi, &c."

Rule 5, *column* 5 (*subdivision of caste, &c.*). If the caste has been entered in column 4, enter here the subdivision. For Bráhmans the main subdivision or tribe will be entered, *e. g.*, Kanaujia, Sanadh, Gaur, Sarwariya, &c.; for Rájputs, Banias, Ahirs, &c., the clan or subcaste, *Kaum bans* or *baran*, e. g., Panwar, Chauhan, Agarwal, Oswal, Gwalbans, &c. Ordinarily the entry for this column will be the answer given to a question such as, kaun Bráhman? kaun Bania? kaun Pathan? If Native Christians recognise any caste, the caste should be entered, or they may be entered as Portuguese, Madrasi, &c."

"Some races may not return subdivisons, and in their case, the entry in column 4 should be repeated, but this column must not be left blank."

"*Rule* 6, *column* 6 (*male or female*).—Enter here for each person as either male or female, even though you have written the word' female' in column 1 already."

"*Rule* 7, *column* 7 (*age*).—Enter the number of years each person has completed. For infants less than one year old, enter the word 'infant.'"

"If a person cannot state his or her age exactly, the enumerator should ask the relations or refer to some well-known event of local importance, or, if the person be present, make a guess at the age from the appearance. He must never insist on seeing any female who is not voluntarily produced before him."

"*Rule* 8, *column* 8 (*marriage, &c.*).—Enter each person, whether infant, child, or grown-up, as either married, unmarried, or widowed."

"Children who have been married should be entered as married, even though they may not have begun to actually live with their wives or husbands. Persons who have been married, but have no wife or husband living, should be entered as widowed. The enumerator must accept the statement made by the person, or in the case of children, by their relatives. This column must not be left blank for any one of whatever age."

"*Rule* 9, *column* 9 (*parent tongue*).—Enter the language which each person returns as ordinarily spoken in the household of that person's parents. The language ordinarily spoken throughout these provinces, except in the Himalayan districts, will be entered as Hindustani."

"*Rule* 10, *column* 10 (*birthplace*).—Enter the district and state in which each person was born, and if the person be not born in the North-Western Provinces or Oudh, add the name of the province of birth."

If the person be born out of India, enter the country, as China, Kabul, Ceylon. The names of villages, tahsíls, &c., are not to be given."

" *Rule* 11, *column* 11 (*occupation or means of subsistence*).—**Read this rule very carefully and ask the supervisor about all cases which seem doubtful to you.**—Enter here the exact occupation or means of livelihood of all males and females who do work or live on private property, such as house rent, shares, &c. In the case of children and women who do not work, enter the occupation of the head of their family, or of the person who supports them, adding the word 'dependent,' but do not leave this column unfilled for any one, even an infant. If a person have two or more occupations, enter only the chief one, except when a person owns or cultivates land in addition to another occupation, when both should be entered. If a person be temporarily out of employ, enter the last or ordinary occupation."

"No vague terms should be used, such as 'service,' 'Government service,' 'shop-keeping,' 'writing' or 'labour' &c., but the exact service, the goods sold, the class of writing or labour, must be stated. When a person's occupation is connected with agriculture, it should be stated whether the land is cultivated in person or all let to tenants; if he be an agricultural labourer, it should be stated whether he be engaged by the month or year or is a daily field labourer. Women who earn money by occupations independent of their husbands, such as selling firewood, cowdung cakes, grass, by grinding flour or doing house work for wages, should be shown under those occupations. If a person makes the articles he sells, he should be entered as 'maker and seller' of them. If a person lives on alms, it should be stated whether he is a religious mendicant or an ordinary beggar. When a person is in Government, railway, or municipal service, the special service should be entered first, and the word Government or municipal, &c., after, as clerk, Government; sweeper, municipal; labourer, railway."

" *Rule* 12, *column* 12 (*instruction*).—Enter in this column against each person, whether grown-up, child or infant, either *learning, literate, illiterate.* Enter all those as *learning* who are under instruction, either at home or at school or college. Enter as literate those who are able to both read and write any language, but are not under instruction as above. Enter as illiterate those who are not under instruction, and who do not know how to both read and write, or who can read but not write, or can sign their own name but not read."

" *Rule* 13, *column* 13 (*language known by literate*).—Enter here the language which those shown as *literate* in column 12 can both read and write, and if a person knows how to read and write English as well as a vernacular, enter 'English also.'

"This column is not to be filled up for those shown in column 12 as learning or illiterate, and except where English is known, only one language should be entered, that which he knows best."

" *Rule* 14, *column* 14 (*infirmities*).—If any person be blind of both eyes, or deaf and dumb from birth, or insane, or suffering from corrosive leprosy, enter the name of the infirmity in this column."

" Do not enter those blind of one eye only, or who have become deaf and dumb after birth, or who are suffering from white leprosy only."

These rules, which could not themselves be lengthened without the risk of confusing the weaker vessels amongst the enumerators, were supplemented by instructions to supervisors on the points on which after having the enumeration instructions acted on, I found further elucidation called for. The instructions to enumerators that if a Hindu could not name his sect, he should be asked the name of the divinity he especially worshipped was due to a suggestion by Mr. W. Crooke, Collector of Mirzapur. The result will be referred to in another chapter of the report. The instructions to supervisors are on record for the information of later census officers and need not be repeated here. Further supplementary instructions were issued in a circular dated 29th January 1891, after some progress had been made in the final record. It may be referred to as showing the points on which the actual working of the rules showed mistakes to be likely. The forms and instructions for the use of each census officer were issued in a compact form. Superintendents and superior officers had a copy of a Census Manual supplied to them, containing all instructions issued. Supervisors were supplied with a hand-book containing :—

" 1*st*.—A statement giving details as to the boundaries of blocks included in his circle and the names of the enumerators."

" 2*nd*—Instructors to supervisors regarding the duties especially due from them."

" 3*rd*.—A copy of the instructions to emunerators and specimens of all forms which have to be filled up by enumerators."

4*th*.—A blank form of supervisor's abstract to be filled up by supervisors, immediately after the final enumeraticn, from the enumerator's abstracts and forwarded to charge superintendents.

5*th*.—A set of exemplar questions, such as should ordinarily be asked in filling up the schedules.

They were subsequently provided each with a copy of a catechism drawn up by Mr. Bullock, then Collector of Bijnor, in which the census instructions were repeated in a way likely to attract attention in the form of question and answer. It was the consideration of the cost which prevented Mr. Bullock's very useful catechism being circulated to all enumerators, to whom it would certainly have been of service.

Enumetators were each provided with a strongly bound book or books containing—

1*st*.—A sheet of instructions to enumerators as to their duties and rules for filling up the enumerator's schedule.

2*nd*.—A specimen schedule with entries completed to exemplify how the schedules are to be filled up.

3*rd*.—A block list containing a detailed list copied from the village or ward list, of all houses, &c., within the block, which have to be visited by the enumerator in the course of his enumeration. The entries in the block lists will, as prescribed in Rule 32, be made under the instructions of the supervisor, generally by the enumerator himself, or when necessary, by the patwári or the supervisor.

4*th*.—Blank schedules sufficient to allow one for each house or other place to be visited by the enumerator and to provide some margin for houses containing more residents than eight, that being the greatest number which can be entered in a single schedule.

5*th*.—A blank form for an abstract to be filled up by the enumerator immediately after the final enumeration.

28. **Amendments suggested in census rules**.—Officers were after the census called on to suggest alterations which experience had shown to be necessary on the rules for enumeration. Certain of the alterations suggested may conveniently be noted here. Those of them which are of special importance will find more detailed notice in other parts of the report.

In regard to the instructions regarding the record of castes, sub-castes and sects, several district reports have suggested that fuller instructions should have been given in the rules. The most extensive suggestion, that made by the Collector of Allahabad, was that exhaustive lists of all religions, castes, sub-castes, sects and mother-tongues should have been supplied to each superintendent, who should, when any entry not in the list was found, enquire specially as to whether it was correct and collect information regarding it—similar suggestions were made from Mainpuri, Agra and Etáwah. As regards the census which is past, it is enough to point out that there were, when it was taken, no materials whatsoever available from which such lists at least as regards sects, sub-castes and occupations could be made. As regards the future census, I very much doubt the expediency of circulating any such guiding lists. The lists would be regarded as standard and the result would be to deprive future Census Officers of an opportunity of correcting or adding to the information already collected. Such lists can safely be used only when the abstracted returns of a census come into the hands of a superior officer, who would know how to utilize them. For such officers they will be available in the tables of the present census.

The Collector of Etáwah, as already mentioned, recommends the preparation of a census map, and makes another useful suggestion which might be incorporated in the instructions to District Officers at next census. It is that a census order book should be kept up in each district, so that a record of all the numerous orders which have to be issued for the guidance of census subordinates and of all the points in which difficulties occur in district census administration may be on record for the use of succeeding Collectors in succeeding enumerations. Several officers point out that the record of the age of children under one year of age by the use of the word *bachcha* has led to a considerable error in the age tables. The subject will be referred to in connection with the age tables. Suggestions as to payment of superintendents, supervisors and enumerators have already been referred to.

On the other hand, the Collector of Farukhabad, a gentleman who went in most thoroughly for census work in his own district, was of opinion that "clear and definite as the instructions were, they aimed at too much." The Collector of Moradabad similarly remarks that the forms err on the side of over-elaboration. The questions thus raised are large ones, which will have to be dealt with in consideration of the value of the information acquired by certain of the census tables. There can be little doubt, I believe, that once is enough to attempt to collect statistics in regard to some of the information embodied in the tables of the present census.

29. **The use of the Kayathi character.**—Instruction to enumerators and forms of census schedules were issued in English and in the Urdu and Devanagri characters. District Officers were consulted as to whether it would be necessary or useful to issue instructions in the Kayathi character, which is largely employed in the eastern districts. Replies were almost unanimous in asserting that such an issue was unnecessary, that all enumerators, though they habitually wrote Kayathi, could read Devanagri. The specimens of Kayathi handwriting received from various districts showed further that the employ-

ment of the character in printed forms to be issued for the use of all districts was impossible. The Kayathi character varies from district to district so much that the patwári who writes the Kayathi of one tract could not read with any accuracy that used even in a neighbouring district In some districts, Kayathi was simply a current form of Devanagri, as full in its list of letters and as accurate in its spelling as that character; elsewhere it degenerated into a roughly phonetic system in which all distinction of long and short vowels is overlooked and in a majority of words no account is taken of vowels at all.

30. **The characters in which enumerators records were written.**—Though forms were not for these reasons printed in Kayathi (or Hindi as it is commonly called in contradistinction to Nagri) it was the only character which could be written by the large majority of enumerators in many districts and particularly in Oudh. Appendix IV shows the characters reported as used by enumerators from the various districts. The total figures are—

Enumerators using English	...	...	...	...	...	863
Ditto ditto Urdu	...	...	...	...	...	54,244
Ditto ditto Nagri	...	...	...	...	...	80,118
Ditto ditto Kayathi	...	...	...	...	...	40,197

These returns decidedly underestimate the use of the Kayathi character. Basti, for instance, returns 7,506 enumerators using Nagri and only 201 using the Kayathi. The great majority of the patwáris in the district to my personal knowledge write their village records in Kayathi, and I have no doubt the census record was written in the same way, and that Basti had at least as large a proportion of enumerators' books in Kayathi as Gorakhpur, where enumerators are equally divided between the two characters. Again, Azamgarh returns no Kayathi books and Ballia only 568, whilst the neighbouring and similar Gházipur shows 2,273 writing Kayathi against 900 writing Nagri.

I consider that it is fairly certain that Kayathi was, in the province as a whole, very nearly as much employed as Nagri. This fact constituted a very real addition to the work of abstraction. The Kayathi character was rarely as clear and legible as Nagri, and its use delayed work by abstractors as well as gave rise to doubt of the entire accuracy of the abstracts.

It is very possible for district officers to discourage the use of the Kayathi character effectively. Patwáris nearly all learn Nagri in their boyhood in the Government schools, and only lapse into Kayathi after they leave school. It would be perfectly possible to insist on all the younger patwaris at least writing Devanagri, and when Kayathi disappears from the patwári's book, it will, I have no doubt, not be long in disappearing from ordinary use. For my own part, I believe that it would be possible within a generation to introduce into general use a character very nearly as current as the Persian and far more legible, I mean the Roman character. A fifth character, which does not appear in the returns, was, as I found in at least one district, not absent from the census offices, the mahajáni, a very modified form of Hindi which required special men to read it. This character was however employed only to an inappreciable extent, and was, where employed, modified to such an extent, to suit the comprehension of persons outside the trading guild, that the enumerator felt he was entitled to call his production Hindi.

The best average work from a census point of view was, without doubt, done by the Urdu-writing enumerators. Where Urdu and Hindi are found together, the man who knows Urdu has almost invariably a better practical education. Where care was taken that the Urdu employed should not be too "shikast," the Urdu work was very satisfactory. The preliminary record written out at leisure was, in general, as legible as could be desired, but the corrections made on the final night, rapidly written in, were however often so illegible as to give trouble in the abstraction office. The work done by the enumerators who wrote English was not satisfactory; they were mostly railway employés, foreigners to the province, and the caste and sect entries made by them were wrong in a considerable proportion. Attempts to translate vernacular names for occupations also gave trouble.

31. **Drafts of the enumeration record.**—The rules as to instruction of enumerators provided that each enumerator should fill up draft schedules for ten houses and have them inspected and corrected by his supervisor before he set to work with the final census record. Printed forms on thin paper were provided for these drafts. With men of ordinary education and intelligence such preliminary instruction with occasional subsequent references to superior authority ought to have been enough to secure a correct record, but a good many district officers were so impressed with the necessity of having all entries made by enumerators tested by the superior staff, that they directed that a complete rough draft should be made on plain paper of all entries for an enumerator's block. These entries were in some districts tested throughout by the supervisors and each of them to some extent tested by charge superintendents. There could be no more effective way of securing as far as possible the entire accuracy of the record. The expense of prescribing such a draft for general adoption at next census would not be prohibitive. Rs. 10,000 would provide and distribute the necessary forms. All the enumerators in six districts of the province had to undertake the extra work implied at the present census. In other districts, many of the superintendents and supervisors had such drafts made by their own enumerators. I would suggest it as a question for decision before next census whether such a draft should not then be prescribed for all enumerators. An alternative would be to alter the dates prescribed for the preparation of the final record in rural tracts from the 15th to the 30th January to somewhat earlier dates and to prescribe the complete preliminary draft in towns only. It was found that there was so little movement in the months of January and February in rural tracts that alterations owing to this cause had very infrequently to be made on the census night. The dates could therefore be moved into December without producing any risk of the record being badly cut about owing to the movement of population. This would allow January and February for testing by the district and superior census staff. Records badly cut about owing to mistakes of the enumerators could be rewritten. This would save the good enumerators from the extra work of writing out their record twice and would probably be very nearly as effective as the preliminary draft in ensuring good work. It would not be absolutely as satisfactory, as alterations would of course be somewhat more numerous than in a record rewritten just

before the census. As regards towns, I consider it would be inexpedient to put the dates for the preparation of the final record further away from the census day, and that to secure a good record a preliminary draft should be prepared for all houses. It is absolutely impossible in a town of any size for superintendents, even if devoting all their time to census work, to test each enumerator's work in the fourteen days which on the present occasion intervened between the completion of the record and the final census.

32. **The testing of the enumeration record.**—Throughout the whole of the months of December, January and February, the entire strength of the district staff, in addition to the specially appointed Census Officers, were employed in testing either draft or faired enumeration records. The testimony of district reports as to the general correctness of the record so tested is almost unanimous. In regard to the record of the numbers of the people the remarks of District Officers bear very explicit evidence to the effect that the record approaches as close to entire accuracy as it possibly can; that in fact the omissions, though they may be proved by age statistics, cannot be detected by testing on the spot; that the parda-nashin woman or unmarried girl, who is omitted from the record, is undiscoverable by the enumerator or superior Census Officer in any way. This, considering the readiness with which the people answered all questions and the interest they displayed in the operations, appears extraordinary, but it is the only conclusion which one who has tested census records at all extensively can come to. The result of the census in showing in equality of the sexes is almost as certain in the best administered district as in the worst. I myself tested enumeration in fully half the districts of the province after the record had begun to take final shape. The total omissions I discovered were very few indeed, and were not at all markedly greater amongst females than amongst males. The testimony of other officers is similar. The Jaunpur report quotes a remark by Mr. Moreland, the Census Officer, on this subject—," I tested the work of some 500 enumerators when in camp. I think the actual enumeration was extremely well done. In only two cases did I find that any person had been omitted." The Deputy Commissioner of Fyzabad remarks—," In numbering houses no places were omitted where there was any likelihood of people passing the night, and it can be confidently said that on the night of enumeration no one escaped enumeration except *perhaps* a few parda-nashin women." The Collector of Benares says,—" all reports point to the great accuracy of the work. A careful numbering and an energetic house-to-house testing could not but produce a good result." The Collector of Muzaffarnagar says,—" I may therefore confidently say that the census returns for this district are, as to numbers at least, substantially correct, and that there is no reason to believe that there has been any extensive omission either of males or females. Remarks to the same effect are made in almost all other districts.

Mistakes in details, discovered and corrected in testing, are noted by almost all districts to have occurred, especially in regard to the entries in the sect, sub-caste and occupation columns. Remarks on the subject will more properly find place in the chapters on these subjects.

33. **The final enumeration.**—The final enumeration came off on the night of the 26th February 1891. The date fixed was in every way a suitable

one. There was moon enough to give all the light possible, and yet it was distant enough from the date of the full moon to allow the movement due to the bathing in the Ganges, which takes place on every full moon, to have almost entirely ceased. The day was nct auspicious for Hindu marriages and was not close to any auspicious day. There was therefore no considerable movement of marriage parties to be provided for. It was far enough advanced in the cold weather to allow ample time for preparation and yet not so far advanced as even in the hottest districts to make it likely that officers would be driven in from the subsequent testing by the heat of the weather. Even in the districts in which it was found most difficult to get persons to perform the more monotonous and laborious duties of enumerators connected with the preparation of the record, there was no reluctance or backwardness on the part of the enumerators in carrying through the final correction necessary to show the population as it stood on the appointed night. The enumerators for the time regarded themselves as the heroes of the hour, and their work was carried through with something like enthusiasm. I spent the night unexpectedly in Cawnpore, and found that even in the Cantonments, with the census administration of which there had, at an earlier stage, been cause to find fault, the final enumeration was carried through with the greatest promptitude and good-will, and that even after spending several hours of the night wandering about correcting the final record, enumerators began on the spot to prepare the abstracts which had to be promptly communicated to the district authorities.

34. **The attitude of the people.**—The attitude of the people was throughout entirely satisfactory. A few districts, Rae Bareli, Bijnor, Dehra Dún, Bulandshahr, Cawnpore report that rumour amongst the lowest classes connected the census with taxation, with a water tax in the last named; but, only in the wilder parts of Mirzapur, did any of the wilder scares which connected themselves with the earlier censuses, find place. A rumour was, there, said to be current that it was intended to deport persons to Burma for sacrifice at the laying of the foundation of some Government fort there. From Benares and Hardwár only was there reported any difficulty in obtaining answers to the questions, and there only from a few persons, Gorkhas in the first named city and outlandish pilgrims from hill states in the other. All other Districts Officers report that the census was regarded by the body of the people either with apathy or with positive interest. Many of the reports give evidence of a keen interest taken by the people in the enumeration. The Deputy Commissioner of Gonda notes how they ran out to meet inspecting officers with the wooden number tickets in their hands, and that there was in his district no friction of any sort between any one of 5,386 Census Officers and the people. The Collector of Farrukhabad says,—" there was no friction or difficulty, the work went on smoothly." Elsewhere, the willingness with which the people met the enumerators with lights, is noted. This last fact was brought prominently to my notice in Cawnpore. Even in this, the largest trading city of the provinces, where the personal influence of Government officers might be supposed to be least, all doors were kept open and all streets were lighted by lamps at every door, till the enumerators had passed.

35. **The preliminary abstraction.**—Two days were allowed to supervisors after the final enumeration to correct the entries made by enumerators on the

final round. Enumerators were instructed immediately after this testing to prepare abstracts showing the number of houses and the population, male and female, residents and visitors, for their blocks through supervisors and charge superintendents to the Tahsíldárs. Seven days were allowed to District Officers for the collection and collation of these returns. After this not later than the 7th March, except in Kumaun and Garhwál, the district totals had to be telegraphed to Allahabad and Simla. It was by a mistake, as it can only be called, that an extension to the 12th March was allowed to the Kumaun districts. The Deputy Commissioner of Kumaun, the officer of most experience in the Himalayan districts, insisted that this extension was absolutely necessary and had it sanctioned. On the 7th March he proved it unnecessary by telegraphing his own totals, whilst the Deputy Commissioner of Garhwál, who had been neutral as to the need for the extension, availed himself of it, although I have no doubt the thoroughness with which all census arrangements were made in his district would have, had he thought it necessary, enabled him to report his totals at the same time as other districts. Mr. P. J. White, Deputy Commissioner of Sultánpur, reported his district totals by the morning of the 1st March. The late General Azim-ud-din, in charge of the Rámpur census, followed a good second on the afternoon of the 1st March, Mr. L. C. Porter, Census Officer at Hardoi, Mr. Steel at Farukhabad and Messrs. Lambe Bullock and LaTouche at Jalaun, Bijnor and Aligarh, all telegraphed their totals on the 2nd March. Except Garhwál which reported on the 10th, there was no district in the provinces which had not telegraphed its figures by the evening of the 7th March. In both Garhwál and Kumaun, the difficulties to be overcome were great. A fall of snow had taken place just before the date fixed for submission of the returns, and the roads in the northern parts of these districts were almost impassable. The provincial total population, according to these telegrams, was reported to be 46,922,690 for British districts and 799,160 for Native States. As compared with the final figures the population of the British districts was 17,605 or ·037 per cent. too high, that of Native States, 6,669 or ·84 per cent. too high. Statements sent by post a few days later amended the telegraphic reports to some extent.

Appendix V compares the figures so reported for each district with those finally found to be correct. The highest proportion of error was in Benares ·7 per cent. and in Kumaun ·69 per cent. In the great majority of districts the error was inappreciable. These abstracts were prepared under great pressure as to the time their preparation was to occupy and would have been more correct had more time been allowed. Their conparative correctness is however enough to show that any simple abstraction of census figures can be promptly carried out through enumerators at a cost practically *nil*, and with a correctness, to all intents and purposes, as great as that attained by the elaborate processes of the census office.

The course of the general arrangements for enumeration have now been indicated. Enumeration in tracts or circumstances in which special variations of the rules were necessary may be briefly referred to.

36. **The Railway Census.**—The Railway Census was, under the orders of the Government of India, carried out entirely by the railway staff, who

provided and trained the enumerators and took the entire census within the railway fencing. As a rule, the work was satisfactorily done. On the Oudh and Rohilkhand Railway, Mr. F. E. G. Walton, Chief Engineer, was in charge and had all preliminary arrangements carried out in a most complete way. On the Bengal and North-Western Railway Mr. J. Walker, Traffic Superintendent, though later in starting work, carried it through finally no less satisfactorily. The officer in charge of the census in Farukhabad specially mentioned the services rendered by the local railway officers in charge there. At Allahabad on the East Indian Railway, Mr. J. Craven and his Assistant Mr. Huddlestone, took pains in having the preliminary arrangements and training of the staff effectively carried out. On the other hand, there were railway administrations in which it was found difficult in the extreme to get census work taken in hand and in which arrangements remained unsatisfactory to the last. As a rule, the railway authorities provided and trained a full staff of well-educated enumerators, but the fact that the majority of them were not natives of the province and were not well acquainted with the caste, sects or even occupation of the province, prevented the record in railway blocks from being on the average as correct as outside the railway boundaries. The census of persons in trains was carried through by a staff of special enumerators, provided at all stations for persons who alighted from trains and at certain fixed stations for trains which passed at sunrise on the 27th. This record written in great haste afterwards gave trouble in the abstraction offices and has perhaps added to our lists of sub-castes a number of names which are not likely to be recognized hereafter. On some of the lines there was some trouble in obtaining the preliminary abstracts and the records, so much so that several Collectors have suggested that in future the superintendence of arrangements on railway lines be left to the district authorities, the railway authorities being only called on to provide the necessary enumerators. I do not however believe that this plan would work as well as that prescribed by the rules. All that is wanted is that the training of the railway enumerators should be closely supervised by the district officials, and that Collectors should be instructed to provide enumerators where the railway authorities found it difficult so obtain natives of Upper India for the work. The returns, when finally ready, should be made over to the local Census Officers direct, without the intervention of any of the railway superior officers being necessary.

37. **The census in cantonments.**—Enumeration of the military lines in cantonments was carried out by the military authorities. So far as the troops were concerned, the enumeration was well enough done, but that of the native servants and camp-followers of British regiments was in general very badly done, the entries being frequently incomprehensible. Discovery of the meaning of one of them was due to the ingenuity of the Census Commissioner for India, when the return reached his office. It was from Cawnpore: several regimental servants were entered as speaking a mother tongue Mori. The interpretation was Moorish, the term by which a Mess Sergeant would generally denominate the mother tongue of the Muhammadan Mess servants. Here, again, a closer connection between the district authorities and the enumerators is necessary. No natives of India should, as a rule, be enumerated by officers or men of British regiments. The enumeration

of cantonments outside military lines was done in the usual way under the orders of the Cantonment Magistrates. The enumerators were of the usual class, and the work in all respects in most cantonments similar to that in the neighbouring municipalities.

38. **Enumeration of travellers.**—Special arrangements were made for the enumeration of persons travelling by boat or road during the night of the census. Enumerators were stationed at intervals along all lines of road and at all ferries, and, as they enumerated a traveller, supplied him with a ticket to prevent re-enumeration. On the Pánjab frontiers, by special arrangement the North-Western Provinces men enumerated all travellers leaving this side, whilst the Panjáb men enumerated all crossing from the Panjáb. A supply of tickets for distribution to men entering the North-Western Provinces from the Panjáb was sent to the Deputy Commissioners of bordering Panjáb districts. As already mentioned, the date fixed for the final census was a suitable one, and there was therefore very little trouble given by large assemblages at fairs. A few of the worshippers at the Magh Mela still lingered at Allahabad and on the roads leading away from it, but were nowhere in great numbers. At Ajudhya there was not a very large assemblage for which special enumerators were provided. The Kumbh Mela at Brindaban was one of the most considerable of the gatherings to be dealt with, but was not extensive enough to be really troublesome. At Hardwár the number of pilgrims was so small as to be enumerated by the ordinary staff. For a province full of holy places, this list of religious fairs is a small one.

The Boat Census.—A very important part of the operations in the Lower Provinces was here, except on the lower reaches of the Gogra and Ganges, not of importance. On these rivers, enumerators were kept at the ghát̃s for twenty-four hours, it being believed that none of the boats in these provinces go on for more than twenty-four hours, without drawing up at a landing place. In districts in which these rivers formed the boundary between the North-Western Provinces and Behar, it was arranged that boats going up the river should be enumerated by the Behar men, those going down by North-Western Provinces' enumerators.

39. **Enumeration in forest and desert tracts.**—A variation of the general rule, that the final enumeration of the population should be on the night of the 26th February was permitted by the Government of India in forest and desert tracts, where a day final census was permitted. The tracts in which this variation was permitted in the North-Western Provinces were, except in the Kumaun and Garhwál districts, not extensive. They consisted of—

(*a*) defined forest tracts in the Himalayan and Sub-Himalayan parts of—

(1) Dehra Dún.
(2) Bijnor.
(3) Tarái.
(4) Pilibhít.
(5) Sahéranpur.

(*b*) outlying gate houses and gangsmen's huts on the Indian Midland Railway in Jhánsi and three forest tracts in the same district.

(c) a number of villages in the wilder parts of the Robertsganj, Dudhi and Chunár tahsíls of the Mirzapur district.

(d) a few of the larger swamps in the Basti district in which persons engaged in hot weather rice cultivation lived in scattered huts.

In these tracts the population is scattered about in small camps or villages, and owing to the fear of wild beasts or the inaccessibility of the places where the people to be enumerated were to be found, enumerators could not be expected to visit them in the night.

The following statement gives an estimate of the population so enumerated by day outside the Kumaun and Garhwál districts and the Native State of Garhwál :—

District.	Total population.		
	Males.	Females.	Total.
Debra Dún ...	29,171	21,909	51,080
Sahâranpur...	829	372	1,201
Bijnor ...	3,763	2,883	6,646
Pilibhít ...	3,329	1,648	4,977
Mirzapur ...	13,333	12,468	25,801
Jhánsi ...	167	114	281
Basti ...	254	11	265
Tarái ...	843	246	1,089
Total ...	51,689	39,651	91,340

40. **The Census in the Himalayas.**—In the Himalayan parts of the Kumaun Division a still wider variation from the rules was considered necessary, for several reasons. The only season in which many of the villages in either district contain their full resident population is the end of the rains and beginning of the cold weather. Immediately after this in the outer tracts, the migration to the Bhábar sets in, and the residents in the higher villages below the Himalayan peaks are driven southwards with their cattle by the snow. On the 26th February, many of the villages in the tracts which migrate to the Bhá-are nearly empty and the upper patties are a waste of deep snow absolutely uninhabited. In the hot weather a large proportion of the men are employed in the hill stations as *jhampanies* and the like, and the Bhotias of the upper patties are absent in Thibet on their trading tours. It is therefore clear that a census which is to ascertain for executive purposes the ordinary resident population of the villages should be taken in October, and that the February census would be of value only for Imperial purposes and to show the extent of the periodic migration. These considerations led to a modification of the rules regarding the dates at which the preliminary record was to be made. It was resolved that the preliminary record in Kumaun and Garhwál should be made, except in towns and in the Bhábar, in October, and that in towns a special hot weather census should be taken in addition to that to be taken later for Imperial purposes. The special rules for Kumaun and Garhwál provided that the figures of the preliminary record should be abstracted by the patwári staff to show the resident population of the hill villages when at their fullest. The final correction in the hill tracts and the ordinary census

in the Bhábar taken as usual in February would show the extent of the migration and the cold weather population of patties and villages. Owing to the way in which the population is scattered over a wide, and, particularly in February, scattered tract, Kumaun and Garhwál are vastly more difficult fields for enumeration than any of the sub-Himalayan forest tracts ; and added to this, is the still more serious difficulty that the state of education made it impossible for the districts to produce the requisite number of enumerators educated enough to work alone. Garhwál had 1,128 enumerators for an area of 5,629 square miles ; Kumaun showed in the returns 5,987 enumerators, but by far the greater part of these were purely nominally so. They were lambardárs, who had to depend on the patwári to do all the entries for them. As a matter of fact, Mr. Giles informed me in January that he had only 600 genuine enumerators for the 7,151 square miles of district. It was necessary therefore to allow time for the patwári to work over the 40 square miles, which in these districts form a patwári's circle, during the time fixed for the final correction. The period of one day allowed in other forest tracts was, in these districts, extended to ten days. Settlement operations were in progress in Garhwál and Kumaun, had sent a number of patwáris to help. For census purposes it was necessary to provide and pay substitutes, so that in these two districts Rs. 641-0-0 were expended in payment of supervisors, as well as Rs. 100 for payment of enumerators in the Bhábar. The census in both Kumaun and Garhwál was from the paucity of available enumerators, the nature of the country, and the migratory habits of the population, an extremely difficult one, but from what I saw of the enumeration record, it was well done in both districts. The prompt way in which the preliminary abstracts were made up has been already mentioned.

41. **Enumeration in Native States, Rampur.**—Census operations in Rámpur were conducted almost precisely as in a British district, the late *vice* President, General Azim-ud-din, corresponding direct with the Superintendent, Census Operations. The usual progress reports were sent and work in Rámpur reported and watched in the usual way. I visited Rámpur in December after all the preliminary arrangements had been completed and found that they had been made carefully and judiciously. The preparation of the lists of numerators and estimates of the books required for them had taken more than usual care, a preliminary rough census having been made in order that the estimate of persons to be enumerated and paper to be used by each enumerator should be accurate. The only variation from the rules observed was in the number of enumerators and blocks. The blocks were considerably larger on an average than in any British district, but with so low a standard of education as in the rural parts of Rámpur, this was absolutely inevitable, particularly as a number of the patwáris were employed at the time on the survey of the State. As far as possible, this defect was remedied by the appointment of a specially strong superior staff. Two special paid inspectors were employed and travelling allowance given to a number of the headquarters staff whilst on tour inspecting census work. The State itself printed forms for the original draft made by the enumerators and employed the Imperial forms for the fair copies only. I suggested in consequence of the size of the blocks that a day census should be taken to allow the enumerators more time to get round their

blocks. The Vice President, however, considered this unnecessary, and owing to the strict injunctions laid on the village headmen and chaukidárs to assist the enumerators in their rounds, it proved to be so. Mounted officers of the Rámpur Military Force were employed on the census night in addition to the regular census staff in all parts of the State in making rounds to see that all enumerators were at their posts. Rámpur, as already mentioned, was second in reporting its totals by telegraph, much ahead of any other Native State in India.

42. **Tehri-Garhwal.**—The Native State of Garhwál was enumerated under the instructions of the Commissioner of Kumaun. The returns for the State were received regularly and satisfactorily. No final report was, however, submitted, and in stating that the census was conducted on the same lines as in British Garhwál, I rely on information given me by the Deputy Commissioner of Garhwál, who, under the Commissioner's orders, inspected the arrangements in patties bordering on his districts. The officer in charge of the census was Babu Raghunath Bhattacharji, the Private Secretary to the Regent.

43. **Enumeration by private schedules.**—A special form of enumeration which requires mention was that by private schedules. The instructions on the subject were as follows :—

"Europeans and Eurasians will be supplied with special European schedules which they will fill up for themselves, their families and their European servants. The necessary instructions will be printed on the reverse of the schedule. Such Europeans and Eurasians as can in 'the opinion of the District Officer be trusted to enumerate their native servants and dependents also will be supplied with blank forms in English in all respects similar to the enumerators' schedules, and brief instuctions as to how they are to be filled up. Native gentlemen who wish to have private schedules for themselves and their families and who undertake to have them filled up in English or Urdu will be provided with household schedules and instructions similar to those last mentioned in either language. No private schedules will be issued in Hindi."

The opinions of officers vary greatly as to the effectiveness of this form of enumeration. In many districts the issue of private schedules was kept to the lowest possible limits, whilst in others it was fairly freely used. The total number of such schedules issued as per returns received was as follows :—

In English	4,117
In Urdu	3,436

Details by districts are given in Appendix VI. The Dehra Dún return was blank, although no doubt such schedules were issued there also. On the whole, I believe that the Urdu schedules were well done. The gentlemen to whom they were issued were all of superior station and education. They valued the privilege and consequently did their best to deserve it. I am of opinion that, within certain well-defined limits as to the status and education of persons to whom such schedules are to be issued, the system might be extended to some extent. Too extensive use of these schedules would give trouble in abstraction, as the locse schedules often get loose from the book to which they are tacked. The schedules issued to Europeans were not as well filled up as they might have been. In not a few instances there were complaints by District

Officers that Europeans to whom schedules had been issued had, with trouble, been compelled to fill them up. How little regard was paid to the instructions printed on the schedules by many Europeans will sufficiently appear from an inspection of the European sect tables, where in spite of exhortations in the instructions that exact sect designations should be entered, it was found necessary to enter large numbers of persons as Protestant unspecified, and so on. All that can be done is to insist at next census on these schedules being examined by the person who collects them. Enumeration by enumerators would be impossible as in the few cases Europeans were enumerated by natives, the returns were incomprehensible.

44. The cost of the enumeration.—The following statement compares the cost of enumeration at the present and at last census under each of the principal heads, excluding superintendence, the figures under which for enumeration and compilation cannot conveniently be distinguished.

Heads.	1881.			1891.		
	Rs.	a.	p.	Rs.	a.	p.
Establishment including pay of enumerators and supervisors	19,103	14	7	14,572	9	11
Contingent charges in districts	6,229	10	6	6,932	7	9
Total district charges ...	25,333	9	1	21,505	1	8
Cost of forms { Printing and binding	28,813	3	6	40,217	10	10
Cost of forms { Distribution to districts	2,698	7	11	7,686	14	11
Total forms ...	31,511	11	5	47,904	9	9
GRAND TOTAL ...	56,845	4	6	69,409	11	5

The total cost in 1891 was Rs. 12,564-6-11 in excess of that in 1881.

Under the head of district charges there has been a considerable saving. The details as shown in the form of account prescribed by the Government of India are as follows :—

		Rs.	a.	p.
1	District office establishment, including amounts paid to supervisors and enumerators ...	14,572	9	11
2	Contingent charges of establishment	1,689	7	11
3	House numbering	114	4	9
4	Lights, ink, paper for drafts, &c., ...	2,464	12	2
5	Special travelling allowance	250	9	9
6	Freight of schedules, &c., from stations and landing places	2,413	5	2
	Total	21,505	1	8

The expenditure was very unequally distributed in the different districts. Appendix VII shows the expenditure in each district, together with the incidence of expenditure on population. It varies from 1,447-5-2 or Rs. 2-9-1 per 1,000 in Kumaun, where the heavy charges are due to the necessity for payment of supervisors and enumerators to Rs. 180-15-4 or as. 1-7 per thousand in Basti.

The only item in the above account of district charges in which any retrenchment can be thought possible, in a future census, is that for the pay ment of district office establishment. District Officers were authorized to entertain, from the 1st August till the abstraction office was opened, one muharrir on Rs. 15 a month, and for each tahsíl one muharrir on Rs. 12 a month, from the time the distribution of enumeration forms began, until the completed enumeration record was despatched to headquarters. They were specially enjoined to be economical even in these appointments, and a good many districts did not employ the full staff sanctioned. District Officers were, after the census, asked whether they considered that in future this paid staff could be dispensed with. A few districts (Muttra, Dehra, Etáwah, Ballia and Agra) all of them except Agra and Etáwah "light," considered either that the tahsíl muharrirs or the whole of the paid staff might be abolished; but all other officers consulted pronounced without hesitation that the staff allowed was the minimum possible. I fully agree with this opinion. In a district or tahsíl with average work, it would be absolutely impossible for the staff besides their usual work and the extra work imposed on almost all of them as Census Officers to undertake the heavy clerical work necessary in connection with the distribution of forms, fairing of census registers, issue of census orders, and the like. Even were it possible it should not be attempted, as a good paid man whose special work is to keep census arrangements up to date, and who cannot have the excuse of alleging that he was prevented from doing so by his other work, is in my opinion absolutely necessary both at the sadar and at tahsíls. In two districts English clerks were allowed, in consideration of the specially heavy work in the district English office. I doubt whether for purely census work they were necessary. In Meerut a paid general superintendent was allowed. In connection with the subject the following remarks by Mr. Rose, the Collector of Farrukhabad, may be quoted :—

"The enumeration staff must always in a large measure be provided by official departments, and the agency which is most largely employed must necessarily be the village patwáris. The patwári prepares the schedules not only of the block of which he is the appointed enumerator, but in many instances of every block in his circle. The enumerators actually appointed often have not the necessary education and intelligence to fill up with any approach to accuracy a somewhat complicated form. They are well able with previous instruction to verify and if necessary to modify the entries in the schedule, to bring them into accordance with existing facts on the night of the census; but this is a much less difficult matter than the preliminary preparation of the schedule. I found much difficulty in Mainpuri in obtaining non-official agency with the necessary qualifications for the work in the interior of a sparsely-populated district; and this remark will apply to Farrukhabad with much the same force as to Mainpuri; it is not easy to find men of education and intelligence. At the same time I am not prepared to suggest that at any future census the agency for enumeration should be a paid agency. On the other hand, I am distinctly of opinion that the agency employed *in supervision* should be paid. The District Officer knows better than any one else the difficulties which arise in his administration by the employment during several months of a lage number of his officials upon work which is outside the limits of their ordinary duties. It simply means that their ordinary duties are neglected. To take, for instance, the kanúngos and patwáris. The village papers were not filed for the simple reason that the field work of these officials was in abeyance because of their employment in census work. It was necessary and it was inevitable, but at the same time when congratulations are freely bestowed upon the slight amount of expenditure with which the important results of the census have been attained, it is well to remember that the general administration has suffered by the economy."

Another suggestion was made by the officer in charge of census in Etáwah who believed that the amount sanctioned for the clerical staff should be devoted to the payment of a General Superintendent for census work as in Meerut.

The question raised has already been referred to in para. 24. There can be no doubt that by the combination of census and current revenue work the patwári and kanúngo staff were worked very hard indeed during the census year, but I cannot consider that some delay in filing patwári's papers in a particular year can be regarded as an injury to administration. I believe that the form which relief should take is the curtailment of the patwári and kanúngo's special work in the census year and not in the payment of a special census supervising staff. The greatest enthusiast for village papers cannot allege that the omission of the khasra rounds in a single year out of ten would in any way injure the value of the patwári's papers for the next Settlement Officer.

45. **Reasons for the higher expenditure in 1891.**—The items in which the expenditure in enumeration in 1891 exceeded that in 1881 are those relating to the preparation and supply of forms, a subject which calls for somewhat detailed remarks.

46. **The enumeration forms.**—The forms printed for enumeration purposes during the late census were as follows :—

Serial No.	Name of form.	Printed in—
1	Manual of Census Rules	English and Urdu.
2	Instructions to Supervisors	English, Urdu and Nagri.
3	Parwanas of appointment for Superintendents	Ditto.
4	,, ,, ,, Supervisors	Ditto.
5	,, ,, ,, Enumerators	Ditto.
6	Letters of commendation to Superintendents	Urdu and Nagri.
7	,, ,, ,, Supervisors	Ditto.
8	,, ,, ,, Enumerators	Ditto.
9	Household schedules for Europeans and Eurasians with instructions on reverse ...	English.
10	,, ,, ,, persons other than Europeans and Eurasians with instructions on reverse.	English and Urdu.
11	Blank enumeration schedules in the ordinary form	English, Urdu and Nagri.
12	Enumerators' books containing 12 schedules	Ditto.
13	,, ,, ,, 24 ,, ...	Ditto.
14	,, ,, ,, 48 ,, ...	Ditto.
15	Books containing 24 schedules for the enumeration of regiments, &c. ...	English.
16	Tickets for boats and travellers enumerated	English, Urdu and Nagri.
17	Catechism for the use of Supervisors on the duties of enumerators	Urdu and Nagri.

The list was a very much more extensive one than at the previous census, when, besides the manual of census rules supplied to superior officers, the only instructions printed were those for enumerators, which had to serve the purposes of instruction of both Supervisors and Superintendents.

Forms of parwanas of appointment, of letters of commendation and draft schedules were now also printed for the first time. The consequence was that charges for forms other than those supplied to enumerators for their final record were almost

			Rs.	a.	p.
Cost of Census Manuals	... ...	Urdu ...	472	15	0
,, Supervisor ,,	... ...	,, ...	942	0	0
,, ,, ,,	... ...	Hindi ...	1,400	15	3
,, Parwanas of appointment	...	...	905	11	5
,, Letters of commendation	...	...	571	3	5
,, Catechisms ...	... ...	Urdu ...	389	13	0
,, ,, ...	... ...	Hindi ...	150	4	4
,, Draft schedules	... ...	...	2,059	9	0
		Total ...	6,892	7	5

entirely new. The total amount as detailed in the accompanying statement was Rs. 6,892-7-5, a large part of the increase in expenditure on forms.

The reasons why the cost of forms for the special use of enumerators should have been so much greater now than in 1881 are entirely connected with the forms themselves, and the way in which, according to the standard instructions to enumerators, they were to be filled up.

		Rs.	a.	p.
1881	... ...	28,813	3	6
1891	... ...	33,325	3	5
Excess	...	4,511	15	11

A. The books issued to enumerators were in every way more complete and more calculated to stand severe usage without risk of damage than those issued in 1881. At that census there were issued a loose sheet of instructions and a varying number of loose forms to each enumerator and he had to tack them together himself. The 1891 enumerator's book was strongly bound in a cartridge cover, on which was provided space for all details as to the identity of the block and enumerator. It contained a sheet of instructions, a form for a list of houses, a specimen completed schedule and form for enumerator's abstract, besides the blank schedules to be filled in in enumeration. At the rates at which the Calcutta Jail Press charged these improvements would add 30 per cent. on books of full size to the cost of the enumeration forms. The percentage of additional cost is considerably larger for the smaller sizes of books. The improved style of form therefore in itself would account for more than the difference in expenditure if the rates charged had been the same. Some margin was however left by the low rates for printing charged by the Calcutta press. This was more than swallowed up by the following reasons for a high expenditure of forms.

B. The rules as to filling up the enumeration schedules provided that a schedule which contained space for eight names was to be provided for each house, even though there was only a single resident in it; when there were more than eight persons in a house, a second schedule had to be devoted entirely to this house, even though there were only nine persons in it. It is clear that in at least half the schedules so filled up more space must have been left than was necessary for the additions to be made on the census night. Again, it was provided in the rules that a blank page should be left for each empty house or other place in which a person might possibly be found on the census night. The waste so caused varied very considerably. In an ordinary agricultural village it was practically *nil*, in some towns it was, partly owing to misunderstandings, very large.

C. The use of the book form as adopted for the provinces was in itself a cause of waste. The Census Commissioner issued a warning before printing was undertaken against making the books too bulky. The necessity for this warning was amply apparent in abstraction work, where the trouble experienced in detecting mistakes in the abstraction of the contents of the larger books was many times greater than it would have been had the books been divided into two and each half abstracted separately. The largest book adopted for the province therefore contained only 24 sheets of blank forms or 48 schedules. The smaller books contained 24 and 12 schedules respectively. Ordinarily these smaller books were intended to be used as supplements to the larger ones and the majority of them might therefore not have contained the instructions, block list or specimen schedules. As, however, a not inconsiderable number of enumerators whose blocks were small required only small books, it was considered best to prevent multiplication of the different descriptions of books to insert the additional pages in all books. There was waste too in the number of schedules due to the book form. An enumerator with 24 houses required, besides a schedule for each house, a margin for houses containing more than eight persons and which therefore occupied two pages. He had to be supplied with an additional book of 12 schedules, though he probably only needed two or three. The amount of the waste thus caused can only be roughly estimated for the province by ascertaining it for a given number of blocks. For 80 blocks in the Rae Bareli district, I find that 214 sheets of instructions, &c., were superfluous, and that 368 schedules were issued besides those estimated to be actually required. The waste under this head is therefore 9·32 per cent. of the whole number of forms issued.

47. **The district indents for enumeration forms.**—The various reasons given why the forms of the present census should be more costly than those of 1881 have made it clear that the additional cost of printing was in no way due to avoidable waste by the excessive issue to districts of forms not required, and that indeed the excess so issued at the present census was much less than at last. The way, in fact, in which the indents were to be prepared made it almost impossible that there should be any very great waste where the instructions were properly carried out. The circle list showed for each block the exact number of houses, and columns were provided against the entries for each block in which were accurately calculated the number of books required, allowing one schedule for each house, plus a prescribed percentage of margin for houses with more than eight persons. In several districts and in Rámpur State even this process was considered not exact enough, and a rough preliminary census was made by the patwáris, and the number of persons in each house noted, so that the exact number of schedules to be filled up was known before the indent was sent. I consider that in the great majority of districts there was little or no avoidable waste of forms. Such waste was not however absent. The most carefully managed districts used about 1·3 or fewer schedules per house, 240 or fewer schedules per thousand of population; *e.g.*, Jhánsi used 1·2 schedules per house and Jaunpur 1·3 or thereabout. Average districts used 1·5 schedules per house, 300 schedules per 1,000 of population. The various causes already enumerated rendered such an expenditure reasonable, but where this rate was much exceeded there must, except in special circumstances, have been waste. As an example of such special circumstances, Benares city may be quoted. There 2½ schedules were indented for for each house, owing to the large population per house in the city, the large number of unoccupied houses to be provided for, and the number of shops in which a single person had to be enumerated. Excessive indents were however not uncommon. Muttra, for instance, took 388 schedules per thousand of population. In Çawnpore 33,852 schedules were sold unused as waste paper, eight per cent. of the whole supply issued to the district. It is almost

impossible for the Census Superintendent to check indents from districts accurately. He has not the accurate information before him the district officer should have; and even if he had, it would be impossible for him to refuse an urgent supplementary indent not clearly absurd, when the district officer immediately before the census declares it to be absolutely necessary. With forms carefully indented for and issued in due time, there should be no need for urgent supplementary indents, but as in the best managed districts one or more of the responsible subordinates *will* go behind hand with his work, there is no probability of its being considered possible at any future census to refuse to meet indents after a certain date.

48. **Proposals as to enumeration forms for next Census.**—In connection with the arrangements for next census, it must be considered how far the advantages of the present system can be secured without so great an increase in cost. The subject was considered at a conference of Census Superintendents held in October 1891 in Simla, and the conclusions arrived at were that the advantages of having a separate page for each house were outweighed by the additional cost so imposed in the census budget. It was recommended that after the entries for a house were ended, two or three blank lines should be left and the entries for the next house begun. If this change was made, the depth of the schedule might be increased so as to allow the record of a larger number of names on one page and so save proportionate space in headings. That the schedules should be strongly bound together is so indispensable to prevent confusion and mistakes in the abstraction office, that reversion to the old system of issuing loose schedules to be tacked together by the enumerators would be distinctly a retrograde step. The Calcutta binding was however unnecessarily good. The wiring and cloth back rendered it so strong that to open a book was a work of trouble. Merely securing the pages together so that there should be no fear of its then getting loose unintentionally could be effected without the use of wire. The books printed for me at Allahabad were tacked together with thread and cloth bound, and there were no complaints of the binding coming loose, nor indeed were the majority of office Superintendents aware that they were less securely bound than those from Calcutta. Binding such as that done by the Allahabad Press could certainly be done by local binders at district headquarters; and if this were arranged it would be possible to bind the books after the preparation of the circle list, and after it was known how many schedules each enumerator would require in his book. The rates to be paid in districts for such binding would be no higher than in the press. By issuing forms to the districts, to be bound together according to the requirements of each individual enumerator, we should save entirely the waste of schedules referred to as having been caused by the issue of bound books, and the form of indent would be so much simplified as to leave the provincial Superintendent a far fuller check over district indents than he could have under the present system.

49. **The enumeration printing.**—The great body of the printing for enumerators was done in Calcutta, according to the arrangements made by the Government of India. The work was well and cheaply done. That the

press, whilst undertaking to supply forms for several provinces, should have been able to issue forms as rapidly as it did, reflects the greatest credit on the administrative powers of the Superintendent of Government Printing, Bengal, who was in charge. It was however inevitable that there should, to some extent, be a block, and when the original preliminary indent sent by my office was exhausted, there was some delay in printing and issuing up to the demand of the second indent, prepared in accordance with the district final indents. As later on in the cold weather supplementary indents continued to be received from districts, the heavy strain on the Calcutta Press and the time taken by consignments reaching these provinces, made it absolutely necessary to have forms set up in type and issued from the Local Government Press. These emergent indents in the local press were well done, and late as some of the latest indents were, many being received throughout the first half of February, Colonél Dodd, by night work in the press, was able to supply all the forms required in time to reach the districts and be distributed before the final census. The cost of carriage from Calcutta raised the expenditure in this respect from Rs. 2,698-7-11 in 1881 to Rs. 7,686-14-11 in 1891.

All things considered, I should strongly recommend that the provincial printing should at next census be done in the provincial press. Work should be started in April, and if the method of binding above recommended is adopted, the last lot of forms should be in the latest district by the end of October. Rates to be paid for census printing may, as on the present occasion, be effectively ascertained and prescribed by the Census Commissioner for India.

50. **The cost of superintendence**—The cost of superintendence is not shown in the above statement of accounts. It was somewhat larger in 1891 than in 1881. The difference is entirely due to the fact that the 1891 figures contain an item of Rs 2,750-0-0 for the pay of a substitute on district work for the provincial Superintendent whilst on census duty. This charge was not imposed on the census budget in 1881. The details of the cost of superintendence to the end of the financial year 1890-91 was as follows:—

	Rs.	a.	p.
Provincial Superintendent's deputation allowance	4,211	3	3
Pay of substitute of Superintendent	2,750	0	0
Travelling allowance of Superintendent	2,296	8	0
Superintendent's office establishment	1,080	3	3
Travelling allowance of ditto	269	10	6
Office contingences for ditto	1,535	8	6
Rent of Superintendent's office	131	0	0
Total ...	12,274	1	6

51. **Abstraction, Tabulation and Compilation**.—The processes by which the census figures were prepared for presentation in the final tables are three, technically known as Abstraction, Tabulation and Compilation.

Abstraction in the present census was the condensation item by item into twelve abstraction sheets of the information contained in the enumeration schedules for each block or book.

Tabulation was the collection for tahsils of the totals of the abstraction sheets by means of tabulation registers.

Compilation included the rearrangement and combination of the tabulation totals into the finally corrected statements published with this report.

Abstraction and tabulation were conducted in district offices by means of a specially appointed staff under the control of District Officers, subject to the general supervision of the Superintendent, Census Operations. Compilation was effected in a central office by the Census Superintendent in communication with District Officers.

52. **The change of system in abstraction.**—The system on which this part of census operations was carried out was entirely different from that employed in these provinces at last census.

It was outlined by the Agra Conference held in December 1889, and explained more in detail by the circulars of the Census Commissioner for India, along with which specimens of the forms proposed were circulated to Provincial Superintendents. The actual detailed rules issued to District Officers were drawn up by me, after the working of the system had been experimented upon in all details. At last census abstraction was done by a group of men working together at the same time on the same block. One man read out each entry to the rest, who abstracted each on to his own sheet such particulars as were required for the table towards which he was working. The men worked together and periodically corrected their results by those arrived at by the other abstractors. The abstraction results were at once posted in the tabulation registers in a way calculated only to obtain means of obtaining the totals under each head without any provision for checking in details. The tabulated totals were combined into the final tabular forms by the district staff and only the figures finally obtained reported to the Census Superintendent. The system had been worked out in all its details by Mr. White himself and provided a remarkably quick and cheap method of attaining the final totals. The drawback, however, was that whilst every opportunity was afforded to the men working in each stage to consult the final totals acquired by their fellow workers and alter results so as to agree with those attained by the other men, there was and could be no effective provision whatsoever to guard against fraudulent combination on the part of the men employed. To any one who has had experience of the way in which work is done by Indian muharrirs working at high pressure, this objection was a fatal one. Even with the system of the present census, where fraudulent combination was possible only with the connivance of the superior and highly paid officers in charge of the district offices, there was so much fraud discovered as to convince me that in exceptional cases work by men who compared their results must in India be regarded with the greatest suspicion. Of the system introduced by the present Census Commissioner for India, the main underlying principle was that each abstractor had to prepare his returns separately, and that the comparison of these results with the work of other abstractors which formed the main test of the honesty and correctness of the work, was to be done only by the supervising officials with the assistance of a

The abstraction system of 1891.

separate staff appointed for the purpose. As the tabulation registers were intended to be fair and permanent records, and therefore it was necessary as far as possible to secure correctness in the entries originally made, it was impossible to carry out the system of isolation to the same extent in tabulation as in abstraction. The value of the system is, however, shown by the fact that though tabulation offers far less temptation to fudging than abstraction does, it was in the tabulation, where muharrirs might have access each to the other's records, that the only instances of dishonest work so extensive as to be destructive of the value of the results were discovered during the present census operations. Comparatively costly as the present system has proved, there can, I think, if entire accuracy of results is valued, be no hesitation in continuing it at next census, rather than in reverting to the cheaper system of 1881.

53. **The abstraction work.**--Preparation for abstraction work was begun immediately after the preliminary abstracts had been prepared and submitted by the enumeration staff. A Deputy or Assistant Collector was in each district placed in charge of the census office, except in Agra, where Munshi Sheo Narain, Rai Bahádur, who had already on behalf of the Collector supervised the whole of the district enumeration, undertook the charge of the abstraction office also. An office Superintendent previously approved by the provincial Superintendent was appointed on pay varying from Rs. 40 to Rs. 80. The subordinate staff consisted of a record-keeper, four or more supervisors for each district, and a number of abstractors fixed for each district, more in view of the budget provision than the work to be done. The subject will be again referred to. Work had by the first of April been started in most districts. The abstractors were, after the system had been a short time in operation, divided into ten groups, each of which abstracted the figures for one of the general abstraction sheets. Each two groups were under a supervisor, through whose hands the abstracted sheets passed to the office Superintendent and his testing staff. The test was conducted mainly by collecting together in a test sheet the figures attained for each block on each sheet. The total figures for all sheets checked each other. The figures for age periods attained on one sheet when combined to some extent checked those for age periods in other sheets. Figures for castes acquired on three different sheets for different tables checked each other. The figures for religions checked each other on four different sheets. Thus for all the work on the most important and complicated abstraction sheets a very effective test of the accuracy of the work done was provided by this comparison. For sheets the details of which were not effectively so tested, reabstraction to the extent of ten per cent. was done; and for all sheets including those the accuracy of which was ascertained by the comparison test, reabstraction was ordered to an extent sufficent to provide against the possibility of the abstractors combining. In regard to the returns for infirmities, the figures for many districts were so surprising, as compared with those for 1881, that for these sheets almost complete reabstraction was ordered after the original registers had been completed. The result was in almost every case to affirm the substantial correctness of the original

figures. Testing, it was originally supposed, could be done by the Superintendent and an assistant muharrir, but before work had long been started it was found necessary to appoint a special tester for each two lakhs of population, and even this staff had to be somewhat increased in most districts. A scale of work determined on, in consultation with the Superintendent, Lower Provinces, was fixed, and before the work had long been in hand, the staff in all districts was working up to it. In spite of the full tale of work being done and these additions to the staff, it was found that, owing to the allowance of abstractors provided for in the budget being too small, abstraction work took fully five months in an ordinary district, instead of the three and a half for which pay of abstractors was provided. However, by the end of August, this part of the work was everywhere, except in Kumaun, complete, and, in my opinion, formed after inspection either by myself or by my personal assistant in every district of the province, well and accurately done. It would be useless to give in detail an account of the process of abstraction. The rules have been printed and are available for reference. As an instance of the complexity of some of the abstraction sheets, it may be mentioned that the sub-caste sheet for one of the blocks of Hardwár town was thirteen feet long when completed, and that six and seven feet of length was not uncommon for caste sheets. The sheet which in every way gave most trouble was that in which the information as to civil condition of castes was collected. As there is little probability of this work being again undertaken, it requires no closer reference.

54. **Tabulation**.—Tabulation was intended to follow abstraction after a short interval during which lists of castes, sub-castes, sects, birth-places, mother-tongues and occupations prepared during abstraction should be examined by myself or my office with a view to preventing tabulation separately of entries which should have been combined. On the whole, if at next census tabulation is to be done in districts, I should not recommend this being again attempted. The work for the Superintendent himself, whilst lists were coming in from each tahsíl of the province, was almost impossibly heavy. The combinations which could, on the information available, be ordered for castes and sects, were not very numerous. For mother-tongues the entries were never so numerous as to make combination before tabulation necessary. For birth-places and occupations, the combinations so ordered were very numerous; but though the tabulation registers were rendered more correct by having the combinations effected during the preparation of the registers, the delay caused by having to send and receive back lists and the frequency with which mistakes were made by the tabulator in combining, and the trouble and delay caused in discovering such mistakes have led me to be strongly of opinion that tabulation should follow immediately on abstraction and show the uncorrected and uncombined abstraction results. All corrections and combinations should be reserved to the compilation stage of the work. To allow combination to be done in districts otherwise than on lists furnished by the Census Superintendent, is, it was clearly proved, absolutely impossible. It was permitted by the present rules to the small extent of allowing District Officers to combine names of occupations which were absolutely identical. The rule was as follows:—

"The words used by different enumerators to describe the same trades will in all probability be numerous, and to prevent utterly useless multiplication of the headings in column 1 of the sheet, it is provided that the Deputy Collector in charge of the office may draw up for the orders of the Collector a list of expressions used for each trade which he considers to be absoultely synonymous. The Collector may on this report order that the entries may be abstracted together. A copy of the list as approved by the Collector should be sent at once to the Superintendent, Census Operations. It must be borne in mind that such combination is to be allowed only when the difference in the two terms used is purely lingual or verbal; that when the meaning is not precisely the same, or when more detail of any kind is given in one term than the other, each should be abstracted separately. Where any doubt is entertained the order passed will be to abstract separately: as an example, the occupations described as kheti and kashtkari may be abstracted together, but the entries kashtkari and kashtkarí asli should be abstracted separately."

Than this nothing could be more guarded, yet it has led in several districts to the obliteration of all distinctions between Government servants, Collectors, Judges, patwáris, village chaukidárs, all being lumped together. Elsewhere a variety of mistakes were so introduced. It would be possible from the record of combination of occupations made in my office at the present census to print and circulate to district offices in a future census the combinations to be allowed, but in view of the impossibility of getting abstractors or tabulators to learn up and work on lists so extensive, I think it better that the tabulation registers should be more or less redundant than that the value of the occupation tables should be impared. Tabulation was estimated to cost about one-third as much as abstraction, but in practice it was found to be in consequence of the elaboration of the caste and occupation details, almost as expensive and very much more troublesome. It was conducted by means of twenty-five registers, of which fourteen were general, containing entries for every block in the provinces and the others contained entries only for those blocks in which there were any statistics of the nature they referred to. These registers were all prepared on a uniform plan, so that all the blocks which occurred on a given page of one register appeared also on the same page or set of pages of all other general registers. The blocks were properly arranged by villages, thánas, parganas and tahsíls, so that the figures for any one of the census tables can by reference to the vernacular registers be ascertained for the smallest or any recognized revenue or executive sub-division of a district. The tabulation for the first fifteen of the imperial tables, though bulky in some cases, gave little trouble, as the statistics for the whole of a tahsíl fell under headings not more numerous than could be arranged in a single page or opposing pair of pages, and the totals could be carried forward from page to page. The registers which did give trouble were those for castes and occupations, in which for each set of blocks which appeared on a single page of register I, there were often entries enough to occupy in the caste and occupation registers the columns for many pages. In these registers the set of villages which occupied a single page of register I, were treated as independent of all others, and the totals for them collected along the bottom of the set of pages. The totals for all sets were collected by means of separate totalling sheets. So prepared, all these registers were extremely bulky and complex. The civil condition by caste register, which required a separate register for each caste, and the correctness of which could not be tested till the final totals were arrived at, was especially bulky and troublesome.

55. **The testing of tabulation registers.**—All general registers were tested page by page as they progressed. The rules stated that the form of test sheet prescribed for abstraction sheets might be used for the purpose, but in future it would be better to print a separate test sheet more suited for the larger figures which occur in the tabulation registers. It should be definitely prescribed that such a test sheet should be filled up for every total in each register.

56. **The census office work in districts.**—The operations of abstraction and tabulation were conducted at very varying rates of speed and of cost by the different districts. In general, the work done was as ascertained by the test in compilation to be thoroughly honest and satisfactory. In two districts there were exceptions of importance to this remark. In Kumaun the work of tabulation must throughout be pronounced unsatisfactory. All registers were received in a most untidy form, and mistakes were frequently detected in all of them. The caste registers were deprived of most of their value by unauthorized conbinations and omissions, and the occupation registers were found in compilation to have been so completely fudged as to be absolutely valueless. In the greater part of the district the occupation registers were deprived of all value by the reckless combinations dishonestly effected on the face of the abstraction sheets to save trouble; whilst in one tahsíl the abstraction sheets were thrown entirely aside and an absolutely imaginary register prepared to give for each block the totals which another register proved to be correct. The whole of the Kumaun occupation work had to be redone at a late stage in compilation and caused much delay. The matter has been brought to the attention of the Commissioner of Kumaun, who has investigated it and issued orders punishing the parties in fault. Allahabad was the only other district in which dishonest work was found to have affected the entire value of a register. The Christian sect and race registers were here fudged in a much more intelligent way than those in Kumaun, but quite as completely. The fraud was so well carried out that it was detected only when the great difference between the details in the figures for the present and past censuses led me to examine in detail the entries for certain specified blocks. As a result, the abstraction sheets were sent for from the district, and it was fouud that abstraction had been properly done to start with, but that a large proportion of the sheets had apparently been lost. Imaginary sheets were fudged instead of those lost, and the figures from them carried into the tabulation registers. The Collector's attention was called to the matter and the dishonest tabulators dismissed from Government service.

Fudging to a very minor extent was detected in Bulandshahr and Mirzapur. In the former it was of trifling extent, a small village had by mistake been omitted from one of the last pages of the registers. The mistake was discovered by the Superintendent and corrected in the earlier registers, but was apparently forgotten before the totals of certain later registers were acquired. When the totals were found, they were of course wrong to the extent of the population of the village omitted, and were put right by means of arbitrary corrections in another village. The fudging was not carried out to such an extent as to appreciably injure the totals, and the fact that the amount to be fudged was exactly the population of the small village omitted, showed how correctly the Bulandshahr registers had been prepared, except in this one respect. In Mirzapur, the fudging discovered consisted in the arbitrary insertion of persons dependent on certain trades into the register, apparently to give an occupation total more in accordance with the census official's idea of what was proper than the registers themselves gave. How incorrect was his idea of the proper total appeared from the fact that the superfluity of persons of the occupations selected for this act of favouritism in that particular tahsíl at once attracted notice when embodied in a provincial return. In Farukhabad some bad work, not considered after full enquiry to be dishonest, was done in the entries made in the registers for the Central Jail block, which did not correspond with those in the abstraction sheets.

Mistakes not attributable to dishonest work but causing suspicion of the carefulness of the work were detected in Aligarh, Farukhabad, Allahabad, Jhánsi, Gházipur, Muttra, Bareilly and the inevitable Kumaun, and to a less extent in Bijnor, Etáwah, Moradabad, Hardoi and Gonda.

The tabulation registers were subjected to a very severe test in the preparation of the provincial village directory, in the course of which the figures for every village were rearranged by religion, age periods and occupation. The result was to show that, on the whole, they were very correct : mistakes were certainly detected in village totals in a comparatively large number of instances, but they were almost entirely mistakes such as did not affect the totals of the imperial tables. They were mainly due to entries for one village having been made in the line or lines appropriate to another. The totals for columns at the bottom of the pages from which the imperial returns were compiled were carried forward correctly, but the cross totals for villages were wrong. The instances in which the mistakes were so considerable as to necessitate the abstraction sheets for a village being referred to were few. In every instance *in which the abstraction sheet was sent for it was found to be correct and the mistake introduced in Tabulation.*

Except in the districts mentioned, the work was found to be honest throughout, and, in general, careful. The ultimate test of the success of the work in the different districts therefore is the cost of the work and the expedition with which the registers were prepared. The table given below compares the dates on which the work of tabulation was completed and the total cost of the work in each district, excluding paper, pencils and rubbers, and in some cases binding of registers.

Abstract No. 4, comparing the dates of completion of tabulation work and the total cost in the districts of the provinces.

Serial number.	District or State.	Date of close of Census office.	Order of merit of district in point of expedition.	Total cost. Rs.	a.	p.	Cost per 1,000 of population. Rs.	a.	p.	Order of merit as regards cost.
1	Debra Dún	31st December 1891 ...	16	3,205	11	0	19	0	11	49
2	Sahárunpur	10th October 1891 ...	1	5,592	12	8	5	9	4	2
3	Muzaffarnagar	31st December 1881 ...	16	6,516	3	7	8	6	10	37
4	Meerut	28th November 1891 ...	6	7,799	0	1	5	9	8	3
5	Bulandshahr	23rd November 1891 ...	5	7,132	0	4	7	8	1	28
6	Aligarh	7th January 1892 ...	17	7,441	10	3	7	2	1	22
	Total, Meerut Division ...	...		37,687	5	11	7	1	2	

***Abstract No. 4, comparing the dates of completion of tabulation work and the total cost in districts of the provinces*—(concluded).**

Serial number.	District or State.	Date of close of Census office.	Order of merit district in point of expedition.	Total cost. Rs.	a.	p.	Cost per 1,000 of population. Rs.	a.	p.	Order of merit as regards cost.
7	Muttra	8th March 1892 ...	32	5,510	13	10	7	11	6	30
8	Agra	15th December 1891 ...	11	7,589	8	0	7	8	11	29
9	Farukhabad	30th November 1891 ...	7	6,442	3	0	7	8	0	27
10	Mainpuri	10th December 1891 ...	10	5,631	3	2	8	6	2	35
11	Etáwah	31st December 1891 ...	16	5,428	10	10	7	7	4	24
12	Etah	11th January 1892 ...	18	5,158	15	11	7	5	6	23
	Total, Agra Division ...	...		35,761	6	9	7	8	0	
13	Bareilly	23rd January 1892 ...	24	6,701	8	8	6	7	0	10
14	Bijnor	23rd December 1891 ...	13	5,638	5	5	7	1	7	20
15	Budaun	15th January 1892 ...	19	7,410	6	11	8	0	0	34
16	Moradabad	9th December 1891 ...	9	7,363	12	10	6	3	10	9
17	Sháhjahánpur	10th February 1892 ...	28	8,009	12	8	8	11	6	39
18	Pilibhít	21st November 1891 ...	4	4,135	5	11	8	6	3	36
	Total, Rohilkhand Division ...	...		39,259	4	5	7	5	6	
19	Cawnpore	21st January 1892 ...	23	9,565	1	0	7	14	6	31
20	Fatehpur	16th January 1892 ...	20	6,090	0	6	8	11	4	38
21	Bánda	31st January 1892 ...	26	7,008	9	6	9	14	10	44
22	Hamírpur	13th October 1891 ...	2	4,530	12	2	8	13	0	40
23	Allahabad	31st December 1891 ...	16	11,610	1	9	7	7	11	26
24	Jhánsi	31st December 1891 ...	16	5,805	12	4	14	2	8	47
25	Jalaun	15th November 1891 ...	3	4,406	8	1	11	1	9	45
26	Lalitpur	29th December 1891 ...	15	2,708	13	4	9	14	0	43
	Total, Allahabad Division ...	...		51,725	10	8	8	15	8	
27	Benares	20th December 1891 ...	12	6,534	12	8	7	1	4	19
28	Mirzapur	31st December 1891 ...	16	7,108	6	2	6	1	10	5
29	Jaunpur	29th February 1892 ...	31	8,197	8	11	6	7	8	11
30	Gházipur	23rd January 1892 ...	24	7,181	15	4	6	10	7	14
31	Ballia	20th January 1892 ...	22	6,709	4	10	7	1	9	21
	Total, Benares Division ...	...		35,731	15	11	6	10	5	
32	Gorakhpur	11th April 1892 ...	33	20,921	9	8	6	15	9	18
33	Basti	15th February 1892 ...	29	11,128	13	7	6	3	8	8
34	Azamgarh	25th January 1892 ...	25	11,519	14	8	6	10	7	15
	Total, Gorakhpur Division ...	...		43,570	5	11	6	11	1	
35	Kumaun	7th February 1892 ...	27	5,023	6	11	8	15	8	41
36	Garhwál	31st January 1892 ...	26	5,402	1	11	13	3	10	46
37	Tarái	18th January 1892 ...	21	3,158	9	3	14	15	10	48
	Total, Kumáun Division ...	...		13,584	2	1	11	7	10	
	Total, N.-W. Provinces ...	...		257,320	3	8	7	8	2	
38	Lucknow	7th February 1892 ...	27	7,258	1	4	9	6	0	42
39	Unao	10th February 1892 ...	28	7,567	11	9	7	14	11	32
40	Rae Bareli	24th December 1891 ...	14	6,457	1	7	6	3	7	7
41	Sitapur	31st December 1891 ...	16	7,230	8	10	6	11	6	16
42	Hardoi	7th January 1892 ...	17	7,277	9	5	6	8	7	12
43	Kheri	19th February 1892 ...	30	7,211	5	5	7	15	8	33
	Total, Lucknow Division ...	...		43,002	6	4	7	5	5	
44	Fyzabad	15th January 1892 ...	19	7,571	8	9	6	3	6	6
45	Gonda	15th January 1892 ...	19	8,496	0	9	5	13	2	4
46	Bahraich	16th January 1892 ...	20	7,493	12	6	7	7	10	25
47	Sultánpur	24th December 1891 ...	14	7,389	9	8	6	13	10	17
48	Partábgarh	15th November 1891 ...	8	4,939	11	8	5	6	9	1
49	Bara Banki	7th December 1891 ...	8	7,448	14	5	6	9	3	13
	Total, Fyzabad Division ...	...		43,334	9	9	6	6	0	
	Total, Oudh ...	...		86,337	0	1	6	13	2	
	Total, N.-W. P. and Oudh ...	...		3,43,657	3	9	7	5	2	

Districts started work very much together about the 1st April. The first to close was Sahâranpur, the Superintendent of which was transferred to my office, taking register 16 with him, untabulated, about four days' work if the whole staff had been put on to it. Hamírpur, closing on the 13th October in the same circumstances with register 16 incomplete, was a good second. After this there was a considerabl intervale till Jalaun and Partábgarh closed on the same day, the 15th November. The Pilibhít office closed on the 21st November; Bulandshahr on the 23rd; Meerut on the 28th and Farukhabad on the 30th. With these is entitled to be ranked Bara Banki, the conclusion of work in which was delayed to the 7th December by my transferring the office Superintendent to Sháhjahánpur to take charge of the office there in which work had fallen seriously behind.

The office Superintendents of all these districts, which were all of them satisfactory in quality of work as well as in quickness, deserve the greatest credit for their management of their subordinates. The following offices closed in December:—

Dehra Dún	...	...	...	...	31st December.
Muzaffarnagar	...	...	...	...	,, ,,
Agra	...	...	...	...	15th ,,
Mainpuri	...	...	...	...	10th ,,
Etáwah	...	...	...	...	31st ,,
Bijnor	...	...	...	...	23rd ,,
Moradabad	...	...	...	...	9th ,,
Jhánsi	...	...	...	...	31st ,,
Allahabad	...	...	...	...	,, ,,
Benares	...	...	...	...	20th ,,
Mirzapur	...	...	...	...	31st ,,
Rae Bareli	...	...	...	...	24th ,,
Sitapur	...	...	...	...	31st ,,
Sultánpur	...	...	...	...	24th ,,

and in all of these, except Dehra, where the cost was excessive, and Allahabad already referred to, the work was on the whole creditable.

The last districts to close were Basti, Kheri, Jaunpur, Muttra, Gorakhpur; of these Basti and Gorakhpur, the largest districts in the provinces, and those most subdivided, had valid reasons for being last. Basti is a small town and not likely to provide a sufficient staff of good muharrirs for a few months' work. Gorakhpur, though a large town, is not large as compared with the number of muharrirs required for the very large district. The patwáris in both districts on whose assistance the District Officer might ordinarily rely are amongst the worst in the provinces. In both districts the work was in point of quality excellent.

57. **Cost of Census work in districts.**—In regard to comparative cost, the gross outlay in each district excluding forms, pencils and in some cases binding, varied from Rs. 5-6-9 per thousand in Partábgarh to Rs. 19-0-11 in Dehra. Sahâranpur (Rs. 5-9-4), Meerut (Rs. 5-9-8), Gonda (Rs. 5-13-2) cost below Rs. 6; and Mirzapur, Fyzabad, Rae Bareli, Basti, Moradabad, Bareilly, Jaunpur, Hardoi, Bara Banki, Ghâzipur, Azamgarh, Sitapur, Sultánpur,

Gorakhpur, between Rs. 6 and Rs. 7 per one thousand. Benares with work more difficult than any of the above followed close with Rs. 7-1-4 per thousand, and Bijnor and Ballia with average cost under Rs. 7-2-0. In the above we have eastern districts and western districts, large districts and small districts, urban districts aud rural districts, districts in all parts of the provinces, except Bundelkhand and the Himalayas. The districts of the Gangetic plain, which remain, are mostly small and outlying, where it was found difficult to procure a full staff of well-educated men. In Allahabad with an average cost of Rs. 7-7-11 and Cawnpore with Rs. 7-14-6 the complexity of the city work and the amount of English work in the former are reasons for a somewhat high rate. In Lucknow the cost was Rs. 9-6-0 per thousand, but the work was certainly the most intricate in the provinces, and was, as I ascertained by several inspections, most carefully done. Sháhjahánpur gives the highest cost of the Gangetic districts, although the place is one in which good muharrirs are available to any reasonable extent. This was the inevitable result of the confusion into which the original Superintendent allowed his work to fall. It reflects the greatest credit on M. Kamta Pershád, the Bara Banki Superintendent, that, deputed to Sháhjahánpur in October, he was able to complete the work there by the 10th February.

The Bundelkhand and Kumaun districts come all together at the bottom of the list. As regards cost, Hamírpur is best with Rs. 8-13-0. Jhánsi was last in Bundelkhand with Rs. 14-2-8. The cost in the Himalayan districts was :—

	Rs.	a.	p.
Kumaun	8	15	8
Garhwál	13	3	10
Tarái	14	15	10
Dehra Dún	19	0	11

Kumaun may be put aside as the work prescribed was not done. The reason for the high cost in the other districts, both in Bundelkhand and the Himalayas, was partly the high cost of supervision owing to the low district population but mostly the low standard of eduction amongst the muharrirs of these districts. In both Jhánsi and Jalaun the District Officers, whilst the Census offices were open, were men who were likely to get the largest possible amount of work from their subordinates, and I must conclude that a high rate is inevitable in Bundelkhand districts. It is certainly so in the Kumaun Division, where the clerical ability of the pahari is very inferior indeed in work which requires quickness. In Garhwál, Mr. Partridge, the Deputy Commissioner, and M. Aziz-uddin, the Deputy Collector in charge of Census, took keen interest in the work, and the office Superintendent was a specially good man. In the Tarái, too, Mr. Roberts, who kept the Census in his own hands, exercised close supervision. I am led therefore to believe that good work in Bundelkhand must cost Rs. 9 or 10 per thousand and in Kumaun Rs. 13 or 14. In other districts it should not, except in exceptional cases, such as that of Lucknow, have exceeded Rs. 7-8-0 a thousand persons. The tendency to exceed this amount is, as already remarked, greatest in small districts, where the supply of muharrirs is small. Looking at the results of my inspections of some of these districts, I am at a loss to say how the arrangements made could have been amended. In Muzaffarnagar, for instance, the registers of which were inspected by the Census Commissioner, the work was throughout kept well in hand; it was well done in all respects, sending me registers of the neatest, absolutely free from such mistakes as I could detect. The cost was Rs. 8-6-10, but I should be loath to say that this fact implies any blame whatsoever on the office Superintendent or the superior offices of the district.

It is somewhat invidious to call attention to the work of a few districts where the working of the majority has been thoroughly good, but the expedition and low cost at which the records of certain districts were completed gives them a distinct claim to mention. Sahâranpur, under a particularly able Superintendent, Lála Chauharja Parshád, fully supported by Mr. Holmes, the Collector, was the first office to close and second in point of cost, and gave me good work. Partábgarh, with Munshi Himmat Sahai as office Superintendent, and Colonel Quin as District Officer, gave the lowest cost, and closed third, giving work in all respects satisfactory. Meerut, with Lála Hazari Lál as office Superintendent and Mr. Whiteway as District Officer, and Bara Banki with Lála Kamta Parshád, office Superintendent, and Colonel Grigg as District Officer, also deserve very special mention. The entire Census work in Agra was under the sole charge of Munshi Sheo Narain, Rai Bahádur, Secretary to the Municipal Board. His experience in earlier Census work and well-recognized administrative ability led the Collector to place him in charge of both enumeration and abstraction, instead of one of the regular district staff. The work was throughout done in a thoroughly satisfactory manner.

58. **The Patwari as an abstractor.**—Before closing my remarks on district abstraction and tabulation work, I desire to give especial prominence to the fact that the statement of cost of operations gives clear testimony as to the value of the patwári in Census operations. He is not so sharp as a good muharrir, but he is infinitely better than the average untrained apprentice who can be picked up for Census offices.

The result is that every district which employed patwáris to any considerable extent is in the first half of the list showing cost of operations, excepting only Hamírpur, in which work was a rupee cheaper than in any other Bundelkhand district. The rules recommended that patwáris should be employed to as large an extent as possible, but many District Officers were against it and it was not insisted on. In future, it should be borne in view that the experience of this Census shows that the patwári is a far cheaper and more honest abstractor than the average muharrir employed.

59. **Compilation.**—Compilation work presented features of difficulty in regard only to castes and occupations. In both of these it was, owing to the transfers from one head to another which were found to be necessary, extremely complex, and the presentation of the elaborate tables for castes and occupations in the final form was found to be a work which occupied my staff and myself for months. An attempt to obtain the correct provincial totals directly in the final form ended disastrously after occupying many

weeks in searching for errors, and it was only when a fresh start was made and the divisional figures, obtained horizontally as well as by adding the columns, were combined for the province, and compared, item by item, with those obtained vertically that the tables in the final form could be guaranteed absolutely correct. The caste tables are, in the detail with which caste subdivisions have been shown, incomparably more complex than in the other provinces of which the reports have so far reached me.

60. Cost of Census operations.—Appendix VIII shows the census accounts year by year in detail, and Appendix IX the gross and net amounts expended in districts and in the Central offices. The gross amounts differ from the net by—

1*st*—The amount of a municipal contribution of Rs. 14,185-2-3, which, under the orders of the Accountant-General, was allowed as a deduction from census accounts.

2*nd*.—Certain deductions from the census bills, owing to the Government of India having in July 1891 directed that for Government servants deputed to census work, only the pay of officiating substitutes *plus* deputation allowance should be charged against census.

3*rd*.—Income from sale of furniture, &c.

The total cost was Rs. 483,130-11-10 against Rs. 280,145-2-5 at last census.

The details under the main heads are as follows :—

Head.		Items.
		Rs. a. p.
Enumeration		69,409 11 5
Abstraction, tabulation and compilation		...
Establishment charges	Rs. 3,31,052-13-10	} 3,76,162 4 10
Printing and distribution of forms	„ 45,109-7-0	
Superintendence		...
Personal charges	„ 26,276 11-0	} 37,558 11 7
Office charges	„ 11,282-0-7	
Grand Total ...		4,83,130 11 10

The heads of the only accounts preserved of the 1881 Census are different, and for comparison with 1881 these sums must be rearranged.

Head.	1881.	1891.
	Rs. a. p.	Rs. a. p.
Enumeration	56,845 4 6	69,409 11 5
Abstraction and compilation establishment	179,446 13 6	3,42,334 14 5
Abstraction, &c., printing	28,486 4 3	45,109 7 0
Superintendence	15,366 12 2	26,276 11 0
Total ...	2,80,145 2 5	4,83,130 11 10

The enumeration figures have already been referred to. On the preparation of the final tables there was an excess charge in the present Census of Rs. 1,62,888-0-11.

This large increase in expenditure has already been the subject of a correspondence with the Government of India, and it need just now be only pointed out that a comparison with the charges at last census, when the system on which the work was done and the work to be done were entirely different, must be misleading in the extreme. At last census, owing to the system by which the muharrirs worked in groups, and to the fact that in at least the great majority of districts it was not considered necessary to have the statistics tabulated in a form to which reference could permanently be made, the cost of census operations in these provinces was a fraction of what it was elsewhere. In the present census work has here been done on a system uniform with that employed in the other provinces of India. It contrasted with that employed at last census in the following respects (1) every possible provision was made against one man's availing himself of the results of another's work to fudge his own or of several combining to fudge; (2) the work of the district offices was thoroughly tested in the headquarters office and prepared by men who knew that such a test was to follow; (3) the work of the district offices was finally tabulated in a form in which information can be had regarding every item that went to make up the district totals in the final tables; (4) the work of the present census was so much greater in quantity and complexity as to make an increase of cost of at least 50 per cent. on abstraction and cent. per cent. on tabulation and compilation necessary. Nearly the whole of the large expenditure of Rs. 3,42,334 shown for office establishment and contingencies was, as detailed in Appendix VIII, expended in districts. Of how severely the district staff was worked all the district reports give the most conclusive evidence. That from Gonda (Colonel Barrow) may be quoted—

"The staff employed was overworked: not only was work carried on on all Sundays and gazetted holidays, but work was literally carried on from "early morn to dewy eve." If holidays had been allowed and ordinary office hours kept, this work (abstraction) would have taken six instead of only four months."

This was the case everywhere. In fact, census work was regarded as a kind of slavery to be endured because it did not last long and would give to the person who endured it a claim on the district officer for permanent employment. It is possible that the cost was raised in a few offices by the Superintendents having been overwhelmed by the magnitude of their task and to some extent lost hold over their men, but where the cost was highest the same long hours and unremitting work were endured.

The real test of the cost of the work is comparison with other provinces. It cost Rs. 10-3-0 per thousand of population in the North-Western Provinces and Oudh, less, I believe, than in any other province except Bengal. It must be remembered, too, in connection with this subject that in the North-Western Provinces the difference between the net and the gross cost of census is very small. The Government of India order allowing permanent employés to be transferred to census work, debiting the census budget with the pay of an officiating substitute instead of their full pay, issued only in July, after arrangements had been made, by which only a very small proportion of patwáris were deputed to census work. The local Accountant-General had in the meantime declined to sanction the debit of patwáris' pay to district budgets and officiating allowances only to census. Had this not been so, it would have been possible in almost all districts, as in Meerut, to employ patwáris to a large extent and thereby to reduce the expenditure charged against census by probably Rs. 2 per thousand of population. This was the case in the Meerut district only. The gross cost of census establishment was there Rs. 7,799-0-1 ; Rs. 2,106-4-7 were recovered on account of the difference between the pay of substitutes and of permanent officials, thereby reducing the net cost of work in Meerut to Rs. 5,692-11-6 or Rs. 4-1-5 per thousand. As pointed out above, it was understood here that the census was to bear the gross cost of the offices, and our saving by the subsequent ruling of the Government of India was only Rs. 19,536-9-10, a fact which must be taken into consideration in comparing the cost here and in other provinces. The work done, too, was to say the least of it, as complicated and extensive as it could be in any other province, and much more so than in most. The registers supplied to districts were except in Kumaun complete, well written on good paper, and fairly well bound ; the cost being necessarily thus raised beyond what it would be if tahsíl totals were acquired without any attempt to preserve a fair record of the details.

61. **Printing for abstraction and tabulation.**—The increase in the cost of paper and printing was necessarily implied by the increase in work, and the fact that the tabulation registers were now prepared on a very much more elaborate system than at last census. The census printing for abstraction was all done by the Government Press, and in general most satisfactorily done. For tabulation it was largely done by the Newal Kishore Press. In the paper employed and way in which the printing was done the work of this press was excellent, but it proved unequal to turning out forms for the more elaborate registers fast enough to supply emergent indents, and several of the forms had to be set up in the Government Press.

The difference in the cost of superintendence is due to the fact that Rs. 5,750 were charged against census for the pay of a substitute for the provincial Superintendent, and that an assistant inspecting officer was employed at a cost of Rs. 3,330-9-6. Travelling allowance was also increased by the last reason and cost Rs. 5,688-14-3 against Rs. 3,966-12-2 at last census.

62. **Abstraction and tabulation at next census.**—The system of abstraction and tabulation to be adopted at next census must depend entirely on the amount and complexity of the work to be done. The members of the conference of Census Superintendents held at Simla after the census were unanimously of opinion that no information should be collected at next census as regards caste or sect, and suggested that it would be unnecessary to collect information regarding mother-tongues or occupations. I am strongly of opinion that the information on all these subjects embodied in the tables of the present census is as full and comprehensive as it could well be, and

that it would be waste of time and money to repeat these tables at next census. If these tables are omitted, the work remaining is free from all difficulty or complexity and could be run through by district offices in three months at a low cost more efficiently than by any other arrangement. If, however, the work to be done approaches in complexity that now done, I should recommend a modification of the system by adopting in part that of the Panjáb. I do not consider that district offices are, as a whole, by any means the best suited to carry out work of such complexity as tabulation of castes or occupations. In the best offices the work was as cheaply and efficiently carried out as was possible, but in many, the Superintendents appear at times to have lost control over their staff and to have allowed matters to come almost to a standstill. Abstraction on a future occasion as at present should be done in district offices under Superintendents of the rank of kanúngos and on lower pay than those employed in the present census. The abstraction sheets when tested should be transferred to divisional offices each under a selected Deputy Collector. In these divisional offices the test of the abstraction work should be repeated and such reabstraction as is considered necessary ordered in the districts and tabulation should after retest and reabstraction be carried out. These offices would be directly under the orders of the Census Superintendent and visited by him once a fortnight, so that all combinations necessary could be carried out under his direct orders before tabulation. The tabulation registers would then correspond in all particulars with the final tables and the work of compilation be reduced to a minimum. I believe that the result of this change of system would be that, complete control in all details of district work being possible, and tabulation being conducted by a picked staff under the best supervision, the work would be superior in point of quality and less expensive than at present. It was the tabulation which cost most in the present census, and in divisional offices it ought to cost no more all over than it did at present in the best managed district offices. An essential of the present plan, if it is adopted, is to provide supervising Deputy Collectors of the very best calibre; men of lower rank have not in general sufficient authority over their immediate subordinates, and would in many instances be reluctant to find fault, even when it was necessary, with the work done in the districts. The pay of the Deputy Collectors for nine divisional offices would be a considerable item, but I have no doubt that the money would be saved over and over again in the outturn of work done, and that the tabulation registers themselves would be more valuable for purposes of reference than at present.

The devotion with which the subordinate staff struggled to carry out in an inadequate time the work entrusted to them has been mentioned. Money rewards were rendered impossible by the state of the census budget, but a reward which would be valued very much more highly by many of the best men has been suggested by District Officers and approved by Government, *viz.*, exemption from the middle class examination. A list of men recommended for such exemption is being forwarded to Government with this report. I have accepted the recommendations of District Officers except where unduly extensive, except in the case of Kumaun, from which I think no exemptions should be sanctioned.

Chapter II.—GENERAL REMARKS ON THE RESULTS OF THE CENSUS OF 1891.

63. **Brief Topographical description of the Provinces.**—The North-West Provinces and Oudh with the two Native States, the administration of which is supervised by the Local Government, comprising in all an area of 112,612 square miles, include nearly the whole of the tract which was known to the Muhammadan chroniclers as "Hindustan." They occupy and are nearly confined to the basin of the Jumna, Ganges and Ghogra rivers, from the sources of the two former in the snows of the inner Himalayas to where united as one great stream they pass into the province of Behar. The three British districts of Kumaun, Garhwál and Dehra Dún and the Native State of Garhwál form the Himalayan part of the province, a compact parallelogram about 180 miles in length from north-west to south-east. The remaining districts of the province lie in or south of the Gangetic plain, bounded to the north by the outer Himalayas for a distance of close on 500 miles and reaching away from them to an average distance of about 200 miles.

64. **The Tarai.**—The line of separation between the Himalayan and Gangetic tracts is both ethnically and topographically the best marked line of division in the provinces. I would place this line ethnically at least in the narrow tract of swamp and marsh which extends almost across the province and is known as the Tarái, rather than at the immediate foot of the hills. In the Doab the actual Tarái has long since disappeared and the cultivators of the plains have occupied the whole of the country up to the foot of the Sewaliks, but elsewhere there is still a dividing line of swamp or at least unhealthily moist forest land through which the clearing and improvements of the plains cultivators have not yet been able to work their way. This line is separated from the foot of the hills by a tract of varying width known where most marked as the Bhábar, which, inaccessible so far from the plains, has been occupied by the hill men. The invariable characteristic of the Bhábar tract is its waterlessness. The impermeable stratum of clay, on which the water available in the plains lies, apparently sinks rapidly from the foot of the hills and has been overlaid by a layer at times over 300 feet deep of porous material, sometimes shale, sometimes sandy soil. In the rains the hill torrents pass over this with apparently no great diminution of their volume, but the quantity of water delivered in the rest of the year by the smaller streams sinks through the porous soil to the substratum, which brings it to the surface in the Tarái, in which almost all the smaller rivers of the province have their permanent sources. This waterless tract exists in the Doab, but owing to the absence of the Tarái and the fact that the overlying soil is culturable though somewhat sandy, it is less markedly different from the rest of the area to the south, and is not there known by the distinctive name of Bhábar. The waterless character is however just as well marked here as in

The Bhábar.

the Kumaun Bhábar. The camping ground of Badshahibagh on the Chakráta road is just outside one of the Siwalik gorges. In the gorge stands a village well with water at 15 feet. In the encamping ground 150 yards away the Military Works Department have sunk a well cylinder 125 feet without getting a drop of water. The Hindan and other rivers of the Upper Doab rise ten miles south of the hills in the tract corresponding to the Tarái.

65. **The Duns.**—North of this Western Bhábar, but outside the Himalayas proper and separated from the plains by the outlying range of the Siwaliks and its continuation in the Bijnor district, lies an elevated plateau statistically of rising importance. The greater part, that to the west of the Ganges, is Dehra Dún, elevated some 2,000 feet above the sea, and therefore enjoying a very much cooler climate than the outer plains. It has been settled largely in grants to Europeans within comparatively recent times, and here only in the provinces we have the hill and plains tribes in actual contact.

66. **The Himalayan tract.**—Regarded from a census point of view the Himalayan area proper consists of three zones. The first, that of the outer Himalayas, is occupied by mountains from 5,000 to 8,500 feet high rising abruptly from the plain and sinking abruptly on the northern sides into deep and narrow valleys. The rainfall is excessive, 80 to 90 inches on an average ; the slopes are rarely gentle enough to allow space for cultivation, and the climate, except at comparatively great heights, unhealthy. Population is therefore scanty in this zone and the greater part is occupied by dense forest. Inside the outer Himalayas comes the second or populated zone where the hills are comparatively low, the valleys wider and the streams more permanent, although the rainfall, 47 inches at Almora, is low as compared with that in the outer range. Further northwards we pass into the third zone, the higher valleys of the inner Himalayas. These are for the most part uninhabitable for six months in the year and occupied temporarily in the hot weather by cowherds, wood cutters and the semi-nomad tribes of Bhotyas who carry on our commerce with Thibet.

67. **The plains districts.**—The Himalayan portions of the province, though occupying an area of 13,973 square miles, are as regards population comparatively unimportant, and by far the greater part of a report on the census of the North-West must concern itself almost exclusively with the figures for the districts of the plains. These districts are as regards physical aspect, climate and population, on the whole, very much more homogeneous than any other of the larger provinces in India, but there are differences in these respects which affect population to a no tinconsiderable extent, and therefore require mention.

68. **Bundelkhand and Mirzapur.**—The parts of the province which are most diverse from the ordinary type, are those which lie to the south of the Jumna before its junction with the Ganges at Allahabad and south of the Ganges eastwards from Allahabad. The former tract, comprising the districts of Bánda, Hamírpur, Jalaun, Jhánsi and Lalitpur, forms part of the ancient

province of Bundelkhand. These districts lie for the most part in a plain, narrow to the south-east, where the Vindyan hills reach within a short distance of the river, but widening northwards, the line of hills running almost due east and west and the Jumna flowing from north-west to south-east. The plain rises gradually from an elevation of 450 feet above the sea in Bánda and Jalaun to 1,500 feet in the Lalitpur plateau. Bundelkhand ranks without doubt as the poorest and most backward part of the plains of the North-West Provinces. The soil, in places the rich black cotton growing "mar," is in general comparatively infertile, sometimes sandy, more often rocky. The country is much cut up by deep ravines by which the drainage is carried into the Jumna and its tributaries. In the southern parts, even north of the Vindyan hills, isolated rocky hills and spurs from the main range render a large part of the area unculturable. The rainfall, averaging from 30 inches in Jalaun to 40 in Lalitpur, is more than usually precarious. Irrigation, though in comparatively small areas possible from ancient drains natural streams and a modern canal, is in general little practised. The crops grown are generally of the poorest description and the cultivation more than usually backward. Bundelkhand is therefore throughout peculiarly subject to drought, and part of it is unusually subject to floods. Of late years the damage done by the spread of kans, a deep-rooted grass, has been great and must be referred to in connection with the question of the movement of population. The climate is regarded as in general healthy, but the cold weather, even in the comparatively elevated Lalitpur, is shorter than in the Ganges valley, while the heat in the hot weather is great and constantly sustained.

The highlands of Mirzapur and Allahabad rising southwards from the Ganges east of Allahabad are not unlike Bundelkhand in character, but the plain on the Ganges is far more uniformly fertile than any part of Bundelkhand, whilst the southern parts are less closely populated and therefore less dependent on the seasons and of less importance in a census report.

69. **The Gangetic plain.**—The remainder of the province, with the exception of a few parganas in the Agra and Allahabad Divisions, is included between the Jumna and Ganges and the outer Himalayas. It consists of a great alluvial plain with a slight slope southwards from the Himalayas and eastwards towards the Bay of Bengal. How slight the slope is, may be gathered from the elevation of a few points. Mohand, at the foot of the Siwaliks in Sahâranpur, and Haldwáni, three miles from the foot of the Himalayas in Kumaun, both in the Bhábar, are 1,500 feet above the sea level. South of the Bhábar the level is usually slightly over 1,000 feet above the sea. Agra, where the Jumna bends from its southerly course to a south-easterly one, is 526 feet above the sea. Allahabad is 340 feet, and Ballia, where the Ganges leaves the province, 220 feet. The central part of the province is divided into a succession of horn-shaped tracts by the rivers which issue from the Himalayas, almost all with a southerly course to start with, gradually trending round to an easterly course before they join the main river in the south of the province. Except in the case of the three great rivers, the Jumna, Ganges and Gnogra, the rivers are little regarded as territorial boundaries. The tracts between the

Jumna and Ganges and beyond the Ghogra are alône known by separate names, the former, the Doab, the latter, Sarwar or Sarjupar.

The level of the Gangetic plain is broken naturally only by the river beds, sunk in general well below the level. The fertility is so uniform and so great as to constitute it the richest part of India. None of the districts can be considered as of inferior soil, but in some the extent of soil impregnated with saltpetre and in consequence unproductive, is so considerable as to affect the total productive power, whilst in others there are considerable tracts of land subject to damage from damp in wet years. Except in these usarous or swampy tracts, which are nowhere very extensive, the province is throughout the rains and cold weather a sea of rich cultivation, broken only by the groves of mixed mango, bamboo and other trees required for fruit or timber by which the villages are in general surrounded. In the hot weather these groves are the only relief to the eye from the wide extent of bare fallow land, which after giving two harvests recovers to a wonderful extent its productive powers simply from the influence of a few months of fierce sunshine and the abundant rains which follow.

The origin of the Gangetic plain is still a matter of dispute amongst geologists. It is considered by some that the soil forming the plain was deposited whilst the rivers from the Himalayas flowed into a great inland sea. The absence of all trace of marine deposits tends however to disprove this theory, and probably the better explanation is that the plain was deposited by fluvial action. This theory is supported by changes which have occurred within historical times. In Behat in Sahâranpur district we have a town which existed within the Christian era buried 17 feet below the present level under alluvial soil. In the districts beyond the Ghogra we have even now the process of formation going on before our eyes. The rivers there, not yet sunk into permanent channels, overlay their banks and bed year after year with a deposit which raises the banks on both sides distinctly above the level of the surrounding country, until in some year of unusually high flood the stream cuts its way into the low grounds outside its banks and there again in a different course begins the elevating process.

70. **The rainfall**.—The variations in rainfall in the province are considerable. Proximity either to the Himalayas or to the Bengal monsoon implies a comparatively high rainfall, whilst the districts most distant from either have the lowest fall. Agra and Muttra, each with an average of about 26 inches, have the minimum fall. Eastwards the rainfall gradually increases. It is 29 in Cawnpore, 31 in Allahabad, 37 in Ghâzipur. Northwards from Agra we have a rise as we approach the Himalayas, slower at first, more abrupt and more considerable close to the hills. Bulandshahr gets just over 26 inches ; Meerut, 28 ; Muzaffarnagar, 32 ; Sahâranpur, 36. Along the foot of the Himalayas we have a rise similar to that along the Jumna and Ganges. Starting with 36 inches in Sahâranpur, we get 40 in Bareilly, 45 in Bahraich, and the maximum for the plains districts is 48½ at Gorakhpur. The average rainfall for the province is 36 inches.

71. **The climate** varies with the rainfall and the latitude. Agra is again our starting point. The climate as enjoying, owing to its dryness and position, the widest range of temperature. The heat is greatest here in the hot weather and in the winter the cold is but little less than in most northern districts of the Doab. As the humidity increases eastward the range of temperature lessens and in Ballia the keen cold and the fierce heat of the western districts are alike absent, and we have a climate similar to that of Behar. Sahâranpur, furthest north, has a long and cool cold weather, whilst the humidity of the soil, together with its proximity to the Himalayas, prevents any very high temperature in the hot weather. Eastwards the range diminishes to Gorakhpur, where we again have a climate like that of Behar, but with an average temperature decidedly lower than that of Ballia.

72. **The history of the provinces.**—The History of Hindustan is that of India. It was the site of the Aryan settlements in the earliest times of which, in the Vedas, we have any record. At the time of Alexander's invasion it was the centre of the great Buddhist kingdom of the Gupta dynasty from which Buddhism spread over China, Eastern India and Central Asia. Buddhism, in its birthplace, was stamped out by modern Hinduism, and from the same centre as Buddhism was spread over India the religion which has taken its place. The original home of Hinduism is still regarded as sacred, wherever Hinduism is influential and the places in the province, which are visited periodically by pilgrims from all over India are very numerous. Chief amongst them are the Himalayan shrines near the sources of the Ganges and Jumna, Hardwár, where the Ganges leaves the hills, Muttra and Brindaban on the Jumna, Prag (Allahabad) where the Jumna, Ganges and mythical Sarsuti unite, Kashi (Benares) and Bindhachal on the lower reaches of the Ganges, and Ajudhiya on the Sarju (Ghogra). Places of pilgrimage less famed are dotted everywhere along the banks of the Ganges, and in the northern forests and Bundelkhand there are many shrines devoted in general to the worship of gods of a non-Aryan type adopted by the all-embracing Hinduism.

In those pre-Muhammadan times, in which we begin to have the slight foundations of genuine Indian history, Hindustan was the site of the great Hindu kingdoms. Since the Muhammadan conquest, an empire centering in Agra and Dehli, the letter bordering on the province and properly belonging to it, extended its authority over the whole or nearly the whole of the present British India. With the death of Aurangzeb in 1707 began for the provinces a period of gradually increasing disintegration and disorder which ended in the establishment of the British power. Rohilkhand, Oudh and Bundelkhand became independent of the Mughal power and its authority was weakened elsewhere. The Mahrattas, checked for a time by their defeat at Panipat in 1761, were gradually establishing their authority in those districts which longest remained subject to the Emperor, when their course of conquest and misrule was interrupted by the gradual British advance from Bengal. In 1763 the effect of the battle of Buxar extended British influence to Allahabad, though it was not till 1775, that the eastern districts of Benares, Jaunpur and Ghâzipur were finally ceded to them. In 1801 the whole of the

Oudh dominions in the lower Doab together with Rohilkhand were ceded by treaty to the British, and in 1803 Lord Lake's campaign against Sindhia brought the whole of the rest of the North-Western Provinces under British rule. For 30 years after annexation the provinces remained under the Bengal Government, but in 1835 the Lieutenant-Governorship of the North-Western Provinces was established, including the whole of the present provinces except Jhánsi, with the addition of the Dehli Commissionership and the Narbada territories. In 1853 Jhánsi was added to the provinces. Dehli and Hissar were transferred to the Panjáb in 1858, and the Sagar and Narbada territories formed into a separate Government in 1859. Oudh was annexed in 1856, but the two provinces were not brought under the same Government till 1876.

73. **Epidemic disease**.—Since the British annexation the provinces have, except for a few months in the Mutiny of 1857, been free from what for many years before had been the chief agencies controlling the material increase of population, war and misrule; but the operation of agencies little less powerful, famine and epidemic disease, has still to be considered. Of the two the more powerful, in a series of years, is epidemic disease, and in particular cholera, small-pox and fever. Fever is by far the most important. The districts of the provinces are naturally very unequally subject to this disease. The tract which is regarded as its particular home is that lying along the foot of the hills, but in a series of wet years it is little less effective in controlling population in the districts of the Doab. The subject will be again referred to more at length in connection with the movement of population and the age tables. The victories which can be reported by the British Administration against epidemic disease are not numerous. Vaccination has made some progress, but not so much as to produce any clearly-defined decrease in the small-pox death rate. Sanitation, except in towns, has made no great progress, and as regards drainage, though much has been done of late years, the action taken has been confined to those tracts in which the swampiness was considered to be increasing.

74. **The irrigation system**.—Against famine and scarcity, on the other hand, a great record progress can be shown. Like the rest of India, the North-West Provinces and Oudh have been periodically visited by scarcity due to failure of the annual rains. Measures of protection, direct in the extension of the area in which food-crops can grow, and of artificial irrigation, and indirect in provision of means of communication with areas outside the famine influence, have been undertken on perhaps a larger scale than in any other part of India. Their efficiency has been tried more than once during the past decade, in years in which the rainfall was greatly below average. Irrigation in three forms is practised in the provinces.

1st.—From canals, fed mostly by the large perennial rivers and in all cases provided by the Government.

2nd.—From wells, almost invariably dug through the upper strata of the soil into a stratum in which a perennial supply of water can be obtained.

3*rd*.—From tanks and streams. The sources of supply in the first two methods do not fail in the dryest years, and they are therefore the only absolutely efficient means of protection against scarcity. The third form of irrigation, except in a comparatively small area, where perennial hill streams are tapped, is apt to fail when it is most wanted ; but it is fortunately confined almost entirely to those damper districts in which the rainfall is least likely to fail.

The canal system provides an almost complete safeguard against an extensive failure of the spring crops or of the more valuable autumn crops in those parganas and areas in which it has been provided. From Sahāranpur to Cawnpore all the districts of the Doab, except Farukhabad, have been so safeguarded, except in those parganas the configuration or surroundings of which render the introduction of canal water impossible or inexpedient.

The extension of the canal system during the past ten years is shown in the following statement :—

Abstract No. 5, showing the extension of canal-irrigation.

Canals.		1881-82.				1890-91.				
		Main Canal, branches and navigation channels.	Distributaries.	Escapes and drainage cuts.	Total.	Main Canal, branches and navigation channels.	Distributaries.	Escapes and drainage cuts.	Total.	Increase.
Upper Ganges Canal	...	460	2,543	900	3,903	456	2,523	1,034	4,013	110
Lower ditto	...	531	1,623	252	2,406	557	2,097	540	3,194	788
Agra Canal	...	165	348	20	533	134	565	49	748	215
Eastern Jumna Canal	...	130	618	292	1,040	129	643	343	1,115	75
Betwa Canal	...	...	...	...	...	168	341	29	538	538
Minor Canals	...	20	397	...	417	20	537	8	565	148
Total	...	1,306	5,529	1,464	8,299	1,464	6,706	2,003	10,173	1,874
		Increase			...	158	1,177	539	1,874	...

This extension does not, however, as the quantity of water available is limited, mean that a corresponding increase in canal-irrigation has taken place. It in general means simply that the benefits of canal-irrigation have been extended to a wider area by decreasing the very high proportion of water allowed to a smaller one.

The system of well-irrigation extends throughout the provinces and even in canal-irrigated districts competes with canal-irrigation in certain localities and for certain crops. A considerable proportion of well-irrigation is from wells dug into the soil without any protecting cylinder. The number of such wells can be largely increased on demand, and decrease considerably in a series of wet years, partly because they are less wanted, partly because the dampness of the soil causes the wells to fall in. Well-irrigation was, therefore, at the period at which the census was taken below average and much below what is possible.

The total cultivated area and the total area irrigated from wells, canals and other sources are compared in the following statement.

Abstract No. 6, comparing the cropped, irrigated and dry areas in the province.

Cultivated area.					
Irrigated.				Dry.	Total.
Wells.	Canals.	Other sources.	Total.		
Acres. No.	Acres. No.	Acres. No.	Acres. No.	Acres. No.	Acres. No.
4,812,586	1,615,495	3,384,131	9,812,212	24,329,459	34,141,671

Regarded as a protection against famine in India, all irrigation is subject to a very noteworthy limitation. The amount of moisture required by the ordinary autumn crops, and in particular the millets, is so great that they cannot be grown satisfactorily by artificial irrigation. The plants, if water enough is supplied to the roots, grow up strong and heathy, but the yield of grain given is insignificant. The same is the case with cotton, one of the most valuable of the autumn crops, and that which pays the autumn rent in many districts. The plants with artificial moisture are strong and healthy, but without moisture in the air, the yield of cotton is very small or *nil*. The failure of the food-supply derived from the autumn crop cannot, therefore, be averted by irrigation, although by the growth of substitute crops its effect can, to some extent, be mitigated. Such a failure, though it would mean much scarcity and distress, would rarely imply actual famine, unless followed by a failure of the spring crop. It is in regard to the spring crop that the value of irrigation is of interest, and I have, therefore, in the accompanying irrigation map (No. 1) shown only the proportion borne by the irrigated to the non-irrigated area in the spring crop. Tank-irrigation, dependent in itself largely on the rainfall, has been distinguished from well and canal-irrigation ; as already pointed out, well-irrigation is at a minimum in the year for which the map has been made.

Irrigation has for many years uniformly been increasing and assuming a more permanent form. It is susceptible of immense further progress by the introduction of canal systems dependent for their supply of water on streams not yet tapped and by the extension of well-irrigation, which is possible almost everywhere in the provinces. Plans on a very large scale for the extension of the canal system have already been drawn up and the scheme of the Sarju canal will no doubt be carried out at some future time when the finance of the country permits.

75. The cultivated area.—As regard extension of cultivation, the limit has been more nearly approached. The abstract in the margin compares the actually cultivated area with that available for extension of cultivation. The forest land, 6725· square miles of it in the Himalayas, cannot be considered as available without fear of subsequent loss, as the province has already been denuded of timber of the more valuable kinds, and the retention of the forests for the supply of timber is absolutely necessary. The rest of the area shown as available for cultivation includes all grove and grazing land in the provinces, and a very large part of it could not be brought under the plough without ultimate injury to the climate and livestock of the province. In quality of soil, too, a large part of the land classed as culturable is very inferior. It is improbable that at the present moment more than 10 per cent. could be added to the cultivated area. The fact that of late years the cultivated area has actually retrograded shows that in many districts the limit of area of cultivation has been nearly approached.

	Cultivated (including new fallow).	Available for cultivation.		Not available for cultivation.	Area for which returns are not available.	Total.
		Fallow and grove.	Forest.			
	Acres.	Acres.	Acres.	Acres.	Acres.	Acres.
N.-W. Provinces ...	27,679,159	6.452,491	6,693,805	6,682,606	5,794,851	53,302,912
Percentage ...	51·92	12·10	12·56	12·53	10·89	...
Oudh	9,386,617	1,857,462	2,028,098	2,226,703	...	15,498,880
Percentage ...	60·57	11·98	13·08	14·37	...	...
Total ...	37,065,776	8,309,953	8,721,903	8,909,309	5,794,851	68,801,792
Percentage ...	53·87	12·08	12·68	12·95	8·42	...

Whilst, however, the cultivated area has been at a standstill, there has been a considerable increase of late years in the cropped area owing to the increase in the practice of double-cropping the best land. During the rains in the beginning of the Indian agrecultural year the cultivator of the North-Western Provinces grows millets, pulse, rice, maize or cotton over nearly 59 per cent. of the cultivated area. In the cold weather, again, he grows wheat, barley, gram, peas or other spring crops over about 60 per cent. of the area, in addition to certain of the rains crops such as arhar and sugarcane, which stand through both harvests. In the hot weather less than one per cent. grows melons or vegetables. In all, 20 per cent. of the cultivated area in the North-Western Provinces of late years grows two crops, whilst a part of the richest land near towns or large villages grows three crops year after year. In Oudh the proportion of double-cropped land is still higher, and in two of the Oudh districts it exceeds 40 per cent. of the actually-cropped area. The question as to whether this double-cropping is injurious to the soil and whether it can be expected to extend still further, is one on which experts differ. The complaints made by cultivators themselves, that the fertility of the soil is being reduced, are constant and loud, especially in canal-irrigated districts; but there can, I think, be little doubt that the weight of expert opinion is against the supposition that the fertility of the soil, where properly treated, is reduced by double-cropping.

[To face Page 82.

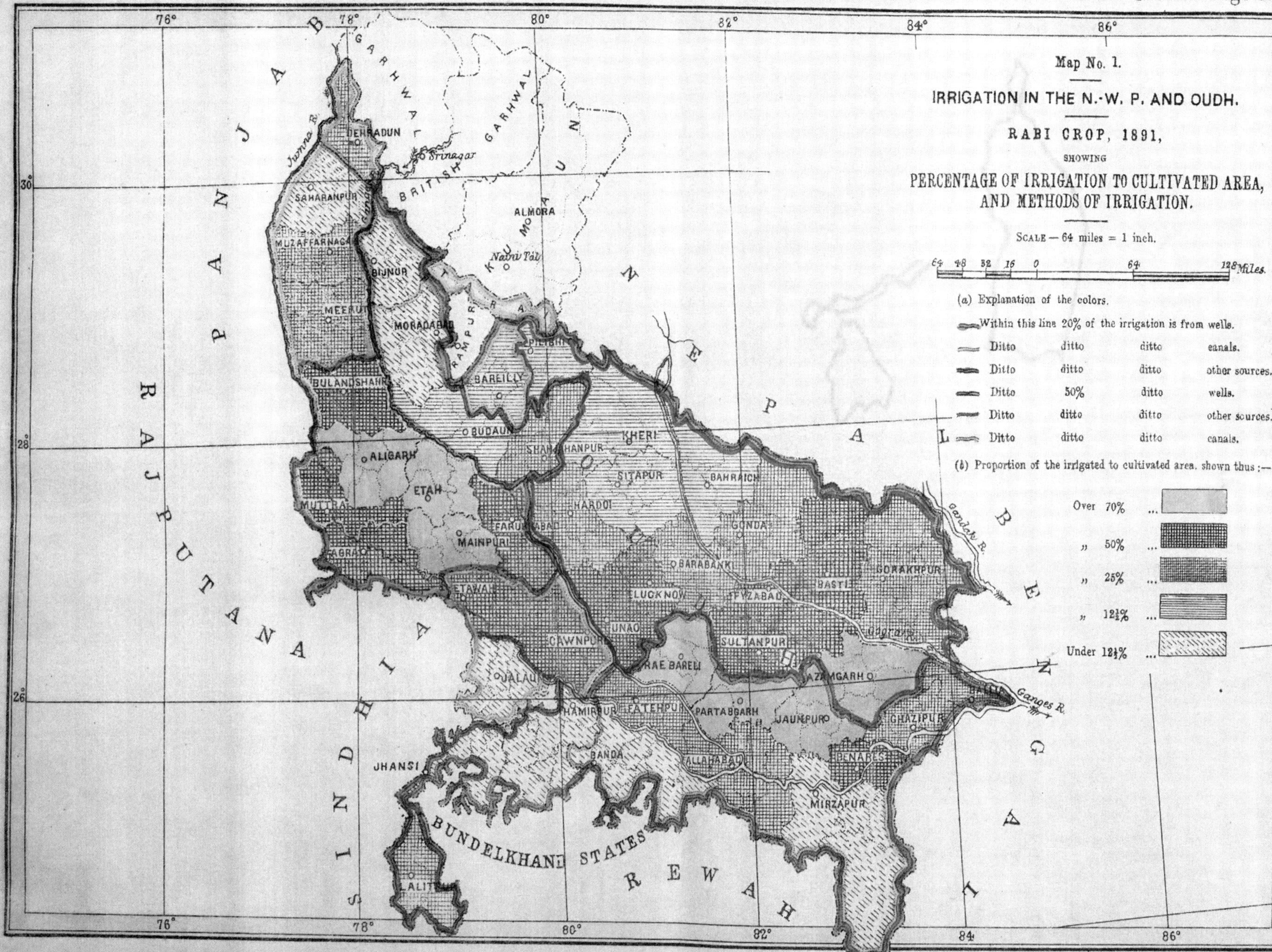

The marginal statement is of interest as showing the relative importance of the crops usually grown in the provinces.

	Percentage on total cropped area.
Wheat	11·7
Rice	16·6
Other cereals	25·2
Millets	15·5
Pulses	16·3
Other food-crops	2·0
Sugarcane	2·9
Cotton	3·6
Indigo	0·8
Opium	0·6
Tea	0·0
Fodder crops	1·7
Other non-food-crops ...	3·1
Total ...	100·

It happily rarely occurs that a drought extends throughout more than a portion of Upper India at the same time, and when in spite of irrigation there has been a loss of a considerable part of the food-supply of a district, the most important aid that can be given to the people is that afforded by easy means of communication with districts or parts in which the food-supply is ample. The means of communication prevalent throughout this part of India in times previous to the present century was away from certain large rivers, almost confined to carriage by pack-animals; and throughout part of Oudh and trans-Gogra districts of the North-West this still remains the standard mode of local transport. In Oudh, this fact is due to the comparative newness of the system of excellent roads which now connect adjacent districts there. In the "Sarjupar" districts the maintenance of roads is, owing to the nature of the soil and the number of perennial streams, more expensive than elsewhere, and the roads for which the standard allotments have been provided consequently in worse order than in other districts in the Himalayas. Elsewhere all local traffic is carried on by means of wheeled conveyances. In the western districts the system of village roads is very complete, and only villages situated in river ravines are beyond the reach of carts.

Boat traffic, never very extensive in the North-West Provinces and Oudh, is now gradually diminishing and is only extensive in the Ganges below Allahabad and the Gogra below Bahrámghat. There is still some traffic in the rains in the upper reaches of these rivers and on the Rapti, Gomti, Jumna and a few other rivers. The upper part of the Ganges Canal and the Agra Canal carry a modest amount of boat traffic, but in no part of the provinces can boat carriage be looked on as to any considerable extent available for the purposes of famine relief.

The sole means of extra provincial communication in case of urgency are the railways with which the provinces are now well-provided, and which are yearly being extended. The East Indian Railway and Oudh and Rohilkhand Railway traverse the province from east to the north-west corner, the one serving all districts south of the Ganges except Bundelkhand, Farukhabad and Etah; the other, a similarly large tract north of the Ganges and south of the Gogra. Bundelkhand is now traversed in all directions by the Indian Midland Railway. Three systems of narrow gauge railways, which it is hoped will soon be linked, give means of communication to the trans-Gogra districts, to the north of Oudh and Rohilkhand, and to those central districts which are separated from the Oudh and Rohilkhand Railway by the Ganges and from the East Indian Railway by distance. Extensions of all these railways, except the East Indian Railway, are now in progress and within a few years there will be no part of the provinces outside the Himalayan districts unprovided with railway communication.

The following statement shows the improvement in railway communication within the last ten years :—

Length of railway lines open in 1880.

East Indian Railway main lines	607	
Branch lines	30	637
Oudh and Rohilkhand Railway main lines ...	419	
Branch lines	128	547
Scindia State Railway		20
North-Western Railway		107
Metre gauge lines ... Muttra to Háthras		29
Metre gauge lines ... Agra to Achnera...		18
Total ...		1,358

Length of railway lines open in 1890.

Broad gauge.	East Indian Railway	618
	Oudh and Rohilkhand	706
	North-Western	107
	Indian Midland	435
	Total ...	1,866
Metre gauge.	Lucknow, Sitapur, Bareilly	199
	Rohilkhand and Kumaun	67
	Bengal and North-Western	309
	Cawnpore-Achnera	240
	Rájputána-Malwa (Agra to Achnera)	18
		833
	Total ...	2,699

One effect of the great improvement in communication and particularly in railway communication as effected within the late years has been the reduction of the price of standard grains to almost a uniform standard in most of the districts of the province. The effect is most graphically shown in the diagram (No. 1) on the opposite page taken from a memo. by the Director of Land Records and Agriculture, and showing the highest and lowest price of wheat in the different districts of the province.

76. **Executive Divisions.**—The provinces on the date of the census consisted of 49 districts and two native states, the former grouped into

[To face page 85.

Diagram No. 1, illustrating the highest and lowest average prices of wheat in the different districts of the province in each year from 1861 *to* 1891.

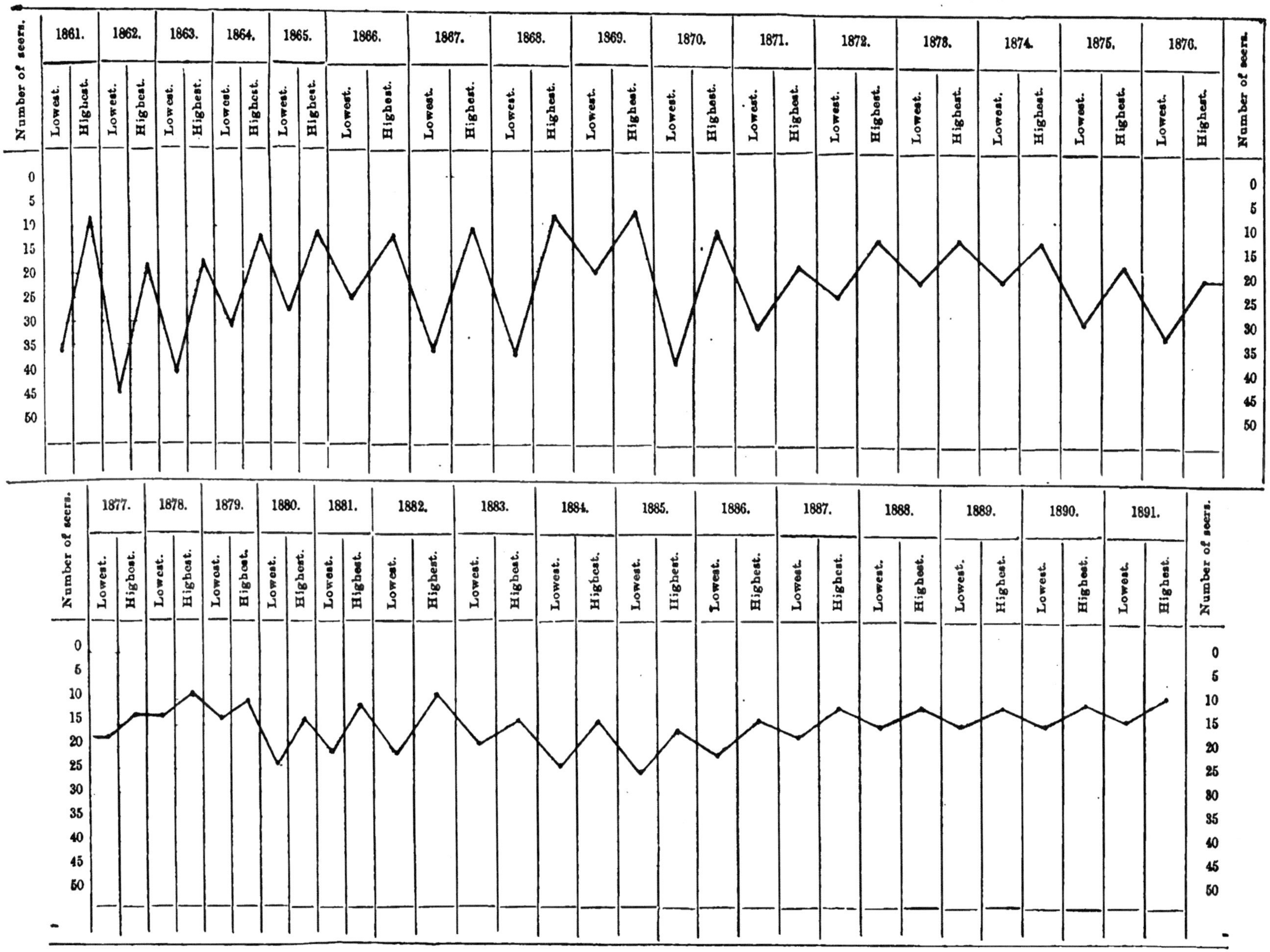

eleven divisions. Soon after the date of the census a rearrangement of the executive divisions of the provinces took place by which the Jhánsi Division was abolished, a new Gorakhpur Division established and the four divisions of Oudh combined into two. A year afterwards the Lalitpur district was abolished and the Tarái and Kumaun districts rearranged as those of Naini Tal and Almora. The new distribution of Commissionerships has been shown in all tables, but the rearrangement, so far as the districts were concerned, could not be given effect to in the imperial tables, because the entries for the birthplace table according to the new distribution could not be ascertained from the enumerator's schedule prepared while the former arrangement was in force. The imperial tables, therefore, show the districts as they stood on the day of the census and the divisions as now arranged. The supplementary provincial tables prepared for executive purposes show all districts and sub-divisions as they stood at the date of publication of the tables and where alterations have taken place after the 26th February 1891 differ from the imperial returns.

77. **The changes in area.**—Before proceeding to the consideration of the census figures proper for the province, the statement of areas in column 1 of table I requires mention. The figures are taken from the latest report of the Board of Revenue available when the table was completed, and show corrections on the survey areas due to resurvey and to transfers by alluvion and diluvion as well as for executive purposes up to the end of September 1890. They show for the whole of the British districts an area of 107,502·8 square miles against 106,103·9 at last census. The difference in the total area, 1,398·9 square miles is almost entirely due to the more accurate measurements of late surveys and occurs almost entirely in the districts the figures for which in 1881 and 1891 are compared in the marginal table.

Abstract No. 7, showing the variations in area of certain districts.

District.	Area in 1881.	Area in 1891.	Increase.
Kumaun	6,000	7,151	1,151
Garhwál	5,500	5,629	129
Jhánsi	1,566	1,640	74
Tarái	938	963	25
Total ...	14,004	15,383	1,379

The figures for Kumaun in 1881 were merely estimates, and are now replaced by figures supplied by the Survey of India. The change in the Tarái also is due to remeasurement, not to alteration of area. In Jhánsi there has been a real increase owing to transfer from Scindia's territory in exchange for the Gwalior Fort and Morar Cantonment. The alterations in none of the other districts have been sufficiently great to deserve notice.

78. **The total population.**—The total population of the 112,612 square miles which form the Lieutenant-Governorship, including native states, was according to the census 47,697,576 persons of whom 46,905,085 reside in British districts and the remainder 792,491 in the two native states. The population of the British districts closely corresponds to that of the German Empire, the area being, however, only half as much or somewhat less than that of the Austrian provinces of the Austro-Hungarian Empire or that of the Italian Kingdom.

The table in the margin in which the population of the provinces is compared with that of the leading countries of the world and of the other larger provinces of India shows the position of the Lieutenant-Governorship as regards population. In India the North-Western Provinces follow the Bengal Lieutenant-Governorship at a considerable interval, but are proportionately even further ahead of any other province. Outside the British Empire, of the great empires and nations of the world only China, Russia and the United States of America exceed the North-Western Provinces and Oudh in population. The population of the United Kingdom only slightly exceeds that of the North-Western Provinces without Oudh. The North-Western Provinces alone contain double the population of Spain, whilst Oudh alone has double the population of countries so historically important as Egypt and Belgium, the latter of which is exceeded in population by two of the divisions of the province. Switzerland, Greece and Denmark all have population considerably lower than that of the single district of Gorakhpur, whilst Norway is but slightly more important in point of population than Basti, the second of the North-Western Provinces districts. Of the two native states attached to the province, Rámpur has a somewhat lower population than New Zealand or than an English county of average size such as Hampshire or Essex; the Rája of Tehri Garhwál rules over about as many mountaineers as the Prince of Montenegro.

Abstract No. 8, comparing the population of the N.-W. Provinces and Oudh with that of certain foreign countries.

Country.	Population.	Country.	Population.
China	404,180,000	Spain	17,550,246
India	284,614,210	Central Previnces with fendatories.	12,944,805
Russia	113,354,649		
Bengal Lieutenant-Governorship.	74,643,366	**Oudh**	12,650,831
		Central Provinces, British districts.	10,784,294
United States of America.	62,622,650		
		Burma	8,098,014
North-Western Provinces and Oudh with feudatories.	47,697,576	Egypt	6,817,265
		Fyzabad Division ...	6,794,272
		Gorakhpur Division,	6,508,526
North-Western Provinces and Oudh, British Districts.	46,905,085	Belgium	6,093,798
		Lucknow Division ...	5,856,559
		Ireland	5,174,836
German Empire ...	46,855,704	Sweden	4,565,668
Japan	39,607,234	Portugal	4,550,699
Bengal Proper ...	38,277,339	Holland	4,548,596
France	37,930,759	Canada	4,324,810
Austria and Hungary ...	37,786,346	Scotland	4,033,103
United Kingdom ...	35,026,108	Ceylon	3,008,239
North-West Provinces.	34,254,254	**Gorakhpur district** ...	2,994,057
		Switzerland ...	2,933,334
England and Wales ...	29,001,018	Greece	2,187,208
Itlay	28,459,628	Norway	1,806,900
Prussia	28,318,470	**Basti district** ...	1,785,844
Bombay with feudatories.	26,916,342	**Kumaun Division** ...	1,181,567
		New South Wales ...	1,122,200
Panjáb with feudatories,	25,130,127	New Zealand ...	578,482
Java	22,819,174	**Rampur State** ...	551,249
Panjáb, British districts,	20,866,847	**Tehri Garhwal** ...	241,242
Bombay, British districts,	18,857,044	Montenegro ...	236,000

79. **The density of the population.**—The census figures for the province are, however, more striking still, when considered in view of the density of population per square mile of area throughout the greater part of the provinces. Before comparing the figures for the province in this respect effectively with those of other countries, it is necessary to some extent to analyse them into their component parts, but in the first place the distribution of gross density within the province itself may be referred to. The accompanying abstract shows the districts arranged in order of density, and the map No. 2 gives a more graphic idea of the location of the more densely populated tracts than a statement can.

[To face page 87.

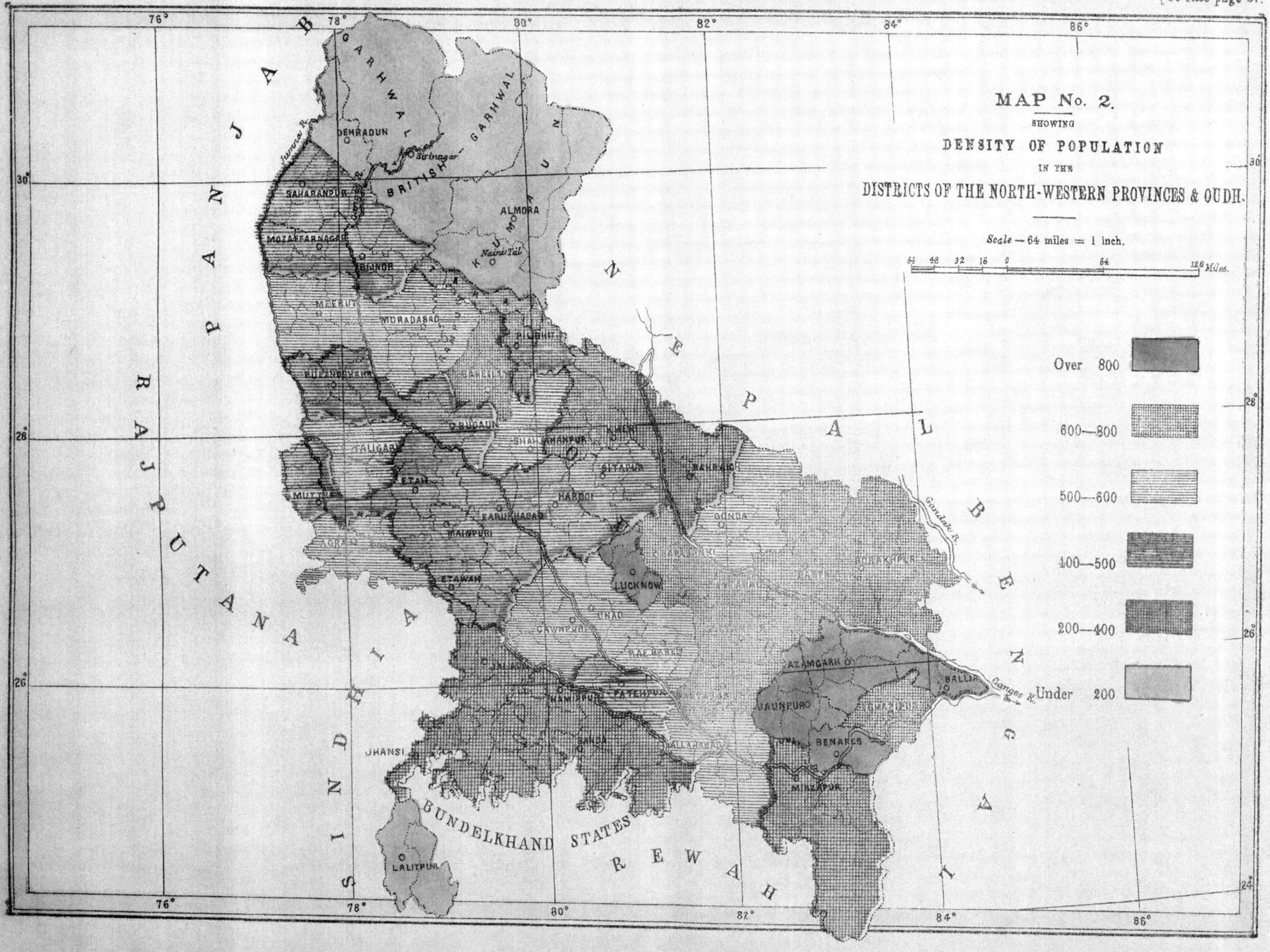

Abstract No. 9, showing the divisions, districts and states of the provinces in order of density of population.

Serial number.	District or Division.	Density per square mile.	Serial number.	District or Division.	Density per square mile.
1	2	3	1	2	3
1	Benares	913·7		Lucknow Division	486·5
2	Jaunpur	816·0	28	Hardoi	478·9
3	Ballia	805·7	29	Sitapur	476·9
4	Azamgarh	804·6		Meerut Division	471·4
5	Lucknow	800·6		Agra Division	470·1
6	Gházipur	737·3	30	Muzaffarnagar	466·1
7	Fyzabad	703·7	31	Budaun	459·0
	Gorakhpur Division	685·7	32	Mainpuri	448·0
8	Gorakhpur	654·3	33	Sahåranpur	446·5
9	Bareilly	652·6		N.-W. Provinces and Oudh	436·4
10	Bara Banki	649·9	34	Etáwah	430·3
11	Basti	645·1	35	Fatehpur	428·1
12	Partábgarh	633·4	36	Bijnor	418·2
13	Sultánpur	629·2		North-Western Provinces	411·3
14	Rao Bareli	591·7	37	Etah	403·3
15	Meerut	587·2	38	Bahraich	373·2
16	Rámpur State	583·3	39	Pilibhít	353·8
	Fyzabad Division	558·0		Allahabad Division	333·4
17	Agra	543·9	40	Kheri	304·7
18	Allahabad	542·6	41	Jalaun	267·9
19	Unao	536·4	42	Jhánsi	249·6
20	Aligarh	534·3	43	Bánda	230·6
21	Sháhjahánpur	526·6	44	Hamírpur	224·4
	Oudh	522·5	45	Mirzapur	222·4
22	Moradabad	516·7	46	Tarái	218·7
	Benares Division	515·5		Native States	155·1
23	Cawnpore	511·9	47	Dehra Dún	140·9
24	Gonda	506·6	48	Lalitpur	140·8
25	Farukhabad	499·1		Kumaun Division	85·9
26	Bulandshahr	497·0	49	Kumaun	78·8
27	Muttra	495·2	50	Garhwál	72·4
	Rohilkhand Division	489·7	51	Tehri Garhwál State	57·9

The distribution of districts according to the gross density is disturbed to a considerable extent by the position of the large cities which, though most of them serve as trade centres for several districts, are included only in the one district in which they are situated. The district of Benares heads the list with density of 913 persons per square mile. Benares, Jaunpur, Azamgarh and Ballia all with densities over 800 per square mile and Gházipur with 737 per square mile form the western part of the most densely populated part of India, possibly of the most densely populated part of the world in which the population is not to a great extent due to the presence of large cities. The neighbouring districts of Behar, ethnologically and geographically very similar to those just mentioned, form the eastern part of this densely populated tract. The density reaches its maximum in the district of Sarun with 930 persons to the square mile, followed closely by Muzaffarpur with 903, whilst Darbhanga and Patna have both over 800. Similarity of circumstances as regards climate and population and recent rapid growth appears to indicate that Gorakhpur and Basti, which at present owing to the population to the north being comparatively scanty, show only 654 and 645 persons per square mile, will within a few decades belong to the most densely populated group. At present with the eastern and central Oudh districts of Lucknow (excluding the city) Bara Banki, Fyzabad, Sultánpur and Partábgarh and northern part of Allahabad, they form the second zone in which the population ranges from 600 to 800. Of the western districts of the province only Bareilly with 652 persons per square mile belongs to this zone. Rae Bareli, Unao, Gonda, Cawnpore on the borders of the densely populated eastern tract, and Agra, Aligarh, Meerut, Moradabad and Sháhjahánpur, scattered amongst more scanty populated western districts, are the remaining districts which are denser in population than the average. All the rest of the west of the Gangetic plain is below average, and in a strip from the Tarái to Bahraich along the foot of the hills the density is much below average. With still lower densities we have two well-marked tracts, (1) Bundelkhand and Mirzapur, south of the Jumna and Ganges, with densities varying from 268 in Jalaun to 141 in Lalitpur, and (2) the Himalayan tract varying from 141 in Dehra Dún to 58 in Tehri Garhwál.

To recapitulate briefly : the eastern half of the Gangetic plain is populated above the average, the density gradually increasing eastwards to a limit over 900 ; the western half of the Gangetic valley is below average in density but with a few scattered districts above it. Bundelkhand and Mirzapur are far below average and the Himalayas scantily populated. Abstract No. 10, and the diagram No. II compare the densities of the districts of the North-Western Provinces and Oudh with those of selected foreign countries. It at once attracts notice that the countries or counties the density of which in

Abstract No. 10, *comparing the density of population in the North-Western Provinces and Oudh with that of other foreign countries and Indian provinces.*

Serial number.	Name of country, &c.	Area in square miles.	Population.	Density per square mile.
1	2	3	4	5
1	Lanarkshire ...	889	904,412	1,017·3
2	**Benares**	1,009·5	921,943	913·7
3	Brabant (south) ...	1,268	1,074,765	847·5
4	**Jaunpur** ...	1,549·8	1,264,949	816·0
5	**Ballia**	1,169·7	942,465	805·7
6	**Lucknow** ...	967	774,163	800·6
7	North Holland ...	1,070	819,283	765·6
8	**Gorakhpur Division** ...	9,491·4	6,508,526	685·7
9	**Gorakhpur** ...	4,576·1	2,994,057	654·8
10	**Bara Banki** ..	1,740·2	1,130,906	649.9
11	**Basti**	2,767	1,785,844	645·2
12	Kent	1,555	977,706	629·0
13	**Rae Bareli** ..	1,751·2	1,036,521	591·7
14	**Meerut**	2,369·7	1,391,458	587·2
15	**Rampur State** ..	945	551,249	583·3
16	**Fyzabad Division** ...	12,176·6	6,794,272	558·6
17	Sakony	5,856	3,182,003	543·0
18	**Allahabad** ...	2,852·3	1,548,787	542·6
19	Belgium	11,373	6,098,798	536·0
20	**Shahjahanpur** ...	1,744·1	918,551	526·6
21	Egypt	12,976	6,817,265	525·
22	**Oudh**	24,217	12,650,831	522·6
23	**Benares Division** ...	10,414	5,368,774	515·5
24	**Farukhabad** ...	1720·3	858,687	499·1
25	England and Wales ...	58,186	29,001,018	498·
26	**Bulandshahr** ...	1,911·1	949,914	497·0
27	**Rohilkhand Division**	10,907·8	5,343,674	489·7
28	**Lucknow Division** ...	12,040·4	5,856,559	486·5
29	Channel Islands ...	295	141,260	479·
30	Yorkshire	6,067	2,886,564	476·
31	Bengal (excluding feudatories) ...	151,543	71,846,987	470·8
32	**Meerut Division** ...	11,326·3	5,326,883	470·3
33	**Agra Division** ...	10,139·2	4,767,759	470·1
34	**Muzaffarnagar** ...	1,658·2	772,874	466·1
35	Java	50,848	22,819,174	449·
36	**Saharanpur** ..	2,242	1,001,280	446·5
37	**N.-W. P. and Oudh** (excluding feudatories)...	107,502·8	46,905,085	436·4
38	**N.-W. P. and Oudh** (including feudatories)...	1,12,611·8	47,697,576	423·6
39	Bijnor	1,898·4	794,070	418·2
40	**N.-W. Provinces** ...	83,285·8	34,254,254	411·3
41	Bengal (including feudatories) ...	187,377	74,643,366	398·3
42	**Holland**	12,648	4,548,596	360·
43	**Allahabad Division** ...	1,726·4	5,757,121	333·4
44	Northamptonshire ...	984	301,695	306·6
45	**Kheri**	2,964·8	903,615	304·7
46	United Kingdom ...	121,481	35,026,108	288·
47	Japan	147,655	39,607,234	268·
48	**Jalaun**	1479·6	396,361	267.9
49	Madras (including feudatories).	150,798	39,331,062	260.8
50	Madras (excluding feudatories).	141,189	35,630,440	252·4
51	**Jhansi**	1,640	409,419	249·6
52	Italy	114,410	28,459,628	249·
53	Devon	2,586	604,397	233·7
54	**Mirzapur** ...	5,228	1,161,508	222·4
55	German Empire ...	211,168	46,853,704	222·
56	Prussia	136,075	28,318,470	208·
57	Panjáb (ixcluding feudatories).	106,899	20,866,847	188·5
58	France	204,092	37,930,759	186·
59	India	1,588,276	284,614,210	179·8
60	Panjáb (including feudatories).	145,198	25,130,127	172·7
61	Ireland	33,583	5,174,636	159·
62	Denmark	14,124	2,185,859	155·

[To face page 89.

DIAGRAM No. II.

COMPARING THE AVERAGE DENSITY OF POPULATION OF THE DIVISIONS OF THE N.-W. P. AND OUDH, AND VARIOUS FOREIGN COUNTRIES.

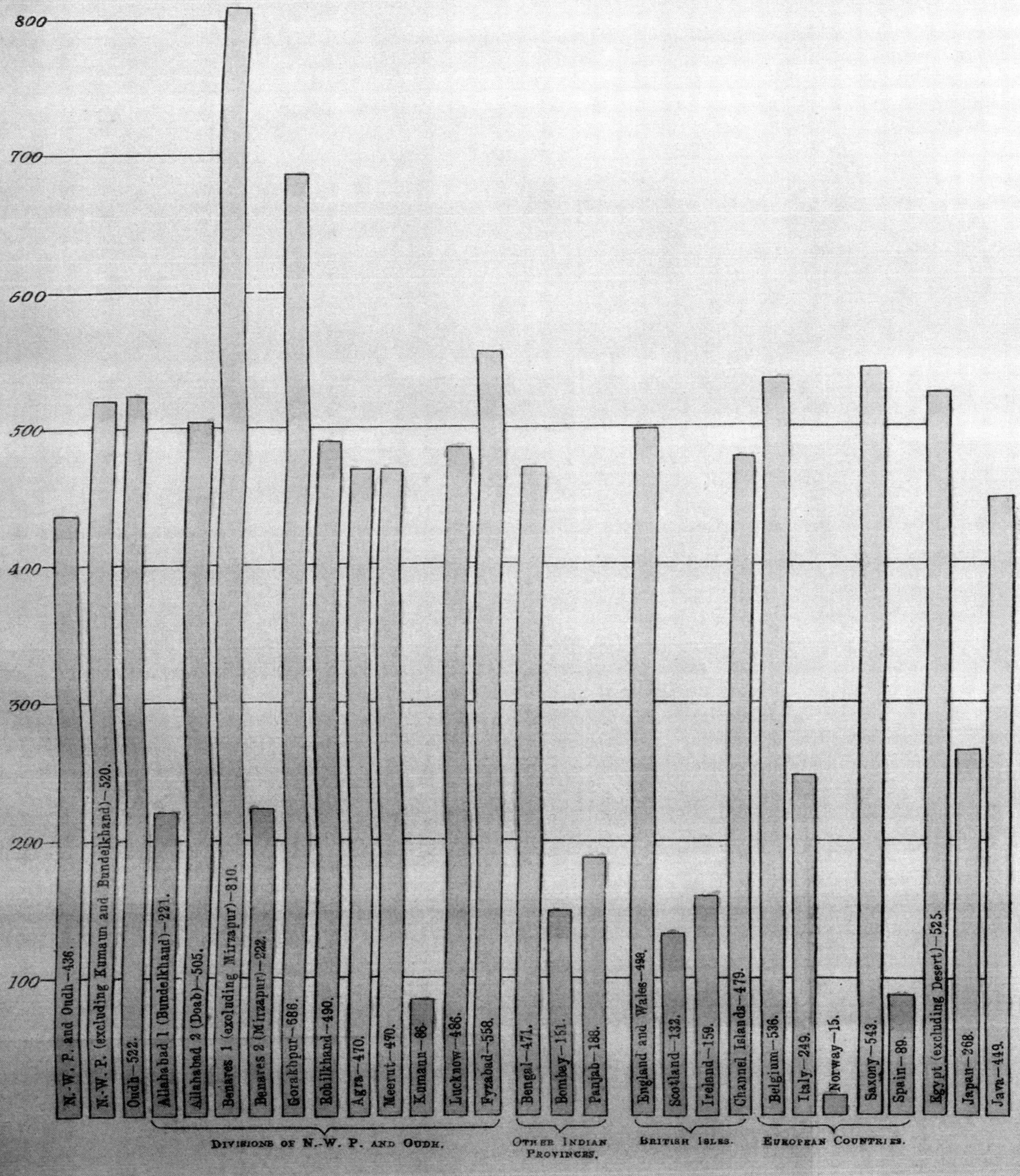

Serial number.	Name of country, &c.	Area in square miles.	Population.	Density per square mile.
1	2	3	4	5
63	Bombay (excluding feudatories).	125,064	18,857,040	151·1
64	**Lalitpur**	1,947·4	274,200	140·8
65	Bombay (including feudatories).	194,109	26,916,342	138·3
66	East Lothian ...	280	38,502	137·5
67	Scotland	30,417	4,033,103	132·
68	Jamaica	4,424	585,582	132·
69	Central Provinces (excluding feudatories)	86,501	10,784,294	124·6
70	Ceylon	25,364	3,008,239	118·
71	Central Provinces (including feudatories).	115,936	12,944,805	111·4
72	China	4,179,560	404,180,000	96·
73	King's County ...	772	72,852	94·3
74	**Kumaun Division** ...	13,742·7	1,181,567	85·9
75	**Kumaun** ..	7,151	563,181	78·8
76	**Tehri Garhwal State**	4,164	241,242	57·9
77	Burma (excluding feudatories).	171,430	7,722,053	45·05
78	Russia in Europe ...	2,130,462·5	95,870,810	45·
79	Burma (including feudatories).	211,430	8,098,014	38.3
80	Norway	123,205	1,806,900	15·

population approaches that of the more populated districts of the North-Western Provinces and Oudh are of limited extent and urban in character to a far greater extent than the most urban districts in these provinces. The density of the average Gangetic districts of the province is approached amongst European countries only in comparatively inextensive areas and in Belgium, England and Wales, Saxony and several others of the smaller German principalities, whilst Holland, Italy, Prussia, France are far below the majority of even the more scantily populated districts. It is throughout clear that the states which thus in density compare with the North-Western Provinces are distinctly urban in character. Lanarkshire, heading the list given with a population somewhat denser than in any North-Western Provinces district, contains the great city of Glasgow with a dozen other towns entitled to be considered important. Brabant, with a population as dense as our densest districts, has nearly half of it in the single town of Brussels. North Holland has similarly more than half in Amsterdam. Kent with a density of 629 includes part of the suburbs of London and is dotted over with towns of importance. Saxony, the most densely populated kingdom of Europe, contrasts with the North-Western Provinces in being essentially a mining and manufacturing country, 58 per cent. of the population being engaged in these occupations and a large part of them resident in large towns. Belgium, next amongst European countries, is also a mining and manufacturing country, containing 26 towns each with a population of over 20,000 and with nearly a million distributed between five only of these towns. So it is with all other countries, the names of which are high in the list given. To realize the full effect of the North-Western Provinces figures for density it is, therefore, necessary to separate the town from the rural population.

80. **The proportion of urban and rural population.**—It has already been stated (para. 14) what a town is for the purposes of the present census. In this definition are included all places with a population of over 5,000, though the extent of population may be the only claim possible to the name of town, and all areas to which the Chaukidári Act has been applied, that is, in general, almost every place in the provinces whatever its size that has any claim to a properly urban character. It is certain that in the North-

Western Provinces returns there is a larger population properly rural included in the urban area than there is of urban omitted from it. With so wide a definition of town the percentage of urban to total population is only 11·3 all over the provinces The figures for districts are given in abstract No. 11.

Abstract No. 11, showing the percentage of urban and rural population in the districts of the provinces.

Serial number.	District.	Percentage of urban population.	Percentage of rural population.
1	Dehra Dún	22·7	77·3
2	Saháranpur	20·3	79·7
3	Muzaffarnagar	16·3	83·7
4	Meerut	20·8	79·2
5	Bulandshahr	17·0	83·0
6	Aligarh	19·5	80·5
	Total, Meerut Division ...	19·1	80·9
7	Muttra	20·7	79·3
8	Agra	20·9	79·1
9	Farukhabad	16·1	83·9
10	Mainpuri	6·8	93·2
11	Etáwah	8·6	91·4
12	Etah	15·4	84·6
	Total, Agra Division ...	15·1	84·9
13	Bareilly	16·5	83·5
14	Bijnor	21·8	78·2
15	Budaun	10·8	89·2
16	Moradabad	20·6	79·4
17	Sháhjahánpur	13·1	86·9
18	Pilibhít	11·6	88·4
	Total, Rohilkhand Division ...	16·2	83·8
19	Cawnpore	17·7	82·3
20	Fatehpur	6·4	93·6
21	Bánda	5·8	94·2
22	Hamírpur	13·5	86·5
23	Allahabad	14·2	85·8
24	Jhánsi	24·1	75·9
25	Jalaun	13·2	86·8
26	Lalitpur	7·4	92·6
	Total, Allahabad Division ...	13·2	86·8
27	Benares	25·5	74·5
28	Mirzapur	10·0	90·0
29	Jaunpur	5·8	94·2
30	Gházipur	10·9	89·1
31	Ballia	10·8	89·2
	Total, Benares Division ...	12·0	88·0

Serial number.	District.	Percentage of urban population.	Percentage of rural population.
32	Gorakhpur	5·6	94·4
33	Basti	1·9	98·1
34	Azamgarh	5·2	94·8
	Total, Gorakhpur Division ...	4·5	95·5
35	Kumaun	5·1	94·9
36	Garhwál	·9	99·1
37	Tarái	10·2	89·8
	Total, Kumaun Division ...	4·6	95·4
	Total, N.-W. Provinces ...	12·7	87·3
38	Lucknow	39·7	60·3
39	Unao	8·2	91·8
40	Rae Bareli	3·0	97·0
41	Sitapur	7·0	93·0
42	Hardoi	9·4	90·6
43	Kheri	4·3	95·7
	Total, Lucknow Division ...	10·8	89·2
44	Fyzabad	11·4	88·6
45	Gonda	4·4	95·6
46	Bahraich	3·9	96·1
47	Sultánpur	·8	99·2
48	Partábgarh	1·8	98·2
49	Bara Banki	5·3	94·7
	Total, Fyzabad Division ...	4·8	95·2
	Total, Oudh ...	7·6	92·4
	Total, N.-W. P. and Oudh ...	11·3	88·7
50	Rámpur	18·7	81·3
51	Tehri Garhwál	...	100·
	Total, Native States ...	13·0	87·0

The percentage is highest in Lucknow, where a large city is surrounded by a small district and the urban population is, therefore, 39 per cent. of the whole. Benares comes second with 25 per cent. urban, Jhánsi third with 24 per cent ; after this come a group of Doab or other western districts with 20 per cent. more or less of town population. The eastern districts of the North-Western Provinces, on the other hand, have only in general about 10 per cent. of town population. In Oudh the average is still lower, half of the districts having less than 5 per cent. The town population in Oudh is probably somewhat understated, as the Town Chaukidári Act has not been so generally applied as in the North-Western Provinces. The real proportion in Oudh is, however, markedly lower than in the North-Western Provinces. The Oudh

[To face page 92.

DIAGRAM No. III.

COMPARING THE DENSITY OF POPULATION, AND PROPORTION OF TOWN AND RURAL POPULATION IN ENGLAND AND WALES, AND THE N.-W. P. AND OUDH.

The whole column represents total density per square mile. *rural* population is shown by green; *town* population by pink.

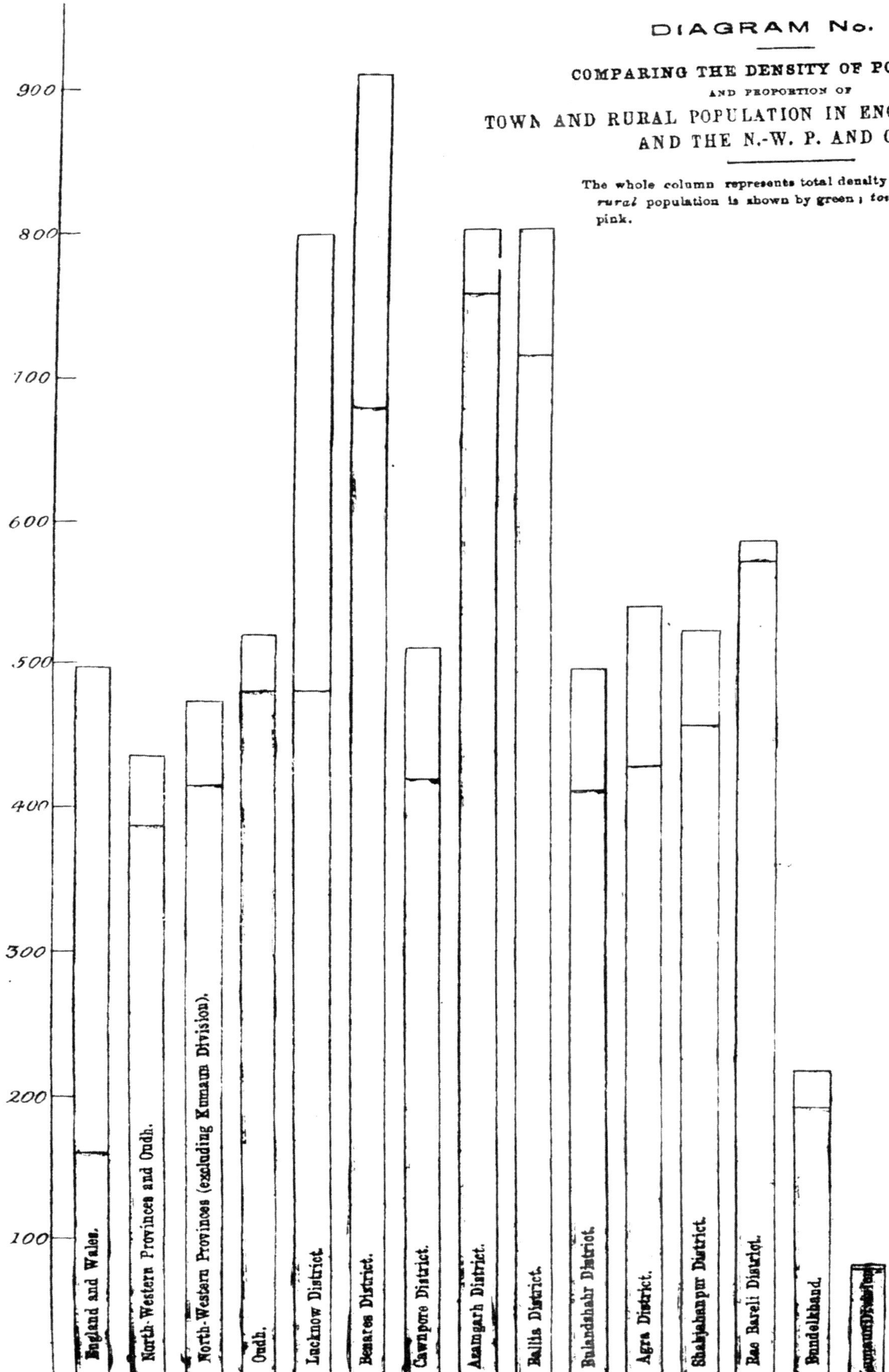

Government was not one in which great trading towns were likely to spring up away from the headquarters of the Government. Not only the traders but the landowners preferred as much as possible to deal with Oudh affairs from just across the border. The zone of the North-Western Provinces which is next to Oudh is in consequence studded with towns or smaller centres of trade whose transactions extended far into Oudh.

The figures for European countries afford a complete contrast to this. The exact proportion of rural and urban population is available only for England and Wales, where it was shown by the 1881 census report to be 32·1 per cent. rural and 67·9 per cent. urban. How complete a contrast the constitution of the population of the North-Western Provinces affords in this respect to that of European countries is clearly shown by diagram No. 3, in which the density of rural and town population is shown separately and contrasted with that in England and Wales. The density of rural population in England and Wales was only 160 per square mile all over. It is remarked with regard to the English distribution of population, that any county which showed a population materially over 200 per square mile owed it to the existence of considerable towns within its area. Contrasting with this we have in the North-Western Provinces and Oudh all over a rural density of 386; in Oudh alone of 483; in the Gorakhpur Division of 655. The districts are shown in order of density of rural population in abstract No. 12, and the general distribution of density in

The density of rural population.

Abstract No. 12, showing the divisions, districts and states of the provinces in order of density of rural population.

Serial number.	District.	Density per square mile.	Serial number.	District.	Density per square mile.
1	2	3	1	2	3
1	Azamgarh	762·6	28	Bulandshahr	412·6
2	Jaunpur	762·0		Rohilkhand Division	410·6
3	Ballia	718·9	29	Moradabad	410·3
4	Benares	679·9	30	Budaun	409·6
5	Gházipur	657·1	31	Fatehpur	400·9
	Gorakhpur Division	655·0		Agra Division	399·4
6	Basti	632·9	32	Etáwah	393·1
7	Fyzabad	624·1	33	Muttra	392·6
8	Sultánpur	624·1	34	Muzaffarnagar	390·0
9	Partábgarh	622·2		N.-W. Provinces and Oudh	386·0
10	Gorakhpur	617·9		Meerut Division	381·2
11	Bara Banki	615·1		N.-W. Provinces	359·0
12	Rae Bareli	574·3	35	Bahraich	358·5
13	Bareilly	545·0	36	Sahàranpur	356·1
	Fyzabad Division	531·1	37	Etah	341·0
14	Unao	492·5	38	Bijnor	326·9
15	Gonda	484·3	39	Pilibhít	312·6
	Oudh	483·8	40	Kheri	291·7
16	Lucknow	482·9		Allahabad Division	289·5
17	Rámpur State	474·1	41	Jalaun	282·4
18	Allahabad	465·8	42	Bánda	217·2
19	Meerut	465·3	43	Mirzapur	200·0
20	Sháhjahánpur	458·1	44	Tarái	196·3
	Benares Division	453·6	45	Hamírpur	194·1
21	Sitapur	443·6	46	Jhánsi	189·5
22	Hardoi	433·7		Native States	134·9
	Lucknow Division	433·7	47	Lalitpur	130·3
23	Aligarh	430·7	48	Debra Dún	108·8
24	Agra	430·1		Kumaun Division	82·0
25	Cawnpore	421·4	49	Kumaun	74·7
26	Farukhabad	418·8	50	Garhwál	71·7
27	Mainpuri	417·7	51	Tehri Garhwál	57·9

the map accompanying (No. 3). The general character of the map is not altered, but the effect due to the accidental presence of large trading centres having been removed, the variations are less abrupt than when the total density was considered. The eastern districts of the Gangetic plain and Central and East Oudh are all above average in density. The western and Doab districts with the exception of a strip from Meerut to Sháhjahánpur interrupted in Moradabad are all below average. They are much below average in a strip below the Himalayas and in three districts of the Agra Division. Kumaun and Bundelkhand districts are all below 250 in rural density.

81. **Instances of great density of population of pargana areas.**—The instances in which, over an area less extensive than a district but extensive enough to obliterate accidental disturbances due to the residence of agriculturists or others being frequently at a distance from their work, the density of population in rural tracts in the North-Western Provinces approaches or exceeds the average for the most densely populated Behar districts are few. The marginal parganas show over all a density of 900 or over; of these Bareilly, Sháhjahánpur, Cawnpore, Chail (Allahabad), Dehat Amanat (Benares), Haveli Jaunpur, Gházipur, Nizamabad (Azamgarh), Mau (Azamgarh), Haveli Oudh (Fyzabad), Lucknow, owe their high density mainly to their containing within their boundaries towns either large or large relatively to the size of the pargana. The densest agricultural parganas in the provinces are :—

Pagana.	Density.
Dehat Amanat (Benares) ...	4,744
Lucknow	2,262
Cawnpore	1,227
Mau (Azamgarh) ...	1,223
Gházipur	1,182
Haveli Jaunpur	1,140
Ballia	1,088
Chail (Allahabad) ..	1,060
Haveli Oudh (Fyzabad) ...	1,060
Sheopur (Benares) ...	1,055
Mirzapur Chauhari(Allahabad)	1,021
Sháhjahánpur	992
Lakhnesar (Ballia) ..	970
Bareilly	957
Dehma (Gházipur) ...	947
Nizamabad (Azamgarh) ...	920
Muhammadabad (Gházipur) ..	917
Rari Jaunpur	908

	Density.
Mirzapur Chaubari in Allahabad	1,021
Sheepur in Benares	1,055
Rari in Jaunpur	908
Muhammadabad in Gházipur	917
Dehma in Gházipur	947
Ballia	1,083

The density is of particular interest only in Mirzapur Chauhari, a small pargana in Allahabad, projecting into the Oudh district of Partábgarh. It is there due to the fact that the Oudh cultivators during the Nawábi found it convenient to settle in British villages whilst cultivating across the border. The old census reports show a density of 1,200 in this pargana, which has gradually fallen since annexation owing to the cultivators moving back into their own villages. Such an increase in density was noted to have existed in a narrow strip along the Oudh border, but it is now traceable only in this one pargana. The Oudh parganas elsewhere show a density not materially or uniformly below that in the North-Western Provinces parganas bordering on them.

82. **Towns and villages—the distinction.**—The total number of towns in the provinces is 484 and of villages 105,716. Definitions of both terms have been given. A line of demarcation by population only, unless pitched

[To face page 93.

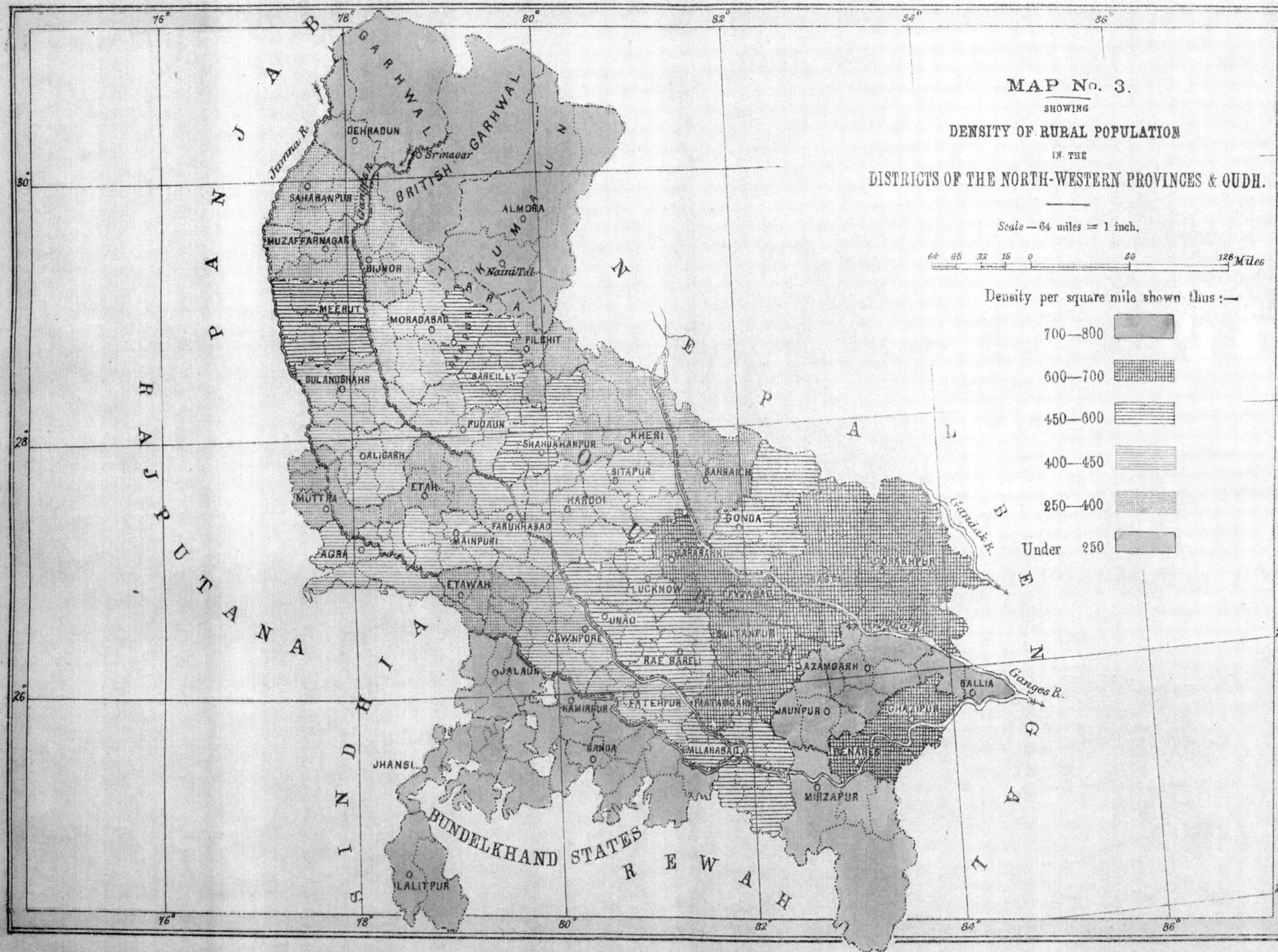

very high, would be impracticable, as mere extent of population, unless very considerable, does not in itself afford in India as in England an indication as to whether the character of the population is in the main rural or urban in character. The most prevalent type of Indian village consists of a stretch of cultivated or culturable land, a square mile or more in extent, with a central inhabited site containing the homes of the whole of the agriculturists who cultivate the land. The area of villages is sometimes so extensive that if the central homestead is adhered to, it is so populous that in England it would rank as a small town, even though it has very little indeed of the urban character so far as the occupations of its inhabitants are concerned. As however such populous villages afford a convenient centre for the homes of the petty itinerant grain and cloth vendors and for the artizans necessary to supply the few wants of the rural population, the larger villages always contain a small proportion of traders and artizans. The line of demarcation begins to be passed where, when owing to the increase of traders and manufacturers not dependent on the village lands, the cess for the payment of village watchmen, charged on the land revenue and therefore proportionate to the area of the village lands becomes insufficient to provide for watch and ward. It then becomes necessary to apply the special Act which allows the imposition of a house tax for payment of watchmen in trading towns and bazárs. Such a tax is rarely or never imposed on cultivators, and its existence is therefore evidence as good as could be supplied of the urban character of a great part of the population, and justifies the retention in our list of towns of places with population so small as many of those shown in Table IV. In Oudh the Act has been less extensively applied than in the North-Western Provinces, as the limitation of the landlord's liability for watch and ward to an amount not exceeding the yield of six per cent. cess, has never been definitely recognized. We have there in consequence a number of places with population under 5,000 which are distinctively urban in character but have not been included in the lists of towns.

83. **The towns of the provinces.**—*The typical country town.*—As already indicated by the low percentage of urban to rural population, the Hindu inhabitant of the North-Western Provinces and Oudh is now little given to dwelling in large towns, although his traditions tell of towns to which the largest of to-day are but as villages. The typical town of the province is the exaggerated village, the development of which has been above indicated. Its origin is due to there being a large area included within the mauza boundaries implying a large agricultural population to start with. It is in general the centre of a pargana and contains a number of families of the classes which were the administrators of the pargana in former days, when the paragana was the centre of administration. Owing to its convenient position, a considerable proportion of the wealthier traders and money-lenders and of the artizan classes have their homes in it. If favourably situated for trade with distant towns, it grows to a certain extent, but in general it depends on the pargana only, of which it is the traditional centre, and is large or small according to the size of the pargana and the extent to which it monopolizes the pargana trade. Such are the majority of towns of medium size in the list in Table IV.

Shikarpur in Bulandshahr may be mentioned as a specific instance. It has a total population of 11,596, of whom 2,261 are agriculturists depending on its five square miles of rich soil. It is the headquarters of the family which owns most of the pargana and of a number of Muhammadan families who under grants from the Dehli kings had at one time acquired a considerable share in it. It is the home of the Kayath families who are the pargana patwáris and owns almost the only bazár and settlement of weavers in the pargana. Kandla in Muzaffarnagar may be mentioned as another instance. With a total population of 9,487, it has 2,929 agriculturists, 1,305 traders, 124 of the professional classes, 1,297 artizans, 2,063 labourers, mostly agricultural. Kairana, a neighbour to Kandla, may be instanced as a pargana town which owes part of its development to trade with the outer world and to its being the headquarters of the tahsíl and the site of a Munsiffi, but in all essentials it is similar. Agriculturists there are 3,390, traders 3,794, professionals 436, artizans 4,101, labourers 2,335, the total population being 18,420. It is unnecessary to multiply instances. The composition of the population of almost all the towns of medium and small size will be found on analysis to be similar.

84. **The important towns.**—Of the larger towns the causes which in the great majority of instances produce a large town in England, namely, natural position and facilities for manufactures or trade are in India little operative. Here the town in general attracts the trade and not the trade the town. There are thirty seven towns in the provinces which, each with a population over 20,000, are entitled to be reckoned as important. Of these there are only six the importance of which can be considered to be solely or mainly due to the natural growth of trade. These are Cawnpore, Mirzapur, Koel, Etáwah, Háthras, Khurja. Cawnpore owes its position both as regards its lead in the grain trade of India and its manufactures of leather and cotton cloth almost entirely to the power of English capital and enterprize, which had full scope under the protection of an important British Cantonment, the oldest in the western part of the provinces. The other towns mentioned are centres of native Indian trade, Mirzapur of the cotton trade with Central India, and the others of the local grain and cotton trade. The great majority of the rest of the thirty-seven towns owe their importance to the having been the capitals, according to their degree, of Muhammadan kings or leaders. Lucknow, the largest town in the provinces, was created by the whim of an Oudh Nawáb, who preferred the site to that of Fyzabad. Agra in the same way grew into importance when chosen to succeed Delhi as the capital of the Mughal Empire. Fyzabad, apart from Ajudhia, owes its origin and importance entirely to its having been an Oudh capital. Bareilly, Sháhjahánpur, Farukhabad, Rámpur, Moradabad, Sahåranpur, Ghåzipur, Jaunpur, Sambhal, Budaun, Amroha, Chandausi, Bahraich, Bánda, Shahabad and probably Pilibhít all owe their position and importance to their having been selected as capitals by Musalmán leaders of power varying with the size of the cities they founded and left behind them. The descendants of the leaders by whose aid they held their provinces still form the aristocracies of most of these towns. Their rapid growth was due to the fact that the surplus wealth of the provinces occupied was drawn into these permanent camps

and attracted to them the handicraftsmen and traders who now form the bulk of their inhabitants. Bahraich and Amroha only amongst the towns mentioned have had the added assistance in rising due to their being places of pilgrimage for low caste Hindus. For towns of the first magnitude markedly Hindus in their population or origin, the *raison d'etre* is almost invariably religious sanctity. Benares, Kashi to the Hindus, the second town in the provinces, is so because it is to the majority of Hindus the most sacred place in them, the spot specially favoured by Mahadeo. Allahabad owes its original importance to its being at the junction of two sacred rivers, a resting place of Rám and the home of Bharat Rishi. The military importance of the position and the fact that it has been for thirty years the headquarters of the Local Government have of course also aided its development. Ajudhya which includes two-fifths of the population of the Fyzabad municipality, owes its size and importance entirely to its sacred character as the capital of Ráma. Muttra and Brindaban are towns of importance because remembered as the favourite haunts of Krishna. Hardwár is so because there the sacred Ganges issues on the plain of Hindustán. Gorakhpur, though mainly important as the trading and administrative headquarters of a district which included formerly most of the present division, owes its origin to its sacred character as the home of Gorakh-Nath. Their remain as towns the origin of which has not been accounted for distinctly by any of the above mentioned causes, Jhánsi, which rose as the capital of a Hindu State, Meerut as the site of an important British cantonment, and Sitapur, Fatehpur and Nagina, none of them important and above 20,000, probably only because they are or were the capitals of British districts. With populations between 10,000 and 20,000 there are 67 towns in the provinces; these are for the most part either capitals of British districts or old pargana towns which have risen beyond the usual size either because they managed to attract to a special extent a share of the general trade or because some of their manufactured products have attained more than a local celebrity.

Three hundred and six places with a population below 10,000 have been classed as towns (native states included). At least 100 of them are in population below the size attained by many of the larger purely agricultural villages, but the fact that in all these small towns the Chaukidári Act has been applied is evidence enough of their urban character.

85. **Size of towns compared with those in other countries.**—A statement comparing as to population the towns of the provinces with those in other countries may be of interest. The provinces contain no towns of the first rank, but the number of those in the second rank is larger than is usual in India. The abstract in the margin shows the position of the principal towns of the provinces as regards population by comparison with well-known European and other foreign towns. Lucknow, the largest, is considerably smaller than Sheffield or Rome, but larger than Belfast, Munich or Edinburgh. Benares, the second town, is slightly smaller than Antwerp or Bristol. Cawnpore stands nearly on a level with Lisbon and Newcastle. Allahabad stands below Genoa, almost equal to Riga. Agra is very nearly the same size as Florence and Stockholm. Bareilly ranks with Aberdeen and Meerut with

Athens. It is unnecessary to carry the detailed comparison further. Abstract No. 13 compares the population of all towns over 20,000 with those of known foreign towns of similar size.

Abstract No. 13, comparing the towns of the North-Western Provinces and Oudh containing a population of over 20,000 with those of the world.

Town.	Population.	Town.	Population.
1	5	1	2
Rome	300,470	Brest	70,780
Lucknow	273,028	Leith	69,700
Barcelona	272,480	Verona...	68,740
Munich...	261,980	York	66,980
Edinburgh	261,260	**Gorakhpur**	63,620
Bucharest	221,800	**Saharanpur**	63,194
Bristol	221,660	**Koil**	61,485
Antwerp	221,360	**Muttra**	61,195
Benares	219,467	Orleans	60,830
Alexandria	208,750	Calais	58,970
Rotterdam	203,470	**Jhansi**	53,779
Cawnpore	188,712	Geneva	52,640
Lisbon	187,400	Great Yarmouth	49,320
Brussels	182,275	Boulogne	45,920
Riga	175,330	Oxford...	45,740
Allahabad	175,246	**Ghazipur**	44,970
Florence	169,000	**Jaunpur**	42,819
Stockholm	168,780	**Hathras**	39,181
Agra	168,662	**Etawah**	38,793
Venice	132,830	**Sambhal**	37,226
Aberdeen	121,900	**Budaun**	35,372
Bareilly	121,039	**Amroha**	35,230
Singapore	120,980	**Pilibhit**	33,799
Blackburn	120,060	Dover	33,420
Yokohama	119,780	**Brindaban**	31,611
Meerut	119,390	Lancaster	31,040
Athens	114,350	Perth	30,760
Strasburg	111,990	**Hardwar Union**	29,125
Norwich	100,960	**Chandausi**	28,111
Utrecht	85,250	**Khurja**	26,349
Plymouth	84,180	**Dehra Dun**	25,684
Mirzapur	84,130	Peterborough	25,170
Nancy	79,050	**Bahraich**	24,046
Fyzabad	78,921	**Banda**	23,071
Shahjahanpur	78,522	**Nagina**	22,150
Farukhabad	78,032	Waterford	21,690
Nice	77,480	**Sitapur**	21,380
Rampur State	76,733	Lucerne	20,570
Cork	75,070	**Fatehpur**	20,179
Algiers	74,790	Tobolsk	20,170
Moradabad	72,921	**Shahabad (Hardoi)**	20,153
Padua	72,170		

86. **Density of population in towns.**—The tables of last census contained information regarding the area and density of population in all towns. The results, however, were so unsatisfactory, owing to variations in the figures for areas, that, as the information was not necessary for any of the imperial tables, it was considered better for the purposes of acquiring accurate general information on the subject to ask District Officers to make special arrangements for an accurate measurement of the area of one selected town in each district. The figures returned are shown in Appendices X, XI and XII. The first shows the area and population of the whole town as demarcated for the purposes of the Municipal or Town Acts, a certain proportion of land outside the town site and not under houses being necessarily included. In a large number of instances the area so defined is doubled or trebled by the inclusion of British cantonments or civil stations, all of which occupy an area altogether disproportioned to their population. Appendix No. XI

shows the returns for the real native town excluding all cantonments and civil stations and all land not occupied by houses which is outside the natural town limits; open spaces inside towns, not common in India, are included. Appendix No. XII shows the area and population of a muhalla in each town specially selected and measured as being known to be one of the densest. The returns now presented are prepared with all possible care, many of them having been returned to districts for correction, but as in general no perfectly accurate surveys have been made of town areas as they now stand, it is more than possible that mistakes have occurred, in some instances, in the record of areas. We are, however, safe in accepting the concurrent evidence of returns from a number of districts.

The figures in Appendix No. X showing the density for the whole area executively included in the towns, are so much affected by what may be described as accidental additions to the areas that they deserve little notice. In Agra, for instance, the municipal area includes the whole of the great waste spaces within the ancient city walls and between Agra and Tajganj, which were formerly the sites of houses when Agra was the Mughal capital, but are now altogether outside the modern city. The table demonstrates in general only the liberality with which the cantonments and civil stations of the province have been laid out and the absence of crowding in them. The table of greatest interest is that in Appendix No. XI, showing the area and population of the native towns selected as important or typical. The figures for 46 towns are given. The average density is 76 persons per acre for the North-Western Provinces, 44 persons per acre for Oudh, and 64 persons per acre for the whole of the provinces.

Abstract No. 14, showing towns classified according to density of population.

Name.	Large towns over* 50,000.	Medium towns,* 15,000 to 50,000.	Small towns* under 15,000.
Over 100 in density per acre—			
Meerut	167	...	...
Shikarpur	...	...	101
Agra	150	...	...
Kásganj	...	119	...
Budaun	...	113	...
Moradabad	157	...	...
Cawnpore	187	...	...
Benares	101	...	...
Naini Tal	...	...	227
Medium density—60 to 100 per acre—			
Farukhabad	75·32	...	...
Etáwah	...	75·63	...
Bareilly	66·68	...	...
Bisalpur	...	...	85·38
Hamírpur	...	...	69·67
Allahabad	63·72	...	...
Jhánsi	...	75·16	...
Kunch	...	...	62·11
Mirzapur	81·11	...	...
Ballia	...	81·02	...
Gajpur	...	...	60·31
Mehndaval	...	...	87·93
Haldwani	...	...	73·60
Unao	...	...	60·37
Sitapur	...	77·35	...
Lakhimpur	...	...	66·06
Sultánpur	...	...	95·18
Nawábganj	...	...	67·65
Tanda (Rámpur)	...	...	73·1

* The population taken into consideration is that of the compact native city excluding outlying hamlets cantonments and civil stations.

Abstract No. 14, *showing towns classified according to density of population*—(concluded).

Name.	Large towns over* 50,000.	Medium towns,* 15,000 to 50,000.	Small towns* under 15,000.
Low density—under 60 per acre—			
Debra	...	...	55·1
Deoband	...	56·45	...
Kandhla	...	...	54·32
Koil	37·63	...	...
Shikohabad	...	...	51·41
Nagina	...	55·37	...
Sháhjahánpur	51·53	...	...
Fatehpur	...	57·37	...
Bánda	...	36·2	...
Tálbehat	...	...	51·1
Jaunpur	...	27·15	...
Azamgarh	...	55·72	...
Lucknow	46·47	...	...
Rae Bareli	...	...	44·15
Sandila	...	26·27	...
Fyzabad	...	53·53	...
Gonda	...	...	59·7
Bahraich	...	19·53	...

Of the large towns included in the list, five give densities over 100, four densities between 60 and 100, and three below 60. The circumstances of all the three last are special. Lucknow contains within the city the palaces and gardens of the old Oudh nobility as well as a number of open areas separating the present muhallas. Sháhjahánpur, lying in a strip between two rivers, is a long narrow town in which owing to its shape the space within the city area not under houses is very large. Koil includes a far outlying muhalla of Jaiganj, and the space between the main town and Jaiganj has apparently been included in the area. Allahabad too (density 63·72) can, owing to the existence of large open spaces between the muhallas, hardly be regarded as typical. There remain eight large towns which are typical; the highest density shown all over is 187 in Cawnpore and the lowest 67 in Bareilly. Between the towns of medium and small size there is apparently little difference in density. In Bahraich 19·53, the density is abnormally low, as a large space is occupied by groves and tombs. The circumstances of Jaunpur, traversed by the river and with much space occupied by the old fort and old mosques and tombs, are similar. In Bánda and Sandila also there are probably special circumstances. Rae Bareli, with a density of 44·15, is a scattered little town with extensive open spaces. The density of the usual towns of medium or small size in the provinces therefore ordinarily varies from 50 persons per acre to 100 or more. In my opinion the average for a larger number of towns would probably be nearer the higher limit than the lower. Shikarpur with a density of 100 has already been cited as a typical country town, and is probably typical in this respect also in the west, whilst Ballia or Mehndawal with 81 to 88 density, are typical in the east. The low average density of Oudh towns is noticeable. Most of the smaller Oudh towns owe a good part of their growth to recent development during which due care has been taken to secure wide roads or open spaces.

* The population taken into consideration is that of the compact native city excluding outlying hamlets, cantonments and civil stations.

The densities above shown for the towns of the province contrast to some degree unfavourably with those for even the larger English towns as shown in the marginal abstract. In one respect the greater density in the small towns must be considered an advantage so long as the sanitary arrangements of the towns remain as limited as they now are. The high density allows every part of the town to be comparatively close to where the pure air of heaven circulates outside and makes impossible the secluded but open spaces which are always the foulest part of a native town.

Towns.	Population.	Persons to an acre.
London	4,215,192	56·0
Brighton	118,186	47·0
Portsmouth	137,917	31·9
Norwich	92,848	12·4
Plymouth	77,127	52·5
Bristol	223,695	48·3
Wolverhampton	80,847	23·8
Birmingham	441,095	52·5
Leicester	143,153	44·7
Notthingham	224,230	22·5
Derby	94,006	27·2
Birkenhead	97,703	25·4
Liverpool	592,991	113·8
Bolton	112,354	46·7
Manchester	377,529	87·9
Salford	218,658	42·3
Oldham	134,158	28·4
Blackburn	116,844	16·8
Preston	102,283	27·5
Huddersfield	90,034	8·6
Halifax	79,207	21·0
Bradford	224,507	20·8
Leeds	345,080	16·0
Sheffield	316,288	16·1
Hull	196,855	24·9
Sunderland	129,684	42·8
Newcastle	157,048	29·2
Cardiff	104,580	14·2

To how great an extent the density is exaggerated in the more closely populated muhallas appears from Appendix XII. The marginally noted towns return muhallas with densities over 200. These high densities are almost entirely in the large towns. Towns of smaller size return for their more populous muhallas in general densities from 100 to 200. The density of muhallas as of towns is markedly lower on the average in Oudh than in the North-West. I have no reason to believe that these great densities are exaggerated. On the other hand, it is more than probable that the lower densities quoted are not of those of the densest muhallas. As there is no record of the areas of muhallas, those shown in the statement had to be specially measured and were selected beforehand without any accurate knowledge. In not a few districts they were so badly selected that I had to send back returns, pointing out that the density of the most thickly populated muhalla was below that for the town as a whole. It is extremely probable that even in many of those towns in which this obvious error was not committed, the muhalla selected was not one of the densest.

Dehra	225
Deoband	208
Agra	360
Etáwah	282
Budaun	244
Moradabad	439
Cawnpore	445
Allahabad	335
Naini Tal	342
Lucknow	264

The difficulty of the selection of such a muhalla is illustrated by one point in the tables. Most persons who have seen something of the various towns of the province would, if asked to pick out that in which the population was densest, at once refer to Benares, where the network of narrow lanes from which all light is shut out by the lofty houses on either side, would appear to indicate a population far denser than in any other city of the provinces. Yet Benares returns as the density of one of its densest muhallas only 192 persons per acre, and the return was compiled with a degree of care which goes far to prove its correctness. The figures for Naini Tal, the summer headquarters of the Government and its principal sanitarium, deserve notice. They show as *the cold weather* density in the upper bazár 342 persons per acre and in the lower bazár 169 persons per acre. The densities in the season when, besides the permanent residents who give the densities quoted, each house is crowded with itinerant dealers and hill coolies must be very much greater.

87. **The density in villages.**—The sketch given of the degree to which a small town in the provinces differs from an agricultural village, makes it clear that in density many of the larger villages are but little behind the smaller towns. I have no figures from which the density of population in village sites can be directly calculated, but it is fairly certain that it is not much below the 50 persons per acre which ordinarily forms the limit in towns. To this resemblance between towns and villages in India and the almost entire absence of proper sanitary arrangements in villages is due the comparatively small difference in the death-rate in towns and in villages. The Sanitary Commissioner's figures for the last ten years show for villages a death-rate 32·5 per thousand and for towns 38·7, that is in towns there are 119 deaths for each hundred in villages for equal numbers living. The registration of deaths in towns is probably better and the real difference still less. The difference is considerably less than it was in England before town sanitation was improved within the last century. It is less than it was even in 1861-70 when there were in English towns 126 deaths against 100 for an equal rural population. It is greater than at the present day in England the latest ratios I have seen being 111 town deaths to 100 country deaths.

88. Distribution of the population between large and small towns and villages.

The total town population in British districts was 5,314,328 against 41,590,757 who reside in villages. Table III gives some interesting information regarding the number of people who live in large or small towns or villages and the number of towns and villages of differents sizes for the districts of the province for which the abstract in the margin shows the provincial totals and percentages. The average population for a town or village for the whole of the provinces is 442 persons and for villages excluding towns, 393 persons.

Abstract No. 15, showing the distribution of the population according to the size of towns and villages in which they reside.

Towns and villages, with population.	Number.	Population.	Percentage of total population.
1—199 ...	48,426	4,203,642	8·9620
200—499 ...	35,690	11,626,946	24·7883
500—999 ...	18,439	12,629,088	26·9248
1,000—1,999 ...	6,662	8,927,709	19·0336
2,000—2,999 ...	1,160	2,780,851	5·9287
3,000—4,999 ...	518	1,922,849	4·0994
5,000—9,999 ...	202	1,335,028	2·8462
10,000—14,999 ...	43	522,190	1·1133
15,000—19,999 ...	24	416,195	·8873
20,000—49,999 ...	19	579,249	1·2349
50,000 and over ...	17	1,961,348	4·1815
Total ...	106,200	46,905,085	100

The bulk of the population, however, live in villages of a size above this average. Of the total population, almost exactly one-third live in villages with a population under 500, whilst two-thirds live in towns or villages with a population over 500, and nearly two-fifths live in towns or villages of population 1,000 or over. There is, in respect both of the size of the villages and of the population of the average village, a steady decrease met with in passing from the west to the east of the province. It is exhibited in abstract No. 16. The Meerut Division

Abstract No. 16, showing the proportion of the population resident in villages of different sizes.

Division.	Average size of village.	Average population of village.	Proportion of population in villages 0—499.	Proportion of population in villages 500—999.	Proportion of population in towns and villages 1,000 and over.
1	2	3	4	5	6
Meerut Division	1·42	549·92	21·05	24·59	54·36
Agra Division	1·24	500·57	26·19	24·67	49·14
Rohilkhand Division	1·05	392·61	35·76	27·71	36·53
Allahabad, Doab	1·01	501·75	31·88	26·28	41·84
Allahabad, Bundelkhand	·40	555·71	25·27	25·96	48·77
Benares (Mirzapur)	·82	270·00	54·32	23·64	22·04
Benares (other districts)	1·82	443·50	31·75	26·12	42·13
Gorakhpur Division	·49	325·07	47·51	26·40	26·09
Kumaun Division	1·35	110·51	83·71	9·03	7·26
North-West Provinces	1·02	367·18	35·07	25·31	39·62
Lucknow Division	1·18	512·63	27·03	28·89	44·08
Fyzabad Division	·86	458·89	32·90	33·37	33·73
Oudh	·99	481·46	30·18	31·29	38·53
North-Western Provinces and Oudh ...	1·01	393·42	33·75	26·93	39·32

has a village of the average of 1·42 square miles with an average population per village and town of 669. This decreases fairly steadily moving eastwards through the Gangetic plain till in the Gorakhpur Division the average area of the village is ·49 and the average population 343. The figures are lowest in the district of Basti with an average area per village of ·403 and a population of 260. Bundelkhand, Mirzapur and Kumaun all of them scantily populated and with comparatively very large areas of unculturable waste are exceptional with villages of far more than average size and far less than average population. As regards the extremes of the series in the Gangetic plain a difference in the circumstances under which the village boundaries orginated is at once suggested by existing circumstances.

Abstract No. 17, showing the average area and population per town and village in the districts of the provinces.

Serial number of district.	District.	Average area of towns and villages in square miles.	Average population per town and village.	Average population per village.
1	Dehra Dún	2·69	382·12	299·29
2	Sahâranpur	1·36	613·15	494·70
3	Muzaffarnagar	1·84	858·75	732·58
4	Meerut	1·54	902·96	730·73
5	Bulandshahr	1·27	629·08	530·72
6	Aligarh	1·01	540·24	441·09
	Total, Meerut Division ...	1·42	669·62	549·92
7	Muttra	1·69	839·03	676·58
8	Agra	1·58	833·72	663·77
9	Farukhabad	1·06	502·45	423·66
10	Mainpuri	1·20	537·87	503·94
11	Etáwah	1·13	487·69	447·36
12	Etah	1·27	473·73	406·61
	Total, Agra Division ...	1·24	584·71	500·57

Abstract No. 17, *showing the average area and population per town and village in the ditricts of the provinces*—(concluded).

Serial number of district.	District.	Average area of towns and villages in square miles.	Average population per town and village.	Average population per village.
13	Bareilly	·81	538·10	451·96
14	Bijnor	·88	372·64	292·46
15	Budaun	1·09	498·71	447 95
16	Moradabad	·93	479·82	383·37
17	Sháhjahánpur	·86	450·93	392·96
18	Pilibhít	1·31	461·81	402·34
	Total, Rohilkhand Division ...	1·05	465·68	392·61
19	Cawnpore	1·20	612·19	506·12
20	Fatehpur	1·14	489·61	461·01
21	Bánda	2·55	588·19	556·39
22	Hamírpur	2·99	672·41	590·22
23	Allahabad	·81	440·48	379·35
24	Jhánsi	2·46	613·82	471·74
25	Jalaun	1·72	460·35	402·80
26	Lalitpur	2·86	403·24	375·08
	Total, Allahabad Division ...	1·56	519·03	453·12
27	Benares	·51	462·82	345·27
28	Mirzapur	1·21	269·68	242·98
29	Jaunpur	·49	396·04	373·70
30	Gházipur	·56	412·36	369·05
31	Ballia	·68	548·26	492·35
	Total, Benares Division ...	·75	388·31	342·65
32	Gorakhpur	·60	395·31	374·21
33	Basti	·40	260·21	255·36
34	Azamgarh	·46	368·89	350·50
	Total, Gorakhpur Division ...	·49	343·51	325·07
35	Kumaun	1·20	94·98	89·63
36	Garhwál	1·54	111·36	110·40
37	Tarái	1·65	361·18	325·38
	Total, Kumaun Division ...	1·35	115·70	110·51
	Total, N.-W. Provinces ...	1·02	418·57	367·18
38	Lucknow	1·06	847·01	517·17
39	Unao	1·07	572·07	529·08
40	Rae Bareli	1·01	598·45	581·39
41	Sitapur	·97	461·95	431·39
42	Hardoi	1·28	590·56	587·71
43	Kheri	1·73	528·12	507·42
	Total, Lucknow Division ...	1·18	572·10	512·63
44	Fyzabad	·64	453·41	403·30
45	Gonda	1·02	515·45	494·82
46	Bahraich	1·42	530·98	510·43
47	Sultánpur	·69	435·39	432·02
48	Partábgarh	·66	425·45	409·78
49	Bara Banki	·84	547·12	519·87
	Total, Fyzabad Division ...	·86	480·66	458·89
	Total Oudh ...	·99	519·24	481·46
	Total, N.-W. Provinces and Oudh ...	1·01	441·67	393·42
50	Rámpur	·62	363·62	296·73
51	Tehri Garhwál	5·19	300·80	300·80
	Total, Native States ...	2·20	341·89	298·14

In the western villages the soil is in general owned by strong coparcenary bodies of the peasant proprietor type, all of them assisting in the cultivation or management of the much subdivided village. They know, except in the vaguest way, of no previous proprietors and own to no grant from a Rája. The small proprietors consider that they own from the same time and with the same original rights as do the great proprietors. In the east, on the other hand, throughout a whole pargana we have almost all the small proprietors acknowledging that they derive their title from the gift of such a Rája, who conquered and took the land from preceding inhabitants often stated to be Bhars. The Rajá's fellow clansmen got their shares generally in large villages and are to this day known far more distinctly than in the west as the aristocrats of the pargana. The great bulk of the small villages are held as grants from the Rájas or Babus by Bráhmans, Bhats and other dependents. The difference, in fact, somewhat resembles that between Saxon England, where each freeholder had held his land for immemorial generations, and Norman England, as it would be had the church been represented by thousands of acquisitive Bráhmans and had personal services been rendered by hereditary servants for whose maintenance it was customary to provide in land. The subject is a most interesting one. I have not had the advantage of seeing it discussed in detail, and my personal experience is almost entirely confined to the extremes of the province and to Oudh, where original ownerships have become overlaid and almost obliterated by the changes which occurred under the rule of the Nawábs whilst might was right.

89. **Inhabited sites.**—It has already been stated that the system by which all the inhabitants of a village (mauza) lived in one central abadi was generally adhered to in the present day only in the western districts, and that elsewhere the homestead had been broken up by the migration of a proportion of the cultivators to outlying hamlets where they live close to their own fields. The process is one which would naturally follow on increasing density of population and consequent need for high cultivation. The natural manure which the lands immediately round an inhabited site obtains from the habits of the people is of great importance in Indian agriculture, especially in the eastern and more minutely cultivated lands. Two causes have been operative in forwarding or retarding the process of migration to outlying hamlets, (A) the caste of the general mass of cultivators, and (B) the amount of security enjoyed previous to British rule by the actual cultivators.

(A) The high-caste cultivator, with in general some reserve resources derived from his ownership of the soil and never so careful as to the *minutiæ* of cultivation as his low-caste fellow agriculturist, long adheres to the central abadi. Thus Rájputs of one clan generally live together in the same abadi, whilst Kurmis, Kachhis, Koeris, Muraos and other close cultivating castes generally adopt the system under which a village is dotted over with hamlets. Chamárs, too, almost everywhere have forsaken the central abadi, because they prefer to be amongst themselves, and other castes prefer not to have them. (B) The security afforded by a large central abadi during the Mahratta times probably ensured its long continuance in the Doab districts. All was fish that came to a Mahratta net, and the smallest cultivator was not below the notice of their plunderers. This cause was operative only where the Mahrattas reached. In Oudh, though the proprietors plundered each other of their lands, they were most careful not to interfere with or drive away the actual cultivators on whom the income from the lands depended. On the contrary, the strongest and therefore in one direction the most lawless of the Oudh Talukdárs were invariably those who most efficiently protected their tenants and encouraged new tenants to settle on waste lands. Abstract No. 18 shows the number of inhabited sites and average population per inhabited site for each district in the province, and gives the proportion borne by the number of inhabited sites to that of the number of villages and towns.

Abstract No. 18, *showing the number of inhabited sites in the districts of the provinces.*

Serial number of district.	District.	Number of inhabited sites.	Average population per inhabited site.	Number of inhabited sites per village.
1	2	3	4	5
1	Dehra Dún	870	193·26	2·01
2	Sahâranpur	2,129	470·31	1·32
3	Muzaffarnagar	1,524	507·14	1·73
4	Meerut	2,310	602·36	1·53
5	Bulandshahr	1,877	506·08	1·26
6	Aligarh	3,266	319·40	1·71
	Total, Meerut Division ...	11,976	444·79	1·53
7	Muttra	2,009	355·11	2·40
8	Agra	3,882	258·58	3·25
9	Farukhabad	4,220	203·49	2·48
10	Mainpuri	4,298	177·33	3·05
11	Etáwah	3,900	186·57	2·62
12	Etah	3,122	204·56	2·14
	Total, Agra Division ...	21,431	222·47	2·65
13	Bareilly	2,419	430·22	1·26
14	Bijnor	2,424	327·58	1·14
15	Budaun	2,546	363·69	1·38
16	Moradabad	3,281	359·46	1·34
17	Sháhjahánpur	2,897	317·07	1·43
18	Pilibhít	1,353	358·73	1·29
	Total, Rohilkhand Division ...	14,919	358·18	1·31
19	Cawnpore	4,371	276·75	2·22
20	Fatehpur	3,598	194·32	2·53
21	Bánda	2,319	304·37	1·94
22	Hamírpur	1,190	431·70	1·58
23	Allahabad	11,493	134·75	3·28
24	Jhánsi	959	426·92	1·46
25	Jalaun	862	459·79	1·01
26	Lalitpur	812	337·68	1·19
	Total, Allahabad Division ...	25,604	224·86	2·32
27	Benares	6,745	136·69	3·39
28	Mirzapur	7,496	154·95	1·74
29	Jaunpur	11,361	111·84	3·56
30	Gházipur	6,635	162·46	2·55
31	Ballia	2,838	332·67	1·66
	Total, Benares Division ...	35,070	153·09	2·54

Abstract No. 18, showing the number of inhabited sites in the districts of the provinces —(concluded).

Serial number of district.	District.	Number of inhabited sites.	Average population per inhabited site.	Number of inhabited sites per village.
1	2	3	4	5
32	Gorakhpur	16,906	177·10	2·24
33	Basti	11,982	149·04	1·75
34	Azamgarh	11,653	148·34	2·49
	Total, Gorakhpur Division ...	40,541	160·54	2·12
35	Kumaun	...	...	...
36	Garhwál	...	...	...
37	Tarái	977	215·53	1·68
	Total, Kumaun Division ...	977	215·53	1·68
	Total, N.-W. Provinces ...	150,518	220·93	2·10
38	Lucknow	1,993	388·46	2·21
39	Unao	4,699	202·94	2·80
40	Rae Bareli	8,538	121·40	4·94
41	Sitapur	6,503	165·37	2·80
42	Hardoi	5,149	216·20	2·75
43	Kheri	4,461	202·56	2·62
	Total, Lucknow Division ...	31,343	186·85	3·07
44	Fyzabad	8,587	141·72	3·21
45	Gonda	14,363	101·60	5·09
46	Bahraich	9,011	111·02	4·71
47	Sultánpur	10,581	116·78	4·28
48	Partábgarh	9,832	92·65	4·50
49	Bara Banki	6,959	162·51	3·38
	Total, Fyzabad Division ...	59,333	144·59	4·21
	Total, Oudh ...	90,676	139·52	3·73
	Total, N.-W. Provinces and Oudh ...	241,194	194·47	2·51
50	Rámpur	...	...	...
51	Tehri Garhwál	...	...	...
	Total, Native States ...	...	...	...

The figures for Kumaun and Garhwál have not been inserted. They were made up for Garhwál, showing in all 12,636 inhabited sites or 3·45 to each village. The Commissioner of Kumaun, however, considered that the actual number of inhabited sites was considerably larger, and so large that there was little chance of obtaining an accurate return. The Garhwál return must therefore be regarded as a minimum for that district. In Kumaun the number of inhabited sites is probably still larger. The scanty areas available for cultivation are separated by intervals so extensive and by paths so inaccessible that each cultivator must live on his own lands, and in general their cottages are scattered all over the hillside.

The population of the average hamlet varies from 602 in Meerut, to 92 in Partábgarh. It is highest in the Meerut and Rohilkhand Divisions, where the misrule before annexation was greatest, the pressure of population least and the proportion of cultivators of good caste and means enough to have cart carriage at their disposal, greatest. It is lowest in the Fyzabad, Benares and Gorakhpur Divisions, where the pressure of population is greatest. The difference between the east and west of the province in this respect is very great and has a marked effect on the aspect of the country. In the western districts a traveller passes through wide open tracts with the groves surrounding villages widely separated. In the east the view is narrowed in every direction by little scattered patches of grove surrounding petty hamlets.

90. **The population per inhabited house.**—The total number of inhabited houses in the province was 8,225,191 against 6,866,503 in 1881; the reason for the increase has been given. This gives an average population per house of 5·703 persons against 5·38 in England in 1881. District averages are given in abstract No. 19 in the margin. The enclosures, which raised the average house population at last census so greatly in the western districts, having been broken up into their component houses, there now remains no marked difference between the average house population in the east and west of the province. It is somewhat lower than elsewhere in the Fyzabad and Allahabad Divisions and highest in Gorakhpur and Benares. In point of fact, the population throughout the province is far too homogeneous for any differences to exist in a distinct degree in the house population. It has from the first been recognised that these figures have little value as regards India in general. The extent to which the population lives in the open air removes most of the objections taken in Europe on sanitary grounds to a high average house population.

Abstract No. 19, showing average population per house in the districts of the provinces.

Serial number.	District.	Average population per house.
1	Dehra Dún	5·33
2	Sahāranpur	4·90
3	Muzaffarnagar	6·89
4	Meerut	5·49
5	Bulandshahr	5·58
6	Aligarh	5·92
	Total, Meerut Division	5·62
7	Muttra	5·49
8	Agra	5·46
9	Farukhabad	6·48
10	Mainpuri	5·78
11	Etáwah	6·00
12	Etah	6·35
	Total, Agra Division	5 89
13	Bareilly	5·80
14	Bijnor	5·61
15	Budaun	5·69
16	Moradabad	5·79
17	Sháhjahánpur	6·34
18	Pilibhít	6·15
	Total, Rohilkhand Division	5·87
19	Cawnpore	5·18
20	Fatehpur	5·07
21	Bánda	4·97
22	Hamírpur	5·57
23	Allahabad	5·19
24	Jhánsi	4·97
25	Jalaun	5·68
26	Lalitpur	6·00
	Total, Allahabad Division	5·20
27	Benares	6·80
28	Mirzapur	5·62
29	Jaunpur	5 69
30	Gházipur	5·90
31	Ballia	6·89
	Total, Benares Division	6·07
32	Gorakhpur	5·94
33	Basti	6·05
34	Azamgarh	6·11
	Total, Gorakhpur Division	6 00

91. **The house population in towns.**—The returns for the eight largest towns give the following

Abstract No. 19, showing average population per house in the districts of the Provinces—(concluded).

Serial number.	District.	Average population per house.
35	Kumaun	6·22
36	Garhwál	5·66
37	Tarái	5·15
	Total, Kumaun Division ...	5·81
	Total, N.-W. Provinces ...	5·76
38	Lucknow	5·19
39	Unao	5·68
40	Rae Bareli	5·35
41	Sitapur	6·18
42	Hardoi	6·09
43	Kheri	5·78
	Total, Lucknow Division ...	5·72
44	Fyzabad	5·21
45	Gonda	5·80
46	Bahraich	5·53
47	Sultánpur	4·12
48	Partábgarh	5·28
49	Bara Banki	5·31
	Total, Fyzabad Division ...	5·40
	Total, Oudh ...	5·55
	Total, N.-W. P. and Oudh ...	5·70
50	Rámpur	5·54
51	Tehri Garhwál...	7·25
	Total, Native States ...	5·97

average house population for each of them :—

1. Agra ... 5·58	5. Lucknow, 4·78
2. Meerut ... 5·74	6. Benares... 7·29
3. Allahabad ... 4·95	7. Farukhabad ... 5·51
4. Bareilly... 6·55	8. Fyzabad... 4·57

Except in the cases of Bareilly and Benares these averages are not materially different from those given for the districts as a whole. Bareilly has little to distinguish its distribution of population from that of the other towns named, and it is possible that the high average shown is due to the fact that enclosures were less uniformly numbered by houses included than in other towns. For Benares, the high house population is real and due to the way in which lofty houses are packed together in the muhallas along the river bank. No figures have been worked out in the present census for families. It might be of some interest if at next census some attempt was made to discover how far and where the old Hindu system under which families remained joint for several generations has been preserved.

92. **The areality.**—It may be interesting before concluding my remarks on the general relation of population to area to present some of the leading figures in a somewhat different light. So far I have mainly referred to the incidence of population on area. A few figures relating to the incidence of area on population may be given. The areality or mean area per person for the provinces as a whole was 1·467. For each of the divisions of the provinces the areality per person, per household and per inhabited site is given in the abstract in the margin.

Abstract No. 20, showing the areality in the Divisions of the Provinces.

Division.	Per. person.	Per. house.	Per inhabited site.
Meerut Division ...	1·360	7 651	605 28
Agra " ...	1·393	8·013	302·77
Rohilkhand " ...	1·306	7·666	467·89
Allahabad (Doab) ...	1·267	6·500	226·00
" (Bundelkhand) ...	2·899	15·404	1,085·40
Benares (Mirzapur) ...	2·878	16·180	445·94
" (other districts) ...	·805	4·999	122 81
Gorakhpur Division ...	·933	5·612	149·83
Kamaun " ...	7·448	43·231	...
N.-W. Provinces ...	1·556	8·967	354·15
Lucknow Division ...	1·315	7 528	245·84
Fyzabad " ...	1·146	6·197	131·33
Oudh ...	1·225	6·795	170·92
N.-W. P. and Oudh. ...	1·467	8·364	285·25

93. The proximity.—The proximity per person, per house and per inhabited site is given in yards in abstract No. 21. Some words of explanation may be required. The *proximity* is, on the hypothesis of equal distribution, the distance to be traversed in passing from one person to another, one house to another, or one inhabited site to another. Thus a postman who had to deliver 1,000 letters to 1,000 persons in the Benares Division would have to traverse only 38 miles, whilst in Meerut his distance would be 49 miles. Again, a postman who had to deliver letters in one thousand houses would have to travel 95 miles in the Eastern Division and 117 in the Doab; or in delivering letters in 100 inhabited sites he would have in the east to travel only 47 miles and in the west no less than 104.

Abstract No. 21, showing proximity per person, &c., in the Divisions of the Provinces.

Division.	Yards per person.	Yards per house.	Yards per inhabited site.
Meerut	87·21	206·79	1,839·2
Agra	88·22	211·62	1,300·8
Rohilkhand	85·44	206·99	1,617·1
Allahabad (Doab) ...	84·16	192·81	1,121·8
„ (Bundelkhand) ...	127·28	293·41	2,462·9
Benares (Mirzapur) ...	126·82	300·71	1,578·7
„ (other districts) ...	67·06	167·16	828·4
Gorakhpur	72·22	177·11	915·1
Kumaun	203·96	491·58	...
N.-W. Provinces ...	93·25	223·86	1,406·8
Lucknow	84·76	205·12	1,172·1
Fyzabad	80·06	186·11	856·7
Oudh	82·74	194·87	977·4
N.-W. Provinces and Oudh ...	90·55	216·21	1,262·6

Chapter III.—THE AGE TABLES.

94. **The population recorded in each age period.**—The assistance of the age tables is so necessary in the examination of most of the further problems connected with population that I propose to depart from the order maintained in the tables and to devote this chapter to the examination and so far as possible to the correction of the returns for ages from the provinces.

The total entries for each age-period as recorded in the enumerators' schedules are shown in the abstract in the margin. The most summary inspection of these figures will indicate that certain errors partly due to unintentional and partly to intentional inaccuracy in the information given to enumerators have to be allowed for. The subject was most carefully worked out by Mr. E. White and Professor Hill at last census, and their conclusions reviewed by a professional statistician for the Census Commissioner for India. It is, therefore, just now sufficient to indicate the conclusions they arrived at and their effects on the figures of the present census and how far they must be modified by the additional information now at our disposal, when for the first time we can compare fully the results of two successive and accurate censuses.

Abstract No. 22, showing the ages as recorded in the enumerators' schedules.

Age-periods.	Total.	Males.	Females.
Under 1 year ...	1,640,597	830,066	810,531
1 year ...	734,492	360,761	873,731
2 ...	1,236,490	600,975	635,515
3 ...	1,472,377	715,315	757,062
4 ...	1,341,086	672,519	668,567
Total (0—4) ...	6,425,042	3,179,636	3,245,406
5—9 ...	6,141,328	3,226,065	2,915,263
10—14 ...	4,960,853	2,833,968	2,126,885
15—19 ...	3,688,735	2,035,364	1,653,371
20—24 ...	4,117,468	2,085,145	2,032,323
25—29 ...	4,135,360	2,107,592	2,027,768
30—34 ...	4,223,047	2,167,572	2,055,475
35—39 ...	2,602,125	1,372,271	1,229,854
40—44 ...	3,340,760	1,708,371	1,632,389
45—49 ...	1,554,030	829,501	724,529
50—54 ...	2,342,786	1,174,361	1,168,425
55—59 ...	707,157	368,823	338,334
60 and over ...	2,666,394	1,214,932	1,451,462
Total ...	46,905,085	24,303,601	22,601,484

95. **Figures showing the exact age of 100,000 persons.**—Much valuable information as to the nature of the errors usually made in enumeration of ages can be derived from consideration of the entries of ages in the following statement showing for blocks the total population of which exactly equalled 100,000, the exact number of entries made for each year of age.

Abstract No. 23, showing the exact ages recorded for 100,000 persons.

Age.	Total.	Males.	Females.	Age.	Total.	Males.	Females.
1	2	3	4	1	2	3	4
Infants ...	3,645	1,846	1,799	11 years ...	1,401	774	627
1 year ...	1,552	795	757	12 ,, ...	3,047	1,809	1,238
2 years ...	2,565	1,214	1,351	13 ,, ...	1,193	701	492
3 ,, ...	3,184	1,577	1,607	14 ,, ...	1,651	944	707
4 ,, ...	2,759	1,400	1,359	15 ,, ...	1,999	1,134	865
5 ,, ...	3,120	1,627	1,493	16 ,, ...	2,316	1,298	1,018
6 ,, ...	2,698	1,424	1,274	17 ,, ...	757	442	315
7 ,, ...	2,565	1,324	1,241	18 ,, ...	2,351	1,304	1,047
8 ,, ...	2,685	1,467	1,218	19 ,, ...	698	369	329
9 ,, ...	1,837	972	865	20 ,, ...	4,428	2,161	2,267
10 ,, ...	3,320	1,869	1,451	21 ,, ...	642	856	286

Abstract No. 23, showing the exact ages recorded for 100,000 *persons*—(concluded).

Age.	Total.	Males.	Females.	Age.	Total.	Males.	Females.
1	2	3	4	1	2	3	4
22 years ...	2,183	1,159	1,024	61 years ...	71	47	24
23 " ...	490	271	219	62 " ...	161	75	86
24 " ...	1,100	560	540	63 " ...	36	22	14
25 " ...	5,393	2,725	2,668	64 " ...	69	27	42
26 " ...	1,005	567	438	65 " ...	524	243	281
27 " ...	575	321	254	66 " ...	45	25	20
28 " ...	1,534	719	815	67 " ...	38	19	19
29 " ...	352	185	167	68 " ...	62	32	30
30 " ...	5,907	2,896	3,011	69 " ...	51	16	35
31 " ...	294	178	116	70 " ...	869	400	469
32 " ...	1,716	937	779	71 " ...	27	13	14
33 " ...	405	265	140	72 " ...	60	37	23
34 " ...	533	293	240	73 " ...	8	6	2
35 " ...	3,009	1,602	1,407	74 " ...	14	6	8
36 " ...	1,041	556	485	75 " ...	185	85	100
37 " ...	283	157	126	76 " ...	11	6	5
38 " ...	762	347	415	77 " ...	7	4	3
39 " ...	318	180	138	78 " ...	19	5	14
40 " ...	5,706	2,828	2,878	79 " ...	21	13	8
41 " ...	208	118	90	80 " ...	393	154	239
42 " ...	689	384	305	81 " ...	6	3	3
43 " ...	130	71	59	82 " ...	12	6	6
44 " ...	258	140	118	83 " ...	...	...	...
45 " ...	2,342	1,262	1,080	84 " ...	3	3	...
46 " ...	277	128	149	85 " ...	24	13	11
47 " ...	182	106	76	86 " ...	1	1	...
48 " ...	452	223	229	87 " ...	7	4	3
49 " ...	139	73	66	88 " ...	8	4	4
50 " ...	4,285	2,032	2,253	89 " ...	3	1	2
51 " ...	135	57	78	90 " ...	70	36	34
52 " ...	352	201	151	91 " ...	...	...	...
53 " ...	86	53	33	92 " ...	4	2	2
54 " ...	117	53	64	93 " ...	...	...	...
55 " ...	984	522	462	94 " ...	...	...	...
56 " ...	171	85	86	95 " ...	13	6	7
57 " ...	101	62	39	96 " ...	1	1	...
58 " ...	196	100	96	97 " ...	2	2	...
59 " ...	63	32	31	98 " ...	4	4	...
60 " ...	2,952	1,343	1,609	99 " and over ...	33	*14	†19
				Total ...	100,000	51,933	48,067

NOTE.—Out of *14; 12 of 100 years, 1 of 101 years, and 1 of 107 years; and out of †19; 17 of 100 years, 1 of 105 years, and 1 of 115 years.

It may of course be assumed that the figures in this table should, if the death-rate in the province were steady and the record correct, show a series steadily decreasing from the smallest to the highest age shown. Examination of the table, however, shows a series anything but continuous.

We may omit for the present mention of ages below five, the details for which have been worked out for the entire population of the provinces and which can best be considered in view of the provincial figures, as they are less likely to be affected by accidental and local causes of variation than those in the abstract. It will be seen that the age-period five, by which is indicated over five and under six, shows a population disproportionately larger than that either preceding or following; that eight, again, is high whilst nine is very low. In the next decade 10, 12, 15, 16, 18 show figures disproportionately large as compared with the other ages in the period. Age 19 shows by far the smallest number yet observed. Passing into the third decade, age 20 has considerably the largest number which has yet occurred; 22 is fairly full, and 25 is higher even than 20; the remaining age-periods all having a low proportion. In the fourth decade, 30 has the highest population shown in the whole of the statement; 32 is not excessively low, and 35 is high; whilst all the other ages in the decade show figures which are only a fraction of those for 30 and 35. In the remaining age-periods, the multiples of ten still more markedly absorb the population for other age-periods, whilst multiples of five continue to do so to an extent decreasing as compared with those of ten as ages advance. At the very foot of the table we have as compared with 4 in 98 and none in 99, 29 of 100. All this indicates very vividly what might have been expected from the ignorance of their correct ages, which it is well known always prevails amongst illiterate persons, and far more so in India than in any other country where accurate censuses are made. A comparison of the figures for males and females in the above statement shows that inaccurate as the record for men is, it is infinitely more so for women, all the inequalities being exaggerated in the returns for the latter.

96. **Corresponding figures in England.**—It may be interesting as exemplifying the enormous difference between what is considered ignorance on this subject in England and the dense ignorance of India to reproduce a statement given in the English Census Report for 1881 to show the extent to which ages are known there.

Age as returned.	Number of deaths.	Age as returned.	Number of deaths.	Age as returned.	Number of deaths.	Age as returned.	Number of deaths.
0 ...	71,888	29 ...	2,235	58 ...	2,110	87 ...	1,234
1 ...	27,908	30 ...	2,762	59 ...	1,932	88 ...	1,195
2 ...	14,983	31 ...	1,960	60 ...	3,394	89 ...	661
3 ...	9,524	32 ...	2,410	61 ...	2,113	90 ...	693
4 ...	6,731	33 ...	2,331	62 ...	2,578	91 ...	387
5 ...	4,713	34 ...	2,332	63 ...	2,770	92 ...	384
6 ...	3,433	35 ...	2,420	64 ...	2,742	93 ...	312
7 ...	2,837	36 ...	2,207	65 ...	2,891	94 ...	197
8 ...	2,337	37 ...	2,276	66 ...	3,016	95 ...	189
9 ...	2,120	38 ...	2,286	67 ...	3,031	96 ...	138
10 ...	1,815	39 ...	1,970	68 ...	2,700	97 ...	110
11 ...	1,667	40 ...	2,965	69 ...	2,247	98 ...	76
12 ...	1,640	41 ...	1,736	70 ...	3,348	99 ...	43
13 ...	1,663	42 ...	2,334	71 ...	2,361	100 ...	37
14 ...	1,899	43 ...	1,882	72 ...	3,236	101 ...	13
15 ...	1,816	44 ...	2,075	73 ...	2,892	102 ...	16
16 ...	2,175	45 ...	2,560	74 ...	2,886	103 ...	11
17 ...	2,303	46 ...	1,976	75 ...	3,081	104 ...	12
18 ...	2,511	47 ...	1,997	76 ...	2,818	105 ...	7
19 ...	2,643	48 ...	2,173	77 ...	3,243	106 ...	4
20 ...	2,663	49 ...	1,897	78 ...	2,812	107 ...	3
21 ...	2,800	50 ...	2,716	79 ...	2,071	108 and upwards.	2
22 ...	2,867	51 ...	1,701	80 ...	2,810		
23 ...	2,747	52 ...	2,168	81 ...	1,852	Unknown.	874
24 ...	2,738	53 ...	1,977	82 ...	2,263		
25 ...	2,607	54 ...	1,985	83 ...	1,843		
26 ...	2,684	55 ...	2,391	84 ...	2,167		
27 ...	2,580	56 ...	2,341	85 ...	1,770		
28 ...	2,542	57 ...	2,116	86 ...	1,468	Total ...	335,956

The difference between this and the table above given for the North-Western Provinces speaks for itself as to the difficulties to be overcome in Indian enumeration and correction of age-periods. It is, however, a difference in degree only, and with certain additions and variations the causes referred to in the English report as affecting the accuracy of the returns apply here also.

97. **The causes affecting the accuracy of the age returns.**—These causes are thus detailed in the English report :—

"In the first place, very many persons, especially among the illiterate classes, do not know what their precise age may be. They keep their date of birth in mind for the earlier part of their life, up to 20 years or so, but after this they lose reckoning, and can only make an approximate statement. Such persons have a strong tendency to return their age as some exact multiple of 10, 30, 40, 50, 60, &c., as the case may be, though in reality they may be a year or two on one or the other side of that precise age. There is also a similar tendency, though in a far less degree, to return the unknown age as 35, 45, 55, or other uneven multiple of five."

"A second cause of erroneous statement as to age is the confusion made by many persons between the year of age in which they are living and the number of years they have completed; for instance, between 'in the 21st year of life' and '21 years old.'"

"The ages of children under five were abstracted at the Census Office by single years; and there can be no doubt that, owing to this confusion as to the proper mode of expression, the number of infants enumerated as under one year of age is very considerably below the mark, very many infants having been returned as one year old who really were only ten or nine, or even fewer, months of age. The returns of children in the second, third, fourth and fifth years of life respectively are also probably far from correct; but here the amount of error will not be so great as in the first year, for, though a certain number in each case will have been pushed on a year beyond their proper place, yet this loss will have been more or less fully compensated by gain from the year below. The total number for the whole quinquennium will almost certainly be understated, because some children in the fifth year of life will have been returned as five years old."

"A third cause of inaccuracy in the age returns is the tendency of old persons, when uncertain as to their exact age, to exaggeration. In consequence of this tendency, very little trust should be put in the quinquennial or even the decennial totals after 85."

"There remains yet another form of inaccuracy in the age returns, which differs from those as yet mentioned in being of a wilful character. Many persons, and notably many women, desirous of being thought to be younger than they really are, return themselves as under 25 or as under 30 when their true age is even considerably beyond these limits."

"On the other hand, we find reason to believe from careful examination of the age tables that a not inconsiderable number of girls who are not yet 15 return themselves as being of that or of more advanced age, probably with the view of getting more readily taken as servants."

The first of these causes operates in India in the same way as in England, but to an infinitely greater degree. The ignorance here is so great that in perhaps the majority of cases amongst the lower classes and especially amongst the women of the lower classes it is better to rely on the enumerator's intelligent observation and in many cases on his personal knowledge of the persons enumerated than on their own statements as to their ages. All officers who have enumerated persons of the lower classes have come across instances in which grey-headed old men have, when asked their ages, said in a hesitating way—"It will be more than 20." A somewhat ludicrous instance came to my notice in the Rae Bareli district. A sweeper recorded his age as 32, this being probably nearly correct: at the same time his mother, a decrepid old woman, reported hers to be 30. The instructions to enumerators, to provide as far as possible against gross mistakes of this kind, directed that, if a person could not state his or her age exactly, the enumerator should ask the relations or refer to some well-known event of local importance, or if the person were present make a guess at the age from the appearance. The district reports show that the subject received all the attention possible from the supervising staff and that the returns, inaccurate as they are, are as accurate as it is possible to expect in the present state of knowledge in India.

98. **Methods in which these defects have to be remedied.**—The method by which both for the figures of the English census and in India the gross inequalities in the age returns due to the preference for round numbers are obviated is by grouping the returns into periods of five or ten years. In the English report it was recommended that the age figures should be grouped in decades of which the multiples of ten should be in the centre, that is from 5 to 14, 15 to 24, and so on. As, however, in all earlier Indian Census Reports the decades which commence with multiples of 10 have been adopted, it is necessary, for the sake of uniformity and to facilitate comparison of figures, to retain this arrangement. In the earlier ages grouping by periods of five years will be found necessary for certain purposes, and, as the tendency to show the ages of young people in exact multiples of ten is very much less than in the higher ages, such a grouping will be correct enough.

Grouping the figures of abstract No. 23 into periods of five and ten years we get the totals shown in the following statement :—

Age.	Males.		Females.	
0—4	6,832	13,646	6,873	12,964
5—9	6,814		6,091	
10—14	6,097	10,644	4,515	8,089
15—19	4,547		3,574	
20—24	4,507	9,024	4,336	8,678
25—29	4,517		4,342	
30—34	4,569	7,411	4,286	6,857
35—39	2,842		2,571	
40—44	3,541	5,333	3,450	5,050
45—49	1,792		1,600	
50—54	2,396	3,197	2,579	3,293
55—59	801		714	
60 and over.	2,678	2,678	3,136	3,136

It will be seen that for males especially, in the arrangement by decades, the series is regular enough to make it possible to regard it as *primâ facie* correct. Great irregularities still exist in the series for women, which it may be possible to correct to some extent by comparison with the figures for males.

The effect of the second cause of error referred to in the quotation from the English report given was not observed at last census of the North-Western Provinces, but it can undoubtedly be traced in the North-Western Provinces returns and it will be necessary by examination of the figures for both censuses and by comparison with the figures for the Panjáb where the rule of enumeration was different to estimate its extent.

The third cause of error, exaggeration of age by old people, affects the returns of the North-Western Provinces most markedly in the case of women. It was allowed for by Mr. Edmund White at last census and will similarly be allowed for now.

Intentional misrepresentation of age by women hardly exists in India, it is believed, in the form in which it takes in England. There are in particular no unmarried women over 20 in the country, and the tendency on the part of women over 20 to intentionally understate their ages is, therefore, practically absent. Misrepresentation of the age of women, however, takes a far more serious form in regard to unmarried girls aged from 10 to 19 and extends beyond the misrepresentation of ages into actual intentional concealment of their existence. This leads to the most serious inaccuracy that can be discovered in the enumeration of an Indian province, and it will be the most important part of this chapter to estimate its amount. The inaccuracy of the enumeration is also, it is believed, added to by the low estimation in which old women and especially old widows are held. It is so often considered useless to try to remember their existence as to make a distinct difference in the census returns.

A special cause of inaccuracy believed by Mr. White to exist in Indian age returns in addition to those found in English returns may be referred to. It is considered that causes producing an accurate return of ages for a particular year have a disturbing effect on the uniformity of the returns.

"The fact of a person having been born in a year of great calamity is generally remembered in his family. This is especially the case of persons born in the year 1857-58, when the disturbances following the mutiny of the native army occurred. Persons born in that year will have been accurately entered by the enumerators as 23 years of age. The ratio of the number in the group 20—24 to the number in the group 25—29 will tend to be greater than it should be, because, while many of the latter group will have been wrongly classed in the former, the reverse error will have been too small to compensate it completely. Evidently there may be many other occurrences well remembered in certain localities which will have a similar disturbing influence on the age returns. It appears, then, that if the age distribution is to be accepted on the ground simply that errors cancel one another, it must be received as correct only within very wide limits."

This suggestion is not as a fact borne out by actual figures. Thus, to take the special instance of the mutiny quoted by Mr. White, we should have expected in his statement of the ages of 1,000 persons (page 5 of 1881 report) some excess in the age 23; but as a matter of fact there are only three persons shown of that age, whilst 88 are shown as aged 25. Again, in the return of 100,000 persons given above on pages 109—110 we should have expected some excess in age 33, which has, however, only 405 persons against 533 in 34 and 3,009 in 35. Again, the famine of 1868 ought, as it is well remembered through the greater part of the provinces, to have given an excess in age 23, whereas the figures for 23 are 490 against 2,183 for 22 and 1,100 for 24. *Primâ facie* I should be inclined to agree with Mr. White. Returns of such ages ought to be in excess but why they are not may, I think, be explained. In the first place the accuracy made possible by reference to such a date is not confined to the single year. It is just as easy for a person enumerated to fix his birth by the mutiny if he were born a few years before or a few years after it as if in the mutiny year. As a matter of fact I have frequently had old men tell me that a son was two or three years old in the year of the mutiny or born two or three years after it, or a man say that his moustache was beginning to grow or had well grown in the time of the mutiny. The influence of such a date is, therefore, spread over several years and not confined to one. A second reason for the absence of the effect anticipated in the returns is that in the great majority of instances the enumerator is too much in a hurry to make the particular enquiries necessary to elicit this information and that the great calamities likely to be generally remembered amongst the population or by the enumerators are not so far removed from the census year as to influence the record of any except the younger people amongst whom mistakes so gross as to attract the attention of an enumerator are less common.

99. **The ages of males below ten.**—The abstract accompanying compares for males the population up to 10 recorded in the present census under each age-period with those in the corresponding periods at the censuses of 1881 and the corresponding percentages in 1872.

Abstract No. 24, comparing for males the ages under 10 for 1872, 1881 *and* 1891.

Age.	1872.	1881.		1891.	
	Percentage to total population.	Population.	Percentage to total population.	Population.	Percentage to total population.
0 ...	4·5	599,666	2·6	830,066	3·41
1 ...	2·4	524,679	2·2	360,761	1·48
2 ...	3·0	440,262	1·9	600,975	2·47
3 ...	2·9	609,581	2·6	715,315	2·95
4 ...	3·3	638,955	2·8	672,519	2·77
0—4 ...	16·1	2,813,143	12·1	3,179,636	13·08
5—9 ...	13·2	3,062,624	13·4	3,226,065	13·27
0—9 ...	29·3	5,875,767	25·5	6,405,701	26·35

The main features in the returns for 1881 and 1891 are similar. There are violent variations in the population at different ages even under five and the numbers in the group 5—9 are much in excess of what they might be expected to be were the birth-rate uniform and the enumeration of ages absolutely correct. How violent the variations are can best be seen by comparing the percentages above given with those in the following statement for the English census returns and those deducted from the corrected life table prepared for the North-Western Provinces at last census under the orders of the Census Commissioner for India and printed in the Census Report for India, page 186.

The latter figures are those with which comparison may most correctly be made, as the death-rate for children is in India admittedly far higher than in England. Mr. White was unable to apply any test to these figures by means of the registered births in the province, but by an elaborate examination of the death returns he believed it proved that the census returns accurately showed the population as it stood, that the lowness of his returns for ages 2 and 0 and for the whole period 0—4 showed that the "procreative energy of the people," to quote a phrase made use of in the same connection by the 1881 Panjáb Superintendent, was exhausted by the famine of 1877 and the fever of 1879 to such an extent that the minor population born in the following years was a fourth less than it naturally would be and the total infant popu-

Age.	English census.	North-Western Provinces Life Table.	
	Percentage.	Actual deduced population.	Percentage.
0 ...	2·9	812,728	3·34
1 ...	2·7	710,639	2·93
2 ...	2·8	659,394	2·71
3 ...	2·7	627,553	2·58
4 ...	2·7	605,235	2·49
0—4 ...	13·9	3,415,549	14·05
5—9 ...	12·4	2,838,621	11·68

lation for the five years about a fifth less than normal. The famine and fever no doubt had, as the birth returns now show, a pronounced effect on the birth-rate of the years immediately following. Something of the same kind has happened on a very much less pronounced scale in the past 10 years when the *births* for the first five years considerably exceed those for the last five years. But the effect on the population was by no means so pronounced as Mr. White's conclusions would point to. He omitted to take into consideration that the children born in 1878 were not exposed to the effects of the famine of 1877 as were those of the preceding years and that, therefore, with even a very low birth-rate the surviving children of that year would not comparatively be at all so few. The agreement of the figures of the present census with those of Mr. White's so far as the proportion between the population from 0—4 and 5—9 was in itself a reason for suspicion as to the correctness of his reasoning as we have not in the last five years had any calamities in any way comparable with those preceding the last census. The conclusion, I have come to, is that in both censuses a considerable mistake has resulted from recording the age of children on their last birth-day. The popular tendency is to state the current and not the completed year, many children of one year of age are accordingly stated to be in the second year and shown as two. Many of those of two are shown as three and so on. This process at last census commenced in the first year of life. On the present occasion the facility with which the word "infant" (bachcha) could be quoted and entered led to a full return for the first year of life and allowed the process of exaggeration of age to begin abruptly from the second.

The correctness of this conclusion is proved in my opinion by comparison of the Panjáb figures for 1881, when the system of record of ages was the same as in the North-Western Provinces, with those for the Panjáb in 1891, when the current and not the completed year was recorded. The figures are given in abstract No. 25 for the Panjab as a whole and the Delhi and Umbala Divisions separately as the vital circumstances of the latter are similar to those of the North-Western Provinces. The 1891 figures for the Panjáb have probably as regards age 0 been increased more than is correct by the use of the word infant.

Abstract No. 25, showing the percentages on total population in Panjáb in 1881 *and* 1891 *of age-periods between* 0 *and* 9.

Age-periods.	1881.	1891. Delhi and Umbala Divisions.	1891. Panjáb.
0 year	3·17	4·23	4·09
1 „	1·75	2·79	2·93
2 years... ...	2·12	2·71	3·00
3 „	2·57	2·63	3·02
4 „	2·77	3·01	3·28
Total under five years.	12·38	15·37	16·32
5-9 years ...	13·94	12·45	14·06
Total 0-9 years ...	26·32	27·82	30·38

Some idea of the extent of the error for at least the first two years of life thus introduced may be gathered from the Sanitary Commissioner's birth and death returns. The children aged under one in the census may be assumed to be those born in 1880 less those who died before enumeration. The deaths to be deducted were during an average life-period of six months of the first year of life. By English returns the deaths during the first six months are to those of the last six as 1,325 to 617 (Newsholme Vital Statistics, page 105). Births in 1890 were 920,356, deaths to be deducted about $\frac{1325}{1942}$ of total deaths under one, that is 142,463. Population under one according to Sanitary Commissioner's returns was therefore 777,893. We have to allow for omissions in the birth record and the census figure is, therefore, probably not much if at all in excess of what is correct. The figures for the second year of life according to the Sanitary Commissioner's returns cannot be so exactly ascertained as the deaths for the period 1—2 are not specially recorded. By a process similar to the above I estimate them to be about 640,000. The census return for age 1—2 is, therefore, at least 270,000 too small. Part of this missing amount is possibly owing to the use of the word "bachcha" included in age 0, but the amount so included is necessarily very small and the deficit has been mainly added to the period 2. By a similar mistake of enumeration, and owing to the special attractiveness of the age period 3, a fully larger number was lost at the end of age 2 to that of 3. This inaccuracy would tend to increase with the age and be greatest owing to the attraction of the round number 5, where the first five years of life end and the second quinquennial period begins. I calculate that at least 270,000 children were shown in period 5—9 instead of in that for 0—4.

In the ages from five and upwards this transfer from one year to another ceases to be at all so regular, the attraction of certain favourite years becoming more pronounced: 10 is by far the greatest favourite in the first 20 years of life, and the return on pages 109—110 makes it perfectly certain that it draws from nine, as well as much more largely from ages higher than 10. There should, therefore, be a correction, probably not materially smaller than that between the first two quinquennial periods, to be made between the second and the third periods. This brings us to the consideration of the periods from 10 upwards which, it has been already shown, it is absolutely futile to consider, unless combined in decades.

100. **The age-periods for males above 10.**—The following statement shows the total male population for 1881 and 1891 arranged in decades with the percentage borne by each decade to the total male population, and also the proportion of the corresponding age-periods in 1872.

Abstract No. 26.

Decade.	1872.	1881.		1891.	
	Proportion to total male population.	Population.	Percentage to total male population.	Population.	Proportion to total male population.
0— 9 ...	29·3	5,875,767	25·5	6,405,701	26·35
10—19 ...	21·3	4,707,432	20·6	4,869,332	20·03
20—29 ...	19·1	4,076,612	17·8	4,192,737	17·25
30—39 ...	14·2	3,320,001	14·5	3,539,843	14·57
40—49 ...	8·9	2,341,880	10·2	2,537,872	10·45
50 and upwards ...	7·2	2,590,864	11·4	2,758,116	11·35
Total ...	100·0	22,912,556	100·0	24,303,601	100·0

It requires little to demonstrate, that the age-periods above 50 cannot be safely considered separately; above that age people are considered aged in India, and the invariable tendency is to exaggerate the return of their age.

We had already seen that a transfer from the second to the first decade of probably nearly 270,000 persons is necessary, and for the same reasons each succeeding decade gains improperly at the expense of that preceding. In correcting for this error the ultimate loser is the age-period from fifty upwards, intermediate age-periods probably being comparatively correct. Though, after 30 the numbers affected by errors of enumeration are fewer, this is nearly counterbalanced by the fact that the proportion of error increases with the age. The net result is, therefore, that some 270,000 persons should be transferred from the age-period over 50 to that under 10. The figures so amended give the male population present in the provinces on the night of the census. A a very material alteration has, however, to be made before these figures could, except in comparison with those for a previous census, be used for the preparation of life statistics. It would be necessary to allow for the excess of emigration over immigration which, as will appear from the chapter on birth-places, amounts for males to 484,169; a number of importance when it is considered that it mainly belongs to two or three age-decades.

101. **The age-periods for females.**—We may now turn to the age-periods for females. The following statement shows the actual numbers now and at last census for each year to four, for the quinquennial periods 0—4 and 5—9 and for all decades thereafter.

Abstract No. 27.

Age-period.	1872.	1881.		1891.	
	Proportion.	Population.	Proportion.	Population.	Proportion.
0 year	4·7	593,526	2·8	810,531	3 58
1 "	2·7	526,198	2·5	373,731	1·65
2 years	3·5	463,432	2·2	635,515	2·81
3 "	2·9	635,661	3·0	757,062	3·35
4 "	3·2	609,039	2·9	668,567	2·96
0—4 "	17·0	2,827,856	13·4	3,245,406	14·35
5—9 "	11·8	2,704,963	12·7	2,915,263	12·90
0—9 "	28·8	5,532,819	26·1	6,160,669	27·25
10—19 "	19·1	3,643,956	17·2	3,780,256	16·73
20—29 "	20·4	3,942,628	18·6	4,060,091	17·96
30—39 "	14·6	3,078,191	14·5	3,285,329	14·54
40—49 "	9·1	2,220,811	10·5	2,356,918	10·43
50 and upwards	8·0	2,776,909	13·1	2,958,221	13 09
Total ...	100·0	21,195,313	100·0	22,601,484	100·0

The following table comparing the absolute numbers of males and females at each period and giving for each age-period the percentage of males and females now and at 1881 and 1872 will also be found useful :—

Abstract No 28.

Age-period.	Numbers in every 100 of population.						Actual number, 1891.	
	1872.		1881.		1891.			
	Males.	Females.	Males.	Females.	Males.	Females.	Males.	Females.
0 year	51·96	48·04	50·25	49·75	50·60	49·40	830,066	810,531
1 "	50·02	49·98	49·93	50·07	49·12	50·88	360,761	373,731
2 years	50·60	49·40	48·72	51·28	48·60	51·40	600,975	635,515
3 "	52·63	47·37	48·95	51·05	48·58	51·42	715,315	757,062
4 "	54·87	45·13	51·20	48·80	50·14	49·86	672,519	668 567
0—4 "	52·09	47·91	49·87	50·13	49·49	50·51	3,179,636	3,245,406
5—9 "	56·07	43·93	53·10	46·90	52·53	47·47	3,226,065	2,915,263
0—9 "	53·81	46·19	51·50	48·50	50·98	49·02	6,405,701	6,160,669
10—19 "	56·15	43·85	56·37	43·63	56·30	43·70	4,869,332	3,780,256
20—29 "	51·66	48·34	50·84	49·16	50·80	49·20	4,192,737	4,060,091
30—39 "	52·67	47·33	51·89	48·11	51·86	48·14	3,539,843	3,285,329
40—49 "	52·74	47·26	51·33	48·67	51·85	48·15	2,587,872	2,356,918
50—59 "	50·17	49·83	50·59	49·41	50·60	49·40	1,543,184	1,506,759
60 and over			45·48	54·52	45·57	54·43	1,214,932	1,451,462
Total ...	53·32	46·68	51·95	48·05	51·81	48·19	24,303,601	22,601,484

The distribution in 1881 and 1891, so far as the proportion between males and females is concerned, is similar almost throughout.

In the age-periods below five, considering females only, the variations from year to year are almost precisely the same as for males and there is, therefore, the same reason to believe that whereas the age-period 0 has a full or somewhat too full population shown, succeeding years each lose to that following them. The record of female births by the Sanitary Commissioner is admittedly and demonstrably so incomplete that the estimate of the correctness or error of the age-period figures made from the female birth and death figures cannot be nearly so exact as for males. These figures would give for the age-period 0, 702,839 females and for age period 1, 613,000. A comparison of these figures with the actuals as enumerated corroborates in general the result deduced from the similar comparison in the case of males. Age-period 0 is full, possibly too full; age-period 1 loses largely to 2 and for similar reasons 2 to 3 and so on. At the age of 4 a change begins to be evident. Females, who for ages 2 and 3 are shown in excess of males, here fall below them; and, as the table on pages 109—110 shows, continues below them for all ages in the following five years. Passing beyond 5 to 9 into the decade 10—19, we find an enormous decrease in the number of females and a consequent fall in the number of females per cent. as compared with males. That this is not due to the death-rate a reference to the age-period 20—29 at once shows. Here we again find the normal proportion of males and females and a female population actually larger than that in the preceding age-period. The main question connected with the correction of the female age-figures is connected with this. I need not recapitulate at length the absolutely conclusive arguments by which Mr. White demonstrated that the deficit from 19 to 20 was due to omissions in enumeration. It could not be due to exaggeration of female ages, because *primâ facie* we know that there can be no tendency to such exaggeration at periods at which the age is well known, and because there is no corresponding excess of females in the age-periods succeeding 10—19. It is not due to any great extent to understatement of female ages, because the lower age-periods have no excess of females. There appears to be three causes of error which affect the returns for the female population below 20 :

1st, the tendency as in males to substitute the current for the completed year ;

2nd, a decided tendency on the part of the parents to understate ages, especially from four upward ;

3rd, a tendency to actually omit girls under 20 from enumeration. The cause of the two last errors is well known. The marriage of a female child is always expensive. The parent considers it his duty to consider the matter from the time she reaches five, and it becomes urgent about ten. Dreading the approach of the time when it will be necessary to marry the girl, he invariably understates her age, and if she is so old that her age cannot be understated sufficiently, prefers to omit mention of her to admitting he has an unmarried daughter of 15 or over. In the quinquennial period 0—4, we have seen that the age-period 1 loses, as in the case of males, probably 270,000 to later periods, besides the amount it has possibly lost to 0. For age periods 2, 3 and 4 there are gains and losses counterbalancing to some extent, 2 loses to 3, 3 to 4, and 4 to 5 owing to the substitution of the current for the completed year. On the other hand, 5 loses to 4, 4 to 3 and 3 to 2 to a diminishing extent owing to the tendency to understate female ages. On the whole, it is probable that the quinquennial period loses to that succeeding but not to the full extent of 270,000 lost by age 1. It is possible only to make a guess at the actual loss. It is probably about 170,000. For the age—period 5 to 9 we may consider that the first and second causes of error mentioned above counterbalance each other to a still greater extent, and that out of the 270,000 due to the period from that over 10 on account of the first cause of error only 100,000 is permanently lost by the period. The figures for the decade as a whole are, therefore, 270,000 short. Mr. White estimated the proper population for the second decade by working back from the third and deducing the proportion of variation between different age-periods for females from that for males. It appears to be safer to assume the correctness of Mr. Hardy's Life Table for the North-Western Provinces than to arbitrarily assume a relation between the male and female birth-rates in those periods in which these rates are most unduly discrepant. I propose, therefore, to deduce the proper population for the age 10—19 from the return for last census for 0—9 with the assistance of the Life Table.

Population, 1881.		Deduced population, 1891.	
Age.	Population.	Age.	Population.
0	593,526	10	418,700
1	526,198	11	409,600
2	463,432	12	379,900
3	635,661	13	536,200
4	609,039	14	414,700
5—9	2,704,963	15—19	2,328,700
Total 0—9	5,532,819	Total 10—19	4,487,800

The details of the calculation are given in the margin. The total so deduced is 4,487,800, but we have already seen that the age-period 0—9 loses by quoting the current for the completed year to the extent of probably 270,000 in the present census, and to a proportionate extent at last census. Assuming that the loss at last census from this cause was such as to account for 200,000 survivors we have as the proper female population for age-period 10—19 roughly 4,690,000. This shows that 910,000 females have been omitted from this age-period alone.

For the age-periods from 20 onwards, Mr. White points out that the percentage of men and women to total population varies from 50·8 and 49·2 in the third decade to 51·9 and 48·1 in the fourth decade, and, after remaining nearly constant through the fifth decade; alter to 48·2 and 51·8 in the period 50 and upwards. He considers that this indicates the existence of an error in the enumeration :—

Age-period.	Males.		Females.	
	Population.	Per 100 of total population.	Population.	Per 100 of total population.
20—29 ...	4,192,737	50·8	4,060,091	49·2
30—39 ...	3,539,843	51·9	3,285,329	48·1
40—49 ...	2,537,872	51·8	2,356 918	48·2
50 and upwards ...	2,758,116	48·2	2,958,221	51·8
Total ...	13,028,568	50·72	12,660,559	49·28

The percentages are almost precisely the same now as at last census. Mr. White argues that because, the percentages for the third decade of life almost exactly equal those for the total of the decades shown above, it is impossible that the proportion of *enumerated* women to *enumerated* men should fall off for two decades and then abruptly increase. It is well known that the death-rate for women over the child-bearing age is lower than that for men, and therefore an increase in the number of aged women as compared with aged men was to be expected; but the eccentricity of the variations indicatad in the table above appears to leave little doubt that the figures as corrected by Mr. White are more nearly accurate than those enumerated. It has been already remarked that large omissions of aged women have taken place, and it may readily be believed that those omissions were so considerable as to reduce the number of old women enumerated to below that of old men. I correct, therefore, as indicated by Mr. White on page 15 of his report. The excess in the number of old women in the period for 50 and over is 278,412, and this has to be allotted 161,925 to age 30—39 and 116,487 to age 40—49.

We have also to carry from the age-period for 50 upwards as in the case of men an allowance for the overstatement of ages due to insertion of the current year of life and the attraction of the round numbers which begin each decade. It is, judging from the deductions above made from the Sanitary Commissioner's figures, at the very lowest 270,000, an amount which as shown for males should be transferred almost entirely from the last age-period. We thus have the following corrected statement of ages for women :—

Age-period.	Population.	Percentage to total population.
0—4	3,415,406	14·53
5—9	3,015,263	12·82
10—19	4,690,000	19·95
20—29	4,060,091	17·27
30—39	3,447,254	14·66
40—49	2,473,405	10·52
50 and upwards	2,409,809	10·25
Total ...	23,511,228	100·00

A last correction has to be made arbitrarily for omissions in age-periods other than that in 10—19. Mr. White pointed out that the circumstances under which the enumeration of women was made were such as to make greater comparative omission, even apart from the marriage question, absolutely certain. They are most of them hidden away out of sight, and aged widows in especial little thought of. All the evidence we have of omissions in enumeration point to omissions of women as alone being possible to any great extent. Mr. White estimated the amount of omission to be one per cent. in all age-periods to the last and 2 per cent. in the period for 50 onwards.

I consider this considerably below the mark. I believe that in the age-period 5—9 there is a high percentage of omissions for the same reason as in 10—19; that the omissions in this age-period are at least 4 per cent. For the age-periods from 10 to 49 Mr. White's addition of 1 per cent. to the amended figures is probably quite full enough, but in the period for 50 and upwards there is every reason to believe that four per cent. of omissions is not too high an estimate. On the other hand, there is no reason to believe that from 0—4 before the parda or marriage age the omission of girls is material. I propose to arbitrarily amend the figures above given as suggested.

102. **Corrected age tables.**—We now have the following finally corrected age table for males and females :—

Age-period.	Males.	Females.	Females to 100 males.	Percentage of age group to total males.	Percentage of age group to total females.
0—4 ...	3,449,636	3,415,406	99·24	14·19	14·31
5—9 ...	3,226,065	3,135,971	97·21	13·27	13·13
0—9 ...	6,675,701	6,551,377	98·14	27·46	27·44
10—19 ...	4,869,332	4,736,900	97·28	20·04	19·84
20 ...	4,192,737	4,100,691	97·81	17·25	17·18
30 ...	3,539,843	3,481,726	98·36	14·57	14·58
40 ...	2,537,872	2,498,139	98·43	10·44	10·46
50 and over ...	2,488,116	2,506,201	100·73	10·24	10·50
Total ...	24,303,601	23,875,034	98·24	100·00	100·00

Comparison of the figures so arrived at with those for a corresponding population of males and females according to the life table in the census report for India, already referred to, may be of interest. It must be remembered that the series in the corrected figures just now calculated are as regards males still far from a natural series, owing to the fact that no allowance has been made for temporary emigrants from the province. The figures for the calculated population of the provinces by the life tables are as shown in the accompanying statement.

Age-period.	Males.	Females.	Total.
0—4	3,415,566	3,332,376	6,747,942
5—9	2,838,635	2,836,367	5,675,002
0—9	6,254,201	6,168,743	12,422,944
10—19	5,124,646	5,093,646	10,218,292
20—29	4,271,958	4,149,168	8,421,126
30—39	3,385,740	3,216,815	6,602,555
40—49	2,536,205	2,422,022	4,958,227
50 and over	2,730,851	2,824,640	5,555,491
Total ...	24,303,601	23,875,034	48,178,635

103. **The proportion of the sexes.**—The proportion of the sexes found in the corrected age statistics is 98·24 to 100 males. This, as Mr. White points out, is probably a minimum proportion, the actually existing proportion being if anything higher. The proportion shown in the actual census figures was 92·99 females to 100 males or in other words 518 males and 482 females

out of a total 1,000, persons. The appended statement (abstract No. 29) shows the corresponding proportions for each district in the provinces :—

Abstract No. 29, showing the proportion of males and females in the districts of the Provinces.

Serial number of district.	District and Division.	Percentage on total population of— Males.	Females.
1	Dehra Dún	59·7	40·3
2	Sahâranpur	54·0	46·0
3	Muzaffarnagar	54·1	45·9
4	Meerut	53·7	46·3
5	Bulandshahr	52·8	47·2
6	Aligarh	53·6	46·4
	Total, Meerut Division ...	53·8	46·2
7	Muttra	53·6	46·4
8	Agra	53·8	46·2
9	Farukhabad	54·1	45·9
10	Mainpuri	54·7	45·3
11	Etáwah	54·5	45·5
12	Etah	54·6	45·4
	Total, Agra Division ...	54·2	45·8
13	Bareilly	53·4	46·6
14	Bijnor	52·7	47·3
15	Budaun	53·8	46·2
16	Moradabad	52·9	47·1
17	Sháhjahánpur	54·0	46·0
18	Pilibhit	53·2	46·8
	Total, Rohilkhand Division ...	53·3	46·7
19	Cawnpore	53·6	46·4
20	Fatehpur	51·5	48·5
21	Bánda	50·6	49·4
22	Hamírpur	50·7	49·3
23	Allahabad	50·5	49·5
24	Jhánsi	52·4	47·6
25	Jalaun	51·5	48·5
26	Lalitpur	51·6	48·4
	Total, Allahabad Division ...	51·5	48·5
27	Benares	50·7	49·3
28	Mirzapur	49·6	50·4
29	Jaunpur	50·2	49·8
30	Ghâzipur	49·3	50·7
31	Ballia	48·0	52·0
	Total, Benares Division ...	49·6	50·4
32	Gorakhpur	50·009	49·991
33	Basti	50·8	49·2
34	Azamgarh	50·2	49·8
	Total, Gorakhpur Division ...	50·3	49·7
35	Kumaun	52·4	47·6
36	Garhwâl	49·1	50·9
37	Tarái	54·8	45·2
	Total, Kumaun Division ...	51·7	48·3
	Total, N.-W. Provinces ...	52·0	48·0

Abstract No. 29—(concluded).

Serial number of district.	District and Division.	Percentage on total population of— Males.	Females.
38	Lucknow	52·6	47·4
39	Unao	51·3	48·7
40	Rae Bareli	49·5	50·5
41	Sitapur	52·7	47·3
42	Hardoi	53·6	46·4
43	Kheri...	53·3	46·7
	Total, Lucknow Division ...	52·3	47·7
44	Fyzabad	50·3	49·7
45	Gonda	51·1	48·9
46	Bahraich	52·3	47·7
47	Sultánpur	49·3	50·7
48	Partábgarh	48·9	51·1
49	Bara Banki	51·0	49·0
	Total, Fyzabad Division ...	50·6	49·4
	Total, Oudh ...	51·3	48·7
	Total, N.-W Provinces and Oudh ...	51·8	48·2
50	Rámpur	52·8	47·2
51	Tehri Garhwál	49·1	50·9
	Total, Native States ...	51·7	48·3

It will be observed that seven districts and one State, and one Commissionership as a whole, show in contrast to the general average, females in excess of males, and that several other districts all in the east of the provinces show the number of females in excess of the proportion calculated in our corrected population statement. The districts and state with females in actual excess are Mirzapur, Gházipur, Ballia, Garhwál, Rae Bareli, Sultánpur, Partábgarh, and Tehri Garhwál. This naturally leads to the question whether in these districts or state the concealment of women referred to above as extensive in the provinces occurs or whether these districts have returned a full proportion of women under each age-period. The following statement comparing for each Commissionership the proportionate number of men and women enumerated under each age-period at once indicates a distinction between the Kumaun Division and the rest of the provinces.

Abstract No. 30.

Age-periods.	Meerut Division.		Agra Division.		Rohilkhand Division.		Allahabad Division.		Benares Division.		Gorakhpur Division.		Kumaun Division.		Lucknow Division.		Fyzabad Division.	
	Males.	Females.	Males.	Females.	Males.	Females.	Males.	Females.	Males.	Females.	Males.	Females.	Males.	Females.	Males.	Females.	Males.	Females.
0—4 ...	1,215	1,359	1,133	1,298	1,339	1,504	1,164	1,268	1,329	1,406	1,459	1,582	1,350	1,478	1,333	1,489	1,427	1,500
5—9 ...	1,182	1,185	1,190	1,211	1,312	1,240	1,334	1,332	1,484	1,341	1,504	1,399	1,263	1 295	1,298	1,296	1,367	1,268
0—9 ...	2,397	2,544	2,323	2,509	2,651	2,744	2,498	2,600	2,813	2,747	2,963	2,981	2,613	2,773	2,631	2,785	2,794	2,771
10—19 ...	2,118	1,849	2,114	1,765	2,073	1,710	2,023	1,732	2,013	1,604	1,930	1,586	2,118	1,978	1,892	1,595	1,890	1,517
20—29 ...	1,845	1,921	1,860	1,975	1,747	1,768	1,721	1,782	1,582	1,715	1,694	1,750	1,806	1,747	1,718	1,810	1,633	1,730
30—39 ...	1,599	1,432	1,558	1,600	1,434	1,381	1,557	1,573	1,391	1,478	1,399	1,465	1,425	1,362	1,434	1,404	1,398	1,430
40—49 ...	1,036	1,025	1,094	1,092	1,039	1,027	1,125	1,105	1,045	1,056	989	97[illegible]	999	951	1,034	1,028	1,017	1,065
50 and upwards.	1,095	1,229	1,081	1,159	1,126	1,370	1,076	1,218	1,156	1,340	1,025	1,257	1,039	1,189	1,296	1,378	1,288	1,487
Total ...	10,000	10,000	10,000	10,000	10,000	10,000	10,000	10,000	10,000	10,000	10,000	10,000	10,000	10,000	10,000	10,000	10,000	1,0 00

104. **Special circumstances in Garhwal.**—The distinction is most marked in Garhwál, the age-periods for which as shown in the accompanying statement contrast in several respects with those for the provinces as a whole :—

Abstract No. 31.

Age-period.	Garhwal.		N.-W. Provinces and Oudh.	
	Males.	Females.	Males.	Females.
0—4	703	736	678	692
5—9	661	664	691	621
0—9	1,364	1,400	1,369	1,313
10—19	1,098	1,015	1,038	803
20—29	834	877	894	865
30	663	676	755	700
40	485	499	541	503
50 and upwards.	468	621	588	631
Total ...	4,912	5,088	5,185	4,815

It is evident that there is here no material deficit in the returns for women in the age-period 10-19. The circumstances of both this district and of Tehri Garhwál, in which there is no confinement of women within the parda, and almost all women move about almost as freely as men, would of itself suggest these districts to be likely to be exceptional. Kumaun shows figures very much more in accordance with the standard, but in it there has been a sufficient accretion of plains people and plains influence to account for the difference. The age statistics of Garhwál (and the remarks apply equally to Tehri Garhwál) have been so thoroughly discussed by Mr. Partridge in his report on the census that I cannot do better than transcribe the following extract :—

" The following is a statement of the distribution by ages of the people of Garhwál."

Age-periods.	Year.	Absolute numbers.		Ratio of the sexes in each age-group.	
		Males.	Females.	Males.	Females.
Infants	1891	7,664	8,027	48·8	51·2
	1881	4,933	5,239		
1 year	1891	3,476	3,643	48·8	51·2
	1881	4,048	4,174		
2 years	1891	5,584	5,860	48·8	51·2
	1881	4,017	4,325		
3 "	1891	5,861	6,406	47·5	52·5
	1881	4,723	5,333		
4 "	1891	6,068	6,015	50·2	49·8
	1881	5,183	5,219		
5— 9 years	1891	26,964	27,079	49·9	50·1
	1881	23,997	23,800		
10—14 "	1891	25,018	22,645	52·5	47·5
	1881	22,566	20,588	52·3	47·7
15—19 "	1891	19,785	18,768	51·3	48·7
	1881	17,023	16,063	51·5	48·5
20—24 "	1891	17,803	18,619	48·9	51·1
25—29 "	"	16,206	17,126	48·6	51·4
30—34 "	"	15,845	16,586	48·9	51·1
35—39 "	"	11,214	10,989	50·5	49·5
40—44 "	"	12,139	13,171	47·9	52·1
45—49 "	"	7,631	7,206	51·4	48·6
50—54 "	"	7,969	9,509	45·5	54·5
55—59 "	"	8,447	8,935	46·7	53·3
60 and over	"	7,645	11,855	39·2	60·8
Total ...	"	200,319	207,499	49·1	50·9

"Now looking at this table, it will be seen that while females outnumber the males in the total population, they outnumber them also in 12 out of the 17 age-periods shown in the table. The five periods in which the males outnumber the females are—

Age-periods.	Year.	Absolute numbers.		Ratio of the sexes in each age-group.	
		Males.	Females.	Males.	Females.
4 years	1891	6,068	6,015	50·2	49·8
	1881	5,183	5,219		
10—14 years	1891	25,018	22,645	52·5	47·5
	1881	22,566	20,688		
15—19 "	1891	19,785	18,768	51·3	48·7
	1881	17,023	16,063		
35—39 "	1891	11,214	10,989	50·5	49·5
45—49 "	"	7,631	7,206	51·4	48·6

"I propose to discuss now the explanations."

"Taking first the figures for the children of four years old, the difference between the total number of boys and the total number of girls is so very small as not to require any explanation."

"The reason why the number of women whose ages are returned at from 35—39 is below the number of men shown in this age-period, is clearly because a larger proportion of the men who were 37, 38 or 39 years old returned themselves at their exact ages, as compared with the proportion of women of these ages who returned themselves or were returned by their husbands as 40 years old."

"It is clear from the figures that a number of men who were really 37, 38 or 39 years old, and who should have come into the 35—39 group returned themselves at 40, a round number, and come into the 40—44 group. I say it is clear, because they cannot in the nature of things be 925 (12,139 minus 11,214) more men alive in the district between 40 and 44 than between 35 and 39."

"But while a number of men did this, the number of women who did it was still greater (*vide* the figures for the 40—44 group). This is exactly what might have been expected, looking at the utter illiterateness and ignorance of the women in the district, and the vagueness of their male relations as to their age when getting on to or past middle life."

"The same thing is found again in the 45—49 group. It would have been extraordinary if it had not been. A number of men who were really 47, 48 or 49 years old returned themselves as 50, but a still larger number of women who were really 47, 48 or 49 were returned at 50. This accounts for the excess of males shown in the 45—49 group."

"I am now left with the two groups 10—14 and 15—19. It is the excess of males in these groups which requires thought and consideration."

"I will repeat the figures here—"

Age-periods.	Year.	Absolute numbers.		Ratio of the sexes.	
		Males.	Females.	Males.	Females.
10—14 years ...	1891	25,018	22,645	52·5	47·5
	1881	22,566	20,588	52·3	47·7
	1872	17,245	14,985	53·5	46·5
15—19 years ...	1891	19,785	18,768	51·3	48·7
	1881	17,023	16,063	51·5	48·5
	1872	16,182	15,482	51·1	48·9

"I do not lay much stress on the absolute figures of the 1872 Census, as I have very little faith in the accuracy of that census. The reason why I insert them is to show that for these two age-periods males were returned in excess of females in that year too in much the same proportion as they have been in 1891."

"Now what is the reason of the excess of males over females shown in the 1891 figures for these two age-periods? First, is the number of females returned in these two age-periods approximately correct or not?"

"I assume that the figures are correct in regard to the absolute number of females of all ages recorded in the district. I assume this because there is not the least reason to suspect any concealment of females of any age. On this assumption then, if the number of females returned in these two age-periods is below the correct number, it must be—"

"(*a*) That the ages of girls between 10 and 19 have been overstated; or

"(*b*) that the ages of girls between 10 and 19 have been understated; or

" that both these causes conjointly have been at work."

"But, as Mr. Plowden pointed out on page LIV of his report on the 1872 Census, in either of these events, the falling off in these two terms (10—14 and 15—19), would be found recouped by a corresponding increase either (*a*) in the term immediately following the age-period 15—19, *i.e.*, in the 20—24 age-period, or (*b*) in the term immediately preceding the age-period 10—14, *i.e.*, in the 5—9 age-period."

"Now I find no evidence of any such increase in the number of females either (*a*) in 20—24 age-period or (*b*) in the 5—9 age-period."

"Nor can I conceive any reason why in this district the ages of girls between 10 and 19 should be purposely either overstated or understated. I arrive then at the conclusion that the number of females shown in these two age-periods is approximately correct."

"I may remark in passing that Mr. White too (paragraph 21, page 19 of his report on the 1881 Census) arrived at the conclusion that there was 'no deficiency in the number of females included in the second decade,' and that, therefore, the low ratio of females to males in the second decade must be due to an excess of the males in the class and not to any defect of the males."

"The next point is, is the number of males returned in these two age-periods correct or not?"

"I reply at once. "No." There is no difficulty whatever in showing this. The number of males who should correctly have been returned in the 10—14 group in 1891 is the number living of those returned as under five years old in 1881, plus the number of the survivors of these latter who were not counted at the 1881 Census. Now the number of males under five years of age returned at the 1881 Census was 22,904."

"Using the life table for males given on page XVI of the appendices to the 1881 Report, I find on the supposition that I am using the table correctly that—

"of the	4,933	male infants returned in 1881 about ... ... might be expected to be living in 1891.	2,900
"	4,048	children between 1 and 2 years.	3,070
"	4,017	between 2 and 3 years	3,350
"	4,723	between 3 and 4 years	4,132
"	5,183	between 4 and 5 years	4,626
Total,	22,904		18,078

"Of these the 22,904 male children under five years of age enumerated in 1881, 18,078 may be expected to have been alive in 1891."

"Say we add another 3,000 for the survivors of some 3,500 male children under five years old alive in 1881 but not enumerated at that census, we get above 21,000, which is still a long way from the 25,018 we have to deal with."

"To deal in the same way with the female children under five years old enumerated in 1881 as has been just done with the male children, I find that, 24,290 female children under five years of age were enumerated in 1881."

"of the	5,239	girls then enumerated as under one year might be expected to be alive in 1891.	3,141
"	4,174	between 1 and 2	3,174
"	4,325	between 2 and 3	3,563
"	5,333	between 3 and 4	4,596
"	5,219	between 4 and 5	4,617
"Total,	24,290		1,9091

"Of the 24,290 female children under five years of age enumerated in 1881 there, 19,091 may be expected to have been alive in 1891. Adding another 3,000 or so, as the survivors of some 3,500 female children under five years of age omitted and not counted in 1881, we get nearly the total (22,645) of females between 10 and 14 shown in 1891."

"This confirms what I wrote above that the number of females shown in the age-period 10-14 is in my opinion approximately correct. It can be shown in another way too that the number of children under five years old must have been returned at considerably under the mark in 1881. For in that year the number of children of both sexes returned as under five years of age was 47,194. In 1891 it was 58,664 or an increase of 11,670. There is no reason that I know of why the number of children of under five should have increased in the 10 years in a higher proportion than that of the population generally. The rate at which the total population increased in the 10 years has been shown to be 17·99 per cent. If the total of children under five returned in 1881 had been correct, they would, increasing at the rate of 17·99 per cent., have numbered now in 1891 some 8,400 more than they did in 1881; as a matter of fact, the returns show them to have been 11,670 more; ergo the 1881 figures are very materially too low."

"Where, then, to return to the point immediately under discussion is the reason of the excess of males in the period 10-14?"

"In 1881 a similar excess had to be explained and Mr. White wrote (para. 21, page 19 of his 1881 report). 'This excess of males in the second decade I am unable to explain; it apparently arises from the inclusion of boys below 10 in the group above, perhaps due to a preference of the age 12 for boys, more marked than in the case of girls.'"

"I cannot say that I see much, if any, evidence in the 1891 figures of an inclusion of boys below 10 in the group 10—14. I should rather suggest that a large number of boys really over 15 have been entered in the group 10—14 either (*a*) intentionally or (*b*) unintentionally; (*a*) if intentionally, that the boy whose age was so understated might escape for two or three years having to do duty as a coolie or bring in wood, grass, &c., when his village was required to furnish such and such a number of coolies for Government work or to bring in supplies for some officer of Government, 16 being the age at which a youth is supposed to be liable to be called on to carry a load as a coolie or furnish bardaish (= supplies) when his village is indented on for utár (forced) coolies or supplies; (*b*) if unintentionally, because youths of 15, 16, 17, and sometimes even 18 in this district, very often look perfect boys (in contradistinction to girls of these ages, who nearly always look their full ages), and the enumerators, when the lads did not know their own ages and their parents were equally ignorant (as will have been very often the case with low castes) may have considerably underestimated the lads' ages. As bearing on the intentional understatement,

I may quote from para. 5 of a letter from the then Senior Assistant Commissioner of Garhwál, printed on pages 11 and 12 of appendix D of volume I of Mr. Plowden's report on the 1865 Census. It was found that the number of females under 16 fell short of the number of males under 16 by nearly 29 per cent. On this Mr. Gardner remarked—'the explanation of this is easy: as males under 16 are exempted from certain public burdens, every young man whose age would make it possible is put down as under 16.'"

"It remains for me to explain the excess of males in the age-period 15—19. The excess as it stands is not very large (19,785 males to 18,768 females), but if my explanation as to the excess of males in the 10—14 group be correct, the excess of males in the 15—19 group will be larger than it appears. Part of it, however, can be explained by the presence in Lansdowne Cantonment of some 500 young Gurkha recruits whose wives, if they are married, were in Nepal, not in this district, and by the presence in the reserved forests when the census was taken of some 300 young (between 15—19) Muhammadan sawyers and wood—cutters from the plains. For the rest, I can only suggest that the death-rate among females between 15 and 19 must, for obvious reasons, be much higher than that among males of the some age. Before I pass on I may remark that the figures look as if some young women of 18 and 19 had been included in the 20—24 age-period."

"I give below a comparative statement similar to that given by Mr. White in para. 21 of his report on the 1881 Census, showing the percentage on the total number of females represented by the number of females in each decade."

Age.	Absolute numbers.		Percentage on total number.	
	1881.	1891.	1881.	1891.
0—9	48,090	57,090	27·5	27·5
10—19	36,651	41,413	21·0	20·0
20—29	29,520	35,745	16·9	17·2
30—39	23,349	27,575	13·3	13·3
40—49	16,145	20,377	9·2	9·8
50 and upwards	21,119	25,299	12·1	12·2
Total ...	174,874	207,499	100	100

"Mr. White was wrong, I think, in believing that at the 1881 Census there were many women between the ages of 20 and 29 away from Garhwál at the time of the census. I am not aware that Garhwáli women ever leave the district temporarily in the cold weather, or at any other time of the year."

105. **Other districts showing an excess of females.**—The circumstances of the other seven districts which show an excess of females are entirely different. An examination of the comparative figures for an exemplar portion of these districts with those for the province in general and selected districts showing a high disproportion of the sexes will make it clear that the exceptionally high proportion of men to women is not due to the absence of concealment in them. The following abstract compares the distribution of 10,000 persons in the Benares Division and the Gorakhpur district both with a high proportion of women with that in the North-Western Provinces and Oudh and in Bijnor, Pilibhít and Etah, all showing more than average disproportion of the sexes.

Abstract No. 32.

Age-period.	N.-W. Provinces and Oudh.			Benares Division.			Gorakhpur district.			Bijnor district.			Pilibhit district.			Etah district.		
	Males.	Females.	Total.	Males.	Females.	Total.	Males.	Females.	Total.	Males.	Females.	Total.	Males.	Females.	Total.	Males.	Females.	Total.
0—9 ...	1,369	1,313	2,682	,395	1,385	2,780	1,502	1,522	3,024	1,391	1,303	2,694	1,407	1,372	2,839	1,197	1,086	2,283
10—19 ...	1,038	803	1,841	998	839	1,837	954	797	1,751	1 092	836	1,928	1,047	740	1,787	1,207	823	2,030
20—29 ...	894	865	1,759	785	864	1,649	872	900	1,772	888	808	1,696	939	812	1,751	1,046	901	1,947
30—39 ...	755	700	1,455	690	744	1,434	710	719	1,429	716	620	1,336	797	673	1,470	864	672	1,536
40—49 ...	541	503	1,044	518	532	1,050	480	463	943	533	480	1,013	557	474	1,031	602	506	1,108
50 and over	588	631	1,219	574	676	1,250	482	599	1,081	646	687	1,333	517	605	1,122	542	554	1,096

This statement at once makes it clear that it is not in the age-period 10—19 that the excess of women is to be looked for, but in the other age-periods. On the other hand, the figures for males in the age-periods from 20 to 50 may at once be observed to be markedly low in the Benares Division as compared with the North-Western Provinces and Oudh and the other districts selected, and that it is in a deficit in the male population and not in an excess in the female that the difference in the proportion must be looked for. Some assistance will be derived from presenting the above figures in a somewhat different aspect, showing the age distribution for each area of 10,000 males and 10,000 females.

Abstract No. 33, *showing the age distribution of* 10,000 *males and* 10,0000 *females.*

Age-period.	North-Western Provinces and Oudh.	Benares Division.	Gorakhpur district.	Bijnor district.	Pilibhit district.	Etah district.
			Males.			
0—9 ...	2,636	2,813	3,002	2,641	2,755	2,194
10—19 ...	2,004	2,013	1,908	2,074	1,967	2,210
20—29 ...	1,725	1,582	1,744	1,686	1,764	1,917
30—39 ...	1,456	1,391	1,420	1,360	1,497	1,582
40—49 ...	1,044	1,045	962	1,011	1,046	1,104
50 and over ...	1,135	1,156	964	1,228	971	993
Total ...	10,000	10,000	10,000	10,000	10,000	10,000
			Females.			
0—9 ...	2,726	2,747	3,043	2,752	2,936	2,390
10—19 ...	1,673	1,664	1,594	1,766	1,582	1,812
20—29 ...	1,794	1,715	1,801	1,708	1,737	1,984
30—39 ...	1,454	1,478	1,438	1,310	1,438	1,479
40—49 ...	1,043	1,056	926	1,013	1,014	1,116
50 and over ...	1,310	1,340	1,198	1,451	1,293	1,219
Total ...	10,000	10,000	10,000	10,000	10,000	10,000

It is clear that the Benares Division is largely deficient in males from 20 to 50 years of age. This is readily explained. The high pressure of population in these districts compels a large number of able-bodied males to seek work at a distance, often in other provinces. The same is the case in all the districts named as showing more males than females, and to a proportionately smaller extent in all districts in which the proportion of females to males materially exceeds the provincial average. The slight increase in the proportion of males to females in the present census as compared with that at last census (there are now 92·99 females to 100 males against 92·50 at last census) therefore indicates rather than this form of emigration is increasing that the females have been more fully enumerated now than at last census. Gházipur in the present census passed into the list of districts showing more females than males. The other districts had an excess of females at last census also. The circumstances of Gorakhpur as indicated by the age figures are exceptional. We have there a large defect in aged males, as compared with aged females, and a disproportionately large number of children. The explanation probably is that the population of the district has been largely recruited by the immigration of young married men and women taking with them their aged female relatives. The movement of aged females would probably not be general so long as their husbands were alive and cling to their old holdings. They would, however, probably join their sons as soon as they were left widowed. The effect on the age figures for males of this migration which takes places largely, as birthplace figures show, to outside the province, has already been referred to.

106. **Comparison of proportion of sexes in the European countries.**— A comparison of the proportion of men and women in the North-Western Provinces with that in western countries would *primâ facie* suggest that the concealment of women was greater even than we have already considered proved. The following statement compares the number of females per 1,000 males at each age-period in the North-Western Provinces and India with corresponding figures for England, Scotland, Ireland, France, Germany, Hungary, Italy and Japan.

Abstract No. 34, Comparing the number of females per 1,000 males at each age-period in the North-Western Provinces and other foreign countries.

Age-period.	N.-W. P. and Oudh.	India.	England.	Scotland.	Ireland.	France.	Germany.	Hungary.	Italy.	Japan.
Under 1 year ...	976	1,018	998	982	962	972	983	990	956	...
1 " ...	1,035	1,038	1,004	964	953	973	996	997	962	...
2 " ...	1,057	1,067	1,003	978	973	987	999	1,001	965	...
3 " ...	1,058	1,068	1,006	977	999	991	1,001	1,002	962	...
4 " ...	994	1,004	1,004	977	968	998	996	1,014	978	...
Total under five years,	1,020	1,089	1,008	976	971	984	995	1,000	964	983
5— 9 " ...	904	938	1,006	976	977	996	999	1,003	966	976
10—14 " ...	750	799	997	968	957	985	1,000	1,012	959	976
15—19 " ...	812	943	1,008	994	1,040	999	1,014	1,124	1,025	972
20—24 " ...	975	1,079	1,093	1,063	1,060	1,057	1,086	1,173	1,017	971
25—29 " ...	962	1,003	1,087	1,105	1,120	958	1,048	1,007	1,027	963
30—34 " ...	948	972	1,077	1,117	1,161	985	1,047	1,045	1,027	986
35—39 " ...	896	875	1,069	1,161	1,128	993	1,061	957	1,005	
40—44 " ...	955	950	1,079	1,166	1,128	986	1,065	1,000	1,010	938
45—49 " ...	873	858	1,103	1,204	1,047	1,001	1,078	950	996	
50—54 " ...	995	1,005	1,104	1,215	1,095	1,028	1,098	1,097	1,020	973
55—59 " ...	917	922	1,111	1,224	1,058	1,015	1,187	1,001	986	
60 and over ...	1,194	1,198	1,187	1,377	1,075	1,067	1,171	1,022	980	1,290
Total ...	930	965	1,055	1,076	1,043	1,005	1,048	1,030	995	977

The western countries in general show male births in excess, but the female death-rate is very much comparatively better than males, so that the number of females decreased less rapidly than males, and the total number of females is larger than of males. It is, however, impossible to argue from the circumstances of a western country as to what those of an eastern one should be. The physical circumstances are absolutely different. It is a still a question as to whether physical circumstances which we know to exist in India do not tend to produce a high male birth-rate ; and it is certain that there are, in the neglect of female offspring by a large part of the population, and its low estimation everywhere, special reasons why the female death-rate should be comparatively high. I do not know how far the census of Italy is to be trusted, but if it is fairly correct, the fact that the most oriental in constitution and climate of western nations shows an excess of males might tend to support the theory that male life is in excess in eastern climates. It will be observed that the Italian figures indicate a large absence of males from the country between 15 and 49, so that the actual disproportion of the sexes is larger than that indicated by the census figures.

107. **The low proportion of females in the Agra Division.**—The age-figures for the Agra Division showing, as compared with the North-Western Provinces and Oudh, a low proportion of females under all age-periods, suggest either that there has been either a general concealment of females under all age-periods, even including the earliest, to a much greater extent than in the rest of the provinces, or that there is a real disproportion between the numbers of the sexes there. The circumstances of the division would justify either supposition. The division is the main seat of that objection to female children which leads to infanticide, and the population is more largely composed of those castes to whom female life is most objectionable ; at the same time it is amongst these same clans that female enumeration would be likely to be worst.

ABSTRACT No. 35, *Agra division 10,000 total population.*

Age-periods.	Males.	Females.	Total.
0—9	1,258	1,150	2,408
10—19	1,145	808	1,953
20—29	1,019	905	1,924
30—39	844	687	1,531
40—49	593	500	1,093
50 and over ...	560	531	1,091
Total ...	5,419	4,581	10,000

108. **Proportion of the sexes in the different religions of the province.**—A comparison of the proportionate numbers of the sexes in the different religions of the province is useful only for Hindus, Muhammadans and Jains, as none of the other religions in the province constitutes a group complete in itself. Christians and Sikhs consist largely of persons in the prime of life imported from Europe and the Panjáb, Aryas largely of young men, whose wives and parents have been recorded as Hindus. The figures for the three religions abovenamed are compared with those for the province in the abstract in the margin. It shows that

Abstract No. 36, showing the proportion of persons, male and female, in each age-period for each of the leading religions.

Age-period.	All religions.			Hindus.			Musalmans			Jains.		
	Males.	Females.	Total.	Males	Females.	Total.	Males.	Females.	Total.	Males.	Females.	Total.
0—4 ...	678	692	1,370	677	690	1,367	687	711	1,398	534	535	1,069
5—9 ..	691	621	1,312	689	621	1,310	682	629	1,311	580	511	1,091
0—9 ...	1,369	1,313	2,682	1,366	1,311	2,677	1,369	1,340	2,709	1,114	1,046	2,160
10—19 ...	1,036	808	1,844	1,040	802	1,842	1,028	831	1,859	1,081	823	1,904
20—29 ...	894	865	1,759	897	864	1,761	850	878	1,728	1,014	869	1,883
30—39 ...	755	700	1,455	759	704	1,463	721	681	1,402	840	701	1,541
40—49 ...	541	503	1,044	545	504	1,049	615	490	1,005	642	522	1,164
50 and over	588	631	1,219	582	626	1,208	628	666	1,294	702	646	1,348
Total ...	5,185	4,815	10,000	5,189	4,811	10,000	5,111	4,889	10,000	5,393	4,607	10,000

the proportion of women is fullest amongst Muhammadans. This fact appears to be the net result of opposing causes.

1*st.*—Concealment of women for causes connected with marriage is less amongst Muhammadans.

2*nd.*—Omission of adult women not aged is possibly greater amongst them.

3*rd.*—The absence of adult men from the provinces already remarked on as characteristic of the Benares Division is certainly proportionately greater than amongst Hindus.

For Jains the proportion of women is far lower than amongst Hindus. Concealment owing to causes connected with marriage is less, but, on the whole, concealment of women is considerably greater amongst Jains than in any other religion. This might have been expected. The Jain and his family live more remote from observation than the households of any other religion.

109. **Proportion of the sexes in the leading groups of castes.**—Abstract No. 37 gives the age and sex proportions for each important caste or group of castes in the province. Certain general inferences may be drawn.

1*st.*—The disproportion of the sexes is greatest amongst Jats and after Jats amongst Rajputs. The disproportion exists at all age-periods and indicates, in all probability, partly concealment of women of all ages and partly a real disproportion in the sexes owing to neglect of infant female life.

2*nd.*—Labouring castes show in general the highest proportion of females. *It is due almost invariably to the absence of adult men in large numbers from the province,* the record of females at those ages at which concealment takes place being little if at all better amongst low than amongst high castes.

3*rd.*—The higher castes are the longer lived the lower castes the more prolific. The longest-lived, caste of all is that of the Khatris, the shortest-lived that of the Chamárs. Forest and Hill tribes Chamárs, Julahas, Pasis are markedly prolific; Kayasths, Khatris and Banias have a notably small proportion of children.

110. **Comparison of the age tables with European countries.**—The following abstract in which the ages of 10,000 persons of each sex as enumerated in the census is compared with the corresponding figures for England, France, Germany and Italy may be of interest.

Abstract No. 37, showing the proportion of persons of each sex and age in each important caste or group of castes.

Age-periods.	Total population.			Jat, Hindu.			Rajput, Hindu.			Rajput, Musalman.			Group 2(a), Hindu. Cultivators.			Group 2(b) and 2(c), Hindu. Cattle-breeders, &c.		
	Males.	Females.	Total.	Males.	Females.	Total.	Males.	Females.	Total.	Males.	Females.	Total.	Males.	Females.	Total.	Males.	Females.	Total.
0— 9 years ...	137	131	268	130	103	233	124	112	236	143	135	278	135	128	263	140	129	269
10—14 " ...	60	45	105	64	41	105	63	46	109	59	43	102	60	55	115	63	48	111
15—39 " ...	208	192	400	237	180	417	225	181	406	198	197	395	208	182	390	214	189	403
40 and over ...	113	114	227	131	114	245	128	121	249	110	115	225	115	117	232	107	110	217
Total ...	518	482	1,000	562	438	1,000	540	460	1,000	510	490	1,000	518	482	1,000	524	476	1,000

Age-periods.	Group 3, Forest and hill tribes. Hindu.			Class A, Agricultural. Hindu.			Brahman. Hindu.			Kayesth. Hindu.			Professional. Class B, Hindu.			Bania. Hindu.		
	Males.	Females.	Total.	Males.	Females.	Total.	Males.	Females.	Total.	Males.	Females.	Total.	Males.	Females.	Total.	Males.	Females.	Total.
0— 9 years ...	162	167	329	134	124	258	132	116	248	113	112	225	130	115	245	121	117	238
10—14 " ...	64	52	116	62	50	112	57	48	105	60	48	108	57	48	105	60	47	107
15—39 " ...	182	183	365	214	184	398	208	184	392	216	189	405	210	184	394	216	191	407
40 and over ...	100	90	190	116	116	232	123	132	255	132	130	262	125	131	256	124	124	248
Total ...	508	492	1,000	526	474	1,000	520	480	1,000	521	479	1,000	522	478	1,000	521	479	1,000

Abstract No. 37, showing the proportion of persons of each sex and age in each important caste or group of castes—(continued).

Age-periods.	Khattri, Hindu.			Group 14, Carriers, Hindu.			Class C, Commercial, Hindu.			Group 15, Goldsmith, Hindu.			Group 16, Barber, Hindu.			Group 17, Blacksmith, Hindu.		
	Males.	Females.	Total.	Males.	Females.	Total.	Males.	Females.	Total.	Males.	Females.	Total.	Males.	Females.	Total.	Males.	Females.	Total.
0— 9 years ...	108	105	213	138	110	248	121	116	237	128	124	252	128	125	253	136	132	268
10—14 „ ...	56	43	99	67	46	113	60	47	107	61	47	108	61	45	106	62	48	110
15—39 „ ...	222	178	400	226	189	415	217	190	407	214	181	395	212	196	408	207	182	389
40 and over ...	144	144	288	107	117	224	125	124	249	127	118	245	117	116	233	117	116	233
Total ...	530	470	1,000	538	462	1,000	523	477	1,000	530	470	1,000	518	482	1,000	522	478	1,000

Age-period.	Group 18, Hindu. Carpenter and turner.			Kori, Hindu,			Julaha, Musalman.			Kumhar, Hindu.			Teli, Hindu.			Dhobi, Hindu.		
	Males.	Females.	Total.	Males.	Females.	Total.	Males.	Females.	Total.	Males.	Females.	Total.	Males.	Females.	Total.	Males.	Females.	Total.
0— 9 years ...	130	121	251	135	134	269	151	146	297	136	134	270	136	131	267	141	139	280
10—14 „ ...	60	44	104	55	41	96	59	45	104	60	54	114	62	50	112	63	47	110
15—39 „ ...	215	191	406	211	197	408	192	197	389	200	190	390	205	198	403	201	194	395
40 and over ...	122	117	239	113	114	227	104	106	210	116	110	226	111	107	218	109	106	215
Total ...	527	473	1,000	514	486	1,000	506	494	1,000	512	488	1,000	514	486	1,000	514	486	1,000

Abstract No. 37, showing the proportion of persons of each sex and age in each important caste or group of castes—(concluded.)

Age-periods.	Group 33, Fishermen and boatmen, Hindu.			Kalwar, Hindu.			Chamar, Hindu.			Group 38, Village watchmen, Hindu.			Class D, Artisans and village menials, Hindu.			Class D, Artisans and village menials, Musalman.		
	Males.	Females.	Total.	Males.	Females.	Total.	Males.	Females.	Total.	Males.	Females.	Total.	Males.	Females.	Total.	Males.	Females.	Total.
0— 9 years ...	142	143	285	129	128	257	146	150	296	147	157	304	142	144	286	145	142	287
10—14 " ...	60	47	107	56	48	104	58	40	98	69	47	116	61	40	101	60	46	106
15—39 " ...	190	197	387	197	191	388	198	201	399	196	184	380	204	202	406	197	192	389
40 and over ...	106	115	221	122	129	251	104	103	207	102	98	200	104	103	207	108	110	218
Total ...	498	502	1,000	504	496	1,000	506	494	1,000	514	486	1,000	511	489	1,000	510	490	1,000

Age-periods.	Bhangi, Hindu.			Bhangi, Musalman.			Class E, Vagrant minor artisans, performers, &c. Hindu.			Group 49, Non-Indian asiatic races, Musalman.			Pathan, Musalman.			Sheikh, Musalman.			Sayed, Musalman.		
	Males.	Females.	Total.	Males.	Females.	Total.	Males.	Females.	Total.	Males.	Females.	Total.	Males.	Females.	Total.	Males	Females.	Total.	Males.	Females.	Total.
0— 9 years ...	139	130	269	143	141	284	150	139	289	127	126	253	124	124	248	132	129	261	117	116	233
10—14 " ...	62	48	110	54	48	102	56	48	104	59	46	105	60	47	107	59	45	104	58	47	105
15—39 " ...	218	194	412	184	187	371	174	185	359	203	193	396	202	189	391	205	194	399	195	196	391
40 and over ...	107	102	209	124	119	243	137	111	248	121	125	246	127	127	254	115	121	236	134	137	271
Total ...	526	474	1,000	505	495	1,000	517	483	1,000	510	490	1,000	513	487	1,000	511	489	1,000	504	496	1,000

Abstract No. 38, distribution by age of 10,000 *males.*

Age-period.	N.-W. Provinces and Oudh, reported.	India, 1891.	N.-W. Provinces, amended.	Oudh.	Benares Division.	Agra Division.	England, 1881.	France, 1886.	Germany, 1885.	Italy, 1881.
Under 1 year ...	342	335		375	265	350	298	188	289	284
1 „ ...	148	170		160	148	129	270	177	270	219
2 years ...	247	288	1,419	262	261	183	278	191	259	252
3 „ ...	294	322		310	335	233	273	190	254	242
4 „ ...	277	304		276	320	238	272	184	246	231
Total under 5 years,	1,308	1,419	1,419	1,383	1,329	1,133	1,391	930	1,318	1,228
5—9 years ...	1,328	1,435	1,327	1,334	1,484	1,190	1,241	901	1,210	1,373
10—14 „ ...	1,166	1,147	2,004	1,108	1,269	1,159	1,109	890	1,088	970
15—19 „ ...	838	837		784	744	955	1,003	848	961	912
20—24 „ ...	858	798	1,725	802	764	972	880	922	850	851
25—29 „ ...	867	867		869	818	908	776	732	757	736
30—34 „ ...	892	828	1,457	864	823	1,004	665	690	659	711
35—39 „ ...	564	614		550	568	554	589	675	603	621
40—44 „ ...	703	627	1,044	674	684	775	533	631	555	626
45—49 „ ...	341	370		351	360	318	433	591	488	485
50—54 „ ...	483	405		519	471	477	385	531	408	507
55—59 „ ...	152	188	1,024	173	148	129	302	474	338	378
60 and over ...	500	470		589	538	426	693	1,185	765	902
Total ...	10,000	10,000	10,000	10,000	10,000	10,000	10,000	10,000	10,000	10,000*

Distribution by age of 10,000 *females.*

Age-periods.	N.-W. Provinces and Oudh, reported.	India, 1891.	N.-W. Provinces, amended.	Oudh.	Benares Division.	Agra Division.	England, 1881.	France, 1886.	Germany, 1885.	Italy, 1881.
Under 1 year ...	359	353		392	255	383	282	181	273	278
1 „ ...	165	184		176	157	152	257	171	258	211
2 years ...	281	319	1,431	291	296	219	265	187	248	245
3 „ ...	335	356		344	368	283	260	188	243	234
4 „ ...	296	315		294	330	261	258	183	235	227
Total under 5 years,	1,436	1,527	1,431	1,497	1,406	1,298	1,322	910	1,257	1,190
5—9 years ...	1,290	1,396	1,313	1,280	1,341	1,211	1,184	891	1,159	1,042
10—14 „ ...	941	950	1,984	888	1,022	895	1,048	871	1,044	935
15—19 „ ...	732	817		664	642	869	959	841	934	940
20—24 „ ...	899	892	1,718	848	842	1,025	912	968	844	869
25—29 „ ...	895	901		919	874	951	800	696	760	760
30—34 „ ...	910	834	1,458	891	906	1,004	679	675	661	734
35—39 „ ...	544	556		528	571	495	597	666	618	627
40—44 „ ...	722	617	1,046	718	729	812	545	618	567	626
45—49 „ ...	321	329		330	327	280	453	588	504	485
50—54 „ ...	517	422		545	510	528	402	542	429	520
55—59 „ ...	150	175	1,050	161	140	117	319	478	369	374
60 and over ...	648	584		731	690	520	780	1,256	859	888
Total ...	10,000	10,000	10,000	10,000	10,000	10,000	10,000	10,000	10,000	10,000

* Actual total 300 in excess.

The figures for the North-Western Provinces as amended show as high a proportionate number of children as the most progressive of the countries mentioned, but in the proportion of aged people they are far behind any of the European countries shown. The inference is that the birth-rate is comparatively high, whilst the average age and, therefore, longevity of the population is very low. The comparison will again be referred to in connection with the movement of population.

111. **The average age of the population.**—The average age of the population calculated by the method suggested to Mr. White, and detailed on page 57 of his report, is 25·05 years for males against 24·96 at last census and against an average age of 26·4 for the English Census.

Chapter IV.—THE MOVEMENT OF POPULATION.

112. **The vital history of the decade.**—The period during which the variation of population has to be specially considered in the present report was in all respects, throughout the greater part of the provinces, far more free from violent disturbance than that which intervened between the Census of 1872 and that of 1881. Population during the last half of the earlier period was affected by a famine of unusual magnitude followed, in a large part of the provinces, by the most severe epidemic of fever which is remembered in them. The year 1881, the first after last census, found the provinces recovering from the effects of the fever and beginning a cycle of comparatively favourable years, owing to the effect of which a rise in population might be expected to take place. A brief history of the general statistical and economic history of the decade may be given as a preface to the consideration of the detailed figures showing the variation of the population.

The welfare of an Indian province even in the most minor details depends so absolutely on the rainfall as to make a record of the fall the most important part of the history of the decade. Abstract No. 39 shows the actual rainfall in inches for each of the divisions of the province. A chart is also given to illustrate the excess or defect of the average rainfall for the province. In the earlier years of the decade the rainfall was generally below the average, the deficiency being most marked in 1883, especially in the western and southern districts, some of which were brought within a measurable distance of severe distress. From 1883 onward the rainfall has generally been in excess, in some seasons very considerably so, the only partial break in the series of seasons of heavy rains being in 1889, when in a few divisions the fall was slightly below the average. During the decade therefore, and particularly in those later years which more particularly affect the census returns, the provinces as a whole have escaped from agricultural loss by failure of the monsoon. The effect of the excess of rainfall in particular localities will have, however, to obtain detailed mention :—

Abstract No. 39, showing the average rainfall for ten years in each Division.

Divisions.	1881.	1882.	1883.	1884.	1885.	1886.	1887.	1888.	1889.	1890.	Mean for ten years.	Mean rainfall as deduced from the observations recorded by the Meteorological Department.
Kumaun Division and Dehra Dún.	55·4	58·2	44·1	63·2	71·1	58·3	54·0	63·1	81·4	73·8	62·3	...
Meerut ...	27·3	23·4	20·5	38·3	35·6	32·3	35·8	34·3	27·9	34·6	31·0	29·5
Rohilkhand ...	35·1	38·3	23·9	43·9	51·0	46·5	40·4	49·3	45·1	44·1	41·8	40·3
Agra ...	36·9	25·0	17·8	37·0	37·5	30·9	36·1	39·2	26·0	31·1	31·8	28·8
Allahabad ...	33·5	33·5	29·5	47·1	39·3	41·2	48·8	51·2	37·2	37·5	39·9	35·7
Jhánsi (Bundelkhand).	40·0	39·6	22·2	43·8	41·7	36·6	46·4	43·6	27·3	43·8	38·5	34·4
Benares and Gorakhpur.	41·0	34·4	28·6	39·3	44·0	49·1	39·7	43·1	47·3	57·2	42·4	40·7
Fyzabad ...	30·8	33·6	30·5	39·8	48·0	48·6	42·5	47·7	50·1	57·5	42·9	42·7
Lucknow ...	32·8	21·8	30·2	38·9	43·5	40·8	32·5	49·0	45·5	43·8	37·8	34·7
Mean for the Provinces.	35·8	32·7	27·4	42·7	45·6	43·0	41·1	46·6	43·2	47·5	40·6	...
Mean exclusive of Kumaun and Dehra Dún.	33·8	30·1	25·7	40·7	43·0	41·5	39·8	45·0	39·4	44·9	38·4	36·0

Diagram No. 4, showing the average rainfall of the North-Western Provinces and Oudh (exclusive of the Himalayan Districts and Dehra Dún) from 1881 *to* 1891.

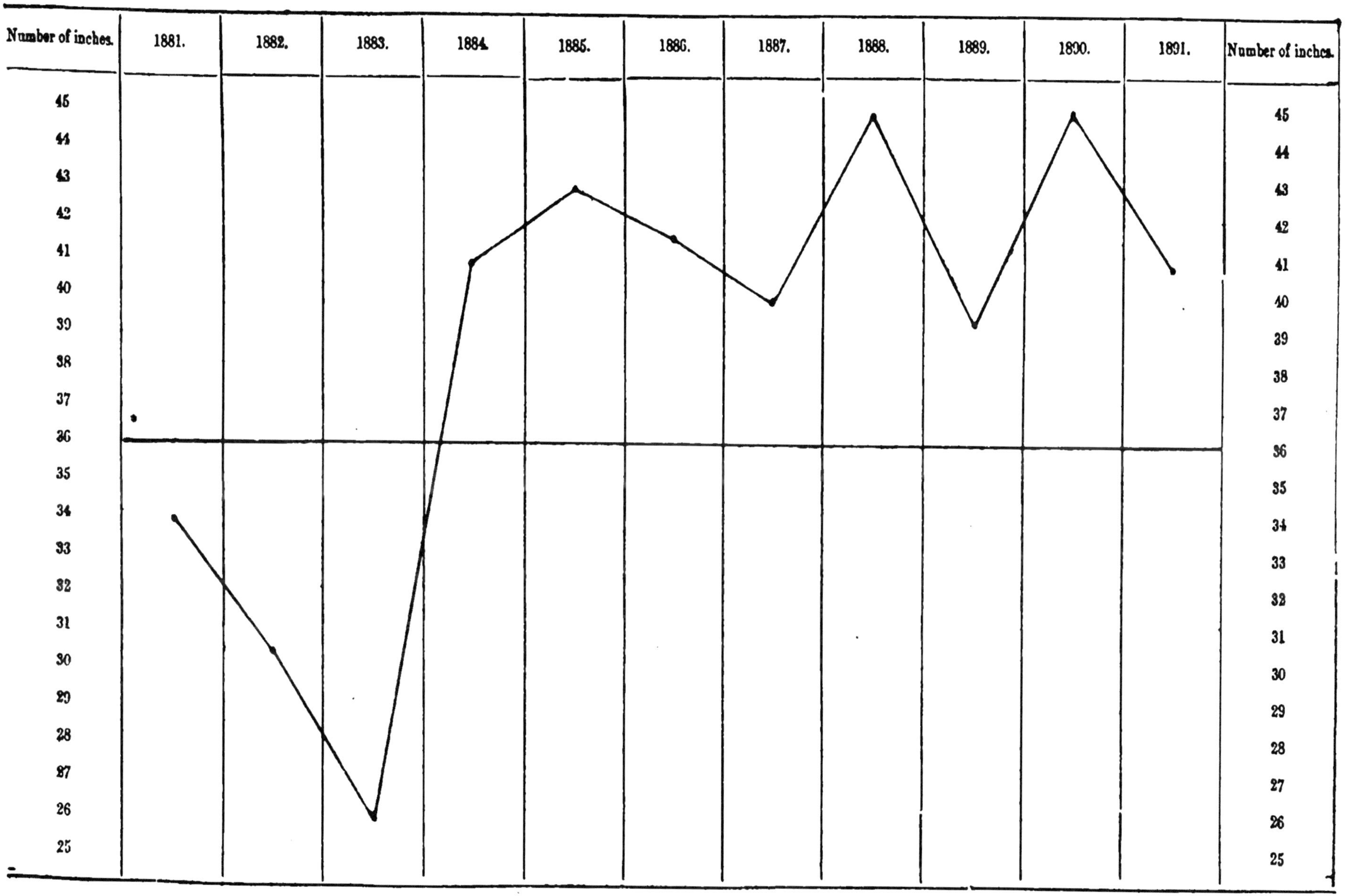

* The thick black line indicates the normal rainfall as deduced from the returns of the Meteorological Department.

To face page 140.]

Diagram No. 5, Illustrating the Provincial ratio of Births and Deaths during the decade.

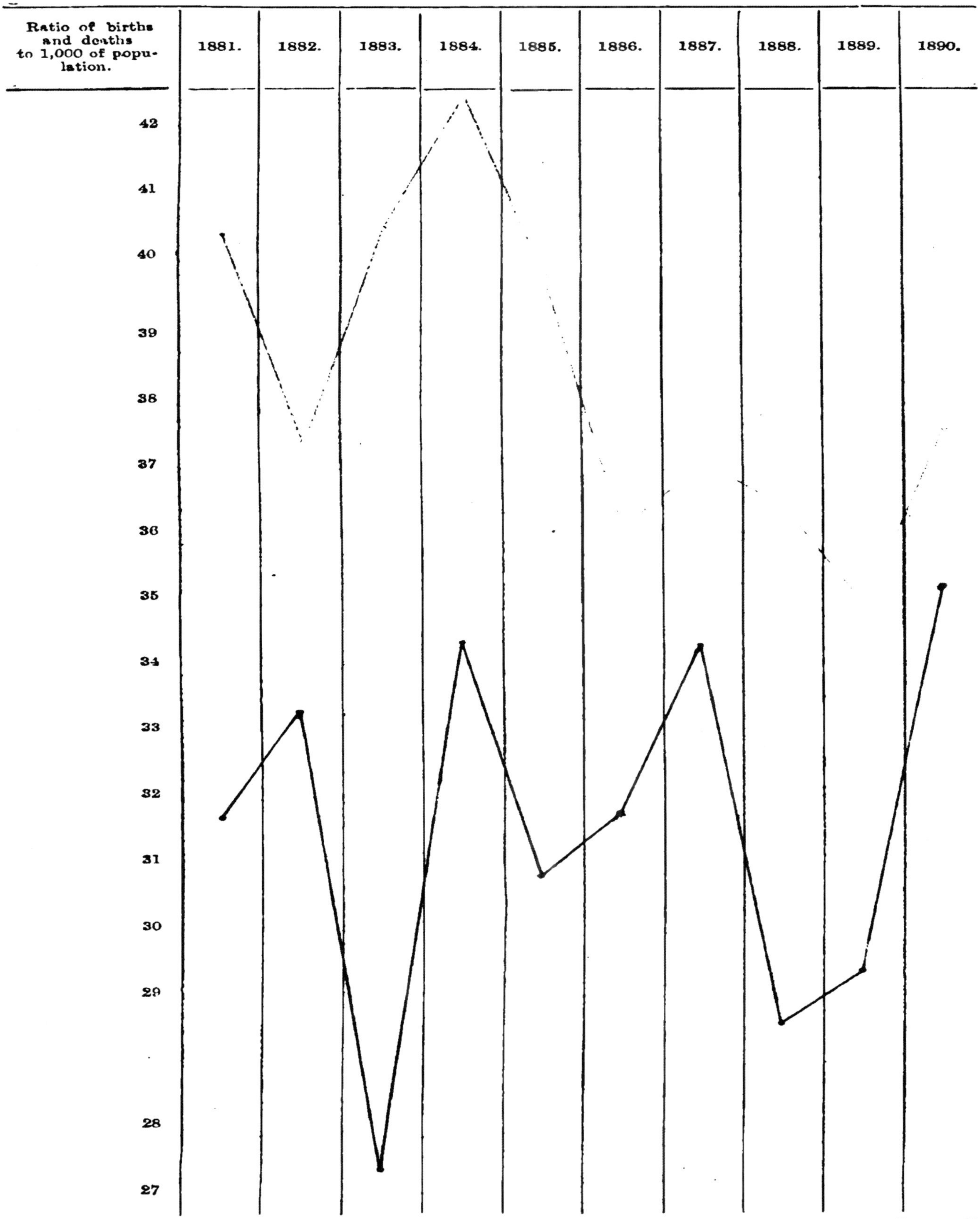

N. B.—The red line indicates the birth rate, and the black line the death rate.

To face page 141.]

The harvests were what might have been expected from such a rainfall. The decade was characterized by a succession of spring harvests in general superior and by an almost as constant a succession of autumn harvests in which the crops either rotted from excessive moisture or were injured by drought in the breaks which almost invariably intervene between periods of exceedingly heavy rainfall. The year 1883-84 was the only one in which both harvests were bad. The rains started with heavy falls in July and September but ceased early, thereby causing immense damage to the autumn crop and to the spring crop which followed, in which practically the whole area sown was in irrigated land. In dry tracts the crops were entirely lost, and the Agra Division narrowly escaped a great calamity. For succeeding years the damage caused to agriculture by the weather is mainly due to excessive or irregular rainfall, and time after time great damage by flooding occurred in lowlying tracts. The result was that the cultivated area, owing to the damp and consequent spread of káns, decreased before the end of the decade in the Agra Division by 200,000 acres and in Bundelkhand by 300,000, a decrease which has more than counterbalanced the increase in sub-Himalayan and Oudh districts.

113. **The public health during the decade.**—The vital statistics recorded by the Sanitary Commissioner for the decade are, as compared with those for the previous 10 years, characterized by a comparative absence of violent fluctuations. These statistics have in the present, as compared with earlier decades, so greatly improved in accuracy that any comparison except as regards fluctuations of the returns for earlier years with those in the past decade would be futile. The total births and deaths recorded in the province during each of the ten years together with the average rates per thousand of estimated population are shown in the accompanying statement and diagram :—

Abstract No. 40.

Year.	Births.		Deaths.	
	Actual numbers.	Per 1,000 of population.	Actual numbers.	Per 1,000 of population.
1881	1,779,473	40·29	1,402,473	31·75
1882	1,656,159	37·21	1,485,127	33·37
1883	1,801,401	40·35	1,216,297	27 24
1884	1,930,961	42·63	1,535,342	34 34
1885	1,819,279	39 73	1,410,639	30·81
1886	1,659,532	36·02	1,467,613	31 86
1887	1,708,735	37·00	1,581,739	34 25
1888	1,687,439	36·83	1,327,113	28·57
1889	1,629,210	34 87	1,372,269	29 37
1890	1,751,168	37·38	1,644,027	35·10
Decennial average ...	1,742,335	38·18	1,446,263	31·66

The births averaging 38·18 per thousand of population for the ten years have invariably been below average in the last five years and invariably above average in the first five. The distinction of causes of death as recorded in these provinces is practically confined to cholera, small-pox and fever, the latter including almost all diseases not cholera or small-pox. Cholera accounts in all for only 4·22 per cent. of the total deaths, but has a large share in determining the variations from year to year in individual districts. Small-pox more constantly present than cholera is hardly less liable to violent outbreaks during which it raises the death-rate to an extent hardly equalled by the more dreaded cholera. For the past 10 years at least the Doab and Agra Divisions have enjoyed comparative immunity from both these diseases, whilst Oudh districts have one and all been subject to violent outbreaks of both. The great bulk of the death-rate is, however, commonly ascribed to fever. The distribution of severe fever during the past 10 years has been very different from that of the first named diseases. It is severe far beyond the average in the Doab, Agra and Rohilkhand, and comparatively light in Oudh and the east, even in the reputedly feverish Gorakhpur and Basti. As to the two last, the statistical reporting appears clearly very bad, probably owing to the continuance of the system by which the work of village watchmen is done by men insufficiently paid by a grant of land and allowed to combine the functions of watchman and cultivator. The average effect, as regards the death-rate in the districts of the province, of cholera, small-pox, fevers, and bowel diseases (so irregularly reported as hardly to warrant mention) is shown in Appendix No. XIII. The figures in the appendix are calculated on the returns of last census, and the total is, therefore, somewhat different from that above given. The effect in each year of the decade of each disease appears from the following abstract:—

Abstract No. 41, showing for each disease the number of deaths per thousand persons.

Year.		Cholera.	Small-pox.	Fevers.	Other causes.	Total.
1		2	3	4	5	6
1881	...	·58	·39	24·95	5·87	31·79
1882	...	2·02	·60	24·90	6·14	33·67
1883	...	·41	3·14	18·82	5·20	27·57
1884	...	·68	4·59	24·35	5·63	35·26
1885	...	1·44	·33	25·48	4·73	31·98
1886	...	·78	·24	27·58	4·66	33·27
1887	...	4·54	·19	25·76	5·34	35·86
1888	...	·42	·56	23·89	5·21	30·08
1889	...	1·09	1·09	23·10	5·81	31·11
1890	...	1·82	1·26	28·21	5·99	37·27

The most unhealthy years of the decade were 1884, when small-pox of a very virulent type was epidemic, 1887, with a severe outbreak of cholera, and 1890, showing the highest death-rate of the ten years owing to cholera and small-pox both being prevalent and influenza (classed as fever) being epidemic in a very severe form. The death-rate except that attributable to fever was on the whole well below average during the ten years. That owing to fever was undoubtedly high, though the great improvement in registration in late years prevents any accurate comparison with previous decades.

114. **Prices during the decade**.—The only other characteristic of the decade which at present requires notice is the vast change which has of late years taken place in the price of food-grains. It is best illustrated by the diagram accompanying No. 6, for which I am indebted to the Director of Agriculture. It will be seen that since 1885, when prices reached the minima for the decade, there has been a steady increase in the price not only of wheat but of other standard food-grains, and that in 1891 prices had reached a level which was only exceeded in the periods during which the famines of 1868 and 1877 affected prices. By natives in general this is attributed to the

Diagram No. 6, Illustrating the average price of wheat and other food-grains in eight typical districts of the North-Western Provinces and Oudh.

The green line represents the price of wheat and the red line that of other food-grains.

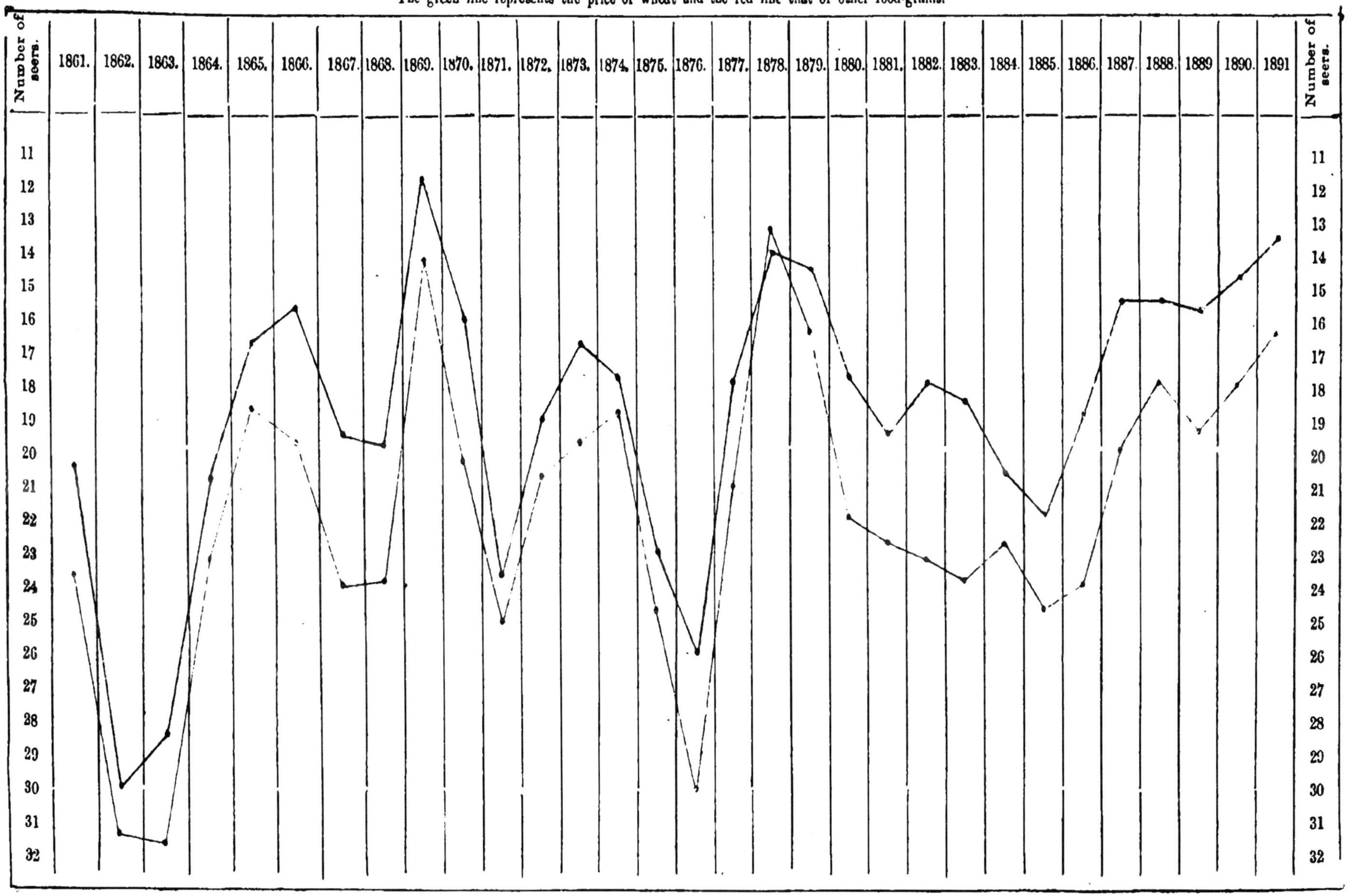

NOTE.—Other food-grains include (1) barley; (2) rice, common; (3) juár; (4) bájra; (5) gram; (6) arhar.

To face page 143.]

large exports, but there can be little doubt that in the main it is primarily due to the fall in the value of the rupee.

115. **The variation of population.**—The total population of the provinces increased so far as appears from a comparison of the census figures for 1881 and 1891 to the extent of 2,797,216; males increased by 1,391,045 and females by 1,406,171. The percentages of increase were for males 6·07, females 6·63, and total population 6·34. This increase was very irregularly distributed over the provinces; four districts and a considerable number of tahsíls show an average decrease over their whole area. On the other hand, four districts show an increase over 15 per cent., the highest increase being 21 per cent. in Garhwál State. Figures showing variations for districts are given in the accompanying abstract No. 42.

	Total.	Males.	Females.
1881	44,107,869	22,912,556	21,195,313
1891	46,905,085	24,303,601	22,601,484
Increase	2,797,216	1,391,045	1,406,171
Percentage of increase	6·34	6·07	6·63

Abstract No. 42, showing percentage of variation of population since 1881 *in the Districts and Divisions of the Provinces.*

Serial number.	District and Division.	Percentage of variation of population.			Remarks.
		Total.	Males.	Females.	
1	2	3	4	5	6
1	Dehra Dún	+16·70	+19·45	+12·86	
2	Sahváranpur	+2·22	+1·87	+2·63	
3	Muzaffarnagar	+1·90	+2·15	+1·62	
4	Meerut	+5·96	+5·93	+6·01	
5	Bulandshahr	+2·71	+1·96	+3·56	
6	Aligarh	+2·15	+1·35	+3·09	
	Total, Meerut Division ...	+3·62	+3·39	+3·87	
7	Muttra	+6·21	+6·01	+6·45	
8	Agra	+2·99	+2·59	+3·46	
9	Farukhabad	—5·39	—5·33	—5·46	
10	Mainpuri	—4·87	—5·72	—3·83	
11	Etáwah	+ ·73	+ ·39	+1·13	
12	Etah	—7·19	—7·37	—6·99	
	Total, Agra Division ...	—1·37	—1·71	—·96	
13	Bareilly	+ ·95	+1·36	+ ·47	
14	Bijnor	+10·65	+9·12	+11·14	
15	Budaun	+2·11	+2·21	+1·99	
16	Moradabad	+2·10	+2·18	+2·01	
17	Sháhjahánpur...	+7·19	+7·66	+6·65	
18	Pilibhít	+7·48	+7·76	+7·15	
	Total, Rohilkhand Division ...	+4·32	+4·41	+4·21	
19	Cawnpore	+2·39	+3·05	+1·65	
20	Fatehpur	+2·25	+3·52	+ ·95	
21	Bánda	+1·03	+ ·71	+1·37	
22	Hamírpur	+1·26	+ ·32	+2·25	
23	Allahabad	+5·06	+5·36	+4·76	
24	Jhánsi*	+22·86	+24·09	+21·55	* Total. Males. Females. 10·07 11·65 8·36 Excluding additions from Scindia's territory.
25	Jalaun	—5·21	—5·58	—4·81	
26	Lalitpur	+10·08	+8·97	+11·29	
	Total, Allahabad Division ...	+3·81	+4·06	+3·55	

Abstract No. 42—(concluded.)

Serial number.	District and Division.	Percentage of variation of population.			Remarks.
		Total.	Males.	Females.	
1	2	3	4	5	6
27	Benares	+3·28	+3·69	+2·85	
28	Mirzapur	+2·17	+1·59	+2·75	
29	Jaunpur	+4·57	+3·85	+5·31	
30	Gházipur	+6·29	+4·85	+7·74	
31	Ballia	+1·91	+ ·45	+3·32	
	Total, Benares Division ...	+3·68	+2·93	+4·44	
32	Gorakhpur	+14·40	+14·64	+14·17	
33	Basti	+9·52	+10·08	+8·95	
34	Azamgarh	+7·78	+6·27	+9·23	
	Total, Gorakhpur Division ...	+11·21	+11·04	+11·38	
35	Kumaun	+14·09	+12·99	+15·32	
36	Garhwál	+17·99	+17·31	+18·66	
37	Tarái	+1·73	+1·89	+1·53	
	Total, Kumaun Division ...	+12·98	+12·04	+13·91	
	TOTAL, N.-W. PROVINCES ...	+4·69	+4·41	+4·99	
38	Lucknow	+11·09	+11·47	+10·69	
39	Unao	+6·07	+6·15	+5·99	
40	Rae Bareli	+8·89	+9·87	+7·95	
41	Sitapur	+12·23	+12·09	+12·37	
42	Hardoi	+12·72	+12·19	+13·33	
43	Kheri	+8·62	+8·31	+8·96	
	Total, Lucknow Division ...	+9·97	+10·06	+9·87	
44	Fyzabad	+12·53	+12·16	+12·91	
45	Gonda	+14·82	+14·69	+14·94	
46	Bahraich	+13·94	+14·02	+13·85	
47	Sultánpur	+12·31	+11·65	+12·96	
48	Partábgarh	+7·53	+5·81	+9·24	
49	Bara Banki	+10·14	+10·22	+10·05	
	Total, Fyzabad Division ...	+12·08	+11·69	+12·47	
	TOTAL, OUDH ...	+11·09	+10·92	+11·27	
	TOTAL, N.-W. PROVINCES & OUDH ...	+6·34	+6·07	+6·63	
50	Rámpur	+1·72	+3·09	+ ·23	
51	Tehri Garhwál	+20·72	+15·67	+26·02	
	TOTAL, NATIVE STATES ...	+6·84	+6·44	+7·27	

To trace accurately the distribution of the areas of increase and decrease it is necessary to take account of sub-divisions of districts—tahsíls everywhere, and where the variations are important of parganas also. The population figures for tahsíls are given in Provincial Table I and the percentages of variation in Appendix No. XIV.

The appended map indicates, as accurately as a small scale map can, the distribution of the movement.

116. **The area of low increase or decrease.**—The area of decrease or very low increase is fairly continuous. Beginning in the Sahâranpur district,

[To face page 144.

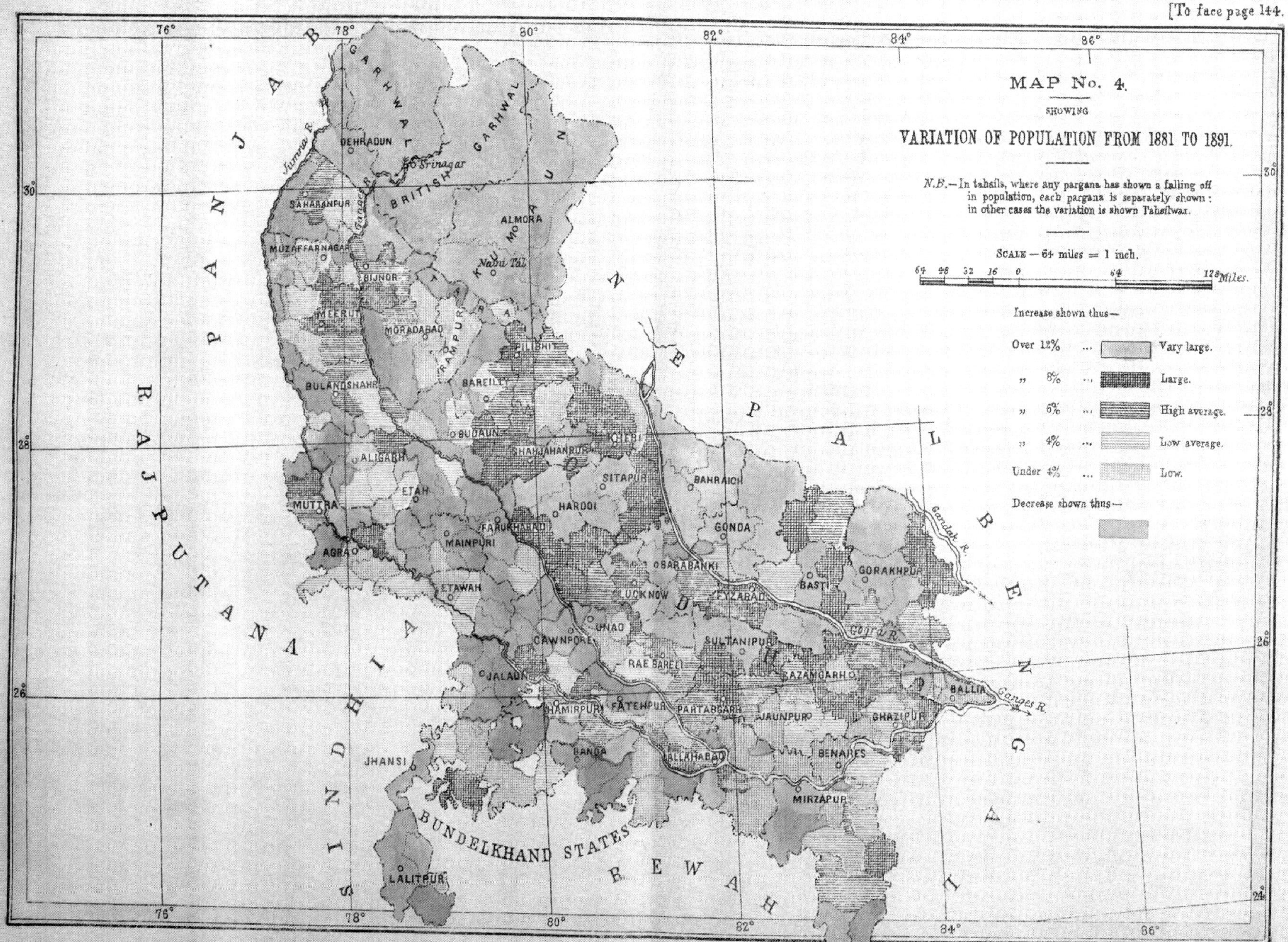

it extends almost without interruption along the Jamna side of the Doáb districts to Muttra and Aligarh, crossing to the Ganges parganas only in the south of Sahāranpur and north of Muzaffarnagar. From Aligarh the tract widens out so as to include nearly the whole of that district and of the Doab east of it, Etah, Mainpuri, Etáwah and Farukhabad being entirely in it. It projects westwards from Etáwah to include the south of the Agra district, leaving Muttra and the north of Agra in the area of more than average increase. From Etah northwards it crosses the Ganges and reaches to the foot of the Himalayas, including the greater part of Budaun, Moradabad, Bareilly and the Tarái and the whole of Rámpur. Southwards and eastwards from Etáwah the tract of low increase or decrease divides so as to leave a strip along the Jamna to Allahabad with increase above the average. South of this strip the whole of Jalaun, the north of Jhánsi and the south of Bánda and Hamírpur are in the low increase tract. North of it there is a similar strip along the Ganges to near Allahabad broken only by the pargana which contains the City of Cawnpore. East of Allahabad, nearly the whole of the eastern districts of the North-Western Provinces except Azamgarh, several parganas of Gházipur and the south of Mirzapur show a rate of increase below average.

117. **The area of high increase.**—This leaves as the region of high increase the Himalayan districts with sub-Himalayan Bijnor and Pilibhít, the whole of Sháhjahánpur and Oudh, the north of Azamgarh, the trans-Ghogra districts of the North-Western Provinces, the south of Mirzapur and Jhánsi, most of Lalitpur and the tracts in the upper Doab on the Ganges and in the lower Doab on the Jamna already mentioned. The uniformity of increase in this tract is according to the pargana figures broken somewhat irregularly along the Ghogra, in the north of Kheri and Sháhjahánpur and on the Ganges in Unao and Rae Bareli by parganas showing a low increase or even a decrease. Every effort has been made to get the pargana figures correct, but as it was impossible at times to ascertain either what was included in a pargana at last census or the detailed last census population of the villages now in a pargana, their accuracy cannot be guaranteed; and where the irregular occurrence of such tracts of low increase cannot be explained, I am inclined to doubt the accuracy of the returns for last census on which the calculations have been founded. The area of very large increase over 12 per cent. is confined to the Himalayas, the north of Bijnor, the trans-Ghogra districts and a strip through the centre of Oudh from Fyzabad to Hardoi.

118. **Examination of the accuracy of enumeration in different districts.**—In examining the details of these variations to ascertain whether they are in all respects genuine or whether there is any reason to suspect bad enumeration at either census I have made use of several tests. The first is a statement comparing the 1881 population with that of the present census aged 10 or more. This statement distinguishes the part of the present population alive at last census from those born since and with which the earlier census is not concerned. It is printed as Appendix No. XV. A large excess in the figures for last census would imply (*a*) a high death-rate

or (*b*) emigration since last census or (*c*) a deficit at the present census or more than one of these causes combined. A low excess would mean (*a*) a low death-rate, (*b*) increased immigration, or (*c*) a deficit in 1881. I regard over-enumeration at either census as very much less probable than under-enumeration at the other. Supplementary tests applied were obtained from (1) a calculation of the population of each district from the Sanitary Commissioner's returns and the census of 1881 as compared with the figures for the present, (2) the Sanitary Commissioner's birth and death-rates; (3) the age-period population of the present census; (4) the figures for migration derived from the birth-place returns. The value of the last mentioned statement is greatly diminished by the fact that for the large extra provincial migration we have no figures by districts. I would suggest that in future the figures for birth-places in at least bordering provinces should be worked out by districts and not by provinces only.

It must not be imagined that the Sanitary Commissioner's returns of births and deaths, greatly as they have improved of late years, are considered so absolutely correct as to be in themselves a test of the correctness of census totals. The looseness of the methods by which they are acquired, contrasted with the exactitude of those employed in the census, forbids this supposition. It, however, appears from their general agreement with the census returns that the figures are *comparatively* so accurate as to be capable of being used as a supplementary test. By comparatively I mean that when the returns of deaths were compared with those of births or those of one district with another the amount of error is in general fairly constant.

119. **Increase in Himalayan districts partly due to better enumeration.**—To begin the application of the tests detailed with the districts of largest increase the low excess of the 1881 population over the 1891 population over ten at once attracts notice in Kumaun and Garhwál. For Garhwál it is clear there was a deficit at last census as compared with the present. The reasons for believing this are clearly worked out in the following extract from Mr. Partridge's report:—

"The mode in which the 1881 Census was carried out in this district was as far as can be discovered as follows:—

"A preliminary census was taken in July, August and September 1880 by 42 patwáris, *i.e.*, there were only 42 enumerators for the whole district. The record so framed was tested by the Naib Tahsíldár, Sub-Deputy Inspector of Schools and the kanúngos in October and November: no final census was taken at all in February 1881. The patwáris were merely ordered to send lists of births and deaths from the close of preliminary census to 17th February 1881, and the preliminary record corrected by these lists became the final record. The results of a census carried out like this cannot have been nearly as accurate as those of a census carried out like that of 1891 are. In my opinion the total returned in 1881 (*viz.*, 345,629) was from 8,000 to 10,000 below the mark, and the figures for 1891 are as accurate as are ever likely to be obtained."

"My reasons for considering the 1881 total too low are as follows:—

"(1) There is no reason in the nature of things why the population of the district should have increased by only 11·4 per cent. in the nine years 1872—1881 and by 17·99 per cent. in the ten years 1881 to 1891. After making all allowance for the fact that the latter period included an extra year, and for the cholera epidemic in 1879, which carried off probably 5,000 or 6,000 people, the 1881 total appears to me distinctly too low. There is practically no immigration into the district and no emigration from it, so these factors may be disregarded."

"(2) I am unable to give the precise number of births and deaths registered in the district from 17th February 1881 to 26th February 1891, but the figures from 1st January 1881 to 31st December 1890 will for my purposes do just as well. I find that in these ten years, 127,297 births were recorded in the district and 84,222 deaths. The natural increase of population thus disclosed is 43,075, but the increase as shown by the census is 62,189 or a difference of 19,114. This difference (19,114) is divided fairly equally between males and females (8,885 males and 10,229 females). Thus:—

"Total of males enumerated in 1881	170,755
"Add number of male children whose births were reported from 1st January 1881 to 31st December 1890	64,607
	235,362
"Deduct number of males whose deaths were reported in the same period	43,928
	191,434

"Deduct this from 200,319, the number of males returned at this census, and the difference is 8,885, while for females we have—

"Total of females enumerated in 1881	174,874
"Add number of female children whose births were reported from 1st January 1881 to 31st December 1890	62,690
	237,564
"Deduct number of females whose deaths were reported in the same period	40,294
	197,270

"Deduct this from 207,499, the number of females returned at this census, and the difference is 10,229.

"The method in which in my opinion this difference of 19,114 should be accounted for is as follows:—

"I should put down some 8,000 to 10,000 of it to defective enumeration at last census, that number of human items having been omitted then, (*a*) of which the greater number were children under 5 and (*b*) in which the majority were of the female sex. The balance I should put down to defective registration in the last 10 years. I am quite prepared to admit that the birth and death registration returns are to some extent defective, but I cannot believe that anything like 19,000 births remained unregistered."

"Therefore, though the increase in population in the last ten years has doubtless been very large, it is not in my opinion as great as the difference between the 1891 and 1881 totals."

"It is clear that the population in this district has a tendency to increase rapidly. This natural tendency was assisted between 1881 and 1891 by a succession of good or at any rate very fair harvests (barring of course the year 1890) and by an absence of epidemic diseases."

I may, in continuation of these remarks, point out that Mr. Partridge should have taken into account only the comparative inaccuracy of the annual vital statistics, and that, therefore, the omissions at last census are probably larger than he suggests. If the death-rate in Garhwál is at all up to the provincial average, and the age classification would indicate that it was above average, the omissions in 1881 would amount to about 20,000 persons.

For Kumaun, with a lower increase and a considerable amount of immigration, the omissions are not proved to have been so large. The population estimated from that of 1881 by adding births and deducting deaths is much lower than the present census figures show it to be, but there can be no doubt that these figures over-estimate the deficit in 1881 and that in Kumaun deaths are better reported than births. With an average death-rate, at least 10,000 possibly 15,000 persons must have been omitted in Kumaun at last census.

This still leaves for Kumaun and Garhwál a rate of increase of 12 per cent. or more. There is reason to believe this is correct. The population of the Himalayan tracts, although in small areas they have recently suffered from scarcity, are comparatively well-to-do; wages are high and prices in the villages by no means comparatively so high. There has been a large extension of cultivation of late years and land is still available. There is no reason to believe that population in the Himalayas has as yet reached its limit. On similar considerations the present census of Tehri-Garhwál shows a deficit of at least 19,000 in the last. It is probably more. The next area of increase which calls for notice is Dehra Dún. The immigration is here so large as sufficiently to explain the rise in population. Similarly in Jhánsi the large apparent rise is due to the extension of a portion of Scindia's territory in the district.

120. **Reasons to believe that the Oudh figures of 1881 were too low.**—The Oudh figures next call for notice. Mr. White considered that the results of the 1881 Census showed that the Oudh Census of 1869 overstated the population. There appears to me to be some reason to believe that the 1881 Census understated it. The proportion of emigrants and immigrants is nearly normal, emigrants being of late years certainly in excess. The death-rate also is normal as both the Sanitary Commissioner's returns and the age tables (see Chapter III) show. All things considered, the ratio borne by the 1881 population to the adult population of 1891 should have been normal. It is however below normal for every district except Partábgarh and Unao. The conclusion to which, after careful consideration, I have been forced to come is, that 250,000 or about 19·8 per cent. of the increase in population in Oudh is due to better enumeration at the present census. It might have been expected. Oudh officers were in 1881 new to the management of an elaborate census, whilst in the North-Western Provinces the experience of 1872 was a guide.

121. **Low enumeration in 1881 in Bijnor.**—The only other district in which there is reason to believe enumeration in 1881 was not full is Bijnor. Here the large comparative increase in females at once indicates better work in 1891. Other reasons incline me to believe that the 1881 figures were about 15,000 short, two-thirds of the difference being in females. In regard to

Bijnor the Sanitary Commissioner's figures with the figures of 1881 show a population 3,213 males more and 5,208 females less than the present census. The comparative agreement of these figures with those of the census in spite of the mistake estimated is easily explained by a comparative excess in the birth-rate for Bijnor. The proportion of minors to total population in Bijnor would indicate a normal birth-rate, whereas that reported is 42 per thousand against 39·5 for the provinces. The Sanitary Commissioner's figures founded on this birth-rate are, therefore, too high, although the birth-rate itself is more than usually correct.

The districts in which a great fall from the 1881 figures in those for adults in 1891 attract notice are Farukhabad, Mainpuri, Etah, Jalaun, Mirzapur, Ballia and Bareilly. In all of these districts either a high recorded death-rate or ascertained emigration, or both, explain the high excess, so that so far as comparison with last census goes, there is no reason to believe that in any district the present census has been defective.

122. **The real increase allowing for differences in enumeration.**—Taking into account the extension of area in the Jhánsi district the total effect of this examination has been to show that the population of the provinces was understated by 343,000 in 1881 and that the real increase for both sexes has been 5·52 per cent. instead of the 6·34 per cent. indicated by the rough comparison.

123. **The causes of the variations**.—These corrections affect only to a slight extent the large variations in the movement of population already indicated in the different parts of the provinces, and it is now necessary to examine in detail the causes, which led to these variations.

The "natural increment" as referred to in connection with movement of population in European countries is a fairly fixed quantity, the causes which lead to abnormally high or low increases in different parts of a country being generally unconnected with the natural increment. It is very different in India where both birth and death-rates vary from year to year and district to district to an extent unknown in Europe. The vessel so to speak answers more freely to her helm. A check in the prosperity of the country implies almost at once a check in the natural increment; an increase in prosperity similarly implies an increase in the natural growth of population.

The other factor in the movement of population, migration, is also, though perhaps smaller in extent, small areas being considered, than in England, more variable than in that country. Emigration in an ordinary plains district almost invariably follows a bad season and is checked by a good one. The reason is obvious, the margin of preparation for bad seasons is far lower than in England and the effect which follows such seasons is, therefore, more sudden.

We have already seen that the principal characteristics, from a vital point of view of the past decade, has been a succession of wet seasons and steady sustained and increasing high prices of food. To these two factors the exceptional variations in population shown by the present census are almost entirely to be attributed. They consist of first, a decrease or low rate of increase in those tracts in which failure of the harvests or injury to public health was induced by excessive moisture ; second, a rapid rate of increase in those tracts in which a high rainfall was advantageous and amongst those classes to whom high prices are beneficial ; third, a movement on the part of those labouring classes whose wages are paid in cash from country tracts and small towns where customary wages are slow to rise to the larger towns or to other provinces where wages are higher. Besides these we have variations due to more permanent causes: first, the movement from the more congested districts into those in which land is still available for cultivation ; second, the movement, due to the decay of certain ancient industries, towards the centres of new industries. These causes explain all the variations noted.

124. **The causes of the decrease and slow increase in certain districts and tahsils—Etawah.**—To take the centre of decrease first, the main reason operative was the unhealthiness and decrease of cultivation due to flooding and spread of jungle grasses, the growth of which is promoted by excessive moisture. The variations in Etáwah, varying from just below average to a considerable decrease, is explained as follows by Mr. Alexander, the Collector :—

" The decrease in the population of the Pachar or lowlying tract in the centre and north of the district is quite in accordance with what I should have expected from my knowledge of the extent to which this tract has suffered from flooding during the last ten years. Previously it had reaped the full advantage of the great facilities from irrigation afforded by the Etáwah and Cawnpore branches of the Ganges Canal, and I have no doubt but that in the previous decade its population had considerably increased, whilst that of the comparatively unirrigated country along and across the Jamna had either remained stationary or actually diminished."

" A cycle of heavy rainfalls has suited the latter tract admirably and its population has consequently increased rapidly. If a cycle of dry years succeeds, the process will, I have no doubt, be again reversed."

125. **Etah.**—The report from Etah, the district which shows the largest decrease in the provinces, gives the following full account of the causes of the fall :—

" During the ten years which have elapsed between the 1881 and 1891 Census there has been a falling off in the population of this district by a little over 7 per cent. Several causes have been at work during this period to retard progress. The mortality from cholera and malarious fevers has been on the increase."

" The retrograde state must be ascribed chiefly to the waterlogged state of a large portion of the district. The two tahsíls that suffered acutely are those of Kásganj and Aliganj. The cause of these misfortunes were, firstly, some five or six years of abnormally heavy rainfall, and, secondly a disastrous flood that swept down the Kali nadi valley in 1885. At first it was the valley of the Kali nadi as also that of the Burhganga further north, which attracted attention. It was clear that the heavy rainfall had done damage, and it was also naturally concluded that a great portion of the rain water, which had fallen on the uplands, must of necessity have found its way down into the valleys, thereby aggravating the evil which already existed down below. The formerly cultivated lands in the Kali nadi valley showed to view a *tabula rasa* for years subsequently ; indeed, it was not till the cold weather of last year, 1891, that cultivation was again undertaken."

" To the north in the Burhganga valley the ground had become saturated and waterlogged, the excess rain water that had come down from above only intensified the evil.

Added to this was the fact that the Burhganga stream, an ancient bed of the Ganges as its name discloses, is a tortuous and sluggish one. It had been left very much to itself during past years; the stream had in places silted up, bunds had been in places formed for purposes of irrigation and not been properly removed. The result was natural. The stream was barely able to carry off normal rainfall, and when the abnormally heavy falls came it could not do its appointed work. The valley lands that used to grow excellent cane and fine rice crops fell bit by bit out of cultivation; mango groves even died off from excess of moisture, and the scene, a couple of years ago, was indeed one of desolation."

"It had, however, been imagined that these evils were confined to the valley lands. Fortunately an officer had been deputed on special duty in the end of 1887, and he discovered that not alone had the valley lands suffered, the uplands also that lay between the two streams had also become desolate. Here, again, heavy rainfall was the primary cause of the trouble, aided by faulty drainage. It was at first assumed on all sides that the canals had brought about the evil. Calmer consideration, however, showed the people's complaints against the canal were grossly exaggerated, canals or their many minor branches had done damage *in places* by obstructing drainage; but to put down, as had been done, *all* the damage to the canals was preposterous. Heavy rainfall was the cause and the effect was the springing of the deadly káns grass. Once it has begun, it spreads rapidly and eats up field after field, throwing acre after acre out of cultivation. It is difficult to eradicate; to do so requires great energy, good strong plough cattle, and capital. Unfortunately it is not an unknown but a recurrent calamity in some parts of this country—in this district, for example, parganas Sirhpura, Sahawar, Patiali and Azamnagar are apt to suffer from it. The people know well what it means; they have little energy, bad cattle and no capital. Government presses for its revenue; the landlord in turn for his rent; tenants lose heart, become apathetic, desert or die; and eventually the evil state of the country presses for consideration. Eventually measures for relief are undertaken, but in the meantime the greater portion of the damage has been done. Villages have broken down, tenants have departed for pastures new, or have become listless and apathetic or have died; cattle too have died off in numbers and the damage has been done. When it is pointed out that the present census shows a decrease of nearly 25,000 in the Kásganj tahsíl or over 11 per cent., and a decrease of nearly 32,000 in the Aliganj tahsíl or over 16 per cent., the above remarks obtain force. The large flood which I have mentioned came down in 1885 was the greatest on record. It came suddenly down the Kali nadi river, which runs through the heart of the district from north-west to south-east. It swept away the Nadrai aqueduct on the Lower Ganges Canal, the masonry bridge on the metalled road between Etah and Kásganj, and the railway bridge at Nadrai. It carried away houses, cattle and property of all kinds. All the villages bordering this river suffered heavily. Next in order of importance among the natural calamities which befell the district was the abnormal increase of cholera and small-pox in 1884 and 1889. The district suffered terribly from both these scourges in those years. The Nadrai aqueduct has been rebuilt and is perhaps the finest in India. It afforded employment, I may add, to thousands of persons about the country who were suffering from want: wages, moreover, were liberal and high, and this large work counteracted and compensated for the evils caused by the flood that carried away its predecessor."

126. **Mainpuri.**—The causes noted in the Mainpuri report are similar. Fever, floods, the spread of káns, the temporary loss of canal-irrigation from the Nadrai aqueduct having been swept away, the isolation of the district from the line of traffic and consequent loss of trade it formerly possessed, led to people being "driven by force of circumstances to seek abroad for the means of sustenance they can no longer find at home. The increasing dearness of the necessaries of life," it is remarked at another part of the

report, "causes much distress to the large classes who live by regular or customary wages on which as yet little impression has been made."

The remarks on the subject are summed up as follows :—

"The decrease of population is largest in tahsíls Mainpuri and Bhongaon, where the stress of the bad seasons and injury from floods and káns has been most severely felt, as also the loss of traffic along the roads. The town of Mainpuri which formerly possessed considerable trade in cotton, oilseeds, cloth and iron has at present absolutely no trade worthy of the name. The Shikohabad tahsíl exhibits the lowest decrease. This has the advantage of the East Indian Railway passing through it and contains the only two markets with any considerable trade. Even here, however, population has not been able to hold its own. Karhal has fared better than any tahsíl in the district, owing to a comparatively light assessment and having been more free from the misfortunes which have affected its neighbours. The revenue is collected with greater ease than in any other tahsíl, indicating a less severe struggle for existence. All that can be said of it, however, is that population has not actually fallen off, the increase of 266 being too insignificant to merit notice."

127. **Farukhabad.**—The Farukhabad district report gives a history of the district year by year too lengthy to extract. Damage by floods, a high rate of mortality due to several visits of cholera and constant fever epídemic, and the decay in the trade and manufactures of Farukhabad itself are the reasons given to explain a decrease in all the tahsíls of the district except Kanauj, and a low rate of increase there.

128. **Bundelkhand.**—From Jalaun, another of the group of districts in which the decrease all over was greatest, the following explanation has been received :—

"The trade of Kalpi and Madhogarh has almost died out and, as a consequence, those engaged in it have in many cases gone elsewhere. There has been a succession of bad seasons and the pressure of high prices thus created has scattered the poorer classes into other districts where the conditions of life were less hard."

"In the tahsíl of Jalaun many muáfis have been resumed, and owing to this there has been a large exodus of the families of the muáfidárs Dakhini Pandits, who have immigrated into Gwaliar. Lastly, I am informed that three years ago cholera, and last year influenza, raged here with great violence and made many victims."

"The result of all these untoward influences has been to best the normal rise of the population and turn it into a decrease."

It is noticeable that whilst the recorded death-rate in the Agra districts was not above normal, it was throughout Bundelkhand, including Jalaun, particularly high during the ten years in question.

In the remainder of Bundelkhand, which showed a decrease, the circumstances were similar. In Hamírpur the decrease was somewhat unexpected and part of it was believed to be due to temporary migration to native states or the northern tahsils of the district. The Bundelkhandies are said to move about in large masses during harvest time from tahsíls in which crops are late to tahsíls where they are early and *vice versá*. The movement was enquired into particularly by a late Collector, Mr. Twigg. The extreme inequality of the variations in Hamírpur makes it probable that the northern tahsíls gained in this way at the expense of the southern. In Bánda some variations are noticeable and the cause is probably the same. The district had suffered considerably from the spread of káns, and alleviating measures had to be undertaken in remission of revenue.

129. **Agra.**—The Agra report gives the following account of the decrease in Fatehpur Sikri and low increase elsewhere in the tahsíls south of the Jamna :—

"The population of the Agra tahsíl and of Keraoli has fallen off. The falling off in the former tahsíl is said to be due partly to the prevalence of fever in the villages bordering on the banks of the canal and partly to the diminution of cultivated area occasioned by the ravages of wild pigs, which has driven tenants to migrate to tracts less exposed to such disadvantages. In the Keraoli tahsíl, in addition to the above causes, the ravages of wild cattle and pigs from the Bhartpur territory reduced the cultivation and consequently the agricultural population to such an extent that Government had to come forward to their assistance in granting remissions and reduction of revenue. A barbed wire fence has now been put up along part of the frontier of the pargana, and this protected line is to be extended. It is hoped that the next census will show an increase both in cultivation and population."

130. **The Jamna parganas in the Upper Doab.**—There remain three tracts of low increase to be mentioned. That to the west may be taken first, a strip along the Jamna from Sahâranpur to Muttra, the northern part of which is irrigated by the Eastern Jamna Canal and the southern by branches of the Ganges Canal. A great part of this tract is lowlying khadir of the Jamna, and it is everywhere subject to flooding from excessive rainfall. The death-rate from fever in part of it was so high some years ago as to attract special attention and procure remedial measures to some extent. The late series of wet years was both as regards health and agricultural prosperity most unfavourable for this tract, and a decrease in population was everywhere anticipated. The decrease has been added to by the decay of a series of towns formerly of importance along the west of Muzaffarnagar and Sahâranpur, but now shut out from all trade, which has been attracted to the tract traversed by the Sindh, Panjáb and Delhi Railway. The greater part of the Muzaffarnagar district is included in the unhealthy tract in which population is at a standstill.

131. **Rohilkhand.**—The decrease in the Rohilkhand tract appears to have been something of a surprise to District Officers and is not satisfactorily accounted for. The greater part of the districts affected are subject to fever and the death-rate for the ten wet years was everywhere abnormally high, 37 in Bareilly and Budaun, 44 in Moradabad, and 53 in the Tarâi, the population in which is only sustained at its present level by constant and extensive immigration. The Rohilkhand districts appear to have been fairly prosperous during the decade, and the high death-rate appears to be the sole explanation of the fall in population.

132. **The Eastern districts.**—Eastwards from these tahsíls in Cawnpore, which are similarly circumstanced to Mainpuri and Etáwah, the areas of actual decrease are few. The part of Cawnpore and Fatehpur near the Ganges has suffered both from flooding and fever epidemic. Further east the only area of extensive decrease is in pargana Mirzapur, where it is due to the decay of the city of Mirzapur, and in Ballia, where it is due to floods from

the Ghogra and to the emigration caused by the great pressure of population on the area. Elsewhere the rate of increase in the eastern districts was almost invariably low, but as reason will be given to believe further on, a low increase is normal and requires neither a want of prosperity nor bad health to explain. It is reduced in the present census by a rise in the emigration to other provinces which, as will be shown in Chapter XI, amounts to 278,642, and of which, as proved by the age figures referred to on page 130 a great proportion comes from the eastern districts. The one point in the low rate of increase in the Benares districts of the North-Western Provinces which calls for particular explanation is the contrast afforded by the low rise in their population to the uniformly large rise in Oudh. The death-rate on the whole was lower and the general health no worse in the eastern districts of the North-Western Provinces than in Oudh. The seasons too were such as suited both tracts.

The district reports treating of the rise in the North-Western Provinces as normal afford me little assistance in arriving at a conclusion on the subject, and the only explanations I can suggest are (1) that as high density of population in Oudh is more recent than in the North-West, the population of the latter province has more completely adapted itself to circumstances in which a large rise in population is likely to be a source of future distress and mortality; (2) the constitution of the population of both tracts is as regards division between urban and rural not altogether the same; Oudh is distinctly less urban than the eastern districts of the North-Western Provinces, and, as will be seen in the remarks on towns, it is the town population which has felt the rise in prices most accutely. It is unfortunate that the figures for foreign emigration cannot be ascertained by districts, otherwise the difference between the rate of natural increment in Oudh and the eastern districts of the North-Western Provinces could probably be proved to be less.

133. **The areas of large increase. The Himalayas.**—Passing to the figures showing large increase, the Himalayan increase has already been alluded to. There were two occasions during the past ten years on which it was considered necessary to assist the population in certain pattis of Kumaun and Garhwál by the importation and sale at rates lower than those prevailing in the localities at the time. The distress was, however, absolutely temporary, and the relief measures made necessary, not by the poverty of the population, but by the inaccessibility of their homes and entire absence of centres of trade, owing to which no sudden demand for food-grains can be met by private enterprise. On the whole, the population of the Himalayas has been prosperous, and except during one eruption of cholera healthy throughout the past ten years. The increase in population has been accompanied by an increase in cultivation, and the area still available is so extensive that it is not likely that the present rate of increase will be checked by natural and ordinary causes for some time.

134. **The sub-Himalayan districts.**—In the sub-Himalayan districts the rise is due to causes easily explained. To the north of all these districts there is still a considerable area available for extension of cultivation, to which emigration from the more crowded parts takes place. South of this

forest area comes a second tract in which the density of population has not yet risen to the figure normal in the more crowded parts of the province and which apparently can ordinarily be maintained with the standard of comfort, if it can be called comfort, to which the low caste cultivator is accustomed. Everywhere in these districts the rental is comparatively low and the proportion of actual cultivators high, so that the recent high prices have allowed a comparatively large margin of profit to the great majority of the people. The large rise in these districts was, therefore, to be expected and it is probable that failing some great calamity it will continue for several decades to come. Basti has, more than any other, been fully settled, but even here the density has not yet risen to the standard of eastern districts, and rents owing to the proximity of large waste areas in Nepál have kept markedly lower than in the neighbouring districts on this side of the Ghogra. Dehra Dún may be specially mentioned. The comparatively cool climate and its freedom from the feverishness of the other sub-Himalayan tracts have made it a favorite settlement for European planters. The area, till lately almost entirely forest, is being rapidly brought under cultivation, an important tea industry has sprung up, and the population unrestrained by the excessive death-rate of other forest tracts is rising rapidly and steadily.

135. **Oudh.**—There remains for mention Oudh, cis-Sarju, throughout the whole of which expect in a pargana or two on the Ghogra and in the Baiswara parganas on the Ganges, the rise has been, even taking into account the under-estimate at last census already referred to much above average. The exceptions mentioned are, in the Ghogra parganas, due to the action of that river, which is apt to alter its bed by several miles in a single season. In Baiswara the ordinary rise is restrained by the large proportion of high caste cultivators amongst whom marriage is late. They have been until very recently suspected of infanticide, and not even now are they free from the suspicion. The parganas too, supply a larger proportion of emigrants than any other part of the Rae Bareli district and have suffered more than usual from the fever epedemic of 1890. The general large rise in Oudh must be attributed in the main to the comparatively favorable seasons and to the high prices which have prevailed. Nearly the whole of Oudh benefits by a wet season, and 75 per cent. of the population are either cultivators or get paid in kind, so that they are either independent of or benefit from a rise in prices. I have no doubt, further, that the recent change in the permanency of Oudh tenures has had to do with the rise. For the whole of the decade now passed the particular attention of District Officers has been directed to prevent arbitrary ejectment of tenants, and even before the Rent Act of 1886 was passed, oppressive action on the part of landlords was minimized by the certainty that such action would tell against them in the provisions of the Bill which was under consideration. The Act when passed has to some extent secured tenants, so far, in the enjoyment of their holdings, and it has, therefore, had on population the same effect as if it were likely to do so in permanency. An inspection of the age and civil condition figures show that Oudh has during the past ten years had some advantage over the North-West as regards both fecundity and longevity. The excess of young people

Abstract No. 43, showing the variations of population in the Districts since 1848.

Serial number.	Districts.	Census of 1848.	Percentage on present population.	Census of 1853.	Percentage on present population.	Census of 1865.	Percentage on present population.	North-Western Provinces Census of 1872 and Oudh Census of 1869	Percentage on present population.	Census of 1881.	Percentage on present population.
1	Dehra Dún	...	...	...	...	102,831	61·27	116,945	69·55	144,070	85·68
2	Sahāranpur	547,353	54·66	801,325	80·02	866,483	86·53	884,017	88·28	979,544	97·82
3	Muzaffarnagar	537,594	69·55	672,861	87·06	682,212	88·27	690,107	89·29	758,444	98·13
4	Meerut	860,736	61·86	1,135,072	81·57	1,199,593	86·20	1,276,104	91·71	1,313,137	94·37
5	Bulandshahr	699,393	73·62	778,342	81·93	800,431	84·26	936,667	98·60	924,822	97·35
6	Aligarh	686,439	65·80	1,041,534	99·83	925,538	88·72	1,073,333	102·88	1,021,187	97 89
	Total, Meerut Division ...	3,331,515	62·54	4,429,134	83·15	4,577,088	85·92	4,977,173	93·43	5,141,204	96·51
7	Muttra	583,705	81·81	718,512	100·71	800,321	112·18	887,689	124·43	671,690	94·15
8	Agra	828,220	82·50	1,001,961	99·81	1,028,544	102·46	1,096,367	109·25	974,656	97·09
9	Farukhabad	753,726	99·54	924,594	107·68	915,943	106·66	918,850	107·01	907,608	105·69
10	Mainpuri	479,599	62·92	634,087	83·19	700,220	91·87	765,845	100·48	801,216	105 13
11	Etáwah	481,224	66·13	610,965	83·96	626,444	86·09	668,641	91·89	722,371	99·27
12	Etah	564,268	80·37	749,361	106·74	614,351	87·50	703,527	100·21	756,523	107·76
	Total, Agra Division ...	3,690,742	77·41	4,639,480	93·11	4,685,823	98·28	5,040,919	105·71	4,834,064	101·40
13	Bareilly	866,262	83·23	1,048,896	100·79	996,929	95·78	1,015,041	97·53	1,030,936	99 05
14	Bijnor	620,546	78·14	695,521	87·59	690,975	87·01	737,153	92·83	721,450	90·85
15	Budaun	693,627	74·93	845,868	91·38	889,810	96·13	934,348	100·94	906,451	97·93
16	Moradabad	997,362	95·77	1,138,461	96·53	1,021,387	86·60	1,122,437	95·17	1,155,173	97·94
17	Sháhjahánpur	750,501	81·70	908,059	98·85	933,979	101·68	949,579	103·38	856,946	93·29
18	Pilibhít	339,482	69·94	407,409	83·93	467,270	96·27	492,098	101·39	451,601	93·04
	Total, Rohilkhand Division ...	4,267,780	79·87	5,044,214	94·40	5,000,350	93·57	5,250 656	98·25	5,122,557	95·86
19	Cawnpore	993,031	82 08	1,174,556	97·09	1,188,862	98·27	1,156,055	95·93	1,181,896	97·65
20	Fatehpur	511,132	73·10	679,787	97·22	680,786	97·37	663,877	94·95	683,745	97·79
21	Bánda	552,526	78·27	743,872	105·39	724,372	102 63	697,684	98·84	698,608	98·97
22	Hamírpur	452,091	88·00	548,604	106·78	520,941	101·41	529,137	103·00	507,337	98·75
23	Allahabad	710,263	45·86	1,379,788	89·09	1,393,183	89·95	1,396,241	90 15	1,474,106	95·18
24	Jhánsi	...	...	...	...	357,442	87·30	317,826	77·62	333,227	81·39
25	Jalaun	...	...	...	...	405,604	102·33	404,447	102·04	418,142	105·49
26	Lalitpur	...	...	...	...	248,146	90·49	212,661	77·55	249,088	90·83
	Total, Allahabad Division ...	3,219,043	68·82	4,526,607	96·78	5,519,336	95·87	5,377,928	93·41	5,545,649	96·33
27	Benares	741,426	80·42	851,757	92·38	793,277	86·04	794,039	86·12	892,684	96·82
28	Mirzapur	831,388	71·66	1,104,315	95·19	1,054,413	90·88	1,015,826	87·56	1,136,796	97·99
29	Jaunpur	798,503	63·13	1,143,749	90·41	1,015,427	80·27	1,025,961	81·10	1,209,663	95 62
30	Ghágipur	726,553	67·40	1,039,529	96 43	891,356	82·69	873,299	81·01	1,014,099	94·08
31	Ballia	526,002	55·81	794,611	84·31	631,636	67·01	686,127	72·79	924,763	98·12
	Total, Benares Division ...	3,623,872	67·50	4,933,961	91·90	4,386,109	81·69	4,395,252	81·86	5,178,005	96·45

32	Gorakhpur	2,376,533	49·71	3,087,874	64·60	3,439,513	71·95	2,019,361	67·44	2,617,120	87·41
33	Basti							1,473,029	82·48	1,630,612	91·30
34	Azamgarh	1,120,682	69·81	1,415,435	81·88	1,205,114	69·71	1,317,626	76·22	1,604,654	92·82
	Total, Gorakhpur Division ...	3,497,215	53·73	4,503,309	69·19	4,644,627	71·36	4,810,016	73·90	5,852,386	89·92
35	Kumaun	...	...	...	...	385,790	68·50	433,314	76·94	493,641	87·65
36	Garhwál	...	...	...	...	248,742	60·99	310,288	76·52	345,629	84·76
37	Tarái	...	...	...	...	165,721	78·70	185,658	88·17	206,993	98·30
	Total, Kumaun Division ...	...	...	...	...	800,253	67·73	929,260	78·65	1,046,263	88·55
	Total, N.-W. Provinces ...	21,630,167	67·96	28,076,705	88·22	29,613,586	86·45	30,781,204	89·86	32,720,128	95·52
38	Lucknow	...	...	...	...	...	...	970,625	125·38	696,824	90·00
39	Unao	...	...	...	...	...	...	724,949	76·01	899,069	94·27
40	Rae Bareli	...	...	...	...	...	...	782,874	75·53	951,905	91·83
41	Sitapur	...	...	...	...	...	...	930,224	86·50	958,251	89·10
42	Hardoi	...	...	...	...	...	...	930,977	83·63	987,630	88·72
43	Kheri	...	...	...	...	...	...	737,732	81·64	831,922	92·06
	Total, Lucknow Division ...	...	...	...	...	...	...	5,077,381	86·69	5,325,601	90·93
44	Fyzabad	...	...	...	...	...	...	1,437,009	118·09	1,081,419	88·86
45	Gonda	...	...	...	...	...	...	1,167,816	80·03	1,270,926	87·09
46	Bahraich	...	...	...	...	...	...	774,437	77·41	878,048	87·76
47	Sultanpur	...	...	...	...	...	...	930,023	86·45	957,912	89·04
48	Partábgarh	...	...	...	...	...	...	936,053	102·75	847,047	92·98
49	Bara Banki	...	...	...	...	...	...	875,876	77·40	1,026,788	90·79
	Total, Fyzabad Division ...	...	...	...	...	...	...	6,120,714	90·08	6,062,140	89·22
	Total, Oudh ...	...	...	...	...	...	...	11,198,095	88·52	11,387,741	90·01
	Total, N.-W. P. and Oudh ...	...	...	...	...	...		41,979,299	89·60	44,107,869	94·03
	Present population of the above area ...	31,824,572		31,824,572		34,254,254		46,905,085		46,905,085	

is most marked in the period 10 to 19 indicating that the Oudh population suffered comparatively far less from the famine and fever of 1877 and 1879 than those of the North-Western Provinces. Oudh shows a slight advance in the proportion of married amongst the population as compared with 1881 and with the North-Western Provinces. Judging from these figures, I would conclude that the rapid increase during the past decade is due not only to present prosperity but to comparative prosperity in the previous decade also.

136. **Movement of population in earlier intercensal periods.**—A statement of great interest is given in the statement accompanying, in which the population of the districts of the province according to earlier census enumerations is compared with that ascertained by the Census of 1891; against each district is given the population enumerated at each census and the proportion borne by that population to the population of 1891. The Census of 1848 gave results undoubtedly far lower than the real population; as already remarked, it was less accurate than the estimate which preceded it in 1826: as for the later enumerations, it may be taken as certain that what error there was, was probably due rather to understatement than to overstatement.

The Census of 1853 showed on the area then enumerated 88 per cent. of the population now on the same area. During the interval between this and the next census in 1865 the country "suffered from terrible calamities; there had been a grievous civil war, a destructive famine, and large portions of the land had been visited by pestilence." The population enumerated in 1865 was less than in 1853 and only 86·45 per cent. of that now on the same area. Between 1865 and 1872 the great famine of 1868 intervened, but the result of a census better in general but very clearly deficient in the Benares Division was to show on the present districts of the North-Western Provinces 89·86 of a the present population. In the meantime the first census of Oudh had been taken showing 88·52 per cent. of the present population than in the Province. The Census of 1881, separated from that preceding by a severe famine and a severe pestilence, showed in the whole of the provinces 94 per cent. of the present population. These figures tend to show a gradual and general rise; but on examining more closely into the details of the figures we find reason to alter this opinion to some extent.

The sub-Himalayan districts and in especial those beyond the Ghogra show a steady increase from census to census. In Oudh the number of enumerations being only three and the period included only twenty-two years, an inference can with less confidence be drawn; but there too there appears to be so far on the whole a slow general increase, except perhaps in the largely urban districts of Lucknow and Fyzabad. The 1869 Census I may remark was considered by Mr. White too high. Elsewhere, it is certain that the population is in a state of fluctuation and that the general rate of increase is very small. Thus in 1853 there were six districts—Muttra, Farukhabad, Etah, Bareilly, Hamírpur, Allahabad—the population in which was then higher than it is now. In 1865 there were seven such districts, three of those last named and Agra, Sháhjahánpur, Bánda and Jalaun. In 1872 no less than eleven districts in the North-Western Provinces had a population higher than they have now. Aligarh had 102·88 per cent. of its present population, the

Agra Division as a whole had a higher population. The districts of Benares Division were in this and probably all preceding censuses greatly underestimated. The first complete enumeration was in 1881, when the population was 96·4 of that now in them. Mr. White demonstrated that the population of the whole of the provinces had not increased during the ten years preceding 1881. It is clear that even including the districts in which there is ample room for increase, the total increase since 1872 has not exceeded 6 per cent. If any trust whatsoever is to be reposed on enumerations elaborately organized and carefully made in previous years, it is more than probable that in the western and Allahabad districts there has been only a trifling increase since the Mutiny, and that the general increase is almost entirely due to the steady increase in the sub-Himalayan districts.

137. **The effect of the variations on the food-supply.**—These facts have a most important bearing on the question which has of late years agitated economic thinkers in India in regard to the sufficiency of the food-supply. It was considered after the most exhaustive examination of the subject which has been made since the report of the Famine Commission that population had increased of late years to such an extent compared with the increase in the cultivated area and productive powers of the soil, that the available surplus of food in an ordinary year was only sufficient for the whole population for the consumption of ten days.

The estimate of the available supply of flood for each person of the populution was made by writers who are recognized authorities in regard to Agricultural statistics, but the facts just indicated appear to make it certain that there is a mistake somewhere. The increase in the area cultivated and the increase in the area irrigated are more or less accurately calculated, and from them it is known that the gross production has increased largely. On the other hand, it appears to me fairly certain that the population is not increasing at all at the rate it is usually supposed, and that in a period of fifty years, with an average share of epidemics and failures of harvests thrown in, the allover increase in the population from Benares to Bulandshahr would be trifling. If this is so, it is certain that the average inhabitant of the country is wealthier and better fed than he was fifty years ago, and that the availtable surplus is larger. Exact enquiries as to the means of subsistence of the lower classes have only been made within comparatively recent times. The information they have elicited shows that for certain classes the supply of food is slender in the extreme, but it is now in my opinion less slender than in former decades. It is the labourer, and not the employer of labour, who now rejects the customary system of payment of wages in kind at rates which have prevailed from time immemorial, and his reason must be that he finds he can do better with the newly-instituted wages in cash; that, therefore, he is better off now than when the rates of payment in kind were instituted.

138. **The movement of population in towns.**—The crisis through which wages in cash are just now, owing to the high price of grain, passing, has, I have no doubt, much to do with the aspect in which the movement of population has next to be considered, *viz.*, the movement in towns as contrasted with

that in the general population. The figures for variations of population in towns given in Table No. IV were prepared as far as possible to show the 1881 population of the present town areas. The definition of town given at last census was different from that now adopted, the number of towns then shown was much smaller and the areas of a large proportion of the towns different. Comparison with the figures in the 1881 report would, therefore, be futile, but the 1881 urban population on the present definition can be obtained from the present table. The total urban population of 1881 according to the table was 5,132,723 or 11·6 per cent. of the whole population. It was in 1891 5,314,328 or 11·3 per cent. The increase was 181,605 in total town population 112,566 in males and 69,039 in females. Some alterations have, however, to be made in these figures before they can be used for purposes of exact comparison, owing to the fact that the 1881 population could not in certain towns be exactly ascertained for the present areas. The most important is in regard to Jhánsi town, which was in Scindia's territory at last census. The population at last census as reported by the Darbár and with the Cantonments and Civil Station included was 32,987. This gives the impossibly large rise in ten years of 20,792, so that it is certain that the statement for 1881 is too low. In comparing 1881 and present figures I propose to exclude Jhánsi. Other towns of which the 1881 population on the present area has not been ascertained are Basti, Balrámpur, Jigna Bazár and Sultánpur, all of which for purposes of consideration of movement I exclude. These exclusions show a total increase of town population of 2·956 per cent. against an increase in the general population of 6·54 per cent.

This result of a much lower increase in towns than in general population has been contributed to by almost every district in the provinces except in Oudh, where 5 out of 12 districts show a considerable increase in towns: a detailed examination of the reasons town by town and district by district is unnecessary because they are everywhere so much the same. Large towns as a rule show an increase. There are in every district one or two of the smaller towns in general favourably situated with regard to the railway, which have shown a considerable increase, whilst the great majority of the others have either decreased or remained absolutely at a standstill. The reasons are—

1st.—The decay of certain native industries and in particular those connected with cotton weaving, the persons carrying on which formed a considerable proportion of the inhabitants of small towns.

2nd.—The decay of old trade marts now losing their importance owing to their being isolated from the railway.

3rd.—A general movement of the labouring classes away from the small towns in which cash payments for labour are slow to rise in proportion to the rise in the price of food-grains.

139. **Remarks on the movement of town population in certain districts.**—The variations in the urban population are shown for all districts in Appendix No. XVII: some of the figures for those districts in which they are noteworthy may be referred to—

Dehra Dún.—The large proportionate rise in town population partly due to the increase in the winter population of Mussoorie, an increase more or less accidental and due to the mildness of the cold weather of 1891. Dehra (population 25,684) itself also shows a large rise. It is more extensively than any other town of its size in the provinces a European settlement, and its importance is rising with that of the Dún.

Sahāranpur.—Is as regards the movement of town population typical. Sahāranpur itself (population 63,194) shows the considerable rise of 4,000 persons. It is the headquarters of the district; it is situated at the junction of the Oudh and Rohilkhand and North-Western Railways with a large railway settlement and workshops; it is the winter headquarters of the remount department, &c., and the site of the principal remount stud in Northern India. There is a steam cotton screw and some iron manufactures in the European style. Hardwár, the population in which varies from time to time with the number of pilgrims who may happen to be there. also shows a rise, and so does Roorkee, a small military cantonment and the site of a Government engineering college and workshops. Two towns, Manglaur and Libarheri, are stationary, and the rest of the towns in the district, 15 of them, show a decrease; the grain and cotton trade on which they formerly flourished having concentrated itself in Sahāranpur.

Muzaffarnagar.—Figures are similar. The headquarters town Muzaffarnagar (population 18,166) shows a rise of 3,086. It is now a very flourishing grain and cotton mart, having drawn to itself all the trade of the district. The west of the district in former years contained a number of flourishing marts of which Shamli, now shrunk to a population of 6,403, was the principal. They are now owing to loss of trade, emigration of cotton weavers and the feverishness of the tract in which they are situated all decaying, so much so that several of them can barely sustain the expensive honor of being ranked amongst towns.

In *Meerut*, the city itself (population 119,390) originally important only because the site of a large cantonment is now becoming an important manufacturing and trading centre. It is the capital of the Upper Doab and the only city in it now of more than district importance. It shows the large rise of 19,825, larger than any other town in the provinces except Cawnpore. One other small town in the district shows an increase, and the rest along with all the Bulandshahr that towns are either at a standstill or decreasing, Khurja is believed to be still a thriving mart and the decrease is somewhat astonishing.

Háthras (population 39,181) is the only town in the Aligarh district which is increasing. It is situated close to a railway junction and owes its rising importance to its being the centre for the local cotton and grain trade.

The rise in the *Muttra* towns is accidental, owing to the presence of an extra regiment in Muttra Cantonment and an assemblage of pilgrims at Brindaban.

In *Agra*, the city (population 168,662) which was formerly the great emporium of trade between Upper India and the Dakkan, appears of late years, since the opening of the Rájputána-Malwa Railway, to be recovering from the stagnation into which the through trade with Calcutta and Bombay had plunged it. It is an important centre of certain native manufactures which have clung to it since it was the Moghal capital.

In *Mainpuri*, all the towns in which have been left on one side by the railway, the urban population is everywhere decreasing. The remark on the subject by the Collector may be quoted.

"The district being a purely agricultural one has been generally declining owing to the loss of traffic along the Grand Trunk Road. The trade of the towns has fallen off from there being no railway communication."

Farukhabad (population 78,032) though recently connected with Cawnpore and Bombay by a branch of the Rájputána-Malwa line, continues to show a decrease in population. It was a well-known centre for cotton weaving and printing, but its weavers and printers are now largely scattered in search of other employment.

Etáwah (population 38,793) is the only other town west of Cawnpore which has increased of late years to any considerable extent. It has attracted all the trade of the district and of Mainpuri to itself and is now a depôt of increasing importance for the trade in grain, cotton and ghi.

In *Etah* the loss of the saltpetre manufacture and of trade is noted as a cause of decrease for the towns there.

In *Rohilkhand* the largest increase is as usual shown by the principal city, Bareilly (population 121,039), which has important sugar manufactories as well as the usual grain trade. Moradabad and Sháhjahánpur, the only other important towns in this part of the province, also show some increase along with Dhampur, Tilhar, Katra, Sambhal and a few other trading towns generally on the railway. The considerable increase in the Bijnor towns has not been explained by the District Officer. It is probable that a considerable part of it is due to better enumeration. Pilibhít is one of the few districts in which the towns are nearly all prosperous and show a considerable increase. It has only very recently been traversed by a railway, and it remains to be seen whether this change will have the effect of injuring the majority of towns to the advantage of Pilibhít and one or two others.

Cawnpore the next town which attracts notice, shows a far larger increase than any other town in the provinces. It has risen from the fifth to the third place amongst the towns of the province during the decade. Its importance as the trading and manufacturing capital of Northern India requires no mention.

The towns of *Bundlekhand* without any exception of importance except Jhánsi and Lalitpur, are decreasing, some of them rapidly. Bánda (population 23,071) a town of former importance as the capital of a native state, has lost its cantonment and is otherwise like the rest of the district in a depressed state, though now that it is traversed by the railway, it may recover. Jhánsi alone has had an important rise. Its extent as already mentioned is uncertain, but it is certain that even excluding the greatly increased cantonment it has been considerable.

In the *east of the provinces* the only rise of importance is that in Allahabad 15,128, thereby raising the population to 175,246. A part of this increase is due to there having been still a number of pilgrims who had attended the Mágh bathing fair in the town, but the city is undoubtedly well-to-do. Besides being the headquarters of Government, it has some resources of its own as a trading and railway centre. Benares (population 219,467) the only city in the provinces which as a centre of native manufactures can rival Lucknow, shows the very small proportional rise of 4,709. There can, I believe, be little doubt that the city is far from being as prosperous as it has been and that high prices have had the effect of causing considerable distress amongst the artizan classes. Mirzapur (population 84,130) formerly the headquarters of the cotton trade with Central India, has, since the direct communication with Bombay deprived it of this trade, been in a decaying state. It has still command of the trade in lac, but, as the fall in population indicates, is in a depressed state. Jaunpur is even more stagnant, its well-known manufacture of rosewater and other scents having been seriously injured by the importation of foreign scents, and the large resident population which depends on "naukri" for a livelihood having found the rise in prices a severe tax. Badshahpur in Jaunpur may be mentioned as a decidedly thriving little town, the census returns for which showing a decrease are believed to be inaccurate owing to the carelessness of the charge Superintendent.

Beyond the Ghogra the towns on the new Bengal and North-Western Railway are all flourishing. Gorakhpur (population 63,620) shows a rise of 3,712; Basti a considerable rise not properly ascertained; Uska in the Basti district, formerly a small bazár, has sprung into importance at the expense of Mehndawal, the old emporium for the trade with Nepál. The latter is separated from the railway by the Rapti and ten miles of as bad a road as any in Asia and is fighting for its spice trade at a great disadvantage.

Turning to *Oudh* we find over all a rise in town population of 7 per cent. against 2·7 per cent. in the North-Western Provinces. The majority of Oudh towns, comparatively very much less numerous than in the North-West, appear to be fairly prosperous. Lucknow, the capital, shows a rise of only 11,725 or 4·49 per cent. Like Benares, it is a great centre of native manufactures, silverware, cotton printing, embroidery, pottery and even spectacles, but as in Benares these manufactures, except perhaps that of the silver-smiths are not prosperous. A considerable proportion of the population of Lucknow consists of families of comparatively well-born Muhammadans who were hangers-on of the ex-royal family. Amongst these, too proud either to work or to beg, and deprived to a great extent of their former means of livelihood, there is a considerable distress. Lucknow has, however, to some extent changed from the old order to the new, and owns paper mills, printing presses, a brewery and some other manufactures in the European style. The large cantonment and civil station also do much to preserve it from decay.

Fyzabad is the only other town of importance in Oudh. In constitution it (excluding Ajudhiya which is purely Hindu) closely resembles Lucknow, but the comparatively large rise of 10·53 per cent. shows that it is in more flourishing circumstances.

140. **Summary of remarks as to movement in towns.**—This brief mention of the principal towns has made clear that, as abovementioned, trade and manufactures are being attracted into a few centres, whilst the majority of small towns are decaying. The sudden decay within the last decade is no doubt due to the great rise in prices consequent on the fall of the rupee, and it cannot be doubted that the effect, temporarily at least, has been to cause great distress in the houses of native artisans and labourers.

The extent to which the rise in population in towns is monopolized by the large trade centres and a few of the smaller towns is made clear by ascertaining what part of the rise has to be allotted to each. The seventeen largest towns in the province (all those above 50,000 except Jhánsi) with a total population of 1,857,611 in 1881 rose to 1,984,297 in 1891, an increase of 126,686 or 6·819 per cent. On a population of 3,237,374 all the other towns during the present decade, showed arise of only 23,262 or ·72 per cent. A considerable number of towns of the second size show large rises whilst the vast majority show either an increase proportionately very low or an actual decrease. In all 256 towns in the provinces show an increase and 234 towns a decrease.

141. **Movement of population in Hill stations.**—A statement appended to table IV shows the movement of summer population in the hill stations of the provinces according to special censuses taken in the season in 1880 and 1890, and a similar appendix to table V shows the constitution of the population of these towns when they are most inhabited. The present population of each and percentage of variation are given in the marginal statement. The variation in Chakráta is accidental, connected with the movement of troops on the dates of the different censuses. Of the other towns, Mussoorie shows much the largest rise, Naini Tal comes next with a rise considerable when it is considered that by far the greater part of the visitors are those who reside there on duty and that there was little change in the departments permitted to reside there in the different years. The appendix to table V is of some interest in connection with the remarks already made as to the density of population in the Naini Tal Bazár. Mussoorie with a far larger number of European residents than Naini Tal has a considerably smaller native population. The percentages of Europeans including Eurasians (the returns for whom are separate only in Naini Tal and Chakráta and altogether incomplete in both of these) and of others than Europeans for

Abstract No. 44, showing the population of Hill stations.

Town.		Population.	Percentage of increase since 1880.
1. Naini Tal	...	13,197	+ 15·23
2. Mussoorie	...	10,086	+ 30·80
3. Ránikhet	...	7,387	+ 11·28
4. Chakráta	...	4,837	+ 164·61
5. Landaur	...	4,190	— 5·37

Abstract No. 45, showing the proportion of Europeans in Hill stations.

Town.		Percentage of Europeans to total population.	Percentage of others than Europeans to total population.
1. Mussoorie	...	25·7	74·3
2. Chakráta	...	33·7	66 3
3. Landaur	...	20·8	79·2
4. Naini Tal	...	15·8	84 2
5. Ránikhet	...	30·4	69 6

the different towns are given in the margin. The cold weather population of those towns as ascertained by the ordinary Census is compared with the hot weather population in the following statement.

Abstract No. 46, comparing the cold-weather and hot-weather population of Hill stations.

Town.	Population in February.	Population in September.	Increase.	Percentage of increase.
Mussoorie	5,142	10,086	4,944	96·1
Chakráta	1,509	4,837	3,328	220·5
Landaur	2,033	4,190	2,157	106·1
Naini Tal	8,455	13,197	4,742	56·1
Ránikhet	2,333	7,387	5,054	216·6

The cold weather population varies largely from year to year owing to the mildness or severity of the winter. That of 1891 is reported from Dehra Dún to have been comparatively mild. In Naini Tal it was certainly the reverse.

Chapter V.—THE VITAL STATISTICS OF THE DECADE.

142. **The vital statistics as collected by the Sanitary Commissioner.**—A test of the correctness of the vital statistics of the province as recorded by the Sanitary Commissioner is afforded by a comparison of the figures for the present and the last census, and I propose to remark briefly on the subject in the present chapter. I have already expressed an opinion that it is futile to expect an absolute test of the accuracy of the census figures from the recorded vital statistics, owing to the very much larger percentage of error to which the latter are exposed from the way in which they are collected. Except in a few towns all such statistics are collected by village or other watchmen, who report occurrences at their fortnightly visits to the police stations to which they are attached. The watchmen are themselves, I suppose almost without exception, absolutely illiterate. They are instructed when they hear of a birth or death to have an entry made by the patwári or some other literate person in a book furnished to them for the purpose. As a matter of fact, the entries in the watchman's book are usually dictated from memory to the police muharrir, who has to enter them in the station mortuary registers; the memorandum book serves only as a means of testing the watchman's work. It may be regarded as certain that a large proportion of error is introduced into these statistics from the first, owing to the watchman's not having received notice of a birth or death or from his having forgotten or neglected to report it. The subsequent totalling of the statistics in the police stations are rarely fully tested and compared with the watchmen's books and the periodical returns submitted, so that an extra percentage of error is here again introduced. The facility with which a native statistician, who is blamed for providing statistics not agreeing with a standard supposed to be correct, can supply statistics that do agree with the standard, makes it very possible that the omissions likely to occur in the watchman's record may be more than provided against in the station returns, and that therefore overstatement is far from impossible. The care taken in all details of the census enumeration and tabulation and the infrequency of cases in which omissions or mistakes in gross numbers are detected is a complete contrast to the procedure in collecting vital statistics, and makes it absolutely certain that the census where it is worst is more correct in regard to resultant numbers than the vital statistics where they are best.

143. **The comparative accuracy of these statistics.**—Vital statistics are however of nearly as much value to indicate the movement of population when they are *comparatively* correct as when they are absolutely so.

By comparatively correct I mean that the error is so regulated in births and deaths, that the difference is the same as if there had been no mistake. Thus if out of 90 births 82 are reported and eight omitted, and out of 70 deaths 62 are reported and eight omitted, the resultant addition to the population is correct in spite of the mistakes. A comparison of the reported vital statistics for the past ten years with the census figures tends to show that this comparative accuracy has been attained to an extent which enables the sanitary authorities to give in an average district almost as entirely correct a statement of the population existing in any intercensal year as if their figures were absolutely correct. In appendix No. XVIII is given a detailed comparison of the population as calculated from that of 1881, by adding births and deducting deaths with that ascertained by the present census.

The net result is as follows :—

Population calculated by vital statistics.			Population ascertained by census.			Excess by vital statistics.			Percentage of excess.		
Total.	Male.	Female.	Total.	Male.	Female.	Total.	Male.	Female.	Total.	Male.	Female.
47,063,933	24,395,093	22,668,840	46,905,085	24,303,601	22,601,484	158,848	91,492	67,356	·339	·377	·298

The Sanitary Commissioner's figures do not of course allow for excess of emigration during the decade, so that the excess of 158,848 shown implies that the results by vital statistics are about 100,000 short of entire resultant accuracy; that is, that on the whole deaths are better reported than births. The correctness of the result in itself implies that the error in the record of births is one-sixth less correct than that of deaths, as the number of births being larger than those of deaths, an exactly proportionate error would show an excess in population. For the province as a whole no greater accuracy so far as this special purpose is concerned can be considered possible than that now attained.

144. **Reasons for the variation from census figures in certain districts.**—In regard to individual districts also the emigration and immigration being taken into account, the accuracy of the Sanitary Commissioner's results is no less marked. To take a few instances ;—the following are the districts in the North-Western Provinces which show the largest deficit in the Sanitary Commissioner's figures as compared with those of census, a deficit explained in each case by the fact that the census included a considerable immigrant population :—

District.	Males.	Females.
Debra Dún	16,662	6,760
Muttra	15,515	14,519
Cawnpore	15,843	8,692
Jhánsi	34,646	26,813
Taráí	18,594	13,686

In Jhánsi 42,638 persons were transferred from Gwalior with Jhánsi city, and a number of villages and the large cantonment is almost entirely new.

In Muttra as we have seen there was a considerable influx of pilgrims on the census night. The migration into Dehra Dún, Cawnpore and the Tarái is well known. Again, the districts in the North-Western Provinces showing the largest excess in the Sanitary Commissioner's figures are those in the Agra Division and Bundelkhand, from which as we have seen there must from agricultural distress have been a considerable emigration, and those in the eastern districts in which it is known emigration to a great percentage does exist.

The figures for the Himalayan districts are less correct; the registration there, as the extremely low birth and death-rates show, is very far out indeed. The age tables for those districts show that they should be fully as high as, if not higher than, for the rest of the province. In Oudh, Fyzabad, Lucknow, Gonda and Bahraich are probably correct in showing excess of immigration, but as shown it is probably too large. The death registration in these and all other Oudh districts, except Unao and Partábgarh, is probably better than that for births. Partábgarh in showing emigration 19,843 men and immigration of 1,563 women is probably very near entire correctness. The result, as a whole, of the comparison has been to show that calculations requiring an estimate of population for intercensal years may safely, and should, be based on the Sanitary Commissioner's returns: allowances for migration can in general be made with comparative accuracy when it is necessary.

145. **The death rate as shown by comparison of Census figures.**—The construction from the census returns of a life table to show the death-rate and expectation of life accurately for each year of life requires the application of statistical processes so elaborate as to require an expert to employ them. I am indebted to Mr. E. J. Kitts for the suggestion of the following simple method of calculating an approximate death-rate for periods of ten years.

The method employed is founded on the hypothesis quoted at page 464 of Farr's vital statistics, under which it is assumed that if *s* deaths occur during a given period they take place at *s* equal intervals. The periods adopted must necessarily be decades as the imperfections of the census age tables prevent any deductions of value from being made on quinquennial periods. Deduction of the death-rates on the method suggested by Mr. Kitts begins with the age period 10—19; for the earlier period reference must be made to the recorded deaths of male children registered under the Infanticide Act. The totals of the population so recorded, the deaths and the percentages of deaths on population for all years for which figures have been published and for the first decade of life are given in the Appendix No. XIX. It was overlooked by Mr. E. White at last census in dealing with these figures, but pointed out by the author of the life table published in the Census Report for India, that the relations between the registered population and the deaths for a given age-period are unusual. The births during a given year are considered to be the population under one for that year, and the whole of the children surviving at the end of the official year are passed on into the next age-period without reference to what their exact ages are; similarly all children surviving at the end of the second official year are passed into the third age-period. The result is that the deaths shown against the population for the age-period under one are not the deaths during a life-period of a year but during an average life-period of six months, children on an average passing into the second age-period at that age. Under the hypothesis quoted the death-rate for the first year of life would be calculated on the deaths shown against the age-period 0 and half the deaths for the age-period 1 year. Similarly the death-rate for the second year of life could be half that shown for age-period 1 year and half that for age-period 2 years, and so on. The errors so introduced would be considerable in the first year of life but gradually less in later years. For our present purpose, to find the death rate for the age-period 0—9, the addition of half the deaths shown against age 10 to that for the first ten years of life will give a death-rate practically accurate. It is therefore 66·39 as shown in the appendix plus an allowance for half the deaths shown in age-period 10 to 11, in all 66·9. For later age-periods I transcribe Mr. Kitts' suggestions to show the method employed in obtaining the death rates to be quoted :—

"Deduct from 0—9 males (1881) the 10—19 males (1891) : this will give the total number of 0—9 males living at the last census and who have died in ten years. These deaths are spread over a life-period of 20 years, *e.g.*, a child born on 16th February 1881 and who died on 18th February 1881 would be in the 1881 census and not in the 1891 census : his age would be 0 : also a child born on 18th February 1871 and who died on 25th February 1891, *i.e.*, age 20, would be in the 0—9 children of 1881 census, and would not be in the 1891 census. If these deaths (which we may call D.) are distributed equally according to the hypothesis on page 464, half will belong to the 0—9 age-period and half to the 10—19 age-period." "Then deduct from 10—19 males 1881 the 20—29 males 1891, and call the remainder (deaths) D^2 : of D^2 half will belong to the 10—19 age-period and half to the 20—29 age-period, and so on : from 40—49 males 1881 deduct the 50—59 males 1891 and the remainder D^5 will be half deaths belonging to 40—49 age-period and half to 50—59 age-period. From 50 *and upwards* 1881 deduct 60 *and upwards* 1891 = D^6 all belonging to 50 and upward age-period."

Hence mortality for 10—19 age-period = $\frac{1}{2}(D+D_2)$

" " 20—29 ... = $\frac{1}{2}(D_2+D_3)$

" " 30—39 ... = $\frac{1}{2}(D^3+D^4)$

" " 40—49 ... = $\frac{1}{2}(D^4+D^5)$

" " 50 and upwards ... = $\frac{1}{2}\ D_5+D_6$

The rate of mortality for each period is calculated on the average population living in that age-period between the two census years ; that is, half the sum of the population of the age-period at both censuses. In this way the figures for the North-Western Provinces only give the death-rates compared in the following table with those calculated from the Sanitary Commissioner's returns for the past ten years on the average population. The figures for Oudh have not been included, because, as the age tables show, the disturbing effect of emigration on certain age-periods is much greater than in the North-Western Provinces, and because, as already pointed out, there is reason to believe there were omissions in the returns for Oudh at last census.

Age-periods.	Male Death-rate per thousand deduced as above.	Male Death-rate by Sanitary Commissioner's returns.
0—9	66·9	62·67
10—19	15·73	9·2
20—29	14·51	14·4
30—39	21·86	18·02
40—49	34·97	26·79
50 and over...	69·50	55·18
All ages	37·38	32·4

The life-rates now deducted are higher to a considerable extent than those calculated from the Sanitary Commissioner's figures for every life-period except one ; that one 20—29 is the one in which they differ most from the rates in Hardie's life table, which shows 21·1 as the death-rate for the mean age of the period. The death-rates for the age-periods are liable to disturbance by accidental causes, but are accurate enough to indicate the probable deficiency in the Sanitary Commissioner's rates. The resultant death-rate for all males is derived from statistics in which the disturbing causes counterbalance to a considerable extent, and the result is therefore probably a nearly correct estimate of the actual death-rate of the province. It is five per thousand higher than that which appears from the Sanitary Commissioner's figures.

The disturbances in the female age-periods are so great and the omissions from those age-periods so irregular that it would be absolutely useless to attempt to work out death-rates for females in this rough way from the census returns. The infanticide figures, too, here cease to be of value, as the death-rate shown is admitted to be too high for the province as a whole. The elaborate calculations made at last census tend to show that the death-rate for females bears to that for males very nearly the relations shown by the rates shown in the Sanitary Commissioner's returns ; that is, they are higher at the periods in which females begin to bear children and lower at other age periods.

146. **The birth-rate.**—The minimum average birth-rate may be deducted from the death-rate. It is higher than the death-rate by the annual proportion of increase per 1,000 ; that is, for the North-West Provinces 4·4. This would make the all-over birth-rate 41·78 against 38·1 shown by the Sanitary Commissioner's figures. 41·78 is, however, as much below the mark as the increase in population has been decreased by means of emigration. Probably a safer estimate of the birth-rate may be obtained by assuming that it is as much higher than the Sanitary Commissioner's birth-rate as the deduced death-rate is above his death-rates at this rate the actual birth-rate would be 43 per 1,000.

Chapter VI.—THE RELIGIONS OF THE PROVINCE.

147. **The distribution by religion.**—With the exception of 22 persons for whom the column for religion was left blank, the population of the province was according to the census distributed between 11 religions; of these four were professed by less than 1,000 persons, of whom none except the three deists are natives of these provinces.

Abstract No. 47.

Religion.	Total.	Males.	Females.
Hindu ...	40,380,168	20,954,923	19,425,245
Musalmán ...	6,346,651	3,243,922	3,102,729
Jain ...	84,601	45,624	38,977
Christian ...	58,441	37,294	21,147
Arya ...	22,053	12,164	9,889
Sikh ...	11,343	8,080	3,263
Buddhist ...	1,387	1,329	58
Parsi ...	342	209	133
Jew ...	60	33	27
Brahmo ...	14	9	5
Deist ...	3	1	2
Unspecified ...	22	13	9
Total ...	46,905,085	24,303,601	22,601,484

148. **Religions entirely foreign.**—The Parsis consist entirely of immigrants from Bombay employed as shopkeepers or traders of sorts in most of the districts of the provinces.

The Jews, few or none of them European, are also shopkeepers, less widely spread throughout the provinces, and most of them in the two districts of Fyzabad and Gorakhpur where they have to some degree settled down.

Brahmos are entirely Bengalis. The movement has never had any disciples amongst the natives of these provinces, and neither now nor at last census has it apparently been important even amongst the Bengali immigrants.

149. **Buddhists.**—Two more of the religions enumerated, though professed by a few persons permanently resident in the provinces, can be briefly disposed of. Buddhists number 1,387 persons in British districts and 107 in Tehri Garhwál; all, except 112 are men and all except the comparatively small numbers shown in Kumaun Garhwál, Tehri-Garhwál and possibly a few of those in Lucknow, are Burmese convicts imprisoned in the jails of the province. The remainder are Bhotiyas, residents either of Tibet or of the upper valleys of the Himalayas in which some trace of Buddhism still lingers. A considerable proportion of the persons who enjoy the monopoly of Indian trade with Tibet are permanent residents of the districts of Kumaun and Garhwál and the Garhwál State. They are considerably more numerous than the Buddhists shown as enumerated in these districts, as for the most part whilst on the Indian side of the passes they profess to be Hindus and Rájput in caste, whilst in Tibet they are strict Buddhists. In the Hindu sect lists 1,649 of them (558 males and 1,091 females) all in Kumaun and Garhwál, appear as worshippers of Buddha (Baudh) or as Lámáists. The mixed form of Buddhism professed by these persons is discribed by Atkinson in the Himalayan Gazetteer as existing in Nipal, but as the returns show and, as is, I believe, well known to District

Officers in Kumaun, it is well recognized in British districts also, although there is not a single Buddhist temple within their area. Their religion is described as a curious admixture of the Buddhist doctrines of the Mahayána and the worship of those Brahmanical deities to whom the later Tantras are devoted (Devi in her more horrible forms) and of indigenous and other Saivite deities. In Buddhist temples in Nipal, images of Kali, Hanuman, Ganesh and Ravana are found side by side with those dedicated to Śakya and other Budhas and Bodhi-sattwas. In this mixed religion is to be found the only trace of Buddhism now left in the sacred country of the Buddhists.

150. **Sikhs.**—Sikhs or persons who call themselves Sikhs ennumerated in these provinces number 11,343, of whom 8,080 are men and 3,263 women. The great majority of the genuine Sikhs in the provinces are employed in the army or in the police force. In the western districts, Hinduism of the Nanakshahi sect is prevalent, and it is probable that many adherents of this sect have recorded themselves as Sikhs, although in fact they are altogether outside the Sikh community. Sikhs are to some extent settlers in these provinces as grantees or immigrants, but Sikhism is in no sense a religion of the province and requires no further reference.

151. **Hinduism.**—There remain as religions which have to a greater or less extent a hold upon the province, Hinduism, Muhammadanism, Jainism, Christianity and Arya Samájism. The proportions borne by the adherents of each of these religions to the total population are shown in the marginal Statement. Hinduism, the indigenous religion of the provinces, still has a firm hold over the vast majority of the residents. Whether all the persons recorded as Hindus in these provinces are really so, in the strictest sense of the word, is not a question to which the census classification gives any answer.

Abstract No. 48,—Showing the distribution of 10,000 persons according to religion

Religion.	Per. 10,000 of total population.	Per. 10,000 males.	Per. 10,000 females.
Hinduism ...	8,609	8,622	8,595
Muhammadanism ...	1,353	1,335	1,373
Jainism ...	18	19	17
Christianity ...	12	15	9
Arya Samájism ...	5	5	4

It was considered inexpedient to attempt any definition of Hinduism, and the instructions to enumerators simply directed that all persons should be recorded as of the religion to which they themselves stated they belonged. The result has been to show that the antagonism with which the animistic religions regard certain of the leading tenets of Hinduism in those parts of India in which they still have a firm hold, has disappeared even from the wildest parts of these provinces, and that all who do not belong to the well-defined folds of the other religions already named, consider themselves Hindus. This result is no doubt due in the main to the facility with which Hinduism includes or at least tolerates all beliefs which do not directly deny Hinduism, but it is to some extent also due to the unconcealed antagonism of monotheistic to idolatrous religions. The Chamárs of the Gangetic plain and the wild tribes of Mirzapur alike preserve themselves free from the influence of perhaps the most universal feature of Hinduism—reverence for the cow; but in the presence of Muhammadanism and Christianity, which condemn with equal freedom the cow worshipper and the ghost worshipper, they consider themselves Hindus and are admitted by strict Hindus to be within the pale of Hinduism. Hinduism as manifested in the sect columns of the census schedules is the subject of a separate chapter. The features in which Hinduism in regard to the proportion of the sexes or conjugal condition presents peculiarities, are referred to in the chapters on these subjects.

It is unnecessary to refer in any great detail to the distribution of Hinduism in the provinces. It includes the majority of the population of every district and in Garhwál and Tehri Garhwál includes over 99 per cent. It is strongest in the Himalayas, Bundelkhand and the Agra and Benares Divisions. It is weakest in Meerut and Rohilkhand and along the foot of the Himalayas. As Hinduism and Muhammadanism include between them over 99 per cent, of the population in almost all the districts of the provinces, its comparative strength may be inferred from the map giving the distribution of Muhammadanism.

152. **Muhammadanism.**—Muhammadanism has been in contact and in conflict with Hinduism in these provinces for 900 years. Its progress has been considerable, in that there are now 6,346,651 Muhammadans in the provinces, of whom probably not more than one-third have a claim in any way valid to be descended from the immigrant Muhammadan conquerors. As compared, however, with the progress made by either Christianity or Muhammadanism in any other country, where in similar circumstances they were in contact with polytheistic religions, it has been altogether inconsiderable. In other countries the monotheistic and proselytizing religions have within a far shorter time altogether obliterated the idolatrous or animistic religions which preceded them. In the North-Western Provinces they still, in spite of considerable assistance from immigration, include less than 14 per cent. of the total population. This difference must, I believe, be attributed partly to the tolerant principles of Hinduism and partly to the influence of the caste system. Hinduism, unlike the Paganism of Europe, offers no direct and intolerant opposition to other religions. It accepts them as true and suitable for people who were born to profess them, and in this way averts from itself the added intensity of attack which is attracted by religions which give condemnation for condemnation and persecution for persecution. The influence of the caste system has probably been still greater. Conversion to another religion implies in general caste-death and the severing of all social relations with the closest relatives of the convert. In a few castes this has not been entirely so. There is much reason to believe that amongst the lower classes of Hindus the caste system as at present constituted, is a comparatively late institution, and that in all probability its influence was far less when first these classes were exposed to the influence of Muhammadanism. Amongst these lower classes therefore Muhammadanism has had its greatest success. Again, amongst Rájputs, Gujars and several other western castes, conversion to Muhammadanism has never implied such absolute rejection from the caste system as in other castes, and as a consequence each of these castes shows an important proportion of Muhammadans.

Abstract No. 49, Showing for each district the distribution of 10,000 persons by religion.

	District.	10,000 total population.			
		Hindu.	Musalmán.	Jain.	Christian.
1	Dehra Dún	8,547	1,184	14	163
2	Sahéranpur	6,668	3,241	61	19
3	Muzaffarnagar	7,020	2,833	121	2
4	Meerut	7,527	2,278	118	40
5	Bulandshahr	8,053	1,884	18	2
6	Aligarh	8,801	1,153	24	4
	Total, Meerut Division ...	7,673	2,214	67	20
7	Muttra	9,060	778	33	12
8	Agra	8,772	1,045	134	47
9	Farukhabad	8,808	1,158	12	10
10	Mainpuri	9,375	545	75	2
11	Etáwah	9,384	582	29	2
12	Etah	8,872	1,040	70	7
	Total, Agra Division ...	9,022	888	62	15
13	Bareilly	7,592	2,356	...	50
14	Bijnor	6,563	8,372	12	11
15	Budaun	8,353	1,601	...	27
16	Moradabad	6,557	3,398	8	28
17	Sháhjahánpur...	8,569	1,407	...	14
18	Pilibhít	8,285	1,700	...	8
	Total, Rohilkhand Division ...	7,574	2,380	4	25
19	Cawnpore	9,127	839	3	25
20	Fatehpur	8,895	1,102	1	1
21	Bánda	9,416	576	4	1
22	Hamírpur	9,348	648	2	...
23	Allahabad	8,866	1,290	4	38
24	Jhánsi	9,302	563	61	46
25	Jalaun	9,351	643	4	2
26	Lalitpur	9,431	217	348	2
	Total, Allahabad Division ...	9,071	881	24	19
27	Benares	9,021	959	1	15
28	Mirzapur	9,342	648	2	4
29	Jaunpur	9,076	919	...	1
30	Gházipur	9,041	953	...	5
31	Ballia	9,294	704	...	...
	Total, Benares Division ...	9,158	832	1	5
32	Gorakhpur	8,988	1,007	...	4
33	Basti	8,456	1,544	...	...
34	Azamgarh	8,695	1,305	...	1
	Total, Gorakhpur Division ...	8,764	1,234	...	2
35	Kumaun	9,757	212	...	28
36	Garhwál	9,897	88	...	14
37	Taráí	6,417	3,572	2	1
	Total, Kumaun Division ...	8,209	768	...	19
	Total, N.-W. Provinces ...	8,572	1,380	24	13
38	Lucknow	7,816	2,084	10	75
39	Unao	9,201	796	...	1
40	Rae Bareli	9,173	830	...	1
41	Sitapur	2,527	1,466	2	7
42	Hardoi	8,969	1,031	...	1
43	Kheri	8,685	1,306	...	6
	Total, Lucknow Division ...	8,764	1,218	2	13
44	Fyzabad	8,841	1,137	1	10
45	Gonda	8,588	1,408	...	2
46	Bahraich	8,297	1,698	...	1
47	Sultánpur	8,912	1,086	...	...
48	Partábgarh	9,000	997	1	1
49	Bara Banki	8,344	1,644	9	1
	Total, Fyzabad Division ...	8,658	1,336	2	3
	Total, Oudh ...	8,704	1,281	2	7
	Total, N.-W. P. and Oudh ...	8,610	1,858	18	12
50	Rámpur	5,623	4,374	3	1
51	Tehri Garhwál	9,938	59	1	...
	Total, Native States ...	6,934	3,060	3	1

[To face Page 144.

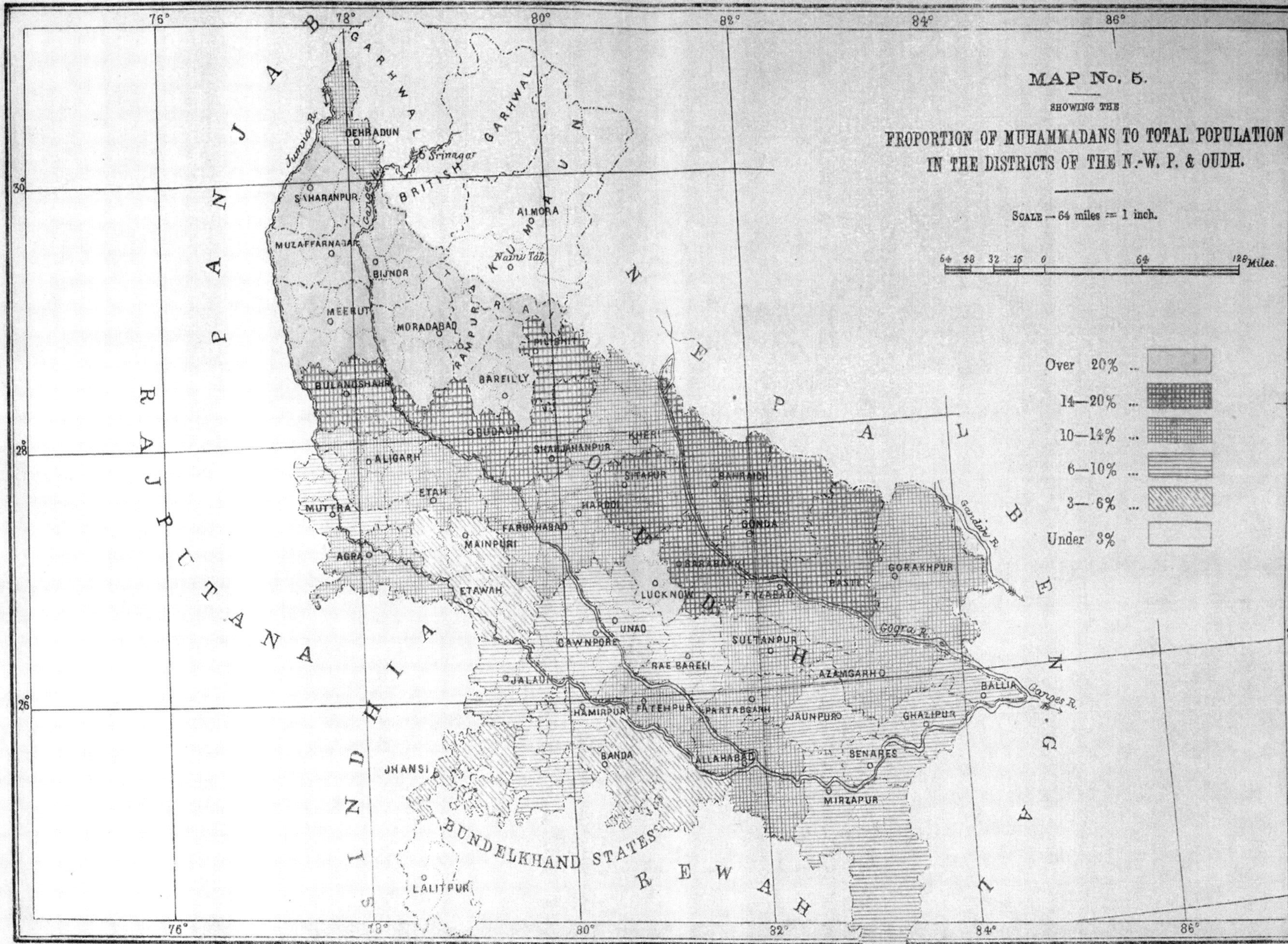

153.—**The distribution of Muhammadanism.**—The distribution of Muhammadanism throughout the provinces is shown in the accompanying map, and in the abstract number 49 on the opposite page showing the proportion to the total population of the adherents of each religion. Its strength varies from 44 per cent. of the total population in Rámpur State to ·6 per cent. in the Garhwál State. It, as the map will show, is far stronger in the half of the provinces which lies nearest the Himalayas. It is weak in the districts on the Ganges to the east, in Bundelkhand and in a central strip from Rae Bareli to Muttra. It is unimportant in the hills.

The reason for these differences one has not to go far to seek. The strong hold of Muhammadanism is in the upper Doab and Rohilkhand, where the invaders settled down not only as conquering rulers but as, to a large extent proprietors of the conquered soil. Further east than Rohilkhand the population of the sub-Himalayan districts is largely new ; the migrating population, cut adrift from home ties and home influences, was greatly exposed to the influence of Muhammadanism, which accordingly has made unusual progress amongst them, even where as in Basti the ruling power has always remained Hindu. Elsewhere the progress made by Muhammadanism varies with the extent of their influence when they ruled the country. Into the Himalayas they never penetrated. In Bundelkhand the intractable Bundelas, aided by the unattractive nature of their country, kept Muhammadan power at a minimum, until in late years the Bánda Nawábs established themselves in that district. From Rae Bareli to Muttra strong and united Rájput clans the proudest and purest in race in the provinces, presented a firm and successful front against Muhammadan encroachment.

154. **Local features of Muhammadanism.**—Certain local features of Muhammadanism which attracted attention in the census deserve notice. They are, 1st the comparative absence of any genuine knowledge of what Muhammadanism is in the lowest class of the population which has called itself Muhammadan, and 2nd the influence still exerted by Hinduism on converts of those classes in which forcible conversion was most common.

Almost all the wandering outcast tribes Nats, Banjaras, Bengalis, Bawariya, &c., and the impure castes of sweepers and Doms,—show a considerable proportion of Muhammadans, but it may be stated with confidence that their Muhammadanism is altogether nominal. They are circumcised and they have ceased to intermarry with Hindus of their castes, but in all other respects they are ignorant of the Muhammadan creed and conform to the precepts of the Muhammadan social law only in refusing the use of the flesh of the pig as food. Many of them continue to worship and sacrifice to Debi or their former low-caste gods, whilst most of them are so ignorant of Muhammadanism as to imagine that in worshipping the five Pirs or some other Muhammadan saint, they are conforming to Muhammadanism. Such Muhammadans, asked to what sect they belonged were of course unable to reply. The less instructed enumerator proceeded to question him as directed for Hindus as to what deity he worshipped, and hence in every district we have entered a list of Muhammadan deities inconsistent with any knowledge of their faith by the persons enumerated.

The list for one tahsíl of Gorakhpur may be quoted in illustration. It is as follows, omitting correct entries or those in which the column was mistaken :—

Imam Hussain.	Chausatti.	Kalka.
Mian Sahib.	Ghózi Mian.	Kalka Phulmati.
Barepir.	Satnami.	Muhammad Sahib.
Panchopir.	Sahja Bi.	

The leaning towards Hinduism amongst converts of a higher class is most marked amongst Rájputs. The great majority of Rájput Muhammadans, though forcibly converted by the threat of ejectment from their land, are now genuine members of their new faith and only acknowledge their Hindu origin by keeping up on certain social occasions some intercourse with their unconverted relatives. Others, however, there are who, though Muhammadan in name, strive to preserve as far as possible the forms and customs of Hinduism. They keep their Hindu names, only substituting the Muhammadan title of Khán for that of Singh. They shave off the beard, cut the hair of the head in the Hindu fashion leaving the top-knot untouched and bathe and cook in conformity with Hindu custom. In matters of creed they are probably to some extent Muhammadan, in matters of form they are Hindus.

155. **Muhammadan sects, Shias and Sunnis.**—The list of genuine Muhammadan sects (omitting entry of all entries made through ignorance and above referred to) is not an extensive one. The detailed figures are given on the margin and the district figures in Appendix No. XX.

Abstract No. 50.

	Total.	Males.	Females.
Sunni	6,049,892	3,095,426	2,954,466
Shia	212,853	103,405	109,448
Ahl-i-Hadis ...	312	119	193
Hanfi	11	9	2
Unspecified ...	83,583	44,963	38,620
Total ...	6,346,651	3,243,922	3,102,729

Sunnis are everywhere most numerous, the numbers of Shias being considerable only in Lucknow, where the Oudh royal family and their relatives and dependents were Shias, and in those districts in which Sayyids are most common. The essential differences between the two sects and the methods of manifesting these differences which make the clashing of sects a danger to the public peace are simply but vividly expressed by a Sunni in the following extract from the Kanoon-i-Islam.

"The Shiahs are likewise termed Tushiah, Muzhubi, Eerani and Teen-Earei."

"The Sunnis are also called Sunnut-Jama-at, Tussunun, and Char-Eari. Between these two sects exists the most inveterate enmity."

"The Shiahs, out of hatred, call the Sunnis Kharji (*i.e.*, Schismatics), because, as they opprobriously affirm, they reject His High Excellency Amir-ul-Mominin Ali, the son of Abu-talib (may God reward him !) So far is this from being the case that all the Sunnis place the utmost faith in His Excellency Ali-un-Murtuza. It is from pure motives of enmity and reproach that they assert such a thing. Moreover, they call them Kafirs or infidels. Independently of the Tassununs being unjustly denominated Kharjis (or Schismatics), there are some real ones of that description, which may be classed under a third head, and unfortunately they are so from their mother's womb, and they utterly abhor His Excellency Ali-un-Murtuza. Therefore, to nickname Sunnis Kharjis, clearly evinces a spirit of ill-will, and a wish to slander. The Sunnis, on the other hand, maliciously term the Shiahs, Rafzis, (*i.e.*, heretics, rejectors or abusers); because they reject the following three companions of the prophet, *viz.*—

"*First.*—His Highness Amir-ul-Muminin Abu Bakar Siddiq, the son of Quhafa (may God reward him!), His Highness the Prophet's (the blessing and peace of God, &c.,) father-in-law, the father of Bibi A-ay-sha (may God reward her!).

"*Second.*—His Highness Amir-ul-Muminin Omar son of Khuttab (may God reward them!), also the prophet's (the blessing, &c.,) father-in-law, and the father of Bibi Hufusa.

"*Third.*—His Highness Amir-ul-Muminin Usman, the son of Afan (may God reward them), His Highness the Prophet's (the blessing, &c.,) son-in-law, and the husband of Bibi Rugia. On the demise of Rugia, the prophet gave him in marriage a second daughter named Oom-e-Kulsum; and owing to this circumstance, Muhammad Mustaffa (the blessing, &c.,) named Usman, Zin Nur-rain, signifying be thou master of two lights (*i.e.*, lights of his eyes) *alias* daughters."

"The Shiahs consider the three abovementioned worthies, and many of the other companions of the prophet, as wicked men, and hold them in the utmost contempt; and in speaking of them, make use of such mean expressions as does not become me to mention. Some of them, in their arithmetical calculations, never utter the number four; and others; instead of using a country cot (or bed) with four legs (called charpai, which means literally four-legged), have one with six, and named it ch'hay-pai (or six legged). Others again, should they ever have allowed the word four inadvertently to escape their tongue, instantly go and gargle their throats; or in meeting a Sunni, should they have kissed his hands (which they do agreeably to their mode of saluting a friend), they perform wazu (or ablutions) immediately after. In some countries they write the names of the three companions on a piece of paper and wear it on the soles of their feet, as the most marked token of disrespect and contempt that they can show towards them."

"Real Rafzis and Kharjis are guilty of many base acts." Among various others, it is customary with the former to celebrate in the month Baqrid, a feast called Gudir, on which occasion they form three hollow images of dough composed of wheaten flour, and fill their cavities with honey; then, using severe terms of abuse, they thrust a knife, first into the body of the one they have named Abu Bakar Siddiq; and, in like manner they stab the second, called Umar; and lastly, poor Usman suffers the same fate; and while the honey flows from the wounded bodies of these dolls, the Shiahs sip a little of it as emblematic of drinking the blood of their enemies; and cut a small bit of the paste, in allusion to the devouring their flesh in rage. The fact is, the Shiahs assert that His Highness Muhammad Mustaffa (the blessing! &c., before his death bestowed the Khilafat (or sovereignty) on Ali; but that immediately after his demise, the other three companions convened a meeting of the nobles and grandees, and with the aid and assistance of men of talents and worth among the Arabs, assigned the right of succession, first, to Siddiq-e-Akbar; then to Umar-e-Adil; next to Usman-e-Gunni; and lastly, to His Highness Ali. Whereas, His Highness Ali was the first legal successor to the royal dignity; and it is for this reason that the Tushiahs hold the three usurpers (as they call them) in such abhorrence."

For the less instructed of Muhammadans and especially amongst Sunnis, the difference between the two sects is little understood, and the enumerator had in general to ascertain the sect by a question as to how the hands were placed in prayer. Sunnis pray with one hand placed over the other on the front of the body, Shias with both hands depressed by the sides.

156. **Ahl-i-Hadis.**—Of the remaining two entries in the abstract above, that of the Ahl-i-Hadis is separate from both Sunnis and Shias. The earlier instructions referred to them by the name of Wahabis by which, after the name of the father of their founder, they are more generally known.

Certain members of the sect in the North-Western Provinces petitioned that the use of the name was not recognized by them and that they should be described as Ahl-i-Hadis or the people of the traditions. This name accordingly appears in general in the schedules. The sect is not now, so far as can be gathered from the schedules, of importance in these provinces, although it was from the North-Western Provinces that Sayyid Ahmad Sháh, of Rae Bareli, the founder of the colony of Wahabi fanatics on the North-West frontier, led his following.

It is more than probable that, as some suspicion of disloyalty to the ruling power popularly attached to certain communities in which the principles of the sect prevail, many adherents of the sect have preferred to conceal the fact, and that the few entries made in the schedules are by leading and well-instructed men who have declared their recognition of the fact that the Government, as not denying them full religious liberty, is one which may lawfully be obeyed by Musalmáns.

The following account of the tenets of the Ahl-i-Hadis is given in the Panjáb Census Report of 1881.

"The Wahabis are Musalmán purists. They accept the six books of traditions as collected by the Sunnis, but reject the subsequent glosses of the father's and the voice of the church, and claim liberty of conscience and the right of private interpretation. They insist strongly upon the unity of God, which doctrine they say has been endangered by the reverence paid by the ordinary Musalmán to Mahomet, to the Imams and to Saints; and forbid the offering of prayer to any prophet, priest or saint, even as a mediator with the Almighty. They condemn the sepulchral honours paid to holy men, and illumination of, visits to, and prostration before, their shrines, and even go so far as to destroy the domes erected over their remains. They call the rest of the Muhammadans Mashrik, or those who associate another with God, and strenuously proclaim that Mahomet was a mere mortal man. They disallow the smoking of tobacco as lawful, and discountenance the use of rosaries or beads. Apparently they insist much upon the approaching appearance of the last Imam Mahdi preparatory to the dissolution of the world. Politically their most important and obnoxious opinion is that they are bound to wage war against all infidels; but it is doubtful whether the Wahabis within the British territory are as fanatical in this respect as their brethren elsewhere. The orthodox deny them the title of Musalmáns."

It may be noted that the opinion just quoted has been expressly repudiated by the modern leaders of the Ahl-i-Hadis. It has been declared by them that they are bound to wage war only against infidels who refuse liberty of conscience to Muhammadans.

The remaining sect entry for Muhammadans is that of one of the great Sunni Schools of doctrine, that founded by Abu Hanifa, known throughout India as the Imam-Azam. Sunnis of the province where they do belong to any particular school are in general Hanifites, but as in general only the main sect was entered, record of adherence to the school is rare.

157. **Increase in Muhammadans.**—Muhammadans in the provinces have increased by 7·15 per cent. during the past decade, Hindus, ncluding Aryans, by only 6·17 per cent. This higher rate of increase or lower rate of decrease has extended throughout every division in the provinces except Kumaun and Benares and through thirty-two out of forty-nine districts. Details as to districts are given in the statement showing proportions of variation of each religion on the following pages.

Abstract No. 51, Showing the percentage of variation by religion.

Serial number.	Districts.	Percentage of variation in Hindus.	Musalmáns.	Jains.	Christians.	Remarks.
	1	2	3	4	5	
1	Dehra Dún	+ 14·77	+ 20·38	+ 74·63	+ 35·46	
2	Sahâranpur	+ 2·18	+ 2·17	− 8·83	+ 10·09	
3	Muzaffarnagar	+ 1·41	+ 2·41	+ ·86	+ 135·19	
4	Meerut	+ 4·99	+ 7·57	− ·44	+ 83 77	
5	Bulandshahr	+ 2 23	+ 2·03	+ 32·78	+ 82·60	
6	Aligarh	+ 1·95	+ 2·56	+ 5·47	+ 60·89	
	Total, Meerut Division ..	+ 3·14	+ 3·90	− ·09	+ 31·86	
7	Muttra	+ 5·68	+ 7·87	+ 50·75	+ 150·29	
8	Agra	+ 2 49	+ 4·63	+ 17·30	− 4·78	
9	Farukhabad	− 6·02	− 1·79	+ 28·75	+ ·25	
10	Mainpuri	− 4·65	− 7·85	− 16·05	− 9.59	
11	Etáwah	+ ·53	+ 2·14	+ 38·73	− 15·19	
12	Etah	− 7 65	− 4·98	− 4·02	+ 344·44	
	Total, Agra Division ...	− 1 72	+ ·22	+ 8·43	+ 9·66	
13	Bareilly	+ ·09	+ 2·96	∞	+ 120 27	
14	Bijnor	+ 7·75	+ 13·59	+ 37·66	+ 20·37	
15	Budaun	+ ·77	+ 6·92	+ 43·13	+ 735·28	
16	Moradabad	+ ·67	+ 4·16	+ 75·48	+ 76·19	
17	Sháhjahánpur	+ 7·06	+ 7·53	∞	− 5·68	
18	Pilibhít	+ 6·66	+ 10·60	∞	+ 1927·78	
	Total, Rohilkhand Division ...	+ 3·16	+ 6·77	+ 56·59	+ 118·27	
19	Cawnpore	+ 1·75	+ 9·09	+ 264·04	− 5·13	
20	Fatehpur...	+ 2·06	+ 3·83	+ 43·24	− 19·32	
21	Bánda	+ 1·10	+ ·09	+ 5·58	− 73·38	
22	Hamírpur	+ 1·29	+ ·16	∞	+ 194·12	
23	Allahabad	+ 5·46	+ 2·38	+ 68·55	− 2·40	
24	Jhánsi	+ 20·34	+ 67·66	+ 10·18	+ 178.07	
25	Jalaun	− 5·54	− ·64	+ 29·23	+ 378·57	
26	Lalitpur	+ 10·68	+ 10·77	− 4·82	+ 152·00	
	Total, Allahabad Division ...	+ 8·61	+ 5·36	+ 3·53	+ 7·66	
27	Benares	+ 8·76	− 1·06	+ 1871·42	− 22·85	
28	Mirzapur	+ 2·19	+ 2·35	+ 40 5	− 33·60	
29	Jaunpur	+ 4·79	+ 2 46	∞	− 22·5	
30	Ghâzipur	+ 6·63	+ 3·15	∞	− 11·11	
31	Ballia	+ 2·42	− 4·28	...	− 53·13	
	Total, Benares Division ...	+ 3·96	+ ·82	+ 118·36	− 23·13	
32	Gorakhpur	+ 14·28	+ 15·48	∞	+ 26 05	
33	Basti	+ 9·55	+ 9·37	...	− 15·38	
34	Azamgarh	+ 7·86	+ 6 84	...	− 3·89	
	Total, Gorakhpur Division ...	+ 11·26	+ 10·84	∞	+ 20·96	
35	Kumaun	+ 14·51	+ 6·29	∞	− 83·09	
36	Garhwál	+ 17·61	+ 73·57	− 97 10	+ 186·78	
37	Tarái	+ 2·42	+ ·03	+ 14·70	+ 109·09	
	Total, Kumaun Division ...	+ 13·95	+ 2·79	− 55·34	− 16·97	
	Total, N.-W. Provinces ...	+ 4·46	+ 5·26	+ 4·85	+ 27·26	

Abstract No. 51—(concluded.)

Serial number.	Districts.	Percentage of variation in				Remarks.
		Hindus.	Musalmáns.	Jains.	Christians.	
	1	2	3	4	5	
38	Lucknow...	+12·03	+ 7·64	+ 135·10	− 8·14	
39	Unao	+ 5·68	+10·55	∞	+ 116·33	
40	Rae Bareli	+ 8·71	+11·03	+ 76·92	+ 17·89	
41	Sitapur	+11·96	+13·60	− 11·03	+ 61·85	
42	Hardoi	+12·81	+11·79	+1200·00	+ 122·67	
43	Kheri	+ 7·84	+13·78	∞	+ 27·20	
	Total, Lucknow Division ...	+ 9·77	+11·32	+ 76·14	+ ·57	
44	Fyzabad	+12·70	+11·18	+3925·00	− 3·91	
45	Gonda	+13·73	+21·88	...	+ 55·97	
46	Bahraich	+13·00	+18·53	+ 29·73	+ 110·17	
47	Sultánpur	+11·99	+15·09	− 100·00	− 3·64	
48	Partábgarh	+ 7·44	+ 8·21	∞	+ 60·42	
49	Bara Banki	+10·36	+ 9·02	+ 8·52	+ 88·46	
	Total, Fyzabad Division ...	+11·69	+14·50	+ 37·24	+ 12·41	
	Total, Oudh ...	+10·79	+13·08	+ 52·00	+ 2·78	
	Total, N.-W. P. & Oudh ...	+ 6·11	+ 7·15	+ 5·81	+ 22·61	
50	Rámpur	+ 2·27	+ ·91	∞	∞	
51	Tehri Garhwál	+20·59	+30·85	∞	+ 55·56	
	Total, Native States ...	+ 9·54	+ 1·05	∞	+ 755·56	

The same phenomenon occurred at last census and attracted attention then. It has been commented upon in several district reports. The usual explanation is the proselytizing character of the Muhammadan religion. The following extract from the Sultánpur report may be quoted as an example of the reasons usually alleged. It is written as may be inferred by a Hindu Deputy Collector.

"This increase is attributed to the following causes—"

"(*a*) Hindu women of loose character often abandoned their religion and accepted Islam."

"(*b*) Persons of low castes when reduced to poverty converted themselves as Muhammadans in the pangs of hunger."

"(*c*) Natural increase by birth."

"(*d*) Adopting orphans as domestic slaves (ghulam)."

"(*e*) Hindus serving with rich Muhammadans are often induced by their masters to embrace the Muhammadan religion."

"(*f*) Hindus in Muhammadan society often accept Islam."

On the other hand a far more thorough examination of the subject by the Collector of Moradabad (Mr. Hardy) leads him to an entirely different conclusion :—

"The Hindus, though nearly double in numbers to the Muhammadans, show an actual increase of less than a third as compared with the latter. I have made many and careful enquiries on the subject, but cannot say that the increase has been satisfactorily explained. It is true that Hinduism is not an actively proselytizing religion and that Muhammadanism is. But the number of converts in the true sense of the word to Muhammadanism is practically *nil*, and though it is true that many outcaste Hindus, especially in the lower castes, drift into Islam as their only refuge from social ostracism, the number of these is not sufficiently large to account satisfactorily for the large Muhammadan increase. Poverty, the eating of alien bread and association with Muhammadan prostitutes and consequent loss of caste, only very partially explain the problem. I endeavoured to find out whether the increase was general or local and the following table gives the results :—"

	Increase as compared with 1881 in Musalmáns.	Decrease.
Moradabad City and Cantonment	4,963	...
Ditto Tahsíl	2,121	...
Bilari ditto	842	...
Chandausi Municipality	759	...
Sambhal Tahsíl	...	5
Ditto Municipality	1,395	...
Amroha Tahsíl	8,992	...
Ditto Municipality	...	253
Hasanpur Tahsíl	...	1,826
Thakurdwara	4,004	...
	18,076	2,084
Net increase ...	15,992	

"The increase, it will be seen, is generally distributed. Hasanpur shows a diminution, but it is common to Hindus whose numbers in that pargana are 6,609 less than in 1881. The Amroha town decrease is due as already explained to cholera. Against the slight decease in Sambhal tahsíl, a Hindu decrease of 4,972 must be set."

"I think the true fact is that more Muhammadan children are born than Hindus, and probably that a larger proportion survives. Our knowledge of the two races would lead us to this supposition." "The Muhammadan is as a rule a stronger man than a Hindu, and his diet is more generous. Marriage is easier for him and less expensive than for his Hindu neighbour, a Muhammadan girl's marriage takes place as a rule later than a Hindu girl's, and no unnatural caste rules compel cohabitation at an age when she is physically immature. The probabilities of her becoming a mother and of her having healthy children are therefore greater." "Should she become a widow she is not debarred from remarriage, as are Hindu widows of the higher castes. The Muhammadan, again, if a widower, finds it easier to remarry than does a Hindu ; all the circumstances are in favour of more Muhammadan children being born, and the fact already noted of their mother's being more fit to bear children is in favor of Muhammadan infant life, to say nothing of the better treatment the Muhammadan girl child as a rule gets in comparison with the Hindu, who, if no longer murdered as was formerly the case among many castes, is still neglected."

"The returns of births and deaths registered are too imperfect to show the actual birth and death-rate percentage among Hindus and Muhammadans, but the following figures are of some value."

"Of the 773,001 Hindus there are 106,045 children under 4, of the 400,705 Muhammadans there are 57,962 children under 4. In other words, there are 137·18 children under 4 to every thousand Hindus to 144 children under 4 amongst as many Muhammadans. Put in another way, there are 57,962 children under 4 living to 400,705 Muhammadans. Given the same number of Hindus, there would only be 54,971 children of the same age. These figures confirm the antecedent theory that the marked Muhammadan increase is due less to proselytism than to the Muhammadans being a more fertile race than the Hindu and to the mortality among their children being less."

158. **Reasons for the increase in Muhammadans.**—These remarks *mutatis mutandis* apply to the province as a whole; and there can be no doubt of the correctness of the conclusion arrived at. A small number of Hindus become Mohammadans owing to their being outcasted, to the influence of Muhammadan women of bad character or to adoption by Muhammadans in times of famine, but the number of such is so small as not materially to affect the religion totals. Of active proselytism by Muhammadans, we have no evidence, although in the present strained state of feeling between the religions owing to the cow-killing question, it is certain that any such proselytism would at once attract notice. On the other hand, the census vital and marriage statistics show a decided tendency on the part of Muhammadans to increase faster than Hindus :—

(1) Owing to the absence of the prohibition of the remarriage of widows, Muhammadans have a slight advantage over Hindus in the proportion of married women of child-bearing age (between fifteen and forty.) The number of such women in 10,000 Hindus is 1,708 in 10,000 Muhammadans 1,726.

(2) Muhammadan women are either decidedly more prolific than Hindu women, or the chances of life for both boys and girls are better amongst Muhammadans than Hindus. The proportion of children under 10 amongst Hindus is 2,677 to 10,000 total population and amongst Muhammadans 2,708.

(3) Muhammadans are, on the whole, longer lived than Hindus. There are amongst 10,000 Hindus, 1,207 persons over 50 and amongst Muhammadans 1,294.

These differences, small as they may appear, are sufficient in 10 years to account for the higher proportion of rise amongst Muhammadans. They might have been expected from *à priori* considerations. Muhammadans permit widow remarriage. They are, on the whole, better off than Hindus, the proportion of the lowest class for whom prosperity means no more than a bare sufficiency of food being greatly less amongst them than amongst Hindus. The waste of female life which undoubtedly still takes place amongst certain classes of Hindus is entirely absent amongst Muhammadans.

159. **Jainism.**—The religion next in the provinces in point of numbers but at a vast distance from Muhammadanism is Jainism, which in the census numbered 84,601 adherents of both sexes. Popularly and as contrasted with Muhammadans and Christians, Jains rank amongst Hindus and as a consequence we have in the population enumerated as Hindus 100 males and 84 females who entered in the sect column Jaini, Saraogi or worshippers of Parasnath. These are in fact ordinary Jains, making the total strength of the religion 84,785 persons or 18 in 10,000 for the whole population.

A very elaborate examination of the Jain philosophy which has earned them a well-deserved claim to the title of Syadvadi, or assertors of impossibilities, is contained in Wilson's sects of the Hindus. The origin of Jainism is universally believed to be connected with Buddhism, the chief tenets of which have been adopted and grotesquely elaborated. The leading principle of Jainism is the reverence paid to holy men who by long and painful preparation have raised themselves to a state of divine perfection and are known as Jinas, conquerors, or Tirthakara, those who have made the pilgrimage and attained Nirvana. The "gems" by which the soul's liberation is effected, are stated to be (*a*) right intuition, (*b*) right knowledge, (*c*) right conduct, the latter consisting in obedience to five rules.

"(1) Do not kill or injure. Strict Jainas carry this to so preposterous an extreme that they strain water before drinking it, sweep the ground with a brush before treading on it, never eat or drink in the dark, and sometimes wear muslin before their mouths to prevent the risk of swallowing minute insects. Moreover, they never eat figs or any fruit containing seed, nor will they even touch flesh meat with their hands."

"(2) Do not tell lies."

"(3) Steal not."

"(4) Be chaste and temperate in thought, word and deed."

"(5) Desire nothing immoderately."

The two Jinas who are now chiefly worshipped are Parasnath the twenty-third and Mahavira the twenty-fourth of those who have attained perfection in the present cycle.

160. **Connection with Hinduism.**—The Jains of the province are almost entirely traders in the principal towns. Their connection with Hinduism in the present day is close. They acknowledge as divine beings subordinate in dignity to the Jinas, Asuras, Nagas, Pisachas, Bhutas, Gandharwas and other gods of present and past ages.

Of this acknowledgment of the Hindu deities we have some proof in the census schedules in which Basdeo, Debi (or Jaini Debi), Siva, Nagsen, Ganpat Nath and Gorakh Nath appear as gods worshipped by Jains. Jains recognize a caste system to some extent modified amongst themselves, but admit Hindu converts into one or other of their "Sachchas," and as are similarly admitted into the Hindu system on renouncing the Jain faith. The conversion of one of the great family of Muthra Seths to Vaishnavaism not long ago created some stir in the Jain community whilst conversions from Hinduism to Jainism in the Mainpuri district created some disturbances amongst Hindus by the great body of whom, as Growse remarks, the "Sky-clad" gods are regarded with unconcealed abhorrence.

161. **Jain sects.**—The Jains recognize two important sects, Svetámbara and Digambara, but the community in these provinces practically belongs entirely to the latter. The points in which a difference exists between the two sects are stated to be 700 in number, of which 84 are of infinite importance. Amongst the latter the following are noted by Wilson :—

"The Svetámbaras decorate the images of the Tirthankaras with earrings, necklaces, armlets, and tiaras of gold and jewels: the Digambaras leave their images without the foreign aid of ornament."

"The Svetámbaras assert that there are twelve heavens and sixty-four Indras: the Digambaras maintain that there are sixteen heavens and one hundred Olympian monarchs."

"The Svetámbaras permit their Gurus to eat out of vessels: the Digambaras receive the food in their open hands from their disciples."

"The Svetámbaras consider the accompaniments of the brush, waterpot, &c., as essential to the character of an asetic: the Digámbaras deny their importance. The Svetámbaras assert that the Angas, or scriptures, are the work of the immediate disciples of the Tirthankaras. The Digambaras, with more reason, maintain that the leading authorities of the Jain religion are the composition of subsequent teachers or Achâryas. The advantage gained by the Digambaras in the last debateable matter, they lose, it is to be apprehended, in the next, when they assert that no women can obtain Nirvana, in opposition to the more gallant doctrine of their rivals, which admits the fair sex to the enjoyment of final annihilation."

The sectarian divisions of the faith are little known to the majority of Jains in these provinces to whom the Svetámbara, though they have temples in Ajudhia and possibly elsewhere, are practically unknown. The entries in the sect column were therefore in general the names of the principal Jinas, Adi Nath, Ajit Nath, Paras Nath, Mahavira or Nim Nath, or the word Saraogi, that by which a secular Jain is distinguished from a Yati (Jati) or member of an ascetic order. The total number of Svetámbaras shown in the provinces was 2,235. It may be assumed that the others are Digambaras.

162. **Increase in Jains.**—Jains especially in Oudh show a considerable increase since last census. It may be readily assumed from the account Mr. White gives of the methods in which Jains were enumerated at last census that the increase is mainly due to better enumeration.

163. **Jain castes.**—The Jain caste lists show that the adherents of the religion are almost entirely Baniyas, 83,976 persons out of the total 84,601 entered originally as Jain in religion being of that caste. The Agarwala, Jaiswar, Khandelwal, Purwar, Palliwal and Oswal sub-castes are the most important. Four hundred and forty-one Rájputs appear, possibly converts but more probably as mostly shown of the Jaiswar sub-caste really belonging to the trading community. There are 32 Bráhmans, Gaur being more numerously represented than any other sub-caste. Gaur Brahmans even though Hindus are employed by Jains as temple attendants and sometimes join the faith of their patrons. The actual conduct of Jain worship is as already stated in the hands of the Jain ascetics or Jati.

164. **Christians.**—Christians show an increase of 10,768 persons or 22·58 per cent. on the figures of last census. The details of variation by race are given in the margin.

Abstract No. 52.

	1881.	1891.	Variation.
Foreign	26,683	27,995	+1,312
Eurasians	7,726	7,040	— 686
Natives	13,264	23,406	+10,142
Total ...	47,673	58,441	10,768

165. **Europeans and Eurasians.**—The figures for Europeans vary so largely, owing to accidental causes connected with the garrison of British regiments in the

province, and those for Eurasians owing to their being largely recorded as Europeans, that little information can be drawn from the figures showing the variation of the race entries. As regards sect, Europeans and Eurasians belong most numerously to the Church of England, Roman Catholics being more numerous than any other Protestant body.

The table below gives the numbers of Europeans and Eurasians of each of the leading sectarian classes without distinction of churches, the figures for which owing to faults in the enumeration records are very incomplete.

Abstract No. 53.

	Total population.
Church of England	21,618
Roman Catholics	8,439
Presbyterians	2,170
Methodists...	1,600
Others	529
Unspecified or insufficiently specified	679
Total ...	35,035

The table showing Christians by race and age gives the following totals :—

Abstract No. 54.

Race.	All ages.			0 to 14 years.		15 to 34 years.		35 to 49 years.		50 years and over.	
	Total.	Males.	Females.	Males.	Females.	Males.	Females.	Males.	Females.	Males.	Females.
Foreign (including Armenian).	27,995	21,426	6,569	2,464	2,302	16,041	2,824	1,886	1,002	1,035	441
Eurasians	7,040	3,485	3,555	1,268	1,347	1,253	1,271	595	507	369	430
Natives of India ...	23,406	12,383	11,023	4,988	4,483	4,507	4,044	1,664	1,413	1,224	1,083
Total ...	58,441	37,294	21,147	8,720	8,132	21,801	8,139	4,145	2,922	2,628	1,954

Of Europeans and Eurasians there were 19,775 males between the ages of 15 and 49, of whom 14,628 were enumerated within military lines and are therefore presumably soldiers or officers in the British army, and 5,147 are, so far as can be judged from the place of enumeration, civilians or employed in civil capacities. The number of volunteers in 1890-91 in the North-Western Provinces and Oudh was 4,181, so that all the available European and Eurasian population has been enrolled except 966, a large part of which must be accounted for in officers and others whose temporary connection with the province or official position prevent their being connected with the volunteer force.

166. **British-born and Foreign European Christians.**—Certain information regarding the ages, occupations and civil condition of British-born and

foreign Christians were prepared in connection with English and foreign Census Operations. They are shown as appendices XXI and XXII. The total number of British-born persons was 17,739 and of persons of foreign nationality 504. Details of the latter are given in Abstract No. 55.

Abstract No. 55, Showing the number of foreigners of non-British nationality in the North-Western Provinces and Oudh.

Nationality.	Total population.		
	Total.	Male.	Female.
American	122	57	65
Austro-Hungarian	10	8	2
Dane	2	1	1
Dutch	14	7	7
French	86	48	38
German	148	71	77
Greek	6	5	1
Italian	38	29	9
Norwegian	1	1	...
Portuguese	52	23	29
Roumanian	1	1	...
Russian	4	2	2
Spanish	7	3	4
Swede	4	2	2
Swiss	8	2	6
Turkish Armenian	1	...	1
Total ...	504	260	244

167. **Native Christians.**—The figures for Native Christians require more detailed comment. They show an increase of no less than 10,142 persons or 76 per cent. An examination of the detailed figures in Table A, Part II, shows that nearly the whole of this large comparative increase has taken place in the adherents of the Episcopal Methodist Church in Rohilkhand. Mr. G. R. C. Williams, Collector of Budaun, remarks on the subject :—

VARIATION BY SECT OF NATIVE CHRISTIANS.

Abstract No. 56.

	1881.	1891.	Variation.	Percentage of variation.
Church of England ...	4,606	5,433	+827	+89·99
Roman Catholic ...	1,782	1,904	+122	+5·43
Presbyterian ...	1,247	1,376	+129	+10·34
Methodists	2,071	13,209	+11,138	+537·80
Others	850	753	—97	—11·15
Unspecified... ...	2,708	731	—1,977	—73·00
Total ...	13,264	23,406	+10,142	+76·46

"The increase in the Christians has been enormous and I attribute it to the three following causes :—"

"(*a*) Births amongst the Christian population already existing at the time of last census and enlisted since"

"(*b*) A keener appreciation on the part of low caste people of the social and material advantages to be obtained by professing Christianity."

"(*c*) Greater energy on the part of the missionaries, whose exertions will probably bring Government face to face with a very serious social problem before many years are over."

The increase as recorded by the census amongst the adherents of this church is 11,138 persons or 537·8 per cent., showing that a sudden and a considerable start has been made in missionary work. It is claimed by the pastors of the church that the increase has been larger than the census figures show. Statistics prepared up to the end of 1891 for the Northern India Conference of the Methodist Episcopal Church show, so far as I can follow their classification, that the Native Christian community attached to that church numbered 32,992 persons, the increase within the year having been 13,500 and the community at the end of 1890, that is, near the date of the census, 19,499. By more than one missionary enumerators were accused of refusing to record persons as Christians. I believe it possible that instances of this kind may have happened. Enumerators may have refused to enter a sweeper as a Christian, for the same reason that they would have refused to enter him as a Shaikh ; that is, that he was arrogating to himself a position and title which it was believed was not his due. Such instances cannot however have been numerous and were certainly not due to any desire to conceal the number of Christians, as enumerators in general regard the acceptance on a large scale of sweepers into the Christian church as a blot on it which if inimical they would be glad to evidence.

Out of the 25,000 persons shown at the end of 1891 as *members* of the Methodist Episcopal Church, no less than 16,000 were probationers. It is cretain, therefore, that the Christian community is in a transition stage and more than probable that the missionaries have got ahead of their enquirers in including them amongst the Christian community.

Returns for other churches are less sensational. The Church of England has comparatively large numbers of Native Christians in Dehra, Sahâranpur, Meerut, Agra, Cawnpore, Allahabad, Benares, Gorakhpur, Kumaun and Lucknow. Roman Catholics are numerous only in Meerut, where the preponderance of males is remarkable and probably due to the excess of boys in the Sardhana orphanage, and in Agra where this church has had a small body of adherents since the days of Akbar. As will appear from a later chapter the Native Christians are, as a whole, the best educated body of natives in the province. The standard of education has somewhat fallen owing to the late low caste additions, and it may be hoped that the position amongst the community which the Native Christians especially of the Anglican Church were, by their superior intelligence and education as well as by more essential qualities, beginning to make for themselves will not be injuriously affected by late accessions. The fact that the American Methodist Church has 6,375 Christian children in their Vernacular Schools and 834 in the Anglo-Vernacular Schools shows that the importance of the subject has not been overlooked. In the Sunday Schools of this church the number of Christians was no less than 15,000, a number which must nearly include the whole minor population.

168. **Aryas.**—Aryas appear for the first time as of a separate religion in the returns of the present census, although for the last eighteen years its influence as a reformed Hindu sect has been extending. Their separate appearance on the present occasion is due to the almost universal desire of the various branches of the Arya Samáj that they should not be recorded as

Hindus, a name which they asserted implied the present degeneracy and the idolatrous beliefs of the representatives of the Arya race.

The number of persons recorded as Aryas in the column for religion was 22,053 of whom 12,164 were males and 9,889 females. To this we have to add, for an estimate of the full strength of the Samáj, 3,405 persons 1,398 males and 2,007 females who were recorded as Hindus in religion and Aryas in sect. This makes the strength of the Samáj as recorded at census 25,458. This total is a mere fraction of the strength in the provinces of each of the older reformed sects of the Hindus and of many of the later. The Arya Samáj has, however, acquired an importance disproportionate to its present members from the high standard of intelligence of the majority of its adherents and the active methods of propagandism adopted.

169. **The history and principles of the Arya Samaj.**—The Samáj was founded by Dayanand Swami, by birth a Bráhman of Gujrat, a man undoubtedly entitled to be reckoned amongst the great teachers who have been produced by a sense of the need for action against the gross idolatry of the masses of the Hindu people. A sense of his mission appears to have been impressed on his mind from his boyhood as he relates of himself that, at the age of fourteen while engaged in service at a shrine of Siva, the idea flashed into his mind on seeing the mice carry away the holy offerings, that the shapeless idol of Siva unable to shake off the rats playing on its head, could be neither the omnipotent and the omniscient Supreme Being, nor a medium of the knowledge of the deity; and, consequently, that it was wholly useless as far as the good of its votaries was concerned.

In 1856, when twenty years of age, he devoted himself to the mission of a religious enquirer and teacher and spent the remaining twenty-seven years of his life travelling over the greater part of Northern India disputing and teaching. He died in 1883 constituting by his will a committee of twenty-three members, of whom the Mahrana of Udepur was president, whose duty was :—

(1) to publish and disseminate the Veda and Vedangas;

(2) to send missionaries to different countries and by their means persuade every one to accept truth and abandon error;

(3) to educate poor people in India (Aryavarta) in the principles of the Arya Samáj as founded by himself. He also left money to be spent in promoting these objects.

The creed of the Arya Samáj is authoritatively emdodied in the following ten propositions :—

(1) God is the fountain of all true knowledge, and the primeval cause of all things knowable.

(2) Worship is alone due to God who is All-truth, All-knowledge, All-beatitude, Incorporeal, Almighty, Just, Merciful, Unbegotten, Infinite, Unchangeable, Without a Beginning, Incomparable, the Support and the Lord of all, All-pervading, Omniscient, Imperishable, Immortal, Exempt from Fear, Eternal, Holy and the Cause of the Universe.

(3) The Vedas are the books of true knowledge, and it is the paramount duty of every Arya to read or hear them read; to teach and preach them to others.

(4) An Arya should always be ready to accept truth and renounce untruth when discovered.

(5) Truth arrived at, after consummate deliberation, should be his guiding principle in all actions.

(6) The primary objected of the Samáj is to do good to the world by improving the physical, intellectual, spiritual, moral and social condition of mankind.

(7) Due love for all and appreciation of justice an Arya should manifest in his behaviour towards others.

(8) He should endeavour to diffuse knowledge and dispel ignorance.

(9) He should not be content with his own improvement but look for it in that of others.

(10) In matters which affect the general social well-being of our race he ought to discard all differences and not allow his individuality to interfere, but in strictly personal matters every one may have his own way.

These propositions are of so indefinite a character that some further elucidation of the subject is required. Daya Nand taught that the four Samhita Vedas are the only true divine revelation; that the Bráhmanas, Upanishads and other later Vedic commentaries are to be accepted as authoritative in expounding the meaning of the Vedas; that the Vedas taught that there was only one god of whom Agni, Aditya, Surya and the other deities named were the servants and instruments, and that adoration was to be offered to one God only, abstracted from all idea of shape and form.

The teachings of science are accepted as facts but all superstitious beliefs regarding the influence of the heavenly bodies or other natural phenomena on the course of events are condemned. Socially the Aryas condemn infant marriage and endeavour to promote education and in especial female education. They acknowledge the existence of caste and the social relations dependent on it, but deny the superiority of one caste to another in religious matters. They are strict vegetarians in theory and practice and condemm taking the life of any animal for the purpose of food. Cow-killing is condemned in especial, not on account of any special reverence due to the cow but on account of its usefulness being more than ordinary. Theoretically the Samáj keeps itself apart from all political movements, but it is doubtful whether individual preachers have adhered to the spirit of the rules of the society on the subject.

170. **The distribution of Arya Samajists in the province.**—The extent to which the principles of the Arya Samáj have been adopted in the different districts of the provinces varies very extensively. In general the adherents of the Samáj are numbered almost entirely amongst those who have received

an English or superior vernacular education; most of them are in Government service or amongst the trading classes. Bulandshahr is the only district in which Aryanism has taken hold to any extent amongst the rural population. This is accounted for by the fact that the headquarters of one of the original Samáj Schools is at Chalesar on the borders of the Bulandshahr and Aligarh districts, and that Daya Nand himself lived for some weeks at Karanbas, a village near Anúpshahr, and met with considerable success in obtaining disciples amongst the Rājputs of the neighbouring villages.

171. **The future of the Samaj.**—Whether the separation between Hindus and Aryas is to be a definite and lasting one is a question on which very different opinions are presented in the district reports. So far, it has not extended to any social separation; caste rules and caste observances are still observed by all Aryas, and though a tendency to intermarry amongst themselves is alleged, there appears to be no inclination to condemn intermarriage with orthodox Hindus. The following remarks are made on the subject by a Hindu, the writer of the Jhánsi district report.

"The separation of Aryas from the rest of the Hindu community, from a religious point of view, is not, on the whole, quite definite. I may safely say that at present Aryanism is an individualistic creed, and, generally speaking, does not extend to entire families or communities. I can assert from personal observation that it is not uncommon that a certain member of a joint Hindu family is an Arya, while his father and uncles, perhaps his brothers and cousins, and certainly his mother, wife, aunts and sisters, still adhere to the orthodox faith. There are but few families in which the ladies have really embraced Aryan doctrines. On the other hand, there are hundreds of Hindus, who, while they repudiate the Arya appellation, entertain doubts with regard to those questions of doctrine, belief, and ritual which constitute the "fundamental division" of Aryas from Hindus. For these reasons I am inclined to think that separation of Aryas from their Hindu brethren is not very well marked."

"The total Arya population of the district consists of":—

Males.	Females.	Total.
85	46	131

"I cannot help remarkiug that the number of females, at least, must have been overstated here as elsewhere. It is a truism to say that women are more conservative than men all the world over, but the saying has special force in the case of native ladies. Native gentlemen might discard old beliefs and customs, and adopt new ideas, but native ladies will be very slow in alienating themselves from time-honoured customs or superstitions. Now at the time of enumeration it must have happened in a number of cases that the Arya members of families must, from a sense of variety or shame, have stated not only themselves as Aryas but every other member of the family, male or female, as well. If every individual of such family were asked to state conscientiously, his or her personal belief, I am sure the number of females could not have borne that ratio to the number of males which it does in the present returns.

It is evidently unsafe, on the basis of the statistics at present available, to predict whether the Arya subdivision is or is not likely to be permanent. As I have already remarked the faith of the Arya reformers, at present, bears the character of a personal or individualistic creed and that, roughly speaking, it does not embrace whole families, or classes of community. On the other hand, the faith is more or less confined to cities and towns and has been received by people who have had more or less of education, and brought up in a certain atmosphere, and the faith has not yet made its way to the masses of the populace in the country.

Judging, however, from the tendency of the times, the general direction of the current in which the thought of the rising generation is drifting and the growing tendency to repudiate the restrictions enforced by the older beliefs, it may be safely said that the Arya subdivision has a fair chance of proving lasting.

All things considered, though Aryanism has, in rejecting idolatry and inculcating observance of a high standard of morals, and at the same time refraining from elevating its founder into an object of worship, advanced beyond most of the Hindu reformed sects in the direction to which religious thought amongst educated Hindus now universally tends, there is reason to believe that in its present form it is not likely to elevate itself into a position different from that of many other Hindu sects. Its organization and the spread of its doctrines through paid propagandists have attracted to it for the present a certain amount of what may turn out to be supposititious interest and importance.

The history of religions, however, contains so many surprises that it may be grossly wrong to predict that this religion is not likely to endure, although it is founded on the divine authority of books which do not bear the interpretation attached to them by it, although it revives in the worship of a Supreme Creator the long forgotten ritual of a tribe of worshippers of the forces of nature, and although it has incorporated or is in a fair way to incorporate in its creed the Hindu notion of the sacredness of the cow for reasons which are of interest solely because it seems incredible that they should affect the beliefs of reasoning and educated men.*

172. **The distribution of religions between town and country.**—The marginal table gives the provincial totals of Table VI showing the urban population by religion. Appendix No. XXIII gives the corresponding figures by districts. Hindus are by far more largely dwellers in rural tracts than in towns. The Muhammadans, who are descendants of immigrant non-Indian races, are as already indicated to a large extent dwellers in towns, and the artizan classes amongst whom the spread of Muhmmadanism has been greatest are urban to a still greater extent. The account already given of Jains and Aryas indicates the reasons for their excess in towns. Amongst Christians and Sikhs, the proportion of imported Government servants resident in headquarters towns and cantonment is disproportionately large.

Abstract No. 57, Showing the distribution of town population by religion.

Religions.	Persons.	Percentage of total town population.	Percentage of total religion.
Hindu	3,415,798	64·27	8·46
Musalmán ...	1,798,903	33·85	28·34
Jain	36,694	·69	43·47
Christian	45,280	·85	78·37
Arya	10,552	·20	47·84
Sikh	6,206	·12	54·71
Others	895	·02	48·96
Total ...	5,314,328	100·00	11·33

* Daya Nand's Gokaruna Nidhi devotes a considerable part of its contents to prove that whereas the flesh of one cow appeases the appetites of only 80 carnivorous persons, it would, if preserved, feed with milk and corn 410,440 persons. A commentator on the same book adds that since a single cow gives a man a profit of Rs. 2,817-8-0, India for want of faith in mathematics loses £ 832,221,316 annually by keeping up the barbarous habit contracted in the days of ignorance. The protection of this species made the ancient kings so rich and consequently so powerful, that the occidental nations consider them to be merely fabulous beings.

Chapter VII.—HINDUISM AND ITS SECTS.

173. **Hinduism.**—The present chapter will give as brief as possible an account of Hinduism in these provinces, as analyzed by the enquiries made in the recent census. The exact definition of what constitutes Hinduism is a task which has proved too much for the most learned and inventive enquirers on the subject. "Hinduism" in the words of Monier Williams "presents for our investigation a complex congeries of creeds and doctrines which in its gradual accumulation may be compared to the gathering together of the mighty volume of the Ganges, swollen by a continual influx of tributary rivers and rivulets, spreading itself over an ever-increasing area of country and finally resolving itself into an intricate Delta of tortuous streams and jungly marshes. Nor is it difficult to account for this complexity. The Hindu religion is a reflection of the composite character of the Hindus, who are not one people, but many. It is based on the idea of universal receptivity. It has ever aimed at accommodating itself to circumstances, and has carried on the process of adaptation through more than three thousand years. It has first borne with and then, so to speak, swallowed, digested and assimilated something from all creeds; or, like a vast hospitable mansion, it has opened its doors to all comers; it has not refused a welcome to applicants of every grade from the highest to the lowest, if only willing to acknowledge the spiritual headship of the Bráhmans and adopt caste rules. In this manner it has held out the right hand of brotherhood to the Fetish-worshipping aborigines of India; it has stooped to the demonolatory of various savage tribes; it has not scrupled to encourage the adoration of the fish, the boar, the serpent, trees, plants, stones and devils; it has permitted a descent to the most degrading cults of the Dravidian races; while at the same time it has ventured to rise from the most grovelling practices to the loftiest heights of philosophical speculation; it has not hesitated to drink in thoughts from the very fountain of truth, and owes not a little to Christianity itself. Strangest of all, it has dissipated the formidable organization which for a long period confronted Bráhmanism, and introduced doctrines subversive to sacerdotalism. It has artfully appropriated Buddhism, and gradually superseded that competing system by drawing its adherents within the pale of its own communion."

The consequence of such a development is that Hinduism includes "a fluctuating mass of beliefs, opinions, usages, observances, social and religious ideas" * the exact details of which it is impossible to reduce to anything like order and in the most diverse aspects of which it is difficult to recognize anything that is common. A belief in the religious superiority of Bráhmans, veneration for the cow and respect for the distinctions of castes are the elements of Hinduism which are most generally recognized as fundamental, but each and all of these has been rejected or is rejected by tribes, castes or sects whose title to be included amongst Hindus is not denied.

174. **The origin of modern Hinduism.**—The uncertainty which attaches to the details of the present condition of Hinduism extends in an intensified

* Barth, Religions of India, page 153.

from to the question of its origin. We have distinct and authentic accounts of the religion of the Aryans when first they entered India. It was that of a nomad and primitive people, a veneration for the personified powers of nature,—Agni, the fire god, Varuna, the sky god, Indra, the rain god, Surya, the sun god, Rudra, the storm god, accompanied by a somewhat elaborate ritual of sacrificial and other observances. The development, from the Vedic beliefs, of Bráhmanism, a purely philosophical religion embodying an elaborate social scheme for the exaltation of the persons whose speculations formulated its beliefs, can be traced; but, when the long successful reaction against Bráhmanism led by the reformer Buddha had at length been vanquished in the country of its birth, we find fully armed and fully developed, in entire possession of the country, the most elaborate and most extraordinary system of inconsistent and grotesque beliefs which the world has seen. The authority of the Vedic Hynms and of the philosophical speculations of the Bráhmans are still acknowledged, but the real beliefs of the new faith as embodied in the Puranas are entirely new, not even the names of the gods now exalted as Supreme occurring in the Vedic Hymns. The new faith was shadowed forth in the epic poems and fully embodied in the Puranas in all those aspects which the Bráhman admits to belong to it. Monier Williams believes that Hinduism—

"Sprung from the later Bráhmanism, because something more was needed for vast populations naturally craving for personal objects of faith and devotion, than the merely spiritual pantheistic creed of Bráhmanism. The chief point which characterizes Hinduism and distinguishes it from Bráhmanism is that it subordinates the purely spiritual Bráhman (nom-Bráhma) with its first manifestation Bráhma to the personal deities Siva and Vishnu or to some form of these deities, while it admits of numerous sects, each sect exalting its own god to the place of the Supreme. Yet we must guard against the idea that Hinduism has superseded Bráhmanism, or that they are mutually antagonistic. The latter system is pantheistic, whereas Hinduism is theistic; but in India forms of pantheism, theism and polytheism are ever interwoven with each other."

175. **The division of Hinduism into sects.**—Of the Neo-Bráhmanic religions it is stated by Barth that the very essence is diversity and its proper manifestation "sect," sect in constant mobility and reduced to such "a state of division that nothing similar to it was ever seen in any other religious system." It is this characteristic of Hinduism which makes it possible to collect information so extensive as has been found to be the case by means of a simple enumeration in a census schedule. The common characteristic of all the so-called sects is the worship of some special divinity exalted above all others. The names of these special deities with some such particulars as are available regarding them and the extent to which they find special worshippers, is the information which in the late census it has been endeavoured to obtain.

The nature of Hinduism as traceable from the ancient texts and the writings of later commentators and leaders of Hindu sectarianism has been very fully dealt with by many European observers. Barth, Monier Williams and other writers have published works on the subject everywhere accessible and to which reference may be made. They trace the gradual development of the Hindu Trinity of Bráhma, Vishnu and Siva, the creator, the preserver and the destroyer and the subsequent expansion of each person of the Trinity into two distinct natures, the passive and the active, the latter called the Sakti and personified as the wife of the person of the Trinity from which it was expanded. The subsequent obliteration of the impersonal Bráhma and the transfer of his attributes to the other gods, the attenuation of the female energy of Vishnu and the expansion of the female energy of Siva left as the leading gods of the present day so far as temple worship and ritual is concerned, Vishnu under one or other of his incarnations, Siva and the Sakti of the third person of the Trinity—Parbatti, Durga, Debi, according to the aspect under which she is considered. Of these Vishnu alone preserves his attributes as a purely Aryan and Bráhmanical deity, Siva has from time to time been identified to some extent with local deities of Dravidian origin, whilst every Dravidian god or goddess adopted into the Hindu system is recognized as a manifestation or form of Debi. The adoption into the Hindu system of Dravidian and aboriginal deities and superstitions has been generally recognized by the writers on the subject. The figures in the following pages will give an idea of how great a hold these superstitions retain on the low class Hindus of the present day.

176. **The instructions as to record of sects.**—The instructions to enumerators and supervisors by which it was intended to obtain the desired record are as follows :—

" Column 3 (sect of religion) enter the sect of religion followed by each person as they return it, as Vaishnava, Vallabhacharya, Kabirpanthi, &c., for Hindus; Sunni, Shiah, &c., for Musalmáns; and for Christians enter whether Church of England, Roman Catholic, Presbyterian, Lutheran, Baptist, American Episcopalian, &c. If a Hindu cannot name his sect, the name of the divinity he especially worships should be entered. (The question will be *Ishta devata kaun hai? or kis devata se mantar lete ho?*). For persons entered in column 2, as Bhils, Gonds, or of other forest tribes, the name of the devata will invariably be entered. If the sect or devata cannot be stated, enter " not returned " in this column, but do not leave it blank."

"The exercise of some intelligence will be necessary on the part of enumerators and supervisors to get this column properly filled up, owing to the ignorance of many Hindus as to the sects to which they belong, and to the fact that most Hindus pay homage to all deities, whether they belong to one particular class or not in paying especial homage to one deity. Of Hindus in general there are reckoned five classes :—Vaishnavas, Saivas, Saktas, Sauras and Ganpatiyas. The first three only are common in the North-Western Provinces, those who worship specially or receive the mantra of Vishnu, of Siva or of the Sakti. The boundaries of these systems are ill-defined; but inside the systems of Vaishnavism and Saivism there are various well-marked sects (sampradaya or panth) whose tenets differ from those of ordinary Hindus and a record of the members of which is desired. Such are amongst Vaishnavas, Vallabhacharya, Rámanandi, Chaitaniya, Bishnois, Kabirpanthi, &c., and amongst Saivas, Lingaits, Pasupatas, &c. There are also amongst Hindus outside the five classes members of various societies (Samáj) who reject the pantheism of ordinary Hindu worship and yet do not entirely reject the Hindu system, *e.g.*, the Arya Samáj or Dayanandis. In the Himalayan districts, again, most Hindus are Smartas, followers of Sankaracharya, worshipping the leading five Hindu deities alike. It is probable that persons of this sect will also be found in the plains. Amongst Jains (Saraogi) two sects are mentioned, Swetambara and Digambara. Amongst Sikhs also sects are numerous. There are Nanakpanthi, Gobind Singhi, Kuka and other Sikh sects. Amongst Muhammadans the sectarian subdivision is well known, and the person enumerated can ordinarily determine at once whether he is a Sunni, a Shia or what."

"On the enumeration being begun, the difficulty of obtaining full details in this column will soon be apparent. This note on sect has been given to guide you as to what is wanted. You will probably find a tendency to enter caste details in this column amongst low caste Hindus. The difference between caste and sect must be clearly realized. The one relates to social status, the other to religious belief. Except in the case of religious ascetics or mendicants, there should be no fear of confusion."

"The enumerator should insert in column 3 the answer he gets from the person enumerated, whether the sect or the devata is mentioned, and not draw inferences from the answer; *e.g.*, if the answer is that Mahadeo is the devata whose mantra is taken, Mahadeo should be entered, not Saiva. In this column it will be well if Christians who are able to write should themselves enter their sects. If the enumerator has to write the sect in vernacular, he must be careful to record the exact pronunciation."

The specimen questions proposed for the use of enumerators were—

" (If the person enumerated is a Hindu, Sikh or a Jain) *Tumhara kya panth hai?* (If he says he does not know.) Tum khas kis devate ko mánte ho? (or) *kis devate se tumhâre yahan mantar liya jata hai?* (or) *Ishta devata kaun hai?*

177. **The meaning to be attached to the word sect.**—The word "sect" used by Monier Williams, Barth and all other late writers on Hinduism, to denote the distinctions introduced by the special devotion of certain worshippers to certain gods was speedily found to be to a great extent a misnomer. It has no equivalent in this meaning in the current Hindi language. The words sampradaya or panth, the proper equivalents of the word sect, are not usually applied to distinguish those who profess themselves the special worshippers of Siva or the special worshippers of Vishnu, unless they belong to what is really a sect, a body of men professing beliefs to some extent different from those of orthodox Hindus in general. The great body of Hindus belong to no sampradaya or panth. They profess their belief in, and reverence for, Bráhma, Vishnu, Siva and all the millions of gods of the Hindu mythology, and worship many of them at their appropriate times and seasons. Of the higher classes a large proportion regard Vishnu or Siva as their "Ishta devata," that is, the god under whose special protection they consider themselves and to whom in consequence they pay special reverence. Of the lower classes many similarly look for special protection to a special form of Debi or to one of those innumerable minor gods which the Bráhmanic system has adopted or tolerated. The fact that this special reverence is paid to one god does not, however, prevent their joining in the worship of other deities or induce them to consider themselves as in any way separated by religious belief from the special worshippers of some other god. It does not even in perhaps the majority of cases imply a belief that their special god is the most powerful of the gods. A proverb quoted in the Panjáb report represents a worshipper ot Guga Pir as replying to a questionas to who was greater, Mahadeo or Guga Pir, with a question as to what it would avail him to say who was greater if he were to be bitten by a snake. The obvious insinuation is that Mahadeo was greater, but that he, immediately subject to the power of Guga Pir, could not venture to say so. The special reverence of one god even to this extent is by no means universal. A considerable proportion of the population were found unable to say they specially reverenced any god, and a still larger proportion replied to the questions put to them,

in a way which implied their rejection of pantheism and polytheism, and their recognition only of one Supreme Being.

178. **The classification of the sect returns.**—The classification of the returns collected in regard to Hindu sects gave an infinity of trouble. The names returned were innumerable, and though enquiries were instituted in every district in the province, very little information was forthcoming in regard to a majority of the names. I have, however, with the information given by the district lists, and sometimes from the indication given by the form of the name itself, been able to classify all into a comparatively few groups, to each of which some reference will be made.

The classification adopted is as follows :—

Class A.—Hindus devoted to no particular deity or sect.
„ B.—Monotheistic.
„ C.—Groups in which Vedic or presectarian influence is apparent.
„ D.—Puranic Vaishnava.
„ E.—Puranic Saiva.
„ F.—Puranic Sakta.
„ G.—Miscellaneous developments and additions.
„ H.—Sectarian subdivisions.

179. **Non-sectarian and unspecified.**—Amongst class A have been placed all who to the question what god they worshipped, replied that they worshipped all the gods ; or who were unable to name any god they worshipped.

Unspecified, 1,486,984.—The class is in point of population shown in the census registers, 773,310 males, 713,674 females, a fairly extensive one ; but it does not from them appear by any means so extensive as might have been inferred from the district accounts of the difficulty with which these sect columns had been filled up for Hindus. In point of fact, I believe that the numbers shown under this head should have been greater ; that the questioning of the enumerators and the example of the better instructed Hindus has induced many who do not in point of fact know what Vaishnavism, Saivism and Saktism is, to record themselves as worshippers of a special god.

180. **The beliefs of the ordinary Hindu.**—The religious beliefs of this section of the Hindus are referred to by a writer who has closely observed the social circumstances of the Hindu peasantry.*

" It is difficult to make out exactly the religious beliefs of the ordinary Hindu peasant. He has practically no belief in the transmigration of souls, but has a vague idea that there is a future life, in which those who are good in this world will be happy in a heaven (Surg), while those who are bad will be wretched in a hell (Narak). His devotional offerings to demons, saints and godlings are meant rather to avert temporal evils or secure temporal blessings than to improve his prospects of the life to come. He has an idea that sin (pap) will bring evil on him and his fellows in this life as well as after death. His instincts as to good and evil are much the same as the ordinary European moral distinctions, only they do not take so wide a range ; instead of extending to the whole human race, or to the whole nation or sect, they extend only to his own tribe, or village, or family. He thinks it wrong to tell a lie unless perhaps to benefit a relative or friend ; he thinks it wicked to

* Wilson, Sirsa Settlement Report, page 138.

injure a man unless he has been injured by him, or to cheat another unless he thinks that that other would cheat him if he got the chance; or to take a bribe without giving the promised consideration for it. He believes vaguely that it is good for him to meditate on the deity, and to show that he is not forgetting him, he mutters "Rám, Rám, Rám," or repeats the name of some other Hindu god when he gets up in the morning, and if he is piously inclined, at other times also, in season and out of season. Notwithstanding all the numerous saints and deities whom he endeavours to propitiate, he has a vague belief that above all there is one Supreme God whom he calls Narayan or Parmeshar, who knows all things and by whom all things were made, and who will reward the good and punish the bad both in this life and in the life to come. There are of course particular sects of Hindus who have developed one phase of these beliefs more strongly than another; some who believe in transmigration of souls; some who have devoted themselves to the worship of one godling more than that of the others; but so far as my experience goes, the moral and religious ideas of the great mass of the Hindu peasantry are as I have above described."

181. **Monotheistic non-sectarian Hindus.**—These remarks apply in part to the next class to be referred to—one which according to the census returns is considerably more extensive and in the future likely to become still more important and numerous, because to some extent indicative of the degree to which Hindu beliefs have been influenced by Muhammadanism and Christianity, an influence likely to increase.

Amongst all classes of the population, and more particularly amongst those castes which are highest and lowest in the Hindu system, the Bráhmans and the Chámars, a frequent answer to the question put to them as to whom they worshipped was "Eswar," "Parmeswar," "Bhagwan" or "Narayan," terms used for God in the abstract, removed from the idea of any special impersonation. It is possible that a few of the persons who entered "Eswar" meant to indicate Siva. It is probable that a few of those who recorded Narayan intended Krishna. It is, however, as certain as careful enquiries by officers in all parts of the provinces can make it, that such replies were intended in general to record belief in one impersonal God, "who made us both" one man added whom I questioned as to what he intended. The feeling which dictates such an entry is widespread amongst the most intelligent of the Hindus and amongst those who have derived their religious ideas from the teachings of Raidas, Kabir and other monotheistic teachers. To this feeling taking a more active form is due the origin of a large number of the numerous reformed sects, regarding some of which information will be collated in the last part of this chapter. Monotheistic belief is, there is reason to believe, gaining ground almost daily, and it is not too much to say that, few as the converts are whom Christian missionaries have gained to their faith, the influence of their belief has reacted upon that of thinking Hindus to an extent of which even the large numbers who have expressed their sole belief in one God is not an excessive indication. Along with the entries for Eswar, Bhagwan, or Narayan have also been included those for Kartár, the Creator; Satnarayan, the true Narayan; Satdeo, the true God; Adjot, the Spirit that was from the beginning; Niraukar, the Formless One; Abnasi, the imperishable one. The name of *Bráhma*, the Creator, was not infrequently recorded with the same intention. The name though that of one of the gods of the Puranic Trinity has, owing to the worship of Bráhma having dropped out of general use, retained its theistic purity of meaning uncontaminated by any connection with the grossly material superstitions which have grown up regarding the two persons now more generally worshipped. Bráhma, like Eswar, now conveys the meaning of the Supreme God.

		Total.	Males.	Females.
Eswar	... ...	3,788,696	2,019,808	1,768,888
Bráhma	... ...	21,535	13,083	8,452
	Total ...	3,810,231	2,032,891	1,777,340

The numbers of worshippers of Eswar or Bráhma are given in the margin. The total 3,810,231 is that of those I have classed as monotheistic.

182. **Pre-Puranic forms of worship.**—The next class, not a large one, consists of those whose tenets preserve at least the memory of Pre-Puranic religion, whilst they do not belong to any one of the modern reformed sects.

Smarta, 402,981.—The largest group in this class is that of the Smartas, followers of Sankarachariya, an early reformer, who, with a view to expound the tenets of the Vedanta philosophy, wandered from his birthplace in the Dakhan to the Himalayas "teaching and holding disputations with the professors of other religions wherever he went." The following account of his tenets is given by Professor Wilson :—

"His leading tenet is the recognition of Bráhma Parabráhma as the sole cause and supreme ruler of the universe and as distinct from Siva, Vishnu, Bráhma or any individual member of the pantheon. With this admission, and having regard to the weakness of those human faculties which cannot elevate themselves to the conception of the inscrutable first cause, the observance of such rites and the worship of such deities as are either prescribed by the Vedas or the works not incompatible with their authority were left undisturbed by Sankara. They even received to a certain extent his particular sanction, and certain divisions of the Hindu faith were, by his express permission, taught by some of his disciples, and are, consequently, regarded by the learned Bráhmans in general as the only orthodox and allowable forms in the present day. For thus Sankara addressed his disciples :—"In the present impure age, the bud of wisdom being blighted in iniquity, men are inadequate to the apprehension of pure unity; they will be apt, therefore, again to follow the dictates of their own fancies, and it is necessary for the preservation of the world and the maintenance of civil and religious distinctions, to acknowledge those modifications of the divine spirit which are the work of the Supreme."

The worship of special gods thus tolerated by Sankarachariya, himself a Vedantist, has become the main faith of the majority of those who in the present day call themselves his followers. They define their special faith as consisting in a belief in all the five principal gods, Siva, Vishnu, Suraj, Sakti, and Ganpati, to whose special worship separate sects of Hindus after Sankarachariya devoted themselves. The name Smarta is derived from Smriti, that which is remembered and handed down by tradition in the religious books subsequent to the Vedas to which Sankarachariya expressed his adherence.

Smartas are scattered over the provinces in small numbers except in Kumaun, the great temples in which are said to have been founded by Sankara, and where the influence of his teachings is extensive to the present day. The Maháráshtra and other imported Bráhmans of the Himalayas are probably Smartas in spirit as in name, but for the great majority of the

Khasiya Bráhmans and Rájputs, the entry was probably made in imitation of that made by their teachers. Their belief is probably little different from that of those who repose their prime trust in Goril or Chattarpal or any other of the gods of that curious blending of Animism, Bráhmanism and Buddhism which forms the Hinduism of the Himalayas and of which an interesting account is given in the second volume of the Himalayan Gazetteer.

Saura, 41,904.—*Sauras* or worshippers of the sun god, Suriya or Aditya, members of one of the sects said to be founded by Sankarachariya and now as a separate sect almost extinct in these provinces, are scattered in small numbers over the provinces, being proportionately more numerous in Kumaun and Oudh. Although worship of the sun as a special tutelary deity is so comparatively rare, Suraj Narayan is regularly worshipped by all high caste Hindus by fasting on Sundays (Adityawar) from sunrise to sunset.

Agni worshippers, 9,774.—Another Vedic deity remembered by the Vedic name is Agni, the fire god, who is worshipped by all Hindus along with other gods in marriage ceremonies and at other social events, but is regarded as a special presiding deity only by a few Aganhotri Bráhmans, whose worship of the fire god is described in the following extract from the Benares Gazetteer :—

"A Bráhman and his wife sit by the side of a hearth face to face, having the hearth between them. This ceremony with hom (pouring ghi into the fire) and incantations three times a day continues till one of the pair dies. The fire is not allowed to die out, but if this accidentally happens, it is renewed with a certain ceremony."

The Agnihotra ceremony is also performed by Aryas. Other Vedic gods Vayu, Indra, &c., are remembered by Hindus at family festivals, but the occurrence of the special worship of such gods indicated by 550 persons is probably due to the reaction towards Vedic religion, of which we have the most visible proof in the figures for the Aryas. The entry in the schedules was mostly "Vedic gods."

Planet worshippers, 45,962.—We have the last remnant of Vedic worship to be mentioned in the worship of the planets, though the beliefs with which the special worship is connected are now distinctly Puranic. At the great festivals of the Hindus a small offering is made to all the planets at once ; but, excepting on these occasions, they are never worshipped together. They are, however, frequently worshipped separately by the sick or unfortunate, who suppose themselves to be under the baneful influence of one or other of them. At these times they are worshipped one after the other in regular succession. Seven of the planets give names to the days of the week ; the other two represent the ascending and descending nodes. Surya and Chandra (Soma) have already been noted as amongst the Vedic deities. Of special planet worshippers 45,962 have been shown at census.

183. **The general distinctions between Vaishnavas and Saivas.**—The classes of special worshippers so far referred to are merely isolated remnants scattered amongst the masses of the population. Our classification next brings up for consideration the cultus which is the essence of Puranic Hinduism, the special worship of Vishnu and of Siva, no longer regarded each as the comple-

ment of the other, but each by his own worshippers as including in his one person all the attributes of godhead and as the one Great God to whom all others are inferior. The essential difference between the two systems is well expressed by Monier Williams in the following remarks :—

"They represent different lines of religious thought; such lines expressing a contrast rather than an opposition. So far indeed from any necessary opposition between the systems, they are necessary complements of each other. For the worship of the composite deity Rudra-Siva is nothing but the expression of the awe felt by human beings in the presence of the two mutually complementary forces of disintegration and reintegration; while the worship of the personal god Vishnu in his descents upon earth in human form is nothing but the expression of the very natural interest felt by man in his own preservation and in the working of the physical forces which resist dissolution."

The outward distinctive signs of Vaishnavism and Saivism in the "tilak" or sectarian marks made on the forehead are for Vishnu an upright white mark of sandal wood and for Siva three horizontal marks made with ashes. A rosary of 108 beads of tulsi wood or lotus berries is worn by Vaishnavites, whilst Saivites wear 32 or 64 of the rough seeds of the Rudraksh. Vishnu is usually worshipped under the form of one of his incarnations represented by the complete image of a well-formed human being; Siva is almost invariably worshipped through the symbol of the *linga*. The offerings at the temples of the two gods are essentially different. The image of Krishna or Ráma is clothed, bathed, fed with offerings of cooked and uncooked grain. The food offered to Vishnu is eaten by all. To Siva, leaves, flowers, uncooked rice and water are offered and the remnants are eaten only by the attendant Goshains of the temple.

184. **Vaishnavism.**—The classification of worshippers of Vishnu in a scheme consistent in itself and such as to fit in with a combined account of Hinduism in general I have found difficult. I have determined to give in the first place the figures for those Vaishnavas who, so far as can be judged from the entries in the schedules, belong to none of the reformed Vaishnava sects but are Vaishnava rather from trust in Vishnu than from adherence to any special sectarian tenets. Such worshippers of Vishnu, as I take it, belong to the general system of orthodox Hinduism from which the reformed sects are to a considerable degree apart owing to their special beliefs.

The reformed Vaishnavite, as well as reformed Saivite sects, will be considered after conclusion of the general remarks on Hinduism. It is certain, however, that to some extent the entries for the members of reformed sects have been included under the general term Vaishnavite, so that the sectarian figures are probably much too low.

Vishnu's preserving and restoring power has been manifested to the world in a series of "Avataras" literally descents in which a portion of his divine essence was "embodied in a human or supernatural form possessed of superhuman powers. All these Avataras became manifest to correct some great evil or effect some great good in the world." It is in general the more personal form of Vishnu as embodied in one of these incarnations that receives the direct worship of his votaries.

"Nevertheless in his antecedent condition as Vishnu, this deity has a material character and individuality of his own quite irrespective of his incarnations. He is described as living in Vaikuntha—a locality, as we have seen, more inaccessible and less easy to identify with any definite spot on earth than Siva's abode, Kailasa. He has a wife, Lakshmi or Sri, the goddess of fortune and beauty, who is fabled to have sprung, with other precious things, from the froth of the ocean when churned by the gods and demons. And as Vishnu in his non-avatara condition lives a life which has fewer features in common with humanity than that of Siva, so is his wife Lakshmi less human than Siva's wife Parvati. In fact, the more human side of both the god and goddess is reserved for their descents in human form, Vishnu as Ráma and Krishna, Lakshmi as Sita and Rukmini. Nevertheless some details of Vishnu's separate personality as distinct from his Avataras may be gathered from the Puranas. For example, we are told that he has a peculiar auspicious mark (Sri-vatsa) on his breast. He has four arms, and holds a symbol in each of his four hands; namely a wheel or circular weapon (Chakra) called Sudarsana, a conch-shell (Sankha) called Panchajanya, a club (Gada) called Kaumodaki, and a lotus-flower (Padama). Of these the circular symbol may possibly have been borrowed from Buddhism. If so, it was originally significant of the wheel of the Buddhistic law, or of the cosmical cycles peculiar to that system. Or bearing in mind Vishnu's connection with the sun, we may reasonably regard it as emblematical of the sun's circular course in the heavens. In the later mythology it is supposed to represent a missile weapon hurled by Vishnu, like a quoit, at the demons who are ever plotting evil against gods and men, and with whom he is always at war. Similarly the conch-shell is blown by him like a trumpet in his battles; its miraculous sound filling his enemies with terror and helping him to secure victory. The club is also used in Vishnu's conflicts with his demon-foes. Moreover, he is armed with a wonderful bow called Sárnga and a sword Nandaka. He has a jewel on his wrist named Syamantaka, and another on his breast called Kaustubha. When he has occasion to move through space he is borne on the mythical bird Garuda, closely related to the sun and compared to an eagle, but represented as semi-human in form and character, with a bird-like face. Possibly this Garuda may be a personification of the sky or ethereal element which supports Vishnu—identified with the sun—one of whose names is 'air-borne' (Váyu-Váhana). It is noteworthy that Garuda, like the Krishna form of Vishnu, is the destroyer of serpents which typify destruction and evil. Yet serpents have also their contrary character, and even divine attributes; for at the dissolution of the Universe and between the intervals of creation, Vishnu, as the Supreme Being, reclines in profound repose on the thousand-headed serpent Sesha—typical of infinity—while his wife Lakshmi chafes his feet, and out of his navel grows the lotus which supports Bráhma, the active agent in reproducing the world. Finally, Vishnu has the river Ganges issuing from one of his feet, whence it flows through the sky before it falls on the head of the god Siva."

Worshippers of Vishnu, 3,733,518 : *Worshippers of Badri Nath*, 6,910.—As worshippers of Vishnu specifying neither their adherence to a separate sect nor a separate incarnation 3,733,518 persons have been recorded at census, and 6,910 persons have recorded their faith in Vishnu as Badri Nath, lord of Badri, sacred to Vishnu in memory of the austerities performed by him there in his dual form of Nara and Narayana.

Worshippers of Nara Sinha 164,555.—Special worshippers of nearly all of the recognized Avataras of Vishnu have occurred in the census schedules. For the following, which may be mentioned in the order in which they are said to have taken place, the numbers recorded are important. The first of importance was the fourth descent, that in the form of Nara Sinha, or, as it is called in the North-Western Provinces, Nar Singh, the man lion. It was undertaken to deliver the world from the tyranny of a demon who by the favour of Bráhma had become invulnerable and who attempted to kill his son Prahlada for worshipping Vishnu. The demon whilst impiously scoffing at the idea of the omnipresence of the god and asking whether he was in a stone pillar of the hall, was suddenly confronted by the god, half-man and half-lion, and torn to pieces.

Worshippers of Parasrám, 118,080.—The sixth incarnation, that of Paras Ráma, or Ráma with the axe, was born of Bráhman parentage to deliver the Bráhmans from the arrogant dominion of the Kshatriyas, from whom he twenty-one times cleared the earth and with whose blood he filled five large lakes. Of "Parasráma" 118,080 worshippers have been recorded.

Worshippers of Ráma, 1,099,111.—The seventh incarnation was that of Ráma, or Rám Chandar, the Kshatriya hero, whose story is the subject of the Rámayan, and is reacted annually in one of the most popular of Hindu festivals, the Rámlila. The story is well known and need not be repeated. The hold which it still has over the country may be inferred from the fact that the name of Rám twice repeated is the ordinary form of salutation throughout Northern India, except amongst Bráhmans who salute each other with the word "Namaskar" and are saluted by others with "Palagan." "It is noteworthy" says Monier Williams, that the Ráma legends have always retained their purity, and, unlike those of Bráhma, Krishna, Siva and Durga, have never been mixed up with indecencies and licentiousness. In fact, the worship of Ráma has never degenerated to the same extent as that of some of these other deities." Ráma and his wife were pure; there was nothing in their characters suggestive of license; and if "the husband of one wife" and the devoted and affectionate wife had come to be associated with impure ideas, they must have lost all that gave them a title to veneration.

The Rámayan which celebrates the adventure of Ráma is to this day, in its modern recension by Tulsi Das, the most popular of the Hindu religious poems. The worship of the great-minded Ráma and the pure and gentle Sita still prevails to a great extent throughout the provinces and especially in the Oudh districts, but of the number of worshippers, outside the sects devoted to the worship of Ráma, 1,099,111 cannot be relied on as an accurate indication for two reasons. It is subject to a large deduction owing to the fact that the name Rám is, like Bhagwan, Ishwar or Narayan, used commonly to indicate the deity as one and supreme. A large number of the persons included here should, therefore, probably be included in the second class referred to on pages 197-198. In certain districts where the number of worshippers of Ráma is greatly in excess of that in the neighbours, this is almost certainly the case, and it is probably so elsewhere to some extent. On the other hand, no doubt a proportion of the worshippers of Rám Chandar have been included under the general term Vaishnava.

Hanuman worshippers, 937,493.—How innate in the Hindu character is the search for the grotesque and the impossible is exemplified by the great extent to which the worship of Ráma has been specially connected with the name of his ally Hanuman or Mahabir, the monkey chief, of whom no less than 937,493 special worshippers have been recorded.

"He was son of Pavana, 'the wind', by Anjana, wife of a monkey named Kesari. He was able to fly, and is a conspicuous figure in the Rámayana. He and the other monkeys who assisted Ráma in his war against Ravana were of divine origin, and their powers were superhuman. Hanuman jumped from India to Ceylon in one bound; he tore up trees, carried away the Himalayas, seized the clouds, and performed many other wonderful exploits. His form is as vast as a mountain and as tall as a gigantic tower. His complexion is yellow and glowing like molten gold. His face is as red as the brightest ruby; while his enormous tail spreads out to an interminable length. He stands on a lofty rock and roars like thunder. He leaps into the air, and flies among the clouds with a rushing noise, whilst the ocean waves are roaring and splashing below. In one of his fights with Ravana and the Rakshasas, they greased his tail and set it on fire, but to their own great injury, for with it he burnt down their capital city, Lanka. This exploit obtained for him the name Lanka-dahi. His services to Ráma were great and many. He acted as his spy and fought most valiantly. He flew to the Himalayas, from whence he brought medicinal herbs with which he restored the wounded and he killed the monster Kala Nemi and thousands of Gandharvas who assailed him. He accompanied Ráma on his return to Ajodhya, and there he received from him the reward of perpetual life and youth. The exploits of Hanuman are favourite topics among Hindus from childhood to age, and paintings of them are common. He is called Marut putra, and he has the patronymics Anili, Marut, &c., and the metronymic Anjáneya. He is also Yoga-Chara, from his power in magic or in the healing art, and Rájata-dyuti 'the brilliant.' Among his other accomplishments, Hanuman was a Grammarian; and the Rámayana says,—'The chief of monkeys is perfect, no one equals him in Sástras, in learning, and in ascertaining the sense of the scriptures (or in moving at will). In all sciences, in the rules of austerity, he rivals the preceptor of the gods.'"

The worship of Hanuman is general throughout the provinces and in the eastern districts is very extensive. Monkeys are regarded as his representatives and food given to them is regarded as an offering to the god and injury done to them as injury to the god. The worship of Hanuman is general amongst all classes, but is probably most general amongst the lower castes by whom his powers as a magician and as the great "Bir" are held in the greatest reverence.

Other companions of Ráma are specially worshipped to an inconsiderable extent. Lachhman, his faithful brother, who gave his life for the king, has 381 worshippers, whilst the other companions of Ráma, including the gentle Sita (Janki) herself and his brother Bharat have 7,984.

Worshippers of Krishna, 684,372—The eighth incarnation of Vishnu, that in which he descended to earth as Krishna, is that to which his worship is most generally directed. Under the name of Krishna in all probability a large proportion of the worshippers shown as Vaishnava unspecified should be included. The actual number of worshippers who wrote Krishna, Sri-Krishna or Krishan Narayan in the schedules was 684,372. Of the legendary adventures of Krishna the most interesting account available is that by the late Mr. F. S. Growse in his memoir on the Muttra district from which the following summary is extracted :—

"It is certain that Krishna was celebrated as a gallant warrior prince for many ages before he was metamorphosed into the amatory swain who now, under the title of Kanhaiya, is worshipped throughout India. He is first mentioned in the Mahábhárat, the most voluminous of all Sanskrit poems, consisting in the printed edition of 91,000 couplets.

There he figures simply as the king of Dwarka and ally of the Pándavs; nor in the whole length of the poem, of which he is to a great extent the hero, is any allusion whatever made to his early life, except in one disputed passage. Hence it may be presumed that his boyish frolics at Muttra and Brindaban, which now alone dwell in popular memory, are all subsequent inventions. They are related at length in the Harivansa, which is a comparatively modern sequel to the Mahábhárat, and with still greater circumstantiality in some of the later Puranas, which probably in their present form date no further back than the tenth century after Christ. So rapid has been the development of the original idea when once planted in the congenial soil of the sensuous east, that, while in none of the more genuine Puranas, even those specially devoted to the inculcation of Vaishnava doctrines, is so much as the name mentioned of his favourite mistress, Radhá, she now is jointly enthroned with him in every shrine and claims a full half of popular devotion. Among ordinary Hindus the recognized authority for his life and exploits is the Bhágavat Purána, or rather its tenth book, which has been translated into every form of the modern vernacular. The Hindi version, entitled the Prem Ságar, is the one held in most repute."

Worshippers of Balarám, 31,412.—Of the companions of Krishna the figures for worshippers, his brother and playmate Balaráma, have been separately compiled and show 31,412 persons.

Companions of Krishna, 101,570.—Of other companions of Krishna including his mistress Radha, with whom so much of the later Krishnavite literature is connected, 101,570 persons have been entered as special worshippers.

Worshippers of minor incarnations of Vishnu, 55,095.—The minor incarnations of Vishnu are worshipped by 55,095 persons. The incarnations, which find an important place in the census lists, are those of "the Varaha, the boar under which form Vishnu after a struggle of 1,000 years recovered the earth from the bottom of the sea to which it had been dragged by a demon and of the Vamana or dwarf by whom Bali the Daitya king was shorn of his dominion over the three worlds. Rája Bali himself, to this day regarded as a model of devotion, austerity and generosity, and possibly in sympathy with the limitation of his kingdom by unfair means to the lower regions has separate worshippers, but owing to the similarity of name to that of an Ahír god the number is unascertainable."

Worshippers of Saligram, 261,610.—The household worship of Vishnu is usually addressed to the Saligráma an ammonite brought from Nipal and connected with the god by the following legend. :—

"A reason for the sacredness of the Shalgráma is found in the Bhagwata Purana. Sani commenced his reign with a request to Bráhma to become subject to him, Bráhma referred him to Vishnu, who asked him to call upon him the next day. When he called, finding that Vishnu had transformed himself ino a mountain, he became a worm named Vajrakita, and afflicted Vishnu for twelve years. At the expiration of that time Vishnu resumed his proper shape, and ordered that henceforth the stones of this mountain (Gandaki) should be worshipped as representatives of himself."

"The Bráhmans usually worship Vishnu in this form in their daily 'puja' at home. In the hot season a vessel of water is suspended over the Saligráma, and the water continually dropping on it keeps it cool; another vessel is placed under it to catch the water, which is drunk in the evening by the worshipper. The marks of it are shown to men when dying, in the belief that the concentration of the mind on them at this time will ensure the soul a safe passage to Vishnu's heaven."

"The popular belief is that in this mountain there are multitudes of insects which perforate the stones; and they when perforated, falling into the river Gandaka, are taken out by means of nets. The more common ones are about the size of a watch, and their price varies according to their size, hollowness, and inside colouring, according to which peculiarities special names are given. For the rarer kinds as much as Rs. 2,000 are given; and when it is remembered that it is believed that the possessor of one of these ammonites, and a shell called Dukshinávartá (*i.e.*, a shell whose convolutions are towards the right), can never be poor, it is not to be wondered at that large prices should be paid for them. As it is also believed that in parting with them they invite misfortune, it is natural that those possessing should wish to retain them; to sell them for gain is regarded as a most dishonourable deed."

Of Vishnu in the form of the Saligráma 261,610 persons are worshippers.

Worshippers of Lakshmi, 1,458.—Amongst the other entries specially connected with the worship of Vishnu are those of 1,458 persons, worshippers of Lakshmi, the Sakti of Vishnu, but now held in universal honour as the goddess of abundance and fortune. In Griffith's Rámayana the following description of Lakshmi or Sri is given :—

"When many a year had fled,
"Up floated, on her lotus bed,
"A maiden fair and tender-eyed,
"In the young flush of beauty's pride.
"She shone with pearl and golden sheen,
"And seals of glory stamped her queen:
"On each round arm glowed many a gem,
"On her smooth brows a diadem.
"Rolling in waves beneath her crown
"The glory of her hair rolled down.
"Pearls on her neck of price untold,
"The lady shone like burnished gold.
"Queen of the gods, she leapt to land,
"A lotus in her perfect hand,
"And fondly, of the lotus sprung,
"To lotus-bearing Vishnu clung.
"Her, gods above and men below,
"As Beauty's Queen and Fortune know."

Lakshmi, few as her special worshippers are, is numerously worshipped under the outward form of a rupee in the most attractive of the Hindu festivals, the Diwali, on which in every Hindu house in the provinces a larger or smaller number of lamps are illuminated in honour of Sri Lakshmiji.

Worshippers of Mahábhárat Heroes, 3,957.—More closely connected with the worship of Vishnu than of Siva is that of the Mahábhárat heroes, the five Pandu warriors who waged a long war against the power and treachery of their rivals the Kurus. Of these the mighty Bhimsen and the Apollo-like Arjan are the favourites, but the wise Judhistar also finds special worshippers. Altogether 3,957 persons worship the Pandu brothers.

Worshippers of Tulsi, 1,139—*Worshippers of Garur,* 163.—The tulsi a plant worshipped mostly by followers of Vishnu, and from the wood of which the beads worn by Vaishnavites are made, has 1,139 special worshippers, probably as an embodiment of the god. The only remaining entry connected with Vishnu is that of 163 worshippers of Garur or Garuda, the mythical bird half-vulture half-man upon which Vishnu rides. He is the great enemy of snakes and bad men, both of whom he devours.

The total number of persons so far recorded as special worshippers of Vishnu, his incarnations or of gods specially connected with him is 7,208,808.

185. **Saivism,** *Saivas,* 8,101,617.—Worshippers of Siva form in every way a more compact body than those just referred to. 8,101,617 persons have recorded themselves simply as Saiva or as worshippers of Siva by one of the one thousand and eight general names which the devotion of his followers has attributed to him. He is Mahadeo or Maheswara, the Great God ; Ishwar, the supreme lord ; Chandra Shekara, he who wears a moon on his forehead ; Bhuteswara, the lord of Ghosts; Nilkantha, the blue-necked ; Gangadhara, he who holds the Ganges ; Digambara, the clothed with space ; Sambhu or Sankara (Shankar), the auspicious ; Bhairava, the destroyer ; Biswanath or Biseswara (Bisheshar), the lord of all ; Hara, the seizer ; Ugra, the fierce ; Aghora, the horrible ; Bhagwat, the divine. From these names may be gathered something as to the various characters attributed to the god. The essential difference between Vishnu and Siva has already been referred to. The former is the god of faith, taking an interest in and providing for the welfare of the universe. In his worship consists, as Monier Williams points out, the only approach in Hinduism to religion in the Western sense. Siva is the god of power, a god to be feared only, removed in all his characters from the weakness of an interest in mankind. Siva as depicted in the later Hindu writings assumes a "very bewildering variety of personalities, but in the words of the author just referred to, "there are really five chief characters of the god who stand out prominently from his general protraiture—

"1st. He is the universal destroyer, annihilating not only men and all created beings but good and evil demons and even Bráhma, Vishnu and all the inferior gods. In this character he is called Bhairawa, the terrible one ; Smasana-Vasin, the dweller in burial grounds. Imps and demons are his ready servants, ferocity and irascibility his normal condition of mind."

"2nd. In the second place, Siva is the impersonation of the eternal reproductive power of nature, perpetually reintegrating after disintegration. It is specially in this personality that he is called the eternally blessed one, 'the causer of blessings' (Siva, Sada Siva, Sankar and Sambhu), and it is in this character that he is now generally worshipped all over India under the well-known and often misunderstood symbol of the Linga."

"*3rd.*—In the third place, Siva is the great typical ascetic and self-mortifier (Yogi, Tapasvi), who has attained the highest perfection in meditation and austerity (whence his names Mahátapah, Maháyogi). In this character he appears quite naked (Dig-Ambara) with only one face, like an ordinary human being, with ash-besmeared body and matted hair (whence his name Dhurjati) sitting in profound meditation under a Banian tree (=Vata or Bar tree), and often, like the contemplative Buddha, under a canopy formed by a serpent's head. There he is supposed to remain passionless, motionless, immovable as the trunk of a tree (sthanu), and perhaps rooted to the same spot for millions of years."

"It is in this character that he teaches men by his own example the power to be acquired by mortification of the body, suppression of the passions, and abstract contemplation, as leading to the loftiest spiritual knowledge and ultimately effecting union with himself in Kailása."

"*4th.*—In the fourth place, the god Siva is a contemplative philosopher and learned sage, the revealer of grammar to the greatest of Indian grammarians, Panini. This, in fact, is one of many proofs that at least one form of Saivism is as much the peculiar system of Bráhmans, learned men, and the higher classes of the Hindu community. Siva is the god of the Bráhmans, Krishna (Vishnu) of the Kshatriyas, Bráhma of the Vaisyas, and Ganesa of Sudras."

"*5th.*—In the fifth place, Siva is exactly the opposite of an ascetic and philosopher. He is a wild and jovial mountaineer (Kiráta), addicted to hunting and wine-drinking, fond of dancing (Nritya-priyah, also called Natesvara, 'lord of dancers'), often dancing with his wife the Tándava dance, and surrounded by dwarfish, buffoon-like troops (Guna) of attendants, who, like their master, are fond of good living and occasionally inebriated by intoxicating liquors. The worshippers of Siva in this character usually (but not invariably) belong to the sect called Saktas, who are devoted to the wife of the god, and are given to self-indulgence and sensual gratification. Their religious books are called Tantras, and their tenets will be explained under the head of Saktism."

It might have been expected that so great a variety of character in the god would have led to a corresponding variety in Saivite sects, but as a matter of fact the absence of anything like abstract religious beliefs in the worship of Siva has preserved Saivism far more united than Vaishnavism, and the so-called Saivite sects are in reality more separate orders of ascetics than separate sects. They are separated from each other by matters of outward form not of inward faith. Saivism affords little foundation for a reformer, and hence almost all attempts at reform have sprung from Vaishnavism.

Worshippers of local Mahadeos, 16,128.—The only group of Siva worshippers which it has been considered necessary to show separately is that which evidences the inclusion to some extent in the character of Siva of the attributes of aboriginal gods or demons—16,128 are recorded as worshippers of local and special Mahadeos, the usurpers of the position formerly occupied by some aboriginal "deo" of fame. The contrast between this number and that shown for local Debis shows to how slight an extent Siva is, as compared with Debi, identified with local gods.

Worshippers of Bhairon, 173,679.—Worshippers of inferior gods connected with Siva form a separate class of some importance. By far the most generally worshipped is Bhairon. In the Puranas a Bhairava was an inferior manifestation of a terrible character, but the Bhairon of these days enjoys a perfectly separate entity as one of Siva's attendants and more particularly as the Kotwal of Benares, Siva's sacred city. He is usually represented as armed with a club and riding upon a dog, but there are at least five different forms of Bhairon known by the separate names of—(1) Kal Bhairon, (2) Bhut Bhairon, (3) Nand Bhairon, (4) Suth Bhairon, (5) Batuk Bhairon. His worshippers, chiefly amongst the lower classes of Saivites, are numerous in Benares and neighbouring districts.

Worshippers of Ganesa, 78,188.—Ganesa (Ganesh or Ganpat), the reputed son of Siva and Parbati, is another Saivite deity who has in late days arrived at greater dignity than was allotted to him in the Puranas. He is the god of wisdom and remover of obstacles.

He has, says Sir William Jones, "the same characteristics as Janus of the Latins. All sacrifices and religious ceremonies, all serious compositions in writing, and all worldly affairs of importance are begun by pious Hindus with an invocation to Ganesa; a word composed of Isa, the governor or leader, and Gana, a company (of deities). Instances of opening business auspiciously by an ejaculation to him might be multiplied with ease. Few books are begun without the words, 'salutation to Ganesa'; and he is first invoked by Bráhmans who conduct the trial by ordeal or perform the ceremony of the homa or sacrifice to fire."

His general appearance is well known. He is represented as a short fat man of a yellow colour with a protuberant belly, four hands and the head of an elephant. An invocation to Ganesh precedes all worship by high caste Hindus, and Bhadon Sudi 4th is held specially sacred in his honour.

Worshippers of Parbati, 8,584.—Worshippers of Parbati, although she has been identified with Durga, have been included here, as the goddesses know by the names of Uma and Parbati have nothing whatsoever in common with the dread Kali. Uma is the name by which the consort of Siva is first known. After she had for her husband's sake immolated herself by entering the sacrificial fire and earned the name of "Sati," a true and virtuous woman, she was born again as Parvati, the daughter of Himawat. In this form she is the constant companion of her husband, and but few independent actions are attributed to her. The number of her worshippers is 8,584 only.

Nandi-Worshippers, 137.—The last divinity to be mentioned in connection with Siva is Nandi, the bull on which Siva rides and whose image is familiar, waiting in reverence outside all Saiva temples. Nandi is credited with 137 special worshippers.

186. **Saktism.**—From Saivism we pass to the third great division of modern Hinduism—Saktism.

It is first met with in the Puranas as the worship of force (Sakti) personified as goddesses, the female counterparts of each of the gods of the Hindu Triad. In the later Puranas special laudation is accorded to the active power of the Sakti and especially of the Sakti of Siva, but Saktism in its present development is distinctly post-Puranic. The special scriptures of the Sakti worshippers are the Tantras which in the words of Monier Williams inculcate "an exclusive worship of Siva's wife as the source of every kind of supernatural faculty and mystic craft." The influence of the Tantras never appears to have been extensive in Hindustan amongst the mass of the people, and the grosser forms of Sakti worship in which the goddess is gratified by free course being allowed to all the sensual appetites, regardless of social rules and restrictions, have never attracted notice except as connected with a comparatively small number of professional devotees regarded with horror by the people in general. It is probably amongst these that 1,576 persons have been found to record themselves as Bami, Vama-Margi, followers of the left hand path, that is, persons who avowedly devote themselves to the worship of the female side of the deity in accordance with the teaching of the Tantras. For

Bami, 1,576.

the great mass of the people, however, the worship of Debi though conducted with oblations of blood and wine is unconnected with licentious orgies. The goddess worshipped as Debi (Devi) is in appearance the dread and blood-thirsty goddess of Tantras, black and hideous, of a terrible countenance dripping with blood, encircled with snakes hung round with skulls and human heads ; but the aspect of Saktism most in evidence in these provinces is one which suggests an origin very different from the semi-philosophical development above referred to. The aspect of the goddess Debi, the number, location, and nature of her shrines, the form of worship usually adopted and the caste of the great mass of her worshippers all suggest that her worship is derived by uninterrupted descent from that of the non-Aryan and probably pre-Aryan demon gods. It is in this origin we have the explanation of the contrast between the various forms of Devi, and of the identification of this repulsive goddess with the loving Uma or the wise Parbati. The gradual acceptance of worshippers of these gods into the Hindu system made it necessary to find a place for them in the Hindu mythology and the various Dravidian Devis, unlike as they were to Parbati, were in consequence recognized as one with the wife of Siva. Legends regarding them were incorporated to some extent in the later Puranas. The worship has, however, as already remarked, retained much of its old form. Devi is worshipped not at the centres of Hinduism nor in celebrated shrines, but in lonely and defined spots hidden away in the northern forests, or at long-recognized shrines, scattered over the country, round which the preservation of a patch of jangal mimics the appearance of the place where a forest demon was worshipped there under her forest name. By her worshippers at each shrine she is known by the local name the Bhawani of Ahorwa, the Debi of Tarkulwa, the Debi of Patan, the Debi who lives on Nanda. Everything indicates that under the one name have been collected a large number of different deities. The worship of Debi is rarely conducted by Bráhmans or members of a recognized religious order. Like her worshippers, her priests are of low caste and non-Aryan ancestry—Malis, Ahírs, Pasis, Bhars, and the like. The offerings largely take the form of sacrifice of living animals, goats, pigs and buffaloes—the head of which along with as much of the forequarters as the executioner can slice away with the head being the perquisite of the attandants at the shrine, and the rest eaten by the persons who have made the offering.

Bindhachal Devi...	...	41,385
Jwalamai ...	...	116,769
Chandi Devi ...	...	1,326
Other local Devis	...	412,056
Total	...	571,536

The most celebrated of the Devis of this province is that of Bindhachal, a shrine on the Ganges near Mirzapur ; Jwalamai, the Devi of Nagarkot in the Kangra Valley; the Devi of the Chandi hill which looks down from across the Ganges on Hardwár, and of Patan, a shrine in the Nepal Taráí. Altogether 571,536 persons have recorded themselves as worshippers of Devi with the addition of some local name. Of Devi under that name or the general names of Bhawani, Kali, Durga, Chamunda (the slayer of Chand and Mund). Ashtbhuji (who rose from the foam), no less than 9,507,409 persons are recorded as special worshippers—a larger number than have declared for any other deity in the Hindu system. Devi worshippers under all names numbered 10,080,521, of whom 5,150,143 were males and 4,930,378 females.

187. **Miscellaneous divinities of modern Hinduism.**—In class VII have been collected a number of groups of worshippers of deities not so distinctly connected as those just mentioned with any of the great Puranic deities, but many of whom are regarded as forms of Devi.

188. **Gods of disease.**—Most closely connected with Devi of any of these groups are the gods of disease. The worship of these gods is common at all times and in especial when epidemic disease is prevalent in the neighbourhood.

Sitala worshippers, 119,139.—The principal, as the most dreaded, is Sitala or Mata, the goddess of Small-pox, represented as a woman riding on a dog or an ass. She is ordinarily worshipped in Asárh and Chet of every year, and when any one is ill of small-pox or after a recovery from it offerings are made to her. Amongst the lower classes she, as the most dreaded form of Devi, is likely to be recorded as specially worshipped with a view to her propitiation.

Cholera worshippers, 9,539.—*Hatthi*, the goddess of cholera, originally represented like Sitala as one of the seven daughters of Rája Ben, is worshipped when the disease is prevalent. Another cholera goddess is Marimai, who is to be propitiated by the offering of (1) a pumpkin, (2) a cock, (3) a he-goat, (4) a ram, (5) a male buffalo, (6) a woman, or (7) a man.

Hardaul Rája, 5,034.—The worship of Hardaul or Hardeo Rája or Hardaul Lála is frequent throughout the provinces for the purpose of averting epidemic disease and in especial cholera. It is mentioned in the Gonda Gazetteer as prevalent in that district. It is shown in the census returns as prevailing to some extent throughout Oudh and the districts of the Allahabad Division, the name being usually given as Hardeo. Elliot, Glossary vol. I, page 269, gives the following account of the worship :—

"Hardaur is the name given to the oblong mounds raised in villages, and studded with flags, for the purpose of averting epidemic diseases, and especially the cholera morbus. It is called after Hardaul Lála, the son of Bir Singh Deo, from whom are descended the Rájas of Dattia. The natives have a firm persuasion that the cholera broke out in Lord Hastings' camp, in consequence of beef having been killed for the European soldiers within the grove where repose the ashes of this Bundelkhand Chief. So rapid has been the extension of this worship, that it now prevails throughout the upper and central Doáb, a great part of Rohilkhand, and to the banks of the Sutlej. To the eastward, the worship of Hulka Devi (the Goddess of Vomiting) has been prevalent since the same period."

Agwan, 25,069.—Agwan, the return of whose worshippers is considerable in the eastern districts, has not been fully identified. The word simply means a leader and may apply to the pujari in any temple. One district note states that Agwan is a disease god, the son of Rája Ben, and, therefore, brother to the seven small-pox sisters.

189. **Serpent worship.**—Serpent worship, one of the most widespread primitive cults, has without doubt been incorporated by Hinduism from the aboriginal tribes which it adopted into its system. The extent to which it has been interwoven into the Puranic legends is a proof of the great extent to which Hinduism is an offspring of the Indian soil and not derived from the

Aryan religion of the Vedas. Vishnu is represented as sleeping on the thousand-headed serpent, Sheshnág, the head of the serpent forming a canopy over him. The linga of Siva is often represented as protected with serpents coiled round it. The names which occur in the census schedules are many of them connected with the Mahábhárat legend which narrates how Manasa, the sister of Vasuki, the king of snakes, married an eminent sage and had by him a son, Astika, who saved the serpent race when menaced with extinction by Janamejaya offering up a sacrifice to procure the extinction of all snakes. Astik, the saviour of the snake race, has 41,351 worshippers. Farukhabad, where Janamejaya made his sacrifice, contributes 3,683 to this number; the rest are mostly in Oudh. The names of other serpent gods, Sheshnág, Vasuki, &c., also occurred in the schedules, but in the return are contained under the general name Nága or Nágdeota.

Naga worshippers, 25,366, *Guga Pir,* 122,991.—A large part of the entries under the above Puranic names are probably made by Agarwala Baniyas who claim descent from Vasuki, the Nága king, and who are specially devoted to serpent worship, calling themselves *Nága upashiki.* Serpent worship is, however, general amongst all classes on Nág Panchmi, the fifth day of Sawan, when in every house offerings of clarified butter and sugar are made to a rude "geru" drawing of a snake on the wall. The most generally worshipped of snake gods in the west and everywhere by Agarwala Baniyas is Guga Pir or as he is also called Zahir Pir or Zahir Diwan. An account of this divinity is given by Elliot (Glossary, I, 256). His connection with snake worship or claims to saintship are not very distinct. The most generally received accounts of his life represent him either a Chauhan Ráj-put as contemporary of Pirthi Rája and as having fought with desperate valour against the Muhammadans with that king or as having fallen with forty-five sons and sixty nephews opposing Mahmud Ghaznavi. The local Hissar tradition states that in a quarrel about land he killed his two brothers, and to avoid his mother's curse wished that the earth might open and swallow him up, horse and all. A voice from heaven declared that he could not have this satisfaction until he repeated the Kalima and became a Muhammadan. "He appears to have had no difficulty in doing this, upon which the earth opened and he leaped into its bosom." Be his origin what it may, it is neither as a suicide nor as an opponent of the Muhammadans that he is now worshipped, but as a god able and willing when propitiated to protect against snakes.

As Monier Williams points out, snakes are regarded in India as embodiments of the contradictory ideas of destruction and regeneration, malevolence and benevolence, demonism and divinity, death and immortality. The divinity worshipped on the Nág Panchmi is beneficent, but the idea mainly connected with the snake gods of the lower classes is fear. The gods regarded by the Agarwalas as ancestral and Guga Pir are probably often regarded as beneficent. The especial snake gods of the lower classes are, however, worshipped entirely through fear. The return of special worshippers for such gods was with one exception small, and as the name generally given was general, *e.g.*, Sámp deota, they have been included in *Nága,* a general term for snake gods. Ahiran, a snake god, worshipped in Sultánpur by daily offerings of red lead, water and rice, has also been so included.

Sokha, 18,578.—An exceptionally large number of persons worship Sokha, stated to be the spirit of a Bráhman killed by a snake, which is now supposed to have the power of inflicting death by snakebite on persons who do not propitiate him. He is worshipped with this view largely in the Benares and Gorakhpur Divisions. The prejudice against killing snakes appears not to be so widely felt in the North-Western Provinces as elsewhere. Doing so is associated with a certain amount of fear, but it appears to be connected more especially with the snake attacked and his mate. If a snake is struck and not killed he is believed to be certain to return to bite his assailant.

190. **Animism in the Hindu system.**—We have seen that under the name of Debi most of the low caste gods of importance have been incorporated into the Hindu system and have to a great extent lost their identity in being so incorporated. In the next class we have mostly to deal with divinities or devils not so fully identified with Debi, who, though many of whom are of aboriginal or Dravidian origin, are in spite of Bráhmanical influence and absorptiveness still largely worshipped by the mass of the low caste people of the provinces as distinct from the great Hindu gods. These objects of worship belong to two markedly distinct classes—those regarded as superhuman in their origin, local, household, forest, and field gods, and those who owe their origin to the virtues, the vices, or the misfortunes of human beings, whose ghosts remain to bless or most generally to plague mankind after their death. The second class is as regards number of special worshippers far more important than the other and it may be dealt with first.

191. **Ghost worship.**—It owes its origin to a variety of superstitions regarding what follows after death. In general, persons who have died a violent or sudden death and have not received due funeral rites become ghosts for the most part malevolent. The spirits of persons noted for evil doing in their lives become after even a natural death the impersonations of the vices they practised in their lives. Men who have married become ghosts if they die without having begotten or adopted a son. On the other hand the ranks of benevolent spirits are very constantly recruited by the addition of the ghosts of men who have been eminent for holiness or well-doing in their lives. The list of those ghostly spirits which are specially worshipped to a noteworthy extent in these provinces is a somewhat lengthy one. I have divided the list into two groups according to their origin. The first is of purely Indian origin. In the second, the influence of Muhammadan reverence for the early martyrs of their faith was the originating principle.

Bráhm worshippers, 406,787.—Of spirits of Hindu origin the most important class as regards special worship are "Bráhms" or the spirits of Bráhmans who have died a violent death or who have committed suicide, in general to revenge themselves for some act of injustice committed against them. It is to the present day an act so common amongst Bráhmans to attempt to attain any object particularly desired by gradually starving themselves that a section in the Penal Code had to be specially provided to punish this form of unlawful influence. Bráhms are worshipped at the spot where they died by all and sundry, but are especially feared by the families of the persons who are either actually or according to Hindu ideas responsible for their deaths, and are accordingly specially worshipped by them. Bráhm worshippers occur to some extent in western districts, but the main seat of such worship is in Oudh and the east of the North-Western Provinces. The Rájput occupation of the Bais parganas is said to have caused a large number of Bráhman deaths, and the brickwork "chaura" or "asthan" raised over the spot where a Brahman died is very common in Bais villages. Rae Bareli, Lucknow, and Unao, therefore, show the largest number of Bráhm-worshippers in the provinces. The stories connected with the death of such Bráhmans are in general so much alike that to quote one or two will be a sufficient indication of their nature. Perhaps of all such spirits that most worshipped in North-Eastern Oudh, is the Bráhm of Ratan Pande, whose story is told in the Gonda Gazetteer. The race referred to in the quotation is that of Kalhans Rájas of Gonda.

"The last of the race, Rája Achal Narain Singh, stands out clearly in tradition as an example of the divine vengeance which overtakes lust and tyranny. His last act in a career of unbridled oppression was to carry off to his fort at Lurhia Ghát, near Khurasa, the virgin daughter of a small Bráhman zamíndár in the Burhapara pargana. The outraged father pleaded as vainly as the father of Chryseis for reparation, and his vengeance was as dramatic and more complete. For twenty-one days he sat under a tamarind tree at the door of the ravisher, refusing meat and drink, till death put an end to his sufferings. His wife, who had followed him, died at the same time from grief. Before his spirit fled, he pronounced a curse of utter extinction on the family of his oppressor, modifying it only in favour of the offspring of the younger Ráni, who alone had endeavoured to induce him to break his fast, and to whom he promised that her descendants, the present Rájas of Babhnipair, should succeed to a small ráj; but that as his eyes had fallen in from hunger, so should they be always blind. His ghost went to the river Sarju, and implored her assistance in avenging himself on the Rája, but she referred him to her elder sister, the Ganges, who said she was too distant to interfere effectually, and referred him back to the Sarju. At last that stream, the faithful friend of Bráhmans, consented to help him, on the condition that he would get the Rája into his power by inducing him to accept some present. He went to the Rája's family priest, and gave him a sacred cord, with the direction that he was to invest his enemy with it. Achal Narain Singh put it on, and then asked where it had come from. When told from the hands of Ratan Pande, his conscience struck him, and he cast it away in terror. But it was too late; the present had been accepted, and a few days later, on the 13th of the light half of Aghan, a lofty wave rushed up from the Sarju through the Mahádeva pargana, and on its crest sat the angry wraith of Ratan Pande. When it reached Lurhia Ghát it broke, and overthrew the Rája's fortress, carrying away everything in indiscriminate ruin, and leaving not a member of his household alive. A deep lake is still shown, under which it is said that in the hot weather the fisherman can strike with his punt-pole the ruined towers of the old palace; and all around the shore are large brick mounds, the remains of ancient mansions, and the palm and date trees of former gardens. Coins are occasionally disinterred by the rains, and I have myself found a copper piece there of a mint which I could not recognise myself or identify in Prinsep. It would of course be a vain task to attempt to disentangle the elements of fact from this singular tradition; but the story is told with a circumstantiality and vividness which render it hard to imagine that it is purely an invention or even an ordinary myth. The exact date is given, the descendants of the avenging Bráhman are still in existence, and the scene of the asserted disaster was certainly at one time the site of a populous town. The Mahádeva pargana is seamed all over with the channels of rivers which have dried up or changed their course, and there is no difficulty in believing either that a Bráhman did starve himself to death at the Rája's gateway, or that the palace was destroyed by some extraordinary natural convulsion, possibly an earthquake, which drove the waters of the Tirhi into a new channel."

Another account of the death of a Bráhm, whose worship is spreading largely over the eastern districts, is given in the following note from *Northern India Notes and Queries* for June 1892 :—

"In Chayanpur Babua, in the Arrah district, there is a platform in honour of Harshu Bráhm. There was once a King Sahbaran there. He built a great palace. Harshu Pánde was his family priest. He had four sons. They built a house higher than the Rája's palace. One day the Rája and Ráni were asleep on the roof of the palace, and they saw a light high up on Harshu's house. The Rája told the Ráni that this was the house of their family priest. Next day the Ráni got her courtiers to hint to the Rája that his family priest by building his house as high as that of the Rája showed his intention of contending with his master. So the Rája was angry and sent workmen, who knocked down Harshu's house. He was so grieved that he sat dharna at the palace door for twenty-two days without food or drink. No one could induce him to go away. Finally the king's daughter implored him to drink, and Harshu drank a little water from her hand. Sugar had been mixed in the water. When he drank this, Harshu said: You said you would give me only water; why did you give me sherbet? She said she gave it to him only to relieve his thirst. He blessed her, and told her that her progeny would increase and the Rája be destroyed. Then Harshu died. When they went to take his corpse to Benares they saw him standing there with his wooden sandals on. He said he had become a Bráhm, and whoever worshipped him would get his desires fulfilled. Now his altar is worshipped with fire sacrifice, Bráhmanical cords, and sweets. If any one obtains his wish he offers a golden Bráhmanical cord and a silken waist string, and feeds Bráhmans in his name."

The legends are all more or less similar, and it is unnecessary to quote further. The names classified in the list of Bráhms are almost innumerable. The information available about them varies from a full and circumstantial account like that given for Ratan Pande or which might be given for Hari Rám, the Ráj Bráhm of the Basti district, down to that derived from the name only, the Bráhmanical character of which was taken to show that the particular Baba referred to was a Bráhm. The total number of Bráhm worshippers according to the census statements was 406,787, large numbers of whom belong to the Rájput caste, the members of which are most likely to incur persecution from a murdered or injured Bráhman. The forms of death selected by suicide Bráhmans are diversified in the extreme. Of all I have heard the most horrible and most likely to impress the imagination of the persons against whom it was directed was that of a Bráhman in the Partábgarh district, who when turned out of his land, to avenge himself, gathered a heap of cowdung in the centre of one of the fields and lay down on it till he was eaten by worms. This happened sixty years ago, but his fields still stand a waste of jangal grass in the middle of rich cultivated land, and neither Hindu nor Muhammadan will put a hand to a plough to till them. Whether Bráhms are to be classed amongst malevolent or beneficent spirits is a question which would probably be answered differently by different worshippers. Those families to whose account a Bráhman's death is due probably regarded him as malevolent but elsewhere a beneficent interest is taken by Bráhms in human affairs. Ratan Pande is said to be the tutelary deity of many Gonda villages.

Other ghosts, 394,830.—Spirits of persons of other castes are not known by distinctive names, but are for the most part known by the general names of Bhút or Pret. Spirits of low caste persons, especially Ahírs, are often called *Bir*, although this name also applies to beings of supernatural origin. Ghosts of low caste women become *churels*, a particularly malevolent and active form of evil spirit, physically distinguishable from living women only by the feet being turned backwards. Of such ghosts unspecified and most of them unidentified 394,830 persons have been shown as special worshippers. It is possible that a number of worshippers of local gods not ghosts have for want of information been included here. Under the head of Bir, 22,553 worshippers have been classed. The information on the subject of each is in general scanty, to the effect that this Bir is the ghost of a Nat and that of an Ahír, that this is honoured with offerings of ganja and that with offerings of food. Birs are, I believe, distinctly maleficent.

Burhe Baba, 54,849.—Burhe Baba is a divinity largely worshipped in the western districts. He is said to have been a Gadariya, distinguished from other Gadariyas by a knowledge of Sanskrit. No trace of his education is visible in his conduct after death. He occupies himself in sending itch, ringworm, or boils to the children of those who offend him. He is, however, placable and contented with little.

Kashi Dass, 172,599.—Kashi Dass is reported to be another spirit god particularly worshipped by Ahírs throughout the eastern districts. It is uncertain whether he was a Bráhman or an Ahír in life. His worshippers number 172,599.

Jokhaiya, 87,061.—A low caste spirit, extensively reverenced in Etáwah and neighbouring districts is Jokhaiya, of whom the following account is given in the District Gazetteer for Mainpuri :—

"Pendhat is noted, however, for the large gatherings which take place there at the shrine of Jokhaiya and at the temple in Magh and Asárh. There is no fixed day, but the Sundays in the latter fortnights of those months called Jat are chosen. The story runs that during the war between Pirthiráj and Jaichand of Kanauj, an Ahír was bringing his wife from home, and with him were a Bráhman and a low caste man, a Bhangi or a Dhanak. The three men joined in the fight and were killed. The Bhangi fell first, and the other two fell at some distance from him. Even when dead their headless trunks (rund) continued the fight. The Bhangi became a bhut (or spirit) under the name Jokhaiya, and the place where he fell is called Jokhaiya to this day. Droves of pigs are grazed here, and at the time of the great gathering the swineherds will kill one of them for a trifle and let the blood flow on the spot. At the other place, where the Bráhman and Ahír fell, there is a temple, and cocoanuts and the like are offered. People come in thousands from the surrounding districts, even from Farukhabad, which touches the opposite side of the district, to pay their devotions here. The great object of the journey is to obtain offspring and have an easy childbirth. The mela is also said to have a good influence on the winter rains or mahawat. The worship of Jokhaiya is also noticed under the Etáwah district."

Worship of Ghosts of Magicians.—Of the remaining spirits worshipped, the most important class is that of the ghosts of sorcerers, fear of whose malevolence has shown itself the predominating religious feeling of 174,304 people. The majority of the sorcerers are Muhammadans, and greatest of all is Sheikh Saddu, of Amroha fame, of whom the following account is given in the Moradabad Gazetteer :—

"Sheikh Saddu or Sadr-ud-din was a former crier (Mu'azzin) of the mosque, and the popular explanation given of the renown attached to his memory is that he practised magic. What is said to be the tomb of Saddu is pointed out under the central arch; that of his mother, Ghasia, is under the northern, and that of a demon, Zen Khán, said to have assisted Saddu, is under the southern arch. The ceremonies observed consist in offering oblations to all three and in touching the chain (called Murrads'). The credulous worshippers believe that Sheikh Saddu had two demons in his service, who ministered to his lusts by bringing young and beautiful females to the magician. He is said to have finally been destroyed by these fiends, who dashed out his brains against the roof. Perhaps the legendary account may contain a glimmering of truth, and the so-called saint may have met his deserts for licentiousness not unknown among persons of his class."

The fear which the evil of his life inspired has led to his ghost being propitiated by large numbers of low caste Hindus throughout Rohilkhand. Worshippers of other Muhammadans reputed to be sorcerers are numerous in the eastern districts. In all the population so recorded amounts to 174,304.

Satti worship, 8,533.—The spirits of women who immolated themselves with their husbands are everywhere worshipped, and 8,533 persons have recorded themselves as regarding such spirits as tutelary deities. The cult appears from the returns to be spread throughout the province.

Bagaha, 7,784, *Sapaha*, 156.—Two small classes of worshippers remain for mention before we pass to the next group. They are the ghosts of persons killed by tigers and snakes, propitiation of whom is believed to protect from a similar death. Worship of the former is general throughout Oudh and the Gorakhpur districts. In Gorakhpur, Gonda, or Bahraich it might have been expected, but it seems extraordinary that such worship has retained its hold in Sultánpur. Probably the comparative rarity of such a death in the southern districts of late years made it appear the more impressive and preserved its memory the longer. The worship of persons killed by snakes appears in small numbers in several of the eastern and Bundelkhand districts.

192. **Worship of Muhammadan Saints.**—We now pass to the mention of the worship of a class of spirits who are amongst the last whom it might be supposed would be worshipped as beneficent deities by Hindus of these provinces.—I mean that of the Muhammadan "Shahids" who fell in battle against the Hindus whilst the country was being overrun. This cult has spread to an extent hardly credible amongst all classes in the eastern districts. Even the Bráhman makes his daily offerings of food and water to the spirits of the great Pir and his associates, and for the low caste man the household worship of the five Pirs is in many districts his sole religious trust. The adoption into the Hindu system as divinities considered beneficent of those men who were most instrumental in the overthrow of the Hindu kingdoms, the subjection of Hindus to an alien rule, and the conversion to Muhammadanism, forcibly in many instances, of large numbers of

Hindu worshippers is not the least bewildering of the many puzzles connected with Hinduism. The cult probably spread through its early adoption by low caste converts who, altogether uninstructed in the principles of Muhammadanism and searching for concrete objects of worship of the nature of those they had abandoned, found their gods in the dead heroes, whom genuine Muhammadans reverenced as martyrs who had fallen on behalf of the faith. Hinduism and especially low caste Hinduism is the least bigoted of religions as regards the objects of worship of other faiths, and it is easy to imagine how the worship of the low caste Muhammadans at shrines dotted all over the country and known by all extended to the low-caste and thence to all Hindus. The five Pirs are not the only Muhammadan martyrs who are worshipped. On the contrary all are esteemed worthy of worship. Every tomb reputed to be that of a "Shahid Mard" has its lamps burning on Fridays. The names of those who have been recorded in the census as specially worshipped are almost innumerable.

The cult is, however, far more extended and far more special in the case of five Pirs than of any other Muhammadan saints. Who the five were is a question variously answered by worshippers in every district. It would be useless to attempt to reproduce a description of the legends which have grown up in connection with the worship, a somewhat elaborate account of which has been recently published by Mr. R. Greeven. It is sufficient to say that the worship centres in Sayyid Salar Masaud Ghazi or Ghazi Mian, sister's son to Mahmud Sabaktagin, who was defeated and killed in 1034 A.D., near Bahraich, whilst leading an expedition against Sohildeo, a Bhar, Tharu or Rájput Rája of Gonda. Of the other Pirs variously quoted from district to district as belonging to the five, some can be identified with companions of Sayyid Salar, whilst others have been introduced into the legends since the adoption of the worship by Hindus. Thus the names of well known Hindu gods, like Kalka and Bhairon, appear in some lists. Amongst the Pirs believed to be identified with the companions of Sayyid Salar are the Hatheli Pir said to be Ghazi Mian's sister's son, Mian Rajjab or Rajjab Salar, and Sikandar Diwana the Búahna Pir, all buried at Bahraich, and Sabu Salar, father of the prince of martyrs, buried near Bara Banki. Amina Satti, a Hindu Ráni, Suthan and Palihar are connected with Ghazi Mian by almost all the legends connected with his story, but have not been identified with any of his historical associates.

The Musalmán origin of the worship even when adopted into the households of Hindus is never forgotten. The offerings to the Pirs are taken by Musalmán dafalis or drummers, who go about reciting the ballads regarding the Pirs, and the great annual pilgrimage to the Pirs' tombs in Bahraich brings profit only to the Muhammadan guardians of the tomb. The ceremonies observed in worshipping the Pirs are not materially different from those with which the Kare gore deo or other low caste gods are worshipped, but there is a distinction of importance in the fact that whilst the worship of the Kare Gore Deo is ignored by high caste Hindus the sanctity of the Pirs is acknowledged.

The number of persons who recorded themselves as special worshippers of the five Pirs was 1,690,985, almost entirely in the Gorakhpur and Benares

Divisions. Most of the Pirs included in any list of the Panchon Pir have been shown also as separately worshipped. Those the number of whose worshippers was most important are given in the margin. Closely connected with the worship of the five Pirs is that of Sanwar or Kunwar Dhir, though his name is not included in any lists of the five I have seen. He is stated by a note from Gházipur to be worshipped like the five Pirs with the assistance of a Dafali. His worshippers are numerous in Gorakhpur, Basti, and Ballia.

Amina Satti	8,202
Búahna Pir	51,617
Hateli Pir	2,777
Palihar	39,954

Other Muhammadan saints are worshipped all over the provinces. A large number of the returns were made under the general names of Shahid Mard, Shahid Pir or the like, but the actual names which occur in the schedules are very numerous. Amongst them occur the names of Bibi Fatima and Bibi Zohra, the latter identified with the Amina Satti of the Pachpiriyas. She is said by the Bara Banki legend to have been cured of blindness by Saiyid Salar and after to have married and died with him at Bahraich. A brick of her tomb was carried to Rudauli in Bara Banki, and a bed is now annually offered to her by sweepers, who are her principal worshippers. The names of Muhammad and of Ali and Imam Husain, themselves "Shahids," occur frequently; all the leading Muhammadan saints of India find Hindu worshippers. Saiyid Abdul Kadir Jilani appears by the names of Miran Pir, Piran-i-Pir, Pir-i-azam, Pir-i-Dastgir, Kadirya Pir. Khwaja Muin-ud-din Chishti appears as the Khwaja Pir. Shah Bazi-ud-din buried at Makhanpur on the Ganges appears as Zinda Shah Madar or Shah Madar. He is a favourite object of worship amongst the lower classes of Hindus, as his worshippers are said to be secure against the bite of snakes and scorpions. Kahárs are in the habit of shouting his name "Dam madar" as an invocation for protection when passing through forest. Pir Jalil of Lucknow, Pir Muhammad of Jaunpur, Jalal-ud-din Bukhhari *urf* Shah Makhdum Ashraf are amongst the other names of note. The total number of worshippers of Pirs not associated with Ghazi-Mian is 501,571.

Sakhi Sarwar, 8,429.—Besides these 8,429 persons were recorded in the western districts as worshippers of the Sarwar Pir or Sakhi Sarwar, a Panjáb saint mostly worshipped by Jats. He appears with a very much slighter historical foundation to be the Panjáb Ghazi Mian, and legends are there current, like those of Saiyid Salar in these provinces, of the doings of his mare, his wife, and his friends and enemies. Bhairon appears to be associated with Sakhi Sarwar in the Panjáb as here with Ghazi Mian. Of Muhammadan saints of all kinds no less than 2,333,643 persons have professed themselves special worshippers—a number which shows that this branch of Hinduism in these provinces has reached an importance such that Ghazi Mian and his fellow saints can fairly be recognised as rivals to the greatest of the orthodox Hindu gods.

193. **Ancestral and caste gods.**—The next class of worshippers to be referred to are those of ancestral or caste gods, a group intermediate between the distinctly "Ghost deities" just mentioned and those of supernatural origin who follow.

Chitra Gupta, 1,967.—The best known of the ancestral gods is perhaps Chitra Gupta, the reputed ancestor, and hereditary deity, of the Kayasth caste. In the Puranas Chitra Gupta was the scribe of Yama, the Judge of the dead. He is worshipped by Kayasths daily as their ancestor, and especially three times a year after the Diwali, on the Holi, and on the Dasehra. The form of worship is described in the following extract :—

"Chitragupta, according to the regular ritual, is invoked at meals. After grace is said each person places either four or five small mouthfuls (grása) of food on the ground on the right side of his place. These are called simply *ahuti* or offerings, or sometimes *Chitrahuti* offerings to Chitr or Chitragupta. While placing the mouthful he should say 'Homage to Chitra to Chitragupta, to Yama, to Yamadharma, to *Bhur bhuwah swah*.' After the dinner is over these morsels are left to be eaten by cats, if there are any in the house, or together with the leaf plates and whatever is left in them, they are thrown out to dogs or other animals."

The number of special worshippers of Chitragupta are few, as Kayaths are in general orthodox Saivites or Vaishnavites and worship Chitragupta with simply a somewhat greater degree of reverence than other castes use to the spirits of their ancestors. Other ancestral gods occur rarely by special names, but under such names as Kuldeota or Bare Purakh, 7,575 persons have shown themselves as special worshippers of their ancestors. Special worship of ancestors is rare ; the only form their worship ordinarily takes is in pouring out in the daily "puja" some water in their honour between the fingers and the thumb of the right hand, that for the recognised gods being poured down the palm of the hand.

Caste deities are in number not a few, but in general not to a great extent specially worshipped. One of the most important is Nathu, the special tutelary deity of the Guriya Kahárs, who is said to have been buried alive under the foundation of the fort at Akbarpur in Fyzabad, where a fair is held in his honour. Nathu has had 124,170 worshippers recorded. Chák Deo, the god of the Wheel, has special worshippers amongst the Kumhárs. Bharbhujas have a special caste deity "Chanda Khartal," whom they worship to some extent, and in whose honour a fair is annually held at Shahabad in Hardoi, at which in the presence of the god the assembled Bhurjis settle their disputes for the year. All such minor caste gods with 4,862 worshippers have been shown together in the table.

Biskarma, 18,805.—Amongst the caste gods may be classed Visvakarma (Biskarma) the omnificent, the Puranic architect of the universe. The Mahabharata describes him as "the lord of the arts, executor of a thousand handicrafts, the carpenter of the gods, the fashioner of all ornaments, the most eminent of artizans, who formed the celestial chariots of the deities, on whose crafts men subsist, and whom, a great and immortal god, they continually worship."

This deity is regarded by Lohárs and Barhais as their especial god, and 18,805 persons have recorded themselves as devoted to his worship.

194. **Low caste gods,** *Kare-Gore Deo,* 756,151.—Very much important as a general cult tean the worship of such special caste gods is that of the worship of certain deities by low castes. Ordinarily their gods have become Devis, but a few have been considered beneath Bráhmanical notice and have

had their worship continued in the simple low caste form by the offering of food and drink without further formality. Most important of these are the Kare-Gore Deo, the black and white gods, extensively and daily worshipped throughout Oudh by the majority of Chamárs and other low castes. The information obtained on the subject is vague and limited. The godlings are supposed to reside in a corner of the house in which a pice has been buried and are worshipped daily by offerings of food. I have been unable to get any satisfactory information as to the origin of the worship. One account connects the Kare-Gore Deo with Kali Singh and Guga Pir; another with two Muhammadan saints, Kalu and Ghori, said to be buried in the Partábgarh district; but the worshippers themselves only know that the cult has been handed down to them by their ancestors. 756,151 persons, mostly in Oudh and the Allahabad Doab districts have been recorded as worshippers of the Kare-Gore Deo.

Bal Raja, 76,395.—Bal Rája as especially worshipped by Ahírs and Bhárs, has been included in this group, although like many other low caste gods, his worship is connected with the idea of protection from snake bite. The Rája was while in life one of two Bhar brothers who ruled at Dalmau and Rae Bareli, and who were conquered and slain by the advancing Muhammadan conquerors in the time of Ibrahim Sharki of Jaunpur. It is said that, in their memory, the women of the Bharautiya sub-caste of Ahírs still in time of mourning abstain from wearing anklets. The worship of Bal Rája is most general in Rae Bareli, where Bal lived died, and Basti, where Bhárs are numerous, and exists to some extent throughout all Eastern Oudh districts. Altogether Bal Rája has 76,395 worshippers.

Kalupanthi, 266,161.—Another low caste god, extensively worshipped in the Meerut Division, is Kalu Kahár, of whom a legend quoted in the Muzaffarnagar Gazetteer relates that he was born of a Kahár girl who by magical charms compelled King Solomon to marry her, with the result that she brought forth a son, Babu Kalu, now worshipped extensively by Kahárs, Chamárs, Sainis, Gadariyas, and other low castes. The fetish is represented as a stick decorated with peacock's feathers, and like other low caste gods is worshipped by petty offerings of food.

Lálbeg 265,967.—Lálbeg, the sweeper god, is another divinity worshipped by a special class, of importance as regards numbers. He is the special deity of the Lálbegi Bhangis and has had 265,967 special worshippers recorded. There are various accounts of Lálbeg, or the Lálguru, as he is called by Hindu sweepers. Elliot identifies him with the Rakshas Aronakirta. Another account identifies him under the name Ishk Lál with the Lál Bhiksu of Buddhism. Again, he is believed to be identical with Bálmik, the author of the Rámayan, whilst the account usually given by Musalmán sweepers is that he is the Lál Pir, a follower of Abdul Kadir Jilani. The caste admits and obtains not a few recruits from outside who are admitted after offering a quantity of mince pies, "chura," to Lálbeg and the brotherhood.

Madain, 2,639.—Whether *Madain*, the god of Wine, should be regarded as specially a low caste god or as belonging to the class of demons with whom he would be classed by most Hindus is an open question. He is, though feared by Oudh Chamárs as far more terrible than any other god, little acknowledged as a special tutelary god, his worshippers being in general ashamed to admit that they regard him as their god, although they regard a false oath sworn by Madain as more certain to attract retribution than one by any other god in the Pantheon. Madain, well known and well feared as he is, has therefore only 2,639 special worshippers.

195. **Demon gods.**—With Madain we have passed into the class of beings believed to be supernatural in origin and not simply the ghosts of dead human beings. He is, as I have said, generally classed amongst demons, and the remaining entries in this class may now be mentioned.

Kerarbír Deo, 31,408.—The largest number of special worshippers are those of Kerarbir Deo, after whom a muhalla of Jaunpur is named. The following account is given in an interesting article on Jaunpur in the *Calcutta Review* of October 1865 :—

"Thus much, however, may be written boldly, that in the earliest times the region of Jaunpur was held by the Bhurs, that aboriginal people of whose civilization we catch glimpses by no means suiting our idea of them as derived from the sight of their outcast descendants. Yet what trace they have left of their long occupation it is hard to say. Along Burna bank are the sites of large cities, destroyed by fire, perhaps when Bráhmanism won its final victories; on Gumti bank stood vast temples which perished in the first inroad of the Musalmán; but what founders, and what antiquity these cities and temples boasted none can now say, yet a local legend gives a hint of one stage of the great conflict, when the aborigines were falling, yet not wholly subdued. When the great Rám Chandar ruled in Ajudhia there dwelt in the neck of Gumti, where now Jaunpur stands, the giant demon Kerar. And, whereas the highways were unsafe by reason of his violence, Rám Chandar in person marched against him, and having vanquished him in single combat, left the giant's trunk lying as a memorial and a warning, but flung his limbs and head to the corners of heaven. Yet over the trunk the demon's followers built a temple, there paying divine honours to their lost lord. Thus the legend; but we, translating it, suspect the truth to be that in some battle here the Bhur hero fell before the might of the invader, and the honour his sorrowing clansmen paid to his remains in time so impressed his enemies that they, giving a different reason, in time paid the same worship. Feroz found here a temple dedicated to Kerarbir within the lands of mauza Kerar. The Hindus named the new fort Kerarkot, and the ground adjoining to the north is still known as muhalla Kerara. An equally probable interpretation of the myth is that Kerar names, not a single hero, but a clan of Bhurs. Elliott names Kerar as a still existing Bhur state. Kerakat, the eastern pargana of Jaunpur, may be by some thought to derive its name (Quasi-Kerarkot) from the same clan. Still under the southern wall of the fort is the shrine of Kerarbir, partly covered by the stones of the fallen wall, but still the scene of worship, whose offerings are supposed to be some Rs. 20 or Rs. 25 a month, a sum probably doubled for a few days after the failure of the first mine which was to blow up that corner of the fort, for, somewhat to the annoyance of the engineer, the natives said that Kerar was stronger than the English powder. The object worshipped is a large stone bearing a rude resemblance to the upper part of a human trunk, smeared thickly with turmeric and the like, so that it is impossible to say what kind of stone it may be."

Kerarbir Deo has 31,408 worshippers in Jaunpur, Benares, the Gorakhpur Division, and some Oudh districts.

Masan, 1,929, the demon of the burning ghát, has 1,929 special worshippers in the eastern districts. He usually "possesses numerous small memorials at all burning gháts. Persons possessed without any assignable cause are for the time being said to be under his influence. Masan is supposed to be of a black colour and hideous appearance; he comes from the remains of a funeral pyre and chases people passing by, who sometimes die from fright, others linger for a few days, and some even go mad." Burglars use ashes from a burning ghát in the name of Masan to prevent the persons being robbed from being awakened. Persons possessed by the demon are supposed to waste away, and in early accounts of the suppression of infanticide in Sahâranpur it is mentioned that all the female children who died of neglect and ill-treatment were stated by their parents to be possessed by Masan.

A more classical demon is *Mahka Suror Bhainsa Sur*, worshipped by 13,141 persons in the eastern districts. The classical name was Maheshasura. The Mahabharat narrates that he was killed by Skanda. The Vamana Purana gives the following account of his defeat and death at the hands of Durga:—

Puranic Demons.

"Siva gave her his trident Vishnu a discus, Varuna a conch-shell, Agni a dart, Vayu a bow, Surya a quiver full of arrows, Indra a thunderbolt, Kuvera a mace, Brahma a rosary and water-pot, Kala a shield and sword, Visvakarma a battle-axe and other weapons. Thus armed and adored by the gods, Katyayini proceeded to the Vindhya hills. Whilst there the Asuras Chanda and Manda saw her, and being captivated by her beauty, they so described her to Mahisha, their king, that he was most anxious to obtain her. On asking for her hand, she told him she must be won in fight. He came and fought. At length Durga dismounted from her lion and sprang upon the back of Mahisha, who was in the form of a buffalo, and with her tender feet so smote him on the head that he fell to the ground senseless, when she cut off his head with her sword."

Worshippers of other demons have been classed together, giving a total of 154,215. The names included have been numerous and many of them unidentified except by the name ending in Sur. Of those identified one of the best known is Agia Baital or Dano, a terrible demon, who, sallying forth at dusk to his usual food of dung beetles, tempts unwary travellers from the path and leads them into the recesses of the forest till their reason fails them. Kansa and Ravana, the well known demons of the Ramayan, also occur as specially worshipped, and so do Sumbha and Nisumbha, demons, who, according to one of the Puranas, having by austerities and self torture continued for several thousand years obtained immortality, imagined themselves superior to the gods until they were destroyed in single combat by Durga. Why demons so described should obtain special worshippers appears extraordinary and the only at all likely explanation I have heard suggested is that the low caste worshippers identify Rawan, Kans, and Sumbha like Kerarbir with demi-gods of earlier races, amongst whose descendants their worship is still kept up, although all authentic account of them is lost.

196. **Village, Forest and Local gods.**—The next group is a very distinct one, including the special worshippers of a number of divinities distinctly outside the Puranic system, and possibly more intimately connected with the ghost worship of pre-Aryan tribes than with the Hindu system—I mean the village, forest, and other local gods

connected with agriculture and pasturage. The deohar or village gods form a very distinct group, to whose honour in almost every village petty offerings are made at appointed seasons at the mounds "thán" sacred to each in almost every village in the Province. The principal of the village gods is Bhumiya, the earth. The name is of Sanskrit origin, and as the attributes of the goddess are those of the Vedic Pirthwi, the mother of all beings, it is apparent that the worship of Bhumiya is in direct continuation of that offered in Vedic times to Prithwi. In dignity, however, the god has sadly fallen. He is now simply the "zamíndár," the landholder, the tutelary patron of cultivation and of boundaries, propitiated by the humblest offerings of the fruits of the earth. He is described by Atkinson as beneficent, employed in protecting the growing or grown crops from hail, blight, and wild animals whilst in the field, and afterwards in the granary from rats and insects. He finds time, however, to interest himself in the general welfare of the village, and as a reward partakes in the good things provided on all occasions of rejoicing. Of Bhumiya 85,731 persons are shown as special worshippers. They are scattered all over the provinces, Kumaun and Oudh furnishing a somewhat larger proportion of them than the rest of the North-West Provinces. A somewhat but less clearly beneficent godling is Kalsen, whose worshippers number 33,087, mostly in Rohilkhand and Kumaun. Another Deohar godling, has 3,785 worshippers in Lucknow and Sitapur. Whilst the village gods just named are the tutelary deities of settled villages, those most reverenced in the wilder tracts are the forest gods Banaspati and Samai, most generally worshipped by Bhars and other semi-aboriginal castes. Samai is worshipped as a Devi with offerings of blood. To Banaspati Mai the offerings are more Hindu in character, consisting of grain and ghi, afterwards made over to a Brahman. Of the gods just named and other forest gods, the number of worshippers are shown in the margin. They are most general in the eastern districts and in Kumaun.

Samai	37,584
Banaspati	16,489
Other forest gods... ...	17,340

Local or village gods not yet identified with Devi are worshipped to a considerable extent throughout the province in much the same form as Bhumiya. The total number of worshippers was no less than 367,591. Of the gods so worshipped the names of many like Chatrpal, Nagarsen, and Bholanath, &c. are well known, but regarding the great majority all I have been able to learn is that they are of the Deohar class.

197. **Rivers and river gods.**—Before passing to a brief mention of the returns for reformed sects, there remains for notice a somewhat miscellaneous group of objects of worship consisting of river gods, holy places, and deified devotees.

For the former group the figures in the statement are shown in the margin. By far the most important is the Ganges, a well-known object of worship amongst Hindus, whose reverence for her appears from their regarding an oath on Ganges water as the most binding that can be taken. Bathing in the Ganges is believed

Ganga	284,594
Jamna	8,316
Saraswati	5,311
Khwaja Khizr	7,730
Other river gods ...	13,594

to have the effect of cleansing from all sin, present, past and future. It is beneficial at all times, but more especially so at the time of full moon. Of all full moons the most propitious is that which ends the month of Katik, when not a small proportion of the population of the provinces assembles on the bank of the Ganges to plunge into the stream at the time the moon reaches its full size. The Ganges by this name has 284,594 worshippers, and under the name of Bhagirathi 5,293 more. Many other rivers in the province are sacred, but the Jamna is the only other local river divinity that has worshippers enough to deserve separate classification. Of the mythical Saraswati 5,311 worshippers are shown. It is probable that these are due less to her position as a river goddess than to those attributes which she acquired as the patroness of the ceremonies performed on the margin of her holy waters, and subsequently as the inspirer of the hymns recited at these ceremonies. She is now known mainly as the goddess of speech and learning, the inventress of the Sanskrit language, and patroness of arts and sciences.

A river god not specially connected with any one stream, and whose worship rather belongs to the Panjáb than to these provinces, is Khwájá Khizr. He is popularly represented as a venerable Muhammadan riding on a fish. He is said by Ibbetson to be properly the Muhammadan saint, to whom the care of travellers is allotted, but is now in the western Doab and in the Pánjáb the Hindu god of Water, worshipped by offerings of ghí and cakes presented to Bráhmans at the village well or pond. Khwaja Khizr has 7,730 worshippers, all in the western districts, and all probably amongst the Kahárs or Mallahs, whose avocations are specially connected with water.

198. **Worshippers of holy places.**—Of the various holy places of Hinduism 56,702 persons appear as worshippers. The greatest of these is Káshi, on whose sanctity generation after generation of Hindus have relied to procure them instant transfer after death to a happier life. Other places which occur in the schedules are Ajudhiya, the centre of the worship of Ráma ; Chitrkot, in the Bánda district, also connected with Ráma's travels ; Kailas, the Himalayan home of Siva ; Gobardhan, the scene of Krishna's boyhood ; Haridwár ; Prag (Allahabad) ; Soron and Bithur, sacred places on the Ganges ; and Gaya in Behar, a place of pilgrimage at which offerings are made for the salvation of the worshippers' ancestors.

199. **Worshippers of deified devotees.**—Deified devotees, saints and teachers have 274,900 worshippers. The majority of these are Vedic or Puranic sages. Vasishtha, a Vedic sage, author of several of the hymns of the Veda, has been declared to be their tutelary deity by 6,886 persons, included in the above. Narad, another Vedic Rishi ; Valmiki, the author of the Rámayan ; Vyasa, the "arranger" of the Vedas ; Kalidasa, the great Sanskrit Dramatist, also appear in the schedules amongst the devotees worshipped. With them are joined names so recent as those of Sur Das and Tulsi Das, the two great stars of the modern Hindi poetic firmament, who, the one in praise of Krishna and the other of Ráma, are believed between them to have exhausted the possibilities of the poetic art. Tulsi Das, though not known as

the founder of a religious sect, has through his translation of the Rámayan had a great and most beneficial influence in the religious life of Northern India :—

"The book is in every one's hands, from the court to the cottage, and is read or heard and appreciated alike by every class of the Hindu community, whether high or low, rich or poor, young or old. It has been interwoven into the life, character, and speech of the Hindu population for more than three hundred years, and is not only loved and admired by them for its poetic beauty, but is reverenced by them as their scriptures. It is the Bible of a hundred millions of people, and is looked upon by them as much inspired as the Bible is considered inspired by the English clergyman. Pandits may talk of the Vedas and of the Upanishads, and a few may even study them ; others may say they pin their faith on the Puranas ; but to the vast majority of the people of Hindustan, learned and unlearned alike, their sole norm of conduct is the so-called Tulsi-Krit Rámayan. It is indeed fortunate for Hindustan that this is so, for it has saved the country from the tantric obscenities of Saivism. Ráma Nand was the original saviour of Upper India from the fate which has befallen Bengal, but Tulsi Das was the great apostle who carried his doctrine east and west and made it an abiding faith. The religion he preached was a simple and sublime one, a perfect faith in the name of God. But what is most remarkable in it, in an age of immorality, when the bonds of Hindu society were loosened and the Mughal empire being consolidated, was its stern morality in every sense of the word. Tulsi was the great preacher of one's duty towards one's neighbour. Valmiki praised Bharat's sense of duty, Lachman's brotherly affection, and Sita's wifely devotion, but Tulsi taught them as an example."

200. **Miscellaneous Puranic gods.**—A group of worshippers of miscellaneous Puranic gods or heroes concludes the enumeration of worshippers of special gods not belonging to defined sects. The number is 2,596. None of the names entered is of general importance. Rája Sagar, a Rája of Ajudhiya of the solar race, indefinitely connected by Puranic legend with the origin of the Ganges, and Dharmarája, the Puranic Judge of the dead, are the best known names included.

201. **Sectarian sub-Divisions, Saiva.**—There now remain for mention those Hindu sects properly so called, incorporation in one or other of which implies adherence to certain defined doctrines. All Hindu sects strictly so called are either Vaishnavite or profess doctrines more akin to Vaishnavism than to Saivism. Certain entries have, however, appeared in the sect column pertaining to Saivism which require mention here, as they have been treated by Wilson and other writers on the subject as sects in somewhat the same sense as the word bears when applied to Vaishnavite sects. The entries for which figures have been abstracted from the sect columns are given in the margin. In point of fact these entries simply indicate Saivite ascetic orders, distinguished from each other in general purely by matters of outward observance and not of belief. They would be made only by professional ascetics and not by ordinary adherents of Saivism. It is no more correct to call them sectarian divisions than it would be to call Franciscan and Dominican friars separate Christian sects. It is in the sub-caste column in which under the general instructions full details of these orders must be looked for. The figures so far as distinctly Saivite are abstracted in the margin. The Dasnami Goshains contribute the best instructed and most respectable body of Saivite

Aughar	5,319
Aghori	1,006
Alakhnami... ...	10,886
Gorakhpanthi ...	28,816
Minor Saivite sects ...	1,870

Goshain Dasnami	103,320
" unspecified	38,477
Jogi { Aughar, Gorakhpanti, unspecified and others. }	78,387
Sanjogi	4,538
Sanniyasi	4,406
Aghori	630

ascetics. They are recruited from the twice born castes and include a number of men of learning, the leading exponents of the philosophical side of Saivism. Wilson distinguishes three and a half of the ten orders as "Dandis" adhering strictly to the precepts of the founder Sankaracharaj in regard to their neglect of worldly possessions and cares. The remaining six and a half members of the Dasnami class, although considered as having fallen from the purity of practice necessary to the Dandi, are still, in general, devoted to their religious profession, and are usually denominated Atits. The chief points of difference between them and the preceding are their abandonment of the staff; their use of clothes, money, and ornaments; their preparing their own food, and their admission of members from any order of Hindus. They are often collected in Maths, as well as the Dandis, but they mix freely in the business of the world; they carry on trade and often accumulate property, and they frequently officiate as priests at the shrines of the deities. Some of them even marry, but in that case they are distinguished by the name Sanjogi from the other Atits. Goshains of the latter six and a half classes are most numerous in these provinces.

Jogis, the next most important group of Saivite ascetics, derive the name from Yoga school of philosophy, which maintains as its leading tenet the possibility of acquiring complete control over material substances by the practice of ascetic practices. To attain perfection in the object of Yoga practices is considered to require a protracted existence and continuation in several births, and to be impossible in the Kali age; but ascetic practices, though thus impotent, are not infrequently continued. The principal group of Jogis is that of Kanphatas, who acknowledge as their founder Gorakh Nath and are distinguished by having their ears bored and rings inserted in them at the time of their initiation. The Gorakhpanthi Jogis belong to a distinct order, in general living together in "Maths" and are respectable as compared with a variety of other classes included under the name Jogi, many of whom are rather mountebanks and fortune tellers than religious ascetics. Popularly, Jogis are divided into classes by the particular form of asceticism practised. Those who go naked are Nagas or Abdhut; those who raise one or both hands to the sky are Urdbahu; those who turn the face to the sky Akasmukhi. Other Saivite orders of importance shown in the returns are Aughar, Alakhnami, Aghori, and Sarbhangi. The first named are usually regarded as Jogis and pretend to some magical powers. They are both in appearance and in observances of a far lower class than the Kanphata. Their bodies are smeared with ashes, and in regard to food and drink they incline to much that is filthy and disgusting. These latter observances are exaggerated in the Aghori, a class now happily nearly extinct. Aghoris keep themselves in a state of perpetual intoxication and eat the flesh of all animals, even of a human dead body. They rub their body with, and eat and drink, the foulest substances, affecting to regard them as delicious food and tasteful liquor.

In the Alakhnami we have more of our approach to a tenet of belief than is usual in Saivite ascetic order. Their belief is that religion consists in contemplation of Siva as "Alakh" or incomprehensible. Rája Siva

Parshád in the Benares Gazetteer gives the following brief account of the Alakhnami :—

"A coat of blanketing and a long cap form his dress. The members of the sect live by mendicancy, which they follow in a very peculiar and deserving manner. Their practice is to pronounce the word Alakh once, and if during that time anything is given them, they take it; if not, they go through the same form elsewhere."

Minor Saivite Sects, 1870.—Jangamas, ascetics of the Linyagat school, who worship Siva under the symbol of the Linga, Paramhans are those who are vowed neither to speak nor to raise their hands in eating, and other minor classes, are included together under the heading minor Saiva sects, of whom 1,870 persons were shown in the sect returns.

202. **Vaishnava, unitarian and miscellaneous sects.**—With the next class, that of Vaishnava sects, begins Hindu sectarianism properly so called, those distinguished from ordinary orthodox Hinduism by matters of belief. Growse traces the origin of these sects in the following remarks :—

"So far as it is possible to compare natural with revealed religion, the course of Hinduism and Christianity has been identical in character; both were subjected to a violent disruption, which occurred in the two quarters of the globe nearly simultaneously, and which is still attested by the multitude of uncouth fragments into which the ancient edifice was disintegrated as it fell. In the west, the revival of ancient literature and the study of forgotten systems of philosophy stimulated enquiry into the validity of those theological conclusions which previously had been unhesitatingly accepted, from ignorance that any counter theory could be honestly maintained by thinking men. Similarly, in the east, the Muhammadan invasion and the consequent contact with new races and new modes of thought brought home to the Indian moralist that his old basis of faith was too narrow; that the division of the human species into the four Manava castes and an outer world of barbarians was too much at variance with facts to be accepted as satisfactory, and that the ancient inspired oracles, if rightly interpreted, must disclose some means of salvation applicable to all men alike, without respect to colour or nationality. The professed object of the reformers was the same in Asia as in Europe, to discover the real purpose for which the Second Person of the Trinity became incarnate; to disencumber the truth, as He had revealed it from the accretions of later superstition; to abolish the extravagant pretensions of a dominant class, and to restore a simpler and more severely intellectual form of public worship."

That they are confined to the Vaishnava side of Hinduism may be readily inferred from the account of the worship of Vishnu given above. Salvation by faith is the central belief of the reformed sects. Faith can attach itself only to a God believed to take a direct and personal interest in the welfare of mankind.

It has already been pointed out that returns for sects tend to lose to a large extent to the general heading Vaishnava. This is especially the case amongst the older Sampradaya, whose beliefs approach most closely to the common standard of Vaishuavism, and it is inevitable where the sectarian name approaches closely in form that of the general subdivision of Hinduism.

These facts explain the low figures shown for the original Vaishnava Sampradaya in the returns and the entire disappearance of one Sampradaya which is known to exist—the *Sri-Vaishnava* founded by Rámanuj in the 11th or 12th century. They are by no means important in these provinces, but attracted some attention of late years by the conver-

Original Vaishnava Sampradaya,		
Nimbarak Vaishnava	...	14,905
Madhvachariya	...	3,226

sion to their beliefs from Jainism of two of the family of the Muttra Seths. The doctrine which is the foundation of their creed is that Vishnu, the one Supreme God, though invisible as cause, is as effect visible in a secondary form in creation. They differ in one material respect from the rest of the older Vaishnava sects in refusing to believe that reverence is due to Radha. The sect is represented in these provinces mainly by persons connected with the Seths' temple at Muttra, all belonging to one of the two sects into which the Sampradaya are divided. The sects are the Tenkalai and the Vadakalai. The account of the difference in their belief given by Growse is interesting as illustrative of the matters to which in the classical reformed sects enquiry and argument are usually directed :—

"The doctrinal points of difference are as follows. The Tenkalai maintain that the female energy of the godhead, though divine, is still a finite creature that serves only as a mediator or minister (Purasha-Kára) to introduce the soul into the presence of the deity; while the Vadakalai regard it as infinite and uncreated, and in itself a means (Upaya) by which salvation can be secured. The second point of difference is a parallel to the controversy between the Calvinists and Armenians in the Christian Church. The Vadakalai, with the latter, insist on the concomitancy of the human will in the work of salvation, and represent the soul that lays hold of God as a young monkey which grasps its mother in order to be conveyed to a place of safety. The Tenkalai, on the contrary, maintain the irresistibility of divine grace and the utter helplessness of the soul, till it is seized and carried off like a kitten by its mother from the danger that threatens it. From these two curious but apt illustrations the one doctrine is known as the Markata-Kishora-Nyáya, the other as the Marjala-Kishora-Nyáya; that is to say, the young monkey theory or the kitten theory."

The Nimbarak Vaishnavas.—The second of the original Sampradaya, founded by Bhaskarachariya, includes a large number of the Vaishnava hermits scattered throughout part of the province, each withdrawn from the world in his own little patch of sacred grove. The name, meaning the sun is in a ním tree, is derived from an incident in the life of the founder when the sun delayed setting to allow a guest of Bhaskaracharya, vowed to eat only in the day, time enough to enjoy his food. Their tenets appear to be obscure and have never been committed to writing. They believe in salvation by faith and by contemplation of the one infinite and invisible God. The reward of faith is not, as with most Hindu sects, final extinction, but final enjoyment of the visible presence of the deity. Radha and Krishna as separate personalities are mere symbols of divine love, and like the symbols adopted by other religions disappear, whilst the essential love for and trust in a Supreme God remains.

The Madhva Vishnavas.—Founded by Madhvacharya, a native of Southern India, the third Jampradaya, includes in these provinces a scattered and not very numerous body of adherents. Their distinctive tenet is the assertion of an essential duality between the Jivatma or principle of life, and the Paramátma or Supreme Being identified with Vishnu. They consequently deny the doctrine of absorption into the universal spirit after death. Ten duties form the moral code of the Madhvas—truth, good counsel, mild speaking, study, liberality, kindness, protection, clemency, freedom from envy, and faith. The usual rites of Hindu worship are followed, images of Siva as well as of Vishnu being admitted to the Madhva temple, but rites are of value only as evidencing a desire to conciliate Vishnu.

Vallabhachariyas 13,183.—The faith of one early Sampradaya, the Vishnu Swami, has disappeared in its original form, but the name has to some extent been appropriated by the followers of Vallabhacharya, a southern Bráhman of this Sampradaya who at Gokal and Benares introduced a new devotion in honor of Krishna in which the god is adored as a child Balkrishna or Bal Gopal. As taught by Vallabhacharya, the doctrines of the sect are unexceptionable. Sin of all kinds is washed away by a union with God. Krishna is the refuge of all, and to the holy Krishna, man must dedicate his bodily faculties, his life, his soul, his belongings, with his wife, his house, his children, and his whole substance. The scandal which has attached itself to the name of the sect is due to a development of this doctrine, apparently in the time of Gokal Nath, the grandson of Vallabhachariya, which identifies the Goshain with the divinity. By the act of dedication a man submits to the pleasure of the Goshain as God's representative not only his worldly wealth but the virginity of his daughter or newly married wife. Under this teaching the Vallabhacharyas have become the epicureans of the east and assert that the ideal life is attained through social enjoyment. Members of the sect are invariably family men and engage freely in secular pursuits.

A sect represented in the provinces and having its principal temples in Brindaban, but which does not appear in the census schedules to any appreciable extent, is that of the *Bengali* or *Gauriya Vaishnavas,* founded by Chaitanya in the beginning of the sixteenth century. Its disappearance from the schedules is no doubt due to the fact that in Muttra it is considered to be sufficiently described by the use of the word Vaishnava. The special tenets of the Bengali Vaishnavas are the identification of Vishnu with the Supreme God and in his possession of "sensible and real attributes," as contrasted with Vedanta belief in the negative properties of God, the identity of Krishna and Chaitanya as embodiments of the God; and the all-sufficiency of faith, such faith being adequately expressed by the mere repetition of the name. The connection of Krishna with Radha occupies an important position in the Gauriya Vaishnava creed. Chaitanya taught the equality of all castes, but this doctrine has not been fully acted on by his successors.

Hari Dasi, 1094.—Lineally descended from the sect of Chaitanya, but indigenous in its growth, is that of Hari Das, a saintly Sanadh Bráhman of the Muttra district, whose miraculous powers are stated to have attracted the belief of the Emperor Akbar. The tenets of the school are not materially different from those of the Vaishnava sects just spoken of. The modern representatives of the Goshains, of this sect, all of them now family men, though Hari Das himself was a celibate, appear to have little claim to respect, either for their learning or the purity of their morals.

Radhaballabhi 34,795.—Of more importance in the provinces than either of the above is the Radhaballabhi sect, founded by Hari Vans, a Gaur Bráhman of Sahâranpur, originally a Madhavachariya Vaishnava, but whose natural passions led him to devote his devotion in a very secondary degree to Krishna himself and mainly to Krishna's mistress, Radha, who was deified as the goddess of Lust. In the writings of Hari Vans, "the language of the brothel is," in the words of Growse, "borrowed for temple use. But strange to say, the Goshains, who accept as their gospel Hari Vans's sensuous ravings, are respectable men who contrast favourably both in sobriety of life and intellectual acquirements with the professors of sects based on more respectable authorities."

Ramanandi, 421,433.—The sects so far mentioned have their headquarters in the home of Krishna and regard that god as the chief incarnation of Vishnu. That next to be mentioned, much more important in its hold over worshippers who are not professional ascetics, addresses its devotions particularly to Ráma Chandra and has its capital in Ajudhiya. Rámanand was a disciple of Rámanuja, but made it his avowed object in founding a new sect to liberate his followers from the fetters of the earlier sect in matters both of form and doctrine. The Rámanandi tenets are, therefore, beyond their assertion of the superiority of Ráma and the necessity for the worship of Ráma and Sita, somewhat indefinite. It was probably this fact which has led to the foundation of separate sects by so many of the followers of Rámanand, Kabir, Raidas, Sena, and others. Throughout the adherents to the original sect and those of the later developments, a purer tone of belief than amongst the sects devoted to Krishna is manifest. The original Rámanandis are largely, especially in Oudh, Rájputs. The later sects have many of their followers amongst the lower castes, Rámanand having taught liberation from caste as well as from other ceremonial observances and chosen many of his leading disciples from men of the lower castes. Nabhaji, a follower of Rámanand and the writer of the Bhakt Mala, the lives of the saints, the work of highest authority amongst the Vaishnava sects, is said to have been a Dom, Kabir a weaver, Sena a barber, Raidas a Chamár. The principal gospel of the Rámanandis is the Rámayan of Tulsi Das, a work regarding which it has already been remarked that Northern India owes to it much of the freedom it enjoys from the licentiousness which has disgraced many of the sects connected with the worship of Radha Krishan or of the Sakti of the Tantras.

The sects which were founded by followers of Rámanand are somewhat numerous. Their followers are probably more fully enumerated than those of the parent sect, both because their tenets are more distinctly defined and because several of them have taken special hold amongst certain defined castes.

Kabir Panthi	...	318,262
Raidasi	...	417,127
Sena Panthi	...	4,325
Namdeo Panthi	...	10,358
Dadu Panthi	...	5,010
Nanak Shahi	...	336,168

The first mentioned, Kabir Panthi, is important both from the number of its adherents and because Nanak the founder of a much more important sect was a follower of Kabir. Kabir, said to have been a Bráhman by birth but adopted by a weaver, was originally a follower of Rámanand, but preached the doctrine of emancipation with a boldness and freedom from superstitious beliefs which completely separated his followers from the general body of Rámanandis, and leaves it doubtful as to whether the sect founded by him should be included amongst Vaishnava sects. "With an unprecedented boldness Kabir assailed the whole system of idolatrous worship, and ridiculed the learning of the Pandits and doctrines of the Sastras in a style peculiarly well suited to the genius of his countrymen to whom he addressed himself, whilst he also directed his compositions to the Musalmán, as well as to the Hindu faith, and with equal severity attacked the *Mulla* and *Korán*. The effect of his lessons, as confined to his own immediate followers, will be shown to have been considerable, but their indirect effect has been still greater, several of the popular sects being little more than ramifications from his stock, whilst *Nanak Shah*, the only Hindu reformer who has established a national faith, appears to have been chiefly indebted for his religious notions to his predecessor Kabir. This sect therefore claims particular attention." Kabir himself, though constant in condemning the prevailing idolatry of the Hindu system, appears himself to have laid down no distinct principles of belief for the guidance of his followers. The consequence has been that to some extent the modern leaders of the sect, though in form of worship completely separated from other Hindus, have adopted many notions from the earlier and more orthodox Vaishnava sects. They admit of but one God, the Creator of the world; they assert that he has a body formed of the five elements of matter and a soul endowed with the three qualities of being. He is free from the defects of human nature and from all restraint as to shape and form, but in other respects the pure man is his living resemblance and after-death his associate and équal. The Supreme Being was alone for many ages, but then to renew the world, became manifest in a female form, the deceiving Maya, from whom the Hindu Trinity and Saktis and all the mistaken notions current amongst mankind originate. The true Kabir Panthi, however, refuses any reverential homage to Maya or the gods whom she created. For him the essence of religion is the true knowledge of Kabir, a knowledge to which both Hindus and Muhammadans are strangers. The moral code of the Kabir Panthis inculcates humanity, including absolute respect for all life, truth, retirement from worldly passions and desires, and submission to the guru or spiritual guide, the latter, however, to be dependent on the pupil's conviction of the worthiness of the guru. The influence of the teachings of Kabir has extended far beyond the limits of his own sect. It has led to the foundation of not a few later important sects and influences, possibly to a still greater extent, the thoughts of Hindus not outwardly separated from the general body of Hindu worshippers. Kabir Panthi ascetics are numerous and in outward appearance not very different from the Gorakhpanthi Jogis, by whom some connection in religious feeling is admitted.

An interesting development of the principles of Kabir we have in the tenets of the Dadupanthis, followers of Dadu, a cotton cleaner or Dhuna of Ahmadabad, but who settled in Ajmir, round which his sect is now strongest. The following interesting account of this sect was given in the *Pioneer* of the 26th March 1892:—

"Dadu, who, like Nanak aud Kabir, gave his name to his followers, was born in Ahmadabad about 1544, and died in Naraina (50 miles W. by S. of Jeypore) in A. D. 1603. His biographer, Jan Gopal, in 2,864 lines, tells how he spent that life in the country between Ahmadabad and Dehli and Agra, teaching, discussing and making many disciples. He appears to have lived a good deal in Amer, the old capital of Jeypore. He had frequent interviews with Akbar at Sikri, and some wonderful stories are told of him there. Dadu's name as a reformer comes along with Kabir, Nanak, Namdéo, Lál Das, and many more. They all protested against abuses that had sprung up in Hinduism, and sought, with more or less success, to get back to the original and simple truths about God, man, and the way of return to Him. These teachings are embodied in his Bani, which is to the Dadupanthi what the Granth is to the Sikh or Nanak Panthi. It contains 20,000 lines. About half the book is made up of sacred songs, while the other half has 37 short discussions on such subjects as 'The Divine Teacher,' 'Remembrance of God,' 'The pain of separation from Him,' 'The Meeting,' 'Mind,' 'Birth,' 'Maya,' 'Truth,' 'Prayer,' &c. Dadu at his death left many disciples; but of these only 152 were initiated. Of these, again, only 52 wrote much and spread the reformed doctrine far and wide. I know not the present number of his followers. They themselves say, when asked, 'Thousands,' 'Many.'

"The Dadupanthis, like most other religious communities in India, have a two-fold division: (1) the exoteric and (2) the esoteric. The exoteric, or uninitiated, are the householders; disciples of the initiated or Shamisdhu order. These grihasthis read, believe, and practice certain of the doctrines of the Bani, and furnish the Dadupanthi Shami with lodging and food when he visits their villages. They are not put out of caste for becoming Dadupanthi Chelas, and so retain all their marriage and social rites and privileges. They retain as a rule their janeo, or holy thread, and other charms, and frequently are found in the temples at idol worship. They attend the Dadupanthi Melas at times. I saw this year several of this class at the mela at Naraina, which is just over. They are the working bees in the Dadupanthi hive, and often provide large sums of money for feasts and other expenses.

"The esoteric or initiated, are called Shami, or master; Sadhu, perfect, pious, holy; sant, saint; guru, teacher; and such like. They renounce the world and live 'a life of single blessedness.' The vows of celibacy and of chastity are clearly laid down and strictly enforced. I find the initiated follow these five professions :—

"(1) **Teachers or gurus.**—Their duty is to teach the Bani and keep their chelas in the right way. Some of these men are good scholars and have a great following of initiated disciples, who go with them about the country. I have seen as many as 50 with one man. They study with him the Bam and also some Sanskrit books, grammar, rhetoric and philosophy. They visit large towns and stay days or weeks as arrangements can be made. Others of them are very sorry fellows indeed, with no education and no influence. They usually go about alone and beg their food from door to door. They wear the Bhagwan kapra, or salmon coloured cloth, and use the mata, which they ought not to do. They find they cannot get on without these."

"(2) **Money-lenders.**—Two of our wealthiest Jeypore citizens are Dadupanthi money-lenders. They are reported to be rich. They have fine gardens outside and large clean houses inside the city. They give money on interest much as other Seths do."

"(3) **Doctors.**—His Highness the Mahárája has a most respected Dadupanthi doctor in daily attendance on the Court. He is well up in native medicine, which he learned from books, and from his predecessor. None of these now study in our colleges. They know little surgery. They are not trained in our sense of the term, but they know Sanskrit shloks, descriptive of diseases, and the remedies to be applied, and many believe in them."

"(4) I am told that it is not below the dignity of the initiated to open a small shop and sell oil, salt and such like. I have not seen this, however. They do keep cows and sell milk."

"(5) The Dadupanthi soldiers of Nága. There are over 5,000 or more in the service of the Jeypore Durbar alone. This does not represent their full number, for there must be young men in the camp, and old too, unfit for service. Their pay is *one anna* per able-bodied man a day; and with this they clothe and feed themselves. They live in seven camps or villages well out on the borders of the State. These they guarded in olden times. Now they visit those villages that have not paid up their rent. On great State occasions they are summoned to the capital. They are never all out on duty. Those who are out get two annas a day, and those left at home cultivate land, breed camels, lend money, and such like, and thus help the common fund. It is said that this soldier saint took his origin from Bhim Singh, a younger brother of a Bikanir King, becoming Dadu's disciple. Dadu made him take up and use the sword and shield he had laid at his feet. The then King of Jeypore, Bhagwan Das, gave him some allowances from the treasury, and he was soon surrounded by more soldier saints. In lawless times they would have many opportunities of enriching themselves. They have done good work in Jeypore for the State. They were faithful to us in the Mutiny. They are nice, simple men, but hardly now deserve the name of soldier."

"There are thus seven villages and many, many houses in Jeypore without women in them. There are no female Nágas, nor villages without men. The ranks of the Nágas are filled up by adoption from all the higher Hindu castes. They are not so numerous as of old. In lawless times they got recruits where they could. The loot of villages gave them wealth, and many a father has reduced his debt by throwing a son or two into the bargain."

Rai Das was another of the pupils of Rámanand who founded a separate sect, whose purity of belief ranks it with or above that founded by Kabir, although its adherents are almost entirely amongst the lowest of the people, the Chamárs, from whom Rai Das himself sprung. In spite of his low birth the purity and influence of his teaching earned him a mythical position in the Bhaktmala or lives of the Vaishnava saints as a Bráhmchari reborn, and disciples even amongst Rájputs so proud as the Ranas of Chittor.

The belief of his followers of to-day, so far as can be ascertained, is purely theistic. They acknowledge one supreme omnipotent and all-seeing God to whom alone worship is due. Their numbers as shown in the schedules are considerable, but they are not improbably still more numerous as many of them are likely to be included amongst those who return themselves as worshippers of Parmeswar.

The persons recorded as *Senapanthi* in these provinces are probably all or nearly all of the same caste as the founder of the sect, a Nai, who was included amongst Rámanand's disciples. The Bhakt Mala relates that Sena, the barber of the Rája of Bandhogarh, was a devout worshipper of Vishnu, but that his devotion to his religious duties prevented on one occasion his appearance at the proper time in attendance on his earthly master Vishnu to save his votary from punishment for this neglect appeared himself in the form of Sena and performed his duties undetected by the Rája until Sena himself appeared with many excuses for his absence. The recollection of the divine fragrance which flowed from the barber showed the Rája what had happened and the barber was elevated to the position of the Rája's guru. Sena's present followers in these provinces are probably to a considerable extent more a subcaste than a genuine sect. They appear in the caste lists as the "Sainbansi" subcaste of Nais. From a doctrinal point of view, however, record as Senapanthi implies, as in the other sects sprung from that of Rámanand, a belief in the superior power of one Supreme God.

In every way the most important of the sects in which the influence of Rámanand and Kabir is traced is that founded by Nanak from which the Sikh faith was developed by a later disciple. Nanakpanthi Hindus number in all 336,168 persons and are found all over the provinces, but are by far more numerous in the western districts in which for the upper agricultural classes this is almost the only reformed faith professed.

"It appears to be a well-ascertained fact that this great teacher was born, not in Lahore itself, but in a neighbouring village, called Talvandi, on the river Ravi, not far from Lahore, in the year 1469, a few years before Chaitanya in Bengal and Martin Luther in Europe. Of course the various biographies of Nanak, called Janam Sákhis, and written in the Panjábi dialect, are filled with myths and stories of miraculous events, invented to justify the semi-deification of the founder of the sect soon after his death. That all the Hindu gods appeared in the sky and announced the birth of a great saint (Bhagat) to save the world, is not quite capable of proof, nor can we quite accept as a fact another statement of his chroniclers, that one day angels seized him while bathing and carried him bodily into the presence of the deity, who presented him with a cup of nectar and charged him to proclaim the One God, under the name of Hari, upon earth. But we need not disbelieve the statement that at an early age he became a diligent student of Vaishnava religious books, and that in his youth he imitated the example of other incipient reformers, wandering to various shrines in search of some clue to the labyrinth of Hinduism. It is even affirmed that his travels included the performance of a hajj to Mecca, and that on being reproved by the Kazi for lying down with his feet towards the Ka'bah, he replied, 'put my feet in that direction where the house of God is not."

"Nanak, however, laid no claim to be the originator of a new religion. His teaching was mainly founded on that of his predecessors, especially on that of Kabir, whom he constantly quoted. He was simply a guru, or teacher, and his followers were simply Sikhs or disciples. But he was also a reformer who aimed, as other reformers had done before him, at delivering Hinduism, and especially the Vaishnavism of Northern India, from its incubus of caste, superstition and idolatry. Yet it does not appear that Nanak directly attacked caste or denounced it in violent language. He simply welcomed persons of all ranks as his followers, and taught that the Supreme Being was no respecter of persons."

"The plain fact was that Nanak found himself in a part of India where Muhammadans formed the majority of the population. Though himself originally a Hindu, he became partially Islamized, to the extent at least of denouncing idolatry. His idea was to bring about a union between Hindus and Muhammadans on the common ground of a belief in One God. Yet the creed of Nanak was really more pantheistic than monotheistic. God, he said, is Supreme Lord over all (Paramesvara). He may be called Bráhma, or by other names, such as Govinda, &c., but his especial name is Hari (=Vishnu). This Supreme Being does not create the universe out of nothing, but evolves it out of Himself. It is a kind of expansion of His own essence which takes place for His own amusement (khelá). Such expansion being made up of the three Gunas, Sattva, Rájas, and Tamas, in perfect equilibrium. It is Illusion or Máyá which disturbs this equilibrium and causes the apparent separation between God, the world and the human soul: all this is pure Bráhmanism. We find also that, except in denouncing idolatry, Nanak differed very little from a pure Vaishnava, for he taught that in the present age of the world (the Kali Yuga) the repetition of the name of Hari is the only means of salvation. Notwithstanding the merit to be gained by benevolent works and religious ceremonies, and that the knowledge of this name is only to be acquired through a properly ordained teacher (guru). It is curious, too, that a religious movement which commenced in an effort to draw the adherents of Sikhism and Muhammadanism together, should have ended in exciting the bitterest animosity between them. Nanak's death is known to have occurred on the 10th of October 1538. One of his sons expected to succeed him, but to the surprise of those who were present at his death, he passed over his own son and nominated as second guru his disciple Lahaná, whose name had been changed to Angáda because of his devotion. He had, so to speak, given up his person (angá) to the service of his master. This appears to have been his chief merit. He was quite illiterate, though tradition makes him the inventor of the peculiar alphabet called Guru-mukhi (a modification of the Devanágri) in which the

Sikh Bible was written. Angáda nominated Amardás to succeed him as third guru. Seven others were appointed to the succession in a similar manner. These make up the ten chief gurus of the Sikh religion. They were, four, Rámdas; five, Arjun; six, Hargovind; seven, Harraí; eight Harkisan (for Har-Krishna); nine, Teg-Bahádur; and ten, Govind Sinh."

With the fourth guru, Rámdas, the Nanakshahi faith began to assume a different character. Rámdas and his son Arjan understood the power of wealth and organization, and under them the faith began to assume political importance. This led to opposition and persecution by the Muhammadan Government, till the suicide of the ninth guru, Teg Bahádur, whilst being subjected to cruel tortures by the order of Aurangzeb, led Govind Sinh, his son, to swear his followers to undying feud against Muhammadanism. Henceforward the followers of Govind Sinh were Sikhs, and their history belongs to that of the neighbouring province. In the North-Western Provinces the sect remained in the position it was left by Nanak, and whilst proud to acknowledge a connection with the faith of the warlike Sikhs, it is far more distinctly a branch of Hindu Vaishnavism. Nanakshahi Hindus in these provinces have been recorded as 336,168 in number. It is probable that not a few of the persons included amongst Sikhs in the western districts are really Nanakpanthi Hindus.

Namdeopanthi, 10,358.—Namdeopanthis are somewhat similarly situated to the Senapanthi. Namdeo was a follower of Rámanand, a Chhipi or cotton printer by caste, who founded a sect to which what has now become a subcaste of his fellow Chhipis somewhat extensively belong. The unity of the deity and the uselessness of ceremonial appear to be the leading characteristics of the creed. Like Raidasi Chamárs and Senapanthi Nais, the Namdeopanthi cotton-printers have been separated from their caste-fellows by the superior purity of their beliefs and now form a separate subcaste, shown in the caste returns as Namdeobansi. Writings by Namdeo form a part of the Sikh Granth or sacred scripture.

Satnami, 152,734.—Of the other sects remaining for mention, by far the most important in these provinces is that of the Satnami worshippers of the true name, founded by Jagjivandas, a Rájput of the Bara Banki district, who died in the beginning of the present century. He is said to have been the disciple of a Saivite Goshain, but of the sect he founded the doctrines are disdistinctly Vaishnavite. Proselytizing was carried on extensively after Jagjiwandas' death by fourteen well-known disciples mostly Rájputs and Bráhmans, but amongst whom were numbered two Kurmis, a Chamár and a Mochi. The influence of the sect is great amongst low-caste people, more especially in the Central Provinces. In the North-Western Provinces and Oudh it is most general in Bara Banki, Gonda, Bahraich, Basti, Rae Bareli Sitapur and other districts not far removed from the home of the founder. To a less extent it occurs throughout the province; indeed there is no province in Northern India in which Satnamis do not occur. The following account of the tenets of the sect is given by Wilson :—

"These profess to adore the true name alone, the One God, the Cause and Creator of all things, *Nirgun*, or void of sensible qualities, without beginning or end."

"They borrow, however, their notions of creation from the Vedanta philosophy, or rather from the modified form in which it is adapted to vulgar apprehension. Worldly existence is illusion, or the work of Máyá, the primitive character of Bhavani, the wife of Siva. They recognise accordingly the whole Hindu Pantheon, and, although they profess to worship but one God, pay reverence to what they consider manifestations of his nature visible in the *Avatárs*, particularly *Ráma* and *Krishna*."

"Unlike the *Sadhs* also, they use distinctive marks, and wear a double string or silk bound round the right wrist. Frontal lines are not invariably employed, but some make a perpendicular streak with ashes of a burnt offering made to *Hanuman*."

"Their moral code is something like that of all Hindu quietists, and enjoins indifference to the world, its pleasures or its pains, implicit devotion to the spiritual guide, clemency and gentleness, rigid adherence to truth, the discharge of all ordinary, social or religious obligations, and the hope of final absorption into the one spirit which pervades all things."

To feed the needy, to wound no one's feelings, to work with the plough till midday, and to spend the rest of the day in prayer and rest are the moral precepts of the sect. Strictly speaking, the Satnami should not worship idols, but a good deal of tolerance is extended towards local superstitions. Incense is burnt to Hanuman under the name of Mahabir. Rámchandar is also an object of reverence. Meat, masur and intoxicating liquors are forbidden and so is the "baingan," the fruit of the egg-plant. The latter prohibition is stated to be in memory of a miracle by which the founder converted a "baingan" into meat for the consumption of a relative, the Rája of Gonda, who insisted on being provided with animal food. Caste is observed and in social ceremonies the usual family customs are adhered to. The number shown under the head Satnami is 152,734. The great majority are followers of Jagjivandas, but a more restricted sect is entirely included, that of the *Sadhs*, a body of Hindu unitarians most numerous in Farukhabad and Mirzapur, who, though identical in name with the sect just described, are absolutely distinct and in point of fact are not Vaishnava, strictly so called. The sect was founded by Birbhan, a resident of Narnaul near Delhi, in 1858. The substance of their creed is given in twelve "hukms" quoted as follows by Wilson :—

1. "Acknowledge but one God, who made and can destroy you, to whom there is none superior, and to whom alone therefore is worship due; not to earth, nor stone, nor metal, nor wood, nor trees, nor any created thing. There is but one Lord, and the Word of the Lord. He who meditates on falsehoods, practices falsehood and commits sin, and he who commits sin falls into Hell."

2. "Be modest and humble; set not your affections on the world; adhere faithfully to your creed and avoid intercourse with all not of the same faith; eat not of a stranger's bread."

3. "Never lie nor speak ill at any time to or of anything, of earth or water, of trees or animals. Let the tongue be employed in the praise of God. Never steal, nor wealth, nor land, nor beasts, nor pasture: distinguish your own from another's property, and be content with what you possess. Never imagine evil. Let not your eyes rest on improper objects, nor men, nor women, nor dances, nor shows."

4. "Listen not to evil discourse, nor to anything but the praises of the Creator, nor to tales, nor gossip, nor calumny, nor music, nor singing, except hymns; but then the only musical accompaniment must be in the mind."

5. "Never covet anything, either of body or wealth: take not of another. God is the giver of all things; as your trust is in Him so shall you receive."

6. "When asked what you are, declare yourself a *Sadh*; speak not of caste; engage not in controversy; hold firm your faith; put not your hope in men."

7. "Wear white garments; use no pigments, nor collyrium, nor dentifrice, not *menhdi*, nor mark your person, nor your forehead with sectarial distinctions, nor wear chaplets or rosaries or jewels."

8. "Never eat nor drink intoxicating substances, nor chew pán, nor smell perfumes, nor smoke tobacco, nor chew nor smell opium; hold not up your hands, bow not down your head in the presence of idols or of men."

9. "Take no life away, nor offer personal violence, nor give damnatory evidence, nor seize anything by force."

10. "Let a man wed one wife, and a woman one husband; let not a man eat of a woman's leavings, but a woman may of a man's, as may be the custom. Let the woman be obedient to the man."

11. "Assume not the garb of a mendicant, nor solicit alms, nor accept gifts. Have no dread of necromancy, neither have recourse to it. Know before you confide. The meetings of the Pious are the only places of pilgrimage, but understand who are the Pious before you so salute them.

12. "Let not a Sadh be superstitious as to days, or to lunations, or to months, or the cries or appearances of birds or animals: let him seek only the will of the Lord."

The principles of these commandments are founded on the unitarianism of Kabir, Nanak, Dadu and other similar writers with possibly some assistance from Christianity. In notions as to the constitution of the universe, the existence of the inferior deities and the object of all devotion—liberation from life on earth, Sadhs do not differ from other Hindus. Caste was originally ignored in the Sadh community and converts received from all classes of the population. They have now, however, ceased to receive converts and form a close caste organization in themselves, the poorer members of which are assisted by the wealthier. A considerable proportion of the Sadhs are wealthy traders, amongst the poorer classes they are largely cotton printers. They have not preserved in its entirety the high standard of honesty and charity inculcated in their commandments, and are believed to reckon amongst their ranks quite as large a proportion of persons, whose standard of conduct in such respects is low, as does any other religion or sect in the North-West Provinces. It is unfortunate that they appear as a caste in Farukhabad only, where the numbers in the caste return are 1,866. They are known to be fairly numerous in Mirzapur and to be found to some extent elsewhere.

Apapanthi 4,267, Munna Dasi 2,636.

The remainder of the sects included as Vaishnava are more or less unimportant and may be dealt with briefly. The *Apapanthi* sect was founded a century ago by Munna Das, a goldsmith ascetic of Mandwa, a village in the Kheri district, to whose miraculous powers an escape from drought which threatened the country was believed to be due and who has since had a not inconsiderable number of followers in the district of his birth and Sitapur and Bahraich. It does not appear that the tenets taught by Munna Das to any considerable extent differ from those of the usual Vaishnava sects. *Anantpanthi* with a following of only 170 persons appears in Rae Bareli and Sitapur. It is a monotheistic reformed sect, the name of which implies a worship of Him who is without beginning or end.

Charandasi, 599.—Charandasi is a Panjáb sect of a more orthodox Vaishnava character than those just described. In these provinces it has only 599 followers. It was founded by Charandas, a merchant of the Dhusar caste, who lived in Delhi in the reign of the second Alamgir. They regard Krishna as the universal source and inculcate his worship combined with that of Radha. Professor Wilson gives the following account of their tenets :—

"Reverence of the Guru, and assertion of the pre-eminence of faith above every other distinction are also common to them with other Vaishnava sects, from whom probably they only differ in requiring no particular qualification of caste, order, nor even of sex, for their teachers : they affirm, indeed, that originally they differed from other sects of Vaishnavas in worshipping no sensible representations of the deity, and in excluding even the Tulsi plant and Saligrám stone from their devotions : they have, however, they admit, recently adopted them, in order to maintain a friendly intercourse with the followers of Rámanand : another peculiarity in their system is the importance they attach to morality, and they do not acknowledge faith to be independent of works : actions, they maintain, invariably meet with retribution or reward : their moral code, which they seem to have borrowed from the Madhvas, if not from a purer source, consists of ten prohibitions. They are not to lie, not to revile, not to speak harshly, not to discourse idly, not to steal, not to commit adultery, not to offer violence to any created thing, not to imagine evil, not to cherish hatred, and not to indulge in conceit or pride. The other obligations enjoined are, to discharge the duties of the profession or caste to which a person belongs, to associate with pious men, to put implicit faith in the spiritual preceptor, and to adore Hari as the original and indefinable cause of all, and who, through the operation of Máyá, created the universe, and has appeared in it occasionally in a mortal form, and particularly as Krishna at Brindaban."

"The followers of Charan Das are both clerical and secular ; the latter are chiefly of the mercantile order ; the former lead a mendicant and ascetic life, and are distinguished by wearing yellow garments and a single streak of sandal, or gopichandana, down the forehead ; the necklace and rosary are of tulsi beads : they wear also a small pointed cap, round the lower part of which they wrap a yellow turban. Their appearance in general is decent, and their deportment decorous ; in fact, although they profess mendicity, they are well supported by the opulence of their disciples ; it is possible, indeed, that this sect, considering its origin, and the class by which it is professed, arose out of an attempt to shake off the authority of the Gokulastha Goshains."

Eswaranandi, 3,966.—Eswaranandi (Sateswari) like Satnami is a sect founded by an Oudh religious thinker in protest against the idolatry and superstition of the beliefs prevailing around him. Eswaranand was a resident of Pura Nand in the Partábgarh district, the son of a religious ascetic. He spent his 85 years of life in obtaining converts to a faith in no way distinguishable by points of doctrine from those of the other Vaishnava Unitarian sects. The number of the sect shown at census was 3,966, principally in the Gonda district.

Parnami, 21,113.—Persons of the similar *Parnami* sect, considerably more numerous (21,113), are found mostly in Gonda, Bahraich, Rae Bareli and Gorakhpur. It is said to have been founded a century ago by a Vaishnava ascetic of Gwalior and spread by the agency of his disciples into Oudh, where they have many lay adherents. The principles of the sect add to those beliefs usual to reformed Vaishnava sects the special one that all the vicissitudes of human life, including birth and death, tend to promote the general welfare, that in fact "whatever is is best."

Prannathi, 65.—The Prannathi sect shows for the province only 65 persons. It appears from Growse's Mathura, that at the time it was written they owned a single representative in that district. The founder of the sect was a Bundelkhand Rájput. His religion was an attempt to effect a compromise between Hinduism, Muhammadanism and Christianity. It condemned idolatry, but found truth to some extent in all religions, and alike looked forward to the recoming of Moses, of Christ, and of Muhammad. A full account of part of the religious books of this very minor sect is given at page 230 *et. seq.* of Growse's Mathura.

Mohandasi, 1,118.—Of somewhat similar principles is the sect founded by Mohan Sain or Mohan Das, a religious ascetic of the Fyzabad district, by which the Muhammadan faith is adopted as foundation of their beliefs, but qualified in many respects by adherence to the Hindu system and the Hindu mythology. The sect numbers 1,118 persons.

Siva Naraini, 24,814.—*Siva Narainis* are considerably more important, especially in Gházipur, Ballia and Gorakhpur, which are close to the birthplace of the founder. They are Unitarians in the strictest sense of the word, paying no regard to any of the objects of Hindu or Muhammadan reverence. They originally received proselytes from both Hindus and Muhammadans and even it is believed from the lowest order of Christians.

"Truth, temperance and mercy are the cardinal virtues of this sect, as well as of the Sadhs; polygamy is prohibited, and sectarial marks are not used: conformity to the external observances of the Hindus or Muhammadans, independently of religious rites, is recommended, but latitude of practice is not unfrequent; and the Siva Narayanis of the lower orders are occasionally addicted to strong potations."

"The sect derives its appellation from that of its founder, Siva Narayan, a Rájput of the Nerivana tribe, a native of Chandavan, a village near Gházipur: he flourished in the reign of Muhammad Sháh, and one of his works is dated Samvat 1791, or A. D. 1735. The sect is strongest amongst Rájputs, but Kahárs and other low caste men are also admitted to a considerable extent.

Radhá Swami, 188.—*Radhá Swami* with 188 adherents, in Muttra mostly, is believed to be a sect founded by Rai Salig Rám, the late Postmaster-General, regarding the tenets of which I have no information.

Swami Naraini, 235.—*Swami Narainis* are shown as numbering 235 persons in these provinces. The founder of the sect, Sahjanand by name, was born in Chapiá Swami Narain in the Gonda district, but his religious work was entirely accomplished in the Bombay Presidency, and the adherents of the sect in these provinces are confined to those connected with a magnificent temple which has been built in the birthplace of the founder. Swami Narain acquired great wealth during his ministry, which, with the leadership of the sect, was bequeathed by him to his relatives in Gonda, who are now the "Mahárájas" of the faith. The institution of the sect was intended as a protest against the licentiousness of the Vallabhacharyas, to whom Sahjanand originally belonged. Radha and Krishna receive the same honour as in the Vallabhacharya faith, Swami Narain himself being added as the third member of the Trinity. Further details regarding the sect, which is influential in Bombay, are given in Monier Williams' Bráhmanism and Hinduism.

Gobindpanthi, 4,605.—More important in these provinces is the less known *Gobindpanthi* sect, whose adherents number 4,605 persons. It was founded by Gobind Das, a mendicant, buried at Ahrauli in the Fyzabad district, in whose honor an annual fair attended by several thousand worshippers is held in Aghan. The beliefs of the sect are theistic, but beyond this I am unable to give any details.

In the margin are given the numbers of adherents of two Ballia Rájput sects, of whom the local Gazetteer gives the following account:—

Nath Bábá	... ...	1,227
Bhikha Sahib	... ...	1,277

"The first of these takes its designation from the founder, whose original name was Amar Singh. He is supposed by Dr. Oldham to have lived 200 years ago, and to have been a deified hero of the Sengar tribe. The local tradition about him is as follows:—He became an ascetic at five years of age; and after 24 years of wandering life, spent mostly in the Panjáb, returned to his people. His divine power was manifested by the singular phenomenon of his cooking-fire remaining unextinguished in the rain, and his identity was proved by a miraculous renewal of lactation in his aged mother. He is represented as a guardian deity, interfering in various ways, and with constant success, on behalf of his votaries. Their successful resistance to the Rájas of Benares, and the restoration of the pargana to them by the English Government, are regarded as instances of the power and influence of Náth Bábá. Every third year in the month of Baisakh a festival is held in his honour at Rasra, the peculiar feature of which is the large offerings of cakes then made. His worship consists principally of adoration of various relics. His shrine is supported, among other offerings, by the voluntary contribution of one pie in the rupee on the Government revenue of pargana Lakhnesar. The zamíndárs, indeed, were willing to have this recorded and made a legal claim upon them, but the Government declined to have anything to do with its collection or legal recognition, and it continues to be a voluntary offering."

"Similar to Náth Bábá among the Sengars is Bhika Sháh among the Kausik Rájputs of Kopachit. The history and tenets of the sect are given as follows, by Bhola Nath, a kanúngo of the Ballia tahsíl. There was a devotee in Dehli whose name was Sháh Muhammad Yari. In his time a certain zamíndár of Bhirkura, named Mardan Sinh, was arrested for default in payment of revenue and sent by the Viceroy (Subadár) to Dehli, where he was imprisoned. A servant who had attended Mohan Sinh paid visits in his leisure hours to Muhammad Yari Sháh. One day the devotee enquired what he was and where he lived. On this the servant narrated the circumstances of his master's imprisonment and of his own presence there. 'Go and tell your master,' said the devotee, 'that he will be set free to-morrow by the order of the Minister of State, and that he should then present himself to me.' Mardan Sinh was actually released the next day, and, as directed, attended on Muhammad Yari Sháh. After several days' attendance and devotion, the devotee expressed himself satisfied, and directed Mardan Sinh to proceed to his own country, and there worship the Atma, and show mercy to the poor and hungry."

"He also gave him a *seli,* or necklace of black silk, worn as a distinguishing mark by the chief who sits on the *gaddi* when he has occasion to go to his disciples. Mardan Sinh was further instructed by Muhammad Yari Sháh to observe the following simple ceremony at the time of making a disciple: a *kanthi,* or sacred garland, is put round his neck, and the disciple is strictly enjoined to repeat constantly the invocation 'Rám, Rám,' and never to take life or tyrannize over any one. Mardan Sinh on his return to Bhirkura made one Bhika his disciple, and the latter finally settled in Baragaon. This happened some 400 years ago, and the Bhika Shábi gaddi (seat) was thus founded. It may be noticed with regard to the above account that a Muhammadan fakir is represented as enjoining the repetition of the strictly Hindu formula 'Rám, Rám.' If the legend is a correct statement of fact, the circumstance is an interesting illustration of the partial amalgamation of Muhammadan and Hindu forms, which we know was the aim of some Vaishnava reformers."

Darya Dasi, 2,310.—A similar sect in the Gházipur district was founded by one Darya Das, a Vaishnava mendicant of the Koeri caste, whose followers now number 2,310.

Bishnois, 49,559.—The last sect to be specially mentioned is in many respects an important one, that of the Bishnois. They number altogether 49,559 persons, mostly in Bijnor. It is by no means certain that the figures given are entirely correct, owing to the identity of the name Bishnoi in the Persian character with Baishnavi, as Vaishnavi is often written and its close resemblance to the corrupt form of Bishni, by which name Hindu Baniyas often describe themselves by way of contrast to "Jaini' fellow-caste men. The Bishnoi sect had its origin in the bordering districts of the Panjáb. The following account of it is taken from the Sirsa Settlement report :—

"The name Bishnoi is evidently derived from the prominence they give in their creed and worship to the god Vishnu, though they themselves say it is derived from the twenty-nine (Bis-Nau) articles of their creed as prescribed by the founder of the sect. It is said that any member of the higher Hindu castes can become a Bishnoi, but in this district at least they are almost all Ját or Khati by tribe, and retain the language, dress and other characteristics of the Bagris ; but they try to sink their tribe in their religion and give their caste as Bishnoi merely. The account they give of the founder of their sect is as follows :—At Pinpásar, a village south of Bikaner in the Jodhpur territory, there lived a Rájput Panwar, named Laut, who had attained the age of sixty years and had no son. One day a neighbour going out to sow his field met Laut, and deeming it a bad omen to meet a childless man, turned back from his purpose. This cut Laut to the quick, and he went out to the jungle and bewailed his childlessness until evening, when a faqir appeared to him and told him that in nine months he should have a son, and after showing his miraculous power by drawing milk from a calf, vanished from his sight. At the time named a child miraculously appeared in Laut's house and was miraculously suckled by his wife Hánsá. This happened in Sambat 1508 (A. D. 1451). For seven years the boy, who was an incarnation (*autar*) of Vishnu, played with his fellows, and then for 27 years he tended cattle, but all this time he spoke no word. His miraculous powers were shown in various ways, such as producing sweets from nothing for the delectation of his companions, and he became known as *Achambha* (the wonder), whence his name of Jhámba, by which he is generally known. After 34 years a Bráhman was sent for to get him to speak, and on his confessing his failure, Jhámbaji again showed his power by lighting a lamp by simply snapping his fingers, and uttered his first word. He then adopted the life of a teacher and went to reside on a sandhill some 30 miles south of Bikaner, where after 51 years he died and was buried instead of being burnt like an ordinary Hindu. He did not marry, but devoted himself to the life of an ascetic teacher. His sayings (*sabd*) to the number of 120 were written down by his disciples, and have been handed down in a book (*pothi*) which is written in the Nagri character and in a Hindu dialect similar to Bágri, seemingly a Márwári dialect. The "twenty-nine" precepts given by him for the guidance of his followers are as follows :—For thirty days after childbirth and five days after a menstrual discharge a woman must not cook food. Bathe in the morning. Commit not adultery. Be content. Be abstemious and pure. Strain your drinking-water. Be careful of your speech. Examine your fuel in case any living creature be burnt with it. Show pity to living creatures. Keep duty present to your mind as the Teacher bade. Do not steal. Do not speak evil of others. Do not tell lies. Never quarrel. Avoid opium, tobacco, bhang, and blue clothing. Flee from spirits and flesh. See that your goats are kept alive (not sold to Musalmáns who will kill them for food). Do not plough with bullocks. Keep a fast on the day before the new moon. Do not cut green trees. Sacrifice with fire. Say prayers. Meditate. Perform worship and attain heaven. And the last of the twenty-nine duties prescribed by the Teacher—Baptize your children if you would be called a true Bishnoi."

"Some of these precepts are not strictly obeyed: for instance, although ordinarily they allow no blue in their clothing, yet a Bishnoi, if he is a servant of the British Government, is allowed to wear a blue uniform; and Bishnois do use bullocks, though most of their farming is done with camels. They also seem to be unusually quarrelsome (in words) and given to use bad language. But they abstain from tobacco, drugs and spirits, and are noted for their regard for animal life, which is such that not only will they not themselves kill any living creature, but they do their utmost to prevent others from doing so. Consequently their villages are generally swarming with antelope and other animals, and they forbid their Musalmán neighbours to kill them and try to dissuade European sportsmen from interfering with them. They wanted it made a condition of their settlement that no one should be allowed to shoot on their land, but at the same time they asked that they might be assessed at lower rates than their neighbours, on the ground that the antelope, being thus left undisturbed, do more damage to their crops; but I told them this would lessen the merit (*pun*) of their good actions in protecting the animals and they must be treated just as the surrounding villages were. They consider it a good deed to scatter grain (chiefly bajra and moth) to pigeons and other birds, and often have a large number of half-tame birds about their villages. The day before the new moon they observe as a Sabbath and fast-day, doing no work in the fields or in the house. They bathe and pray three times a day, in the morning, afternoon and in the evening, saying "Bishno, Bishno," instead of the ordinary Hindu, Rám, Rám. Their clothing is the same as that of other Bagris, except that their women do not allow the waist to be seen and are fond of wearing black woollen clothing. They are more particular about ceremonial purity than ordinary Hindus are, and it is a common saying that if a Bishnoi's food is on the first of a string of 20 camels and a man of another caste touches the last camel of the string, the Bishnoi will consider his food defiled and throw it away. They do not revere Bráhmans, but have priests (Sadh) of their own, chosen from among the laity. They do not burn their dead, but bury them below the cattle-stall or in a place frequented by cattle such as a cattle-pen. They observe the Holi in a different way from other Hindus. After sunset on that day they fast till the next forenoon, when after hearing read the account of how Prahlad was tortured by his infidel father Hárnaksh for believing in the god Vishnu until he was delivered by the god himself in his incarnation of the lion-man, and mourning over Prahlad's sufferings, they light a sacrificial fire and partake of consecrated water, and after distributing impurified sugar (*gur*) in commemoration of Prahlad's delivery from the fire into which he was thrown, they break their fast. Bishnois go on pilgrimage to the place where Jhámbaji is buried, south of Bikaner, where there is a tomb (*mat*) over his remains and a temple (*mandir*) with regular attendants (*pujari*). A festival takes place here every six months in Asauj and Phagan, when the pilgrims go to the sandhill on which Jhámbaji lived, and there light sacrificial fires (*hom*) of jandi wood in vessels of stone and offer a burnt offering of barley, til, ghi and sugar, at the same time muttering set prayers. They also make presents to the attendants of the temple and distribute *moth* and other grains for peacocks and pigeons which live there in numbers. Should any one have committed an offence, such as having killed an animal, or sold a cow or goat to a Musalmán, or allowed an animal to be killed when he could have prevented it, he is fined by the assembled Bishnois for the good of the temple and the animals kept there. Another place of pilgrimage is a tomb called Chhámbola in the Jodhpur country, where a festival is held once a year in Chait."

A somewhat different but probably incorrect account of the sect is given in the Bijnor Gazetteer in which Jhámbaji is identified with Shaikh Makhdum Jahania Jahangasht, a Muhammadan saint of Márwár. In Bijnor the Bishnois are mostly Baniya and in the use of the Muhammadan salutation *salám alaikum* and the title Shaikhji appear to differ from those of the Panjáb. The Bijnor Bishnois account for this by saying they murdered a Muhammadan Kazi who prevented their burning a widow, and were glad to compound the offence by pretending to adopt Muhammadanism. The separation between the Bishnois and other Hindus is, though decreasing, still considerable, and religious prejudices on either side are still apt to give trouble.

Minor and undefined sects, 38,093.—Sects which have not been identified or which occur only to a very minor extent in these provinces number 38,093 persons, and are shown together as the last entry in the table.

203. **Sectarian distribution of population.**—The following abstract gives the total of each of the groups and classes referred to above and shows the proportion included in each of the total Hindu population. Roughly, Sakti worshippers are 25 per cent. of the total population. They are closely allied to and would popularly be combined with the 16 per cent. who are animistic. Altogether over 41 per cent. of the population belongs to the class whose religion is directly descended from that of the non-Aryan aboriginies of India. Next in importance as regards numbers are the Vaishnavas, those at the furthest extreme in religious matters from the animists. Vaishnavas, including reformed sects, include over 22 per cent. of the population; next in numbers with just under 21 per cent. are the Saivas. Less than 10 per cent. profess themselves monothestic and non-sectarian. Less than 4 per cent. were unable to specify their beliefs, and the remainder over 2 per cent. belong to various small groups not specially connected with either of the main divisions of Hinduism.

Abstract No. 58.—Showing the population and proportion to the total number of Hindus of the great sectarian classes.

Class.	Group.	Population.	Percentage of total Hindu population.
Class I.—Belonging to no sectarian subdivision.	...	1,486,984	3·68
Class II.—Monotheistic ...	...	3,810,231	9·44
Class III.—Pre-Puranic beliefs ...	...	501,171	1·25
Class IV.—Worshippers of Puranic deities connected with Vishnu.	Group (a) Worshippers of Vishnu and Badri Nath.	3,740,428	9·26
	„ (b) Worshippers of incarnations of Vishnu and of gods and demi-gods connected therewith.	3,468,380	8·59
	Class IV ...	7,208,808	17·85
Class V.—Worshippers of Puranic deities connected with Siva.	Group (a) Worshippers of Siva and local and special Mahadeo.	8,117,745	20·11
	„ (b) Worshippers of gods and demi-gods connected with Siva.	260,588	·64
	Class V ...	8,378,333	20·75
Class VI.—Worshippers of Puranic Saktis.	...	10,080,521	24·96

Abstract No. 58.—*Showing the population and proportion to the total number of Hindus of the great sectarian classes*—(concluded).

Class.	Group.	Population.	Percentage of total Hindu population.
Class VII.—Developments and additions to Saktism.	Group (*a*) Worshippers of gods of disease ...	158,780	·39
	" (*b*) Snake-worshippers	203,286	·51
	" (*c*) Worshippers of spirits of deceased persons who have died a violent death	1,329,456	3·29
	" (*d*) Worshippers of Muhammadan saints,	2,333,643	5·78
	" (*e*) Worshippers of caste and ancestral gods.	157,379	·39
	" (*f*) Other gods worshipped by special classes.	1,370,883	3·39
	" (*g*) Demon-worshippers	203,332	·51
	" (*h*) Worshippers of village, forest and local gods.	561,607	1·39
	" (*i*) Worshippers of river and river gods...	319,545	·79
	Class VII. ...	6,637,911	16·44
Class VIII.—Worshippers of other Puranic gods and demi-gods and objects of reverence.	...	334,198	·83
Class IX.— ...	Group (*a*) Sectarian subdivisions, Saivite ...	47,897	·12
	" (*b*) Vaishnava, Unitarian and miscellaneous sects.	1,888,862	4·67
	Class IX ...	1,936,759	4·79
Not properly Hindus ...	...	5,252	·01
	Total ...	40,380,168	100·00

Chapter VIII—THE CIVIL CONDITION OF THE POPULATION.

204. **The tables showing conjugal condition.**—Statistics regarding the civil condition of the population are prepared in a very elaborate form in Tables VIII and D. In the former the population is classified by civil condition for each religion with the same full detail of age as in the age tables. In the latter all castes and races in the province are shown as single, married, or widowed for the age-periods 0 to 9, 10 to 14, 15 to 39, 40 and over.

Table VIII is of value in these provinces only in so far as the conjugal condition of the whole population and of Hindus, Muhammadans and Jains are concerned; of the other religions, none constitute self-contained groups; statistics regarding them are complicated by the absence of children or wives connected with the population recorded in other religions or other countries. These tables show a conjugal condition of the population very different from anything of which we have experience elsewhere. Of the whole population, including minors, 50·5 per cent. are shown as married, leaving slightly less than half the total population as single and widowed, 38·1 of the former, 11·4 of the latter. How considerable a contrast this presents to the English constitution of population appears from Abstract No. 60 in which the proportion borne by the population of each of the civil conditions to the total of each sex, is compared for the North-Western Provinces and England. The comparison shows the North-Western Provinces figures for single much lower than in England; those for married proportionably higher; whilst those for widowed are greatly in excess, especially for women, for whom the proportion of the total sex in this condition is considerably more than double as many as in England.

Abstract No. 59, showing for North-Western Provinces and Oudh, the marriage statistics as returned in the schedules together with their proportions to total population.

	Gross numbers.			Percentage on total population.		
	Total.	Males.	Females.	Total.	Males.	Females.
Single ...	17,884,471	10,944,547	6,939,924	38·13	23·33	14·80
Married ...	23,694,436	11,820,598	11,873,838	50·52	25·21	25·31
Widowed ...	5,326,178	1,538,456	3,787,722	11·35	3·28	8·07

Abstract No. 60, comparing the marriage statistics of North-Western Provinces and Oudh with those of England.

	Males.			Females.		
	Single.	Married.	Widowed.	Single.	Married.	Widowed.
N.-W. Provinces and Oudh.	4,503	4,863	634	3,069	5,254	1,677
England ...	6,193	3,465	342	5,923	3,327	750

Abstract No. 61, showing the percentage per 10,000 of each sex of the single, married and widowed at each age-period.

	N.-W. Provinces and Oudh.			England.		
	Single.	Married.	Widowed.	Single.	Married.	Widowed.
			Males.			
0—14 ...	3,448	344	9	3,740	...	...
15—24 ...	641	1,014	41	1,683	199	2
25—34 ...	243	1,413	103	457	964	20
35—44 ...	95	1,041	132	155	926	40
45—54 ...	45	636	143	79	681	59
55 and over ...	31	415	206	79	695	221
Total, Males ...	4,503	4,863	634	6,193	3,465	342
			Females.			
0—14 ...	2,975	679	13	3,555	...	...
15—24 ...	59	1,513	59	1,541	325	3
25—34 ...	18	1,595	195	432	1,007	39
35—44 ...	9	902	355	176	874	94
45—54 ...	4	393	439	102	607	145
55 and over ...	4	172	616	117	514	469
Total, Females ...	3,069	5,254	1,677	5,923	3,827	750

Attention is thus at once drawn to the three phenomena of most importance and interest in connection with marriage statistics in India—(1) infant marriage, (2) the universality of marriage, (3) enforced widowhood. In considering all these phenomena, a comparison by ages of each civil condition as presented in the marginal table abstract No. 61, is necessary.

205. **Infant marriage.**—In England and Wales there are no persons married before 15 and only 5 males and 24 females in 10,000 of each sex married under 20. In North-Western Provinces and Oudh, on the contrary, out of 10,000 males 344 are married below 15 and 420 more between 15 and 20. For females the corresponding figures are still higher, 679 and 667. Table VIII shows that marriage is occasionally practised in India almost immediately after the birth of a child; 1,971 persons are shown as married in the first year of life. The numbers steadily rise for succeeding years until 13,076 boys and 20,517 girls are shown as married under 4. Marriage of children under four is happily exceptional, but it exists in nearly all parts of the province, and in all branches of the population; the proportion of such marriages amongst Muhammadans not being materially different from those amongst Hindus. It is, I believe, confined to the lowest classes of the population, and amongst Muhammadans probably to a great extent is amongst sweepers, whose ideas of Muhammadanism are, as already remarked, indefinite in the extreme. It is said to be an occasional custom amongst certain castes to betroth children before they are born conditionally on their turning out of opposite sexes. The custom of marriage of infants under 4, though prevailing to some extent everywhere, is specially prevalent in certain districts, Dehra Dún, Sahâranpur, Agra, Fatehpur, Bánda, Allahabad showing specially large numbers in the western districts, whilst the eastern districts both of Oudh and North-Western Provinces all show a proportion of such marriages considerably above average. From 5 to 9 marriage becomes important, nearly 433 per 10,000 of the male population of that age-period being married and 999 per 10,000 of the female population. Between 10 and 14 nearly nine-tenths of the female population

Abstract No. 62, showing for married the absolute numbers of males and females aud their proportion to 10,000 of same sex and age-periods.

Age-periods.	Absolute numbers of males and females married.		Proportion to 10,000 of same sex and age-periods.	
	Males.	Females.	Males.	Females.
0 year ...	857	1,114	10	13
1 „ ...	857	1,172	24	31
2 „ ...	1,883	2,713	31	43
3 „ ...	3,382	5,504	47	73
4 „ ...	6,097	10,014	90	149
0—4 „ ...	13,076	20,517	41	63
5—9 „ ...	139,773	291,373	433	999
Total, 0—9 „ ...	152,849	311,890	238	506
10—14 „ ...	684,952	1,221,870	2,417	5,744
15—19 „ ...	1,020,582	1,507,733	5,014	9,119
20—24 „ ...	1,443,669	1,911,378	6,923	9,404
25—29 „ ...	1,654,290	1,856,524	7,849	9,155
30—34 „ ...	1,778,861	1,747,479	8,206	8,501
35—39 „ ...	1,135,619	988,812	8,256	8,040
40—44 „ ...	1,393,582	1,050,977	8,157	6,438
45—49 „ ...	661,188	434,907	7,970	6,002
50—54 „ ...	885,634	454,625	7,541	3,891
55—59 „ ...	263,152	142,643	7,134	4,216
60 and over ...	746,220	245,005	6,142	1,688
Total ...	11,820,598	11,873,838	4,863	5,253

pass into the married state, but considerably more than one-half of the males still remain unmarried. Between 15 and 19 there are 15 married females for each one unmarried, whilst at the end of the period only 60 per cent. of the males have been married. By 24, practically the whole of the female population have been married, almost the whole of those unmarried at this and later ages being women whose avocations preclude marriage or whose physical or mental health forbids it. Of men, considerably more than a fourth are unmarried up to 24, whilst an appreciable but diminishing number remain unmarried through all subsequent age-periods.

Abstract No. 63, *showing the distribution of* 10,000 *Hindus according to sex and age.*

Age-periods.	Single.		Married.		Widowed.		Total.	
	Males.	Females.	Males.	Females.	Males.	Females.	Males.	Females.
1	2	3	4	5	6	7	8	9
0—4 ...	674·0	685·2	2·9	4·3	·1	·2	677·0	689·7
5—9 ...	656·8	554·8	31·8	64·9	1·0	1·3	689·6	621·0
10—14 ...	448·4	178·8	153·2	269·0	3·6	4·8	605·2	452·6
15—19 ...	204·4	18·4	223·2	321·5	6·9	9·5	434·5	349·4
20—24 ...	120·1	5·1	310·3	405·8	14·4	20·0	444·8	430·9
25—29 ...	76·2	3·6	354·2	396·2	21·6	33·2	452·0	433·0
30—34 ...	52·8	3·5	379·9	372·7	32·4	63·6	465·1	439·8
35—39 ...	26·8	1·9	242·0	211·5	25·4	50·7	294·2	264·1
40—44 ...	25·3	1·8	297·3	222·9	44·3	124·3	366·9	349·0
45—49 ...	11·5	·7	140·8	92·4	25·8	62·3	178·1	155·4
50—54 ...	13·5	1·1	186·6	94·8	49·4	150·9	249·5	246·8
55—59 ...	4·6	·4	55·5	30·0	18·4	41·5	78·5	71·9
60 and over,	12·3	1·1	154·2	50·9	87·5	254·9	254·0	306·9
Total ...	2,326·7	1,456·4	2,531·9	2,536·9	330·8	817·2	5,189·4	4,810·5

For Muhammadans the distribution is not materially different from that for Hindus, which dominates the total tables. The proportion of each sex unmarried at the earlier age-periods is somewhat greater than amongst Hindus, whilst at the later age-periods the proportion of men unmarried is distinctly lower, and that of single women distinctly higher. This is what might be expected. It is well known that a considerable proportion of men remains unmarried amongst Hindus of several castes, and that a large proportion of the prostitutes and dancing girls who have not been born to the occupation either are or become Muhammadans; in the latter case to escape from the absolute social death that befalls them amongst Hindus of the caste in which

Abstract No. 64, *showing the distribution of* 10,000 *Musalmáns according to sex and age.*

Age-periods.	Single.		Married.		Widowed.		Total.	
	Males.	Females.	Males.	Females.	Males.	Females.	Males.	Females.
1	2	3	4	5	6	7	8	9
0—4 ...	684·3	705·8	2·5	4·4	·3	·3	687·1	710·5
5—9 ...	662·8	582·3	17·4	45·8	·8	1·1	681·0	629·2
10—14 ...	495·3	247·4	101·7	209·5	2·7	3·1	599·7	460·0
15—19 ...	239·8	42·7	182·0	321·7	5·9	6·9	427·7	371·3
20—24 ...	122·8	13·2	291·1	419·8	13·6	15·4	427·5	448·4
25—29 ..	60·1	8·9	342·9	395·2	20·1	24·9	423·1	429·0
30—34 ...	35·8	8·9	376·7	374·1	28·8	47·9	441·3	430·9
35—39 ...	16·3	4·3	242·5	207·3	21·5	88·8	280·3	250·4
40—44 ...	13·3	5·1	297·7	233·2	37·3	105·6	348·3	343·9
45—49 ...	5·1	1·8	141·5	95·0	20·6	52·0	167·2	148·8
50—54 ...	6·9	3·6	205·0	111·9	45·6	150·0	257·5	265·5
55—59 ...	2·2	1·1	60·1	33·3	16·7	39·0	79·0	73·4
60 and over	7·1	4·2	191·7	60·8	92·7	262·4	291·5	327·4
Total ...	2,351·8	1,629·3	2,452·8	2,512·0	306·6	747·4	5,111·2	4,888·7

they were born. For Jains, the general outlines are the same, but whilst the age of marriage is somewhat higher than amongst Hindus, the male population is more completely married at 24 and the female at 20 than in any other religion. The number of both males and females who remain unmarried after these ages is low, though in the case of women not so much lower as might have been expected from the entire absence of women of the dancing girl class amongst the Jains.

Abstract No. 65, showing the distribution of 10,000 *Jains according to sex and age.*

Age-periods.	Single.		Married.		Widowed.		Total.	
	Males.	Females.	Males.	Females.	Males.	Females.	Males.	Females.
1	2	3	4	5	6	7	8	9
0—4 ...	532·9	532·2	·5	2·2	·6	·2	534·0	534·6
5—9 ...	568·6	483·6	10·5	26·0	·7	·9	579·8	510·5
10—14 ...	460·6	192·9	115·3	218·4	2·7	5·9	578·6	417·2
15—19 ...	247·4	13·6	244·8	370·6	9·6	22·3	501·8	406·5
20—24 ...	172·6	3·6	332·9	413·1	28·0	44·4	533·5	461·1
25—29 ...	120·5	2·3	322·7	340·6	37·4	65·2	480·6	408·1
30—34 ...	99·5	2·9	337·0	311·8	58·0	110·5	494·5	425·2
35—39 ...	56·3	2·0	237·9	193·6	51·5	80·2	345·7	275·8
40—44 ...	57·8	1·0	253·0	196·9	83·8	158·9	394·6	356·8
45—49 ...	33·1	1·0	151·9	83·8	62·8	80·7	247·8	165·5
50—54 ...	33·3	1·3	150·7	86·6	101·4	173·0	285·4	260·9
55—59 ...	13·5	·1	62·6	31·3	52·8	54·0	128·9	85·3
60 and over	26·1	1·3	111·4	39·8	150·1	258·4	287·6	299·6
Total ...	2,422·2	1,237·8	2,331·2	2,314·7	639·4	1,054·6	5,392·8	4,607·1

Of the total population above 15 who are single, married and widowed, the marginal table shows the proportion in the North-Western Provinces and Oudh and in England for 10,000 of each sex.

		Single.	Married.	Widowed.
N.-W. Provinces and Oudh	Males ...	1,702	7,292	1,006
	Females...	150	7,224	2,626
England	Males ...	3,918	5,532	550
	Females...	3,674	5,164	1,162

To sum up, we have seen 1st, that whilst marriage begins almost immediately after birth for some castes amongst both Hindus and Muhammadans, it is most general for males just before the age of twenty and for females just before fifteen ; 2nd, that after 30 for males and 19 for women, only a small fraction of the total population remains unmarried ; 3rd, that marriage is but slightly later amongst Muhammadans than amongst Hindus, and that it is, on the whole, more universal in the former than in the latter religion. The difference between the ages at which Hindus and Muhammadans are usually married is probably, amongst Hindus of good caste, fully more than compensated for by the fact that the bride does not usually go to her husband's house until a subsequent ceremony "gauna" is completed, usually after signs of puberty appear and at an interval generally of three, five or seven years after the marriage. Hindu marriages are not therefore finally completed till usually three years after they have been celebrated. Amongst Muhammadans the bride goes to live with the bridegroom's family immediately after marriage, which, in the words of a Muhammadan author, is usually celebrated "when the youth is eighteen and the young lady thirteen or fourteen at the most. Many are married at an earlier age, when, in the opinion of the parents, an eligible match is to be secured. And in some cases, where the parents on both sides have the union of their children at heart, they contract them at six or seven years old, which marriage they solemnly bind themselves to fulfil when the children have reached a proper age. Under these circumstances the children are allowed to live in the same house, and often form an attachment for each other, which renders their union a life of real happiness."

There is no reason to believe that in these provinces the age of consummation of marriage is earlier amongst Hindus than Muhammadans, or that the premature consummation, the religious necessity for which was of late so much insisted on in Bengal, takes place at least amongst any except the very lowest castes.

206. **Widow marriage.**—The figures for widowed present several features of great interest. The distinction between the different religions is here much more marked than in the earlier conjugal condition. Of 10,000 of the total Hindu population, 331 males and 817 females are widowed; 306 males and 747 females amongst Muhammadans; and no less than 639 males and 1,054 females amongst Jains. It is clear, therefore, that both males and females, but particularly the latter, remarry more extensively amongst Muhammadans than Hindus, and very much more frequently amongst Hindus than amongst Jains. As regards females, this is exactly what might have been expected from what is known of the social circumstances of the three religions. Muhammadans permit remarriage alike amongst males and females and the excess of female widowed is due to the same reasons as the excess in England. The higher proportion of widowed of both sexes as compared with England is of course mainly due to the higher proportion of marriages. The somewhat higher proportion of excess amongst Muhammadan widows over Muhammadan widowers as compared with English figures is probably due to the greater facilities an English widow enjoys for remarriage. Amongst Hindus, as is well known, remarriage is in the higher caste permitted only for males. The castes which do not permit widow remarriage are roughly one-fourth of the whole, so that Hindus as regards female remarriage occupy a position between Muhammadans and Jains but nearer the former than the latter. The latter are practically as regards such matters Hindus of high caste and permit no widow remarriage, hence the high proportion of widows.

	Gross numbers.	Percentage.
Not permitting widow remarriage ...	9,713,087	24·05
Permitting widow remarriage ...	30,667,081	75·95
Total, Hindus ...	40,380,168	100·00

The figures for males are noteworthy; they tend to show that in those religions and castes which enforce widowhood on their women, the men also remarry to a considerably less extent than in those in which widow remarriage is permitted. This was to be expected, as early marriage and enforced widowhood for females would ordinarily necessitate for a widower a marriage very unequal in point of age, and therefore even amongst a people so given to unequal marriages as Hindus comparatively difficult and comparatively objectionable.

A comparison of the number of widowers and widows in each age-group for the Hindu and Muhammadan religions is instructive. It shows how the number of Hindu widows almost at once begins to rise above that of widowers, whilst amongst Muhammadans the numbers continue fairly close to the age of thirty, when it is more difficult for a woman to remarry than a man, and the number of widows to widowers consequently rises suddenly.

Abstract No. 66, showing widows to 1,000 widowers at each age-group for Hindus and Muhammadans.

	0—9.	10—19.	20—29.	30—39.	40—49.	50 and over.
Hindus	1,364	1,354	1,479	1,976	2,663	2,880
Muhammadans ...	1,228	1,158	1,199	1,724	2,720	2,913

207. **The fecundity of the population.**—A comparison of the fecundity of Indian with that of European women may be interesting. The tables show in all 8,011,921 married women between the ages of 15 and 40, which may be assumed to be the limits of the reproductive period in India. The actual births during the year of census as reported by the Sanitary Commissioner were 1,751,168; we have seen that his returns are probably considerably too low, and that the actual birth-rate was about 43 per cent., giving a total number of births 2,016,915 for the above number of child-bearing women or 251 births for each 1,000 wives. The corresponding English rate for the census of 1881 was 292.

Some rough comparative indication of the usual difference in age between husbands and wives amongst Hindus and Muhammadans may be derived from a calculation of the mean age of husbands and wives in the method referred to on page 139. For Hindus the mean age of husbands is 34·48 and of wives 28·95. For Muhammadans the figures are 36·31 and 29·89. The calculation for women is disturbed by the uncertainty attaching to the ages of women, but it is not in error to at all the same extent as that for all women, as the omissions of women in the age-period in which they are most numerous occur mainly for unmarried women. The English mean age of the married was 43·1 for males and 40·7 for females, being of course owing to later marriage and longer life, considerably higher than in this country. A comparison of the marriage statistics for the present census and for that of 1881 is given in the accompanying abstracts. The variations shown

Abstract No. 67, comparing the marriage statistics for the present and the 1881 censuses; per 10,000 of each sex.

	Males.		Females.	
	1881.	1891.	1881.	1891.
Single	4,522	4,503	3,015	3,070
Married	4,848	4,864	5,277	5,254
Widowed	630	633	1,708	1,676

Abstract No. 68, comparing by age the marriage statistics for the present and the 1881 censuses per 10,000 of each sex and civil condition.

		0—14.	15—24.	25—39.	40—49.	50 and over.
Males.						
Single	1881...	7,700	1,425	620	132	123
	1891...	7,660	1,422	650	147	121
Married	1881...	657	1,969	3,998	1,739	1,637
	1891...	709	2,085	3,865	1,738	1,603
Widowed	1881...	183	898	2,559	1,893	4,467
	1891...	141	643	2,387	2,088	4,741
Females.						
Single	1881...	9,669	225	66	20	20
	1891...	9,690	191	73	22	24
Married	1881...	1,293	2,850	3,906	1,245	706
	1891...	1,292	2,880	3,868	1,251	709
Widowed	1881...	79	366	1,851	2,251	5,453
	1891...	76	353	1,768	2,260	5,543

are in all respects trifling, showing that in so far as affecting the census returns the results of the late agitation against early marriage that we have heard so much of is absolutely *nil*. In connection with this question the figures for married Aryas may be advantageously compared with those for Hindus. It must be borne in mind that a comparatively large number of Aryas have been included within that religion of late years, and that on being included the connections already made remain. The figures for males are complicated by the inclusion of a number of educated young men as yet comparatively free from family burdens, to such an extent that no inference can be drawn from them. For females also, there is a large excess of young women under 25, but in spite of this there is reason in the large deficit in the married under 14, to believe that to some extent the Aryas do act upon their belief in the inexpediency of early marriage.

Abstract No. 69, *showing Married Aryas* 10,000 *of each sex.*

	0—14.	15—24.	25—39.	40—49.	50 and over.
Males	523	3,021	4,065	1,345	1,046
Females	798	3,912	3,689	1,045	606

208. **Local variations in marriage statistics.**—Before passing to the consideration of the figures for civil condition of castes, the comparative topographical distribution of the characteristics of civil condition may be referred to. The accompanying tables show for each of the divisions of the province, 1st the distribution by civil condition of 10,000 persons of each sex, and 2nd the distribution by age of 10,000 persons of each sex and civil condition. These must be examined in view of the Divisional comparison of ages given at an earlier page. Thus the noticeably high proportion of females single in the Gorakhpur Division is due to the large proportion of children in that division. It is not so noticeable for men because of the unusually high proportion of men who are married in that division. These tables show that the proportion of men who remain unmarried after 25 is noticeably higher in the Meerut, Agra and Allahabad Divisions than elsewhere and considerably lower in Gorakhpur than in any other division. The proportion of females unmarried after 24 is every where very low. Infant marriage both of males and females is most rife in Benares and Allahabad, Gorakhpur and Fyzabad following at some interval. Widow remarriage leading to a low proportion of widows and especially of widows under 40 is commonest in Gorakhpur, Oudh, and the largely Musalmán divisions of Rohilkhand and Meerut.

Abstract No. 70, *showing the distribution by civil condition of* 10,000 *persons of each sex.*

Divisions.	Single.		Married.		Widowed.	
	Males.	Females.	Males.	Females.	Males.	Females.
Meerut	4,358	2,928	4,817	5,436	825	1,636
Agra	4,766	2,862	4,430	5,225	804	1,913
Rohilkhand	4,725	3,104	4,599	5,259	676	1,637
Allahabad	4,281	2,848	5,012	5,323	707	1,829
Benares	4,408	2,997	5,024	5,174	568	1,829
Gorakhpur	4,337	3,328	5,200	5,198	463	1,474
Kumaun	4,853	3,351	4,634	5,059	513	1,590
N.-W. Provinces	4,484	3,037	4,853	5,259	663	1,704
Lucknow	4,722	3,290	4,690	5,142	588	1,568
Fyzabad	4,410	3,051	5,071	5,320	519	1,629
Oudh	4,557	3,160	4,892	5,240	551	1,600
N.-W. Provinces and Oudh	4,503	3,070	4,864	5,254	633	1,676

Abstract No. 71, *showing the distribution of* 10,000 *persons of each sex and civil condition by age. Single.*

Divisions.	0—14.		15—24.		25—39.		40—49.		50 and over.	
	Males.	Females.	Males.	Females.	Males.	Females.	Males	Females.	Males.	Females.
Meerut Division ...	7,374	9,701	1,603	209	720	58	170	15	133	17
Agra " ...	6,953	9,710	1,920	157	804	80	187	27	136	26
Rohilkhand " ...	7,371	9,699	1,683	195	682	61	150	21	114	24
Allahabad " ...	7,549	9,672	1,330	177	768	93	196	29	157	29
Benares " ...	8,098	9,706	1,078	176	577	76	148	22	99	20
Gorakhpur " ...	8,519	9,740	959	169	404	60	67	15	51	16
Kumaun " ...	7,452	9,556	1,932	325	493	77	74	23	49	19
N.-W. Provinces ...	7,649	9,701	1,442	186	649	70	148	21	112	22
Lucknow Division ...	7,429	9,603	1,547	245	696	90	160	29	168	33
Fyzabad " ...	7,909	9,710	1,202	172	616	73	135	20	138	25
Oudh	7,676	9,660	1,369	206	655	81	147	24	153	29
N.-W. Provinces and Oudh	7,660	9,690	1,422	191	650	73	147	22	121	24

Abstract No. 72, *showing the distribution of* 10,000 *persons of each sex and civil condition by age. Married.*

Divisions.	0—14.		15—24.		25—39.		40—49.		50 and over.	
	Males.	Females.	Males.	Females.	Males.	Females.	Males.	Females.	Males.	Females.
Meerut Division ...	635	1,131	2,412	3,258	3,950	3,742	1,630	1,189	1,373	680
Agra " ...	368	1,172	2,153	3,341	4,222	3,841	1,858	1,143	1,399	503
Rohilkhand " ...	514	1,185	2,116	3,036	3,915	3,744	1,799	1,289	1,656	746
Allahabad " ...	932	1,559	2,067	2,776	3,864	3,889	1,758	1,205	1,379	571
Benares " ...	995	1,628	1,984	2,658	3,639	3,833	1,721	1,207	1,661	674
Gorakhpur " ...	902	1,348	2,187	2,730	3,739	3,932	1,661	1,241	1,511	749
Kumaun " ...	323	1,209	2,026	3,260	4,120	3,693	1,848	1,174	1,683	664
N.-W. Provinces ...	731	1,344	2,150	2,953	3,883	3,831	1,735	1,213	1,501	659
Lucknow Division ...	442	993	1,855	2,835	3,973	4,014	1,808	1,346	1,922	812
Fyzabad " ...	820	1,282	1,948	2,561	3,693	3,930	1,696	1,359	1,843	868
Oudh	651	1,152	1,906	2,685	3,818	3,967	1,746	1,353	1,879	843
N.-W. Provinces and Oudh	709	1,292	2,085	2,880	3,865	3,868	1,738	1,251	1,603	709

Abstract No. 73, *showing the distribution of* 10,000 *persons of each sex and civil condition by age. Widowed.*

Divisions.	0—14.		15—24.		25—39.		40—49.		50 and over.	
	Males.	Females.	Males.	Females.	Males.	Females.	Males.	Females.	Males.	Females.
Meerut Division ...	101	68	716	513	2,480	1,899	2,153	2,294	4,550	5,226
Agra " ...	74	68	706	542	2,651	2,197	2,260	2,544	4,309	4,649
Rohilkhand " ...	104	68	693	365	2,583	1,542	2,070	2,104	4,600	5,921
Allahabad " ...	208	93	613	362	2,439	2,095	2,258	2,492	4,482	4,958
Benares " ...	218	102	632	305	2,238	1,888	2,010	2,317	4,902	5,888
Gorakhpur " ...	181	79	676	266	2,348	1,625	2,082	2,206	4,713	5,824
Kumaun " ...	88	89	672	504	2,557	1,877	2,079	2,190	4,604	5,334
N.-W. Provinces ...	140	80	675	389	2,466	1,878	2,148	2,326	4,571	5,327
Lucknow Division ...	95	48	512	282	2,144	1,531	1,892	2,089	5,357	6,050
Fyzabad " ...	191	73	564	228	2,113	1,897	1,891	2,058	5,241	6,244
Oudh	143	62	538	251	2,128	1,455	1,892	2,073	5,299	6,159
N.-W. Provinces and Oudh	141	76	648	353	2,387	1,768	2,088	2,260	4,741	5,543

Abstract No. 74, showing distribution of 10,000 persons of each caste by age and civil condition.

Caste, group and class.	Male. Married. 0 to 9.	10 to 14.	15 to 39.	40 and over.	Total.	Unmarried. 0 to 9.	10 to 14.	15 to 39.	40 and over.	Total.	Widower. 0 to 9.	10 to 14.	15 to 39.	40 and over.	Total.	Total male.
Jat, Hindu ...	19	150	1,423	863	2,455	1,287	483	752	109	2,631	1	6	180	340	527	5,613
Rájput, Hindu ...	16	97	1,337	806	2,256	1,221	528	811	209	2,769	1	4	100	270	375	5,400
„ Musalmán ...	19	82	1,414	860	2,375	1,402	510	494	36	2,442	3	3	70	206	282	5,099
Group 2A, Hindu, Cultivators ...	48	171	1,529	880	2,628	1,304	428	435	54	2,221	2	3	111	217	333	5,182
„ 2B. and C, Hindu, Cattle breeders, graziers and sheep breeders.	44	172	1,617	809	2,642	1,354	454	431	40	2,279	1	4	97	217	319	5,240
Group 3, Hindu, Forest and hill tribes ...	38	123	1,427	826	2,414	1,577	511	313	23	2,424	2	4	77	155	238	5,076
Class A, Hindu, Agricultural ...	38	154	1,511	839	2,542	1,304	462	526	84	2,376	1	4	106	233	344	5,262
Bráhman, Hindu ...	23	105	1,296	816	2,240	1,301	458	682	126	2,567	1	2	102	291	396	5,203
Kayasth, Hindu ...	10	67	1,326	849	2,252	1,122	526	727	143	2,518	1	4	108	328	441	5,211
Class B, Hindu, Professional ...	21	102	1,301	820	2,244	1,276	466	690	137	2,569	1	3	104	295	403	5,216
Baniya, Hindu ...	17	138	1,507	843	2,505	1,190	456	516	88	2,250	1	4	139	324	468	5,223
Khatri, Hindu ...	8	80	1,497	929	2,514	1,073	472	596	137	2,278	1	4	125	376	506	5,298
Group 14, Hindu, Carriers ...	10	57	1,169	740	1,976	1,366	603	965	83	3,017	1	4	133	250	388	5,381
Class C, Hindu, Commercial ...	17	132	1,489	840	2,478	1,193	464	538	90	2,285	1	4	138	323	466	5,229
Group 15, Hindu, Goldsmith ...	17	113	1,460	870	2,460	1,258	497	553	82	2,390	1	4	132	311	448	5,298
„ 16, Hindu, Barber ...	24	126	1,545	849	2,544	1,259	479	463	60	2,261	1	3	109	263	376	5,181
„ 17, Hindu, Blacksmith ...	29	176	1,565	883	2,653	1,332	441	394	43	2,210	1	4	107	248	360	5,223
„ 18, Hindu, Carpenter and turner ...	17	121	1,554	891	2,583	1,282	480	477	52	2,291	1	4	113	275	393	5,267
Kori, Hindu ...	29	133	1,601	861	2,624	1,317	410	401	48	2,176	1	4	112	219	336	5,136
Julaha, Musalmán ...	33	138	1,502	847	2,520	1,465	448	344	21	2,278	1	2	74	180	257	5,055
Kumhar, Hindu ...	65	192	1,608	893	2,758	1,291	402	297	25	2,015	3	7	97	245	352	5,125
Teli, Hindu ...	32	168	1,601	874	2,675	1,323	453	344	25	2,145	2	4	102	209	317	5,137
Dhobi, Hindu ...	33	155	1,586	857	2,631	1,377	468	336	27	2,208	1	4	93	204	302	5,141
Group 33, Hindu, Fishermen, boatmen, palki-bearers, cooks, &c.	32	135	1,469	839	2,475	1,382	460	349	33	2,224	1	4	87	192	284	4,983
Kalwár, Hindu ...	28	129	1,499	934	2,590	1,261	429	383	55	2,128	1	3	88	230	322	5,040
Chamár, Hindu ...	42	181	1,561	842	2,626	1,418	392	323	20	2,153	1	5	97	188	291	5,070
Group 38, Hindu, Village watchmen ...	46	254	1,550	823	2,673	1,424	426	339	21	2,210	2	8	74	170	254	5,137
Class D, Hindu ... } Artisans and village menials	37	173	1,593	824	2,627	1,384	428	360	26	2,198	1	3	90	187	281	5,106
Do. Musalman ... } Artisans and village menials	26	131	1,512	858	2,527	1,424	469	369	24	2,286	2	3	81	200	286	5,099
Bhangi, Hindu ...	24	148	1,637	783	2,592	1,366	467	411	32	2,276	1	5	133	254	393	5,261
„ Musalmán ...	23	96	1,408	996	2,523	1,408	441	338	28	2,215	...	4	89	220	313	5,051
Class E, Hindu, Vagrant minor artisans, performers, &c. ...	41	123	1,227	1,143	2,534	1,458	436	427	38	2,359	7	4	84	186	281	5,174
Group 49, Non-Indian Asiatic races ...	14	69	1,358	945	2,386	1,257	523	577	42	2,399	1	2	98	219	320	5,105
Pathan Musalmán ...	14	66	1,328	994	2,402	1,223	528	615	49	2,415	1	2	83	230	316	5,133
Sheikh „ ...	14	73	1,394	908	2,389	1,301	520	548	35	2,404	1	2	107	204	314	5,107
Sayed „ ...	12	56	1,256	1,016	2,340	1,135	528	620	61	2,344	1	2	81	269	353	5,037

Abstract No. 74, showing distribution 10,000 persons of each caste by age and civil condition—(concluded).

Castes, group and class.	Female.															
	Married.					Unmarried.					Widow.					Total female.
	0 to 9.	10 to 14.	15 to 39.	40 and over.	Total.	0 to 9.	10 to 14.	15 to 39.	40 and over.	Total.	0 to 9.	10 to 14.	15 to 39.	40 and over.	Total.	
Jat, Hindu	32	221	1,645	478	2,376	993	184	16	4	1,197	1	5	143	665	814	4,387
Rájput, Hindu	45	211	1,523	463	2,242	1,079	242	51	9	1,381	2	6	237	732	977	4,600
" Musalmán	39	189	1,750	492	2,470	1,312	238	51	6	1,607	2	3	166	653	824	4,901
Group 2A, Hindu, Cultivators	83	363	1,628	534	2,608	1,193	182	28	5	1,408	2	5	159	636	802	4,818
" 2B. and C., Hindu, Cattle-breeders, graziers and sheep-breeders.	90	304	1,719	492	2,605	1,204	169	25	5	1,403	2	4	145	601	752	4,760
Group 3, Hindu, Forest and hill tribes	64	182	1,642	491	2,379	1,607	330	71	6	2,014	2	5	119	405	531	4,924
Class A, Hindu, Agricultural	74	301	1,638	502	2,515	1,168	194	32	6	1,400	2	6	171	644	823	4,788
Bráhman, Hindu	39	256	1,522	503	2,320	1,114	223	36	1	1,374	2	5	276	820	1,103	4,797
Kayasth, Hindu	24	139	1,544	514	2,221	1,090	331	87	7	1,515	1	5	263	784	1,053	4,789
Class B., Hindu, Professional	39	243	1,522	503	2,307	1,110	232	45	4	1,391	2	5	270	809	1,086	4,784
Baniya, Hindu	41	267	1,640	510	2,458	1,124	193	30	7	1,354	1	6	238	720	965	4,777
Khatri, Hindu	24	231	1,520	572	2,347	1,017	193	30	11	1,251	4	8	233	859	1,104	4,702
Group 14, Hindu, Carriers	25	140	1,536	453	2,154	1,076	313	87	12	1,488	1	7	267	702	977	4,619
Class C. Hindu, Commercial	39	260	1,631	510	2,440	1,117	199	33	8	1,357	1	7	239	727	974	4,771
Group 15, Hindu Goldsmith	52	235	1,560	547	2,394	1,182	227	37	7	1,453	2	7	209	637	855	4,702
" 16, Hindu, Barber	44	245	1,761	522	2,572	1,201	198	31	6	1,436	2	5	167	637	811	4,819
" 17, Hindu, Blacksmith	59	286	1,644	517	2,506	1,259	189	32	7	1,487	2	4	139	639	784	4,777
" 18, Hindu, Carpenter and turner	42	248	1,708	550	2,548	1,170	192	28	8	1,398	1	5	170	611	787	4,733
Kori, Hindu	73	249	1,793	540	2,655	1,267	162	34	6	1,469	2	6	140	592	740	4,864
Julaha, Musalmán	84	268	1,792	516	2,660	1,370	185	81	14	1,650	2	3	95	535	635	4,945
Kumhar, Hindu	134	336	1,741	519	2,730	1,200	191	22	5	1,418	2	11	138	576	727	4,875
Teli, Hindu	70	310	1,779	490	2,649	1,239	186	60	8	1,493	2	5	145	569	721	4,863
Dhobi, Hindu	73	282	1,775	519	2,649	1,318	183	34	8	1,543	2	4	130	531	667	4,859
Group 33, Hindu, Fishermen, boatmen, palki-bearers, cooks, &c.	61	266	1,777	542	2,646	1,360	198	39	6	1,603	2	5	155	606	768	5,017
Kalwár, Hindu	57	277	1,722	570	2,626	1,224	193	29	8	1,454	2	6	158	714	880	4,960
Chamar, Hindu	89	274	1,842	482	2,687	1,404	130	20	6	1,560	1	4	137	541	683	4,930
Group 38, Hindu, Village watchmen	174	285	1,696	501	2,656	1,392	176	32	6	1,606	2	12	115	472	601	4,863
Class D., Hindu ... } Artisans and village menials	78	248	1,852	471	2,649	1,362	143	27	4	1,536	2	4	144	559	709	4,894
Do., Musalmán .. } Artisans and village menials ...	68	250	1,765	541	2,624	1,344	209	60	11	1,624	1	4	109	539	653	4,901
Bhangi, Hindu	64	276	1,788	526	2,654	1,232	196	32	6	1,466	1	5	127	486	619	4,739
" Musalmán	45	204	1,669	636	2,554	1,361	277	63	10	1,711	...	2	138	544	684	4,949
Class E., Hindu, Vagrant minor artisans, performers, &c. ...	63	255	1,575	589	2,482	1,320	224	83	17	1,644	2	4	187	507	700	4,826
Group 49, Non-Indian Asiatic races	33	162	1,677	537	2,409	1,226	293	95	16	1,630	1	2	155	698	856	4,895
Pathan, Musalmán	29	158	1,638	542	2,367	1,208	307	88	16	1,619	1	3	163	714	881	4,867
Sheikh "	38	174	1,703	518	2,433	1,255	273	89	16	1,633	1	2	147	677	827	4,893
Sayed "	21	115	1,640	606	2,382	1,134	354	148	21	1,657	1	2	176	745	924	4,963

209. **Caste variations in marriage statistics.**—An abstract for the principal castes and groups of castes of the table showing civil condition by caste is given in abstract No. 74.

The proportions given are for 10,000 of each caste. The result of this elaborate table is only to confirm what was already known of the majority of castes. It shows us that the largest proportion of males who remain permanently unmarried is amongst Jats, Rájputs, Bráhmans, Kayaths, Khatries and to a less extent amongst Baniyas. It shows that marriage is latest for men in these castes also whilst it is earliest for the low caste cultivators, forest and hill tribes, Julahas, Kumhars, Telis, Dhobis, Fishing castes, Chamárs, Pasis and vagrant castes, the highest figure of all being for Kumhars. The figures for women are in certain respects both more pronounced and more important than for men. For women the largest numbers permanently unmarried amongst respectable Hindus are amongst Rájputs and Khatris. The high proportion amongst the former may have to do with the claim made by many of the dancing castes to be Rájputs. Why it should be high amongst Khatris I have been unable to ascertain or imagine. Banjaras and vagrant Hindu castes show proportionately much larger numbers. Amongst the Muhammadans the higher the caste, the higher the proportion of women not married at all. Female infant marriage is most extensive amongst cultivating castes, grazing castes, forest and hill tribes, Koris, Julahas, Kumhars, Telis, Dhobis, Chamárs, Pasis, sweepers and vagrant castes. Of the whole, Pasis are easily first, Kumhars following a close second. Widows are most numerous amongst Bráhmans, Rájputs, Kayaths, Banyas, Khatris and Sayyids, easily the highest proportion being amongst Khatris and Bráhmans. The lowest proportion of widows is amongst the forest and hill tribes and after them amongst sweepers, Pasis, Julahas and Chamárs in all of which castes woman is peculiarly a helpmate for man. As I have said, almost all of these facts, though never before reduced to figures, were fairly well known. The table in which they are incorporated was by far the most troublesome and expensive of those prepared. It is perhaps well it has been done once, that the trouble, expense and vexation of preparing it should be a matter of past and not of future history.

Chapter IX.—EDUCATION.

210. **The tables showing Education.**—Two tables were prepared in regard to education at the present census. The first table IX shows in three age-periods and for each religion the number of persons learning, literate and illiterate. The second table C shows for each caste in the province the number of persons learning, literate in English, literate in other languages but not in English and illiterate.

The instructions to enumerators on the subject of the education entries indicate the meaning it was desired to attach to each of the terms employed.

"Rule 12, column 12 (instruction). Enter in this column against each person, whether grown-up, child or infant, either learning, literate or illiterate. Enter all those as learning who are under instruction, either at home or at school or college. Enter as literate those who are able to both read and write any language, but are not under instruction as above. Enter as illiterate those who are not under instruction, and who do not know how to both read and write, or who can read but not write, or can sign their own names but not read."

"Rule 13, column 13 (language known by literate). Enter here the language which those shown as literate in column 12 can both read and write, and if a person knows how to read and write English, as well as vernacular, enter "English" also."

"This column is not to be filled up for those shown in column 12 as learning or illiterate, and except where English is known, only one language should be entered, that which he knows best."

211. **Reasons to believe the return of learners inaccurate.**—The figures recorded at the present census for learning, literate and illiterate are compared with those at last census in the accompanying statement. It will be at once observed that whereas there is a large decrease in the number of learning there is a large increase in the number of literate, the differences being so large as to indicate a change in some essential point of classification. Returns prepared annually by the Department of Public Instruction in which not only all the pupils in Government schools are enumerated, but an estimate made of the other learners throughout the districts of the province give some assistance in tracing the cause of the variation. These returns show the total number of male learners as 275,651 against 238,441 enumerated at census, and 13,870 female learners against 8,404 at census. The district returns examined in detail show that the census figures are most in defect in those districts in which the number of pupils at private institutions is largest. This gives a clue to the apparent reason for the

Abstract No. 75, comparing the last census figures for learning, literate and illiterate with those recorded at the present census.

Education.	1891.		1881.	
	Males.	Females.	Males.	Females.
Learning	238,441	8,404	299,225	9,771
Literate	1,257,149	38,468	1,038,458	21,590
Illiterate	22,808,011	22,554,612	21,579,873	21,168,952

error. In the instructions the word school was translated Madrasa. It was overlooked that the word Madrasa was in the vernacular of the common people used only to designate a Government school. The consequence has been that a large number of pupils learning at private institutions have not been shown as learning and either omitted or included in literate. Similar omissions took place, I am informed, in the Panjáb for the same reason at the present census and in several other provinces at the last census and possibly now. It was believed that at last census record of pupils was omitted owing to want of specification in the instructions. It will in future be necessary therefore to specify still further and make express use of the words "Maktab" and "Patsala" to include vernacular schools as patronized by Muhammadans and Hindus.

The return for learners at the present census therefore loses most of its comparative value. That of the Educational Department, though nearer the truth, does not supply the deficiency, as it is materially lower than the returns at last census, though it appears probable that the actual number of learners as well as the actual number of literate has increased. This mis-enumeration appears to have affected different classes of the population differently. For Hindu males the number of learners out of 10,000 persons is only 98. For Muhammadans it is 154, whilst the proportion of literate is somewhat lower than for Hindus. For Jains the proportion of learning to literate is nearly the same as for Hindus, whilst for Aryas it is even higher than for Muhammadans. From figures varying so greatly no general inferences of value can be drawn. Muhammadans and Aryas either make use of Government schools to a much larger extent than Hindus and Jains or their superior knowledge of Urdu has enabled them more correctly to interpret the word "Madrasa." For Aryas the extremely high proportion of male learners to literate males shows that a number of young men whose education is not yet completed have recorded themselves as Aryas whilst their parents are amongst Hindus. The question whether children learning at private schools have been omitted or simply included amongst literate is of importance. Amongst Hindus it appears certain that some proportion has been omitted, as even to put the average age of beginning education so late as ten does not fully account for the difference between the difference of the literate and learning in the two age-periods of 0-14 and 15 to 24. It is probable that children learning at private schools who could not be said to be able to read and write have been actually omitted, and that others have been in general included in literate. The total number of omissions cannot have been great, as Hindus learning and literate combined show a larger proportionate advance on the figures of last census than do the figures for the whole population. Subsequent remarks in regard to the proportion of literate and illiterate must be understood to be subject to correction on this account.

212. **The proportion of literate persons in the population.**—The total number of persons literate and learning in the provinces was 1,495,590 males 46,872 females against an illiterate population of 22,808,011 males and 22,554,612 females; that is to say, out of 10,000 males 615 were literate or learning and 9,385 illiterate; out of 10,000 females 21 were literate or learning and 9,979 illiterate. The proportions are compared with those

for other Indian provinces in the marginal abstract. The North-Western Provinces and Oudh enjoys the distinction of being the most illiterate of the great provinces of India, it is surpassed in this respect only by the backward Central Provinces.

Abstract No. 76, comparing for North-Western Provinces and Oudh the proportion of illiteracy with those for other Indian provinces.

Provinces.	No. of illiterate per 10,000.
North-Western Provinces and Oudh	9,385
Bengal	8,921
Madras	8,512
Bombay	8,686
Panjáb	9,258
Central Provinces	9,431
Assam	9,244
Burma	5,505
Hyderabad	9,285
Mysore	8,947

As compared with European figures the illiteracy of the North-Western Provinces is still more striking. The proportion of illiterate for several European countries is shown in the margin. The most illiterate country shown, Portugal, is better than the North-Western Provinces by 188 males per 1,000 and by 105 females for the same total. For England and Wales the figures have unfortunately not been collected in any census, but an indication of the amount of the illiteracy has been obtained from a record of the number of persons who cannot write their own names at marriage. This will compare fairly enough with the North-Western Provinces figures for males and females after their education is complete; that is from 25 upwards.

Abstract No. 77, showing per 1,000 the proportions of illiterate males and females in several European and foreign countries.

Country.	Males.	Females.
Ireland	446	499
Italy	623	764
Austria	479	533
Hungary	592	717
Portugal	750	892
Ceylon	731	971
New South Wales	312	333
Victoria	245	245
Queensland	324	309
South Australia	283	289
New Zealand	252	275
Chili	719	779

	Proportion of illiterate per 1,000 of each sex.	
	Males.	Females.
England and Wales	96	1,15
Scotland	46	82
North-Western Provinces and Oudh ...	9,16	9,98
France	1,43	2,26

213. **Education by religion.**—The record of illiteracy is however very different in the different classes of the population. Whilst the North-Western Provinces is in general education greatly below the level of the least educated country of Europe, there are certain classes educated to such an extent as to compare favourably enough with many European countries. This variation in literacy is very considerable in the different religions of the country, the comparative figures for which are given in the abstract accompanying. Hindus, by whom

Abstract No. 78, showing literate and learning per 10,000 of each sex and religion.

Religion.	Males.	Females.
Hindu	592	13
Musalmán	606	26
Jain	4,865	92
Christian	7,376	5,385
Arya	5,058	764
Sikh	3,300	138
Others	5,991	4,914

[To face page 259.

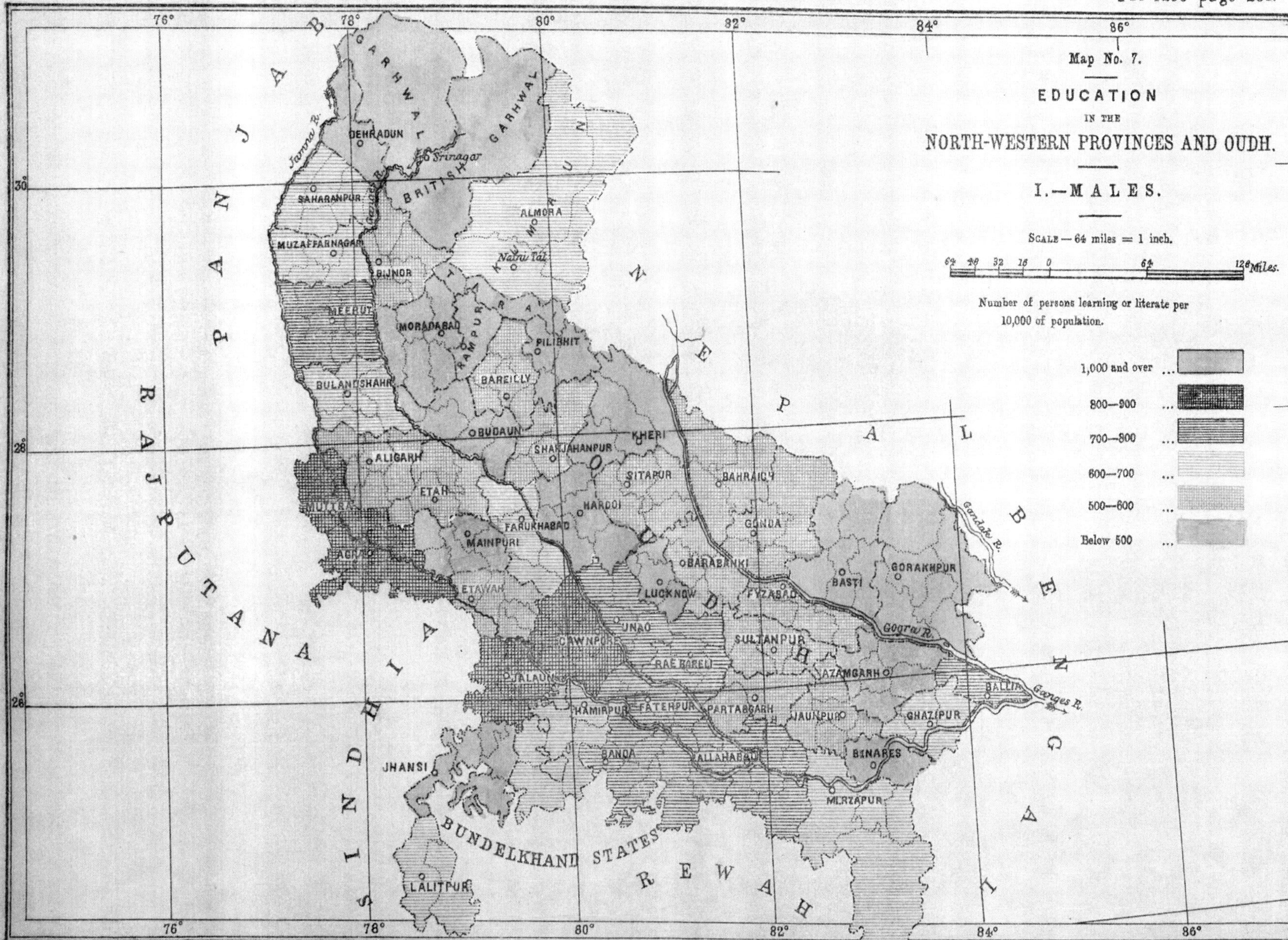

the statistics for general education are owing to their large numbers dominated, are themselves well below average in point of education. Excluding children under five, Hindus have 8,103 males and 8,553 females illiterate against 8,077 and 8,543 for the population as a whole. Musalmáns are decidedly above average, the number of illiterate males and females being 8,049 and 8,520 besides children under five. The remaining classes of the population are distinctly more literate, as a whole; the comparatively small body of Christians, including the Europeans in India, is of course incomparably more literate than any other religion, and even if foreign and Eurasian Christians are excluded, the Native Christian community is, considering both sexes, better educated than any other religion except amongst the foreigners included under other religions. Out of 10,000 total population they have the comparatively small number of 5,750 illiterate men and 6,631 illiterate women, thus showing the community as a whole to be better educated than the Italians. The standard of education amongst Native Christians has been greatly lowered by the late additions to the faith, large numbers of whom are, as has already been shown, from the lowest classes. Native Christians excluding the additions made within the last decade are by their general education well fitted to take a much higher place in the community than they now enjoy. Best educated as a whole after the Native Christians and with the male population better educated than in that class are the Aryas, who including children under five have rather more than half the total male population educated, and excluding children under five nearly three-fifths. For women the proportion of illiteracy is high, but it is far better than for any other religion except Christians. They have 764 literate and learning women per 10,000 against 21 in the general population. Jains follow after Aryas with a somewhat smaller proportion of literate men and a very much smaller proportion of literate women. The figures are 4,865 against 5,058 for literate men, and 92 against 764 literate women in 10,000 of each sex. After Jains come Sikhs largely imported and better educated than the average in their own country. From Sikhs there is a great drop both in males and females educated to Muhammadans and Hindus.

214. **Education by districts.**—The distribution of the population by localities naturally shows very much less variation than that by religion, but it is still considerable. The accompanying abstract shows the districts arranged in order of literacy and the proportion of illiterate males and females in 10,000 in each. As regards males the first six districts are: (1) Benares, (2) Dehra Dún, (3) Garhwál, (4) Jhánsi, (5) Lucknow, (6) Muttra. Two of these districts are centres of Hindu religion and owe their literacy to this fact; Dehra Dún owes its position to the large European population and Jhánsi partly to the large European population and partly to the generally high standard of education in Bundelkhand; Lucknow is high owing to the high standard of intelligence in the city, to which the large European population contributes. The position taken by Garhwál by virtue of the education of a purely agricultural population is noteworthy. The six most uneducated districts or states are: (1) Rámpur, (2) Kheri, (3) Budaun, (4) Tarái, (5) Hardoi and (6) Basti. Rámpur is considerably more illiterate than any British district, and as the literacy is there more confined to the capital than in British districts, the difficulty in obtaining enumerators already referred to may be

understood. The distribution of literacy is shown in the accompanying map No. 6. Kumaun, as a whole, is the most literate division, followed close by Allahabad and Benares. Oudh is less literate on the average than the North-Western Provinces, but the two most illiterate divisions are in the North-West Provinces, Rohilkhand and Gorakhpur.

Abstract No. 79, showing the districts of the provinces arranged in order of literacy and the proportion of illiterate males and females in 10,000 of each.

District.	Number of illiterate males in 10,000.	District.	Number of illiterate females in 10,000.
Benares	8,787	Dehra Dún	9,803
Debra Dún	8,809	Benares	9,910
Garhwál	8,944	Lucknow	9,924
Jhánsi	8,985	Agra	9,942
Lucknow	9,007	Allahabad	9,956
Muttra	9,099	Jhánsi	9,967
Agra	9,168	Farukhabad	9,970
Jalaun	9,177	Kumaun	9,970
Cawnpore	9,185	Muttra	9,973
Ballia	9,252	Cawnpore	9,973
Meerut	9,269	Ballia	9,976
Rae Bareli	9,271	Sahárandpur	9,977
Allahabad	9,276	Meerut	9,977
Bánda	9,280	Bareilly	9,977
Unao	9,291	Moradabad	9,977
Fatehpur	9,294	Mirzapur	9,978
Kumaun	9,306	Gházipur	9,979
Farukhabad	9,332	Sháhjahanpur	9,981
Hamírpur	9,333	Etah	9,982
Muzaffarnagar	9,334	Gorakhpur	9,983
Gházipur	9,349	Rae Bareli	9,983
Mirzapur	9,350	Etáwah	9,984
Bulandshahr	9,367	Bijnor	9,984
Sahárанpur	9,387	Budaun	9,984
Lalitpur	9,392	Bulandshahr	9,985
Etiwah	9,406	Mainpuri	9,985
Bara Banki	9,407	Tarái	9,985
Fyzabad	9,426	Sitapur	9,986
Bahraich	9,439	Pilibhít	9,987
Sitapur	9,448	Fyzabad	9,987
Etah	9,452	Jaunpur	9,988
Jaunpur	9,455	Muzaffarnagar	9,989
Sultánpur	9,473	Aligarh	9,989
Bijnor	9,474	Partabgarh	9,989
Bareilly	9,483	Bara Banki	9,989
Gonda	9,484	Rampur	9,989
Partabgarh	9,489	Garhwál	9,990
Aligarh	9,492	Hardoi	9,990
Sháhjahánpur	9,494	Bahraich	9,990
Gorakhpur	9,503	Jalaun	9,991
Tehri-Garhwál	9,515	Lalitpur	9,991
Moradabad	9,521	Unao	9,991
Azamgarh	9,532	Fatehpur	9,992
Mainpuri	9,554	Bánda	9,992
Pilibhít	9,559	Basti	9,992
Basti	9,562	Azamgarh	9,992
Hardoi	9,584	Hamírpur	9,993
Tarái	9,590	Kheri	9,993
Budaun	9,619	Gonda	9,994
Kheri	9,637	Sultánpur	9,995
Rampur	9,711	Tehri Garhwál	9,996

The figures for literate women are in general very small, so much so as to be much more affected than those for men by the inclusion of European women. Dehra Dún, Benares, Agra, Allahabad, Ballia, Lucknow, are easily the most literate, whilst the lowest proportion of literate women is to be found in several of the Oudh and Bundelkhand districts. All this appears much more fully in the accompanying maps Nos. 7 and 8. The figures for female education in certain districts are so low as to give rise to the suspicion suggested to me by a Hindu that women, even when they are literate, do not in view of Hindu prejudices, wish to so record themselves. The returns of the Educational Department show 13,870 girls learning, and if this is under the mark in the same proportion as for boys, the number of learning is so large as to account for a much larger literate population amongst women than has been shown.

215. **English education.**—The returns of the present census collect for the first time some interesting information as to the number of persons literate in English. The result is shown by districts and religions in an appendix to Table C. In the whole of the provinces and for all religions only 43,364 males and 6,578 females have been shown as literate in English. The figures by religions with the proportion to 10,000 total population for each sex and religion are shown in the margin. From these have to be excluded 19,326 literate males and 5,360 literate females of foreign or Eurasian birth, so that the whole number of the native population in these provinces who are literate in English is only 24,038 males and 1,218 females. The proportion is far higher amongst Native Christians than in any other religion to which natives of the province belong. They have literate in English 1,192 males and 953 females per 10,000 of each sex. Aryas follow second with 393 males and 5 females. Sikhs, Jains, Musalmáns, Hindus follow in the order named, the latter with only four persons per 10,000 of both sexes literate in English. It is understood, of course, that this does not include persons learning English, who are probably considerably more numerous in proportion.

Abstract No. 80, showing population literate in English.

Religion.	Males.		Females.	
	Actual numbers.	Per 10,000 of population.	Actual numbers.	Per 10,000 of population.
Hindu ...	17,465	8	118	...
Musalman ...	4,189	13	39	...
Jain ...	266	59	1	...
Christian ...	20,801	5,578	6,412	8,033
Arya ...	478	393	5	5
Sikh ...	14	17	...	...
Other religions ...	151	948	3	128
Total ...	43,364	18	6,578	3

216. **The increase in Education.**—The total number of males of all religions and all ages learning and literate at last census was 1,332,683. The increase in persons educated or being educated was therefore 162,907 males or 12·2 per cent. against an increase in the total male population of 6·07 per cent. Similarly for females the actual number educated or being educated was at the present census 46,872 or ·21 per cent., an increase over the figure of last census of 15,511 persons and 49·4 per cent. Education has, therefore, on the whole, considerably improved. . The improvement extends to all religions except Christians, for whom as already remarked the proportion of educated persons has fallen. It is unfortunate that the imperfection of our returns for learners prevents an examination of how far this rate of progress is being sustained. For Muhammadans for whom the numbers of learners are most completely given, it appears that education is advancing steadily, the number of illiterate in the age-period 15 to 24 being considerably lower than in the later periods. For Hindus the opposite is the case, but owing to the omissions in learners, little reliance can be placed on any inference drawn from them.

217. **Education by caste.**—Table C. gives details as to the education in English and vernacular of all the castes of the province. The proportionate figures for 100 males and 100 females for each of the most important castes or groups of castes are given in the accompanying statement. The distinction between the various Muhammadan artizan castes is so slight that the proportions

for only one of them, *Julahas*, has been given separately in addition to those for the totals of the group. Amongst men, easily the most generally educated caste in the province are the Kayasths, who have only 3,898 illiterate males in 10,000. They are followed at some distance by Khatris 5,168 illiterate per 10,000 and Native Christians 5,750 illiterate. After these and close together come Banyas and Sayyids, each with between 73 and 74 per cent. of illiterate. Bráhmans are next with 82 per cent. illiterate. The only other castes of importance with less than 90 per cent. of illiterate are Kalwars, Sheikhs, Pathans and Sunars. Hindu Rájputs, are just over 90 per cent. ; Musalmán Rájputs are considerably more illiterate, the percentage for them being 95. At the other end of the scale, Dhobis appear to be the most illiterate caste in the province, and none of the low castes have two literate persons per hundred, most of them have less than one. For women the order is somewhat different. Native Christians are easily first ; Khatris are next, Kayasths third and Sayyids fourth, no other caste having more than one woman in a hundred educated.

Abstract No. 81, *showing for the most important castes or groups of castes the proportionate education figures per* 100 *of each sex.*

Class, group or castes.	Male.					Female.				
	Learning.	English.	Other languages.	Illiterate.	Total.	Learning.	English.	Other languages.	Illiterate.	Total.
Jat, Hindu	·813	·039	2·685	96·463	100	·0078	·0006	·0276	99·9640	100
Rájput, Hindu	·187	·071	8 376	90·366	100	·025	·001	·804	99·670	100
Rájput, Musalmán	·98	·03	3·89	95·10	100	·02	..	·13	99·85	100
Group 2A, Hindu, Cultivators ...	·20	·01	1·34	98·45	100	·00	·00	·01	99·99	100
Group 2B and 2C, Hindu, Cattle-breeders, graziers and sheep-breeders.	·11	·00	·56	99·33	100	·00	·00	·00	100·00	100
Group 3, Hindu, Forest and hill tribes.	·28	...	·86	98·86	100	...	...	·002	99·998	100
Class A, Hindu, Agricultural ...	·42	·02	2·73	96·83	100	·01	·(0	·07	99·92	100
Bráhman, Hindu	2·527	·227	15·192	82·054	100	·039	·002	·287	99·672	100
Kayasth, Hindu	11·949	2·052	47·019	38·980	100	·182	·011	2·767	97·090	100
Class B, Hindu, Professional ...	3·24	·38	17·43	78·95	100	·05	·00	·50	99·45	100
Bania, Hindu	3·56	30	22·66	73·48	100	·12	·00	·32	99 56	100
Khatri, Hindu	9·890	5·302	33·132	51·676	100	·420	·028	2·575	96·977	100
Group 14, Hindu, Carriers ...	·46	·00	2·72	96·82	100	·01	...	·01	99·98	100
Class C, Hindu, Commercial ...	3·65	·44	22·18	73·73	100	·13	·00	·39	99·48	100
Group 15, Hindu, Goldsmith ...	1·98	·12	10·85	87·05	100	·02	...	·11	99·87	100
Group 16, Hindu, Barber ...	·18	·01	·81	99·00	100	·00	...	·00	100·00	100
Group 17, Hindu, Blacksmith ...	·18	·02	1·58	98·22	100	·0^	...	·00	100 00	100
Group 18, Hindu, Carpenter and turner.	·27	·04	1·32	98·37	100	·00	...	·02	99·98	100
Kori, Hindu	·068	·009	·491	99·432	100	·0007	·0015	·0057	99·9921	100
Julaha, Musalmán	·520	·038	1·860	97·587	100	·014	...	·043	99·943	100
Kumbár, Hindu	·063	·006	·306	99 625	100	·000	...	·006	99·994	100
Teli, Hindu	·291	·009	2·090	97·610	100	·006	...	·014	99·980	100
Dhobi, Hindu	·02	·01	·22	99·75	100	...	...	·007	99·993	100
Group 33, Hindu, Fishermen, boatmen, palki-bearers, cooks, &c.	·00	·02	·74	99·24	100	·00	...	·00	100 00	100
Kalwár, Hindu	2·33	·07	14·44	83·16	100	·015	·000	·067	99·918	100
Chamár, Hindu	·153	·003	1·163	98·681	100	·001	...	·002	99·997	100
Group 38, Hindu, Village watchmen.	·05	·00	·35	99·60	100	·01	...	·01	99 98	100
Class D, Hindu, Artisans and village menials.	·22	·01	1·49	98·28	100	·00	·00	·01	99·99	100
Class D, Musalmán, Artisans and village menials.	·45	·02	1 39	98·14	100	·01	·00	·08	99·96	100
Bhangi, Hindu	·078	·008	·414	99 500	100	·002	...	·021	99 977	100
Do., Musalmán ...	·11	·01	·62	99·26	100	·01	...	·03	99·96	100
Class E, Hindu, vagrant, minor artisans, performers, &c.	·12	·03	·63	99·22	100	·00	·00	·03	99·97	100
Group 49, Non-Indian Asiatic races.	3·24	·31	8·91	87·54	100	·14	·00	·45	99·41	100
Native Christians	17·98	11·91	12·68	57·48	100	14·16	9·53	10·00	66·31	100
Eurasians	15·12	55·41	8·26	21·21	100	12·43	45 57	7 20	34·80	100

In English education Native Christians are easily first, Native Christian women being better educated in English than men in any other caste. Khatris are easily second, and Kayasths easily third; Sayyids follow with one third of the proportion for Kayasths, and after them come Banyas with less than half the Sayyid proportion, and Sheikhs, with somewhat more than a third of the proportion for Sayyids. Pathans, Bráhmans, and Sunars are the only other castes in which one male in a thousand knows English. The proportion of women knowing English reaches one in 10,000 only for Khatris and Kayasths (Native Christians of course being excepted).

218. **Eurasian education**.—Eurasians have not been referred to in the above remarks, but the education figures for them are especially interesting in connection with the question of employment for this growing class of the population. The proportions for males and females are shown in the abstract in the margin. Of the proportion shown as illiterate, probably 17 per cent. for each sex are children whose education has not yet been begun, 14·5 per cent. being the usual proportion under five, and education usually not beginning to any material extent till after six. Allowing for this, the figures for Eurasian males show a proportion not only better beyond comparison than any caste of native Hindustanis, but considerably better than that quoted above for England and to some extent better than that for Scotland. Eurasian women, less generally educated than English or Scotch women, are considerably better in this respect than those of France. It must be remembered too that there is a strong tendency on the part of the Native Christians to show themselves as Eurasians, and that many of the best educated Eurasians are shown as Europeans. These changes affect the returns for Eurasian education injuriously—so that in point of fact it is probably even better educated than would appear from the tables. The percentage of Eurasians who are literate in languages other than English is swollen by the entries of those who profess a French, Portuguese or other foreign nationality and have entered French, Portuguese or other foreign language as that in which they are literate. It probably owes part of the proportion to the inclusion of Native Christians amongst Eurasians.

Abstract No. 82, showing for Eurasians the proportion of education.

	Learning.	Literate in English.	Literate in other languages.	Illiterate.
Males ...	15·12	55·41	8·26	21·21
Females ...	12·43	45·57	7·20	34·80

Chapter X.—MOTHER TONGUES.

219. **The classification of languages.**—Under the instructions of the Government of India, the languages of the persons enumerated in the different provinces have been classified territorially so as to correspond to some extent with the entries in the birth-place, table XI. They have accordingly for these provinces been arranged in four groups—

A. Vernaculars of India.

B. Languages of Asiatic countries beyond India.

C. European languages.

D. Other languages and unspecified.

The Indian vernaculars have been subdivided into seven sub-groups according to the provinces or parts of India in which they are spoken.

220. **Languages of the provinces.**—The first of these sub-groups, languages of the North-Western Provinces and Oudh, is the only one which is of any considerable importance to the present report. The languages so included and the population which has returned them as, in the words of the definition adopted in the instructions to enumerators, " ordinarily spoken in the households of their parents " are as follows :—

Abstract No. 83.—*Showing persons returned under each of the languages of the province.*

Language.	Total.	Males.	Females.
Hindustani	45,882,262	23,771,140	22,111,122
Pahari unspecified	77,374	44,069	33,305
Kumauni	429,166	221,405	207,761
Garhwáli	407,450	198,668	208,782
Jaunsari	78	62	16
Nipali	18,035	12,111	5,924
Total ...	46,814,365	24,247,455	22,566,910

Out of a total population of 46,905,085, only 90,720 persons have been enumerated as speaking mother tongues other than those above mentioned.

221. **The term Hindustani why used.**—The mother tongue returned by the vast majority of the population was Hindustani. For the uniform use of this word in the schedules, the provincial instructions to enumerators are responsible to a great extent. The words of the instructions were " the language ordinarily spoken throughout these provinces except in the Himalayan districts will be entered as Hindustani."

The word Hindustani was selected to mean in its widest sense, the language of Hindustan including both the Urdu of the towns and the Hindi of the villages. It is sufficient justification of the selection of the word that it is that which has been used both by Forbes and by Fallon, the former of whom has made Urdu the foundation of his dictionary, whilst the latter has made the inclusion of the village Hindi spoken by rustics and women a chief feature of his work.

Objection may however be taken to the instructions above quoted on wider and more important grounds than the mere selection of the word by which the language of the provinces was to be designated. It will no doubt be objected that these directions preclude the possibility of obtaining from the census schedules, a satisfactory record of the population by which each of the different dialects of the province is spoken. Full consideration was given to this objection before the instructions were issued, and I trust that it will easily be made clear that no record of dialects worthy of the name could be obtained from the census enumeration.

The most recent list, according to the ideas of linguistic specialists, of the dialects and languages of the North-Western Provinces and Oudh, which I have been able to discover, is contained in a communication in 1887 by Mr. G. A. Grierson to the Government of Bengal suggesting a systematic survey of the vernaculars of India. Mr. Grierson's list is professedly a rough one and an obvious mistake in it, so far as these provinces are concerned, is the omission of the special dialects of Bundelkhand and Baghelkhand, which Mr. Grierson shows only for Central India and of a number of those of the semi-nomad tribes of the Tarái, which he shows in the Nipal list. Amending the list to this extent, we get for the provinces excluding the Himalayas the following list :—

Languages.	*Dialects.*
Hindi.	Standard including archaic, mediæval and modern, also various lingua francas, such as Hindustani, Dakhini and Portuguese.
	Braj.
	Kosali.
	Kanauji.
	Tharu.
	Bhogsa.
Bihari.	Baiswari.
	Bhojpuri.
	Bundeli.
	Bhageli.

This list except in its somewhat greater elaboration and in its assuming Bihari as the name of the eastern language of these provinces, agrees with that given by a scholar of admitted authority, Dr. Hœrnle, in his "Introduction to the Grammar of Eastern Hindi" and quoted by Mr. E. White in the 1881 report for these provinces. The mention of Dakhini and Portuguese Hindustani as languages of the North-Western Provinces is probably a part of the roughness of the list. It is when we compare this long list of dialects with the dialectic variations for which the people themselves are likely to give separate names that the hopelessness of collecting in a census of these provinces any linguistic information whatsoever becomes apparent.

When it is considered that 200,000 Census Officers were employed in taking the census, many of them very imperfectly educated, it is apparent that disregard of rules must be frequent, and accordingly from the list of instances in which the rule directing that Hindustani should be recorded as the language of these provinces was disregarded, we get some imformation of value as to the popular idea of the diversity of language in the province.

222. **The variations popularly recognized**—.The languages recorded in the schedules which were after abstraction combined with Hindustani in the tables were as follows :—

Urdu.	Banjari.
Purbi.	Churuwali.
Jaunpuri.	Sanskrit.
Hindi.	Moori.
Desi.	

Of these Banjari and Churuwali were recorded for very few persons respectively. They are not in any sense recognized dialects and were recorded only by a fractional proportion of the castes after the names of which they are called. Sanskrit is of course no longer a language spoken in any household. Moori was an entry made by a European Sergeant in Cawnpore for the language of a few Hindustanis he enumerated. The occurrence, which was frequent, of the word Desi, is an interesting illustration of the fact I am endeavouring to prove. To the persons for whom it was recorded as well as the enumerators who recorded it the language of the provinces was clearly regarded as one. Purbi and Jaunpuri are different terms used for the same idea. The word Purbi or Purabiya, as the more general, may be allowed to stand for both.

There remains as our popular record of dialectic variations Urdu, Purbi and Hindi. Had the instructions been to record the language each person said he spoke, the list would not have been much more extensive. Braj Bhasha would probably occur in a few instances. Pachhade " boli" would occur in the eastern districts as the dialect of emigrants from the west. As a rule, however, the record would be absolutely indefinite and useless from the great excess of entries of the names Desi or Hindi.

It would be possible by indicating a line of questioning to be followed by the enumerators to obtain more explicit entries, but these would be of the recognized name of the " des" or locality and not of any general dialectic names such as those given by Mr. Grierson. From the Doab we should have entries of Doabi, Sahâranpuri, Muzaffarnagri, from Rohilkhand of Rohilkhandi, Katehriya, Moradabadi or the indefinite term Khari Boli. From the east, to judge by the replies I have received from districts, the entries would be generally Purbi, Azamgarhia, Mirzapuria, Sarwariya, and the like. It is unnecessary to multiply instances. We should have a record of localities not of dialects. I am aware that in so concluding I am expressing an opinion contrary to that expressed by several gentlemen of authority on the subject, but after enquiring from District Officers and others in all parts of the provinces I can come to no other conclusion. The result would be to leave us exactly where we started, as the classification of the innumerable local names we should have in the schedules would have to be accomplished by outside assistance.

223. **The Variations of Hindi recognized by travelled natives.**—As a matter of fact, if information is desired as to what natives themselves consider their general dialectic classification, we have to enquire in general outside and not in the areas themselves. The dialect varies with the most extraordinary

rapidity from place to place. Thus in Basti I have been informed that the dialect (*boli*) changes every five *kos*, the supposed change in dialect being simply a change in one or two standard agricultural words.

The people are quick to recognize the slightest difference from the language spoken by themselves and amongst their immediate neighbours, and note every petty variation as a change in dialect. It is only where they can refer to a dialect markedly different from their own that they are able to generalize and class a group of the ever-varying local idioms under a general dialectic name. The dialects so recognized would, so far as I can ascertain from the replies of my correspondents, be as follows. A rough indication of the population for each is appended :—

Abstract No. 48.

Districts.	Dialect.	Population.
Upper Doab	Pachhadi Hindi or Doabi ...	4,660,022
Agra, Muttra and part of Aligarh	Braj Bhasha	2,215,893
Etawáh, Etah, Mainpuri and part of Farukhabad ...	Antarvedi, or possibly Braj Bhasha, of which it is a variation.	2,933,313
Cawnpore, and part of Farukhabad and Unao	Kanaujia	1,987,408
Rohilkhand and Tarái	Rohilkhandi or the Khari boli ...	5,554,242
Most of Unao, Rae Bareli and part of Lucknow and possibly Fatehpur.	Baiswari	1,916,870
The rest of Oudh	Awadhi	10,772,634
Bundelkhand	Bundelkhandi	2,299,532
The districts east of Allahabad	Purbi	8,106,793
The Trans-Gogra districts of the North-Western Provinces ...	Sarwar ki boli	4,779,901
The south of Mirzapur and Allahabad...	Baghelkhandi	539,343
		45,765,951

The above with the well-recognized difference between the Urdu of educated Muhammadans and the desi or Hindi of the Hindu villagers are, so far as I can ascertain, the *general* dialectic variations which are recognized by the better informed amongst the people themselves.

I am indebted to the Reverend J. D. Bates of Allahabad for a letter on the subject, the great interest of which is my reason for printing it in extenso, especially as the geographical distribution of dialects has not, so far as I can ascertain, been satisfactorily dealt with in any printed volume :—

"The list of dialects of the Hindi language put forth by Mr. Grierson is correct, as far as it goes, to wit :—

Braj	Western Hindi.
Kosali	
Kanauji	
Baiswari	Eastern Hindi.
Bhojpuri	
Bundeli	

"The statement, however, that these technical designations are merely employed for convenience by European scholars, but are absolutely unknown (as names of dialects) to the people themselves is *not* correct. I do not mean that any and every native who speaks any given dialect, is *ipso facto* aware of its particular designation, for the ignorance of the people is great: but any native whose intelligence is above that of the poor clodhopper can tell that *his* lingo is Braj or Bhojpuri, or what not. If any "*man from the country*" (not a city man), whose speech is some dialect of the Hindi were asked what was his language, not one in fifty would say "Hindi" (they do not generally know their language by that name) but he would answer 'Baiswari' 'Braj,' or what not. The average man, in fact *does* know the special designation of his mother-dialect. The designations given to the dialects by specialists are not inventions. The terms "eastern" and "western" as applied to this language, are translations of words technically applied by the people themselves. But at this point also, as at every point in connection with this subject, one has to hold himself prepared for complications: for there is a distinct difference between 'Purbi' and '*old* Purbi,' as there is also between the Western Hindi of to-day (*Pachhaon ki boli*) and that of the "Prithi-ráj Rásan" of Chand Bardai (12th cent. A.D.). The lines between the linguistic aspects of the several dialects are very clear: the difficulty is rather the geographical one. For what has happened is this: the several dialects of Hindi have got all muddled up together; whence it happens that the part of the country in which any given dialect is spoken, cannot be adequately expressed in terms of geography. Beames, Hœrnle, Grierson, Kellogg, and others have all severally tried so to express the facts, but they have all of them done so with this reservation, that the said geographical limitations assigned by them each to the several dialects are approximate only. The difficulty has arisen mainly from the great amount of intercourse continually going on among the people (and more and more so as the years advance) on account of the necessity of travelling. There has hence come to be an ever-increasing fusion of the peoples of the various districts; and with this fusion there has been of necessity a good deal of fusion and confusion of their tongues. This it is which makes the fixing of the geographical limits of their curious dialects such a problematical task."

'The so-called 'Standard Hindi' of the English writers on Hindi Grammar is a thing unknown to the native people: it is not in truth the lingo spoken by any of them. The expression is commonly held to be a translation of the term 'Khari boli,' but it is doubtful whether the letter *r* here is really र or ड़, a point on which even the natives themselves are not agreed, whence they are not at all clear as to what the expression means as applied to the Hindi language. English writers apply it to that stiff, straight-laced type of the language which is framed on the model of the Muhammadan Urdu. I do not blame the said English writers, for I have never yet been able to see how else the thing is to be done. For when one constructs a work purporting to be a grammar of a language which is made up of a congeries of dialects having no particular and universal form which can be regarded as the type common to all of them, he *must* fix upon some one type for himself, otherwise his grammar is a grammar of a dialect and not a grammar of the language in its entirety. The general type, then, which has been usually fixed upon by such writers has been this objectionable Urduized type, which is, as a matter of fact, the type usually spoken by English people, when they wish to speak what they fancy to be 'Hindi.' Hence the opinion has spread abroad that Hindi is nothing else than Urdu written in the Devanagri characters; that, in other words, there is no such language as Hindi (!) It is this type of the language (this manufactured type of it) that makes it so difficult for the natives to understand what we wish to say when speaking in Hindi (as it is called): they are in great measure driven to conjecture what it is we mean. The reason is that the grammars, from which educated foreigners get at the language, are constructed on this artificial and pedantic model. The Eurasian and the uneducated English adventurer, who comes out to India, who both of them learn the language without books, speak more genuine and intelligible Hindi than do we who have learned a dozen languages before we set foot in the country. Some of our educated fellow countrymen (scholars both here and at home) have given it as their opinion that there is no such language as 'Hindi' at all; and their official status has given great weight to the dogma, for they are men *who ought to know*. But no mistake could be greater: a man holding such an opinion has only to go out into the villages some twenty miles from the Anglicized and Muhammadanized influence of the speech of the larger cities, and he will at once discover that the people (the *οἱ πολλοί* of Plato and his great disciple) speak a lingo which is a *terra incognita* to him: that lingo is Hindi (in one or another of its seven, or as some say, nine dialects)."

"So mixed up have the numerous dialects come to be, that in this single district of Allahabad, every one of the six mentioned by Grierson and localized by him is current; and such is also the case with most of the other districts, excepting those at the geographical extremes from one another. Theoretically, the dialect of this district is Bhojpuri; but such a statement must be received with a great deal of reservation. When it happens that the districts are separated by very broad rivers, there is not much difficulty in assigning the geographical limits of their respective dialects. (The dialect of Tirhut, for example, is very markedly different from that of the Monghyr district, on the other side of the river there.)"

"Speaking broadly, one does not fully realize the application of the terms 'eastern' and 'western' till he comes to associate with the villagers at the geographical extremes. If from the Sahâranpur district he were to remove direct to (say) the district of Monghyr, he would find the dialectic differences so strongly marked that he would often find himself at a loss to understand what a man says. The differences are mainly in the inflections; and there are also differences in the vocabularies and even in the genders. Many words are used in the 'western' Hindi that are not known in the 'eastern', and *vice versâ*; and many words are used in the one district in senses which in the other district they do not carry: while a word which is masculine in the east is often feminine in the west and *vice versâ*, and so the game goes on. And all this, which applies to east and west, applies also to north and south, so much so, that the lingo of the man from Bundelkhand would be as little intelligible to the man of Kumaun as French would be to the untravelled Italian"

"Coming then to the more practical portion of your letter, 'as to the classification of the population of these provinces according to dialect,'—the best account of which I have any knowledge is that given by Kellogg in his 'Hindi Grammar,' which appeared under the patronage of the Government of these Provinces in 1876. As I said above, Grierson's is good *as far as it goes*, but unfortunately it does not include all the phenomena. But, indeed, any theory on this complicated subject (a subject in which the native scholar cannot help us as we need) must, after all, be but an *approximation* to the facts. And every theory would need to be worked out in continual remembrance of such considerations as those mentioned above."

These remarks of Mr. Bates express clearly the qualifications necessary in accepting the list of dialects above given. The language ordinarily varies *rapidly but imperceptibly* from place to place, and it is only in the centre of the area allotted to each dialect that its general characteristics can be ascertained and the difference between it and its neighbouring dialects accurately estimated. Mr. Bates, it appears to me, whilst starting with the assertion that dialectic variations are well recognized by educated natives, gives ample reason to believe that, as I have above asserted, they recognize rather the locality than the dialect.

224. **A possible connection between dialectic variations and the distribution of Brahmans.**—The general character of the dialectic variations in the different parts of the provinces appears to be closely connected with the class of Bráhmans who are predominant in each part. The map on page 318 showing distribution of Bráhmans indicates with certain qualifications

the general allocation of the dialects. The qualifications are the differences introduced by Muhammdan influence in Rohilkhand and the Upper Doab, and that due to the separation for several generations of Oudh from the East.

In this way we should have the distribution of dialects as follows :—

Dialect				Country
Pachhadi	...	...	...	In the country of Gaur Bráhmans.
Braj	...	...	...	In that of the Sanadh.
Rohilkhandi	...	...	...	
Kanaujiya	...	...	...	In the Kanaujiya country.
Baiswari	...	...	...	
Western Awadhi	...	...	...	
Awadh Purbi	...	...	...	In that of Sarwariyas.
Purbi ...	...	...	...	
Bundeli	...	...	...	In that of Jijhautiya Bráhmans.

225. **The other languages of the provinces.**—The other languages of the provinces are those spoken in the Himalayas or in that Sub-Himalyan tract, the people of which are traditionally recognized as connected with the Himalayan rather than the plains castes. The languages shown are Kumauni, Garhwáli, Jaunsari and Nipali, the latter has been included, as the language spoken by the forest tribes on the Nipal border is so usually called. The use of the general word Pahari instead of the specific names has occurred to such an extent as to make it necessary to add a column for Pahari unspecified. The entries for Dehra Dún in this column have been reolassed by the Superintendent of the Dún as follows :—

Jaunsari	...	...	...	...	47,517
Garhwáli	...	...	...	...	7,732
Unascertainable		...	...	...	5,663

The great majority of entries for the Tarái in this column should properly have been under Kumauni; those for Gorakhpur, Gonda and Bahraich under Nipali. For the other plains districts the majority should be under Kumauni, but the exact proportion cannot be estimated. The reclassification indicated gives the following figures for each language :—

Kumauni	...	...	...	...	440,213
Garhwáli	...	...	...	...	415,182
Jaunsari	...	...	...	...	47,595
Nipali	...	...	...	...	21,924
Unspecified	...	...	...	...	7,189

The exact dialectic allocation of the Pahari dialects has apparently never been fully enquired into. That recognized by the people themselves and which accordingly has been shown in the schedules is according to the present executive distribution of the area. The Tarái dialects, believed to be so markedly different from the ordinary pahari as to entitle them to be shown as separate dialects, have either not appeared under specific names in the schedules or have appeared for so few persons as to make it useless to retain them.

226. **Languages of other Indian provinces.**—Passing to the languages of other provinces recorded as spoken by persons resident in them, a few

remarks appear necessary. The inadequacy of all the entries, especially for languages or dialects closely akin to those of the provinces, is another proof of the assertion already made, that it is impossible in the Census schedules to collect any proper record of the distribution of dialects. Behar dialects do not occur in the schedules for the North-Western Provinces. For Rájputána we have such figures as 9 persons speaking Mewati, 3 speaking Rangari, 12 Mewari, 10 Dadari, a dialect of Jaipur; whilst the birth-place tables show that persons born in the localities in which these dialects are spoken are numerous. Even for languages not closely allied to those of the provinces, the entries in the language column of the schedule are inaccurate as compared with those in the birth-place column. It has been found that even for Afghans born in Afghanistan or Kashmiris born in Kashmir, Hindustani frequently appears as the language entry. The main reason is probably want of close enquiry by the enumerator, but for the Kashmiris at least the fact that Urdu was and is the aristocratic language of India has probably much to do with the entry of that language against their names.

The following explanations as to the languages which occur may be of use.

Marwari is spoken by a class of money-lenders and traders scattered over the provinces. They are residents of Marwar, and still keep up a close connection with their native country. The North-Western Provinces and Oudh are their oyster which they very efficiently open by dint of higher interest and harder dealings than any local money-lender, even a Rastogi, can pretend to. *Mewati*, *Rangari*, *Bagri*, *Mewari*, *Dadari* are Rájputána dialects very insufficiently recorded.

Of the languages of the Pánjáb and Scinde, those which call for notice are *Sindhi and Dogri* and the Simla Hill State dialects. Sindhi is recorded in Muzaffarnagar and Sahāranpur as the mother tongue of certain settlers in these districts who are reported to have come from Scinde a century ago, and to have since intermarried amongst themselves and to still speak Sindhi in their own homes. They are by occupation usually either fishermen or cultivators. Dogri is the language recorded in Sahāranpur by what are locally known as Kashmiri Gujars. They are a class of nomad herdsmen, who trace their origin from Jammu and still speak Dogri amongst themselves. They move in the cold weather into the Sewaliks with their buffaloes, and retire again to the higher hills in Jaunsar or the Simla Hill States as the hot weather comes on. They have absolutely no communication with the residents of the surrounding villages, except when, once a week, a Bania visits them to buy their ghi and to sell them wheat flour they want.

Dialects of the Simla Hill States were reported from Native Garhwál only. The detailed names in the schedules were Utrochi, Bashahri and Keonthali, the languages of Teroch, Bisahr and Keonthal.

Bengali requires no mention, except to direct attention to the high proportion of women in Muttra and Benares, in both of which it is customary for Bengalis, especially women, to settle down.

Uriya.—Is spoken by temple priests in Brindaban and pilgrims to Muttra or Brindaban from Orissa.

Burmese.—The entries are almost entirely for prisoners in the jails of the Agra, Farukhabad, Bareilly, Allahabad, Benares and Lucknow districts. There are large numbers in each of the Central Jails, and they occasionally appear to be sent to District Jails to teach the other prisoners wood-carving. The entries for women under Burmese are entirely due to mistakes. Those against Agra, should be under Hindustani, those for Sitapur under Bengali.

Assamese and Manipuri are entries by pilgrims, or political détenus. Several members of the ex-royal family of Manipur are settled in Brindaban, and large numbers under the head Manipuri are for them and their attendants.

Gujrati and Marathi.—The greater part of the entries are for pilgrims in Benares, but the former is largely spoken by the traders temporarily settled like Marwaris in the province, and the latter by men in Government or other employment in Bundelkhand.

Tamil and Telegu.—The majority of the entries are by pilgrims; the rest are by scattered Madrasi domestic servants.

227. Foreign languages.—*Persian.*—A few entries are by Persians scattered over the country; but the great majority are by the Afghan détenus in Dehra Dún and their followers and by Afghan political pensioners in Meerut and elsewhere. Persian is the language spoken in the western part of Afghanistan, Pushtu being that only of the Pathan tribes.

Chinese.—There are a few Chinese employed in tea gardens in Kumaun, but the great majority of the entries in the schedules mean simply Bhotiya or Tibetan spoken by the nomad traders of the Upper Himalayas, who carry on the Indian trade with Tibet. The same class shows 1,089 entries under Tibetan. This last includes some entries from Tehri-Garhwál under the name Jadh, which the Secretary to the Darbár reports to be the language of a low caste race residing on the frontier of Tibet and the Tehri State. He states that these people are subjects of Tibet, and temporarily settle here during the snow season as petty traders.

The only European language which requires mention is *Portuguese.* Of the persons who entered Portuguese in the schedules only one claims to have been born in Portugal. The others are born either in Goa or British India. In regard to race, one enters European, seven Portuguese, seven Eurasian and the others native or Goanese. In occupation one is a priest; 12 are railway drivers or carriage examiners, positions likely to be occupied by Eurasians; three subsist by mission alms, and three are menial servants. I am not acquainted with the constitution of society in Goa; but if the relation between Native Goanese and Portuguese Eurasians is similar to that between Native Christians and English Eurasians in these provinces, the former speaking vernacular and the latter English as their mother tongue, the chances are that the majority of the entries of Portuguese mean Portuguese and not Goanese, but that some entries are very clearly euphemisms for Goanese.

Other entries in the language table require no mention. The following table shows the proportions borne by each group of languages to the total population.

Abstract No. 85, showing the proportions borne by each group of languages to total population.

Languages.	Percentage on total population.
Vernaculars of the North-Western Provinces and Oudh	99·806
Other Indian vernaculars	·120
Languages of Asiatic countries beyond India	·004
European languages	·070
Other languages	·000
Unspecified	·000
Total ...	100·

Chapter XI.—THE BIRTH PLACES OF THE PEOPLE.

228. **The Birth place figures.**—The record of the birth places of the people is of importance, chiefly as affording some measure of the migration of the population from one district of the province to another, from and to other provinces of India, and from foreign countries. Table XI shows the population enumerated in each district distributed according to the districts of these provinces or the other provinces of India or foreign countries in which they were born. The figures for immigration are, of course, as comprized within the population enumerated in a district, complete by districts It is unfortunate that those for emigration are less complete owing to the fact that in provinces outside the North-Western Provinces, tabulation was not done for North-Western Provinces districts separately, but only for each of the joint provinces as a whole. It would be a somewhat extensive task to tabulate the entries for a province according to the districts, not only in that, but in distant provinces; but the interest attaching to the figures is so great that I trust that in neighbouring provinces, at least, it will be considered possible to do so at next census. The gross figures for the population of the North-Western Provinces and Oudh, as enumerated by birth place, are as follows:—

1.	Born in the district of enumeration	41,770,401
2.	Born in a neighbouring district in this province	3,741,714
3.	Born in a neighbouring district of another province	508,468
4.	Born in distant districts of the province	588,626
5.	Born in distant districts of other provinces	266,865
6.	Born in Asia beyond India	2,842
7.	" " Europe	18,130
8.	" " Africa	355
9.	" " America	767
10.	" " Australasia	62
11.	" " At Sea	19
12.	Birth place unspecified	6,836
	Total	46,905,085

The figures are given by districts in Appendix No. XXV, rearranged from Table XI. For emigrants the figures corresponding to 1, 2 and 4 are available in Table XI itself. Those corresponding to 3 are available for the Panjab, Rajputana, Central Provinces and Bengal in returns received from these provinces. For Central India no such return is available, but the figures may be estimated to be not very different from the corresponding immigration. For 5 and later heads above we have for districts no corresponding return for emigrants. Those for 5, however, are available for the province as a whole. The extent of emigrants to foreign countries is so small as not to be important.

The people of the provinces, are, as a whole, little given to migration. 89·05 per cent. of them were enumerated in the district in which they were born, and no less than 98·25 per cent. of the population enumerated in the province were born in one or other of the districts of it. These proportions contrast with those given in the English Census Report for 1881 for England, from which it appears that the proportion of the population of the most stationary counties in England, born and enumerated in those counties, was equal to the average for the whole of the North-Western Provinces, whilst most counties show a far greater amount of movement. The figures for various counties are quoted for the sake of comparison. The percentage of the total English population born in England was 95·6 against 98·25 for the North-Western Provinces. When, however, we proceed to analyze the figures for migration in the North-Western Provinces and eliminate the figures representing a local migration produced by special causes operative in India, the amount of genuine economical migration will be found to be comparatively very much smaller.

Abstract No. 86, showing the proportion of the population enumerated in certain counties of England who were born in that county.

County.	Number born in county of 1,000 enumerated therein.
London...	629
Surrey	478
Kent	720
Middlesex	357
Cambridgeshire	782
Norfolk	880
Devonshire	820
Cornwall	894
Gloucestershire	736
Rutlandshire	675
Lincolnshire	822
Lancashire	741
Yorkshire	817
Northumberland	737
Cumberland	764
Cardiganshire	898
Denbighshire	740

229. **Migration within the district of birth.**—Of migration within the boundaries of a district, the census tables either afford us no indication in general or only such a rough indication as is derived from a comparison of the increase or decrease in different parts of a district. Such a rough indication was believed by the Collector of Hamírpur to have been given by the high rate of increase in the north of his district as compared with the decrease in the south. Such migrations are stated usual, especially at harvest time in Bundelkhand; the labourers of a tract in which the harvest is late moving in masses into another where the harvest is early or *vice versá*, such a migration is probably common elsewhere than in Bundelkhand, where, as often happens, harvests of different parts of a district ripen at different times. The 26th February was too early for harvest operations in any part of the Doab, otherwise the deficit along the Jumna tract where the harvest is late might have been partly so explained. In the districts on the Gogra, where, as has already been noticed, one or two parganas show a decrease or low rate of increase, it is possible that this cause has been operative, as in the damp Gogra tract crops ripen later and require less attention before ripening than do crops in the upland away from the river.

230. **Local migration in Kumaun and Garhwal.**—The census rules were to some extent altered, to provide for a measure of a well-known local migration in Kumaun, that from the upper valleys into the central zone and from the outer valleys into the Bhábar. It is probable that in the statement given as Appendix No. XXVI, this movement is somewhat inadequately represented, as the preliminary record made late in October was probably not quite early enough to anticipate all movements into the Bhábar. The movement in Kumaun is double; the first part is due to the abandonment of the upper pattis at the approach of the winter snow, the second to

the movement from the outer pattis into the Bhábar which is uninhabitable during the rains. The first movement left the greater part of the highlying patti of Darma in Kumaun uninhabited, the total population of the patti being reduced from 8,232 in August to 2,513 in February. It caused a great fall in the population of Johar in Kumaun (15,299 to 10,788) and Painkhanda in Garhwál (9,394 to 5,804). It led to a similar rise in the population of the adjoining pattis to the south, Askot (9,566 to 12,170), Sira (12,341 to 13,496), Danpur (36,107 to 38,680) all in Kumaun and Dasoli (12,328 to 13,775), Nagpur (48,942 to 50,907) in Garhwal. The population of the central pattis in both districts is left untouched, as the second movement, that to the Bhábar, is in general from the outer Himalayan parganas only. The second movement is highly marked in Kumaun only. It reduces the population of Kali Kumaun from 55,642 to 33,551, that of Dhiyani Rao from 13,960 to 6,875, of Chakhata from 39,183 to 21,895, Mahryuri from 4,165 to 925, Ramgarh from 4,305 to 550, Kota from 5,016 to 3,964, Pali from 125,389 to 118,020; Kutauli from 8,102 to 2,482, and other parganas in a smaller degree. All these parganas combine to swell the Bhábar population from 42,469 to 105,549. In Garhwál the second movement is slight, but the duns of Tallasalan fill up at the expense of the inner parganas, raising the population of the pargana from 43,659 to 51,093. On the whole, Kumaun loses between the first and second causes, owing to the hill stations being largely abandoned. Garhwál gains from an influx of wood-cutters into the forests below the hills and from the return of coolies from Simla, Mussoorie, Naini Tal and other hill stations.

231. **Movement between neighbouring districts.**—Of such migrations within districts except in Kumaun and Garhwál, the census tables give no measure. So soon as the migration extends beyond the district of birth, we have, however, a fairly accurate measure in the birth-place tables. The abstract (No. 87) on the opposite page shows the proportionate amount of such migration for each district, division and province as a percentage on the total population enumerated. The causes to which the migrations shown are to be attributed are partly religious, partly social and partly economical. The religious movement is important in the present census only as regards Muttra and Benares, in both of which a considerable number of persons from a distance constantly reside, and in the former of which there was at the time of the census a considerable temporary gathering. It is to this cause that the high excess of immigrants over emigrants in both these districts is to be attributed. The effect of this religious migration in other districts on the 26th February was small. In Allahabad a few pilgrims remained after the Maghmela, and in the districts round Allahabad a few pilgrims were probably enumerated on their way home. The social cause of migration is by far the most important in its numerical result. It is the custom for all high castes and for most low castes to take their wives from a clan or caste sub-division outside that to which they themselves belong. This in general necessitates their looking for their wives at some distance, and in the case of Rajputs, whose gradations of rank are numerous, and amongst whom the clans in general occupy fairly extensive continuous tracts of country, it often necessitates their wives being brought from a considerable distance. A very sum-

Abstract No. 87, comparing percentages of emigration and immigration for districts.

Serial number of district.	District.	Born and resident.	Immigrants from neighbouring districts.	Immigrants from distant districts of the province.	Immigrants from distant parts of India.	Immigrants from foreign countries.	Immigrants unspecified.	Total, immigrants.	Emigrants to neighbouring districts.	Emigrants to distant districts of the province.	Emigrants to distant parts of India.	Total, emigrants in India.
1	Dehra Dún	67·04	15·85	10·68	5·784	·5924	·0475	32·9589	1·62	·71		
2	Sahâranpur	92·59	4·43	1·88	1 019	·0674	·0353	7·4317	6·16	·84		
3	Muzaffarnagar	85·27	12·72	·97	1·020	·0041	·0196	14·7837	9·37	·89		
4	Meerut	86·84	9·37	2·07	1·446	·2519	·0007	13·1386	6·79	1·28		
5	Bulandshahr	86·17	11·85	1·44	·4920	·0345	·0116	13·8281	10·76	1·19		
6	Aligarh	85·31	11·27	2·73	·6850	·0089	...	14·6939	12·48	2·54		
	Total, Meerut Division ...	86·65	9·96	2·15	1·121	·1056	·0120	13·3486	8·70	1·27		
7	Muttra	78·53	16·60	1·67	3·065	·0843	·0382	21·4575	11·12	2·24		
8	Agra	82·53	13·87	2·47	1·119	·0964	·0483	17·6037	8·21	2·83		
9	Farukhabad	87·04	11·41	1·04	·659	·0513	·0329	13·1932	13·89	1·71		
10	Mainpuri	83·87	13·78	1·49	·8261	·0049	·0169	16·1179	12·52	2·16		
11	Etáwah	85·35	12·95	1·21	·4791	·0075	·0057	14·6523	11·68	·80		
12	Etah	84·04	14·50	1·07	·3659	·0055	·0163	15·9577	17·63	1·70		
	Total, Agra Division ...	83·59	13·77	1·54	1·028	·0449	·0278	16·4107	12·27	1·97		
13	Bareilly	83·18	14·24	2·00	·3490	·2268	·0061	16·8219	11·61	3·38		
14	Bijnor	95·00	4·28	·55	·1699	·0030	...	5·0029	9·21	·66		
15	Budaun	88·82	10·39	·49	·2625	·0049	·0269	11·1743	13·49	·94		
16	Moradabad	90·76	7·77	1·21	·2317	·0164	·0049	9·2330	10·31	1·83		
17	Sháhjahánpur	89·09	9·55	1·14	·1652	·0536	...	10·9088	20·06	1·38		
18	Pilibhít	84·22	13·44	2·19	·1148	·0061	·0226	15·7735	10 001	·559		
	Total, Rohilkhand Division ...	88·69	9·79	1·21	·2285	·0589	·0090	11·2964	12·70	1·61		
19	Cawnpore	85·94	8·81	3·91	1·131	·1306	·0721	14·0537	7·12	2·09		
20	Fatehpur	90·24	8·99	·55	·2098	·0017	...	9·7515	8·18	·80		
21	Bánda	90·58	8·25	·88	·2227	·0039	·0620	9·4186	9·36	1·00		
22	Hamírpur	85·40	13·69	·48	·4245	·0031	·0001	14·5977	14·23	·32		
23	Allahabad	94·03	3·69	1·11	1·036	·1248	·0014	5·9622	5·45	1·49		
24	Jhánsi	76·92	18·17	2·98	1·605	·2574	·0644	23·0768	17·46	·83		
25	Jalaun	87·19	9·15	·80	2·843	·0083	·0022	12·8035	12·97	·67		
26	Lalitpur	91·48	4·94	·61	2·953	·0094	·0025	8·5149	10·48	·20		
	Total, Allahabad Division ...	88·87	8·33	1·63	1·057	·0813	·0028	11·1011	9·01	1·20		
27	Benares	87·38	9·24	1·43	1·880	·0612	...	12·6112	6·44	1·31		
28	Mirzapur	92·83	5·76	·45	·9246	·0045	·0209	7·1600	5·92	·55		
29	Jaunpur	92·39	6·91	·52	·1338	·0066	·0401	7·6105	9·52	2·35		
30	Ghâzipur	92·62	6·84	·22	·2976	·0134	·0054	7·3764	7·27	·86		
31	Ballia	93·22	6·49	·11	·1604	·0072	·0050	6·7726	8·53	·26		
	Total, Benares Division ...	92·23	7·006	·534	·6456	·0171	·0179	8·2206	7·62	1·12		

Abstract No. 87, comparing percentages of emigration and immigration for districts—(continued).

Serial number of district.	District.	Born and resident.	Immigrants from neighbouring districts.	Immigrants from distant districts of the province.	Immigrants from distant parts of India.	Immigrants from foreign countries.	Immigrants unspecified.	Total, immigrants.	Emigrants to neighbouring districts.	Emigrants to distant districts of the province.	Emigrants to distant parts of India.	Total, emigrants in India.
32	Gorakhpur	91·99	6·85	·73	·4171	·0056	·0003	8·0030	3·39	·33		
33	Basti	94·85	4·43	·65	·0525	·0066	...	5·1391	9·49	·30		
34	Azamgarh	94·38	5·38	·12	·1071	·0078	·0001	5·6150	8·35	·45		
	Total, Gorakhpur Division ...	93·41	5·79	·55	·2347	·0065	·00018	6·58138	6·38	·36		
35	Kumaun	93·22	3·95	1·82	·9113	·0786	·0131	6·7730	2·27	·81		
36	Garhwál	96·67	1·89	·15	·2829	·0193	·0009	2·3431	3·31	·20		
37	Tarái	51·78	47·00	1·06	·1239	·0061	·0199	48·2099	10·43	·03		
	Total, Kumaun Division ...	87·37	10·91	1·11	·5541	·0452	·0101	12·6294	4·08	·46		
	Total, N.-W. Provinces ...	89·03	8·96	1·24	·6954	·0510	·0147	10·9611	9·10	1·18	2·23	12·51
38	Lucknow	82·13	11·50	4·71	1·277	·3647	·0104	17·8621	9·39	6·00		
39	Unao	90·99	7·83	1·00	·1679	·0028	·0079	9·0086	9·58	1·03		
40	Rae Bareli	90·82	8·45	·71	·2472	·0038	·0013	9·4123	6·91	1·16		
41	Sitapur	90·21	8·57	1·04	·1235	·0517	·0025	9·7877	11·44	·63		
42	Hardoi	91·96	7·50	·47	·0642	·0013	·00008	8·03558	9·74	·48		
43	Kheri	83·25	14·52	2·09	·1154	·0028	·0136	16·7418	6·17	·26		
	Total, Lucknow Division ...	88·60	9·53	1·51	·2925	·0944	·0054	11·4323	8·93	1·43		
44	Fyzabad	88·86	8·88	1·82	·3125	·0708	·0441	11·1274	8·32	2·00		
45	Gonda	90·23	9·21	1·07	·1674	·0077	·0046	10·4497	6·04	1·14		
46	Bahraich	87·12	10·20	2·45	·1724	·0058	·0518	12·8800	4·06	·48		
47	Sultánpur	89·55	9·40	·90	·1142	·0068	·0244	10·4454	8·36	2·71		
48	Partábgarh	88·89	10·22	·73	·1552	·0036	·0057	11·1145	7·48	1·48		
49	Bara Banki	92·78	6·54	·56	·0939	·0062	·0018	7·2019	9·96	1·11		
	Total, Fyzabad Division ...	89·53	9·15	1·10	·1694	·0178	·0214	10·4586	7·36	1·49		
	Total, Oudh ...	89·10	9·32	1·30	·2264	·0371	·0140	10·8975	8·10	1·44	1·447	10·99
	Total, N.-W. P. and Oudh ...	89·05	9·06	1·25	·5688	·0742	·0145	10·9675	8·82	1·26	2·02	12·10
50	Rampur	87·81	8·52	1·31	·1350	·0257	...	9·9907	13·84	·91		
51	Tehri Garhwál	99·60	·190	·6	·1426	...	...	·9326	1·096	·034		
	Total, Native States ...	91·40	7·52	·92	·1373	...	...	8·5773	9·96	·64		

mary examination of the birth-place tables will show, that by far the greatest part of the movement recorded is between neighbouring districts, that it is to a considerable extent reciprocal, if not, between, each two districts, then between each group of districts, and that the great majority of the persons who have moved from a district of birth to a neighbouring district are women. By far the greatest proportion of this movement into neighbouring districts is due to the marriage custom just referred to. Its effects are not confined to women only, as a bride coming from one wealthy house to another is followed by a lot of servants and hangers-on, or a bride coming from a needy to a wealthy house is followed by needy brothers and cousins. On the other hand, a bridegroom marrying into a well-to-do family, particularly if there are no sons, frequently transfers himself and his belongings to the house of his wife's father. There is thus a constant and considerable movement of men in consequence of such marriages. The extent of the movement may best be illustrated by selecting a typical district and giving the figures. Rae Bareli a district without any manufacturing towns inhabited by a closely packed population of its own, and, therefore, presenting no attractions to settlers from an economical point of view, but as largely populated by Rajput clans of higher status than those in neighbouring distiets is as suitable a district to select as any. Appendix No. XXV shows the following immigrants in Rae Bareli :—

	Total.	Male.	Female.	Percentage.
Born in contiguous districts	87,374	27,537	59,837	8·43
Born in distant districts of the province	7,391	3,298	4,093	·71
Born in other provinces of India	2,557	1,245	1,312	·25

Other figures may be neglected. On the other hand, Rae Bareli sends out :—

	Total.	Male.	Female.	Percentage.
To neighbouring districts	71,463	24,442	47,021	6·89
To distant districts of the province	12,053	7,433	4,620	1·16

and to distant provinces an unascertained number. In examining the details, we see that Rae Bareli sends to and receives from contiguous and neighbouring districts a large number of persons with females always, except in the case of emigrants to Lucknow and Cawnpore, largely in excess. The result is that so far as the movement in the provinces is concerned, Rae Bareli gains 3,095 males and 12,816 females, although it sends out a not inconsiderable excess number of emigrants, mostly male, to distant districts of the province. All motive for migration into Rae Bareli from an economical point of view is absent, and it is clear that the movement is almost entirely due to the social cause.

To ascertain how far migration is due to causes connected with the prosperity or want of prosperity of a district, this social migration must be eliminated for Rae Bareli and other districts of alike status. This may be easily done without risk of great error by setting down all migration from and to neigbouring districts as due to this cause. In a district like Cawnpore, however, this introduces a considerable amount of error. The Cawnpore figures if referred to will show that in the population it sends to its neighbours, women are always greatly in excess, but that this is not always the case in regard to the immigrants it receives. Even in the case of Cawnpore, however, the movement from neighbouring districts is generally mostly of women, and, therefore, mostly due to intermarriage. All over we are well within the mark if we estimate that for the majority of districts the movement between contiguous districts is that due to marriage customs.

232. **Movement between distant districts of the province.**—Eliminating this we have next to consider the movement amounting to 1·25 per cent. of the whole population between distant districts of the province, by far the greater part, of which is due to economical causes. Even here, however, we have no exact indication of the condition of each district owing to the fact that custom as to the direction of migration varies largely in different parts of the province. Rae Bareli, for instance, is shown by the age figures to be one of the districts in which emigration of males is highest in the provinces, and yet the excess of emigration over immigration as shown by the birth-place table is only ·45 per cent. on the total population. This at once, from a knowledge of the circumstances of the district, is seen to be due to the fact that economical emigration from Rae Bareli is in an unusually large proportion to distant provinces, the district supplying the Madras and Bombay armies with a large proportion of their high caste recruits and sending large numbers of low caste men to a distance as Commissariat employés and in similar employments. The birth-place table does not, therefore, give an exact indication of the relative economic position of each district, but it gives an indication accurate enough in the main of the group to which economically each district belongs, whether it is emigrant or immigrant. These figures give the marginally noted lists of districts. At least two districts in which the figures are misleading may be picked out at once. Etáwah and Jalaun shown as immigrant are undoubtedly emigrant. The cause of the appearance of Etáwah on the wrong side of the list is that the economic movement is even as regards distant districts swamped by the marriage movement. The district is the main home of the Chauhan clan, who intermarry with other clans in the most distant parts of the provinces. For Jalaun the cause of the misplacement is, that the emigration, which was

Abstract No. 88, showing the districts of the province classified as emigrant and immigrant considering only presumably economic movements.

	Immigrant.		Emigrant.
1	Dehra Dún.	1	Muttra.
2	Sahâranpur.	2	Agra.
3	Muzaffarnagar.	3	Farukhabad.
4	Meerut.	4	Mainpuri.
5	Bulandshahr.	5	Bareilly.
6	Aligarh.	6	Bijnor.
7	Etáwah.	7	Budaun.
8	Etah.	8	Moradabad.
9	Pilibhít	9	Sháhjahánpur.
10	Cawnpore.	10	Fatehpur.
11	Jhánsi.	11	Bánda.
12	Jalaun.	12	Hamírpur.
13	Lalitpur.	13	Allahabad.
14	Benares.	14	Mirzapur
15	Gorakhpur.	15	Jaunpur.
16	Basti.	16	Ghâzipur.
17	Kumaun.	17	Ballia.
18	Tarái.	18	Azamgarh.
19	Sitapur.	19	Garhwál.
20	Kheri	20	Lucknow.
21	Bahraich.	21	Unao.
22	Rampur.	22	Rae Bareli.
23	Tehri Garhwál.	23	Hardoi.
		24	Fyzabad.
		25	Gonda.
		26	Sultanpur.
		27	Partabgarh.
		28	Bara Banki.

considerable, was to native states almost entirely. As regards the other districts they appear to be accurately enough placed. For 29 districts the social circumstances are such as to lead to emigration; 20 receive an excess of immigrants.

233. **Movement to and from other provinces of India.**—Before passing to the consideration of the movement to and from other provinces it may be interesting to give statements similar to those contained in the last Census Report showing the gross emigration and immigration. The districts are in the following abstracts (Nos. 89 and 90) ranged in order according to the extent of each movement.

Abstract No. 89, showing percentage of total emigrants to population of each district.

Serial number.	Name of district or division.	Percentage.	Serial number.	Name of district or division.	Percentage.
1	Sháhjahánpur	22·04		North-Western Provinces ...	10·28
2	Etah	19·33		Allahabad Division	10·21
3	Jhánsi	18·29		North-Western Provinces and Oudh	10·08
4	Farukhabad	15·60		Meerut Division	9·968
5	Lucknow...	15·39	29	Bijnor	9·871
6	Aligarh	15·02	30	Basti	9·788
7	Bareilly	14·99	31	Muzaffarnagar	9·757
8	Rámpur	14·75		Oudh	9·541
9	Mainpuri...	14·68	32	Cawnpore	9·210
10	Hamírpur	14·55	33	Fatehpur...	8·981
11	Budaun	14·43	34	Partabgarh	8·961
	Rohilkhand Division	14·31		Fyzabad Division	8·847
	Agra Division	14·24	35	Azamgarh	8·799
12	Jalaun	13·64	36	Ballia	8·786
13	Muttra	13·36		Benares Division	8·742
14	Etáwah	12·48	37	Ghúzipur...	8·128
15	Moradabad	12·14	38	Rae Bareli	8·075
16	Sitapur	12·07	39	Meerut	8·066
17	Bulandshahr	11·95	40	Benares	7·751
18	Jaunpur	11·87	41	Gonda	7·176
19	Sultanpur	11·07	42	Allahabad	6·941
20	Bara Banki	11·07	43	Sahúranpur	6·904
21	Agra	11·04		Gorakhpur Division	6·737
22	Lalitpur	10·68	44	Mirzapur...	6·470
23	Unao	10·61	45	Kheri	6·427
	Native States	10·60		Kumaun Division	4·542
24	Pilibhít	10·56	46	Bahraich...	4·542
25	Tarái	10·46	47	Gorakhpur	3·724
26	Bánda	10·36	48	Garhwál	3·506
	Lucknow Division	10·36	49	Kumaun	3·075
27	Hardoi	10·32	50	Dehra Dún	2·330
28	Fyzabad	10·32	51	Tehri Garhwál	1·130

Abstract No. 90, showing percentage of total immigrants to population of each district.

Serial number.	District.	Percentage.	Serial number.	District.	Percentage.
1	Tarái	48·2099		North-Western Provinces and Oudh	10·9675
2	Dehra Dún	32·9539		North-Western Provinces	10·9611
3	Jhánsi	23·0718	27	Sháhjahánpur	10·9088
4	Muttra	21·4575	28	Oudh	10·8975
5	Lucknow	17·8621		Fyzabad Division	10·4586
6	Agra	17·6037		Gonda	10·4497
7	Bareilly	16·8219	29	Sultanpur	10·4454
8	Kheri	16·7418	30	Sitapur	9·7877
	Agra Division	16·4107	31	Fatehpur	9·7515
9	Mainpuri	16·1179	32	Bánda	9·4186
10	Etah	15·9577	33	Rae Bareli	9·4123
11	Pilibhít	15·7735	34	Moradabad	9·2330
12	Muzaffarnagar	14·7387	35	Unao	9·0086
13	Aligarh	14·6939		Native States	8·6010
14	Etáwah	14·6523	36	Lalitpur	8·5149
15	Hamírpur	14·5977	37	Hardoi	8·0355
16	Cawnpore	14·0537	38	Gorakhpur	8·0030
17	Bulandshahr	13·8281	39	Jaunpur	7·6105
	Meerut Division	13·3486	40	Sahárunpur	7·4317
18	Farukhabad	13·1932	41	Gházipur	7·3764
19	Meerut	13·1386	42	Bara Banki	7·2019
20	Bahraich	12·8800	43	Mirzapur	7·1600
21	Jalaun	12·8045	44	Kumaun	6·7730
	Kumaun Division	12·6294	45	Ballia	6·7726
22	Benares	12·6112		Gorakhpur Division	6·5813
23	Rámpur	12·1807	46	Allahabad	5·9622
	Lucknow Division	11·4323	47	Azamgarh	5·6150
	Rohilkhand Division	11·2964	48	Basti	5·1391
24	Budaun	11·1743	49	Bijnor	5·0029
25	Fyzabad	11·1274	50	Garhwál	2·3431
26	Partabgarh	11·1145	51	Tehri Garhwál	·3926
	Allahabad Division	11·1011			

Abstract No. 91, showing migration between this and other provinces of India.

Province or State.	Immigration.			Emigration.			Excess.			Deficit.		
	Total.	Neighbouring districts.	Distant districts.	Total.	Neighbouring districts.	Distant districts.	Total.	Neighbouring districts.	Distant districts.	Total.	Neighbouring districts.	Distant districts.
Aden ...	14	...	14	1,539	...	1,539	...	...	...	1,525	...	1,525
Ajmere Merwara.	...	...	...	17,687	...	17,687	...	...	...	17,687	...	17,687
Andamans ...	75	...	75	8,940	...	8,940	...	...	...	8,865	...	8,865
Assam ...	1,790	...	1,790	57,851	...	57,851	...	...	...	56,061	...	56,061
Baroda ..	...	...	...	7,476	...	7,476	...	...	...	7,476	...	7,476
Bengal ...	205,915	155,203	50,712	364,925	110,756	254,169	44,447	44,447	...	203,457	...	203,457
Berar ...	392	...	392	28,359	...	28,359	...	...	...	27,967	...	27,967
Bhutan ...	204	...	204	...	...	...	204	...	204	...	...	...
Bombay ..	7,079	...	7,079	85,732	...	85,732	...	...	...	78,653	...	78,653
Burma ...	1,610	...	1,610	18,233	...	18,233	...	...	...	16,623	...	16,623
Central India,	229,220	195,232	33,988	288,914	195,232	93,682	...	...	...	59 694	...	59,694
Central Provinces.	12,177	4,146	8,031	123,004	14,939	108,065	...	...	...	110,827	10,793	100,034
Coorg ...	7	...	7	12	...	12	...	...	...	5	...	5
French and Portuguese Settlements.	53	...	53	...	...	...	53	...	53	...	...	...
Hyderabad ..	1,981	...	1,981	12,667	...	12,667	...	...	...	10,686	...	10,686
Kashmir ..	1,403	...	1,403	860	...	860	543	...	543	...	...	...
Madras ..	1,717	...	1,717	4,174	...	4,174	...	...	...	2,457	...	2,457
Mysore ...	98	...	98	440	...	440	...	...	...	342	...	342
Nepal ..	41,132	...	41,132	...	...	...	41,132	...	41,132	...	...	...
Punjab ...	142,315	78,946	63,369	245,805	95,301	150,504	...	...	...	103,490	16,355	87,135
Quetta ..	...	...	...	4,312	...	4,312	...	...	...	4,312	...	4,312
Rajputana ...	128,151	82,741	45,410	99,924	1,048	98,876	81,693	81,693	...	53,466	...	53,466
Total ...	775,388	516,208	259,065	1,365,854	417,276	948,578	168,072	126,140	41,932	758,593	27,148	731,445

The figures for migration between this and neighbouring provinces are also given above The immigration is ·5688 per cent. of the provincial population enumerated, the emigration 2·024 per cent. That to neighbouring districts not in any way differing from that of similar extent in the provinces is distinguished from the genuine migration to and from distant districts.

On the whole, the North-West Provinces send out 590,521 more persons than they receive, affording by their absence and by the considerable sums they bring or send back to the more congested districts, a relief the extent of which would be difficult to calculate. The districts from which these emigrants are taken are mainly those which contribute to the inter-provincial economic migration. They belong in social standing to all classes of the population, but are most largely drawn from the class which furnishes Hindustani soldiers and the lowest classes both amongst Hindus and Muhammadans who work as domestic servants, grooms and the like. A brief account of the motives for these migrations may be given where they are important.

To the *Andamans* we send 3,482 males and 458 females, partly prisoners, partly policemen and sepoys and receive back a few Hindustani children born in the islands.

Assam.—Receives the large number of 57,851 persons from the North-Western Provinces, mostly coolie labourers, but also to some extent sepoys and policemen. It sends 1,790 persons, of whom the great majority are pilgrims at Muttra where the Manipuri princes have settled or in Benares. The rest are the returned children of the coolie labourers or soldiers.

Bengal.—Excluding the interchange of brides and their relations with Behar and Chota Nagpur, Bengal sends to these provinces the largest number of migrants they receive. Those from Behar are mostly labourers from Bengal proper. Bengali clerks and law agents with their families are scattered throughout every district in the province having penetrated even into Garhwál. They are most largely employed in the Railway and Military Offices, but are in not inconsiderable numbers as pleaders in the principal towns and in Civil Government employ as clerks. Both Muttra and Benares, the two principal sacred places in the provinces, have large colonies of Bengalies both amongst the priests and worshippers. Bengali women, more devout than their male relations, are in excess in both places. On the other hand, Bengal is a favourite field of employment for the surplus population of these Provinces, who from the Eastern and Oudh districts migrate in large numbers to work as messengers, doorkeepers, policemen, grooms, and domestic servants. Probably a considerable proportion of the persons shown as born in Bengal in the smaller districts are the children who return from Bengal with such emigrants.

Bombay sends 7,079 persons to these provinces. They are largely shown as residing in the smaller districts and probably not a small part of them are the children of the North-Western Provinces emigrants to Bombay. Of genuine natives of Bombay there are as usual a number of pilgrims and priests at Benares and Muttra, and a good many Gujrati money-lenders scattered over the country in the larger towns.

Our emigrants to Bombay are more important in point of number. They are mainly soldiers in the Bombay army which recruits largely in these provinces taking men of castes who would not obtain admission into Bengal regiments; others are traders, mechanics, messengers, porters and the like, in Bombay itself and the other considerable towns.

Central India is the only province that sends an excess of emigrants to any extent considerable into the North-Western Provinces. A large part are marriage emigrants and of the rest messengers and labourers are probably in the majority as regards numbers. There are also not a few Mahratta Brahmans employed as clerks, &c., in the Bundelkhand and other border districts. On the other hand, the North-Western Provinces districts send to the Central Provinces a large number of labourers and a very much more important class in the employés of all ranks of the Native Governments.

To the *Central Provinces*, the North-Western Provinces and Oudh have contributed a large number of cultivating emigrants, and it is probable that the majority of the 12,177 persons enumerated in the North-Western Provinces as born in the Central Provinces are the children of such emigrants returned to their native places.

Hyderabad is a favourite resort of the educated natives of the North-Western Provinces in the search for employment. The Hyderabad Contingent is largely recruited in these Provinces, and the State also employs many Hindustanis as soldiers. The immigrants from Hyderabad are almost entirely children born of Hindustani parents in that State.

Kashmir is the native home of a body of Pandits, who, particularly in Oudh, hold a considerable number of posts of all degrees of importance in Government service and elsewhere, wherever it is likely that a quick wit and a clear head, can, with the assistance of a considerable faculty for accumulation, procure their advancement. They are the majority of the persons born in Kashmir in the North-Western Provinces. It is problematic whether they were to the extent shown born in Kashmir, as colonies of them have been settled in Lucknow and Delhi for several generations. The Kashmir born of Saháranpur and Dehra Dún have already (page 270) been mentioned. They are Gujar herdsmen in the Siwaliks.

With *Madras*, the North-Western Provinces has but little intercourse. They send a certain proportion of soldiers to the Madras army and receive back their children and a few Madrasi servants.

Nepal.—From Nepal 41,132 immigrants are shown. Along the Tarái line from Pilibhít to Gorakhpur a large proportion of the so-called immigrants belong to the semi-nomad tribes who live along the border, sometimes in Nepal and sometimes in our border. A numerous class is also the children of cultivators from the North-Western Provinces and Oudh who hold land in the Nepal Tarái to a considerable extent, whilst still keeping their permanent homes in the British districts. In Benares the Nepal born are political refugees and pilgrims. In the Tarái they are coolie labourers for the most part. They are so to a great extent in Kumaun also,

Elsewhere the Nepalese shown are almost entirely Gurkha soldiers in British Regiments and their families many of whom live with them. Returns of the North-Western Provinces emigrants to Nepal are not available, but the number is not inconsiderable. Land in the Nepal Tarái can be rented at a few annas a bigha, and in spite of a profound dread of the Gurkhali, this tempts the cultivator from border districts annually to venture across into the Nepal Tarái to raise a cold weather harvest and then return to his home.

To the *Panjáb*, the North-Western Provinces and Oudh send 245,805 emigrants and receive 142,315—a large proportion in both numbers are due to intermarriage across the Jumna, but of genuine Panjábi immigrants there is a large number employed as soldiers and policemen throughout the provinces. The class sent by the North-Western Provinces to the Panjáb is in general of a rank below the sepoy, grooms, commissariat drivers, and water-carriers and the like.

The last province which occurs in the list is *Rajputana*. There is the usual interchange of marriage relations. Rajputana also furnishes the western districts with messengers, a few sepoys, and large numbers of labourers. The most important class, however, which immigrates from Rájputana are the Marwari baniyas, who have already been referred to in connection with the language table. The classes of emigrants from the North-Western Provinces to Rajputana are not materially different from those received, but perhaps include a larger proportion of educated men employed in the service of the Native Governments.

234. **Movement between the North-Western Provinces and Oudh and foreign countries.**—Immigration from Asiatic countries beyond India is not important. It has been already referred to in connection with the language table and the remarks apply here also. From countries beyond Asia the only immigrants of importance are the British military forces and civil staff and a comparatively small proportion of merchants, manufacturers, and planters.

Of the emigrants sent out to foreign countries we have no return. The only movement of any importance is that of registered emigrants to the West Indian Islands and Natal. A return of the numbers recruited for this migration in the North-Western Provinces and Oudh for the past ten years as indicated in the margin, with the numbers recruited from the North-Western Provinces in Bengal where they are available. In all 78,318 persons were recruited in these provinces within ten years preceding the Census. Probably where recruitment in other Provinces is included, about 90,000

Abstract No. 92, showing the numbers recruited in the North-Western Provinces and Oudh for the past ten years.

Year.	Recruited in North-Western Provinces and Oudh.	Natives of North-Western Provinces and Oudh, including those recruited in other Provinces.
1881-82	10,000	Not available.
1882-83	8,526	Ditto.
1883-84	8,599	9,804
1884-85	8,461	Not available.
1885-86	2,854	Ditto.
1886-87	4,271	Ditto.
1887-88	4,275	4,973
1888-89	5,905	7,203
1889-90	8,995	11,629
1890-91	16,432	19,133

natives of these provinces emigrated to these colonies. The usual term of engagement is for five years and most of the emigrants return after either five or ten years. In all probability the emigrants from the North-Western Provinces in the colonies are not in excess of the number recruited in ten years.

The figures for the returned children of such emigrants given in Part F of the table, indicate the districts which mostly supply the emigrants. They almost entirely come from the Benares, Gorakhpur and Fyzabad Divisions. The only other form of emigration from these provinces at all in evidence is that to the Muhammadan sacred cities of Medina and Mekka. The numbers which go every year from the provinces, and of persons resident in Mekka, are not inconsiderable, but I have seen no estimate of their numbers.

235. **Excess of emigration over immigration.**—Emigration and immigration have now been considered in detail. It remains to compare the total population of the province as enumerated with the number of persons who are born in the provinces, and, therefore, though not all resident, nearly all natives of it :—

	Residents in the Province.	Natives in birth of the Province.
Born and resident in the Provinces	46,100,741	46,100,741
From and to the rest of India	775,333	1,365,354
Foreign countries	22,175	*86,000
Total	46,898,249	47,552,595
Excess born in the North-Western Provinces and Oudh	...	654,346

The excess of North-Western Provinces emigrants to almost all Provinces and to foreign countries is some index of the congested state of population in the Provinces, and especially in those eastern districts from which most of the emigrants come.

The amount of emigration in India at the end of the present decade is compared with that in 1881 in the accompanying statement :—

Abstract No. 93, showing the emigration in India at the beginning and end of the present decade.

	1881.			1891.		
	Total.	Males.	Females.	Total.	Males.	Females.
Immigrant from other Provinces ...	729,676	301,482	428,194	775,333	323,002	452,331
Emigrant to other Provinces	1,087,212	633,411	453,801	1,365,854	807,171	558,683
Excess of emigration	357,536	331,929	25,607	590,521	484,169	106,352
Increase in excess in 1891	...	...	...	232,985	152,240	80,745

The total excess is greater in 1891 by 232,985 persons. A large proportion of the immigrants are women and children. The majority of the emigrants are adult men. The age figures for the Province are, therefore, on the whole somewhat deficient in adult men from 20 to 45.

The effect of this fact on the age tables, death rates and the Sanitary Commissioner's statistical returns has already been referred to.

* Estimate.

Chapter XII.—THE INFIRMITIES OF THE PROVINCE.

236. **Instructions as to record of infirmities.**—The instructions to enumerators in regard to the record of infirmities were as follows:—

"If any person be blind of both eyes, or deaf and dumb from birth, or insane, or suffering from corrosive leprosy, enter the name of the infirmity in column 14 (Infirmities). Do not enter those blind of one eye only, or who have become deaf and dumb after birth, or who are suffering from white leprosy only."

In abstraction it was directed that 10 per cent. of the books should be reabstracted for the purpose of discovering whether any mistakes had been made in regard to the abstraction of infirmities. After the returns reached me and had been compiled, the variations met with were so remarkable, that I considered it advisable to direct complete reabstraction for all infirmities in those districts in which the variations, either plus or minus, were noteworthy. The result was in all cases to reaffirm the substantial accuracy of the figures originally reported, and it may therefore be taken as certain that the figures in the tables present accurately the results enumerated in the present Census. District Officers were asked in submitting their final reports to procure a note on the subject of the infirmities and their variations since last Census from Civil Surgeons. The result has been somewhat disappointing, except in one or two instances. Little examination of any value was made of the statistics by Civil Surgeons. To an enquirer anxious in a matter of vital statistics to place faith in the remarks made by the professional vital statisticians of the province, the extent to which contradictory reasons were given to explain variations in different districts, and the confidence with which, on the ground of his own narrow experience as a medical practitioner, each correspondent condemns or affirms the value of the statistics at either Census, are somewhat bewildering. A few reports from which quotations will be given are of value. To the Civil Surgeons of Bijnor and Sháhjahánpur in particular I am indebted for interesting memoranda.

Part I.—INSANES.

237. **The figures for Insanity.**—The marginal statement compares the total number of insanes recorded in the provinces at this and the two preceding censuses. The North-Western Provinces show a decreased number of insanes as compared with both preceding censuses. In Oudh the total figures are almost precisely the same as in 1881. In comparing the age-periods for insanes it will be observed (abstract No. 94) that whilst there is an increase in the absolute and

Abstract No. 94, comparing the total number of insanes recorded in the provinces at this and the two preceding censuses.

		Total.	Males.	Females.
North-Western Provinces ...	1872 ...	4,801	3,443	1,358
	1881 ...	4,809	3,323	1,486
	1891 ...	4,043	2,791	1,252
Oudh	1881 ...	1,538	1,044	494
	1891 ...	1,538	1,056	482
North-Western Provinces and Oudh.	1881 ...	6,347	4,367	1,980
	1891 ...	5,581	3,847	1,734

proportionate number of insanes for children under 10 and for women from 20 to 29, there is a decrease in every other age-period. Before any opinion can be pronounced as to the correctness of these figures, enquiry is necessary as to the usual causes of insanity in India. In this connection the following remarks by the Civil Surgeon of Bijnor commenting on the figures for that district may be quoted.

Abstract No. 95, showing proportion of insanes at each period to 10,000 of total population in 1881 and 1891.

Age.	1881.		1891.	
	Males.	Females.	Males.	Females.
0—4	0 1	0·03	0·18	0 07
5—9	0·4	0·2	0·45	0·20
10—14	1·1	0·7	0·91	0 55
15—19	1·8	1·3	1·52	0·80
20—29	2·8	1·0	2·24	0·?7
30—39	3·1	1·3	2·47	1·08
40—49	3·0	1·6	2 75	1·25
50—59	2 9	1·7	2·21	1 87
60 and over.	2 6	1·5	1·85	1·06
Total ...	1·9	0·9	1 58	0·77

238. **Remarks by the Civil Surgeon, Bijnor on Insanity.**—" I venture to offer a scheme of classification before forming an opinion as to the most likely cause in each of the cases whose distribution by age is given in the above table."

" There is (1) one case at 4 years of age which is most probably—

A. Insanity of early developement.

Causes.—Idiocy from brain deficiency.

Ditto sense deficiency.

Ditto inability to develope.

Imbecility from inability to develope fully.

" There are nine cases between the ages of 5 and 10 years which might be termed—

B. Insanity of childhood.

Forms of insanity of childhood—

Mania.
Melancholia.
Moral perversion.

Causes of insanity of childhood—

From congenital causes.
From epilepsy.
From injury or brain disease.

There are 25 cases between the ages of 14 and 20 years which might be termed—

C. Insanity of adolescence, due to—

Onset of sexuality.
Stress of work.
Phthisis, &c.

(Nervous system only fit for low pressure.)

Symptoms.—Mania with conceit, emotional melancholia and hypochondriasis, with liability to recur, and tendency to mental weakness.

There are 63 cases between the ages of 24 and 49 years which might be termed :—

D. Insanity of maturity.

Mania.
Melancholia.
Dementia.
General paralysis due to strain or excess.

" In this last group of cases there seems to be a greater tendency to insanity between the ages of 40 and 44 years, as both males and females are attacked in largest numbers at this time of life, the climacteric period. "

" There are 20 cases between the ages of 50 and 60 years and over, which might be termed—

E. Insanity of age.

Mania ...	...	All tend to dementia.
Melancholia	...	
Dementia	...	

" The last group of all might be termed—

F. Insanity of climacteric.

(*a*) In women { Delusions. Persecutions. Hallucinations.

(*b*) In men : often hypochondriacal, due to visceral breakdown.

" The above causes might account for cases of insanity in both men and women between the ages of 40 and 44 years. "

" Having given the above scheme of classification of the cases in Table XII to explain the causes and factors in the production of unsound mind in their distribution by age, it remains for me to specially note the causes which operate in this district generally.

N.B.—1. " *The increase in the population.*— Since the taking of the previous census (1881) the increase in population has caused, no doubt, a harder struggle for existence amongst the labouring classes generally and higher pressure in life as the result of education and civilizing influences among the middle classes who are highly ambitious for position and better circumstances. All the above causes tend to act harmfully on the mind and body chiefly through the mind and emotional feelings. The wear and tear of life is greater, and incapacitates the individual physically as well as mentally, since the mind and body act and react upon one another. " *Mens sana in corpore sano.*" The incapacitated and the physically and mentally weak go to the wall in the battle for existence, and the nervous system breaks down and insanity is the result."

2. " *The use of intoxicants.*—Such as alcohol and *cannabis indica* (bhang and ganja) is resorted to to a great extent generally in India, and this district is no exception to the practice. The intoxicants are taken for various purposes, *viz.*, to sharpen the mental faculties, to produce pleasureable feelings, to increase appetite and improve digestion, to give courage and energy, to deaden pains and calm hunger, to increase virile power, to drown cares and anxieties, to produce homicidal and suicidal tendencies. "

" These might all be classified under the head of Toxic Insanity, when the individual loses all control over himself, and is a nuisance and danger to others.

3. *Insanity during the child-bearing period.*—Puerperal insanity, and also through fevers and visceral inflammations, which deserve separate notice, as there must be some cases attributable to these causes."

4. " *Heredity.*—Also must produce some cases."

On the same subject the Civil Surgeon of Sháhjahánpur says—

" The popular belief is that a large number of cases of insanity is due to debility following fever or starvation. *I have never heard it attributed to opium*, but a good many cases are attributed to drinking alcohol, or to indulgence in some form of *cannabis indica.*

" The *Indian hemp* plant is used as an intoxicant in various forms, *viz.*, bhang, the whole plant pounded into a paste with water and sugar. Some eat this in the form of pills, some drink it as an infusion. *Ganja*, the leaves and twigs are pressed together, dried and smoked like tobacco. *Churrus* is the dried juice of the whole plant, exuded ; it is smoked with or without tobacco. *Majoon* or *hashish* is a sort of sweetmeat made from an infusion of the leaves, mixed with sugar; it is chewed and swallowed like toffy."

239. **Causes of insanity.**—Dr. Cleghorn's interesting note on the Census of 1872 in the North-West Provinces quotes the same causes for insanity in India. It may be taken as clear that the causes mainly operative are (1) heredity, (2) intemperance, (3) chronic want of food, (4) stress of mental work or anxiety, (5) in women, uterine disorders and enforced widowhood.

It is estimated that in England recoveries from insanity amount to 40 per cent. of those cases, generally of acute mania the most incurable form of madness, which are sent to lunatic asylums, and that of the milder forms of insanity not sent to asylums probably 70 per cent. recover. It is therefore clear that, given a change in the causes operative to produce insanity, the population affected will change considerably in a decade. As it happens, we have in the caste statement for the present Census some indication of the causes principally operative of late years. The castes with population above 100,000, which amongst Hindus show the largest proportion of insanes are (1) Bharbhunja, (2) Bania, (3) Kayasth, (4) Sunar, (5) Bhat, (6) Fakir, (7) Bráhman, (8) Dom. Of these, three are trading castes, for whom the leading special cause of anxiety may be readily believed to be mental anxiety. Three are literate castes, two at least of which stand highest in intellectual power amongst the castes of the province. For Bráhmans at least intemperance cannot be considered to be operative. The leading cause of insanity for these three castes is, therefore, probably intellectual strain. There remain two castes probably, taken all, in all the most intemperate in the provinces. The figures for Doms are, however, affected by locality to a great extent, as they are almost all Himalayan in residence. Of castes with lower averages the spirit-drinking castes show a percentage of insanes in general slightly above average. The lowest percentages are amongst the temperate and hardworking agriculturists—Játs, Kurmis, Kachis and the like; Chamárs, the caste most likely to be affected by want of food, show a percentage below average. Again, amongst Muhammadans, the Sayyids and Pathans stand out with percentages of insane far above average, the first easily the most intellectual, the second possibly the most intemperate of Muhammadan castes. Muhammadans, as a rule, show a higher percentage of insane than Hindus, and Jains a still higher rate. The caste statements therefore tend to show that the causes of insanity most operative of late years are (1) mental strain (2) intemperance. The influence of the latter is far less marked than that of the former.

240. **Variation in the proportion of insanity in 1881 and 1891.**—Turning again to the comparative statement showing percentages of insanity for each age-period we find that heredity, to which early insanity must mainly be ascribed, and uterine diseases affecting women most largely from 20 to 24, show in the returns of the present census an increased effect, and that insanity due to other causes shows a decrease. From the known history of the provinces and the fact that insanity due to chronic insufficiency of food cannot be traced in the caste returns in Table XIIA, such a decrease might have been expected. The conclusion I draw from a consideration of all

[To face page 281.

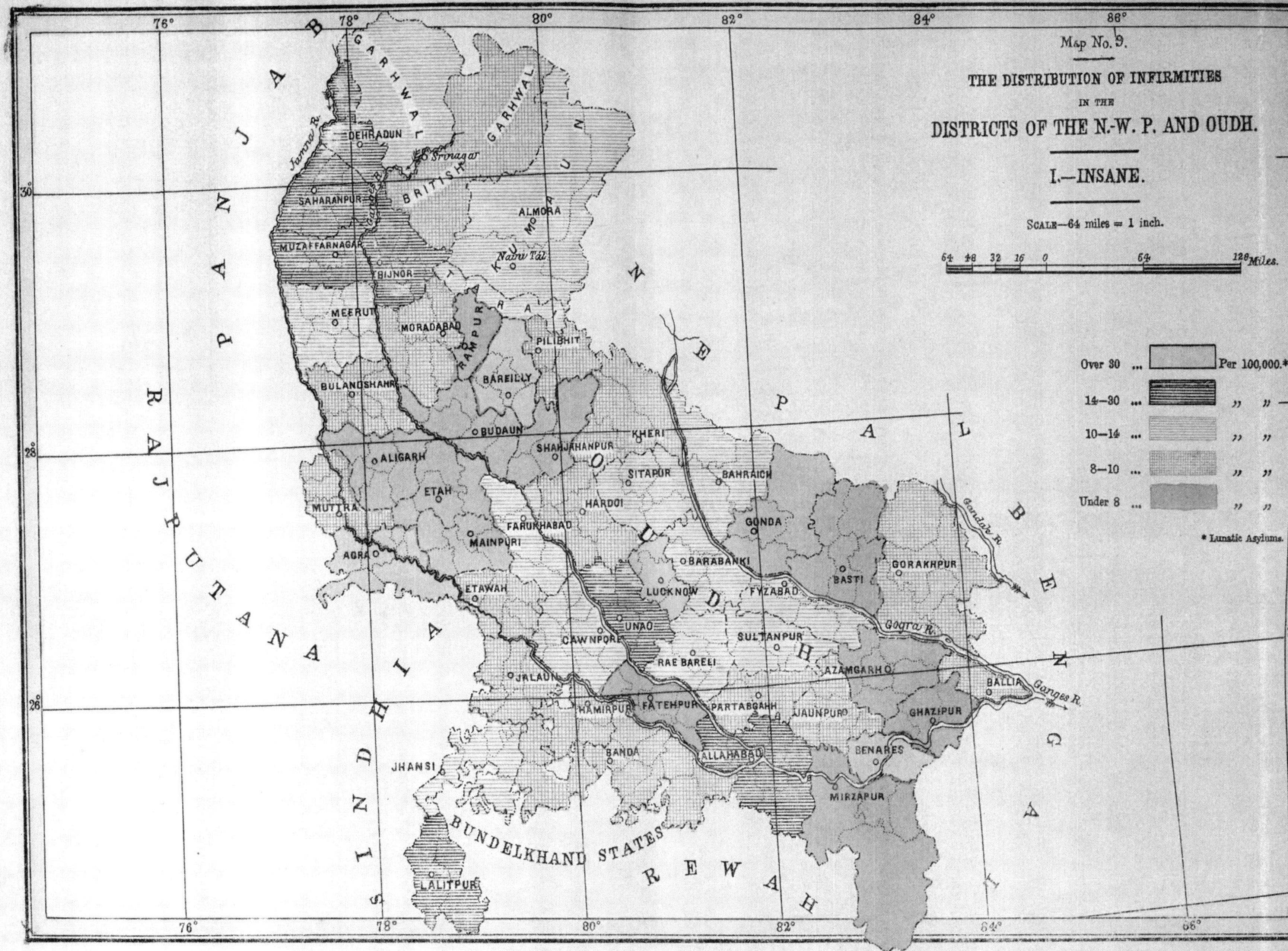

connected facts is that there has been within the past decade a considerable decrease in insanity, certainly not over-estimated by the comparison of the figures for the two censuses, and therefore at least 12 per cent. on the total insane population of 1881. The decrease has been spread over the provinces fairly evenly, the increases shown for certain districts, excluding those containing lunatic asylums, being in general only such as to bring them, in the percentage of insanity shown, more in line with their neighbours. There is one exception in Allahabad, the proportion of insane in which was high at last census and is now still higher. The fact is probably due to local accidental causes connected with the assemblage of pilgrims at the Magh Mela, who are likely to be followed by wandering beggars of weak intellect.

241. **Local distribution of insanity.**—In considering the distribution of insanity in districts of the provinces (see map No. 9) no clear connection between prevalence of insanity and climate or locality can be traced. Four districts in the province each contain a lunatic asylum, and accordingly show a very much higher percentage of insanity than the others. They are Bareilly, Agra, Benares and Lucknow. The death-rate amongst the lunatics in the asylums for a period of three years averaged 95 per thousand, between two and three times as much as that for the population in general, and nearly five times as much as the death-rate for the population above ten, amongst whom most of the persons in asylums must be. The death-rate is in itself enough to ensure a nearly complete change in the insane population in the course of ten years.

The average number of inmates in each asylum in 1890-91.

Bareilly	316
Agra	210
Benares	290
Lucknow	197

Apart from the asylum districts and excluding Allahabad already referred to, the largest proportion of lunacy is found in Central Oudh, the adjoining districts of Cawnpore and Farukhabad, and in a group of districts in the north-west of the provinces reaching along the foot of the hills to the Tarái. The lowest proportion of lunacy is in the eastern districts, Fatehpur and the Central Doab. I am unable to trace any underlying principle in this distribution. The consumption of drugs manufactured from hemp is considered accountable for a considerable proportion of temporary insanity of the kind which most commonly comes to the notice of District Officers, that in which mania is a prominent symptom. An attempt made to trace some correspondence between the consumption of drugs in districts, as indicated by the drug income and the total amount of insanity, failed to show any correspondence whatsoever. The cases in which the consumption of drugs and proportion of insanity were at opposite ends of the two scales for the same district were quite as numerous as those in which the two sets of statistics agreed in being high or low. The proportion of insane to total population along with the proportion of variation since 1881 are shown in Appendix No. XXVII.

242. **Comparison of proportion of insanity in the two sexes.**—The incidence of the recorded insane on total population shows rather more than double as much insanity amongst males as amongst females. This is in contrast to the English figures, which show 3,353 insane females per million

against 3,148 insane males. The disproportion exists in all districts including Garhwál, the only district in the provinces in which the enumeration of females was correct. It is still larger in the admissions to the lunatic asylums, where roughly three men are admitted for one woman. There can, I think, be no doubt that female insanity has to some extent been concealed, but there is no reason to believe that as in England insanity amongst women is as great as amongst men. The circumstances producing insanity are in India far more unequally distributed between the sexes than in England. The women of India are little affected either by mental anxiety, intellectual strain or intemperance.

ABSTRACT No. 96.

Showing the number of insane persons of each religion now and in 1881.

	Number.						Percentage on total religion.					
	1881.			1891.			1881.			1891.		
	Total.	Males	Females.	Total.	Males.	Females.	Total.	Males.	Females.	Total.	Males.	Females.
Hindu ...	5,133	3,594	1,539	4,623	3,186	1,437	·0135	·0081	·0084	·0114	0152	·0074
Musalmán ...	1,174	750	424	936	648	288	·0198	·0248	·0146	·0147	·0200	·0093
Jain ...	15	11	4	10	7	3	·0188	·0261	·0108	·0118	·0153	·0076
Christian ...	25	12	13	12	6	6	·0524	·0385	·0790	·0205	·0161	·0284
Other religions ...	...	...	...	...	...	...	...	...	...	...	...	...
Total ...	6,347	4,367	1,980	5,581	3,847	1,734	·0144	·0191	·0093	·0119	·0158	·0077

243. **Insanity in the different religions.**—The figures for Native Christians cannot be regarded as having any bearing on the subject, both because the total insane number only nine, and because there are so many orphan refuges in charge of Christian Missionaries, into which insane children would be apt to drift, to be classed for the future as Christians. The accompanying statement comparing the amount of insanity in each religion is of interest for other religions. It shows 147 insane Muhammadans against 114 insane Hindus, the excess taking place alike amongst males and females. Male Jains show a slightly larger proportion of insanity than Hindus; female Jains a slightly smaller proportion. The number of insane Jains is, however, so small that no inference of any value can be drawn from the comparison. Why the proportion of insanes should be larger amongst Muhammadans than Hindus is doubtful. They are somewhat more educated than Hindus. The danger of consanguineous marriages is probably somewhat greater amongst them. On the other hand, as a class they indulge less in either spirits or hemp drugs than Hindus do. Opium, which they do indulge into a greater extent than Hindus, has invariably been asserted not to produce insanity.

244. **Insanity in different castes.**—A statement comparing insanity amongst different castes deduced from Table XIIA has already been referred to. It is given in Appendix, No XXVIII and shows the percentage of insane for all castes with a population of over 100,000. For smaller castes the percentages must be regarded as useless, as the addition of one or two insane persons would affect the percentage materially. Sayyads show a far higher percentage of insane than any other group amongst either the Muhammadans

or the Hindus. The lowest proportion of insane is amongst the Hindu cultivating castes, several of which are amongst the spirit-drinking castes, and singularly enough amongst Muhammadan Rájputs, for whom the proportion of insane, 4 per 10,000, contrasts with that for Hindu Rájputs, 14 per 10,000. I have nothing to add to the inferences already drawn from the caste returns, that education and business anxieties are the most prominent causes of insanity, and that after them the intemperate use of drugs is probably most effective. Neither spirit-drinking to the extent to which it is possible for a low-caste Hindu to indulge in it, nor chronic starvation appear from the caste statement to have had any effect on the returns for the present Census.

245. **Comparison with European countries.**—The contrast between the proportion of insane persons in India, and in European countries as indicated in the margin is very striking indeed. That there are omissions in the Indian record of persons whose insanity is not of a very pronounced type is certain. Such omissions occur to a very large extent even in the English Census lists. The last published English Census report noted that on attempting to trace in the Census schedules the names of insane children as received from a private asylum, it was found that mention of the infirmity had in half the undoubted cases been omitted by the parents. In India probably the omissions are proportionately more extensive and extend to the adult population as well as to minors. An Indian cultivator's standard of the brain power necessary to save from idiocy would possibly be lower than that adopted in England. But, all possible omissions considered, it is certain that the proportion of insane in the North-West Provinces is not one-tenth of that in England. The proportion according to our returns amounts to almost exactly one-tenth in the case of our most highly educated and intellectual caste, and to one-thirtieth or thereby in the ordinary cultivating castes of the country.

Abstract No. 97, comparing the proportion of insanes recorded in these provinces with those of European countries.

Country.	Insane per 10,000 population.	
	Males.	Females.
North-West Provinces ...	1·58	·76
England and Wales	31	33
Scotland	38	39
Ireland	38	34
Italy	8	6
Austria	22	19
Hungary	22	18
Portugal	23	17
Victoria	37	31
New Zealand	33	22
U. S. America	35	32

Part II.—DEAF-MUTES.

246. **The variation in the proportion of deaf-mutism.**—The total number of deaf-mutes recorded in the present Census was 32,896, of whom 21,225 were males and 11,671 females. This represents an increase over the figures of last Census of 5,247 persons, 3,597 males and 1,650 females. The instructions to enumerators provided that only those persons who had been deaf and dumb from birth should be recorded. This, though a good working rule for persons who are not experts in surgery, is inaccurate, as an indication of the record actually made, as it is impossible to distinguish in practice between deaf-mutism, which is congenital and that which has been acquired

before a child has learned to speak. Statistics quoted in the 1881 English Census report show that in England about 37 per cent. of the cases of deaf-mutism recorded are not congenital, and that in Bavaria 80 per cent. of deaf-mutism is congenital, and 20 per cent. acquired, 16 per cent. before the age of 5, and the rest after that age. There is reason, to be referred to hereafter, to believe that in India the proportions are very different. The matter has now only been referred to make clear what has or should have been recorded. The increase in deaf-mutes in the present Census contrasts with the decrease recorded in other infirmities, and it has just to be decided how far it is real or due to incomplete enumeration at last Census or excess of enumeration at the present. On this question the most reliable information we have is contained in the distribution by age-periods of deaf-mutes at the Census of 1881 and for the present Census. The statement in the margin compares the proportion borne by deaf-mutes to the total population for each age-period now and in 1881. It may be observed from this abstract and from comparison of the 1881 and 1891 Tables that there is both an actual and a proportionate increase in the entries under all age-periods except the last. It also appears, if the 1891 figures for each age-period are compared with those of 1881 for a period ten years lower, that the 1891 figures are in general in excess of those for 1881. The inference is clear that the increase has not been a real one, and that either there have been omissions in 1881 or that persons have been wrongly included in 1891 to a greater extent than at the earlier Census. The idea that persons not deaf and dumb from infancy, but who have become deaf in after-life may have been included, at once suggests itself. Deafness is a disease that is most prevalent in late life and that remains through life. It is therefore clear that if such cases have been included, the proportion of persons afflicted will rise from age-period to age-period reaching their maximum in the latest age-period. Referring to the age abstract above given, there appears at once to be reason to believe that persons who are simply deaf have to some extent been included in the

Abstract No. 98, comparing the total number of deaf-mutes recorded in the provinces at this and the two preceding censuses.

		Total.	Males.	Females.
North-Western Provinces ...	1872 ...	7,942	5,506	2,436
	1881 ...	20,162	12,874	7,288
	18·1 ...	22,977	14,822	8,155
Oudh	1881 ...	7,487	4,754	2,733
	1891 ...	9,919	6,403	3,516
North-Western Provinces and Oudh	1881 ...	27,649	17,628	10.021
	1891 ...	32,896	21,225	11,671

Abstract No. 99, showing proportion of deaf-mutes at each age-period to 10,000 of total population in 1881 and 1891.

Age.	1881.		1891.	
	Males.	Females.	Males.	Females.
0—4	2·2	1·5	2 90	1·76
5—9	7·3	4 7	9·24	5·63
10—14	9·1	6·3	10·16	6·30
15—19	9·7	5·0	10·82	6·21
20—29	8·8	4·3	9·69	5·15
30—39	7·0	3·8	8·68	4 83
40—49	7·1	4·4	8·43	5·27
50—59	8·0	5 9	9·36	6·26
60 and over	14·5	10·4	12·52	8·45
Total ...	7·7	4·7	8 73	5·16

age-periods from 50 and upwards, but, at the same time, it is clear that they have been included to a still greater extent in 1881, the figures in the last age-period of which are actually higher than those in the last age-period now. Those wrongly included now number, if the life-period of a deaf mute be not far from as good as that of a person not so afflicted, about 1,300 persons, more if the death-rate amongst deaf-mutes is materially above the normal. It appears, however, that no part of the rise can be explained by excess of wrongful inclusion in 1891, but that rather it is added to by the more numerous incorrect inclusions in 1881. A reference to the figures for districts will give us some clue to the explanation. It will be seen that variations are many of them violent, and that they generally result in doing away with equally violent variations from district to district in the 1881 figures; *e.g.*, the largest proportion of variation is in Azamgarh. The number of deaf and dumb shown at last Census was 259; that at the present Census 1,005. Azamgarh has now 58 deaf-mutes per 100,000 of population against 68 in Basti and 60 in Ballia. It is clear that the figures for Azamgarh at last Census were inadequate. The next largest variation is in Sultánpur, 329 to 821. Sultánpur has now 76 per 100,000 against 64 in Bara Banki and 67 in Fyzabad. It is somewhat higher than either of its neighbours now, but was clearly far too low at last Census. On the other hand, there are somewhat violent decreases Moradabad has fallen from 1,264 to 510. It now shows 43 per 100,000 against 52 in its neighbour Budaun. It is clear that it was proportionately much too high at last Census. On the whole, the results of the variations have been to make the variations from district to district far less abrupt than they were at last Census. It is probable therefore that the large rise exhibited is mainly due to omissions at last Census.

247. **Extent of concealment of deaf-mutism.**—Deaf-mutism is an infirmity about which, unlike insanity, there is in general no chance of there being two opinions, and therefore it might well be expected to be more fully recorded than insanity. There does, however, occur a form of concealment of a nature which the English report terms excusable. It is referred to in the following extract:—

> "There is no reason to suppose that the returns of the deaf and dumb were vitiated, as were those of idiots and imbeciles, by distinctly wilful omissions. But there can be no doubt that here also many excusable omissions were made in the first age-period, that is, among children under five years of age. Parents are often not aware of the deafness of their infants; and, even when an impartial observer would have no doubt as to the fact, the parent, not unnaturally, hopes on against hope, and will not publicly acknowledge as a fact what he as yet refuses to accept as a certainty even to himself."

The amount of the concealment may be estimated as indicated in the English report by supposing that the proportion of deaf and dumb in the age-periods in which concealment takes place was the same as in the subsequent age-periods for which the returns are correct. In this procedure an error of excess, due to the fact that the death of a deaf and dumb child is more probable than that of a sound child is corrected by an error of defect due to the fact that some children do not become deaf and dumb till after five. There is probably some defect in the age-period—10 to 14; but it is trifling and may be neglected. The omissions in the earlier age-periods would, preserving the same proportion of males and females as in the later age-periods, imply a total defect of 5,466 persons, considerably more than can be supposed to have been added in later life of persons deaf, but not dumb. The enumeration as shown in the tables, therefore, probably errs in defect rather than excess.

248. **The local distribution of deaf-mutism.**—The district figures are compared in detail for all three Censuses in Appendix No. XXIX, which also shows the percentage of variations between the figures of 1881 and 1891.

Deaf-mutism (see map No. 10) appears from a comparison of the proportion borne by persons afflicted to total population in different districts to be to a much greater extent than other infirmities peculiarly prevalent in certain localities. The Himalayan districts, including Dehra Dún, show considerably the largest incidence. They are closely followed by the Sub-Himalayan districts in the north of Oudh and beyond the Gogra, and at some little interval by those of Bundelkhand. Three Oudh districts, Sitapur, Fyzabad and Sultánpur, close to the south of the Sub-Himalayan districts and a strip from the Tarái through Bijnor to Muzaffarnagar complete the area in which deaf-mutism is most prevalent; Sahâranpur and Pilibhít alone break the series of Sub-Himalayan districts showing a high incidence. The districts of minimum incidence are scattered through the centre of the provinces from Moradabad to Mirzapur, including Moradabad, Rámpur (the infirmity statistics for which appear unreliable) Aligárh, Mainpuri, Sháhjahánpur, Hardoi, Fatehpur and Mirzapur.

The English Census showed a considerable excess of deaf-mutism in the mountainous countres of England. This fact is even more clearly visible in the returns for the North-Western Provinces, as all that are to any extent mountainous are amongst those in which the proportion of deaf-mutism is highest. Along with the mountainous districts amongst those which show the highest figures are those which though not mountainous are by reputation the most malarious in the provinces. It is probable that in the distribution of the infirmity, we have an indication of the principal causes in these provinces. Where congenital, its origin is believed by surgeons to be closely allied to insane necrosis, so that it might be expected to be most important in those districts in which insanity was most prevalent. In the North-Western Provinces, however, insanity is below average in most of the districts in which deaf-mutism is most prevalent. The distribution of the latter indeed approaches more closely to that of leprosy than to any other infirmity. This distribution appears to warrant the belief that in these provinces deaf-mutism is less frequently congenital than in England, and much more frequently due to those zymotic diseases to which 40 per cent. of the English deaf-mutism is due. The prevalence of such disease to an unusual extent in the insanitary villages of the Himalayas and Bundelkhand and amongst the damp malarious forests of the Sub-Himalayan tract can easily be believed and in fact is known to exist.

249. **Comparison with deaf-mutism in European countries.**—The comparative extent of deaf-mutism in these provinces and elsewhere in India

[To face Page 296.

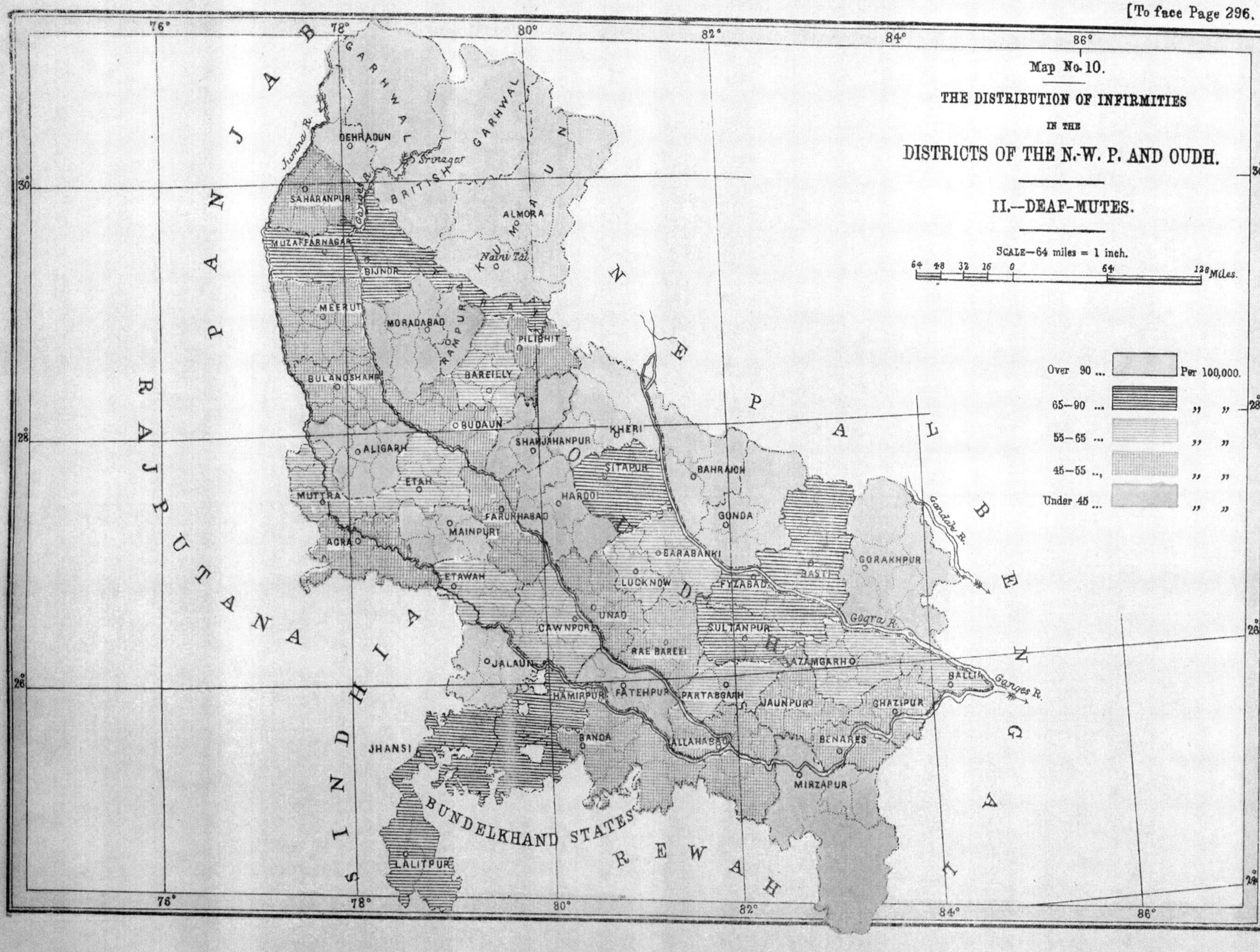

and in European countries is shown in the marginal abstract. Unlike the closely allied insanity, it is more prevalent in India than in most European countries. Successive English Census returns show a steady decrease. In 1861 there were for the United Kingdom one deaf and dumb person in 1,484; in 1871 one in 1,742; in 1881 one in 1,794. The gradual but pronounced improvement is believed to be due to improved and extended sanitary measures and to improved medical knowledge. The time has not yet come when improved medical knowledge can be believed to be approaching the homes of Indian children, but improvement in sanitation is possible to an extent far greater than in England.

Abstract No. 100, *comparing the proportion of deaf-mutes recorded in these provinces with other Indian provinces and Foreign countries.*

Country.	Number of deaf-mutes per 100,000 of population.
North-Western Provinces and Oudh	70
Bengal	94
Panjáb	97
Madras	76
England and Wales	55
Scotland	25
Ireland	75
Italy	55
Austria	130
Hungary	130
Portugal	25
Ceylon	15
Victoria	35
New Zealand	20
U. S. America	65

250. **Comparative deaf-mutism in the sexes.**—The disproportion between the sexes already noticed for insanes extends also to deaf-mutes, but to a somewhat smaller extent. For each 100 male deaf-mutes there are 55 females so afflicted. The English figures show an inequality also, there being for 100 males only 80 females. The inequality is still greater in Austria, with 73 females to 100 males. Deaf-mutism does not appear to be concealed to any considerable extent in adults, and though the figures for females are probably to some extent too low, there is no reason to believe, as in the case of lepers, that they are greatly in defect.

251. **Deaf-mutism by religion.**—The accompanying statement shows the figures for deaf-mutes distributed by religion for the last two censuses and the proportions borne by the deaf-mutes, males and females, of each religion to the total of each sex. Muhammadans show a higher proportion both of males and females who are deaf-mutes than do Hindus. Jains are distinctly better than either of the religions just mentioned. The excess in Muhammadans is due to their being in excess in the Sub-Himalayan districts, which are most affected; the defect in Jains is probably due to their superior sanitary surroundings as a whole; they are generally well-to-do, comparatively well-housed, well-clad and well-looked after

Abstract No. 101, *showing the number of deaf-mutes of each religion now and in* 1881.

Religion.		Number.			Percentage on total religion.		
		Total.	Males.	Females.	Total.	Males.	Females.
Hindu	1881 ...	23,715	15,259	8,456	·0623	·0770	·0464
	1891 ...	27,892	18,115	9,777	·0691	·0864	·0503
Musalmán	1881 ...	3,864	2,324	1,540	·0652	·0769	·0531
	1891 ...	4,944	3,075	1,869	·0779	·0948	·0602
Jain	1881 ...	36	27	9	·0450	·0640	·0242
	1891 ...	25	18	7	·0295	·0394	·0180
Christian	1881 ...	33	17	16	·0692	·0545	·0972
	1891 ...	35	17	18	·0599	·0456	·0851
Other religions.	1881 ...	1	1	...	·0252	·0335	...
	1891 ...	...	...	...	...	...	...
Total...	1881 ...	27,649	17,628	10,021	·0627	·0769	·0473
	1891 ...	32,896	21,225	11,671	·0701	·0873	·0516

when children. Christians, the returns for whom are of little value, are better than Hindus and Muhammadans as regards males, worse as regards females. The figures are affected no doubt, as in the case of insanes, by the number of deaf-mutes in, or brought up in, Christian Orphanages.

252. **Deaf-mutism by caste.**—In the caste figures for this infirmity there is little that is noticeable. The largest proportion is amongst Doms, largely a hill caste, and the most insanitary of hill castes. Gonds are next, a somewhat inexplicable fact, as they live mostly in the eastern districts in which the infirmity is little prevalent. The close cultivating castes, Kurmis, Muraos, Koeries, in general show a proportion above average. It is not unreasonable to suppose that this is due to their fondness for their manure heaps. Rájputs and Bráhmans are above average, no doubt because of the large numbers of them in the hill and Sarjupar districts. Banias, in this *as in every other infirmity*, show a proportion above average. Chamárs have a proportion of deaf-mutes much below average, a fact which may possibly be due to their living for the most part in small abadies separate from the main village. Pasis are also well below average. For Muhammadans, Pathans, Sheikhs, and Julahas have the largest proportions. It appears clear that deaf-mutism varies with locality far more than with castes, and that no definite principles can be gathered from the caste return.

Part III.—THE BLIND.

253. **Decrease in blindness since last Census.**—The total number of blind persons in the province as enumerated at the present Census was 109,913. Males and females were nearly in equal numbers, the former being somewhat in excess. The enumeration showed a decrease since last Census of 19,925 blind persons or 15·34 per cent. of the whole. The decrease was largest amongst females, being for them 13,729, or 20 per cent. against 6,196 or 10 per cent. in males. A comparision of the age-table for blind at each Census shows that there has been an actual and comparative increase in the figures for both males and females under 5, and that in the other age-periods there has been a comparative decrease gradually increasing until it is greatest and very considerable in the highest age-periods. Subsequent remarks will show that a considerable decrease might

Abstract No. 102, *comparing the total number of blind persons recorded in the provinces at this and the two preceding censuses.*

Province or country.		Total.	Males.	Females.
North-Western Provinces ...	1872 ...	66,751	37,360	29,391
	1881 ...	92,797	44,826	47,971
	1891 ...	74,190	37,872	36,318
Oudh	1881 ...	37,041	16,834	20,207
	1891 ...	35,723	17,592	18,131
North-Western Provinces and Oudh.	1881 ...	129,838	61,660	68,178
	1891 ...	109,913	55,464	54,449

Abstract No. 103, *showing now and in* 1881, *the proportion of blind persons at each age-period to* 10,000 *of total population.*

Age-period.	1881.		1891.	
	Males.	Females.	Males.	Females.
0—4	6·9	4·8	9·19	5·39
5—9	13·2	10·1	12·73	8·74
10—14	17·4	13·8	15·57	12·08
15—19	19·7	15·5	18·50	13·50
20—29	20·8	17·0	19·09	14·59
30—39	22·5	24·8	20·45	21·56
40—49	30·3	41·7	26·33	31·41
50—59	54·6	73·9	41·49	53·07
60 and over	143·4	184·0	97·94	116·73
Total ...	26·9	32·2	22·82	24·09

have been anticipated, but an examination of the district figures gives reason to believe that in a few districts the decrease is larger than can be explained by the causes operative. I regard as not considerable the danger of an excess in the entries to any considerable extent at last Census by inclusion of persons blind of one eye, as the Hindustani words to express complete blindness and blindness in one eye are altogether different, and the word "andha" would rarely or never be applied where "kana" was meant. I cannot help suspecting that in Aligarh, Mirzapur, Unao, and perhaps Gorakhpur and Basti, there may have been some defect in the present enumeration, as the decreases shown in these districts have had the effect of bringing the incidence of blindness in them below that in their neighbours. The error was, however, by no means so considerable as to affect total results. By far the greater part of the decrease is real and can be explained.

254. **The causes of blindness.**—The causes of blindness have been more thoroughly enquired into by the Civil Surgeons of the province than those of any other infirmity, as in almost every district of the province a large proportion of the surgical operations performed are for the removal of cataract—Dr. Temple Wright's remarks on the subject may be quoted, though I should be sorry to hold myself responsible for certain of the opinions expressed.

"No doubt blindness is partly caused by small-pox, but I really do not think small-pox is so destructive to sight as starvation; and such is the opinion of all of my brother-officers with whom I have conversed on the subject."

"The poorer classes of natives *never get enough food,* even when they are in ordinary health, and when they are ill from *fever* the commonest form of disease, they *cannot eat,* so they (if they don't die) go about in a chronic state of debility.

"The eye contains some of the most delicate tissues in the whole body, and besides its general debility which it shares with the rest of the fever-stricken body, it has its own special cause of debility in the pain caused by the light, not only from the sun, but also when reflected from the ground, from water, from walls and clothes.

"After an attack of fever, I myself felt the glare of the sunlight, whether direct or reflected, far more intolerable than before I had fever.

"After fevers, the commonest disorders in India are indigestion and bowel complaints, which are accompanied by disagreeable taste in the mouth."

"To obtain a better taste, the poor Indian, uninstructed in physiology, eats pan and drinks tobacco (as he phrases it) very frequently without any food in his stomach, but though the taste in the mouth may be improved, the vitality of the stomach and heart is diminished. Dyspepsia notoriously is decreased by giving hydrochloric acid to aid the stomach in dissolving the food.

"But common table salt, *chloride of sodium,* is a Government monopoly, and the price charged in effect puts such a *heavy tax on it, that neither the people nor the cattle get enough salt to keep them in health.*"

255. **Small-pox as a cause of blindness.**—Dr. Cleghorn, in his note on the infirmity figures of the 1872 Census, points out that before introduction of vaccination into England, 35 per cent. of the cases of blindness were due to small-pox, and believes that the proportion in India was the same in 1872. Vaccination has increased largely since, and it is probable that the proportion is now, all ages together, somewhat smaller. The appended statement shows the average incidence of deaths by small-pox on the total population

of each district for the last twenty-two years. The variations are large. Oudh, the most backward part of the provinces as regards vaccination, is the home of small-pox. Small-pox is above average in Bundelkhand, Meerut and Rohilkhand. The Agra and Benares Divisions are freest from it after Kumaun, in which the incidence is very small indeed.

Abstract No. 104, *showing the ratio of deaths from small-pox in each district : average for the past* 22 *years.*

Serial number.	District.	Total.	Average.	Remarks.
1	Dehra Dún	1·42	·06	
2	Sahāranpur	31·47	1·43	
3	Muzaffarnagar	32·82	1·49	
4	Meerut	8·90	·40	
5	Bulandshahr	27·37	1·24	
6	Aligarh	27·10	1·23	
7	Muttra	8·85	·40	
8	Agra	14·80	·67	
9	Farukhabad	22·42	1·02	
10	Mainpuri	16·48	·75	
11	Etáwah	26·89	1·22	
12	Etah	26·70	1·21	
13	Bareilly	37·55	1·53	
14	Bijnor	45·48	2·07	
15	Budaun	39·51	1·80	
16	Moradabad	35·73	1·62	
17	Sháhjahánpur	36·74	1·67	
18	Pilibhít	13·85	1·08	
19	Cawnpore	26·07	1·19	
20	Fatehpur	26·84	1·22	
21	Bánda	22·16	1·01	
22	Hamírpur	25·35	1·15	
23	Allahabad	22·65	1·03	
24	Jhánsi	36·85	1·68	
25	Jalaun	13·79	·63	
26	Lalitpur	50·18	2·28	
27	Benares	8·40	·38	
28	Mirzapur	22·30	1·01	
29	Jaunpur	18·24	·83	
30	Gházipur	17·85	·81	
31	Ballia	5·34	·45	
32	Gorakhpur	36·51	1·66	
33	Basti	27·47	1·25	
34	Azamgarh	19·08	·87	
35	Kumaun	1·72	·08	
36	Garhwál	·65	·03	
37	Tarái	11·81	·54	
38	Lucknow	43·85	1·99	
39	Unao	56·09	2·55	
40	Rae Bareli	48·47	2·20	
41	Sitapur	47·89	2·18	
42	Hardoi	48·47	2·20	
43	Kheri	32·80	2·49	
44	Fyzabad	28·14	1·28	
45	Gonda	53·07	2·41	
46	Bahraich	53·27	2·42	
47	Sultánpur	28·76	1·31	
48	Partábgarh	45·36	2·06	
49	Bara Banki	43·78	1·99	
	Total, N.-W. P. and Oudh ...	29·92	1·36	

The incidence of blindness, as will be seen, roughly corresponds, but the agreement between district figures for small-pox and those for blind is so far from close that small-pox cannot be regarded as the chief cause operative in producing blindness.

Dr. Cleghorn's remarks on the chief cause believed to be operative are as follows :—

" Even after deducting 35 per cent. as due to small-pox, there still remains one blind person in every 707 of the population, a ratio much greater than is found in all European countries except Norway. Sufficient reasons to account for this excess are to be found in the general poverty of the lower classes, the inferior quality of their food (especially in fatty and saline principles), overcrowding in unventilated houses, the general prevalence of malarial fevers and enlargements of the spleen, and the presence of the leprosy taint. All of these conditions are highly favourable to the developement of cataract and inflamatory affections of the eye. Intense sunlight, leading to overstimulation of the retina, and the irritating smoke from cow-dung, the common fuel of the country, may be mentioned as exciting causes of eye disease of general application in these provinces."

256. **Reasons for the decrease in blindness.**—One important reason for a decrease in the number of blind during the present decade is that this, the main cause of blindness in the provinces, has been, as the history of the province shows, less operative in the present than in preceding decades. The decade has been, on the whole, except in certain districts, one of more than average prosperity. There has been no famine as in 1868 and 1877, no severe fever epidemic as in 1879. It is natural, therefore, to suppose that the additions to the blind population during the past decade have been fewer than in former periods, and that a part of the decrease has been so caused.

The second cause of decrease, less conjectural and probably more operative than the first, is the great increase in the application of improved surgical methods to eye disease in the provinces. The statement in the margin shows for each of the ten years of the decade the number of cataract operations performed in the dispensaries of the provinces The total number of operations was 54,535, of which 47,081 or 86 per cent. were either completely successful or gave relief. In the previous decade we have against this operations in European dispensaries probably less than one-third as numerous and a proportion of the cases now taken to English surgeons treated by "sattiahs" or native eye surgeons; it can have been only a comparatively small proportion, because the sattiah is expensive, and the English surgery costs nothing. The highest percentage of temporary success achieved by the sattiah's methods even in England was 50 per cent. In India the percentage of success must have been lower still, and as the presence of the depressed lens left in the eye by the sattiah's operation frequently causes inflammation and total destruction of the eye, the relief given was often temporary even in the percentage of successful cases. All things considered, there can be little doubt that the excess of successful eye operations within the present decade is not less than 25,000 more than in previous decades. This in itself is more than the total gross decrease in blind. Allowing for the operation of the first cause quoted, it is clear that a proportionate decrease not less than that shown in the tables might have been expected.

Abstract No. 105, showing for each of the ten years of the decade the number of cataract operations performed in the dispensaries of the provinces.

Year.	Performed during the year.	Cured or relieved.	Discharged otherwise.
1881 ...	2,640	2,097	551
1882 ...	3,521	2,775	658
1883 ...	4,641	3,788	812
1884 ...	6,084	5,101	896
1885 ...	6,048	5,299	838
1886 ...	5,506	4,790	684
1887 ...	5,625	4,843	724
1888 ...	6,022	5,352	668
1889 ...	6,784	6,060	610
1890 ...	7,664	6,976	648
Total ...	54,535	47,081	7,089

The age figures agree with the explanations given of the cause of decrease. It is greatest in the later age-periods amongst those persons most liable to cataract and most likely to seek relief in hospitals.

Abstract No. 106, showing blind persons per 100,000 on total population.

No.	District	
1	Dehra Dún	167·73
2	Saháranpur	268·46
3	Muzaffarnagar	347·80
4	Meerut	261·95
5	Bulandshahr	250·55
6	Aligarh	167·28
	Total, Meerut Division ...	252 09
7	Muttra	368·79
8	Agra	278·88
9	Farukhabad	190·06
10	Mainpuri	223·18
11	Etáwah	246·98
12	Etah	220·63
	Total, Agra Division ...	254 00
13	Bareilly	268·57
14	Bijnor	347·32
15	Budaun	265·34
16	Moradabad	317·02
17	Sháhjahánpur	180·61
18	Pilibhit	227·46
	Total, Rohilkhand Division ...	271 56
19	Cawnpore	306·96
20	Fatehpur	314·38
21	Bánda	325·43
22	Hamírpur	385·81
23	Allahabad	167·28
24	Jhánsi	374·44
25	Jalaun	230·09
26	Lalitpur	275·35
	Total, Allahabad Division ...	277·55
27	Benares	155·97
28	Mirzapur	113·99
29	Jaunpur	97·40
30	Gházipur	245·94
31	Ballia	125·73
	Total, Benares Division ...	145·85
32	Gorakhpur	102·77
33	Basti	127·06
34	Azámgarh	168·00
	Total, Gorakhpur Division ...	126·76
35	Kumaun	163·89
36	Garhwál	169·20
37	Tarái	222·74
	Total, Kumaun Division ...	176·22
	Total, N.-W. Provinces ...	216·59
38	Lucknow	380·93
39	Unao	297·60
40	Rae Bareli	363·43
41	Sitapur	362·75
42	Hardoi	215 68
43	Kheri	282·09
	Total, Lucknow Division ...	314·27
44	Fyzabad	320·65
45	Gonda	121·16
46	Bahraich	198·92
47	Sultánpur	328·50
48	Partábgarh	266·22
49	Bara Banki	327·08
	Total, Fyzabad Division ...	254·89
	Total, Oudh ...	258·68
	Total, N.-W. Provinces and Oudh ...	234·33
50	Rampur	131·16
51	Tehri Garhwál	124·77
	Total, Native States ...	129·81

[To face page 303.

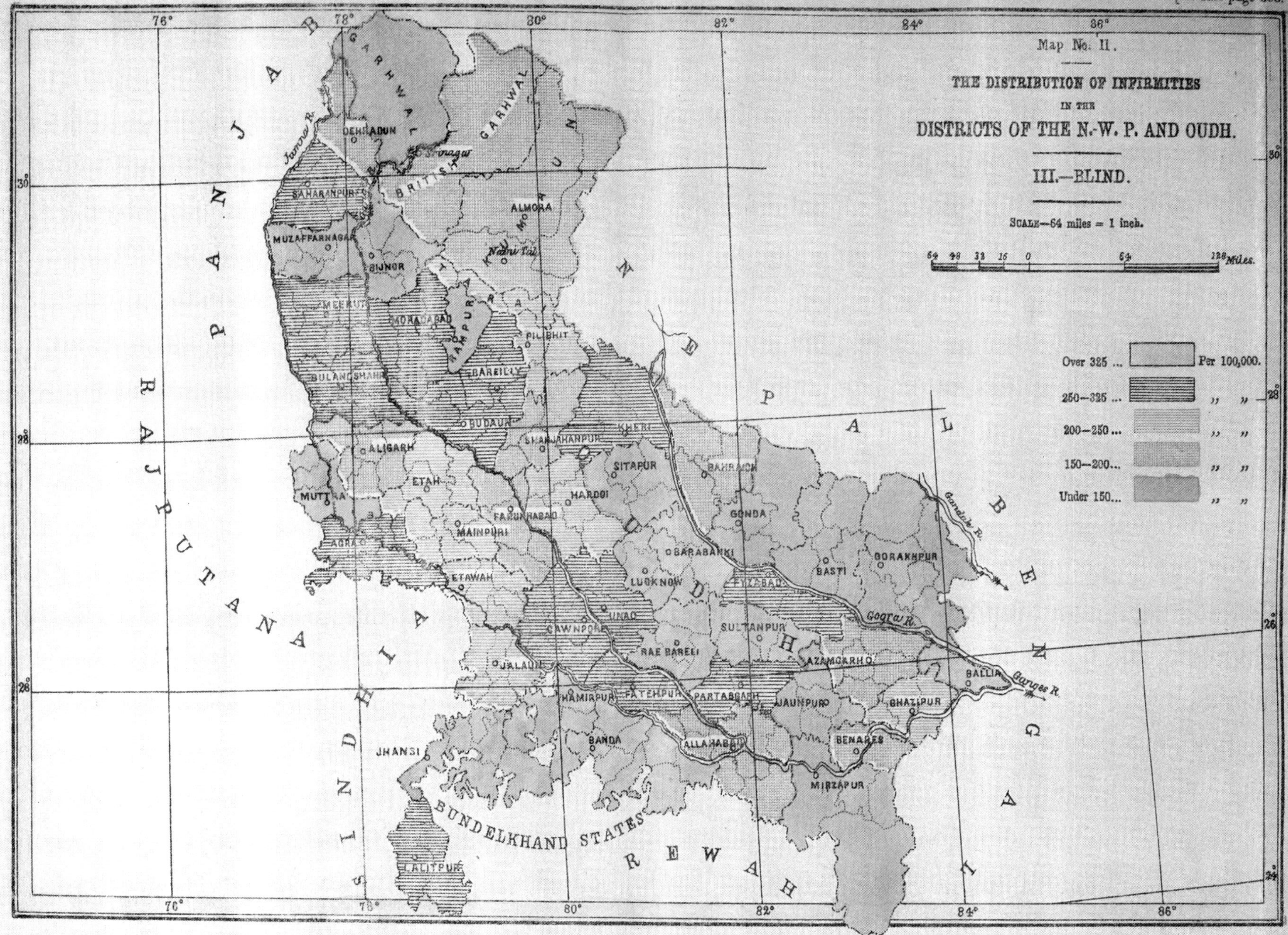

257. **The local distribution of blindness.**—The distribution of blind in the provinces is shown in the accompanying map (No. 11) and abstract No. 106. The infirmity is greatly in excess in Oudh Cis-Gogra, except Hardoi, in Bundelkhand, the Upper Doab and Rohilkhand. It is least in the eastern and Trans-Gogra districts and in the Himalayas. Cawnpore and Fatehpur lying between Oudh and Bundelkhand, and Agra and Muttra bordering on Native States have also a proportion of blind above average. The distribution as already stated agrees roughly with the distribution of epidemic small-pox.

258. **Proportion of blindness in the sexes.**—Blindness is an infirmity which there is no tendency to conceal, and is therefore as fully recorded amongst females as amongst males. The proportion of blindness was greatest amongst females, there being 2,409 blind females per million against 2,282 blind males. This is in opposition to English statistics, which show 953 blind males and 809 blind females per million of each sex. English statisticians consider that in view of the greater liability of males to disease causing blindness such a disproportion of the sexes might have been expected. In India, however, it can only be said of the men of the better classes that they are more exposed to risk of blindness than their female relatives. Low caste women, as a rule share their husbands' labours in the sunshine and are more exposed than they to the constant iritant effect of cow-dung smoke.

Referring to the caste statement, we find that for the higher castes the excess of blind males though less than in England is marked. Thus for the military and dominant group, in general well-to-do and whose women do not in general labour in the fields, there are 4,850 blind men for 3,827 blind women; amongst Bráhmans there are 5,729 blind men against 4,862 blind women; amongst the trading castes 1,996 blind men against 1,664 blind women; amongst Sayyids 319 blind men against 255 blind women. On the other hand, of low castes whose wives work in the fields we have for the cultivating group 6,974 males blind against 7,140 women; for fishermen 2,448 males and 2,650 females, for the Pasi group 1,569 males, 1,692 females; for Chamárs 6,627 males, 7,683 females. It appears from a comparison of the figures for the sexes that amongst people of good position males are more exposed to blindness than females; that amongst the poorer classes whose wives do not work in the fields, men and women are alike exposed to blindness and that amongst those classes whose women do work in the fields, the women are most exposed to risk.

259. **Blindness in different religions.**—The comparative figures for religions are what might have been expected from these remarks. Hindus and Muhammadans all over show much the same proportion of blindness; but amongst Hindus it is considerably in excess for women whilst amongst Muhammadans the proportion for each sex is nearly the same.

Jains show far fewer blind than either of the first mentioned religions and the proportion for women amongst them is still lower. For Christians the total proportion of blindness is below average, but it is above average for women, no doubt from accidental causes.

Abstract No. 107, *showing the number of blind persons of each religion now and in* 1881.

	Number.						Percentage on total religion.					
	1881.			1891.			1881.			1891.		
	Total.	Males.	Females.	Total.	Males.	Females.	Total.	Males.	Females.	Total.	Males.	Females.
Hindu	110,085	52,021	58,064	94,802	47,754	47,048	·2893	·2626	·3183	·2348	·2279	·2422
Musalman ...	19,457	9,489	9,968	14,902	7,600	7,302	·3285	·3139	·3437	·2348	·2343	·2358
Jain	190	108	82	62	42	20	·2376	·2558	·2208	·0733	·0906	·0513
Christian ...	98	41	57	124	57	67	·2056	·1314	·3464	·2122	·1528	·3168
Other religions ...	8	1	7	23	11	12	·2016	·3349	·7128	·0653	·0503	·0896
Total ...	129,838	61,660	68,178	109,913	55,464	54,449	·2943	·2691	·3217	·2343	·2282	·2409

260. **Blindness in different castes.**—The caste figures for blind convey less definite ideas in regard to the distribution of blindness than might have been expected owing to the very well marked territorial distribution of the infirmity. The influence of locality is so considerable as to operate to a greater extent than that of occupation or social condition. The Gonds resident in the east where blindness is least, show an incidence of blindness well below average, whilst that of the kindred Kahars scattered over the provinces is well above average. Bhuinhars, a caste of high standing resident entirely in the east, show the lowest percentage of blindness, whilst Bráhmans and Rájputs of similar social position show incidences which though below average are very materially higher than that for Bhuinhars. The highest percentage of blindness shown by any considerable caste is that for Kories, who are largely resident in Bundelkhand, a centre for small-pox and blindness. Their occupation, that of weaving, requiring close optical attention has no doubt also great influence, as we find the high incidence of blindness repeated for the corresponding class amongst Muhammadans, that of Julahas. Certain general principles may be inferred from the caste table. Low castes show higher percentages than high castes, agricultural and labouring castes higher than those whose avocations do not imply exposure to sun and weather. Education does not imply a high proportion of blindness, as the best educated castes, Kayasths, Sayyids and Bráhmans, show percentages considerably below normal. It is remarkable that in this as in all other infirmities Banias show a proportion of infirm considerably above average. The percentages of blindness for all castes with more than 100,000 persons are shown in Appendix No. XXVIII.

261. Comparison with foreign countries.—The prevalence of blindness in these and other Indian provinces is compared with that of certain European countries in the statement given in the margin. The incidence in these provinces though slightly below the Indian average, is *far* higher than in any European country for which I have seen the figures, excepting only Finland, where the incidence of blindness approaches to that in India.

Abstract No. 108, Blind per million living of each sex.

	Males.	Females.
North-Western Provinces and Oudh ...	2,282	2,409
Bengal	1,001	1,020
Panjáb	3,379	3,678
Bombay	1,495	1,478
Madras	1,005	1,039
England and Wales	953	809
Scotland	865	827
Ireland	1,141	1,219
Denmark	776	793
Norway	1,318	1,411
Sweden	767	843
Finland	1,514	2,938
German Empire	884	881
Hungary	1,280	1,123
Holland	499	394
Belgium	982	641
France	948	726
Spain	1,242	1,011
Italy	1,106	925

It could hardly have been otherwise. The risk to which Indian eyesight is exposed, is in every way greater than in European countries. Small-pox is far more prevalent. The average Hindu is from insufficient food and insanitary surroundings far less likely to be in a state of health in which his eyesight can resist the greater risk implied in exposure to the sun in this country. It is singular that in Europe the proportion of women blind is higher than that of men only in Ireland and in the northern Scandinavian countries. England, Scotland and all the southern countries of Europe give an incidence higher on men than on women.

Part IV.—LEPERS.

262. The figures for leprosy.—The figures for leprosy in all provinces in India have so recently been examined by the Leprosy Commission that little need be said on the subject. The returns for the province show as in all other infirmities, except deaf-mutism a decrease on those for last Census. The total number now enumerated was 16,895 against 17,822 at last Census, a decrease of 5 per cent. proportionately smaller in males and larger in females. The diagnosis of leprosy is a matter which requires considerable medical knowledge, and it is clear that statistics collected by means of a census must be subject to a considerable risk of error from unintentional mistakes as well as intentional omissions. One of the most likely of these unintentional mistakes is the record of leucoderma, white leprosy in English and sometimes known by the name of kachcha korh or false leprosy

Abstract No. 109, comparing the total number of lepers recorded in the provinces at this and the two preceding censuses.

		Total.	Males.	Females.
North-Western Provinces ...	1872 ...	10,099	8,160	1,939
	1881 ...	13,379	10,666	2,713
	1891 ...	11,592	9,410	2,182
Oudh	1881 ...	4,443	3,787	656
	1891 ...	5,303	4,540	763
North-Western Provinces and Oudh.	1881 ...	17,822	14,453	3,369
	1891 ...	16,895	13,950	2,945

in Urdu. Particular care was taken in the instructions at the present Census to guard against this, and it is possible that a part of the decrease was due to cases of leucoderma having been included at last Census. The only inference I can draw from a comparison of the figures for ages of lepers at both censuses is that something of this kind happened. In the present Census the proportion of lepers at each age gradually increases to a maximum for men between 50 and 54 and for women five years later. This appears to be what might be expected for real lepers. The young are less liable to it, so that its incidence gradually increases up to or some time after the age at which it usually makes its appearance. As leprosy less frequently makes its first appearance in old age and as it is a disease which rapidly shortens the life of those afflicted with it, the proportion of lepers is bound to decrease in the higher age-periods. This is what is indicated by the returns for the present Census. On the contrary, those for last Census rise to a maximum at the highest age-period as they would if leucoderma, a disease which does not shorten life, were included to a considerable extent. I have no hesitation, both from a consideration of the age-tables and of the variations in districts, in general resulting in doing away with abrupt contrasts between the figures for neighbouring districts, in pronouncing the present Census tables more correct returns of leprosy than those of the preceding Census. These considerations leave the question as to whether leprosy has increased or not undecided. The fact that the lowest age-period shows an increase might indicate that it had increased, but the numbers in that age-period are so small and so subject to accidental variations due to concealment, that no safe inference can be drawn from it. Failing further evidence, we must accept the gross result derived from a comparison of the figures for 1881 and 1891 and believe that it has decreased.

Abstract No. 110, *showing now and in* 1881 *the proportion of lepers at each age-period to* 10,000 *of total population.*

Age-periods.	1881.		1891.	
	Males.	Females.	Males.	Females.
0—4	0·1	0·1	·25	·10
5—9	0·4	0·3	·25	·21
10—14	1·0	0·7	·55	·36
15—19	2·2	1·2	1·55	·77
20—29	4·2	1·2	3·63	1·03
30—39	9·1	1·8	8·84	1·77
40—49	16·1	3·0	15·13	2·63
50—59	19·5	3·9	18·10	3·38
60 and over	20·0	4·9	16·73	3·57
Total ...	6·3	1·6	5·74	1·30

263. **Considerations suggesting a decrease.**—The conclusions of the Leprosy Commission are for the most part negative; but it appears to be their opinion that leprosy is in general neither hereditary nor due to communication from person to person, but that it for the most part originates *de novo* in the subject when certain predisposing conditions due to bad health, bad food and bad sanitary conditions combine. There is reason to believe that, on the whole, of late years the conditions affecting health in these provinces have improved, and that if the conclusions of the Sanitary Commissioners are accurate, leprosy would tend to diminish as the Census figures tend to show it has.

264. **Leprosy by locality.**—The distribution by locality of lepers is in some respects well marked. The Himalayan districts stand apart from all others with more than four times the proportion of lepers that are

[To face page 306.

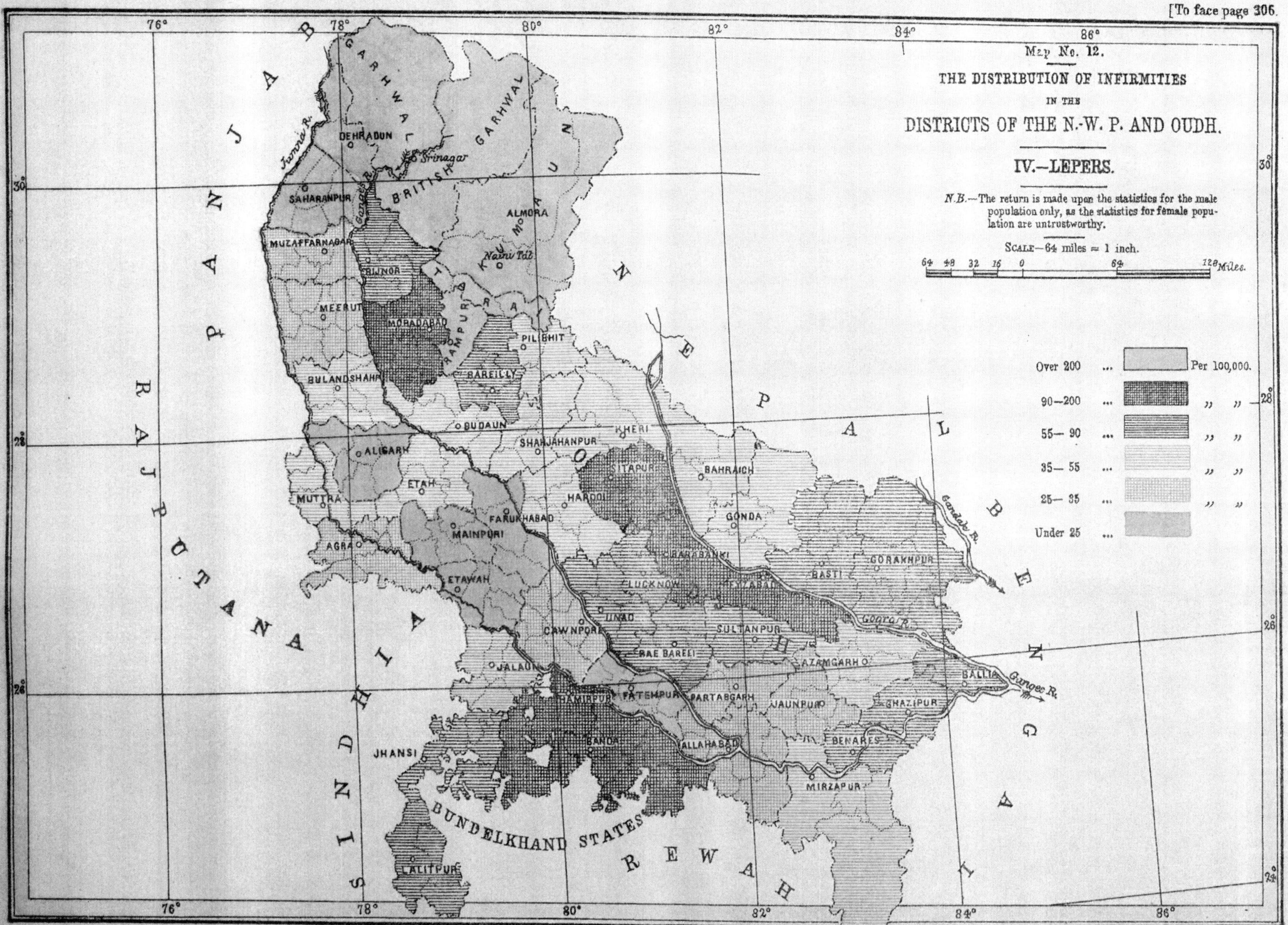

to be found elsewhere. A strip along the south bank of the Gogra including Fyzabad Bara Banki and Sitapur, the two adjoining districts of Bánda and Hamírpur, and Moradabad form a second group with nearly double the average number of lepers. The other districts above average adjoin those just mentioned or reach along the Bihar border. The minimum districts are those wholly or partly in the Doab and Partábgarh and Jaunpur. A strip from Bulandshahr to Gonda is just below average. No marked characteristics are common to those tracts in which leprosy is in excess. The physical conditions of life in the Himalayas and Bundelkhand are to some extent similar, but leprosy appears to be consistent only in preferring these two localities. In the Gangetic districts the arrangement appears thoroughly irregular. At any rate I have been unable to trace any features common to the leprosy tract in either the natural character of the country or the caste or condition of the inhabitants which are not equally common to the tracts in which leprosy is far below average. The Leprosy Commissioners apparently have been unable to trace any clear connection between climates, locality and incidence of leprosy. Their one conclusion on this subject, that leprosy is greatest in a dry climate is certainly not borne out in detail by the distribution in the North-Western Provinces.

165. **Leprosy in the sexes.**—The proportion of male lepers to total male population is 5·74 to 100,000; that of female lepers 1·30 to 100,000. The disease is one which would be concealed where it was possible to conceal it, and in all probablity a very large number of cases have been omitted. Leprous women in the plains who confine themselves to their homes, and whose leprosy is not therefore well known, would rarely be recorded as lepers. The circumstances are different in the hills, where few women are parda-nashin, and where in consequence the existence of leprosy must be nearly as well known for a woman as a man. It is in Garhwál one might hope to have the proportion of male and female lepers best shown ; even there, male lepers are more than twice as numerous as females. There is nothing in the details for the returns for these provinces which would indicate less inequality in the sexes than this, and so far as the gross returns are concerned, nothing in the figures for other provinces of India. Some concealment in Garhwál amongst women is possible, but it can hardly be great. It is probable therefore that men are more liable to leprosy than women.

Abstract No. 111, *showing the number of lepers of each religion now and in* 1881.

	Number.						Percentage on total religion.					
	1881.			1891.			1881.			1891.		
	Total.	Males.	Females.	Total.	Males.	Females.	Total.	Males.	Females.	Total.	Males.	Females.
Hindu	15,304	12,588	2,716	14,891	12,337	2,554	·0402	·0635	·0149	·0369	·0589	·0131
Musalmán	2,427	1,811	616	1,839	1,506	333	·0410	·0599	·0212	·0290	·0464	·0107
Jain	18	17	1	19	16	3	·0225	·0403	·0027	·0225	·0351	·0077
Christian	73	37	36	146	91	55	·1532	·1186	·2188	·2498	·2440	·2601
Other religions ...	...	...	...	...	...	...	...	...	...	...	...	...
Total ...	17,822	14,453	3,369	16,895	13,950	2,945	·0404	·0631	·0159	·0360	·0574	·0130

266. **Leprosy by religions.**—The returns for distribution of leprosy by religion and caste are affected to so large an extent by the large proportion of lepers in the hill districts that it is necessary to deduct them from the returns before the incidence can be considered effectively. This deduction being made, the percentages for the different religions are as follows :—

	Number.			Percentage on total religion.		
	Total.	Male.	Female.	Total.	Male.	Female.
Hindu	12,871	10,869	2,002	·0328	·0531	·0106
Musalmán	1,835	1,503	332	·0291	·0467	·0107
Jain	19	16	3	·0225	·0352	·0077
Christian	20	16	4	·0374	·0460	·0213
Total ...	14,745	12,404	2,341	·0322	·0523	·0106

Muhammadans show a lower incidence than Hindus, probably to some extent because, on the whole, their social position and surroundings are better. Jains have a considerably lower proportion of lepers than either Hindus or Muhammadans for probably the some reasons. The returns for Christians are peculiarly misleading, because the Kumaun leper asylums are under the charge of Christian Missionaries, and a large proportion of the lepers in them have declared themselves Christians ; nevertheless it has been argued from the incidence of leprosy on hill Christians that the real proportion of lepers in India was far higher than that reported.

267. **Leprosy by caste.**—Turning to the caste percentages given in Appendix No. XXVIII, we find that the castes which give the highest percentages of lepers are those named in the margin; amongst them are all the principal fishing and cultivating castes, except in the first group, Mallahs, and in the second Kisans and Koeries. It also includes castes of the highest position, Bráhmans and Rájputs. It does not include Chamárs, for whom the incidence is 30. The only inference, it appears to me possible to draw, is that the influence of locality is greater than that of social surroundings.

Caste		Caste		Caste	
Mali ...	69	Kahar ...	39	Brahman ...	34
Murao ...	69	Kalwar ...	39	Lohar ...	34
Kewat ...	54	Rajput ...	38	Barhai ...	34
Bhat ...	51	Kurmi ...	38	Baniya ...	33
Gond ...	46	Pasi ...	37	Fakir ...	32
Dom ...	42	Kumhar ...	36	Ahár ...	32
Kori ...	42	Bhar ...	35	Bhangi ...	32
Dhobi ...	40	Nai ...	35	Kachhi ...	32
				Teli ...	32

268. **Leprosy in other provinces of India.**—The incidence of leprosy in this is compared with that of the other provinces of India in the margin. The provinces are in this respect average.

Abstract No. 112, comparing the incidence of leprosy in these provinces with those of other provinces of India.

Province.	Percentage.
North-Western Provinces	3·64
Assam	12·38
Bengal	6 17
Berar	12·74
Bombay	5·39
Burma	13 87
Central Provinces	4·97
Coorg	1·33
Madras	3·54
Panjáb	2·09

Chapter XIII.—THE CASTES, RACES AND TRIBES OF THE PROVINCES.

269. **The Caste Tables.**—The tables regarding castes which have been prepared in the present census are as follows :—

(1) Table XVI, part A.—Showing for the Hindu, Muhammadan, Jain, Sikh and Arya religions, all caste or tribal divisions together with such subdivisions as are of provincial importance, or are found in a few or more districts of the province.

(2) Table XVI, part B.—Showing such subdivisions as, though locally important, occur in a few districts of the province.

(3) A caste index showing the names of all sub-divisions of castes recorded in the census schedules.

(4) Tables XIIA., XIIIA., XIVA., XVA.—Showing the distribution of the infirmities, regarding which information has been collected in the census amongst the castes or tribes of each religion.

(5) Table C.—Showing the extent to which education prevails amongst the castes and tribes of the province.

(6) Table D.—Showing the conditions as regards civil condition of each caste in the province.

The Government of the North-Western Provinces and Oudh has recently appointed a selected officer Honorary Director of Ethnographical Research in these provinces, and it is understood that he is collecting material for an exhaustive work on the origin and customs of the various castes of the province. I do not, therefore, propose to include in the present chapter any remarks on the subject, except to embody for the use of the Department of Ethnology, such information as it was found necessary to collect from districts for the preparation of the caste tables and as may be wanted to explain the arrangement of the tables. Table XVI and the caste index have been specially prepared in view of their being used by the Director of Ethnological research, and are, therefore, arranged alphabetically, to admit of such rearrangement and classification as he may think necessary. It was absolutely impossible for me, in general, to determine by any other test, than that of numbers, what was to be considered a separate caste, and what were the genuine subdivisions of each caste. I have, therefore, followed the general rule for table XVI of preserving separate all castes, the identity of which was not ascertained beyond doubt, and of showing as separate all subdivisions of castes which occur in several districts, or contain in any one district more than 200 persons. It is probable that a number of the castes shown as separate in table XVI are branches of a single caste. It is certain that for many castes the subdivisional names recorded are sometimes synonyms and sometimes cross, so that persons really of the same subdivision may appear under one of several headings. I started with the idea that it would be possible to ascertain by enquiry from districts what the real subdivisions of castes were, but the number of the names which occurred in the census registers and the scantiness and inconsistency of the information received on the subject from districts, made it clear that a consistent and exhaustive record of caste subdivisions could only be made with the assistance of specialists in every district, and after enquiries extending over several years. Table XVI is, therefore, prepared except for the best known castes direct from the census registers without material alteration so far as the sub-caste entries are concerned. It involved no little trouble to reduce the original caste lists to even the extent to which they have been reduced. The number of synonyms and occupational names which appeared in the original registers was very extensive, and the contradictory information regarding them coming from different districts made it a matter of much difficulty to find their proper places. With regard to the caste tables on infirmities, education and civil condition, the circumstances are somewhat different. The exact boundaries of a caste are here of less importance than identity of function and circumstances, and I have, therefore, used greater liberty in dealing with the returns. In these tables the different castes have been classified in accordance with a scheme of classification drawn up by the Census Commissioner for India, and which, though in regard to artizan classes somewhat unnecessarily detailed for a provincial classification, is, as finally amended, more consistent and more successful in bringing allied castes into at least the same group than any other I have seen. It is founded on the traditional occupation of the different castes.

270. **Classification of castes by traditional occupation.**—The classification and total numbers, male and female for each caste and group of castes, along with the number of sub-caste names which occur in the census registers are shown in the caste abstract printed as Appendix No. XXX. The other caste tables are arranged on the same system to bring together castes for which the various statistics given are likely to be similar. They are referred in the chapters on the special subjects which they illustrate.

The following table gives an abstract of the figures for each group and shows the proportion borne by the group to the total population of the provinces.

271. **Distribution of different castes.**—The province is, as a whole, much more uniform in regard to ethnological characteristics than any other province in Northern India. The great castes Bráhmans, Chamárs, Rájputs and Ahírs extend all over the province. Most of the servile and trading castes do so also, and the cultivating castes, though the names change, are so much alike in all essentials as to be more closely connected than the branches of many other castes. The chief exceptions to this rule of general distribution are the Jats, Bhuinhars and Pasis. The two former confined to opposite ends of the province and entirely separate from other castes, the latter in its various branches spread over all the east and centre of the provinces, but with nothing to correspond with Doab. The distribution of the leading castes or groups of castes is shown in the appended maps Nos. 13, 14, 15 and 16.

To face page 310.

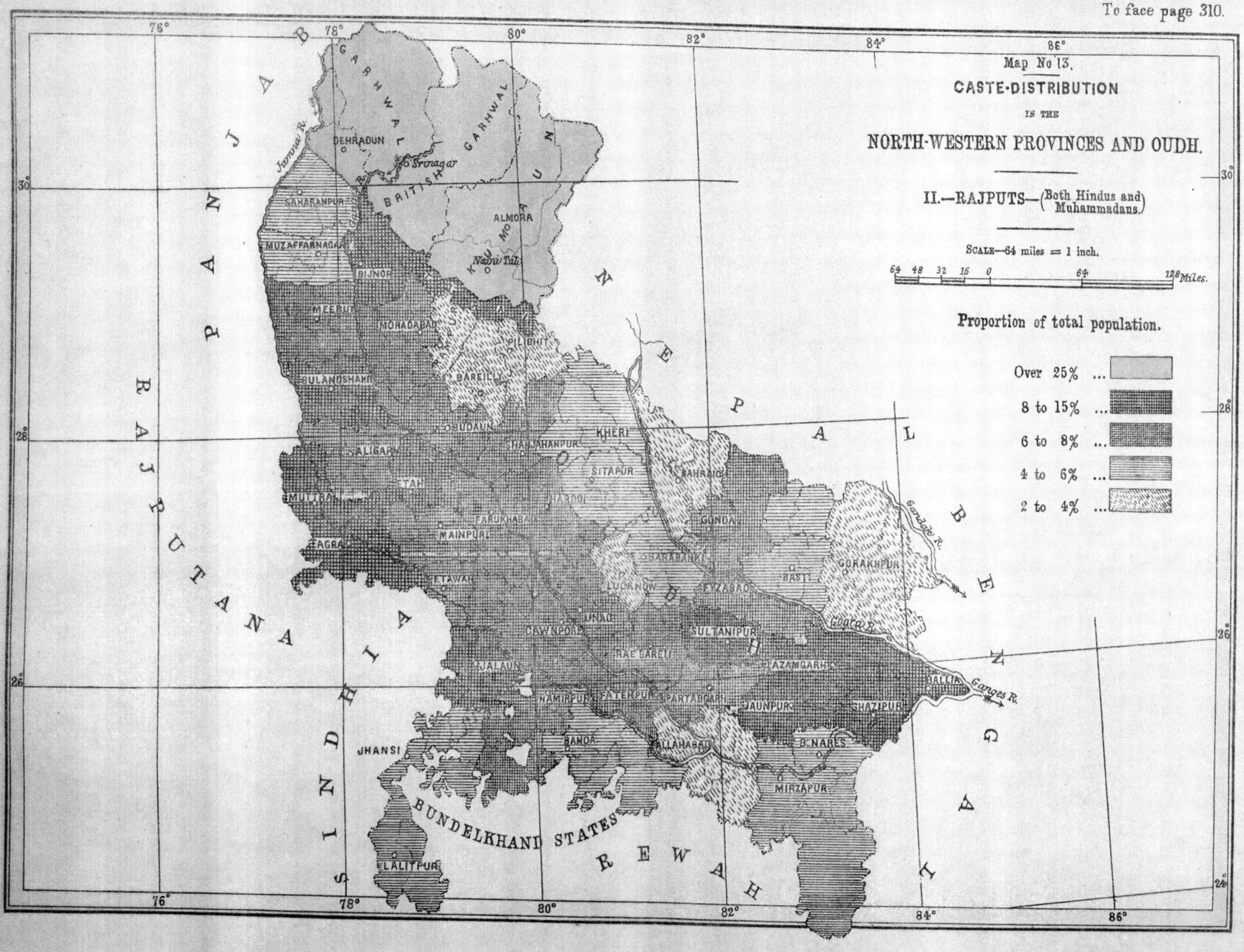

Abstract No. 113, showing abstract of the figures for each group and the proportion borne by the group to the total population.

Class.	Group.	Castes included.	Population.				Proportion of group to total population and to population of each religion.			
			Total group.	Hindus.	Musalmáns.	Others.	Total population	Hindus.	Musalmáns	Others.
1	2	3	4	5	6	7	8	9	10	11
Class A.—Agricultural.	1. Military and dominant ...	Bhuinhar, Jat, Rájput and Taga	4,682,263	4,251,310	418,141	12,812	9·98	10·53	6·58	7·19
	2(*a*). Cultivators ...	Barai, Bhar, Bhurtiya, Dangi, Gara, Golapurab, Jhojha, Kachhi Kamboh, Khagi, Kirar, Kisan, Koeri, Kurmi, Kunjra, Lodha, Mali, Meo, Mewati, Murao, Rain, Rawa, Ror, and Saini.	6,587,021	6,345,547	241,215	259	14·04	15·72	8·81	·15
	2(*b*). Cattle-breeders and graziers	Ahar, Ahir, Dogar, Gaddi, Ghosi, and Gujar	4,585,968	4,441,125	144,494	349	9·78	11·00	2·27	·19
	2(*c*). Sheep breeders ...	Gadariya	929,463	929,059	378	26	1·98	2·30	·01	·01
	3. Forest and hill tribes ...	Baiswar, Bhil, Bhoksa, Bhuinyan, Cheru, Goli, Gond, Kharwar, Kol, Korwar, Mahra, Majhwar, Manjhi, Musahar, Soiri, Sonthal and Tharu.	193,731	193,731	...	...	·41	·47	...	...
		Total, Class A. ...	16,978,446	16,160,772	804,228	13,446	36·19	40·02	12 67	7·54
Class B.—Professional.	4. Priests	Bráhman, and Mahábráhman	4,744,890	4,739,711	...	5,179	10·12	11·74	...	2·91
	5. Devotees	Fakir	623,506	284,621	338,474	411	1·33	·70	5·33	·23
	6. Genealogists	Bhat	161,144	131,471	29,463	210	·34	·33	·47	·11
	7. Writers	Kayasth	514,327	511,426	...	2,901	1·11	1 27	...	1·63
	8. Astrologers	Joshi	35,069	35,049	...	20	·07	·08	...	·01
	9. Musicians and ballad-singers,	Dafali, Dhari, Dom, Mirasi, and Panwaria	72,272	...	72,272	...	·15	...	1·14	...
	10. Dancers and singers ...	Barwa, Beriya, Bhagat, Gandharp, Hurkiya, Kathik, Paturiya, Radha and Tawaif.	52,965	27,908	25,053	4	·11	·07	·39	...
	11. Actors	Bhand	4,014	14	4,000	...	·01	...	·06	...
		Total, Class B. ...	6,208,187	5,730,200	469,262	8,725	13·24	14·19	7·39	4·89
Class C.—Commercial.	12. Traders	Baniya, Bhatiya, Bohra, Dhusar Bhargava and Khattri ...	1,428,977	1,338,020	...	90,957	3·05	3·31	...	51·02
	13. Pedlars	Bisati and Bamaiya	5,054	3,872	1,110	72	·01	·01	·02	·04
	14. Carriers	Ahiwasi, Baidguar, Banjara, Belwar, Naik and Rahwari ...	86,674	59,032	27,373	269	·18	·15	·43	·15
		Total, Class C. ...	1,520,705	1,400,924	28,483	91,298	3 24	3·47	·45	51·21

Abstract No. 113, *showing abstract of the figures for each group and the proportion borne by the group to the total population*—(concluded).

Class.	Group.	Castes included.	Population. Total group.	Population. Hindus.	Population. Musalmans.	Population. Others.	Proportion of group to total population and to population of each religion. Total population.	Hindus.	Musalmáns.	Others.
1	2	3	4	5	6	7	8	9	10	11
Class D.—Artizans and village menials.	15. Goldsmith	Sonar	255,629	255,008	320	301	·55	·63	·01	·17
	16. Barber	Nai	862,273	668,087	193,937	249	1·84	1·65	3·06	·14
	17. Blacksmith	Lohar and Nalband	592,649	525,910	66,633	106	1·26	1·30	1·05	·06
	18. Carpenters and turners ...	Barhai and Kharadi	560,821	499,791	60,297	733	1·20	1·23	·95	·41
	18(*a*). Painter	Rangsaz	1,486	87	1,399	...	...	...	·02	...
	19. Mason	Raj	6,633	3,165	3,468	...	·01	·01	·05	...
	20. Brass and coppersmiths,	Jastgar, Kalaigar, Kasera, Rangdhar and Thathera ...	28,921	28,109	796	16	·06	·07	·01	·01
	21. Tailor	Darzi	228,926	82,210	146,703	13	·49	·20	2·31	·01
	22. Grain-parchers and confectioners.	Bharbhuja and Halwai	406,462	365,898	40,553	11	·87	·90	·64	·01
	23. Perfume and drug preparers and sellers and betel-leaf sellers.	Gandhi nd Tamboli...	74,801	73,721	1,048	32	·16	·18	·02	·02
	24(*a*). Weavers	Julaha, Kori and Pankha	1,806,483	926,151	880,231	101	3·85	2·30	13·88	·06
	24(*b*) Calenderers and dyers ...	Chhipi and Rangrez	70,320	23,257	47,006	57	·15	·05	·74	·03
	25. Washermen	Dhobi	658,745	579,783	78,947	15	1·41	1·43	1·25	·01
	26. Cotton-cleaners... ...	Dhuna and Kadhera	453,743	51,753	401,987	3	·97	·12	6·33	...
	27. Oil-pressers	Teli	934,080	741,427	192,604	49	1·99	1·84	3·03	·03
	28. Potters	Kumhar	713,000	702,805	10,189	6	1·52	1·74	·16	...
	29. Glass and lac workers ...	Churihar, Lakhera, Manihar and Potgar	100,023	6,058	93,948	17	·21	·01	1·48	·01
	29(*a*) Bead-stringers ...	Patwa	30,977	30,812	165	...	·07	·08	...	...
	29(*b*). Fireworks makers ...	Atishbaz	534	...	534	...	...	...	·01	...
	30. Salt and earthworkers ...	Bayar, Beldar, Dhangar, Ghasiyara and Luniya	469,659	469,395	259	5	1·00	1·16	...	...
	31. Goldsmiths' refuse collectors,	Niyaria	258	65	193	...	...	...	...	...
	32. Iron smelters ...	Agaria and Sann	1,195	1,195	...	...	...	...	...	...
	33. Fishermen, boatmen, palki-bearers, cooks, &c.	Bargah, Bargi, Bari, Bhatiyara, Bhishti, Gond, Gorcha, Kahar, Kewat, Lorha, Mallah, Mukeri, Nanbai and Sejwari.	2,215,611	2,085,640	129,782	189	4·72	5·16	2·04	·10
	33(*a*). Rice-huskers ...	Barwar and Kuta	6,408	6,408	...	...	·01	·01	...	...
	34(*a*). Distillers	Kalwar	348,790	347,037	1,454	299	·74	·86	·02	·17
	34(*b*) Toddy-drawers ...	Bind and Tarmali	77,013	77,013	...	...	·16	·17	...	...
	35. Butchers	Chik, Kassab and Khatik	347,871	199,069	148,790	12	·74	·49	2·34	·01
	36. Lime-burners	Sunkar	1,396	1,396	...	...	...	·00	...	...
	37. Leather-workers ...	Chamar, Dabgar, Dhalgar and Mochi	5,829,707	5,825,470	3,801	436	12·43	14·42	·06	·24
	38. Village-watchmen ...	Arakh, Balahar, Boriya, Dhanuk, Dhari, Khangar, Kotwar, Pahriya and Pasi.	1,521,836	1,521,835	...	1	3·24	3·76	...	...

	39. Scavengers	Bhangi and Domar	430,983	413,226	17,843	414	·92	1·02	·28	·23
		Total, Class D.	19,037,233	16,511,781	2,522,387	8,065	40·58	40·89	39·74	1·72
Class E.—Vagrant minor artizans and performers, &c.	40. Grindstone makers and stone quarriers.	Khumra	5,198	...	5,198	...	·01	...	·08	...
	41. Knife-grinders ...	Saikalgar	4,206	704	3,446	56	·01	·00	·06	·03
	42. Mat-makers and cane-splitters.	Bansphor, Basor, Dharkar, Dom, Dorha, Dusadh, Kharot, Pankhiya and Tarkihar.	435,261	434,222	1,039	...	·93	1·08	·02	...
	43. Hunters and fowlers ...	Aberiya, Baheliya, Bandi, Bengali, Gandhila, Gidhiya and Kanjar...	73,010	70,801	2,197	12	·16	·18	·03	·01
	44. Miscellaneous and disreputable livers.	Badhik, Barwar, Bawaria, Bhantu, Dalehra, Habura, Harjala, Hijra, Sainsi, and Siyarmar.	16,450	15,090	1,360	...	·03	·04	·02	...
	45. Turners and acrobats ...	Nat	63,584	42,880	20,702	2	·13	·10	·33	...
	46. Castes foreign to the Province.	Sat gop and Sud	324	324	...	...	...	...	...	...
		Total, Class E. ...	598,033	564,021	33,942	70	1·28	1·40	·54	·04
Class F.—Races, nationalities and sectarian communities.	47. Indian Nationality not returned by caste.	Bhotiya, Mandraji, Mahrata and Pindari	8,257	8,256	1	...	·01	·02	...	...
	48. Sectarian castes ...	Naumuslim and Sadh	90,314	1,870	88,444	...	·19	...	1·39	...
	49. Non-Indian Asiatic races ...	Biloch, Iraki, Mughal, Pathan, Sheikh, Syed and Turk ...	2,382,786	...	2,382,786	...	5·09	...	37·55	...
	50. Non-Asiatic races ...	Armenians, Europeans and Habshi	28,189	...	194	27,995	·06	...	...	15·71
	51. Eurasians	Eurasians	7,040	...	...	7,040	·02	...	...	3·95
	52. Christian converts ...	Native Christians	23,406	...	...	23,406	·05	...	...	13·13
	53. Castes unspecified ...	Castes unspecified	22,489	2,344	16,924	3,221	·05	·01	·27	1·81
		Total, Class F. ...	2,562,481	12,470	2,488,349	61,662	5·47	·03	39·21	34·60

272. **Statement showing variations in castes unreliable.**—An examination of the variations in the population of different castes is rendered difficult by the fact that certain castes are so closely connected that the figures for one vary at the expense of the other, and because of the number of not very well ascertained combinations made at last census. The following statement compares the variations for all Hindu castes with a population of 100,000 or more. Muhammadan castes are still less defined, and no comparison of the variations in their numbers can be made with the figures of last census.

Abstract No. 141, *comparing the variations for Hindu castes with a population of* 100,000, *or more.*

Caste.	Total population of 1881.	Total population of 1891.	Increase.		Decrease.		Remarks.
			Actual.	Percentage.	Actual.	Percentage.	
Bráhman	4,655,204	4,719,882	64,678	1·595	...	...	
Rájput	3,127,207	3,253,020	125,813	4·023	...	...	Including Chauhan.
Baniya	1,282,682	1,279,246	...	...	3,436	·268	Including Kandu.
Ahár...	257,670	244,166	...	...	13,504	5·240	Confused with Ahírs.
Ahír...	3,584,185	3,916,846	332,661	9·272	...	...	*Cf.* Ahár.
Barhai	497,207	498,985	1,778	·357	...	...	
Bhangi	426,243	397,197	...	...	29,046	6·812	*Cf.* Dom, largely included in 1881.
Bhar	349,113	417,745	68,632	1·966	...	...	
Bharbhunja	301,086	301,196	110	·036	...	...	
Bhát...	129,921	131,471	1,550	1·193	...	...	
Bhuinhar	188,080	221,027	32,947	17·520	...	...	Liable to inclusion in Bráhmans.
Chamár	5,360,548	5,816,053	455,505	8·494	...	...	
Dhánuk	119,341	146,189	26,848	22·490	...	...	
Dhobi	518,872	579,783	60,911	11·739	...	...	*Cf.* Bhangi.
Dom...	176,615	270,560	93,945	53·193	...	...	
Fakír	343,535	284,621	...	...	58,914	17·150	
Gadariya	860,220	929,059	68,839	8·002	...	...	
Gujar	269,036	280,113	11,077	4·117	...	...	
Ját	672,068	677,854	5,786	·860	...	...	*Cf.* Kurmi.
Kachhi including Koeri, Murao and Saini in 1891.	1,941,663	2,007,953	66,290	3·414	...	...	
Kahár including Gond in 1891	1,209,350	1,308,955	99,605	8·236	...	...	
Kalwar	345,365	347,037	1,672	·484	...	...	
Kayasth	513,495	511,426	...	...	2,069	·402	
Khatik	152,030	189,639	37,609	24·740	...	...	
Kori...	843,422	919,649	76,227	9·057	...	...	
Kumhár	633,989	702,805	68,816	10·850	...	...	
Kurmi including Kisan in 1891	2,075,026	2,370,112	295,086	14·240	...	...	
Lodha	1,000,599	1,029,213	28,614	2·860	...	...	
Lohár	496,547	525,910	29,363	5·913	...	...	
Luniya	378,619	412,817	34,198	9·032	...	...	
Máli	236,355	245,876	9,521	4·028	...	...	
Mallah including Kewat and Chain in 1891.	660,748	709,871	49,123	7·437	...	...	Including Chain in 1881.
Nái	639,957	668,087	28,130	4·395	...	...	
Pási	1,033,184	1,219,311	186,127	18·016	...	...	
Sunar	247,485	255,008	7,523	3·039	...	...	
Taga	101,615	99,409	...	...	2,206	2·171	
Tamboli including Barai in 1891.	209,777	227,062	17,285	8·240	...	...	
Teli	685,123	741,427	56,304	8·218	...	...	

[To face Page 314.

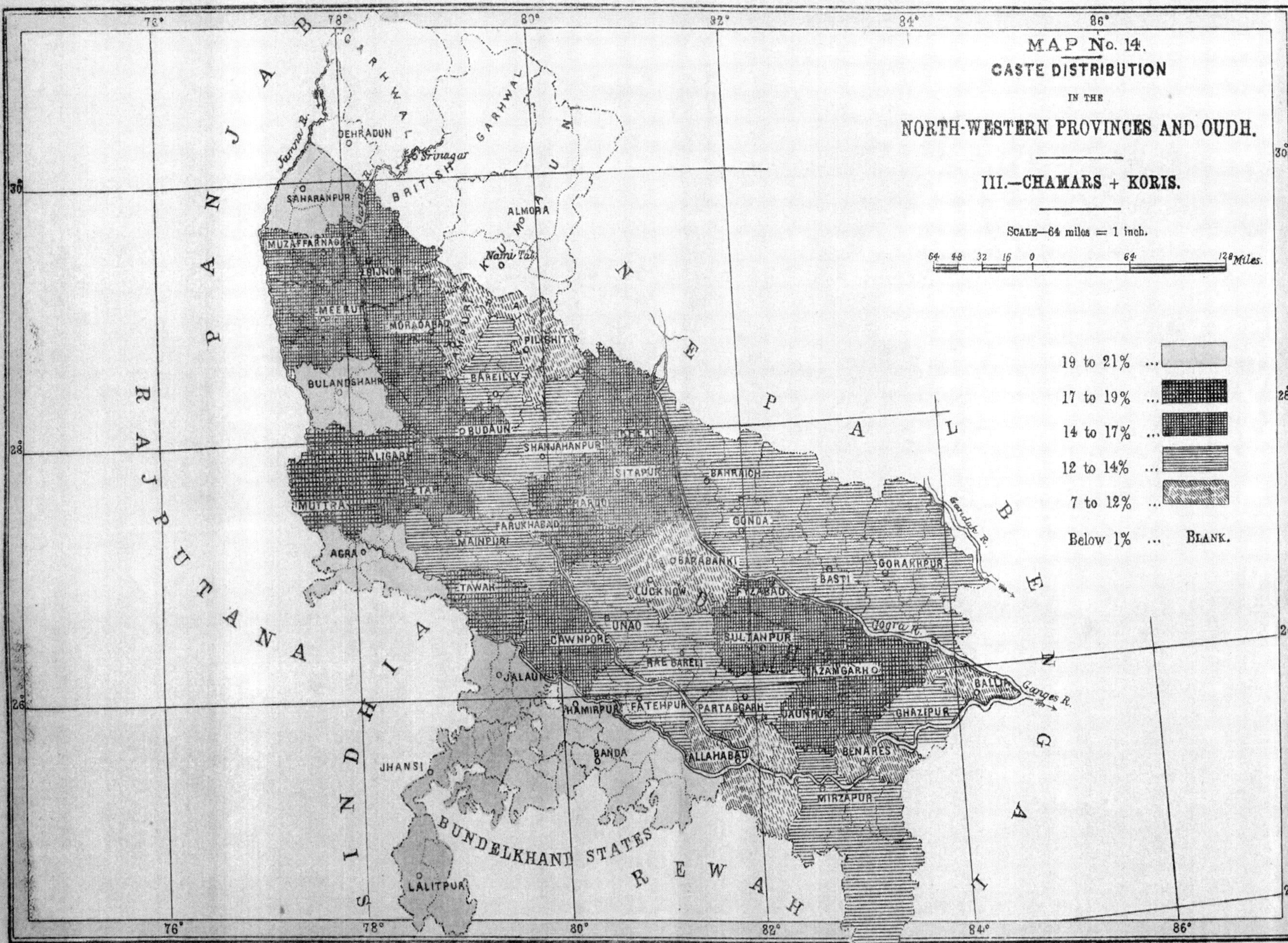

273. **Remarks on various castes.**—In regard to the preparation of the tables and especially table XVI, the following remarks may be of use to those who have occasion to use them. They embody in general the results of enquiries I found it necessary to make from districts. I follow the same order as in table XVI itself.

Agariya.—The first caste which occurs requires mention. It, as now shown, contains only the numbers of an aboriginal tribe in Mirzapur. In former census returns a number of Agariyas in Bulandshahr were invariably included. Enquiry on the present occasion elicited the reply that they were a separate caste intermarrying with persons of the same caste ; that they were of Rájput descent and emigrants from Moradabad. In Moradabad no trace of the caste could be found, and a further enquiry as to where their marriages were arranged led to the information being obtained that they married in Aligarh, Etah and Agra ; that in Aligarh they were known as Gole Thákurs and in Agra as Nuneras. They are in fact Luniyas (see remarks on that caste).

Ahár.—The similarity of the name in Urdu and in pronunciation to Ahír led to what were on inspection detected as clearly mistakes in the table as originally compiled. The figures were circulated to districts, and it is hoped those now presented are accurate. It was shown by the replies from districts that some confusion existed in the returns for last census.

Ahír.—A number of the persons here included as Ahírs were returned as a separate caste, Ghosi, from Hamírpur, Jhánsi, Jalaun and Bánda. They were reported from the districts to be separate from Ahírs : as, however, the main Ahír : sub-castes do not intermarry, they would readily be considered absolutely separate castes ; and as it was certain that the Ghosis of Bundelkhand were the same caste as were returned from Cawnpore, Fatehpur, &c., as Ahír sub-caste Ghosi, they have been combined under that sub-caste. There were no Ahírs of the Ghosi subdivision in the original lists of the districts named, so that the figures for the so-called Ghosi caste are readily ascertainable. The subdivisions of Ahírs shown in the statement undoubtedly cross ; but the information received on the subject on this and all other castes was so vague and contradictory, that it was considered better to present the figures as originally returned and not to attempt combinations. The Ghosis just named are probably Nandbans.

Ahiwasi.—Does not occur at last census, having probably been included amongst Bráhmans. An account of the caste is given in Growse's Muttra Memoir, page 11. They are hereditary carriers and dealers in salt, but also officiate as temple priests.

Arakh.—Is a branch of the great Pasi tribe, and the large variations in the total population of the caste since last census is probably due to the fact that a larger proportion was then included in Pasi. There are now 16,210 persons shown under Pasi as of the Arakh sub-caste. I have in all such castes followed the uniform rule that, unless identity was absolutely certain the returns were printed as received and without transfer from one caste to another.

Badhik.—Was at last census included in Baheliya, a caste from which it is perfectly separate. The caste is very much more numerous than the statement shows. They call themselves Rájputs and have no doubt been entered as Chauhans. The Gorakhpur returns show no Badhiks, although a considerable number have been settled there.

Baheliya.—At last census included Aheriya, Badhik, Beriya, Boriya, Chirimar and several other castes now shown separately and believed to be perfectly separate.

Balahar.—Is an occupational term. The persons so shown are probably either Basor or Bhangi.

Bandi.—Is mentioned by Crooke as a bird-catching caste of the Tarái. In that district they have been included as a sub-caste of Hill Doms.

Baniya.—The Bishnoi sub-caste are, for the most part those Baniyas who belong to the Bishnoi sect referred to in the chapter on sects. Bishnois have, however, for the most part entered a proper sub-caste name, whilst, on the other hand, most of the entries here in Muzaffarnagar and Meerut are probably due to Agarwala Baniyas often describing themselves as "Bishni," meaning Vaishnava.

Baniya Dusar.—In the census returns for 1872, this sub-caste was shown as Dhusar. The returns for the present census as originally received showed both Dhusar and Dusar separately for some districts, whilst in others large numbers which could only belong to the Dusar subdivision were tabulated as Dhusars. Enquiry on the subject was made in all districts and the figures regrouped in accordance with the result. The Dhusar, who claim a Bráhmanical origin and, according to Todd, perform Bráhmanical functions in their original home in Rájputana,—have been shown as a separate caste, Dhusar Bhargava. They include many men of distinction in the provinces. On the other hand, Dusar is a sub-caste of Baniyas of low standing, permitting widow remarriage, who have no connection whatsoever with the Bhargava caste. They are stated to be a branch of Umars descended from a second wife, hence the name Dusar. It is possible that the figures as shown are still not correct. Dhusars, comparatively strong in the western districts, are not likely to be as numerous as the returns show in Allahabad. A second reason for confusion as to Dhusar was introduced by many of the caste showing themselves as Bráhmans, whilst Bhargava is also a sub-caste of Sarwariya Bráhmans. It appears probable that many of the latter have been included in Dhusar.

Baniya Jhamaiya.—This is a sectarian not a caste subdivision, and the numbers are in all probability not reliable. Jhamaji was the founder of the Bishnoi sect; but, so far as I have been able to ascertain, the sect in the central districts does not preserve the same rigorous separation from other Hindus as in Bijnor and Moradabad.

Baniya Mahajan.—The word is frequently quoted as a caste name by a group of Baniya sub-castes of the lowest status. It is used also by Kalwars, and it is possible that some Kalwars have been included here.

[To face page 316.

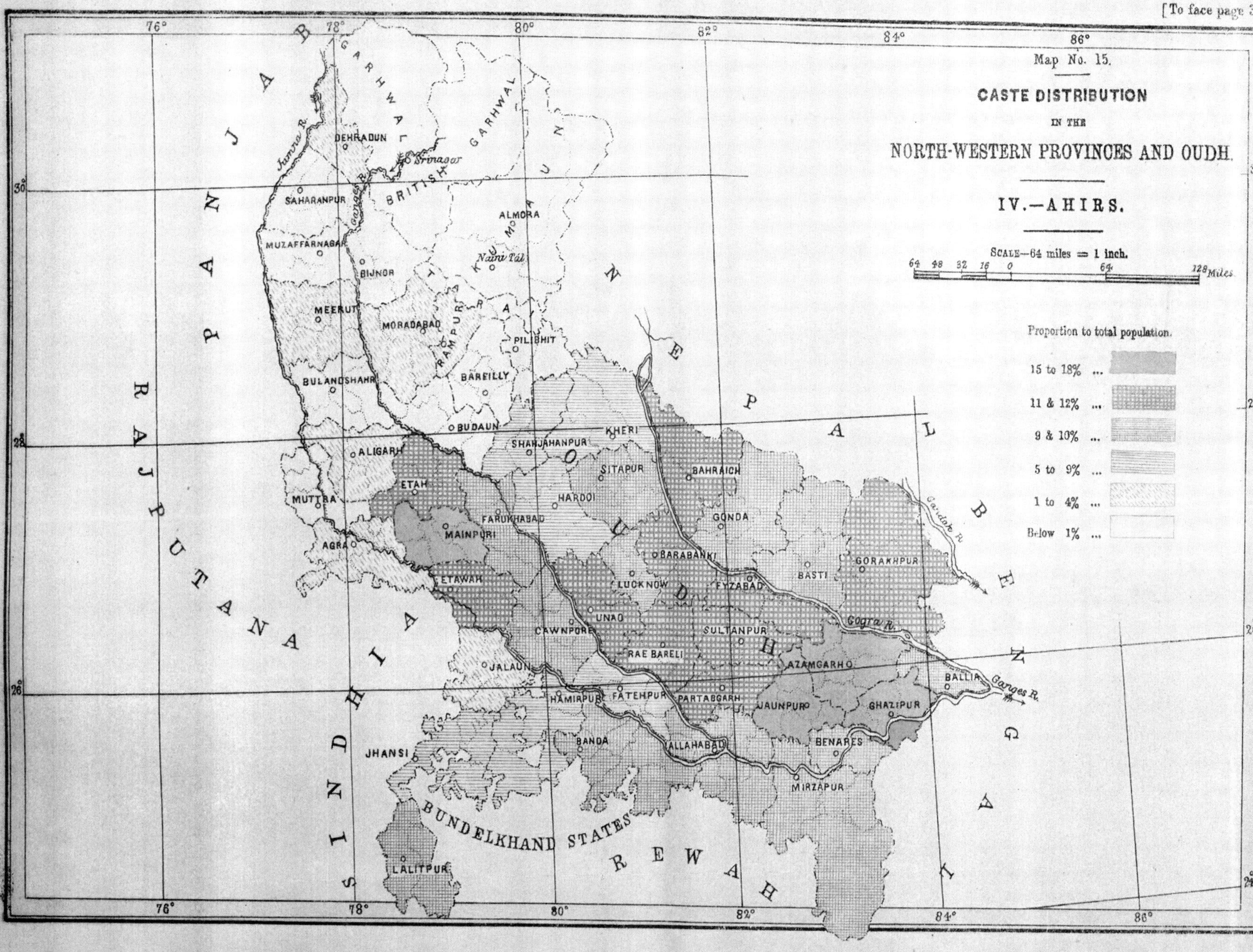

The use of the word Baniya as a caste designation has been objected to by a critic of a former census report, but without, so far as I can see, sufficient justification. It is true that under the name Baniya are quoted a number of castes to all intents and purposes absolutely separate and varying in status from the high caste Agarwala or Oswal to the very low caste Kandu or Umar ; but the popular use of the word Baniya to include all is so universal, that any attempt to enumerate without employing this name would be certain to result in the greatest confusion. The Baniya is not the only caste by any means in which the different branches are absolutely endogenous and separate.

Banjara.—The minor Banjara subdivisions as enumerated showed names like Badi and Brijbasi, which would appear to indicate a close connection with Nats. Some enquiry was made on the subject by Mr. Vincent Smith, who, however, was unable to find evidence of any direct connection between the castes.

Bansphor.—The caste name is occupational and the persons shown as Dhanuk probably really belong to that caste. Many of the others are Dharkars for whom Bansphor is shown as a sub-caste. In fact, probably both Dharkar and Bansphor are castes of recent formation not yet completely severed from the parent Dhanuks and Doms.

Barai.—The Barai and Tamboli castes are, judging from the census returns, originally altogether the same, and even now in general, undistinguishable. Some districts, however, report that Barais and Tambolis do not intermarry, and it is probable that a process of separation is going on, the actual pân cultivator calling himself Barai whilst the dealer is gradually being separated as the Tamboli caste. The returns are printed as received from districts.

Bargah and *Bargi.*—Are given as tabulated in districts. They are probably Baris, but Bargah is used as a title by Ahírs also.

Barhai.—The close correspondeuce between the Barhai and Lohar subdivisions indicates a close connection between the castes. They were probably originally the same, and now not far apart. Working in metal, however, always tends to depress a caste in the Hindu social system, and Barhais and Lohars are now distinguished by the fact that, whilst a high caste Hindu will drink from a Barhai, he refuses to do so from a Lohar.

Barwar.—Apparently includes two castes—rice-pounders, not of the best reputation, in Rohilkhand, and professional thieves in Gonda and elsewhere in prison. The latter Barwar always professes to belong to another caste, and the numbers in the return are probably much below the mark.

Bawariya.—Is another caste of which the returns are probably incomplete.

Beldar.—Was at last census included in Luniya, to which in all probability a considerable number belong. The combination is not, however, safe, as Chamárs, who take to earthwork on roads and railways, at once become Beldars in caste. Kharot, shown as a subdivision of Beldar in Gorakhpur and Basti, also appears as a separate caste. From the latter district they were reported to be a caste of mat-weavers.

Belwar.—Is a caste of carriers and cattle-dealers closely resembling the Naiks and probably of similar origin. They occur in many more districts than have returned them. From Gonda it is reported that the Belwars there recorded themselves as Sanadh Bráhmans.

Bengalí.—Should include only the wandering tribe of that name, but probably includes also natives of Bengal whose caste was improperly omitted in the schedules. I am indebted to the District Superintendent of Police, Muzaffarnagar, for the following notes on Bengalis. They are also known as Singhiwalas from the horn cup which they use for cupping. The blood is usually drawn from the soles of the feet with a view to getting rid of the superabundant heat of the disposition. They believe they are called Bengalis because they learned to cup in Bengal. Part of the caste is Musalmán in name, but in name only, as all sacrifice to Devi. Socially they are Hindus of the lowest grade like Nats and Kanjars, but are altogether unconnected with these castes.

Bhagat.—Is a dancing girl caste of the Agra Division. It is reported to be a caste, not simply an occupational name.

Bhand.—Includes only 14 Hindus. It is not a Hindu caste, and was properly entered from the occupation of the persons enumerated.

Bhangi.—At last census included Basor and Domar, now shown separately.

Bharbhunja.—Shows Kandu as a subdivision. Kandus, a Bania sub-caste, frequently are grain-parchers by trade and hence the entry. The other subdivisions evidence the claim the Bharbhunjas like the Darzis make that they are Kayasths.

Bhatiya.—Are traders in several of the Doab districts, though only shown in Muttra. They claim to be Bhatti Rájputs in Aligarh, and most are so entered. Bulandshahr reported that they were Khattris and had been so shown. In Etah the name appears to be applied to another caste who are purohits of Gahoi Baniyas. They do not occur in the census tables as Bhatiyas.

A somewhat indefinite account of the *Bind* caste is given in Crooke's Ethnographical handbook. The census returns suggest some connection with the Gonds of Gházipur and Ballia.

Boriya.—Is another branch of the Pasi caste. It probably should have been included in the corresponding subdivision of that caste.

Bráhman.—The allocation of the different Bráhman sub-castes is well defined and is shown in the accompanying map No. 17.

Chain.—The persons shown as Chain, Kewat, Mallah, and possibly many of those included in Kahar, probably belong to the same caste or group of castes. The actual relations which exist between them and their sub-castes are, however, far from certainly ascertained and all have been shown as

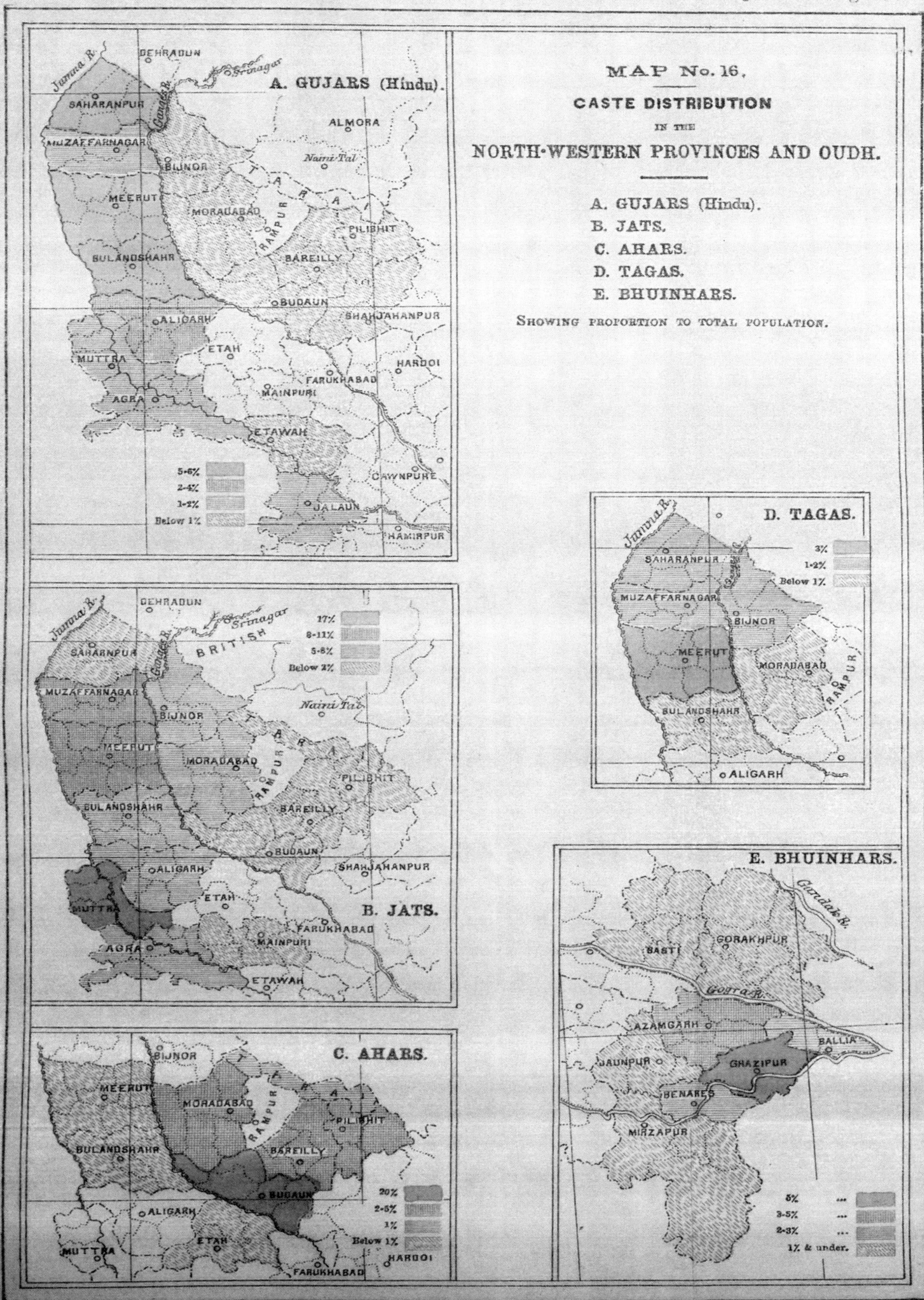
MAP No. 16.
CASTE DISTRIBUTION
IN THE
NORTH-WESTERN PROVINCES AND OUDH.
A. GUJARS (Hindu).
B. JATS.
C. AHARS.
D. TAGAS.
E. BHUINHARS.
SHOWING PROPORTION TO TOTAL POPULATION.
A. GUJARS (Hindu).
5-6%
2-4%
1-2%
Below 1%
B. JATS.
17%
8-11%
5-8%
Below 2%
C. AHARS.
20%
2-5%
1%
Below 1%
D. TAGAS.
3%
1-2%
Below 1%
E. BHUINHARS.
5%
3-5%
2-3%
1% & under.
DEHRADUN
SAHARANPUR
MUZAFFARNAGAR
MEERUT
BULANDSHAHR
ALIGARH
MUTTRA
AGRA
ETAWAH
MAINPURI
ETAH
FARUKHABAD
BIJNOR
MORADABAD
RAMPUR
BAREILLY
PILIBHIT
BUDAUN
SHAHJAHANPUR
HARDOI
CAWNPURE
JALAUN
HAMIRPUR
ALMORA
Naini Tal
Srinagar
Jumna R.
Ganges R.
BRITISH
BASTI
GORAKHPUR
Gandak R.
Gogra R.
AZAMGARH
BALLIA
JAUNPUR
GHAZIPUR
BENARES
MIRZAPUR

enumerated. It appears fairly certain that under the names of Kewat, Chain and Mallah are included a group of endogenous fishing and boating castes who, not having any direct relations, but still recognizing some connection with each other, use an occupational term to denote the group to which they belong.

Dhanuk, *Dom*, *Dusadh* } are castes which, from the census returns, appear to be closely connected. The distinction has so far not been defined, and each is shown as a separate caste, though the others occur as sub-castes.

Dorha.—With a total population of 68 is reported by Kheri to be a separate caste and to come originally from Gonda or Bahraich, which districts return none of them. They are rope-makers by occupation. If the account of the caste given by the district is to be relied on, they are considerably higher in the social stage than the Kanjars who are the principal rope-making tribe. They permit widow remarriage and divorce and drink spirits, but do not eat pork or vermin. Dorha is reported to be a separate caste, though the numbers are so small as to make it unlikely. They make ropes and bamboo baskets, and were it not that they are reported to abstain from eating pork might be identified with Dharkars.

Fakir.—The compilation for the mendicant classes gave great trouble. The general word Fakir, not properly applicable to a Hindu mendicant at all, was commonly used without further specification. The words Goshain Bairagi, Jogi, Saniyasi, were apparently used by a considerable proportion of the enumerators as interchangeable, each appearing as a subdivision of the others. A large proportion of the subdivisional names reported were absolutely unrecognizable. Thus out of 71 subdivisions found in the schedules for Bairagi only 18 were recognized by the leading Bairagis of Ajudhiya as being names of genuine Bairagi sects. The others were either not traced or did not belong to Bairagis at all. It was found impossible to compile an exhaustive or even a consistent list of the different entries returned, and the table had to take its present form in which the entries in the caste columns are preserved, even though the entries in the sub-caste columns were inconsistent with them, it being more probable that the first was right than the second. Thus an entry Jogi Dasnami would stand amongst Jogi unspecified. The small number of entries under Goshain Gokulastha and Brindrabani shows how unsatisfactorily the schedules in this respect were drawn up. Though the subdivisional names are universally used, all have disappeared under Goshain unspecified. It may be interesting to note the names of those Dasnami subdivisions which occur. They are Giri, Puri, Bharthi, Ban (Vana), Jati, Bodla, Asrama, Parbat (Parbata). The lists of the ten classes vary. The names which do not occur in the census schedules and are entered in one list or another of the ten classes are Saraswati, Aranya, Tirtha and Sagara. Two of these may possibly be identical with two in the census list.

Gandharp is reported from Gházipur and Benares to be a separate caste, of which some of the women become dancers and prostitutes, being out-casted on becoming so. The caste succession is kept up by women who marry and remain in caste.

Gidhiya.—Is reported from the Taráì to be a bird-catching caste. They are probably Baheliyas.

Gole.—The persons shown in this column are Luneras, and might have been included in that caste.

Gond.—A caste of domestic servants which occur in somewhat large numbers in the Benares Division, must be distinguished from the aboriginal Gonds, who alone are mentioned in Mr. Crooke's Glossary. Relations between the Binds and the Gonds have already been suggested.

Gorcha.—Is another caste reported from Kheri only and, like Doriha, said to have emigrated from Gonda and Bahraich. They claim to be descended from Kalhans Rájputs of pargana Gwarich. They are reported to be of much the same status as the Dorha, permitting widow remarriage but not eating pork. They are by occupation fishermen and mat-makers.

Harjala.—Or Harjaliya are reported from several districts. A wandering tribe who could not be traced when the subsequent enquiries were made, but who were believed in Sháhjahánpur to subsist by begging from Ahírs and Lodhas.

Hijra and *Jastgar* are neither of them properly caste entries. The latter are probably Thathere.

Joshi.—The hill Joshi, a genuine Bráhman, is not included in this caste.

Kachhi, Koeri, Murao.—Are believed to be very closely allied castes, if not identical. The sub-caste names here, many of them common to cultivating castes entirely distinct, give less assistance than elsewhere, but each of the names occurs as a sub-caste of each of the others.

Kayasth.—The subdivision Srivastab includes many of the Hindu Darzis. Some enquiry made in Allahabad and Oudh regarding Khemadoz, a class of Darzis, who used to make tents, elicited the information that most were shown as Kayasths in the caste returns. They are of course not recognized by genuine Kayasths from whom they are separated definitely by permitting widow remarriage.

Kharadi.—Is an instance of a caste in course of formation. They tend to become separate from Barhais, but are not yet distinctly recognized as separate.

Kharot.—Though following Crooke, it has been shown as a separate caste where so returned, is clearly the same as the Kharot shown as a subdivision of Kewat.

Khattri.—For this caste the subdivisions shown are what are distinguished by themselves as the "Al." There also exists a cross topographical subdivision which was stated by Khattris whom I consulted on the subject to be accidental, that determining marriage relations being the "Al" solely.

Kisan.—Lodha occurs as a subdivision, and the two castes are probably the same. The population statistics in several districts show a large fall in Lodha as compared with neighbouring districts, a fall which is explained by part of the caste having been transferred to Kisan.

[To face page 318.

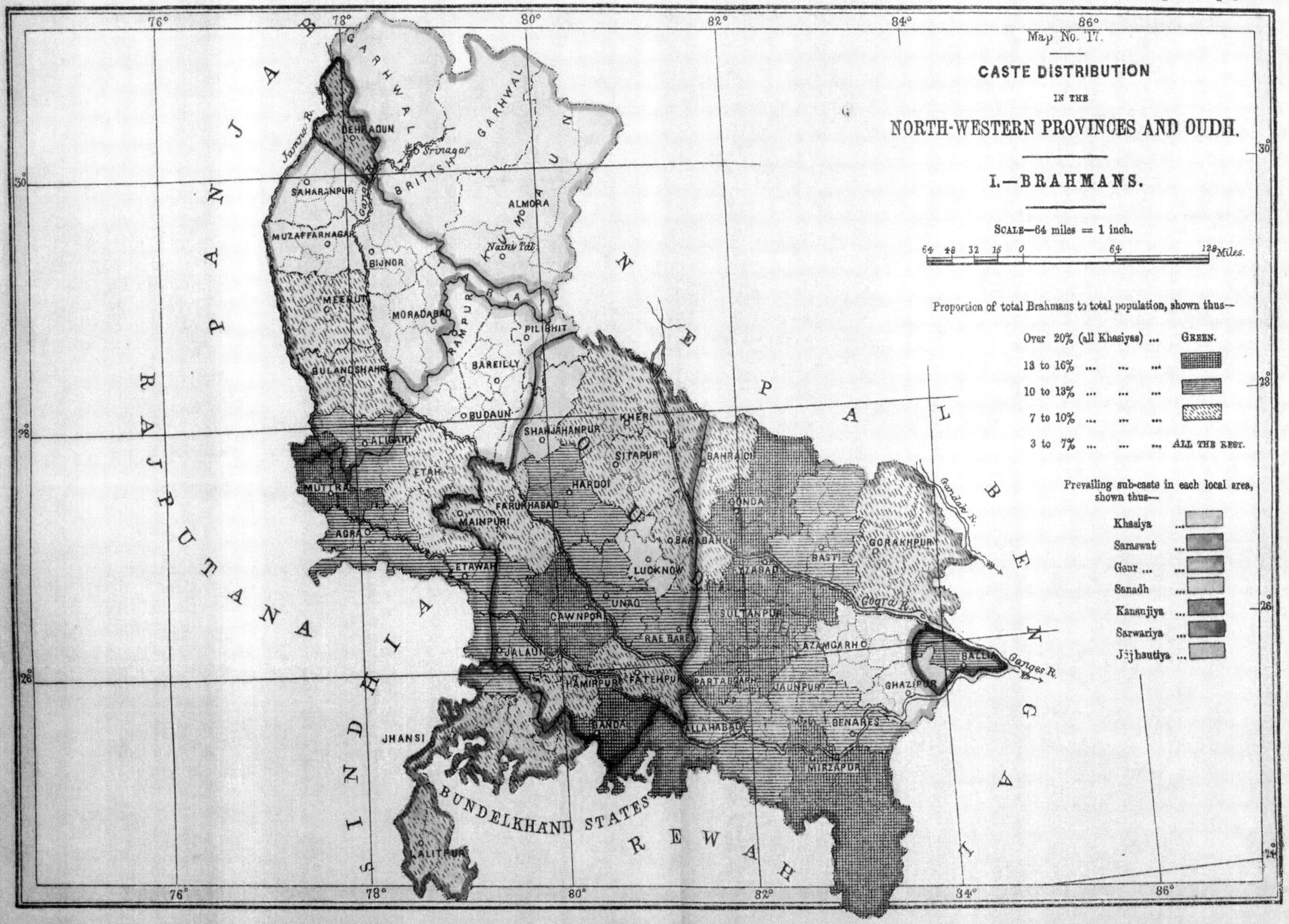

Lakhera.—Entries for persons shown as of castes Lakhera, Kancher, Manihar, Churihar and Potgar, appeared with such irregularity from different districts that it was considered necessary to make enquiry on the subject. The result was that Lakheras and Kanchers have been combined, but Manihars although probably identical kept separate. The accounts given by members of the caste of their origin are very various and sometimes ingenious. One account is that, like the Patwas, with whom they are connected, they where originally Kayaths. According to another account they were made from the dirt washed from Parbatti before her marriage with Siva, created by the god to make bangles for his wife and hence called Deobansi. Again, it is stated that they were created by Krishna to make bangles for the Gopies. The most elaborate account of their origin given states that they were originally Jadobansi Rájputs, who assisted the Kurus to make a fort of lac in which the Pandus were to be treacherously burnt. For this treachery they were degraded and compelled eternally to work in lac or glass. They are in status ordinary low caste Hindus permitting widow remarriage and divorce, drinking wine, but not eating pork. They make tiklis as well as lac and glass bangles.

Lorha.—Is a rope-making caste shown in Sahéranpur only.

Luniya and *Lunera or Nunera* were originally shown separately, the former in the east and the latter generally in the west; but each appeared to such an extent as a sub-caste of the other that there was no advantage in preserving the distinction.

Mahábráhman.—The numbers shown are very much below the mark, the majority of the caste has been included in Bráhmans, the Mahábráhman being very reluctant to use the distinguishing prefix in giving his caste.

Mahra.—An aboriginal caste of the Eastern Dún, did not occur separately at last census, and is not shown in Crooke's handbook. The following notes from Dehra Dún may therefore be of interest :—

" The *Mahras* are the aboriginal inhabitants and occupy all the unhealthy villages in the Eastern Dún, where no one else can live. These are also Rájputs and are closely allied to the Bhoksas of the Rohilkhand Tarái and Tharus of the Oudh Tarái : they are clearly all one and the same race. " The Mahras have few traditions except that their ancestors were Rájputs. They present many points of resemblance to the Bhoksas, though neither will acknowledge any connection with the other. They are of settled habits, dwellers in swamps and cultivators of rice and are proof against malaria. They do not admit outsiders into the caste. They are timid and are averse to intercourse with strangers. They marry generally on attaining puberty. They are in their habits and customs Hindus of the ordinary low caste type, and Gaur Bráhmans are employed by them as priests for marriage and funeral ceremonies. Remarriage of the widows is permitted. The widow is not obliged to marry her husband's elder or younger brother. They eat pork and fowls and drink spirits like most of the dwellers in the Tarái swamps. Some of them are hunters and catch game, and others are good fishermen."

Mandraji—Means Madrasi, shown without specification of caste.

Mukeri.—Is a Muhammadan caste of some extent; similarity of occupation has led two Hindus to show themselves as of this caste.

Naik.—Is a caste of good status of zamíndárs and cattle dealers. They are believed to be of Banjara origin, but have now settled down; and, as they are well-to-do, allege a Bráhmanical origin. In Basti they showed themselves as Bráhmans.

Niariya.—Is also an occupational term and so is *Paturiya*. It includes in general most women who are prostitutes or dancing girls, and whose caste occupation is not dancing.

Potgar.—Is reported from Partábgarh to be a separate caste engaged in manufacturing beads. They are stated to be of Rájput descent and still, unlike the Lakheras, to preserve high caste ways, wearing the janeo and not allowing widow remarriage.

Rájput.—A comparison of the numbers of each clan recorded for each district with those at last census disclosed variations so considerable as to necessitate a general enquiry on the subject. In some cases the variations appear to be due to the fact that Rájput women after marriage are sometimes recorded as of their husband's and sometimes as of their father's caste, the latter being probably the proper entry. Other variations were so large as to be inexplicable. There were some districts in which the figures given for each clan at last census bore no relation whatsoever to those now ascertained. Every effort was made by comparison in detail with district figures to get the present lists correct as to numbers and names. The spurious Chauhans of the North-Western districts are shown amongst Chauhan Rájputs. They almost all so described themselves and it was impossible to discriminate between them and the genuine Chauhans.

Rámaiya.—Is a pedlar caste of Bijnor and neighbouring districts. The following extract from a letter by Mr. F. S. Bullock on this caste may be given:—

"The Rámaiyas have for years past been settled down in the Bijnor district in the Chandpur and Dhampur tahsíls. Altogether they are to be found in 35 or 40 villages, but chiefly in large groups in the villages of Nurpur, Rohunagli, Nahilpur and Harupur. I believe this to be the only district in India in which they have settled down in any number, but they live in a few villages in the Panjáb, *viz.*, in Delhi, Amritsar and Patiala, one village (Chilkhana) in Sahåranpur, two villages (Chandpur and Soron) in Aligarh, and in Bettiah and Bhagalpur in Bengal. They are pedlars by profession and sell precious stones and boxwala goods, such as mirrors, combs, soap, candles and stones.

"They call themselves Sikhs by religion and they worship Guru Nanak, and say they came from the Panjáb. Some shave their heads, and some do not. In fact, they appear to have two sects and account for it thus—Guru Nanak had two sons—

Srichand.	Luchmi Das.
Sadu branch.	Sikh branch.

"The descendants of Srichand shave and look like Hindus, but they are a drunken lot and eat meat, but do not worship the cow. They travel all over India, chiefly in the Deccan, while the Sikh clan travel chiefly in the Panjáb. About 600 of them live in Nurpur, which is the largest collection of them in one village, I believe, in India.

"The population in Bijnor is 3,042, *viz.*, 2,154 females and 888 males. The difference is easily accounted for, as the men travel about and earn their living, while the women stay at home. They do not cultivate. They are well off and make lots of money by 'carpet bagging.'"

Rangrez and *Rangsaz.*—Are both occupational names. The former are probably Chhipi, the latter Barhai or Lakhera.

Sani or *Saini.*—Was at last census combined with Mali. They are, however, stated by Mr. J. O. Miller, lately Settlement Officer at Muzaffarnagar, to preserve themselves absolutely distinct and have in consequence been shown separately. The sub-caste names shown for both castes are the same, and it is probable that the absolute separation Mr. Miller attests is comparatively late.

Satgop and *Sud.*—Are foreign castes, and the persons shown in the return pilgrims.

Saun.—Is a caste of Hill Khas Rájputs, shown separately in the Tarái only.

Siyarmer.—Should have been included in Kanjar.

Tarmali.—Is either Bind or Pasi.

274. **Muhammadan castes ill-defined.**—The boundaries of the Muhammadan castes are ill-defined, as there is, on one hand, a tendency to constitute every occupation a caste, and, on the other, for all low-caste Muhammadans to enrol themselves amongst Pathans or Sheikhs. So far as it was possible, members of artizan castes, who included themselves amongst Sheikhs by such names as Sheikh Nurbaf (Julaha) or Sheikh Khwaja Mansuri (Dhuna), have been incorporated in the castes to which they belong, but a large number have shown themselves as Sheikh Siddiki or Sheikh Kureshi and not a few as Pathan Ghori. Those who have done so are undistinguishable from the genuine members of these classes.

Chapter XIV.—THE OCCUPATIONS OF THE PEOPLE.

275. **The enumeration of persons dependent on each occupation.**—It has already been mentioned that in the present census the principle on which the occupation tables have been prepared has been changed. The present tables show the number of persons dependent on each occupation without distribution of workers and non-workers, whereas at last census the entries showed the actual number of workers, only the gross number of the non-workers being shown as unoccupied. The enumerator's record distinguished workers and non-workers, but the distinction was ignored in the subsequent abstraction and tabulation. It has been considered by several officers that this implied a distinct loss of available information, but personally I believe in the soundness of the course prescribed by the Government of India. The complexity of the operations of tabulation and compilation of the occupation returns was great as they stood, and had the number of entries been doubled with the cost and the intricacy of the work would have been greatly increased. There is, moreover, the greatest reason to doubt whether the distinction between workers and non-workers was in enumeration observed with such an amount of accuracy as to make returns preserving the distinction valuable.

The record of occupations in enumeration gave considerably more trouble than any other part of the schedule. The instructions to enumerators and supervisors were as follows :—

"Enter here the exact occupation or means of livelihood of all males and females who do work or live on private property, such as house-rent, shares, &c. In the case of children and women who do no work, enter the occupation of the head of their family, or of the person who supports them, adding the word "dependent," but do not leave this column unfilled for any one, even an infant. If a person have two or more occupations, enter only the chief one, except when a person owns or cultivates land in addition to another occupation, when both should be entered. If a person be temporarily out of employ, enter the last or ordinary occupation."

"No vague terms should be used, such as "service," "Government service," "shop-keeping," "writing," or labour," &c.; but the exact service, the goods sold, the class of writing or labour, must be stated. When a person's occupation is connected with agriculture, it should be stated whether the land is cultivated in person or all let to tenants; if he be an agricultural labourer, it should be stated whether he be engaged by the month or year or is a daily field labourer. Women who earn money by occupations independent of their husbands, such as selling firewood, cowdung cakes, grass, by grinding flour or doing house work for wages, should be shown under those occupations. If a person makes the articles he sells, he should be entered as "maker and seller" of them. If a person lives on alms, it should be stated whether he is a religious mendicant or an ordinary beggar. When a person is in Government, Railway, or Municipal service, the special service should be entered first, and the word Government or Municipal, &c., after, as clerk, Government; sweeper, Municipal; labourer, Railway."

"The greatest care must be taken in understanding and getting the enumerators to understand how the entries in this column must be made."

"(1). The object is to record the immediate source of the income by which each and every person is supported. The question by which the answer to be recorded can ordinarily be obtained is—"By what trade or by what source of income are you supplied? ("kaunse pesha se, ya kaunsi amdani se, guzar karte ho?" or more familiarly "tumhare yahán kya kám hota hai?" The entry will be the same whether the trade is actually carried on by the person enumerated or by his other relative or guardian, except that in the latter case the word "dependent" will be affixed. Some care will probably be necessary to guard against the record by domestic servants of their master's trade or source of income. Old servants may be likely to class themselves with the members of their master's family."

"(2). In recording occupation the most specific terms possible must be used, regarding shopkeepers the wares they deal in must be specified. Regarding persons serving in the army or civil service, their rank and the branch to which they belong. Pensions from either the military or civil service should be specified. Special attention is needed to the record of occupations of agricultural classes. Their connection with the land should be shown in the most specific way and by the name which is used locally, *e.g.*, the proprietor of a revenue-free estate should be shown as muafidár and not simply zamíndár. Sub-tenants will be distinguished from tenants-in-chief. Gardeners (bághban, mali, &c.) and market gardeners (kunjra, &c.) should be distinguished from ordinary cultivators."

"(3). With regard to agricultural labourers, care must be taken to distinguish those more or less permanently employed, *e.g.*, those known as halwaha, hali, charwáhá, baldi, or by the general name of "kamera," from those who are employed by the day or by the job, and usually known as mazdúr or mehnati. To distinguish the latter from city labourers, they should be shown as khet ka mazdúr."

"(4). Note that the second occupation of agriculturists and of those only is to be entered."

The errors usually found in enumerators' work were in general due to a tendency, almost insuperable, to record occupations in far too general terms. There was also a tendency, due to the rule that second occupations of agriculturists were to be shown, to record two occupations where agriculture was not one, thus making it difficult to ascertain in abstraction which was the chief occupation. A uniform rule had to be observed, and it was therefore prescribed that when this happened the occupation first entered was to be regarded as the chief one. This was probably correct in the majority of instances, and any errors due to it would be likely to balance each other.

276. **Tabulation and final occupation tables.**—Occupation entries were tabulated in alphabetical order without any combination of items not absolutely identical being permitted. The re-classification of the entries according to the prescribed scheme shown in the final tables was entirely done in compilation in the Central office. For this purpose classification registers were opened in English and vernacular. The entries for several districts were first classified by me in English. A vernacular copy of my entries was made over to each Superintendent in charge of a group of occupation moharrirs, with the orders that the compilation sheets were to be prepared according to the register for all entries which occurred in it, but that new entries were to be reported to me before their classification was entered. In this way a complete classification of the occupation entries has been recorded and the volumes are available for use or comparison at next census.

The work was one of no small labour, many of the terms used in districts not occurring in any dictionary, and their meaning having to be ascertained from the districts.

The tables regarding occupations accompanying the provincial report are three.

XVIIA. showing the distribution of the urban, rural and total population of the British districts and native states of the province according to occupation and age.

XVIIB. showing the distribution of the population of each district and state by occupation without distinction of age.

XVIIC. showing for the British districts and native states the second occupation of agriculturists.

277. **The classification of occupations.**—The general scheme of classification was prescribed by the Census Commissioner for India with a view to making comparison with standard English records of occupation as far possible as Indian peculiarities allowed. It was modified in minor details as work proceeded. The provincial tables omit all heads in the original scheme in which there were no entries for the province. The general scheme of classification is indicated in the following extract from a circular by the Census Commissioner :—

"In the first place, the aggregate of the various means of liveihood are divided into the following main classes :—

A.—Government.

B.—Pasture and agriculture.

C.—Personal services.

D.—The preparation and supply of material substances.

E.—Commerce and the transport of persons, goods and messages, the storage of goods.

F.—Professions—learned, artistic and minor.

G.—Indefinite occupations and means of subsistence independent of occupation.

"Subordinate to the seven classes come 24 orders, as shown marginally, bracketed according to their respective main heads. The first few explain themselves; as regards the seventh, eighth, ninth, tenth and eleventh, the object the article or service is intended for is placed more prominently than the material dealt with. On the other hand, from the twelfth to the seventeenth, the latter is regarded as more characteristic of the occupation than the object for which the prepared article is intended. The distinction is, of course, conventional only and not economic, as in both orders the makers and the sellers of an article are combined, and it is only in the eighteenth order that special mention is made of those who return themselves as exclusively engaged in distribution."

Orders.

Class	Orders
A.	I.—Administration. II.—Defence. III.—Foreign and feudatory state service.
B.	IV.—Cattle-breeding, &c. V.—Agriculture.
C.	VI.—Personal services.
D.	VII.—Food and drink. VIII.—Light, firing and forage. IX.—Buildings. X.—Vehicles and vessels. XI.—Supplementary requirements. XII.—Textile fabrics and dress. XIII.—Metals and precious stones. XIV.—Glass, pottery and stoneware. XV.—Wood, cane and leaves. XVI.—Drugs, gums, &c. XVII.—Leather.
E.	XVIII.—Commerce. XIX.—Transport and storage.
F.	XX.—Learned and artistic professions. XXI.—Sports and amusements.
G.	XXII.—Complex occupations. XXIII.—Indefinite. XXIV.—Independent of work.

The classification next passes into sub-orders, and where still further definition is thought necessary, into groups subordinate to the sub-orders.

Sub-orders and groups.

Under the 77 sub-orders have been arranged the occupations of the province in 419 heads. An examination of these entries in detail would be one which would require a report in itself and I propose to make only a few remarks pointing out the salient features in the distribution of population by occupation.

278. **Causes producing inaccuracy in occupation tables.**—Before doing so attention may be drawn to certain general considerations which affect the consistency or exhaustiveness of the occupation classification of the province.

I.—I have already referred to the tendency to undue generalization. I regret that it took place not only in enumeration but in certain tabulation offices and has led to its being necessary to omit details for a good many occupations in the districts in which it was extensive.

II.—The omission of record of domestic and secondary occupations was inevitable unless the record of two or more occupations for each person was enjoined, a course almost impossible in view of the enormous addition to the complexity of the returns.

The domestic trades most usual in these provinces may be mentioned. Tat-making, tazia-making, artificial flower-making, kite-making, thread-making, sewing, chikan and other embroidery, are often carried on as domestic work by men. They are, except tat-making, usual only amongst Muhammadans.

The absence of domestic sewing amongst Hindus is no doubt partly accounted for by the fact that the dress of a low caste Hindu woman, in the eastern districts especially, wants little or no sewing, and that of a man not much, as compared with a Muhammadan. There is no doubt, however, that caste prejudices have great influence in the matter. The poverty of a considerable number of Muhammadan families who consider themselves "sharif" leads to their employing themselves largely on such occupations, especially in Lucknow; but they rarely admit that they carry on these occupations as a means of earning a livelihood—Kahars do net-making as a domestic trade.

Chikan and other embroidery (kamdani),
Net-work (kamarbands mostly),
Baskets of munj and sink,
Fan-making,
Vermicelli (siwain)-making,
Sewing,
Stocking-knitting (a late accomplishment),
Spinning,
Cotton-cleaning,
} are domestic trades often carried on by women.

III.—The record for occupations which depend upon the season of year must necessarily be complete in a census taken on a fixed date. As an example of importance, indigo-manufacture may be mentioned. In certain districts it gives employment to a very large number of persons during the rains, but in February the factories are for the most part standing empty and in consequence only a few permanant employés are shown in the census returns.

IV.—Native terminology, unless qualified to an extent untrained enumerators could hardly be expected to attempt, renders inevitable some want of detail and certain arbitrary variations between some of the occupation columns. Thus a cattle-breeder would probably be described in an enumerator's schedules by exactly the same expression as is used to describe his cowherd. Again, the word usually employed to describe both the estate of a wealthy landholder is that which is properly appropriate to an independent native state, and the servants of both are therefore confused. The word sepoy (sipahi) is used both for a soldier and a messenger.

V.—The English report notes the impossibility of preparing a scheme of classification in which certain columns would not to some extent clash with other. This is equally the case in India, particularly as the present scheme of classification, though modified in important particulars to suit India, in some cases distinguishes occupations which in these provinces are regarded as the same and, on the other hand, to a smaller extent combines occupations regarded by native custom as essentially different.

An Appendix, XXXI, has been added showing the heads of occupation the entries in which cross to an important extent.

279. **Additional occupations of agriculturists.**—Second occupations of agriculturists have, as already noted, been recorded. It is important to notice that in the general Tables A and B persons dependent partly on agriculture and partly on another occupation are entered under the latter and not the former. The additions to be made to each head of agriculture are shown in Table XVII-C. Thus a pleader who is also a landholder appears in Tables A and B as a pleader, whilst Table C shows that he, with a certain number of other pleaders, are also landholders. The figures for all occupations other than agriculture are complete. Those for agriculture to include persons partly dependent must have the entries in Table C added to them. General appendices to this chapter show—

(1) (Appendix XXXII.) The proportion of the town population dependent on each class, order or sub-order of occupation and the proportions in which occupations are distributed between towns and rural tracts.

(2) (Appendix XXXIII.) The extent to which the age distribution of the various classes of occupations vary from the general age distribution.

280. **Persons dependent on the service of Government.**—The first of the great classes into which the population has been distributed is that of persons in the service of Government or dependent on such persons. The functions of Government in India extend far beyond the primary duties usually associated with the idea of Government. Public education, engineering, agricultural training, medical practice, vaccination, are all branches of

Government service in India to a far greater extent than in any European country. It was desired for the sake of uniformity that the persons to be shown under class A should, so far as possible, exclude those dependent on these extensions of the responsibilities of Government and be confined to those who fulfil the essential functions of protection and defence. Engineers, surveyors, teachers and medical men in the service of Government should, therefore, be shown under separate heads provided for each of these professions, and only the agents of Government in administration and defence included under this head. There is, however, reason to believe that the attraction of the general term "Government service" has drawn many persons from the special heads into class A.

The class is naturally a large one. The functions of Government in India are widely extended, owing to the fact that the Government is the supreme proprietor of the soil, and in that character maintains elaborate records and accounts of the produce of the soil and the rental transactions between landholders and tenants. The extent to which offences against property are rendered possible in India by the comparative want of protection afforded by earthen walls and unlocked doors also necessitates an extension of the police system in the provision of watch and ward for every small village to which in England we have no parallel. On the other hand, the provision of officials of classes corresponding to those in England is, for equal populations, very much smaller in India, so that, as a whole, Government service includes a smaller proportion of the population than it does in England.

The total population dependent on Government service was 926,661, of whom 530,442 were males of all ages. These amount to 197 persons in 10,000 of the total population. They are shown for the provinces under 7 sub-orders and 18 occupations. The sub-orders distinguish service of the Imperial Government, Local and Municipal service and village service. To the native all are Government service alike, and in not a few districts all distinctions have been obliterated and officers, clerks, messengers, policemen, village accountants and village watchmen shown together as Government sevants. In this case all have been shown under occupation No. 4, the rank to which the majority of servants of the Imperial Government belong. The third order, service of foreign and feudatory states, is probably insufficient, as the term "Naukari riyasat" is applied alike to the service of large zamindars and of independent chiefs. All for whom this entry was made without further specification were considered to be servants of ordinary proprietors of land.

There is a noticeable absence of both women and children amongst the persons in Government service, the reason being that women and children are mostly left at home, members of an undivided family of whom the resident heads are agriculturists. There is, therefore, a tendency, even though one or more of the family are in Government service, for those at home to record themselves as agriculturists. This is especially the case for soldiers. Though the actual garrison of the province is large, a number of men probably greatly exceeding the actual garrison in number are employed as soldiers in other provinces. The proportion of women and children should, therefore, were it not for the reason just given, be high in proportion to the number of men. Economically the variations in the numbers or circumstances of Government service are of little interest. They are as a body less exposed either to poverty or riches than any of the other classes of population.

281. **Agricultural population.**—Class B includes by far the largest and most important and numerous part of the population—that dependent on agriculture or pasturage in the widest sense of these words. This class contains within its two orders and six sub-orders a population of no less than 28,912,897 or 6,165 per 10,000 of the total population of the provinces. The totals under the two orders included are :—

Connected with the pasturage or management of stock ...	343,476
Agricultural, including growers of special products, labourers and persons employed in agricultural management and supervision	28,521,117

These figures do not, however, include the whole population more or less directly dependent on agriculture. Table C, as already stated, shows the number of persons dependent on land-owning or cultivation in addition to some other occupation and should, with a view to considering the comparative importance of agiculture in the country, be taken into account.

Another addition of importance has, in my opinion, to be made here. Occupation No. 406 shows 3,911,020 persons who were recorded as dependent on general labour, of whom 455,637 live in towns and 3,455,383 in villages; such persons described themselves no doubt accurately as general labourers, as they do any kind of work which turns up. It is however certain that the majority of them depend more on agricultural labour than on labour of any other sort. They from time to time find work in building earthen walls, thatching houses, road-making and fetching and carrying for petty traders in villages, but on much the greater number of days in a year they are engaged in field work, the only form of work which to any great extent is always to be found in the villages of the province. The vast majority of these general labourers in villages are, therefore, nearly as much dependent on agricultural labour as those who have so recorded themselves. Another addition not of great importance is that of the 73,767 persons who record themselves as blanket-weavers. They are almost exclusively of exactly the same class as that which records itself as sheep-breeders, and it is purely a matter of accident under which name a man enters himself. Blanket-weaving is in these provinces exclusively a domestic occupation carried on in times of leisure by the sheep-breeders.

We are now in a position to show the total number of persons dependent wholly or in part on agriculture or pasturage. They may in view of their connection with the land be redistributed so as to bring together those of similar economic condition. The North-Western Provinces and Oudh are essentially agricultural. Pastural pursuits are, except in tracts so comparatively unimportant in the matter of population as to be negligeable in a view of the circumstances of the province, entirely an adjunct of agriculture and may be so shown. We have therefore the following redistribution of population above mentioned :—

Proprietors of land	3,910,470
Cultivators	25,118,250
Labourers	5,767,019
Total, wholly or partly dependent on agriculture ...	34,795,739

Persons deriving the whole or a part of their means of subsistence from agriculture, therefore, form 74·2 per cent. of the total population—a population greatly higher than in any European country. The proportion as appears from Appendix No. XXXIV. varies greatly in the different parts of the province. Kumaun is almost exclusively agricultural ; after Kumaun the Eastern Divisions of Gorakhpur, Oudh and Benares are the most exclusively agricultural, whilst in the Western Division of Meerut the proportion of agriculturists falls to a percentage not unlike that of a non-manufacturing European country or county. It is therefore the case that, excluding Kumaun, the area statistics for which are not reliable, where the area per head available for cultivation is smallest, the proportion of persons dependent on agriculture is largest.

The density of the agricultural population on the cultivated area is greatest in Azamgarh, Jaunpur and the neighbouring Oudh districts.

Abstract No. 115, showing density of agricultural population on cultivated area.

District.	Density.	District.	Density.
Garhwál	2,030·6	Hardoi	637·8
Kumaun	1,283·2	Mainpuri	629·4
Azamgarh	1,244·1	Sháhjahánpur	628·3
Kumaun Division	1,134·8	Bareilly	623·6
Jaunpur	1,054·8	Fatehpur	618·2
Sultánpur	1,042·4	Kheri	600·8
Fyzabad	1,038·5	Pilibhít	574·6
Partábgarh	999·3	Bahraich	573·5
Mirzapur	980·5	Etah	570·1
Gorakhpur Division	952·5	Agra Division	569·9
Benares Division	942·2	Rohilkhand Division	564·5
Benares	897·0	Budaun	556·5
Gorakhpur	894·7	Sitapur	550·4
Rae Bareli	894·3	Moradabad	531·4
Ballia	893·5	Agra	514·3
Gházipur	860·6	Allahabad Division	505·9
Basti	849·8	Bijnor	478·7
Fyzabad Division	819·5	Meerut	468·3
Bara Banki	800·4	Lalitpur	467·7
Lucknow	799·6	Bulandshahr	460·3
Unao	794·3	Tarái	451·7
Oudh	753·2	Meerut Division	448·01
Gonda	711·5	Aligarh	433·9
Allahabad	698·5	Sahéranpur	429·9
Dehra Dún	685·9	Muttra	427·2
Lucknow Division	681·4	Bánda	416·9
North-Western Provinces and Oudh ...	677·5	Muzaffarnagar	410·2
Farukhabad	676 7	Jhánsi	390·2
Cawnpore	666·2	Hamírpur	307·4
Etáwah	657·8	Jalaun	297·7
North-Western Provinces	651·3		

It steadily and rapidly decreases westwards, and in Muttra and Sahâranpur is not one-third of what it is in Azamgarh. The circumstances of the agricultural population, their liability to distress from failure of harvests, and their state now as compared with that in previous periods of Indian history have already been fully enquired into during the present year, and

I have nothing to add to the conclusions arrived at by the Director of Agriculture in a memorandum lately submitted to Government. How a cultivator in Azamgarh manages to subsist on half an acre, whilst in Sahāranpur an acre and a half is required, is a question on which much might be written. It appears certain, 1st, that the western cultivator with his larger holding lives better and has a far higher standard of comfort than the majority of persons of the same occupation in the east; 2nd, that the eastern cultivator is far more dependent than the western on crops which yield a high return for a small area. From the opium cultivation in particular he derives an amount of assistance in subsisting on his land the importance of which it is difficult to overrate. In many districts it is the opium which pays the rent, and without the opium the rent could not be paid; 3rd, the eastern cultivator is less exclusively dependent on agriculture than his compatriot in the west. Emigration from the eastern districts in search of temporary employment is, as already pointed out, very extensive and in many families subsistence is only possible with the assistance derived from the emigrant members.

282. **Other classes of occupations.**—The other classes of occupations are of infinitely less importance in the provinces than that just referred to, and may be briefly referred to.

The third class in the census returns is that showing persons dependent on personal services for their livelihood, who include 5½ per cent. of the total population. The occupations under this class, important in the North-West Provinces, are barbers, washermen, water-carriers, indoor servants and sweepers and scavengers. The extent to which even the poorest of the population is dependent on the services of this class is a peculiarity of Indian society for which caste prejudices are mainly responsible. The barber, the washerman and in many districts the sweeper receives his petty fees in grain from every cultivator in his village, and amongst classes above the lowest the water-carrier and domestic servant is employed to an extent incomparably greater than amongst the corresponding classes in England. Paid for the most part in grain, these village servants are no less dependent on the harvests than the cultivators themselves. In status and modes of life they are not materially different from cultivators of the lower grades.

Class D, that of persons dependent on the preparation and supply of material substances, includes two classes whose circumstances are widely different, dealers and producers. It was inevitable that they should be shown together, as owing to the confusion already referred in Indian terminology between the producer and the vendor, the schedule entries cannot be relied upon to distinguish the two classes of occupation accurately. It is possible, however, roughly to separate them. Manufacturers in India are almost invariably of the petty class who sell as well as make their wares, but the real means of subsistence is the production, the vending being an accident. Roughly, out of the total 7,898,769 persons in class D, 2,554,085 derived their livelihood entirely from dealing in articles produced by others, whilst 5,344,684 persons are mainly dependent on the production or manufacture of their wares. The persons in the first subdivision are closely allied to those shown as commercial in class E. Altogether, including shopkeepers of all kinds as well as bankers and merchants properly so called, commercial occupations in these provinces support 3,726,260 persons or 7·9 per cent. of the total population. Naturally in a country into which the extended needs of civilization have little penetrated, the class which supplies articles of food and drink is by far the most extensive under this head. On such occupations 2,296,661 persons are dependent, 1,173,244 being connected with the supply of vegetable food, mostly dealers in or vendors of grain. The commercial population is that about the comparative prosperity of which least doubt can be entertained. Trade beyond doubt is greatly increasing, and whilst it may be believed that pressure of population and subdivision of land is injuriously affecting the circumstances of landholders and cultivators, there can be no hesitation in believing that the trader is in the provinces yearly advancing in wealth and importance, that whilst the Thákur may be falling into the background the Baniya steadily increases his wealth and importance.

Of the 5,344,684 persons above noted as manufacturers or producers, the circumstances are very different. They form 11·4 per cent. of the total population. The groups which are most important in point of numbers are—

Oil-pressers	568,443
Makers of bangles, necklaces, &c.	190,617
Workers in cotton	1,524,739
Tailors	349,935
Workers in gold, silver, &c.	248,686
Carpenters	391,765
Blacksmiths	319,540
Potters	466,390
Cane-workers	205,405
Workers in leather	361,783

Of these the two most important groups, the oil-pressers and workers in cotton, have felt the competition of European goods severely. The native cotton manufactures of the country are being undersold by manufacture in Europe or on European methods and the large class which has so far hereditarily depended on these manufactures is now in process of finding some other occupation and, as already remarked in connection with the movement of the population in towns, suffering severely whilst undergoing it.

In class F persons dependent on professional income only three classes included are of importance numerically—

(1) Ministers of religion	156,100
(2) Religious mendicants	251,988
(3) Dancers, singers and players	88,777

The first mainly consists of Hindu priests with whom should also be numbered most of the 78,203 persons dependent on astrology. Those included in the first class are the "purohits" or family priests, a class contemptuously regarded amongst Brahmans. The Pandit or astrologer assumes to himself a much higher position. The vast difference between the 234,303 persons recorded as dependent on these occupations and the 4,719,882 Brahmans in the provinces is instructive as showing how comparatively rarely the Brahman exercises what is ordinarily regarded as his hereditary function. It is probable, however, that the number of priests is, owing to the fact that the occupation is looked down on by Brahmans in general, greatly understated. Almost all of them hold some land and prefer to be recorded as landholders or cultivators and to omit all mention of the professional income.

The large class of 251,988 religious mendicants is distinguished by no clear line from the still larger group, 573,966, shown as dependent on general mendicancy under class G. Amongst the better class of Muhammadans it is vigorously denied that the professional mendicants who are their co-religionists can be regarded as in any way ministers of or connected with religion. Amongst Hindus of the better class the feeling is not very materially different, although the connection of the wandering mendicant with religious offices is more generally admitted.

There remains for mention under class G only the important group of unskilled labourers, on whom 3,959,896 persons are shown as dependent. They are mostly, as already stated, employed on agricultural labour and, with the 3,006,785 persons shown as exclusively agricultural labourers, form the very poorest class of the population. For many of them it appears certain that two full meals a day is a luxury enjoyed only in years of prosperity. They are those who most promptly become dependent on Government for a bare livelihood in times of famine. At the same time it is no less certain that in a year of ordinary prosperity there is far less severe distress amongst this class than is constantly prevalent amongst the substratum of the population of a European country. The wants of the Indian poor are few as compared with those of Europeans, principally because the climate removes, except to a comparatively small extent, the need for protection against cold and wet.

APPENDICES.

APPENDIX I.

Return of Census Agency—Town Blocks.

Serial number.	District or State.	Number of Superintendents. District staff.	Other departments.	Non-officials.	Total.	Number of Supervisors. Patwáris.	Other district staff.	Other departments.	Non-officials.	Unspecified.	Total.	Number of Ennumerators. Patwáris.	Other officials.	Zamindárs.	Zamindárs' Agents.	School boys.	Other non-officials.	Unspecified.	Total.
1	2	3	4	5	6	7	8	9	10	11	12	13	14	15	16	17	18	19	20
1	Dehra Dún ...	2	1	...	3	...	8	5	5	...	18	...	63	...	8	5	105	...	181
2	Sahâranpur ...	11	5	1	17	12	4	21	45	...	82	12	78	184	49	59	472	...	854
3	Muzaffarnagar	9	...	2	11	7	14	7	17	...	45	28	109	85	18	29	295	...	564
4	Meerut	Included in rural.																	
5	Bulandshahr	2	...	...	2	12	37	1	16	...	66	13	93	62	43	48	410	...	669
6	Aligarh	4	...	5	9	1	15	2	59	...	77	20	...	40	25	10	626	...	721
	Total, Meerut Division	28	6	8	42	32	78	36	142	...	288	73	343	371	143	151	1,908	...	2,989
7	Muttra	...	3	...	3	1	22	20	2	...	45	10	146	19	9	11	301	...	496
8	Agra	2	...	11	13	...	22	39	35	...	96	11	269	6	9	111	391	...	797
9	Farukhabad	2	2	1	5	...	12	14	31	...	57	6	112	33	42	29	393	...	615
10	Mainpuri	...	...	1	1	...	2	1	10	...	13	...	84	...	1	...	88	...	123
11	Etáwah	1	...	...	1	...	13	2	6	...	21	2	65	6	3	1	116	...	193
12	Etah	14	...	...	14	2	14	...	31	...	47	13	89	79	25	5	216	...	427
	Total, Agra Division	19	5	13	37	3	85	76	115	...	279	42	765	143	89	157	1,455	...	2,651
13	Bareilly	9	6	4	19	10	30	10	7	...	57	18	64	51	24	25	464	...	646
14	Bijnor	3	5	3	11	11	23	12	10	...	56	9	93	116	34	40	312	...	604
15	Budaun	1	...	...	1	...	...	3	8	...	11	...	18	37	...	...	63	...	118
16	Moradabad	5	1	...	6	15	20	42	31	...	108	9	159	172	15	50	502	...	907
17	Sháhjahánpur	...	3	1	4	2	...	11	32	...	45	...	119	69	23	15	223	...	449
18	Pilibhit	...	...	1	1	2	9	5	5	...	21	1	79	17	20	1	71	...	189
	Total, Rohilkhand Division	18	15	9	42	40	82	83	93	...	298	37	532	462	116	131	1,635	...	2,913
19	Cawnpore	4	2	3	9	...	24	28	20	...	72	...	179	...	...	...	560	...	789
20	Fatehpur	1	...	1	2	...	7	1	7	...	15	5	19	18	6	2	136	...	186
21	Bánda	...	3	2	5	2	11	4	5	...	22	...	126	11	12	5	60	...	214
22	Hamírpur	...	...	...	...	14	3	24	5	...	46	33	36	14	8	...	180	...	266
23	Allahabad	14	...	18	32	...	15	24	77	...	116	10	66	...	1	...	909	...	986
24	Jhánsi	1	4	2	7	2	1	1	8	...	12	5	44	8	1	59	414	...	531
25	Jalaun	2	...	...	2	...	13	4	7	...	24	7	74	15	17	84	84	...	231

No.	District																		
26	Lalitpur	2	1	...	3	...	3	2	2	...	7	5	22	1	2	...	58	...	88
	Total, Allahabad Division ...	24	10	26	60	18	77	88	131	...	314	65	566	67	42	150	2,351	...	3,241
27	Benares	2	1	6	9	...	30	8	45	...	78	...	...	...	...	...	...	740	740
28	Mirzapur	1	2	...	3	...	9	4	20	...	33	16	111	8	12	1	197	...	345
29	Jaunpur	...	...	2	2	...	3	4	18	...	25	...	24	28	16	9	212	...	289
30	Gházipur	2	...	...	2	12	16	1	3	...	32	4	176	...	3	...	228	...	411
31	Ballia	1	...	...	1	11	9	10	15	...	45	2	19	58	9	61	302	...	451
	Total, Benares Division ...	6	3	8	17	23	67	22	101	...	213	22	330	94	40	71	939	740	2,236
32	Gorakhpur	...	2	3	5	...	4	...	21	...	25	...	35	...	...	2	241	...	278
33	Basti	...	...	...	...	...	12	3	3	...	18	...	47	9	3	17	152	...	228
34	Azamgarh	...	1	...	1	4	...	11	16	...	81	6	37	...	1	1	351	...	396
	Total, Gorakhpur Division ...	...	3	3	6	4	16	14	40	...	74	6	119	9	4	20	744	...	902
35	Kumaun	20	1	3	24	...	57	10	2	...	69	...	166	...	...	...	1	...	167
36	Garhwál	...	1	...	1	...	...	2	...	...	2	...	6	...	...	...	7	...	13
37	Taráí	2	...	...	2	...	5	2	...	...	7	1	25	8	...	...	31	...	65
	Total, Kumaun Division ...	22	2	3	27	...	62	14	2	...	78	1	197	8	...	...	39	...	245
	TOTAL, N.-W. PROVINCES ...	117	44	70	231	120	467	333	624	...	1,544	246	2,852	1,154	434	680	9,071	740	15,177
38	Lucknow	1	...	8	9	...	41	84	5	...	130	2	472	...	...	...	815	...	1,289
39	Unao	2	1	1	4	3	11	15	9	...	38	8	83	52	18	23	175	...	359
40	Rae Bareli	...	1	1	2	...	1	4	6	...	11	3	22	...	...	...	111	...	136
41	Sitapur	1	3	2	6	...	9	7	12	...	28	3	93	22	27	26	117	...	288
42	Hardoi	2	...	4	6	1	15	7	17	...	40	1	90	174	41	39	61	...	406
43	Kheri	1	...	...	1	2	4	4	6	...	16	3	66	5	19	4	61	...	158
	Total, Lucknow Division ...	7	5	16	28	6	81	121	55	...	263	20	826	258	105	92	1,340	...	2,636
44	Fyzabad	3	1	3	7	...	22	14	20	...	56	16	241	31	30	...	172	...	490
45	Gonda	1	1	2	4	...	8	...	11	...	19	...	60	...	13	...	109	...	182
46	Bahraich	1	...	...	1	...	1	2	18	...	21	1	71	2	43	4	65	...	186
47	Sultánpur	...	...	1	1	...	1	3	...	...	4	...	24	2	3	...	29	...	58
48	Partabgarh	1	...	...	1	...	...	2	1	...	3	...	22	...	...	1	9	...	32
49	Bara Banki	3	...	...	3	...	3	19	6	...	28	7	119	33	14	4	76	...	253
	Total, Fyzabad Division ...	9	2	6	17	...	35	40	56	...	131	24	537	68	103	9	460	...	1,201
	TOTAL, OUDH ...	16	7	22	45	6	116	161	111	...	394	44	1,363	321	208	101	1,800	...	3,837
	TOTAL, N.-W. P. & OUDH ...	133	51	92	276	126	583	494	735	...	1,938	290	4,215	1,475	642	781	10,871	740	19,014
50	Rampur	...	6	...	6	1	...	9	13	...	23	5	112	5	2	2	96	...	222
51	Tehri Garhwál	...	...	...	...	...	...	...	...	...	...	...	...	...	...	...	...	...	...
	TOTAL, NATIVE STATES ...	...	...	...	...	...	...	...	...	...	...	...	...	...	...	...	...	...	...

APPENDIX II.

Return of Census Agency—Rural Blocks.

Serial number.	District or State.	Number of Superintendents.				Number of Supervisors.						Number of Enumerators.							
		District staff.	Other departments.	Non-officials.	Total.	Patwáris.	Other district staff.	Other departments.	Non-officials.	Unspecified.	Total.	Patwáris.	Other officials.	Zamindárs.	Zamindárs' Agents.	School boys.	Other non-officials.	Unspecified.	Total.
1	2	3	4	5	6	7	8	9	10	11	12	13	14	15	16	17	18	19	20
1	Dehra Dún ...	3	...	...	3	55	...	10	...	...	65	...	58	167	32	2	274	...	533
2	Saháranpur ...	4	...	1	5	145	26	20	67	...	258	662	142	524	107	189	1,053	...	2,677
3	Muzaffarnagar ...	10	...	1	11	137	14	8	58	...	217	306	77	417	74	80	1,236	...	2,190
4	Meerut, including town ...	39	24	...	63	388	60	27	82	...	557	398	85	1,507	75	147	2,025	...	4,237
5	Bulandshahr ...	26	...	...	26	276	1	...	14	...	291	246	160	211	149	36	2,012	...	2,804
6	Aligarh ...	40	...	...	40	20	...	...	268	...	288	600	400	800	500	80	440	...	2,820
	Total, Meerut Division ...	122	24	2	148	1,021	101	65	489	...	1,676	2,212	912	3,626	937	534	7,040	...	15,261
7	Muttra ...	12	...	...	12	110	23	80	24	...	187	407	163	372	93	67	1,001	...	2,103
8	Agra ...	15	...	...	15	85	46	74	92	...	297	618	182	284	96	266	1,627	...	3,073
9	Farukhabad ...	14	...	...	14	88	38	35	90	...	251	479	93	657	246	61	825	...	2,361
10	Mainpuri ...	15	...	...	15	...	48	58	162	...	268	492	165	156	77	...	2,109	...	2,999
11	Etáwah ...	12	...	...	12	158	23	13	29	...	223	254	108	624	184	61	1,199	...	2,330
12	Etah ...	...	...	...	...	35	68	34	77	...	214	527	60	430	111	7	980	...	2,116
	Total, Agra Division ...	68	...	...	68	476	246	244	474	...	1,440	2,777	771	2,423	807	462	7,741	...	14,981
13	Bareilly ...	10	...	...	10	88	47	33	153	...	271	565	90	591	252	92	1,855	...	2,945
14	Bijnor ...	12	3	...	15	139	15	20	44	...	218	369	113	417	122	34	1,169	...	2,214
15	Budaun ...	10	...	...	10	181	...	50	84	...	315	444	170	916	414	...	1,109	...	3,053
16	Moradabad ...	18	...	...	18	244	25	10	25	...	304	519	66	352	276	96	2,024	...	3,333
17	Sháhjahánpur ...	...	14	...	14	532	...	...	...	...	532	7	127	318	196	8	1,852	...	2,503
18	Pilibhít ...	14	...	...	14	112	5	6	15	...	138	256	21	176	597	...	297	...	1,347
	Total, Rohilkhand Division ...	64	17	...	81	1,246	92	119	321	...	1,778	2,160	587	2,770	1,857	225	7,796	...	15,395
19	Cawnpore ...	36	...	1	37	63	70	72	207	...	412	714	118	740	186	18	2,681	...	4,452
20	Fatehpur ...	22	1	1	24	26	27	34	130	...	217	588	121	602	109	9	906	...	2,235
21	Bánda ...	22	...	...	22	165	53	27	56	...	301	598	154	1,082	203	20	1,029	...	3,086
22	Hamírpur ...	17	...	...	17	35	16	44	55	...	150	469	29	113	48	...	940	...	1,599
23	Allahabad ...	54	...	11	65	71	86	52	318	...	472	700	63	120	75	...	4,231	...	5,189
24	Jhánsi ...	25	11	...	36	7	49	38	67	...	151	242	61	166	18	...	817	...	1,304
25	Jalaun ...	9	...	3	12	16	43	21	72	...	152	886	103	88	59	828	430	...	1,394
26	Lalitpur ...	3	...	...	3	25	22	31	43	...	121	204	14	101	6	5	667	...	997
	Total, Allahabad Division ...	188	12	16	216	408	316	319	933	...	1,976	3,901	658	2,912	704	380	11,701	...	20,256

27	Benares	10	...	...	10	229	...	59	32	...	320	...	...	...	...	...	...	2,734	2,734
28	Mirzapur	15	13	1	29	252	39	7	212	...	510	269	144	882	397	31	3,127	...	4,850
29	Jaunpur	29	...	7	36	97	7	6	302	...	412	466	12	341	68	4	3,198	...	4,089
30	Ghâzipur	24	...	1	25	340	14	1	81	...	436	161	112	162	132	...	2,726	166	3,459
31	Ballia	12	...	1	13	266	...	29	68	...	363	206	12	1,227	61	140	1,970	...	3,616
	Total, Benares Division ...	90	13	10	113	1,184	60	102	695	...	12,041	1,102	280	2,612	658	175	11,021	2,900	18,748
32	Gorakhpur	59	7	13	79	624	62	118	293	...	1,097	762	132	4,203	881	73	4,882	...	10,833
33	Basti	26	...	...	26	1,093	37	3	16	...	1,149	9	96	5,635	87	165	1,961	...	7,953
34	Azamgarh	...	...	...	...	161	...	75	316	...	552	682	33	184	22	...	3,988	...	4,909
	Total, Gorakhpur Division ...	85	7	13	105	1,878	99	196	625	...	2,798	1,453	261	10,022	940	238	10,781	...	23,695
35	Kumaun	32	1	4	37	80	363	...	...	...	443	...	146	4,902	...	...	779	...	5,827
36	Garhwál	7	3	...	10	40	3	31	17	...	91	...	85	...	...	...	1,030	...	1,115
37	Tarái	8	...	...	8	29	34	1	2	...	66	197	143	71	40	57	99	...	607
	Total, Kumaun Division ...	47	4	4	55	149	400	32	19	...	600	197	374	4,973	40	57	1,908	...	7,549
	Total, N.-W. Provinces ...	664	77	45	786	6,362	1,314	1,077	3,556	...	12,309	13,802	3,843	29,338	5,943	2,071	57,988	2,900	115,885
38	Lucknow	17	4	...	21	19	6	21	92	...	138	288	108	82	31	10	798	...	1,312
39	Unao	16	...	...	16	112	10	64	119	...	305	480	58	1,032	115	94	1,249	...	3,028
40	Rae Bareli	15	...	...	15	22	10	79	208	...	319	668	62	266	96	...	2,348	...	3,440
41	Sitapur	18	2	1	21	87	11	56	169	...	323	661	102	356	333	38	1,820	...	3,310
42	Hardoi	17	2	4	23	263	1	6	201	...	471	550	53	1,550	279	57	1,597	...	4,086
43	Kheri	13	...	...	13	175	4	18	155	...	352	311	93	168	213	...	2,347	...	3,132
	Total, Lucknow Division ...	96	8	5	109	678	42	244	944	...	1,908	2,958	476	3,454	1,067	199	10,154	...	18,308
44	Fyzabad	31	2	...	33	53	54	42	199	...	348	540	159	836	4	9	1,987	...	3,535
45	Gonda	21	1	...	22	61	...	...	403	...	464	825	...	596	326	...	2,948	...	4,695
46	Bahraich	2	2	9	13	30	14	55	268	...	367	583	72	137	269	2	2,507	...	3,570
47	Sultanpur	27	...	3	30	7	83	66	150	...	306	766	72	1,228	186	23	1,592	...	3,867
48	Partabgarh	16	6	9	31	...	...	...	...	275	275	...	...	...	...	...	...	2,992	2,992
49	Bara Banki...	17	...	...	17	45	7	124	154	...	330	705	106	715	417	63	1,550	...	3,556
	Total, Fyzabad Division ...	114	11	21	146	196	158	287	1,174	275	2,090	3,419	409	3,512	1,202	97	10,584	2,992	22,215
	Total, Oudh ...	210	19	26	255	874	200	531	2,118	275	3,998	6,377	885	6,966	3,269	296	20,738	2,992	40,523
	Total, N.-W. P. and Oudh ...	874	96	71	1,041	7,236	1,514	1,608	5,674	275	16,307	20,179	4,728	36,304	8,212	2,367	78,726	5,892	156,408
50	Rampur	...	21	...	21	6	...	85	40	...	131	329	63	20	24	5	309	...	750
51	Tehri Garhwal	...	...	...	...	...	...	...	...	...	...	...	...	...	...	...	...	...	...
	TOTAL, NATIVE STATES ...	...	...	...	...	...	...	...	...	...	...	...	...	...	...	...	...	...	...

APPENDIX III.

Return of Census Agency—All blocks.

Serial number.	District or State.	Number of Superintendents. District staff.	Number of Superintendents. Other departments.	Number of Superintendents. Non-officials.	Number of Superintendents. Total.	Number of Supervisors. Patwáris.	Number of Supervisors. Other district staff.	Number of Supervisors. Other departments.	Number of Supervisors. Non-officials.	Number of Supervisors. Unspecified.	Number of Supervisors. Total.	Number of Enumerators. Patwáris.	Number of Enumerators. Other officials.	Number of Enumerators. Zamindárs.	Number of Enumerators. Zamindárs' agents.	Number of Enumerators. School boys.	Number of Enumerators. Other non-officials.	Number of Enumerators. Unspecified.	Number of Enumerators. Total.
1	2	3	4	5	6	7	8	9	10	11	12	13	14	15	16	17	18	19	20
1	Dehra Dún	5	1	...	6	55	8	15	5	...	83	...	121	167	40	7	379	...	714
2	Sahāranpur	15	5	2	22	157	30	41	112	...	340	674	220	708	156	248	1,525	...	3,531
3	Muzaffarnagar	19	...	3	22	144	28	15	75	...	262	334	186	502	92	109	1,531	...	2,754
4	Meerut	39	24	...	63	388	60	27	82	...	557	308	85	1,507	75	147	2,025	...	4,237
5	Bulandshahr	28	...	...	28	288	38	1	30	...	357	259	243	273	192	84	2,422	...	3,473
6	Aligarh	44	...	5	49	21	15	2	327	...	365	620	400	840	525	90	1,066	...	3,541
	Total, Meerut Division ...	150	30	10	190	1,053	179	101	631	...	1,964	2,285	1,255	3,997	1,080	685	8,948	...	18,250
7	Muttra	12	3	...	15	111	45	50	26	...	232	417	309	391	102	78	1,302	...	2,599
8	Agra	17	...	11	28	85	68	113	127	...	393	629	451	290	105	377	2,018	...	3,870
9	Farukhabad...	16	2	1	19	88	50	49	121	...	308	485	205	690	288	90	1,218	...	2,976
10	Mainpuri	15	...	1	16	...	50	59	172	...	281	492	249	156	78	...	2,147	...	3,122
11	Etáwah	13	...	...	13	158	36	15	35	...	244	256	173	530	187	62	1,315	...	2,523
12	Etah	14	...	...	14	37	82	34	108	...	261	540	149	509	136	12	1,196	...	2,542
	Total, Agra Division ...	87	5	13	105	479	331	320	589	...	1,719	2,819	1,536	2,566	896	619	9,196	...	17,632
13	Bareilly	19	6	4	29	48	77	43	160	...	328	583	154	642	276	117	1,819	...	3,591
14	Bijnor	15	8	3	26	150	38	32	54	...	274	378	206	533	156	74	1,471	...	2,818
15	Budaun	11	...	...	11	181	...	53	92	...	326	444	188	953	414	...	1,172	...	3,171
16	Moradabad	23	1	...	24	259	45	52	56	...	412	528	225	524	291	146	2,526	...	4,240
17	Sháhjahánpur	...	17	1	18	534	...	11	32	...	677	7	246	387	219	18	2,075	...	2,952
18	Pilibhít	14	...	1	15	114	14	11	20	...	159	257	100	193	617	1	368	...	1,536
	Total, Rohilkhand Division ...	82	32	9	123	1,286	174	202	414	...	2,076	2,197	1,119	3,232	1,973	356	9,431	...	18,308
19	Cawnpore	40	2	4	46	63	94	100	227	...	484	714	292	740	186	18	3,241	...	5,191
20	Fatehpur	23	1	2	26	26	34	35	137	...	232	593	140	520	115	11	1,042	...	2,421
21	Bánda	22	3	2	27	167	64	31	61	...	323	598	280	1,093	215	25	1,089	...	3,300
22	Hamírpur	17	...	...	17	49	19	68	60	...	196	502	65	127	51	...	1,120	...	1,865
23	Allahabad	68	...	29	97	71	51	76	390	...	588	710	129	120	76	...	5,140	...	6,175
24	Jhánsi	26	15	2	43	9	50	39	65	...	168	247	105	174	19	59	1,231	...	1,836
25	Jalaun	11	...	3	14	16	56	25	79	...	176	393	177	103	76	412	464	...	1,625
26	Lalitpur	5	1	...	6	25	25	33	45	...	128	209	36	102	8	5	725	...	1,086
	Total, Allahabad Division ...	212	22	42	276	426	393	407	1,064	...	2,290	3,966	1,224	2,979	746	530	14,052	...	23,497

27	Benares	12	1	6	19	229	30	62	77	...	398	...	...	...	...	...	...	3,474	3,474
28	Mirzapur	16	15	1	32	252	48	11	232	...	543	285	255	890	409	32	3,324	...	5,195
29	Jaunpur	29	...	9	38	97	10	10	320	...	437	466	86	369	84	13	3,410	...	4,378
30	Ghazipur	26	...	1	27	352	30	2	84	...	468	165	288	162	185	...	2,954	166	3,870
31	Ballia	13	...	1	14	277	9	39	83	...	408	208	31	1,285	70	201	2,272	...	4,067
	Total, Benares Division ...	96	16	18	130	1,207	127	124	796	...	2,254	1,124	610	2,706	698	246	11,960	3,640	20,984
32	Gorakhpur	59	9	16	84	624	66	118	314	...	1,122	762	167	4,203	831	75	5,078	...	11,111
33	Basti	26	...	...	26	1,093	49	6	19	...	1,167	9	143	5,644	90	182	2,113	...	8,181
34	Azamgarh	...	1	...	1	165	...	86	832	...	683	688	70	184	23	1	4,339	...	5,305
	Total, Gorakhpur Division ...	85	10	16	111	1,882	115	210	665	...	2,872	1,459	380	10,031	944	258	11,525	...	24,597
35	Kumaun	52	2	7	61	80	420	10	2	...	512	...	312	4,902	...	...	780	...	5,994
36	Garhwal	7	4	...	11	40	3	33	17	...	93	...	91	...	...	...	1,037	...	1,128
37	Tarái	10	...	...	10	29	39	3	2	...	73	198	168	79	40	57	180	...	672
	Total, Kumaun Division ...	69	6	7	82	149	462	46	21	...	678	198	571	4,981	40	57	1,947	...	7,794
	Total, N.-W. Provinces ...	781	121	115	1,017	6,482	1,781	1,410	4,180	...	13,853	14,048	6,695	30,492	6,377	2,751	67,059	3,640	131,062
38	Lucknow	18	4	8	30	19	47	105	97	...	268	290	580	82	31	10	1,608	...	2,601
39	Unao	18	1	1	20	115	21	79	128	...	343	488	141	1,084	133	117	1,424	...	3,387
40	Rae Bareli	15	1	1	17	22	11	83	214	...	330	671	84	266	96	...	2,459	...	3,576
41	Sitapur	19	5	3	27	87	20	63	181	...	351	664	195	378	360	64	1,937	...	3,598
42	Hardoi	19	2	8	29	264	16	13	218	...	511	551	143	1,724	320	96	1,658	...	4,492
43	Kheri	14	...	...	14	177	8	22	161	...	368	314	159	178	232	4	2,408	...	3,290
	Total, Lucknow Division ...	103	13	21	137	684	123	365	999	...	2,171	2,978	1,302	3,707	1,172	291	11,494	...	20,944
44	Fyzabad	34	3	3	40	53	76	56	219	...	404	556	400	867	34	9	2,159	...	4,025
45	Gonda	22	2	2	26	61	8	...	414	...	483	825	60	596	339	...	3,057	...	4,877
46	Bahraich	3	2	9	14	30	15	57	286	...	388	584	143	139	312	6	2,572	...	3,756
47	Sultánpur	27	...	4	31	7	84	69	150	...	310	766	96	1,230	189	23	1,621	...	3,925
48	Partábgarh	17	6	9	32	...	...	2	1	275	278	...	22	...	...	1	9	2,992	3,024
49	Bara Banki	20	...	...	20	45	10	148	160	...	358	712	225	748	431	67	1,626	...	3,809
	Total, Fyzabad Division ...	123	13	27	163	196	193	327	1,230	275	2,221	3,443	946	3,580	1,305	106	11,044	2,992	23,416
	Total, Oudh ...	226	26	48	300	880	316	692	2,229	275	4,392	6,421	2,248	7,287	2,477	397	22,538	2,992	44,360
	Total, N.-W. P. and Oudh ...	1,007	147	163	1,317	7,362	2,097	2,102	6,409	275	18,245	20,469	8,943	37,779	8,854	3,148	89,597	6,632	175,422
50	Rampur	...	27	...	27	7	...	94	53	...	154	334	175	25	26	7	405	...	972
51	Tehri Garhwál	...	...	...	...	...	...	...	...	...	...	...	...	...	...	...	...	...	...
	TOTAL, NATIVE STATES ...	...	...	...	...	...	...	...	...	...	...	...	...	...	...	...	...	...	...

APPENDIX IV.

Showing the number of Enumerators writing each character.

Serial number.	Name of district.	Town. English.	Town. Urdu.	Town. Nagri.	Town. Kayathi.	Town. Total.	Rural. English.	Rural. Urdu.	Rural. Nagri.	Rural. Kayathi.	Rural. Total.	Total. English.	Total. Urdu.	Total. Nagri.	Total. Kayathi.	Total. Total.
1	2	3	4	5	6	7	8	9	10	11	12	13	14	15	16	17
1	Dehra-Dun	36	145	...	...	181	...	157	376	...	533	36	302	376	...	714
2	Sahāranpur	22	832	...	...	854	3	2,475	199	...	2,677	25	3,307	199	...	3,531
3	Muzaffarnagar	2	562	...	...	564	2	2,013	175	...	2,190	4	2,575	175	...	2,754
4	Meerut	...	...	...	...	...	24	3,677	536	...	4,237	24	3,677	536	...	4,237
5	Bulandshahr	2	641	26	...	669	7	2,114	683	...	2,804	9	2,755	709	...	3,473
6	Aligarh	1	700	20	...	721	9	1,911	900	...	2,820	10	2,611	920	...	3,541
	Total, Meerut Division ...	63	2,880	46	...	2,989	45	12,347	2,869	...	15,261	108	15,227	2,915	...	18,250
7	Muttra	8	345	143	...	496	2	77	2,024	...	2,103	10	422	2,167	...	2,599
8	Agra	31	714	52	...	797	7	56	3,010	...	3,073	38	770	3,062	...	3,870
9	Farukhabad	3	543	69	...	615	...	743	1,618	...	2,361	3	1,286	1,687	...	2,976
10	Mainpuri	...	123	...	...	123	9	441	2,549	...	2,999	9	564	2,549	...	3,122
11	Etáwah	1	165	27	...	193	...	72	2,258	...	2,330	1	237	2,285	...	2,523
12	Etah	...	386	41	...	427	...	804	1,311	...	2,115	...	1,190	1,352	...	2,542
	Total, Agra Division ...	43	2,276	332	...	2,651	18	2,193	12,770	...	14,981	61	4,469	13,102	...	17,632
13	Bareilly	...	632	14	...	646	...	2,822	123	...	2,945	...	3,454	137	...	3,591
14	Bijnor	6	598	...	...	604	5	2,129	80	...	2,214	11	2,727	80	...	2,818
15	Budaun	...	118	...	...	118	6	2,807	240	...	3,053	6	2,925	240	...	3,171
16	Moradabad	5	897	5	...	907	...	3,222	111	...	3,338	5	4,119	116	...	4,240
17	Sháhjahánpur	3	446	...	...	449	...	1,339	1,164	...	2,503	3	1,785	1,164	...	2,952
18	Pilibhit	5	183	1	...	189	...	1,048	299	...	1,347	5	1,231	300	...	1,536
	Total, Rohilkhand Division ...	19	2,874	20	...	2,913	11	13,367	2,017	...	15,395	30	16,241	2,037	...	18,308
19	Cawnpore	5	724	10	...	739	7	265	4,177	3	4,452	12	989	4,187	3	5,191
20	Fatehpur	...	110	76	...	186	21	222	1,992	...	2,235	21	332	2,068	...	2,421
21	Bánda	4	140	70	...	214	3	134	2,949	...	3,086	7	274	3,019	...	3,300
22	Hamirpur	3	78	185	...	266	1	4	1,594	...	1,599	4	82	1,779	...	1,865
23	Allahabad	216	596	174	...	986	12	993	4,184	...	5,189	228	1,589	4,368	...	6,175
24	Jhánsi	24	163	344	...	531	40	20	1,244	...	1,304	64	183	1,588	...	1,835
25	Jalaun	9	140	48	34	231	...	7	726	661	1,394	9	147	774	695	1,625
26	Lalitpur	9	1	78	...	88	3	3	991	...	997	12	4	1,069	...	1,085
	Total, Allahabad Division ...	270	1,952	985	34	3,241	87	1,648	17,857	664	20,256	357	3,600	18,842	698	23,497

No.	District																
27	Benares	...	62	397	281	...	740	3	125	2,606	...	2,734	65	522	2,887	...	3,474
28	Mirzapur	...	10	210	125	...	345	...	94	4,756	...	4,850	10	304	4,881	...	5,195
29	Jaunpur	...	5	264	20	...	289	3	601	3,485	...	4,089	8	865	3,505	...	4,378
30	Gházipur	...	1	265	...	145	411	3	428	900	2,128	3,459	4	693	900	2,273	3,870
31	Ballia	...	...	...	392	59	451	...	16	3,091	509	3,616	...	16	3,483	568	4,067
	Total, Benares Division	...	78	1,136	818	204	2,236	9	1,264	14,838	2,637	18,748	87	2,400	15,656	2,841	20,984
32	Gorakhpur	...	...	278	...	...	278	17	336	5,195	5,285	10,833	17	614	5,195	5,285	11,111
33	Basti	...	1	152	75	...	228	...	321	7,481	201	7,953	1	473	7,506	201	8,181
34	Azamgarh	...	2	314	80	...	396	5	484	4,420	...	4,909	7	798	4,500	...	5,305
	Total, Gorakhpur Division	...	3	744	155	...	902	22	1,141	17,046	5,486	23,695	25	1,885	17,201	5,486	24,597
35	Kumaun	...	6	1	160	...	167	...	...	5,827	...	5,827	6	1	5,987	...	5,994
36	Garhwál	...	...	...	13	...	13	...	...	1,115	...	1,115	...	...	1,128	...	1,128
37	Tarái	...	...	1	64	...	65	...	302	305	...	607	...	303	369	...	672
	Total, Kumaun Division	...	6	2	237	...	245	...	302	7,247	...	7,549	6	304	7,484	...	7,794
	Total, N.-W. Provinces	...	482	11,864	2,593	238	15,177	192	32,262	74,644	8,787	115,885	674	44,126	77,237	9,025	131,062
38	Lucknow	...	36	1,253	...	...	1,289	6	684	622	...	1,312	42	1,937	622	...	2,601
39	Unao	...	22	322	15	...	359	...	259	973	1,796	3,028	22	581	988	1,796	3,387
40	Rae Bareli	...	2	131	...	3	136	...	440	118	2,882	3,440	2	571	118	2,885	3,576
41	Sitapur	...	14	262	...	12	288	...	622	106	2,582	3,310	14	884	106	2,594	3,598
42	Hardoi	...	1	393	...	12	406	8	423	223	3,432	4,086	9	816	223	3,444	4,492
43	Kheri	...	3	141	...	14	158	1	404	2	2,725	3,132	4	545	2	2,739	3,290
	Total, Lucknow Division ...	...	78	2,502	15	41	2,636	15	2,832	2,044	13,417	18,308	93	5,334	2,059	13,458	20,944
44	Fyzabad	...	39	438	...	13	490	...	877	90	2,568	3,535	39	1,315	90	2,581	4,025
45	Gonda	...	...	182	...	...	182	40	137	...	4,518	4,695	40	319	...	4,518	4,877
46	Bahraich	...	9	161	...	16	186	2	364	...	3,204	3,570	11	525	...	3,220	3,756
47	Sultánpur	...	...	58	...	...	58	...	507	...	3,360	3,867	...	565	...	3,360	3,925
48	Partábgarh	...	...	32	...	...	32	...	148	433	2,411	2,992	...	180	433	2,411	3,024
49	Bara-Banki	...	3	250	...	...	253	3	1,630	299	1,624	3,556	6	1,880	299	1,624	3,809
	Total, Fyzabad Division	...	51	1,121	...	29	1,201	45	3,663	822	17,635	22,215	96	4,784	822	17,714	23,416
	Total, Oudh	...	129	3,623	15	70	3,837	60	6,495	2,866	31,102	40,523	189	10,118	2,881	31,172	44,360
	Total, N.-W. P. and Oudh	...	611	15,487	2,608	308	19,014	252	38,757	77,510	39,889	156,408	863	54,244	80,118	40,197	175,422
50	Rámpur	...	...	222	...	...	222	...	750	...	...	750	...	972	...	...	972
51	Tehri Garhwál	...	...	...	...	...	...	...	...	...	...	...	...	...	...	...	...
	TOTAL, NATIVE STATES	...	...	...	...	...	...	...	...	...	...	...	...	...	...	...	...

APPENDIX V.

Showing the population of the districts of the North-Western Provinces and Oudh, according to both the preliminary and the final returns.

Serial number.	Name of district.	Population by preliminary abstract.	Final population.	Error in excess.	Error in decrease.	Percentage of error.
1	2	3	4	5	6	7
1	Dehra Dún	168,196	168,185	61	...	+·036
2	Sahâranpur	1,001,453	1,001,280	173	...	+·017
3	Muzaffarnagar	773,204	772,874	330	...	+·042
4	Meerut	1,390,362	1,391,458	...	1,096	—·078
5	Bulandshahr	950,476	949,914	562	...	+·059
6	Aligarh	1,041,219	1,043,172	...	1,953	—·187
	Total, Meerut Division ...	5,324,910	5,326,833	...	1,923	—·361
7	Muttra	713,093	713,421	...	328	—·045
8	Agra	1,004,401	1,003,796	605	...	+·060
9	Farukhabad	858,376	858,687	...	311	—·036
10	Mainpuri	762,628	762,163	465	...	+·061
11	Etáwah	727,289	727,629	...	340	—·046
12	Etah	701,933	702,063	...	130	—·018
	Total, Agra Division ...	4,767,720	4,767,759	...	39	—·001
13	Bareilly	1,042,745	1,040,691	2,054	...	+·197
14	Bijnor	793,712	794,070	...	358	—·045
15	Budaun	925,026	925,598	...	572	—·061
16	Moradabad	1,179,862	1,179,398	464	...	+·039
17	Sháhjahánpur	918,419	918,551	...	132	—·014
18	Pilibhit	485,967	485,366	601	...	+·123
	Total, Rohilkhand Division ...	5,345,731	5,343,674	2,057	...	+·038
19	Cawnpore	1,207,955	1,209,695	...	1,740	—·143
20	Fatehpur	697,363	699,157	...	1,794	—·256
21	Bánda	705,989	705,832	157	...	+·022
22	Hamírpur	514,104	513,720	384	...	+·074
23	Allahabad	1,550,347	1,548,737	1,610	...	+·103
24	Jhánsi	409,791	409,419	372	...	+·090
25	Jalaun	396,491	396,361	130	...	+·032
26	Lalitpur	274,229	274,200	29	...	+·010
	Total, Allahabad Division ...	5,756,269	5,757,121	...	852	—·147
27	Benares	928,633	921,943	6,690	...	+·725
28	Mirzapur	1,158,638	1,161,508	...	2,870	—·247
29	Jaunpur	1,267,143	1,264,949	2,194	...	+·173
30	Gházipur	1,084,729	1,077,909	6,820	...	+·632
31	Ballia	943,000	942,465	585	...	+·056
	Total, Benares Division ...	5 382,148	5,368,774	13,369	...	+·249
32	Gorakhpur	2,993,732	2,994,057	...	325	—·011
33	Basti	1,789,948	1,785,844	4,104	...	+·229
34	Azamgarh	1,733,509	1,728,625	4,884	...	+·282
	Total, Gorakhpur Division ...	6,517,189	6,508,526	8,663	...	+·133
35	Kumaun	566,847	563,181	3,666	...	+·697
36	Garhwál	406,635	407,818	...	1,183	—·290
37	Tarái	210,827	210,568	259	...	+·123
	Total, Kumaun Division ...	1,184,309	1,181,567	2,742	...	+·232
	Total, N.-W. Provinces ...	34,278,271	34,254,254	24,017	...	+·070
38	Lucknow	774,415	774,163	252	...	+·032
39	Unao	949,041	953,636	...	4,595	—·481
40	Rae Bareli	1,036,174	1,036,521	...	347	—·033
41	Sitapur	1,075,010	1,075,418	...	408	—·037
42	Hardoi	1,114,117	1,113,211	906	...	+·081
43	Kheri	906,623	903,615	3,008	...	+·332
	Total, Lucknow Division ...	5,855,380	5,856,559	...	1,179	—·020
44	Fyzabad	1,217,477	1,216,959	518	...	+·042
45	Gonda	1,461,866	1,459,229	2,637	...	+·180
46	Bahraich	1,003,613	1,000,432	3,181	...	+·317
47	Sultánpur	1,075,378	1,075,851	...	473	—·043
48	Partábgarh	910,866	910,895	...	29	—·003
49	Bara Banki	1,128,151	1,130,906	...	2,755	—·243
	Total, Fyzabad Division ...	6,797,351	6,794,272	3,079	...	+·045
	Total, Oudh ...	12,652,731	12,650,831	1,900	...	+·015
	TOTAL, N.-W. P. AND OUDH ...	46,931,002	46,905,085	25,917	...	+·055
50	Rampur	558,276	551,249	7,027	...	+1·274
51	Tehri Gárhwal	240,889	241,242	...	353	—·146
	Total, Native States ...	799,165	792,491	6,674	...	+·342

APPENDIX VI.

Showing the number of private schedules issued.

Serial number.	Name of district.	Town. English.	Town. Urdu.	Rural. English.	Rural. Urdu.	Total. English.	Total. Urdu.
1	2	3	4	5	6	7	8
1	Dehra Dún	...	...	...	...	...	...
2	Saháranpur	100	19	1	...	101	19
3	Muzaffarnagar	8	3	...	...	8	3
4	Meerut	1,000	400	...	...	1,000	400
5	Bulandshahr	25	75	4	25	29	100
6	Aligarh	25	15	...	...	25	15
	Total, Meerut Division ...	1,158	512	5	25	1,163	537
7	Muttra	37	...	...	...	37	...
8	Agra	574	45	2	1	576	46
9	Farukhabad	30	4	2	5	32	9
10	Mainpuri	3	...	8	2	11	2
11	Etáwah	25	59	1	27	26	86
12	Etah	17	105	5	99	22	204
	Total, Agra Division ...	686	213	18	134	704	347
13	Bareilly	89	...	2	...	91	...
14	Bijnor	10	...	...	...	10	...
15	Budaun	...	...	30	5	30	5
16	Moradabad	25	107	1	...	26	107
17	Sháhjahánpur	43	17	1	1	44	18
18	Pilibhít	5	11	...	...	5	11
	Total, Rohilkhand Division ...	172	135	34	6	206	141
19	Cawnpore	98	...	...	1	98	1
20	Fatehpur	13	66	33	9	46	75
21	Bánda	...	29	3	33	3	62
22	Hamírpur	15	...	6	...	21	...
23	Allahabad	246	26	13	142	259	168
24	Jhánsi	83	15	192	1	275	16
25	Jalaun	6	2	...	...	6	2
26	Lalitpur	9	1	...	...	9	1
	Total, Allahabad Division ...	470	139	247	186	717	325
27	Benares	99	149	...	...	99	149
28	Mirzapur	9	...	12	...	21	...
29	Jaunpur	15	30	5	30	20	60
30	Gházipur	43	...	...	...	43	...
31	Ballia	3	1	...	...	3	1
	Total, Benares Division ...	169	180	17	30	186	210
32	Gorakhpur...	87	109	115	1	202	110
33	Basti	12	23	...	4	12	27
34	Azamgarh	2	376	5	1,002	7	1,378
	Total, Gorakhpur Division ...	101	508	120	1,007	221	1,515
35	Kumaun	120	...	48	...	168	...
36	Garhwál	8	...	12	...	20	...
37	Tarái	3	14	4	6	7	20
	Total, Kumaun Division ...	131	14	64	6	195	20
	Total, N.-W. Provinces ...	2,887	1,701	505	1,394	3,392	3,095
38	Lucknow	513	5	1	9	514	14
39	Unao	12	36	...	3	12	39
40	Rae Bareli...	4	2	...	...	4	2
41	Sitapur	35	10	1	...	36	10
42	Hardoi	8	...	...	6	8	6
43	Kheri	5	...	...	...	5	...
	Total, Lucknow Division ...	577	53	2	18	579	71
44	Fyzabad	68	72	3	71	71	143
45	Gonda	39	...	...	...	39	...
46	Bahraich	13	21	1	32	14	53
47	Sultánpur	7	...	1	3	8	3
48	Partábgarh	7	26	1	5	8	31
49	Bara Banki	5	30	1	10	6	40
	Total, Fyzabad Division ...	139	149	7	121	146	270
	Total, Oudh ...	716	202	9	139	725	341
	TOTAL, N.-W. P. AND OUDH ...	3,603	1,903	514	1,533	4,117	3,436
50	Rampur	7	5	...	...	7	6
51	Tehri Garhwál	...	...	...	...	...	...
	Total, Native States ...	...	...	...	...	...	...

APPENDIX VII.

Showing the expenditure on enumeration in each district together with the incidence of expenditure on population.

Serial number.	Name of district.	Total expenditure on enumeration.	Incidence per 1,000 of population.	Remarks.
		Rs. a. p.	Rs. a. p.	
1	Dehra Dún	207 15 2	1 3 9	
2	Sahéranpur	243 3 5	0 3 10	
3	Muzaffarnagar	483 3 1	0 10 0	
4	Meerut	616 5 11	0 7 0	
5	Bulandshahr	280 5 5	0 4 8	
6	Alígarh	371 7 3	0 5 8	
	Total, Meerut Division ...	2,202 8 3	0 6 7	
7	Muttra	320 12 7	0 7 2	
8	Agra	345 13 7	0 5 3	
9	Farukhabad	505 0 6	0 9 4	
10	Mainpuri	797 12 10	1 9 3	
11	Etáwah	544 6 1	0 11 10	
12	Etah	594 0 9	0 13 6	
	Total, Agra Division ...	3,107 14 4	0 10 5	
13	Bareilly	429 4 11	0 6 7	
14	Bijnor	258 14 10	0 5 2	
15	Budaun	339 14 11	0 5 10	
16	Moradabad	492 13 9	0 6 8	
17	Sháhjahánpur	219 14 0	0 3 9	
18	Pilibhít	229 10 10	0 7 6	
	Total, Rohilkhand Division ...	1,970 9 3	0 5 1	
19	Cawnpore	500 10 10	0 6 9	
20	Fatehpur	563 11 1	0 12 10	
21	Bánda	451 2 2	0 10 2	
22	Hamírpur	426 1 10	0 13 3	
23	Allahabad	585 3 10	0 5 4	
24	Jhánsi	374 3 0	0 14 7	
25	Jalaun	331 3 8	0 13 4	
26	Lalitpur	202 1 0	0 11 9	
	Total, Allahabad Division ...	3,434 5 5	0 9 6	
27	Benares	349 15 11	0 6 0	
28	Mirzapur	443 9 8	0 6 1	
29	Jaunpur	336 0 9	0 4 3	
30	Ghézipur	422 7 10	0 6 3	
31	Ballia	340 6 8	0 5 9	
	Total, Benares Division ...	1,892 8 10	0 5 7	
32	Gorakhpur	857 14 2	0 4 7	
33	Basti	180 15 4	0 1 7	
34	Azamgarh	330 6 0	0 3 0	
	Total, Gorakhpur Division ...	1,369 3 6	0 3 4	
35	Kumaun	1,447 5 2	2 9 1	
36	Garhwál	512 6 6	1 4 1	
37	Taréi	441 3 3	2 1 7	
	Total, Kumaun Division ...	2,400 14 11	2 0 6	
	Total, N.-W. Provinces ...	16,378 0 6	0 7 7	
38	Lucknow	650 14 5	0 13 5	
39	Unao	366 10 0	0 6 1	
40	Rae Bareli...	384 6 2	0 5 11	
41	Sitapur	543 15 9	0 8 1	
42	Hardoi	292 5 4	0 4 2	
43	Kheri	388 3 4	0 6 10	
	Total, Lucknow Division ...	2,626 7 0	0 7 2	
44	Fyzabad	404 10 10	0 5 4	
45	Gonda	365 1 9	0 4 0	
46	Bahraich	228 1 9	0 3 7	
47	Sultánpur	369 9 5	0 5 6	
48	Partábgarh	289 8 11	0 5 1	
49	Bara Banki...	322 13 6	0 4 6	
	Total, Fyzabad Division ...	1,979 14 2	0 4 8	
	TOTAL OUDH ...	4,606 5 2	0 5 9	
	TOTAL, N.-W. PROVINCES AND OUDH ...	20,984 5 8	0 7 1	
50	Central Office	520 12 0	...	
	GRAND TOTAL ...	21,505 1 8	...	

APPENDIX VIII.

Showing the Census Accounts year by year in detail.

Main-head.		Sub-head.	1890-91. Revised estimate.	1890-91. Actuals. Sub-head.	1890-91. Actuals. Main-head.	1891-92. Revised estimate.	1891-92. Actuals. Sub-head.	1891-92. Actuals. Main-head.
1		2	3	4	5	6	7	8
			Rs. a. p.	Rs. a. p.	Rs. a. p.	Rs. a. p.	Rs. a. p.	Rs. a. p.
Part A. Enumeration.	I.—District charges.	1. District establishment ...	...	14,572 9 11	...	...	...	...
		2. Contingent charges of establishment.	...	1,689 7 11	...	...	...	...
		3. House numbering ...	...	114 4 9	...	...	...	...
		4. Lights, ink and paper for drafts, &c.	...	2,464 12 2	...	...	...	...
		5. Remuneration of Census officers	...	...	...	...	...	...
		6. Special travelling allowance ...	...	210 15 6	...	...	39 10 3	...
		7. Freight of schedules, &c., from stations and landing places.	...	2,413 5 2	...	...	...	...
		Total I, District charges ...	23,017 10 0	...	21,465 7 5	39 10 3	...	39 10 3
	II.—Enumeration printing.	8. Paper for schedules, &c., at press. 9. Printing and binding ...	...	38,868 6 8	...	...	1,349 4 2	...
		10. Despatching from press ...	...	7,686 14 11	...	...	...	...
		Total II, paper and printing A. ...	39,790 0 0	...	46,555 5 7	1,100 0 0	...	1,349 4 2
		Total, Enumeration ...	62,807 10 0	...	68,020 13 0	1,139 10 3	...	1,388 14 5
Part B.—Abstraction and compilation.	III.—Tabulation office.	11. Office rent	...	...	...	...	2,640 13 3	...
		12. Office furniture and repairs, &c.	...	1,443 10 3	...	...	984 7 11	...
		13. Record establishment ...	...	128 14 8	...	...	15,021 0 1	...
		14. Correspondence and accounts establishment.	...	...	...	...	...	...
		15. Menial establishment ...	...	5 14 4	...	...	6,453 2 2	...
		16. Working staff including Superintendence-officials.	...	719 11 2	...	...	3,15,187 4 10	...
		17. Ditto Clerks specially entertained.	...	...	...	...	285 5 1	...
		18. Travelling allowance to and from the office.	...	89 6 6	...	...	854 5 6	...
		19. Freight of schedules, &c., to office	...	142 9 0	...	...	1,979 2 6	...
		20. Petty stationery and contingencies.	...	975 12 9	...	...	6,221 11 5	...
		Total III, Tabulation office ...	4,700 0 0	...	3,505 14 8	3,14,000 0 0	3,49,627 4 9	...
		Deductions	...	...	...	...	—35,161 9 9	...
		Net amount chargeable to tabulation &c.	4,700 0 0	...	3,505 14 8	3,14,000 0 0	...	3,14,465 11 0
	IV.—Tabulation printing.	21. Papers for sheets, registers, and tables at press. 22. Printing of forms, tables, and reports.	...	8,649 8 3	...	...	34,466 8 9	...
		23. Freight of sheets, &c., to office ...	...	516 14 0	...	...	1,248 12 6	...
		Total IV, Paper and printing B. ...	10,000 0 0	...	9,166 6 3	42,900 0 0	...	35,715 5 3
		Total, Compilation ...	14,700 0 0	...	12,672 4 11	3,56,900 0 0	...	3,50,181 0 3
Part C.—Superintendence.	V.—Superintendent's personal charges.	24. Provincial Superintendent's deputation allowance.	...	4,211 3 3	...	...	4,608 0 0	...
		25. Pay of substitute of Superintendent.	...	2,750 0 0	...	...	3,000 0 0	...
		26. „ Assistant inspecting officer	...	...	...	...	2,338 13 6	...
		27. Travelling allowance of Superintendent and of assistant inspecting officer.	...	2,296 8 0	...	...	3,183 11 3	...
		Total V, Superintendent's personal charges.	7,450 0 0	...	9,257 11 3	11,000 0 0	...	13,130 8 9
	VI.—Superintendent's office.	28. Superintendent's office establishment.	...	1,080 3 3	...	...	2,671 1 0	...
		29. Travelling allowance for establishment.	...	269 10 6	...	...	717 6 6	...
		30. Office contingencies for establishment.	...	1,535 8 6	...	...	1,626 0 11	...
		31. Rent of Superintendent's office...	...	131 0 0	...	...	490 0 0	...
		Total VI, Superintendent's office	3,060 0 0	...	3,016 6 3	6,000 0 0	...	5,504 8 5
		Total, Superintendence ...	10,510 0 0	...	12,274 1 6	17,000 0 0	...	18,635 1 2
		GRAND TOTAL ...	88,017 10 0	...	92,967 3 5	3,75,039 10 3	...	3,70,204 15 10

APPENDIX VIII.

Showing the Census Accounts year by year in detail—(concluded).

Main-head.	Sub-head.	1892-93. Revised estimate.	1892-93. Actuals. Sub-head.	1892-93. Actuals. Main-head.	Total. Revised estimate.	Total. Actuals. Sub-head.	Total. Actuals. Main-head.
1	2	9	10	11	12	13	14
		Rs. a. p.	Rs. a. p.	Rs. a. p.	Rs. a. p.	Rs. a. p.	Rs. a. p.
Part A. Enumeration. I.—District charges.	1. District establishment ...	...	...	...	...	14,572 9 11	...
	2. Contingent charges of establishment.	...	...	...	...	1,689 7 11	...
	3. House numbering ...	...	...	...	...	114 4 9	...
	4. Lights, ink and paper for drafts, &c.	...	...	...	...	2,464 12 2	...
	5. Remuneration of Census officers	...	...	...	...	...	...
	6. Special travelling allowance ...	...	...	...	...	250 9 9	...
	7. Freight of schedules, &c., from stations and landing places.	...	...	...	...	2,413 5 2	...
	Total I, District charges ...	...	...	...	23,057 4 3	...	21,505 1 8
II.—Enumeration printing.	8. Paper for schedules, &c., at press. 9. Printing and binding ...	...	...	...	...	40,217 10 10	...
	10. Despatching from press ...	...	...	...	...	7,686 14 11	...
	Total II, paper and printing A. ...	...	...	...	40,890 0 0	...	47,904 9 9
	Total, Enumeration ...	...	...	...	63,947 4 3	...	69,409 11 5
Part B.—Abstraction and compilation. III.—Tabulation office.	11. Office rent	...	460 0 0	...	...	3,100 13 3	...
	12. Office furniture and repairs, &c.	...	...	...	...	2,428 2 2	...
	13. Record establishment ...	...	1,088 1 9	...	...	16,238 0 6	...
	14. Correspondence and accounts establishment.	...	...	...	...	...	...
	15. Menial establishment ...	...	138 4 4	...	...	6,597 4 10	...
	16. Working staff including Superintendence-officials.	...	11,079 4 7	...	...	3,26,986 4 7	...
	17. Ditto Clerks specially entertained.	...	100 0 0	...	...	385 5 1	...
	18. Travelling allowance to and from the office.	...	228 5 9	...	...	1,172 1 9	...
	19. Freight of schedules, &c., to office	...	664 4 11	...	...	2,786 0 5	...
	20. Petty stationery and contingencies.	...	643 11 6	...	...	7,841 3 8	...
	Total III, Tabulation office ...	15,052 2 10	14,402 0 10	...	3,33,752 2 10	3,67,535 4 3	...
	Deductions	...	—1,320 12 8	...	...	—36,482 6 5	...
	Net amount chargeable to tabulation, &c.	15,052 2 10	...	13,081 4 2	3,33,752 2 10	...	3,31,052 13 10
IV.—Tabulation printing.	21. Papers for sheets, registers, and tables at press. 22. Printing of forms, tables, and reports.	...	227 11 6	...	...	43,343 12 6	...
	23. Freight of sheets, &c., to office...	...	...	...	...	1,765 10 6	...
	Total IV, Paper and printing B. ...	6,000 0 0	...	227 11 6	58,900 0 0	...	45,109 7 0
	Total, Compilation ...	21,052 2 10	...	13,308 15 8	3,92,652 2 10	...	3,76,162 4 10
Part C.—Superintendence. V.—Superintendent's personal charges.	24. Provincial Superintendent's deputation allowance.	...	2,688 0 0	...	...	11,507 3 3	...
	25. Pay of substitute of Superintendent.	...	...	...	...	5,750 0 0	...
	26. „ Assistant inspecting officer	...	991 12 0	...	...	3,330 9 6	...
	27. Travelling allowance of Superintendent and of assistant inspecting officer.	...	208 11 0	...	...	5,688 14 3	...
	Total V, Superintendent's personal charges.	4,728 3 10	...	3,888 7 0	23,178 3 10	...	26,276 11 0
VI.—Superintendent's office.	28. Superintendent's office establishment.	...	1,743 11 2	...	...	5,494 15 5	...
	29. Travelling allowance for establishment.	...	200 11 0	...	...	1,187 12 0	...
	30. Office contingencies for establishment.	...	581 11 9	...	...	3,743 5 2	...
	31. Rent of Superintendent's office...	...	235 0 0	...	...	856 0 0	...
	Total VI, Superintendent's office ...	2,708 1 6	...	2,761 1 11	11,768 1 6	...	11,282 0 7
	Total, Superintendence ...	7,436 5 4	...	6,649 8 11	34,946 5 4	...	37,558 11 7
	GRAND TOTAL ...	28,488 8 2	...	19,958 8 7	4,91,545 12 5	...	4,83,130 11 10

APPENDIX IX.

Showing the gross and net amounts expended on account of Abstraction and Tabulation in the districts of the North-Western Provinces and Oudh.

	District.	1890-91.	1891-92.	1892-93.	Total.	Deduction.	Net charges.
		Rs. a. p.	Rs. a. p.	Rs. a. p.	Rs. a. p.	Rs. a. p.	Rs. a. p.
1	Dehra Dún	102 14 9	3,062 12 3	40 0 0	3,205 11 0	386 8 3	2,819 2 9
2	Sahárанpur	145 14 6	5,433 14 2	13 0 0	5,592 12 8	675 2 2	4,917 10 6
3	Muzaffarnagar	24 8 6	6,452 6 1	39 5 0	6,516 3 7	319 6 0	6,196 13 7
4	Meerut...	119 12 6	7,648 11 7	30 8 0	7,799 0 1	2,895 9 4	4,903 6 9
5	Bulandshahr	7 2 4	7,124 14 0	...	7,132 0 4	857 14 0	6,274 2 4
6	Aligarh	68 0 6	7,841 2 9	32 7 0	7,441 10 3	1,259 7 0	6,182 3 3
	Total, Meerut Division ...	468 5 1	37,063 12 10	155 4 0	37,687 5 11	6,393 14 9	31,293 7 2
7	Muttra...	7 0 0	5,493 9 10	10 4 0	5,510 13 10	695 7 8	4,815 6 2
8	Agra	341 3 7	7,218 4 5	30 0 0	7,589 8 0	1,339 5 6	6,250 2 6
9	Farukhabad	42 15 5	6,386 11 7	12 8 0	6,442 3 0	573 15 6	5,868 8 6
10	Mainpuri	13 6 8	5,569 12 6	48 0 0	5,631 3 2	220 1 0	5,411 2 2
11	Etáwah	30 9 3	5,390 9 7	7 8 0	5,428 10 10	591 2 6	4,837 8 4
12	Etah	...	5,128 15 11	30 0 0	5,158 15 11	1,375 11 10	3,783 4 1
	Total, Agra Division ...	435 2 11	35,187 15 10	188 4 0	35,761 6 9	4,795 12 0	30,965 10 9
13	Bareilly	47 12 9	6,628 11 11	25 0 0	6,701 8 8	555 1 10	6,146 6 10
14	Bijnor	199 0 4	5,313 5 10	125 15 3	5,638 5 5	490 4 3	5,148 1 2
15	Budaun	22 5 2	7,320 13 9	67 4 0	7,410 6 11	599 12 2	6,810 10 9
16	Moradabad	121 0 6	7,209 7 0	33 5 4	7,363 12 10	1,075 7 9	6,288 5 1
17	Sháhjahánpur	33 14 9	7,975 13 11	...	8,009 12 8	813 1 6	7,196 11 2
18	Pilibhít	8 15 2	4,104 6 9	22 0 0	4,135 5 11	520 15 9	3,614 6 2
	Total, Rohilkhand Division ...	433 0 8	38,552 11 2	273 8 7	39,259 4 5	4,064 11 3	35,204 9 2
19	Cawnpore	75 3 3	9,479 13 9	10 0 0	9,565 1 0	902 11 3	8,662 5 9
20	Fatehpur	29 0 6	6,034 10 10	26 5 2	6,090 0 6	344 2 5	5,745 14 1
21	Bánda	66 1 9	6,811 8 7	130 15 2	7,008 9 6	174 14 3	6,833 11 3
22	Hamírpur	34 13 7	4,492 0 7	3 14 0	4,530 12 2	321 11 2	4,209 1 0
23	Allahabad	70 7 2	11,518 10 7	21 0 0	11,610 1 9	1,368 10 4	10,241 7 5
24	Jhánsi	11 3 11	5,757 13 9	36 10 8	5,805 12 4	676 3 0	5,129 9 4
25	Jalaun	12 7 0	4,374 1 1	20 0 0	4,406 8 1	623 1 8	3,783 6 5
26	Lalitpur	29 11 1	2,679 2 3	...	2,708 13 4	98 4 6	2,610 8 10
	Total, Allahabad Division ...	329 0 3	51,147 13 5	248 13 0	51,725 10 8	4,509 10 7	47,216 0 1
27	Benares	52 2 9	6,455 1 11	27 8 0	6,534 12 8	1,587 8 9	4,947 3 11
28	Mirzapur	51 15 0	6,997 12 6	58 10 8	7,108 6 2	768 4 5	6,340 1 9
29	Jaunpur	103 6 0	8,064 2 11	30 0 0	8,197 8 11	1,199 11 7	6,997 13 4
30	Gházipur	33 12 0	7,148 3 4	...	7,181 15 4	530 6 6	6,651 8 10
31	Ballia	23 7 4	6,685 13 6	...	6,709 4 10	1,068 9 1	5,640 11 9
	Total, Benares Divison ...	264 11 1	35,351 2 2	116 2 8	35,731 15 11	5,154 8 4	30,577 7 7
32	Gorakhpur	161 14 9	20,488 11 10	270 15 1	20,921 9 8	542 0 0	20,379 9 8
33	Basti	7 13 0	11,088 2 2	37 14 5	11,128 13 7	550 13 4	10,578 0 3
34	Azamgarh	76 9 0	11,357 8 10	85 12 10	11,519 14 8	177 3 9	11,342 10 11
	Total, Gorakhpur Division ...	246 4 9	42,929 6 10	394 10 4	43,570 5 11	1,270 1 1	42,300 4 10
35	Kumaun	100 14 8	4,899 12 2	22 12 1	5,023 6 11	183 11 0	4,839 11 11
36	Garhwál	22 13 7	5,366 12 4	12 8 0	5,402 1 11	26 3 0	5,375 14 11
37	Tarái	44 12 0	3,113 13 3	...	3,158 9 3	1,044 0 2	2,114 9 1
	Total, Kumaun Division ...	168 8 3	13,380 5 9	35 4 1	13,584 2 1	1,253 14 2	12,330 3 11
	TOTAL, N.-W. PROVINCES ...	2,345 1 0	2,53,613 4 0	1,361 14 8	257,320 3 8	27,432 8 2	229,887 11 6
38	Lucknow	...	7,218 1 4	40 0 0	7,258 1 4	1,869 13 4	5,388 4 0
39	Unao	34 5 8	7,502 1 5	31 4 8	7,567 11 9	184 6 9	7,433 5 0
40	Rae Bareli	287 7 7	6,145 8 4	24 1 8	6,457 1 7	1,126 2 10	5,330 14 9
41	Sitapur...	56 9 10	7,143 15 0	30 0 0	7,230 8 10	311 10 4	6,918 14 6
42	Hardoi...	115 15 8	7,152 7 1	9 2 8	7,277 9 5	1,329 4 9	5,948 4 8
43	Kheri	58 2 2	7,123 3 3	30 0 0	7,211 5 5	483 7 2	6,727 14 3
	Total, Lucknow Division ...	552 8 11	42,285 4 5	164 9 0	43,002 6 4	5,254 13 2	37,747 9 2
44	Fyzabad	100 10 5	7,468 14 4	2 0 0	7,571 8 9	799 11 8	6,771 13 1
45	Gonda	245 14 11	8,246 12 6	3 5 4	8,496 0 9	694 1 7	7,801 15 2
46	Bahraich	36 15 11	7,454 1 11	2 10 8	7,493 12 6	582 11 9	6,911 0 9
47	Sultánpur	86 12 11	7,282 4 2	20 8 7	7,389 9 8	684 7 10	6,705 1 10
48	Partábgarh	63 1 10	4,869 4 6	7 5 4	4,939 11 8	410 5 0	4,529 6 8
49	Bara Banki	74 12 9	7,358 6 2	10 11 6	7,443 14 5	623 11 3	6,820 3 2
	Total, Fyzabad Division ...	608 4 9	42,679 11 7	46 9 5	43,334 9 9	3,795 1 1	39,539 8 8
	TOTAL, OUDH ...	1,160 13 8	84,965 0 0	211 2 5	86,337 0 1	9,049 14 3	77,287 1 10
	TOTAL, N.-W. P. & OUDH ...	3,505 14 8	338,578 4 0	1,573 1 1	343,657 3 9	36,482 6 5	307,174 13 4
	General compilation charges. Allahabad ...	...	8,961 9 0	8,775 13 3	17,737 6 3	...	17,737 6 3
	General compilation charges. Naini Tal ...	...	2,087 7 9	3,237 10 4	5,325 2 1	...	5,325 2 1
	General compilation charges. Rae Bareli ...	...	...	815 8 2	815 8 2	...	815 8 2
	TOTAL, GENERAL CHARGES ...	...	11,049 0 9	12,828 15 9	23,878 0 6	...	23,878 0 6
	GRAND TOTAL ...	3,505 14 8	349,627 4 9	14,402 0 10	367,535 4 3	36,482 6 5	331,052 13 10

APPENDIX X.

Showing the density of population in the typical towns of the provinces.

(Total Area.)

Serial number.	District.	Town.	Total area. A. R. P.	Total population.	Density.
1	Dehra Dún	Dehra	2,315 0 0	21,881	9·45
2	Sahāranpur	Deoband	5,313 0 0	19,250	3·62
3	Muzaffarnagar	Kandhla	218 0 0	9,487	43·52
4	Meerut	Meerut	2,215 1 17	78,637	88·21
5	Bulandshahr	Shikarpur	115 0 0	11,596	100·83
6	Aligarh	Koil	2,326 0 0	61,485	26·43
	Total, Meerut Division		12,502 1 17	197,336	15·78
7	Muttra	*Nil.*	...	...	...
8	Agra	Agra	10,898 0 0	145,361	13·34
9	Farukhabad	Farukhabad	2,185 0 0	78,009	33·41
10	Mainpuri	Shikohabad	497 0 0	9,717	19·55
11	Etáwah	Etáwah	2,524 1 24	38,793	15·37
12	Etah	Kasganj	371 0 0	16,050	43·26
	Total, Agra Division		16,470 1 24	282,930	17·18
13	Bareilly	Bareilly	4,922 0 0	107,785	21·89
14	Bijnor	Nagina	530 0 0	22,150	41·79
15	Budaun	Budaun	427 0 0	35,372	82·84
16	Moradabad	Moradabad	1,673 2 2	72,068	43·06
17	Sháhjahánpur	Sháhjahánpur	2,421 3 35	76,977	31·78
18	Pilibhít	Bisalpur	149 0 35	9,221	61·79
	Total, Rohilkhand Division		·10,123 2 32	323,578	31·96
19	Cawnpore	Cawnpore	2,947 0 0	163,779	55·58
20	Fatehpur	Fatehpur	762 0 0	20,179	26·48
21	Bánda	Bánda	3,060 0 0	23,071	7·54
22	Hamírpur	Hamírpur	833 0 0	7,081	8·50
23	Allahabad	Allahabad	26,550 0 0	162,895	6·14
24	Jhánsi	Jhánsi	3,602 0 29	44,544	12·37
25	Jalaun	Kunch	705 1 21	13,408	19·01
26	Lalitpur	Talbehat	113 0 32	5,795	51·10
	Total, Allahabad Division		38,572 3 2	440,752	11·43
27	Benares	Benares	6,213 0 0	213,168	34·31
28	Mirzapur	Mirzapur	3,776 0 0	84,130	22·28
29	Jaunpur	Jaunpur	4,577 0 0	42,819	9·33
30	Ghāzipur	*Nil.*	...	...	...
31	Ballia	Ballia	1,803 0 0	16,372	9·08
	Total, Benares Division		16,369 0 0	356,489	21·78
32	Gorakhpur	Gajpur	534 0 0	4,284	8·02
33	Basti	Mehndawal	125 0 0	10,991	87·93
34	Azamgarh	Azamgarh	1,425 0 0	19,442	13·64
	Total, Gorakhpur Division		2,084 0 0	34,717	16.66
35	Kumaun	Naini Tal	2,898 0 7$\frac{10}{11}$	7,883	2·72
		Haldwani	473 1 14$\frac{3}{8}$	4,947	5·08
36	Garhwál	*Nil.*	...	...	...
37	Tarái	*Nil.*	...	...	...
	Total, Kumaun Division		3,371 1 22$\frac{11}{88}$	12,830	3·81
	TOTAL, N.-W. PROVINCES		99,493 2 17$\frac{11}{88}$	1,648,627	16·63
38	Lucknow	Lucknow	16,009 0 0	249,511	15·59
39	Unao	Unao	4,597 0 0	12,831	2·79
40	Rae Bareli	Rae Bareli	4,471 1 13	18,798	4·22
41	Sitapur	Sitapur	964 0 0	17,149	17·79
42	Hardoi	Sandila	657 0 0	16,813	25·59
43	Kheri	Lakhimpur	982 2 0	8,073	8·22
	Total, Lucknow Division		27,671 3 13	323,175	11·68
44	Fyzabad	Fyzabad	8,330 0 0	72,686	8·73
45	Gonda	Gonda	1,353 1 19	17,423	12·87
46	Bahraich	Bahraich	1,745 0 0	24,046	13·79
47	Sultánpur	Saltanpur	836 0 0	8,751	10·47
48	Partábgarh	*Nil*	...	...	...
49	Bara Banki	Nawábganj	1,455 3 35	14,432	9·92
	Total, Fyzabad Division		13,720 1 14	137,338	10·01
	TOTAL, OUDH		41,392 0 27	460,513	11·13
	TOTAL, N.-W. P. AND OUDH		140,885 3 4$\frac{11}{88}$	2,109,140	14·97
50	Rampur	Tanda	126 0 0	8,772	69·62
51	Tehri Garhwál	*Nil.*	...	...	...
	TOTAL, NATIVE STATES		126 0 0	8,772	69·62

APPENDIX XI.

Showing the density of population in the typical towns of the provinces.

City Area.

Serial number.	District.	Town.	City area. A.	R.	P.	City population.	Density.
1	Dehra Dún	Dehra	130	0	0	7,168	55·10
2	Sahâranpur	Deoband	341	0	0	19,250	56·45
3	Muzaffarnagar	Kandhla	173	0	0	9,398	54·32
4	Meerut	Meerut	288	2	17	48,692	167·67
5	Bulandshahr	Shikarpur	115	0	0	11,596	100 83
6	Aligarh	Koil	1,407	0	20	55,211	37·63
	Total, Meerut Division ...	...	2,454	2	37	151,310	61·64
7	Muttra	*Nil.*	No return submitetd.				
8	Agra...	Agra	500	0	0	75,158	150·32
9	Farukhabad	Farukhabad	867	0	0	65,308	75·32
10	Mainpuri	Shikohabad	189	0	0	9,717	15·41
11	Etáwah	Etáwah	490	0	19	36,443	75·63
12	Etah...	Kasganj	135	0	0	16,050	118·89
	Total, Agra Division ...	...	2,181	0	19	202,671	92·63
13	Bareilly	Bareilly	1,471	0	0	98,089	66·68
14	Bijnor	Nagina	400	0	0	22,150	55·37
15	Budaun	Budaun	312	0	0	35,372	113·37
16	Moradabad	Moradabad	460	1	10	72,068	156 56
17	Sháhjahánpur	Sháhjahánpur	1,449	0	25	75,258	51·53
18	Pilibhít	Bisalpur	108	0	0	9,221	85·38
	Total, Rohilkhand Division ...	...	4,200	1	35	312,158	74·32
19	Cawnpore	Cawnpore	787	0	0	137,825	187·01
20	Fatehpur	Fatehpur...	313	0	0	17,958	57·37
21	Bánda	Banda	606	1	1·5	21,946	36·19
22	Hamírpur	Hamírpur	92	0	0	6,410	69·67
23	Allahabad	Allahabad	1,470	2	0	93,703	63·72
24	Jhánsi	Jhánsi	493	1	0	37,075	75·16
25	Jalaun	Kunch	215	3	23	13,408	62·11
26	Lalitpur	Talbehat	113	0	32	5,795	51·101
	Total, Allahabad Division ...	...	4,041	0	16·5	334,120	82·68
27	Benares	Benares	860	0	0	86,920	101·07
28	Mirzapur	Mirzapur...	687	2	21	55,767	81·11
29	Jaunpur	Jaunpur	888	0	0	24,109	27·15
30	Gházipur	*Nil.*	...			...	...
31	Ballia...	Ballia	192	0	0	15,556	81·02
	Total, Benares Division ...	...	2,627	2	21	182,352	69·63
32	Gorakhpur	Gajpur	71	0	0	4,282	60·31
33	Basti	Mehndawal	125	0	0	10,991	87·93
34	Azamgarh	Azamgarh	327	0	29·7	18,230	55·72
	Total, Gorakhpur Division ...	...	523	0	29·7	33,503	64·04
35	Kumaun	Naini Tal	22	2	38 6/11	5,172	227·43
		Haldwani	63	1	8	4,659	73·60
36	Garhwál	*Nil.*	...			...	...
37	Tarái	*Nil.*	...			...	...
	Total, Kumaun Division ...	...	86	0	6 6/11	9,831	114·26
	Total, North-Western Provinces ...	...	16,114	1	4·7	1,225,945	76·08
38	Lucknow	Lucknow...	5,012	0	16	232,935	46·47
39	Unao	Unao	154	0	0	9,297	60·37
40	Rae Bareli	Rae Bareli	297	2	17	13,001	44·15
41	Sitapur	Sitapur	211	1	30	16,354	77·35
42	Hardoi	Sandila	640	0	0	16,813	26·27
43	Kheri	Lakhimpur	87	1	18	5,771	66·06
	Total, Lucknow Division ...	...	6,402	2	1	294,171	45·94
44	Fyzabad	Fyzabad	735	0	0	39,347	53·53
45	Gonda	Gonda	239	1	24	14,293	59·70
46	Bahraich	Bahraich	1,199	3	0	23,426	19·53
47	Sultánpur	Sultanpur	53	2	20	5,354	95·18
48	Partábgarh	*Nil.*	...			...	...
49	Bara Banki	Nawabganj	193	2	20	13,099	67·65
	Total, Fyzabad Division ...	...	2,421	1	24	95,519	39·45
	Total, Oudh ...	...	8,823	3	25	389,690	44·16
	Total, N.-W. Provinces ...	...	24,938	2	29·7	1,615,635	64·78
50	Rampur	Tanda	120	0	0	8,772	73·10
51	Tehri Garhwál	*Nil.*	...			...	...
	TOTAL, NATIVE STATES ...	...	120	0	0	8,772	73·10

APPENDIX XII.

Showing the density of population in the typical towns of the provinces.

(Selected Mohallas.)

Serial number.	District.	Town.	Area of densest Mohalla.	Population of densest Mohalla.	Density.
			A. R. P.		
1	Dehra Dun	Dehra	7 0 0	1,578	225·43
2	Sahâranpur	Deoband	2 2 13	538	208·43
3	Muzaffarnagar	Kandhla	9 0 0	1,297	144·11
4	Meerut	Meerut	22 3 25	3,896	170·10
5	Bulandshahr	Shikarpur	10 0 0	1,672	167·20
6	Aligarh	Koil	28 2 0	2,369	83·12
	Total, Meerut Division		79 3 38	11,350	141·89
7	Muttra	*Nil*	...	...	...
8	Agra	Agra	6 0 0	2,164	360·67
9	Farukhabad	Farukhabad	12 0 0	1,021	85·08
10	Mainpuri	Shikobabad	29 0 0	2,135	73·62
11	Etáwah	Etáwah	2 2 20	742	282·67
12	Etah	Kásganj	34 0 0	4,505	132·50
	Total, Agra Division		83 2 20	10,567	126·36
13	Bareilly	Bareilly	22 0 0	3,179	144·50
14	Bijnor	Nagina	25 0 0	1,551	62·04
15	Budaun	Budaun	1 1 30	352	244·87
16	Moradabad	Moradabad	1 1 34	648	439·66
17	Shâhjahânpur	Shâhjahânpur	54 3 15	2,918	53·11
18	Pilibhit	Bisalpur	10 2 0	1,034	98·48
	Total, Rohilkhand Division		115 0 39	9,672	83·99
19	Cawnpore	Cawnpore	14 0 0	6,227	444·79
20	Fatehpur	Fatehpur	14 0 0	2,091	149·36
21	Bánda	Bánda	47 3 0	3,223	67·49
22	Hamirpur	Hamirpur	25 0 0	2,018	80·72
23	Allahabad	Allahabad	15 0 0	5,037	335·80
24	Jhánsi	Jhánsi	20 2 7	1,605	77·46
25	Jalaun	Kunch	12 0 32	993	81·39
26	Lalitpur	Talbehat	31 0 16	1,753	56·46
	Total, Allahabad Division		179 2 15	22,947	127·77
27	Benares	Benares	13 2 18	2,622	192·61
28	Mirzapur	Mirzapur	42 3 26	5,786	134·83
29	Jaunpur	Jaunpur	34 0 0	1,060	81·18
30	Ghazipur	*Nil*	...	...	...
31	Ballia	Ballia	61 0 0	5,160	84·59
	Total, Benares Division		151 2 4	14,628	96·54
32	Gorakhpur	Gajpur	5 0 0	306	61·20
33	Basti	Mehndawal	10 0 0	1,582	158·20
34	Azamgarh	Azamgarh	25 2 19·5	1,934	75·48
	Total, Gorakhpur Division		40 2 19·5	3,822	94·09
35	Kumaun	Naini Tal { Upper Bazar	7 2 26 10/11	2,623	342·06
		Naini Tal { Lower Bazar	15 0 11 7/11	2,549	169·10
		Naini Tal { Haldwani	3 2 1 3/5	307	87·46
36	Garhwál	*Nil.*	...	...	...
37	Tarái	*Nil.*	...	...	...
	Total, Kumaun Division		26 1 8/55	5,479	208·72
	TOTAL, N.-W PROVINCES		676 8 15·6	78,465	155·09
38	Lucknow	Lucknow	17 0 0	4,492	264·24
39	Unao	Unao	21 0 0	1,457	69·36
40	Rae-Bareli	Rae Bareli	120 0 37	5,883	48·93
41	Sitapur	Sitapur	91 0 0	8,935	98·19
42	Hardoi	Sandila	262 0 0	7,839	29·92
43	Kheri	Lakhimpur	28 2 22	2,246	78·43
	Total, Lucknow Division		539 3 19	30,852	57·14
44	Fyzabad	Fyzabad	2 3 22	247	85·54
45	Gonda	Gonda	22 0 11	1,606	72·77
46	Bahraich	Baharaich	90 2 20	3,761	41·50
47	Sultánpur	Sultánpur	9 1 37	1,065	112·33
48	Partábgarh	*Nil.*	...	...	...
49	Bara Banki	Nawábganj	12 2 0	1,886	150·88
	Total, Fyzabad Division		137 2 10	8,565	62·26
	TOTAL OUDH		677 1 29	39,417	58·19
	TOTAL, N.-W. PROVINCES AND OUDH		1,354 1 4·6	117,882	86·95
50	Rampur	Tanda	18 0 35	1,626	89·25
51	Tehri Garhwál	*Nil.*	...	...	...
	TOTAL, NATIVE STATES		18 0 35	1,626	89·25

APPENDIX XIII.

Showing the average death-rate from different causes for ten years.

Division.	Serial number.	District.	Cholera.	Small-pox.	Fevers.	Dysentery and diarrhœ.	All causes.
MEERUT ...	1	Dehra Dún	·48	·04	14·94	6·28	22·35
	2	Sahéranpur	·24	·38	38·01	3·52	37·93
	3	Muzaffarnagar	·12	·28	32·95	·87	34·70
	4	Meerut	·22	·10	35·97	·80	38·52
	5	Bulandshahr	·93	·80	33·66	1·23	37·06
	6	Aligarh	·65	·75	28·46	1·68	32·46
AGRA ...	7	Muttra	·42	·18	26·55	1·63	28·66
	8	Agra	·69	·46	26·57	1·34	32·78
	9	Farukhabad	·71	·90	31·83	·66	37·17
	10	Mainpuri	·42	·73	27·36	·18	31·62
	11	Etáwah	·70	1·19	27·17	1·10	32·80
	12	Etah	·50	·84	27·97	·22	33·80
ROHILKHAND	13	Bareilly	1·73	1·14	30·81	1·94	37·55
	14	Bijnor	.37	1·15	24·19	3·75	32·66
	15	Budaun	·95	1·97	29·67	1·69	37·10
	16	Moradabad	1·07	·90	35·14	3·34	44·60
	17	Shéhjahánpur	1·97	1·19	24·91	2·94	36·12
	18	Pilibhít	2·64	1·36	29·85	·71	35·58
ALLAHABAD ...	19	Cawnpore	·86	·73	30·20	2·87	40·81
	20	Fatehpur	1·31	1·33	28·16	1·45	38·56
	21	Bánda	2·08	·70	23·92	1·96	34·18
	22	Hamírpur	1·63	·68	24·04	9·06	42·22
	23	Allahabad	1·07	·70	21·47	1·02	28·05
	24	Jhánsi	2·67	2·10	22·19	5·33	42·75
	25	Jalaun	2·17	·61	25·60	3·32	39·90
	26	Lalitpur	·71	2·14	11·33	7·54	36·75
BENARES ...	27	Benares	1·71	·81	22·34	2·03	30·88
	28	Mirzapur	1·40	·70	22·87	0·65	29·95
	29	Jaunpur	1·20	·64	21·31	·12	25·39
	30	Gházipur	1·65	·37	23·61	·54	27·64
	31	Ballia	1·68	·41	20·61	·11	24·51
GORAKHPUR...	32	Gorakhpur	1·69	1·28	15·38	1·59	27·40
	33	Basti	2·18	1·30	19·48	·26	28·13
	34	Azamgarh	1·56	·46	19·79	1·86	27·25
KUMAUN ...	35	Kumaun	2·17	·10	13·64	5·20	25·00
	36	Garhwál	·57	·01	12·49	9·97	24·36
	37	Tarái	1·42	·57	44·58	4·58	52·78
LUCKNOW ...	38	Lucknow	1·70	2·57	25·96	1·12	33·98
	39	Unao	1·10	3·03	24·88	·96	33·98
	40	Rae Bareli	2·57	3·04	24·41	·18	33·62
	41	Sitapur	1·93	2·40	25·92	·53	32·27
	42	Hardoi	1·02	2·95	24·69	·38	31·59
	43	Kheri	2·70	4·79	24·81	·10	30·08
FYZABAD ...	44	Fyzabad	1·48	1·40	22·92	1·12	29·21
	45	Gonda	2·23	3·10	21·61	·11	30·71
	46	Bahraich	2·04	2·60	21·18	·10	30·19
	47	Sultánpur	1·97	1·68	21·65	·89	30·66
	48	Partábgarh	1·52	2·61	18·08	1·07	31·63
	49	Bara Banki	2·01	2·66	23·28	·75	34·56
		Total, N.-W. P. and Oudh ...	1·38	1·24	24·71	1·53	32·50

APPENDIX XIV.

Showing percentages of variations of population in the tahsíls of the North-Western Provinces and Oudh.

Serial number of tahsíl.	Name of district.	Name of tahsíl.	Percentage of variation on total population.
1	Dehra Dún	Dehra	+18·78
2		Kalsi	+12·37
3	Sahâranpur	Sahâranpur	+6·91
4		Deoband	−2·57
5		Roorkee	+5·8007
6		Nukúr	−4·45
7	Muzaffarnagar.	Muzaffarnagar ...	+1·87
8		Kairana	−1·03
9		Jánsath	+5·27
10		Burhana	+1·79
11	Meerut ...	Meerut	+11·98
12		Ghaziabad	+·95
13		Mowana	+11·28
14		Bághpat	+·64
15		Sardhana	+5·81
16		Hápur	+6·08
17	Bulandshahr	Anúpshahr	+4·307
18		Bulandshahr	+7·05
19		Sikandarabad	−4·96
20		Khúrja	+4·03
21	Aligarh ...	Atrauli	+11·97
22		Aligarh	+·93
23		Iglás	−8·73
24		Khair	−5·995
25		Háthras	+4·403
26		Sikandra Rao	+4·16
27	Muttra ...	Muttra (Sadr)... ...	+6·63
28		Chhata	+10·22
29		Kosi	−7·77
30		Mát	−6·27
31		Mahaban	+14·25
32		Sadabad	+14·44
33	Agra ...	Etmádpur	+8·84
34		Firozabad	+8·35
35		Báh	+4·41
36		Fatehabad	+3·52
37		Agra (Sadr)	+2·23
38		Keraoli	−6·72
39		Khairagarh	+4·88

Serial number of tahsíl.	Name of district.	Name of tahsíl.	Percentage of variation on total population.
40	Farukhabad	Kanauj	+2·02
41		Tirwa	−1·67
42		Cibramau	−9·5
43		Farukhabad (Sadr) ...	−4·01
44		Kaimganj	−3·77
45		Aligarh	−3·77
46	Mainpuri ...	Mainpuri	−6·64
47		Bhongaon	−7·31
48		Karhal	+·03
49		Shikohabad	−3·305
50		Mustafabad	−4·28
51	Etáwah ...	Etáwah	+2·49
52		Bharthna	+5·29
53		Bidhuna	−2·67
54		Phaphund	−3·83
55		Auraiya	−·01
56	Etah ...	Etah	+·006
57		Kásganj	−11·42
58		Aliganj	−16·41
59		Jalesar	+1·77
60	Bareilly ...	Faridpur	+7·79
61		Bareilly	+4·46
62		Aonla	−·09
63		Mirganj	−5·59
64		Baheri	−5·44
65		Nawabganj	+6·03
66	Bijnor ...	Bijnor	+7·89
67		Najibabad	+17·45
68		Nagina	+7·69
69		Dhámpur	+7·03
70		Chándpur	+11·72
71	Budaun ...	Gunnaur	+7·53
72		Bisauli	−2·14
73		Sahaswan	+·04
74		Budaun	+1·96
75		Dataganj	+4·87

APPENDIX XIV.

Showing percentages of variations of population in the tahsils of the North-Western Provinces and Oudh—(continued).

Serial number of tahsíl.	Name of district.	Name of tahsíl.	Percentage of variation on total population.
76	Moradabad	Moradabad	+3·85
77		Thakurdwára	+10·56
78		Bilari	+·09
79		Sambhal	—1·003
80		Amroha	+6·99
81		Hasanpur	—5·02
82	Sháhjahánpur.	Sháhjahánpur... ...	+8·38
83		Jalalabad	+9·24
84		Tilhar	+10·398
85		Powayan	+1·54
86	Pilibhít ...	Bisalpur	+6·42
87		Pilibhít	+8·597
88		Puranpur	+7·08
89	Cawnpore ...	Akbarpur	—6·96
90		Bilhaur	—·58
91		Bhognipur	+9·64
92		Cawnpore	+12·18
93		Derapur	—2·006
94		Rasulabad	—2·58
95		Narwal	—2·99
96		Shiurajpur	—1·93
97		Ghátampur	+3·88
98	Fatehpur ...	Fatehpur	—1·21
99		Kalianpur	—·33
100		Kora	+8·33
101		Gházipur	+2·46
102		Khakhreru	+9·84
103		Khagá	+·83
104	Bánda ...	Bánda	—6·36
105		Pailani	+6·64
106		Baberu	+12·74
107		Kamasin	+2·53
108		Mau	—1·29
109		Karwi	+2·78
110		Badausa	—2·52
111		Girwan	—3·52

Serial number of tahsíl.	Name of district.	Name of tahsíl.	Percentage of variation on total population.
112	Hamírpur ...	Hamírpur	+7·61
113		Maskara	—5·12
114		Ráth	—7·69
115		Kulpahar	+1·58
116		Mahoba	+5·06
117		Mandha	+14·66
118	Allahabad ...	Allahabad	+7·67
119		Sirathu	+5·304
120		Manjhanpur	—9·48
121		Soraon	+1·07
122		Phulpur	+2·23
123		Handia	+1·26
124		Karchhana	+8·64
125		Bara	+10·46
126		Meja	+1·57
127	Jhánsi ...	Jhánsi	+17·86
128		Mau	+8·00009
129		Garotha	+1·17
130		Moth	+4·13
131		Lalitpur	+13·45
132		Mehroni	+5·86
133	Jalaun ...	Orai	—6·46
134		Kálpi	—3·96
135		Jalaun	—9·16
136		Kunch	+·95
137	Benares ...	Benares	+3·19
138		Gangapur	+·52
139		Chandauli	+4·505
140	Mirzapur ...	Mirzapur	—1·41
141		Chunar	+1·59
142		Robertsganj	+6·83
143		Kourh	+2·89
144		Chakia	+5·13
145	Jaunpur ...	Jaunpur	+4·058
146		Mariahu	+4·62
147		Machhlishahr	+2·48
148		Khutahan	+6·6996
149		Kerakat	+4·802

APPENDIX XIV.

Showing percentages of variations of population in the tahsíls of the North-Western Provinces and Oudh—(concluded).

Serial number of tahsíl.	Name of district.	Name of tahsíl.	Percentage of variation on total population.	Serial number of tahsíl.	Name of district.	Name of tahsíl.	Percentage of variation on total population.
150	Gházipur ...	Gházipur	+5·71	187	Rae Bareli	Rae Bareli	+11·44
151		Korantadih	+11·84	188		Dalmau	+5·06
152		Zamania	+9·29	189		Dirgbijaiganj	+12·92
153		Saidpur	+3·22	190		Salon	+6·88
154	Ballia ...	Ballia	+2·16	191	Sitapur ...	Sitapur	+13·08
155		Rasra	+·09	192		Sidhauli	+11·85
156		Bansdih	—2·005	193		Misrikh	+13·82
157	Gorakhpur...	Bansgaon	+6·796	194		Biswan	+10·32
158		Maharajganj	+39·85	195	Hardoi ...	Hardoi	+17·22
159		Padrauna	+8·17	196		Sandila	+10·76
160		Hata	+16·37	197		Bilgram	+8·66
161		Deoria	+7·62	198		Shahabad	+14·39
162		Gorakhpur (Sadr) ...	+14·72	199	Kheri ...	Lakhimpur	+10·56
163	Basti ...	Domariaganj	+11·72	200		Muhamdi	+11·04
164		Bánsi	+7·05	201		Nighasan	+4·13
165		Haraiya	+5·15	202	Fyzabad ...	Fyzabad	+8·81
166		Basti	+12·63	203		Akbarpur	+15·26
167		Khalilabad	+11·39	204		Tanda	+17·48
168	Azamgarh ...	Deogaon	+10·62	205		Bikapur	+8·599
169		Nizamabad	+3·904	206	Gonda ...	Gonda	+15·09
170		Mahul	+10·43	207		Tarabganj	+6·21
171		Sagri	+4·998	208		Utraula	+20·55
172		Muhammadabad ...	+10·008	209	Bahraich ...	Bahraich	+14·65
173	Almora ...	Champawat	+20·43	210		Kaisarganj	+12·35
174		Almora	+14·39	211		Nanpara	+15·04
175	Garhwál ...	Pauri	+17·99	212	Sultánpur ...	Sultanpur	+13·43
176	Naini Tal ...	Rudarpur	−2·49	213		Musafirkhana	+13·56
177		Kilpuri	+15·197	214		Amethi	+10·30
178		Kashipur	−2·407	215		Kadipur	+11·49
179		Bhabar	+9·94	216	Partábgarh	Partabgarh	+9·17
180	Lucknow ...	Lucknow	+8·17	217		Patti	+6·22
181		Mohanlalganj	+16·21	218		Kunda	+7·15
182		Malihabad	+14·699	219	Bara Banki	Nawábganj	+14·58
183	Unao	Unao	+2·66	220		Haidargarh	+14·304
184		Safipur	+8·32	221		Ramsanheighat ...	+6·43
185		Purwa	+5·26	222		Fatehpur	+8·98
186		Mohan	+7·88				

APPENDIX XV.

Comparing the 1881 *population with that of the present census aged* 10 *or more.*

Division.	Serial number.	District.	Population over 10.	Population 1881.	Excess of (5) over (4).	Percentage of excess on 5.
1	2	3	4	5	6	7
MEERUT.	1	Dehra Dún	130,095	144,070	18,975	9·70
	2	Sahárаupur	753,307	979,544	226,237	23·09
	3	Muzaffarnagar	583,487	758,444	174,957	23·06
	4	Meerut	1,047,403	1,313,137	265,734	20·23
	5	Bulandshahr	714,115	924,822	210,707	22·78
	6	Aligarh	785,953	1,021,187	235,234	23·03
AGRA.	7	Muttra	538,754	671,690	132,936	19·79
	8	Agra	751,457	974,656	223,199	22·89
	9	Farukhabad	658,260	907,608	249,348	27·47
	10	Mainpuri	580,195	801,216	221,021	27·58
	11	Etáwah	549,256	722,371	173,115	23·96
	12	Etah	541,774	756,523	214,749	28·38
ROHILKHAND.	13	Bareilly	759,443	1,030,936	271,493	26·33
	14	Bijnor	580,133	721,450	141,817	19·58
	15	Budaun	688,530	906,451	217,921	24·04
	16	Moradabad	872,530	1,155,173	282,643	24·46
	17	Sháhjahánpur	674,920	856,946	182,026	21·24
	18	Pilibhít	347,546	451,601	104,055	23·04
ALLAHABAD.	19	Cawnpore	927,151	1,181,396	254,245	21·52
	20	Fatehpur	530,523	683,745	153,222	22·40
	21	Bánda	518,936	698,608	179,672	25·71
	22	Hamírpur	380,154	507,337	127,183	25·06
	23	Allahabad	1,145,703	1,474,106	328,403	22·27
	24	Jhánsi	301,105	333,227	32,122	9·63
	25	Jalaun	296,906	418,142	121,236	28·99
	26	Lalitpur	189,967	249,088	59,121	23·73
BENARES.	27	Benares	677,153	892,684	215,531	24·14
	28	Mirzapur	838,168	1,136,796	298,628	26·27
	29	Jaunpur	907,683	1,209,663	301,980	24·96
	30	Gházipur	776,856	1,014,099	237,243	23·39
	31	Ballia	676,257	924,763	248,506	26·87
GORAKHPUR.	32	Gorakhpur	2,088,812	2,617,120	528,308	20·18
	33	Basti	1,252,462	1,630,612	378,150	23·19
	34	Azamgarh	1,233,366	1,604,654	371,288	23·13
KUMAUN.	35	Kumaun	408,716	493,641	84,925	17·20
	36	Garhwál	295,111	345,629	50,518	14·61
	37	Tarái	159,870	206,993	47,123	22·76
		Total, North-Western Provinces ...	25,162,117	32,720,128	7,558,011	23·09
LUCKNOW.	38	Lucknow	578,319	696,824	118,505	17·00
	39	Unao	698,578	899,069	200,491	22·30
	40	Rae Bareli	758,793	951,905	193,112	20·28
	41	Sitapur	776,318	958,251	181,933	18·98
	42	Hardoi	802,836	987,630	184,794	18·71
	43	Kheri	657,922	831,922	174,000	20·91
FYZABAD.	44	Fyzabad	880,616	1,081,419	200,803	18·56
	45	Gonda	1,041,961	1,270,926	228,965	18·01
	46	Bahraich	722,330	878,048	155,718	17·73
	47	Sultánpur	777,578	957,912	180,334	18·82
	48	Partábgarh	652,977	847,047	194,070	22·91
	49	Bara Banki	828,370	1,026,788	198,418	19·32
		Total, Oudh ...	9,176,598	11,387,741	2,211,143	19·41
		Total, North-Western Provinces and Oudh ...	34,338,715	44,107,869	9,769,154	22·14
NATIVE STATES.	50	Rampur	415,000	541,914	126,914	23·41
	51	Tehri Garhwál	172,814	199,836	27,022	13·52
		Total, Native States ...	587,814	741,750	153,936	20·75

APPEN

Showing the death returns by districts

Serial number.	District.	1881. Males.	1881. Females.	1882. Males.	1882. Females.
1	Debra Dún	1,748	1,246	1,823	1,269
2	Sahóraupur	19,793	17,610	18,890	16,485
3	Muzaffarnagar	12,942	11,016	12,655	10,411
4	Meerut	26,146	22,854	24,293	20,741
5	Bulandshahr	15,611	13,142	14,692	12,631
6	Aligarh	14,979	12,366	13,469	10,932
	Total, Meerut Division ...	91,219	78,234	85,822	72,469
7	Muttra	10,144	7,997	10,108	8,311
8	Agra	14,268	12,141	15,773	13,922
9	Farukhabad	15,785	13,218	15,263	13,109
10	Mainpuri	12,196	10,112	12,593	10,592
11	Etáwah	12,018	10,220	11,845	9,320
12	Etah	11,873	9,952	12,105	10,449
	Total, Agra Division ...	76,284	63,640	77,682	65,703
13	Bareilly	19,177	17,510	27,908	25,801
14	Bijnor	9,859	8,748	11,555	10,115
15	Budaun	18,414	12,069	18,055	16,259
16	Moradabad	20,591	18,831	26,085	23,551
17	Sháhjahánpur	13,323	11,119	18,016	16,518
18	Pilibhít	7,980	6,550	12,017	11,224
	Total, Rohilkhand Division ...	84,344	74,827	113,586	103,468
19	Cawnpore	25,633	23,345	26,082	23,552
20	Fatehpur	12,858	11,426	14,578	13,600
21	Bánda	10,785	8,661	14,518	11,799
22	Hamírpur	9,285	7,138	10,562	9,000
23	Allahabad	22,177	19,740	23,620	19,830
24	Jhánsi	6,774	5,797	6,889	5,963
25	Jalaun	8,875	7,199	7,068	5,777
26	Lalitpur	4,404	3,984	4,454	3,986
	Total, Allahabad Division ...	100,791	87,290	107,721	93,507
27	Benares	16,797	15,618	19,616	17,405
28	Mirzapur	17.955	16,534	22,206	18,832
29	Jaunpur	18,257	15,972	20,317	16,578
30	Gházipur	18,435	16,997	18,002	15,177
31	Ballia	16,523	15,800	14,118	11,337
	Total, Benares Division ...	87,967	80,921	94,259	79,329
32	Gorakhpur	52,420	47,772	45,762	39,507
33	Basti	28,675	26,679	25,649	22,946
34	Azamgarh	27,247	24,352	28,814	23,468
	Total, Gorakhpur Division ...	108,851	98,803	100,225	85,921
35	Kumaun	5,648	4,659	5,545	4,605
36	Garhwál	4,016	3,509	4,204	3,707
37	Tarái	5,445	4,353	6,546	5,797
	Total, Kumaun Division ...	15,109	12,521	16,295	14,109
	TOTAL, NORTH-WESTERN PROVINCES ...	564,065	496,236	595,590	514,506
38	Lucknow	11,436	10,251	14,372	13,075
39	Unao	14,031	13,389	14,026	12,435
40	Rae Bareli	12,930	12,873	16,207	15,037
41	Sitapur	15,062	11,923	22,658	19,722
42	Hardoi	13,516	10,842	15,585	13,531
43	Kheri	13,958	11,211	15,063	13,035
	Total, Lucknow Division ...	80,933	70,489	97,911	86,885
44	Fyzabad	20,650	18,676	20,132	17,411
45	Gonda	18,734	17,064	16,564	14,447
46	Bahraich	13,783	11,224	11,711	9,667
47	Sultánpur	16,579	15,667	18,480	15,826
48	Partábgarh	13,192	13,252	15,885	14,575
49	Bara Banki	16,499	15,430	18,467	17,120
	Total, Fyzabad Division ...	99,437	91,313	101,239	89,046
	TOTAL, OUDH ...	180,370	161,802	199,150	175,881
	TOTAL, N.-W. PROVINCES AND OUDH ...	744,435	658,038	794,740	690,387

DIX XVI.

for the years 1881 *to* 1890.

1883.		1884.		1885.		1886.	
Males.	Females.	Males.	Females.	Males.	Females.	Males.	Females.
1,643	1,134	1,679	1,201	1,622	1,340	1,705	1,237
15,999	13,947	29,002	26,999	20,892	18,200	17,451	14,561
12,189	10,154	18,550	16,594	15,791	13,300	15,505	11,193
21,400	18,290	29,490	27,754	29,355	26,826	28,191	24,679
13,535	11,543	17,132	15,489	25,789	24,604	20,533	18,064
12,064	10,007	22,918	20,023	21,053	18,628	18,211	15,209
76,830	65,075	118,766	108,060	114,502	102,898	99,596	84,943
8,463	6,931	12,459	10,820	10,145	8,180	9,763	7,916
15,964	13,594	21,041	18,959	16,471	14,388	15,396	13,349
16,346	14,255	22,415	20,469	20,963	18,031	17,480	14,813
12,990	10,287	15,932	13,167	15,829	12,043	12,789	9,877
11,176	8,636	13,331	11,278	14,659	12,203	13,469	10,936
10,106	8,223	17,131	14,635	15,576	12,486	13,576	10,235
75,045	61,926	102,309	89,328	93,643	77,331	82,473	67,126
16,118	14,171	19,385	17,730	20,397	18,296	32,063	26,724
10,760	9,710	12,229	11,820	13,188	12,730	15,154	13,325
15,233	13,678	19,000	17,179	21,878	19,584	23,826	20,040
18,708	16,420	27,065	26,542	29,422	28,319	37,340	33,879
14,747	13,379	15,903	14,727	16,335	15,559	19,533	17,352
8,059	6,679	7,985	6,861	6,966	5,933	9,258	7,708
83,625	74,037	102,467	94,859	108,186	100,421	137,174	119,028
25,214	22,850	31,097	28,543	25,185	23,673	22,916	20,621
11,640	10,678	16,359	15,425	11,321	11,297	10,408	9,616
14,357	12,169	15,561	13,115	8,792	7,458	9,446	7,875
10,667	9,436	14,898	14,183	8,639	7,430	9,150	8,258
17,285	13,969	18,789	15,343	17,327	14,918	18,383	15,803
6,203	5,389	8,209	7,579	5,274	4,413	6,156	5,499
7,106	6,018	10,464	9,832	7,605	6,308	6,913	5,989
3,590	3,235	4,018	3,853	4,037	3,792	5,242	4,747
96,062	83,744	119,395	107,878	88,180	79,289	88,614	78,408
13,026	10,692	12,125	10,105	13,349	11,752	14,579	13,404
15,947	13,300	17,025	14,945	14,631	12,563	17,107	15,148
13,992	11,928	16,607	13,833	14,100	11,879	21,117	18,102
10,862	9,043	13,364	11,636	14,478	13,594	19,030	17,674
10,144	8,398	12,061	10,002	11,518	10,101	10,529	8,520
63,971	53,361	71,182	60,521	68,076	59,889	82,362	72,848
31,083	25,682	40,947	34,833	36,634	31,345	32,265	27,286
18,483	16,186	32,210	29,709	21,757	20,712	25,435	24,348
15,517	12,544	21,044	18,009	24,116	22,240	29,454	26,615
65,083	54,412	94,201	82,551	82,507	74,297	87,144	78,249
5,030	4,194	6,269	5,494	5,409	5,231	5,483	5,315
4,239	3,890	3,684	3,542	4,204	3,950	3,764	3,431
5,413	4,592	5,907	5,097	4,719	3,934	5,950	5,479
14,682	12,676	15,860	14,133	14,332	13,115	15,197	14,226
475,298	405,231	624,180	557,325	569,426	507,240	592,560	514,827
14,972	13,658	12,068	10,758	13,438	13,201	13,324	12,522
14,155	13,033	15,268	13,828	12,462	11,567	14,970	13,741
15,566	14,923	17,140	16,123	17,564	17,364	15,204	14,255
15,141	13,175	14,177	11,555	13,223	12,374	16,301	14,179
17,760	15,897	18,551	16,097	14,931	13,325	16,072	13,557
11,435	9,910	13,209	10,834	10,771	9,050	11,906	9,686
89,029	80,596	90,413	79,195	82,389	76,881	87,837	77,940
14,560	11,754	16,365	13,411	16,941	14,187	18,882	15,978
17,220	15,210	26,968	23,726	10,359	17,547	22,129	19,999
12,467	10,634	10,173	16,457	12,683	11,103	12,952	11,190
12,009	9,932	15,677	13,418	13,749	11,884	16,798	14,796
11,783	10,795	17,918	16,487	13,899	12,749	14,367	13,289
20,535	19,244	12,926	11,703	15,593	15,009	17,745	16,324
88,574	77,569	109,027	95,202	92,224	82,479	102,873	91,576
177,603	158,165	199,440	174,397	174,613	159,360	190,710	169,516
652,901	563,396	823,620	731,722	744,039	666,600	788,270	684,343

APPEN

Showing the death returns by districts

Serial number.	District.	1887. Males.	1887. Females.	1888. Males.	1888. Females.
1	Dehra Dún	2,245	1,723	1,772	1,263
2	Sahéranpur	21,406	18,364	16,271	13,183
3	Muzaffarnagar	13,118	10,610	12,503	10,444
4	Meerut	31,970	28,536	23,989	19,728
5	Bulandshahr	23,822	20,626	16,832	13,663
6	Aligarh	23,014	18,966	18,751	14,575
	Total, Meerut Division ...	115,570	98,825	90,118	72,856
7	Muttra	13,239	10,878	12,911	9,915
8	Agra	18,246	16,260	15,994	13,653
9	Farukhabad	19,927	16,795	15,819	12,805
10	Mainpuri	12,595	9,898	11,604	9,550
11	Etáwah	15,393	12,776	10,956	9,270
12	Etah	15,056	11,087	15,313	11,870
	Total, Agra Division ...	94,455	77,694	82,397	67,063
13	Bareilly	18,218	14,663	17,649	15,081
14	Bijnor	12,939	11,060	11,421	9,508
15	Budaun	18,725	15,775	17,063	14,863
16	Moradabad	27,482	24,176	24,808	22,296
17	Sháhjahánpur	16,738	14,274	16,289	13,998
18	Pilibhít	9,119	7,055	9,111	6,799
	Total, Rohilkhand Division ...	103,216	87,003	96,341	82,545
19	Cawnpore	31,977	28,841	21,590	20,099
20	Fatehpur	16,464	14,460	12,504	12,114
21	Bánda	15,158	13,267	13,240	11,467
22	Hamírpur	15,396	14,576	11,861	10,025
23	Allahabad	26,959	20,609	21,295	19,018
24	Jhánsi	12,464	11,392	7,029	5,958
25	Jalaun	14,249	13,425	9,195	7,963
26	Lalitpur	6,406	5,889	4,337	3,796
	Total, Allahabad Division ...	135,073	122,459	101,051	90,440
27	Benares	15,473	13,865	16,349	14,569
28	Mirzapur	21,563	19,134	18,700	17,048
29	Jaunpur	16,180	12,961	13,660	10,915
30	Gházipur	13,957	12,184	12,655	11,706
31	Ballia	11,861	9,757	9,589	8,257
	Total, Benares Division ...	79,034	67,901	70,953	62,495
32	Gorakhpur	38,022	33,363	33,181	29,001
33	Basti	24,906	23,335	19,686	18,227
34	Azamgarh	20,491	18,073	19,678	17,691
	Total, Gorakhpur Division ...	83,419	74,771	72,545	64,919
35	Kumaun	6,667	6,287	6,443	5,498
36	Garhwál	4,979	4,693	4,778	4,433
37	Tarái	6,348	5,429	5,505	4,518
	Total, Kumaun Division ...	17,994	16,409	16,726	14,449
	TOTAL, NORTH-WESTERN PROVINCES ...	628,761	545,062	530,131	454,767
38	Lucknow	16,910	14,527	12,937	12,401
39	Unao	20,739	19,690	16,004	15,712
40	Rae Bareli	20,425	19,762	14,252	13,576
41	Sitapur	17,323	14,846	16,368	14,441
42	Hardoi	17,969	15,389	16,461	14,436
43	Kheri	13,095	10,795	14,741	12,471
	Total, Lucknow Division ...	105,461	95,009	90,753	83,037
44	Fyzabad	16,799	14,080	16,395	14,600
45	Gonda	24,797	22,469	17,485	15,638
46	Bahraich	12,868	10,502	13,400	11,548
47	Sultánpur	18,014	16,238	13,763	12,253
48	Partabgarh	13,001	11,595	12,967	12,083
49	Bara Banki	24,068	23,015	14,537	13,756
	Total, Fyzabad Division ...	109,547	97,899	88,547	79,878
	TOTAL, OUDH ...	215,008	192,908	179,300	162,915
	TOTAL, N.-W. PROVINCES AND OUDH ...	843,769	737,970	709,431	617,682

DIX XVI.

for the years 1881 *to* 1890—(concluded).

1889.		1890.		Total.		
Males.	Females.	Males.	Females.	Total.	Males.	Females
1,857	1,336	2,923	1,942	32,708	19,017	13,691
16,244	13,826	24,447	21,570	375,140	200,395	174,745
12,945	10,759	19,088	17,345	265,107	143,281	121,826
24,340	20,164	28,822	24,729	502,297	267,996	234,301
17,393	14,351	20,663	17,396	347,511	186,002	161,509
21,384	16,836	21,959	17,571	342,910	187,797	155,113
94,163	77,272	117,902	100,553	1,865,673	1,004,488	861,185
13,840	10,780	14,784	11,764	209,343	115,851	93,492
18,412	15,059	20,604	16,870	320,363	172,168	148,195
15,845	12,686	21,172	17,051	334,047	180,815	153,232
12,027	9,098	15,310	12,259	240,748	133,865	106,883
12,939	10,193	16,760	13,274	240,652	132,546	108,106
14,644	10,888	16,776	12,971	254,947	142,156	112,791
87,707	68,699	105,406	84,189	1,600,100	877,401	722,699
16,276	14,017	19,376	17,603	388,163	206,567	181,596
11,025	9,291	15,917	13,891	284,245	124,047	110,198
14,132	11,460	17,756	15,043	335,032	179,082	155,950
21,849	19,165	29,542	27,447	504,368	263,742	240,626
13,529	11,378	20,067	17,843	310,622	164,475	146,147
7,814	6,328	10,966	9,891	164,303	89,275	75,028
84,625	71,639	113,624	101,718	1,936,733	1,027,188	909,545
21,889	19,186	27,235	24,277	493,755	258,768	234,987
12,425	11,721	17,649	17,251	262,794	135,206	127,588
14,369	11,999	14,146	12,116	240,298	130,372	109,926
10,489	9,080	12,851	11,095	214,019	113,798	100,221
29,363	25,378	26,395	24,358	407,559	218,593	188,966
6,848	5,783	9,190	7,909	140,718	75,036	65,682
8,053	6,571	10,049	8,465	167,124	89,577	77,547
6,162	5,721	5,571	5,010	92,234	48,221	44,013
109,598	95,439	123,086	110,481	2,018,501	1,069,571	948,930
15,112	13,113	13,437	11,452	281,838	149,863	131,975
18,890	16,180	19,291	17,178	344,177	183,315	160,862
14,476	11,974	19,372	17,117	309,337	168,078	141,259
14,626	12,532	13,227	11,937	281,116	148,636	132,480
12,547	11,271	13,602	12,321	228,256	122,492	106,764
75,651	65,070	78,929	70,005	1,444,724	772,384	672,340
34,953	30,886	39,022	34,933	718,906	384,288	334,608
19,375	18,193	21,897	20,218	458,626	238,073	220,553
21,729	19,607	24,899	22,556	438,144	232,989	205,155
76,057	68,686	85,818	77,707	1,615,666	855,350	760,316
9,418	9,227	9,028	7,958	123,408	64,940	58,468
4,609	4,171	5,451	4,968	84,222	43,928	40,294
6,187	5,285	6,074	5,305	107,883	58,074	49,789
20,214	18,683	20,553	18,231	315,513	166,962	148,551
548,015	465,488	645,718	562,884	10,796,910	7,673,344	5,023,566
14,317	13,026	15,569	14,611	266,373	138,343	128,030
18,064	16,620	18,544	17,214	305,492	158,263	147,229
15,292	13,496	18,878	18,513	319,440	163,518	155,922
17,203	14,685	18,211	15,178	307,745	165,667	142,078
17,911	14,727	19,821	16,839	313,207	168,567	144,640
12,953	10,446	19,629	16,145	250,343	136,760	113,583
95,740	83,000	110,662	98,500	1,762,600	931,118	831,482
16,149	13,968	20,669	18,558	330,165	177,542	152,623
18,812	16,555	24,533	21,348	390,604	206,601	184,003
13,795	12,035	20,350	17,214	264,756	143,182	121,574
12,324	11,174	17,805	17,538	293,924	155,198	138,726
11,528	11,518	14,402	13,647	268,932	138,942	129,990
22,568	20,600	21,050	19,559	355,748	183,988	171,760
95,176	85,850	118,809	107,864	1,904,129	1,005,453	898,676
190,916	168,850	229,061	206,364	3,666,759	1,936,571	1,730,188
738,931	633,338	874,779	769,248	14,463,639	7,709,915	6,753,724

APPENDIX XVII.

Showing the variations in the urban population.

Serial number.	District.	Town population in 1881. Total.	Town population in 1881. Males.	Town population in 1881. Females.	Town population in 1891. Total.	Town population in 1891. Males.	Town population in 1891. Females.	Total, increase per cent.	Males, increase per cent.	Females, increase per cent.	Total, decrease per cent.	Males, decrease per cent.	Females, decrease per cent.
1	Dehra Dún	29,285	18,509	10,776	38,245	25,147	13,078	30·59	35·86	21·54	...	...	...
2	Sahāranpur	206,395	111,409	94,986	202,839	111,478	91,361	...	·06193	...	1·722	...	3·816
3	Muzaffarnagar	128,973	69,144	59,829	126,009	67,959	58,050	...	...	...	2·298	1·713	2·973
4	Meerut	269,220	146,531	122,639	288,786	157,864	130,922	7·267	7·734	6·711	...	...	...
5	Bulandshahr	167,152	87,641	79,811	161,268	84,300	76,968	...	...	...	3·520	3·812	3·198
6	Aligarh	197,210	104,693	92,517	202,137	107,314	94,823	2·498	2·503	2·492	...	...	...
	Total, Meerut Division ...	998,235	537,927	460,308	1,019,284	554,062	465,222	21·09	3·000	1·067	...	...	...
7	Muttra	136,550	72,202	64,348	147,748	78,712	69,086	8·237	9·016	7·363	...	...	...
8	Agra	200,476	108,627	91,849	209,928	112,703	97,225	4·714	3·752	5·853	...	...	...
9	Farukhabad	139,422	71,195	68,227	138,049	71,723	66,326	...	·7416	...	·9850	...	2·786
10	Mainpuri	64,757	35,819	28,938	52,114	27,836	24,278	...	...	...	19·52	22·52	16·10
11	Etáwah	61,131	33,020	28,111	62,851	33,332	29,519	2·813	·9448	5·008	...	...	...
12	Etah	122,779	64,296	58,483	108,411	57,189	51,222	...	...	...	11·70	11·05	12·41
	Total, Agra Division ...	725,115	385,159	339,956	719,151	381,495	337,656	...	...	...	·8225	·9513	·6765
13	Bareilly	164,289	84,441	79,848	171,567	90,368	81,199	4·430	7·021	1·691	...	...	...
14	Bijnor	160,531	81,077	79,454	173,465	87,508	85,957	8·057	6·597	8·184	...	...	...
15	Budaun	96,294	49,293	47,001	99,570	50,581	48,989	3·402	2·613	4·229	...	...	...
16	Moradabad	237,327	121,350	115,977	242,815	123,181	119,634	2·312	1·508	3·153	...	...	...
17	Sháhjahánpur	119,340	59,908	59,432	120,455	60,893	59,562	·9343	1·644	·2187	...	...	...
18	Pilibhít	49,029	24,529	24,500	56,519	28,899	27,620	15·27	17·81	12·73	...	...	...
	Total, Rohilkhand Division ...	826,810	420,598	406,212	864,391	441,430	422,961	4·545	4·953	4·123	...	...	...
19	Cawnpore	179,947	101,408	78,539	213,780	119,959	93,821	18·80	18·29	19·45	...	...	...
20	Fatehpur	46,161	23,440	22,721	44,430	22,585	21,845	...	...	...	3·750	3·647	3·855
21	Bánda	48,904	25,170	23,734	41,058	20,447	20,611	...	...	...	16·04	18·76	13·15
22	Hamírpur	72,417	36,617	35,800	69,283	34,696	34,587	...	...	...	4·327	5·246	3·388
23	Allahabad	209,561	110,509	99,052	219,884	116,572	103,312	4·926	5·486	4·300	...	...	...
24	Jhánsi	82,123	42,240	39,883	98,540	53,238	45,302	19·99	26·09	13·58	...	...	...
25	Jalaun	55,954	28,193	27,761	52,371	26,795	25,576	...	...	...	6·403	4·958	7·870
26	Lalitpur	18,964	9,824	9,140	20,274	10,471	9,803	6·907	6·585	7·253	...	...	...
	Total, Allahabad Division ...	714,031	377,401	336,630	759,620	404,763	354,857	6·384	7·250	5·414	...	...	...

27	Benares	231,404	118,461	112,943	235,552	123,066	112,486	1·792	3·887	...	...	...	·4063
28	Mirzapur	119,543	58,792	60,751	116,676	58,020	58,656	...	...	...	2·398	1·313	3·448
29	Jaunpur	75,075	37,178	37,897	73,980	37,028	86,952	...	...	...	2·398	1·313	5·876
30	Gházipur	110,782	54,084	56,698	117,279	57,100	60,179	5·864	5·576	6·139	...	...	...
31	Ballia	105,016	50,322	54,694	101,539	48,531	53,008	...	...	...	8·311	3·559	3·082
	Total, Benares Division ...	641,820	318,837	322,983	645,026	323,745	321,281	·4995	1·539	...	...	...	·5269
32	Gorakhpur	164,545	83,011	81,534	166,183	83,984	82,199	·9955	1·172	·8156	...	...	...
23	Basti	24,893	13,137	11,756	34,367	19,125	1,5242	38·05	45·58	29·65	...	...	...
34	Azamgarh	88,006	44,394	43,612	90,383	45,489	44,894	2·700	2·466	2·937	...	...	...
	Total, Gorakhpur Division ...	277,444	140,542	136,902	290,933	148,598	142,385	4·860	5·732	3·968	...	...	...
35	Kumaun	27,760	18,355	9,405	28,904	18,713	10,191	4·121	1·950	8·357	...	...	...
36	Garhwál	2,100	1,046	1,054	3,740	2,405	1,335	78·09	129·9	26·66	...	...	...
37	Tarái	21,622	11,384	10,238	21,524	11,128	10,396	...	...	1·543	·4532	2·248	...
	Total, Kumaun Division ...	51,482	30,785	20,697	54,168	32,246	21,922	9·102	4·746	5·918	...	...	...
	Total, North-Western Provinces ...	4,234,937	2,211,249	2,023,688	4,352,573	2,286,339	2,066,234	2·777	3·395	2·102	...	...	...
38	Lucknow	294,101	155,059	139,042	307,155	162,639	144,516	4·438	4·888	3·937	...	...	...
39	Unao	70,796	35,338	35,458	78,015	39,772	38,243	10·19	22·54	7·854	...	...	...
40	Rae Bareli	27,313	13,625	13,688	30,724	15,999	14,725	12·48	17·42	7·575	...	...	...
41	Sitapur	72,432	37,584	34,848	75,028	39,731	35,297	3·584	5·712	1·288	...	...	...
42	Hardoi	94,812	48,655	46,157	105,003	54,310	50,693	10·74	11·62	9·822	...	...	...
43	Kheri	36,766	20,015	16,751	38,461	20,563	17,898	4·610	2·737	6·847	...	...	...
	Total, Lucknow Division ...	596,220	310,276	285,944	634,886	336,014	301,372	6·401	7·329	5·396	...	...	...
44	Fyzabad	128,037	67,173	60,864	138,524	73,189	65,335	8·191	8·956	6·874	...	...	...
45	Gonda	55,137	29,545	25,592	64,269	34,565	29,704	16·61	16·99	16·06	...	...	...
46	Bahraich	34,244	18,017	16,227	39,289	20,765	18,524	14·73	15·25	14·15	...	...	...
47	Sultánpur	9,374	5,277	4,097	8,751	4,919	3,832	...	...	...	6·646	6·784	6·468
48	Partábgarh	15,389	7,999	7,390	16,049	8,608	7,441	4·289	7·613	·6901	...	...	...
49	Bara Banki	59,385	30,177	29,208	60,487	30,880	29,607	1·855	2·932	1·366	...	...	...
	Total, Fyzabad Division ...	301,566	158,188	143,378	327,369	172,926	154,443	8·556	9·317	7·717	...	...	...
	Total, Oudh ...	897,786	468,464	429,322	961,755	505,940	455,815	7·125	7·999	6·171	...	...	...
	Total, N.-W. Provinces and Oudh ...	5,132,723	2,679,713	2,453,010	5,314,328	2,792,279	2,522,049	3·538	4·200	2·814	...	...	...
50	Rampur	101,111	50,222	50,889	103,188	54,478	48,710	2·054	8·474	...	...	...	4·291
51	Tehri Garhwál	...	...	...	...	...	...	...	...	...	...	...	...
	TOTAL, NATIVE STATES ...	101,111	50,222	50,889	103,188	54,478	48,710	2·054	8·474	...	...	...	4·291

APPENDIX XVIII.

Giving a detailed comparison of the population as calculated from that of 1881 *by adding births and deducting deaths.*

Serial number.	1	2		3		4		5		6	
	District.	Population in 1881.		Population by adding births and deducting deaths.		Actual population in 1891.		Excess of 3 over 4.		Excess of 4 over 3.	
		Males.	Females.	Males.	Females.	Males.	Females.	Males.	Females.	Males.	Females.
1	Dehra Dún	83,985	60,085	83,662	61,051	100,324	67,811	...	...	16,662	6,760
2	Sahéranpur	530,427	449,117	543,019	463,988	540,351	460,929	2,668	3,059	...	...
3	Muzaffarnagar ...	409,436	349,008	416,230	353,682	418,228	354,646	...	...	1,998	964
4	Meerut	705,437	607,700	742,787	635,112	747,244	644,214	...	...	4,457	9,102
5	Bulandshahr	491,958	432,864	508,466	448,730	501,621	448,293	6,845	437	...	...
6	Aligarh	551,279	469,908	567,624	494,238	558,748	484,429	8,881	9,809	...	...
	Total, Meerut Division ...	2,772,522	2,368,682	2,861,788	2,456,801	2,866,511	2,460,322	...	...	4,723	3,521
7	Muttra	360,967	310,723	367,145	316,242	382,660	330,761	...	...	15,515	14,519
8	Agra	526,801	447,855	555,888	476,894	540,459	463,337	15,429	13,557	...	...
9	Farukhabad	490,508	417,100	482,115	415,957	464,340	394,347	17,775	21,610	...	...
10	Mainpuri	442,094	359,122	436,107	364,466	416,799	345,364	19,308	19,102	...	...
11	Etáwah	395,224	327,147	398,630	340,927	396,775	330,854	1,855	10,073	...	...
12	Etah	413,689	342,834	402,728	345,638	383,203	318,860	19,525	26,778	...	...
	Total, Agra Division ...	2,629,283	2,204,781	2,642,613	2,260,124	2,584,236	2,183,523	58,377	76,601	...	...
13	Bareilly	548,010	482,926	571,659	507,891	555,480	485,211	16,179	22,680	...	...
14	Bijnor	383,258	338,192	421,425	370,650	418,212	375,858	3,213	...	...	5,208
15	Budaun	487,351	419,100	512,896	449,513	498,134	427,464	14,762	22,049	...	...
16	Moradabad	610,291	544,882	635,209	571,500	623,572	555,826	11,637	15,674	...	...
17	Sháhjahánpur... ...	460,064	396,882	502,120	440,034	495,306	423,245	6,814	16,789	...	...
18	Pilibhít	239,787	211,814	252,292	228,680	258,402	226,964	...	1,666	6,110	...
	Total, Rohilkhand Division	2,728,761	2,393,796	2,895,601	2,568,218	2,849,106	2,494,568	46,495	73,650	...	...
19	Cawnpore	628,891	552,505	632,249	552,911	648,092	561,603	...	...	15,843	8,692
20	Fatehpur	347,587	336,158	359,386	341,385	359,821	339,386	...	2,049	435	...
21	Bánda	354,377	344,231	367,509	361,418	356,894	348,938	10,615	12,480	...	...
22	Hamírpur	259,778	247,559	266,978	258,603	260,603	253,117	6,375	5,486	...	...
23	Allahabad	741,730	732,376	765,356	752,882	781,509	767,228	...	...	16,153	14,846
24	Jhánsi	172,884	160,343	179,882	168,078	214,528	194,891	...	...	34,646	26,813
25	Jalaun	216,145	201,997	214,878	204,907	204,090	192,271	10,788	12,636	...	...
26	Lalitpur	129,799	119,289	146,792	137,054	141,436	132,764	5,356	4,290	...	...
	Total, Allahabad Division	2,851,191	2,694,458	2,933,030	2,777,238	2,966,973	2,790,148	...	...	33,943	12,910
27	Benares	450,784	441,900	460,336	451,056	467,453	454,490	...	...	7,117	3,434
28	Mirzapur	567,304	569,492	600,108	604,707	576,341	585,167	23,767	19,540	...	...
29	Jaunpur	611,407	598,256	652,160	642,918	634,950	629,999	17,210	12,979	...	...
30	Gházípur	507,117	500,982	540,430	538,008	531,701	546,208	8,729	...	...	8,120
31	Ballia	450,605	474,158	489,199	508,792	452,611	489,854	36,588	18,938	...	...
	Total, Benares Division ...	2,587,217	2,590,788	2,742,233	2,745,621	2,663,056	2,705,718	79,177	39,903	...	...
32	Gorakhpur	1,306,123	1,310,997	1,491,456	1,504,324	1,497,284	1,496,773	...	7,551	5,828	...
33	Basti	824,251	806,361	950,726	923,484	907,337	878,507	43,389	44,977	...	...
34	Azamgarh	816,429	788,225	879,288	848,523	867,611	861,014	11,677	...	...	12,491
	Total, Gorkhpur Division ...	2,946,803	2,905,583	3,321,470	3,276,331	3,272,232	3,236,294	49,238	40,037	...	...
35	Kumaun	261,054	232,587	262,689	232,852	294,957	268,224	...	...	32,268	35,372
36	Garhwál	170,755	174,874	191,434	197,271	200,319	207,499	...	...	8,885	10,228
37	Tarái	113,315	93,678	96,866	81,422	115,460	95,108	...	...	18,594	13,686
	Total, Kumaun Division ...	545,124	501,139	550,989	511,545	610,736	570,831	...	...	59,747	59,286
	Total, N.-W. Provinces ...	17,060,901	15,659,227	17,947,724	16,595,878	17,812,850	16,441,404	134,874	154,474	...	...
38	Lucknow	365,305	331,519	388,706	350,248	407,201	366,962	...	...	18,495	16,714
39	Unao	461,167	437,902	505,889	473,801	489,512	464,124	16,377	9,767	...	...
40	Rae Bareli	466,906	484,999	511,646	520,318	512,980	523,541	...	...	1,334	3,223
41	Sitapur	505,986	452,265	561,556	506,054	567,182	508,231	...	...	5,627	2,177
42	Hardoi	531,704	455,926	595,185	517,323	596,497	516,714	...	609	1,312	...
43	Kheri	445,019	386,908	478,775	421,000	482,035	421,580	...	...	3,260	580
	Total, Lucknow Division ...	2,776,087	2,549,514	3,041,756	2,788,834	3,055,407	2,801,152	...	...	13,651	12,318
44	Fyzabad	546,174	535,245	592,469	583,635	612,602	604,357	...	...	20,183	20,722
45	Gonda	650,771	620,155	738,825	697,665	746,403	712,826	...	...	7,578	15,161
46	Bahraich	459,187	418,861	506,276	464,682	523,567	476,865	...	...	17,291	12,183
47	Sultánpur	475,125	482,787	524,832	524,648	530,486	545,365	...	...	5,654	20,717
48	Partábgarh	420,730	426,317	465,014	464,161	445,171	465,724	19,843	...	...	1,563
49	Bara Banki	523,581	503,207	578,197	549,337	577,115	553,791	1,082	...	...	4,454
	Total, Fyzabad Division ...	3,075,568	2,986,572	3,405,613	3,284,128	3,435,344	3,358,928	...	...	29,731	74,800
	TOTAL, OUDH ...	5,851,655	5,536,086	6,447,369	6,072,962	6,490,751	6,160,080	...	...	43,382	87,118
	TOTAL, N.-W. P. & OUDH	22,912,556	21,195,313	24,395,093	22,668,840	24,303,601	22,601,484	91,492	67,356	...	...

APPENDIX XIX.

Showing the deaths of children aged from 0 to 9 amongst the population registered under the Infanticide Act.

Age period.	Males.			Females.		
	Population.	Deaths.	Death rate per 1,000.	Population.	Deaths.	Death rate per 1,000
0 year	53,595	12,179	227·24	49,859	12,011	240·90
1 "	42,468	4,957	116·72	37,928	5,152	135·84
2 years	41,631	2,848	68·41	33,026	3,090	93·56
3 "	37,073	1,603	43·23	26,623	1,711	64·26
4 "	35,967	1,196	33·25	23,346	1,043	44·67
5 "	35,078	849	24·19	20,401	742	36·37
6 "	34,266	688	20·07	17,776	472	26·55
7 "	34,781	539	15·49	16,463	344	20·89
8 "	35,715	416	11·62	15,499	275	17·74
9 "	36,081	396	10·97	14,755	241	16·33
Total ...	386,655	25,670	66·39	255,676	25,081	98·10

APPENDIX XX.

Showing by districts the different sects of Muhammadans.

Serial number.	Districts.	Total.		Sunni.		Shia.		Ahl-i-Hadis.		Hanfi.		Unspecified.	
		Males.	Females.	Males.	Females.	Males.	Females.	Males.	Females.	Males.	Females.	Males.	Females.
1	2	3	4	5	6	7	8	9	10	11	12	13	14
1	Dehra Dún	12,660	7,236	12,354	7,131	306	105	...	...	...	...	...	...
2	Sahóranpur	171,120	153,312	168,933	151,161	2,187	2,151	...	...	...	...	...	...
3	Muzaffarnagar	116,504	102,486	109,676	95,610	6,413	6,671	...	...	...	...	415	205
4	Meerut	167,391	149,580	164,818	147,218	2,810	2,152	...	...	...	...	263	210
5	Bulandshahr	92,762	86,257	89,029	82,572	3,418	3,432	...	...	...	...	315	253
6	Aligarh	63,397	56,941	61,292	54,426	2,105	2,515	...	...	...	...	...	...
	Total, Meerut Division ...	623,834	555,812	606,102	538,118	16,739	17,026	...	...	...	...	993	668
7	Muttra	33,545	29,112	32,170	28,105	663	537	...	...	...	...	712	470
8	Agra	55,184	49,249	52,593	46,947	1,283	1,164	...	...	...	...	1,308	1,138
9	Farukhabad	50,226	49,250	47,263	46,139	1,384	1,555	...	...	...	...	1,579	1,556
10	Mainpuri	21,921	19,608	21,322	19,065	849	847	...	...	...	...	250	196
11	Etáwah	22,164	20,161	20,537	18,784	609	580	4	5	...	...	1,014	792
12	Etah	38,478	34,475	36,311	32,676	605	499	...	...	...	...	1,562	1,300
	Total, Agra Division ...	221,518	201,855	210,196	191,716	4,893	4,682	4	5	...	...	6,425	5,452
13	Bareilly	127,754	117,285	125,538	115,420	2,171	1,838	...	...	...	...	45	27
14	Bijnor	135,684	131,478	132,474	128,011	3,210	3,467	...	...	...	...	...	...
15	Budaun	77,277	71,012	76,551	70,197	349	426	...	...	...	...	377	389
16	Moradabad	206,740	193,965	191,886	179,174	5,341	6,242	...	...	...	...	9,513	8,549
17	Shâhjahánpur	66,563	62,703	65,688	62,101	183	180	...	...	...	...	692	422
18	Pilibhít	42,840	39,646	41,842	39,029	181	131	...	...	...	...	817	486
	Total, Rohilkhand Division ...	656,858	616,089	633,979	593,932	11,435	12,284	...	...	...	...	11.444	9,873
19	Cawnpore	54,177	47,364	52,100	45,447	2,052	1,877	...	...	...	...	25	40
20	Fatehpur	38,207	38,854	34,952	35,747	1,543	1,838	...	...	...	...	1,712	1,269
21	Bánda	20,104	20,558	18,670	19,250	313	298	...	...	...	...	1,121	1,010
22	Hamírpur	16,309	16,972	15,894	16,618	179	165	...	...	...	...	236	189
23	Allahabad	98,431	101,422	92,267	95,055	4,497	4,926	...	...	...	...	1,667	1,441
24	Jhánsi	12,585	10,482	11,946	10,033	333	165	...	...	...	...	306	284
25	Jalaun	12,732	12,769	11,920	12,054	124	96	...	...	...	...	688	619
26	Lalitpur	3,126	2,820	2,967	2,701	52	25	...	...	...	...	107	94
	Total, Allahabad Division ...	255,671	251,241	240,716	236,905	9,093	9,890	...	...	...	...	5,862	4,946

27	Benares	45,190	48,211	43,173	41,870	2,017	1,841	...	...	...	...	...	...
28	Mirzapur	37,453	37,787	34,364	34,615	1,104	1,053	...	...	...	...	1,985	2,119
29	Jaunpur	55,935	60,349	48,884	52,625	7,065	7,684	...	...	...	...	46	40
30	Gházipur	48,119	54,607	44,467	50,658	1,885	2,119	8	8	9	2	1,750	1,820
31	Ballia	30,630	35,723	29,141	33,996	430	517	...	...	...	...	1,059	1,210
	Total, Benares Division ...	217,387	231,677	200,029	213,264	12,501	13,214	8	8	9	2	4,840	5,189
32	Gorakhpur	150,849	150,781	148,226	148,407	615	499	...	...	...	...	2,008	1,875
33	Bastí	139,691	136,038	136,019	132,385	1,603	1,717	...	...	...	...	2,069	1,936
34	Azamgarh	109,738	115,901	101,145	106,741	5,746	6,428	...	...	...	...	2,847	2,732
	Total, Gorakhpur Division ...	400,278	402,720	385,390	387,533	7,964	8,644	...	...	...	...	6,924	6,543
35	Kumaun	7,954	4,015	4,341	2,537	661	256	...	...	...	...	2,962	1,222
36	Garhwál	2,908	697	1,608	480	1,028	125	...	...	...	...	272	92
37	Tarái	41,035	34,172	40,819	34,057	90	66	...	...	...	...	126	50
	Total, Kumaun Division ...	51,897	38 884	46,768	37,074	1,769	446	...	...	...	...	3,360	1,364
	TOTAL, N.-W. PROVINCES ...	2,427,443	2,298,278	2,323,180	2,198,542	64,394	65,686	12	13	9	2	39,848	34,035
38	Lucknow	80,878	80,491	64,683	60,528	15,513	19,318	...	...	...	...	682	645
39	Unao	38,497	37,123	36,914	35,676	1,014	1,230	...	...	...	...	569	517
40	Rae Bareli	41,627	44,338	40,390	42,799	1,287	1,539	...	...	...	...	...	...
41	Sitapur	81,209	76,430	78,971	73,705	1,804	1,828	...	...	...	...	1,034	897
42	Hardoi	59,390	55,284	56,247	51,758	3,143	3,526	...	...	...	...	...	...
43	Kheri	62,414	55,643	61,138	54,698	716	631	...	...	...	...	560	314
	Total, Lucknow Division ...	364,015	349,609	337,743	319,164	23,427	28,072	...	...	...	...	2,845	2,373
44	Fyzabad	68,214	70,247	59,283	61,851	8,678	8,139	107	180	...	...	146	77
45	Gonda	104,995	100,430	103,920	99,448	1,075	982	...	...	...	...	...	...
46	Bahraich	88,215	81,583	86,129	79,606	1,190	1,174	...	...	...	...	896	803
47	Sultánpur	55,477	61,369	53,596	59,309	1,290	1,485	...	...	...	...	591	575
48	Partábgarh	43,652	47,186	42,937	46,432	378	323	...	...	...	...	337	431
49	Bara Banki	91,911	94,027	88,638	90,114	2,973	3,587	...	...	...	...	300	326
	Total, Fyzabad Division ...	452,464	454,842	434,503	436,760	15,584	15,690	107	180	...	...	2,270	2,212
	TOTAL, OUDH ...	816,479	804,451	772,246	755,924	39,011	43,762	107	180	...	...	5,115	4,585
	TOTAL, N.-W. P. AND OUDH ...	3,243,922	3,102,729	3,095,426	2,954,466	103,405	109,448	119	193	9	2	44,963	38,620
50	Rámpur	125,065	116,042	124,949	115,932	116	110	...	...	...	...	...	...
51	Tehri Garhwál	711	714	425	411	135	122	...	...	...	...	151	181
	TOTAL, NATIVE STATES ...	125,776	116,756	125,374	116,343	251	232	...	...	...	...	151	181

APPEN

Return of Brit

Birth-places.

Birth-place.	Total.	Male.	Female.
England	13,308	11,942	1,366
Scotland	1,586	1,425	161
Ireland	2,696	2,327	369
Wales	108	92	16
Channel Islands	6	5	1
Isle of Man	35	32	3
Total ...	17,739	15,823	1,916

Civil condition

Civil condition.	Under one year.		One year.		Two years.		Three years.		Four years.		Total 0—4 years.		5—9 years.		10—14 years.	
	Male.	Female.	Male.	Female.	Male.	Female.	Male.	Female.	Male.	Female.	Male.	Female.	Male.	Female.	Male.	Female.
Single	20	8	23	27	39	30	36	36	39	37	157	138	142	131	81	64
Married ...	...	...	...	...	...	...	...	...	...	...	...	...	...	...	...	...
Widowed ...	...	...	...	...	...	...	...	...	...	...	...	...	...	...	...	...
Total ...	20	8	23	27	39	30	36	36	39	37	157	138	142	131	81	64

Infir

Infirmity.	Total afflicted.			0—4 years.		5—9 years.		10—14 years.		15—19 years.		20—24 years.	
	Total.	Male.	Female.	Male.	Female.	Male.	Female.	Male.	Female.	Male.	Female.	Male.	Female.
Insane	...	...	...	...	...	...	...	...	...	...	...	...	...
Deaf-mute	...	...	...	...	...	...	...	...	...	...	...	...	...
Blind	...	...	...	...	...	...	...	...	...	...	...	...	...
Leper	1	1	...	...	...	...	...	...	...	...	...	...	...

DIX XXI.

ish-born subjects.

Occupations.

Class.	0—4 years. Male.	0—4 years. Female.	0—4 years. Total	5—14 years. Male.	5—14 years. Female.	5—14 years. Total.	15 years and over. Male.	15 years and over. Female.	15 years and over. Total.	Total. Male.	Total. Female.	Total. Total.
A.—Government	131	104	235	138	122	260	14,134	797	14,930	14,402	1,023	15,425
B.—Pasture and Agriculture ...	3	5	8	4	4	8	83	47	130	90	56	146
C.—Personal services	...	6	6	2	8	10	29	86	115	31	100	131
D.—Preparation and supply of material substances.	2	2	4	4	1	5	110	48	158	116	51	167
E.—Commerce, transport, storage ...	7	8	15	21	27	48	433	185	618	461	220	681
F.—Professions	10	13	23	27	28	55	515	313	828	552	354	906
G.—Indefinite and independent ...	4	...	4	27	5	32	140	107	247	171	112	283
Total ...	157	138	295	223	195	418	15,443	1,583	17,026	15,823	1,916	17,739

by age.

15—19 years. Male.	15—19 years. Female.	20—24 years. Male.	20—24 years. Female.	25—29 years. Male.	25—29 years. Female.	30—34 years. Male.	30—34 years. Female.	35—39 years. Male.	35—39 years. Female.	40—44 years. Male.	40—44 years. Female.	45—49 years. Male.	45—49 years. Female.	50—54 years. Male.	50—54 years. Female.	55—59 years. Male.	55—59 years. Female.	60 years and over. Male.	60 years and over. Female.	Total. Total.	Total. ale.	Total. Female.
466	96	7,383	78	4,470	65	828	25	240	17	73	13	27	10	15	6	5	4	6	3	14,543	13,893	650
2	18	101	206	268	318	399	228	346	162	223	97	211	58	127	35	51	14	70	13	2,947	1,798	1,149
...	...	3	3	8	6	24	5	14	22	21	11	15	10	14	19	10	7	23	34	249	132	117
468	114	7,487	287	4,746	389	1,251	258	600	201	317	121	253	78	156	60	66	25	99	50	17,739	15,823	1,916

mities.

25—29 years. Male.	25—29 years. Female.	30—34 years. Male.	30—34 years. Female.	35—39 years. Male.	35—39 years. Female.	40—44 years. Male.	40—44 years. Female.	45—49 years. Male.	45—49 years. Female.	50—54 years. Male.	50—54 years. Female.	55—59 years. Male.	55—59 years. Female.	60 years and over. Male.	60 years and over. Female.
...	...	...	...	...	...	...	...	...	...	...	...	...	...	...	...
...	...	...	...	...	...	...	...	...	...	...	...	...	...	...	...
...	...	...	...	...	...	...	...	...	...	...	...	...	...	...	...
...	...	...	...	...	...	...	...	1	...	...	...	...	...	...	...

APPENDIX

Return of foreigners of

OCCUPA

Class.	All nationalities. Total.	Male.	Female.	Nation: American. Male	Female.	Austro-Hungarian. Male.	Female.	Dane. Male.	Female.	Dutch. Male.	Female.	French. Male.	Female.
A.—Government	57	37	20	6	5	2	...	...	...	1	1	3	4
B.—Pasture and agriculture	21	13	8	...	1	...	...	...	...	...	...	7	3
C.—Personal services	17	4	13	1	2	...	...	...	...	...	...	1	2
D.—Preparation and supply of material substances...	62	38	24	4	2	...	1	...	...	...	...	6	...
E.—Commerce, transport and storage	72	49	23	7	4	1	...	1	...	3	3	9	...
F.—Professions	228	99	129	37	50	5	1	...	1	1	2	20	23
G.—Indefinite and independent	47	20	27	2	1	...	...	...	...	2	1	2	6
Total ...	504	260	244	57	65	8	2	1	1	7	7	48	38

AGE

Nationality.	Total, population. Total.	Male.	Female.	Under 1 year. Male.	Female.	1 year. Male.	Female.	2 years. Male.	Female.	3 years. Male.	Female.	4 years. Male.	Female.	Total, 0—4 years. Male.	Female.	5—9 years. Male.	Female
American	122	57	65	1	2	3	...	2	2	3	1	...	1	9	6	3	4
Austro-Hungarian	10	8	2	...	...	...	...	...	1	...	...	...	...	...	1	...	...
Dane	2	1	1	...	...	...	...	...	...	...	...	...	...	...	...	.	.
Dutch	14	7	7	...	1	...	...	...	2	...	...	...	..	...	3	1	1
French...	86	48	38	...	...	2	1	2	...	1	1	3	...	8	2	3	6
German	148	71	77	1	...	...	...	...	1	...	1	1	...	2	2	2	4
Greek	6	5	1	...	...	...	...	...	...	...	...	...	...	...	...	...	..
Italian	38	29	9	...	...	...	...	...	1	1	1	...	...	1	2	3	1
Norwegian	1	1	...	...	...	...	...	...	...	...	...	...	...	...	...	...	...
Potuguese	52	23	29	...	...	1	...	...	...	...	2	1	...	2	2	2	6
Roumanian	1	1	...	...	...	...	...	...	...	...	...	...	...	...	...	...	...
Russian	4	2	2	...	...	...	...	...	...	...	...	...	...	...	...	...	.
Spanish	7	3	4	...	...	...	...	...	...	...	...	...	...	...	...	...	1
Swede	4	2	2	...	...	...	...	...	...	...	...	...	...	...	...	...	...
Swiss	8	2	6	...	...	...	...	...	...	...	...	...	...	...	...	...	...
Turkish Armenian	1	...	1	...	...	...	...	...	...	...	...	...	...	...	...	...	...
Total ...	504	260	244	2	3	6	1	4	7	5	6	5	1	22	18	14	23

BIRTH

Nationality.	Total population. Total.	Male.	Female.	A.—North-Western Provinces and Oudh. Male.	Female.	B.—India outside North-Western Provinces and Oudh. Male.	Female.	C.—Other Asiatic countries. Male.	Female.	D.—Coun: Austria. Male.	Female.	France. Male.	Female.	Germany. Male.	Female.	Greece. Male.	Female.
American	122	57	65	9	9	8	7	...	1	...	...	...	...	...	...	...	...
Austro-Hungarian	10	8	2	...	...	...	...	...	...	8	1	...	...	...	...	...	...
Dane	2	1	1	1	...	...	1	...	...	...	...	...	...	...	...	...	...
Dutch	14	7	7	1	6	3	1	1	...	...	...	...	...	...	...	...	...
French	86	48	88	12	6	24	23	...	...	...	...	12	8	...	...	...	...
German	148	71	77	9	11	15	6	...	...	...	...	...	...	47	56	...	...
Greek	6	5	1	...	1	4	...	...	...	...	...	...	...	...	...	1	...
Italian...	38	29	9	4	4	6	3	...	...	...	...	...	...	...	...	...	1
Norwegian	1	1	...	...	...	...	...	...	...	...	...	...	...	...	...	...	...
Portuguese	52	23	29	2	3	17	25	...	...	3	...	1	...	...	...	...	...
Roumanian	1	1	...	...	...	...	...	...	...	...	...	...	...	...	...	...	...
Russian	4	2	2	...	...	...	...	...	...	...	...	...	...	...	...	...	...
Spanish	7	3	4	...	...	2	3	...	...	...	...	1	...	...	...	...	...
Swede	4	2	2	...	...	...	...	...	...	...	...	...	...	...	...	...	...
Swiss	8	2	6	...	1	...	...	...	...	...	...	...	...	...	...	...	...
Turkish Armenian	1	...	1	...	...	...	...	...	...	...	...	...	...	...	...	...	...
Total ...	504	260	244	88	42	79	70	1	1	11	1	14	8	47	56	1	1

XXII.

Non-British nationality.

TIONS.

alities.

German.		Greek.		Italian.		Norwegian.		Portuguese.		Roumanian.		Russian.		Spanish.		Swede.		Swiss.		Turkish Armenian.	
Male.	Female.	Male.	Female.	Male.	Female.	Male.	Female.	Male.	Female.	Male.	Female.	Male.	Female.	Male.	Female.	Male.	Female.	Male.	Female.	Male.	Female.
10	5	...	...	9	1	...	...	4	...	1	...	...	1	...	1	...	1	1	1	...	...
4	4	...	...	...	...	...	...	1	...	...	...	1	...	...	...	...	...	...	...	...	...
2	7	...	...	...	1	...	...	...	1	...	...	...	...	...	...	...	...	...	...	...	...
18	15	...	...	5	...	...	...	5	2	...	...	...	1	...	...	...	...	...	3	...	...
14	3	3	...	1	1	...	...	9	11	...	...	...	...	...	...	1	1	...	...	...	...
16	38	...	1	11	4	1	...	4	4	...	...	1	...	1	3	1	...	1	1	...	1
7	5	2	...	8	2	...	...	...	11	...	...	...	...	2	...	...	...	...	1	...	...
71	77	5	1	29	9	1	...	23	29	1	...	2	2	3	4	2	2	2	6	...	1

PERIODS.

10—14 Years.		15—19 Years.		20—24 Years.		25—29 Years.		30—34 Years.		35—39 Years.		40—44 Years.		45—49 Years.		50—54 Years.		55—59 Years.		60 Years and over.	
Male.	Female.	Male.	Female.	Male.	Female.	Male.	Female.	Male.	Female.	Male.	Female	Male.	Female.	Male.	Female.	Male.	Female.	Male.	Female.	Male.	Female.
4	3	3	1	1	2	7	17	12	9	5	5	1	3	4	8	3	2	4	3	1	2
...	...	...	...	...	...	...	1	4	...	1	...	...	...	3	...	...	...	...	...	...	...
...	...	...	...	1	...	...	...	...	...	...	...	...	1	...	...	...	...	...	...	...	...
...	...	...	1	...	...	...	1	...	...	2	...	1	1	1	...	1	...	...	...	1	...
3	2	4	2	6	4	3	6	1	3	2	3	2	2	5	1	5	4	2	...	4	3
7	2	4	5	7	12	10	10	7	8	13	7	4	7	3	10	3	5	3	1	6	4
...	...	...	...	1	...	2	...	1	1	...	...	...	...	...	...	...	...	...	...	1	...
2	1	1	1	1	2	3	1	2	...	4	...	...	...	5	1	4	...	...	...	3	...
...	...	...	...	...	...	1	...	...	...	...	...	...	...	...	...	...	...	...	...	...	...
...	10	2	2	2	3	2	1	1	1	6	1	3	...	1	1	1	1	...	...	1	1
...	...	...	...	...	...	1	...	...	...	...	...	...	...	...	...	...	...	...	...	...	...
...	...	...	1	...	...	...	1	...	...	2	...	...	...	...	...	...	...	...	...	...	...
1	...	2	...	...	...	...	3	...	...	...	...	...	...	...	...	...	...	...	...	...	...
...	...	...	...	1	...	...	...	...	1	...	...	...	...	...	1	1	...	...	...	...	...
...	2	...	1	...	...	...	1	...	...	...	...	...	2	1	...	...	...	...	...	1	...
...	...	...	...	...	...	...	...	...	...	...	1	...	...	...	...	...	...	...	...	...	...
17	20	16	14	20	23	29	42	28	23	35	17	11	16	23	22	18	12	9	4	18	10

PLACES.

tries in Europe.

Holland.		Italy.		Norway.		Roumania.		Russia.		Spain.		Sweden.		Switzerland.		Total D.		E.—Africa.		F.—America.		G.—Australasia.		H.—At Sea.	
Male.	Female.	Male.	Female.	Male.	Female.	Male.	Female.	Male.	Female.	Male.	Female.	Male.	Female.	Male.	Female.	Male.	Female.	Male.	Female.	Male.	Female.	Male.	Female.	Male.	Female.
...	...	1	...	...	...	...	...	...	...	...	...	...	...	...	...	1	...	...	...	39	48	...	...	...	...
...	...	...	...	...	...	...	...	...	...	...	...	...	...	...	...	8	1	...	1	...	...	...	...	...	...
...	...	...	...	...	...	...	...	...	...	...	...	...	...	...	...	...	...	...	...	...	...	...	...	...	...
2	...	...	...	...	...	...	...	...	...	...	...	...	...	...	...	2	...	...	...	...	...	...	...	...	...
...	...	...	...	...	...	...	...	...	...	...	...	...	...	...	...	12	8	...	...	...	...	...	...	...	1
...	...	...	...	...	...	...	...	...	...	...	...	...	...	...	...	47	57	...	2	...	1	...	...	...	...
...	1	...	...	...	...	...	...	...	...	...	...	...	...	...	...	1	...	...	...	...	...	...	...	...	...
...	...	19	1	...	...	...	...	...	...	...	...	...	...	...	...	19	2	...	...	...	...	...	...	...	...
...	...	...	...	1	...	...	...	...	...	...	...	...	...	...	...	1	...	...	...	...	...	...	...	...	...
...	...	...	...	...	...	...	...	...	...	...	...	...	...	...	...	4	...	...	...	...	1	...	...	...	...
...	...	...	...	...	...	1	...	...	...	...	...	...	...	...	...	1	...	...	...	...	...	...	...	...	...
...	...	...	...	...	...	...	...	2	2	...	...	...	...	...	...	2	2	...	...	...	...	...	...	...	...
...	...	...	...	...	...	...	...	...	...	...	1	...	...	...	...	1	1	...	...	...	...	...	...	...	...
...	...	...	...	...	...	...	...	...	...	...	...	2	1	...	1	2	2	...	...	...	...	...	...	...	...
...	...	...	...	...	...	...	...	...	...	...	...	...	...	2	3	2	3	...	...	...	...	...	...	...	...
...	...	...	...	...	...	...	...	...	...	...	...	...	...	...	...	...	...	...	...	...	1	...	...	...	...
2	1	20	1	1	...	1	...	2	2	...	1	2	1	2	4	103	76	...	3	39	51	...	...	...	1

APPENDIX XXIII.

Showing the total Urban population by religion in the districts of the Provinces.

Serial number.	Name of district.	Total.	Hindu.	Musalman.	Jain.	Christian.	Arya.	Sikh.	Others.
1	Dehra Dún	38,245	26,238	8,790	193	2,133	475	413	3
2	Sahâranpur	202,839	103,576	92,122	4,531	1,888	234	480	8
3	Muzaffarnagar	126,009	67,497	55,095	2,988	127	218	84	...
4	Meerut	288,786	172,043	101,906	7,236	5,298	1,334	968	1
5	Bulandshahr	161,268	97,431	61,640	1,045	153	976	23	...
6	Aligarh	202,137	144,014	55,716	1,416	461	454	62	14
	Total, Meerut Division ...	1,019,284	610,799	375,269	17,409	10,060	3,691	2,030	26
7	Muttra	147,798	121,435	23,548	1,040	841	134	798	2
8	Agra	209,928	139,489	60,376	4,386	4,047	837	498	295
9	Farukhabad	138,049	96,342	39,653	903	540	355	16	240
10	Mainpuri	52,114	35,606	13,886	2,347	71	125	79	...
11	Etáwah	62,851	44,448	17,214	1,028	115	28	16	2
12	Etah	108,411	70,726	35,199	1,667	406	369	42	2
	Total, Agra Division ...	719,151	508,046	189,876	11,371	6,020	1,848	1,449	541
13	Bareilly	171,567	92,429	75,181	1	3,484	239	226	7
14	Bijnor	173,465	65,943	104,808	971	556	1,045	142	...
15	Budaun	99,570	50,806	47,299	144	543	773	5	...
16	Moradabad	242,815	106,066	133,728	675	1,294	1,022	27	3
17	Sháhjahánpur	120,455	62,240	56,921	15	817	360	101	1
18	Pilibhít	56,519	33,003	23,083	...	204	229	...	...
	Total, Rohilkhand Division ...	864,391	410,487	441,020	1,806	6,898	3,668	501	11
19	Cawnpore	213,780	160,615	49,398	410	3,014	259	44	40
20	Fatehpur	44,430	29,401	14,923	77	13	12	4	...
21	Bánda	41,058	31,972	8,768	214	56	20	25	3
22	Hamírpur	69,283	56,315	12,872	...	48	29	11	8
23	Allahabad	219,884	148,131	65,433	281	5,860	...	155	24
24	Jhansi	98,540	80,771	14,119	969	1,578	126	921	56
25	Jalaun	52,371	40,582	11,638	68	66	11	2	4
26	Lalitpur	20,274	16,519	2,131	1,574	30	...	19	1
	Total, Allahabad Division ...	759,620	564,806	179,282	3,593	10,665	457	1,181	136
27	Benares	235,552	181,999	52,178	109	1,210	...	52	4
28	Mirzapur	116,676	97,745	18,149	228	359	30	165	...
29	Jaunpur	73,980	44,803	29,093	6	77	...	1	...
30	Gházipur	117,279	88,827	28,101	27	269	34	17	4
31	Ballia	101,539	85,908	15,619	...	10	...	...	2
	Total, Benares Division ...	645,026	499,282	143,140	370	1,925	64	235	10
32	Gorakhpur	166,183	126,448	39,265	43	399	...	...	28
33	Basti	34,367	26,589	7,661	...	57	60	...	...
34	Azamgarh	90,383	47,992	42,347	...	43	...	...	1
	Total, Gorahkpur Division ...	290,933	201,029	89,273	43	499	60	...	29
35	Kumaun	58,904	22,915	5,351	...	629	...	...	9
36	Garhwál	3,740	3,437	246	...	57	...	...	...
37	Tarái	21,524	12,068	9,317	38	6	88	7	...
	Total, Kumaun Division ...	54,168	38,420	14,914	38	692	88	7	9
	Total, N.-W. Provinces ...	4,352,573	2,832,369	1,432,774	34,630	36,759	9,876	5,403	762
38	Lucknow	307,155	181,249	118,477	752	5,726	476	853	122
39	Unao	78,015	53,339	24,533	8	103	9	23	...
40	Rae Bareli	30,724	17,666	12,836	22	115	...	85	...
41	Sitapur	75,028	39,860	34,140	215	703	64	41	5
42	Hardoi	105,003	65,386	39,459	13	132	...	13	...
43	Kheri	38,461	24,789	13,510	10	67	60	25	...
	Total, Lucknow Division ...	634,386	382,289	242,955	1,020	6,846	609	540	127
44	Fyzabad	138,524	89,894	47,013	149	1,242	55	171	...
45	Gonda	64,269	43,987	20,092	...	165	...	25	...
46	Bahraich	39,289	18,922	20,181	46	94	12	31	3
47	Sultánpur	8,751	5,461	3,250	...	40	...	...	...
48	Partábgarh	16,049	9,988	5,879	126	45	...	11	...
49	Bara Banki	60,487	32,888	26,759	723	89	...	25	3
	Total, Fyzabad Division ...	327,369	201,140	123,174	1,044	1,675	67	268	6
	Total, Oudh ...	961,755	583,429	366,129	2,064	8,521	676	808	133
	Total, N.-W. P. and Oudh ...	5,314,328	3,415,798	1,798,903	36,694	45,280	10,552	6,206	895
50	Rámpur	103,188	33,351	69,633	136	45	23	...	...
51	Tehri Garhwál	...	...	...	...	...	...	...	...
	TOTAL, NATIVE STATES ...	103,188	33,351	69,633	136	45	23	...	...

APPENDIX XXIV.

Showing the numbers returned as belonging to each Hindu sect or class of worshippers.

Class.	Group.	Sect or deity worshipped.	Total.	Male.	Female.
I.—Belonging to No. Sectarian Sub-division.	...	...	1,486,984	773,310	713,674
II.—Monotheistic ...	...	Ishwar worshippers	3,788,696	2,019,808	1,768,888
		Brahma „	21,535	13,083	8,452
		Total, Class II ...	3,810,231	2,032,891	1,777,840
III.—Pre-Puranic beliefs	...	Smarthas	402,981	200,567	202,414
		Suriya worshippers	41,904	22,328	19,576
		Agni „	9,774	5,412	4,362
		Other Puranic gods	550	336	214
		Planet	45,962	21,883	24,079
		Total, Class III ...	501,171	250,526	250,645
IV.—Worshippers of Puranic deities connected with Vishnu.	4(*a*).	Worshippers of :—			
		Vishnu	3,733,518	1,958,727	1,774,791
		Badri Nath	6,910	3,860	3,050
		Total, 4(*a*) ...	3,740,428	1,962,587	1,777,841
	4(*b*).	Worshippers of incarnations of Vishnu and of gods and demi-gods connected therewith.	164,555	84,831	79,724
		Nar Singh	1,18,080	58,843	59,237
		Parasram	1,099,111	575,793	523,818
		Ram	937,493	488,899	448,594
		Hanuman	381	209	172
		Lachhman	7,984	4,489	3,495
		Companions of Ram (Sita and Bharat) ...	684,372	369,470	314,902
		Krishna	31,412	16,898	14,514
		Balarama	101,570	60,169	41,401
		Companions of Krishna	3,144,958	1,659,601	1,485,357
		Minor incarnations of Vishnu	55,095	27,369	27,726
		Salagram	261,610	132,006	129,604
		Lakshmi	1,458	569	889
		Mahabharat Heroes	3,957	2,215	1,842
		Tulsi	1,139	497	642
		Gorur	163	76	87
		Total, 4(*b*) ...	3,468,380	1,822,233	1,646,147
		Total, Class IV ...	7,208,808	3,784,820	3,423,988

APPENDIX XXIV.

Showing the numbers returned as belonging to each Hindu sect or class of worshippers—(continued).

Class.	Group.	Sect or deity worshipped.	Total.	Male.	Female.
V.—Worshippers of Puranic deities connected with Siva.	5(*a*).	Worshippers of :—			
		Siva	8,101,617	4,246,568	3,855,049
		Local and special Mahadeo	16,128	8,129	7,999
		Total, 5(*a*) ...	8,117,745	4,254,697	3,863,048
	5(*b*).	Worshippers of gods and demi-gods connected with Siva.			
		Bhairon	173,679	89,419	84,260
		Ganesha	78,188	40,199	37,989
		Parbati	8,584	4,172	4,412
		Nandi	137	68	69
		Total 5(*b*) ...	260,588	133,858	126,730
		Total, Class V ...	8,878,333	4,388,555	3,989,778
VI.—Worshippers of Puranic Saktis.		Sakti (Local) :—			
		Bami	1,576	880	696
		Worshippers of Local Devis	571,536	298,892	272,644
		" of Devi under a general name ...	9,507,409	4,850,371	4,657,038
		Total, Class VI ...	10,080,521	5,150,143	4,930,378
VII.— ...	7(*a*).	Development and additions of Saktism. Worshippers of gods of diseases.			
		Sitla	119,139	59,879	59,260
		Cholera	9,538	3,964	5,574
		Hardaul Raja	5,034	2,505	2,529
		Agwan	25,069	12,568	12,501
		Total 7(*a*) ...	158,780	78,916	79,864
	7 (*b*).	Snake Worshippers :—			
		Astik	41,351	21,253	20,098
		Nag	25,366	13,500	11,866
		Gugapir...	122,991	65,289	57,702
		Sokha	13,578	6,394	7,184
		Total, 7(b) ...	203,286	106,436	96,850

APPENDIX XXIV.

Showing the numbers returned as belonging to each Hindu sect or class of worshippers—(continued).

Class.	Group.	Sect or deity worshipped.	Total.	Male.	Female.
VII.—(*continued*) ...	7(c)	Worshippers of spirits of deceased persons who have died a violent death.			
		Brahms	406,787	203,500	203,287
		Other evil spirits (Pret churel and undefined)	394,830	204,814	190,016
		Bir	22,553	11,931	10,622
		Burhe Babu	54,849	27,378	27,471
		Kasbi Das	172,599	91,229	81,370
		Jokhaiya	87,061	47,789	39,272
		Sorcerers	174,304	91,981	82,323
		Satti	8,533	4,077	4,456
		Bagha	7,784	3,370	4,414
		Sapha	156	79	77
		Total, 7(c) ...	1,329,456	686,148	643,308
	7(d)	Worshippers of Muhammadan Saints—			
		Pachpiria	1,690,985	843,057	847,928
		Amina Satti	8,202	3,837	4,365
		Brihnapir	51,617	25,355	26,262
		Hathele Pir	2,777	1,595	1,182
		Palihar	39,954	19,660	20,294
		Sanwar Dhir	30,108	15,620	14,488
		Other Muhammadan Saints	501,571	252,700	248,871
		Sarwar Pir	8,429	5,180	3,249
		Total, 7(d) ...	2,333,643	1,167,004	1,166,639
	7(e)	Worshippers of caste and ancestral gods—			
		Chitragupta	1,967	1,066	901
		Other ancestral deities	7,575	4,185	3,390
		Nathu	124,170	61,254	62,916
		Minor caste gods	4,862	2,501	2,361
		Biswakarma	18,805	9,568	9,237
		Total, 7(e) ...	157,379	78,574	78,805
	7(f)	Other gods worshipped by special classes—			
		Low caste gods	6,209	3,305	2,904
		Karegore Deo	756,151	879,372	376,779
		Balraju	76,395	88,752	37,643
		Kalupanthi	266,161	137,787	128,374
		Lalbeg	265,967	141,477	124,490
		Total, 7(f) ...	1,370,883	700,693	670,190

APPENDIX XXIV.

Showing the numbers returned as belonging to each Hindu sect or class of worshippers—(continued).

Class.	Group.	Sect or deity worshipped.	Total.	Male.	Female.
VII.—(*concluded*) ...	7(*g*)	Demon worshippers—			
		Madain	2,639	1,296	1,343
		Kerarbir Deo	31,408	15,783	15,625
		Masan	1,929	912	1,017
		Mahkasur or Bhainsasur	13,141	6,522	6,619
		Demons...	154,215	80,701	73,514
		Total, 7(*g*) ...	203,332	105,214	98,118
	7(*h*)	Worshippers of village, forest and local gods—			
		Bhumiya	85,731	45,006	40,725
		Kalsen	33,087	17,300	15,787
		Mahngi Tappa	3,785	2,089	1,696
		Sammai	37,584	17,264	20,320
		Banaspati	16,489	8,589	7,900
		Other forest gods	17,340	8,681	8,659
		Local or village gods	367,591	185,024	182,567
		Total, 7(*h*) ...	561,607	283,953	277,654
	7(*i*)	Worshippers of river and river gods—			
		Ganga	284,594	152,466	132,128
		Jumna	8,316	4,478	3,838
		Saraswati	5,311	1,589	3,722
		Khwaja Khizr	7,730	4,088	3,642
		Other river gods	13,594	6,900	6,685
		Total, 7(*i*) ...	319,545	169,530	150,015
		Total, Class VII ...	6,637,911	3,376,468	3,261,443
VIII.—Worshippers of other Puranic gods and demi-gods, and objects of reverence.	...	Worshippers of :—			
		Holy places	56,702	30,625	26,077
		Deified devotees	274,900	138,593	136,307
		Miscellaneous Puranic gods	2,596	1,365	1,231
		Total, Class VIII ...	334,198	170,583	163,615
IX.	9(*a*)	Sectarian Sub-divisions saivite—			
		Aughar	5,319	2,861	2,458
		Aghori	1,006	570	436
		Alakhnami	10,886	5,601	5,285
		Gorakhpanthi	28,816	15,409	13,407
		Minor Saivite sects	1,870	1,596	274
		Total, 9(*a*) ...	47,897	26,037	21,860

APPENDIX XXIV.

Showing the numbers returned as belongiug to each Hindu sect or class of worshippers—(concluded).

Class.	Group.	Sect or deity worshipped.	Total.	Male.	Female.
IX.—(*concluded*) ...	9(*b*)	Vaishnava, unitarian and miscellaneous sects :—			
		Nimbarak Vaishnava	14,905	8,166	6,739
		Madhvachariya	3,226	1,701	1,525
		Vallabhachariya	13,183	6,574	6,609
		Haridasi	1,094	576	518
		Radha Vallabhi	34,795	19,082	15,713
		Ramanandi	421,433	222,281	199,152
		Kabirpanthi	318,262	167,208	151,^54
		Raidasi	417,127	225,176	191,951
		Sainpanthi	4,325	2 316	2,009
		Namdeopanthi	10,358	5,795	4,563
		Dadupanthi	5,010	2,729	2,281
		Nanakshahi	336,168	172,330	163,838
		Satnami	152,734	83,032	69,702
		Apapanthi	4,267	2,227	2,040
		Munnadasi	2,636	1,442	1,194
		Anantpanthi	170	81	89
		Charandasi	599	374	225
		Eshwaranandi	3,966	1,991	1,975
		Parnami	21,113	10,721	10,392
		Prannathi	65	36	29
		Mohandasi	1,118	544	574
		Shiva Naraini	24,814	12,526	12,558
		Radha Swami	188	93	95
		Swami Naraini	235	210	25
		Gobindpanthi	4,605	2,323	2,282
		Nath Baba	1,227	629	598
		Bhika Sahib	1,277	683	594
		Dariyadasi	2,310	1,170	1,140
		Bishnoi	46,559	26,977	22,582
		Minor and undefined sects	38,093	20,801	17,292
		Total, 9(*b*) ...	1,888,862	999,524	889,338
		Total, Class IX ...	1,936,759	1,025,561	911,198
Not properly Hindus ...	...	Baudh	1,649	558	1,091
		Arya Samajist	3,405	1,398	2,007
		Brahmo Samajist	7	4	3
		Atheist	7	6	1
		Jain (Sorsogi)	184	100	84
		Total, Not properly Hindus ...	5,252	2,066	3,186
		GRAND TOTAL ...	40,380,168	20,954,923	19,425,245

APPEN.

Summary of

Serial number.	District or State.	Total Population.			A.—Born in district or state where enumerated.		
		Total.	Male.	Female.	Total.	Male.	Female.
1	Dehra Dún	168,135	100,324	67,811	112,787	61,558	51,179
2	Sahāranpur	1,001,280	540,351	460,929	926,880	505,836	421,044
3	Muzffarnagar	772,874	418,228	354,646	659,002	379,433	279,569
4	Meerut	1,391,458	747,244	644,214	1,208,650	678,336	530,314
5	Bulandshahr	949,914	501,621	448,293	818,524	460,702	357,822
6	Aligarh	1,043,172	558,743	484,429	889,864	498,803	391,061
	Total, Meerut Division ...	5,326,833	2,866,511	2,460,322	4,615,657	2,584,668	2,030,989
7	Muttra	713,421	382,660	330,761	560,284	330,346	229,938
8	Agra	1,003,796	540,459	463,337	827,321	473,920	353,401
9	Farukhabad	858,687	464,340	394,347	747,422	427,094	320,328
10	Mainpuri	762,163	416,799	345,364	639,266	378,776	260,490
11	Etáwah	727,629	396,775	330,854	621,000	354,567	266,433
12	Etah	702,063	383,203	318,860	590,013	348,531	241,482
	Total, Agra Division ...	4,767,759	2,584,236	2,183,523	3,985,306	2,313,234	1,672,072
13	Bareilly	1,040,691	555,480	485,211	865,602	504,863	360,739
14	Bijnor	794,070	418,212	375,858	754,338	401,583	352,756
15	Budaun	925,598	498,134	427,464	822,103	461,257	360,846
16	Moradabad	1,179,398	623,572	555,826	1,070,399	583,099	487,300
17	Shábjahánpur	918,551	495,306	423,245	818,325	455,117	363,208
18	Pilibhít	485,366	258,402	226,964	408,777	223,015	185,762
	Total, Rohilkhand Division ...	5,343,674	2,849,106	2,494,568	4,739,544	2,628,933	2,110,611
19	Cawnpore	1,209,695	648,092	561,603	1,039,654	567,469	472,185
20	Fatehpur	699,157	359,821	339,336	630,925	335,881	295,044
21	Bánda	705,832	356,894	348,938	639,343	330,758	308,585
22	Hamírpur	513,720	260,603	253,117	438,717	236,678	202,039
23	Allahabad	1,548,737	781,509	767,228	1,456,364	742,195	714,169
24	Jhánsi	409,419	214,528	194,891	314,911	176,125	138,786
25	Jalaun	396,361	204,090	192,271	345,596	187,500	158,096
26	Lalitpur	274,200	141,436	132,764	250,851	132,644	118,207
	Total, Allahabad Division ...	5,757,121	2,966,773	2,790,148	5,116,361	2,709,250	2,407,111
27	Benares	921,943	467,453	454,490	805,629	421,873	383,756
28	Mirzapur	1,161,508	576,341	585,167	1,078,295	545,629	532,666
29	Jaunpur	1,264,949	634,950	629,999	1,168,682	612,908	555,774
30	Gházipur	1,077,909	531,701	546,208	998,300	512,194	486,106
31	Ballia	942,465	452,611	489,854	878,570	441,345	437,225
	Total, Benares Division ...	5,368,774	2,663,056	2,705,718	4,929,476	2,533,949	2,395,527
22	Gorakhpur	2,994,057	1,497,284	1,496,773	2,754,277	1,384,320	1,369,957
33	Basti	1,785,844	907,337	878,507	1,693,939	872,784	821,155
34	Azamgarh	1,728,625	867,611	861,014	1,631,551	848,155	783,396
	Total, Gorakhpur Division ...	6,508,526	3,272,232	3,236,294	6,079,767	3,105,259	2,974,508
35	Kumaun	563,181	294,957	268,224	525,012	268,750	256,262
36	Garhwál	407,818	200,319	207,499	398,252	192,907	205,345
37	Tarái	210,568	115,460	95,108	109,040	60,681	48,359
	Total Kumaun Division ...	1,181,567	610,736	570,831	1,032,304	522,338	509,966
	Total, N.-W. Provinces ...	34,254,254	17,812,850	16,441,404	30,498,415	16,397,631	14,100,784
38	Lucknow	774,163	407,201	366,962	635,851	339,477	296,374
39	Unao	953,636	489,512	464,124	867,673	460,703	406,970
40	Rae Bareli	1,036,521	512,980	523,541	939,145	480,867	458,278
41	Sitapur	1,075,413	567,182	508,231	970,108	522,013	448,095
42	Hardoi	1,113,211	596,497	516,714	1,023,749	558,823	464,926
43	Kheri	903,615	482,035	421,580	752,301	403,049	349,252
	Total, Lucknow Division ...	5,856,559	3,055,407	2,801,152	5,188,827	2,764,932	2,42,3.895
44	Fyzabad	1,216,959	612,602	604,357	1,081,470	560,173	521,297
45	Gonda	1,459,229	746,403	712,826	1,307,705	679,352	628,353
46	Bahraich	1,000,432	523,567	476,865	871,569	456,377	415,192
47	Sultánpur	1,075,851	530,486	545,365	963,398	499,103	464,295
48	Partábgarh	910,895	445,171	465,724	809,655	418,021	391,634
49	Bara Banki	1,130,906	577,115	553,791	1,049,362	547,403	501,959
	Total, Fyzabad Division ...	6,794,272	3,435,344	3,358,928	6,083,159	3,160,429	2,922,730
	Total, Oudh ...	12,650.831	6,490,751	6,160,080	11,271,986	5,925,361	5,346,625
	Total, N.-W. Provinces and Oudh ...	46,905,085	24,303,601	22,601,484	41,770,401	22,322,992	19,447,409
50	Rámpur	551,249	291,092	260,157	484,052	263,124	220,928
51	Tehri Garhwál	241,242	118,378	122,864	240,275	117,738	122,537
	TOTAL, NATIVE STATES ...	792,401	409,470	383,021	724,327	380,862	343,465

DIX XXV.

Table XI.

B.—Born in district or state immediately contiguous to that where enumerated.						C.—Born in remote districts or states of the same province.		
(a.) In the same province or agency.			(b.) In another province or agency.					
Total.	Male.	Female.	Total.	Male.	Female.	Total.	Male.	Female.
22,758	15,822	6,936	3,895	2,689	1,206	17,945	12,045	5,900
32,486	11,626	20,860	11,826	4,025	7,801	18,919	11,124	7,795
92,055	28,732	63,323	7,211	1,842	5,369	6,536	3,729	2,807
108,370	30,853	77,517	21,974	6,987	14,987	28,830	16,245	12,585
97,944	28,439	69,505	14,610	4,400	10,210	43,723	5,327	8,396
116,342	42,589	73,753	1,252	504	748	28,476	12,926	15,550
469,955	158,061	311,894	60,768	20,447	40,321	144,429	61,396	53,033
75,554	20,804	54,750	42,905	14,552	28,353	11,925	6,157	5,768
75,525	23,547	51,978	63,541	23,040	40,501	24,737	12,467	12,270
98,003	29,907	68,096	...	...	...	8,968	4,552	4,416
105,014	30,269	74,745	...	...	...	11,420	4,360	7,060
80,666	30,865	49,801	13,561	5,476	8,085	8,819	4,042	4,777
101,891	30,424	71,467	...	...	...	7,433	2,660	4,773
536,658	165,816	370,837	120,007	43,068	76,989	73,302	34,238	39,064
148,235	33,957	114,278	...	...	...	12,797	11,892	8,905
33,996	12,930	21,066	...	...	...	4,363	2,833	1,530
96,147	32,875	63,272	...	...	...	4,623	2,469	2,154
91,593	32,513	59,080	...	...	...	14,422	6,149	8,273
87,756	33,158	54,598	...	...	...	10,459	5,696	4,763
65,026	28,419	36,607	239	178	61	10,627	6,319	4,308
522,753	173,852	348,901	239	178	61	65,291	35,358	29,933
106,606	43,563	63,043	...	...	...	47,296	27,099	20,197
62,847	21,281	41,566	...	...	...	3,906	1,983	1,923
32,563	12,753	19,810	25,697	8,626	17,071	6,191	3,574	2,617
36,821	12,222	24,599	33,500	9,378	24,122	2,484	1,433	1,051
57,201	19,503	37,698	...	...	...	17,176	10,239	6,937
14,283	4,905	9,378	60,105	19,301	40,804	12,231	8,720	3,511
25,202	7,496	17,706	11,055	3,658	7,397	8,193	1,495	1,698
1,081	461	620	12,465	4,289	8,176	1,672	1,183	489
336,604	122,184	214,420	142,822	45,252	97,570	94,149	55,726	38,423
73,562	23,932	49,630	11,598	2,728	8,870	18,246	8,458	4,788
48,682	14,075	34,607	18,267	7,989	10,278	5,220	3,038	2,182
87,454	17,411	70,043	...	...	...	6,528	3,700	2,828
52,069	13,422	38,647	21,700	2,814	18,886	2,428	1,436	992
32,613	7,005	25,608	28,541	3,042	25,499	1,113	693	420
294,380	75,845	218,535	80,106	16,573	63,533	28,535	17,325	11,210
130,479	62,363	68,116	74,537	31,174	43,363	22,090	12,713	9,377
74,316	26,580	47,736	4,801	2,547	2,254	11,731	4,729	7,002
93,057	17,613	75,444	...	...	...	2,027	993	1,034
297,852	106,556	191,296	79,338	33,721	45,617	35,848	18,435	17,413
16,568	10,045	6,523	5,687	4,886	801	10,265	7,373	2,892
7,717	5,765	1,952	...	...	...	612	567	45
95,250	51,083	44,167	8,720	2,063	1,657	2,242	1,445	797
119,535	66,893	52,642	9,407	6,949	2,458	13,119	9,385	3,734
2,577,732	869,207	1,708,525	492,687	166,188	326,499	424,673	231,863	192,810
80,056	36,889	52,167	...	...	...	36,464	21,845	14,619
74,664	24,137	50,527	...	...	...	9,595	3,802	5,793
87,374	27,537	59,837	...	...	...	7,891	3,298	4,093
92,112	38,148	53,964	...	...	...	11,280	5,618	5,662
83,477	34,421	49,056	...	...	...	5,254	2,787	2,467
128,822	65,344	63,478	2,393	1,406	987	18,907	11,400	7,507
555,505	226,476	329,029	2,393	1,406	987	88,891	48,750	40,141
108,083	38,988	69,095	...	...	...	22,204	9,965	12,239
129,235	57,474	71,761	4,247	1,963	2,284	15,580	6,523	9,057
102,882	52,452	50,430	9,141	5,058	4,083	14,537	8,252	6,285
101,174	26,540	74,634	...	...	...	9,713	4,058	5,660
93,127	23,462	69,665	...	...	...	6,614	2,874	3,740
73,976	26,065	47,911	...	...	...	6,414	2,992	3,422
608,477	224,981	383,496	13,388	7,021	6,367	75,062	34,659	40,403
1,163,982	451,457	712,525	15,781	8,427	7,354	163,953	83,409	80,544
3,741,714	1,320,664	2,421,050	508,468	174,615	333,853	588,626	315,272	273,354
59,115	23,636	35,479	...	...	...	7,196	3,815	3,881
71	43	28	388	206	182	164	128	36
59,186	23,679	35,507	388	206	182	7,360	3,943	3,417

APPEN

Summary of

Serial number.	District or State.	D.—Born in remote parts of India.			E.—Born in other countries of Asia.					
					(a) Contiguous to India.			(b) Remote from India.		
		Total.	Male.	Female.	Total.	Male.	Female.	Total.	Male.	Female.
1	Dehra Dún	9,724	7,469	2,255	483	879	104	54	26	28
2	Sah'ranpur	10,206	7,042	3,164	27	22	5	12	10	2
3	Muzaffarnagar	7,886	4,397	3,489	7	4	3	8	7	1
4	Meerut	20,120	11,635	8,485	164	108	56	6	4	2
5	Bulandshahr	4,674	2,432	2,242	117	96	21	187	181	6
6	Aligarh	7,145	3,855	3,290	24	22	2	29	17	12
	Total, Meerut Division ...	59,755	36,830	22,925	822	631	191	296	245	51
7	Muttra	21,878	10,082	11,796	5	5	...	7	6	1
8	Agra	11,220	6,555	4,665	153	128	25	32	29	3
9	Farukhabad	3,570	2,301	1,269	37	14	23	...	...	...
10	Mainpuri	6,296	3,348	2,948	9	9	...	1	...	1
11	Etáwah	3,486	1,764	1,722	1	1	...	5	3	2
12	Etah	2,572	1,516	1.056	11	10	1	8	6	2
	Total, Agra Division ...	49,022	25,566	23,456	216	167	49	53	44	9
13	Bareilly	3,632	2,452	1,180	27	21	6	38	18	20
14	Bijnor	1,349	853	496	7	6	1	6	3	3
15	Budaun	2,430	1,380	1,050	7	7	...	7	6	1
16	Moradabad	2,732	1,635	1,097	35	27	8	7	4	3
17	Sháhjahánpur	1,518	886	632	17	13	4	31	21	10
18	Pilibhít	557	394	163	11	10	1	6	5	1
	Total, Rohilkhand Division ...	12,218	7,600	4,618	104	84	20	95	57	38
19	Cawnpore	13,686	8,169	5,517	76	67	9	28	21	7
20	Fatehpur	1,467	666	801	4	4	...	5	4	1
21	Bánda	1,572	992	580	10	7	3	2	1	1
22	Hamírpur	2,181	877	1,304	5	5	...	1	1	...
23	Allahabad	16,040	7,934	8,106	15	6	9	17	7	10
24	Jhánsi	6,571	4,363	2,208	57	48	9	6	6	...
25	Jalaun	11,273	3,917	7,356	11	11	...	...	...	...
26	Lalitpur	8,098	2,835	5,263	13	13	...	4	2	2
	Total, Allahabad Division ...	6,888	29,753	31,135	191	161	30	63	42	21
27	Benares	17,343	9,948	7,395	37	25	12	6	5	1
28	Mirzapur	10,748	5,485	5,263	4	4	...	1	1	...
29	Jaunpur	1,693	740	953	11	7	4	17	14	3
30	Gházipur	3,208	1,727	1,481	6	6	...	6	2	4
31	Ballia	1,512	480	1,032	4	...	4	1	1	...
	Total, Benares Division ...	34,504	18,880	16,124	62	42	20	31	23	8
32	Gorakhpur	12,495	6,585	5,910	30	29	1	22	15	7
33	Basti	938	642	296	11	9	2	...	...	...
34	Azamgarh	1,852	776	1,076	12	10	2	10	7	3
	Total, Gorakhpur Division ...	15.285	8,008	7,282	53	48	5	32	22	10
35	Kumaun	5,132	3,561	1,571	253	170	83	...	...	...
36	Garhwál	1,154	1,016	138	58	50	8	...	...	...
37	Tarái	261	157	104	9	7	2	...	...	...
	Total, Kumaun Division ...	6,547	4,734	1,813	320	227	93	...	...	...
	Total, N.-W. Provinces ...	208,219	130,866	107,353	1,768	1,360	408	570	433	137
38	Lucknow	9,887	6,571	3,316	104	68	36	75	39	36
39	Unao	1,601	823	778	6	4	2	3	2	1
40	Rae Bareli	2,557	1,245	1,312	12	7	5	6	6	...
41	Sitapur	1,329	872	457	38	26	12	25	17	8
42	Hardoi	715	455	260	7	6	1	...	...	...
43	Kheri	1,043	761	282	7	5	2	9	5	4
	Total, Lucknow Division ...	17,132	10,727	6,405	174	116	58	118	69	49
44	Fyzabad	3,803	2,583	1,220	39	27	12	41	17	24
45	Gonda	2,281	990	1,291	20	20	...	1	1	...
46	Bahraich	1,725	1,173	552	12	11	1	12	7	5
47	Sultánpur	1,229	670	559	16	13	3	18	8	10
48	Partábgarh	1,414	773	641	18	13	5	4	4	...
49	Bara Banki	1,062	605	457	22	19	3	9	5	4
	Total, Fyzabad Division ...	11,514	6,794	4,720	127	103	24	85	42	43
	Total, Oudh ...	28,646	17,521	11,125	301	219	82	203	111	92
	Total, N.-W. P. and Oudh ...	266,865	148,387	118,478	2,069	1,579	490	778	544	229
50	Rámpur	744	418	326	65	49	16	71	45	26
51	Tehri Garhwál	344	263	81	...	...	...	...	...	...
	TOTAL, NATIVE STATES ...	1,088	681	407	65	49	16	71	45	26

DIX XXV.

Table XI.—(concluded).

F.—Born in other continents.			G.—Born at Sea.			H.—Birth-place unspecified.		
Total.	Male.	Female.	Total.	Male.	Female.	Total.	Male.	Female.
459	289	170	...	...	...	80	47	33
636	530	106	...	...	...	288	186	152
17	10	7	...	...	...	152	74	78
3,329	3,068	261	5	4	1	10	4	6
24	10	14	...	...	...	111	34	77
40	27	13	...	...	...	...	...	...
4,505	3,934	571	5	4	1	641	295	346
590	557	33	...	...	...	273	151	122
782	576	206	...	...	...	485	197	288
403	360	43	1	...	1	283	112	171
28	17	11	...	...	...	129	20	109
49	34	15	...	...	...	42	23	19
20	15	5	...	...	...	115	41	74
1,872	1,559	313	1	...	1	1,327	544	783
2,295	2,237	58	1	1	...	64	39	25
11	5	6	...	...	...	...	...	...
32	14	18	...	...	...	249	126	123
151	126	25	1	1	...	58	18	40
445	415	30	...	...	...	...	...	...
13	10	3	...	...	...	110	52	58
2,947	2,807	140	2	2	...	481	235	246
1,476	1,326	150	...	...	...	873	378	495
3	2	1	...	...	...	...	...	...
16	12	4	...	...	...	438	171	267
10	8	2	...	...	...	1	1	...
1,901	1,617	284	...	...	...	23	8	15
988	906	82	3	3	...	264	151	113
22	10	12	...	...	...	9	3	6
9	6	3	...	...	...	7	3	4
4,425	3,887	538	3	3	...	1,615	715	900
522	484	38	...	...	...	...	...	...
48	30	.18	...	...	...	243	90	153
56	30	26	...	...	...	508	140	368
132	75	57	1	...	1	59	25	34
63	22	41	..	...	...	48	23	25
821	641	180	1	...	1	958	278	580
114	77	37	3	2	1	10	6	4
108	46	62	...	...	...	...	...	...
114	56	58	...	...	...	2	1	1
336	179	157	3	2	1	12	7	5
190	128	62	...	...	...	74	44	30
21	12	9	...	...	...	4	2	2
4	3	1	...	...	...	42	21	21
215	143	72	...	...	...	120	67	53
15,121	13,150	1,971	15	11	4	5,054	2,141	2,913
2,641	2,276	365	4	1	3	81	35	46
18	10	8	...	...	...	76	31	45
22	14	8	...	...	...	14	6	8
494	475	19	...	...	...	27	13	14
8	5	3	...	...	...	1	...	1
10	8	2	...	...	...	123	57	66
3,193	2,788	405	4	1	3	822	142	180
782	654	128	...	...	...	537	195	342
92	52	40	...	...	...	68	28	40
35	20	15	...	...	...	519	217	302
40	15	25	...	...	...	263	84	179
11	6	5	...	...	...	52	18	34
40	20	20	...	...	...	21	6	15
1,000	767	233	...	...	...	1,460	548	912
4,193	3,555	688	4	1	3	1,782	690	1,092
19,314	16,705	2,609	19	12	7	6,836	2,831	4,005
6	5	1	...	...	...	...	...	...
...	...	...	...	...	...	...	...	...
6	5	1	...	...	...	...	...	...

APPENDIX XXVI.

Comparing the population of the preliminary and General Censuses in the districts of Kumaun and Garhwál.

District.	Name of pargana and tahsíl.	Population in October 1890.			Population on the General Census day.		
		Total.	Males.	Females.	Total.	Males.	Females.
Kumaun.	Kali Kumaun	55,642	29,247	26,395	33,551	17,025	16,526
	Sira	12,341	6.401	5,940	13,496	6,937	6,559
	Shor	28,859	14,751	14,108	30,871	15,645	15,226
	Askot	9,566	4,879	4,687	12,170	6,001	6,169
	Darma	8,232	4,351	3,881	2,513	1,227	1,286
	Tahsíl Champawat ...	114,640	59,629	55,011	92,601	46,835	45,766
	Baramandal	85,439	46,206	39,233	69,218	35,276	33,942
	Chaugarkha	38,592	20,232	18,360	37,212	18,960	18,252
	Danpur	26,107	18,972	17,135	38,680	20,271	18,409
	Gangoli	31,597	16,636	14,961	33,271	17,207	16,064
	Johar	15,299	8,011	7,288	10,788	5,501	5,287
	Pali	125,389	62,966	62,423	118,020	57,896	60,124
	Phaldakot	16,969	8,402	8,567	11,711	6,167	5,544
	Tahsíl Almora ...	349,392	181,425	147,967	318,900	161,278	157,622
	Chakhata	39,183	24,660	14,523	21,895	14,920	6,975
	Kota	5,016	2,555	2,461	3,964	2,108	1,856
	Dhaniakot	11,569	6,084	5,485	9,440	4,787	4,653
	Rámgarh	4,305	2,155	2,150	550	354	196
	Kotauli	8,102	4,076	4,026	2,482	1,245	1,237
	Mahryuri	4,165	2,083	2,082	925	551	374
	Dhayanirao	13,960	7,205	6,755	6,875	3,571	3,304
	Kumaun Bhábar	42,469	24,298	18,171	105,549	59,308	46,241
	Tahsíl Bhábar ...	128,769	73,116	55,653	151,680	86,844	64,836
	Total, District Kumaun ...	592,801	314,170	278,631	563,181	294,957	268,224
	Urban	**33,070**	**22,630**	**10,440**	**28,904**	**18,713**	**10,191**
	Rural	**559,731**	**291,540**	**268,191**	**534,277**	**276,244**	**258,033**
Garhwál.	Dewalgarh	29,025	14,089	14,936	29,895	14,623	15,272
	Barasyun	63,151	30,732	32,419	63,229	30,590	32,639
	Ganga Salan	49,214	24,098	25,116	47,510	22,674	24,836
	Nagpur	48,942	23,995	24,947	50,907	24,629	26,278
	Chandpur	40,110	19,452	20,658	40,706	19,548	21,158
	Talla Salan	43,659	22,210	21,449	51,093	27,993	23,100
	Malla Salan	47,756	23,352	24,404	47,594	22,954	24,640
	Chandkot	26,767	12,922	13,775	26,573	12,621	13,952
	Painkhanda	9,394	4,616	4,778	5,804	2,875	2,929
	Dasoli	12,328	6,040	6,288	13,775	6,633	7,142
	Budhan	30,509	15,171	15,338	30,732	15,179	15,553
	Total tahsíl Pauri and District Garhwál ...	400,855	196,747	204,108	407,818	200,319	207,499
	Urban	**3,529**	**2,211**	**1,318**	**3,740**	**2,405**	**1,335**
	Rural	**397,326**	**194,536**	**202,790**	**404,078**	**197,914**	**206,164**

APPENDIX XXVII.

Showing the proportion of total insane population and variation since last census.

Serial number.	District.	Proportion per 100,000 to total population.	Proportion of variation since 1881.	Remarks.
1	Dehra Dún	22·0	+2·70	
2	Sahâranpur	14·0	—23·52	
3	Muzaffarnagar	15·0	—23·71	
4	Meerut	11·0	—9·65	
5	Bulandshahr	9·1	—28·92	
6	Aligarh	6·9	—39·49	
	Total, Meerut Division ...	11·6	—22·48	
7	Muttra	8·8	+108·22	
8	Agra	30·0	+15·26	
9	Farukhabad	12·0	—38·37	
10	Mainpuri	7·9	—51·37	
11	Etáwah	9·4	—26·84	
12	Etah	6·9	—51·48	
	Total, Agra Division ...	13·5	—16·62	
13	Bareilly	38·0	—6·14	
14	Bijnor	15·0	+35·95	
15	Budaun	7·2	—12·98	
16	Moradabad	8·4	—41·17	
17	Sháhjahánpur	7·3	—58·38	
18	Pilibhít	8·0	+5·23	
	Total, Rohilkhand Division ...	14·8	—17·34	
19	Cawnpore	11·0	—27·77	
20	Fatehpur	6·7	—48·35	
21	Bánda	9·0	—76·97	
22	Hamírpur	8·1	—2·32	
23	Allahabad	14·0	+27·52	
24	Jhánsi	12·0	+2·04	
25	Jalaun	8·6	—64·58	
26	Lalitpur	16·0	+109·04	
	Total, Allahabad Division ...	11·3	—31·76	
27	Benares	40·8	+28·23	
28	Mirzapur	6·0	—27·67	
29	Jaunpur	9·0	—12·05	
30	Gházipur	7·6	+17·14	
31	Ballia	8·4	—37·98	
	Total, Benares Division ...	13·9	—·26	
32	Gorakhpur	8·3	—4·96	
33	Basti	7·3	—4·41	
34	Azamgarh	5·6	+127·90	
	Total, Gorakhpur Division ...	7·3	+8·16	
35	Kumaun	10·0	—29·62	
36	Garhwál	9·8	—25·92	
37	Tarái	11·0	+140·00	
	Total, Kumaun Division ...	10·3	—16·55	
	Total, N.-W. Provinces ...	11·8	—15·92	
38	Lucknow	40·0	+32·06	
39	Unao	15·0	+2·14	
40	Rae Bareli	12·0	—12·58	
41	Sitapur	11·0	+12·26	
42	Hardoi	8·2	—34·50	
43	Kheri	8·8	—23·07	
	Total, Lucknow Division ...	14·9	+·11	
44	Fyzabad	11·0	+52·17	
45	Gonda	7·9	+33·72	
46	Bahraich	10·0	—22·13	
47	Sultánpur	10·0	+60·56	
48	Partábgarh	8·3	—38·21	
49	Bara Banki	11·0	—27·60	
	Total, Fyzabad Division ...	9·8	—·15	
	Total, Oudh ...	12·2	...	
	Total, N.-W. P. and Oudh ...	11·9	—12·07	
50	Rámpur	6·7	—51·31	
51	Tehri Garhwál	11·0	—6·66	
	TOTAL, NATIVE STATES ...	8·2	—38·67	

APPENDIX XXVIII.

Showing for castes numbering above 100,000, *the percentage of insanes, deaf-mutes, blind persons and lepers.*

Serial number.	Caste.	Total number of caste.	Insanes.		Deaf-mutes.		Blind persons.		Lepers.	
			Number.	Percentage.	Number.	Percentage.	Number.	Percentage.	Number.	Percentage.
	1	2	3	4	5	6	7	8	9	10
			HINDU CASTES.							
1	Ahar	244,166	30	·012	133	·054	717	·294	77	·032
2	Abir	3,916,845	383	·010	2,580	·066	8,250	·211	1,120	·029
3	Baniya	1,279,246	270	·021	1,056	·083	3,431	·268	429	·033
4	Barai	153,421	12	·008	114	·074	335	·218	42	·027
5	Barhai	498,985	53	·011	451	·090	1,098	·220	173	·035
6	Bhangi	397,197	40	·010	175	·044	1,229	·309	128	·032
7	Bhar	417,745	20	·005	30	·007	725	·174	147	·035
8	Bharbhunja	301,196	46	·024	236	·078	959	·318	82	·027
9	Bhat	131,471	24	·018	100	·076	420	·319	67	·051
10	Bhuinhar	221,027	30	·014	159	·072	258	·117	64	·029
11	Brahman	4,719,882	719	·015	3,700	·078	10,591	·224	1,842	·039
12	Chamar	5,815,053	585	·010	3,272	·056	14,310	·246	1,723	·030
13	Dhanuk	146,189	12	·008	74	·051	368	·247	35	·024
14	Dhobi	579,783	53	·009	422	·073	1,417	·244	231	·040
15	Dom	270,560	31	·015	579	·214	391	·147	509	·188
16	Fakir	284,621	53	·017	201	·071	747	·262	108	·038
17	Gadariya	929,059	69	·007	446	·048	2,206	·237	240	.026
18	Gujar	280,113	27	·010	119	·042	675	·241	66	·023
19	Jat	677,854	59	·009	293	·043	1,820	·268	132	·019
20	Kachhi	703,367	76	·011	348	·049	1,833	·261	227	·032
21	Kahar	1,184 451	56	·013	799	·067	3,159	·267	468	·039
22	Kalwar	347,037	48	·014	240	·069	749	·216	134	·039
23	Kayasth	511,426	102	·020	349	·068	991	·194	135	·026
24	Kewat	315,852	19	·006	180	·057	761	·241	171	·054
25	Khatik	189,639	10	·005	52	·027	307	·162	42	·022
26	Kisan	364,455	16	·004	168	·046	642	·176	69	·019
27	Koeri	540,245	49	·009	678	·125	789	·137	159	·029
28	Kori	919,649	111	·012	603	·066	3,243	·359	422	·046
29	Kumhar	702,505	83	·012	413	·059	1,584	·225	253	·036
30	Kurmi	2,005,657	157	·008	1,429	·071	4,359	·217	753	·638
31	Lodha	1,029,213	86	·008	751	·073	2,922	·284	303	·029
32	Lohar	525,910	61	·012	396	·075	1,263	·240	188	·036
33	Luniya	403,318	27	·007	356	·088	658	·163	108	·025
34	Mali	245,876	35	·014	85	·035	653	·265	171	·069
35	Mallah	365,379	38	·010	164	·045	491	·134	96	·036
36	Murao	664,616	63	·009	627	·094	1,531	·230	231	·069
37	Nai	668,087	74	·011	564	·084	2,220	·355	237	·035
38	Pasi	1,219,311	87	·007	592	·048	2,557	·210	449	·037
39	Rajput	3.253,020	400	·012	2,493	·077	5,741	·176	2,076	·064
40	Sunar	255,008	48	·019	223	·087	585	·229	68	·027
41	Teli	741,427	85	·011	614	·083	1,855	·250	235	·032
42	Gond	115,643	14	·012	160	·138	261	·226	53	·046
			MUSALMAN CASTES.							
1	Dhuna	401,987	42	·010	265	·066	815	·202	151	·038
2	Darzi	146,703	20	·014	102	·069	372	·254	23	·016
3	Fakir	388,474	45	·013	193	·057	787	·218	93	·027
4	Julaha	880,231	91	·010	768	·087	2,216	·252	272	·031
5	Kassab	148,516	19	.013	72	·048	408	·275	43	·029
6	Nai	193,937	30	.015	140	·072	480	·247	50	·026
7	Pathan	700,398	149	·021	763	·108	1,752	·250	236	·033
8	Rajput	375,833	...	·004	288	·077	444	·118	75	·020
9	Sayed	242,811	81	·033	174	·072	574	·236	62	·026
10	Sheikh	1,382,566	197	·012	210	·091	4,009	·308	491	·037
11	Teli	192,604	19	·010	102	·053	413	·214	48	·025

APPENDIX XXIX.

Showing by districts the number of deaf-mutes in 1872, 1881 and 1891.

Serial number.	District.	1872.	1881.	1891.	Percentage of variation between 1881 and 1891.
1	Dehra Dún	98	326	490	+50·30
2	Sahéranpur	83	507	537	+5·91
3	Muzaffarnagar	143	554	519	−6·31
4	Meerut	145	520	669	+28·65
5	Bulandshahr	151	364	437	−20·05
6	Aligarh	167	360	380	+5·55
	Total, Meerut Division ...	787	2,631	3,032	+15·23
7	Muttra	165	205	399	+94·62
8	Agra	311	352	542	+53·97
9	Farukhabad	151	452	467	+3·31
10	Mainpuri	148	310	283	−8·70
11	Etáwah	84	304	455	+49·67
12	Etah	197	370	395	+6·75
	Total, Agra Division ...	1,056	1,993	2,541	+27·49
13	Bareilly	410	515	639	+24·07
14	Bijnor	164	556	536	−3·59
15	Budaun	244	448	487	+8·70
16	Moradabad	442	1,264	510	−59·65
17	Sháhjahánpur	264	380	338	−11·05
18	Pílibhít	...	218	264	+21·10
	Total, Rohilkhand Division ...	1,524	3,381	2,774	−17·95
19	Cawnpore	247	563	771	+36·94
20	Fatehpur	128	308	194	−35·97
21	Bánda	270	383	362	−5·48
22	Hamírpur	106	280	386	+37·85
23	Allahabad	266	835	754	−9·70
24	Jhánsi	32	124	297	+139·51
25	Jalaun	63	169	358	+111·83
26	Lalitpur	35	89	189	+112·35
	Total, Allahabad Division ...	1,147	2,746	3,311	+20·57
27	Benares	151	468	444	−5·12
28	Mirzapur	125	491	482	−1·83
29	Jaunpur	77	296	693	+134·12
30	Gházipur	293	400	491	+22·75
31	Ballia	...	357	569	+59·38
	Total, Benares Division ...	646	2,012	2,679	+33·15
32	Gorakhpur	772	3,550	4,348	+22·47
33	Basti	204	1,414	1,221	−13·64
34	Azamgarh	204	259	1,005	+288·03
	Total, Gorakhpur Division ...	1,180	5,223	6,574	+52·86
35	Kumaun	864	1,285	1,293	+·62
36	Garhwál	676	793	608	−23·33
37	Tarái	62	98	165	+68·36
	Total, Kumaun Division ...	1,602	2,176	2,066	−5·05
	Total, N.-W. Provinces ...	7,942	20,162	22,977	+13·96
38	Lucknow	...	301	484	+60·79
39	Unao	...	402	446	+10·94
40	Rae Bareli	...	506	590	+16·60
41	Sitapur	...	450	701	+55·75
42	Hardoi	...	352	452	+28·46
43	Kheri	...	940	1,080	+14·89
	Total, Lucknow Division ...	...	2,951	3,753	+27·17
44	Fyzabad	...	453	820	+81·01
45	Gonda	...	1,265	1,406	+11·14
46	Bahraich	...	1,456	1,656	+27·47
47	Sultanpur	...	329	828	+149·54
48	Partabgarh	...	258	535	+107·36
49	Bara Banki	...	775	728	−6·06
	Total, Fyzabad Division ...	...	4,536	6,166	+35·93
	Total, Oudh ...	...	7,487	9,919	+32·48
	Total, N.-W. Provinces and Oudh ...	...	27,649	32,896	+18·97
50	Rámpur	...	469	104	−77·82
51	Tehri Garhwál	...	348	289	−16·95
	TOTAL, NATIVE STATES ...	...	817	393	−51·89

APPENDIX XXX.

Showing the classification of castes by traditional occupation.

Class.	Group.	Castes, tribes, &c.	Number of sub-castes.	Strength. Total.	Strength. Males.	Strength. Females.	Religion.
A.—Agricultural.	1. Military and dominant.	Bhuinhar	458	221,027	109,852	111,175	Hindu.
		Do.	...	4	4	...	Arya.
		Jat	1,791	677,854	380,494	297,360	Hindu.
		Do.	106	14,190	7,771	6,419	Musalman.
		Do.	...	724	411	313	Arya.
		Do.	...	6,058	4,691	1,367	Sikh.
		Rájput	1,689	3,253,020	1,756,411	1,496,609	Hindu.
		Do.	698	375,833	191,604	184,229	Musalman.
		Do.	...	431	229	202	Jain.
		Do.	...	3,710	2,068	1,642	Arya.
		Do.	...	849	534	315	Sikh.
		Taga	155	99,409	56,274	43,135	Hindu.
		Do.	55	28,118	14,767	13,351	Musalman.
		Do.	...	1,036	604	432	Arya.
	Total, Group 1	Hindu	4,093	4,251,310	2,303,031	1,948,279	
		Musalman	769	418,141	214,142	203,999	
		Jain	...	431	229	202	
		Arya	...	5,474	3,087	2,387	
		Sikh	...	6,907	5,225	1,682	
		Total ...	4,862	4,682,263	2,525,714	2,156,549	
	2 (a) Cultivators	Barai	147	153,421	77,720	75,701	Hindu.
		Bhar	153	417,745	206,274	211,471	Do.
		Bhurtiya	8	423	233	190	Do.
		Dangi	67	2,363	1,239	1,124	Do.
		Gara	51	51,088	27,227	23,861	Musalman.
		Golapurab	76	9,723	5,315	4,408	Hindu.
		Jhojha	75	26,847	13,958	12,889	Musalman.
		Kachhi	560	703,367	371,893	331,474	Hindu.
		Do.	...	1	1	...	Arya.
		Kamboh	89	6,222	3,408	2,814	Hindu.
		Do.	5	2,322	1,100	1,222	Musalman.
		Do.	...	6	3	3	Arya.
		Do.	...	28	24	4	Sikh.
		Khagi	135	43,435	23,028	20,412	Hindu.
		Kirar	55	18,363	9,934	8,429	Do.
		Kisan	98	364,455	194,845	169,610	Do.
		Koeri	140	540,245	272,845	267,400	Do.
		Kurmi	1,488	2,005,657	1,035,002	970,655	Do.
		Do.	...	140	88	52	Arya.
		Do.	...	5	2	3	Sikh.
		Kunjra	94	85,529	43,792	41,737	Musalman.
		Lodha	515	1,029,213	534,580	494,633	Hindu.
		Do.	...	12	7	5	Arya.
		Mali	853	245,876	129,394	116,482	Hindu.
		Do.	...	54	28	26	Arya.
		Do.	...	3	2	1	Jain.
		Do.	...	10	9	1	Sikh.
		Meo	97	10,642	5,733	4,909	Hindu.
		Mewati	347	60,332	31,875	28,457	Musalman.
		Murao	232	664,916	347,899	317,017	Hindu.
		Rain	7	146	74	72	Do.
		Do.	50	15,097	7,957	7,140	Musalman.
		Rawa	44	25,451	13,875	11,576	Hindu.
		Ror	80	4,459	2,513	1,946	Do.
		Saini	86	99,425	52,611	46,814	Do.
	Total, Group 2(a)	Hindu	4,880	6,345,547	3,288,410	3,057,137	
		Musalman	622	241,215	125,909	115,306	
		Jain	...	3	2	1	
		Arya	...	213	127	86	
		Sikh	...	43	35	8	
		Total ...	5,502	6,587,021	3,414,483	3,172,538	
	2 (b) Cattle breeder and grazier.	Ahar	976	244,166	133,348	110,818	Hindu.
		Do.	...	1	1	...	Arya.
		Ahír	1,767	3,916,846	2,039,906	1,876,940	Hindu.
		Do.	...	193	113	80	Arya.
		Do.	...	1	1	...	Jain.
		Do.	...	60	40	20	Sikh.

APPENDIX XXX.

Showing the classification of castes by traditional occupation—(continued).

Class.	Group.	Castes, tribes, &c.	Number of sub-castes.	Strength. Total.	Strength. Males.	Strength. Females.	Religion.
A.—Agricultural—(*concluded*).	2(*b*) Cattle breeder and grazier—(*concluded*).	Dogar	...	340	179	161	Musalman.
		Gaddi	255	51,970	27,282	24,688	Do.
		Ghosi	111	27,760	14,200	13,560	Do.
		Gujar	1,178	280,113	160,573	119,540	Hindu.
		Do.	380	64,424	33,570	30,854	Musalman.
		Do.	...	27	14	13	Arya.
		Do.	...	67	45	22	Sikh.
	Total, Group 2 (*b*)	Hindu	3,921	4,441,125	2,333,827	2,107,298	
		Musalmán	746	144,494	75,231	69,263	
		Jain	...	1	1	...	
		Arya	...	221	128	93	
		Sikh	...	127	85	42	
		Total ...	4,667	4,585,968	2,409,272	2,176,696	
	2 (*c*) Sheep breeders.	Gadarya	1,313	929,059	480,273	448,786	Hindu.
		Do.	8	378	197	181	Musalmán.
		Do.	...	14	12	2	Arya.
		Do.	...	12	6	6	Sikh.
	Total, Group 2(*c*)	Hindu	1,313	929,059	480,273	448,786	
		Musalmán	8	378	197	181	
		Arya	...	14	12	2	
		Sikh	...	12	6	6	
		Total ...	1,321	929,463	480,488	448,975	
	3. Forest and Hill Tribes.	Baiswar	...	1,898	961	937	Hindu.
		Bhil	7	190	117	73	Do.
		Bhoksa	5	1,208	646	562	Do.
		Bhuinyan	...	849	447	392	Do.
		Cheru	6	4,883	2,458	2,425	Do.
		Goli	1	21	11	10	Do.
		Gond	105	8,861	4,135	4,726	Do.
		Kharwar	...	176	86	90	Do.
		Kol	52	68,556	34,342	34,214	Do.
		Korwar	...	33	16	17	Do.
		Mahra	17	699	399	300	Do.
		Majhwar	2	16,268	8,018	8,250	Do.
		Manjhi	5	6,122	3,123	2,999	Do.
		Musahar	137	40,662	20,779	19,883	Do.
		Soiri	6	17,822	9,084	8,738	Do.
		Sonthal	1	1	1	...	Do.
		Tharu	73	25,492	13,720	11,772	Do.
	Total, group 3 ...	Hindu	417	193,731	98,343	95,388	
	Total, Class A. ...	Hindu	14,624	16,160,772	8,503,884	7,656,888	
		Musalman	2,145	804,228	415,479	383,749	
		Jain	...	435	232	203	
		Arya	...	5,922	3,354	2,568	
		Sikh	...	7,089	5,351	1,738	
		Total ...	16,769	16,978,446	8,928,300	8,050,146	
B.—Professional	4. Priests ...	Brahman	902	4,719,882	2,455,791	2,264,091	Hindu.
		Do.	...	5,031	2,823	2,208	Arya.
		Do.	...	32	14	18	Jain.
		Do.	...	116	86	30	Sikh.
		Mahabrahman ...	30	19,829	10,302	9,527	Hindu.
	Total, Group 4 ...	Hindu	932	4,739,711	2,466,093	2,273,618	
		Jain	...	32	14	18	
		Arya	...	5,031	2,823	2,208	
		Sikh	...	116	86	30	
		Total ...	932	4,744,890	2,469,016	2,275,874	

APPENDIX XXX.

Showing the classification of castes by traditional occupation—(continued).

Class.	Group.	Castes, tribes, &c.	Number of sub-castes	Strength. Total.	Males.	Females.	Religion.
B.—Professional—(*continued*).	5. Devotees ...	Fakir	,1291	284,621	158,303	126,318	Hindu.
		Do.	524	338,474	175,347	163,127	Musalman.
		Do.	...	12	9	3	Jain.
		Do.	...	233	127	106	Arya.
		Do.	...	166	104	62	Sikh.
	Total, Group 5 ...	Hindu	1,291	284,621	158,303	126,318	
		Musalman	524	338,474	175,347	163,127	
		Jain	...	12	9	3	
		Arya	...	233	127	106	
		Sikh	...	166	104	62	
		Total ...	1,815	623,506	333,890	289,616	
	6. Genealogists...	Bhat	968	131,471	67,417	64,054	Hindu.
		Do.	161	29,463	14,767	14,696	Musalman.
		Do.	...	9	7	2	Jain.
		Do.	...	90	44	46	Arya.
		Do.	...	111	86	25	Sikh.
	Total, Group 6 ...	Hindu	968	13,471	67,417	64,054	
		Musalman	161	29,463	14,767	14,696	
		Jain	...	9	7	2	
		Arya	...	90	44	46	
		Sikh	...	111	86	25	
		Total ...	1,129	161,144	82,321	78,823	
	7. Writers ...	Kayasth	230	511,426	266,525	244,901	Hindu.
		Do.	...	2,887	1,555	1,332	Arya.
		Do.	...	14	9	5	Sikh.
	Total, Group 7 ...	Hindu	230	511,426	266,525	244,901	
		Arya	...	2,887	1,555	1,332	
		Sikh	...	14	9	5	
		Total ...	230	514,327	268,089	246,238	
	8. Astrologers ...	Joshi	451	35,049	18,214	16,835	Hindu.
		Do.	...	20	12	8	Arya.
	Total, Group 8 ...	Hindu	451	35,049	18,214	16,835	
		Arya	...	20	12	8	
		Total ...	451	35,069	18,226	16,843	
	9. Musicians and ballad singers.	Dafali	67	42,075	21,616	20,459	Musalman.
		Dharbi	14	1,322	691	631	Ditto.
		Dom Mirasi... ...	201	28,363	14,318	14,045	Ditto.
		Panwariya	...	512	242	270	Ditto.
	Total, Group 9 ...	Musalmans	282	72,272	36,867	35,405	
	10. Dancers and singers.	Barwa	4	1,631	780	851	Hindu.
		Beriya	250	14,420	6,417	8,003	Do.
		Do.	12	893	381	512	Musalman.
		Bhagat	...	485	252	233	Hindu.
		Gandharp	23	664	309	355	Do.
		Hurkiya	21	801	455	346	Musalman.
		Kathik	378	2,034	983	1,051	Hindu.
		Paturya	49	4,710	1,864	2,846	Do.
		Do.	...	4	1	3	Sikh.
		Radha	71	3,964	2,018	1,946	Hindu.
		Do.	8	390	189	201	Musalman.
		Tawaif	216	22,969	8,394	14,575	Ditto.
	Total, Group 10...	Hindu	775	27,908	12,623	15,285	
		Musalman	257	25,053	9,419	15,634	
		Sikh	...	4	1	3	
		Total ...	1,032	52,965	22,043	30,922	

APPENDIX XXX.

Showing the classification of castes by traditional occupation—(continued).

Class.	Group.	Castes, tribes, &c.	Number of sub-castes.	Strength. Total.	Males.	Females.	Religion.
B.—Professional (*concluded*).	11. Actors and mimes.	Bhand	2	14	10	4	Hindu.
		Do.	31	4,000	2,045	1,955	Musalman.
	Total, Group 11...	Hindu	2	14	10	4	
		Musalman	31	4,000	2,045	1,955	
		Total ...	33	4,014	2,055	1,959	
	Total, Class B....	Hindu	4,649	5,730,200	2,989,185	2,741,015	
		Musalman	1,255	469,262	238,445	230,817	
		Jain	...	53	30	23	
		Arya	...	8,261	4,561	3,700	
		Sikh	...	411	286	125	
		Total ...	5,904	6,208,187	3,232,507	2,975,680	
C.—Commercial	12. Traders ...	Baniya	759	1,279,246	668,153	611,093	Hindu.
		Do.	...	83,976	45,290	38,686	Jain.
		Do.	...	5,740	3,077	2,663	Arya.
		Do.	...	90	52	38	Sikh.
		Bhatiya	20	265	129	136	Hindu.
		Bohra	17	1,131	614	517	Do.
		Dhusar Bhargava ...	2	12,279	6,557	5,722	Do.
		Khatri	761	45,099	23,895	21,204	Do.
		Do.	...	516	283	233	Arya.
		Do.	...	635	372	263	Sikh.
	Total, Group 12...	Hindu	1,559	1,338,020	699,348	638,672	
		Jain	...	83,976	45,290	38,686	
		Arya	...	6,256	3,360	2,896	
		Sikh	...	725	424	301	
		Total ...	1,559	1,428,977	748,422	680,555	
	13. Pedlar ...	Bisati	...	107	52	55	Hindu.
		Do.	4	852	422	430	Musalman.
		Ramaiya	22	3,765	1,372	2,393	Hindu.
		Do.	...	72	38	34	Sikh.
		Do.	5	258	107	151	Musalman.
	Total, Group 13...	Hindu	22	3,872	1,424	2,448	
		Musalman	9	1,110	529	581	
		Sikh	...	72	38	34	
		Total ...	31	5,054	1,991	3,063	
	14. Carriers ...	Ahiwasi	22	9,502	4,630	4,872	Hindu.
		Baidguar	7	420	177	243	Musalman.
		Banjara	253	39,875	22,328	17,547	Hindu.
		Do.	98	26,953	13,457	13,496	Musalman.
		Do.	...	23	14	9	Arya.
		Do.	...	246	119	127	Sikh.
		Belwar	31	6,194	3,243	2,951	Hindu.
		Naik	6	2,563	1,217	1,346	Do.
		Rahwari	61	898	345	553	Do.
	Total, Group 14	Hindu	373	59,032	31,763	27,269	
		Musalman	105	27,373	13,634	13,739	
		Arya	...	23	14	9	
		Sikh	...	246	119	127	
		Total ...	478	86,674	45,530	41,144	

APPENDIX XXX.

Showing the classification of castes by traditional occupation—(continued).

Class.	Group.	Castes, tribes, &c.	Number of sub-castes.	Strength.			Religion.
				Total.	Males.	Females.	
C.—Commercial—(*concluded*).	Total, Class C. ...	Hindu	1,954	1,400,924	732,585	668,389	
		Musalman	114	28,483	14,163	14,320	
		Jain	...	83,976	45,290	38,686	
		Arya	...	6,279	3,374	2,905	
		Sikh	...	1,043	581	462	
		Total ...	2,068	1,520,705	795,943	724,762	
D.—Artisan and village menial.	15. Goldsmith ...	Sonar	1,627	255,008	185,081	119,927	Hindu.
		Do.	...	3	2	1	Jain.
		Do.	...	240	128	112	Arya.
		Do.	...	58	34	24	Sikh.
		Do.	3	320	163	157	Musalman.
	Total, Group 15	Hindu	1,627	255,008	135,081	119,927	
		Musalman	3	320	163	157	
		Jain	...	3	2	1	
		Arya	...	240	128	112	
		Sikh	...	58	34	24	
		Total ...	1,630	255,629	135,408	120,221	
	16. Barber ...	Nai	888	668,087	346,106	321,981	Hindu.
		Do.	197	193,937	98,488	95,449	Musalman.
		Do.	...	19	11	8	Jain.
		Do.	...	71	36	35	Arya.
		Do.	...	159	96	63	Sikh.
	Total, Group 16	Hindu	888	668,087	346,106	321,981	
		Musalman	197	193,937	98,488	95,449	
		Jain	...	19	11	8	
		Arya	...	71	36	35	
		Sikh	...	159	96	63	
		Total ...	1,085	862,273	444,737	417,536	
	17. Blacksmith...	Lohar	736	525,910	274,670	251,240	Hindu.
		Do.	114	66,204	34,915	31,289	Musalman.
		Do.	...	28	17	11	Arya.
		Do.	...	78	45	33	Sikh.
		Nalband	6	429	204	225	Musalman.
	Total, Group 17	Hindu	736	525,910	274,670	251,240	
		Musalman	120	66,633	35,119	31,514	
		Arya	...	28	17	11	
		Sikh	...	78	45	33	
		Total ...	856	592,649	309,851	282,798	
	18. Carpenters and turners.	Barhai	859	498,985	262,817	236,168	Hindu.
		Do.	79	59,899	31,281	28,618	Musalman.
		Do.	...	81	53	28	Arya.
		Do.	...	652	525	127	Sikh.
		Kharadi	17	806	404	402	Hindu.
		Do.	3	398	214	184	Musalman.
	Total, Group 18	Hindu	876	499,791	263,221	236,570	
		Musalman	82	60,297	31,495	28,802	
		Arya	...	81	53	28	
		Sikh	...	652	525	127	
		Total ...	958	560,821	295,294	265,527	

APPENDIX XXX.

Showing the classification of castes by traditional occupation—(continued).

Class.	Group.	Castes, tribes, &c.	Number of sub-castes.	Strength. Total.	Strength. Males.	Strength. Females.	Religion.
D.—Artisan and village menial—(*continued*).	18(*a*) Painters ...	Bangsaz	26	87	56	31	Hindu.
		Do.	20	1,399	707	692	Musalman.
	Total, Group 18(*a*)	Hindu	26	87	56	31	
		Musalman	20	1,399	707	692	
		Total ...	46	1,486	763	723	
	19 Mason ...	Raj	49	3,165	1,590	1,575	Hindu.
		Do.	27	3,468	1,633	1,835	Musalman.
	Total, Group 19	Hindu	49	3,165	1,590	1,575	
		Mussulman	27	3,468	1,633	1,835	
		Total ...	76	6,633	3,223	3,410	
	20.—Brass and coppersmiths.	Jastgar	...	13	7	6	Hindu.
		Kalaigar	4	89	49	40	Musalman.
		Kasera	53	7,273	3,795	3,478	Hindu.
		Rangdhar	6	185	99	86	Musalman.
		Thathera	309	20,823	10,976	9,847	Hindu.
		Do.	5	522	266	256	Musalman.
		Do.	...	16	10	6	Sikh.
	Total, Group 20	Hindu	362	28,109	14,778	13,331	
		Musalman	15	796	414	382	
		Sikh	...	16	10	6	
		Total ...	377	28,921	15,202	13,719	
	21.—Tailor ...	Darzi	526	82,210	43,195	39,015	Hindu.
		Do.	146	146,703	74,016	72,687	Musalman.
		Do.	...	2	2	...	Arya.
		Do.	...	11	7	4	Sikh.
	Total, Group 21	Hindu	526	82,210	43,195	39,015	
		Musalman	146	146,703	74,016	72,687	
		Arya	...	2	2	...	
		Sikh	...	11	7	4	
		Total ...	672	228,926	117,220	111,706	
	22.—Grain parchers and confectioners.	Bharbhunja ...	364	301,196	158,102	143,094	Hindu.
		Do.	40	9,009	5,015	3,994	Musalman.
		Do.	...	10	6	4	Arya.
		Do.	...	1	1	...	Sikh.
		Halwai	334	64,702	33,394	31,308	Hindu.
		Do.	57	31,544	16,350	15,194	Musalman.
	Total, Group 22	Hindu	698	365,898	191,496	174,402	
		Musalman	97	40,553	21,365	19,188	
		Arya	...	10	6	4	
		Sikh	...	1	1	...	
		Total ...	795	406,462	212,868	193,594	

APPENDIX XXX.

Showing the classification of castes by traditional occupation—(continued).

Class.	Group.	Castes, tribes, &c.	Number of sub-castes.	Strength. Total.	Males.	Females.	Religion.
D.—Artisan and village menial—(*continued*).	23. Perfume and drug preparers and sellers and betel-leaf sellers.	Gandhi	1	80	41	39	Hindu
		Do.	9	778	404	374	Musalman.
		Tamoli	244	73,641	38,278	35,363	Hindu.
		Do.	...	270	133	137	Musalman.
		Do.	...	1	1	...	Jain.
		Do.	...	31	17	14	Arya.
	Total, Group 23...	Hindu	245	73,721	38,319	35,402	
		Musalman	9	1,048	537	511	
		Jain	...	1	1	...	
		Arya	...	31	17	14	
		Total ...	254	74,801	38,874	35,927	
	24(*a*) Weavers ...	Julaha	244	880,231	445,016	435,215	Musalmán.
		Kori	1,040	919,649	472,337	447,312	Hindu.
		Do.	...	28	19	9	Arya.
		Do.	...	73	49	24	Sikh.
		Pankha	5	6,502	3,215	3,287	Hindu.
	Total, Group 24(*a*)	Hindu	1,045	926,151	475,552	450,599	
		Musalman	244	880,231	445,016	435,215	
		Arya	...	28	19	9	
		Sikh	...	73	49	24	
		Total ...	1,289	1,806,483	920,636	885,847	
	24(*b*) Calenderers and dyers.	Chhipi	202	23,249	12,246	11,003	Hindu.
		Do.	21	11,871	6,097	5,774	Musalman.
		Do.	...	24	14	10	Arya.
		Do.	...	33	30	3	Sikh.
		Rangrez	1	8	4	4	Hindu.
		Do.	81	35,135	18,294	16,841	Musalman.
	Total, Group 24(*b*)	Hindu	203	23,257	12,250	11,007	
		Musalman	102	47,006	24,391	22,615	
		Arya	...	24	14	10	
		Sikh	...	33	30	3	
		Total ...	305	70,320	36,685	33,635	
	25. Washerman	Dhobi	925	579,783	298,032	281,751	Hindu.
		Do.	216	78,947	40,800	38,147	Musalman.
		Do.	...	6	5	1	Arya
		Do.	...	9	7	2	Sikh.
	Total, Group 25...	Hindu	925	579,783	298,032	281,751	
		Musalman	216	78,947	40,800	38,147	
		Arya	...	6	5	1	
		Sikh	...	9	7	2	
		Total ...	1,141	658,745	338,844	319,901	
	26. Cotton cleaners.	Dhuna	152	401,987	202,825	199,162	Musalman.
		Kadhera	559	51,753	27,268	24,485	Hindu.
		Do.	...	3	2	1	Arya.
	Total, Group 26...	Hindu	559	51,753	27,268	24,485	
		Musalman	152	401,987	202,825	199,162	
		Arya	...	3	2	1	
		Total ...	711	453,743	230,095	223,648	

APPENDIX XXX.

Showing the classification of castes by traditional occupation—(continued).

Class.	Group.	Castes, Tribes, &c.	Number of sub-castes.	Strength. Total.	Strength. Males.	Strength. Females.	Religion.
D.—Artisan and village menial—(*continued*).	27. Oil pressers...	Teli	742	741,427	380,839	360,588	Hindu.
		Do.	239	192,604	101,384	91,220	Musalman.
		Do.	...	1	1	...	Arya.
		Do.	...	48	29	19	Sikh.
	Total, Group 27	Hindu	742	741,427	380,839	360,588	
		Musalman	239	192,604	101,384	91,220	
		Arya	...	1	1	...	
		Sikh	...	48	29	19	
		Total ..	981	934,080	482,253	451,827	
	28. Potters ...	Kumhar	773	702,805	360,146	342,659	Hindu.
		Do.	52	10,189	5,219	4,970	Musalman.
		Do.	...	2	2	...	Jain.
		Do.	...	2	2	...	Arya.
		Do.	...	2	1	1	Sikh.
	Total, Group 28	Hindu	773	702,805	360,146	342,659	
		Musalman	52	10,189	5,219	4,970	
		Jain	...	2	2	...	
		Arya	...	2	2	...	
		Sikh	...	2	1	1	
		Total ...	825	713,000	365,370	347,630	
	29. Glass and lac-workers.	Churihar	...	703	363	340	Hindu.
		Do.	111	28,250	13,914	14,336	Musalman.
		Lakhera	125	3,678	1,898	1,780	Hindu.
		Do.	...	85	43	42	Musalman.
		Manihar	19	1,585	814	771	Hindu.
		Do.	130	65,613	33,875	31,738	Musalman.
		Do.	...	1	1	...	Arya.
		Do.	...	16	10	6	Sikh.
		Potgar	...	92	43	49	Hindu.
	Total, Group 29	Hindu	144	6,058	3,118	2,940	
		Musalman	241	93,948	47,832	46,116	
		Arya	...	1	1	...	
		Sikh	...	16	10	6	
		Total ...	385	100,023	50,961	49,062	
	29(*a*) Bead stringers.	Patwa	294	30,812	15,724	15,088	Hindu.
		Do.	2	165	83	82	Musalman.
	Total, Group 29(*a*)	Hindu	294	30,812	15,724	15,088	
		Musalman	2	165	83	82	
		Total ...	296	30,977	15,807	15,170	
	29(*b*) Fireworks maker.	Atishbaz	6	534	272	262	Musalman.
	Total, Group 29(*b*)	Musalman	6	534	272	262	
	30. Salt and earth-workers.	Bayar	5	18,821	9,237	9,584	Hindu.
		Beldar	183	37,238	18,918	18,320	Do.
		Do.	3	61	29	32	Musalman.
		Dhangar	9	519	259	260	Hindu.

APPENDIX XXX.

Showing the classification of castes by traditional occupation—(continued).

Class.	Group.	Castes, tribes, &c.	Number of sub-castes.	Strength. Total.	Males.	Females.	Religion.
D.—Artisan and village menial—(*continued*).	30. Salt and earth-workers—(*concluded.*)	Ghasiyara	...	198	94	104	Musalman.
		Luniyan	808	412,817	207,473	205,344	Hindu.
		Do.	...	5	3	2	Sikh.
	Total, Group 30	Hindu	1,005	469,395	235,887	233,508	
		Musalman	3	259	123	136	
		Sikh	...	5	3	2	
		Total ...	1,008	469,659	236,013	233,646	
	31. Goldsmiths' refuse collectors.	Niariya	1	65	24	41	Hindu.
		Do.	1	193	109	84	Musalman.
	Total, Group 31	Hindu	1	65	24	41	
		Musalman	1	193	109	84	
		Total ...	2	258	133	125	
	32. Iron smelters	Agarya	1	938	481	457	Hindu.
		Saun	63	257	138	119	Do.
	Total, Group 32 ...	Hindu	64	1,195	619	576	
	33. Fishermen, boatmen, palki bearers, cooks, &c.	Bargah	9	918	450	468	Hindu.
		Bargi	46	1,076	544	532	Do.
		Bari	503	69,708	34,917	34,791	Do.
		Bhatiyara	52	30,658	15,908	14,750	Musalman.
		Bhishti	126	80,147	40,996	39,151	Do.
		Chain	39	28,610	14,644	13,966	Hindu.
		Gond	...	115,643	54,954	60,689	Do.
		Do.	...	8	4	4	Sikh.
		Gorchha	3	963	475	488	Hindu.
		Kahar	823	1,184,451	600,258	584,193	Do.
		Do.	24	6,928	3,438	3,490	Musalman.
		Do.	...	1	1	...	Jain.
		Do.	...	120	63	57	Arya.
		Do.	...	60	53	7	Sikh.
		Kewat	296	315,882	159,313	156,569	Hindu.
		Lorha	...	2,622	1,382	1,240	Do.
		Mallah	625	365,379	171,688	193,691	Do.
		Do	22	3,629	1,725	1,904	Musalman.
		Mukeri	...	2	...	2	Hindu.
		Do.	22	6,243	3,060	3,183	Musalman.
		Nanbai	6	2,177	1,110	1,067	Do.
		Sejwari	18	386	187	199	Hindu.
	Total, Group 33	Hindu	2,362	2,085,640	1,038,812	1,046,828	
		Musalman	252	129,782	66,237	63,545	
		Jain	...	1	1	...	
		Arya	...	120	63	57	
		Sikh	...	68	57	11	
		Total ...	2,614	2,215,611	1,105,170	1,110,441	
	33(*a*) Rice huskers.	Barwar	23	2,379	1,130	1,249	Hindu.
		Kuta	65	4,029	2,000	2,029	Do.
	Total, Group 33(*a*)	Hindu	88	6,408	3,130	3,278	

APPENDIX XXX.

Showing the classification of castes by traditional occupation—(continued).

Class.	Group.	Castes, tribes, &c.	Number of sub-castes.	Strength. Total.	Males.	Females.	Religion.
D.—Artisan and village menial—(*continued*).	34(*a*) Distillers ...	Kalwar	619	347,037	174,924	172,113	Hindu.
		Do.	...	26	19	7	Sikh.
		Do.	12	1,454	724	730	Musalman.
		Do.	...	273	145	128	Arya.
	Total, Group 34(*a*)	Hindu	619	347,037	174,924	172,113	
		Musalman	12	1,454	724	730	
		Arya	...	273	145	128	
		Sikh	...	26	19	7	
		Total ...	631	348,790	175,812	172,978	
	34(*b*) Toddy-drawers.	Bind	67	76,986	37,320	39,666	Hindu.
		Tarmali	...	27	12	15	Do.
	Total, Group 34(*b*)	Hindu	67	77,013	37,332	39,681	
	35 Butchers ...	Chik	270	9,430	4,980	4,450	Hindu.
		Kassab	131	148,516	76,457	72,059	Musalman.
		Khatík	816	189,639	101,232	88,407	Hindu.
		Do.	7	4	2	2	Arya.
		Do.	...	8	3	5	Sikh.
		Do.	...	274	157	117	Musalman.
	Total, Group 35	Hindu	1,086	199,069	106,212	928,57	
		Musalman	138	148,790	76,614	72,176	
		Arya	...	4	2	2	
		Sikh	...	8	3	5	
		Total ...	1,224	347,871	182,831	165,040	
	36 Lime-burners	Sunkar	44	1,396	710	686	Hindu.
	Total, Group 36	Hindu	44	1,396	710	686	
	37 Leather workers.	Chamár	1,146	5,816,053	2,948,446	2,867,607	Hindu.
		Do.	...	174	86	88	Arya.
		Do.	...	260	130	130	Sikh.
		Dabgar	8	1,353	699	654	Hindu.
		Do.	1	129	60	69	Musalman.
		Dhalgir	8	45	19	26	Hindu.
		Mochi	150	8,019	4,248	3,771	Hindu.
		Do.	27	3,672	1,931	1,741	Musalman.
		Do.	...	2	2	...	Sikh.
	Total, Group 37	Hindu	1,312	5,825,470	2,953,412	2,872,058	
		Musalman	28	3,801	1,991	1,810	
		Arya	...	174	86	88	
		Sikh	...	262	132	130	
		Total ...	1,340	5,829,707	2,955,621	2,874,086	
	38. Village Watchmen.	Arakh	178	80,574	41,177	39,397	Hindu.
		Baláhar	85	2,359	1,206	1,153	Do.
		Baniya	57	26,909	14,157	12,752	Do.
		Dhánuk	320	146,189	77,427	68,762	Do.
		Do.	...	1	...	1	Sikh.
		Dhari	40	12,972	6,554	6,418	Hindu.
		Khangár	602	32,929	16,525	16,404	Do.
		Kotwar	...	97	44	53	Do.
		Pahriya	28	495	269	226	Do.
		Pasi	305	1,219,311	624,442	594,869	Do.
	Total, Group 38	Hindu	1,515	1,521,835	781,801	740,034	
		Sikh	...	1	...	1	
		Total ...	1,515	1,521,836	781,801	740,035	

APPENDIX XXX.

Showing the classification of castes by traditional occupation—(continued).

Class.	Group.	Castes, tribes, &c.	Number of sub-castes.	Strength. Total.	Males.	Females.	Religion.
D.—Artisan and village menial—(*concluded*).	39. Scavengers ...	Bhangi	1,859	397,197	208,918	188,279	Hindu.
		Do.	47	17,335	8,756	8,579	Musalman.
		Do.	...	1	1	...	Arya.
		Do.	...	413	231	182	Sikh.
		Domar	244	16,029	7,989	8,040	Hindu.
		Do.	...	8	5	3	Musalman.
	Total, Group 39	Hindu	1,603	413,226	216,907	196,319	
		Musalman	47	17,343	8,761	8,582	
		Arya	...	1	1	...	
		Sikh	...	413	231	182	
		Total ...	1,650	430,983	225,900	205,083	
	Total, Class D. ...	Hindu	20,484	16,511,781	8,431,211	8,080,570	
		Musalman	2,451	2,522,387	1,286,318	1,236,069	
		Jain	...	26	17	9	
		Arya	...	1,100	600	500	
		Sikh	...	1,939	1,289	650	
		Total ...	22,935	19,037,233	9,719,435	9,317,798	
E.—Vagrant, minor artisans and performers, &c.	40. Grindstone-makers and stone quarriers.	Khumra	13	5,198	2,683	2,515	Musalman.
	Total,, Group 40...	Musalman	13	5,198	2,683	2,515	
	41. Knife grinders.	Saikalgar	25	704	360	344	Hindu.
		Do.	8	3,446	1,635	1,811	Musalman.
		Do.	...	56	30	26	Sikh.
	Total, Group 41	Hindu	25	704	360	344	
		Musalman	8	3,446	1,635	1,811	
		Sikh	...	56	30	26	
		Total ...	33	4,206	2,025	2,181	
	42. Mat-makers and cane splitters.	Bansphor	94	17,221	8,897	8,324	Hindu.
		Do.	2	112	56	56	Musalman.
		Basor	373	25,447	12,803	12,644	Hindu.
		Dharkar	230	29,639	14,682	14,957	Do.
		Dom	354	270,560	144,865	125,695	Do.
		Dorha	...	68	33	35	Do.
		Dusadh	90	82,913	39,878	43,035	Do.
		Kharot	3	5,641	2,780	2,861	Do.
		Pankhiya	...	913	444	469	Musalman.
		Tarkihar	37	2,733	1,457	1,276	Hindu.
		Do.	2	14	9	5	Musalman.
	Total, Group 42	Hindu	1,181	434,222	225,395	208,827	
		Musalman	4	1,039	509	530	
		Total ...	1,185	435,261	225,904	209,357	

APPENDIX XXX.

Showing the classification of castes by traditional occupation—(continued).

Class.	Group.	Castes, tribes, &c.	Number of sub-castes.	Strength. Total.	Males.	Females.	Religion.
E.—Vagrant, minor artisans and performers, &c.—(*concld.*).	43. Hunters, fowlers, &c.	Aheriya	64	19,768	10,514	9,254	Hindu.
		Bahelia	213	32,094	16,682	15,412	Do.
		Do.	12	1,660	856	804	Musalman.
		Do.	...	1	...	1	Sikh.
		Bandi	4	110	66	44	Hindu.
		Bengali	54	1,070	560	510	Do.
		Do.	4	280	136	144	Musalman.
		Do.	...	3	1	2	Sikh.
		Gandhila	4	134	70	64	Hindu.
		Giddhiya	...	17	13	4	Do.
		Kanjar	196	17,608	9,182	8,426	Do.
		Do.	6	257	136	121	Musalman.
		Do.	...	8	5	3	Sikh.
	Total, Group 43...	Hindu	535	70,801	37,087	33,714	
		Musalman	22	2,197	1,128	1,069	
		Sikh	...	12	6	6	
		Total ...	557	73,010	38,221	34,789	
	44. Miscellaneous and disreputable livers.	Badhik	4	126	78	48	Hindu.
		Barwar	...	2,703	1,243	1,460	Do.
		Bawariya	19	2,490	1,217	1,273	Do.
		Do.	...	239	119	120	Musalman.
		Bhantu	1	372	164	208	Hindu.
		Dalerah	44	2,233	1,138	1,095	Do.
		Habura	31	2,596	1,317	1,279	Do.
		Harjala	4	275	138	137	Do.
		Hijra	...	7	4	3	Do.
		Do.	9	1,118	749	369	Musalman.
		Sainsi	41	4,287	2,332	1,955	Hindu.
		Do.	...	3	2	1	Musalman.
		Siyarmar	...	1	1	...	Hindu.
	Total Group (44)	Hindu	144	15,090	7,632	7,458	
		Musalman	9	1,360	870	490	
		Total ...	153	16,450	8,502	7,948	
	45 Tumblers and acrobats.	Nat	386	42,880	21,251	21,629	Hindu.
		Do.	205	20,702	10,487	10,215	Musalman.
		Do.	...	2	2	...	Sikh.
	Total Group (45)	Hindu	386	42,880	21,251	21,629	
		Musalman	205	20,702	10,487	10,215	
		Sikh	...	2	2	...	
		Total ...	591	63,584	31,740	31,844	
	46. Castes foreign to the Province.	Satgop	4	177	54	123	Hindu.
		Sud	10	147	68	85	Do.
	Total Group (46)	Total, Hindu	14	324	116	208	
	Total Class E. ...	Hindu	2,284	564,021	291,841	272,180	
		Musalman	248	33,942	17,312	16,630	
		Sikh	...	70	38	32	
		Total ...	2,532	598,033	309,191	288,842	

APPENDIX XXX.

Showing the classification of castes by traditional occupation—(continued).

Class.	Group.	Castes, tribes, &c.	Number of sub-castes.	Strength. Total.	Males.	Females.	Religion.
Class F. ... Races, nationalities and sectarian communities.	47.—Indian nationalities not returned by caste.	Bhotiya	4	7,467	3,670	3,797	Hindu.
		Mandraji	1	81	27	4	Do.
		Mahratta	54	782	345	387	Do.
		Pindari	...	26	13	13	Do.
		Do.	...	1	1	...	Musalman.
	Total Group (47)	Hindu	59	8,256	4,055	4,201	
		Musalman	...	1	1	...	
		Total ...	59	8,257	4,056	4,201	
	48.—Sectarian castes.	Naumuslim... ...	203	88,444	45,562	42,882	Musalman.
		Sadh	1	1,870	953	917	Hindu.
	Total group (48)	Musalman	208	88,444	45,562	42,882	
		Hindu	1	1,879	953	917	
		Total ...	204	90,314	46,515	43,799	
	49.—Non-Indian Asiatic races.	Biloch	73	13,672	7,088	6,584	Musalman.
		Iraki	14	11,677	5,442	6,235	Do.
		Mughal	409	76,673	38,421	38,252	Do.
		Pathan	1,770	700,393	359,538	340,855	Do.
		Sheikh	851	1,332,566	680,494	652,072	Do.
		Syed	555	242,811	122,322	120,489	Do.
		Turk	...	4,994	2,816	2,178	Do.
	Total Group (49) ...	Musalman	3,672	23,82,786	1,216,121	1,166,665	
	50. Non-Asiatic races.	Armenians	...	54	34	20	Christian.
		European	...	27,941	21,392	6,549	Do.
		Habshi	13	194	99	95	Musalman.
	Total Group (50)	Musalman	13	194	99	95	
		Christian	...	27,995	21,426	6,569	
		Total ...	13	28,189	21,525	6,664	
	51. Eurasians ...	Eurasians	...	7,040	3,485	3,555	Christian.
	Total Group (51) ...	Christian	...	7,040	3,485	3,555	
	52. Christian converts.	Native Christians ...	...	23,406	12,383	11,023	Christian.
	Total group (52) ...	Christian	...	23,406	12,383	11,023	
	53. Castes unspecified.	Castes unspecified ...	...	2,344	1,259	1,085	Hindu.
		Ditto ...	...	16,924	10,422	6,502	Musalman.
		Ditto ...	...	111	55	56	Jain.
		Ditto ...	...	491	275	216	Arya.
		Ditto ...	...	791	535	256	Sikh.
		Ditto ...	...	1,387	1,329	58	Buddhist.
		Ditto ...	...	342	209	133	Parsi.
		Ditto ...	...	60	33	27	Jew.
		Ditto ...	...	14	9	5	Brambo.
		Ditto ...	...	3	1	2	Deist.
		Ditto ...	...	22	13	9	Unspecified.

APPENDIX XXX.

Showing the classification of castes by traditional occupation—(concluded).

Class.	Group.	Castes, tribes, &c.	Number of sub-castes.	Strength. Total.	Males.	Females.	Religion.
Class F. ... Races, nationalities and sectarian communities.—(*concld.*).	Total Group ...	Hindu	...	2,344	1,259	1,085	
		Musalman	...	16,924	10,422	6,502	
		Jain	...	111	55	56	
		Arya	...	491	275	216	
		Sikh	...	791	535	256	
		Jew	...	60	33	27	
		Christian	...	...	...	...	
		Parsi	..	342	209	133	
		Buddhist	...	1,387	1,329	58	
		Bramho	...	14	9	5	
		Deist	...	3	1	2	
		Unspecified	...	22	13	9	
		Total ...	...	22,489	14,140	8,349	
	Total, Class F ...	Hindu	80	12,470	6,267	6,203	
		Musalman	3,882	2,488,349	1,272,205	1,216,144	
		Jain	...	111	55	56	
		Arya	...	491	275	216	
		Sikh	...	791	535	256	
		Christian	...	58,441	37,294	21,147	
		Jew	...	60	33	27	
		Parsi	...	342	209	133	
		Buddhist	...	1,387	1,329	58	
		Bramho	...	14	9	5	
		Deist	...	3	1	2	
		Unspecified	...	22	13	9	
		Total ...	3,962	2,562,481	1,318,225	1,244,256	
	Provincial Total for N.-W. P. and Oudh.	Hindu	44,075	40,380,168	20,954,923	19,425,245	
		Musalman	10,095	6,346,651	3,243,922	3,102,729	
		Jain	...	84,601	45,624	38,977	
		Christian	...	58,441	37,294	21,147	
		Arya	...	22,053	12,164	9,889	
		Sikh	...	11,343	8,080	3,263	
		Buddhist	...	1,387	1,329	58	
		Parsi	...	342	209	133	
		Jew	...	60	33	27	
		Bramho	...	14	9	5	
		Deist	...	3	1	2	
		Unspecified	...	22	13	9	
		Total ...	54,170	46,905,085	24,303,601	22,601,484	

APPENDIX XXXI.

Showing the occupations which are likely to be confused with each other in the Census Schedules.

Number of occupation in table.	Name of occupation.	Remarks.
17 and 18 50	Feudatory state menial service ... ... Agents and managers of landed estates	The word "riyasat" is applied either to a feudatory state or to any important land-holder's estate.
20 22 68 69	Cattle breeders and dealers ... ... Buffalo breeders and dealers ... ... Cow and buffalo keepers, and milk and butter sellers ... Ghí preparers and sellers	The cattle and buffalo breeder is almost invariably the same, and it is only by accident that breeders of buffaloes only are entered. The other occupations cross each other largely, 68 and 69 both refer to a single class.
26 197	Sheep and goat breeders and dealers ... ... Blanket makers and sellers	Both occupations are exercised invariably by the same persons.
37 38	Field servants ... ... Field labourers	The enumerators record often gives too little specification to distinguish between these too classes.
38 406	Field labourers ... ... General labourers	The class of persons whose usual labour is field labour, should be shown in 38, but the enumerator frequently argued that they were ready to do any kind of labour and should therefore be entered as general labourers.
40 101	Betel-vine growers .. .. Betal-leaf and areca-nut sellers	The same person often does both and it is an accident which he enters.
42	Indigo planters	The general term in use is Godam níl; Kothi níl. Tijarat níl, is also frequently used. No distinction is drawn in these terms between a person who is a planter or a worker, but not a planter. In English the word planter includes also persons who only buy plants.
43 82	Market gardeners ... ... Vegetable sellers	Kunjrás almost invariably both grow and sell vegetables. Koeris generally both grow and sell.
44 169	Gardeners, seeds-men (Baghban) ... ... Flower garland makers and sellers	The occupations both belong to the mali.
50 60 339	Managers of landed estates ... ... Door-keepers, &c. ... ... Messengers, unspecified	"Sipahi" is the general term for the Subordinate Collector of rent, the door-keeper in a land holder's house and the messenger. Sipahi zamindár I have classed under 50. Fauj talukdár in 60. Sipahi in 339.
234	Gold and silver workers	Boring for ear-rings is a "jaj-mani" of sunars. So that the imperial heading ear-borers does not occur in these provinces.
56 329 58	Water carriers ... ... Palki, &c., bearers ... ... Indoor servants	Pani bharna goes under 56, kahari under 329, khidmatgár under 58. It is absolutely a chance which word is entered in the schedules. Kahari is a general term which includes all three occupations.
57 80 58	Cooks ... ... Baker ... ... Indoor servant	Khana pakana, roti pakana under 57. Nanbai under 80. Khidmatgár under 58, but may for Muhammadans mean cook; bawarchi has been classed in 57, which includes the heading in the imperial table of dealers in cooked food.
73 74 335	Fishermen and fish curers ... ... Fish dealers ... ... Boatmen	The first two are absolutely the same. They are apt to affect 335.
75 77	Grain dealers ... ... Pulse and flour preparers and sellers	Anaj. Ata dal. Parchun. } Bechna. } All are corresponding terms, but the distinction is neither clear nor well observed.
83 86 100	Fruit sellers, (mewa farosh) ... ... Sweetmeat pedlars (khwanche wale) ... ... Grocers and general condiment dealers	All sell cocoanuts. The entry "naryal bechna" would probably mean "hukka" sellers.
84 85	Confectioners and sweetmeat sellers ... ... Sweetmeat pedlars	84 swallows up 85. In many districts cooks who are also fishermen, &c. are unknown.
89 91	Country spirit distillers and sellers ... ... Foreign wine and spirit dealers	91 is swallowed up in 89, for want of specification in schedules. All spirit licenses are "thekas," and "thekadar" is the word in use for a farmer, so that farmers of liquor, Opium, &c., cannot be shown as a separate class.
95 96	Sugar manufactures and sellers ... ... Molasses, &c., sellers	There is no line of distinction. The sugar manufacturer also sells the molasses.

APPENDIX XXXI.

Showing the occupations which are likely to be confused with each other in the Census Schedules—(continued).

Number of occupation in table.	Name of occupation.	Remarks.
100	General condiment dealers	Assafœtida selling shown in imperial scheme does not exist as a separate occupation.
98	Venegar sellers	Sirka bechna. / Achar bechna. Go together and it is an accident which entry is made.
99	Pickle sellers	
106	Oil pressers and sellers	Are the same.
107	Oil cake sellers	
110	Kerosine oil sellers	Not usual as a separate occupation. Pansaries and purchanies sell kerosine oil.
109	Torch makers and sellers	The word mashalchi will generally mean an indoor servant who with hindustanies looks after the lamps, and with English people washes dishes.
68	Indoor servants	
114	Firewood and grass gatherers	"Indhan" applies both to cowdung and small firewood. All the occupations given are intermixed in the vernacular terms usually employed.
115	Firewood dealers	
117	Cowdung preparers and sellers	
122	Thatch dealers	
118	Hay contractors	
262	Timber and bamboo dealers	
119	Brick and tile burners	Tiles are made and burnt by kumhars, and 259 includes tile makers for the most part. The most common toy is of earthenware, and 259 includes many persons who might come under 155.
259	Potters	
120	Tilers and Tile-turners	
155	Toy makers	
121	Stone quarry owners, &c.	The only stone at all general is kankar. Kankar diggers along with tank diggers and road labourers are often entered as general labourers.
402	Tank diggers	
403	Road labourers	
406	General labourers	
124	Stone workers	124 is apt to include 260 altogether, and all makers of stone mortars.
260	Grind stone and mill stone makers	
261	Pestle and mortar makers	
125	Masons	Raj or memar is the usual word for the person who does both brick-work and plastering.
126	Plasterers	
127	Mud-wall and roof makers	406 includes in common parlance the other two.
406	General labourers	
402	Tank diggers	
132	Cart and carriage makers	251 and 264 include part of the population belonging to 132. The only part of cart making regarded as a special trade is the wheel making.
251	Blacksmiths	
264	Carpenters	
180	Agricultural implement makers	180 loses to both the others.
251	Blacksmiths	
264	Carpenters	
268	Chik (screen) makers	"Pal banana" applies to both sail making and chik (screen) making. Boatmen are almost invariably their own sail makers, and this occupation does not occur. Ordinary tailors occasionally make sails.
137	Paper makers	Stationer as a separate occupation does not exist. Paper and ink is usually sold by bisaties, and pens by Booksellers.
138	Stationers	
150	Turners	All usually come under the general name of Barhai.
263	Wood cutters	
264	Carpenters	
265	Coopers and box makers	
170	Artificial flower makers	Are the same. The atish-baz is the professional tazia maker. Artificial flowers and tazias are also made by the persons who wish to use them. The latter are rarely made for sale.
189	Fireworks makers	
169	Tazia makers	
163	Lac Bangle makers	The general term "churi banana" usually occurs, and has been included in 165. The churihar or manihar also fits on the bangles, so that bangle fitting does not occur as a separate occupation.
165	Glass Bangle makers	
187	Ammunition dealers	187 is apt to include 188 and 189. The atish-baz and the gunpowder maker are the same.
188	Gunpowder makers and sellers	
189	Fireworks makers	

APPENDIX XXXI.

Showing the occupations which are likely to be confused with each other in the Census Schedules—(concluded).

Number of occupation in table.	Name of occupation.	Remarks.
207 216 211 212	Braid and ribbon makers ... ... Tape makers ... ... Cotton spinners ... ... Cotton weavers	The general word is fita banana. The work is done by the same man, except as a domestic trade.
217	Tent manufacturers	Not now recognized as a separate trade. Tent makers are included under 223 tailors in general. Khemadoz now exists as a caste, but not as a profession.
219 220 221	Hemp rope makers... ... ... Sacking, &c. makers ... ... Net makers	All run into each other. In country districts, ropes and tát are mostly made by the cultivators. Kanjars also make ropes. Nets are made by fishermen.
226	Hosiers	This is a branch of the universal "bisat-khana" 310.
233 234	Gold and silver dealers ... ... Gold and silver workers	233 is rare apart from 234. Gold assaying does not occur apart from either of the others.
244	General workers in brass, copper, &c.	No one has entered himself as a worker in brass only, or copper only. The usual metal is an alloy, and in general a man works in brass, copper or alloy as required.
266 267	Basket weavers, &c. ... ... Mat makers	These entries cross and cannot be distinguished.
269	Leaf plate makers	This is done usually by the Bari khidmatgár.
275 276 277 279	Collectors of forest produce	The same man may do all.
280 373	Chemists ... ... Dispensary service	May be confused.
292 293 294 295 296	Tanners, curriers and hide sellers ... Shoe makers ... ... Leather dyers ... ... Water bag makers ... ... Hide and horn dealers	These are all in general the occupations of chamars, and proper specification under the different heads is impossible.
300 301	Bankers ... ... Bill discounters	No distinct line of demarcation is recognized.
306 307 308	Merchants' clerks ... ... Shop keepers' clerks ... ... Shop keepers' servants	The general word Saudagar applies to all, and dukan to the wholesale warehouse, as much as to the parchuni shop.
342	Porters	Is little recognized as a separate occupation, most are under general labourers.
361 356 363	Lawyers' clerks ... ... Public scribes ... ... Petition writers	All cross.
365	Practitioners by diploma	Is often blank—may have gone into 366 under the translation "Hikmat karna".
395 396 397	Exhibitors of puppets (kat putli) ... ... Conjurers and fortune tellers ... ... Acrobats	"Nats" do all and are likely to enter bazigar as a general term.
401 402 406	Well sinkers ... ... Tank diggers ... ... General labour	Are apt to cross. Between 401 and 402 there is no permanent distinction.
405 406	Rice pounding ... ... General labour	405 looses to 406. Rice pounding is usually a domestic occupation. In all cases it is a temporary occupation only likely to occur in the new rice season.

APPENDIX XXXII.

howing the proportion of population dependent on each class, order and sub-order of occupations and the proportion in towns for each class.

Class.	Order.	Sub-order.	Total. Population.	Total. Per 10,000 of total population	Town. Population.	Town. Percentage of town to total population.
		1. Service of the Imperial and Provincial Governments.	386,986	83		
		2. Service of local and municipal bodies ...	15,174	3		
		3. Village service	440,837	94		
	1	Administration	842,997	180	245,154	29·08
		4 Army	72,460	15		
		5. Navy and marine	...	...		
	2	Defence	72,460	15	51,694	71·34
		6. Administrative service	11,057	2		
		7. Army and marine	147	...		
	3	Foreign and Feudatory state service ...	11,204	2	4,873	43·49
A ...	...	Government	926,661	197	301,721	32·56
		8. Stock breeding and dealing	377,247	81		
		9. Subsidiary services to stock	14,533	3		
	4	Live stock	391,780	84	48,304	3·26
		10. Interest in land...	25,036,230	5,337		
		11. Agricultural labourers	30,06,785	641		
		12. Growers of special products and trees ...	130,347	28		
		13. Agricultural training and supervision ...	347,755	75		
	5	Agriculture	28,521,117	6081	1,013,452	3·55
B ...	...	Pasture and Agriculture	28,912,897	6,165	1,061,756	3·67
		14. Personal and domestic services ...	2,205,162	470		
		15. Non-domestic establishment ...	10,879	2		
		16. Sanitation	319,592	68		
	6	Personal, house-hold and sanitary services ...	2,535,633	540	618,424	24·39
C ...	...	Personal services	2,535,633	540	618,424	24·39
		17. Animal food	280,328	60		
		18. Vegetable food	1,625,324	347		
		19. Drink, condiments and narcotics ...	391,009	83		
	7	Food and Drink, &c.	2,296,661	490	968,147	29·96
		20. Lighting	570,134	122		
		21. Fuel and forage...	200,730	43		
	8	Light, Firing and forage	770,864	165	137,783	17·87

APPENDIX XXXII.

Showing the proportion of population dependent on each class, order and sub-order of occupations and the proportion in towns for each class—(continued).

Class.	Order.	Sub-order.	Total. Population.	Total. Per 10,000 of total population.	Town. Population.	Town. Percentage of town to total population.
		22. Building materials	29,200	6		
		23. Artificers in building	120,262	26		
	9	Buildings	149,462	32	88,467	59·19
		24. Railway plapt	1,109	...		
		25. Carts, carriages, &c.	13,714	3		
		26. Slips and boats	263	...		
	10	Vehicles and vessels	15,086	3	10,032	66·50
		27. Paper, &c.	2,994	1		
		28. Books and prints, &c.	12,104	3		
		29. Watches, clocks and scientific instruments	1,720	...		
		30. Carving, engraving, &c.	2,982	1		
		31. Toys, curiosities, &c.	11,166	2		
		32. Music and musical instruments ...	1,079	...		
		33 Necklaces, bracelets, beads, sacred theads, &c.	190,617	41		
		34. Furniture	2,332	...		
		35. Harness	3,847	1		
		36. Tools and machinery	67,301	4		
		37. Arms and ammunition	11,444	2		
	11	Supplementary requirements	307,586	65	97,950	31·84
		38. Wool and Fur	79,115	17		
		39. Silk	14,936	3		
		40. Cotton	1,524,739	325		
		41. Jut, flax, coir, &c, ...	46,892	10		
		42. Dress	524,502	111		
	12	Textile fabrics and dress	2,190,184	466	546,699	24·96
		43. Gold, silver and precious stones ...	248,686	53		
		44. Brass, copper and bell metal ...	56,495	12		
		45. Tin, zinc, mercury and lead... ...	9,391	2		
		46. Iron and steel	328,939	70		
	13	Metals and precious stones	643,511	137	169,698	26·37
		47. Glass and chinaware	1,561	...		
		48. Earthen and stoneware	471,265	101		
	14	Glass pottery and stoneware	472,826	101	52,125	13·88
		49. Timber and wood	425,711	91		
		50. Cane work, matting and leaves ...	205,405	44		
	15	Wood, cane and leaves	631,116	135	93,950	14·88
		51. Gums wax and similar forest produce ...	12,286	3		
		52. Drugs, dyes, pigments, &c.	47,404	10		
	16	Drugs, gums, dyes, &c.	59,690	13	19,902	33·34

APPENDIX XXXII.

Showing the proportion of population dependent on each class, order and sub-order of occupations and the proportion in towns for each class—(concluded).

Class.	Order.	Sub-order.	Total. Population.	Total. Per 10,000 of total population.	Town. Population.	Town. Percentage of town to total population.
		53. Leather, &c.	861,783	77		
	17	Leather, horns, bones and grease	861,783	77	98,071	27·10
D ...	...	Preparation and supply of material substances ...	7,898,769	1,684	2,002,824	25·35
		54. Dealers in money and securities ...	238,571	51		
		55. General merchandise	20,015	4		
		56. Dealings unspecified	133,920	29		
		57. Middlemen	91,163	19		
	18	Commerce	483,669	103	186,486	38·55
		58. Railway	55,941	12		
		59. Road	462,647	98		
		60. Water	43,170	9		
		61. Messages	45,196	10		
		62. Storage and weighing	81,552	18		
	19	Transport and storage	688,506	147	206,262	29·95
E ...	...	Commerce, transport, storage	1,172,175	250	392,748	33·50
		63. Religion	412,449	88		
		64. Education	63,478	14		
		65. Literature	15,464	3		
		66. Law	40,589	9		
		67. Medicine	59,393	12		
		68. Engineering and surveying	10,488	2		
		69. Other sciences	78,278	17		
		70. Pictorial art and sculpture	535	...		
		71. Music, acting, dancing	88,777	19		
	20	Learned and artistic professions	769,454	164	297,189	38·62
		72. Sport	9,387	2		
		73. Exhibition and games	8,444	2		
	21	Sport and amusements	17,831	4	4,547	25·50
F ...	...	Professions	787,285	168	301,736	38·32
		74. Unskilled labour	3,959,896	844		
		75. Undefined, &c.	21,388	5		
	23	Indefinite	3,981,284	849	484,534	12·17
		76. Property and alms	595,527	127		
		77. Supported at the public charge ...	94,854	20		
	24	Independent of work	690,381	147	150,585	21·81
G ...	...	Indefinite and Independent	4,671,665	996	635,119	13·59
		TOTAL, NORTH-WESTERN PROVINCES AND OUDH,	46,905,085	10,000	5,314,328	11·34

APPENDIX XXXIII.

Showing the age distribution of the various classes of occupations.

Class.	Total.				Males.				Females.			
	0—4 years.	5—14 years.	15 years and over.	Total.	0—4 years.	5—14 years.	15 years and over.	Total.	0—4 years.	5—14 years.	15 years and over.	Total.
A.—Government	1,301	2,118	6,581	10,000	1,143	1,998	6,859	10,000	1,511	2,277	6,212	10,000
B.—Pasture and agriculture	1,392	2,427	6,181	10,000	1,321	2,557	6,122	10,000	1,468	2,285	6,247	10,000
C.—Personal services	1,339	2,276	6,385	10,000	1,275	2,384	6,341	10,000	1,411	2,157	6,432	10,000
D.—Preparation and supply of material substances ...	1,351	2,272	6,377	10,000	1,327	2,417	6,256	10,000	1,377	2,125	6,498	10,000
E.—Commerce, transport, storage	1,378	2,151	6,471	10,000	1,388	2,142	6,520	10,000	1,428	2,167	6,405	10,000
F.—Professions	1,134	2,071	6,795	10,000	1,090	2,161	6,749	10,000	1,182	1,974	6,844	10,000
G.—Indefinite and independent	1,335	2,362	6,303	10,000	1,284	2,542	6,174	10,000	1,388	2,173	6,439	10,000
TOTAL, POPULATION ...	1,370	2,367	6,263	10,000	1,308	2,494	6,198	10,000	1,436	2,231	6,333	10,000

APPENDIX XXXIV.

Showing the proportion to divisional populations of the population of the classes.

Divisions.	Class A. Government.	Class B. Pasture and agriculture.	Class C. Personal services.	Class D. Preparation and supply of material substances.	Class E. Commerce, transport, storage.	Class F. Professions.	Class G. Indefinite and independent.	Total.
Meerut Division	1·95	48·89	9·36	22·19	2·75	2·51	12·85	100
Agra Division	2·13	56·33	6·58	19·84	3·01	2·56	9·55	100
Rohilkhand Division	2·07	59·90	6·18	20·73	2·31	1·85	9·96	100
Allahabad Division	2·53	58·60	5·05	18·14	2·27	1·79	11·62	100
Benares Division	1·44	63·83	3·67	15·45	2·62	1·32	11·67	100
Gorakhpur Division	1·66	67·93	4·11	13·65	2·11	·76	9·78	100
Kumaun Division	·89	83·71	2·16	6·49	·90	·80	5·05	100
North-Western Provinces	1·92	60·36	5·62	17.74	2·43	1·71	10·22	100
Lucknow Division	2·42	64·10	5·47	14·97	2·58	2·00	8·46	100
Fyzabad Division	1·88	65·99	4·29	13·94	2·77	1·22	9·91	100
Oudh	2·13	65·12	4·83	14·41	2·69	1·58	9·24	100
North-Western Provinces and Oudh	1·97	61·64	5·40	16·85	2·50	1·68	9·96	100

PROVINCIAL TABLE I.

SHOWING THE VARIATIONS IN THE POPULATION OF THE TAHSILS SINCE THE PREVIOUS CENSUS.

The variations in the population of the

PROVINCIAL TABLE I.

Serial number of district.	Name of district.	Serial number of tahsíl.	Name of tahsíl.	Total. Census, 1881.	Total. Census, 1891.	Total. Increase + or decrease −.
1	2	3	4	5	6	7
1	Dehra Dún ...	1	Dehra	98,953	117,438	+18,485
		2	Kalsi	45,117	50,697	+5,580
			Total ...	144,070	168,135	+24,065
2	Sahâranpur ...	3	Sahâranpur	292,293	312,498	+20,205
		4	Deoband	211,058	205,627	−5,431
		5	Roorkee	274,571	290,498	+15,927
		6	Nukúr	201,622	192,657	−8,965
			Total ...	979,544	1,001,280	+21,736
3	Muzaffarnagar ...	7	Muzaffarnagar	202,707	206,496	+3,789
		8	Kairána	202,233	200,157	−2,076
		9	Jánsath	183,854	193,533	+9,679
		10	Burhana	169,650	172,688	+3,038
			Total ...	758,444	772,874	+14,430
4	Meerut ...	11	Meerut	291,170	326,054	+34,884
		12	Ghâziabad	244,815	247,141	+2,326
		13	Mowána	159,832	177,868	+18,036
		14	Bâghpat	258,000	259,656	+1,656
		15	Sardhana	159,422	168,692	+9,270
		16	Hápur	199,898	212,047	+12,149
			Total ...	1,313,137	1,391,458	+78,321
5	Bulandshahr ...	17	Anúpshahr	213,294	222,481	+9,187
		18	Bulandshahr	262,901	281,928	+19,027
		19	Sikandarabad	236,066	224,368	−11,698
		20	Khúrja	212,561	221,137	+8,576
			Total ...	924,822	949,914	+25,092
6	Aligarh ...	21	Atrauli	146,536	164,073	+17,537
		22	Aligarh	227,654	229,767	+2,113
		23	Iglas	111,379	107,227	−4,152
		24	Khair	160,264	150,658	−9,606
		25	Háthras	199,481	208,264	+8,783
		26	Sikandra Rao	175,873	183,185	+7,312
			Total ...	1,021,187	1,043,172	+21,985
7	Muttra ...	27	Muttra (Sadar)	220,307	234,914	+14,607
		28	Chháta	84,598	93,243	+8,645
		29	Kosi	65,293	60,222	−5,071
		30	Mát	95,446	89,451	−5,995
		31	Mahaban	116,829	133,488	+16,659
		32	Sadabad	89,217	102,103	+12,886
			Total ...	671,690	713,421	+41,731
8	Agra ...	33	Etmádpur	141,267	153,761	+12,494
		34	Firozabad	108,521	112,153	+3,632
		35	Bah	120,529	125,848	+5,319
		36	Fatehabad	104,762	108,446	+3,684
		37	Agra (Sadar)	266,765	272,718	+5,953
		38	Keraoli	114,678	106,977	−7,701
		39	Kheragarh	118,134	123,893	+5,759
			Total ...	974,656	1,003,796	+29,140
9	Farukhabad ...	40	Kanauj	114,912	117,229	+2,317
		41	Tirwa	171,546	168,673	−2,873
		42	Chibramau	122,782	111,114	−11,668
		43	Farukhabad (Sadar) ...	255,127	244,896	−10,231
		44	Káimganj	167,156	143,557	−23,599
		45	Aligarh	76,085	73,218	−2,867
			Total ...	907,608	858,687	−48,921

Tahsíls since the previous Census.

PROVINCIAL. TABLE I.

Males.			Females.			Serial number of tahsíl.
Census, 1881.	Census, 1891.	Increase + or decrease –.	Census, 1881.	Census, 1891.	Increase + or decrease –.	
8	9	10	11	12	13	14
58,585	71,889	+13,304	40,368	45,549	+5,181	1
25,400	28,435	+3,035	19,717	22,262	+2,545	2
83,985	100,324	+16,339	60,085	67,811	+7,726	
155,318	165,426	+10,108	136,975	147,072	+10,097	3
115,347	112,685	–2,662	95,711	92,942	–2,769	4
151,524	159,227	+7,703	123,047	131,271	+8,224	5
108,238	103,013	–5,225	93,384	89,644	–3,740	6
530,427	540,351	+9,924	449,117	460,929	+11,812	
110,864	113,613	+2,749	91,843	92,883	+1,040	7
108,479	107,701	–778	93,754	92,456	–1,298	8
98,677	103,922	+5,245	85,177	89,611	+4,434	9
91,416	92,992	+1,576	78,234	79,696	+1,462	10
409,436	418,228	+8,792	349,008	354,646	+5,638	
158,590	178,105	+19,515	132,580	147,949	+15,369	11
131,400	132,078	+678	113,415	115,063	+1,648	12
85,575	94,317	+8,742	74,257	83,551	+9,294	13
138,603	140,303	+1,700	119,397	119,353	–44	14
85,855	90,539	+4,684	73,567	78,153	+4,586	15
105,414	111,902	+6,488	94,484	100,145	+5,661	16
705,437	747,244	+41,807	607,700	644,214	+36,514	
112,625	117,271	+4,646	100,669	105,210	+4,541	17
139,175	148,045	+8,870	123,726	133,883	+10,157	18
127,442	119,878	–7,564	108,624	104,490	–4,134	19
112,716	116,427	+3,711	99,845	104,710	+4,865	20
491,958	501,621	+9,663	432,864	448,293	+15,429	
79,116	87,644	+8,528	67,420	76,429	+9,009	21
123,029	122,475	–554	104,625	107,292	+2,667	22
60,319	57,628	–2,691	51,060	49,599	–1,461	23
85,607	80,138	–5,469	74,657	70,518	–4,139	24
107,109	111,709	+4,600	92,372	96,555	+4,183	25
96,099	99,149	+3,050	79,774	84,036	+4,262	26
551,279	558,743	+7,464	469,908	484,429	+14,521	
117,905	125,990	+8,085	102,402	108,924	+6,522	27
44,985	49,672	+4,687	39,613	43,571	+3,958	28
34,002	31,738	–2,264	31,291	28,484	–2,807	29
50,978	47,407	–3,571	44,468	42,044	–2,424	30
64,037	72,319	+8,282	52,792	61,169	+8,377	31
49,060	55,534	+6,474	40,157	46,569	+6,412	32
360,967	382,660	+21,693	310,723	330,761	+20,038	
77,137	83,200	+6,063	64,130	70,561	+6,431	33
59,287	60,292	+1,005	49,234	51,861	+2,627	34
63,524	66,937	+3,413	57,005	58,911	+1,906	35
56,835	58,744	+1,909	47,927	49,702	+1,775	36
144,267	146,817	+2,550	122,498	125,901	+3,403	37
61,596	57,667	–3,920	53,082	49,310	–3,772	38
64,155	66,802	+2,647	53,979	57,091	+3,112	39
526,801	540,459	+13,658	447,855	463,337	+15,482	
61,970	62,642	+672	52,942	54,587	+1,645	40
94,541	92,332	–2,209	77,005	76,341	–664	41
66,617	60,159	–6,458	56,165	50,955	–5,210	42
136,417	131,858	–4,559	118,710	113,038	–5,672	43
88,779	76,836	–11,943	78,377	66,721	–11,656	44
42,184	40,513	–1,671	33,901	32,705	–1,196	45
490,508	464,340	–26,168	417,100	394,347	–22,753	

The variations in the population of the

PROVINCIAL TABLE I.

Serial number of district.	Name of district.	Serial number of tahsíl.	Name of tahsíl.	Total. Census, 1881.	Census, 1891.	Increase + or decrease —.
1	2	3	4	5	6	7
10	Mainpuri	46	Mainpuri	183,334	171,152	—12,182
		47	Bhongaon	210,768	195,368	—15,400
		48	Karhal	100,031	100,297	+266
		49	Shikohabad	144,882	140,093	—4,789
		50	Mustafabad	162,201	155,253	—6,948
			Total	801,216	762,163	—39,053
11	Etáwah	51	Etáwah	193,211	198,023	+4,812
		52	Bharthna	161,446	169,979	+8,533
		53	Bidbuna	138,149	134,459	—3,690
		54	Phaphúnd	111,585	107,307	—4,278
		55	Auraiya	117,980	117,861	—119
			Total	722,371	727,629	+5,258
12	Etah	56	Etah	226,892	227,030	+138
		57	Kásganj	216,646	192,009	—24,637
		58	Aliganj	193,800	161,994	—31,806
		59	Jalesar	118,925	121,030	+2,105
			Total	756,263	702,063	—54,200
13	Bareilly	60	Farídpur	111,141	119,805	+8,664
		61	Bareilly	285,731	298,482	+12,751
		62	Aonla	197,636	195,950	—1,686
		63	Mírganj	100,939	95,300	—5,639
		64	Baheri	218,487	206,805	—11,682
		65	Nawábganj	117,002	124,349	+7,347
			Total	1,030,936	1,040,691	+9,755
14	Bijnor	66	Bijnor	124,096	133,887	+9,791
		67	Najibabad	133,561	156,873	+23,312
		68	Nagína	170,075	183,147	+13,072
		69	Dhámpur	170,039	181,988	+11,949
		70	Chándpur	123,679	138,175	+14,496
			Total	721,450	794,070	+72,620
15	Budaun	71	Gunnaur	117,535	126,388	+8,853
		72	Bisauli	187,658	183,640	—4,018
		73	Sahaswán	192,391	192,989	+598
		74	Budaun	222,312	226,673	+4,361
		75	Dátaganj	185,876	195,908	+10,032
			Total	905,772	925,598	+19,826
16	Moradabad	76	Moradabad	231,863	240,795	+8,932
		77	Thákurdwára	109,596	121,174	+11,578
		78	Bilári	229,784	231,947	+2,163
		79	Sambhal	248,107	245,619	—2,488
		80	Amroha	174,014	186,183	+12,169
		81	Hasanpur	161,809	153,680	—8,129
			Total	1,155,173	1,179,398	+24,225
17	Sháhjahánpur	82	Sháhjahánpur	252,028	273,146	+21,118
		83	Jalálabad	145,915	159,392	+13,477
		84	Tilhar	214,488	236,791	+22,303
		85	Powáyan	245,454	249,222	+3,768
			Total	857,885	918,551	+60,666
18	Pilibhít	86	Bisalpur	179,350	190,864	+11,514
		87	Pilibhít	183,344	199,297	+15,953
		88	Puranpur	88,907	95,205	+6,298
			Total	451,601	485,366	+33,765

Tahsils since the previous Census.

PROVINCIAL TABLE I.

Males.			Females.			Serial number of tahsil.
Census, 1881.	Census, 1891.	Increase + or decrease —.	Census, 1881.	Census, 1891.	Increase + or decrease —.	
8	9	10	11	12	13	14
101,783	93,782	—8,001	81,551	77,370	—4,181	46
116,391	107,109	—9,282	94,377	88,259	—6,118	47
55,720	54,675	—1,045	44,311	45,622	+1,311	48
79,316	76,477	—2,839	65,566	63,616	—1,950	49
88,884	84,756	—4,128	73,317	70,497	—2,820	50
442,094	416,799	—25,295	359,122	345,364	—13,758	
105,319	107,503	+2,184	87,892	90,520	+2,628	51
88,736	92,857	+4,121	72,710	77,122	+4,412	52
76,275	73,926	—2,349	61,874	60,533	—1,341	53
61,193	58,644	—2,549	50,392	48,663	—1,729	54
63,701	63,845	+144	54,279	54,016	—263	55
395,224	396,775	+1,551	327,147	330,854	+3,707	
125,298	123,468	—1,830	101,594	103,562	+1,968	56
117,769	105,106	—12,663	98,877	86,903	—11,974	57
105,801	89,060	—16,741	87,999	72,934	—15,065	58
64,672	65,569	+897	54,253	55,461	+1,208	59
413,540	383,203	—30,337	342,723	318,860	—23,863	
60,254	65,453	+5,199	50,887	54,352	+3,465	60
152,341	160,805	+8,464	133,390	137,677	+4,287	61
104,433	103,903	—530	93,203	92,047	—1,156	62
52,907	49,750	—3,157	48,032	45,550	—2,482	63
115,144	108,982	—6,162	103,343	97,823	—5,520	64
62,931	66,587	+3,656	54,071	57,762	+3,691	65
548,010	555,480	+7,470	482,926	485,211	+2,285	
66,179	71,310	+5,181	57,917	62,577	+4,660	66
71,678	82,135	+10,457	61,883	74,738	+12,855	67
90,554	96,156	+5,602	79,521	86,991	+7,470	68
89,190	95,475	+6,285	80,849	86,513	+5,664	69
65,657	73,136	+7,479	58,022	65,039	+7,017	70
383,258	418,212	+34,954	338,192	375,858	+37,666	
63,665	68,478	+4,813	53,870	57,910	+4,040	71
99,988	98,563	—1,425	87,670	85,077	—2,593	72
104,010	104,180	+170	88,381	88,809	+428	73
118,218	120,297	+2,079	104,094	106,376	+2,282	74
101,106	106,616	+5,510	84,770	89,292	+4,522	75
486,987	498,134	+11,147	418,785	427,464	+8,679	
121,656	126,025	+4,369	110,207	114,770	+4,563	76
58,559	64,268	+5,709	51,037	56,906	+5,869	77
121,434	123,416	+1,982	108,350	108,531	+181	78
130,441	129,303	—1,138	117,666	116,316	—1,350	79
90,845	97,811	+6,966	83,169	88,372	+5,203	80
87,356	82,749	—4,607	74,453	70,931	—3,522	81
610,291	623,572	+13,281	544,882	555,826	+10,944	
133,206	144,664	+11,458	118,822	128,482	+9,660	82
79,990	87,392	+7,402	65,925	72,000	+6,075	83
116,160	128,783	+12,623	98,328	108,008	+9,680	84
131,221	134,467	+3,246	114,233	114,755	+522	85
460,577	495,306	+34,729	397,308	423,245	+25,937	
96,158	102,602	+6,444	83,192	88,262	+5,070	86
96,111	104,764	+8,653	87,233	94,533	+7,300	87
47,518	51,036	+3,518	41,389	44,169	+2,780	88
239,787	258,402	+18,615	211,814	226,964	+15,150	

The variations in the population of the

PROVINCIAL TABLE I.

Serial number of district.	Name of district.	Serial number of tahsíl.	Name of tahsíl.	Total. Census, 1881.	Total. Census, 1891.	Total. Increase + or decrease —.
1	2	3	4	5	6	7
19	Cawnpore ...	89	Akbarpur	109,910	102,256	—7,654
		90	Bilhaur	100,654	100,051	—603
		91	Bhognipur	88,081	96,575	+8,494
		92	Cawnpore	289,333	324,628	+35,295
		93	Derapur	124,746	122,244	—2,502
		94	Rasúlabad	102,168	99,537	—2,631
		95	Narwal	101,830	98,784	—3,046
		96	Shiurájpur	150,728	147,823	—2,905
		97	Ghátampur	113,946	117,797	+3,851
			Total ...	1,181,396	1,209,695	+28,299
20	Fatehpur ...	98	Fatehpur	177,596	175,452	—2,144
		99	Kalianpur	119,182	118,786	—396
		100	Kora	81,164	87,925	+6,761
		101	Gházipur	90,170	92,389	+2,219
		102	Khakhreru	78,686	86,525	+7,839
		103	Khaga	136,947	138,080	+1,133
			Total ...	683,745	699,157	+15,412
21	Bánda ...	104	Bánda	120,578	112,912	—7,666
		105	Pailani	83,033	88,544	+5,511
		106	Baberu	85,229	96,284	+11,055
		107	Kamasin	81,238	83,297	+2,059
		108	Mau	74,622	73,658	—964
		109	Karwi	85,318	87,687	+2,369
		110	Badausa	79,939	77,922	—2,017
		111	Girwan	88,651	85,528	—3,123
			Total ...	698,608	705,832	+7,224
22	Hamírpur ...	112	Hamírpur	75,398	81,133	+5,735
		113	Muskara	79,817	75,735	—4,082
		114	Ráth	106,013	97,862	—8,151
		115	Kulpahar	125,578	127,567	+1,989
		116	Mahoba	70,626	74,200	+3,574
		117	Maudha	49,905	57,223	+7,318
			Total ...	507,337	513,720	+6,383
23	Allahabad ...	118	Allahabad	318,059	342,446	+24,387
		119	Sirathu	123,386	129,932	+6,546
		120	Manjhanpur	120,283	131,688	+11,405
		121	Soraon	184,894	186,876	+1,982
		122	Phúlpur	173,001	176,851	+3,850
		123	Handia	184,754	187,089	+2,335
		124	Ḳarchhana	124,094	134,818	+10,724
		125	Bara	53,430	63,816	+10,386
		126	Meja	192,205	195,221	+3,016
			Total ...	1,474,106	1,548,737	+74,631
24	Jhánsi ...	127	Jhánsi	113,058	145,680	+32,622
		128	Mau	107,151	115,724	+8,573
		129	Garotha	87,897	88,926	+1,029
		130	Moth	56,755	59,089	+2,334
		131	Lalitpur	138,516	157,153	+18,637
		132	Mehroni	110,572	117,047	+6,475
			Total ...	613,949	683,619	+69,670
25	Jalaun ...	133	Orai	72,380	67,702	—4,678
		134	Kálpi	82,003	78,754	—3,249
		135	Jalann	161,916	147,090	—14,826
		136	Kúnch	101,843	102,815	+972
			Total ...	418,142	396,361	—21,781

PROVINCIAL TABLE I.

Tahsíls since the previous Census.

Males.			Females.			Serial number of tahsíl.
Census, 1881.	Census, 1891.	Increase + or decrease —.	Census, 1881.	Census, 1891.	Increase + or decrease —.	
8	9	10	11	12	13	14
59,235	54,887	—4,348	50,675	47,369	—3,306	89
54,617	53,675	—942	46,037	46,376	+339	90
44,536	50,846	+6,310	43,545	45,729	+2,184	91
159,063	178,830	+19,767	130,270	145,798	+15,528	92
66,285	65,345	—940	58,461	56,899	—1,562	93
55,342	54,117	—1,225	46,826	45,420	—1,406	94
52,492	51,261	—1,231	49,338	47,523	—1,815	95
79,485	77,763	—1,722	71,243	70,060	—1,183	96
57,836	61,368	+3,532	56,110	56,429	+319	97
628,891	648,092	+19,201	552,505	561,603	+9,098	
90,959	90,183	—776	86,637	85,269	—1,368	98
61,416	62,017	+601	57,766	56,769	—997	99
40,898	45,299	+4,401	40,266	42,626	+2,360	100
46,318	48,119	+1,801	43,852	44,270	+418	101
39,284	44,075	+4,791	39,402	42,450	+3,048	102
68,712	70,128	+1,416	68,235	67,952	—283	103
347,587	359,821	+12,234	336,158	339,336	+3,178	
62,233	56,942	—5,291	58,345	55,970	—2,375	104
42,147	45,350	+3,203	40,886	43,194	+2,308	105
41,917	47,961	+6,044	43,312	48,323	+5,011	106
41,346	42,317	+971	39,892	40,980	+1,088	107
37,948	37,506	—442	36,674	36,152	—522	108
43,702	44,506	+804	41,616	43,181	+1,565	109
40,526	39,255	—1,271	39,413	38,667	—746	110
44,558	43,057	—1,501	44,093	42,471	—1,622	111
354,377	356,894	+2,517	344,231	348,938	+4,707	
37,936	42,018	+4,082	37,462	39,115	+1,653	112
41,396	38,538	—2,858	38,421	37,197	—1,224	113
54,147	48,799	—5,348	51,866	49,063	—2,803	114
64,468	64,647	+179	61,110	62,920	+1,810	115
36,518	37,770	+1,252	34,108	36,430	+2,322	116
25,313	28,831	+3,518	24,592	28,392	+3,800	117
259,778	260,603	+825	247,559	253,117	+5,558	
162,947	176,851	+13,904	155,112	165,595	+10,483	118
61,728	65,431	+3,703	61,658	64,501	+2,843	119
60,216	66,925	+6,709	60,067	64,763	+4,696	120
90,867	90,801	—66	94,027	96,075	+2,048	121
86,221	87,701	+1,480	86,780	89,150	+2,370	122
93,664	94,126	+462	91,090	92,963	+1,873	123
62,698	68,961	+6,263	61,396	65,857	+4,461	124
26,928	32,651	+5,723	26,502	31,165	+4,663	125
96,461	98,062	+1,601	95,744	97,159	+1,415	126
741,730	781,509	+39,779	732,376	767,228	+34,852	
59,388	79,788	+20,400	53,670	65,892	+12,222	127
54,931	59,003	+4,072	52,220	56,721	+4,501	128
45,591	45,618	+27	42,306	43,308	+1,002	129
28,950	30,119	+1,169	27,805	28,970	+1,165	130
72,606	81,768	+9,162	65,910	75,385	+9,475	131
57,193	59,668	+2,475	53,379	57,379	+4,000	132
318,659	355,964	+37,305	295,290	327,655	+32,365	
37,176	34,621	—2,555	35,204	33,081	—2,123	133
41,690	40,521	—1,169	40,313	38,233	—2,080	134
85,092	76,148	—8,944	76,824	70,942	—5,882	135
52,187	52,800	+613	49,656	50,015	+359	136
216,145	204,090	—12,055	201,997	192,271	—9,726	

The variations in the population of the

PROVINCIAL TABLE I.

Serial number of district.	Name of district.	Serial number of tahsíl.	Name of tahsíl.	Total. Census, 1881.	Census, 1891.	Increase + or decrease —.
1	2	3	4	5	6	7
26	Benares ...	137	Benares	562,518	580,467	+17,954
		138	Gangapur	89,473	89,934	+461
		139	Chandauli	240,698	251,542	+10,844
			Total ...	892,684	921,943	+29,259
27	Mirzapur ...	140	Mirzapur	377,331	372,015	—5,316
		141	Chunár	182,669	185,582	+2,913
		142	Robertsganj	226,318	241,779	+15,461
		143	Kourh	283,027	291,218	+8,191
		144	Chakia	67,451	70,914	+3,463
			Total ...	1,136,796	1,161,508	+24,712
28	Jaunpur ...	145	Jaunpur	257,309	278,482	+21,173
		146	Mariáhu	242,214	253,402	+11,188
		147	Machhlishahr	238,759	244,677	+5,918
		148	Khutahan	268,822	286,832	+18,010
		149	Kerakat	202,559	201,556	−1,003
			Total ...	1,209,663	1,264,949	+55,286
29	Ghásipur ...	150	Ghásipur	332,408	350,823	+18,415
		151	Korantadih	272,684	304,979	+32,295
		152	Zamánia	225,949	246,930	+20,981
		153	Saidpur	169,720	175,177	+5,457
			Total ...	1,000,761	1,077,909	+77,148
30	Ballia ...	154	Ballia	345,815	353,289	+7,474
		155	Rasra	304,994	307,645	+2,651
		156	Bansdih	287,292	281,531	—5,761
			Total ...	938,101	942,465	+4,364
31	Gorakhpur ...	157	Bansgaon	422,858	451,606	+28,748
		158	Mahárájganj	365,702	511,450	+145,748
		159	Padrauna	559,838	605,551	+45,713
		160	Háta	371,284	430,069	+58,785
		161	Deoria	481,145	517,793	+36,648
		162	Gorakhpur (Sadar) ...	416,293	477,588	+61,295
			Total ...	2,617,120	2,994,057	+376,937
32	Basti ...	163	Domariaganj	280,254	313,090	+32,836
		164	Bánsi	338,839	362,724	+23,885
		165	Haraiya	334,378	351,609	+17,231
		166	Basti	335,551	377,935	+42,384
		167	Khalilabad	341,590	380,486	+38,896
			Total ...	1,630,612	1,785,844	+155,232
33	Azamgarh ...	168	Deogaon	239,425	264,851	+25,426
		169	Nizámabad	278,611	289,488	+10,877
		170	Mahul	312,146	344,723	+32,577
		171	Sagri	447,455	469,817	+22,362
		172	Muhammadabad	327,017	359,746	+32,729
			Total ...	1,604,654	1,728,625	+123,971
34	Almora ...	173	Champawat	76,895	92,601	+15,706
		174	Almora	278,780	318,900	+40,120
			Total ...	355,675	411,501	+55,826
35	Garhwál ...	175	Pauri	345,629	407,818	+62,189
			Total ...	345,629	407,818	+62,189

Tahsíls since the previous Census.

PROVINCIAL TABLE I.

Males.			Females.			Serial number of tahsíl.
Census, 1881.	Census, 1891.	Increase + or decrease —.	Census, 1881.	Census, 1891.	Increase + or decrease —.	
8	9	10	11	12	13	14
285,417	296,936	+11,519	277,096	283,531	+6,435	137
45,339	45,317	—22	44,134	44,617	+483	138
120,028	125,200	+5,172	120,670	126,342	+5,672	139
450,784	467,453	+16,669	441,900	454,490	+12,590	
186,145	183,490	—2,655	191,186	188,525	—2,661	140
90,265	91,031	+766	92,404	94,551	+2,147	141
113,975	120,477	+6,502	112,343	121,302	+8,959	142
142,902	145,092	+2,190	140,125	146,126	+6,001	143
34,017	36,251	+2,234	33,434	34,663	+1,229	144
567,304	576,341	+9,037	569,492	585,167	+15,675	
129,809	139,196	+9,387	127,500	139,286	+11,786	145
123,212	126,830	+3,618	119,002	126,572	+7,570	146
119,079	122,903	+3,824	119,680	121,774	+2,094	147
136,199	144,622	+8,423	132,623	142,210	+9,587	148
103,108	101,399	—1,709	99,451	100,157	+706	149
611,407	634,950	+23,543	598,256	629,999	+31,743	
168,751	176,339	+7,588	163,657	174,484	+10,827	150
135,634	148,415	+12,781	137,050	156,564	+19,514	151
109,943	119,394	+9,451	116,006	127,536	+11,530	152
85,603	87,553	+1,950	84,117	87,624	+3,507	153
499,931	531,701	+31,770	500,830	546,208	+45,378	
164,269	165,596	+1,327	181,546	187,693	+6,147	154
154,038	152,888	—1,150	150,956	154,757	+3,801	155
139,484	134,127	—5,357	147,808	147,404	—404	156
457,791	452,611	—5,180	480,310	489,854	+9,544	
210,046	222,512	+12,466	212,812	229,094	+16,282	157
184,228	261,719	+77,491	181,474	249,731	+68,257	158
279,566	303,206	+23,640	280,272	302,345	+22,073	159
185,782	215,496	+29,714	185,502	214,573	+29,071	160
237,623	254,229	+16,606	243,522	263,564	+20,042	161
208,878	240,122	+31,244	207,415	237,466	+30,051	162
1,306,123	1,497,284	+191,161	1,310,997	1,496,773	+185,776	
141,616	158,572	+16,956	138,638	154,518	+15,880	163
171,209	183,916	+12,707	167,630	178,808	+11,178	164
169,783	179,065	+9,282	164,595	172,544	+7,949	165
170,017	193,309	+23,292	165,534	184,626	+19,092	166
171,626	192,475	+20,849	169,964	188,011	+18,047	167
824,251	907,337	+83,086	806,361	878,507	+72,146	
122,793	133,346	+10,553	116,632	131,505	+14,873	168
141,426	145,315	+3,889	137,185	144,173	+6,988	169
159,423	174,532	+15,109	152,723	170,191	+17,468	170
226,037	233,002	+6,965	221,418	236,815	+15,397	171
166,750	181,416	+14,666	160,267	178,330	+18,063	172
816,429	867,611	+51,182	788,225	861,014	+72,789	
39,472	46,835	+7,363	37,423	45,766	+8,343	173
143,250	161,278	+18,028	135,530	157,622	+22,092	174
182,722	208,113	+25,391	172,953	203,388	+30,435	
170,755	200,319	+29,564	174,874	207,499	+32,625	175
170,755	200,319	+29,564	174,874	207,499	+32,625	

The variations in the population of the

PROVINCIAL TABLE I.

Serial number of district.	Name of district.	Serial number of tahsíl.	Name of tahsíl.	Total. Census, 1881.	Total. Census, 1891.	Total. Increase + or decrease —.
1	2	3	4	5	6	7
36	Naini Tal ...	176	Rudarpur	83,030	80,965	—2,065
		177	Kilpuri	48,990	56,435	+7,445
		178	Káshipur	74,973	73,168	—1,805
		179	Bhabar	137,966	151,680	+13,714
			Total ...	344,959	362,248	+17,289
			Total, N.-W. P. ...	32,751,762	34,254,254	+1,502,492
37	Lucknow ...	180	Lucknow	414,570	448,461	+33,891
		181	Mohanlálganj	129,209	150,160	+20,951
		182	Malihabad	153,045	175,542	+22,497
			Total ...	696,824	774,163	+77,339
38	Unao ...	183	Unao	187,891	192,894	+ 5,003
		184	Safipur	194,001	210,141	+16,140
		185	Purwa	278,527	293,152	+14,625
		186	Mohan	238,650	257,449	+18,799
			Total ...	899,069	953,636	+54,567
39	Rae Bareli ...	187	Rae Bareli	199,095	221,875	+22,780
		188	Dalmau	262,499	275,786	+13,287
		189	Digbijaiganj	245,079	276,740	+31,661
		190	Salon	245,232	262,120	+16,888
			Total ...	951,905	1,036,521	+84,616
40	Sitapur ...	191	Sitapur	257,514	291,190	+33,676
		192	Sidhauli	240,602	269,122	+28,520
		193	Misrikh	213,671	243,207	+29,536
		194	Biswan	246,464	271,894	+25,430
			Total ...	958,251	1,075,413	+117,162
41	Hardoi ...	195	Hardoi	261,107	306,071	+44,964
		196	Sandila	250,406	277,359	+26,953
		197	Bilgram	259,292	281,747	+22,455
		198	Sháhabad	216,825	248,034	+31,209
			Total ...	987,630	1,113,211	+125,581
42	Kheri ...	199	Lakhimpur	330,707	365,622	+34,915
		200	Muhamdi	232,909	258,617	+25,708
		201	Nighasan	268,306	279,376	+11,070
			Total ...	831,922	903,615	+71,693
43	Fyzabad ...	202	Fyzabad	290,942	316,586	+25,644
		203	Akbarpur	209,694	241,702	+32,008
		204	Tanda	314,768	369,781	+55,013
		205	Bikapur	266,015	288,890	+22,875
			Total ...	1,081,419	1,216,959	+135,540
44	Gonda ...	206	Gonda	351,185	404,172	+52,987
		207	Tarabganj	363,012	385,560	+22,548
		208	Utraula	556,729	669,497	+112,768
			Total ...	1,270,926	1,459,229	+188,303
45	Bahraich ...	209	Bahraich	311,352	356,958	+45,606
		210	Kaisarganj	295,975	332,193	+36,218
		211	Nánpára	270,721	311,281	+40,560
			Total ...	878,048	1,000,432	+122,384

Tahsils since the previous Census.

PROVINCIAL TABLE I.

Males.			Females.			Serial number of tahsil.
Census, 1881.	Census, 1891.	Increase + or decrease —.	Census, 1881.	Census, 1891.	Increase + or decrease —.	
8	9	10	11	12	13	14
45,917	44,861	—1,056	37,113	36,104	—1,009	176
27,051	31,576	+4,525	21,939	24,859	+2,920	177
40,347	39,023	—1,324	34,626	34,145	—481	178
78,332	86,844	+8,512	59,634	64,836	+5,202	179
191,647	202,304	+10,657	153,312	159,944	+6,632	
17,076,877	17,812,850	+735,973	15,674,885	16,441,404	+766,519	
219,327	238,406	+19,079	195,243	210,055	+14,812	180
65,893	76,949	+11,056	63,316	73,211	+9,895	181
80,085	91,846	+11,761	72,960	83,696	+10,736	182
365,305	407,201	+41,896	331,519	366,962	+35,443	
96,263	98,934	+2,671	91,628	93,960	+2,332	183
102,889	111,336	+8,447	91,112	98,805	+7,693	184
136,906	144,148	+7,242	141,621	149,004	+7,383	185
125,109	135,094	+9,985	113,541	122,355	+8,814	186
461,167	489,512	+28,345	437,902	464,124	+26,222	
98,203	110,966	+12,763	100,892	110,909	+10,017	187
128,471	135,041	+6,570	134,028	140,745	+6,717	188
119,081	137,090	+18,009	125,998	139,650	+13,652	189
121,151	129,883	+8,732	124,081	132,237	+8,156	190
466,906	512,980	+46,074	484,999	523,541	+38,542	
135,475	153,725	+18,250	122,039	137,465	+15,426	191
127,217	141,791	+14,574	113,385	127,331	+13,946	192
113,710	129,794	+16,084	99,961	113,413	+13,452	193
129,584	141,872	+12,288	116,880	130,022	+13,142	194
505,986	567,182	+61,196	452,265	508,231	+55,966	
142,184	165,564	+23,380	118,923	140,507	+21,584	195
132,372	146,818	+14,446	118,034	130,541	+12,507	196
140,396	150,803	+10,407	118,896	130,944	+12,048	197
116,752	133,312	+16,560	100,073	114,722	+14,649	198
531,704	596,497	+64,793	455,926	516,714	+60,788	
175,987	194,145	+18,158	154,720	171,477	+16,757	199
125,194	138,708	+13,514	107,715	119,909	+12,194	200
143,838	149,182	+5,344	124,468	130,194	+5,726	201
445,019	482,035	+37,016	386,903	421,580	+34,677	
148,170	160,872	+12,702	142,772	155,714	+12,942	202
107,065	122,697	+15,632	102,629	119,005	+16,376	203
159,426	186,861	+27,435	155,342	182,920	+27,578	204
131,513	142,172	+10,659	134,502	146,718	+12,216	205
546,174	612,602	+66,428	535,245	604,357	+69,112	
178,938	205,533	+26,595	172,247	198,639	+26,392	206
186,630	196,553	+9,923	176,382	189,007	+12,625	207
285,203	344,317	+59,114	271,526	325,180	+53,654	208
650,771	746,403	+95,632	620,155	712,826	+92,671	
161,801	186,047	+24,246	149,551	170,911	+21,360	209
155,387	173,193	+17,806	140,588	159,000	+18,412	210
141,999	164,327	+22,328	128,722	146,954	+18,232	211
459,187	523,567	+64,380	418,861	476,865	+58,004	

The variations in the population of the

PROVINCIAL TABLE I.

Serial number of district.	Name of district.	Serial number of tahsíl.	Name of tahsíl.	Total. Census, 1881.	Census, 1891.	Increase + or decrease —.
1	2	3	4	5	6	7
46	Sultánpur ...	212	Sultánpur	291,767	330,964	+39,197
		213	Musáfirkhána	221,229	251,221	+29,992
		214	Amethi	198,734	219,208	+20,474
		215	Kadipur	246,182	274,458	+28,276
			Total ...	957,912	1,075,851	+117,939
47	Partábgarh ...	216	Partábgarh	280,685	306,427	+25,742
		217	Patti	255,697	271,592	+15,895
		218	Kunda	310,665	332,876	+22,211
			Total ...	847,047	910,895	+63,848
48	Bara Banki ...	219	Nawábganj	212,058	242,975	+30,917
		220	Haidargarh	170,381	194,752	+24,371
		221	Ram Sanehighat... ...	354,706	377,527	+22,821
		222	Fatehpur	289,643	315,652	+26,009
			Total ...	1,026,788	1,130,906	+104,118
			Total, Oudh ...	11,387,741	12,650,831	+1,263,090
			TOTAL, N.-W. P. AND OUDH...	44,139,503	46,905,085	+2,765,582

Tahsíls since the previous Census.

PROVINCIAL TABLE I.

Males.			Females.			Serial number of tahsíl.
Census, 1881.	Census, 1891.	Increase + or decrease —.	Census, 1881.	Census, 1891.	Increase + or decrease —.	
8	9	10	11	12	13	14
144,482	162,215	+17,733	147,285	168,749	+21,464	212
106,984	122,268	+15,284	114,245	128,953	+14,708	213
96,861	106,512	+9,651	101,873	112,696	+10,823	214
126,798	139,491	+12,693	119,384	134,967	+15,583	215
475,125	530,486	+55,361	482,787	545,365	+62,578	
138,003	148,426	+10,423	142,682	158,001	+15,319	216
129,579	134,223	+4,644	126,118	137,369	+11,251	217
153,148	162,522	+9,374	157,517	170,354	+12,837	218
420,730	445,171	+24,441	426,317	465,724	+39,407	
109,870	125,970	+16,100	102,188	117,005	+14,817	219
84,028	97,081	+13,053	86,353	97,671	+11,318	220
177,477	188,763	+11,286	177,229	188,764	+11,535	221
152,206	165,301	+13,095	137,437	150,351	+12,914	222
523,581	577,115	+53,534	503,207	553,791	+50,584	
5,851,655	6,490,751	+639,096	5,536,086	6,160,080	+623,994	
22,928,532	24,303,601	+1,375,069	21,210,971	22,601,484	+1,390,513	

PROVINCIAL TABLE II.

SHOWING THE POPULATION OF THE TAHSILS DISTRIBUTED ACCORDING TO RELIGION.

The Population of the Tahsíls distri

PROVINCIAL TABLE II.

Serial number of district.	Name of district.	Serial number of tahsíl.	Name of tahsíl.	Total Population.			Hindu.		
				Both sexes.	Males.	Females.	Both sexes.	Males.	Females.
1	2	3	4	5	6	7	8	9	10
1	Debra Dún ...	1	Dehra ...	117,438	71,889	45,549	94,148	57,281	36,867
		2	Kalsi ...	50,697	28,435	22,262	49,570	27,646	21,924
			Total ...	168,135	100,324	67,811	143,718	84,927	58,791
2	Sahâranpur ...	3	Sahâranpur ...	312,498	165,426	147,072	188,063	100,332	87,731
		4	Deoband ...	205,627	112,685	92,942	154,835	85,278	69,557
		5	Roorkee ...	290,498	159,227	131,271	199,651	110,340	89,311
		6	Nukúr ...	192,657	103,013	89,644	124,945	67,796	57,149
			Total ...	1,001,280	540,351	460,929	667,494	363,746	303,748
3	Muzaffarnagar,	7	Muzaffarnagar ...	206,496	113,613	92,883	145,793	80,553	65,240
		8	Kairána ...	200,157	107,701	92,456	137,829	74,702	63,127
		9	Jansath ...	193,533	103,922	89,611	135,426	73,103	62,323
		10	Burhana ...	172,688	92,992	79,696	123,515	66,976	56,539
			Total ...	772,874	418,228	354,646	542,563	295,334	247,229
4	Meerut ...	11	Meerut ...	326,054	178,105	147,949	225,284	122,294	102,990
		12	Gháziabad ...	247,141	132,078	115,063	192,838	103,751	89,087
		13	Mowána ...	177,868	94,317	83,551	133,991	71,566	62,425
		14	Bághpat ...	259,656	140,303	119,353	211,845	114,654	97,191
		15	Sardhana ...	168,692	90,539	78,153	125,025	67,365	57,660
		16	Hápur ...	212,047	111,902	100,145	158,667	84,064	74,603
			Total ...	1,391,458	747,244	644,214	1,047,650	563,694	483,956
5	Bulandshahr...	17	Anúpshahr ...	222,481	117,271	105,210	183,537	97,137	86,400
		18	Bulandshahr ...	281,928	148,045	133,883	212,656	112,061	100,595
		19	Sikandarabad ...	224,368	119,878	104,490	188,084	100,922	87,162
		20	Khúrja ...	221,137	116,427	104,710	180,660	95,504	85,156
			Total ...	949,914	501,621	448,293	764,937	405,624	359,313
6	Aligarh ...	21	Atrauli ...	164,073	87,644	76,429	138,613	74,308	64,305
		22	Aligarh ...	229,767	122,475	107,292	189,142	101,156	87,986
		23	Iglas ...	107,227	57,628	49,599	101,079	54,403	46,676
		24	Khair ...	150,656	80,138	70,518	139,421	74,125	65,296
		25	Háthras ...	208,264	111,709	96,555	188,799	101,341	87,458
		26	Sikandra Rao ...	183,185	99,149	84,036	161,676	87,855	73,821
			Total ...	1,043,172	558,743	484,429	918,730	493,188	425,542
7	Muttra ...	27	Muttra ...	234,914	125,990	108,924	207,851	110,658	97,193
		28	Chháta ...	93,243	49,672	43,571	83,128	44,175	38,953
		29	Kosi ...	60,222	31,738	28,484	52,260	27,637	24,623
		30	Mát ...	89,451	47,407	42,044	83,631	44,355	39,276
		31	Mahaban ...	133,488	72,319	61,169	125,646	68,182	57,464
		32	Sadabad ...	102,103	55,524	46,569	93,869	51,151	42,718
			Total ...	713,421	382,660	330,761	646,385	346,158	300,227
8	Agra ...	33	Etmádpur ...	153,761	83,200	70,561	140,105	76,022	64,083
		34	Firozabad ...	112,153	60,292	51,861	100,059	53,915	46,144
		35	Bah ...	125,848	66,937	58,911	120,465	64,040	56,425
		36	Fatehabad ...	108,446	58,744	49,702	101,309	54,930	46,379
		37	Agra (Sadr) ...	272,718	146,817	125,901	206,680	111,206	95,474
		38	Keraoli ...	106,977	57,667	49,310	95,112	51,187	43,925
		39	Kheragarh ...	123,893	66,802	57,091	115,589	62,345	53,244
			Total ...	1,003,796	540,459	463,337	879,319	473,645	405,674
0	Farukhabad ...	40	Kanauj ...	117,229	62,642	54,587	97,981	52,777	45,204
		41	Tirwa ...	168,673	92,332	76,341	157,959	86,632	71,327
		42	Chibraman ...	111,114	60,159	50,955	99,709	54,333	45,376
		43	Farukhabad (Sadr)	244,896	131,858	113,038	208,942	113,372	95,570
		44	Káimganj ...	143,557	76,836	66,721	122,078	66,701	55,377
		45	Aligarh ...	73,218	40,513	32,705	69,525	38,492	31,033
			Total ...	858,687	464,340	394,347	756,194	412,307	343,887

buted according to Religion.

PROVINCIAL TABLE II.

Musalmán.			Jain.			Christian.			Others.			Serial number of tahsíl.
Both sexes.	Males.	Females.	Both sexes.	Males.	Females.	Both sexes.	Males.	Females.	Both sexes.	Males.	Females.	
11	12	13	14	15	16	17	18	19	20	21	22	23
19,118	12,100	*7,018*	**182**	123	*59*	**2,513**	1,374	*1,139*	**1,477**	1,011	*466*	1
778	560	*218*	**52**	38	*14*	**230**	130	*100*	**67**	61	*6*	2
19,896	12,660	*7,236*	**234**	161	*73*	**2,743**	1,504	*1,239*	**1,544**	1,072	*472*	
121,372	63,370	*58,002*	**1,955**	1,086	*869*	**792**	422	*370*	**316**	216	*100*	3
48,908	26,356	*22,552*	**1,710**	951	*759*	**9**	5	*4*	**165**	95	*70*	4
88,544	47,290	*41,254*	**465**	266	*199*	**1,170**	832	*338*	**668**	499	*169*	5
65,608	34,104	*31,504*	**1,954**	1,022	*932*	**3**	1	*2*	**147**	90	*57*	6
324,432	171,120	*153,312*	**6,084**	3,325	*2,759*	**1,974**	1,260	*714*	**1,296**	900	*396*	
58,670	31,841	*26,829*	**1,297**	775	*522*	**80**	49	*31*	**656**	395	*261*	7
60,271	31,839	*28,432*	**1,527**	828	*699*	**13**	12	*1*	**517**	320	*197*	8
55,480	29,319	*26,161*	**2,441**	1,381	*1,060*	**21**	13	*8*	**166**	107	*59*	9
44,569	23,505	*21,064*	**4,131**	2,271	*1,860*	**13**	7	*6*	**459**	232	*227*	10
218,990	116,504	*102,486*	**9,396**	5,255	*4,141*	**127**	81	*46*	**1,798**	1,054	*744*	
92,843	49,990	*42,853*	**1,538**	880	*658*	**4,600**	3,685	*915*	**1,789**	1,256	*533*	11
53,019	27,620	*25,399*	**301**	172	*129*	**232**	118	*114*	**751**	417	*334*	12
42,253	21,849	*20,404*	**87**	53	*34*	**47**	23	*24*	**1,490**	826	*664*	13
40,202	21,478	*18,724*	**7,139**	3,884	*3,255*	**46**	28	*18*	**424**	259	*165*	14
35,679	18,840	*16,839*	**7,159**	3,921	*3,238*	**442**	203	*239*	**387**	210	*177*	15
52,975	27,614	*25,361*	**156**	83	*73*	**68**	44	*24*	**181**	97	*84*	16
316,971	167,391	*149,580*	**16,380**	8,993	*7,387*	**5,435**	4,101	*1,334*	**5,022**	3,065	*1,957*	
37,304	19,255	*18,049*	**221**	112	*109*	**47**	25	*22*	**1,372**	742	*630*	17
67,813	35,155	*32,658*	**87**	48	*39*	**88**	46	*42*	**1,284**	735	*549*	18
35,410	18,490	*16,920*	**455**	244	*211*	**42**	22	*20*	**377**	200	*177*	19
38,492	19,862	*18,630*	**521**	267	*254*	**33**	18	*15*	**1,431**	776	*655*	20
179,019	92,762	*86,257*	**1,284**	671	*613*	**210**	111	*99*	**4,464**	2,453	*2,011*	
25,042	13,096	*11,946*	**201**	113	*88*	**56**	38	*18*	**161**	89	*72*	21
38,861	20,414	*18,447*	**762**	390	*372*	**297**	152	*145*	**705**	363	*342*	22
6,106	3,202	*2,904*	**42**	23	*19*	...	...	...	...	...	...	23
11,191	5,985	*5,206*	**40**	24	*16*	...	...	...	**4**	4	...	24
18,493	9,853	*8,640*	**942**	502	*440*	**19**	8	*11*	**11**	5	*6*	25
20,645	10,847	*9,798*	**520**	265	*255*	**93**	55	*38*	**251**	127	*124*	26
120,338	63,397	*56,941*	**2,507**	1,317	*1,190*	**465**	253	*212*	**1,132**	588	*544*	
24,708	13,470	*11,238*	**584**	329	*255*	**831**	689	*142*	**940**	844	*96*	27
9,878	5,356	*4,522*	**207**	119	*88*	**5**	4	*1*	**25**	18	*7*	28
7,004	3,595	*3,409*	**934**	484	*450*	**5**	4	*1*	**19**	18	*1*	29
5,694	2,976	*2,718*	**37**	21	*16*	...	...	...	**89**	55	*34*	30
7,640	4,029	*3,611*	**171**	89	*82*	**5**	3	*2*	**26**	16	*10*	31
7,733	4,119	*3,614*	**470**	250	*220*	...	...	...	**31**	14	*17*	32
62,657	33,545	*29,112*	**2,403**	1,292	*1,111*	**846**	700	*146*	**1,130**	965	*165*	
10,467	5,498	*4,969*	**2,812**	1,485	*1,327*	**249**	124	*125*	**128**	71	*57*	33
9,328	4,818	*4,510*	**2,576**	1,432	*1,144*	**16**	11	*5*	**174**	116	*58*	34
3,727	2,012	*1,715*	**1,638**	873	*765*	...	...	...	**18**	12	*6*	35
5,962	3,166	*2,796*	**1,116**	607	*509*	**7**	5	*2*	**52**	36	*16*	36
56,349	29,635	*26,714*	**3,828**	2,076	*1,752*	**4,469**	2,810	*1,659*	**1,392**	1,090	*302*	37
11,046	6,045	*5,001*	**773**	407	*366*	**16**	8	*8*	**30**	20	*10*	38
7,554	4,010	*3,544*	**719**	426	*293*	**1**	1	...	**30**	20	*10*	39
104,433	55,184	*49,249*	**13,462**	7,306	*6,156*	**4,758**	2,959	*1,799*	**1,824**	1,365	*459*	
18,747	9,618	*9,129*	**354**	173	*181*	...	...	...	**147**	74	*73*	40
10,455	5,561	*4,894*	**83**	38	*45*	...	...	...	**176**	101	*75*	41
11,342	5,792	*5,550*	**33**	19	*14*	**13**	7	*6*	**17**	8	*9*	42
34,159	17,318	*16,841*	**408**	213	*195*	**801**	500	*301*	**586**	455	*131*	43
21,096	9,924	*11,172*	**161**	89	*72*	**7**	4	*3*	**215**	118	*97*	44
3,677	2,013	*1,664*	**9**	5	*4*	**7**	3	*4*	...	...	...	45
99,476	50,226	*49,250*	**1,048**	537	*511*	**828**	514	*314*	**1,141**	756	*385*	

PROVINCIAL TABLE II.

Serial number of district.	Name of district.	Serial number of tahsil.	Name of Tahsil.	Total population. Both sexes.	Males.	Females.	Hindu. Both sexes.	Males.	Females.
1	2	3	4	5	6	7	8	9	10
10	Mainpuri ...	46	Mainpuri ...	171,152	93,782	77,370	159,519	87,455	72,064
		47	Bhongaon ...	195,368	107,109	88,259	187,390	102,911	84,479
		48	Karhal ...	100,297	54,675	45,622	94,315	51,530	42,785
		49	Shikohabad ...	140,093	76,477	63,616	128,373	70,300	58,073
		50	Mustafabad ...	155,253	84,756	70,497	144,697	79,167	65,530
			Total ...	762,163	416,799	345,364	714,294	391,363	322,931
11	Etáwah ...	51	Etáwah ...	198,023	107,503	90,520	178,382	97,253	81,129
		52	Bharthna ...	169,979	92,857	77,122	164,406	89,825	74,581
		53	Bidhuna ...	134,459	73,926	60,533	127,457	70,215	57,242
		54	Phaphúnd ...	107,307	58,644	48,663	100,974	55,336	45,638
		55	Auraiya ...	117,861	63,845	54,016	111,644	60,615	51,029
			Total ...	727,629	396,775	330,854	682,863	373,244	309,619
12	Etah ...	56	Etah ...	227,030	123,468	103,562	207,675	113,241	94,434
		57	Kásganj ...	192,009	105,106	86,903	167,392	91,932	75,460
		58	Aliganj ...	161,994	89,060	72,934	142,677	78,909	63,768
		59	Jalesar ...	121,030	65,569	55,461	105,089	57,234	47,855
			Total ...	702,063	383,203	318,860	622,833	341,316	281,517
13	Bareilly ...	60	Farídpur ...	119,805	65.453	54,352	103,446	56,585	46,861
		61	Bareilly ...	298,482	160,805	137,677	197,475	107,502	89,973
		62	Aonla ...	195,950	103,903	92,047	160,978	85,675	75,303
		63	Mírganj ...	95,300	49,750	45,550	77,743	40,622	37,121
		64	Baheri ...	206,805	108,982	97,823	148,789	78,810	69,979
		65	Nawábganj ...	124,349	66,587	57,762	101,172	54,260	46,912
			Total ...	1,040,691	555,480	485,211	789,603	423,454	366,149
14	Bijnor ...	66	Bijnor ...	133,887	71,310	62,577	94,146	50,944	43,202
		67	Najibabad ...	156,873	82,135	74,738	98,898	53,010	45,888
		68	Nagína ...	183,147	96,156	86,991	117,210	62,531	54,679
		69	Dhámpur ...	181,988	95,475	86,513	113,323	60,652	52,671
		70	Chándpur ...	138,175	73,136	65,039	98,314	52,761	45,553
			Total ...	794,070	418,212	375,858	521,891	279,898	241,993
15	Budaun ...	71	Gunnaur ...	126,388	68,478	57,910	112,521	61,024	51,497
		72	Bisauli ...	183,640	98,563	85,077	156,876	84,218	72,658
		73	Sahaswán ...	192,989	104,180	88,809	160,938	87,311	73,627
		74	Budaun ...	226,673	120,297	106,376	170,167	91,770	78,397
		75	Dátaganj ...	195,908	106,616	89,292	172,677	94,322	78,355
			Total ...	925,598	498,134	427,464	773,179	418,645	354,534
16	Moradabad ...	76	Moradabad ...	240,795	126,025	114,770	135,312	71,972	63,340
		77	Thákurdwára ...	121,174	64,268	56,906	78,768	41,936	36,832
		78	Bilári ...	231,947	123,416	108,531	169,580	90,350	79,230
		79	Sambhal ...	245,619	129,303	116,316	162,059	86,294	75,765
		80	Amroha ...	186,183	97,811	88,372	111,692	60,378	51,314
		81	Hasanpur ...	153,680	82,749	70,931	115,590	62,793	52,797
			Total ...	1,179,398	623,572	555,826	773,001	413,723	359,278
17	Sháhjahánpur,	82	Sháhjahánpur ...	273,146	144,664	128,482	211,128	113,872	97,256
		83	Jalálabad ...	159,392	87,392	72,000	145,638	80,346	65,292
		84	Tilhar ...	236,791	128,783	108,008	205,288	111,978	93,310
		85	Powáyan ...	249,222	134,467	114,755	225,082	121,192	103,890
			Total ...	918,551	495,306	423,245	787,136	427,388	359,748
18	Pilibhít ...	86	Bisalpur ...	190,864	102,602	88,262	170,960	91,793	79,167
		87	Pilibhít ...	199,297	104,764	94,533	145,982	77,587	68,395
		88	Puranpur ...	95,205	51,036	44,169	85,178	45,737	39,441
			Total ...	485,366	258,402	226,964	402,120	215,117	187,003

buted according to Religion.

PROVINCIAL TABLE II.

Musalman.			Jain.			Christian.			Others.			Serial number of tahsíl.
Both sexes.	Males.	Females.	Both sexes.	Males.	Females.	Both sexes.	Males.	Females.	Both sexes.	Males.	Females.	
11	12	13	14	15	16	17	18	19	20	21	22	23
10,139	5,479	4,660	1,131	650	481	122	63	59	241	135	106	46
7,580	3,973	3,607	343	190	153	3	2	1	52	33	19	47
4,881	2,552	2,329	1,100	592	508	...	...	...	1	1	...	48
10,644	5,560	5,084	943	537	406	2	2	...	131	78	53	49
8,285	4,357	3,928	2,243	1,219	1,024	5	4	1	23	9	14	50
41,529	21,921	19,608	5,760	3,188	2,572	132	71	61	448	256	192	
17,783	9,190	8,593	1,699	956	743	115	71	44	44	33	11	51
5,234	2,854	2,380	319	165	154	15	8	7	5	5	...	52
6,977	3,693	3,284	8	8	...	...	...	...	17	10	7	53
6,223	3,252	2,971	8	4	4	3	3	...	99	49	50	54
6,108	3,175	2,933	83	45	38	1	1	...	25	9	16	55
42,325	22,164	20,161	2,117	1,178	939	134	83	51	190	106	84	
17,126	9,018	8,108	2,041	1,108	933	141	70	71	47	31	16	56
23,381	12,509	10,872	283	148	135	313	169	144	640	348	292	57
18,976	9,957	9,019	199	105	94	57	40	17	85	49	36	58
13,470	6,994	6,476	2,422	1,303	1,119	9	7	2	40	31	9	59
72,953	38,478	34,475	4,945	2,664	2,281	520	286	234	812	459	353	
16,147	8,763	7,384	...	...	...	127	76	51	85	29	56	60
96,489	49,883	46,606	1	1	...	3,843	2,977	866	674	442	232	61
34,193	17,779	16,414	...	...	...	776	447	329	3	2	1	62
17,333	8,997	8,336	...	...	...	224	131	93	...	...	...	63
57,812	30,067	27,745	3	1	2	198	103	95	3	1	2	64
23,065	12,265	10,800	...	...	...	103	56	47	9	6	3	65
245,039	127,754	117,285	4	2	2	5,271	3,790	1,481	774	480	294	
38,565	19,783	18,782	92	43	49	405	198	207	679	342	337	66
57,415	28,834	28,581	236	127	109	66	35	31	258	129	129	67
64,058	32,633	31,425	134	72	62	126	86	40	1,619	834	785	68
67,693	34,279	33,414	531	281	250	121	84	37	320	179	141	69
39,431	20,155	19,276	5	3	2	190	89	101	235	128	107	70
267,162	135,684	131,478	998	526	472	908	492	416	3,111	1,612	1,499	
13,706	7,355	6,351	...	...	...	69	43	26	92	56	36	71
26,083	13,986	12,097	31	17	14	425	225	200	225	117	108	72
31,300	16,467	14,833	198	112	86	469	247	222	84	43	41	73
54,768	27,600	27,168	...	...	...	1,222	663	559	516	264	252	74
22,432	11,869	10,563	...	...	...	396	215	181	403	210	193	75
148,289	77,277	71,012	229	129	100	2,581	1,393	1,188	1,320	690	630	
103,710	53,062	50,648	304	170	134	944	526	418	525	295	230	76
42,312	22,280	20,032	...	...	...	5	2	3	89	50	39	77
61,634	32,653	28,981	196	100	96	307	177	130	230	136	94	78
82,255	42,317	39,938	256	136	120	670	358	312	379	198	181	79
73,338	36,820	36,518	125	60	65	946	513	433	82	40	42	80
37,456	19,608	17,848	121	66	55	435	233	202	78	49	29	81
400,705	206,740	193,965	1,002	532	470	3,307	1,809	1,498	1,383	768	615	
60,499	29,806	30,693	15	8	7	993	733	260	511	245	266	82
13,585	6,945	6,640	21	12	9	69	45	24	79	44	35	83
31,225	16,643	14,582	...	...	...	176	100	76	102	62	40	84
23,957	13,169	10,788	...	...	...	90	48	42	93	58	35	85
129,266	66,563	62,703	36	20	16	1,328	926	402	785	409	376	
19,705	10,697	9,008	...	...	...	188	106	82	11	6	5	86
52,809	26,887	25,922	...	...	...	166	95	71	340	195	145	87
9,972	5,256	4,716	11	4	7	11	10	1	33	29	4	88
82,486	42,840	39,646	11	4	7	365	211	154	384	230	154	

The Population of the Tahsíls distri

PROVINCIAL TABLE II.

Serial number of district.	Name of district.	Serial number of tahsil.	Name of tahsil.	Total Population.			Hindu.		
				Both sexes.	Males.	Females.	Both sexes.	Males.	Females.
1	2	3	4	5	6	7	8	9	10
19	Cawnpore ...	89	Akbarpur ...	102,256	54,887	47,369	95,620	51,433	44,187
		90	Bilhaur ...	100,051	53,675	46,376	91,635	49,385	42,250
		91	Bhognipur ...	96,575	50,846	45,729	87,696	46,363	41,333
		92	Cawnpore ...	324,628	178,830	145,798	269,902	148,305	121,597
		93	Derapur ...	122,244	65,345	56,899	116,115	62,119	53,996
		94	Rasúlabad ...	99,537	54,117	45,420	94,387	51,456	42,931
		95	Narwal ...	98,784	51,261	47,523	94,672	49,142	45,530
		96	Shiurájpur ...	147,823	77,763	70,060	141,713	74,532	67,181
		97	Ghatampur ...	117,797	61,368	56,429	112,250	58,436	53,814
			Total ...	1,209,695	648,092	561,603	1,103,990	591,171	512,819
20	Fatehpur ...	98	Fatehpur ...	175,452	90,183	85,269	153,621	79,237	74,384
		99	Kaliánpur ...	118 786	62,017	56,769	108,519	56,804	51,715
		100	Kora ...	87 925	45,299	42,626	81,766	42,244	39,522
		101	Gházipur ...	92,389	48,119	44,270	86,239	44,947	41,292
		102	Khakhreru ...	86,525	44,075	42,450	75,820	38,869	36,951
		103	Khaga ...	138,080	70,128	67,952	115,958	59,413	56,545
			Total ...	699,157	359,821	339,336	621,923	321,514	300,409
21	Bánda ...	104	Bánda ...	112,912	56,942	55,970	101,640	51,458	50,182
		105	Pailani ...	88,544	45,350	43,194	82,461	42,297	40,164
		106	Baberu ...	96,284	47,961	48,323	89.709	44,707	45,002
		107	Kamasin ...	83,297	42,317	40,980	80,904	41,036	39,868
		108	Mau ...	73,658	37,506	36,152	71,324	36,300	35,024
		109	Karwi ...	87,687	44,506	43,181	84,433	42,931	41,502
		110	Badausa ...	77,922	39,255	38,667	75,207	37,887	37,320
		111	Girwan ...	85,528	43,057	42,471	79,001	39,909	39,092
			Total ...	705,832	356,894	348,938	664,679	336,525	328,154
22	Hamírpur ...	112	Hamírpur ...	81,133	42,018	39,115	76,642	39,690	36,952
		113	Muskara ...	75,735	38,538	37,197	71,988	36,652	35,336
		114	Ráth ...	97,862	48,799	49,063	91,135	45,589	45,546
		115	Kulpahar ...	127,567	64,647	62,920	121,406	61,563	59,843
		116	Mahoba ...	74,200	37,770	36,430	69,884	35,655	34,229
		117	Maudha ...	57,223	28,831	28,392	49,160	25,013	24,147
			Total ...	513,720	260,603	253,117	480,215	244,162	236,053
23	Allahabad ...	118	Allahabad ...	342,446	176,851	165,595	255,463	132,285	123,178
		119	Sirathu ...	129,932	65,431	64,501	110,310	55,960	54,350
		120	Manjhanpur ...	131,688	66,925	64,763	118,410	60,340	58,070
		121	Soraon ...	186,876	90,801	96,075	161,432	78,906	82,526
		122	Phúlpur ...	176.851	87,701	89,150	155,740	77,532	78,208
		123	Handia ...	187,089	94,126	92,963	169,299	85,614	83,685
		124	Karchhana ...	134,818	68,961	65,857	124,410	63,590	60,820
		125	Bara ..	63,816	32,651	31,165	61.585	31,469	30,116
		126	Meja ...	195,221	98,062	97,159	185,285	93,088	92,197
			Total ...	1,548,737	781,509	767,228	1,341,934	678,784	663,150
24	Jhánsi ...	127	Jhánsi ...	145,680	79,788	65,892	129,376	69,692	59,684
		128	Mau ...	115,724	59,003	56,721	109.840	56,096	53,744
		129	Garotha ...	88,926	45,618	43,308	85.054	43,569	41,485
		130	Moth ...	59,089	30,119	28.970	56,534	28,830	27,704
		131	Lalitpur ...	157,153	81,768	75,385	148,112	77,041	71,071
		132	Mehroni ...	117,047	59,668	57,379	110,483	56,428	54,055
			Total ...	683,619	355,964	327,655	639,899	331,656	307,743
25	Jalaun ...	133	Orai ...	67,702	34,621	33,081	61,496	31,533	29,963
		134	Kalpi ...	78,754	40,521	38,233	71,742	37,092	34,650
		135	Jalaun ...	147,090	76,148	70,942	140,181	72,611	67 570
		136	Kúnch ...	102,815	52,800	50,015	97,185	49,983	47,202
			Total ...	396,361	204,090	192,271	370,604	191,219	179,385

buted according to Religion.

PROVINCIAL TABLE II.

Musalmán.			Jain.			Christian.			Others.			Serial number of tahsil.
Both sexes.	Males.	Females.	Both sexes.	Males.	Females.	Both sexes.	Males.	Females.	Both sexes.	Males.	Females.	
11	12	13	14	15	16	17	18	19	20	21	22	23
6,498	3,371	3,127	...	...	...	11	6	5	127	77	50	89
8,368	4,264	4,104	...	...	...	9	6	3	39	20	19	90
8,798	4,436	4,362	4	2	2	1	1	...	76	44	32	91
51,009	28,029	22,980	410	242	168	2,995	2,071	924	312	183	129	92
6,128	3,225	2,903	...	...	...	...	...	...	1	1	...	93
5,038	2,603	2,435	...	...	...	...	...	...	112	58	54	94
4,072	2,098	1,974	...	...	...	6	5	1	34	16	18	95
6,084	3,220	2,864	...	...	...	14	6	8	12	5	7	96
5,546	2,931	2,615	1	1	...	...	...	...	...	...	...	97
101,541	54,177	47,364	415	245	170	3,036	2,095	941	713	404	309	
21,748	10,898	10,850	1	1	...	67	38	29	15	9	6	98
10,263	5,209	5,054	...	...	...	...	...	...	4	4	...	99
6,083	3,015	3,068	76	40	36	...	...	...	...	...	...	100
6,150	3,172	2,978	...	...	...	...	...	...	...	...	...	101
10,704	5,205	5,499	1	1	...	...	...	...	...	...	...	102
22,113	10,708	11,405	5	3	2	4	4	...	...	...	...	103
77,061	38,207	38,854	83	45	38	71	42	29	19	13	6	
10,917	5,298	5,619	216	102	114	55	31	24	84	53	31	104
6,076	3,050	3,026	5	1	4	...	...	...	2	2	...	105
6,572	3,251	3,321	...	...	...	...	...	...	3	3	...	106
2,379	1,270	1,109	...	...	...	2	2	...	12	9	3	107
2,277	1,176	1,101	50	24	26	...	...	...	7	6	1	108
3,223	1,559	1,664	2	...	2	15	8	7	14	8	6	109
2,707	1,361	1,346	5	4	1	1	1	...	2	2	...	110
6,511	3,139	3,372	6	3	3	1	1	...	9	5	4	111
40,662	20,104	20,558	284	134	150	74	43	31	133	88	45	
4,457	2,304	2,153	...	...	...	15	11	4	19	13	6	112
3,746	1,885	1,861	...	...	...	1	1	...	...	...	...	113
6,718	3,205	3,513	5	2	3	...	...	...	4	3	1	114
6,054	3,029	3,025	101	52	49	...	...	...	6	3	3	115
4,244	2,069	2,175	1	1	...	33	21	12	38	24	14	116
8,062	3,817	4,245	...	...	...	1	1	...	...	...	...	117
33,281	16,309	16,972	107	55	52	50	34	16	67	43	24	
80,630	40,700	39,930	309	156	153	5,866	3,590	2,276	178	120	58	118
19,582	9,450	10,132	37	18	19	3	3	...	...	...	...	119
13,219	6,559	6,660	59	26	33	...	...	...	...	...	...	120
25,436	11,893	13,543	...	...	...	8	2	6	...	...	...	121
21,111	10,169	10,942	...	...	...	...	...	...	...	...	...	122
17,790	8,512	9,278	...	...	...	...	...	...	...	...	...	123
10,081	5,064	5,017	5	4	1	52	33	19	270	270	...	124
2,228	1,180	1,048	3	2	1	...	...	...	...	...	...	125
9,776	4,904	4,872	155	66	89	4	3	1	1	1	...	126
199,853	98,431	101,422	568	272	296	5,933	3,631	2,302	449	391	58	
12,378	7,182	5,196	921	504	417	1,874	1,379	495	1,131	1,031	100	127
4,770	2,334	2,436	1,104	567	537	1	1	...	9	5	4	128
3,566	1,884	1,682	304	163	141	...	...	...	2	2	...	129
2,353	1,185	1,168	192	100	92	2	1	1	8	3	5	130
3,951	2,114	1,837	4,997	2,551	2,446	56	34	22	37	28	9	131
1,995	1,012	983	4,549	2,214	2,335	7	3	4	13	11	2	132
29.013	15,711	13,302	12,067	6,099	5,968	1,940	1,418	522	1,200	1,080	120	
6,062	3,015	3,047	78	41	37	54	29	25	12	3	9	133
6,958	3,401	3,557	39	18	21	11	8	3	4	2	2	134
6,870	3,510	3,360	34	22	12	1	1	...	4	4	...	135
5,611	2,806	2,805	17	9	8	1	1	...	1	1	...	136
25,501	12,732	12,769	168	90	78	67	39	28	21	10	11	

PROVINCIAL TABLE II.

Serial number of district.	Name of district.	Serial number of tahsíl.	Name of tahsíl.	Total Population. Both sexes.	Total Population. Males.	Total Population. Females.	Hindu. Both sexes.	Hindu. Males.	Hindu. Females.
1	2	3	4	5	6	7	8	9	10
26	Benares ...	137	Benares ...	580,467	296,936	*283,531*	514,655	262,386	*252,269*
		138	Gangapur ...	89,934	45,317	*44,617*	86,118	43,404	*42,714*
		139	Chandauli ...	251,542	125,200	*126,342*	230,957	115,245	*115,712*
			Total ...	921,943	467,453	*454,490*	831,730	421,035	*410,695*
27	Mirzapur ...	140	Mirzapur ...	372,015	183,490	*188,525*	346,068	170,507	*175,561*
		141	Chunar ...	185,582	91,031	*94,551*	170,992	83,851	*87,141*
		142	Robertsganj ...	241,779	120,477	*121,302*	232,651	115,891	*116,760*
		143	Kourh ...	291,218	145,092	*146.126*	270,109	134,754	*135,355*
		144	Ckakia ...	70,914	36,251	*34,663*	65,412	33,411	*32,001*
			Total ...	1,161,508	576,341	*585,167*	1,085,232	538,414	*546,818*
28	Jaunpur ...	145	Jaunpur ...	278,482	139,196	*139,286*	244,164	122,843	*121,321*
		146	Mariáhu ...	253,402	126,830	*126,572*	240.221	120,434	*119,787*
		147	Machhlishahr ...	244,677	122.903	*121,774*	225,539	113,678	*111,861*
		148	Khutahan ...	286,832	144,622	*142,210*	248,018	125,959	*122,059*
		149	Kerakat ...	201,556	101,399	*100,157*	190,563	95,982	*94,581*
			Total ...	1,264,949	634,950	*629,999*	1,148,505	578,896	*569,609*
29	Gházipur ...	150	Gházipur ...	350,823	176,339	*174,484*	317,097	159,954	*157,143*
		151	Korantadih ...	304,979	148.415	*156,564*	276,427	135,164	*141,263*
		152	Zamánia ...	246,930	119,394	*127.536*	217,722	106,149	*111,573*
		153	Saidpur ...	175,177	87,553	*87,624*	163,094	81,870	*81,224*
			Total ...	1,077,909	531,701	*546,208*	974,340	483,137	*491,203*
30	Ballia ...	154	Ballia ...	353,289	165,596	*187,693*	331,433	155,475	*175,958*
		155	Rasra ...	307,645	152,888	*154,757*	282,839	141,306	*141,533*
		156	Bansdih ...	281,531	134,127	*147,404*	261,823	125,187	*136,636*
			Total ...	942,465	452,611	*489,854*	876,095	421,968	*454,127*
31	Gorakhpur ...	157	Bánsgaon ...	451,606	222,512	*229,094*	423,335	208.532	*214,803*
		158	Maharájganj ...	511,450	261,719	*249,731*	454,329	232,628	*221,701*
		159	Padrauna ...	605,551	303,206	*302,345*	514,359	257,202	*257,157*
		160	Hata ...	430,069	215,496	*214,573*	393,225	197,055	*196,170*
		161	Deoria ...	517,793	254,229	*263.564*	474,674	233,272	*241,402*
		162	Gorakhpur (Sadar)	477,588	240,122	*237,466*	431,242	217,068	*214,174*
			Total ...	2,994,057	1,497,284	*1,496,773*	2,691,164	1,345,757	*1,345,407*
32	Basti ...	163	Domariaganj ...	313,090	158,572	*154,518*	237,747	120,691	*117,056*
		164	Bánsi ...	362,724	183,016	*178,808*	302,121	153,087	*149,034*
		165	Haraiya ...	351,609	179,065	*172,544*	323,390	164,701	*158,689*
		166	Basti ...	377,935	193,309	*184,626*	331,697	169,553	*162,144*
		167	Khalilabad ...	380,486	192,475	*188,011*	315,034	159,543	*155,491*
			Total ...	1,785,844	907,337	*878,507*	1,509,989	767,575	*742,414*
33	Azamgarh ...	168	Deogaon ...	264,851	133,346	*131,505*	246,936	124,693	*122,243*
		169	Nizambad ...	289,488	145,315	*144,173*	235,298	119,010	*116,288*
		170	Mahul ...	344,723	174,532	*170,191*	304,224	154,852	*149,372*
		171	Sagri ...	469,817	233,002	*236,815*	416,352	207,182	*209,170*
		172	Muhammadabad...	359,746	181,416	*178,330*	300,101	152,096	*148,005*
			Total ...	1,728,625	867,611	*861,014*	1,502,911	757,833	*745,078*
34	Almora ...	173	Champáwat ...	92,601	46,835	*45,766*	92,145	46,703	*45,442*
		174	Almora ...	318,900	161,278	*157,622*	316,612	159,956	*156,656*
			Total ...	411,501	208,113	*203,388*	408,757	206,659	*202,098*

buted according to Religion.

PROVINCIAL TABLE II.

Musalmán.			Jain.			Christian.			Others.			Serial number of tahsíl.
Both sexes.	Males.	Females.	Both sexes.	Males.	Females	Both sexes.	Males.	Females.	Both sexes.	Males.	Females.	
11	12	13	14	15	16	17	18	19	20	21	22	23
64,101	33,381	30,720	138	86	52	1,263	793	470	310	290	20	137
3,816	1,913	1,903	...	...	...	...	...	...	...	...	...	138
20,484	9,896	10,588	...	...	...	101	59	42	...	...	...	139
88,401	45,190	43,211	138	86	52	1,364	852	512	310	290	20	
25,473	12,751	12,722	271	132	139	155	77	78	48	22	26	140
14,126	6,989	7,137	5	1	4	227	92	135	232	98	134	141
9,033	4,537	4,496	5	1	4	82	45	37	8	3	5	142
21,106	10,336	10,770	...	...	...	1	1	...	2	2	...	143
5,502	2,840	2,662	...	...	...	...	...	...	...	...	...	144
75,240	37,453	37,787	281	134	147	465	215	250	290	125	165	
34,229	16,303	17,926	...	...	...	89	50	39	...	...	...	145
13,181	6,396	6,785	...	...	...	...	...	...	...	...	...	146
19,130	9,219	9,911	6	4	2	1	1	...	1	1	...	147
38,812	18,661	20,151	...	...	...	2	2	...	...	...	...	148
10,992	5,416	5,576	...	...	...	1	1	...	...	...	...	149
116,344	55,995	60,349	6	4	2	93	54	39	1	1	...	
33,202	16,085	17,117	4	3	1	284	147	137	236	150	86	150
28,508	13,228	15,280	23	14	9	21	9	12	...	...	...	151
28,936	13,125	15,811	...	...	...	268	118	150	4	2	2	152
12,080	5,681	6,399	...	...	...	3	2	1	...	...	...	153
102,726	48,119	54,607	27	17	10	576	276	300	240	152	88	
21,839	10,108	11,731	...	...	...	15	11	4	2	2	...	154
24,806	11,582	13,224	...	...	...	...	...	...	...	...	...	155
19,708	8,940	10,768	...	...	...	...	...	...	...	...	...	156
66,353	30,630	35,723	...	...	...	15	11	4	2	2	...	
28,264	13,975	14,289	...	...	...	7	5	2	...	...	...	157
57,079	29,073	28,006	...	...	...	41	17	24	1	1	...	158
91,157	45,980	45,177	...	...	...	34	23	11	1	1	...	159
36,841	18,438	18,403	...	...	...	2	2	...	1	1	...	160
43,105	20,946	22,159	...	...	...	14	11	3	...	...	...	161
45,184	22,437	22,747	44	26	18	1,078	566	512	40	25	15	162
301,630	150,849	150,781	44	26	18	1,176	624	552	43	28	15	
75,343	37,881	37,462	...	...	...	...	...	...	...	...	...	163
60,591	30,820	29,771	...	...	...	12	9	3	...	...	...	164
28,219	14,364	13,855	...	...	...	...	...	...	...	...	...	165
46,126	23,696	22,430	...	...	...	54	30	24	58	30	28	166
65,450	32,930	32,520	...	...	...	...	...	...	2	2	...	167
275,729	139,691	136,038	...	...	...	66	39	27	60	32	28	
17,915	8,653	9,262	...	...	...	...	...	...	...	...	...	168
54,130	26,272	27,858	...	...	...	59	32	27	1	1	...	169
40,496	19,677	20,819	...	...	...	3	3	...	...	...	...	170
53,456	25,816	27,640	...	...	...	9	4	5	...	...	...	171
59,642	29,320	30,322	...	...	...	3	...	3	...	...	...	172
225,639	109,738	115,901	...	...	...	74	39	35	1	1	...	
126	59	67	...	...	...	330	73	257	...	...	...	173
1,893	1,116	777	5	4	1	376	192	184	14	10	4	174
2,019	1,175	844	5	4	1	706	265	441	14	10	4	

PROVINCIAL TABLE II.

Serial number of district.	Name of district.	Serial number of tahsíl.	Name of tahsíl.	Total Population. Both sexes.	Total Population. Males.	Total Population. Females.	Hindu. Both sexes.	Hindu. Males.	Hindu. Females.
1	2	3	4	5	6	7	8	9	10
35	Garhwál ...	175	Pauri ...	407,818	200,319	207,499	403,603	197,106	206,497
			Total ...	407,818	200,319	207,499	403,603	197,106	206,497
36	Naini Tal ...	176	Rudarpur ...	80,965	44,861	36,104	42,156	23,575	18,581
		177	Kilpuri ...	56,435	31,576	24,859	46,376	25,867	20,509
		178	Káshipur ...	73,168	39,023	34,145	46,628	24,865	21,763
		179	Bhabar ...	151,680	86,844	64,836	140,815	79,581	61,234
			Total ...	362,248	203,304	159,944	275,975	153,888	122,087
			Total, N.-W. P. ...	34,254,254	17,812,850	16,441,404	29,364,955	15,290,070	14,074,885
37	Lucknow ...	180	Lucknow ...	448,461	238,406	210,055	316,916	170,927	145,989
		181	Mohanlálganj ...	150,160	76,949	73,211	136,162	70,148	66,014
		182	Malihabad ...	175,542	91,846	83,696	151,947	80,075	71,872
			Total ...	774,163	407,201	366,962	605,025	321,150	283,875
38	Unao ...	183	Unao ...	192,894	98,934	93,960	180,577	92,481	88,096
		184	Safipur ...	210,141	111,336	98,805	183,041	97,422	85,619
		185	Purwa ...	293,152	144,148	149,004	277,039	136,243	140,796
		186	Mohan ...	257,449	135,094	122,355	236,794	124,730	112,064
			Total ...	953,636	489,512	464,124	877,451	450,876	426,575
39	Rae Bareli	187	Rae Bareli ...	221,875	110,966	110,909	204,350	102,262	102,088
		188	Dalmau ...	275,786	135,041	140,745	263,193	128,890	134,303
		189	Digbijaiganj ...	276,740	137,090	139,650	252,781	125,543	127,238
		190	Salon ...	262,120	129,883	132,237	229,966	114,496	115,470
			Total ...	1,036,521	512,980	523,541	950,290	471,191	479,099
40	Sitapur ...	191	Sitapur ...	291,190	153,725	137,465	234,157	124,450	109,707
		192	Sidhauli ...	269,122	141,791	127,331	230,022	121,525	108,497
		193	Misrikh ...	243,207	129,794	113,413	223,735	119,527	104,208
		194	Biswan ...	271,894	141,872	130,022	228,766	119,683	109,083
			Total ...	1,075,413	567,182	508,231	916,680	485,185	431,495
41	Hardoi ...	195	Hardoi ...	306,071	165,564	140,507	283,812	153,750	130,062
		196	Sandila ...	277,359	146,818	130,541	243,331	129,312	114,019
		197	Bilgram ...	281,747	150,803	130,944	255,265	137,159	118,106
		198	Sháhabad ...	248,034	133,312	114,722	215,931	116,776	99,155
			Total ...	1,113,211	596,497	516,714	998,339	536,997	461,342
42	Kheri ...	199	Lakhimpur ...	365,622	194,145	171,477	313,839	166,951	146,888
		200	Muhamdi ...	258,617	138,708	119,909	224,555	120,789	103,766
		201	Nighasan ...	279,376	149,182	130,194	246,461	131,476	114,985
			Total ...	903,615	482,035	421,580	784,855	419,216	365,639
43	Fyzabad ...	202	Fyzabad ...	316,586	160,872	155,714	272,000	138,379	133 621
		203	Akbarpur ...	241,702	122,697	119,005	216,504	110,252	106,252
		204	Tánda ...	369,781	186,861	182,920	318,512	161,424	157,088
		205	Bikapur ...	288,890	142,172	146,718	269,815	133,167	136,648
			Total ...	1,216,959	612,602	604,357	1,076,831	543,222	533,609
44	Gonda ...	206	Gonda ...	404,172	205,533	198,639	352,909	179,514	173,395
		207	Tarabganj ...	385,560	196,553	189,007	356,615	181,710	174,905
		208	Utraula ...	669,497	344,317	325,180	543,990	280,043	263,947
			Total ...	1,459,229	746,403	712,826	1,253,514	641,267	612,247

buted according to Religion.

PROVINCIAL TABLE II.

Musalmán.			Jain.			Christian.			Others.			Serial number of tahsíl.
Both sexes.	Males.	Females.	Both sexes.	Males.	Females.	Both sexes.	Males.	Females.	Both sexes.	Males.	Females.	
11	12	13	14	15	16	17	18	19	20	21	22	23
3,605	2,908	697	2	1	1	573	289	284	35	15	20	175
3,605	2,908	697	2	1	1	573	289	284	35	15	20	
38,799	21,279	17,520	...	...	...	9	6	3	1	1	...	176
10,049	5,703	4,346	...	...	...	8	6	2	2	...	2	177
26,359	14,058	12,306	39	22	17	6	4	2	136	79	57	178
9,950	6,779	3,171	...	...	...	895	476	419	20	8	12	179
85,157	47,814	37,343	39	22	17	918	492	426	159	88	71	
4,725,721	2,427,443	2,298,278	82,134	44,334	37,800	49,129	31,002	18,127	32,315	20,001	12,314	
123,921	62,383	61,538	752	398	354	5,750	3,942	1,808	1,122	756	366	180
13,925	6,760	7,165	1	1	...	19	13	6	53	27	26	181
23,523	11,735	11,788	44	20	24	...	...	...	28	16	12	182
161,369	80,878	80,491	797	419	378	5,769	3,955	1,814	1,203	799	404	
12,149	6,368	5,781	...	...	...	79	38	41	89	47	42	183
27,087	13,907	13,180	8	4	4	4	2	2	1	1	...	184
16,086	7,890	8,196	...	...	...	8	4	4	19	11	8	185
20,598	10,332	10,266	...	...	...	15	9	6	42	23	19	186
75,920	38,497	37,423	8	4	4	106	53	53	151	82	69	
17,304	8,569	8,735	2	1	1	129	70	59	90	64	26	187
12,590	6,148	6,442	...	...	...	1	1	...	2	2	...	188
23,945	11,537	12,408	1	1	...	9	5	4	4	4	...	189
32,126	15,373	16,753	20	8	12	6	4	2	2	2	...	190
85,965	41,627	44,338	23	10	13	145	80	65	98	72	26	
56,191	28,621	27,570	36	25	11	697	559	138	109	70	39	191
38,890	20,156	18,734	177	91	86	9	7	2	24	12	12	192
19,452	10,254	9,198	...	...	...	11	8	3	9	5	4	193
43,106	22,178	20,928	21	10	11	...	...	...	1	1	...	194
157,639	81,209	76,430	234	126	108	717	574	143	143	88	55	
22,160	11,758	10,402	1	1	...	80	46	34	18	9	9	195
34,013	17,500	16,513	...	...	...	15	6	9	...	...	...	196
26,447	13,625	12,822	12	7	5	23	12	11	...	...	...	197
32,054	16,507	15,547	...	...	...	49	29	20	...	...	...	198
114,674	59,390	55,284	13	8	5	167	93	74	18	9	9	
51,565	27,076	24,489	8	6	2	87	41	46	123	71	52	199
33,644	17,670	15,974	2	2	...	411	245	166	5	2	3	200
32,848	17,668	15,180	...	...	...	7	5	2	60	33	27	201
118,057	62,414	55,643	10	8	2	505	291	214	188	106	82	
42,949	21,341	21,608	150	74	76	1,238	896	342	249	182	67	202
25,180	12,435	12,745	11	3	8	7	7	...	...	...	...	203
51,262	25,433	25,829	...	...	...	4	1	3	3	3	...	204
19,070	9,005	10,065	...	...	...	5	...	5	...	...	...	205
138,461	68,214	70,247	161	77	84	1,254	904	350	252	185	67	
51,110	25,948	25,162	...	...	...	128	57	71	25	14	11	206
28,910	14,827	14,083	...	...	...	35	16	19	...	...	...	207
125,405	64,220	61,185	...	...	...	85	43	42	17	11	6	208
205,425	104,995	100,430	...	...	...	248	116	132	42	25	17	

The Population of the Tahsíls distri

PROVINCIAL TABLE II.

Serial number of district.	Name of district.	Serial number of tahsíl.	Name of tahsíl.	Total Population. Both sexes.	Total Population. Males.	Total Population. Females.	Hindu. Both sexes.	Hindu. Males.	Hindu. Females.
1	2	3	4	5	6	7	8	9	10
45	Bahraich ...	209	Bahraich ...	**356,958**	186,047	*170,911*	**305,156**	159,396	*145,760*
		210	Kaisarganj ...	**332,193**	173,193	*159,000*	**275,989**	144,349	*131,640*
		211	Nánpára ...	**311,281**	164,327	*146,954*	**248,556**	131,065	*117,491*
			Total ...	**1,000,432**	523,567	*476,865*	**829,701**	434,810	*394,891*
46	Sultánpur ...	212	Sultánpur ...	**330,964**	162,215	*168,749*	**284,649**	140,368	*144,281*
		213	Musáfirkhána ...	**251,221**	122,268	*128,953*	**210,586**	103,348	*107,238*
		214	Amethi ...	**219,208**	106,512	*112,696*	**207,903**	100,986	*106,917*
		215	Kadipur ...	**274,458**	139,491	*134,967*	**255,814**	130,277	*125,537*
			Total ...	**1,075,851**	530,486	*545,365*	**958,952**	474,979	*483,973*
47	Partábgarh ...	216	Partábgarh ...	**306,427**	148,426	*158,001*	**272,731**	132,229	*140,502*
		217	Patti ...	**271,592**	134,223	*137,369*	**243,950**	120,696	*123,254*
		218	Kunda ...	**332,876**	162,522	*170,354*	**303,154**	148,480	*154,674*
			Total ...	**910,895**	445,171	*465,724*	**819,835**	401,405	*418,430*
48	Bara Banki ...	219	Nawábganj ...	**242,975**	125,970	*117,005*	**193,290**	101,082	*92,208*
		220	Haidargarh ...	**194,752**	97,081	*97,671*	**173,953**	87,031	*86,922*
		221	Ram Sanehi ghát,	**377,527**	188,763	*188,764*	**315,268**	158,753	*156,515*
		222	Fatehpur ...	**315,652**	165,301	*150,351*	**261,229**	137,689	*123,540*
			Total ...	**1,130,906**	577,115	*553,791*	**943,740**	484,555	*459,185*
			Total, Oudh ...	**12,650,831**	6,490,751	*6,160,080*	**11,015,213**	5,664,853	*5,350,360*
			TOTAL, N.-W. P. AND OUDH.	**46,905,085**	24,303,601	*22,601,484*	**40,380,168**	20,954,923	*19,425,245*

buted according to Religion.

PROVINCIAL TABLE II.

Musalmán.			Jain.			Christian.			Others.			Serial number of tahsil.
Both sexes.	Males.	Females.	Both sexes.	Males.	Females.	Both sexes.	Males.	Females.	Both sexes.	Males.	Females.	
11	12	13	14	15	16	17	18	19	20	21	22	23
51,566	26,505	*25,061*	47	32	*15*	95	55	*40*	94	59	*35*	209
56,087	28,768	*27,319*	1	1	...	8	5	*3*	108	70	*38*	210
62,145	32,942	*29,203*	...	...	...	21	13	*8*	559	307	*252*	211
169,798	88,215	*81,583*	48	33	*15*	124	73	*51*	761	436	*325*	
46,271	21,823	*24,448*	...	...	...	44	24	*20*	...	...	...	212
40,630	18,917	*21,713*	...	...	...	5	3	*2*	...	...	...	213
11,305	5,526	*5,779*	...	...	...	...	...	...	...	...	...	214
18,640	9,211	*9,429*	...	...	...	4	3	*1*	...	...	...	215
116,846	55,477	*61,369*	...	...	...	53	30	*23*	...	...	...	
33,493	16,094	*17,399*	127	63	*64*	65	30	*35*	11	10	*1*	216
27,639	13,524	*14,115*	3	3	...	...	...	...	...	...	...	217
29,706	14,034	*15,672*	...	...	...	12	6	*6*	4	2	*2*	218
90,838	43,652	*47,186*	130	66	*64*	77	36	*41*	15	12	*3*	
49,251	24,667	*24,584*	343	166	*177*	76	47	*29*	15	8	*7*	219
20,793	10,047	*10,746*	1	1	...	5	2	*3*	...	...	...	220
61,758	29,751	*32,007*	447	228	*219*	35	19	*16*	19	12	*7*	221
54,136	27,446	*26,690*	252	144	*108*	31	19	*12*	4	3	*1*	222
185,938	91,911	*94,027*	1,043	539	*504*	147	87	*60*	38	23	*15*	
1,620,930	816,479	*804,451*	2,467	1,290	*1,177*	9,312	6,292	*3,020*	2,909	1,837	*1,072*	
6,346,651	3,243,922	*3,102,729*	84,601	45,624	*38,977*	58,441	37,294	*21,147*	35,224	21,838	*13,386*	

PROVINCIAL TABLE III.

SHOWING THE NUMBER OF VILLAGES AND TOWNS IN EACH TAHSIL CLASSIFIED BY POPULATION.

The number of villages and towns in each

PROVINCIAL TABLE III.

Seral number of district.	Name of district.	Serial. number of tahsíl.	Name of tahsíl.	With less than 200 inhabitants.	With from 200 to 499 inhabitants.	With from 500 to 999 inhabitants.	With from 1,000 to 1,999 inhabitants.
1	2	3	4	5	6	7	8
1	Dehra Dún	1	Debra	274	85	26	6
		2	Kalsi	1	5	9	17
			Total ...	275	90	35	23
2	Sahéranpur	3	Sahéranpur	133	172	189	44
		4	Deoband	60	117	77	44
		5	Roorkee	123	145	103	49
		6	Nukúr	133	162	70	19
			Total ...	449	596	1 389	156
3	Muzaffarnagar	7	Muzaffarnagar	60	75	70	39
		8	Kairána	62	86	57	22
		9	Jánsath	46	59	76	37
		10	Burhana	14	43	41	27
			Total ...	182	263	244	125
4	Meerut	11	Meerut	34	95	84	60
		12	Gháziabad	83	118	74	53
		13	Mowána	72	51	82	34
		14	Bághpat	34	58	52	53
		15	Sardhana	13	26	28	32
		16	Hápur	58	101	94	34
			Total ...	294	449	414	266
5	Bulandshahr	17	Anúpshahr	89	153	82	35
		18	Bulandshahr	62	141	105	49
		19	Sikandarabad	106	155	107	31
		20	Khúrja	76	154	88	25
			Total ...	333	603	382	140
6	Aligarh	21	Atrauli	69	126	68	25
		22	Aligarh	85	165	73	23
		23	Iglas	71	77	37	22
		24	Khair	62	121	242	31
		25	Háthras	104	135	84	29
		26	Sikandra Rao	35	94	70	35
			Total ...	426	718	574	165
7	Muttra	27	Muttra (Sadar)	49	74	59	22
		28	Chháta	20	29	28	17
		29	Kosi	5	14	16	13
		30	Mat	45	41	32	19
		31	Mahaban	53	67	41	24
		32	Sadabad	20	47	34	18
			Total ...	192	272	210	113
8	Agra	33	Etmadpur	28	53	49	81
		34	Firozabad	42	88	28	24
		35	Bah	50	72	52	24
		36	Fatehabad	21	63	53	16
		37	Agra (Sadar)	18	45	50	22
		38	Keraoli	35	64	47	17
		39	Kheragarh	32	46	37	26
			Total ...	226	431	316	160
9	Farukhabad	40	Kanauj	61	78	53	16
		41	Tirwa	64	90	60	31
		42	Chibramau	92	90	41	16
		43	Farukhabad (Sadar) ...	140	140	72	30
		44	Káimganj	190	139	43	15
		45	Aligarh	94	69	38	9
			Total ...	641	606	307	117

tahsíl classified by population.

PROVINCIAL TABLE III.

With from 2,000 to 2,999 inhabitants.	With from 3,000 to 4,999 inhabitants.	With from 5,000 to 9,999 inhabitants.	With from 10,000 to 14,999 inhabitants.	With from 15,000 to 19,999 inhabitants.	With from 20,000 to 49,999 inhabitants.	With 50,000 and over inhabitants.	Total number of villages and towns.	Serial number of tahsíl.	Remarks.
9	10	11	12	13	14	15	16	17	18
5	1	1	...	...	1	...	399	1	
8	1	...	...	...	...	...	41	2	
13	2	1	...	...	1	...	440		
7	2	...	...	...	...	1	498	3	
4	3	1	...	1	...	...	307	4	
7	2	1	2	...	1	...	433	5	
5	4	1	...	1	...	...	395	6	
23	11	3	2	2	1	1	1,633		
11	5	2	...	1	...	...	263	7	
14	5	3	...	1	...	...	250	8	
9	5	4	...	...	...	...	236	9	
15	7	4	...	...	...	...	151	10	
49	22	13	...	2	...	...	900		
8	1	1	...	...	...	1	284	11	
12	8	2	1	...	...	...	351	12	
6	4	3	...	...	...	...	252	13	
21	7	4	1	...	...	...	230	14	
10	11	2	1	...	...	...	123	15	
8	4	1	1	...	...	...	301	16	
65	35	13	4	...	...	1	1,541		
9	2	3	...	...	...	...	373	17	
6	6	2	1	1	...	...	373	18	
6	2	...	...	1	...	...	408	19	
7	4	1	...	...	1	...	356	20	
28	14	6	1	2	1	...	1,510		
6	2	...	...	1	...	...	297	21	
3	1	2	...	...	...	1	353	22	
5	2	...	...	...	...	...	214	23	
4	2	...	...	...	...	...	462	24	
3	3	...	...	...	1	...	359	25	
5	6	...	1	...	...	...	246	26	
26	16	2	1	1	1	1	1,931		
6	7	...	...	...	1	1	219	27	
5	6	...	...	...	...	...	105	28	
5	2	1	...	...	...	...	56	29	
3	2	1	...	...	...	...	143	30	
8	2	3	...	...	...	...	198	31	
4	4	2	...	...	...	...	129	32	
31	23	7	...	...	1	1	850		
11	6	1	...	...	...	...	179	33	
4	...	...	...	1	...	...	187	34	
5	2	1	...	...	...	...	206	35	
8	1	...	...	...	...	...	162	36	
7	2	...	...	...	...	1	145	37	
4	2	1	...	...	...	...	170	38	
6	8	...	...	...	...	...	155	39	
45	21	3	...	1	...	1	1,204		
3	1	...	...	1	...	...	213	40	
8	4	2	...	...	...	...	259	41	
1	1	2	...	...	...	...	243	42	
6	...	...	...	...	...	1	389	43	
4	1	2	...	...	...	...	394	44	
1	...	...	...	...	...	...	211	45	
23	7	6	...	1	...	1	1,709		

The number of villages and towns in each

PROVINCIAL TABLE III.

Serial number of district.	Name of district.	Serial number of tahsíl.	Name of tahsíl.	With less than 200 inhabitants.	With from 200 to 499 inhabitants.	With from 500 to 999 inhabitants.	With from 1,000 to 1,999 inhabitants.
1	2	3	4	5	6	7	8
10	Mainpuri	46	Mainpuri	61	94	56	81
		47	Bhongaon	151	131	57	36
		48	Karhal	62	76	48	10
		49	Shikohabad	82	123	56	23
		50	Mustafabad	84	93	65	25
			Total ...	440	517	282	125
11	Etáwah	51	Etáwah	123	134	67	25
		52	Bharthna	74	121	72	32
		53	Bidhuna	103	98	62	26
		54	Phaphúnd	83	95	47	13
		55	Auraiya	97	115	58	19
			Total ..	480	563	306	115
12	Etah	56	Etah	153	174	85	46
		57	Kásganj	161	141	59	14
		58	Aliganj	193	176	81	16
		59	Jalesar	24	58	43	25
			Total ...	531	549	268	101
13	Bareilly	60	Farídpur	129	120	55	16
		61	Bareilly	121	183	81	21
		62	Aonla	59	130	94	28
		63	Mírganj	14	63	59	18
		64	Baheri	75	199	100	31
		65	Nawábganj	97	124	70	13
			Total ...	495	819	459	127
14	Bijnor	66	Bijnor	182	130	32	9
		67	Najíbabad	206	138	52	8
		68	Nagína	232	143	75	15
		69	Dhámpur	265	169	60	12
		70	Chándpur	186	141	47	9
			Total ...	1,071	721	266	53
15	Budaun	71	Gunnaur	53	119	74	15
		72	Bisauli	80	146	75	34
		73	Sahaswán	178	166	78	25
		74	Budaun	114	160	81	29
		75	Dátaganj	126	153	82	30
			Total ...	551	744	390	193
16	Moradabad	76	Moradabad	57	112	94	27
		77	Thákurdwára	67	117	59	15
		78	Bilári	81	171	108	28
		79	Sambhal	119	218	102	22
		80	Amroha	244	202	47	10
		81	Hasanpur	294	180	38	10
			Total ...	862	1,000	443	112
17	Sháhjahánpur	82	Sháhjahánpur	156	177	101	28
		83	Jalálabad	133	126	67	20
		84	Tilhar	197	212	108	25
		85	Powáyan	261	255	112	36
			Total ...	747	770	388	109
18	Pilibhít	86	Bisalpur	101	197	102	21
		87	Pilibhit	92	194	83	14
		88	Puranpur	114	69	38	8
			Total ...	307	460	223	43

tahsil classified by population.

PROVINCIAL TABLE III.

With from 2,000 to 2,999 inhabitants.	With from 3,000 to 4,999 inhabitants.	With from 5,000 to 9,999 inhabitants.	With from 10,000 to 14,999 inhabitants.	With from 15,000 to 19,999 inhabitants.	With from 20,000 to 49,999 inhabitants.	With 50,000 and over inhabitants.	Total number of villages and towns.	Serial number of tahsil.	Remarks.
9	10	11	12	13	14	15	16	17	18
9	...	2	...	1	...	...	**254**	46	
16	1	2	...	...	...	...	**394**	47	
4	1	1	...	...	...	...	**202**	48	
2	2	1	...	...	...	...	**289**	49	
7	2	2	...	...	...	...	**278**	50	
38	6	8	...	1	...	...	**1,417**		
5	2	...	...	...	1	...	**357**	51	
6	4	...	...	...	...	...	**309**	52	
3	1	...	...	...	...	...	**293**	53	
2	1	1	...	...	...	...	**242**	54	
1	...	1	...	...	...	...	**291**	55	
17	8	2	...	...	1	...	**1,492**		
3	3	2	...	...	...	...	**466**	56	
5	5	1	1	1	...	...	**388**	57	
1	2	...	...	...	...	...	**469**	58	
6	1	1	1	...	...	...	**159**	59	
15	11	4	2	1	...	...	**1,482**		
1	...	1	...	...	...	...	**322**	60	
7	...	...	...	...	...	1	**414**	61	
7	2	1	1	...	...	...	**322**	62	
2	1	...	...	...	...	...	**157**	63	
6	1	...	...	...	...	...	**412**	64	
1	2	...	...	...	...	...	**307**	65	
24	6	2	1	...	...	1	**1,934**		
1	1	3	...	1	...	...	**359**	66	
2	1	...	1	1	...	...	**409**	67	
2	...	3	...	...	1	...	**471**	68	
...	...	3	1	1	...	...	**511**	69	
2	3	...	1	...	...	...	**389**	70	
7	5	9	3	3	1	...	**2,139**		
2	...	1	...	...	...	...	**264**	71	
5	3	1	...	...	...	...	**344**	72	
3	1	1	...	1	...	...	**453**	73	
5	3	1	...	...	1	...	**394**	74	
4	3	3	...	...	...	...	**401**	75	
19	10	7	...	1	1	...	**1,856**		
2	4	1	...	...	...	1	**298**	76	
3	1	1	...	...	...	...	**263**	77	
4	4	1	...	...	1	...	**393**	78	
4	...	1	1	...	1	...	**468**	79	
1	2	1	...	...	1	...	**508**	80	
2	2	2	...	...	...	...	**528**	81	
16	13	7	1	...	3	1	**2,458**		
1	2	...	...	...	...	1	**466**	82	
6	2	1	...	...	...	...	**355**	83	
2	1	2	...	1	...	...	**548**	84	
3	...	1	...	...	...	...	**668**	85	
12	5	4	...	1	...	1	**2,037**		
2	...	1	...	...	...	...	**424**	86	
2	1	1	...	...	1	...	**388**	87	
8	2	...	...	...	...	...	**239**	88	
12	3	2	...	...	1	...	**1,051**		

The number of villages and towns in each

PROVINCIAL TABLE III.

Serial number of district.	Name of district.	Serial number of tahsíl.	Name of tahsíl.	With less than 200 inhabitants.	With from 200 to 499 inhabitants.	With from 500 to 999 inhabitants.	With from 1,000 to 1,999 inhabitants.
1	2	3	4	5	6	7	8
19	Cawnpore	89	Akbarpur	54	77	44	20
		90	Bilhaur	28	53	44	24
		91	Bhognipur	64	107	47	10
		92	Cawnpore	66	78	44	26
		93	Derapur	88	112	60	17
		94	Rasúlabad	33	53	43	23
		95	Narwal	42	70	31	27
		96	Shiurájpur	146	81	57	29
		97	Ghátampur	58	95	55	17
			Total ...	579	726	425	193
20	Fatehpur	98	Fatehpur	158	124	62	24
		99	Kalianpur	49	97	47	17
		100	Kora	45	84	28	18
		101	Ghâzipur	43	56	28	14
		102	Khakhreru	49	65	38	11
		103	Khága	153	108	41	27
			Total ...	497	534	244	106
21	Bánda	104	Bánda	20	42	25	20
		105	Pailáni	25	39	25	23
		106	Baberu	19	35	35	23
		107	Kamásin	50	60	34	21
		108	Mau	65	62	28	12
		109	Karwi	77	63	36	17
		110	Badausa	34	40	35	17
		111	Girwan	61	57	36	19
			Total ...	351	398	254	152
22	Hamírpur	112	Hamírpur	35	42	20	20
		113	Muskara	28	15	26	14
		114	Ráth	32	33	40	26
		115	Kulpahár	91	68	44	26
		116	Mahoba	10	37	31	10
		117	Maudha	20	22	24	13
			Total ...	216	217	185	109
23	Allahabad	118	Allahabad	82	117	78	26
		119	Sirathu	79	78	67	21
		120	Manjhanpur	73	103	64	23
		121	Soraon	146	165	89	31
		122	Phúlpur	192	200	77	18
		123	Handia	268	207	88	20
		124	Karchhana	123	135	64	19
		125	Bárá	125	85	28	4
		126	Meja	254	220	81	21
			Total ...	1,342	1,310	636	188
24	Jhánsi	127	Jhánsi	74	76	45	14
		128	Mau	43	49	41	27
		129	Garotha	49	57	47	18
		130	Moth	41	40	21	13
		131	Lalitpur	162	120	65	25
		132	Mehroni	129	97	55	16
			Total ...	498	489	274	113
25	Jalaun	133	Orai	44	21	23	14
		134	Kálpi	62	53	25	14
		135	Jalaun	175	146	58	20
		136	Kúnch	73	66	37	14
			Total ...	354	286	188	62

tahsil classified by population.

PROVINCIAL TABLE III.

With from 2,000 to 2,999 inhabitants.	With from 3,000 to 4,999 inhabitants.	With from 5,000 to 9,999 inhabitants.	With from 10,000 to 14,999 inhabitants.	With from 15,000 to 19,999 inhabitants.	With from 20,000 to 49,999 inhabitants.	With 50,000 and over inhabitants.	Total number of villages and towns.	Serial number of tahsil.	Remarks.
9	10	11	12	13	14	15	16	17	18
3	1	...	...	...	...	...	199	89	
5	...	1	...	...	...	...	155	90	
3	...	...	...	...	...	...	231	91	
4	7	1	...	...	...	1	227	92	
4	...	...	...	...	...	...	281	93	
3	3	...	...	...	...	...	158	94	
4	1	...	...	...	...	...	175	95	
5	1	...	...	...	...	...	319	96	
4	2	...	...	...	...	...	231	97	
35	15	2	...	...	...	1	1,976		
6	3	...	...	...	1	...	378	98	
6	1	2	...	...	...	...	219	99	
2	3	...	...	...	...	...	175	100	
7	4	...	...	...	...	...	152	101	
4	2	...	...	...	...	...	169	102	
2	4	...	...	...	...	...	335	103	
27	17	2	...	...	1	...	1,428		
6	2	1	...	...	1	...	117	104	
8	1	...	...	...	...	...	121	105	
5	4	...	...	...	...	...	121	106	
2	...	...	...	...	...	...	167	107	
1	1	1	...	...	...	...	170	108	
3	1	...	...	...	...	...	197	109	
2	2	...	...	...	...	...	130	110	
3	1	...	...	...	...	...	177	111	
30	12	2	...	...	1	...	1,200		
1	2	2	...	...	...	...	122	112	
4	3	1	...	...	...	...	91	113	
4	...	...	1	...	...	...	136	114	
5	3	1	...	...	...	...	238	115	
4	1	2	...	...	...	...	95	116	
1	1	1	...	...	...	...	82	117	
19	10	7	1	...	...	...	764		
8	2	1	...	...	...	1	315	118	
7	1	...	...	...	...	...	354	119	
3	1	...	...	...	...	...	268	120	
4	...	1	...	...	...	...	436	121	
3	1	1	...	...	...	...	492	122	
2	...	...	...	...	...	...	585	123	
2	1	...	...	...	...	...	343	124	
...	...	...	...	...	...	...	242	125	
2	4	...	...	...	...	...	582	126	
31	10	3	...	...	...	1	3,516		
2	...	1	...	...	...	1	213	127	
...	2	...	...	1	...	...	163	128	
1	...	1	...	...	...	...	173	129	
...	3	...	...	...	...	...	118	130	
4	...	1	1	...	...	...	378	131	
3	2	...	...	...	...	...	302	132	
10	7	3	1	1	...	1	1,347		
2	2	1	...	...	...	...	107	133	
2	...	...	1	...	...	...	157	134	
3	2	1	...	...	...	...	400	135	
6	...	...	1	...	...	...	197	136	
13	4	2	2	...	...	...	861		

The number of villages and towns in each

PROVINCIAL TABLE III.

Serial number of district.	Name of district.	Serial number of tahsíl.	Name of tahsíl.	With less than 200 inhabitants.	With from 200 to 499 inhabitants.	With from 500 to 999 inhabitants.	With from 1,000 to 1,999 inhabitants.
1	2	3	4	5	6	7	8
26	Benares	137	Benares	415	359	159	55
		138	Gangapur	129	102	34	15
		139	Chandauli	316	239	125	26
			Total ...	860	700	318	96
27	Mirzapur	140	Mirzapur	522	299	118	30
		141	Chunar	280	208	72	15
		142	Robertsganj	850	311	72	14
		143	Kourh	564	370	128	17
		144	Chakia	296	99	17	2
			Total ...	2,512	1,287	407	78
28	Jaunpur ...	145	Jaunpur	324	249	107	32
		146	Mariáhu	259	255	126	40
		147	Khutahan	264	267	131	38
		148	Machhlishahr	234	229	126	32
		149	Kerakat	166	144	100	41
			Total ...	1,247	1,144	590	183
29	Gházipur	150	Gházipur	457	255	130	52
		151	Korantadih	413	206	109	40
		152	Zamánia	119	100	70	46
		153	Saidpur	300	150	82	26
			Total ...	1,289	711	391	164
30	Ballia	154	Ballia	204	113	99	53
		155	Rasra	296	199	119	69
		156	Bansdih	247	121	80	43
			Total ...	747	433	298	165
31	Gorakhpur	157	Bánsgaon	950	522	152	45
		158	Mahárájganj	389	536	277	70
		159	Padrauna	388	515	259	98
		160	Háta	249	426	213	55
		161	Deoria	520	488	204	68
		162	Gorakhpur (Sadar)... ...	389	436	184	54
			Total ...	2,885	2,923	1,289	390
32	Basti	163	Domariaganj	479	491	103	25
		164	Bansi	695	470	109	30
		165	Haraiya	830	482	115	25
		166	Basti	933	549	95	16
		167	Khalilabad	748	482	130	31
			Total ...	3,685	2,474	552	127
33	Azamgarh	168	Deogaon	317	202	128	54
		169	Nizamabad	373	278	107	39
		170	Mahul	376	358	165	44
		171	Sagri	655	424	165	76
		172	Muhammadabad	458	231	126	60
			Total ...	2,179	1,493	691	273
34	Almora	173	Champáwat	1,287	65	...	...
		174	Almora	3,151	326	7	...
			Total ...	4,438	391	7	...
35	Garhwál	175	Pauri	3,134	488	88	1
			Total ...	3,134	488	88	1

tahsíl classified by population.

PROVINCIAL TABLE III.

With from 2,000 to 2,999 inhabitants.	With from 3,000 to 4,999 inhabitants.	With from 5,000 to 9,999 inhabitants.	With from 10,000 to 14,999 inhabitants.	With from 15,000 to 19,999 inhabitants.	With from 20,000 to 49,999 inhabitants.	With 50,000 and over inhabitants.	Total number of villages and towns.	Serial number of tahsíl.	Remarks.
9	10	11	12	13	14	15	16	17	18
6	3	...	...	...	...	1	998	137	
1	...	...	...	...	...	...	281	138	
6	...	...	1	...	...	...	713	139	
13	3	...	1	...	...	1	1,992		
5	3	...	...	...	...	1	978	140	
1	...	...	2	...	...	...	578	141	
3	...	...	...	...	...	...	1,250	142	
5	1	...	...	...	...	...	1,085	143	
2	...	...	...	...	...	...	416	144	
16	4	...	2	...	...	1	4,307		
6	1	...	...	...	1	...	720	145	
...	1	...	...	...	...	...	681	146	
8	4	1	...	...	...	...	713	147	
2	...	2	...	...	...	...	625	148	
3	1	...	...	...	...	...	455	149	
19	7	3	...	...	1	...	3,194		
9	2	...	...	...	1	...	906	150	
10	9	2	...	...	...	...	789	151	
12	4	3	3	...	...	...	357	152	
4	...	...	...	...	...	...	562	153	
35	15	5	3	...	1	...	2,614		
23	9	6	1	1	...	...	509	154	
8	4	1	...	...	...	...	696	155	
9	7	6	1	...	...	...	514	156	
40	20	13	2	1	...	...	1,719		
6	2	3	...	...	...	...	1,680	157	
5	1	...	...	...	...	...	1,278	158	
17	4	4	...	...	...	...	1,285	159	
5	4	1	...	...	...	...	953	160	
14	1	4	1	...	...	...	1,300	161	
11	3	...	...	...	...	1	1,078	162	
58	15	12	1	...	...	1	7,574		
...	1	...	...	...	...	...	1,099	163	
5	2	1	...	...	...	...	1,312	164	
1	1	...	...	...	...	...	1,454	165	
4	2	...	1	...	...	...	1,600	166	
5	1	...	1	...	...	...	1,398	167	
15	7	1	2	...	...	...	6,863		
2	2	...	...	...	...	...	705	168	
5	2	...	...	1	...	...	805	169	
7	...	...	...	...	...	...	950	170	
8	6	2	...	...	...	...	1,336	171	
9	1	3	1	1	...	...	890	172	
31	11	5	1	2	...	...	4,686		
...	...	...	...	...	...	...	1,352	173	
1	...	1	...	...	...	...	3,486	174	
1	...	1	...	...	...	...	4,838		
1	...	...	...	...	...	...	3,662	175	
1	...	...	...	...	...	...	3,662		

The number of villages and towns in each

PROVINCIAL TABLE III.

Serial number of district.	Name of district.	Serial number of tahsíl.	Name of tahsíl.	With less than 200 inhabitants.	With from 200 to 499 inhabitants.	With from 500 to 999 inhabitants.	With from 1,000 to 1,999 inhabitants.
1	2	3	4	5	6	7	8
36	Naini Tal	176	Rudarpur	100	94	37	10
		177	Kilpuri	75	85	25	2
		178	Káshipur	64	61	22	2
		179	Bhabar	936	156	31	2
			Total	1,175	396	115	16
			Total, N.-W. Provinces	36,490	26,521	12,748	4,594
37	Lucknow	180	Lucknow	66	120	79	32
		181	Mohanlálganj	40	83	68	25
		182	Malihabad	111	153	82	27
			Total	217	356	229	84
38	Unao	183	Unao	75	102	59	37
		184	Safipur	90	155	78	33
		185	Purwa	139	218	105	46
		186	Mohan	120	211	97	40
			Total	424	686	339	156
39	Rae Bareli	187	Rae Bareli	75	138	82	38
		188	Dálmau	171	232	121	39
		189	Digbijaiganj	52	109	107	77
		190	Salon	129	163	87	49
			Total	427	642	397	203
40	Sitapur	191	Sitapur	217	247	186	27
		192	Sidhauli	140	200	158	40
		193	Misrikh	250	247	122	25
		194	Biswan	93	205	155	44
			Total	700	899	571	136
41	Hardoi	195	Hardoi	115	145	121	79
		196	Sandila	74	141	101	66
		197	Bilgram	132	172	111	56
		198	Sháhabad	185	201	102	32
			Total	506	659	435	233
42	Kheri	199	Lakhimpur	180	226	197	68
		200	Muhamdi	190	242	132	39
		201	Nighasan	113	109	112	67
			Total	483	577	441	174
43	Fyzabad	202	Fyzabad	148	150	85	47
		203	Akbarpur	231	252	119	35
		204	Tanda	399	358	162	43
		205	Bikapur	184	230	147	55
			Total	962	990	513	180
44	Gonda	206	Gonda	178	315	198	69
		207	Tarabganj	112	178	162	88
		208	Utraula	408	573	428	72
			Total	698	1,066	788	229
45	Bahraich	209	Bahraich	172	257	199	55
		210	Kaisarganj	160	251	160	62
		211	Nánpára	114	188	180	54
			Total	446	696	589	171

tahsíl classified by population.

PROVINCIAL TABLE III.

With from 2,000 to 2,999 inhabitants.	With from 3,000 to 4,999 inhabitants.	With from 5,000 to 9,999 inhabitants.	With from 10,000 to 14,999 inhabitants.	With from 15,000 to 19,999 inhabitants.	With from 20,000 to 49,999 inhabitants.	With 50,000 and over inhabitants.	Total number of villages and towns.	Serial number of tahsíl.	Remarks.
9	10	11	12	13	14	15	16	17	18
1	...	...	...	...	...	...	242	176	
...	...	...	...	...	...	...	187	177	
3	...	1	1	...	...	...	154	178	
...	1	2	...	...	...	...	1,128	179	
4	1	3	1	...	...	...	1,711		
861	376	163	32	20	16	15	81,836		
8	1	1	...	...	...	1	308	180	
6	3	2	...	...	...	...	227	181	
4	1	1	...	...	...	...	379	182	
18	5	4	...	...	...	1	914		
7	6	...	1	...	...	...	287	183	
7	2	3	...	...	...	...	368	184	
9	9	1	1	...	...	...	528	185	
7	7	2	...	...	...	...	484	186	
30	24	6	2	...	...	...	1,667		
6	4	2	...	1	...	...	346	187	
7	5	1	...	...	...	...	576	188	
14	5	...	...	...	...	...	364	189	
7	10	...	1	...	...	...	446	190	
34	24	3	1	1	...	...	1,732		
...	1	...	2	...	1	...	631	191	
4	1	1	...	...	...	...	544	192	
3	2	...	...	...	...	...	649	193	
4	2	1	...	...	...	...	504	194	
11	6	2	2	...	1	...	2,328		
8	5	1	1	...	...	...	475	195	
15	4	...	...	1	...	...	402	196	
8	1	2	2	...	...	...	484	197	
2	1	...	...	...	1	...	524	198	
33	11	3	3	1	1	...	1,885		
6	1	2	...	...	...	...	680	199	
1	3	1	...	...	...	...	608	200	
11	8	3	...	...	...	...	423	201	
18	12	6	...	...	...	...	1,711		
11	5	2	...	...	...	1	449	202	
4	...	...	...	...	...	...	641	203	
5	2	1	...	1	...	...	971	204	
6	1	...	...	...	...	...	623	205	
26	8	3	...	1	...	1	2,684		
9	2	...	...	1	...	...	772	206	
15	7	2	...	...	...	...	564	207	
7	4	2	1	...	...	...	1,495	208	
31	13	4	1	1	...	...	2,831		
4	1	1	...	...	1	...	690	209	
11	4	...	...	...	...	...	648	210	
10	1	1	...	...	...	...	548	211	
25	6	2	...	...	1	...	1,886		

The number of villages and towns in each

PROVINCIAL TABLE III.

Serial number of district.	Name of district.	Serial number of tahsíl.	Name of tahsíl.	With less than 200 inhabitants.	With from 200 to 499 inhabitants.	With from 500 to 999 inhabitants.	With from 1,000 to 1,999 inhabitants.
1	2	3	4	5	6	7	8
46	Sultánpur	212	Sultánpur	314	312	146	58
		213	Musáfirkhána	103	149	115	52
		214	Amethi	110	187	111	45
		215	Kadipur	281	292	136	34
			Total ...	808	940	507	184
47	Partábgarh	216	Partábgarh	221	295	130	44
		217	Patti	326	311	135	24
		218	Kunda	197	271	145	63
			Total ...	744	877	410	131
48	Bara Banki	219	Nawábganj	82	161	107	36
		220	Haidargarh	100	136	92	34
		221	Ramsanehighát	123	234	180	76
		222	Fatehpur	216	260	143	41
			Total ...	521	781	522	187
			Total, Oudh ...	6,936	9,169	5,691	2,068
			TOTAL, N.-W. P. & OUDH ...	43,426	35,690	18,439	6,662

tahsíl classified by population.

PROVINCIAL TABLE III.

With from 2,000 to 2,999 inhabitants.	With from 3,000 to 4,999 inhabitants.	With from 5,000 to 9,999 inhabitants.	With from 10,000 to 14,999 inhabitants.	With from 15,000 to 19,999 inhabitants.	With from 20,000 to 49,999 inhabitants.	With 50,000 and over inhabitants.	Total number of villages and towns.	Serial number of tahsíl.	Remarks.
9	10	11	12	13	14	15	16	17	18
6	1	1	...	...	...	...	**832**	212	
11	4	...	...	...	...	...	**434**	213	
4	...	...	...	...	...	...	**457**	214	
4	1	...	...	...	...	...	**748**	215	
25	6	1	...	...	...	...	**2,471**		
7	1	1	...	...	...	...	**699**	216	
3	1	...	...	...	...	...	**800**	217	
10	3	...	...	...	...	...	**689**	218	
20	5	1	...	...	...	...	**2,188**		
7	5	1	1	...	...	...	**390**	219	
6	4	...	...	...	...	...	**372**	220	
10	5	1	1	...	...	...	**630**	221	
5	8	2	...	...	...	...	**675**	222	
28	22	4	2	...	...	...	**2,067**		
299	142	39	11	4	3	2	**24,364**		
1,160	518	202	43	24	19	17	**106,200**		

PROVINCIAL TABLE IV.

SHOWING THE EDUCATIONAL POSITION OF EACH TAHSIL IN THE NORTH-WESTERN PROVINCES AND OUDH.

Showing the Educational position of each Tahsíl in the N.-W. Provinces and Oudh.

PROVINCIAL TABLE IV.

Serial number of district.	Name of district.	Serial number of tahsíl.	Name of tahsíl.	Total by Education. Learning. Males.	Learning. Females.	Literate. Males.	Literate. Females.	Illiterate. Males.	Illiterate. Females.	Age-period, 5 to 14. Total males.	Learning.	Literate.	Illiterate.
1	2	3	4	5	6	7	8	9	10	11	12	13	14
1	Debra Dún.	1	Dehra ... Urban ...	1,011	236	4,470	720	17,772	11,398	3,623	696	223	2,704
			Rural ...	813	67	4,764	217	43,059	32,911	9,720	532	117	9,071
			Total ...	1,824	303	9,234	937	60,831	44,309	13,343	1,228	340	11,775
		2	Kalsi ... Urban ...	57	18	464	62	1,373	664	211	39	8	164
			Rural ...	19	5	364	11	26,158	21,502	6,374	10	14	6,350
			Total ...	76	23	828	73	27,531	22,166	6,585	49	22	6,514
			Total ... Urban ...	1,068	254	4,934	782	19,145	12,062	3,834	735	231	2,868
			Rural ...	832	72	5,128	228	69,217	54,413	16,094	542	131	15,421
			Total ...	1,900	326	10,062	1,010	88,362	66,475	19,928	1,277	362	18,289
2	Sahâranpur.	3	Sahâranpur ... Urban ...	1,537	85	4,730	453	27,909	28,390	6,841	1,014	190	5,637
			Rural ...	935	17	3,604	46	126,621	118,081	33,650	723	184	32,793
			Total ...	2,472	102	8,334	499	154,620	146,471	40,491	1,737	324	38,430
		4	Deoband ... Urban ...	510	6	1,766	32	13,682	13,991	3,300	328	108	2,864
			Rural ...	422	9	2,721	13	93,584	78,891	23,324	297	99	22,928
			Total ...	932	15	4,487	45	107,266	92,882	26,624	625	207	25,792
		5	Roorkee ... Urban ...	1,106	54	6,293	246	33,686	29,172	7,586	551	181	6,854
			Rural ...	716	2	3,623	17	113,803	101,780	30,264	561	138	29,565
			Total ...	1,822	56	9,916	263	147,489	130,952	37,850	1,112	319	36,419
		6	Nukúr ... Urban ...	592	16	2,225	49	17,352	18,867	4,379	394	71	3,914
			Rural ...	419	7	1,934	16	80,491	70,689	20,771	290	93	20,388
			Total ...	1,011	23	4,159	65	97,843	89,556	25,150	684	164	24,302
			Total ... Urban ...	3,745	161	15,014	780	92,719	90,420	22,106	2,287	550	19,269
			Rural ...	2,492	35	11,882	92	414,499	369,441	108,009	1,871	464	105,674
			Total ...	6,237	196	26,896	872	507,218	459,861	130,115	4,158	1,014	124,943
3	Muzaffarnagar.	7	Muzaffarnagar Urban ...	621	22	2,647	94	13,467	12,043	3,279	436	69	2,774
			Rural ...	888	4	3,736	23	92,254	80,697	23,439	614	104	22,721
			Total ...	1,509	26	6,383	117	105,721	92,740	26,718	1,050	173	25,495
		8	Kairána ... Urban ...	676	9	2,512	69	21,035	22,133	5,419	493	73	4,853
			Rural ...	578	2	3,289	13	79,611	70,230	19,801	467	113	19,221
			Total ...	1,254	11	5,801	82	100,646	92,363	25,220	960	186	24,074
		9	Jánsath ... Urban ...	569	10	1,670	31	11,910	12,373	3,161	428	34	2,699
			Rural ...	1,129	23	3,542	71	85,093	77,108	21,494	842	108	20,544
			Total ...	1,698	33	5,212	102	97,012	89,476	24,655	1,270	142	23,243
		10	Burhana ... Urban ...	300	1	1,348	14	11,200	11,251	2,835	218	42	2,575
			Rural ...	694	...	3,704	6	75,751	68,424	19,264	558	162	18,544
			Total ...	994	1	5,047	20	86,951	79,675	22,099	776	204	21,119
			Total ... Urban ...	2,166	42	8,172	208	57,021	57,800	14,694	1,575	218	12,901
			Rural ...	3,289	29	14,271	113	332,709	296,454	83,998	2,481	487	81,030
			Total ...	5,455	71	22,443	321	390,330	354,254	98,692	4,056	705	93,931

Showing the Educational position of each Tahsíl in the N.-W. P. and Oudh—(*continued*).

PROVINCIAL TABLE IV.

Serial number of district.	Name of district.	Serial number of tahsíl.	Name of tahsíl.		Total by Education. Learning. Males.	Learning. Females.	Literate. Males.	Literate. Females.	Illiterate. Males.	Illiterate. Females.	Age—period, 5 to 14. Total males.	Learning.	Literate.	Illiterate.
1	2	3	4		5	6	7	8	9	10	11	12	13	14
	Meerut.	11	Meerut ...	Urban ...	2,594	*202*	12,488	*903*	59,383	*56,470*	**14,767**	1,891	296	12,580
				Rural ...	692	*2*	3,660	*12*	99,288	*90,360*	**24,487**	551	113	23,823
			Total ...		3,286	*204*	16,148	*915*	158,671	*146,830*	**39,254**	2,442	409	36,403
		12	Gháziabad ...	Urban ...	559	*14*	2,793	*75*	19,028	*19,763*	**4,900**	463	67	4,370
				Rural ...	613	*4*	4,223	*24*	104,862	*95,183*	**26,216**	473	129	25,614
			Total ...		1,172	*18*	7,016	*99*	123,890	*114,946*	**31,116**	936	196	29,984
		13	Mowána ...	Urban ...	338	*10*	1,014	*22*	10,659	*11,089*	**2,803**	263	22	2,518
				Rural ...	733	*3*	2,508	*14*	79,065	*72,463*	**19,725**	560	85	19,080
			Total ...		1,071	*13*	3,522	*36*	89,724	*83,502*	**22,528**	823	107	21,598
		14	Bághpat ...	Urban ...	383	*2*	2,528	*18*	19,163	*18,524*	**4,913**	316	83	4,514
				Rural ...	788	...	5,184	*19*	112,257	*100,790*	**27,809**	620	212	26,977
			Total ...		1,171	*2*	7,712	*37*	131,420	*119,314*	**32,722**	936	295	31,491
		15	Sardhana ...	Urban ...	360	*71*	1,633	*36*	13,737	*13,930*	**3,708**	284	59	3,360
				Rural ...	514	*14*	3,674	*19*	70,621	*64,083*	**17,538**	411	150	16,977
			Total ...		874	*85*	5,307	*55*	84,358	*78,013*	**21,241**	695	209	20,337
		16	Hápur ...	Urban ...	309	*6*	1,606	*17*	9,289	*9,820*	**2,313**	239	39	2,035
				Rural ...	1,065	*8*	4,304	*31*	95,329	*90,263*	**23,797**	844	141	22,812
			Total ...		1,374	*14*	5,910	*48*	104,618	*100,083*	**26,110**	1,083	180	24,847
			Total ...	Urban ...	4,543	*305*	22,062	*1,071*	131,259	*129,546*	**33,399**	3,456	566	29,377
				Rural ...	4,405	*31*	23,553	*119*	561,422	*513,142*	**139,572**	3,459	830	135,283
			Total ...		8,948	*336*	45,615	*1,190*	692,681	*642,688*	**172,971**	6,915	1,896	164,660
	Bulandshahr.	17	Anúpshahr ...	Urban ...	654	*8*	2,276	*78*	13,890	*15,256*	**3,526**	480	59	2,987
				Rural ...	838	*14*	3,619	*86*	95,994	*89,768*	**23,986**	616	120	23,250
			Total ...		1,492	*22*	5,895	*164*	109,884	*105,024*	**27,512**	1,096	179	26,237
		18	Bulandshahr...	Urban ...	1,067	*33*	2,829	*123*	20,206	*20,904*	**5,008**	767	69	4,172
				Rural ...	1,463	*22*	4,930	*75*	117,550	*112,726*	**29,295**	1,104	139	28,052
			Total ...		2,530	*55*	7,759	*198*	137,756	*133,630*	**34,303**	1,871	208	32,224
		19	Sikandarabad	Urban ...	566	*10*	2,142	*121*	14,017	*15,512*	**3,542**	438	52	3,052
				Rural ...	403	*1*	3,403	*43*	99,347	*88,803*	**23,735**	287	106	23,342
			Total ...		969	*11*	5,545	*164*	113,364	*104,315*	**27,277**	725	158	26,394
		20	Khúrja ...	Urban ...	750	*11*	2,772	*48*	23,131	*24,864*	**5,807**	547	56	5,204
				Rural ...	632	*20*	3,426	*33*	85,716	*79,734*	**21,005**	515	99	20,391
			Total ...		1,382	*31*	6,198	*81*	108,847	*104,598*	**26,812**	1,062	155	25,595
			Total ...	Urban ...	3,037	*62*	10,019	*370*	71,244	*76,536*	**17,883**	2,232	236	15,415
				Rural ...	3,336	*57*	15,378	*237*	398,607	*371,031*	**98,021**	2,522	464	95,035
			Total ...		6,378	*119*	25,397	*607*	469,851	*447,567*	**115,904**	4,754	700	110,450

Showing the Educational position of each Tahsíl in the N.-W. P. and Oudh—(*continued*).

PROVINCIAL TABLE IV.

Serial number of district.	Name of district.	Serial number of tahsíl.	Name of tahsíl.	Total by Education. Learning. Males.	Learning. Females.	Literate. Males.	Literate. Females.	Illiterate. Males.	Illiterate. Females.	Age—period, 5 to 14. Total males.	Learning.	Literate.	Illiterate.
1	2	3	4	5	6	7	8	9	10	11	12	13	14
6	Aligarh.	21	Atrauli ... Urban ...	255	*7*	1,018	*43*	10,676	*11,240*	**2,689**	217	64	2,408
			Rural ...	307	*4*	1,868	*24*	73,520	*65,111*	**17,482**	274	128	17,080
			Total ...	562	*11*	2,886	*67*	84,196	*76,351*	**20,171**	491	192	19,488
		22	Aligarh ... Urban ...	1,101	*32*	3,771	*127*	34,962	*34,590*	**8,014**	756	341	6,917
			Rural ...	684	*3*	2,337	*16*	79,620	*72,524*	**18,309**	632	276	17,401
			Total ...	1,785	*35*	6,108	*143*	114,582	*107,114*	**26,323**	1,388	617	24,318
		23	Iglas ... Urban ..	47	...	218	*6*	1,354	*1,490*	**409**	39	20	350
			Rural ...	368	*6*	2,604	*25*	53,037	*48,072*	**12,920**	303	152	12,465
			Total ...	415	*6*	2,822	*31*	54,391	*49,562*	**13,329**	342	172	12,815
		24	Khair ... Urban ...	148	*1*	636	*9*	5,380	*5,571*	**1,450**	126	6	1,318
			Rural ...	446	*3*	2,872	*39*	70,656	*64,895*	**17,390**	391	136	16,863
			Total ...	594	*4*	3,508	*48*	76,036	*70,466*	**18,840**	517	142	18,181
		25	Háthras ... Urban ...	380	*13*	1,060	*43*	27,847	*25,367*	**5,945**	276	62	5,607
			Rural ...	692	*7*	2,199	*39*	79,531	*71,086*	**17,644**	589	106	16,949
			Total ...	1,072	*20*	3,259	*82*	107,378	*96,453*	**23,589**	865	168	22,556
		26	Sikandra Rao Urban ...	423	*25*	1,591	*52*	16,447	*16,207*	**4,180**	323	60	3,797
			Rural ...	445	*5*	2,952	*50*	77,291	*67,697*	**18,744**	359	119	18,266
			Total ...	868	*30*	4,543	*102*	93,738	*83,904*	**22,924**	682	179	22,063
			Total ... Urban ...	2,354	*78*	8,294	*280*	96,666	*94,465*	**22,687**	1,737	553	20,397
			Rural ...	2,942	*28*	14,832	*193*	433,655	*389,385*	**102,489**	2,548	917	99,024
			Total ...	5,296	*106*	23,126	*473*	530,321	*483,850*	**125,176**	4,285	1,470	119,421
7	Muttra.	27	Muttra (Sadar) Urban ...	1,834	*65*	11,295	*510*	42,919	*48,284*	**9,855**	1,331	216	8,308
			Rural ...	560	*1*	3,580	*64*	65,802	*60,000*	**15,457**	457	96	14,904
			Total ...	2,394	*66*	14,875	*574*	108,721	*108,284*	**25,312**	1,788	312	23,212
		28	Chhâta ... Urban ...	113	*1*	474	*10*	5,297	*5,127*	**1,278**	87	12	1,179
			Rural ...	269	*9*	2,477	*21*	41,042	*38,403*	**9,455**	238	106	9,111
			Total ...	382	*10*	2,951	*31*	46,339	*43,530*	**10,733**	325	118	10,290
		29	Kosi ... Urban ...	104	...	654	*7*	3,665	*3,974*	**903**	84	15	804
			Rural ...	164	*1*	1,432	*15*	25,719	*24,487*	**6,074**	143	47	5,884
			Total ...	268	*1*	2,086	*22*	29,384	*28,461*	**6,977**	227	62	6,668
		30	Mát ... Urban ...	...	...	...	...	...	...	...	...	...	...
			Rural ...	611	*2*	2,499	*23*	44,297	*42,019*	**11,023**	534	108	10,381
			Total ...	611	*2*	2,499	*23*	44,297	*42,019*	**11,023**	534	108	10,381
		31	Mahaban ... Urban ...	394	*8*	1,612	*37*	6,648	*7,789*	**1,889**	328	81	1,480
			Rural ...	652	*5*	2,893	*41*	60,120	*53,289*	**14,710**	581	121	14,008
			Total ...	1,046	*13*	4,505	*78*	66,768	*61,078*	**16,599**	909	202	15,488
		32	Sadabad ... Urban ...	143	*10*	403	*30*	3,157	*3,234*	**857**	100	14	743
			Rural ...	482	*4*	1,838	*18*	49,511	*43,273*	**11,928**	402	64	11,462
			Total ...	625	*14*	2,241	*48*	52,668	*46,507*	**12,785**	502	78	12,205
			Total ... Urban ...	2,588	*84*	14,438	*594*	61,686	*68,408*	**14,782**	1,930	338	12,514
			Rural ...	2,738	*22*	14,719	*182*	286,491	*261,471*	**68,647**	2,355	542	65,750
			Total ...	5,326	*106*	29,157	*776*	348,177	*329,879*	**83,429**	4,285	880	78,264

Showing the Educational position of each Tahsíl in the N.-W. P. and Oudh—(*continued*).

PROVINCIAL TABLE IV.

Serial number of district.	Name of district.	Serial number of tahsíl.	Name of tahsíl.	Total by Education. Learning. Males.	Learning. Females.	Literate. Males.	Literate. Females.	Illiterate. Males.	Illiterate. Females.	Age—period, 5 to 14. Total males.	Learning.	Literate.	Illiterate.
1	2	3	4	5	6	7	8	9	10	11	12	13	14
8	Agra.	33	Etmádpur ... Urban ...	52	12	217	11	876	1,016	268	48	11	209
			Rural ...	858	50	3,896	169	77,301	69,303	19,055	714	170	18,171
			Total ...	910	62	4,113	180	78,177	70,319	19,323	762	181	18,380
		34	Firozabad ... Urban ...	304	12	876	27	6,849	7,210	1,910	227	38	1,645
			Rural ...	490	4	1,756	60	50,017	44,548	12,345	413	51	11,881
			Total ...	794	16	2,632	87	56,866	51,758	14,255	640	89	13,526
		35	Bah ... Urban ...	80	...	327	12	1,737	1,828	471	65	16	390
			Rural ...	756	11	3,810	84	60,227	56,976	15,752	666	193	14,893
			Total ...	836	11	4,137	96	61,964	58,804	16,223	731	209	15,283
		36	Fatehabad ... Urban ...	106	9	332	22	1,972	2,129	538	80	9	449
			Rural ...	335	2	2,386	25	53.613	47,515	12,961	275	122	12,564
			Total ...	441	11	2,718	47	55,585	49,644	13,499	355	131	13,013
		37	Agra (Sadar) ... Urban ...	3,825	452	13,576	1,420	73,522	75,867	18,472	2,164	496	15,812
			Rural ...	531	122	2,566	79	52,797	47,961	12,309	412	95	11,802
			Total ...	4,356	574	16,142	1,499	126,319	123,828	30,781	2,576	591	27,614
		38	Keraoli ... Urban ...	144	2	597	11	5,084	5,178	1,258	114	18	1,126
			Rural ...	355	...	2,670	25	48,817	44,094	11,778	282	107	11,389
			Total ...	499	2	3,267	36	53,901	49,272	13,036	396	125	12,515
		39	Kheragarh ... Urban ...	32	...	265	4	1,930	2,003	491	31	17	443
			Rural ...	560	5	3,271	39	60,744	55,040	15,084	503	148	14,433
			Total ...	592	5	3,536	43	62,674	57,043	15,575	534	165	14,876
			Total ... Urban ...	4,543	487	16,190	1,507	91,970	95,231	23,408	2,729	605	20,074
			Rural ...	3,885	194	20,355	481	403,516	365,437	99,284	3,265	886	95,133
			Total ...	8,428	681	36,545	1,988	495,486	460,668	122,692	5,994	1,491	115,207
9	Farukhabad.	40	Kanauj ... Urban ...	294	4	1,149	27	7,320	8,854	2,150	232	40	1,878
			Rural ...	456	3	2,597	47	50,826	45,652	13,193	342	120	12,731
			Total ...	750	7	3,746	74	58,146	54,506	15,343	574	160	14,609
		41	Tirwa ... Urban ...	161	...	848	15	6,151	6,051	1,647	136	21	1,490
			Rural ...	468	...	2,332	37	82,372	70,238	21,683	345	110	21,228
			Total ...	629	...	3,180	52	88,523	76,289	23,330	481	131	22,718
		42	Chibramau ... Urban ...	217	12	717	29	5,245	5,847	1,382	169	12	1,201
			Rural ...	525	8	2,252	47	51,203	45,012	13,085	424	95	12,566
			Total ...	742	20	2,969	76	56,448	50,859	14,467	593	107	13,767
		43	Farukhabad (Sadar). Urban ...	1,559	142	6,513	448	33,068	36,302	8,043	1,196	208	6,639
			Rural ...	969	81	4,228	158	85,521	75,907	21,630	773	166	20,691
			Total ...	2,528	223	10,741	606	118,589	112,209	29,673	1,969	374	27,330
		44	Káimganj ... Urban ...	275	7	799	40	7,407	8,548	2,017	217	26	1,774
			Rural ...	510	20	2,005	34	65,840	58,072	16,944	366	75	16,503
			Total ...	785	27	2,804	74	73,247	66,620	18,961	583	101	18,277

Showing the Educational position of each Tahsil in the N.-W. P. and Oudh—(*continued*).

PROVINCIAL TABLE IV.

Serial number of district.	Name of district.	Serial number of tahsil.	Name of tahsil.	Total by Education. Learning. Males.	Learning. Females.	Literate. Males.	Literate. Females.	Illiterate. Males.	Illiterate. Females.	Age—period, 5 to 14. Total males.	Learning.	Literate.	Illiterate.
1	2	3	4	5	6	7	8	9	10	11	12	13	14
9	Farukhabad—(*concluded*).	45	Aligarh ... Urban ...	...	...	...	...	...	...	...	...	...	...
			Rural ...	326	*7*	1,808	*38*	38,379	*32,660*	**9,245**	273	93	8,879
			Total ...	326	*7*	1,808	*38*	38,379	*32,660*	**9,245**	273	93	8,879
			Total ... Urban ...	2,506	*165*	10,026	*559*	59,191	*65,602*	**15,239**	1,950	307	12,982
			Rural ...	3,254	*119*	15,222	*361*	374,141	*327,541*	**95,780**	2,523	659	92,598
			Total ...	5,760	*284*	25,248	*920*	433,332	*398,143*	**111,019**	4,473	966	105,580
10	Mainpuri.	46	Mainpuri ... Urban ...	626	*20*	2,121	*152*	10,392	*11,135*	**2,593**	452	43	2,098
			Rural ...	427	*8*	2,546	*101*	77,670	*65,954*	**19,839**	328	73	19,438
			Total ...	1,053	*28*	4,667	*253*	88,062	*77,089*	**22,432**	780	116	21,536
		47	Bhongaon ... Urban ...	93	*2*	309	*8*	2,159	*2,499*	**567**	78	9	480
			Rural ...	585	*17*	3,398	*64*	100,565	*85,669*	**25,445**	469	138	24,838
			Total ...	678	*19*	3,707	*72*	102,724	*88,168*	**26,012**	547	147	25,318
		48	Karhal ... Urban ...	83	...	431	*9*	2,862	*2,913*	**758**	66	18	679
			Rural ...	147	*3*	1,268	*36*	49,884	*42,661*	**12,819**	109	41	12,669
			Total ...	230	*3*	1,699	*45*	52,746	*45,574*	**13,577**	175	54	13,348
		49	Shikohabad ... Urban ...	156	*5*	770	*18*	6,523	*6,429*	**1,600**	120	25	1,455
			Rural ...	359	*2*	2,050	*29*	66,619	*57,133*	**16,480**	292	68	16,120
			Total ...	515	*7*	2,820	*47*	73,142	*63,562*	**18,080**	412	93	17,575
		50	Mustafabad ... Urban ...	13	...	201	...	1,097	*1,088*	**289**	12	10	267
			Rural ...	464	*14*	2,638	*53*	80,343	*69,342*	**20,162**	389	64	19,709
			Total ...	477	*14*	2,839	*53*	81,440	*70,430*	**20,451**	401	74	19,976
			Total ... Urban ...	971	*27*	3,832	*187*	23,033	*24,064*	**5,807**	728	100	4,979
			Rural ...	1,982	*44*	11,900	*283*	375,081	*320,759*	**94,745**	1,587	384	92,774
			Total ...	2,953	*71*	15,732	*470*	398,114	*344,823*	**100,552**	2,315	484	97,753
11	Etáwah.	51	Etáwah ... Urban ...	1,036	*35*	3,340	*132*	18,363	*20,343*	**5,022**	732	221	4,069
			Rural ...	539	*4*	3,059	*98*	81,166	*69,908*	**21,422**	459	107	20,856
			Total ...	1,575	*39*	6,399	*230*	99,529	*90,251*	**26,444**	1,191	328	24,925
		52	Bharthna ... Urban ...	145	*2*	500	*17*	2,788	*2,847*	**779**	121	21	637
			Rural ...	758	*4*	3,476	*88*	85,190	*74,164*	**23,306**	637	176	22,493
			Total ...	903	*6*	3,976	*105*	87,978	*77,011*	**24,085**	758	197	23,130
		53	Bidhuna ... Urban ...	...	...	...	...	...	...	...	...	...	...
			Rural ...	646	*6*	2,871	*63*	70,409	*60,464*	**18,768**	537	159	18,072
			Total ...	646	*6*	2,871	*63*	70,409	*60,464*	**18,768**	537	159	18,072
		54	Phaphúnd ... Urban ...	111	*2*	451	*6*	3,143	*3,278*	**829**	93	13	723
			Rural ...	332	*6*	2,162	*30*	52,445	*45,341*	**13,936**	286	140	13,510
			Total ...	443	*8*	2,613	*36*	55,588	*48,619*	**14,765**	379	153	14,233
		55	Auraiya ... Urban ...	100	...	745	*10*	2,610	*2,847*	**672**	83	46	543
			Rural ...	550	*12*	2,803	*54*	57,087	*51,093*	**15,417**	461	151	14,805
			Total ...	650	*12*	3,548	*64*	59,647	*53,940*	**16,089**	544	197	15,848
			Total ... Urban ...	1,392	*39*	5,086	*165*	26,904	*29,315*	**7,302**	1,029	301	5,972
			Rural ...	2,825	*32*	14,371	*333*	346,247	*300,970*	**92,849**	2,380	733	89,736
			Total ...	4,217	*71*	19,407	*498*	373,151	*330,285*	**100,151**	3,409	1,084	95,708

Showing the Educational position of each Tahsíl in the N.-W. P. and Oudh—(*continued*).

PROVINCIAL TABLE IV.

Serial number of district.	Name of district.	Serial number of tahsíl.	Name of tahsíl.	Total by Education. Learning. Males	Learning. Females.	Literate. Males.	Literate. Females.	Illiterate. Males.	Illiterate. Females.	Age—period, 5 to 14. Total males.	Learning.	Literate.	Illiterate.
1	2	3	4	5	6	7	8	9	10	11	12	13	14
12	Etah.	56	Etah ... Urban ...	548	*17*	1,874	*75*	10,078	*11,017*	**2,564**	411	44	2,109
			Rural ...	713	*13*	3,496	*82*	106,759	*92,358*	**25,820**	582	116	25,122
			Total ...	1,261	*30*	5,370	*157*	116,837	*103,375*	**28,384**	993	160	27,231
		57	Kásganj ... Urban ...	881	*43*	3,249	*88*	17,679	*19,330*	**4,957**	709	146	4,102
			Rural ...	375	*19*	2,081	*57*	80,841	*67,366*	**19,267**	289	47	18,931
			Total ...	1,256	*62*	5,330	*145*	98,520	*86,696*	**24,224**	998	193	23,033
		58	Aliganj ... Urban ...	387	*10*	1,215	*45*	11,194	*11,530*	**2,888**	300	36	2,552
			Rural ...	495	*12*	2,025	*51*	73,744	*61,286*	**18,613**	378	71	18,164
			Total ...	882	*22*	3,240	*96*	84,938	*72,816*	**21,501**	678	107	20,716
		59	Jalesar ... Urban ...	246	*6*	1,074	*29*	8,764	*9,032*	**2,059**	182	18	1,859
			Rural ...	372	*9*	1,963	*54*	53,150	*46,331*	**12,929**	291	75	12,563
			Total ...	618	*15*	3,037	*83*	61,914	*55,363*	**14,988**	473	93	14,422
			Total ... Urban ...	2,062	*76*	7,412	*237*	47,715	*50,909*	**12,468**	1,602	244	10,622
			Rural ...	1,955	*53*	9,565	*244*	314,494	*267,341*	**76,629**	1,540	309	74,780
			Total ...	4,017	*129*	16,977	*481*	362,209	*318,250*	**89,097**	3,142	553	85,402
13	Bareilly.	60	Farídpur ... Urban ...	124	*3*	341	*18*	4,244	*4,141*	**1,124**	100	10	1,014
			Rural ...	382	*4*	1,396	*21*	58,966	*50,165*	**14,362**	281	35	14,046
			Total ...	506	*7*	1,737	*39*	63,210	*54,306*	**15,486**	381	45	15,060
		61	Bareilly ... Urban ...	3,055	*156*	9,700	*617*	51,680	*55,831*	**13,062**	2,054	175	10,833
			Rural ...	650	*6*	2,234	*21*	93,486	*81,046*	**22,470**	478	76	21,916
			Total ...	3,705	*162*	11,934	*638*	145,166	*136,877*	**35,532**	2,532	251	32,749
		62	Aonla ... Urban ...	476	*72*	1,075	*33*	10,812	*11,654*	**2,929**	358	8	2,563
			Rural ...	581	*26*	2,147	*35*	88,812	*80,227*	**22,193**	443	69	21,681
			Total ...	1,057	*98*	3,222	*68*	99,624	*91,881*	**25,122**	801	77	24,244
		63	Mírganj ... Urban ...	69	...	71	*3*	1,657	*1,760*	**488**	62	1	425
			Rural ...	314	*3*	912	*16*	46,727	*43,768*	**11,723**	259	17	11,447
			Total ...	383	*3*	983	*19*	48,384	*45,528*	**12,211**	321	18	11,872
		64	Baheri ... Urban ...	17	...	46	...	1,780	*1,886*	**470**	15	1	454
			Rural ...	702	*9*	2,238	*29*	104,199	*95,899*	**26,142**	523	80	25,539
			Total ...	719	*9*	2,284	*29*	105,979	*97,785*	**26,612**	538	81	25,993
		65	Nawábganj ... Urban ...	135	*4*	368	*18*	4,718	*5,008*	**1,221**	95	15	1,111
			Rural ...	362	*6*	1,341	*18*	59,663	*52,713*	**14,658**	267	31	14,360
			Total ...	497	*10*	1,709	*36*	64,381	*57,716*	**15,879**	362	46	15,471
			Total ... Urban ...	3,876	*235*	11,601	*689*	74,891	*80,275*	**19,294**	2,684	210	16,400
			Rural ...	2,991	*54*	10,268	*140*	451,853	*403,818*	**111,548**	2,251	308	108,989
			Total ...	6,867	*289*	21,869	*829*	526,744	*484,093*	**130,842**	4,935	518	125,389

Showing the Educational position of each Tahsíl in the N.-W. P. and Oudh—(*continued*).

PROVINCIAL TABLE IV.

Serial number of district.	Name of district.	Serial number of tahsíl.	Name of tahsíl.	Total by Education. Learning. Males.	Learning. Females.	Literate. Males.	Literate. Females.	Illiterate. Males.	Illiterate. Females.	Age—period, 5 to 14. Total males.	Learning.	Literate.	Illiterate.
1	2	3	4	5	6	7	8	9	10	11	12	13	14
14	Bijnor.	66	Bijnor ... Urban ...	1,022	*103*	2,023	*129*	16,593	*18,009*	**4,502**	696	24	3,782
			Rural ...	428	*13*	1,275	*17*	49,969	*44,306*	**12,042**	337	16	11,689
			Total ...	1,450	*116*	3,298	*146*	66,562	*62,315*	**16,544**	1,033	40	15,471
		67	Najíbabad ... Urban ...	585	*13*	1,443	*53*	15,009	*17,130*	**4,071**	446	28	3,597
			Rural ...	764	*9*	1,908	*29*	62,426	*57,504*	**15,483**	590	35	14,858
			Total ...	1,349	*22*	3,351	*82*	77,435	*74,634*	**19,554**	1,036	63	18,455
		68	Nagína ... Urban ...	714	*18*	1,615	*46*	17,775	*19,956*	**4,795**	512	19	4,264
			Rural ...	613	*11*	1,809	*22*	73,630	*66,938*	**18,778**	475	41	18,262
			Total ...	1,327	*29*	3,424	*68*	91,405	*86,894*	**23,573**	987	60	22,526
		69	Dhámpur ... Urban ...	899	*25*	1,800	*84*	22,048	*24,117*	**5,913**	666	30	5,217
			Rural ...	511	*5*	1,624	*23*	68,593	*62,259*	**16,768**	402	44	16,322
			Total ...	1,410	*30*	3,424	*107*	90,641	*86,376*	**22,681**	1,068	74	21,539
		70	Chándpur ... Urban ...	285	...	517	*10*	5,180	*6,264*	**1,440**	217	3	1,220
			Rural ...	515	*13*	1,686	*37*	64,953	*58,715*	**15,588**	397	30	15,161
			Total ...	800	*13*	2,203	*47*	70,133	*64,979*	**17,028**	614	33	16,381
			Total ... Urban ...	3,505	*159*	7,398	*322*	76,605	*85,476*	**20,721**	2,537	104	18,080
			Rural ...	2,831	*51*	8,302	*128*	319,571	*289,722*	**78,659**	2,201	166	76,292
			Total ...	6,336	*210*	15,700	*450*	396,176	*375,198*	**99,380**	4,738	270	94,372
15	Budaun.	71	Gunnaur ... Urban ...	74	*29*	238	*24*	2,591	*2,585*	**729**	60	5	664
			Rural ...	271	*9*	1,399	*18*	63,905	*55,245*	**15,845**	204	41	15,600
			Total ...	345	*38*	1,637	*42*	66,496	*57,830*	**16,574**	264	46	16,264
		72	Bisauli ... Urban ...	236	*23*	586	*27*	6,198	*6,286*	**1,612**	180	12	1,420
			Rural ...	514	*7*	2,094	*28*	88,935	*78,706*	**22,101**	387	55	21,659
			Total ...	750	*30*	2,680	*55*	95,133	*84,992*	**23,713**	567	67	23,079
		73	Sahaswán ... Urban ...	304	*12*	963	*27*	9,716	*10,381*	**2,597**	244	18	2,335
			Rural ...	376	*12*	1,906	*57*	90,915	*78,320*	**22,498**	287	75	22,136
			Total ...	680	*24*	2,869	*84*	100,631	*88,701*	**25,095**	531	93	24,471
		74	Budaun ... Urban ...	1,345	*91*	2,228	*145*	17,564	*21,426*	**5,106**	1,012	35	4,059
			Rural ...	717	*83*	2,388	*47*	96,055	*84,584*	**23,786**	561	76	23,149
			Total ...	2,062	*174*	4,616	*192*	113,619	*106,010*	**28,892**	1,573	111	27,208
		75	Dátaganj ... Urban ...	186	*15*	482	*33*	7,870	*7,885*	**2,106**	155	13	1,938
			Rural ...	555	*8*	2,154	*40*	95,369	*81,311*	**24,133**	450	61	23,622
			Total ...	741	*23*	2,636	*73*	103,239	*89,196*	**26,239**	605	74	25,560
			Total ... Urban ...	2,145	*170*	4,497	*256*	43,939	*48,563*	**12,150**	1,651	83	10,416
			Rural ...	2,433	*119*	9,941	*190*	435,179	*378,166*	**108,363**	1,889	308	106,166
			Total ...	4,578	*289*	14,438	*446*	479,118	*426,729*	**120,513**	3,540	391	116,582

Showing the Educational position of each Tahsíl in the N.-W. P. and Oudh—(*continued*).

PROVINCIAL TABLE IV.

Serial number of district.	Name of district.	Serial number of tahsíl.	Name of tahsíl.	Total by Education. Learning. Males.	Learning. Females	Literate. Males.	Literate. Females.	Illiterate. Males.	Illiterate. Females.	Age—period, 5 to 14. Total males.	Learning.	Literate.	Illiterate.
1	2	3	4	5	6	7	8	9	10	11	12	13	14
16	Moradabad.	76	Moradabad ... Urban ...	2,026	*268*	4,669	*456*	33,325	*37,367*	**9,101**	1,327	127	7,647
			Rural ...	498	*5*	1,475	*21*	81,032	*76,653*	**20,579**	373	43	20,163
			Total ...	2,524	*273*	6,144	*477*	117,357	*114,020*	**29,680**	1,700	170	27,810
		77	Thákurdwára, Urban ...	114	*1*	271	*13*	3,047	*3,242*	**870**	92	2	776
			Rural ...	399	*1*	1,704	*18*	58,733	*53,631*	**15,159**	325	90	14,744
			Total ...	513	*2*	1,975	*31*	61,780	*56,873*	**16,029**	417	92	15,520
		78	Bilári ... Urban ...	702	*37*	2,740	*126*	19,005	*20,067*	**4,878**	500	76	4,302
			Rural ...	419	*7*	1,907	*32*	98,643	*88,262*	**23,541**	305	62	23,174
			Total ...	1,121	*44*	4,647	*158*	117,648	*108,329*	**28,419**	805	138	27,476
		79	Sambhal ... Urban ...	787	*28*	1,657	*72*	24,429	*26,649*	**6,625**	552	32	6,041
			Rural ...	512	*13*	2,081	*30*	99,837	*89,524*	**24,660**	386	69	24,205
			Total ...	1,299	*41*	3,738	*102*	124,266	*116,173*	**31,285**	938	101	30,246
		80	Amroha ... Urban ...	743	*13*	1,670	*90*	17,914	*21,663*	**4,795**	511	47	4,237
			Rural ...	366	*8*	1,622	*14*	75,496	*66,584*	**18,475**	278	43	18,154
			Total ...	1,109	*21*	3,292	*104*	93,410	*88,247*	**23,270**	789	90	22,391
		81	Hasanpur ... Urban ...	432	*7*	1,120	*8*	8,530	*9,527*	**2,355**	299	34	2,022
			Rural ...	374	*1*	1,598	*19*	70,695	*61,369*	**17,833**	302	38	17,493
			Total ...	806	*8*	2,718	*27*	79,225	*70,896*	**20,188**	601	72	19,515
			Total ... Urban ...	4,804	*354*	12,127	*765*	106,250	*118,515*	**28,624**	3,281	318	25,025
			Rural ...	2,568	*35*	10,387	*134*	487,436	*436,023*	**120,247**	1,969	345	117,933
			Total ...	7,372	*389*	22,514	*899*	593,686	*554,538*	**148,871**	5,250	663	142,958
17	Sháhjahánpur.	82	Sháhjahánpur Urban ...	1,634	*156*	4,707	*260*	32,828	*38,937*	**8,600**	1,168	117	7,315
			Rural ...	866	*20*	2,714	*57*	101,915	*89,052*	**24,757**	654	84	24,019
			Total ...	2,500	*176*	7,421	*317*	134,743	*127,989*	**33,357**	1,822	201	31,334
		83	Jalalabad ... Urban ...	141	*3*	382	*12*	2,900	*3,291*	**784**	105	5	674
			Rural ...	552	*23*	2,336	*41*	81,081	*68,630*	**20,667**	458	92	20,117
			Total ...	693	*26*	2,718	*53*	83,981	*71,921*	**21,451**	563	97	20,791
		84	Tilhar ... Urban ...	515	*26*	1,553	*38*	13,323	*14,201*	**3,621**	410	46	3,165
			Rural ...	619	*19*	2,654	*49*	110,119	*93,675*	**27,754**	476	120	27,158
			Total ...	1,134	*45*	4,207	*87*	123,442	*107,876*	**31,375**	886	166	30,323
		85	Powayan ... Urban ...	148	*6*	471	*38*	2,291	*2,594*	**638**	125	11	502
			Rural ...	740	*11*	5,073	*62*	125,744	*112,044*	**31,860**	604	180	31,076
			Total ...	888	*17*	5,544	*100*	128,035	*114,638*	**32,498**	729	191	31,578
			Total ... Urban ...	2,488	*191*	7,113	*348*	51,342	*59,023*	**13,643**	1,808	179	11,656
			Rural ...	2,777	*73*	12,777	*209*	418,859	*363,401*	**105,038**	2,192	476	102,370
			Total ...	5,215	*264*	19,890	*557*	470,201	*422,424*	**118,681**	4,000	655	114,026
18	Pilibhít.	86	Bisalpur ... Urban ...	200	*4*	772	*27*	5,329	*5,459*	**1,374**	143	13	1,218
			Rural ...	672	...	2,877	*35*	92,752	*82,737*	**23,352**	489	76	22,787
			Total ...	872	*4*	3,649	*62*	98,081	*88,196*	**24,726**	632	89	24,005
		87	Pilibhít ... Urban ...	801	*44*	2,232	*140*	19,565	*21,946*	**5,271**	586	41	4,044
			Rural ...	499	*8*	1,792	*35*	79,875	*72,360*	**19,680**	388	35	19,257
			Total ...	1,300	*52*	4,024	*175*	99,440	*94,306*	**24,951**	974	76	28,901

Showing the Educational position of each Tahsíl in the N.-W. P. and Oudh—(*continued*).

PROVINCIAL TABLE IV.

Serial number of district.	Name of district.	Serial number of tahsíl.	Name of tahsíl.	Total by Education. Learning. Males.	Learning. Females.	Literate. Males.	Literate. Females.	Illiterate. Males.	Illiterate. Females.	Age—period, 5 to 14. Total males.	Learning.	Literate.	Illiterate.
1	2	3	4	5	6	7	8	9	10	11	12	13	14
18	Pilibhít—(*concluded*).	88	Puranpur ... Urban ...	..	...	...	...	...	...	...	...	...	...
			Rural ...	269	...	1,266	14	49,501	44,155	12,074	192	37	11,845
			Total ...	269	...	1,266	14	49,501	44,155	12,074	192	37	11,845
			Total ... Urban ...	1,001	48	3,004	167	24,804	27,405	6,645	729	54	5,862
			Rural ...	1,440	8	5,935	84	222,128	199,252	55,106	1,069	148	53,889
			Total ...	2,441	56	8,939	251	247,022	226,657	61,751	1,798	202	59,751
19	Cawnpore.	89	Akbarpur ... Urban ...	95	1	492	19	3,296	3,260	867	73	11	783
			Rural ...	202	2	2,035	10	48,767	44,077	12,341	161	110	12,070
			Total ...	297	3	2,527	29	52,063	47,337	13,208	234	121	12,853
		90	Bilhaur ... Urban ...	94	1	330	7	2,213	2,515	626	67	9	550
			Rural ...	355	4	2,777	38	47,906	43,811	12,117	297	136	11,684
			Total ...	449	5	3,107	45	50,119	46,326	12,743	364	145	12,234
		91	Bhognipur ... Urban ...	12	...	89	...	766	873	205	9	2	194
			Rural ...	293	1	2,559	19	47,127	44,836	12,006	227	100	11,679
			Total ...	305	1	2,648	19	47,893	45,709	12,211	236	102	11,878
		92	Cawnpore ... Urban ...	2,969	231	17,943	947	88,869	83,513	20,289	2,122	630	17,537
			Rural ...	546	5	3,916	48	64,587	61,054	16,022	454	189	15,379
			Total ...	3,515	236	21,859	995	153,456	144,567	36,311	2,576	819	32,916
		93	Derapur ... Urban ...	37	1	184	3	1,315	1,236	344	27	9	308
			Rural ...	409	1	2,720	48	60,680	55,610	15,940	310	109	15,521
			Total ...	446	2	2,904	51	61,995	56,846	16,284	337	118	15,829
		94	Rasúlabad ... Urban ...	...	...	...	...	...	...	...	...	...	...
			Rural ...	256	3	1,959	25	51,902	45,392	13,428	193	99	13,136
			Total ...	256	3	1,959	25	51,902	45,392	13,428	193	99	13,136
		95	Narwal ... Urban ...	82	...	231	9	942	1,205	295	51	3	241
			Rural ...	478	6	3,001	34	46,527	46,269	11,840	377	145	11,318
			Total ...	560	6	3,232	43	47,469	47,474	12,135	428	148	11,559
		96	Shiurájpur ... Urban ...	...	...	...	...	...	...	...	...	...	...
			Rural ...	709	9	4,539	48	72,515	70,003	18,765	558	210	17,997
			Total ...	709	9	4,539	48	72,515	70,003	18,765	558	210	17,997
		97	Ghátampur ... Urban ...	...	...	...	...	...	...	...	...	...	...
			Rural ...	479	5	3,026	17	57,863	56,407	14,164	375	108	13,681
			Total ...	479	5	3,026	17	57,863	56,407	14,164	375	108	13,681
			Total ... Urban ...	3,289	234	19,269	985	97,401	92,602	22,626	2,349	664	19,613
			Rural ...	3,727	36	26,532	287	497,874	467,459	126,623	2,952	1,206	122,465
			Total ...	7,016	270	45,801	1,272	595,275	560,061	149,249	5,301	1,870	142,078
20	Fatehpur	98	Fatehpur ... Urban ...	496	11	1,520	55	9,330	11,142	2,723	380	82	2,261
			Rural ...	650	2	3,777	49	74,410	74,010	20,361	504	234	19,623
			Total ...	1,146	13	5,297	104	83,740	85,152	23,084	884	316	21,884

Showing the Educational position of each Tahsíl in the N.-W. P. and Oudh—(*continued*).

PROVINCIAL TABLE IV.

Serial number of district.	Name of district.	Serial number of tahsil.	Name of tahsil.		Total by Education. Learning. Males.	Learning. Females.	Literate. Males.	Literate. Females.	Illiterate. Males.	Illiterate. Females.	Age-period, 5 to 14. Total males.	Learning.	Literate.	Illiterate.
1	2	3	4		5	6	7	8	9	10	11	12	13	14
20	Fatehpur—(*concluded*).	99	Kalianpur	Urban	50	...	725	*4*	3,988	*4,114*	**1,006**	36	47	923
				Rural	421	*9*	3,376	*31*	53,457	*52,611*	**13,630**	332	166	13,132
			Total		471	*9*	4,101	*35*	57,445	*56,725*	**14,636**	368	213	14,055
		100	Kora	Urban	196	*1*	836	*23*	4,332	*5,348*	**1,184**	154	35	995
				Rural	385	*3*	2,113	*13*	37,437	*37,238*	**9,480**	335	125	9,020
			Total		581	*4*	2,949	*36*	41,769	*42,586*	**10,664**	489	160	10,015
		101	Gházipur	Urban	...	...	...	...	...	...	...	...	...	...
				Rural	564	*10*	3,132	*27*	44,423	*44,233*	**12,102**	478	200	11,424
			Total		564	*10*	3,132	*27*	44,423	*44,233*	**12,102**	478	200	11,424
		102	Khakhreru	Urban	71	*1*	230	*2*	811	*1,144*	**274**	54	4	216
				Rural	447	*3*	2,403	*20*	40,113	*41,280*	**11,011**	370	102	10,539
			Total		518	*4*	2,633	*22*	40,924	*42,424*	**11,285**	424	106	10,755
		103	Khága	Urban	...	...	...	...	...	...	...	...	...	...
				Rural	806	*10*	3,173	*14*	66,149	*67,928*	**18,393**	668	182	17,543
			Total		806	*10*	3,173	*14*	66,149	*67,928*	**18,393**	668	182	17,543
			Total	Urban	813	*13*	3,311	*84*	18,461	*21,748*	**5,187**	624	168	4,395
				Rural	3,273	*37*	17,974	*164*	315,989	*317,300*	**84,977**	2,687	1,009	81,281
			Total		4,086	*50*	21,285	*238*	334,450	*339,048*	**90,164**	3,311	1,177	85,676
21	Bánda.	104	Bánda	Urban	621	*28*	1,951	*98*	8,872	*11,501*	**2,517**	436	69	2,012
				Rural	583	*2*	2,467	*10*	42,448	*44,331*	**12,158**	484	109	11,565
			Total		1,204	*30*	4,418	*108*	51,320	*55,832*	**14,675**	920	178	13,577
		105	Pailáni	Urban	...	...	...	...	...	...	...	...	...	...
				Rural	582	*4*	2,526	*23*	42,242	*43,167*	**12,241**	480	149	11,612
			Total		582	*4*	2,526	*23*	42,242	*43,167*	**12,241**	480	149	11,612
		106	Baberu	Urban	...	...	...	...	...	...	...	...	...	...
				Rural	486	*13*	2,296	*41*	45,179	*48,269*	**13,368**	425	138	12,805
			Total		486	*13*	2,296	*41*	45,179	*48,269*	**13,368**	425	138	12,805
		107	Kamásin	Urban	...	...	...	...	...	...	...	...	...	...
				Rural	475	*1*	1,997	*14*	39,845	*40,965*	**11,506**	404	106	10,996
			Total		475	*1*	1,997	*14*	39,845	*40,965*	**11,506**	404	106	10,996
		108	Mau	Urban	142	...	617	*10*	2,427	*2,940*	**755**	113	35	607
				Rural	359	...	2,036	*12*	31,925	*33,190*	**9,243**	309	108	8,826
			Total		501	...	2,653	*22*	34,352	*36,130*	**9,998**	422	143	9,433
		109	Karwi	Urban	219	*1*	686	*15*	3,302	*4,268*	**1,054**	164	34	856
				Rural	359	...	2,128	*18*	37,812	*38,879*	**11,212**	292	97	10,823
			Total		578	*1*	2,814	*33*	41,114	*43,147*	**12,266**	456	131	11,679
		110	Badausa	Urban	...	...	...	...	...	...	...	...	...	...
				Rural	436	*1*	1,861	*13*	36,958	*38,653*	**10,704**	375	78	10,251
			Total		436	*1*	1,861	*13*	36,958	*38,653*	**10,704**	375	78	10,251

Showing the Educational position of each Tahsíl in the N.-W. P. and Oudh—(*continued*).

PROVINCIAL TABLE IV.

Serial number of district.	Name of district.	Serial number of tahsíl.	Name of tahsíl.	Total by Education. Learning. Males.	Learning. Females.	Literate. Males.	Literate. Females.	Illiterate. Males.	Illiterate. Females.	Age—period, 5 to 14. Total males.	Learning.	Literate.	Illiterate.
1	2	3	4	5	6	7	8	9	10	11	12	13	14
21	Bánda—(*concluded*).	111	Girwan ... Urban ...	61	...	194	*3*	1,355	*1,747*	**451**	55	5	391
			Rural ...	547	*3*	2,104	*8*	38,796	*40,710*	**11,476**	460	123	10,893
			Total ...	608	*3*	2,298	*11*	40,151	*42,457*	**11,927**	515	128	11,284
			Total ... Urban ...	1,043	*29*	3,448	*126*	15,956	*20,456*	**4,777**	768	143	3,866
			Rural ...	3,827	*24*	17,415	*139*	315,205	*328,164*	**91,908**	3,229	908	87,771
			Total ...	4,870	*53*	20,863	*265*	331,161	*348,620*	**96,685**	3,997	1,051	91,637
22	Hamírpur.	112	Hamírpur ... Urban ...	366	*10*	1,083	*21*	6,943	*7,677*	**1,887**	288	20	1,579
			Rural ...	295	*2*	1,650	*6*	31,678	*31,399*	**8,741**	267	83	8,391
			Total ...	661	*12*	2,733	*27*	38,624	*39,076*	**10,628**	555	103	9,970
		113	Muskara ... Urban ...	36	...	213	...	2,815	*2,918*	**734**	35	13	686
			Rural ...	467	...	1,977	*7*	33,030	*34,272*	**9,120**	396	65	8,659
			Total ...	503	...	2,190	*7*	35.845	*37,190*	**9,854**	431	78	9,345
		114	Ráth ... Urban ...	·117	*1*	631	*9*	5,171	*6,382*	**1,479**	84	25	1,370
			Rural ...	337	*3*	2,140	*22*	40,403	*42,646*	**11,061**	290	91	10,680
			Total ...	454	*4*	2,771	*31*	45,574	*49,028*	**12,540**	374	116	12,050
		115	Kulpahar ... Urban ...	124	*5*	463	*5*	4,824	*5,329*	**1,436**	99	17	1,320
			Rural ...	615	*4*	2,655	*13*	55,966	*57,564*	**15,946**	519	90	15,337
			Total ...	739	*9*	3,118	*18*	60,790	*62,893*	**17,382**	618	107	16,657
		116	Mahoba ... Urban ...	217	*8*	846	*22*	7,673	*8,750*	**2,174**	169	44	1,961
			Rural ...	247	...	1,173	*9*	27,614	*27,641*	**7,665**	217	48	7,400
			Total ...	464	*8*	2,019	*31*	35 287	*36,391*	**9,839**	386	92	9,361
		117	Maudha ... Urban ...	83	...	212	*1*	2,876	*3,449*	**830**	68	5	757
			Rural ...	276	*3*	1,163	*8*	24,221	*24,931*	**6,876**	246	57	6,573
			Total ...	359	*3*	1,375	*9*	27,097	*28,380*	**7,706**	314	62	7,330
			Total ... Urban ...	943	*24*	3,448	*58*	30,305	*34,505*	**8,540**	743	124	7,673
			Rural ...	2,237	*12*	10,758	*65*	212,912	*218,453*	**59,409**	1,935	434	57,040
			Total ...	3,180	*36*	14,206	*123*	243,217	*252,958*	**67,949**	2,078	558	64,713
23	Allahabad.	118	Allahabad ... Urban ...	3,803	*504*	15,248	*1,995*	77,134	*79,325*	**19,146**	2,521	725	15,900
			Rural ...	1,109	*20*	4,022	*43*	75,535	*83,708*	**20,884**	873	239	19,772
			Total ...	4,912	*524*	19,270	*2,038*	152,669	*163,033*	**40,030**	3,394	964	35,672
		119	Sirathu ... Urban ...	230	*4*	743	*11*	4,287	*5,753*	**1,355**	163	49	1,143
			Rural ...	466	*1*	2,881	*16*	56,823	*58,716*	**15,418**	339	220	14,859
			Total ...	696	*5*	3,624	*27*	61,110	*64,469*	**16,773**	502	269	16,002
		120	Manjhanpur ... Urban ...	43	...	232	*1*	1,289	*1,403*	**424**	40	18	366
			Rural ...	422	...	2,966	*10*	61,973	*63,849*	**17,127**	309	194	16,624
			Total ...	465	...	3,198	*11*	63,262	*64,752*	**17,551**	349	212	16,990

Showing the Educational position of each Tahsíl in the N.-W. P. and Oudh—*(continued).*

PROVINCIAL TABLE IV.

Serial number of district.	Name of district.	Serial number of tahsíl.	Name of tahsíl.	Total by Education. Learning. Males.	Learning. Females.	Literate. Males.	Literate. Females.	Illiterate. Males.	Illiterate. Females.	Age—period, 5 to 14. Total males.	Learning.	Literate.	Illiterate.
1	2	3	4	5	6	7	8	9	10	11	12	13	14
23	Allahabad—*(concluded)*.	121	Soraon ... Urban ...	75	...	390	*5*	3,502	*4,391*	**1,007**	61	22	924
			Rural ...	418	*2*	3,639	*63*	82,777	*91,614*	**23,186**	312	234	22,640
			Total ...	493	*2*	4,029	*68*	86,279	*96,005*	**24,193**	373	256	23,564
		122	Phúlpur ... Urban ...	90	*2*	403	*7*	3,983	*4,583*	**1,090**	51	26	1,013
			Rural ...	363	*1*	2,659	*38*	80,203	*84,519*	**22,204**	247	152	21,805
			Total ...	453	*3*	3,062	*45*	84,186	*89,102*	**23,294**	298	178	22,818
		123	Handia ... Urban ...	...	...	...	...	...	...	...	...	...	...
			Rural ...	315	*5*	3,497	*24*	90,314	*92,934*	**25,475**	207	161	25,107
			Total ...	315	*5*	3,497	*24*	90,314	*92,934*	**25,475**	207	161	25,107
		124	Karchhana ... Urban ...	13	...	122	...	1,546	*1,755*	**366**	12	29	325
			Rural ...	507	*11*	3,412	*84*	63,361	*64,007*	**16,904**	341	201	16,362
			Total ...	520	*11*	3,534	*84*	64,907	*65,762*	**17,270**	353	230	16,687
		125	Bára ... Urban ...	...	...	...	...	...	...	...	...	...	...
			Rural ...	360	*3*	1,804	*47*	30,487	*31,115*	**8,394**	269	81	8,044
			Total ...	360	*3*	1,804	*47*	30,487	*31,115*	**8,394**	269	81	8,044
		126	Meja ... Urban ...	124	...	622	*3*	2,693	*3,570*	**841**	92	42	707
			Rural ...	524	*111*	5,027	*383*	89,073	*93,092*	**25,987**	323	416	25,248
			Total ...	648	*111*	5,649	*386*	91,766	*96,662*	**26,828**	415	458	25,955
			Total ... Urban ...	4,378	*510*	17,760	*2,022*	94,434	*100,780*	**24,229**	2,940	911	20,378
			Rural ...	4,484	*154*	29,907	*708*	630,546	*663,054*	**175,579**	3,220	1,898	170,461
			Total ...	8,862	*664*	47,667	*2,730*	724,980	*763,834*	**199,808**	6,160	2,809	190,839
24	Jhánsi.	127	Jhánsi ... Urban ...	996	*63*	7,145	*406*	27,443	*26,733*	**6,988**	663	258	6,067
			Rural ...	349	*10*	2,023	*101*	41,832	*38,579*	**12,195**	301	74	11,820
			Total ...	1,345	*73*	9,168	*507*	69,275	*65,312*	**19,183**	964	332	17,887
		128	Mau ... Urban ...	336	*2*	1,354	*12*	7,939	*10,032*	**2,316**	290	75	1,951
			Rural ...	605	*3*	2,406	*22*	46,363	*46,650*	**13,376**	519	85	12,772
			Total ...	941	*5*	3,760	*34*	54,302	*56,682*	**15,692**	809	160	14,723
		129	Garotha ... Urban ...	79	*1*	400	*3*	2,421	*2,890*	**690**	58	16	616
			Rural ...	569	*3*	2,700	*19*	39,449	*40,392*	**11,481**	475	152	10,854
			Total ...	648	*4*	3,100	*22*	41,870	*43,282*	**12,171**	533	168	11,470
		130	Moth ... Urban ...	155	*3*	672	*20*	4,298	*5,137*	**1,327**	147	39	1,141
			Rural ...	415	*4*	1,576	*8*	23,003	*23,798*	**6,827**	367	62	6,398
			Total ...	570	7	2,248	*28*	27,301	*28,935*	**8,154**	514	101	7,539
		131	Lalitpur ... Urban ...	309	*6*	1,572	*34*	7,077	*8,146*	**2,414**	284	115	2,015
			Rural ...	582	*2*	2,839	*38*	69,389	*67,160*	**22,360**	491	164	21,705
			Total ...	891	7	4,411	*72*	76,466	*75,306*	**24,774**	775	279	23,720

Showing the Educational position of each Tahsíl in the N.-W. P. and Oudh—(*continued*).

PROVINCIAL TABLE IV.

Serial number of district.	Name of district.	Serial number of tahsíl.	Name of tahsíl.		Total by Education. Learning. Males.	Learning. Females.	Literate. Males.	Literate. Females.	Illiterate. Males.	Illiterate. Females.	Age—period, 5 to 14. Total males.	Learning.	Literate.	Illiterate.
1	2	3	4		5	6	7	8	9	10	11	12	13	14
24	Jhánsi—(*concluded*).	132	Mehroni	Urban	35	*1*	166	*2*	1,312	*1,616*	**439**	30	18	391
				Rural	499	*5*	2,626	*55*	55,030	*55,701*	**17,425**	436	181	16,808
			Total		534	*6*	2,792	*57*	56,342	*57,316*	**17,864**	466	199	17,199
			Total	Urban	1,910	*75*	11,309	*477*	50,490	*54,553*	**14,174**	1,472	521	12,181
				Rural	3,019	*27*	14,170	*243*	275,066	*272,280*	**83,664**	2,589	718	80,357
			Total		4,929	*102*	25,479	*720*	325,556	*326,833*	**97,838**	4,061	1,239	92,538
25	Jalaun.	133	Orai	Urban	271	*3*	1,028	*26*	6,529	*7,194*	**1,825**	202	42	1,581
				Rural	271	...	2,014	*11*	24,508	*25,847*	**7,072**	240	127	6,705
			Total		542	*3*	3,042	*37*	31,037	*33,041*	**8,897**	442	169	8,286
		134	Kálpi	Urban	153	*4*	749	*11*	5,408	*6,388*	**1,445**	124	46	1,275
				Rural	274	...	1,960	*18*	31,977	*31,812*	**9,243**	244	118	8,881
			Total		427	*4*	2,709	*29*	37,385	*38,200*	**10,688**	368	164	10,166
		135	Jalaun	Urban	173	...	848	*14*	4,725	*5,439*	**1,474**	147	52	1,275
				Rural	802	*11*	4,110	*63*	65,490	*65,415*	**19,411**	651	260	18,500
			Total		975	*11*	4,958	77	70,215	*70,854*	**20,885**	798	312	19,775
		136	Kunch	Urban	196	...	1,018	*10*	5,697	*6,487*	**1,640**	165	47	1,428
				Rural	386	*1*	2,574	*32*	42,929	*43,485*	**12,486**	317	121	12,048
			Total		582	*1*	3,592	*42*	48,626	*49,972*	**14,126**	482	168	13,476
			Total	Urban	793	*7*	3,643	*61*	22,359	*25,508*	**6,384**	638	187	5,559
				Rural	1,733	*12*	10,658	*124*	164,904	*166,559*	**48,212**	1,452	626	46,134
			Total		2,526	*19*	14,301	*185*	187,263	*192,067*	**54,596**	2,090	813	51,693
26	Benares.	137	Benares	Urban	5,936	*602*	23,648	*2,499*	86,504	*102,304*	**22,168**	3,343	800	18,025
				Rural	2,290	*43*	12,991	*571*	165,567	*177,512*	**51,279**	1,806	868	48,605
			Total		8,226	*645*	36,639	*3,070*	252,071	*279,816*	**73,447**	5,149	1,668	66,630
		138	Gangapur	Urban	...	...	...	...	...	...	...	...	...	...
				Rural	290	...	2,430	*69*	42,597	*44,548*	**12,649**	213	158	12,278
			Total		290	...	2,430	*69*	42,597	*44,548*	**12,649**	213	158	12,278
		139	Chandauli	Urban	219	*7*	1,232	*151*	5,527	*6,923*	**1,498**	166	45	1,287
				Rural	1,275	*25*	6,428	*212*	110,519	*119,024*	**32,200**	986	420	30,794
			Total		1,494	*32*	7,660	*363*	116,046	*125,947*	**33,698**	1,152	465	32,081
			Total	Urban	6,155	*609*	24,880	*2,650*	92,031	*109,227*	**23,666**	3,509	845	19,312
				Rural	3,855	*68*	21,849	*852*	318,683	*341,084*	**96,128**	3,005	1,446	91,677
			Total		10,010	*677*	46,729	*3,502*	410,714	*450,311*	**119,794**	6,514	2,291	110,989
27	Mirzapur.	140	Mirzapur	Urban	1,530	*71*	7,710	*480*	34,350	*43,432*	**9,770**	1,188	595	7,992
				Rural	390	*10*	4,963	*110*	134,547	*144,422*	**39,937**	269	183	39,485
			Total		1,920	*81*	12,673	*590*	168,897	*187,854*	**49,707**	1,452	778	47,477
		141	Chunár	Urban	276	*19*	1,463	*136*	9,610	*11,550*	**2,727**	211	68	2,448
				Rural	725	*5*	4,681	*141*	74,326	*82,700*	**22,618**	591	273	21,754
			Total		1,001	*24*	6,094	*277*	83,936	*94,250*	**25,345**	802	341	24,202

Showing the Educational position of each Tahsil in the N.-W. P. and Oudh—(*continued*).

PROVINCIAL TABLE IV.

Serial number of district.	Name of district.	Serial number of tahsil.	Name of tahsil.	Total by Education. Learning. Males.	Learning. Females.	Literate. Males.	Literate. Females.	Illiterate. Males.	Illiterate. Females.	Age—period, 5 to 14. Total males.	Learning.	Literate.	Illiterate.
1	2	3	4	5	6	7	8	9	10	11	12	13	14
27	Mirzapur—(*concluded*).	142	Robertsganj ... Urban ...	41	...	177	*4*	894	*1,141*	**337**	41	21	275
			Rural ...	516	*7*	4,149	*170*	114,700	*119,980*	**36,245**	379	220	35,646
			Total ...	557	7	4,326	*174*	115,594	*121,121*	**36,582**	420	241	35,921
		143	Kourh ... Urban ...	17	...	289	*4*	1,663	*1,819*	**510**	13	20	477
			Rural ...	538	*4*	8,225	*78*	134,360	*144,221*	**39,720**	394	521	38,805
			Total ...	555	*4*	8,514	*82*	136,023	*146,040*	**40,230**	407	541	39,282
		144	Chakia ... Urban ...	...	...	...	...	...	...	..	...	..	...
			Rural ...	143	*1*	1,674	*29*	34,434	*34,633*	**10,421**	109	127	10,185
			Total ...	143	*1*	1,674	*29*	34,434	*34,633*	**10,421**	109	127	10,185
			Total ... Urban ...	1,864	*90*	9.639	*624*	46,517	*57,942*	**13,344**	1,448	704	11,192
			Rural ...	2,312	27	23,642	*528*	492,367	*525,956*	**148,941**	1,742	1,324	145,875
			Total ...	4,176	*117*	33,281	*1,152*	538,884	*583,898*	**162,285**	3,190	2,028	157,067
28	Jaunpur.	145	Jaunpur ... Urban ...	1,003	*47*	2,716	*136*	19,183	*22,828*	**5,509**	645	187	4,677
			Rural ...	544	*6*	4,654	*182*	111,096	*116,087*	**31,955**	421	346	31,188
			Total ...	1,547	*53*	7,370	*318*	130,279	*138,915*	**37,464**	1,066	533	35,865
		146	Mariáhu ... Urban ...	64	*2*	204	*3*	1,520	*1,830*	**515**	45	6	464
			Rural ...	599	*6*	5,631	*88*	118,812	*124,643*	**35,854**	462	296	35,096
			Total ...	663	*8*	5,835	*91*	120,332	*126,473*	**36,369**	507	302	35,560
		147	Machhlishahr Urban ...	168	...	881	*15*	6,435	*7,554*	**1,828**	119	70	1,639
			Rural ...	335	*1*	4.249	*66*	110,835	*114,138*	**31,087**	242	300	30,545
			Total ...	503	*1*	5,130	*81*	117,270	*121,692*	**32,915**	361	370	32,184
		148	Khutahan ... Urban ...	122	...	620	*3*	2,521	*2,931*	**808**	102	72	634
			Rural ...	731	*4*	5,848	*177*	134,780	*139,095*	**38,281**	587	346	37,348
			Total ...	853	*4*	6,468	*180*	137,301	*142,026*	**39,089**	689	418	37,082
		149	Kerakat ... Urban ...	44	...	217	*3*	1,330	*1,600*	**399**	29	7	363
			Rural ...	696	*3*	5,291	*73*	93,821	*98,478*	**28,078**	556	387	27,135
			Total ...	740	*3*	5,508	*76*	95,151	*100,078*	**28,477**	585	304	27,498
			Total ... Urban ...	1,401	*49*	4,638	*160*	30,989	*36,743*	**9.059**	940	342	7,777
			Rural ...	2,905	*20*	25,673	*586*	569,344	*592,441*	**165,255**	2,268	1,675	161,312
			Total ...	4,306	*69*	30,311	*746*	600,333	*629,184*	**174,314**	3,208	2,017	169,089
29	Gházipur.	150	Gházipur ... Urban ...	1,514	*74*	8,823	*314*	17,740	*21,505*	**5,167**	995	72	4,100
			Rural ...	1,139	*13*	7,183	*186*	144,940	*152,392*	**42,170**	903	348	40,919
			Total ...	2,653	*87*	11,006	*500*	162,680	*173,897*	**47,337**	1,898	420	45,019
		151	Korantadih ... Urban ...	148	*1*	708	*43*	8,010	*10,131*	**2,398**	125	58	2,215
			Rural ...	716	*19*	6,299	*227*	132,534	*146,143*	**38,428**	596	328	37,504
			Total ...	864	*20*	7,007	*270*	140,544	*156,274*	**40,826**	721	386	39,719
		152	Zamánia ... Urban ...	268	*4*	1,651	*32*	19,075	*23,958*	**5,721**	225	113	5,383
			Rural ...	563	8	5,375	*180*	92,462	*103,354*	**27,233**	446	322	26,465
			Total ...	831	*12*	7,026	*212*	111,537	*127,312*	**32,954**	671	485	31,848

Showing the Educational position of each Tahsíl in the N.-W. P. and Oudh—(*continued*).

PROVINCIAL TABLE IV.

Serial number of district.	Name of district.	Serial number of tahsíl.	Name of tahsíl.		Total by Education. Learning. Males.	Learning. Females.	Literate. Males.	Literate. Females.	Illiterate. Males.	Illiterate. Females.	Age-period, 5 to 14. Total males.	Learning.	Literate.	Illiterate.
1	2	3	4		5	6	7	8	9	10	11	12	13	14
29	Ghazipur—(*concluded*).	163	Saidpur	Urban	97	*3*	522	*16*	3,544	*4,098*	**1,027**	90	44	893
				Rural	549	*2*	4,026	*62*	78,816	*83,443*	**23,378**	482	289	22,667
			Total		646	*5*	4,548	*78*	82,359	*87,541*	**24,405**	572	283	23,550
			Total	Urban	2,027	*82*	6,704	*405*	48,369	*59,692*	**14,313**	1,435	287	12,591
				Rural	2,967	*42*	22,883	*655*	448,751	*486,332*	**131,209**	2,427	1,237	127,545
			Total		4,994	*124*	29,587	*1,060*	497,120	*546,024*	**145,522**	3,862	1,524	140,136
30	Ballia.	164	Ballia	Urban	651	*14*	2,607	*119*	17,015	*20,983*	**5,343**	427	237	4,679
				Rural	1,579	*22*	10,647	*527*	133,097	*166,028*	**43,256**	1,286	1,013	40,957
			Total		2,230	*36*	13,254	*646*	150,112	*187,011*	**48,599**	1,713	1,250	45,636
		165	Basra	Urban	211	*6*	1,170	*17*	5,646	*7,421*	**1,818**	155	77	1,586
				Rural	897	*26*	7,231	*138*	137,733	*147,149*	**41,442**	727	464	40,251
			Total		1,108	*32*	8,401	*155*	143,379	*154,570*	**43,260**	882	541	41,837
		166	Bansdih	Urban	374	*9*	1,982	*92*	18,875	*24,347*	**5,945**	323	165	5,457
				Rural	698	*9*	5,791	*216*	106,407	*122,731*	**33,294**	552	393	32,349
			Total		1,072	*18*	7,773	*308*	125,282	*147,078*	**39,239**	875	558	37,806
			Total	Urban	1,236	*29*	5,759	*228*	41,536	*52,751*	**13,106**	905	479	11,722
				Rural	3,174	*57*	23,669	*881*	377,237	*435,908*	**117,992**	2,565	1,870	113,557
			Total		4,410	*86*	29,428	*1,109*	418,773	*488,659*	**131,098**	3,470	2,349	125,279
31	Gorakhpur.	167	Bansgaon	Urban	220	*5*	1,470	*56*	9,379	*11,363*	**2,827**	164	103	2,560
				Rural	1,552	*26*	12,565	*519*	197,326	*217,125*	**60,053**	1,200	798	58,055
			Total		1,772	*31*	14,035	*575*	206,705	*228,488*	**62,880**	1,364	901	60,615
		168	Mahárájganj	Urban	17	*1*	103	*24*	1,327	*1,263*	**377**	16	4	357
				Rural	1,101	*13*	8,411	*148*	250,760	*248,282*	**70,867**	817	462	69,588
			Total		1,118	*14*	8,514	*172*	252,087	*249,545*	**71,244**	833	466	69,945
		169	Padrauna	Urban	74	...	507	*32*	10,045	*10,582*	**2,710**	49	18	2,643
				Rural	817	*4*	7,777	*145*	283,986	*291,582*	**82,155**	563	384	81,208
			Total		891	*4*	8,284	*177*	294,031	*302,164*	**84,865**	612	397	83,856
		160	Háta	Urban	43	*1*	627	*10*	6,211	*6,741*	**1,643**	35	33	1,575
				Rural	478	*8*	7,344	*136*	200,793	*207,677*	**57,971**	364	513	57,094
			Total		521	*9*	7,971	*146*	207,004	*214,418*	**59,614**	399	546	58,669
		161	Deoria	Urban	179	...	2,177	*59*	17,046	*19,463*	**4,839**	148	180	4,511
				Rural	909	*7*	10,987	*405*	222,931	*243,630*	**65,847**	670	737	64,440
			Total		1,088	*7*	13,164	*464*	239,977	*263,093*	**70,686**	818	917	68,951
		162	Gorakhpur (Sadar).	Urban	1,804	*116*	5,426	*388*	27,329	*32,095*	**7,994**	1,223	201	6,570
				Rural	1,299	*73*	8,477	*307*	195,787	*204,487*	**53,354**	974	503	51,877
			Total		3,103	*189*	13,903	*695*	223,116	*236,582*	**61,348**	2,197	704	58,447
			Total	Urban	2,337	*123*	10,310	*569*	71,837	*81,507*	**20,390**	1,635	534	18,221
				Rural	6,156	*131*	55,561	*1,660*	1,351,683	*1,412,783*	**390,247**	4,588	3,397	383,262
			Total		8,493	*254*	65,871	*2,229*	1,422,020	*1,494,290*	**410,637**	6,223	3,931	400,483

Showing the Educational position of each Tahsíl in the N.-W. P. and Oudh—(*continued*).

PROVINCIAL TABLE IV.

Serial number of district.	Name of district.	Serial number of tahsíl.	Name of tahsíl.	Total by Education. Learning. Males.	Learning. Females.	Literate. Males.	Literate. Females.	Illiterate. Males.	Illiterate. Females.	Age-period, 5 to 14. Total males.	Learning.	Literate.	Illiterate.
1	2	3	4	5	6	7	8	9	10	11	12	13	14
32	Basti.	163	Domariaganj ... Urban ...	27	...	205	1	1,299	1,580	371	18	12	341
			Rural ...	501	2	6,400	91	150,140	152,844	42,382	403	470	41,509
			Total ...	528	2	6,605	92	151,439	154,424	42,753	421	482	41,850
		164	Bánsi ... Urban ...	13	...	303	7	3,585	2,726	772	11	23	738
			Rural ...	590	9	6.159	126	173,266	175,940	49,104	450	454	48 200
			Total ...	603	9	6,462	133	176,851	178,666	49,876	461	477	48,938
		165	Haraiya ... Urban ...	...	...	...	...	...	...	...	...	...	...
			Rural ...	475	2	7,202	140	171,388	172,402	45,231	378	473	44,380
			Total ...	475	2	7,202	140	171,388	172,402	45,231	378	473	44,380
		166	Basti ... Urban ...	332	17	1,219	99	6,406	5,557	1,795	211	86	1,548
			Rural ...	542	2	7,110	100	177,700	178,851	47,016	396	358	46,262
			Total ...	874	19	8,329	199	184,106	184,408	48,811	607	394	47,810
		167	Khalilabad ... Urban ...	106	...	642	25	4,988	5,230	1,417	88	31	1,298
			Rural ...	676	3	7,324	131	178,739	182,622	49,841	526	481	48,834
			Total ...	782	3	7,966	156	183,727	187,852	51,258	614	512	50,132
			Total ... Urban ...	478	17	2,369	132	16,278	15,093	4,355	328	102	3,925
			Rural ...	2,784	18	34,195	588	851,233	862,659	233,574	2,153	2,236	229,185
			Total ...	3,262	35	36,564	720	867,511	877,752	237,929	2,481	2,338	233,110
33	Azamgarh.	168	Deogaon ... Urban ...	...	...	...	...	...	...	...	...	...	...
			Rural ...	631	7	5,546	92	127,169	131,406	36,787	519	341	35,927
			Total ...	631	7	5,546	92	127,169	131,406	36,787	519	341	35,927
		169	Nizámabad ... Urban ...	607	15	1,928	115	9,883	10,899	2,785	393	78	2,314
			Rural ...	785	11	5,129	100	126,983	133,033	36,993	655	410	35,928
			Total ...	1,392	26	7,057	215	136,866	143,932	39,778	1,048	488	38,242
		170	Mahul ... Urban ...	45	...	411	...	2,093	2,456	645	42	24	579
			Rural ...	743	5	6,241	120	164,999	167,610	46,743	595	379	45,769
			Total ...	788	5	6,652	120	167,092	170,066	47,388	637	403	46,348
		171	Sagri ... Urban ...	27	...	290	3	2,246	2,758	711	22	20	669
			Rural ...	858	21	9,067	176	220,514	233,857	65,612	688	809	64,115
			Total ...	885	21	9,357	179	222,760	236,615	66,323	710	829	64,784
		172	Muhammadabad. Urban ...	344	11	1,832	72	25,783	28,565	7,684	282	124	7,278
			Rural ...	546	6	5,623	70	147,288	149,606	41,911	461	425	41,025
			Total ...	890	17	7,455	142	173,071	178,171	49,595	743	549	48,303
			Total ... Urban ...	1,023	26	4,461	190	40,005	44,678	11,825	739	246	10,840
			Rural ...	8,563	50	31,606	558	786,953	815,512	228,046	2,918	2,364	222,764
			Total ...	4,586	76	36,067	748	826,958	860,190	239,871	3,657	2,610	233,604

Showing the Educational position of each Tahsíl in the N.-W. P. and Oudh—(*continued*).

PROVINCIAL TABLE IV.

Serial number of district.	Name of district.	Serial number of tahsíl.	Name of tahsíl.		Total by Education. Learning. Males.	Learning. Females.	Literate. Males.	Literate. Females.	Illiterate. Males.	Illiterate. Females.	Age—period, 5 to 14. Total males.	Learning.	Literate.	Illiterate.
1	2	3	4		5	6	7	8	9	10	11	12	13	14
34	Almora.	173	Champawat	Urban	...	...	...	...	...	...	...	...	...	...
				Rural	380	99	1,528	110	44,927	45,557	10,772	295	138	10,344
			Total		380	99	1,528	110	44,927	45,557	10,772	295	138	10,344
		174	Almora	Urban	385	18	2,206	52	3,586	3,912	1,098	278	212	608
				Rural	1,942	19	10,263	58	142,896	153,563	40,470	1,448	825	38,197
			Total		2,327	37	12,469	110	146,482	157,475	41,568	1,726	1,037	38,805
			Total	Urban	385	18	2,206	52	3,586	3,912	1,098	278	212	608
				Rural	2,322	118	11,791	168	187,823	199,120	51,242	1,743	958	48,541
			Total		2,707	136	13,997	220	191,409	203,032	52,340	2,021	1,170	49,149
35	Garhwál.	175	Pauri	Urban	7	2	782	23	1,616	1,310	288	5	100	183
				Rural	2,167	70	18,166	127	177,581	205,967	51,694	1,516	2,001	48,177
			Total		2,174	72	18,948	150	179,197	207,277	51,982	1,521	2,101	48,360
36	Naini Tal.	176	Rudarpur	Urban	...	...	...	...	...	...	...	...	...	...
				Rural	137	4	685	10	44,039	36,090	9,603	94	17	9,492
			Total		137	4	685	10	44,039	36,090	9,603	94	17	9,492
		177	Kilpuri	Urban	...	...	...	...	...	...	...	...	...	...
				Rural	327	7	974	13	30,275	24,839	6,983	268	56	6,659
			Total		327	7	974	13	30,275	24,839	6,983	268	56	6,659
		178	Káshipur	Urban	388	23	1,332	80	9,408	10,293	2,500	325	48	2,127
				Rural	225	4	672	7	26,998	23,738	6,729	190	28	6,511
			Total		613	27	2,004	87	36,406	34,031	9,229	515	76	8,638
		179	Bhabar	Urban	200	99	599	156	10,737	5,954	1,718	136	110	1,472
				Rural	155	31	2,827	139	72,326	58,457	15,939	113	328	15,498
			Total		355	130	3,426	295	83,063	64,411	17,657	249	438	16,970
			Total	Urban	588	122	1,931	236	20,145	16,247	4,218	461	158	3,599
				Rural	844	46	5,158	169	173,638	143,124	39,254	665	429	38,160
			Total		1,432	168	7,089	405	193,783	159,371	43,472	1,126	587	41,759
37	Lucknow.	180	Lucknow	Urban	6,013	483	22,012	2,180	125,163	132,314	27,606	3,842	463	23,301
				Rural	538	9	3,026	34	81,654	75,035	18,724	400	80	18,244
			Total		6,551	492	25,038	2,214	206,817	207,349	46,330	4,242	543	41,545
		181	Mohanlálganj	Urban	119	...	384	12	3,577	4,261	937	98	11	828
				Rural	757	4	3,239	45	68,873	68,889	17,007	600	91	16,316
			Total		876	4	3,623	57	72,450	73,150	17,944	698	102	17,144
		182	Malihabad	Urban	281	7	627	21	4,463	5,238	1,194	226	11	957
				Rural	709	5	2,754	54	83,012	78,371	20,522	532	51	19,939
			Total		990	12	3,381	75	87,475	83,609	21,716	758	62	20,896
			Total	Urban	6,413	490	23,023	2,213	138,203	141,813	29,737	4,166	485	25,086
				Rural	2,004	18	9,019	133	233,539	222,295	56,253	1,532	222	54,499
			Total		8,417	508	32,042	2,346	366,742	364,108	85,990	5,698	707	79,585

Showing the Educational position of each Tahsīl in the N.-W. P. and Oudh—(*continued*).

PROVINCIAL TABLE IV.

Serial number of district.	Name of district.	Serial number of tahsīl.	Name of tahsīl.	Total by Education.						Age—period, 5 to 14.			
				Learning.		Literate.		Illiterate.		Total males	Learning.	Literate.	Illiterate.
				Males.	Females.	Males.	Females.	Males.	Females.				
1	2	3	4	5	6	7	8	9	10	11	12	13	14
38	Unao.	183	Unao ... Urban ...	539	32	1,357	81	5,446	5,376	1,449	356	25	1,068
			Rural ...	918	2	5,423	50	85,251	88,419	23,017	689	218	22,110
			Total ...	1,457	34	6,780	131	90,697	93,795	24,466	1,045	243	23,178
		184	Safipur ... Urban ...	394	3	1,172	18	11,157	12,402	3,018	304	21	2,693
			Rural ...	618	3	4,045	23	93,950	86,356	24,153	467	133	23,553
			Total ...	1,012	6	5,217	41	105,107	98,758	27,171	771	154	26,246
		185	Purwa ... Urban ...	465	2	1,551	24	8,396	11,043	2,474	359	51	2,064
			Rural ...	1,603	3	9,188	127	122,945	137,805	34,172	1,236	425	32,611
			Total ...	2,068	5	10,739	151	131,341	148,848	36,646	1,595	476	34,575
		186	Mohan ... Urban ...	253	2	681	11	8,361	9;249	2,175	197	18	1,960
			Rural ...	883	7	5,634	70	119,282	113,016	30,630	688	251	28,691
			Total ...	1,136	9	6,315	81	127,643	122,265	32,805	885	269	31,651
			Total ... Urban ...	1,651	39	4,761	134	33,860	38,070	9,116	1,216	115	7,785
			Rural ...	4,022	15	24,290	270	421,428	425,596	111,972	3,080	1,027	107,865
			Total ...	5,673	54	29,051	404	454,788	463,666	121,088	4,296	1,142	115,650
39	Rae Bareli.	187	Rae Bareli ... Urban ...	486	23	1,634	114	8,100	8,441	1,968	313	41	1,614
			Rural ...	1,007	22	5,483	134	94,256	102,175	25,002	738	160	24,104
			Total ...	1,493	45	7,117	248	102,356	110,616	26,970	1,051	201	25,718
		188	Dalmau ... Urban ...	...	...	...	...	...	...	...	...	...	...
			Rural ...	1,644	12	9,139	235	124,258	140,498	35,437	1,243	398	33,796
			Total ...	1,644	12	9,139	235	124,258	140,498	35,437	1,243	398	33,796
		189	Digbijaiganj Urban ...	...	...	...	...	...	...	...	...	...	...
			Rural ...	1,094	23	8,991	181	127,005	139,446	33,179	835	471	31,873
			Total ...	1,094	23	8,991	181	127,005	139,446	33,179	835	471	31,873
		190	Salon ... Urban ...	228	2	457	14	5,094	6,131	1,470	171	15	1,284
			Rural ...	926	18	6,360	139	116,818	125,933	31,752	663	215	30,874
			Total ...	1,154	20	6,817	153	121,912	132,064	33,222	834	230	32,158
			Total ... Urban ...	714	25	2,091	128	13,194	14,572	3,438	484	56	2,898
			Rural ...	4,671	75	29,973	689	462,337	508,052	125,370	3,479	1,244	120,647
			Total ...	5,385	100	32,064	817	475,531	522,624	128,808	3,968	1,300	123,545
40	Sitapur.	191	Sitapur ... Urban ...	928	92	3,587	207	20,474	21,317	5,344	607	66	4,671
			Rural ...	799	3	5,214	88	122,723	115,758	31,422	589	171	30,662
			Total ...	1,727	95	8,801	295	143,197	137,075	36,766	1,196	237	35,333
		192	Sidhauli ... Urban ...	208	1	602	15	5,790	6,212	1,370	153	8	1,200
			Rural ...	796	10	5,206	100	129,189	120,993	32,195	619	129	31,447
			Total ...	1,004	11	5,808	115	134,979	127,205	33,565	772	137	32,656
		193	Misrikh ... Urban ...	198	17	824	24	3,370	3,853	1,014	152	28	834
			Rural ...	1,021	16	4,965	95	119,416	109,408	31,376	802	156	30,418
			Total ...	1,219	33	5,789	119	122,786	113,261	32,390	954	184	31,252

Showing the Educational position of each Tahsil in the N.-W. P. and Oudh—(*continued*).

PROVINCIAL TABLE IV.

Serial number of district.	Name of district.	Serial number of tahsil.	Name of tahsil.		Total by Education. Learning. Males.	Learning. Females.	Literate. Males.	Literate. Females.	Illiterate. Males.	Illiterate. Females.	Age-period, 5 to 14. Total males.	Learning.	Literate.	Illiterate.
1	2	3	4		5	6	7	8	9	10	11	12	13	14
40	Sitapur—(*concluded*).	194	Biswan	Urban	193	*3*	521	*28*	3,036	*3,528*	790	138	4	648
				Rural	851	*5*	5,394	*87*	131,877	*126,371*	33,777	618	163	32,996
			Total		1,044	*8*	5,915	*115*	134,913	*129,899*	34,567	756	167	33,644
			Total	Urban	1,527	*113*	5,584	*274*	32,670	*34,910*	8,518	1,050	106	7,362
				Rural	3,467	*34*	20,779	*370*	503,205	*472,530*	128,770	2,628	619	125,523
			Total		4,994	*147*	26,313	*644*	535,875	*507,440*	137,288	3,678	725	132,885
41	Hardoi.	195	Hardoi	Urban	432	*27*	1,269	*87*	8,005	*7,322*	1,940	264	31	1,645
				Rural	676	*6*	4,583	*77*	150,599	*132,988*	38,980	518	179	38,283
			Total		1,108	*33*	5,852	*164*	158,604	*140,310*	40,920	782	210	39,928
		196	Sandila	Urban	288	*8*	829	*42*	7,361	*8,285*	1,898	204	9	1,685
				Rural	579	*1*	4,360	*39*	133,401	*122,166*	33,653	474	182	32,997
			Total		867	*9*	5,189	*81*	140,762	*130,451*	35,551	678	191	34,682
		197	Bilgram	Urban	449	*11*	1,960	*33*	16,809	*18,703*	4,133	354	57	3,722
				Rural	286	*6*	3,478	*47*	127,821	*112,144*	31,321	240	120	30,961
			Total		735	*17*	5,438	*80*	144,630	*130,847*	35,454	594	177	34,683
		198	Sháhabad	Urban	382	*24*	1,351	*55*	15,175	*16,096*	3,931	307	92	3,532
				Rural	477	*21*	3,421	*64*	112,506	*98,462*	128,035	370	187	127,478
			Total		859	*45*	4,772	*119*	127,681	*114,558*	31,966	677	279	31,010
			Total	Urban	1,551	*70*	5,409	*217*	47,350	*50,406*	11,902	1,129	189	10,584
				Rural	2,018	*34*	15,842	*227*	524,327	*465,760*	131,989	1,602	668	129,719
			Total		3,569	*104*	21,251	*444*	571,677	*516,166*	143,891	2,731	857	140,303
42	Kheri.	199	Lakhimpur	Urban	309	*17*	1,459	*64*	9,742	*9,454*	2,245	206	41	1,998
				Rural	513	*8*	5,091	*66*	177,031	*161,868*	42,319	390	256	41,673
			Total		822	*25*	6,550	*130*	186,773	*171,322*	44,564	596	297	43,671
		200	Muhamdi	Urban	122	*2*	456	*12*	2,964	*3,376*	800	82	8	710
				Rural	763	*34*	4,428	*95*	129,975	*116,390*	32,926	535	313	32,078
			Total		885	*36*	4,884	*107*	132,939	*119,766*	33,726	617	321	32,788
		201	Nighasan	Urban	43	*1*	371	*12*	5,097	*4,960*	1,312	34	42	1,236
				Rural	310	*4*	3,632	*36*	139,729	*125,181*	33,486	217	315	32,954
			Total		353	*5*	4,003	*48*	144,826	*130,141*	34,798	251	357	34,190
			Total	Urban	474	*20*	2,286	*88*	17,803	*17,790*	4,357	322	91	3,944
				Rural	1,586	*46*	13,151	*197*	446,735	*403,439*	108,731	1,142	884	106,705
			Total		2,060	*66*	15,437	*285*	464,538	*421,229*	113,088	1,464	975	110,649

Showing the Educational position of each Tahsil in the N.-W. P. and Oudh—(*continued*).

PROVINCIAL TABLE IV.

Serial number of district.	Name of district.	Serial number of tahsil.	Name of tahsil.		Total by Education. Learning. Males.	Learning. Females.	Literate. Males.	Literate. Females.	Illiterate. Males.	Illiterate. Females.	Age—period, 5 to 14. Total males.	Learning.	Literate.	Illiterate.
1	2	3	4		5	6	7	8	9	10	11	12	13	14
43	Fyzabad.	202	Fyzabad	Urban	1,955	*111*	8,300	*497*	39,995	*41,616*	**9,233**	1,164	398	7,676
				Rural	904	*2*	4,595	*43*	105,123	*113,445*	**26,658**	625	518	25,515
				Total	2,859	*113*	12,895	*540*	145,118	*155,061*	**35,891**	1,789	911	33,191
		203	Akbarpur	Urban	155	*1*	455	*15*	3,215	*3,602*	**861**	98	26	737
				Rural	573	*1*	3,687	*35*	114,612	*115,351*	**29,255**	387	133	28,735
				Total	728	*2*	4,142	*50*	117,827	*118,953*	**30,116**	485	159	29,472
		204	Tanda	Urban	324	*3*	1,281	*18*	17,509	*19,472*	**4,652**	255	131	4,266
				Rural	839	*5*	5,049	*53*	161,859	*163,369*	**44,189**	618	233	43,338
				Total	1,163	*8*	6,330	*71*	179,368	*182,841*	**48,841**	873	364	47,604
		205	Bikapur	Urban	...	...	...	...	...	...	...	...	...	...
				Rural	506	*4*	6,549	*71*	135,117	*146,643*	**35,590**	373	307	34,910
				Total	506	*4*	6,549	*71*	135,117	*146,643*	**35,590**	373	307	34,910
			Total	Urban	2,434	*115*	10,036	*530*	60,719	*64,573*	**14,746**	1,517	550	12,670
				Rural	2,822	*12*	19,880	*202*	516,711	*538,925*	**135,692**	2,003	1,191	132,498
				Total	5,256	*127*	29,916	*732*	577,430	*603,498*	**150,438**	3,520	1,741	145,177
44	Gonda.	206	Gonda	Urban	443	*61*	1,837	*109*	10,603	*10,830*	**2,671**	273	33	2,365
				Rural	820	*3*	9,417	*81*	182,413	*187,555*	**48,168**	569	466	47,133
				Total	1,263	*64*	11,254	*190*	193,016	*198,385*	**50,839**	842	499	49,498
		207	Tarabganj	Urban	204	*2*	1,573	*16*	8,687	*8,430*	**2,186**	145	64	1,977
				Rural	508	*16*	10,704	*92*	174,877	*180,451*	**46,095**	346	604	45,145
				Total	712	*18*	12,277	*108*	183,564	*188,881*	**48,281**	491	668	47,122
		208	Utraula	Urban	275	*4*	1,397	*17*	9,546	*10,235*	**2,564**	179	75	2,310
				Rural	688	*2*	10,738	*103*	321,673	*314,819*	**84,433**	492	766	83,175
				Total	963	*6*	12,135	*120*	331,219	*325,054*	**86,997**	671	841	85,485
			Total	Urban	922	*67*	4,807	*142*	28,836	*29,495*	**7,421**	597	172	6,652
				Rural	2,016	*21*	30,859	*276*	678,963	*682,825*	**178,696**	1,407	1,836	175,453
				Total	2,938	*88*	35,666	*418*	707,799	*712,320*	**186,117**	2,004	2,008	182,105
45	Bahraich.	209	Bahraich	Urban	782	*22*	2,143	*122*	12,955	*13,943*	**3,475**	572	63	2,840
				Rural	1,315	*9*	7,468	*95*	161,384	*156,720*	**42,015**	1,042	254	40,719
				Total	2,097	*31*	9,611	*217*	174,339	*170,663*	**45,490**	1,614	317	43,559
		210	Kaisarganj	Urban	...	...	...	...	...	...	...	...	...	...
				Rural	1,344	*17*	8,326	*164*	163,523	*158,819*	**42,260**	1,014	372	40,874
				Total	1,344	*17*	8,326	*164*	163,523	*158,819*	**42,260**	1,014	372	40,874

Showing the Educational position of each Tahsíl in the N.-W. P. and Oudh—(*continued*).

PROVINCIAL TABLE IV.

Serial number of district.	Name of district.	Serial number of tahsíl.	Name of tahsíl.	Total by Education. Learning. Males.	Learning. Females	Literate. Males.	Literate. Females.	Illiterate. Males.	Illiterate. Females.	Age—period, 5 to 14. Total males.	Learning.	Literate.	Illiterate.
1	2	3	4	5	6	7	8	9	10	11	12	13	14
45	Bahraich—(*concluded*).	211	Nánpára ... Urban ...	148	...	571	*21*	4,166	*4,416*	**1,145**	119	12	1,014
			Rural ...	970	*8*	6,349	*58*	152,123	*142,451*	**39,256**	740	220	38,296
			Total ...	1,118	*8*	6,920	*79*	156,289	*146,867*	**40,401**	859	232	39,310
			Total ... Urban ...	930	*22*	2,714	*143*	17,121	*18,359*	**4,620**	691	75	3,854
			Rural ...	3,629	*34*	22,143	*317*	477,030	*457,990*	**128,531**	2,796	846	119,889
			Total ...	4,559	*56*	24,857	*460*	494,151	*476,349*	**128,151**	3,487	921	123,743
46	Sultánpur.	212	Sultánpur ... Urban ...	258	*6*	860	*35*	3,801	*3,791*	**961**	162	36	763
			Rural ...	1,156	*3*	7,436	*49*	148,704	*164,865*	**38,614**	924	533	37,157
			Total ...	1,414	*9*	8,296	*84*	152,505	*168,656*	**39,575**	1,086	569	37,920
		213	Musáfirkhána Urban ...	...	...	...	...	...	...	...	...	...	...
			Rural ...	873	*2*	5,660	*48*	115,735	*128,903*	**29,850**	658	258	28,934
			Total ...	873	*2*	5,660	*48*	115,735	*128,903*	**29,850**	658	258	28,934
		214	Amethi ... Urban ...	...	...	...	...	...	...	...	...	...	...
			Rural ...	413	*12*	5,733	*52*	100,366	*112,632*	**27,334**	284	212	26,838
			Total ...	413	*12*	5,733	*52*	100,366	*112,632*	**27,334**	284	212	26,838
		215	Kadipur ... Urban ...	...	...	...	...	...	...	...	...	...	...
			Rural ...	788	*2*	4,847	*101*	133,856	*134,864*	**35,770**	565	150	35,055
			Total ...	788	*2*	4,847	*101*	133,856	*134,864*	**35,770**	565	150	35,055
			Total ... Urban ...	258	*6*	860	*35*	3,801	*3,791*	**961**	162	36	763
			Rural ...	3,230	*19*	23,676	*250*	498,661	*541,264*	**131,568**	2,431	1,153	127,084
			Total ...	3,488	*25*	24,536	*285*	502,462	*545,055*	**132,529**	2,593	1,189	128,747
47	Partábgarh.	216	Partábgarh ... Urban ...	331	*22*	1,081	*83*	5,493	*5,521*	**1,479**	219	30	1,230
			Rural ...	694	*8*	7,039	*152*	133,788	*152,215*	**39,626**	537	457	38,632
			Total ...	1,025	*30*	8,120	*235*	139,281	*157,736*	**41,105**	756	487	39,862
		217	Patti ... Urban ...	...	...	...	...	...	...	...	...	...	...
			Rural ...	378	*1*	4,214	*83*	129,631	*137,285*	**37,035**	281	172	36,583
			Total ...	378	*1*	4,214	*83*	129,631	*137,285*	**37,035**	281	172	36,583
		218	Kunda ... Urban ...	39	...	125	...	1,539	*1,815*	**437**	29	5	403
			Rural ...	960	*24*	7,881	*177*	151,978	*168,338*	**44,328**	714	369	43,245
			Total ...	999	*24*	8,006	*177*	153,517	*170,153*	**44,765**	743	374	43,648
			Total ... Urban ...	370	*22*	1,206	*83*	7,032	*7,336*	**1,916**	248	35	1,633
			Rural ...	2,032	*33*	19,134	*412*	415,397	*457,838*	**120,989**	1,532	998	118,459
			Total ...	2,402	*55*	20,340	*495*	422,429	*465,174*	**122,905**	1,780	1,033	120,092

Showing the Educational position of each Tahsíl in the N.-W. P. and Oudh—(*concluded*).

PROVINCIAL TABLE IV.

Serial number of district.	Name of district.	Serial number of tahsíl.	Name of tahsíl.	Total by Education. Learning. Males.	Learning. Females.	Literate. Males.	Literate. Females.	Illiterate. Males.	Illiterate. Females.	Age—period, 5 to 14. Total males.	Learning.	Literate.	Illiterate.
1	2	3	4	5	6	7	8	9	10	11	12	13	14
48	Bara Banki.	219	Nawábganj ... Urban ...	581	*11*	2,082	*81*	10,749	*11,966*	**2,642**	384	57	2,201
			Nawábganj ... Rural ...	990	*5*	4,143	*60*	107,425	*104,882*	**26,000**	773	159	25,068
			Total ...	1,571	*16*	6,225	*141*	118,174	*116,848*	**28,642**	1,157	216	27,269
		220	Haidargarh ... Urban ...	...	...	...	...	...	...	...	...	...	...
			Haidargarh ... Rural ...	1,016	*13*	5,327	*116*	90,738	*97,542*	**23,509**	767	208	22,534
			Total ...	1,016	*13*	5,327	*116*	90,738	*97,542*	**23,509**	767	208	22,534
		221	Ram Sanehi-ghát. Urban ...	471	*9*	1,429	*51*	8,645	*10,874*	**2,468**	382	51	2,035
			Ram Sanehi-ghát. Rural ...	1,389	*15*	7,512	*89*	169,317	*177,726*	**41,928**	1,042	347	40,539
			Total ...	1,860	*24*	8,941	*140*	177,962	*188,600*	**44,396**	1,424	398	42,574
		222	Fatehpur ... Urban ...	191	*5*	722	*34*	6,010	*6,576*	**1,498**	159	24	1,315
			Fatehpur ... Rural ...	1,324	*15*	7,032	*95*	150,022	*143,626*	**36,398**	997	288	35,113
			Total ...	1,515	*20*	7,754	*129*	156,082	*150,202*	**37,896**	1,156	312	36,428
			Total ... Urban ...	1,243	*25*	4,233	*166*	25,404	*29,416*	**6,608**	925	132	5,551
			Total ... Rural ...	4,719	*48*	24,014	*360*	517,502	*523,776*	**127,835**	3,579	1,002	123,254
			Total ...	5,962	*73*	28,247	*526*	542,906	*553,192*	**134,443**	4,504	1,134	128,805

PROVINCIAL TABLE V.

SHOWING THE VARIATIONS IN THE POPULATION OF THE PARGANAS SINCE THE PREVIOUS CENSUS.

The variations in the population of the

PROVINCIAL TABLE V.

Serial number of district.	Name of district.	Serial number of pargana.	Name of pargana.	Total. Census, 1881.	Census, 1891.	Increase + or Decrease —.
1	2	3	4	5	6	7
1	Debra Dún ...	1	Western Dún	77,935	89,578	+11,643
		2	Eastern Dún	21,018	27,860	+6,842
		3	Jaunsár Báwar	45,117	50,697	+5,580
			Total ...	144,070	168,135	+24,065
2	Sahāranpur ...	4	Sahāranpur	131,629	137,186	+5,557
		5	Faizabad	48,623	51,817	+3,194
		6	Muzaffarabad	54,275	59,776	+5,501
		7	Haraura	57,766	63,719	+5,953
		8	Manglaur	73,157	74,761	+1,604
		9	Bhagwánpur	67,765	71,097	+3,332
		10	Roorkee	66,236	69,644	+3,408
		11	Jawalapur	67,413	74,996	+7,583
		12	Rámpur	74,810	68,688	—6,122
		13	Nágal	58,029	61,718	+3,689
		14	Deoband	78,219	75,221	—2,998
		15	Nakúr	54,662	52,160	—2,502
		16	Sirsawa	40,293	39,392	- 901
		17	Sultánpur	49,577	46,348	—3,229
		18	Gangoh	57,090	54,757	—2,333
			Total ...	979,544	1,001,280	+21,736
3	Muzaffarnagar ...	19	Muzaffarnagar	61,185	64,310	+3,125
		20	Baghra	50,039	50,872	+833
		21	Chartháwal	39,489	40,140	+651
		22	Purchhapar	40,124	38,952	—1,172
		23	Gordhanpur	11,870	12,222	+352
		24	Shámli	56,182	57,060	+878
		25	Thána Bhawan	43,700	43,560	—140
		26	Jhinjhána	37,661	38,110	+449
		27	Kairána	40,262	41,389	+1,127
		28	Bidauli	24,428	20,038	—4,390
		29	Jauli Jánsath	42,590	45,562	+2,972
		30	Khátauli	56,215	61,335	+5,120
		31	Bhúkarheri	46,957	46,556	—401
		32	Bhúma Sambalhera	38,092	40,080	+1,988
		33	Burhána	44,227	46,019	+1,792
		34	Shikárpur	58,554	60,021	+1,467
		35	Kandhla	66,869	66,648	—221
			Total ...	758,444	772,874	+14,430
4	Meerut	36	Meerut	291,170	326,054	+34,884
		37	Jalálabad	103,595	107,500	+3,905
		38	Dásna	76,147	77,008	+861
		39	Loni	65,073	62,633	—2,440
		40	Hastinapur	82,270	92,585	+10,315
		41	Kithore	77,562	85,283	+7,721
		42	Bághpat	111,572	115,284	+3,712
		43	Kotána	47,550	47,262	—288
		44	Baraut	59,169	59,828	+659
		45	Chapranli	39,709	37,282	—2,427
		46	Sardhana	88,427	91,857	+3,430
		47	Barnawa	70,995	76,835	+5,840
		48	Hápur	89,528	97,342	+7,814
		49	Garhmuktesar	48,724	50,300	+1,576
		50	Sarawa	35,008	37,205	+2,197
		51	Puth	26,638	27,200	+562
			Total ...	1,313,137	1,391,458	+78,321
5	Bulandshahr ...	52	Sikandarabad	86,824	83,754	—3,070
		53	Dankaur	57,939	51,874	—6,065
		54	Dádri	91,303	88,740	—2,563
		55	Khúrja	105,185	103,132	—2,053
		56	Pahásu	53,822	62,064	+8,242
		57	Jewar	53,554	55,941	+2,387
		58	Anúpshahr	67,820	68,179	+359
		59	Ahár	66,578	69,015	+2,437
		60	Dibai	78,896	85,287	+6,391
		61	Baran	90,268	95,063	+4,795
		62	Siyána	70,821	74,610	+3,789
		63	Agauta	60,981	65,826	+4,845
		64	Shikárpur	40,831	46,429	+5,598
			Total ...	924,822	949,914	+25,092

parganas since the previous census.

PROVINCIAL TABLE V.

Males.			Females.			Serial number of pargana.
Census, 1881.	Census, 1891.	Increase + or Decrease —.	Census, 1881.	Census, 1891.	Increase + or Decrease —.	
8	9	10	11	12	13	14
46,077	54,207	+8,130	31,858	35,371	+3,513	1
12,508	17,682	+5,174	8,510	10,178	+1,668	2
25,400	28,435	+3,035	19,717	22,262	+2,545	3
83,985	100,324	+16,339	60,085	67,811	+7,726	
69,963	73,360	+3,397	61,666	63,826	+2,160	4
25,974	27,097	+1,123	22,649	24,720	+2,071	5
28,903	31,400	+2,497	25,372	28,376	+3,004	6
30,478	33,569	+3,091	27,288	30,150	+2,862	7
40,094	40,344	+250	33,063	34,417	+1,354	8
36,793	37,996	+1,203	30,972	33,101	+2,129	9
36,753	37,998	+1,245	29,483	31,646	+2,163	10
37,884	42,889	+5,005	29,529	32,107	+2,578	11
40,604	37,072	—3,532	34,206	31,616	—2,590	12
31,763	33,953	+2,190	26,266	27,765	+1,499	13
42,980	41,660	—1,320	35,239	33,561	—1,678	14
29,443	27,976	—1,467	25,219	24,184	—1,035	15
21,925	21,316	—609	18,368	18,076	—292	16
26,310	24,620	—1,690	23,267	21,728	—1,539	17
30,560	29,101	—1,459	26,530	25,656	—874	18
530,427	540,351	+9,924	449,117	460,929	+11,812	
33,774	35,939	+2,165	27,411	28,371	+960	19
26,881	27,578	+697	23,158	23,294	+136	20
21,643	22,097	+454	17,846	18,043	+197	21
21,901	21,206	—695	18,223	17,746	—477	22
6,665	6,793	+128	5,205	5,429	+224	23
30,600	30,900	+300	25,582	26,160	+578	24
23,177	23,262	+85	20,523	20,298	—225	25
20,001	20,264	+263	17,660	17,846	+186	26
21,462	22,338	+876	18,800	19,051	+251	27
13,239	10,937	—2,302	11,189	9,101	—2,088	28
22,571	24,332	+1,761	20,019	21,230	+1,211	29
29,935	33,003	+3,068	26,280	28.332	+2,052	30
26,061	25,371	—690	20,896	21,185	+289	31
20,110	21,216	+1,106	17,982	18,864	+882	32
23,730	24,776	+1,046	20,497	21,243	+746	33
31,554	32,409	+855	27,000	27,612	+612	34
36,132	35,807	—325	30,737	30,841	+104	35
409,430	418,228	+8,792	349,008	354,646	+5,638	
158,590	178,105	+19,515	132,580	147,949	+15,369	36
55,734	57,119	+1,385	47,861	50,381	+2,520	37
40,020	40,974	+954	36,127	36,034	—93	38
35,646	33,985	—1,661	29,427	28,648	—779	39
44,224	49,181	+4,957	38,046	43,404	+5,358	40
41,351	45,136	+3,785	36,211	40,147	+3,936	41
59,884	62,243	+2,359	51,688	53,041	+1,353	42
25,564	25,471	—93	21,986	21,791	—195	43
31,999	32,361	+362	27,170	27,467	+297	44
21,156	20,228	—928	18,553	17,054	—1,499	45
47,437	49,185	+1,748	40,990	42,672	+1,682	46
38,418	41,354	+2,936	32,577	35,481	+2,904	47
47,340	51,362	+4,022	42,188	45,980	+3,792	48
25,833	26,639	+806	22,891	23,661	+770	49
18,143	19,367	+1,224	16,865	17,838	+973	50
14,098	14,534	+436	12,540	12,666	+126	51
705,437	747,244	+41,807	607,700	644,214	+36,514	
46,344	44,131	—2,213	40,480	39,623	—857	52
31,292	28,102	—3,190	26,647	23,772	—2,875	53
49,806	47,645	—2,161	41,497	41,095	—402	54
55,808	54,158	—1,650	49,377	48,974	—403	55
28,435	32,736	+4,301	25,387	29,328	+3,941	56
28,473	29,533	+1,060	25,081	26,408	+1,327	57
35,889	35,844	—45	31,931	32,335	+404	58
34,871	36,278	+1,407	31,707	32,737	+1,030	59
41,865	45,149	+3,284	37,031	40,138	+3,107	60
48,124	49,945	+1,821	42,144	45,118	+2,974	61
37,173	39,129	+1,956	33,648	35,481	+1,833	62
32,193	34,457	+2,264	28,788	31,369	+2,581	63
21,685	24,514	+2,829	19,146	21,915	+2,769	64
491,958	501,621	+9,663	432,864	448,293	+15,429	

The variations in the population of the

PROVINCIAL TABLE V.

Serial number of district.	Name of district.	Serial number of pargana.	Name of pargana.	Total. Census, 1881.	Total. Census, 1891.	Total. Increase + or Decrease —.
1	2	3	4	5	6	7
6	Aligarh ...	65	Barauli ...	9,288	9,964	+676
		66	Koil ...	193,118	190,263	—2,855
		67	Morthal ...	25,248	29,540	+4,292
		68	Atrauli ...	72,574	81,113	+8,539
		69	Gangiri ...	73,962	82,960	+8,998
		70	Hasangarh ...	65,452	64,827	—625
		71	Gorai ...	45,927	42,400	—3,527
		72	Sikandra Rao ...	118,423	123,247	+4,824
		73	Akrabad ...	57,450	59,938	+2,488
		74	Háthras ...	159,114	167,125	+8,011
		75	Mursán ...	40,367	41,139	+772
		76	Tappal ...	51,562	51,611	+49
		77	Chandaus ...	38,632	35,354	—3,278
		78	Khair ...	70,070	63,691	—6,379
			Total ...	1,021,187	1,043,172	+21,985
7	Muttra ...	79	Muttra ...	220,307	234,914	+14,607
		80	Kosi ...	65,293	60,222	—5,071
		81	Chháta ...	84,598	93,243	+8,645
		82	Mát ...	95,446	89,451	—5,995
		83	Mahaban ...	116,829	133,488	+16,659
		84	Sadabad ...	89,217	102,103	+12,886
			Total ...	671,690	713,421	+41,731
8	Agra ...	85	Agra ...	266,765	272,718	+5,953
		86	Etmádpur ...	141,267	153,761	+12,494
		87	Bah ...	120,529	125,848	+5,319
		88	Fatehabad ...	104,762	108,446	+3,684
		89	Firozabad ...	108,521	112,153	+3,632
		90	Keraoli ...	114,678	106,977	—7,701
		91	Kheragarh ...	118,134	123,893	+5,759
			Total ...	974,656	1,003,796	+29,140
9	Farukhabad ...	92	Kanauj ...	114,912	117,229	+2,317
		93	Tirwa ...	91,994	95,732	+3,738
		94	Sakráwa ...	17,786	16,658	—1,128
		95	Sakatpur ...	26,673	24,685	—1,988
		96	Saurikh ...	35,093	31,598	—3,495
		97	Tálgrám ...	58,325	54,743	—3,582
		98	Chibráman ...	64,457	56,371	—8,086
		99	Muhammadabad ...	21,543	21,695	+152
		100	Pahára ...	114,528	113,367	—1,161
		101	Bhojpur ...	61,043	55,765	—5,278
		102	Shamsabad East ...	58,013	54,069	—3,944
		103	Kampil ...	69,255	64,601	—4,654
		104	Shamsabad West ...	97,901	78,956	—18,945
		105	Imratpur ...	47,214	46,941	—273
		106	Khákhatmau ...	16,595	15,592	—1,003
		107	Paramnagar ...	12,276	10,685	—1,591
			Total ...	907,608	858,687	—48,921
10	Mainpuri ...	108	Mainpuri ...	86,153	81,631	—4,522
		109	Ghiror ...	62,837	57,871	—4,966
		110	Kuráoli ...	34,344	31,650	—2,694
		111	Bhongaon ...	124,204	116,803	—7,401
		112	Bewar ...	19,152	16,142	—3,010
		113	Alipur Patti ...	14,463	13,043	—1,420
		114	Kishni Nabiganj ...	52,949	49,380	—3,569
		115	Karhal ...	55,478	55,301	—177
		116	Barnahal ...	44,553	44,996	+443
		117	Shikohabad ...	144,882	140,093	—4,789
		118	Mustafabad ...	162,201	155,253	—6,948
			Total ...	801,216	762,163	—39,053
11	Etáwah ...	119	Etáwah ...	193,211	198,023	+4,812
		120	Bharthna ...	161,446	169,977	+8,533
		121	Bidhúna ...	138,149	134,459	—3,690
		122	Phaphúnd ...	111,585	107,307	—4,278
		123	Auraiya ...	117,980	117,861	—119
			Total ...	722,371	727,629	+5,258

parganas since the previous census.

PROVINCIAL TABLE V.

Males.			Females.			Serial number of parganas.
Census, 1881.	Census, 1891.	Increase + or Decrease —.	Census, 1881.	Census, 1891.	Increase + or Decrease —.	
8	9	10	11	12	13	14
5,096	5,287	+191	*4,192*	*4,677*	*+485*	65
104,246	101,517	—2,729	*88,872*	*88,746*	*—126*	66
13,687	15,671	+1,984	*11,561*	*13,869*	*+2,308*	67
39,274	43,069	+3,795	*33,300*	*38,044*	*+4,744*	68
39,842	44,575	+4,733	*34,120*	*38,385*	*+4,265*	69
35,522	34,778	—744	*29,930*	*30,049*	*+119*	70
24,797	22,850	—1,947	*21,130*	*19,550*	*—1,580*	71
64,778	66,885	—2,107	*53,645*	*56,362*	*+2,717*	72
31,321	32,264	+943	*26,129*	*27,674*	*+1,545*	73
84,980	89,431	+4,451	*74,134*	*77,694*	*+3,560*	74
22,129	22,278	+149	*18,238*	*18,861*	*+623*	75
27,497	27,481	—16	*24,065*	*24,130*	*+65*	76
20,589	18,808	—1,781	*18,043*	*16,546*	*—1,497*	77
37,521	33,849	—3,672	*32,549*	*29,842*	*—2,707*	78
551,279	558,743	+7,464	*469,908*	*484,429*	*+14,521*	
117,905	125,990	+8,085	*102,402*	*108,924*	*+6,522*	79
34,002	31,738	—2,264	*31,291*	*28,484*	*—2,807*	80
44,985	49,672	+4,687	*39,613*	*43,571*	*+3,958*	81
50,978	47,407	—3,571	*44,468*	*42,044*	*—2,424*	82
64,037	72,319	+8,282	*52,792*	*61,169*	*+8,377*	83
49,060	55,534	+6,474	*40,157*	*46,569*	*+6,412*	84
360,967	382,660	+21,693	*310,723*	*330,761*	*+20,038*	
144,267	146,817	+2,550	*122,498*	*125,901*	*+3,403*	85
77,137	83,200	+6,063	*64,130*	*70,561*	*+6,431*	86
63,524	66,937	+3,413	*57,005*	*58,911*	*+1,906*	87
56,835	58,744	+1,909	*47,927*	*49,702*	*+1,775*	88
59,287	60,292	+1,005	*49,234*	*51,861*	*+2,627*	89
61,596	57,667	—3,929	*53,082*	*49,310*	*—3,772*	90
64,155	66,802	+2,647	*53,979*	*57,091*	*+3,112*	91
526,801	540,459	+13,658	*447,855*	*463,337*	*+15,482*	
61,970	62,642	+672	*52,942*	*54,587*	*+1,645*	92
50,563	52,119	+1,556	*41,431*	*43,613*	*+2,182*	93
9,833	9,083	—750	*7,953*	*7,575*	*—378*	94
14,937	13,694	—1,243	*11,736*	*10,991*	*—745*	95
19,208	17,436	—1,772	*15,885*	*14,162*	*—1,723*	96
31,337	29,524	—1,813	*26,988*	*25,219*	*—1,769*	97
35,280	30,635	—4,645	*29,177*	*25,736*	*—3,441*	98
11,910	11,899	—11	*9,633*	*9,796*	*+163*	99
60,137	60,378	+241	*54,391*	*52,989*	*—1,402*	100
32,755	30,094	—2,661	*28,288*	*25,671*	*—2,617*	101
31,615	29,487	—2,128	*26,398*	*24,582*	*—1,816*	102
33,610	34,278	+668	*35,645*	*30,323*	*—5,322*	103
55,169	42,558	—12,611	*42,732*	*36,398*	*—6,334*	104
26,007	26,012	+5	*21,207*	*20,929*	*—278*	105
9,376	8,644	—732	*7,219*	*6,948*	*—271*	106
6,801	5,857	—944	*5,475*	*4,828*	*—647*	107
490,508	464,340	—26,168	*417,100*	*394,347*	*—22,753*	
47,958	44,589	—3,369	*38,195*	*37,042*	*—1,153*	108
34,894	32,082	—2,812	*27,943*	*25,789*	*—2,154*	109
18,931	17,111	—1,820	*15,413*	*14,539*	*—874*	110
68,331	63,922	—4,409	*55,873*	*52,881*	*—2,992*	111
10,982	9,042	—1,940	*8,170*	*7,100*	*—1,070*	112
7,791	7,005	—786	*6,672*	*6,038*	*—634*	113
29,287	27,140	—2,147	*23,662*	*22,240*	*—1,422*	114
31,111	30,229	—882	*24,367*	*25,072*	*+705*	115
24,609	24,446	—163	*19,944*	*20,550*	*+606*	116
79,316	76,477	—2,839	*65,566*	*63,616*	*—1,950*	117
88,884	84,756	—4,128	*73,317*	*70,497*	*—2,820*	118
442,094	416,799	—25,295	*359,122*	*345,364*	*—13,758*	
105,319	107,503	+2,184	*87,892*	*90,520*	*+2,628*	119
88,736	92,857	+4,121	*72,710*	*77,122*	*+4,412*	120
76,275	73,926	—2,349	*61,874*	*60,533*	*—1,341*	121
61,193	58,644	—2,549	*50,392*	*48,663*	*—1,729*	122
63,701	63,845	+144	*54,279*	*54,016*	*—263*	123
395,224	396,775	+1,551	*327,147*	*330,854*	*+3,707*	

The variations in the population of the

PROVINCIAL TABLE V.

Serial number of district.	Name of district.	Serial number of pargana.	Name of pargana.	Total. Census, 1881.	Total. Census, 1891.	Total. Increase + or Decrease —.
1	2	3	4	5	6	7
12	Etah ...	124	Etah Sakíth	116,609	114,244	—2,365
		125	Saunhar	14,079	11,973	—2,106
		126	Marehra	96,204	100,813	+4,609
		127	Jalesar	118,925	121,030	+2,105
		128	Azamnagar	102,697	81,484	—21,213
		129	Barna	16,256	12,495	—3,761
		130	Patiáli	30,983	21,613	—9,370
		131	Nidhpur	43,864	46,402	+2,538
		132	Olai	29,528	12,191	—17,337
		133	Bilrám	42,619	61,374	+18,755
		134	Pachlana	13,608	12,329	—1,279
		135	Soron	26,362	23,145	—3,217
		136	Sirhpura	34,638	26,435	—8,203
		137	Saháwar Karsána	52,517	41,071	—11,446
		138	Faizpur	17,374	15,464	—1,910
			Total ...	756,263	702,063	—54,200
13	Bareilly	139	Bareilly	285,731	298,482	+12,751
		140	Sháhi	43,828	39,960	—3,868
		141	Ajaon	15,781	14,626	—1,155
		142	Sirauli (South)	36,693	39,927	+3,234
		143	Farídpur	111,141	119,805	+8,664
		144	Nawábganj	117,002	124,349	+7,347
		145	Aonla	81,808	77,938	—3,870
		146	Bulia	23,093	22,934	—159
		147	Sirauli (North)	41,330	40,714	—616
		148	Saneha	56,042	55,151	—891
		149	Richha	100,600	98,905	—1,695
		150	Chaumahla	54,231	53,966	—265
		151	Kabar	39,409	35,680	—3,729
		152	Sarsáwan	24,247	18,254	—5,993
			Total ...	1,030,936	1,040,691	+9,755
14	Bijnor	153	Bijnor	49,966	53,108	+3,142
		154	Daranagar	38,131	40,594	+2,463
		155	Mandawar	35,999	40,185	+4,186
		156	Bashta	26,743	27,788	+1,045
		157	Búrpur	35,404	39,200	+3,796
		158	Chándpur	61,532	71,187	+9,655
		159	Dhámpur	85,033	89,714	+4,681
		160	Seohára	48,142	51,012	+2,870
		161	Nihtor	36,864	41,262	+4,398
		162	Afzalgarh	69,439	69,099	—340
		163	Barhapura	29,067	34,814	+5,747
		164	Nagína	71,569	79,234	+7,665
		165	Akbarabad	22,275	25,815	+3,540
		166	Kíratpur	47,416	54,444	+7,028
		167	Najíbabad	63,870	76,614	+12,744
			Total ...	721,450	794,070	+72,620
15	Budaun	168	Budaun	135,576	141,822	+6,246
		169	Ujháni	86,736	84,851	—1,885
		170	Sahaswán	95,974	98,583	+2,609
		171	Kot	96,417	94,406	—2,011
		172	Asadpur	61,238	67,836	+6,598
		173	Rájpura	56,297	58,552	+2,255
		174	Bisauli	58,164	56,473	—1,691
		175	Satási	47,011	49,668	+2,657
		176	Islámnagar	82,483	77,499	—4,984
		177	Salempur	108,904	120,462	+11,558
		178	Usehat	76,972	75,446	—1,526
			Total ...	905,772	925,598	+19,826
16	Moradabad ...	179	Biléri	229,784	231,947	+2,163
		180	Moradabad	231,863	240,795	+8,932
		181	Sambhal	248,107	245,619	—2,488
		182	Amroha	174,014	186,183	+12,169
		183	Hasanpur	161,809	153,680	—8,129
		184	Thákurdwára	109,596	121,174	+11,578
			Total ...	1,155,173	1,179,398	+24,225

parganas since the previous census.

PROVINCIAL TABLE V.

Males.			Females.			Serial number of parganas.
Census, 1881.	Census, 1891.	Increase + or Decrease —.	Census, 1881.	Census, 1891.	Increase + or Decrease —.	
8	9	10	11	12	13	14
64,584	62,414	—2,170	52,026	51,830	—196	124
7,800	6,631	—1,169	6,279	5,342	—937	125
52,914	54,423	+1,509	43,290.	46,390	+3,100	126
64,672	65,569	+897	54,253	55,461	+1,208	127
56,304	45,019	—11,285	46,393	36,465	—9,928	128
9,033	6,956	—2,077	7,223	5,539	—1,684	129
16,551	11.758	—4,793	14,432	9,855	—4,577	130
23,913	25,327	+1,414	19,951	21,075	+1,124	131
15,975	6,792	—9,183	13,553	5,399	—8,154	132
23,290	33,327	+10,037	19,329	28,047	+8,718	133
7.585	6,808	—777	6,023	5,521	—502	134
13,985	12,390	—1,595	12,377	10,755	—1,622	135
19,199	14,819	—4,380	15,439	11,616	—3,823	136
28,261	22,605	—5,656	24,256	18,466	—5,790	137
9,474	8,365	—1,109	7,900	7,099	—801	138
413,540	383,203	—30,337	342,723	318,860	—23,863	
152,341	160,805	+8,464	133,390	137,677	+4,287	139
22 955	20,801	—2,154	20,873	19,159	—1,714	140
8,139	7,513	—626	7,642	7,113	—529	141
19,208	20,853	+1,645	17,485	19,074	+1,589	142
60,254	65,453	+5,199	50,887	54,352	+3,465	143
62,931	66,587	+3,656	54,071	57,762	+3,691	144
43,118	41,372	—1,746	38,690	36,566	—2,124	145
12,353	12,363	+10	10,740	10,571	—169	146
21,813	21,436	—377	19,517	19,278	—239	147
29,754	29,315	—439	26,288	25,836	—452	148
53,435	52,192	—1,243	47,165	46,713	—452	149
28,589	28,655	+66	25,642	25,311	—331	150
20,510	18,620	—1,890	18,899	17,060	—1,839	151
12,610	9,515	—3,095	11,637	8,739	—2,898	152
548,010	555,480	+7,470	482,926	485,211	+2,285	
26,854	28,378	+1,524	23,112	24,730	+1,618	153
20,292	21,508	+1,216	17,839	19,086	+1,247	154
19,033	21,424	+2,391	16,966	18,761	+1,795	155
14,615	15,084	+469	12,128	12,704	+576	156
18,761	20,717	+1,956	16,643	18,483	+1,840	157
32,281	37,335	+5,054	29,251	33,852	+4,601	158
44,388	47,045	+2,657	40,645	42,669	+2,024	159
25,513	26,865	+1,352	22,629	24,147	+1,518	160
19,289	21,565	+2,276	17,575	19,697	+2,122	161
37,118	36,438	—680	32,321	32,661	+340	162
15,865	18,426	+2.561	13,202	16,388	+3,186	163
37,571	41,292	+3,721	33,998	37,942	+3,944	164
12,021	13,624	+1,603	10,254	12,191	+1,937	165
25,019	27,982	+2,963	22,397	26,462	+4,065	166
34,638	40,529	+5,891	29,232	36,085	+6,853	167
383,258	418,212	+34,954	338,192	375,858	+37,666	
71,100	74,272	+3,172	64,476	67,550	+3,074	168
47,118	46,025	—1.093	39,618	38,826	—792	169
52,223	53,170	+947	43,751	45,413	+1,662	170
51,787	51,010	—777	44,630	43,396	—1,234	171
32,823	36,562	+3,739	28,415	31,274	+2,859	172
30,842	31,916	+1,074	25,455	26,636	+1,181	173
30,829	30,254	—575	27,335	26,219	+1,116	174
25,254	26,646	+1.392	21,757	23,022	+1,265	175
43,905	41,663	—2,242	38,578	35,836	—2,742	176
59,363	65,856	+6,493	49,541	54,606	+5,065	177
41,743	40,760	—983	35,229	34,686	+543	178
486,987	498,134	+11,147	418,785	427,464	+8,679	
121,434	123,416	+1,982	108,350	108,531	+181	179
121,656	126,025	+4,369	110,207	114,770	+4,563	180
130,441	129,303	—1,138	117,666	116,316	—1,350	181
90,845	97,811	+6,966	83,169	88,372	+5,203	182
87,356	82,749	— 4,607	74,453	70,931	—3,522	183
58,559	64,268	+5,709	51,037	56,906	+5,869	184
610,291	623,572	+13,281	644,882	555,826	+10,944	

The variations in the population of the

PROVINCIAL TABLE V.

Serial number of district.	Name of district.	Serial number of pargana.	Name of pargana.	Total. Census, 1881.	Total. Census, 1891.	Total. Increase + or Decrease —.
1	2	3	4	5	6	7
17	Sháhjahánpur ...	185	Sháhjahánpur	146,109	150,137	+4,028
		186	Jamaur	43,851	50,470	+6,619
		187	Kánt	62,068	72,539	+10,471
		188	Powáyan	142,373	144,603	+2,230
		189	Baragaon	45,989	45,664	—325
		190	Khútar	57,092	58,955	+1,863
		191	Tilhar	66,549	78,254	+11,705
		192	Míránpur Katra	8,988	9,885	+897
		193	Jalálpur	43,592	44,110	+518
		194	Nigohi	54,461	58,536	+4,075
		195	Khera Bajhera	40,898	46,006	+5,108
		196	Jalálabad	145,915	159,392	+13,477
			Total ...	857,885	918,551	+60,666
18	Pilibhít ...	197	Bisalpur	179,350	190,864	+11,514
		198	Pilibhít	100,186	110,640	+10,454
		199	Jahánabad	83,158	88,657	+5,499
		200	Puranpur	88,907	95,205	+6,298
			Total ...	451,601	485,366	+33,765
19	Cawnpore ...	201	Akbarpur	109,910	102,256	—7,654
		202	Bilhaur	100,654	100,051	—603
		203	Bhognipur	88,081	96,575	+8,494
		204	Derapur	124,746	122,244	—2,502
		205	Ghátampur	113,946	117,797	+3,851
		206	Rasúlabad	102,168	99,537	—2,631
		207	Narwal	101,830	98,784	—3,046
		208	Shiurájpur	150,728	147,823	—2,905
		209	Cawnpore	289,333	324,628	+35,295
			Total ...	1,181,396	1,209,695	+28,299
20	Fatehpur	210	Fatehpur	112,960	112,672	—288
		211	Haswa	64,636	62,780	—1,856
		212	Bindki	44,351	43,775	—576
		213	Tappa Jár	37,342	38,941	+1,599
		214	Kutia Gunír	37,489	36,070	—1,419
		215	Kora	81,164	87,925	+6,761
		216	Ekdala	65,499	71,851	+6,352
		217	Dhata	13,187	14,674	+1,487
		218	Ayáh Sáh	17,155	15,674	—1,481
		219	Gházipur	46,231	48,365	+2,134
		220	Muttaur	26,784	28,350	+1,566
		221	Kotila	25,067	25,296	+229
		222	Hathgaon	111,880	112,784	+904
			Total ...	683,745	699,157	+15,412
21	Bánda	223	Bánda	120,578	112,912	—7,666
		224	Pailáni	83,033	88,544	+5,511
		225	Baberu	85,229	96,284	+11,055
		226	Girwan	88,651	85,528	—3,123
		227	Badausa	79,939	77,922	—2,017
		228	Karwi	85,318	87,687	+2,369
		229	Kamásin	81,238	83,297	+2,059
		230	Mau	74,622	73,658	—964
			Total ...	698,608	705,832	+7,224
22	Hamírpur	231	Sumerpur	48,853	52,301	+3,448
		232	Hamírpur	26,545	28,832	+2,287
		233	Maudha	49,905	57,223	+7,318
		234	Mahoba	70,626	74,200	+3,574
		235	Panwári-Jaitpur	125,578	127,567	+1,989
		236	Ráth	106,013	97,862	—8,151
		237	Jalálpur	79,817	75,735	—4,082
			Total ...	507,337	513,720	+6,383

parganas since the previous census.

PROVINCIAL TABLE V.

Males. Census, 1881.	Males. Census, 1891.	Males. Increase + or Decrease —.	Females. Census, 1881.	Females. Census, 1891.	Females. Increase + or Decrease —.	Serial number of pargana.
8	9	10	11	12	13	14
75,780	77,885	+2,105	70,329	72,252	+1,923	185
23,806	27,210	+3,404	20,045	23,260	+3,215	186
33,620	39,569	+5,949	28,448	32,970	+4,522	187
76,017	78,187	+2,170	66,356	66,416	+60	188
24,583	24,654	+71	21,406	21,010	—396	189
30,621	31,626	+1,005	26,471	27,329	+858	190
35,792	42,223	+6,431	30,757	36,031	+5,274	191
4,886	5,352	+466	4,102	4,533	+431	192
23,680	23,877	+197	19,912	20,233	+321	193
29,297	31,744	+2,447	25,164	26,792	+1,628	194
22,505	25,587	+3,082	18,393	20,419	+2,026	195
79,990	87,392	+7,402	65,925	72,000	+6,075	196
460,577	495,306	+34,729	397,308	423,245	+25,937	
96,158	102,602	+6,444	83,192	88,262	+5,070	197
52,085	57,920	+5,835	48,101	52,720	+4,619	198
44,026	46,844	+2,818	39,132	41,813	+2,681	199
47,518	51,036	+3,518	41,389	44,169	+2,780	200
239,787	258,402	+18,615	211,814	226,964	+15,150	
59,235	54,887	—4,348	50,675	47,369	—3,306	201
54,617	53,675	—942	46,037	46,376	+339	202
44,536	50,846	+6,310	43,545	45,729	+2,184	203
66,285	65,345	—940	58,461	56,899	—1,562	204
57,836	61,368	+3,532	56,110	56,429	+319	205
55,342	54,117	—1,225	46,826	45,420	—1,406	206
52,492	51,261	—1,231	49,338	47,523	—1,815	207
79,485	77,763	—1,722	71,243	70,060	—1,183	208
159,013	178,830	+19,767	130,270	145,798	+15,528	209
628,891	648,092	+19,201	552,505	561,603	+9,098	
57,819	57,788	—31	55,141	54,884	—257	210
33,140	32,395	—745	31,496	30,385	—1,111	211
23,023	22,924	—99	21,328	20,851	—477	212
19,152	20,346	+1,194	18,190	18,595	+405	213
19,241	18,747	—494	18,248	17,323	—925	214
40,898	45,299	+4,401	40,266	42,626	+2,360	215
32,763	36,494	+3,731	32,736	35,357	+2,621	216
6,521	7,581	+1,060	6,666	7,093	+427	217
8,762	8,152	—610	8,393	7,522	—871	218
23,941	25,189	+1,248	22,290	23,176	+886	219
13,615	14,778	+1,163	13,169	13,572	+403	220
12,552	12,633	+81	12,515	12,663	+148	221
56,160	57,495	+1,335	55,720	55,289	—431	222
347,587	359,821	+12,234	336,158	339,336	+3,178	
62,233	56,942	—5,291	58,345	55,970	—2,375	223
42,147	45,350	+3,203	40,886	43,194	+2,308	224
41,917	47,961	+6,044	43,312	48,323	+5,011	225
44,558	43,057	—1,501	44,093	42,471	—1,622	226
40,526	39,255	—1,271	39,413	38,667	—746	227
43,702	44,506	+804	41,616	43,181	+1,565	228
41,346	42,317	+971	39,892	40,980	+1,088	229
37,948	37,506	—442	36,674	36,152	—522	230
354,377	356,894	+2,517	344,231	348,938	+4,707	
24,518	27,003	+2,485	24,335	25,298	+963	231
13,418	15,015	+1,597	13,127	13,817	+690	232
25,313	28,831	+3,518	24,592	28,392	+3,800	233
36,518	37,770	+1,252	34,108	36,430	+2,322	234
64,468	64,647	+179	61,110	62,920	+1,810	235
54,147	48,799	—5,348	51,866	49,063	—2,803	236
41,396	38,538	—2,858	38,421	37,197	—1,224	237
259,778	260,603	+825	247,559	253,117	+5,558	

The variations in the population of the

PROVINCIAL TABLE V.

Serial number of district.	Name of district.	Serial number of pargana.	Name of pargana.	Total. Census, 1881.	Census, 1891.	Increase + or Decrease —.
1	2	3	4	5	6	7
		238	Jhúsi	68,532	69,309	+777
		239	Sikandra	104,469	107,542	+3,073
		240	Kiwái	85,768	89,006	+3238
		241	Mah	98,986	98,083	—903
		242	Soraon	98,082	101,342	+3,260
		243	Nawábganj	67,634	66,237	—1,397
23	Allahabad	244	Mirzapur Chauhári	19,178	19,297	+119
		245	Khairágarh	192,205	195,221	+3,016
		246	Arail	124,094	134,818	+10,724
		247	Bára	53,430	63,816	+10,386
		248	Kara	123,386	129,932	+6,546
		249	Karári	75,630	84,665	+9,035
		250	Atharban	44,653	47,023	+2,370
		251	Cháil	318,059	342,446	+24,387
			Total ...	1,474,106	1,548,737	+74,631
		252	Jhánsi	113,058	145,680	+32,622
		253	Mau	107,151	115,724	+8,573
		254	Garotha	87,897	88,926	+1,029
		255	Moth	56,755	59,089	+2,334
		256	Lalitpur	61,181	70,189	+9,008
24	Jhánsi	257	Bánsi	21,858	24,389	+2,531
		258	Tálbehat	39,904	46,607	+6,703
		259	Bálábehat	15,573	15,968	+395
		260	Bánpur	43,354	51,012	+7,658
		261	Mehroni	22,100	22,862	+762
		262	Maraura	45,118	43,173	—1,945
			Total ...	613,949	683,619	+69,670
		263	Orai	72,380	67,702	—4,678
25	Jalaun	264	Jalaun	161,916	147,090	—14,826
		265	Kálpi	82,003	78,754	—3,249
		266	Kúnch	101,843	102,815	+972
			Total ...	418,142	396,361	—21,781
		267	Athgaon	25,419	27,471	+2,052
		268	Pandrah	36,396	37,552	+1,156
		269	Jalhúpur	26,816	28,349	+1,533
		270	Dehát Amánat	258,108	261,901	+3,793
		271	Sultánipur	7,919	8,497	+578
		272	Shivapuri	33,728	34,709	+981
		273	Katehar	73,975	78,303	+4,328
		274	Kolo Asla	70,062	72,316	+2,254
26	Benares	275	Kaswar Sarkári	30,090	31,369	+1,279
		276	Barhwal	36,785	39,861	+3,076
		277	Bara	29,307	30,776	+1,469
		278	Dhús	24,529	28,132	+3,603
		279	Ralhupur	29,417	26,658	—2,759
		280	Mahwari	19,445	20,574	+1,129
		281	Majhwar	45,445	47,972	+2,527
		282	Narwan	43,681	45,090	+1,409
		283	Mawai	12,089	12,479	+390
		284	Kaswár Rája	89,473	89,934	+461
			Total ...	892,684	921,943	+29,259
		285	Kantit	341,616	339,280	—2,336
		286	Kaswár	85,715	82,735	—2,980
		287	Haveli Chunár	37,013	35,817	—1,196
27	Mirzapur	288	Bhagwat	24,414	24,867	+453
		289	Kariyát Síkhar	24,203	25,224	+1,021
		290	Taluqa Saktisgarh	16,843	17,250	+407
		291	Bhuili	58,836	59,597	+761
		292	Ahraura	21,360	22,827	+1,467

parganas since the previous census.

PROVINCIAL TABLE V.

Males.			Females.			Serial number of parganas.
Census, 1881.	Census, 1891.	Increase + or Decrease —.	Census, 1881.	Census, 1891.	Increase + or Decrease —.	
8	9	10	11	12	13	14
34,029	34,298	+269	*34,503*	*35,011*	*+508*	238
52,192	53,403	+1,211	*52,277*	*54,139*	*+1,862*	239
43,687	44,666	+979	*42,081*	*44,340*	*+2,259*	240
49,977	49,460	—517	*49,009*	*48,623*	*—386*	241
48,082	49,395	+1,313	*50,000*	*51,947*	*+1,947*	242
33,352	32,153	—1,199	*34,282*	*34,084*	*—198*	243
9,433	9,253	—180	*9,745*	*10,044*	*+299*	244
96,461	98,062	+1,601	*95,744*	*97,159*	*+1,415*	245
62,698	68,961	+6,263	*61,396*	*65,857*	*+4,461*	246
26,928	32,651	+5,723	*26,502*	*31,165*	*+4,663*	247
61,728	65,431	+3,703	*61,658*	*64,501*	*+2,843*	248
37,514	42,691	+5,177	*38,116*	*41,974*	*+3,858*	249
22,702	24,234	+1,532	*21,951*	*22,789*	*+838*	250
162,947	176,851	+13,904	*155,112*	*165,595*	*+10,483*	251
741,730	781,509	+39,779	*732,376*	*767,228*	*+34,852*	
59,388	79,788	+20,400	*53,670*	*65,892*	*+12,222*	252
54,931	59,003	+4,072	*52,220*	*56,721*	*+4,501*	253
45,591	45,618	+27	*42,306*	*43,308*	*+1,002*	254
28,950	30,119	+1,169	*27,805*	*28,970*	*+1,165*	255
32,071	36,390	+4,319	*29,110*	*33,799*	*+4,689*	256
11,521	12,794	+1,273	*10,337*	*11,595*	*+1,258*	257
20,843	24,203	+3,360	*19,061*	*22,404*	*+3,343*	258
8,171	8,381	+210	*7,402*	*7,587*	*+185*	259
22,443	26,106	+3,663	*20,911*	*24,906*	*+3,995*	260
11,459	11,606	+147	*10,641*	*11,256*	*+615*	261
23,291	21,956	—1,335	*21,827*	*21,217*	*—610*	262
318,659	355,964	+37,305	*295,290*	*327,655*	*+32,365*	
37,176	34,621	—2,555	*35,204*	*33,081*	*—2,123*	263
85,092	76,148	—8,944	*76,824*	*70,942*	*—5,882*	264
41,690	40,521	—1,169	*40,313*	*38,233*	*—2,080*	265
52,187	52,800	+613	*49,656*	*50,015*	*+359*	266
216,145	204,090	—12,055	*201,997*	*192,271*	*—9,726*	
12,804	13,751	+947	*12,615*	*13,720*	*+1,105*	267
18,383	18,811	+428	*18,013*	*18,741*	*+728*	268
13,149	13,922	+773	*13,667*	*14,427*	*+760*	269
131,775	136,614	+4,839	*126,333*	*125,287*	*—1,046*	270
3,995	4,314	+319	*3,924*	*4,183*	*+259*	271
17,619	18,563	+944	*16,109*	*16,146*	*+37*	272
36,856	38,692	+1,836	*37,119*	*39,611*	*+2,492*	273
35,611	36,469	+858	*34,451*	*35,847*	*+1,396*	274
15,225	15,800	+575	*14,865*	*15,569*	*+704*	275
18,287	19,898	+1,611	*18,498*	*19,963*	*+1,465*	276
14,312	14,979	+667	*14,995*	*15,797*	*+802*	277
12,389	14,552	+2,163	*12,140*	*13,580*	*+1,440*	278
15,075	13,211	—1,864	*14,342*	*13,447*	*—895*	279
9,692	10,093	+401	*9,753*	*10,481*	*+728*	280
22,579	23,984	+1,405	*22,866*	*23,988*	*+1,122*	281
21,695	22,347	+652	*21,986*	*22,743*	*+757*	282
5,999	6,136	+137	*6,090*	*6,343*	*+253*	283
45,339	45,317	—22	*44,134*	*44,617*	*+483*	284
450,784	467,453	+16,669	*441,900*	*454,490*	*+12,590*	
167,592	167,267	—325	*174,024*	*172,013*	*—2,011*	285
18,553	16,223	—2,330	*17,162*	*16,512*	*—650*	286
18,122	17,221	—901	*18,891*	*18,596*	*—295*	287
12,085	12,202	+117	*12,329*	*12,665*	*+336*	288
11,435	11,738	+303	*12,768*	*13,486*	*+718*	289
8,503	8,789	+286	*8,340*	*8,461*	*+121*	290
29,214	29,553	+339	*29,622*	*30,044*	*+422*	291
10,906	11,528	+622	*10,454*	*11,299*	*+846*	292

The variations in the population of the

PROVINCIAL TABLE V.

Serial number of district.	Name of district.	Serial number of pargana.	Name of pargana.	Total. Census, 1881.	Total. Census, 1891.	Total. Increase + or Decrease —.
1	2	3	4	5	6	7
27	Mirzapur—(*concluded*)	293	Bijaigarh	47,962	53,149	+5,187
		294	Barhar	75,699	79,938	+4,239
		295	Agori	32,713	35,045	+2,332
		296	Singrauli	29,274	33,704	+4,430
		297	Dúdhi	40,670	39,943	—727
		298	Bhadohi	283,027	291,218	+8,191
		299	Kera Mangraur	67,451	70,914	+3,463
			Total ...	1,136,796	1,161,508	+24,712
28	Jaunpur	300	Haveli Jaunpur	141,238	153,756	+12,518
		301	Saremu	21,534	22,720	+1,186
		302	Zafrabad	5,797	6,459	+662
		303	Khapraha	7,967	8,805	+838
		304	Kariyát Dost...	21,850	24,573	+2,723
		305	Rari Jaunpur	58,923	62,169	+3,246
		306	Ghiswa	84,640	86,466	+1,826
		307	Mongra	55,791	57,225	+1,434
		308	Garwara	98,328	100,986	+2,658
		309	Mariáhu	242,214	253,402	+11,188
		310	Chanda	25,981	28,501	+2,520
		311	Rari Khutahan	26,300	28,843	+2,543
		312	Kariyát Mendha	14,141	15,335	+1,194
		313	Ungli	202,400	214,153	+11,753
		314	Kerakat	136,748	146,148	+9,400
		315	Bialsi	65,811	55,408	—10,403
			Total ...	1,209,663	1,264,949	+55,286
29	Gházipur	316	Gházipur	113,608	117,108	+3,500
		317	Karanda	30,161	31,438	+1,277
		318	Pachotar	70,140	77,576	+7,436
		319	Shádiabad	118,499	124,701	+6,202
		320	Saidpur	109,805	112,711	+2,906
		321	Khánpur	22,828	24,232	+1,404
		322	Bahriabad	37,087	38,234	+1,147
		323	Zamania	174,966	192,206	+17,240
		324	Mahaich	50,983	54,724	+3,741
		325	Zahúrabad	74,502	79,953	+5,451
		326	Garha	37,708	46,809	+9,101
		327	Dehma	13,536	14,293	+757
		328	Muhammadabad	146,938	163,924	+16,986
			Total ...	1,000,761	1,077,909	+77,148
30	Ballia	329	Kharíd	186,467	176,627	—9,840
		330	Sikandarpur (East)	100,825	104,904	+4,079
		331	Ballia	197,791	201,570	+3,779
		332	Doaba	88,024	89,545	+1,521
		333	Kopachit (East)	60,000	62,174	+2,174
		334	Bhadaon	28,386	29,592	+1,206
		335	Sikandarpur (West)	184,543	184,192	—351
		336	Kopachit (West)	39,388	41,725	+2,337
		337	Lakhnesar	52,677	52,136	—541
			Total ...	938,101	942,465	+4,364
31	Gorakhpur ...	338	Sylhat	197,191	216,434	+19,243
		339	Sháhjahánpur	95,911	113,361	+17,450
		340	Haveli Hata	78,182	100,274	+22,092
		341	Bhawapár Bansgaon	59,240	63,174	+3,934
		342	Anowla	78,941	93,337	+14,396
		343	Dhuriapár	214,405	230,767	+16,362
		344	Chillupár	70,272	64,328	—5,944
		345	Haveli Maharajganj	249,218	367,527	+118,309
		346	Bináyakpur	39,145	50,970	+11,825
		347	Tilpur	77,339	92,953	+15,614
		348	Sidwa Jobna	559,838	605,551	+45,713
		349	Salempur	481,145	517,793	+36,648
		350	Bhawapár Gorakhpur	46,758	47,127	+369
		351	Haveli Gorakhpur	290,193	341,296	+51,103
		352	Maghar	79,342	89,165	+9,823
			Total ...	2,617,120	2,994,057	+376,937

parganas since the previous census.

PROVINCIAL TABLE V.

Males. Census, 1881.	Males. Census, 1891.	Males. Increase + or Decrease —.	Females. Census, 1881.	Females. Census, 1891.	Females. Increase + or Decrease —.	Serial number of pargana.
8	9	10	11	12	13	14
24,178	26,108	+1,930	23,784	27,041	+3,257	293
37,263	39,353	+2,090	38,436	40,585	+2,149	294
16,672	17,807	+1,135	16,041	17,288	+1,197	295
15,137	17,114	+1,977	14,137	16,590	+2,453	296
20,725	20,095	—630	19,945	19,848	—97	297
142,902	145,092	+2,190	140,125	146,126	+6,001	298
34,017	36,251	+2,234	33,434	34,663	+1,229	299
567,304	576,341	+9,037	569,492	585,167	+15,675	
70,719	76,687	+5,968	70,519	77,069	+6,550	300
10,759	11,820	+561	10,775	11,400	+625	301
2,885	3,174	+289	2,912	3,285	+373	302
4,106	4,439	+333	3,861	4,366	+505	303
11,190	12,389	+1,199	10,660	12,184	+1,524	304
30,150	31,187	+1,037	28,773	30,982	+2,209	305
42,418	43,279	+861	42,222	43,187	+965	306
27,930	29,248	+1,318	27,861	27,977	+116	307
48,731	50,376	+1,645	49,597	50,610	+1,013	308
123,212	126,830	+3,618	119,002	126,572	+7,570	309
13,355	14,462	+1,107	12,626	14,039	+1,413	310
13,451	14,718	+1,267	12,849	14,125	+1,276	311
7,126	7,643	+517	7,015	7,692	+677	312
102,267	107,799	+5,532	100,133	106,354	+6,221	313
70,617	73,777	+3,160	66,131	72,371	+6,240	314
32,491	27,622	+4,869	33,320	27,786	+5,534	315
611,407	634,950	+23,543	598,256	629,999	+31,743	
56,456	58,552	+2,096	57,152	58,556	+1,404	316
14,760	15,095	+335	15,401	16,343	+942	317
36,516	39,458	+2,942	33,624	38,118	+4,494	318
61,019	63,234	+2,215	57,480	61,467	+3,987	319
55,333	56,060	+727	64,472	66,651	+2,179	320
11,473	12,279	+806	11,355	11,953	+598	321
18,797	19,214	+417	18,290	19,020	+730	322
84,502	92,084	+7,582	90,464	100,122	+9,658	323
25,441	27,310	+1,869	25,542	27,414	+1,872	324
38,478	40,257	+1,779	36,024	39,696	+3,672	325
18,200	22,055	+3,855	19,508	24,754	+5,246	326
6,660	7,045	+385	6,876	7,248	+372	327
72,296	79,058	+6,762	74,642	84,866	+10,224	328
499,931	531,701	+31,770	500,830	546,208	+45,378	
89,375	83,283	—6,092	97,092	93,344	—3,748	329
50,109	50,844	+735	50,716	54,060	+3,344	330
93,057	93,434	+377	104,734	108,136	+3,402	331
41,614	41,914	+300	46,410	47,631	+1,221	332
29,598	30,248	+650	30,402	31,926	+1,524	333
14,607	14,875	+268	13,779	14,717	+938	334
92,933	91,284	+1,649	91,610	92,908	+1,298	335
20,347	20,824	+477	19,041	20,901	+1,860	336
26,151	25,905	—246	26,526	26,231	—295	337
457,791	452,611	—5,180	480,310	489,854	+9,544	
98,066	107,377	+9,311	99,125	109,057	+9,932	338
48,550	57,632	+9,082	47,361	55,729	+8,368	339
39,166	50,487	+11,321	39,016	49,787	+10,771	340
29,212	30,986	+1,774	30,028	32,188	+2,160	341
39,746	46,661	+6,915	39,195	46,676	+7,481	342
106,831	113,934	+7,103	107,574	116,833	+9,259	343
34,257	30,931	—3,326	36,015	33,397	—2,618	344
125,019	187,543	+62,524	124,199	179,984	+55,785	345
20,264	26,865	+6,601	18,881	24,105	+5,224	346
38,945	47,311	+8,366	38,394	45,642	+7,248	347
279,566	303,206	+23,640	280,272	302,345	+22,073	348
237,623	254,229	+16,606	243,522	263,564	+20,042	349
23,324	23,272	—52	23,434	23,855	+421	350
145,982	172,569	+26,587	144,211	168,727	+24,516	351
39,572	44,281	+4,709	39,770	44,884	+5,114	352
1,306,123	1,497,284	+191,161	1,310,997	1,496,773	+185,776	

The variations in the population of the

PROVINCIAL TABLE V.

Serial number of district.	Name of district.	Serial number of pargana.	Name of pargana.	Total. Census, 1881.	Total. Census, 1891.	Total. Increase + or Decrease –.
1	2	3	4	5	6	7
32	Basti	353	Basti (East)	109,174	130,058	+20,879
		354	Maghar (West)	57,564	70,985	+13,421
		355	Maholi (West)	105,843	110,334	+4,491
		356	Nagar (East)	62,970	66,563	+3,593
		357	Bánsi (East)...	312,749	332,690	+19,941
		358	Bináyakpur	26,090	30,034	+3,944
		359	Bánsi (West)	103,917	111,571	+7,654
		360	Rasúlpur	176,337	201,519	+25,182
		361	Amorha	190,445	197,107	+6,662
		362	Basti (West)	68,109	77,256	+9,147
		363	Nagar (West)	75,824	77,246	+1,422
		364	Maghar (East)	208,916	238,691	+29,775
		365	Maholi (East)	132,674	141,795	+9,121
			Total ...	1,630,612	1,785,844	+155,232
33	Azamgarh	366	Nizámabad	278,611	289,488	+10,877
		367	Chiriákot	50,557	55,230	+4,673
		368	Kariyat Mittu	13,075	14,746	+1,671
		369	Mawnatbhanjan	24,943	27,624	+2,681
		370	Muhammadabad	238,442	262,146	+23,704
		371	Sagri	178,533	189,295	+10,762
		372	Ghosi	125,885	139,916	+14,031
		373	Gopálpur	49,844	54,645	+4,801
		374	Náthupur	93,193	85,961	–7,232
		375	Atraulia	96,026	102,885	+6,859
		376	Kauria	48,422	52,245	+3,823
		377	Máhul	167,698	189,593	+21,895
		378	Belhábáns	39,884	44,947	+5,063
		379	Bela Daultabad	84,219	91,494	+7,275
		380	Deogaon	115,322	128,410	+13,088
			Total ...	1,604,654	1,728,625	+123,971
34	Almora	381	Káli Kumaun	31,333	33,551	+2,218
		382	Sira	11,409	13,496	+2,087
		383	Shor	25,516	30,871	+5,355
		384	Askot	8,637	12,170	+3,533
		385	Darma	...	2,513	+2,513
		386	Baramandal	60,291	69,218	+8,927
		387	Chaugarkha	29,801	37,212	+7,411
		388	Dánpur	33,424	38,680	+5,256
		389	Gangoli	27,183	33,271	+6,088
		390	Johar	9,424	10,788	+1,364
		391	Pali	106,334	118,020	+11,686
		392	Phuldakot	12,323	11,711	–612
			Total ...	355,675	411,501	+55,826
35	Garhwál	393	Dewalgarh	29,288	29,895	+607
		394	Bara Syun	48,220	63,229	+15,009
		395	Ganga Salan	44,632	47,510	+2,878
		396	Nágpur	42,300	50,907	+8,607
		397	Chándpur	35,489	40,706	+5,217
		398	Talla Salan	37,924	51,093	+13,169
		399	Malla Salan	41,125	47,594	+6,469
		400	Chánndkot	23,408	26,578	+3,170
		401	Painkhanda	7,513	5,804	–1,709
		402	Dasoli	10,043	13,775	+3,732
		403	Budhan	25,692	30,732	+5,040
			Total ...	345,629	407,818	+62,189
36	Naini Tal	404	Káshipur	74,973	73,168	–1,805
		405	Bázpur	33,932	32,554	–1,378
		406	Gadarpur	14,842	18,855	+4,013
		407	Rudarpur	34,256	29,556	–4,700
		408	Kilpuri	11,765	12,447	+682
		409	Nanakmatta	13,575	16,083	+2,508
		410	Bilhari	23,650	27,905	+4,255
		411	Chakhatá	13,028	21,895	+8,867
		412	Kotá	4,074	3,964	–110
		413	Dhaniakot	6,961	9,440	+2,479
		414	Ramgarh	306	550	+244
		415	Kotauli	2,073	2,482	+409
		416	Mahruri	454	925	+471
		417	Dhyanirao	6,984	6,875	–109
		418	Kumaun-Bhabar	104,086	105,549	+1,463
			Total ...	344,959	362,248	+17,289

parganas since the previous census.

Males. Census, 1881.	Males. Census, 1891.	Males. Increase + or Decrease —.	Females. Census, 1881.	Females. Census, 1891.	Females. Increase + or Decrease —.	Serial number of parganas.
8	9	10	11	12	13	14
56,045	67,420	+11,375	53,129	62,633	+9,504	353
29,284	36,315	+7,031	28,280	34,670	+6,390	354
52,837	55,715	+2,878	53,006	54,619	+1,613	355
31,851	33,859	+2,008	31,119	32,704	+1,585	356
158,249	168,756	+10,507	154,500	163,934	+9,434	357
12,960	15,160	+2,200	13,130	14,874	+1,744	358
52,602	56,393	+3,791	51,315	55,178	+3,863	359
89,014	102,179	+13,165	87,323	99,340	+12,017	360
97,323	100,355	+3,032	93,122	96,752	+3,630	361
34,320	39,520	+5,200	33,789	37,736	+3,947	362
38,140	39,190	+1,050	87,684	88,056	+372	363
104,876	120,892	+16,016	104,040	117,799	+13,759	364
66,750	71,583	+4,833	65,924	70,212	+4,288	365
824,251	907,337	+83,086	806,361	878,507	+72,146	
141,426	145,315	+3,889	137,185	144,173	+6,988	366
25,858	28,082	+2,224	24,699	27,148	+2,449	367
6,710	7,516	+806	6,365	7,230	+865	368
12,719	13,662	+943	12,224	13,962	+1,738	369
121,463	132,156	+10,693	116,979	129,990	+13,011	370
90,690	94,736	+4,046	87,843	94,559	+6,716	371
63,793	69,214	+5,421	62,092	70,702	+8,610	372
25,192	27,380	+2,188	24,652	27,265	+2,613	373
46,362	41,672	—4,690	46,831	44,289	—2,542	374
49,672	52,601	+2,929	46,354	50,284	+3,930	375
24,534	26,621	+2,087	23,888	25,624	+1,736	376
85,217	95,310	+10,093	82,481	94,283	+11,802	377
20,660	22,973	+2,313	19,224	21,974	+2,750	378
42,874	45,751	+2,877	41,345	45,743	+4,398	379
59,259	64,622	+5,363	56,063	63,788	+7,725	380
816,429	867,611	+51,182	788,225	861,014	+72,789	
16,081	17,025	+944	15,252	16,526	+1,274	381
5,859	6,937	+1,078	5,550	6,559	+1,009	382
13,081	15,645	+2,564	12,435	15,226	+2,791	383
4,451	6,001	+1,550	4,186	6,169	+1,983	384
...	1,227	+1,227	...	1,286	+1,286	385
30,892	35,276	+4,384	29,399	33,942	—4,543	386
15,416	18,960	+3,544	14,385	18,252	+3,867	387
17,817	20,271	+2,454	15,607	18,409	+2,802	388
14,185	17,207	+3,022	12,998	16,064	+3,066	389
4,803	5,501	+698	4,621	5,287	+666	390
52,418	57,896	+5,478	53,916	60,124	+6,208	391
7,719	6,167	—1,552	4,604	5,544	+940	392
182,722	208,113	+25,391	172,953	203,388	+30,435	
14,234	14,623	+389	15,054	15,272	+218	393
23,638	30,590	+6,952	24,582	32,639	+8,057	394
22,677	22,674	—3	21,955	24,836	+2,881	395
20,993	24,629	+3,636	21,307	26,278	+4,971	396
17,336	19,548	+2,212	18,153	21,158	+3,005	397
18,869	27,993	+9,124	19,055	23,100	+4,045	398
20,081	22,954	+2,873	21,044	24,640	+3,596	399
11,277	12,621	+1,344	12,126	13,952	+1,826	400
3,782	2,875	—907	3,731	2,929	—802	401
5,015	6,633	+1,618	5,028	7,142	+2,114	402
12,853	15,179	+2,326	12,839	15,553	+2,714	403
170,755	200,319	+29,564	174,874	207,499	+32,625	
40,347	39,023	—1,324	34,626	34,145	—481	404
18,592	17,890	—702	15,340	14,664	—676	405
8,150	10,683	+2,533	6,692	8,172	+1,480	406
19,175	16,288	—2,887	15,081	13,268	—1,813	407
6,545	7,236	+691	5,220	5,211	—9	408
7,262	8,877	+1,615	6,313	7,206	+893	409
13,244	15,463	+2,219	10,406	12,442	+2,036	410
8,676	14,920	+6,244	4,352	6,975	+2,623	411
2,462	2,108	—354	1,612	1,856	+244	412
3,538	4,787	+1,249	3,423	4,653	+1,230	413
183	354	+171	123	196	+73	414
1,010	1,245	+235	1,063	1,237	+174	415
240	551	+311	214	374	+160	416
3,629	3,571	—58	3,355	3,304	—51	417
58,594	59,308	+714	45,492	46,241	+749	418
191,647	202,304	+10,657	153,312	159,944	+6,632	

PROVINCIAL TABLE V.

The variations in the population of the

PROVINCIAL TABLE V.

Serial number of district.	Name of district.	Serial number of pargana.	Name of pargana.	Total. Census, 1881.	Total. Census, 1891.	Total. Increase + or Decrease —.
1	2	3	4	5	6	7
37	Lucknow ...	419	Bijnaur	60,065	68,583	+8,518
		420	Kakori	30,535	34,408	+3,873
		421	Lucknow	323,970	345,470	+21,500
		422	Mahona	65,248	75,421	+10,173
		423	Malihabad	87,797	100,121	+12,324
		424	Mohanlálganj	96,878	113,434	+16,556
		425	Nigohan	32,331	36,726	+4,395
			Total ...	696,824	774,163	+77,339
38	Unao ...	426	Unao	34,684	40,899	+6,215
		427	Pariar	14,560	14,406	—154
		428	Sikandarpur	31,416	29,852	—1,564
		429	Harha	107,231	107,787	+506
		430	Bangarmau	92,656	96,318	+3,662
		431	Safipur	68,258	80,393	+12,135
		432	Fatehpur Chaurasi	33,087	33,430	+343
		433	Asoha	20,242	21,542	+1,300
		434	Bihar	12,832	13,713	+881
		435	Bhagwantnagar	25,623	26,499	+876
		436	Patan	5,740	5,815	+75
		437	Panhan	7,566	8,325	+759
		438	Purwa	60,335	68,387	+8,052
		439	Daundia Khera	33,467	33,566	+99
		440	Ghátampur	15,469	15,115	—354
		441	Magrair	16,343	16,938	+595
		442	Maurawan	80,910	88,252	+7,342
		443	Asiwan Rasúlabad	60,119	64,463	+4,344
		444	Auras Mohan	99,359	109,929	+10,570
		445	Jhalotar Ajgain	58,185	60,654	+2,469
		446	Gorinda Parsandan	20,987	22,403	+1,416
			Total ...	899,069	953,636	+54,567
39	Rae Bareli...	447	Rae Bareli	199,095	221,875	+22,780
		448	Inhauna	51,818	59,836	+8,018
		449	Samrauta	52,480	58,305	+5,825
		450	Mohanganj	47,652	50,639	+2,987
		451	Kumhrawan	35,259	39,790	+4,531
		452	Hardoi	13,173	14,769	+1,596
		453	Bachhrawan	44,697	53,401	+8,704
		454	Salon	127,122	130,482	+3,360
		455	Parshadipur	32,026	34,534	+2,508
		456	Rokha	86,084	97,104	+11,020
		457	Dalmau	139,184	148,329	+9,145
		458	Sareni	63,823	66,368	+2,545
		459	Khiron	59,492	61,089	+1,597
			Total ...	951,905	1,036,521	+84,616
40	Sitapur ...	460	Pírnagar	19,692	20,545	+853
		461	Khairabad	57,411	63,041	+5,630
		462	Rámkot	7,666	8,920	+1,254
		463	Sitapur	59,811	71,844	+12,033
		464	Laharpur	88,418	98,667	+10,249
		465	Hargam	24,516	28,173	+3,657
		466	Biswan	105,559	115,504	+9,945
		467	Tambaur	69,744	80,007	+10,263
		468	Kundri (North)	71,161	76,383	+5,222
		469	Bari	54,030	61,291	+7,261
		470	Sadarpur	50,233	58,616	+8,383
		471	Kundri (South)	26,516	27,911	+1,395
		472	Mahmúdabad	78,002	86,805	+8,803
		473	Manwan	31,821	34,499	+2,678
		474	Chandra	34,874	39,826	+4,952
		475	Aurangabad	21,057	21,955	+898
		476	Karauna	16,283	18,794	+2,511
		477	Gundla Mau	21,710	22,868	+1,158
		478	Machhrehta	40,672	47,545	+6,873
		479	Misrikh	41,561	50,374	+8,813
		480	Maholi	37,514	41,850	+4,336
			Total ...	958,251	1,075,413	+117,162

parganas since the previous census.

PROVINCIAL TABLE V.

Males. Census, 1881.	Males. Census, 1891.	Males. Increase + or Decrease —.	Females. Census, 1881.	Females. Census, 1891.	Females. Increase + or Decrease —.	Serial number of pargana.
8	9	10	11	12	13	14
31,615	35,701	+4,086	28,450	32,882	+4,432	419
15,523	17,607	+2,084	15,012	16,801	+1,789	420
172,189	185,098	+12,909	151,781	160,372	+8,591	421
34,180	39,620	+5,440	31,068	35,801	+4,733	422
45,905	52,226	+6,321	41,892	47,895	+6,003	423
49,406	58,091	+8,685	47,472	55,343	+7,871	424
16,487	18,858	+2,371	15,844	17,868	+2,024	425
365,805	407,201	+41,396	331,519	366,962	+35,443	
18,141	21,773	+3,632	16,543	19,126	+2,583	426
7,731	7,746	+15	6,829	6,660	—169	427
16,493	15,399	—1,094	14,923	14,453	—470	428
53,898	54,016	+118	53,333	53,721	+388	429
49,225	51,341	+2,116	43,431	44,977	+1,546	430
35,811	42,086	+6,275	32,447	38,307	+5,860	431
17,853	17,909	+56	15,234	15,521	+287	432
10,338	10,934	+596	9,904	10,608	+704	433
6,086	6,471	+385	6,746	7,242	+496	434
12,393	12,801	+408	13 230	13,698	+468	435
2,655	2,632	—23	3,085	3,183	+98	436
3,692	4,073	+381	3,874	4,252	+378	437
29,845	31,610	+1,765	30,490	31,777	+1,287	438
16,397	16,083	—314	17,070	17,483	+413	439
7,615	7,297	—318	7,854	7,818	—36	440
7,760	8,070	+310	8,583	8,868	+285	441
40,125	44,177	+4,052	40,785	44,075	+3,290	442
31,399	33,753	+2,354	28,720	30,710	+1,990	443
52,236	58,042	+5,806	47,123	51,887	+4,764	444
30,536	31,672	+1,136	27,649	28,982	+1,333	445
10,938	11,627	+689	10,049	10,776	+727	446
461,167	489,512	+28,345	437,902	464,124	+26,222	
98,203	110,966	+12,763	100,892	110,909	+10,017	447
24,693	29,030	+4,337	27,125	30,806	+3,681	448
25,529	28,936	+3,407	26,951	29,369	+2,418	449
23,098	25,041	+1,943	24,554	25,598	+1,044	450
17,456	19,945	+2,489	17,803	19,845	+2,042	451
6,397	7,341	+944	6,776	7,428	+652	452
21,908	26,797	+4,889	22,789	26,604	+3,815	453
63,225	64,251	+1,026	63,897	66,231	+2,334	454
15,930	17,109	+1,179	16,096	17,425	+1,329	455
41,996	48,523	+6,527	44,088	48,581	+4,493	456
68,320	72,979	+4,659	70,864	75,350	+4,486	457
30,899	32,089	+1,190	32,924	34,279	+1,355	458
29,252	29,973	+721	30,240	31,116	+876	459
466,906	512,980	+46,074	484,999	523,541	+38,542	
10,428	10,825	+397	9,264	9,720	+456	460
29,348	32,404	+3,056	28,063	30,637	+2,574	461
4,020	4,756	+736	3,646	4,164	+518	462
32,879	39,624	+6,745	26,932	32,220	+5,288	463
45,988	51,372	+5,384	42,430	47,295	+4,865	464
12,812	14,744	+1,932	11,704	13,429	+1,725	465
55,564	60,673	+5,109	49,995	54,831	+4,836	466
36,732	41,617	+4,885	33,012	38,390	+5,378	467
37,288	39,582	+2,294	33,873	36,801	+2,928	468
28,525	32,142	+3,617	25,505	29,149	+3,644	469
26,729	31,203	+4,474	23,504	27,413	+3,909	470
14,259	14,839	+580	12,257	13,072	+815	471
41,023	45,542	+4,519	36,979	41,263	+4,284	472
16,681	18,065	+1,384	15,140	16,434	+1,294	473
18,986	21,706	+2,720	15,888	18,120	+2,232	474
11,018	11,697	+679	10,039	10,258	+219	475
8,664	10,028	+1,364	7,619	8,766	+1,147	476
11,510	12,128	+618	10,200	10,735	+535	477
21,400	25,085	+3,685	19,272	22,460	+3,188	478
22,167	26,904	+4,737	19,394	23,470	+4,076	479
19,965	22,246	+2,281	17,549	19,604	+2,055	480
505,986	567,182	+61,196	452,265	508,231	+55,966	

The variations in the population of the

PROVINCIAL TABLE V.

Serial number of district.	Name of district.	Serial number of pargana.	Name of pargana.	Total. Census, 1881.	Total. Census, 1891.	Total. Increase + or Decrease —.
1	2	3	4	5	6	7
41	Hardoi ...	481	Bangar	65,652	79,509	+13,857
		482	Gopamau	130,786	152,841	+22,055
		483	Sara (Janubi)	17,842	20,337	+2,495
		484	Bawan	28,957	32,888	+3,931
		485	Barwan	17,870	20,496	+2,626
		486	Alamnagar	18,282	20,820	+2,538
		487	Shábabad	67,182	75,658	+8,476
		488	Sara (Shumali)	16,685	20,189	+3,504
		489	Panderwa Pihani	37,463	40,963	+3,500
		490	Suromannagar	13,096	16,368	+3,272
		491	Pachhoba	30,253	34,647	+4,394
		492	Pali	25,962	29,760	+3,798
		493	Mansúrnagar	7,902	9,629	+1,727
		494	Bilgram	53,580	62,505	+8,925
		495	Sandi	71,252	73,381	+2,129
		496	Katiari	38,317	39,072	+755
		497	Mallawan	75,402	85,706	+10,304
		498	Kachhandau	20,741	21,083	+342
		499	Sandila	151,440	169,203	+17,763
		500	Kallianmal	28,572	30,487	+1,915
		501	Gondwa	58,674	64,369	+5,695
		502	Balamau	11,720	13,300	+1,580
			Total ...	987,630	1,113,211	+125,581
42	Kheri ...	503	Bhur	81,894	89,256	+7,362
		504	Paila	38,005	43,948	+5,943
		505	Srinagar	88,499	92,277	+3,778
		506	Kukra Mailani	14,641	21,747	+7,106
		507	Kheri	107,668	118,394	+10,726
		508	Atwa Piparia	10,575	15,439	+4,864
		509	Aurangabad	32,853	35,334	+2,481
		510	Pasgawan	49,775	55,812	+6,037
		511	Haidarabad	40,761	47,513	+6,752
		512	Kasta	31,671	36,028	+4,357
		513	Muhamdi	55,333	56,889	+1,556
		514	Magdapur	11,941	11,602	—339
		515	Palia	18,277	15,235	—3,042
		516	Dhaurahra	88,334	89,928	+1,594
		517	Firozabad	55,006	61,110	+6,104
		518	Khairigarh	39,444	39,364	—80
		519	Nighasan	67,245	73,739	+6,494
			Total ...	831,922	903,615	+71,693
43	Fyzabad ...	520	Khandasa	67,712	72,340	+4,628
		521	Pachhimráth	198,303	216,550	+18,247
		522	Akbarpur	137,159	160,432	+23,273
		523	Majhaura	72,535	81,270	+8,735
		524	Surhurpur	92,037	106,094	+14,057
		525	Tanda	84,890	99,252	+14,362
		526	Birhar	137,841	164,435	+26,594
		527	Haveli (Oudh)	139,610	153,271	+13,661
		528	Mangalsi	91,954	96,086	+4,132
		529	Amsin	59,378	67,229	+7,851
			Total ...	1,081,419	1,216,959	+135,540
44	Gonda ...	530	Gonda	275,925	319,220	+43,295
		531	Paharapur	75,260	84,952	+9,692
		532	Nawábganj	68,511	78,035	+9,524
		533	Mahadewa	51,492	59,676	+8,184
		534	Digsar	94,833	91,365	−3,468
		535	Guwarich	148,176	156,484	+8,308
		536	Utraula	90,836	113,348	+22,512
		537	Sadullanagar	40,894	53,476	+12,582
		538	Burhapára	31,196	44,553	+13,357
		539	Babhnipair	36,405	45,450	+9,045
		540	Mankapur	46,887	57,123	+10,236
		541	Balrámpur	178,336	198,357	+20,021
		542	Tulsipur	132,175	157,190	+25,015
			Total ...	1,270,926	1,459,229	+188,303

parganas since the previous census.

PROVINCIAL TABLE V.

Males.			Females.			Serial number of parganas.
Census, 1881.	Census, 1891.	Increase + or Decrease —.	Census, 1881.	Census, 1891.	Increase + or Decrease —.	
8	9	10	11	12	13	14
36,392	43,695	+7,303	29,260	85,814	+6,554	481
70.269	81,718	+11,449	60,517	71,123	+10,606	482
9,672	10,932	+1,260	8,170	9,405	+1,235	483
15,607	17,696	+2,089	13,350	15,192	+1,842	484
10,244	11,523	+1,279	7,626	8,973	+1,347	485
10,075	11,359	+1,284	8,207	9,461	+1,254	486
35,492	40,286	+4,794	31,690	35,372	+3,682	487
9,157	10,873	+1,716	7,528	9,316	+1,788	488
19,636	21,529	+1,893	17,827	19,434	+1,607	489
7,249	8,894	+1,645	5,847	7,474	+1,627	490
16,760	19,037	+2,277	13,493	15,610	+2,117	491
14,153	16,073	+1,920	11,809	13,687	+1,878	492
4,230	5,261	+1,031	3,672	4,368	+696	493
28,691	33,496	+4,805	24,889	29,009	+4,120	494
38,799	39,261	+462	32,453	34,120	+1,667	495
21,351	21,338	—13	16,966	17,734	+768	496
39,907	45,071	+5,164	35,495	40,635	+5,140	497
11,648	11,637	—11	9,093	9,446	+353	498
79,791	89,323	+9,532	71,649	79,880	+8,231	499
15,098	16,276	+1,178	13,474	14,211	+737	500
31,138	34,172	+3,034	27,536	30,197	+2,661	501
6,345	7,047	+702	5,375	6,253	+878	502
531,704	596,497	+64,793	455,926	516,714	+60,788	
43,838	47,930	+4,092	38,056	41,326	+3,270	503
20,028	23,080	+3,052	17,977	20,868	+2,891	504
47,095	48,787	+1,692	41,404	43,490	+2,086	505
8,075	12,059	+3,984	6,566	9,688	+3,122	506
56,951	62,289	+5,338	50,717	56,105	+5,388	507
5,656	8,243	+2,587	4,919	7,196	+2,277	508
17,603	18,985	+1,382	15,250	16,349	+1,099	509
26,949	30,062	+3,113	22,826	25,750	+2,924	510
21,969	25,622	+3,653	18,792	21,891	+3,099	511
17,021	19,197	+2,176	14,650	16,831	+2,181	512
29,470	30,449	+979	25,863	26,440	+577	513
6,526	6,150	—376	5,415	5,452	+37	514
10,433	8,358	+2,075	7,844	6,877	—967	515
46,768	47,046	+278	41,566	42,882	+1,316	516
29,098	32.013	+2,915	25,908	29,097	+3,189	517
21,378	20,850	—528	18,066	18,514	+448	518
36,161	40,915	+4,754	31,084	32,824	+1,740	519
445,019	482,035	+37,016	386,903	421,580	+34,677	
33,388	35,564	+2,176	34,324	36,776	+2,452	520
98,125	106,608	+8,483	100,178	109,942	+9,764	521
70,218	81,638	+11,420	66,941	78,794	+11,853	522
36,847	41,059	+4,212	35,688	40,211	+4,523	523
47,142	53,913	+6,771	44,895	52,181	+7,286	524
42,633	49,756	+7,123	42,257	49,496	+7,239	525
69,651	83,192	+13.541	68,190	81,243	+13,053	526
72,296	80,168	+7,872	67,314	73,103	+5,789	527
45,891	47,039	+1,148	46,063	49,047	+2,984	528
29,983	33,665	+3,682	29,395	33,564	+4,169	529
546,174	612,602	+66,428	535,245	604,357	+69,112	
140,793	162,557	+21,764	135,132	156,663	+21,531	530
38,145	42,976	+4,831	37,115	41,976	+4,861	531
36,342	40,903	+4,561	32,169	37,132	+4,963	532
26,537	30,123	+3,586	24,955	29,553	+4,598	533
47,951	45,754	—2,197	46,882	45,611	—1,271	534
75,800	79.773	+3,973	72,376	76,711	+4,335	535
46,653	57,928	+11,275	44,183	55,420	+11,237	536
20,794	27,160	+6,366	20,100	26,316	+6,216	537
15,954	23,065	+7,111	15,242	21,488	+6,246	538
18,687	23,414	+4,727	17,718	22,036	+4,318	539
24,087	29,868	+5,781	22,800	27,255	+4,455	540
90.564	101,236	+10,672	87,772	97,121	+9,349	541
68,464	81,646	+13,182	63,711	75,544	+11,833	542
650,771	746,403	+95,632	620,155	712,826	+92,671	

The variations in the population of the

PROVINCIAL TABLE V.

Serial number of district.	Name of district.	Serial number of pargana.	Name of pargana.	Total. Census, 1881.	Total. Census, 1891.	Total. Increase + or Decrease —.
1	2	3	4	5	6	7
45	Bahraich	543	Hisámpur	144,238	159,189	+14,951
		544	Fakharpur	151,737	173,004	+21,267
		545	Nánpára	168,942	192,092	+23,150
		546	Charda	76,018	88,291	+12,273
		547	Dharmanpur	25,761	30,898	+5,137
		548	Bahraich	122,882	145,906	+23,024
		549	Ikauna	89,626	107,562	+17,936
		550	Bhinga	86,927	90,767	+3,840
		551	Tulsipur	11,917	12,723	+806
			Total	878,048	1,000,432	+122,384
46	Sultánpur	552	Mírápur	153,481	173,954	+20,473
		553	Baraunsa	138,286	157,010	+18,724
		554	Esauli Cis-Amethi	37,347	41,607	+4,260
		555	Esauli Cis-Faizabad	45,995	53,438	+7,443
		556	Jagdispur	90,138	101,514	+11,376
		557	Gaura Jamon	47,749	54,662	+6,913
		558	Amethi	159,618	176,961	+17,343
		559	Asil	39,116	42,247	+3,131
		560	Aldemau	169,392	189,229	+19,837
		561	Chanda	76,790	85,229	+8,439
			Total	957,912	1,075,851	+117,939
47	Partábgarh	562	Partábgarh	235,533	254,979	+19,446
		563	Ateha	45,152	51,448	+6,296
		564	Manikpur	55,474	55,738	+264
		565	Behar	128,344	138,417	+10,073
		566	Rámpur	73,962	81,328	+7,366
		567	Dhingwas	52,885	57,393	+4,508
		568	Patti	255,697	271,592	+15,895
			Total	847,047	910,895	+63,848
48	Bara Banki	569	Partábganj	33,448	38,624	+5,176
		570	Satrikh	22,570	24,659	+2,089
		571	Sidhaur A	30,165	33,469	+3,304
		572	Nawábganj	61,029	67,659	+6,630
		573	Dewa	64,846	78,564	+13,718
		574	Kursi	35,814	45,042	+9,228
		575	Bhitauli	22,839	21,099	—1,740
		576	Mohammadpur	29,814	33,444	+3,630
		577	Rámnagar	80,559	86,213	+5,654
		578	Bado Sarai	27,648	24,855	—2,793
		579	Fatehpur	92,969	104,999	+12,030
		580	Dariabad	128,644	132,997	+4,353
		581	Rudauli	110,262	116,274	+6,012
		582	Mawai Maholara	37,040	39,854	+2,814
		583	Surajpur	57,386	63,956	+6,570
		584	Hasaurhi	21,374	24,446	+3,072
		585	Sidhaur B	61,715	68,217	+6,502
		586	Haidargarh	58,522	68,944	+10,422
		587	Subeha	50,144	57,591	+7,447
			Total	1,026,788	1,130,906	+104,118

Parganas since the previous Census.

PROVINCIAL TABLE V.

Males.			Females.			Serial number of pargana.
Census, 1881.	Census, 1891.	Increase + or Decrease —.	Census, 1881.	Census, 1891.	Increase + or Decrease —.	
8	9	10	11	12	13	14
75,490	82,776	+7,286	68,748	76,418	+7,665	543
79,897	90,417	+10,520	71,840	82,587	+10,747	544
88,587	100,589	+12,002	80,355	91,503	+11,148	545
39,315	46,084	+6,719	36,703	42,257	+5,554	546
14,097	17,704	+3,607	11,664	13,194	+1,530	547
64,378	76,649	+12,271	58,504	69,257	+10,753	548
45,903	55,343	+9,440	43,723	52,219	+8,496	549
44,981	47,203	+2,222	41,946	43,564	+1,618	550
6,539	6,852	+313	5,378	5,871	+493	551
459,187	523,567	+64,380	418,861	476,865	+58,004	
75,264	84,566	+9,302	78,217	89,388	+11,171	552
69,218	77,649	+8,431	69,068	79,361	+10,293	553
17,890	20,068	+2,178	19,457	21,539	+2,082	554
22,484	26,166	+3,682	23,511	27,272	+3,761	555
43,328	49,141	+5,813	46,810	52,373	+5,563	556
23,282	26,893	+3,611	24,467	27,769	+3,302	557
77,607	85,979	+8,372	82,011	90,982	+8,971	558
19,254	20,533	+1,279	19,862	21,714	+1,852	559
87,729	96,882	+9,153	81,663	92,347	+10,684	560
39,069	42,609	+3,540	37,721	42,620	+4,899	561
475,125	530,486	+55,361	482,787	545,365	+62,578	
115,968	123,398	+7,430	119,565	131,581	+12,016	562
22,035	25,028	+2,993	23,117	26,420	+3,303	563
27,444	27,352	—92	28,030	28,386	+356	564
63,321	67,435	+4,114	65,023	70,982	+5,959	565
36,374	39,648	+3,274	37,588	41,680	+4,092	566
26,009	28,087	+2,078	26,876	29,306	+2,430	567
129,579	134,223	+4,644	126,118	137,369	+11,251	568
420,730	445,171	+24,441	426,317	465,724	+39,407	
17,078	19,684	+2,606	16,370	18,940	+2,570	569
11,492	12,614	+1,122	11,078	12,045	+967	570
15,235	17,083	+1,848	14,930	16,386	+1,456	571
32,278	35,567	+3,289	28,751	32,092	+3,341	572
33,787	41,022	+7,235	31,059	37,542	+6,483	573
18,813	23,598	+4,785	17,001	21,444	+4,443	574
12,196	11,161	—1,035	10,643	9,938	—705	575
15,748	17,699	+1,951	14,066	15,745	+1,679	576
42,649	45,641	+2,992	37,910	40,572	+2,662	577
14,276	12,629	—1,647	13,372	12,226	—1,146	578
48,524	54,573	+6,049	44,445	50,426	+5,981	579
66,188	68,218	+2,025	62,456	64,784	+2,328	580
54,173	56,709	+2,536	56,089	59,565	+3,476	581
17,953	19,572	+1,619	19,087	20,282	+1,195	582
28,692	32,137	+3,445	28,694	31,819	+3,125	583
10,471	12,132	+1,661	10,903	12,314	+1,411	584
31,158	34,523	+3,365	30,557	33,694	+3,137	585
28,679	34,362	+5,683	29,843	34,582	+4,739	586
24,191	28,196	+4,005	25,953	29,395	+3,442	587
523,581	577,115	+53,534	503,207	553,791	+50,584	

PROVINCIAL TABLE VI.

SHOWING THE VARIATIONS IN THE POPULATION OF THE POLICE CIRCLES SINCE THE PREVIOUS CENSUS.

Showing the variations in the population of the

PROVINCIAL TABLE VI.

Serial number of district.	Name of district.	Serial number of thána.	Name of thána.	Total population. Census, 1881.	Census, 1891.	Increase + or Decrease —
1	2	3	4	5	6	7
1	Dehra Dún ...	1	Dehra	50,964	60,141	+9,177
		2	Mussoorie	7,697	10,806	+3,109
		3	Sahaspur	22,612	23,577	+965
		4	Rájpur	8,942	9,626	+684
		5	Chakráta	1,327	1,509	+182
		6	Kalsi	43,790	49,188	+5,398
		7	Bhogpur	8,738	13,288	+4,550
			Total ...	144,070	168,135	+24,065
2	Saháranpur ...	1	Saháranpur	135,070	140,164	+5,094
		2	Rámpur	56,577	52,277	—4,300
		3	Behat	52,736	55,849	+3,113
		4	Muzaffarabad	32,034	35,509	+3,475
		5	Mirzapur	17,805	19,632	+1,827
		6	Fatehpur	33,948	41,484	+7,536
		7	Mohand	13,342	13,394	+52
		8	Bhagwánpur	37,769	38,481	+712
		9	Nágal	45,750	47,489	+1,739
		10	Manglaur	64,737	67,527	+2,790
		11	Dausnie	21,674	22,218	+544
		12	Roorkee	64,168	67,999	+3,831
		13	Jawalapur	64,967	70,119	+5,152
		14	Sultánpur	15,501	16,712	+1,211
		15	Badhgaon	36,057	34,601	—1,456
		16	Nanauta	25,646	23,451	—2,195
		17	Deoband	80,357	80,768	+411
		18	Nakúr	53,823	52,217	—1,606
		19	Gangoh	46,830	44,324	—2,506
		20	Sirsawa	29,832	27,278	—2,554
		21	Chilkana	39,183	37,552	—1,631
		22	Bassie	11,738	12,235	+497
			Total ...	979,544	1,001,280	+21,736
3	Muzaffarnagar ...	1	Muzaffarnagar	61,185	64,310	+3,125
		2	Titavi	50,039	50,872	+833
		3	Charthláwal	39,489	40,140	+651
		4	Pur	40,124	38,952	—1,172
		5	Gordhanpur	11,629	12,016	+387
		6	Shámli	56,182	57,060	+878
		7	Thána Bhawan	43,700	43,560	—140
		8	Jhanjhána	32,455	32,633	+178
		9	Kairána	40,262	41,389	+1,127
		10	Bidauli	16,257	13,321	—2,936
		11	Jánsath	39,721	42,659	+2,938
		12	Khatauli	64,154	69,916	+5,762
		13	Bhopa	50,067	49,486	—581
		14	Miranpur	38,092	40,259	+2,167
		15	Burhana	44,227	46,019	+1,792
		16	Shahpur	50,615	51,440	+825
		17	Kandhla	66,869	66,648	—221
		18	Chausana	13,377	12,194	—1,183
			Total ...	758,444	772,874	+14,430
4	Meerut	1	City Station	76,106	90,617	+14,511
		2	Kankar Khora	13,315	13,990	+675
		3	Baxar Khera	25,515	27,799	+2,284
		4	Mau Khas	21,925	25,339	+3,414
		5	Jani	68,328	71,394	+3,066
		6	Dauralá	39,461	43,853	+4,392
		7	Buhukpur	32,687	34,505	+1,818
		8	Kharkhoda	39,173	41,028	+1,855
		9	Begamabad	40,128	41,888	+1,760
		10	Sadar Bazár	24,002	26,844	+2,842
		11	Lalkurti	14,615	18,909	+4,294
		12	Dhaplana	42,564	44,364	+1,800
		13	Pilkhua	31,382	32,194	+812
		14	Gháziabad	45,225	43,276	—1,949
		15	Muradnagar	41,096	42,429	+1,333
		16	Shahdara	20,624	18,867	—1,757
		17	Khekhra	23,628	24,697	+1,069
		18	Loui	22,437	23,736	+1,299
		19	Mowána	64,111	73,301	+9,190
		20	Khánpur	7,049	6,914	—135
		21	Parichhatgarh	45,032	50,328	+5,296
		22	Behsuma	17,268	19,105	+1,837

Police Circles since the previous Census.

PROVINCIAL TABLE VI.

Males. Census, 1881.	Males. Census, 1891.	Males. Increase + or Decrease —	Females. Census, 1881.	Females. Census, 1891.	Females. Increase + or Decrease —	Serial number of thanas.
8	9	10	11	12	13	14
29,701	35,953	+6,252	21,263	24,188	+2,925	1
5,336	7,537	+2,201	2,361	3,269	+908	2
13,105	13,657	+552	9,507	9,920	+413	3
5,031	5,502	+471	3,911	4,124	+213	4
1,045	1,165	+120	282	344	+62	5
24,355	27,270	+2,915	19,435	21,918	+2,453	6
5,412	9,240	+3,828	3,326	4,048	+722	7
83,985	100,324	+16,339	60,085	67,811	+7,726	
71,680	74,839	+3,159	63,390	65,825	+1,935	1
30,815	28,161	—2,654	25,762	24,116	- 1,646	2
27,984	29,182	+1,198	24,752	26,667	+1,915	3
16,776	18,572	+1,796	15,258	16,937	+1,679	4
9,649	10,329	+680	8,156	9,303	+1,147	5
17,816	21,564	+3,748	16,132	19,920	+3,788	6
7,785	7,436	-349	6,557	6,958	+401	7
20,191	20,311	+120	17,578	18,170	+592	8
24,688	25,649	+961	21,062	21,840	+778	9
35,532	36,365	+833	29,205	31,162	+1,957	10
11,932	12,049	+117	9,742	10,169	+427	11
35,705	37,427	+1,722	28,463	30,572	+2,109	12
36,367	39,896	+3,529	28,600	30,223	+1,623	13
8,463	9,131	+668	7,038	7,581	+543	14
20,527	19,558	—969	15,530	15,043	—487	15
13,655	12,443	—1,212	11,991	11,008	—983	16
43,513	44,505	+992	36,844	36,263	—581	17
29,083	28,155	—928	24,740	24,062	—678	18
25,114	23,587	—1,527	21,716	20,737	—979	19
16,141	14,739	—1,402	13,691	12,539	—1,152	20
20,648	19,875	—773	18,535	17,677	—858	21
6,363	6,578	+215	5,375	5,657	+282	22
530,427	540,351	+9,924	449,117	460,929	+11,812	
33,774	35,939	+2,165	27,411	28,371	+960	1
26,881	27,578	+697	23,158	23,294	+136	2
21,643	22,097	+454	17,846	18,043	+197	3
21,901	21,206	—695	18,223	17,746	—477	4
6,521	6,665	+144	5,108	5,351	+213	5
30,600	30,900	+300	25,582	26,160	+578	6
23,177	23,262	+85	20,523	20,298	—225	7
17,185	17,338	+153	15,270	15,295	+25	8
21,462	22,338	+876	18,800	19,051	+251	9
8,941	7,320	—1,621	7,316	6,001	—1,315	10
21,089	22,764	+1,675	18,632	19,895	+1,263	11
34,185	37,605	+3,420	29,969	32,311	+23,42	12
27,687	26,967	—720	22,380	22,519	+139	13
20,110	21,316	+1,206	17,982	18,943	+961	14
23,730	24,776	+1,046	20,497	21,243	+746	15
27,304	27,807	+503	23,311	23,633	+322	16
36,132	35,807	—325	30,737	30,841	+104	17
7,114	6,543	—571	6,263	5,651	— 612	18
409,436	418,228	+8,792	349,008	354,646	+5,638	
41,547	49,592	+8,045	34,559	41,025	+6,466	1
6,946	7,358	+412	6,369	6,632	+263	2
13,369	14,648	+1,279	12,146	13,151	+1,005	3
11,673	13,425	+1,752	10,252	11,914	+1,662	4
36,817	38,154	+1,337	31,511	33,240	+1,729	5
21,022	23,409	+2,387	18,439	20,444	+2,005	6
17,366	18,570	+1,204	15,321	15,935	+614	7
20,551	21,425	+874	18,622	19,603	+981	8
21,615	22,441	+826	18,513	19,447	+934	9
14,374	16,040	+1,666	9,628	10,804	+1,176	10
8,595	11,529	+2,934	6,020	7,380	+1,360	11
22,366	23,616	+1,250	20,198	20,748	+550	12
16,450	16,959	+509	14,932	15,235	+303	13
24,634	23,031	—1,603	20,591	20,245	— 346	14
22,048	22,548	+500	19,048	19,881	+833	15
11,126	10,281	—845	9,498	8,586	—912	16
12,336	13,162	+826	11,292	11,535	+243	17
12,279	12,982	+703	10,158	10,754	+596	18
34,278	38,697	+4,419	29,833	34,604	+4,771	19
3,856	3,881	+25	3,193	3,033	—160	20
23,998	26,768	+2,770	21,034	23,560	+2,526	21
9,416	10,268	+852	7,852	8,837	+985	22

Showing the variations in the population of the

PROVINCIAL TABLE VI.

Serial number of district.	Name of district.	Serial number of thána.	Name of thána.	Total Population. Census, 1881.	Census, 1891.	Increase + or Decrease—
1	2	3	4	5	6	7
4	Meerut—(*concluded*) ...	23	Kithor	32,763	36,469	+3,706
		24	Bághpat	55,579	50,808	—4,771
		25	Baleni	24,512	26,794	+2,282
		26	Lalyana	20,661	21,459	+798
		27	Chaprauli	47,141	45,041	—2,100
		28	Baraut	86,237	90,215	+3,978
		29	Sardhana	68,529	70,691	+2,162
		30	Binauli	32,991	36,285	+3,294
		31	Daha	37,793	40,679	+2,886
		32	Hápur	76,330	81,421	+5,091
		33	Baxar	24,396	26,330	+1,934
		34	Garhmuktesar	30,772	30,173	—599
		35	Bahádurgarh	19,762	19,716	—46
			Total ...	1,313,137	1,391,458	+78,321
5	Bulandshahr ...	1	Jhajhar	50,185	52,779	+2,594
		2	Sikandarabad	62,050	58,189	—3,861
		3	Jarcha	20,451	18,519	—1,934
		4	Khúrja	78,707	75,575	—3,132
		5	Gulaothi	58,385	57,519	—866
		6	Bulandshahr...	78,119	84,452	+6,333
		7	Kasna	19,103	17,176	—1,927
		8	Dankaur	32,304	31,090	—1,214
		9	Surajpur	16,886	14,582	—2,304
		10	Dadri	36,296	39,772	+3,476
		11	Sarái Sadar	14,819	11,120	—3,699
		12	Arnia	23,995	26,110	+2,115
		13	Shikárpur	43,005	50,294	+7,289
		14	Pahasu	49,942	54,892	+4,950
		15	Dibai	62,228	64,253	+2,025
		16	Jewar	37,355	36,807	—548
		17	Anúpshahr	32,422	33,944	+1,522
		18	Jahángirabad	52,111	54,689	+2,578
		19	Ahar	24,532	18,825	—5,707
		20	Khánpur	27,807	33,892	+6,085
		21	Aurangabad	27,705	35,723	+8,018
		22	Siyana	61,148	61,205	+57
		23	Rámghát	15,267	18,507	+3,240
			Total ...	924,822	949,914	+25,092
6	Aligarh ...	1	Jawan	31,752	34,823	+3,071
		2	Somna	29,852	27,989	—1,863
		3	Akrabad	65,407	69,323	+3,916
		4	Koil	139,689	136,549	—3,140
		5	Harduaganj	34,426	33,460	—966
		6	Atrauli	57,831	67,782	+9,951
		7	Barlah	25,904	24,045	—1,859
		8	Dadon	45,259	53,920	+8,661
		9	Gangiri	29,169	30,430	+1,261
		10	Gonda	40,242	40,037	—205
		11	Iglas	70,003	66,048	—3,955
		12	Mursán	44,683	38,048	—6,635
		13	Sikandra Rao	64,548	63,693	—855
		14	Agsauli	22,951	25,657	+2,706
		15	Salempur	14,759	15,575	+816
		16	Hasayin	29,911	37,881	+7,970
		17	Háthras	92,724	104,774	+12,050
		18	Sasni	44,627	42,005	—2,622
		19	Tappal	43,564	40,710	—2,854
		20	Narainpur	17,736	22,668	+4,932
		21	Chandausi	35,397	32,899	—2,498
		22	Khair	40,753	34,856	—5,897
			Total ...	1,021,187	1,043,172	+21,985
7	Muttra ...	1	Ol	19,904	16,860	—3,044
		2	Aring	18,974	21,218	+2,244
		3	Brindaban	26,013	35,287	+9,274
		4	Jait	20,236	21,694	+1,458
		5	Rasúlpur	8,098	7,509	—589
		6	Sonkh	14,900	16,541	+1,641
		7	Sadar Bazár	8,869	10,264	+1,395
		8	Farah	27,269	22,387	—4,882
		9	Gobardhan	16,774	20,068	+3,294
		10	Muttra	67,885	67,764	—121
		11	Chhàta	26,537	35,712	+9,175

Police Circles since the previous Census—(*continued*).

PROVINCIAL TABLE VI.

Males.			Females.			Serial number of thána.
Census, 1881.	Census, 1891.	Increase + or Decrease—	Census, 1881.	Census, 1891.	Increase + or Decrease—	
8	9	10	11	12	13	14
17,292	19,101	+1,809	*15,471*	*17,368*	*+1,897*	23
30,065	27,827	−2,238	*25,514*	*22,981*	*—2,533*	24
13,032	14,282	+1,250	*11,480*	*12,512*	*+1,032*	25
11,130	11,548	+418	*9,531*	*9,911*	*+380*	26
25,172	24,311	−861	*21,969*	*20,730*	*—1,239*	27
46,528	48,772	+2,244	*39,709*	*41,443*	*+1,734*	28
36,793	37,735	+942	*31,736*	*32,956*	*+1,220*	29
17,685	19,370	+1,685	*15,306*	*16,915*	*+1,609*	30
20,618	22,048	+1,430	*17,175*	*18,631*	*+1,456*	31
40,798	42,938	+2,140	*35,532*	*38,483*	*+2,951*	32
12,869	13,917	+1,048	*11,527*	*12,413*	*+886*	33
16,389	16,103	—286	*14,383*	*14,070*	*—313*	34
10,404	10,508	+104	*9,358*	*9,208*	*—150*	35
705,437	747,244	+41,807	*607,700*	*644,214*	*+36,514*	
26,621	28,088	+1,467	*23,564*	*24,691*	*×1,127*	1
33,169	30,532	—2,637	*28,881*	*27,657*	*—1,224*	2
10,911	9,536	—1,377	*9,540*	*8,983*	*—557*	3
41,651	39,659	—1,992	*37,056*	*35,916*	*—1,140*	4
30,887	30,087	—800	*27,498*	*27,432*	*—66*	5
41,724	44,360	+2,636	*36,395*	*40,092*	*+3,697*	6
10,446	9,485	—961	*8,657*	*7,691*	*—966*	7
17,409	16,702	—707	*14,895*	*14,388*	*—507*	8
9,243	7,960	—1,283	*7,643*	*6,622*	*—1,021*	9
19,938	21,433	+1,495	*16,358*	*18,339*	*+1,981*	10
8,206	6,039	—2,167	*6,613*	*5,081*	*—1,532*	11
12,740	13,722	+982	*11,255*	*12,388*	*+1,133*	12
22,918	26,554	+3,636	*20,087*	*23,740*	*+3,653*	13
26,402	28,986	+2,584	*23,540*	*25,906*	*+2,366*	14
32,664	33,838	+1,174	*29,564*	*30,415*	*+851*	15
19,813	19,466	—347	*17,542*	*17,341*	*—201*	16
17,076	18,039	+963	*16,346*	*15,905*	*+559*	17
27,640	28,623	+983	*24,471*	*26,066*	*+1,595*	18
12,896	10,013	—2,883	*11,636*	*8,812*	*—2,824*	19
14,539	17,703	+3,164	*13,268*	*16,189*	*+2,921*	20
14,541	18,609	+4,068	*13,164*	*17,114*	*+3,950*	21
32,035	32,218	+183	*29,113*	*28,987*	*—126*	22
8,489	9,969	+1,480	*6,778*	*8,538*	*+1,760*	23
491,958	501,621	+9,663	*432,864*	*448,293*	*+15,429*	
17,334	18,567	+1,233	*14,418*	*16,256*	*+1,838*	1
16,102	14,873	—1,229	*13,750*	*13,116*	*—634*	2
35,481	37,248	+1,767	*29,926*	*32,075*	*+2,149*	3
75,267	72,740	—2,527	*64,422*	*63,809*	*—613*	4
18,648	17,883	—765	*15,778*	*15,577*	*—201*	5
31,176	35,705	+4,529	*26,655*	*32,077*	*+5,422*	6
13,880	12,715	—1,165	*12,024*	*11,330*	*—694*	7
24,689	29,450	+4,761	*20,570*	*24,470*	*+3,900*	8
15,836	16,336	+500	*13,333*	*14,094*	*+761*	9
21,793	21,417	—376	*18,449*	*18,620*	*+171*	10
37,904	35,579	—2,325	*32,099*	*30,469*	*—1,630*	11
24,441	20,552	—3,889	*20,242*	*17,496*	*—2,746*	12
35,049	34,467	—582	*29,499*	*29,226*	*—273*	13
12,756	14,010	+1,254	*10,195*	*11,647*	*+1,452*	14
8,077	8,487	+410	*6,682*	*7,088*	*+406*	15
16,303	20,461	+4,158	*13,608*	*17,420*	*+3,812*	16
49,277	56,152	+6,875	*43,447*	*48,622*	*+5,175*	17
23,965	22,354	—1,611	*20,662*	*19,651*	*—1,011*	18
23,155	21,640	—1,515	*20,409*	*19,070*	*—1,339*	19
9,504	12,081	+2,577	*8,232*	*10,587*	*+2,355*	20
18,884	17,530	—1,354	*16,513*	*15,369*	*—1,144*	21
21,758	18,496	—3,262	*18,995*	*16,360*	*—2,635*	22
551,279	558,743	+7,464	*469,908*	*484,429*	*+14,521*	
10,614	9,046	—1,568	*9,290*	*7,814*	*—1,476*	1
10,293	11,472	+1,179	*8,681*	*9,746*	*+1,065*	2
13,898	18,392	+4,494	*12,115*	*16,895*	*+4,780*	3
11,031	11,790	+759	*9,205*	*9,904*	*+699*	4
4,349	4,135	—214	*3,749*	*3,374*	*—375*	5
7,929	8,873	+944	*6,971*	*7,668*	*+697*	6
4,749	6,483	+1,734	*4,120*	*3,781*	*—339*	7
15,275	12,178	—3,097	*11,994*	*10,209*	*—1,785*	8
8,877	10,569	+1,692	*7,897*	*9,499*	*+1,602*	9
35,754	35,786	+32	*32,131*	*31,978*	*—153*	10
14,019	18,973	+4,954	*12,518*	*16,739*	*+4,221*	11

Showing the variations in the population of the

PROVINCIAL TABLE VI.

Serial number of district.	Name of district.	Serial number of thána.	Name of thána.	Total population. Census, 1881.	Census, 1891.	Increase + or Decrease —
1	2	3	4	5	6	7
		12	Kosi	49,290	43,488	−5,802
		13	Majhoi	12,028	10,463	−1,565
		14	Barsana	16,752	20,866	+4,114
		15	Sahar	19,393	24,077	+4,684
		16	Shergarh	19,445	15,752	−3,693
		17	Raya	42,981	51,424	+8,443
7	Muttra—(*concluded*) ...	18	Surir	27,335	27,402	+67
		19	Mát	24,686	25,362	+676
		20	Nohjhíl	44,827	38,818	−6,009
		21	Baldeo	56,765	65,458	+8,693
		22	Mahaban	19,146	19,411	+265
		23	Sahpan	25,830	29,464	+3,634
		24	Sadabad	57,753	66,132	+8,379
			Total, ...	671,690	713,421	+41,731
		1	Achhnera	27,280	26,085	−1,195
		2	Etmad-ud-daula	12,981	17,020	+4,039
		3	Tájganj	27,792	29,331	+1,539
		4	Dowki	26,757	26,700	−57
		5	Rakabganj	31,230	36,105	+4,875
		6	Runkuta	17,829	16,535	−1,294
		7	Shamshabad	31,709	32,511	+802
		8	Keraoli	31,931	32,611	+680
		9	Kakuba	24,258	20,184	−4,074
		10	Loha Mandi	34,426	39,395	+4,969
		11	Malpura	26,090	24,430	−1,660
		12	Hariparbat	27,895	25,057	−2,838
		13	Etmadpur	68.933	65,333	−3,600
		14	Abaran	33,362	36,779	+3,417
		15	Khandauli	23,941	30,852	+6,911
		16	Narkhi	40.459	45,009	+4,550
8	Agra ...	17	Bah	37,441	37,368	−73
		18	Batesar	9,979	14,397	+4,418
		19	Pinahat	39,214	38,149	−1,065
		20	Jaitpur	33,895	35,934	+2,039
		21	Iradatnagar	23,091	25,583	+2,492
		22	Fatehabad	34.105	35,500	+1,395
		23	Nibohra	18,062	18,633	+571
		24	Firozabad	69,933	70,654	+721
		25	Fatehpur Sikri	34.911	29,056	−5,855
		26	Kagaraul	23,464	28.357	+4,893
		27	Jagner	39,047	37,797	−1,250
		28	Saiyan	24,289	23.413	−876
		29	Khairagarh	18,947	21.301	+2,354
		30	Chhátta	30,757	27,113	−3,644
		31	Kotwáli	28,539	33.303	+4,764
		32	Sadar Bazár	15,358	15,268	−90
		33	Lalkurti	6,751	8,033	+1,282
			Total ...	974,656	1,003,796	+29,140
		1	Sárai Míran	82,659	87,772	+5,113
		2	Tirwa	77,618	77,686	+68
		3	Gursahaiganj	75,748	70,726	−5,022
		4	Thatia	28,588	34,461	+5,873
		5	Saurikh	76,819	66,922	−9,897
		6	Chibramau	66,167	57,848	−8,319
		7	Káimganj	67,822	60.157	−7,665
		8	Muhammadabad	86,497	85,413	−1,084
9	Farukhabad ...	9	Farukhabad	89,310	79,223	−10,087
		10	Fatehgarh	27,231	29,669	+2,438
		11	Colonelganj	4,889	5.023	+134
		12	Kamálgang	48,841	45,568	−3,273
		13	Shamsabad	40,919	37,402	−3,517
		14	Kampil	34,751	28,548	−6,203
		15	Nawábganj	23,664	19.051	−4,613
		16	Allahganj	19.133	18,388	−745
		17	Aligarh	40,603	40,957	+354
		18	Paramnagar	16,349	13,873	−2,476
			Total ...	907,608	858,687	−48,921
		1	Mainpuri	90,292	82,096	−8,196
		2	Aunchha	27,689	28,157	+468
10	Mainpuri ...	3	Kuraoli	45,817	41,667	−4,150
		4	Barnahal	38,426	40,099	+1,673
		5	Jasrana	62,448	59,557	−2,891

Police Circles since the previous Census—(*continued*).

PROVINCIAL TABLE VI.

Males.			Females.			Serial number of thána.
Census, 1881.	Census, 1891.	Increase + or Decrease—	Census, 1881.	Census, 1891.	Increase + or Decrease—	
8	9	10	11	12	13	14
25,523	22,841	−2,682	23,767	20,647	−3,120	12
6,376	5,605	−771	5,652	4,858	−794	13
8,845	11,014	+2,169	7,907	9,852	+1,945	14
10,141	12,601	+2,460	9,252	11,476	+2,224	15
10,378	8,492	−1,886	9,067	7,260	−1,807	16
23,692	27,993	+4,301	19,289	23,431	+4,142	17
14,634	14,440	−194	12,701	12,962	+261	18
13,366	13,576	+210	11,320	11,786	+466	19
23,786	20,566	−3,220	21,041	18,252	−2,789	20
31,228	35,573	+4,345	25,537	29,885	+4,348	21
10,256	10,233	−23	8,890	9,178	+288	22
14,051	15,910	+1,859	11,779	13,554	+1,775	23
31,903	36,119	+4,216	25,850	30,013	+4,163	24
360,967	382,660	+21,693	310,723	330,761	+20,038	
14,742	14,158	−584	12,538	11,927	−611	1
6,922	9,131	+2,209	6,059	7,889	+1,830	2
14,181	15,022	+841	13,611	14,309	+698	3
14,638	14,504	−134	12,119	12,196	+77	4
16,135	18,618	+2,483	15,095	17,487	+2,392	5
9,729	9,047	−682	8,100	7,488	−612	6
17,242	17,676	+434	14,467	14,835	+368	7
17,290	17,554	+264	14,641	15,057	+416	8
13,189	10,988	−2,201	11,069	9,196	−1,873	9
17,666	20,603	+2,937	16,760	18,792	+2,032	10
14,136	13,448	−688	11,954	10,982	−972	11
16,178	14,252	−1,926	11,717	10,805	−912	12
37,781	35,225	−2,556	31,152	30,108	−1,044	13
17,954	19,761	+1,807	15,408	17,018	+1,610	14
13,492	17,033	+3,541	10,449	13,819	+3,370	15
22,085	24,312	+2,227	18,374	20,697	+2,323	16
19,713	19,853	+140	17,728	17,515	−213	17
5,279	7,634	+2,355	4,700	6,763	+2,063	18
20,916	20,627	−289	18,298	17,522	−776	19
17,616	18,823	+1,207	16,279	17,111	+832	20
12,558	13,871	+1,313	10,533	11,712	+1,179	21
18,380	19,106	+726	15,725	16,394	+669	22
9,936	10,235	+299	8,126	8,398	+272	23
38,209	37,859	−350	31,724	32,795	+1,071	24
18,355	15,471	−2,884	16,556	13,585	−2,971	25
12,557	15,090	+2,533	10,907	13,267	+2,360	26
21,088	20,413	−675	17,959	17,384	−575	27
13,427	12,599	−828	10,862	10,814	−48	28
10,330	11,626	+1,296	8,617	9,675	+1,058	29
16,741	14,510	−2,231	14,016	12,603	−1,413	30
14,888	17,353	+2,465	13,651	15,950	+2,299	31
9,812	9,321	−491	6,546	6,947	+401	32
3,636	4,736	+1,100	3,115	3,297	+182	33
526,801	540,459	+13,658	447,855	463,337	+15,482	
44,124	46,528	+2,404	38,535	41,244	+2,709	1
42,633	42,478	−155	34,985	35,208	+223	2
40,971	38,160	−2,811	34,777	32,566	−2,211	3
15,686	18,768	+3,082	12,902	15,693	+2,791	4
42,562	36,875	−5,687	34,257	30,047	−4,210	5
36,261	31,457	−4,804	29,906	26,391	−3,515	6
35,727	31,976	−3,751	32,095	28,181	−3,914	7
47,366	46,607	−759	39,131	38,806	−325	8
46,168	40,714	−5,454	43,142	38,509	−4,633	9
14,768	16,999	+2,231	12,463	12,670	+207	10
2,802	2,897	+95	2,087	2,126	+39	11
26,204	24,641	−1,563	22,637	20,927	−1,710	12
21,597	19,796	−1,801	19,322	17,606	−1,716	13
18,662	15,448	−3,214	16,089	13,100	−2,989	14
12,793	10,483	−2,310	10,871	8,568	−2,303	15
10,519	10,159	−360	8,614	8,229	−385	16
22,541	22,710	+169	18,062	18,247	+185	17
9,124	7,644	−1,480	7,225	6,229	−996	18
490,508	464,340	−26,168	417,100	394,347	−22,753	
50,112	44,781	−5,331	40,180	37,315	−2,865	1
15,672	15,635	−37	12,017	12,522	+505	2
25,229	22,628	−2,601	20,588	19,039	−1,549	3
21,108	21,941	+833	17,318	18,158	+840	4
34,228	32,664	−1,564	28,220	26,893	−1,327	5

Showing the variations in the population of the

PROVINCIAL TABLE VI.

Serial number of district.	Name of district.	Serial number of thána.	Name of thána.	Total population. Census, 1881.	Census, 1891.	Increase + or Decrease—
1	2	3	4	5	6	7
10	Mainpuri—(*concluded*)	6	Ghiror	48,532	43,341	—5,191
		7	Bhongaon	68,530	69,430	+900
		8	Bewar	54,969	39,249	– 15,720
		9	Kishni Nabiganj	55,682	59,060	× 3,378
		10	Kurra	28,024	29,453	× 1,429
		11	Karhal	47,420	45,218	—2,202
		12	Sirsaganj	81,426	76,278	—5,148
		13	Shikohabad	57,080	57,227	+147
		14	Eka	66,381	60,660	—5,721
		15	Pharha	28,500	30,671	× 2,171
			Total ...	801,216	762,163	—39,053
11	Etáwah ...	1	Etáwah	65,852	66,985	× 1,133
		2	Jaswantnagar	48,664	49,856	+ 1,192
		3	Barhpura	21,282	25,564	+ 4,282
		4	Basrehar	40,300	36,070	—4,230
		5	Baralokpur	24,406	23,535	—8,71
		6	Bharthna	50,903	46,269	—4,634
		7	Bakewar	60,727	70,650	+ 9,923
		8	Sahson	23,505	29,336	+ 5,831
		9	Usrahar	27,310	30,235	+ 2,925
		10	Bidhúna	33,948	33,296	—652
		11	Bela	36,702	37,328	+ 626
		12	Kuder Kote	26,405	24,923	—1,482
		13	Airwa	18,236	17,417	—819
		14	Sahail	23,789	23,569	—220
		15	Chhachhund	26,834	25,181	—1,653
		16	Phaphúnd	44,870	42,346	—2,524
		17	Umri	38,776	37,520	—1,256
		18	Ajitmal	65,721	66,160	+ 439
		19	Auraiya	44,141	41,389	– 2,752
			Total ...	722,371	727,629	+ 5,258
12	Etah ...	1	Etah	65,647	72,911	+ 7,264
		2	Sakít	37,998	35,597	—2,401
		3	Malaon	34,182	30,333	– 3,849
		4	Amanpur	29,592	29,761	+ 169
		5	Marehra	52,181	52,088	—93
		6	Nidhauli Kalan	37,964	38,394	+ 430
		7	Awa	28,278	28,502	+ 224
		8	Jalesar	68,523	71,667	+ 3,144
		9	Umargarh	22,124	20,861	—1,263
		10	Patiáli	45,456	35,544	—9,912
		11	Jaithra	48,403	37,380	—11,023
		12	Aliganj	70,100	56,621	—13,479
		13	Sirhpura	32,744	20,979	—11,765
		14	Sahawar	41,031	31,879	—9,152
		15	Kadirganj	27,887	31,145	+ 3,258
		16	Soron	53,577	46,871	– 6,706
		17	Kásganj	60,576	61,530	+ 954
			Total ...	756,263	702,063	—54,200
13	Bareilly ...	1	Kotwáli	78,674	80,727	+ 2,053
		2	Baradari	48,826	51,796	+ 2,970
		3	Kila	58,722	59,911	+ 1,189
		4	Sadar	10,257	13,254	+ 2,997
		5	Bhutaha	46,030	51,513	× 5,483
		6	Bhojupura	28,281	30,723	× 2,442
		7	Deorania	40,623	38,356	—2,267
		8	Rithaura	17,495	18,418	+ 923
		9	Sháhi	50,769	46,730	– 4,039
		10	Faridpur	58,403	58,019	– 384
		11	Gaini	43,096	42,095	—1,001
		12	Fatehganj West	37,321	37,480	+ 159
		13	Shishgarh	53,591	49,307	– 4,284
		14	Mirganj	39,392	38,663	– 729
		15	Sirauli	47,368	45,753	—1,615
		16	Fatehganj East	23,841	27,550	+ 3,709
		17	Hafizganj	40,808	42,404	× 1,596
		18	Nawábganj	60,828	65,101	+ 4,273
		19	Aonla	62,857	63,922	+ 1,065
		20	Bhamora	49,652	50,015	+ 363
		21	Baheri	78,876	74,221	– 4,655
		22	Richha	55,226	54,733	– 493
			Total ...	1,030,936	1,040,691	× 9,755

Police Circles since the previous Census—(*continued*).

PROVINCIAL TABLE VI.

Males.			Females.			Serial number of thánas.
Census, 1881.	Census, 1891.	Increase + or Decrease—	Census, 1881.	Census, 1891.	Increase + or Decrease—	
8	9	10	11	12	13	14
26,786	23,842	—2,944	*21,746*	*19,499*	*—2,247*	6
37,148	37,586	+ 438	*31,382*	*31,844*	*+ 462*	7
31,035	21,964	—9,071	*23,934*	*17,285*	*—6,649*	8
30,744	32,357	+ 1,613	*24,938*	*26,703*	*+ 1,765*	9
15,724	16,173	+ 449	*12,300*	*13,280*	*+ 980*	10
26,530	24,628	—1,902	*20,890*	*20,590*	*—300*	11
44,698	41,899	—2,799	*36,728*	*34,379*	*—2,349*	12
31,147	31,005	—142	*25,933*	*26,222*	*+ 289*	13
36,390	33,101	—3,289	*29,991*	*27,559*	*—2,432*	14
15,543	16,595	× 1,052	*12,957*	*14,076*	*+ 1,119*	15
442,094	416,799	—25,295	*359,122*	*345,364*	*—13,758*	
35.586	35,731	+145	*30,266*	*31,254*	*+ 988*	1
26,767	27.532	+765	*21,897*	*22,324*	*+ 427*	2
11,227	13,690	× 2,463	*10,055*	*11,874*	*+ 1,819*	3
22,253	19,819	—2,434	*18,047*	*16,251*	*—1,796*	4
13,482	12,932	—550	*10,924*	*10,603*	*—321*	5
28.477	25,449	—3,028	*22,426*	*20,820*	*—1,606*	6
32,916	38,264	× 5,348	*27,811*	*32,386*	*+ 4,575*	7
12.777	16,075	× 3,298	*10,728*	*13,261*	*+ 2,533*	8
15,122	16,675	× 1,553	*12,188*	*13,560*	*+ 1,372*	9
18,636	18,361	—275	*15,312*	*14,935*	*—377*	10
20,164	20,461	× 297	*16,538*	*16,867*	*+ 329*	11
14,903	13,767	—1,136	*11,502*	*11,156*	*—346*	12
10,117	9,645	—472	*8,119*	*7,772*	*—347*	13
12,970	12,873	—97	*10,819*	*10,696*	*—123*	14
14,753	13,957	— 796	*12,081*	*11,224*	*— 857*	15
24,640	22,824	—1,816	*20,230*	*19,522*	*—708*	16
21,186	20,586	—600	*17,590*	*16,934*	*—656*	17
35,644	35,866	× 222	*30,077*	*30,294*	*+ 217*	18
23,604	22,268	—1,336	*20,537*	*19,121*	*—1,416*	19
395,224	396,775	+ 1,551	*327,147*	*330,854*	*+ 3,707*	
36,679	40,010	× 3,331	*28,968*	*32,901*	*+ 3,933*	1
20,756	19,211	—1,545	*17,242*	*16,386*	*—856*	2
18,941	16,707	—2,234	*15,241*	*13,626*	*—1,615*	3
16,253	16,282	× 29	*13,339*	*13,479*	*+ 140*	4
28.543	28,014	—529	*23,638*	*24,074*	*+ 436*	5
21,077	20,929	—148	*16,887*	*17,465*	*+ 578*	6
15,265	15,513	× 248	*13,013*	*12,989*	*— 24*	7
37,069	38,450	× 1,381	*31,454*	*33,217*	*+ 1,763*	8
12,338	11,606	—732	*9,786*	*9,255*	*—531*	9
24,469	19,523	—4,946	*20,987*	*16,021*	*—4,966*	10
26.544	20,955	—5,589	*21,859*	*16,425*	*—5,434*	11
38,290	31,021	—7,269	*31,810*	*25,600*	*—6,210*	12
17,965	11,721	—6,244	*14,779*	*9,258*	*—5,521*	13
22,184	17,594	—4,590	*18,847*	*14,285*	*—4,562*	14
15.179	16,873	× 1,694	*12,708*	*14,272*	*+ 1,564*	15
29,123	25,423	—3,700	*24,454*	*21,448*	*—3,006*	16
32,865	33,371	× 506	*27,711*	*28,159*	*+ 448*	17
413,540	383,203	—30,337	*342,723*	*318,860*	*—23,863*	
41,918	44,110	× 2,192	*36,756*	*36,617*	*—139*	1
25.416	26,834	+ 1,418	*23,410*	*24,962*	*+ 1,552*	2
29,770	30,798	+ 1,028	*28,952*	*29,113*	*+ 161*	3
6,720	9,033	× 2,313	*3,537*	*4,221*	*+ 684*	4
24,990	28,029	× 3,039	*21,040*	*23,484*	*+ 2,444*	5
15,339	16,498	+ 1,159	*12,942*	*14,226*	*+ 1,283*	6
21,758	20,274	—1,484	*18,865*	*18,082*	*—783*	7
9,667	10,101	+ 434	*7,828*	*8,317*	*+ 489*	8
26,705	24,375	—2,330	*24,064*	*22,355*	*—1,709*	9
31,897	31,595	— 302	*26,506*	*26,424*	*—82*	10
22,703	22,145	—558	*20,393*	*19,950*	*— 443*	11
20,058	19,950	—108	*17,263*	*17,530*	*+ 267*	12
27,759	25,635	—2,124	*25,832*	*23,672*	*—2,160*	13
20,541	20,242	—299	*18,851*	*18,421*	*—430*	14
24,794	23,975	—819	*22,574*	*21,778*	*—796*	15
12,801	15,217	+ 2,416	*11,040*	*12,333*	*+ 1,293*	16
22,086	22,882	+ 796	*18,722*	*19,522*	*+ 800*	17
32,503	34,712	+ 2,209	*28,325*	*30,389*	*+ 2,064*	18
33,099	33,820	+ 721	*29,758*	*30,102*	*+ 344*	19
26,654	26,969	+ 315	*22,998*	*23,046*	*+ 48*	20
41,593	39,628	—1,965	*37,283*	*34,593*	*—2,690*	21
29,239	28,658	— 581	*25,987*	*26,075*	*+ 88*	22
548,010	555,480	+ 7,470	*482,926*	*485,211*	*+ 2,285*	

Showing the variations in the population of the

PROVINCIAL TABLE VI.

Serial number of district.	Name of district.	Serial number of thana.	Name of thána.	Total population. Census, 1881.	Census, 1891.	Increase + or Decrease.—
1	2	3	4	5	6	7
14	Bijnor ...	1	Bijnor	49,966	53,108	+3,142
		2	Ambera	31,757	34,547	+2,790
		3	Ganj	6,374	60,47	−327
		4	Mandawar	35,999	40,185	+4,186
		5	Bashta	26,743	27,788	+1,045
		6	Núrpur	35,404	39,200	+3,796
		7	Chándpur	61,532	71,187	+9,655
		8	Dhámpur	48,959	52,856	+3,897
		9	Sherkot	33,280	33,743	+463
		10	Nahtaur	39,658	44,377	+4,719
		11	Seohara	48,142	51,012	+2,870
		12	Afzalgarh	49,845	49,839	−6
		13	Rehar	19,594	19,260	−334
		14	Barhapura	29,067	34,814	+5,747
		15	Nagína	71,569	79,234	+7,665
		16	Kiratpur	55,563	64,124	+8,561
		17	Najibabad	54,847	65,788	+10,941
		18	Nangal	18,146	21,664	+3,518
		19	Shiampur	4,155	4,323	+168
		20	Kauria	850	974	+124
			Total ...	721,450	794,070	+72,620
15	Budaun ...	1	Budaun	105,620	107,639	+2,019
		2	Binawar	35,565	42,956	+7,391
		3	Dataganj	62,931	68,989	+6,058
		4	Kakrala	31,566	29,698	−1,868
		5	Ujhiani	61,382	57,558	−3,824
		6	Gunnaur	62,432	68,291	+5,859
		7	Sahaswán	55,102	61,148	+6,046
		8	Kadir Chauk	25,010	23,832	−1,178
		9	Zarífnagar	35,703	39,714	+4,011
		10	Bilsi	84,405	80,781	−3,624
		11	Islámnagar	61,805	54,706	−7,099
		12	Bisauli	71,519	75,402	+3,883
		13	Rájpura	49,756	49,812	+56
		14	Mirzapur Behta	28,346	25,174	−3,172
		15	Wazírganj	37,287	39,620	+2,333
		16	Sadullaganj	22,880	25,105	+2,225
		17	Hazratpur	30,209	34,649	+4,440
		18	Usehat	44,254	40,524	−3,730
			Total ...	905,772	925,598	+19,826
16	Moradabad ...	1	Chandausi	91,911	89,410	−2,501
		2	Seondara	63,320	65,422	+2,102
		3	Kundarki	43,391	42,944	−447
		4	Moradabad	138,065	102,988	+8,341
		5	Moghalpura		43,418	
		6	Mundha	46,288	50,442	+4,154
		7	Mainather	46,777	49,165	+2,388
		8	Sambhal	108,383	110,647	+2,264
		9	Manpur	50,312	51,422	+1,110
		10	Asmoli	66,651	64,571	−2,080
		11	Bahjoi	56,144	52,430	−3,714
		12	Amroha	120,653	123,206	+2,553
		13	Chhajlet	50,458	58,479	+8,021
		14	Hasanpur	56,876	53,091	−3,785
		15	Bachraon	50,025	46,556	−3,469
		16	Tigri	16,595	19,583	+2,988
		17	Rehra	38,413	34,450	−3,963
		18	Thákurdwára	56,485	62,527	+6,042
		19	Dilari	54,426	58,647	+4,221
			Total ...	1,155,173	1,179,398	+24,225
17	Sháhjahánpur ...	1	Sháhjahánpur	89,305	91,338	+2,083
		2	Sihra Mau South	35,920	41,280	+218
		3	Dhakia	44,621	44,403	+8,422
		4	Sadr Bazár	40,292	41,875	+1,583
		5	Kánt	47,299	53,951	+6,652
		6	Tilhar	62,466	71,536	+9,070
		7	Jalálabad	49,828	57,357	+7,529
		8	Madnapur	34,869	40,480	+5,611
		9	Powayan	72,149	73,364	+1,215
		10	Bánda	66,302	68,044	+1,742
		11	Nigohi	41,480	42,799	+1,319
		12	Khutar	33,911	32,912	−999
		13	Sihra Mau North	25,427	28,206	+2,779

Police Circles since the previous Census—(*continued*).

PROVINCIAL TABLE VI.

Males.			Females.			Serial number of thána.
Census, 1881.	Census, 1891.	Increase + or Decrease —	Census, 1881.	Census, 1891.	Increase + or Decrease—	
8	9	10	11	12	18	14
26,854	28,378	+1,524	*23,112*	*24,730*	*+1,618*	1
16,968	18,392	+1,424	*14,789*	*16,155*	*+1,366*	2
3,324	3,116	−208	*3,050*	*2,931*	*—119*	3
19,033	21,424	+2,391	*16,966*	*18,761*	*+1,795*	4
14,615	15,084	+469	*12,128*	*12,704*	*+576*	5
18,761	20,717	+1,956	*16,643*	*18,483*	*+1,840*	6
32,281	37,335	+5,054	*29,251*	*33,852*	*+4,601*	7
25,712	27,973	+2,261	*23,247*	*24,883*	*+1,636*	8
17,159	17,450	+291	*16,121*	*16,293*	*+172*	9
20,806	23,187	+2,381	*18,852*	*21,190*	*+2,338*	10
25,513	26,865	+1,352	*22,629*	*24,147*	*+1,518*	11
26,740	26,107	—633	*23,105*	*23,732*	*+627*	12
10,378	10,331	—47	*9,216*	*8,929*	*−287*	13
15,865	18,426	+2,561	*18,202*	*16,388*	*+3,186*	14
37,571	41,292	+3,721	*33,998*	*37,942*	*+3,944*	15
29,322	33,026	+3,704	*26,241*	*31,098*	*+4,857*	16
29,054	34,174	+5,120	*25,793*	*31,614*	*+5,821*	17
9,600	11,323	+1,723	*8,546*	*10,341*	*+1,795*	18
2,995	2,834	—161	*1,160*	*1,489*	*+329*	19
707	778	+71	*143*	*196*	*+53*	20
383,258	418,212	+34,954	*338,192*	*375,858*	*+37,666*	
54,891	55,849	+958	*50,729*	*51,790*	*+1,061*	1
19,009	22,955	+3,946	*16,556*	*20,001*	*+3,445*	2
34,284	37,714	+3,430	*28,647*	*31,275*	*+2,628*	3
16,745	15,593	—1,152	*14,821*	*14,105*	*—716*	4
33,743	31,431	—2,312	*27,639*	*26,127*	*−1,512*	5
33,740	36,913	+3,173	*28,692*	*31,378*	*+2,686*	6
29,781	32,757	+2,976	*25,321*	*28,391*	*+3,070*	7
13,484	12,920	—564	*11,526*	*10,912*	*—614*	8
19,473	21,624	+2,151	*16,230*	*18,090*	*+1,860*	9
45,462	43,688	—1,774	*38,943*	*37,093*	*−1,850*	10
32,933	29,502	−3,431	*28,872*	*25,204*	*—3,668*	11
38,030	40,562	+2,532	*33,489*	*34,840*	*+1,351*	12
27,089	27,065	−24	*22,667*	*22,747*	*+80*	13
15,031	13,387	—1,644	*13,315*	*11,787*	*—1,528*	14
20,010	21,183	+1,173	*17,277*	*18,437*	*+1,160*	15
12,389	13,740	+1,351	*10,491*	*11,365*	*+874*	16
16,556	18,899	+2,343	*13,653*	*15,750*	*+2,097*	17
24,337	22,352	—1,985	*19,917*	*18,172*	*—1,745*	18
486,987	498,134	+11,147	*418,785*	*427,464*	*+8,679*	
49,027	47,455	—1,572	*42,884*	*41,955*	*—929*	1
33,370	35,077	+1,707	*29,950*	*30,345*	*+396*	2
22,858	22,770	−88	*20,533*	*20,174*	*—359*	3
72,300	53,522	+3,615	*65,765*	*49,466*	*+4,726*	4
	22,393			*21,025*		5
24,470	26,793	+2,323	*21,818*	*23,649*	*+1,831*	6
24,618	25,999	+1,381	*22,159*	*23,166*	*+1,007*	7
56,284	57,412	+1,128	*52,099*	*53,235*	*+1,136*	8
26,224	27,288	+1,064	*24,088*	*24,134*	*+46*	9
35,481	34,344	—1,137	*31,170*	*30,227*	*—943*	10
29,748	28,070	—1,678	*26,396*	*24,360*	*—2,036*	11
62,776	64,488	+1,712	*57,877*	*58,718*	*+841*	12
26,523	30,944	+4,421	*23,935*	*27,535*	*+3,600*	13
29,697	28,439	—1,258	*27,179*	*24,652*	*—2,527*	14
27,744	24,941	−2,803	*22,281*	*21,615*	*—666*	15
8,865	10,478	+1,613	*7,730*	*9,105*	*+1,375*	16
21,050	18,891	—2,159	*17,363*	*15,559*	*—1,804*	17
30,227	33,017	+2,790	*26,258*	*29,510*	*+3,252*	18
29,029	31,251	+2,222	*25,397*	*27,396*	*+1,999*	19
610,291	623,572	+13,281	*544,862*	*555,826*	*+10,944*	
45,056	46,227	+1,171	*44,249*	*45,111*	*+862*	1
19,323	22,334	+3,011	*16,597*	*18,946*	*+2,349*	2
23,916	24,047	+131	*2,0705*	*20,356*	*+349*	3
21,685	22,445	+760	*18,607*	*19,430*	*+823*	4
25,414	29,136	+3,722	*21,885*	*24,815*	*+2,930*	5
33,544	38,542	+4,998	*28,922*	*32,994*	*+4,072*	6
27,048	30,988	+3,940	*22,780*	*26,369*	*+3,589*	7
19,664	22,331	+2,667	*15,205*	*18,149*	*+2,944*	8
38,489	39,462	+973	*53,660*	*33,902*	*+242*	9
35,456	36,855	+1,399	*30,846*	*31,189*	*+343*	10
22,102	23,159	+1,057	*19,378*	*19,640*	*+262*	11
18,076	17,665	—411	*15,835*	*15,247*	*—588*	12
13,681	15,116	+1,435	*11,746*	*13,090*	*+1,344*	13

Showing the variations in the population of the

PROVINCIAL TABLE VI.

Serial number of district.	Name of district.	Serial number of thána.	Name of thána.	Total population. Census, 1881.	Census, 1891.	Increase + or Decrease —
1	2	3	4	5	6	7
		14	Khudaganj	38,847	39,769	+922
17	Sháhjahánpur—(*concluded*).	15	Jaintipur	41,267	45,223	+3,956
		16	Míranpur Katra	34 266	38,964	+4,698
		17	Kundaria	30,047	33,308	+3,261
		18	Rafiabad	35,038	38,348	+3,310
		19	Mirzapur	34,551	35,394	+843
			Total	857,885	918,551	+60,666
		1	Bisalpur	96,847	102,112	+5,265
		2	Barkhera	45,170	49,903	+4,733
		3	Bilsanda	37,333	38,849	+1,516
18	Pilibhít	4	Pilibhít	83,144	87,121	+3,977
		5	Newria	16,935	23,519	+6,584
		6	Jahánabad	51,736	54,445	+2,709
		7	Amaria	31,529	34,212	+2,683
		8	Puranpur	60,944	61,855	+911
		9	Madho Tanda	27,963	33,350	+5,387
			Total	451,601	485,366	+33,765
		1	Akbarpur	65,710	62,981	—2,729
		2	Gajuer	56,123	49,126	—6,997
		3	Sheoli	59,004	53,722	—5,282
		4	Sachendi	55,633	53,802	—1,831
		5	Kainjri	44,367	43,008	—1,359
		6	Derapur	45,826	47,936	+2,110
		7	Bilhaur	67,309	66,151	—1,158
		8	Kakwan	32,443	37,545	+5,102
		9	Shiurájpur	51,905	50,443	—1,462
		10	Bhognipur	58,352	58,267	—85
		11	Musanagar	25,857	28,275	+2,418
		12	Sikandra	48,084	49,392	+1,308
		13	Mangalpur	47,568	47,992	+424
19	Cawnpore	14	Ghatampur	64,499	61,647	—2,852
		15	Sajeti	23,646	25,115	+1,469
		16	Sarh	35,304	36,641	+1,337
		17	Rasulabad	47,137	45,784	—1,353
		18	Narwal	24,085	28,704	+4,619
		19	Mahárájpur	40,429	44,863	+4,434
		20	Bithúr	44,195	49,962	+5,767
		21	Kotwáli	73,908	69,055	—4,853
		22	Cantonment	25,795	27,903	+2,108
		23	Nawábganj	8,984	9,310	+326
		24	Kaliyánpur	29,315	29,814	+499
		25	Bidhnu	35,167	36,440	+1,273
		26	Colonelganj	23,230	36,754	+13,524
		27	Fílkhana	20,616	21,731	+1,115
		28	Anwarganj	26,905	37,332	+10,427
			Total	1,181,396	1,209,695	+28,299
		1	Kaliyánpur	25,219	24,201	—1,018
		2	Husainganj	52,621	52,820	+199
		3	Fatehpur	70,756	68,280	—2,476
		4	Málwa	31,236	31,615	+379
		5	Asothar	19,027	20,739	+1,712
		6	Tharyaon	55,782	53,986	—1,796
		7	Aung	23,382	23,101	—281
		8	Khajuha	19,533	19,981	+448
		9	Bindki	37,127	36,485	—642
20	Fatehpur	10	Lalauli	30,701	30,311	—390
		11	Jafarganj	19,666	23,551	+3,885
		12	Amauli	23,098	28,440	+5,342
		13	Jahánabad	33,953	33,882	—71
		14	Dhata	16,249	18,453	+2,204
		15	Kishanpur	25,343	27,867	+2,524
		16	Khakreru	38,479	41,662	+3,183
		17	Gházipur	39,105	40,061	+956
		18	Hathgaon	56,332	56,561	+229
		19	Gaunti	24,791	24,859	+68
		20	Khaga	41,345	42,302	+957
			Total	683,745	699,157	+15,412

Police Circles since the previous Census—(*continued*).

PROVINCIAL TABLE VI.

Males.			Females.			Serial number of thana.
Census, 1881.	Census, 1891.	Increase + or Decrease—	Census, 1881.	Census, 1891.	Increase + or Decrease—	
8	9	10	11	12	13	14
21,018	21,462	+444	*17,829*	*18,307*	*+478*	14
22,734	25,064	+2,330	*18,533*	*20,159*	*+1,626*	15
18,597	21,370	+2,773	*15,669*	*17,594*	*+1,925*	16
16,591	18,512	+1,921	*13,456*	*14,796*	*+1,340*	17
19,448	21,196	+1,748	*15,590*	*17,152*	*+1,562*	18
18,735	19,395	+660	*15,816*	*15,999*	*+183*	19
460,577	495,306	+34,729	*397,308*	*423,245*	*+25,937*	
51,978	54,653	+2,675	*44,869*	*47,459*	*+2,590*	1
24,068	26,723	+2,655	*21,102*	*23,180*	*+2,078*	2
20,112	21,226	+1,114	*17,221*	*17,623*	*+402*	3
43,154	45,634	+2,480	*39,990*	*41,487*	*+1,497*	4
8,843	12,286	+3,443	*8,092*	*11,233*	*+3,141*	5
27,496	28,742	+1,246	*24,240*	*25,703*	*+1,463*	6
16,618	18,102	+1,484	*14,911*	*16,110*	*+1,199*	7
32,789	33,236	+447	*28,155*	*28,619*	*+464*	8
14,729	17,800	+3,071	*13,234*	*15,550*	*+2,316*	9
239,787	258,402	+18,615	*211,814*	*226,964*	*+15,150*	
35,314	33,837	—1,477	*30,396*	*29,144*	*—1,252*	1
26,391	26,098	—293	*29,732*	*23,028*	*—6,704*	2
31,354	28,391	—2,963	*27,650*	*25,331*	*—2,319*	3
29,631	28,735	—896	*26,002*	*25,067*	*—935*	4
23,630	23,081	—549	*20,737*	*19,927*	*—810*	5
24,351	25,650	+1,299	*21,475*	*22,286*	*+811*	6
36,157	35,220	—937	*31,152*	*30,931*	*—221*	7
18,264	20,517	+2,253	*14,179*	*17,028*	*+2,849*	8
27,563	26,548	—1,015	*24,342*	*23,895*	*—447*	9
29,351	30,772	+1,421	*29,001*	*27,495*	*—1,506*	10
13,233	14,790	+1,557	*12,624*	*13,485*	*+861*	11
25,079	26,430	+1,351	*23,005*	*22,962*	*—43*	12
25,557	25,641	+84	*22,011*	*22,351*	*+340*	13
32,675	31,996	—679	*31,824*	*29,651*	*—2,173*	14
11,660	13,118	+1,458	*11,986*	*11,997*	*+11*	15
17,937	18,857	+920	*17,367*	*17,784*	*+417*	16
25,712	25,068	—644	*21,425*	*20,716*	*—709*	17
12,735	15,000	+2,265	*11,350*	*13,704*	*+2,354*	18
21,189	23,277	+2,088	*19,240*	*21,586*	*+2,346*	19
24,784	26,339	+1,555	*19,411*	*23,623*	*+4,212*	20
43,720	38,989	—3,731	*30,188*	*30,066*	*—122*	21
14,671	16,880	+1,209	*11,124*	*11,023*	*—101*	22
4,664	4,947	+283	*4,320*	*4,363*	*+43*	23
15,172	15,922	+750	*14,143*	*13,892*	*—251*	24
16,727	18,925	+2,198	*18,440*	*17,515*	*—925*	25
14,548	20,924	+6,376	*8,682*	*15,830*	*+7,148*	26
11,241	11,711	+470	*9,375*	*10,020*	*+645*	27
15,581	20,429	+4,848	*11,324*	*16,903*	*+5,579*	28
628,891	648,092	+19,201	*552,505*	*561,603*	*+9,098*	
13,067	12,536	—531	*12,152*	*11,665*	*—487*	1
26,688	26,777	+89	*25,933*	*26,043*	*+110*	2
36,360	35,382	—978	*34,396*	*32,898*	*—1,498*	3
16,011	16,469	+458	*15,225*	*15,146*	*—79*	4
9,820	10,834	+1,014	*9,207*	*9,905*	*+698*	5
28,642	27,739	—903	*27,140*	*26,247*	*—893*	6
12,074	12,142	+68	*11,308*	*10,959*	*—349*	7
9,751	10,231	+480	*9,782*	*9,750*	*—32*	8
19,374	19,123	—251	*17,753*	*17,362*	*—391*	9
15,582	15,758	+176	*15,119*	*14,553*	*—566*	10
9,944	12,256	+2,312	*9,722*	*11,295*	*+1,573*	11
11,710	14,638	+2,928	*11,388*	*13,802*	*+2,414*	12
17,061	17,493	+432	*16,892*	*16,389*	*—503*	13
8,077	9,521	+1,444	*8,172*	*8,932*	*+760*	14
12,791	14,108	+1,317	*12,552*	*13,759*	*+1,207*	15
19,118	21,204	+2,086	*19,361*	*20,458*	*+1,097*	16
20,180	20,855	+675	*18,925*	*19,206*	*+281*	17
27,912	28,299	+387	*28,420*	*28,262*	*—158*	18
12,211	12,432	+221	*12,580*	*12,427*	*—153*	19
21,214	22,024	+810	*20,131*	*20,278*	*+147*	20
347,587	359,821	+12,234	*336,158*	*339,336*	*+3,178*	

Showing the variations in the population of the

PROVINCIAL TABLE VI.

Serial number of district.	Name of district.	Serial number of thána.	Name of thána.	Total population. Census, 1881.	Census, 1891.	Increase + or Decrease —
1	2	3	4	5	6	7
21	Bánda	1	Bánda	71,691	66,223	—5,468
		2	Khanna	22,701	23,587	+886
		3	Mataundh	20,076	18,208	—1,868
		4	Tindwari	28,852	27,482	—1,370
		5	Murwal	16,636	17,443	+807
		6	Pailani	34,252	32,397	—1,855
		7	Jaspura	22,204	30,214	+8,010
		8	Baberu	44,987	47,464	+2,477
		9	Marka	13,819	18,057	+4,238
		10	Oran	21,777	22,823	+1,046
		11	Bisanda	27,225	29,254	+2,029
		12	Pangara	25,651	24,470	—1,181
		13	Kalinjar	32,729	30,611	—2,118
		14	Khurand	14,129	15,764	+1,635
		15	Girwan	17,456	17,708	+252
		16	Badausa	43,245	39,485	—3,760
		17	Itwan	5,509	5,944	+435
		18	Raipura	29,183	26,290	—2,893
		19	Karwi	37,629	40,583	+2,954
		20	Manikpur	19,380	19,993	+613
		21	Pahari	29,848	28,720	—1,128
		22	Kamásin	34,649	36,777	+2,128
		23	Rájapur	37,219	36,803	—416
		24	Bargarh	9,794	10,996	+1,202
		25	Mau	37,967	38,536	+569
			Total	698,608	705,832	+7,224
22	Hamírpur	1	Sumerpur	26,827	34,019	+7,192
		2	Lálpura	17,632	13,561	—4,071
		3	Hamírpur	20,662	21,656	+994
		4	Kurara	12,173	13,357	+1,184
		5	Sisolar	16,853	19,835	+2,982
		6	Maudha	38,749	43,366	+4,617
		7	Srinagar	22,581	24,161	+1,580
		8	Kabrai	19,036	19,430	+394
		9	Mahoba	29,254	31,506	+2,252
		10	Ajnar	30,949	34'607	+3,658
		11	Pánwari	34,059	33,073	—986
		12	Káshipur	13,073	13,625	+552
		13	Kulpahar	41,555	39,387	—2,168
		14	Jaria	28,378	26,191	—2,187
		15	Chandaut	11,352	10,688	—664
		16	Ráth	59,642	53,938	—5,704
		17	Kharela	14,323	12,333	—1,990
		18	Majhgawan	15,634	15,512	—122
		19	Jalálpur	12,850	12,150	—700
		20	Muskara	25,966	27,858	+1,892
		21	Bewar	15,789	13,467	—2,322
			Total	507,337	513,720	+6,383
23	Allahabad	1	Phúlpur	73,750	73,033	—717
		2	Sarái Inaet	72,641	74,480	+1,839
		3	Handia	77,224	77,959	+735
		4	Sikandra	44,246	46,011	+1,765
		5	Baraut	30,179	32,659	+2,480
		6	Sarái Mamrez	51,180	51,249	+69
		7	Mau Aima	53,690	51,970	—1,720
		8	Soraon	65,275	70,281	+5,006
		9	Nawábganj	60,490	59,095	—1,395
		10	Kheri	23,331	24,308	+977
		11	Moja	36,578	34,662	—1,916
		12	Koraon	49,937	54,247	+4,310
		13	Manda	41,046	39,363	—1,683
		14	Sirsa	41,313	42,641	+1,328
		15	Ghúrpur	33,244	37,213	+3,969
		16	Mutthiganj	14,605	15,620	+1,015
		17	Karchhana	72,368	75,889	+3,521
		18	Bárah	29,468	37,164	+7,696
		19	Dando	19,570	22,498	+2,928
		20	Sheorájpur	14,906	17,679	+2,773
		21	Saini	67,016	67,409	+393
		22	Kohkhiraj	50,353	52,798	+2,445
		23	Manjhanpur	51,564	54,479	+2,915
		24	Pachhim Sarira	43,415	48,097	+4,682

Police Circles since the previous Census—*(continued)*.

PROVINCIAL TABLE VI.

Males.			Females.			Serial number of thána.
Census, 1881.	Census, 1891.	Increase + or Decrease —	Census, 1881.	Census, 1891.	Increase + or Decrease —	
8	9	10	11	12	13	14
36,981	33,332	—3,649	34,710	32,891	—1,819	1
11,620	11,984	+364	11,081	11,603	+522	2
10,373	9,144	—1,229	9,703	9,064	—639	3
14,837	13,937	—900	14,015	13,545	—470	4
8,252	8,673	+421	8,384	8,770	+386	5
17,574	16,553	—1,021	16,678	15,844	—834	6
11,077	15,676	+4,599	11,127	14,538	+3,411	7
22,079	23,606	+1,527	22,908	23,858	+950	8
6,778	9,131	+2,353	7,041	8,926	+1,885	9
10,820	11,496	+676	10,957	11,327	+370	10
13,702	14,489	+787	13,523	14,765	+1,242	11
12,636	12,149	—487	13,015	12,321	—694	12
16,543	15,521	—1,022	16,186	15,090	—1,096	13
7,273	7,996	+723	6,856	7,768	+912	14
8,782	8,907	+125	8,674	8,801	+127	15
22,054	19,971	—2,083	21,191	19,514	—1,677	16
2,836	2,982	+146	2,673	2,962	+289	17
15,041	13,306	—1,735	14,142	12,984	—1,158	18
18,874	20,484	+1,610	18,755	20,099	+1,344	19
10,379	10,405	+26	9,001	9,588	+587	20
15,069	14,418	—651	14,779	14,302	—477	21
17,202	18,680	+1,478	17,447	18,097	+650	22
19,530	18,860	—670	17,689	17,943	+254	23
4,955	5,614	+659	4,839	5,382	+543	24
19,110	19,580	+470	18,857	18,956	+99	25
354,377	356,894	+2,517	344,231	348,938	+4,707	
13,257	17,493	+4,236	13,570	16,526	+2,956	1
9,059	7,016	—2,043	8,573	6,545	—2,028	2
10,659	11,370	+711	10,003	10,286	+283	3
5,973	6,896	+923	6,200	6,461	+261	4
8,644	10,134	+1,490	8,209	9,701	+1,492	5
19,639	21,720	+2,081	19,110	21,646	+2,536	6
11,727	12,426	+699	10,854	11,735	+881	7
9,853	9,933	+80	9,183	9,497	+314	8
14,979	15,937	+958	14,275	15,569	+1,294	9
15,998	17,700	+1,702	14,951	16,907	+1,956	10
17,289	16,537	—752	16,770	16,536	—234	11
6,819	6,930	+111	6,254	6,695	+441	12
21,351	19,931	—1,420	20,204	19,456	—748	13
14,684	13,179	—1,505	13,694	13,012	—682	14
5,774	5,426	—348	5,578	5,262	—316	15
30,139	26,756	—3,383	29,503	27,182	—2,321	16
7,652	6,282	—1,370	6,671	6,051	—620	17
8,072	7,772	—300	7,562	7,740	+178	18
6,623	6,125	—498	6,227	6,025	—202	19
13,360	14,160	+800	12,606	13,698	+1,092	20
8,227	6,880	—1,347	7,562	6,587	—975	21
259,778	260,603	+825	247,559	253,117	+5,558	
37,271	36,721	—550	36,479	36,312	—167	1
35,954	36,762	+808	36,687	37,718	+1,031	2
38,893	38,845	—48	38,331	39,114	+783	3
21,963	22,771	+808	22,283	23,240	+957	4
15,397	16,474	+1,077	14,782	16,185	+1,403	5
26,184	26,078	—106	24,996	25,171	+175	6
26,057	25,212	—845	27,633	26,758	—875	7
32,133	34,298	+2,165	33,142	35,983	+2,841	8
29,923	28,732	—1,191	30,567	30,363	—204	9
11,819	12,484	+665	11,512	11,824	+312	10
18,620	17,618	—1,002	17,958	17,044	—914	11
25,153	27,429	+2,276	24,784	26,818	+2,034	12
20,440	19,715	—725	20,606	19,648	—958	13
20,429	20,816	+387	20,884	21,825	+941	14
16,330	18,551	+2,221	16,914	18,662	+1,748	15
8,328	8,938	+610	6,277	6,682	+405	16
36,200	38,512	+2,312	36,168	37,377	+1,209	17
14,550	18,947	+4,397	14,918	18,217	+3,299	18
9,999	11,597	+1,598	9,571	10,896	+1,325	19
7,620	9,028	+1,408	7,286	8,651	+1,365	20
33,738	34,007	+269	33,278	33,402	+124	21
25,025	26,249	+1,224	25,328	26,549	+1,221	22
25,895	27,729	+1,834	25,669	26,750	+1,081	23
21,829	24,722	+2,893	21,586	23,375	+1,789	24

Showing the variations in the population of the

PROVINCIAL TABLE VI.

Serial number of district.	Name of district.	Serial number of thána.	Name of thána.	Total population. Census, 1881.	Census, 1891.	Increase + or Decrease —
1	2	3	4	5	6	7
23	Allahabad—*(concluded)*	25	Karari	42,207	45,679	+3,472
		26	Saráı Akíl	64,741	75,100	+10,359
		27	Pura Mufti	49,926	50,351	+425
		28	Pipalgaon	27,311	29,340	+2,029
		29	Kotwáli	82,571	89,302	+6,731
		30	Kydganj	14,096	15,026	+930
		31	Dáraganj	14,129	14,111	—18
		32	Colonelganj	31,931	36,767	+4,836
		33	Cantonments...	1,967	1,824	+143
		34	Cannington	6,598	91,66	+2,568
		35	Sadar Bazár	7,266	7,193	—73
			*Raniganj**	13,974	14,079	+105
			Total ...	1,474,106	1,548,737	+74,631
24	Jhánsi ...	1	Jhánsi City	26,782	37,075	+10,293
		2	New Jhánsi	5,776	19,122	+13,346
		3	Sadar Bazár	4,732	9,235	+4,503
		4	Baragaon	18,008	18,597	+589
		5	Barwa Sagar	12,919	14,037	+1,118
		6	Baidora	12,630	13,741	+1,111
		7	Babina	14,082	15,545	+1,463
		8	Chírgaon	25,983	25,426	—557
		9	Raksa	10,525	9,828	—697
		10	Mau	46,309	46,495	+186
		11	Uldan	13,724	17,006	+3,282
		12	Sakrar	15,282	16,289	+1,007
		13	Bonda	6,145	7,859	+1,714
		14	Siaori	25,494	28,075	+2,581
		15	Garotha	22,455	21,464	—991
		16	Kakarbai	14,347	14,594	+247
		17	Pandwaha	16,194	19,650	+3,456
		18	Gur Saráı	17,229	16,530	—699
		19	Moth	17,168	23,073	+5,905
		20	Erich	17,867	18,618	+751
		21	Baghera	15,961	17,160	+1,199
		22	Lalitpur	30,211	35,669	+5,458
		23	Jaklaun	9,496	10,869	+1,373
		24	Birdha	11,024	11,592	+568
		25	Khajuria	8,636	9,947	+1,311
		26	Kailwara	9,025	10,282	+1,257
		27	Jakhora	17,127	19,159	+2,032
		28	Bánsi	10,962	10,150	—812
		29	Talbehat	19,965	23,357	+3,392
		30	Nathi Khera...	12,230	14,424	+2,194
		31	Bar	27,817	28,340	+523
		32	Dudhai	10,227	10,329	+102
		33	Narhat	13,646	14,514	+868
		34	Banpur	15,804	18,644	+2,840
		35	Mehroni	16,267	17,496	+1,229
		36	Sojna	12,135	12,410	+275
		37	Maraura	15,443	13,967	—1,476
		38	Girar	6,935	7,106	+171
		39	Madanpur	7,387	5,945	—1,442
			Total ...	582,315	683,619	+101,304
25	Jalaun ...	1	Orai	35,711	34,365	—1,346
		2	Ait	17,024	15,789	—1,235
		3	Mohana	11,004	9,547	—1,457
		4	Ata	21,904	20,024	1,880
		5	Kunch	48,753	45,177	—3,576
		6	Sayednagar	21,134	21,390	—256
		7	Jalaun	44,476	39,596	—4,880
		8	Kuthaund	26,421	25,679	—742
		9	Hadrukh	29,662	28,199	—1,463
		10	Churkhi	25,654	24,626	—1,028
		11	Madhogarh	29,392	24,166	—5,226
		12	Kálpi	34,315	33,973	—342
		13	Mau	13,559	15,061	+1,502
		14	Reudhar	24,391	24,798	+407
		15	Rámpura	13,251	13,845	+594
		16	Gopálpura	6,023	6,528	+505
		17	Jagamanpur	15,468	13,598	—1,870
			Total ...	418,142	396,361	—21,781

* Criminal jurisdiction vested in

Police Circles since the previous Census—(*continued*).

PROVINCIAL TABLE VI.

Males.			Females.			
Census, 1881.	Census, 1891.	Increase + or Decrease —	Census, 1881.	Census, 1891.	Increase + or Decrease —	Serial number of tháns.
8	9	10	11	12	13	14
21,063	23,022	+1,959	21,144	22,657	+1,513	25
31,213	37,071	+5,858	33,628	38,029	+450	26
24,405	24,540	+135	25,521	25,811	+290	27
13,148	14,191	+1,043	14,163	15,149	+986	28
43,032	46,662	+3,630	39,539	42,640	3,101	29
7,401	8,011	+610	6,695	7,015	+320	30
7,551	7,355	—196	6,578	6,756	+178	31
16,956	20,135	+3,179	14975,	16,632	+1,657	32
1,096	931	—165	871	893	+22	33
4,044	5,487	+1,443	2,554	3,679	+1,125	34
5,094	5,134	+40	2,172	2,059	—113	35
6,977	6,735	—242	6,997	7,344	+347	
741,730	781,509	+39,779	732,376	767,228	+34,852	
13,127	19,220	+6,093	13,655	17,855	+4,200	1
3,354	11,405	+8,051	2,422	7,717	+5,295	2
3,663	7,030	+3,867	1,569	2,205	+636	3
9,364	9,606	+242	8,644	8991	+347	4
6,790	7,360	+570	6,129	6,677	+548	5
6,418	7,373	+955	6,212	6,368	+156	6
7,541	8,174	+633	6,541	7,371	+830	7
12,985	12,945	—40	12,998	12,481	—517	8
5,293	5,301	+8	5,232	4,527	—705	9
23,172	23,276	+104	2,3137	23,219	+82	10
7,078	8,683	+1,605	6,646	8,323	+1,677	11
8,177	8,480	+303	7,105	7,809	+704	12
3,197	4,114	+917	2,948	3,745	+797	13
13,097	14,450	+1,353	12,397	13,625	+1,228	14
11,524	10,933	—591	10,931	10,531	—400	15
7,359	7,664	+305	6,988	6,930	—58	16
8,518	10,081	+1,563	7,676	9,569	+1,893	17
8,720	8,399	—321	8,509	8,131	—378	18
8,788	11,738	+2,950	8,380	11,335	+2,955	19
9,077	9,454	+377	8,790	9,164	+374	20
8,269	8,842	+573	7,692	8,318	+626	21
15,866	18,560	+2,694	14,345	17,109	+2,764	22
5,008	5,603	+595	4,488	5,266	+778	23
5,792	6,009	+217	5,232	5,583	+351	24
4,451	5,066	+615	4,185	4,881	+696	25
4,702	5,377	+675	4,323	4,905	+582	26
9,027	10,132	+1,105	8,100	9,027	+927	27
6,969	5,215	—1,754	3,993	4,935	+942	28
10,444	12,142	+1,698	9,521	11,215	+1,694	29
6,294	7,469	+1,175	5,936	6,955	+1,019	30
13,910	14,605	+695	13,907	13,735	—172	31
5,395	5,467	+72	4,832	4,862	+30	32
7,030	7,424	+394	6,616	7,090	+474	33
8,089	9,484	+1,395	7,715	9,160	+1,445	34
8,379	8,807	+428	7,888	8,689	+801	35
6,318	6,415	+97	5,817	5,995	+178	36
7,982	6,943	—1,039	7,461	7,024	—437	37
3,631	3,676	+45	3,304	3,430	+126	38
3,766	3,042	—724	3,621	2,903	—718	39
302,683	355,964	+53,281	279,632	327,655	+ 48,023	
18,133	17,729	—404	17,578	16,636	—942	1
8,957	8,084	—873	8,067	7,705	—362	2
5,662	4,822	—840	5,342	4,725	—617	3
11,432	10,360	—1,072	10,472	9,664	—808	4
24,727	23,096	—1,631	24,026	22,081	—1,945	5
10,524	10,838	+314	10,610	10,552	—58	6
22,643	20,128	—2,515	21,833	19,468	—2,365	7
14,038	13,306	—732	12,383	12,373	—10	8
15,548	14,527	—1,021	14,114	13,672	—442	9
13,159	12,745	—414	12,495	11,881	—614	10
15,873	12,701	—3,172	13,519	11,465	—2,054	11
17,126	17,315	+189	17,189	16,658	—531	12
7,014	7,811	+797	6,545	7,250	+705	13
12,746	12,813	+67	11,646	11,985	+340	14
7,011	7,825	+314	6,240	6,520	+280	15
3,195	3,353	+158	2,828	3,175	+347	16
8,357	7,137	—1,220	7,111	6,461	—650	17
216,145	204,090	—12,055	201,997	192,271	—9,726	

the Deputy Commsiioner of Partabgarh.

Showing the variations in the population of the

PROVINCIAL TABLE VI.

Serial number of district.	Name of district.	Serial number of thána.	Name of thána.	Total Population. Census, 1881.	Census, 1891.	Increase + or Decrease —
1	2	3	4	5	6	7
26	Benares	1	Baragaon	61,643	64,550	+2,907
		2	Sikraul	57,239	58,560	+1,321
		3	Phúlpur	51,139	54,856	+3,717
		4	Chaubepur	57,586	63,180	+5,594
		5	Rohania	25,074	40,862	+15,788
		6	Adampura	21,190	20,834	—356
		7	Chetganj	28,456	29,768	+1,312
		8	Camp	9,076	8,757	—319
		9	Bhelupur	43,803	39,867	—3,936
		10	Jaitpura	22,883	22,815	—68
		11	Dasasumedh	41,135	41,539	+404
		12	Kotwáli	27,562	27,658	+96
		13	Kalbhairon	30,793	30,980	+187
		14	Cholapur	63,049	63,662	+613
		15	Mirzamurád	111,358	102,513	—8,845
		16	Shakaldiha	41,939	43,711	+1,772
		17	Chandauli	41,861	45,801	+3,940
		18	Saiyidrája	53,553	54,710	+1,157
		19	Balua	43,017	46,264	+3,247
		20	Alinagar	30,267	33,569	+3,302
		21	Rámnagar	30,061	27,487	—2,574
			Total	**892,684**	**921,943**	**+29,259**
27	Mirzapur	1	Marihan	21,228	21,572	+344
		2	Parari	35,686	36,839	+1,153
		3	Kotwáli	113,335	116,222	+2,887
		4	Bindhyachal	39,528	40,278	+750
		5	Gaipurwa	24,135	28,959	+4,824
		6	Hallia	24,815	23,454	—1,361
		7	Drummondganj	13,891	13,079	—812
		8	Lálganj	49,736	48,967	—769
		9	Gopiganj	67,351	69,135	+1,784
		10	Kachhwa	30,982	32,735	+1,753
		11	Chunár	98,769	103,158	+4,389
		12	Mirzapur Khurd	58,805	59,597	+792
		13	Ahraura	22,438	22,827	+389
		14	Pannuganj	49,687	53,149	+3,462
		15	Ghorawal	18,206	18,972	+766
		16	Sháhganj	25,542	27,160	+1,618
		17	Robertsganj	30,307	33,806	+3,499
		18	Chopan	24,850	25,967	+1,117
		19	Kone	8,143	9,078	+935
		20	Khairwa	31,535	33,704	+2,169
		21	Dudhi	39,301	39,943	+642
		22	Bhadohi	53,922	56,113	+2,191
		23	Aurai	100,911	100,048	—863
		24	Suriawan	34,970	34.885	—85
		25	Ujh	37,970	40,947	+2,977
		26	Chakia	80,753	70,914	—9839
			Total	**1,136,796**	**1,161,508**	**+24,712**
28	Jaunpur	1	Kotwáli	114.007	100,401	—13,606
		2	Bakhsha	72,837	83,361	+10,524
		3	Sarái Khoja	71,224	78,184	+6,960
		4	Kerakat	94,511	102,623	+8,112
		5	Gulzárganj	46,117	47,507	+1,390
		6	Bamuiaon	55,301	59,296	+3,995
		7	Badshahpur	51,444	53,242	+1,798
		8	Sujanganj	84,148	84,766	+618
		9	Badlapur	75,635	81,661	+6,026
		10	Rámpur	82,756	88,334	+5,578
		11	Khutahan	58,230	61,560	+3,330
		12	Sarpatha	70,270	66,259	—4,011
		13	Sháhganj	51,883	62,117	+10,234
		14	Chandwak	50,036	53,222	+3,186
		15	Jalálpur	68,776	76,792	+8,016
		16	Machhlishahr	60,958	63,404	+2,446
		17	Mariahu	101,530	102,220	+690
			Total	**1,209,663**	**1,264,949**	**+55,286**
29	Gházipur	1	Gházipur	100,057	103,696	+3,639
		2	Muhammadabad	85,312	89,531	+4,219
		3	Nandganj	47,159	47,293	+134
		4	Karanda	30,161	31,438	+1,277
		5	Birno	59,710	64,449	+4,739

Police Circles since the previous Census—(*continued*).

PROVINCIAL TABLE VI.

Males.			Females.			Serial number of thána.
Census, 1881.	Census, 1891.	Increase + or Decrease —	Census, 1881.	Census, 1891.	Increase + or Decrease —	
8	9	10	11	12	13	14
31,218	32,383	+1,165	*30,425*	*32,167*	*+1,742*	1
30,029	31,313	+1,284	*27,210*	*27,247*	*+37*	2
25,849	27,592	+1,743	*25,290*	*27,264*	*+1,974*	3
28,285	30,830	+2,545	*29,301*	*32,350*	*+3,049*	4
12,565	20,603	+8,038	*12,509*	*20,259*	*+7,750*	5
10,683	10,569	—114	*10,507*	*10,265*	*—242*	6
14,452	15,573	+1,121	*14,004*	*14,195*	*+191*	7
5,141	5,351	+210	*3,935*	*3,406*	*—529*	8
22,165	20,780	—,1385	*21,638*	*19,087*	*—2,551*	9
11,852	11,901	+49	*11,031*	*10,914*	*—117*	10
20,259	20,856	+597	*20,876*	*20,683*	*—193*	11
14,189	14,735	+546	*13,373*	*12,923*	*—450*	12
15,683	16,039	+356	*15,110*	*14,941*	*—169*	13
31,914	32,058	+144	*31,135*	*31,604*	*+469*	14
56,472	51,670	—4,802	*54,886*	*50,843*	*—4,043*	15
20,774	21,804	+1,030	*21,165*	*21,907*	*+742*	16
20,896	22,919	+2,023	*20,965*	*22,882*	*+1,917*	17
26,532	27,155	+623	*27,021*	*27,555*	*+534*	18
21,156	22,571	+1,415	*21,861*	*23,693*	*+1,832*	19
15,343	17,189	+1,846	*14,924*	*16,380*	*+1,456*	20
15,327	13,562	—1,765	*14,734*	*13,925*	*—809*	21
450,784	467,453	+16,669	*441,900*	*454,490*	*+12,590*	
10,608	10,855	+252	*10,625*	*10,717*	*+92*	1
17,522	18,301	+779	*18,164*	*18,538*	*+374*	2
55,634	57,269	+1,635	*57,701*	*58,953*	*+1,252*	3
19,010	19,040	+30	*20,518*	*21,238*	*+720*	4
11,703	14,043	+2,340	*12,432*	*14,916*	*+2,484*	5
12,405	11,859	—546	*12,410*	*11,695*	*—815*	6
7,160	6,556	—604	*6,731*	*6,523*	*—208*	7
25,814	24,638	—1,176	*23,922*	*24,329*	*+407*	8
33,773	34,227	+454	*33,578*	*34,908*	*+1,330*	9
15,859	16,223	+364	*15,123*	*16,512*	*+1,389*	10
47,272	49,950	+2,678	*51,497*	*53,208*	*+1,711*	11
29,720	29,553	—167	*29,085*	*30,044*	*+959*	12
10,975	11,528	+553	*11,463*	*11,299*	*—164*	13
24,973	26,108	+1,135	*24,714*	*27,041*	*+2,327*	14
9, 85	9,389	+304	*9,121*	*9,583*	*+462*	15
12,312	13,282	+970	*13,230*	*13,878*	*+648*	16
15,211	16,682	+1,471	*15,096*	*17,124*	*+2,028*	17
12,894	13,366	+472	*11,956*	*12,601*	*+645*	18
4,008	4,441	+433	*4,135*	*4,637*	*+502*	19
16,184	17,114	+930	*15,351*	*16,590*	*+1,239*	20
20,094	20,095	+1	*19,207*	*19,848*	*+641*	21
27,276	27,990	+714	*26,646*	*28,123*	*+1,477*	22
52,314	50,101	—2,213	*48,597*	*49,947*	*+1,350*	23
16,439	17,040	+601	*18,531*	*17,845*	*—686*	24
17,747	20,440	+2,693	*20,223*	*20,507*	*+284*	25
41,317	36,251	—5,066	*39,436*	*34,663*	*—4,773*	26
567,304	576,341	+9,037	*569,492*	*585,167*	*+15,675*	
56,144	49,778	—6,366	*57,863*	*50,623*	*—7,240*	1
37,769	41,916	+4,147	*35,068*	*41,445*	*+6,377*	2
35,770	39,140	+3,370	*35,454*	*39,044*	*+3,590*	3
47,337	51,755	+4,418	*47,174*	*50,868*	*+3,694*	4
23,373	23,975	+602	*22,744*	*23,532*	*+788*	5
28,308	29,956	+1,648	*26,993*	*29,340*	*+2,347*	6
26,348	27,210	+862	*25,096*	*26,032*	*+936*	7
42,170	42,148	—22	*41,978*	*42,618*	*+640*	8
38,839	41,433	+2,594	*36,796*	*40,228*	*+3,432*	9
42,288	44,171	+1,883	*40,468*	*44,163*	*+3,695*	10
29,348	30,739	+1,391	*28,882*	*30,821*	*+1,939*	11
35,957	33,908	—2,040	*34,313*	*32,351*	*—1,962*	12
25,990	30,924	+4,934	*25,893*	*31,193*	*+5,300*	13
25,383	26,921	+1,538	*24,653*	*26,301*	*+1,648*	14
34,456	38,284	+3,828	*34,320*	*38,508*	*+4,188*	15
30,589	31,636	+1,047	*30,369*	*31,768*	*+1,399*	16
51,338	51,056	—282	*50,192*	*51,164*	*+972*	17
611,407	634,950	+23,543	*598,265*	*629,999*	*+3,1743*	
49,779	51,930	+2,151	*50,278*	*51,766*	*+1,488*	1
42,383	43,779	+1,396	*42,929*	*45,752*	*+2,823*	2
23,477	23,454	—23	*23,682*	*23,839*	*+157*	3
14,760	15,095	+335	*15,401*	*16,343*	*+942*	4
30,779	32,728	+1,949	*28,931*	*31,721*	*+2,790*	5

Showing the variations in the population of the

PROVINCIAL TABLE VI.

Serial number of district.	Name of district.	Serial number of thána.	Name of thána.	Total population. Census, 1881.	Census, 1891.	Increase + or Decrease—
1	2	3	4	5	6	7
		6	Kasimabad	85,635	91,239	+5,604
		7	Mardah	41,156	45,366	+4,210
		8	Shadiabad	82,397	85,715	+3,318
		9	Saidpur	92,262	100,503	+8,241
		10	Sadat	44,455	42,706	−1,749
29	Ghá́zipur—(*concluded*).	11	Zamánia	62,848	69,609	+6,761
		12	Gahmer	54,304	58,178	+3,874
		13	Dildárnagar	48,637	53,638	+5,001
		14	Dhanapur	48,456	51,761	+3,305
		15	Karou	33,440	44,373	+10,933
		16	Narhi	19,938	25,271	+5,333
		17	Korantadih	64,834	73,143	+8,309
			Total ...	1,000,761	1,077,909	+77,148
		1	Bansdih	134,473	127,574	−6,899
		2	Reoti	51,994	49,053	−2,941
		3	Ubhaon	37,261	56,800	+19,539
		4	Sikandarpur	116,645	93,606	−23,039
		5	Nagra	89,499	91,910	+2,411
30	Ballia ...	6	Ballia	138,378	135,203	−3,175
		7	Haldi	59,413	66,367	+6,954
		8	Bairia	88,024	89,545	+1,521
		9	Garwar	98,070	94,223	−3,847
		10	Haldharpur	54,526	59,500	+4,974
		11	Rasra	69,818	78,684	+8,866
			Total ...	938,101	942,465	+4,364
		1	Deoria	88,837	106,516	+17,679
		2	Chaura	47,266	65,839	+18,573
		3	Ruddarpur	137,577	132,923	−4,654
		4	Háta	99,400	124,752	+25,352
		5	Tarkulwa	101,574	122,329	+20,755
		6	Mansúrganj	61,761	81,739	+19,978
		7	Pipraich	61,896	76,224	+14,328
		8	Bansgaon	108,876	141,215	+32,339
		9	Barhalganj	106,404	101,722	−4,682
		10	Rudrapur	88,138	85,331	−2,807
		11	Gola	71,803	74,260	+2,457
		12	Belghát	69,576	74,679	+5,103
		13	Mahrájganj	56,819	88,140	+31,321
		14	Rigauli	59,951	67,304	+7,353
		15	Biraicha	47,949	55,471	+7,522
		16	Panaira	12,216	29,681	+17,465
31	Gorakhpur ...	17	Semra	76,331	112,585	+36,254
		18	Paisia	35,553	51,194	+15,641
		19	Thuthibari	20,989	25,074	+4,085
		20	Kothibhar	87,816	99,514	+11,698
		21	Nichlaul	37,801	45,449	+7,648
		22	Padrauna	104,031	102,085	−1,946
		23	Ramkola	59,664	60,323	+659
		24	Kasia	78,608	95,279	+16,671
		25	Kázipur	79,242	95,519	+16,277
		26	Tariya Sojan	72,773	77,278	+4,505
		27	Bishanpura	50,997	51,313	+316
		28	Barhaj	77,300	74,634	−2,666
		29	Salempur	115,165	117,042	+1,877
		30	Kotwáli	198,006	220,682	+22,676
		31	Sahjanwa	57,403	63,564	+6,161
		32	Barhi	49,088	57,377	+8,289
		33	Khukhendu	85,805	88,573	+2,768
		34	Ghauti	110,505	128,447	+17,942
			Total ...	2,617,120	2,994,057	+376,937
		1	Basti	133,943	136,607	+2,664
		2	Sonha	41,966	59,743	+17,777
		3	Dudhara	49,943	72,354	+22,411
		4	Rudhauli	56,355	62,705	+6,350
		5	Barakoni	87,994	88,378	+384
		6	Budha	45,759	51,049	+5,290
32	Basti ...	7	Kalwari	64,669	67,177	+2,508
		8	Uska	59,212	61,269	+2,057
		9	Bánsi	94,363	101,886	+7,523
		10	Bankata	52,829	56,737	+3,908
		11	Chílhia	98,742	105,174	+6,432
		12	Lotan	38,419	43,428	+5,009
		13	Tilokpur	55,913	52,071	−3,842
		14	Dhebarua	30,420	31,068	+648
		15	Misraulia	45,463	47,198	+1,735

Police Circles since the previous Census—(*continued*).

PROVINCIAL TABLE VI.

Males.			Females.			Serial number of thána.
Census, 1881.	Census, 1891.	Increase + or Decrease—	Census, 1881.	Census, 1891.	Increase + or Decrease—	
8	9	10	11	12	13	14
44,128	46,048	+1,920	41,507	45,191	+3,684	6
21,654	23,038	+1,384	19,502	22,328	+2,826	7
42,379	43,466	+1,087	40,018	42,249	+2,231	8
46,581	50,206	+3,625	45,681	50,297	+4,616	9
22,588	21,489	—1,099	21,867	21,217	—650	10
30,255	33,456	+3,201	32,593	36,153	+3,560	11
25,999	27,753	+1,754	28,305	30,425	+2,120	12
23,444	25,837	+2,393	25,193	27,801	+2,608	13
24,191	25,806	+1,615	24,265	25,955	+1,690	14
16,570	21,361	+4,791	16,870	23,012	+6,142	15
9,722	12,122	+2,400	10,216	13,149	+2,933	16
31,242	34,133	+2,891	33,592	39,010	+5,418	17
499,931	531,701	+31,770	500,830	546,208	+45,378	
64,846	60,804	—4,042	69,627	66,770	—2,857	1
24,529	22,479	—2,050	27,465	26,574	—891	2
18,075	27,196	+9,121	19,186	29,604	+10,418	3
58,074	45,374	—12,700	58,571	48,232	—10,339	4
45,201	45,713	+512	44,298	46,197	+1,899	5
66,370	63,746	—2,624	72,008	71,457	—551	6
26,687	29,688	+3,001	32,726	36,679	+3,953	7
41.614	41,914	+300	46,410	47,631	—1,221	8
49,283	46,178	—3,105	48,787	48,045	—742	9
27,922	30,073	+2,151	26,604	29,427	+2,823	10
35,190	39,446	+4,256	34,628	39,238	+4,610	11
457,791	452,611	—5,180	480,310	489,854	+9,544	
44,423	53,103	+8,680	44,414	53,413	+8,999	1
23,836	33,163	+9,327	23,430	32,676	+9,246	2
68,023	65,364	—2,659	69,554	67,559	—1,995	3
49,904	62,904	+13,000	49,496	61,848	+12,352	4
51,473	62,122	+10,649	50,101	60,207	+10,106	5
30,803	41,377	+10,574	30,958	40,362	+9,404	6
31,184	38,570	+7,386	30,712	37,654	+6,942	7
54.128	69,851	+15,723	54,748	71,364	+16,616	8
52,164	49,040	—3,124	54,240	52,682	—1,558	9
44,359	42,772	—1,587	43,779	42,559	—1,220	10
35,518	36,424	+906	36,285	37,836	+1,551	11
34,851	37,288	+2,437	34,725	37,391	+2,666	12
28,084	44,547	+16,463	28,735	43,593	+14,858	13
30,247	33,916	+3,669	29,704	33,388	+3,684	14
24,184	28,239	+4,055	23,765	27,232	+3,467	15
6,127	15,323	+9,196	6,089	14,358	+8,269	16
38,667	58,141	+19,474	37,664	54,444	+16,780	17
18,231	26,852	+8,621	17,322	24,342	+7,020	18
10,827	13,145	+2,318	10,162	11,929	+1,767	19
44,435	50,484	+6,049	43,381	49,030	+5,649	20
19,009	23,356	+4,347	18,792	22,093	+3,301	21
52,366	51,368	—998	51,665	50,717	—948	22
29,821	30,655	+834	29,843	29,668	—175	23
39,293	47,833	+8,540	39,315	47,446	+8,131	24
39,347	47,096	+7,749	39,895	48,423	+8,528	25
35,721	38,044	+2,323	37,052	39,234	+2,182	26
25,004	25,074	+70	25,993	26,239	+246	27
38,354	37,433	—921	38,946	37,201	—1,745	28
55,969	56,077	+108	59,196	60,965	+1,769	29
99,765	111,506	+11,741	98,241	109,176	+10,935	30
28,598	31,418	+2,820	28,805	32,146	+3,341	31
24,276	28,545	+4,269	24,812	28,832	+4,020	32
42,889	43,842	+953	42,916	44,731	+1,815	33
54,243	62,412	+8,169	56,262	66,035	+9,773	34
1,306,123	1,497,284	+191,161	1,310,997	1,496,773	+185,776	
69,271	70,075	+804	64,672	66,532	+1,860	1
21,387	30,916	+9,529	20,579	28,827	+8,248	2
24,686	36,306	+11,620	25,257	36,048	+10,791	3
28,665	32,111	+3,446	27,690	30,594	+2,904	4
18,994	19,219	+225	19,000	19,159	+159	5
23,050	26,062	+3,012	22,709	24,987	+2,278	6
32,614	34,239	+1,625	32,055	32,938	+883	7
30,344	31,668	+1,324	28,868	29,601	+733	8
47,565	51,581	+4,016	46,798	50,305	+3,507	9
26,451	28,463	+2,012	26,378	28,274	+1,896	10
50,159	53,106	+2,947	48,583	52,068	+3,485	11
19,087	22,023	+2,936	19,332	21,405	+2,073	12
27,986	25,812	—2,174	27,927	26,259	—1,668	13
15,475	15,899	+424	14,945	1,5169	+224	14
23,122	23,954	+832	22,341	23,244	+903	15

Showing the variations in the population of the

PROVINCIAL TABLE VI.

Serial number of district.	Name of district.	Serial number of thána.	Name of thána.	Total population. Census, 1881.	Census, 1891.	Increase + or Decrease —
1	2	3	4	5	6	7
32	Basti—(*concluded*)	16	Chhapia	57,780	66,251	+8,471
		17	Domariaganj	90,678	116,502	+25,824
		18	Parasrámpur	57,399	61,275	+3,876
		19	Paikaulia	62,089	69,093	+7,004
		20	Chhaoni	75,718	78,458	+2,740
		21	Harria	51,945	55,085	3,140
		22	Kaptánganj	70,267	71,747	+1,480
		23	Khalilabad	62,247	70,678	+8,431
		24	Menhdawal	80,527	84,476	+3,949
		25	Dhanghata	58,098	61,303	+3,205
		26	Mahuli	57,874	64,132	+6,258
			Total	1,630,612	1,785,844	+155,232
33	Azamgarh	1	Azamgarh (Kotwali)	74,267	78,911	+4,644
		2	Ahraula	82,822	85,873	+3,051
		3	Jahanaganj	47,241	52,002	+4,761
		4	Sarái Mír	55,501	59,903	+4,402
		5	Kandhrapur	58,327	60,106	+1,779
		6	Gambhirpur	70,504	75,025	+4,521
		7	Mehnagar	52,267	61,104	+8,837
		8	Nizámabad	70,664	72,832	+2,168
		9	Chiriakot	78,940	87,660	+8,720
		10	Maunatbhanjan	97,253	108,205	+10,952
		11	Ghosi	85,580	96,286	+10,706
		12	Muhammadabad	109,895	117,746	+7,851
		13	Dobri	47,427	49,125	+1,698
		14	Raunapar	46,613	49,792	+3,179
		15	Sagri	93,476	101,554	+8,078
		16	Madhuban	99,024	90,776	—8,248
		17	Mahárájganj	72,726	79,224	+6,498
		18	Atraulia	79,153	90,038	+10,885
		19	Barda	41,578	47,143	+5,565
		20	Pawai	42,642	45,301	+2,659
		21	Didarganj	74,115	85,727	+11,612
		22	Tarwa	59,570	58,244	—1,326
		23	Deogaon	65,069	76,048	+10,979
			Total	1,604,654	1,728,625	+123,971
34	Lucknow	1	Banthara	55,196	58,912	+3,716
		2	Goshainganj	58,581	55,631	—2,950
		3	Lucknow	92,511	104,701	+12,190
		4	Mohanlálganj	76,969	104,697	+27,728
		5	Malihabad	99,549	114,984	+15,435
		6	Chauk	56,618	60,160	+3,542
		7	Saadatganj	30,588	31,292	+704
		8	Daulatganj	38,415	37,619	—796
		9	Wazírganj	36,641	39,273	+2,632
		10	Hasanganj	24,406	27,184	+2,778
		11	Dilkusha	21,530	23,517	+1,987
		12	Itaunja	53,870	62,067	+8,197
		13	Ganeshganj	51,950	54,126	+2,176
			Total	696,824	774,163	+77,339
35	Unao	1	Unao	105,849	113,268	+7,419
		2	Safipur	103,768	110,167	+6,399
		3	Ajgain	80,926	84,229	+3,303
		4	Achalganj	66,414	65,367	—1,047
		5	Bara	68,589	70,264	+1,675
		6	Purwa	70,828	73,230	+2,402
		7	Auras	71,719	80,099	+8,380
		8	Bangarmau	81,825	89,785	+7,960
		9	Fatehpur Chaurasi	34,833	35,564	+731
		10	Asoba	46,159	50,188	+4,029
		11	Behar	38,400	40,672	+2,272
		12	Maurawan	64,458	70,195	+5,737
		13	Hasanganj	65,301	70,608	+5,307
			Total	899,069	953,636	+54,567

Police Circles since the previous Census—(*continued*).

PROVINCIAL TABLE VI.

Males.			Females.			Serial number of thánas.
Census, 1881.	Census, 1891.	Increase + or Decrease—	Census, 1881.	Census, 1891.	Increase + or Decrease—	
8	9	10	11	12	13	14
29,332	33,898	+4,566	28,448	32,353	+3,905	16
45,701	59,009	+13,308	44,977	57,493	+12,516	17
29,091	31,142	+2,051	28,308	30,133	+1,825	18
31,199	35,245	+4,046	30,890	33,848	+2,958	19
38,277	39,757	+1,480	37,441	38,701	+1,260	20
26,833	28,317	+1,484	25,112	26,768	+1,656	21
35,253	36,333	+1,080	35,014	35,414	+400	22
31,070	35,747	+4,677	31,177	34,931	+3,754	23
40,543	43,023	+2,480	39,984	41,453	+1,469	24
29,433	31,070	+1,637	28,665	30,233	+1,568	25
28,663	32,362	+3,699	29,211	31,770	+2,559	26
824,251	907,337	+83,086	806,361	878,507	+72,146	
38,083	40,292	+2,209	36,184	38,619	+2,435	1
42,528	43,521	+993	40,294	42,352	+2,058	2
24,311	26,463	+2,152	22,930	25,539	+2,609	3
27,760	29,496	+1,736	27,741	30,407	+2,666	4
29,799	30,320	+521	28,528	29,786	+1,258	5
35,590	37,251	+1,661	34,914	37,774	+2,860	6
26,623	30,613	+3,990	25,644	30,491	+4,847	7
35,909	36,550	+641	34,755	36,282	+1,527	8
40,399	44,768	+4,369	38,541	42,892	+4,351	9
49,654	54,701	+5,047	47,599	53,504	+5,905	10
43,654	47,852	+4,198	41,926	48,434	+6,508	11
55,865	58,922	+3,057	54,030	58,824	+4,794	12
23,945	24,221	+276	23,482	24,904	+1,422	13
23,585	24,994	+1,409	23,028	24,798	+1,770	14
47,424	50,506	+3,082	46,052	51,048	+4,996	15
49,110	43,955	—5,155	49,914	46,821	—3,093	16
36,766	39,868	+3,102	35,960	39,356	+3,396	17
40,691	46,001	+5,310	38,462	44,037	+5,575	18
21,527	23,757	+2,230	20,051	23,386	+3,335	19
21,813	23,077	+1,264	20,829	22,224	+1,395	20
37,512	42,799	+5,287	36,603	42,928	+6,325	21
30,203	29,456	—747	29,367	28,788	—579	22
33,678	38,228	+4,550	31,391	37,820	+6,429	23
816,429	867,611	+51,182	788,225	861,014	+72,789	
28,943	30,539	+1,596	26,253	28,373	+2,120	1
29,793	28,510	—1,283	28,788	27,121	—1,667	2
48,181	55,749	+7,568	44,330	48,952	+4,622	3
39,469	53,774	+14,305	37,500	50,923	+13,423	4
52,120	60,125	+8,005	47,429	54 859	+7,430	5
28,608	30,440	+1,832	28,010	29,720	+1,710	6
15,242	15,809	+567	15,346	15,483	+137	7
19,104	18,803	—301	19,311	18,816	—495	8
18,856	20,505	+1,649	17,785	18,768	+983	9
12,753	14,456	+1,703	11,653	12,728	+1,075	10
14,474	16,019	+,1545	7,056	7,498	+442	11
28,236	32,579	+4,343	25,634	29,488	+3,854	12
29,526	29,893	+367	22,424	24,233	+1,809	13
365,305	407,201	+41,896	331,519	366,962	+35,443	
55,260	59,473	+4,213	50,589	53,795	+3,206	1
54,279	57,600	+3,321	49,489	52,567	+3,078	2
42,339	43,832	+1,493	38,587	40,397	+1,810	3
32,944	32,126	—818	33,470	33,241	—229	4
34,088	33,878	—180	34,501	36,386	+1,855	5
34,812	36,192	+1,380	36,016	37,038	+1,022	6
38,036	42,650	+4,614	33,683	37,449	+3,766	7
42,893	47,769	+4,876	38,932	42,016	+3,084	8
18,855	19,091	+206	15,978	16,473	+525	9
23,389	25,593	+2,204	22,770	24,595	+1,825	10
18,358	19,310	+952	20,042	21,362	+1,320	11
31,897	35,047	+3,150	32,561	35,148	+2 587	12
34,017	36,951	+2,934	31,284	33,657	+2,373	13
461,167	489,512	+28,845	437,902	464,124	+26,222	

Showing the variations in the population of the

PROVINCIAL TABLE VI.

Serial number of district.	Name of district.	Serial number of thána.	Name of thána.	Total Population. Census, 1881.	Census, 1891.	Increase + or Decrease —
1	2	3	4	5	6	7
36	Rae Bareli ...	1	Bachhrawan	81,903	95,642	+13,739
		2	Jagatpur	94,856	104,423	+9,567
		3	Digbijaiganj	102,256	123,939	+21,683
		4	Rae Bareli	119,435	113,229	—6,206
		5	Gurbakshganj	67,464	78,688	+11,224
		6	Mau	86,962	101,452	+14,490
		7	Mohanganj	107,896	119,076	+11,180
		8	Salon	122,640	127,596	+4,956
		9	Dalmau	84,067	83,259	—808
		10	Sareni	84,426	89,217	+4,791
			Total ...	951,905	1,036,521	+84,616
37	Sitapur ...	1	Sidhauli	114,576	131,915	+17,339
		2	Kamálpur	51,626	58,006	+6,380
		3	Sitapur	104,151	108,669	+3,918
		4	Misrikh	90,526	92,299	+1,773
		5	Maholi	77,311	97,304	+19,993
		6	Hargam	42,087	51,002	+8,915
		7	Laharpur	123,783	139,980	+16,197
		8	Biswan	107,255	122,027	+14,772
		9	Tambour	63,573	83,697	+20,124
		10	Thangaon	65,159	62,662	—2,497
		11	Mahmudabad	117,604	127,852	+10,248
			Total ...	958,251	1,075,413	+117,162
38	Hardoi ...	1	Hardoi	106,021	117,384	+11,363
		2	Baghaoli	85,192	94,888	+9,696
		3	Bilgram	83,461	96,526	+13,065
		4	Tandiawan	64,520	74,678	+10,158
		5	Pihani	88,798	101,774	+12,976
		6	Beniganj	43,059	51,163	+8,104
		7	Sháhabad	101,976	113,427	+11,451
		8	Harpálpur	81,044	91,352	+10,308
		9	Pali	56,438	64,416	+7,978
		10	Mallawan	95,727	101,814	+6,087
		11	Sandila	111,370	127,312	+15,942
		12	Atrauli	70,024	78,477	+8,453
			Total ...	987,630	1,113,211	+125,581
39	Kheri ...	1	Bhira	46,374	51,966	+5,592
		2	Gola	77,200	94,022	+16,822
		3	Phulbehar	54,957	58,862	+3,905
		4	Nimgaon	57,345	65,008	+7,663
		5	Lakhimpur	136,900	143,032	+6,132
		6	Nighasan	101,231	101,067	—164
		7	Mitauli	65,197	72,366	+7,169
		8	Muhamdi	75,149	80,682	+5,533
		9	Pasgawan	52,775	59,060	+6,285
		10	Palia	30,714	34,542	+3,828
		11	Dhaurahra	75,076	73,858	—1,218
		12	Isanagar	59,004	69,150	+10,146
			Total ...	831,922	903,615	+71,693
40	Fyzabad ...	1	Ronahi	111,829	118,964	+7,135
		2	Milkipur	102,393	112,497	+10,104
		3	Maharájganj	96,746	109,563	+12,817
		4	Bikapur	120,002	132,616	+12,614
		5	Jalálpur	128,170	144,758	+16,588
		6	Tanda	140,402	165,609	+25,207
		7	Akbarpur	123,920	142,850	+18,930
		8	Rámnagar	108,275	125,767	+17,492
		9	Sadar, or Pura Kalandar ...	77,120	86,463	+9,343
		10	Ajudhia	22,885	24,165	+1,280
		11	Cantonments	5,099	6,235	+1,136
		12	Kotwáli	44,578	47,472	+2,894
			Total ...	1,081,419	1,216,959	+135,540

Police Circles since the previous Census—(*continued*).

PROVINCIAL TABLE VI.

Males.			Females.			Serial number of thána.
Census, 1881.	Census, 1891.	Increase + or Decrease—	Census, 1881.	Census, 1891.	Increase + or Decrease—	
8	9	10	11	12	13	14
40,310	47,949	+7,639	41,593	47,693	+6,100	1
47,004	51,562	+4,558	47,852	52,861	+5,009	2
50,084	61,645	+11,561	52,172	62,294	+10,122	3
59,030	56,757	—2,273	60,405	56,472	—3,933	4
33,109	38,946	+5,837	34,355	39,742	+5,387	5
42,490	50,686	+8,196	44,472	50,766	+6,294	6
51,845	58,475	+6,630	56,051	60,601	+4,550	7
60,860	62,766	+1,906	61,780	64,830	+3,050	8
41,182	40,992	—190	42,885	42,267	—618	9
40,992	43,202	+2,210	43,434	46,015	+2,581	10
466,906	512,980	+46,074	484,999	523,541	+38,542	
60,496	69,357	+8,861	54,080	62,558	+8,478	1
27,194	30,421	+3,227	24,432	27,585	+3,153	2
55,198	58,159	+2,961	49,553	50,510	+957	3
48,096	49,269	+1,173	42,430	43,030	+600	4
41,654	52,241	+10,587	35,657	45,063	+9,406	5
22,240	26,931	+4,691	19,847	24,071	+4,224	6
64,782	73,114	+8,332	59,001	66,866	+7,865	7
56,597	64,078	+7,481	50,658	57,949	+7,291	8
33,036	43,088	+10,052	30,537	40,609	+10,072	9
34,671	33,031	—1,640	30,488	29,631	—857	10
62,022	67,493	+5,471	55,582	60,359	+4,777	11
505,986	567,182	+61,196	452,265	508,231	+55,966	
57,722	64,258	+6,536	48,299	53,126	+4,827	1
46,229	51,081	+4,852	38,963	43,807	+4,844	2
44,387	51,488	+7,101	39,074	45,038	+15,964	3
34,401	39,737	+5,336	30,119	34,941	+4,822	4
47,635	54,443	+6,808	41,163	47,331	+6,168	5
22,826	27,596	+4,770	20,233	23,567	+3,334	6
54,535	60,639	+6,104	47,441	52,788	+5,347	7
44,418	49,785	+5,367	36,626	41,567	+4,941	8
31,029	35,122	+4,093	25,409	29,294	+3,885	9
53,492	53,852	+360	42,235	47,962	+5,727	10
58,155	66,802	+8,647	53,215	60,510	+7.295	11
36,875	41,694	+4,819	33,149	36,783	+3,634	12
				...		
531,704	596,497	+64,798	455,926	516,714	+60,788	
24,843	28,335	+3,492	21,531	23,631	+2,100	1
41,477	50,592	+9,115	35,723	43,430	+7,707	2
29,232	31,108	+1,876	25,725	27,754	+2,029	3
30,047	34,233	+4,186	27,298	30,775	+3,477	4
72,678	75,375	+2,697	64,222	67,657	+3,435	5
54,358	53,523	—835	46,873	47,544	+671	6
34,975	38,695	+3,720	30,222	33,671	+3,449	7
40,737	43,107	+2,370	34,412	37,575	+3,163	8
28,545	31,797	+3,252	24,230	27,263	+3,033	9
17,119	20,385	+3,266	13,595	14,157	+562	10
39,930	38,568	—1,362	35,146	35,290	+144	11
31,078	36,317	+5,239	27,926	32,833	+4,907	12
445,019	482,035	+37,016	386,903	421,580	+34,677	
55,671	58,027	+2,356	56,158	60,937	+4,779	1
50,574	55,380	+4,806	51.819	57,117	+5,298	2
48,999	54,894	+5,895	47,747	54,669	+6,922	3
59,233	65,413	+6,180	60,769	67,203	+6,434	4
65,764	78,835	+8,071	62,406	70,923	+8,517	5
70,585	83,233	+12,648	69,817	82,376	+12,559	6
63,194	72,374	+9,180	60,726	70,476	+9,750	7
54 860	63,731	+8,871	53,415	62,036	+8,621	8
37,810	42,514	+4,704	39,310	43,949	+4,639	9
12,339	13,491	+1,152	10,546	10,674	+128	10
3,725	4,398	+673	1,374	1,837	+463	11
23,420	25,312	+18,92	21,158	22,160	+1,002	12
546,174	612,602	+66,428	535,245	604,357	+69,112	

Showing the variations in the population of the

PROVINCIAL TABLE VI.

Serial number of district.	Name of district.	Serial number of thána.	Name of thána.	Total population. Census, 1881.	Census, 1891.	Increase + or Decrease —
1	2	3	4	5	6	7
41	Gonda ...	1	Andhiari	62,526	75,560	+13,034
		2	Itia Thok	78,531	91,690	+13,159
		3	Ramapur	75,245	82,475	+7,230
		4	Srinagar	48,041	57,069	+9,028
		5	Gonda	116,605	133,920	+17,315
		6	Colonelganj	102,222	111,047	+8,825
		7	Wazirganj	49,917	59,075	+9,158
		8	Nawábganj	55,279	61,825	+6,546
		9	Tarabganj	115,751	114,137	—1,614
		10	Paraspur	61,147	66,535	+5,388
		11	Utraula	114,322	138,433	+24,111
		12	Sadullanagar	59,182	80,096	+20,914
		13	Birpur	45,133	56,905	+11,772
		14	Balrámpur	76,672	82,098	+5,426
		15	Tulsipur	88,170	109,123	+20,953
		16	Lalia	67,841	78,896	+11,055
		17	Pachperwa	54,342	60,345	+6,003
			Total ...	1,270,926	1,459,229	+188,303
42	Bahraich ...	1	Kaisarganj	106,323	116,222	+9,899
		2	Fakharpur	70,754	83,471	+12,717
		3	Piagpur	91,883	109,460	+17,577
		4	Bahraich	111,233	127,494	+16,261
		5	Sisaya	57,991	66,774	+8,783
		6	Kherighát	53,401	52,810	—591
		7	Nánpára	101,058	123,839	+22,781
		8	Malhipur	70,998	80,489	+9,491
		9	Motipur	51,610	55,053	+3,443
		10	Sujauli	13,457	17,531	+4,074
		11	Ikauna	49,618	58,395	+8,777
		12	Bhinga	99,722	108,894	+9,172
			Total ...	878,048	1,000,432	+122,384
43	Sultánpur ...	1	Sultánpur	100,669	114,844	+14,175
		2	Piparpur	67,177	73,693	+6,516
		3	Musáfirkhána	86,891	98,879	+11,988
		4	Lambhua	78,416	87,252	+8,836
		5	Haliapur	57,647	67,411	+9,764
		6	Jaisingpur	71,926	81,077	+9,151
		7	Kurebhar	66,820	75,707	+8,887
		8	Jagdispur	80,959	91,769	10,810
		9	Bazár Sukul	31,024	34,561	+3,537
		10	Gauriganj	59,842	65,084	+5,242
		11	Raipur	97,526	108,574	+11,048
		12	Kadipur	85,348	94,986	+9,638
		13	Dostpur	73,667	82,014	+8,347
			Total ...	957,912	1,075,851	+117,939
44	Partábgarh ...	1	Macandrewganj	121,248	125,576	+4,328
		2	Ràniganj	90,453	96,427	+5,974
		3	Katka Manapur	38,637	42,700	+4,063
		4	Jothwara	133,845	148,214	+14,369
		5	Sangipur	101,846	112,550	+10,704
		6	Kunda	123,088	130,660	+7,572
		7	Sangramgarh	101,492	109,941	+8,449
		8	Patti	128,177	135,345	+7,168
			*Sorson**	212	210	—2
			*Machhlisahahr**	6,343	7,209	+866
			*Sikandra**	681	690	+9
			*Mau**	1,025	1,373	+348
			Total ...	847,047	910,895	+63,848
45	Bara Banki ...	1	Nawábganj	150,909	170,324	+19,415
		2	Zaidpur	91,880	101,686	+9,806
		3	Kursi	80,665	99,893	+19,228
		4	Rámnagar	113,586	117,173	+3,587
		5	Tikaitnagar	118,478	117,839	—639
		6	Fatehpur	122,783	138,443	+15,660
		7	Ramsanehighát	106,051	117,997	+11,946
		8	Bhilsar	133,770	141,016	+7,246
		9	Haidergarh	108,666	126,535	+17,869
			Total ...	1,026,788	1,130,906	+104,118

* Criminal jurisdiction for the population shown as belonging to thánas Sorson, Sikandra and Mau is vested in the Magistrate

Police Circles since the previous Census—(*concluded*).

Males.			Females.			Serial number of thâna.
Census, 1881.	Census, 1891.	Increase + or Decrease—	Census, 1881.	Census, 1891.	Increase + or Decrease—	
8	9	10	11	12	13	14
32,169	39,266	+7,097	30,357	36,294	+5,937	1
39,593	46,176	+6,583	38,938	45,514	+6,576	2
38,422	41,763	+3,341	36,823	40,712	+3,889	3
24,577	29,155	+4,578	23,464	27,914	+4,450	4
60,049	68,348	+8,299	56,556	65,572	+9,016	5
52,146	57,033	+4,887	50,076	54,014	+3,938	6
26,207	30,253	+4,046	23,710	28,822	+5,112	7
29,320	32,499	+3,179	25,959	29,326	+3,367	8
58,528	57,220	—1,308	57,223	56,917	—306	9
31,146	33,598	+2,452	30,001	32,937	+2,936	10
58,654	70,787	+12,133	55,668	67,646	+1,1978	11
29,870	40,845	+10,975	29,312	39,251	+9,939	12
23,102	29,437	+6,335	22,031	27,468	+5,437	13
38,779	41,750	+2,971	37,893	40,348	+2,455	14
45,571	56,275	+10,704	42,599	52,848	+10,249	15
34,833	41,151	+6,318	33,008	37,745	+4,737	16
27,805	30,847	+3,042	26,537	29,498	+2,961	17
650,771	746,403	+95,632	620,155	712,826	+92,671	
55,680	60,329	+4,649	50,643	55,893	+5,250	1
37,180	43,684	+6 504	33,574	39,787	+6,213	2
47,194	56,622	+9,428	44,689	52,838	+8,149	3
58,690	67,027	+8,337	52,543	60,467	+7,924	4
30,657	34,941	+4,284	27,334	31,833	+4,499	5
28,313	27,237	−1,076	26,088	26,573	+485	6
52,157	64,663	+12.506	48,901	59,176	+10,275	7
36,847	41,847	+5,000	34,151	38,642	+4,491	8
27,573	29,562	+1,989	24.037	25,491	+1,454	9
7,322	10,397	+3,075	6,135	7,134	+999	10
25,673	30,356	+4,683	23,945	28,039	+4,094	11
51,901	56,902	+5,001	47,821	51,992	+4,171	12
459,187	523,567	+64,380	418,861	476,865	+58,004	
49,291	55,630	+6,339	51,378	59,214	+7,836	1
33,098	35,788	+2,690	34,079	37,905	+3,826	2
42,003	47,927	+5,924	44,888	50,952	+6,064	3
39,794	43,569	+3,775	38,622	43,683	+5,061	4
28,180	32,982	+4,802	29,467	34,429	+4,962	5
36,499	40,995	+4,496	35,427	40,082	×4,655	6
33,317	37,128	+3,811	33,503	38,579	+5,076	7
38,893	44,505	+5,612	42,066	47,264	+5,198	8
14,958	16,845	+1,887	16,066	17,716	+1650	9
29,399	31,855	+2,456	30,443	33,229	+2,786	10
47,221	52,608	+5,387	50,305	55,966	+5,661	11
44,258	48,803	+4,545	41,090	46,183	+5,093	12
38,214	41,851	+3,637	35,453	40,163	+4,710	13
475,125	530,486	+55,361	482,787	545,365	+62,578	
60,429	61,297	+868	60,819	64,279	+3,460	1
45,379	46,977	+1,598	45,074	49,450	+4,376	2
18,863	20,614	+1,751	19,774	22,086	+2,312	3
65,745	71,475	+5,730	68,100	76,739	+8,639	4
49,678	54,498	+4,820	52,168	58,052	+5,884	5
60,768	63,589	2,821	62,320	67,071	+4,751	6
50,274	54,249	+3,975	51,218	55,692	+4,474	7
65,388	67,721	+2,333	62,789	67,624	+4,835	8
112	112	...	100	98	—2	
3,240	3,627	+387	3,103	3,582	+479	
343	323	—20	338	367	+29	
511	689	+178	514	684	+170	
420,730	445,171	+24,441	426,317	465,724	+39,407	
78,449	88,155	+9,706	72,460	82,169	+9,709	1
46,393	51,606	+5,213	45,487	50,080	+4,593	2
42,203	52,321	+10,118	38,462	47,572	+9,110	3
60,086	61,834	+1,748	53,500	55,339	+1,839	4
61,016	60,439	—577	57,462	57,400	—62	5
64,272	72,272	+8.000	58,511	66,171	+7,660	6
52,672	59,064	+6,392	53,379	58,933	+5,554	7
65,620	68,866	+3,246	68,150	72,150	+4,000	8
52.870	62,558	+9,688	55,796	63,977	+8,181	9
523,581	577,115	+53,534	503,207	553,791	+50,584	

of Allahabad. For the population shown against thâna Machhlishahr it is vested in the Magistrate of Jaunpur.

PROVINCIAL TABLE VI.

Supplement.

SUPPLEMENT.

Showing the variations in the population of the Pattis of the Kumaun Division since the previous Census arranged according to mortuary circles.

Serial number of district.	Name of district.	Name of mortuary circle.	Serial number of patti.	Name of patti.	Total population. Census, 1881.	Total population. Census, 1891.	Total population. Increase + or Decrease —	Males. Census, 1881.	Males. Census, 1891.	Males. Increase + or Decrease —	Females. Census, 1881.	Females. Census, 1891.	Females. Increase + or Decrease —
1	2	3	4	5	6	7	8	9	10	11	12	13	14
46	Almora.	Almora Rural circles.	1	Goriphat	3,895	4,514	+619	2,024	2,330	+306	1,871	2,184	+313
			2	Talla Des	5,529	6,274	+745	2,779	3,171	+392	2,750	3,103	+353
			3	Danpur Malla ...	5,051	5,562	+511	2,554	2,801	+247	2,497	2,761	+264
			4	Danpur Bichla ...	2,904	3,342	+438	1,432	1,678	+246	1,472	1,664	+192
			5	Danpur Talla ...	4,780	5,408	+628	2,518	2,789	+271	2,262	2,619	+357
			6	Dug	3,567	4,208	+641	1,857	2,172	+315	1,710	2,036	+326
			7	Katyur Malla ...	5,122	7,218	+2,096	2,864	4,199	+1,335	2,258	3,019	+761
			8	Katyur Bichla ...	4,414	4,693	+279	2,578	2,423	—155	1,836	2,270	+434
			9	Katyur Talla ...	3,103	3,999	+896	1,661	2,062	+401	1,442	1,937	+495
			10	Nakuri	4,483	4,250	—233	2,353	2,147	—206	2,130	2,103	—27
			11	Darun	5,118	5,588	+470	2,664	2,935	+271	2,454	2,658	+199
			12	Kharain	1,783	2,164	+381	939	1,149	+210	844	1,015	+171
			13	Lakhanpur Malla ...	4,636	5,173	+537	2,370	2,708	+338	2,266	2,465	+199
			14	Lakhanpur Talla ...	3,488	4,592	+1,104	1,754	2,195	+441	1,734	2,397	+663
			15	Rithagarh	2,411	3,551	+1,140	1,254	1,824	+570	1,157	1,727	+570
			16	Rangor	5,616	7,249	+1,633	2,967	3,810	+843	2,649	3,439	+790
			17	Salam Malla ...	3,056	4,649	+1,593	1,592	2,280	+688	1,464	2,369	+905
			18	Salam Talla ...	3,693	4,246	+553	1,876	2,059	+183	1,817	2,187	+370
			19	Bel	5,582	6,737	+1,155	2,867	3,515	+648	2,715	3,222	+507
			20	Bherang	1,835	2,294	+459	931	1,149	+218	904	1,145	+241
			21	Baraun	6,520	7,668	+1,148	3,438	3.988	+550	3,082	3,680	+598
			22	Kamsyar	5,111	6,776	+1,665	2,671	3,531	+860	2,440	3,245	+805
			23	Pungraun	3,500	3,679	+179	1,854	1,846	—8	1,646	1,833	+187
			24	Athigaon	4,635	6,117	+1,482	2,424	3,178	+754	2,211	2,939	+728
			25	Bisaund Malla ...	1,102	1,388	+286	549	663	+114	553	725	+172
			26	Boraraw Palla ...	5,387	6,034	+647	2,778	3,149	+371	2,609	2,885	+276
			27	Boraraw Walla ...	4,252	4,762	+510	2,224	2,389	+165	2,028	2,373	+345
			28	Dwarsyun	1,389	1,068	—321	708	482	—226	681	586	—95
			29	Kairarau	4.009	4,316	+307	2,060	2,211	+151	1,949	2,105	+156
			30	Kaligarh	2,301	2,439	+138	1,153	1,183	+30	1,148	1,256	+108
			31	Khasparja	12,305	13,459	+1,154	6,999	6,722	—277	5,306	6,737	+1,431
			32	Uchyur	3,511	3,797	+286	1,768	1,857	+89	1,743	1,940	+197
			33	Ryuni	1,105	1,064	- 41	531	534	+3	574	530	—44
			34	Syunara Malla ...	4,542	5,385	+843	2,146	2,721	+575	2,396	2,664	+268
			35	Syunara Talla ...	5,048	6,015	+967	2,593	3,125	+532	2,455	2,890	+435
			36	Tikhun Malla ...	3,624	4,585	+961	1,745	2,237	+492	1,879	2,348	+469
			37	Tikhun Talla ...	3,903	4,711	+808	1,887	2,263	+376	2,016	2,448	+432
			38	Athaguli Palla ...	4,343	7,286	+2,943	2,042	3,957	+1,915	2,301	3,329	+1,028
			39	Athaguli Walla ...	3,470	2,909	—561	1,709	1,783	+74	1,761	1,126	—635
			40	Chaugaon	2,660	2,832	+172	1,265	1,364	+99	1,395	1,468	+73
			41	Dhuraphat ...	539	1,666	+1,127	253	828	+575	286	838	+552
			42	Kandarkhua ...	1,914	2,319	+405	944	1,163	+219	970	1,156	+186
			43	Malli Doti ...	7,210	4,894	—2,316	5.257	2,812	—2,445	1,953	2,082	+129
			44	Chaukot Malla ...	7,061	7,931	+870	3,518	3,897	+379	3,543	4,034	+491
			45	Chaukot Bichla ...	7,621	8,887	+1,266	3,765	4,333	+568	3,856	4,554	+698
			46	Chaukot Talla ...	7,497	7,450	—47	3,706	3,646	—60	3,791	3,804	+13
			47	Dora Malla ...	6,497	6,868	+371	3,234	3,390	+156	3,263	3,478	+215
			48	Dora Bichla ...	5,619	5,875	+256	2,741	2,823	+82	2,878	3,052	+174
			49	Dora Talla ...	6,509	7,629	+1,120	3,228	3,789	+561	3,281	3,840	+559
			50	Giwar Palla ...	6,252	6,595	+343	3,140	3,346	+206	3,112	3,249	+137
			51	Giwar Talla ...	6,573	7,342	+769	3,212	3,649	+437	3,361	3,693	+332
			52	Giwar Walla ...	5,228	5,905	+677	2,601	2,981	+380	2,627	2,974	+347
			53	Kaklasaun Malla ...	5,724	6,546	+822	2,741	3,107	+366	2,983	3439	+456
			54	Kaklasaun Talla ...	1,474	1,816	+342	715	895	+180	759	921	+162
			55	Naya Palla ...	4,746	5,360	+614	2,354	2,673	+319	2,392	2,687	+295
			56	Naya Walla ...	3,736	4,514	+778	1,699	2,165	+466	2,037	2,349	+312
			57	Silaur Malla ...	3,693	4,591	+898	1,860	2,206	+346	1,833	2,385	+552
			58	Silaur Talla ...	4,364	4,707	+343	2,142	2,258	+116	2,222	2,449	+227
			59	Salt Malla	6,195	7,247	+1,052	3,032	3,577	+545	3,163	3,670	+507
			60	Salt Palla	4,828	5,348	+520	2,349	2,624	+275	2,479	2,724	+245
			61	Salt Talla	7,127	7,564	+437	3,616	3,717	+101	3,511	3,847	+336
			62	Salt Walla	5,590	5,845	+255	2,765	2,870	+105	2,825	2,975	+150
				Total, Almora Rural Circle.	278,780	318,900	+40,120	1,43,250	61,278	+18,028	135,530	157,622	+2,2092
		Champawat Rural circle.	63	Chalsi	3,690	4,648	+958	1,789	2,297	+508	1,901	2,351	+450
			64	Charal Malla ...	367	448	+81	192	230	+38	175	218	+43
			65	Charal Talla ...	731	500	—231	452	272	—180	279	228	—51
			66	Gumdes	4,926	5,611	+685	2,534	2,770	+236	2,392	2,841	+449
			67	Gungol	...	1,562	1,562	...	791	+791	..	771	+771
			68	Khilpatti Phat ...	1,504	1,880	+376	712	913	+201	792	967	+175
			69	Palbilon Malla ...	977	994	+17	500	504	+4	477	490	+13
			70	Palbilon Talla ...	4,573	4,249	—324	2,430	2,230	—200	2,143	2,019	—124
			71	Pharka	...	16	+16	...	7	+7	...	9	+9
			72	Regruban	5,039	5,696	+657	2,566	2,926	+360	2,473	2,770	+297
			73	Sipti	787	645	—142	434	317	—117	353	328	—25
			74	Sui Bisung ...	226	610	+384	160	370	+210	66	240	+174
			75	Asi	...	355	+355	...	162	+162	...	193	+193
			76	Talli Rao	2,951	1,640	—1,311	1,492	798	—694	1,459	842	—617
			77	Talla Des ...	5,562	4,697	—865	2,820	2,438	—382	2,742	2,259	—483
				Total, Champawat Rural Circle.	31,333	33,551	+2,218	16,081	17,025	+944	15,262	16,526	+1,274

SUPPLEMENT.

Showing the variations in the population of the Pattis of the Kumaun Division since the previous Census arranged according to mortuary circles—(continued).

PROVINCIAL TABLE VI. Supplement.

Serial number of district.	Name of district.	Name of mortuary circle.	Serial number of patti.	Name of patti.	Total population. Census, 1881.	Total population. Census, 1891.	Total population. Increase + or Decrease —.	Males. Census, 1881.	Males. Census, 1891.	Males. Increase + or Decrease —.	Females. Census, 1881.	Females. Census, 1891.	Females. Increase + or Decrease —.
1	2	3	4	5	6	7	8	9	10	11	12	13	14
46	Almora—(concluded).	Sor Rural Circle.	78	Byans	...	115	+115	...	57	+57	...	58	+58
			79	Chandans	...	1,296	+1,296	...	602	+602	...	694	+694
			80	Darma Malla ...	...	217	+217	...	111	+111	...	106	+106
			81	Darma Talla ...	...	885	+885	...	457	+457	...	428	+428
			82	Athbisi Malla ...	1,162	1,044	—118	591	518	—73	571	526	—45
			83	Athbisi Talla ...	1,041	1,118	+77	564	577	+13	477	541	+64
			84	Barabisi	4,092	5,129	+1,037	2 114	2,641	+527	1,978	2,488	+510
			85	Dindihat	2,473	2,902	+429	1,262	1,490	+228	1,211	1,412	+201
			86	Mali	2,641	3,303	+662	1,328	1,711	+383	1,313	1,592	+279
			87	Askot Malla ...	3,228	5,783	+2,555	1,662	2,780	+1,118	1,566	3,003	+1,437
			88	Askot Talla ...	5,409	6,387	+978	2,789	3,221	+432	2,620	3,166	+546
			89	Kharaynt ...	2,751	3,087	+336	1,404	1,617	+213	1,347	1,470	+123
			90	Khark Des ...	935	1,221	+286	480	638	+158	455	583	+128
			91	Mahar ...	4,472	4,827	+355	2,309	2,287	—22	2,163	2,540	+377
			92	Naya Des	2,748	3,245	+497	1,397	1,630	+233	1,351	1,615	+264
			93	Rawal	2,327	3,313	+986	1,152	1,762	+610	1,175	1,551	+376
			94	Seti Malla	432	491	+59	214	245	+31	218	246	+28
			95	Seti Talla	2,892	3,494	+602	1,490	1,783	+293	1,402	1,711	+309
			96	Saun	2,925	3,537	+612	1,508	1,804	+296	1,417	1,733	+316
			97	Waldia Malla ...	979	1,567	+588	543	818	+275	436	749	+313
			98	Waldia Bichla ...	896	984	+88	456	483	+27	440	501	+61
			99	Waldia Talla ...	4,159	5,105	+946	2,128	2,578	+450	2,031	2,527	+496
				Total, Sor Rural Circle	45,562	59,050	+13,488	23,391	29,810	+6,419	22,171	29,240	+7,069
				Total, Almora district ...	355,675	411,501	+55,826	182,722	208,113	+25,391	172,953	203,388	+30,435
47	Garhwál.	Dasoli Painkhanda circle.	1	Painkhanda Malla ...	3,906	2,556	—1,350	1,987	1,260	—727	1,919	1,296	—623
			2	Painkhanda Talla ...	3,607	2,324	—1,283	1,795	1,158	—637	1,812	1,166	—646
			3	Dasoli Malla ...	2,524	3,299	+775	1,229	1,579	+350	12,95	1,720	+425
			4	Dasoli Talla ...	7,519	10,476	+2,957	3,786	5,054	+1,268	3,733	5,422	+1,689
				Total, Dasoli Painkhanda circle.	17,556	18,655	+1,099	8,797	9,051	+254	8,759	9,604	+845
		Badhan circle.	5	Pindárwár ...	7,443	8,911	+1,468	3,690	4,375	+685	3,753	4,536	+783
			6	Pindarpar ...	8,576	10,116	+1,540	4,320	5,077	+757	4,256	5,039	+783
			7	Kapiri ...	2,236	2,770	+534	1,097	1,369	+272	1,139	1,401	+262
			8	Karakot ...	2,885	3,387	+502	1,461	1,650	+189	1,424	1,737	+313
			9	Nandák ...	3,791	4,464	+673	1,903	2,200	+297	1,888	2,264	+376
			10	Khansar ...	761	1,084	+323	382	508	+126	379	576	+197
				Total, Badhan circle	25,692	30,732	+5,040	12,853	15,179	+2,326	12,939	15,553	+2,714
		Nagpur circle.	11	Bamsu	1,483	1,479	—4	673	594	—79	810	885	+75
			12	Maikhanda ...	1,275	1,437	+162	650	726	+76	625	711	+86
			13	Parkandi with Urgam villages.	2,549	3,051	+502	1,254	1,496	+242	1,295	1,555	+260
			14	Kaliphat Malla ...	3,723	4,248	+525	1,878	2,116	+238	1,845	2,132	+287
			15	Kaliphat Talla ...	8,724	10,547	+1,823	4,336	5,074	+738	4,388	5,473	+1,085
			16	Nagpur Talla ...	8,516	10,079	+1,563	4,265	4,894	+629	4,251	5 185	+934
			17	Nagpur Bichla ...	10,591	12,922	+2,331	5,305	6,288	+983	5,286	6,634	+1,348
			18	Nagpur Malla ...	5,439	8,068	+2,629	2,632	3,898	+1,266	2,807	4,170	+1,363
				Total, Nagpur circle	42,300	51,831	+9,531	20,998	25,086	+4,093	21,307	26,745	+5,438
		Chandpur circle.	19	Chandpur Sili ...	5,144	6,151	+1,007	2,490	2,974	+484	2,654	3,177	+523
			20	Sirgur	1,938	2,508	+570	970	1,210	+240	968	1,298	+330
			21	Chandpur Taili ...	5,911	7,049	+1,138	2,873	3,292	+419	3,038	3,757	+719
			22	Lohba	6,734	8,100	+1,366	3,283	3,905	+622	3,451	4,195	+744
			23	Chauthan	4,714	5,049	+335	2,339	2,455	+116	2,375	2,594	+219
			24	Choprakot	7,375	9,092	+1,717	3,577	4 378	+801	3,798	4,714	+916
			25	Dhaijyuli	2,398	2,757	+359	1,168	1,334	+166	1,230	1,423	+193
			26	Ranigadh	1,275	1,392	+117	636	669	+33	639	723	+84
				Total, Chandpur circle	35,489	42,098	+6,609	17,336	20,217	+2,881	18,153	21,881	+3,728

PROVINCIAL TABLE VI.

Supplement.

SUPPLEMENT.

Showing the variations in the population of the Puttis of the Kumaun Division since the previous Census arranged according to mortuary circles—(continued).

Serial number of district.	Name of district.	Name of mortuary circle.	Serial number of patti.	Name of patti.	Total Population. Census, 1881.	Total Population. Census, 1891.	Total Population. Increase + or Decrease —.	Males. Census, 1881.	Males. Census, 1891.	Males. Increase + or Decrease —.	Females. Census, 1881.	Females. Census, 1891.	Females. Increase + or Decrease —.
1	2	3	4	5	6	7	8	9	10	11	12	13	14
47	Garhwál—(continued).	Dewalgarh circle.	27	Chalan Syun ...	4,188	5,161	+973	2,040	2,549	+509	2,148	2,612	+464
			28	Bachhan Syun ...	3,225	4,021	+796	1,637	1,967	+330	1,588	2,054	+466
			29	Dhanpur ...	5,206	6,160	+954	2,571	3,085	+514	2,635	3,075	+440
			30	Bidol Syun ...	1,370	1,707	+337	682	842	+160	688	865	+177
			31	Ghurdur Syun ...	3,829	4,781	+952	1,823	2,306	+483	2,006	2,475	+469
			32	Kandar Syun ...	5,601	6,673	+1,072	2,662	3,205	+543	2,939	3,468	+529
			33	Kathul Syun ...	3,769	4,378	+609	1,773	2,053	+280	1,996	2,325	+329
				Total, Dewalgarh circle	27,188	32,881	+5,693	13,188	16,007	+2,819	14,000	16,874	+2,874
		Barah Syun circle.	34	Nandal Syun ...	3,141	3,940	+799	1,615	2,145	+530	1,526	1,795	+269
			35	Gagwar Syun ...	3,458	4,151	+693	1,663	2,028	+365	1,795	2,123	+328
			36	Paidul Syun ...	4,368	4,677	+309	2,107	2,224	+117	2,261	2,453	+192
			37	Maniyar Syun ...	5,925	7,169	+1,244	2,935	3,425	+490	2,990	3,744	+754
			38	Aswal Syun ...	6,418	7,139	+721	3,090	3,285	+195	3,328	3,854	+526
			39	Kandwal Syun ...	1,709	2,157	+448	848	1,050	+202	861	1,107	+246
			40	Bangarh Syun ...	1,896	2,356	+460	927	1,164	+237	969	1,192	+223
			41	Banel Syun ...	5,015	5,322	+307	2,486	2,563	+77	2,529	2,759	+230
			42	Patwal Syun ...	1,688	1,834	+146	832	886	+54	856	948	+92
			43	Kaphol Syun ...	3,237	3,866	+629	1,606	1,856	+250	1,631	2,010	+379
			44	Khat Syun ...	2,499	2,970	+471	1,206	1,402	+196	1,293	1,568	+275
			45	Idwal Syun ...	3,528	4,404	+876	1,734	2,125	+391	1,794	2,279	+485
			46	Siton Syun ...	4,286	5,186	+900	2,094	2,545	+451	2,192	2,641	+449
			47	Rawat Syun ...	1,052	1,294	+242	495	611	+116	557	683	+126
				Total, Barah Syun circle	48,220	56,465	+8,245	23.638	27,309	+3,671	24,582	29,156	+4,574
		Srinagar circle.	48	Srinagar ...	2,100	2,386	+286	1,046	1,228	+182	1,054	1,158	+104
				Total, Srinagar circle	2,100	2,386	+286	1,046	1,228	+182	1,054	1,158	+104
		Chaund Kot circle.	49	Maundar Syun ...	6,367	6,834	+467	3,048	3,188	+140	3,319	3,646	+327
			50	Mawal Syun ...	4,665	5,360	+695	2,234	2,537	+303	2,431	2,823	+392
			51	Ringwar Syun ...	1,778	1,993	+215	825	921	+96	953	1,072	+119
			52	Jaintol Syun ...	2,082	2,426	+344	1,026	1,211	+185	1,056	1,215	+159
			53	Kimgaddigad ...	3,245	3,881	+636	1,557	1.898	+341	1,688	1,983	+295
			54	Pinglapakha ...	1,466	1,711	+245	735	844	+109	731	867	+136
			55	Gurar Syun ...	3,800	4,368	+568	1,852	2,022	+170	1,948	2,346	+398
				Total, Chaundkot circle	23,403	26,573	+3,170	11,277	12,621	+1,344	12,126	13,952	+1,826
		Malla Salan circle.	56	Talain	4,521	5,330	+809	2,155	2,540	+385	2,366	2,790	+424
			57	Saindhar ...	1,641	1,879	+238	814	920	+106	827	959	+132
			58	Gujru ...	3,811	4,255	+444	1,873	2,076	+203	1,938	2,179	+241
			59	Dhaundyal Syun ...	2,367	2,837	+470	1,151	1,349	+198	1,216	1,488	+272
			60	Sabli ...	6,812	8,052	+1,240	3,300	3,888	+588	3,512	4,164	+652
			61	Meldhar ...	747	787	+40	372	375	+3	375	412	+37
			62	Bangar Syun ...	2,330	2,673	+343	1,149	1,295	+146	1,181	1,378	+197
			63	Kolagad ...	1,498	1,945	+447	764	971	+207	734	974	+240
			64	Khatli ...	9,866	11,502	+1,636	4,797	5,586	+789	5,069	5,916	+847
			65	Iriakot ...	7,532	8,334	+802	3,706	3,954	+248	3,826	4,380	+554
				Total, Malla Salan circle	41,125	47,594	+6,469	20.081	22,054	+2,873	21,044	24,640	+3,596
		Talla Salan circle.	66	Sila Talla ...	1,519	1,940	+421	718	988	+270	801	952	+151
			67	Sila Malla ...	5,078	5,774	+696	2,459	2.843	+384	2,619	2,931	+312
			68	Painun ...	7,069	7,241	+172	3.396	3,445	+49	3.673	3,796	+123
			69	Bijlot Walla ...	4,042	3,374	—668	1,983	1,638	—345	2,059	1,736	—323
			70	Bijlot Palla ...	3,050	4,248	+1,198	1,525	2,052	+527	1,525	2,196	+671
			71	Badalpur Malla ...	5,974	6,823	+849	2,969	3,209	+240	3,005	3,614	+609
			72	Badalpur Talla ...	2,724	2,890	+166	1,318	1,375	+57	1,406	1,515	+109
			73	Kauria Walla ...	1,991	2,248	+257	999	1,130	+131	992	1,118	+126
			74	Kauria Palla ...	336	425	+89	156	202	+46	180	223	+43
			75	Bungi ...	4,308	4,351	+43	2,119	2,101	—18	2,189	2,250	+61
			76	Bhabar villages and Forests Garhwal Division.	1,369	4,285	+2,916	897	2,597	+1,700	472	1,688	+1,216
				Total, Talla Salan circle	37,460	43,599	+6,139	18,539	21,580	+3,041	18,921	22,019	+3,098

SUPPLEMENT.

Showing the variations in the population of the Pattis of the Kumaun Division since the previous Census and arranged according to mortuary circles—(concluded).

PROVINCIAL TABLE VI. Supplement.

Serial number of district.	Name of district.	Name of mortuary circle.	Serial number of patti.	Name of patti.	Total population. Census, 1881.	Total population. Census, 1891.	Total population. Increase + or Decrease —.	Males. Census, 1881.	Males. Census, 1891.	Males. Increase + or Decrease —.	Females. Census, 1881.	Females. Census, 1891.	Females. Increase + or Decrease —.
1	2	3	4	5	6	7	8	9	10	11	12	13	14
47	Garhwál—(concluded).	Ganga Salan circle.	77	Dhangu Malla ...	5,953	6,395	+442	2,904	2,937	+33	3,049	3,458	+409
			78	Dhangu Talla ...	4,806	5,003	+197	2,377	2,416	+39	2,429	2,587	+158
			79	Ajmir	5,189	5,942	+753	2,575	2,838	+263	2,614	3,104	+490
			80	Langur	6,253	7,308	+1,055	3,053	3,478	+425	3,200	3,830	+630
			81	Karoundu Walla ...	1,906	2,115	+209	905	984	+79	1,001	1,133	+130
			82	Karoundu Palla ...	1,666	2,105	+439	810	983	+173	856	1,122	+266
			83	Udaipur Malla ...	3,113	3,583	+470	1,549	1,750	+201	1,564	1,833	+269
			84	Udaipur Bichla ...	6,446	7,029	+583	3,111	3,320	+209	3,335	3,709	+374
			85	Udaipur Talla ...	6,986	8,030	+1,044	3,522	3,968	+446	3,464	4,062	+598
			86	Bhabar villages and forests, Ganges Division.	2,314	5,434	+3,120	1,871	4,744	+2,873	443	690	+247
				Total, Ganga Salan circle	44,632	52,944	+8,312	22,677	27,418	+4,741	21,956	25,526	+3,571
		Kotdwara circle.	87	Kotdwara	464	706	+242	330	492	+162	134	214	+80
				Total, Kotdwara circle	464	706	+242	330	492	+162	134	214	+80
		Lansdowne circle.	88	Lansdowne ...	...	1,354	1,354	...	1,177	1,177	...	177	177
				Total, Lansdowne circle	...	1,354	1,354	...	1,177	1,177	...	177	177
				Total, District Garhwál	345,629	407,818	+62,189	170,755	200,319	+29,564	174,874	207,499	+32,625
48	Naini Tal.	Naini Tal rural circle.	1	Jaspur	30,288	30,125	−163	16,520	16,192	−328	13,768	13,933	+165
			2	Kashipur	44,685	43,043	−1,642	23,827	22,831	−996	20,858	20,212	−646
			3	Bazpur	33,932	32,554	−1,378	18,592	17,890	−702	15,340	14,664	−676
			4	Gadarpur	18,982	18,855	−127	10,471	10,683	+212	8,511	8,172	−339
			5	Rudarpur	30,116	29,556	−560	16,854	16,288	−566	13,262	13,268	+6
			6	Kilpuri	48,990	56,435	+7,445	27,051	31,576	+4,525	21,939	24,859	+2,920
				Total ...	206,993	210,568	+3,575	113,315	115,460	+2,145	93,678	95,108	+1,430
			7	Chakhata	13,028	21,895	+8,867	8,676	14,920	+6,244	4,352	6,975	+2,623
			8	Kota Malla ...	1,269	1,797	+528	698	981	+283	571	816	+245
			9	Kota Talla ...	2,805	2,167	−638	1,764	1,127	−637	1,041	1,040	−1
			10	Malla Kosian ...	1,489	1,048	−441	782	510	−272	707	538	−169
			11	Talla Kosian ...	1,278	1,467	+189	611	747	+136	667	720	+53
			12	Dhaniakot ...	753	1,250	+497	453	745	+292	300	505	+205
			13	Uchakot	1,690	2,309	+619	804	1,166	+362	886	1,143	+257
			14	Chauthan	1,751	3,366	+1,615	888	1,619	+731	863	1,747	+884
			15	Ramgarh Talla ...	13	16	+3	4	7	+3	9	9	...
			16	Ramgarh Malla ...	177	289	+112	114	218	+104	63	71	+8
			17	Agar	116	245	+129	65	129	+64	51	116	+65
			18	Kotauli Malli ...	671	1,148	+477	322	583	+261	349	565	+216
			19	Kotauli Talli ...	845	736	−109	415	360	−55	430	376	−54
			20	Bisaud Talla ...	187	152	−35	94	85	−9	93	67	−26
			21	Bisaud Bichla ...	370	446	+76	179	217	+38	191	229	+38
			22	Mahruri Malli ...	169	15	−154	89	9	−80	80	6	−74
			23	Mahruri Talli ...	200	600	+400	115	366	+251	85	234	+149
			24	Mahrauri Bichli ...	85	310	+225	36	176	+140	49	134	+85
			25	Chaubansi	152	202	+50	75	99	+24	77	103	+26
			26	Chhabbis Dumola ...	1,629	1,602	−27	857	844	−13	772	758	−14
			27	Bisjula	974	1,171	+197	510	571	+61	464	600	+136
			28	Malli Rao	1,145	798	−347	585	380	−140	610	412	−198
			29	Chaugarh	3,084	3,102	+18	1,652	1,671	+19	1,432	1,431	−1
			30	Bhábár Chakhata ...		33,202			18,777			14,425	
			31	Bhábár Chaubansi ...		4,566			2,506			2,060	
			32	Bhábár Chilkia ...	104,086	20,158	+1,468	58,594	11,103	+714	45,492	9,055	+749
			33	Bhábár Kota ...		39,806			22,664			17,142	
			34	Bhábár Talla Des ...		7,817			4,258			3,559	
				Total, Naini Tal Rural Circle.	137,966	151,680	+13,714	78,332	86,844	+8,512	59,634	64,836	+5,202
				Total, District Naini Tal	344,959	362,248	+17,289	191,647	202,304	+10,657	153,312	159,944	+6,632

PROVINCIAL TABLE VII.

SHOWING THE POPULATION OF THE POLICE CIRCLES DISTRIBUTED BY RELIGION.

Showing the population of the Police

PROVINCIAL TABLE VII.

Serial number of district.	Name of district.	Serial number of thána.	Name of thána.	Total population. Both sexes.	Total population. Males.	Total population. Females.	Hindus. Both sexes.	Hindus. Males.	Hindus. Females.
1	2	3	4	5	6	7	8	9	10
1	Debra Dún ...	1	Dehra	60,141	35,953	24,188	47,830	28,454	19,376
		2	Rájpur	9,626	5,502	4,124	8,573	4,866	3,707
		3	Mussoorie	10,806	7,537	3,269	7,916	5,449	2,467
		4	Sahaspur	23,577	13,657	9,920	17,865	10,295	7,570
		5	Kalsi	49,188	27,270	21,918	48,779	26,999	21,780
		6	Chakráta	1,509	1,165	344	791	647	144
		7	Bhogpur	13,288	9,240	4,048	11,964	8,217	3,747
			Total ...	168,135	100,324	67,811	143,718	84,927	58,791
2	Sahâranpur ...	1	Sahâranpur	140,164	74,839	65,325	74,341	40,436	33,905
		2	Rámpur	52,277	28,161	24,116	40,035	21,628	18,407
		3	Behat	55,849	29,182	26,667	34,578	18,169	16,409
		4	Muzaffarabad	35,509	18,572	16,937	23,676	12,379	11,297
		5	Mirzapur	19,632	10,329	9,303	10,193	5,433	4,760
		6	Fatehpur	41,484	21,564	19,920	28,530	14,793	13,737
		7	Mohand	13,394	7,436	5,958	11,061	6,061	5,000
		8	Bhagwánpur	38,481	20,311	18,170	25,000	13,228	11,772
		9	Nágal	47,489	25,649	21,840	36,383	19,646	16,737
		10	Manglaur	67,527	36,365	31,162	47.533	25,879	21,654
		11	Dausnie	22,218	12,049	10,169	15,846	8,647	7,199
		12	Roorkee	67,999	37,427	30,572	40,135	21,990	18,145
		13	Jawálapur	70,119	39,896	30,223	52,602	30,463	22,139
		14	Sultánpur	16,712	9,131	7,581	13,399	7,373	6,026
		15	Badhgaon	34,601	19,558	15,043	30,595	17,339	13,256
		16	Nanauta	23,451	12,443	11,008	18,802	10,042	8,760
		17	Deoband	80,768	44,505	36,263	54,796	30,449	24,347
		18	Nukúr	52,217	28,155	24,062	38,166	20,919	17,247
		19	Gangoh	44,324	23,587	20,737	27,302	14,887	12,415
		20	Sirsáwa	27,278	14,739	12,539	18,520	10,084	8,436
		21	Chilkána	37,552	19,875	17,677	17,361	9,214	8,147
		22	Bassie	12,235	6,578	5,657	8,640	4,687	3,953
			Total ...	1,001,280	540,351	460,929	667,494	363,746	303,748
3	Muzaffarnagar.	1	Muzaffarnagar	64,310	35,939	28,371	40,653	22,819	17,834
		2	Titavi	50,872	27,578	23,294	38,422	20,916	17,506
		3	Charthâwal	40,140	22,097	18,043	28,401	15,707	12,694
		4	Púr	38,952	21,206	17,746	27,673	15,196	12,477
		5	Gordhanpur	12,016	6,665	5,351	10,553	5,859	4,694
		6	Shámli	57,060	30,900	26,160	46,344	25,029	21,315
		7	Thána Bhawan	43,560	23,262	20,298	28,404	15,476	12,928
		8	Jhinjhána	32,633	17,338	15,295	25,175	13,535	11,640
		9	Kairána	41,389	22,338	19,051	20,763	11,300	9,463
		10	Bidauli	13,321	7,320	6,001	8,305	4,596	3,709
		11	Jánsath	42,659	22,764	19,895	27,652	14,808	12,844
		12	Khátauli	69,916	37,605	32,311	49,767	26,798	22,969
		13	Bhopa	49,486	26,967	22,519	34,942	19,199	15,743
		14	Míránpur	40,259	21,316	18,943	29,251	15,636	13,615
		15	Burhána	46,019	24,776	21,243	31,294	16,978	14,316
		16	Sháhpur	51,440	27,807	23,633	37,549	20,481	17,068
		17	Kandhla	66,648	35,807	30,841	48,577	26,235	22,342
		18	Chausána	12,194	6,543	5,651	8,838	4,766	4,072
			Total ...	772,874	418,228	354,646	542,563	295,334	247,229
4	Meerut ...	1	City Station	90,617	49,592	41,025	49,774	27,320	22,454
		2	Kankar Khera	13,990	7,358	6,632	10,644	5,603	5,041
		3	Bazar Khera	27,799	14,648	13,151	19,813	10,495	9,318
		4	Mau Khas	25,339	13,425	11,914	19,266	10,263	9,003
		5	Jani	71,394	38,154	33,240	57,532	30,893	26,639
		6	Daurala	43,853	23,409	20,444	34,318	18,375	15,943
		7	Bubukpur	34,505	18,570	15,935	28,340	15,208	13,132
		8	Kharkhoda	41,028	21,425	19,603	28,715	15,131	13,584
		9	Begamabad	41,888	22,441	19,447	35,359	19,037	16,322
		10	Sadar Bazár	26,844	16,040	10,804	17,232	10,043	7,189
		11	Lál Kurti	18,909	11,529	7,380	9,596	5,476	4,120
		12	Dhaulana	44,364	23,616	20,748	33,411	17,982	15,429
		13	Pilkhua	32,194	16,959	15,235	22,225	11,758	10,467
		14	Gháziabad	43,276	23,031	20,245	31,972	17,155	14,817
		15	Murádnagar	42,429	22,558	19,881	34,176	18,201	15,975
		16	Shahdara	18,867	10,281	8,586	14,654	8,037	6,617
		17	Khekhra	24,697	13,162	11,535	121,130	11,213	9,917
		18	Loni	23,736	12,982	10,754	21,156	11,659	9,497
		19	Mowána	73,301	38,697	34,604	55,989	29,770	26,219
		20	Khanpur	6,914	3,881	3,033	5,869	3,292	2,577
		21	Parichhatgarh	50,328	26,768	23,560	37,991	20,250	17,741
		22	Behsuma	19,105	10,268	8,837	16,631	8,962	7,669
		23	Kithor	36,469	19,101	17,368	24,738	13,152	11,586
		24	Bághpat	50,808	27,827	22,981	42,477	23,309	19,168
		25	Baleni	26,794	14,282	12,512	22,736	12,136	10,600
		26	Lályana	21,459	11,548	9,911	17,111	9,247	7,864

Circles distributed by Religion.

PROVINCIAL TABLE VII.

Muhammadans.			Jains.			Christians.			Others.			Serial number of thána.
Both sexes.	Males.	Females.	Both sexes.	Males.	Females.	Both sexes.	Males.	Females.	Both sexes.	Males.	Females.	
11	12	13	14	15	16	17	18	19	20	21	22	23
10,222	6,283	3,939	134	86	48	907	412	495	1,048	718	330	1
936	566	370	8	8	...	78	39	39	31	23	8	2
1,700	1,318	382	18	10	8	1,113	702	411	59	58	1	3
5,128	3,043	2,085	19	17	2	393	208	185	172	94	78	4
350	231	119	28	19	9	13	6	7	18	15	3	5
428	329	99	24	19	5	217	124	93	49	46	3	6
1,132	890	242	3	2	1	22	13	9	167	118	49	7
19,896	12,660	7,236	234	161	73	2,743	1,504	1,239	1,544	1,072	472	
63,226	32,964	30,262	1,625	880	745	772	418	359	200	146	54	1
11,228	5,977	5,251	975	530	445	...	...	...	39	26	13	2
21,061	10,889	10,172	168	104	64	11	4	7	31	16	15	3
11,722	6,126	5,596	70	43	27	...	...	...	41	24	17	4
9,419	4,883	4,536	19	12	7	1	1	...	...	...	...	5
12,815	6,687	6,128	88	51	37	8	4	4	43	29	14	6
2,323	1,365	958	8	8	...	...	...	...	2	2	...	7
13,435	7,056	6,379	2	2	...	7	3	4	37	22	15	8
10,833	5,849	4,984	123	73	50	6	2	4	144	79	65	9
19,711	10,338	9,373	215	116	99	12	6	6	56	26	30	10
6,330	3,382	2,948	...	...	...	13	7	6	29	13	16	11
26,076	14,129	11,947	183	111	72	1,073	771	302	532	426	106	12
17,390	9,352	8,038	60	33	27	54	37	17	13	11	2	13
3,301	1,749	1,552	...	...	...	11	8	3	1	1	...	14
3,875	2,140	1,735	126	77	49	...	...	...	5	2	3	15
4,429	2,276	2,153	219	124	95	...	...	...	1	1	...	16
25,596	13,846	1,750	369	204	165	3	3	...	4	3	1	17
13,229	6,799	6,430	736	384	352	...	...	...	86	53	33	18
16,847	8,607	8,240	151	80	71	...	...	...	24	13	11	19
8,368	4,441	3,927	380	207	173	3	1	2	7	6	1	20
19,744	10,433	9,311	446	227	219	...	...	...	1	1	...	21
3,474	1,832	1,642	121	59	62	...	...	...	...	...	...	22
324,432	171,120	153,312	6,084	3,325	2,759	1,974	1,260	714	1,296	900	396	
22,394	12,349	10,045	726	438	288	80	49	31	457	284	173	1
12,136	6,478	5,658	283	169	114	...	...	...	31	15	16	2
11,429	6,211	5,218	156	97	59	...	...	...	154	82	72	3
11,136	5,926	5,210	129	70	59	...	...	...	14	14	...	4
1,460	805	655	3	1	2	...	...	...	...	...	...	5
10,098	5,508	4,590	181	102	79	5	4	1	432	257	175	6
14,965	7,682	7,283	148	74	74	8	8	...	35	22	13	7
7,250	3,681	3,569	180	100	80	...	...	...	28	22	6	8
19,715	10,539	9,176	889	480	409	...	...	...	22	19	3	9
4,981	2,703	2,278	35	21	14	...	...	...	...	...	...	10
14,548	7,673	6,875	428	262	166	...	...	...	31	21	10	11
18,204	9,715	8,489	1,802	1,002	800	11	7	4	132	83	49	12
14,282	7,617	6,665	262	151	111	...	...	...	...	...	...	13
10,902	5,622	5,280	94	50	44	10	6	4	2	2	...	14
13,694	7,224	6,470	1,013	563	450	...	...	...	18	11	7	15
13,140	6,920	6,220	692	373	319	...	...	...	59	33	26	16
15,394	8,125	7,269	2,281	1,251	1,030	13	7	6	383	189	194	17
3,262	1,726	1,536	94	51	43	...	...	...	...	...	...	18
218,990	116,504	102,486	9,396	5,255	4,141	127	81	46	1,798	1,054	744	
39,214	21,393	17,821	710	399	311	314	158	156	605	322	283	1
3,240	1,693	1,547	18	12	6	50	28	22	38	22	16	2
7,976	4,146	3,830	3	3	...	...	...	...	7	4	3	3
6,042	3,132	2,910	2	2	...	...	...	...	29	28	1	4
13,311	6,946	6,365	58	39	19	...	...	...	493	276	217	5
9,185	4,844	4,341	178	100	78	21	9	12	151	81	70	6
5,807	3,169	2,638	277	154	123	...	...	...	81	39	42	7
12,295	6,283	6,012	12	6	6	...	...	...	6	5	1	8
6,444	3,359	3,085	2	2	...	6	2	4	77	41	36	9
6,991	4,052	2,939	512	292	220	1,221	882	339	888	771	117	10
6,199	3,379	2,820	58	34	24	2,994	2,608	386	62	32	30	11
10,837	5,571	5,266	2	2	...	1	1	...	113	60	53	12
9,924	5,176	4,748	32	18	14	3	1	2	10	6	4	13
10,885	5,653	5,232	126	62	64	124	68	56	169	93	76	14
8,223	4,331	3,892	7	4	3	4	1	3	19	11	8	15
3,988	2,116	1,872	126	79	47	94	45	49	5	4	1	16
2,835	1,565	1,270	730	382	348	...	...	...	2	2	...	17
2,576	1,319	1,257	4	4	...	...	...	...	...	...	...	18
16,885	8,701	8,184	11	8	3	38	19	19	378	199	179	19
869	485	384	1	1	...	...	...	...	175	103	72	20
11,677	6,158	5,519	...	...	...	...	...	...	660	360	300	21
2,242	1,179	1,063	75	44	31	9	4	5	148	79	69	22
11,629	5,890	5,739	...	...	...	...	...	...	102	59	43	23
6,966	3,751	3,215	1,365	765	600	...	...	...	...	...	...	24
3,883	2,042	1,841	56	36	20	...	...	...	119	68	51	25
4,306	2,275	2,031	29	18	11	...	...	...	13	8	5	26

Showing the population of the Police

PROVINCIAL TABLE VII.

Serial number of district.	Name of district.	Serial number of thána.	Name of thána.	Total population. Both sexes.	Total population. Males.	Total population. Females.	Hindus. Both sexes.	Hindus. Males.	Hindus. Females.
1	2	3	4	5	6	7	8	9	10
4	Meerut—(*concluded*).	27	Chaprauli	45,041	24,311	*20,730*	34,983	18,909	*16,074*
		28	Baraut	90,215	48,772	*41,443*	72,599	39,354	*33,245*
		29	Sardhana	70,691	37,735	*32,956*	46,692	25,173	*21,519*
		30	Binauli	36,285	19,370	*16,915*	30,270	16,236	*14,034*
		31	Daha	40,679	22,048	*18,631*	31,461	17,006	*14,455*
		32	Hapur	81,421	42,938	*38,483*	61,640	32,585	*29,055*
		33	Bagsar	26,330	13,917	*12,413*	19,564	10,439	*9,125*
		34	Garhmuktesar	30,173	16,103	*14,070*	22,148	11,833	*10,315*
		35	Bahadurgarh	19,716	10,508	*9,208*	15,438	8,192	*7,246*
			Total ...	1,391,458	747,244	*644,214*	1,047,650	563,694	*483,956*
5	Bulandshahr ...	1	Jhajhar	52,779	28,088	*24,691*	44,595	23,800	*20,795*
		2	Sikandarabad	58,189	30,532	*27,657*	46,295	24,523	*21,772*
		3	Jarcha...	18,519	9,536	*8,983*	13,835	6,949	*6,886*
		4	Khúrja	75,575	39,659	*35,916*	54,379	28,771	*25,608*
		5	Gulaothi	57,519	30,087	*27,432*	42,450	22,261	*20,189*
		6	Bulandshahr	84,452	44,360	*40,092*	57,939	30,548	*27,391*
		7	Kasna	17,176	9,485	*7,691*	15,930	8,801	*7,129*
		8	Dankaur	31,090	16,702	*14,388*	25,268	13,586	*11,682*
		9	Surajpur	14,582	7,960	*6,622*	12,651	6,918	*5,733*
		10	Dádri	39,772	21,433	*18,339*	35,926	19,333	*16,593*
		11	Sarái Sadar	11,120	6,039	*5,081*	10,144	5,522	*4,622*
		12	Arnia	26,110	13,722	*12,388*	23,256	12,231	*11,025*
		13	Shikárpur	50,294	26,554	*23,740*	41,205	21,774	*19,431*
		14	Pahasu	54,892	28,986	*25,906*	45,509	24,059	*21,450*
		15	Dibai	64,253	33,838	*30,415*	53,084	28,104	*24,980*
		16	Jewar	36,807	19,466	*17,341*	32,083	17,011	*15,072*
		17	Anúpshahr	33,944	18,039	*15,905*	28,525	15,220	*13,305*
		18	Jahángirabad	54,689	28,623	*26,066*	43,334	22,739	*20,595*
		19	Ahar	18,825	10,013	*8,812*	16,251	8,623	*7,628*
		20	Khanpur	33,892	17,703	*16,189*	26,556	13,974	*12,582*
		21	Aurangabad	35,723	18,609	*17,114*	28,632	15,025	*13,607*
		22	Siyana...	61,205	32,218	*28,987*	50,449	26,659	*23,790*
		23	Rámghát	18,507	9,969	*8,538*	17,141	9,193	*7,948*
			Total ...	949,914	501,621	*448,293*	764,937	405,624	*359,313*
6	Aligarh ...	1	Jawan	34,823	18,567	*16,256*	31,541	16,756	*14,785*
		2	Somna	27,989	14,873	*13,116*	26,709	14,185	*12,524*
		3	Akrabad	69,323	37,248	*32,075*	58,755	31,807	*26,948*
		4	Koil	136,549	72,740	*63,809*	106,580	57,061	*49,519*
		5	Harduaganj	33,460	17,883	*15,577*	29,507	15,770	*13,737*
		6	Atrauli	67,782	35,705	*32,077*	57,760	30,493	*27,267*
		7	Barlah	24,045	12,715	*11,330*	19,580	10,403	*9,177*
		8	Dadon	53,920	29,450	*24,470*	46,382	25,438	*20,944*
		9	Gangiri	30,430	16,336	*14,094*	26,063	14,039	*12,024*
		10	Gonda	40,037	21,417	*18,620*	38,075	20,400	*17,675*
		11	Iglas	66,048	35,579	*30,469*	61,936	33,410	*28,526*
		12	Mursán	38,048	20,552	*17,496*	35,325	19,136	*16,189*
		13	Sikandra Rao	63,693	34,467	*29,226*	54,444	29,633	*24,811*
		14	Agsauli	25,657	14,010	*11,647*	23,987	13,126	*10,861*
		15	Salempur	15,575	8,487	*7,088*	14,584	7,952	*6,632*
		16	Hasayin	37,881	20,461	*17,420*	35,162	18,980	*16,182*
		17	Háthras	104,774	56,152	*48,622*	92,651	49,634	*43,017*
		18	Sásni	42,005	22,354	*19,651*	38,878	20,718	*18,160*
		19	Tappál	40,710	21,640	*19,070*	37,629	19,966	*17,663*
		20	Narainpur	22,668	12,081	*10,587*	21,224	11,328	*9,896*
		21	Chandaus	33,899	17,530	*16,369*	30,019	15,970	*14,049*
		22	Khair	34,856	18,496	*16,360*	31,944	16,988	*14,956*
			Total ...	1,043,172	558,743	*484,429*	918,730	493,188	*425,542*
7	Muttra ...	1	Ol	16,860	9,046	*7,814*	14,496	7,806	*6,690*
		2	Aríng	21,218	11,472	*9,746*	19,203	10,363	*8,840*
		3	Brindaban	35,287	18,392	*16,895*	33,807	17,518	*16,289*
		4	Jait	21,694	11,790	*9,904*	20,513	11,130	*9,383*
		5	Rasúlpur	7,509	4,135	*3,374*	7,123	3,922	*3,201*
		6	Sonkh	16,541	8,873	*7,668*	15,783	8,473	*7,310*
		7	Sadar Bazár	10,264	6,483	*3,781*	6,433	3,726	*2,707*
		8	Farah	22,387	12,178	*10,209*	19,595	10,668	*8,927*
		9	Gobardhan	20,068	10,569	*9,499*	17,385	9,104	*8,281*
		10	Muttra	67,764	35,786	*31,978*	57,776	30,458	*27,318*
		11	Chháta...	35,712	18,973	*16,739*	30,396	16,096	*14,300*
		12	Kosi	43,488	22,841	*20,647*	38,686	20,377	*18,309*
		13	Majhoi	10,463	5,605	*4,858*	8,121	4,400	*3,721*
		14	Barsana	20,866	11,014	*9,852*	19,584	10,279	*9,305*
		15	Sahar	24,077	12,601	*11,476*	22,560	11,792	*10,768*
		16	Shergarh	15,752	8,492	*7,260*	13,241	7,151	*6,090*
		17	Raya	51,424	27,993	*23,431*	48,556	26,462	*22,094*
		18	Surir	27,402	14,440	*12,962*	25,054	13,183	*11,871*
		19	Mát	25,362	13,576	*11,786*	24,050	12,866	*11,184*

Circles distributed by Religion—(*continued*).

PROVINCIAL TABLE VII.

Muhammadans.			Jains.			Christians.			Others.			Serial number of thána.
Both sexes.	Males.	Females.	Both sexes.	Males.	Females.	Both sexes.	Males.	Females.	Both sexes.	Males.	Females.	
11	12	13	14	15	16	17	18	19	20	21	22	23
8,412	4,487	3,925	1,470	799	671	22	16	6	154	100	54	27
13,968	7,444	6,524	3,488	1,883	1,605	24	12	12	136	81	55	28
20,077	10,465	9,612	3,180	1,733	1,447	439	200	239	303	164	139	29
4,416	2,244	2,172	1,587	878	709	3	3	...	9	9	...	30
7,101	3,884	3,217	2,116	1,157	959	...	...	...	1	1	...	31
19,569	10,238	9,336	145	77	68	51	34	17	16	9	7	32
6,759	3,474	3,285	...	...	...	7	4	3	...	...	...	33
7,969	4,239	3,730	...	...	...	10	6	4	46	25	21	34
4,271	2,313	1,958	...	...	...	...	...	...	7	3	4	35
316,971	167,391	149,580	16,380	8,993	7,387	5,435	4,101	1,334	5,022	3,065	1,957	
8,077	4,232	3,845	20	11	9	14	9	5	73	36	37	1
11,442	5,781	5,661	304	162	142	18	11	7	130	55	75	2
5,106	2,543	2,563	76	42	34	...	...	...	2	2	...	3
20,325	10,418	9,907	230	110	120	8	4	4	633	356	277	4
15,046	7,813	7,233	3	2	1	3	2	1	17	9	8	5
26,050	13,541	12,509	46	25	21	82	41	41	335	205	130	6
1,243	681	562	...	...	...	...	...	...	3	3	...	7
5,754	3,080	2,674	31	17	14	20	8	12	17	11	6	8
1,929	1,040	889	...	...	...	...	...	...	2	2	...	9
3,822	2,084	1,738	5	3	2	3	2	1	16	11	5	10
956	507	449	20	10	10	...	...	...	...	...	...	11
2,435	1,254	1,181	...	...	...	...	...	...	419	237	182	12
8,957	4,698	4,259	12	7	5	2	2	...	118	73	45	13
8,753	4,604	4,149	137	75	62	...	...	...	493	248	245	14
10,440	5,349	5,091	125	69	56	3	1	2	601	315	286	15
4,544	2,355	2,189	153	81	72	12	6	6	15	13	2	16
5,282	2,753	2,529	55	24	31	20	11	9	62	31	31	17
10,163	5,238	4,925	7	4	3	11	5	6	1,174	637	537	18
2,422	1,301	1,121	1	1	...	...	...	...	151	88	63	19
7,323	3,720	3,603	...	...	...	1	1	...	12	8	4	20
7,054	3,568	3,486	...	...	...	...	...	...	37	16	21	21
10,658	5,496	5,162	26	14	12	1	1	...	71	48	23	22
1,238	706	532	33	14	19	12	7	5	83	49	34	23
179,019	92,762	86,257	1,284	671	613	210	111	99	4,464	2,453	2,011	
2,878	1,596	1,282	4	2	2	6	3	3	394	210	184	1
1,276	685	591	3	2	1	...	...	...	1	1	...	2
10,199	5,259	4,940	344	170	174	...	...	...	25	12	13	3
28,845	15,104	13,741	700	359	341	290	148	142	134	68	66	4
3,721	2,000	1,721	54	27	27	1	1	...	177	85	92	5
9,734	5,051	4,683	164	89	75	9	6	3	115	66	49	6
4,416	2,283	2,133	32	21	11	7	4	3	10	4	6	7
7,496	3,989	3,507	5	3	2	1	1	...	36	19	17	8
4,328	2,270	2,058	...	...	...	39	27	12	...	...	...	9
1,962	1,017	945	...	...	...	...	...	...	...	...	...	10
4,070	2,146	1,924	42	23	19	...	...	...	...	...	...	11
2,713	1,412	1,301	...	...	...	2	1	1	8	3	5	12
8,814	4,608	4,206	149	77	72	93	55	38	193	94	99	13
1,669	883	786	...	...	...	...	...	...	1	1	...	14
988	532	456	3	3	...	...	...	...	...	...	...	15
2,552	1,387	1,165	135	74	61	...	...	...	32	20	12	16
11,316	6,098	5,218	787	411	376	17	7	10	3	2	1	17
3,084	1,607	1,477	48	34	14	...	...	...	...	...	...	18
3,076	1,671	1,405	5	3	2	...	...	...	...	...	...	19
1,442	752	690	2	1	1	...	...	...	...	...	...	20
2,876	1,557	1,319	4	3	1	...	...	...	...	...	...	21
2,883	1,490	1,393	26	15	11	...	...	...	3	3	...	22
120,338	63,397	56,941	2,507	1,317	1,190	465	253	212	1,132	588	544	
2,308	1,208	1,100	39	23	16	...	...	...	17	9	8	1
2,010	1,106	904	3	2	1	...	...	...	2	1	1	2
1,366	802	564	65	41	24	22	14	8	27	17	10	3
1,156	644	512	19	11	8	...	...	...	6	5	1	4
385	212	173	...	...	...	...	...	...	1	1	...	5
739	389	350	18	10	8	...	...	...	1	1	...	6
2,393	1,421	972	4	1	3	723	635	88	711	700	11	7
2,671	1,438	1,233	47	29	18	...	...	...	74	43	31	8
2,584	1,419	1,165	96	45	51	3	1	2	...	...	...	9
9,514	5,057	4,457	285	161	124	83	39	44	106	71	35	10
5,162	2,788	2,374	148	85	63	...	...	...	6	4	2	11
4,140	2,104	2,036	638	338	300	5	4	1	19	18	1	12
2,164	1,124	1,040	178	81	97	...	...	...	...	...	...	13
1,240	708	532	30	18	12	...	...	...	12	9	3	14
1,463	776	687	49	29	20	5	4	1	...	...	...	15
2,399	1,280	1,119	110	60	50	...	...	...	2	1	1	16
2,836	1,518	1,323	28	11	12	...	...	...	9	7	2	17
2,335	1,246	1,089	5	3	2	...	...	...	8	8	...	18
1,304	703	601	...	...	...	...	...	...	8	7	1	19

Showing the population of the Police

PROVINCIAL TABLE VII.

Serial number of district.	Name of district.	Serial number of thána.	Name of thána.	Total population. Both sexes.	Total population. Males.	Total population. Females.	Hindus. Both sexes.	Hindus. Males.	Hindus. Females.
1	2	3	4	5	6	7	8	9	10
7	Muttra—(*concluded*).	20	Nohjhíl	38,818	20,566	18,252	36,567	19,434	17,133
		21	Baldeo	65,458	35,573	29,885	62,551	34,032	28,519
		22	Mahaban	19,411	10,233	9,178	17,212	9,104	8,108
		23	Sahpan	29,464	15,910	13,554	27,076	14,592	12,484
		24	Sadabad	66,132	36,119	30,013	60,617	33,222	27,395
			Total ...	713,421	332,660	330,761	646,385	346,158	300,227
8	Agra ...	1	Achhnera	26,085	14,158	11,927	22,252	11,965	10,287
		2	Etmád-ud-daula	17,020	9,131	7,889	15,633	8,362	7,271
		3	Tájganj	29,331	15,022	14,309	23,851	12,335	11,516
		4	Dowki	26,700	14,504	12,196	25,318	13,745	11,573
		5	Rakábganj	36,105	18,618	17,487	24,164	12,507	11,657
		6	Runkuta	16,535	9,047	7,488	14,712	8,068	6,644
		7	Shamshabad	32,511	17,676	14,835	29,529	16,111	13,418
		8	Keraoli	32,611	17,554	15,057	29,721	16,007	13,714
		9	Kakuba	20,184	10,988	9,196	18,481	10,028	8,453
		10	Loha Mandi	39,395	20,603	18,792	29,118	15,336	13,782
		11	Málpura	24,430	13,448	10,982	23,156	12,741	10,415
		12	Hariparbat	25,057	14,252	10,805	18,928	10,834	8,094
		13	Etmádpur	65,333	35,225	30,108	58,478	31,663	26,815
		14	Aharan	36,779	19,761	17,018	34,017	18,325	15,692
		15	Khandauli	30,852	17,033	13,819	28,021	15,499	12,522
		16	Narkhi	45,009	24,312	20,697	41,331	22,328	19,003
		17	Bah	37,368	19,853	17,515	35,700	18,937	16,763
		18	Batesar	14,397	7,634	6,763	14,181	7,520	6,661
		19	Pinahat	38,149	20,627	17,522	36,769	19,883	16,886
		20	Jaitpur	35,934	18,823	17,111	33,815	17,700	16,115
		21	Iradatnagar	25,583	13,871	11,712	24,213	13,091	11,122
		22	Fatehabad	35,500	19,106	16,394	33,155	17,889	15,266
		23	Nibohra	18,633	10,235	8,398	18,053	9,907	8,146
		24	Fírozabad	70,654	37,859	32,795	62,015	33,349	28,666
		25	Fatehpur Sikri	29,056	15,471	13,585	25,062	13,382	11,680
		26	Kagaraul	28,357	15,090	13,267	25,955	13,770	12,185
		27	Jagner	37,797	20,413	17,384	35,653	19,318	16,340
		28	Saiyan	23,413	12,599	10,814	21,927	11,819	10,108
		29	Kheragarh	21,301	11,626	9,675	19,843	10,843	9,000
		30	Chhatta	27,113	14,510	12,603	20,973	11,294	9,679
		31	Kotwáli	33,303	17,353	15,950	20,330	10,635	9,695
		32	Sadar Bazár	15,268	93,21	5,947	9,801	5,433	4,168
		33	Lál Kurti	8,033	4,736	3,297	5,164	3,026	2,338
			Total ...	1,003,796	540,459	463,337	879,319	473,645	405,674
9	Farukhabad ...	1	Sarái Míran	87,772	46,528	41,244	71,003	37,964	33,039
		2	Tirwa	77,686	42,478	35,208	73,274	40,080	33,194
		3	Gursahaiganj	70,726	38,160	32,566	61,071	33,225	27,846
		4	Thatia	34,461	18,768	15,693	31,127	16,951	14,176
		5	Saurikh	66,922	36,875	30,047	63,190	34,980	28,210
		6	Chibráman	57,848	31,457	26,391	54,416	29,695	24,721
		7	Káimganj	60,157	31,976	28,181	49,672	27,074	22,598
		8	Muhammadabad	85,413	46,607	38,806	81,691	44,614	37,077
		9	Farukhabad	79,223	40,714	38,509	60,442	31,545	28,897
		10	Fatehgarh	29,669	16,999	12,670	24,377	13,987	10,390
		11	Colonelganj	5,023	2,897	2,126	4,028	2,259	1,769
		12	Kamálganj	45,568	24,641	20,927	38,404	20,967	17,437
		13	Shamsabad	37,402	19,796	17,606	31,722	17,135	14,587
		14	Kampil	28,548	15,448	13,100	24,380	13,493	10,887
		15	Nawábganj	19,051	10,483	8,568	17,872	9,846	8,026
		16	Allahganj	18,388	10,159	8,229	16,951	9,360	7,591
		17	Aligarh	40,957	22,710	18,247	39,111	21,704	17,407
		18	Paramnagar	13,873	7,644	6,229	13,463	7.428	6,035
			Total ...	858,687	464,340	394,347	756,194	412.307	343,887
0	Mainpuri ...	1	Mainpuri	82,096	44,781	37,315	75,212	41,031	34,181
		2	Aunchha	28,157	15,635	12,522	27,176	15,085	12,091
		3	Kuraoli	41,667	22,628	19,039	39,468	21,474	17,994
		4	Barnahal	40,099	21,941	18,158	37,700	20,654	17,046
		5	Jasrana	59,557	32,664	26,893	55,680	30,619	25,061
		6	Ghiror	43,341	23,842	19,499	41,329	22,724	18,605
		7	Bhongaon	69,430	37,586	31,844	65,781	35,774	30,007
		8	Bewar	39,249	21,964	17,285	37,995	21,257	16,738
		9	Kishni Nabiganj	59,060	32,357	26,703	56,660	31,046	25,614
		10	Kurra	29,453	16,173	13,280	28,685	15,742	12,943
		11	Karhal	45,218	24,628	20,590	41,730	22,834	18,896
		12	Sirsaganj	76,278	41,899	34,379	71,363	39,128	32,235
		13	Shikohabad	57,227	31,005	26,222	50,656	27,728	22,928
		14	Eka	60,660	33,101	27,559	56,752	31,053	25,699
		15	Pharha	30,671	16,595	14,076	28,107	15,214	12,893
			Total ...	762,163	416,799	345,364	714,294	391,368	322,931

Circles distributed by Religion—(*continued*).

PROVINCIAL TABLE VII.

Muhammadans.			Jains.			Christians.			Others.			Serial number of thana.
Both sexes.	Males.	Females.	Both sexes.	Males.	Females.	Both sexes.	Males.	Females.	Both sexes.	Males.	Females.	
11	12	13	14	15	16	17	18	19	20	21	22	23
2,146	1,074	1,072	32	18	14	...	...	...	73	40	33	20
2,753	1,460	1,293	144	76	68	...	...	...	10	5	5	21
2,187	1,122	1,065	...	...	...	5	3	2	7	4	3	22
2,002	1,107	895	362	202	160	...	...	...	24	9	15	23
5,400	2,844	2,556	108	48	60	...	...	...	7	5	2	24
62,657	33,545	29,112	2,403	1,292	1,111	846	700	146	1,180	965	165	
3,542	2,053	1,489	273	130	143	12	6	6	6	4	2	1
1,303	715	588	58	38	20	25	15	10	1	1	...	2
5,116	2,492	2,624	345	183	162	18	11	7	1	1	...	3
1,169	645	524	207	111	96	6	3	3	...	...	...	4
11,131	5,656	5,475	411	236	175	316	162	154	83	57	26	5
1,455	777	678	365	199	166	...	...	...	3	3	...	6
2,425	1,260	1,165	540	294	246	6	4	2	11	7	4	7
2,669	1,429	1,240	213	113	100	...	...	...	8	5	3	8
1,640	925	715	61	34	27	2	1	1	...	...	...	9
9,547	4,830	4,717	505	277	228	104	72	32	121	88	33	10
1,223	675	548	51	32	19	...	...	...	...	...	...	11
4,234	2,384	1,850	180	103	77	1,428	661	767	287	270	17	12
4,850	2,503	2,347	1,637	872	765	249	124	125	119	63	56	13
2,083	1,072	961	720	356	364	...	...	...	9	8	1	14
2,545	1,376	1,169	286	158	128	...	...	...	...	...	...	15
2,455	1,319	1,136	1,219	661	558	...	...	...	4	4	...	16
1,416	788	628	241	122	119	...	...	...	11	6	5	17
202	106	96	13	7	6	...	...	...	1	1	...	18
931	500	431	448	239	204	...	...	...	6	5	1	19
1,178	618	560	941	505	436	...	...	...	...	...	...	20
829	470	359	537	306	231	1	1	...	3	3	...	21
2,253	1,153	1,100	60	39	21	1	1	...	31	24	7	22
324	188	136	246	135	111	...	...	...	10	5	5	23
6,971	3,548	3,423	1,482	839	643	16	11	5	170	112	58	24
3,944	2,060	1,884	33	19	14	4	2	2	13	8	5	25
2,398	1,317	1,081	4	3	1	...	...	...	...	...	...	26
2,129	1,092	1,037	13	6	7	...	...	...	2	2	...	27
1,157	585	572	327	194	133	...	...	...	2	1	1	28
1,427	764	663	8	5	3	...	...	...	23	14	9	29
5,194	2,710	2,484	853	450	403	22	14	8	71	42	29	30
11,395	5,837	5,558	1,111	586	525	256	143	113	211	152	59	31
4,154	2,762	1,392	60	39	21	823	774	249	430	313	117	32
1,194	575	619	19	15	4	1,469	954	315	187	166	21	33
104,433	55,184	49,249	13,462	7,306	6,156	4,758	2,959	1,799	1,824	1,365	459	
16,358	8,364	7,994	354	173	181	...	...	...	57	27	30	1
4,324	2,359	1,965	31	13	18	...	...	...	57	26	31	2
9,543	4,876	4,667	...	...	...	11	7	4	101	52	49	3
3,273	1,787	1,486	49	22	27	...	...	...	12	8	4	4
3,617	1,823	1,794	3	3	...	...	...	...	112	69	43	5
3,396	1,742	1,654	33	19	14	2	...	2	1	1	...	6
10,311	4,809	5,502	118	65	53	6	3	3	50	25	25	7
3,559	1,901	1,658	77	43	34	4	2	2	82	47	35	8
18,032	8,794	9,238	304	149	155	294	130	164	151	96	55	9
4,806	2,623	2,183	23	19	4	125	66	59	338	304	34	10
618	336	282	4	2	2	371	298	73	2	2	...	11
7,144	3,664	3,480	...	...	...	7	4	3	13	6	7	12
5,609	2,621	2,988	31	20	11	...	...	...	40	20	20	13
4,155	1,950	2,205	12	4	8	1	1	...	...	...	...	14
1,054	564	490	...	...	...	...	...	...	125	73	52	15
1,430	796	634	...	...	...	7	3	4	...	...	...	16
1,837	1,001	836	9	5	4	...	...	...	...	...	...	17
410	216	194	...	...	...	...	...	...	...	...	...	18
99,476	50,226	49,250	1,048	537	511	828	514	314	1,141	756	385	
6,016	3,253	2,763	529	316	213	122	63	59	217	118	99	1
852	477	375	128	72	56	...	...	...	1	1	...	2
1,922	995	927	266	150	116	...	...	...	11	9	2	3
2,222	1,180	1,042	176	106	70	...	...	...	1	1	...	4
3,330	1,729	1,601	546	315	231	...	...	...	1	1	...	5
1,619	903	716	354	194	160	...	...	...	39	21	18	6
3,353	1,650	1,703	275	147	128	1	1	...	20	14	6	7
1,242	700	542	2	2	...	2	1	1	8	4	4	8
2,371	1,295	1,076	5	1	4	...	...	...	24	15	9	9
762	428	334	6	3	3	...	...	...	...	...	...	10
2,557	1,306	1,251	931	488	443	...	...	...	...	...	...	11
4,272	2,401	1,871	550	313	237	1	1	...	92	56	36	12
6,181	3,042	3,139	377	226	151	1	1	...	12	8	4	13
3,018	1,572	1,446	863	464	399	5	4	1	22	8	14	14
1,812	990	822	752	391	361	...	...	...	...	...	...	15
41,529	21,921	19,608	5,760	3,188	2,572	132	71	61	448	256	192	

Showing the population of the Police

PROVINCIAL TABLE VII.

Serial number of district.	Name of district.	Serial number of tháma.	Name of thána.	Total population.			Hindus.		
				Both sexes.	Males.	Females.	Both sexes.	Males.	Females.
1	2	3	4	5	6	7	8	9	10
		1	Etáwah	66,985	35,731	*31,254*	53,154	28,705	*24,449*
		2	Jaswantnagar	49,856	27,532	*22,324*	46,796	25,843	*20,953*
		3	Barhpura	25,564	13,690	*11,874*	24,539	13,112	*11,427*
		4	Basrehar	36,070	19,819	*16,251*	34,859	19,135	*15,724*
		5	Baralokpur	23,535	12,932	*10,603*	22,970	12,629	*10,341*
		6	Bharthna	46,269	25,449	*20,820*	44,681	24,541	*20,140*
		7	Bakewar	70,650	38,264	*32,386*	68,209	36,975	*31,234*
		8	Sahson	29,336	16,075	*13,261*	28,726	15,741	*12,985*
		9	Usrahar	30,235	16,675	*13,560*	29,220	16,128	*13,092*
11	Etáwah	10	Bidhúna	33,296	18,361	*14,935*	31,663	17,474	*14,189*
		11	Bela	37,328	20,461	*16,867*	35,845	19,386	*15,959*
		12	Kuderkot	24,923	13,767	*11,156*	22,841	12,731	*10,110*
		13	Airwa	17,417	9,645	*7,772*	16,806	9,311	*7,495*
		14	Sahail	23,569	12,873	*10,696*	22,803	12,464	*10,339*
		15	Chhachhund	25,181	13,957	*11,224*	24,279	13,444	*10,835*
		16	Phaphúnd	42,346	22,824	*19,522*	38,430	20,846	*17,584*
		17	Umri	37,520	20,586	*16,934*	36,078	19,799	*16,279*
		18	Ajít Mal	66,160	35,866	*30,294*	62,429	33,920	*28,509*
		19	Auraiya	41,389	22,268	*19,121*	39,035	21,060	*17,975*
			Total	727,629	396,775	*330,854*	682,863	373,244	*309,619*
		1	Etah	72,911	40,010	*32,901*	66,671	36,495	*30,176*
		2	Sakít	35,597	19,211	*16,386*	33,274	18,061	*15,213*
		3	Malaon	30,333	16,707	*13,626*	29,087	16,003	*13,084*
		4	Amanpur	29,761	16,282	*13,479*	27,208	14,876	*12,332*
		5	Marehra	52,088	28,014	*24,074*	45,590	24,775	*20,815*
		6	Nidhauli kalan	38,394	20,929	*17,465*	35,101	19,185	*15,916*
		7	Awa	28,502	15,513	*12,989*	25,380	13,764	*11,616*
		8	Jalesar	71,667	38,450	*33,217*	61,217	33,146	*28,071*
12	Etah	9	Umargarh	20,861	11,606	*9,255*	18,492	10,324	*8,168*
		10	Patiáli	35,544	19,523	*16,021*	28,031	15,607	*12,424*
		11	Jaithra	37,380	20,955	*16,425*	35,773	20,035	*15,738*
		12	Aliganj	56,621	31,021	*25,600*	49,440	27,284	*22,156*
		13	Sirhpura	20,979	11,721	*9,258*	19,580	10,934	*8,646*
		14	Sahawar	31,879	17,594	*14,285*	26,829	14,884	*11,945*
		15	Kadirganj	31,145	16,873	*14,272*	28,268	15,366	*12,902*
		16	Soron	46,871	25,423	*21,448*	42,733	23,167	*19,566*
		17	Kásganj	61,530	33,371	*28,159*	50,159	27,410	*22,749*
			Total	702,063	383,203	*318,860*	622,833	341,316	*281,517*
		1	Kotwáli	80,727	44,110	*36,617*	52,520	29,341	*23,179*
		2	Báradari	51,796	26,834	*24,962*	28,829	15,372	*13,457*
		3	Kila	59,911	30,798	*29,113*	35,772	18,776	*16,996*
		4	Sadar	13,254	9,033	*4,221*	7,396	4,584	*2,812*
		5	Bhutaha	51,513	28,029	*23,484*	45,848	24,875	*20,973*
		6	Bhojupura	30,723	16,498	*14,225*	22,165	12,029	*10,136*
		7	Deorania	38,356	20,274	*18,082*	31,227	15,490	*15,737*
		8	Rithaura	18,418	10,101	*8,317*	14,337	7,902	*6,435*
		9	Sháhi	46,730	24,375	*22,355*	37,494	19,589	*17,905*
		10	Farídpur	58,019	31,595	*26,424*	48,275	26,385	*21,890*
		11	Gaini	42,095	22,145	*19,950*	34,774	18,407	*16,367*
13	Bareilly	12	Fatehganj West	37,480	19,950	*17,530*	30,993	16,434	*14,559*
		13	Shishgarh	49,307	25,635	*23,672*	33,679	17,600	*16,079*
		14	Mírganj	38,663	20,242	*18,421*	31,051	16,265	*14,786*
		15	Sirauli	45,753	23,975	*21,778*	36,748	19,281	*17,467*
		16	Fatehganj East	27,550	15,217	*12,333*	24,464	13,517	*10,947*
		17	Hafizganj	42,404	22,882	*19,522*	34,720	18,785	*15,935*
		18	Nawábganj	65,101	34,712	*30,389*	53,204	28,408	*24,796*
		19	Aonla	63,922	33,820	*30,102*	51,381	27,339	*24,042*
		20	Bhamora	50,015	26,969	*23,046*	43,425	23,413	*20,012*
		21	Baheri	74,221	39,628	*34,593*	54,397	29,154	*25,243*
		22	Richha	54,733	28,658	*26,075*	36,904	20,508	*16,396*
			Total	1,040,691	555,480	*485,211*	789,603	423,454	*366,149*
		1	Bijnor	53,108	28,378	*24,730*	33,900	18,511	*15,389*
		2	Amhera	34,547	18,392	*16,155*	26,068	14,010	*12,058*
		3	Ganj	6,047	3,116	*2,931*	3,872	2,055	*1,817*
		4	Mandáwar	40,185	21,424	*18,761*	30,306	16,368	*13,938*
		5	Bashta	27,788	15,084	*12,704*	21,614	11,876	*9,738*
14	Bijnor	6	Nurpur	39,200	20,717	*18,483*	28,520	15,120	*13,400*
		7	Chándpur	71,187	37,335	*33,852*	48,180	25,765	*22,415*
		8	Dhámpur	52,856	27,978	*24,883*	36,642	19,562	*17,080*
		9	Sherkot	33,743	17,450	*16,293*	19,009	10,058	*8,951*
		10	Nahtaur	44,377	23,187	*21,190*	26,276	14,070	*12,206*
		11	Seohara	51,012	26,865	*24,147*	31,396	16,962	*14,434*
		12	Afzalgarh	49,839	26,107	*23,732*	31,851	16,929	*14,922*

Circles distributed by Religion—(*continued*).

PROVINCIAL TABLE VII.

Muhammadans.			Jains.			Christians.			Others.			Serial number of thána.
Both sexes.	Males.	Females.	Both sexes.	Males.	Females.	Both sexes.	Males.	Females.	Both sexes.	Males.	Females.	
11	12	13	14	15	16	17	18	19	20	21	22	23
12,715	6,381	*6,334*	961	545	*416*	113	69	*44*	42	31	*11*	1
2,776	1,532	*1,244*	280	153	*127*	2	2	...	2	2	...	2
569	321	*248*	456	257	*199*	...	...	...	...	...	...	3
1,209	683	*526*	2	1	*1*	...	...	...	...	...	...	4
563	301	*262*	2	2	...	...	...	...	...	...	...	5
1,577	897	*680*	7	7	...	1	1	...	3	3	...	6
2,309	1,222	*1,087*	117	59	*58*	14	7	*7*	1	1	...	7
407	229	*178*	202	104	*98*	...	...	...	1	1	...	8
1,015	547	*468*	...	...	...	...	...	...	...	...	...	9
1,624	878	*746*	8	8	...	...	...	...	1	1	...	10
1,982	1,074	*908*	...	...	...	...	...	...	1	1	...	11
2,082	1,036	*1,046*	...	...	...	...	...	...	...	...	...	12
596	326	*270*	...	...	...	...	...	...	15	8	*7*	13
766	409	*357*	...	...	...	...	...	...	...	...	...	14
900	511	*389*	1	1	...	...	...	...	1	1	...	15
3,840	1,941	*1,899*	7	3	*4*	3	3	...	66	31	*35*	16
1,410	770	*640*	...	...	...	...	...	...	32	17	*15*	17
3,644	1,907	*1,737*	62	30	*32*	...	...	...	25	9	*16*	18
2,341	1,199	*1,142*	12	8	*4*	1	1	...	...	...	...	19
42,325	22,164	*20,161*	2,117	1,178	*939*	134	83	*51*	190	106	*84*	
5,099	2,890	*2,209*	1,090	591	*499*	24	15	*9*	27	19	*8*	1
2,069	1,002	*1,067*	244	143	*101*	...	...	...	10	5	*5*	2
988	565	*423*	242	131	*111*	9	3	*6*	7	5	*2*	3
2,254	1,234	*1,020*	29	20	*9*	...	...	...	270	152	*118*	4
6,306	3,144	*3,162*	81	41	*40*	108	52	*56*	3	2	*1*	5
2,924	1,550	*1,374*	369	194	*175*	...	...	...	...	...	...	6
2,321	1,315	*1,006*	792	426	*366*	...	...	...	9	8	*1*	7
9,519	4,815	*4,704*	902	468	*434*	9	7	*2*	20	14	*6*	8
1,630	864	*7,66*	728	409	*319*	...	...	...	11	9	*2*	9
7,452	3,876	*3,577*	1	1	...	53	36	*17*	7	4	*3*	10
1,567	896	*671*	2	2	...	2	2	...	36	20	*16*	11
6,972	3,624	*3,348*	196	102	*94*	2	2	...	11	9	*2*	12
1,391	782	*609*	7	4	*3*	1	1	...	...	...	...	13
5,006	2,686	*2,320*	2	1	*1*	25	14	*11*	17	9	*8*	14
2,846	1,491	*1,355*	...	...	...	...	...	...	31	16	*15*	15
4,076	2,216	*1,860*	...	...	...	54	34	*20*	8	6	*2*	16
10,533	5,529	*5,004*	260	131	*129*	233	120	*113*	345	181	*164*	17
72,953	38,478	*34,475*	4,945	2,664	*2,281*	520	286	*234*	812	459	*353*	
27,079	14,218	*12,861*	...	...	...	848	347	*501*	280	204	*76*	1
22,888	11,418	*11,470*	1	1	...	77	42	*35*	1	1	...	2
23,955	11,912	*12,043*	...	...	...	103	65	*38*	81	45	*36*	3
3,176	1,973	*1,203*	...	...	...	2,543	2,372	*171*	139	104	*35*	4
5,645	3,141	*2,504*	...	...	...	20	13	*7*	...	...	...	5
8,405	4,384	*4,021*	...	...	...	94	55	*39*	59	30	*29*	6
7,045	4,737	*2,308*	3	1	*2*	78	45	*33*	3	1	*2*	7
4,010	2,160	*1,850*	...	...	...	2	2	...	69	37	*32*	8
9,112	4,725	*4,387*	...	...	...	79	40	*39*	45	21	*24*	9
9,559	5,127	*4,432*	...	...	...	100	54	*46*	85	29	*56*	10
7,189	3,664	*3,526*	...	...	...	132	74	*58*	...	...	...	11
6,246	3,383	*2,863*	...	...	...	241	133	*108*	...	...	...	12
15,555	8,000	*7,555*	...	...	...	73	35	*38*	...	...	...	13
7,560	3,943	*3,617*	...	...	...	52	34	*18*	...	...	...	14
8,787	4,566	*4,221*	...	...	...	218	128	*90*	...	...	...	15
3,069	1,686	*1,383*	...	...	...	17	14	*3*	...	...	...	16
7,630	4,065	*3,565*	...	...	...	49	30	*19*	5	2	*3*	17
11,839	6,274	*5,565*	...	...	...	54	26	*28*	4	4	...	18
12,338	6,347	*5,991*	...	...	...	203	134	*69*	...	...	...	19
6,364	3,443	*2,921*	...	...	...	223	111	*112*	3	2	*1*	20
19,782	10,452	*9,330*	...	...	...	42	22	*20*	...	...	...	21
17,806	8,136	*9,670*	...	...	...	23	14	*9*	...	...	...	22
245,039	127,754	*117,285*	4	2	*2*	5,271	3,790	*1,481*	774	480	*294*	
18,694	9,601	*9,093*	61	32	*29*	223	99	*124*	230	135	*95*	1
8,476	4,379	*4,097*	...	...	...	...	...	...	3	3	...	2
2,140	1,047	*1,093*	28	9	*19*	7	5	*2*	...	...	...	3
9,255	4,756	*4,499*	3	2	*1*	175	94	*81*	446	204	*242*	4
6,036	3,142	*2,894*	...	...	...	131	63	*68*	7	3	*4*	5
10,621	5,571	*5,050*	...	...	...	53	23	*30*	6	3	*3*	6
22,774	11,442	*11,332*	5	3	*2*	6	3	*3*	222	122	*100*	7
15,974	8,272	*7,702*	139	82	*57*	22	12	*10*	79	45	*34*	8
14,513	7,265	*7,248*	96	55	*41*	45	37	*8*	80	35	*45*	9
17,713	8,906	*8,807*	225	112	*113*	22	12	*10*	141	87	*54*	10
19,493	9,836	*9,657*	71	32	*39*	32	23	*9*	20	12	*8*	11
16,915	8,617	*8,298*	59	31	*28*	3	1	*2*	1,011	529	*482*	12

Showing the population of the Police

PROVINCIAL TABLE VII.

Serial number of district.	Name of district.	Serial number of thána.	Name of thána.	Total population. Both sexes.	Total population. Males.	Total population. Females.	Hindus. Both sexes.	Hindus. Males.	Hindus. Females.
1	2	3	4	5	6	7	8	9	10
14	Bijnor—(concluded).	13	Behar	19,260	10,831	8,929	14,113	7,612	6,501
		14	Barhapura	34,814	18,426	16,388	24,414	13,042	11,372
		15	Nagina	79,234	41,292	37,942	46,832	24,948	21,884
		16	Kíratpur	64,124	33,026	31,098	38,367	20,397	17,970
		17	Najíbabad	65,788	34,174	31,614	39,586	21,064	18,522
		18	Nángal...	21,664	11,323	10,341	16,673	8,724	7,949
		19	Shiámpur	4,323	2,834	1,489	3,440	2,189	1,251
		20	Kauria	974	778	196	832	636	196
			Total ...	794,070	418,212	375,858	521,891	279,898	241,993
15	Budaun ...	1	Budaun	107,639	55,849	51,790	70,990	37,829	33,161
		2	Binawar	42,956	22,955	20,001	34,318	18,855	15,963
		3	Dátaganj	68,989	37,714	31,275	61,342	33,518	27,824
		4	Kakrála	29,698	15,593	14,105	21,262	11,397	9,865
		5	Ujhiani	57,558	31,431	26,127	51,276	28,016	23,260
		6	Gunnaur	68,291	36,913	31,378	59,704	32,343	27,361
		7	Sahaswán	61,148	32,757	28,391	44,088	24,082	20,006
		8	Kadirchauk	23,832	12,920	10,912	18,789	10,348	8,441
		9	Zarífnagar	39,714	21,624	18,090	35,452	19,303	16,149
		10	Bilsi	80,781	43,688	37,093	71,023	38,352	32,671
		11	Islámnagar	54,706	29,502	25,204	46,873	25,324	21,549
		12	Bisauli	75,402	40,562	34,840	65,015	34,969	30,046
		13	Rájpura	49,812	27,065	22,747	45,430	24,667	20,763
		14	Mirzapur Behta	25,174	13,387	11,787	22,470	11,954	10,516
		15	Wazírganj	39,620	21,188	18,437	32,577	17,396	15,181
		16	Sadullaganj	25,105	13,740	11,365	22,948	12,557	10,391
		17	Hazratpur	34,649	18,899	15,750	32,087	17,530	14,557
		18	Usehat	40,524	22,352	18,172	37,535	20,705	16,830
			Total ...	925,598	498,134	427,464	773,179	418,645	354,534
16	Moradabad ...	1	Chandausi	89,410	47,455	41,955	69,176	36,762	32,414
		2	Seondara	65,422	35,077	30,345	54,688	29,247	25,441
		3	Kundarki	42,944	22,770	20,174	24,780	13,236	11,544
		4	Moradabad	102,988	53,522	49,466	59,560	31,521	28,039
		5	Mundha	50,442	26,793	23,649	30,972	16,591	14,381
		6	Mainather	49,165	25,999	23,166	32,365	17,147	15,218
		7	Sambhal	110,647	57,412	53,235	60,737	32,208	28,534
		8	Moghalpura	43,418	22,393	21,025	18,750	9,861	8,889
		9	Mánpur	51,422	27,288	24,134	31,545	16,919	14,626
		10	Asmoli	64,571	34,344	30,227	42,447	22,629	19,818
		11	Bahjoi	52,430	28,070	24,360	45,682	24,476	21,206
		12	Amroha	123,206	64,488	58,718	68,588	37,156	31,432
		13	Chhajlait	58,479	30,944	27,535	39,353	21,246	18,107
		14	Hasanpur	53,091	28,439	24,652	35,962	19,504	16,458
		15	Bachráon	46,556	24,941	21,615	34,805	18,956	15,849
		16	Tigri	19,583	10,478	9,105	14,859	7,932	6,927
		17	Behra	34,450	18,891	15,559	29,964	16,401	13,563
		18	Thákurdwára	62,527	33,017	29,510	45,301	23,954	21,347
		19	Dilari	58,647	31,251	27,396	33,467	17,982	15,485
			Total ...	1,179,398	623,572	555,826	773,001	413,723	359,278
17	Sháhjahánpur.	1	Sháhjahánpur	91,338	46,227	45,111	57,228	30,061	27,167
		2	Sehra Mau South	41,280	22,334	18,946	37,676	20,414	17,262
		3	Dhakia...	44,403	24,047	20,356	39,237	21,207	18,030
		4	Sadar Bazár	41,875	22,445	19,430	26,323	14,408	11,915
		5	Kánt	53,951	29,136	24,815	48,289	26,178	22,111
		6	Tilhar	71,536	38,542	32,994	57,489	31,164	26,325
		7	Jalálabad	57,357	30,988	26,369	49,424	27,073	22,351
		8	Madnapur	40,480	22,331	18,149	38,694	21,801	17,893
		9	Powáyan	73,364	39,462	33,902	66,556	35,797	30,759
		10	Banda	68,044	36,855	31,189	63,008	33,987	29,021
		11	Nigohi	42,799	23,159	19,640	37,947	20,525	17,422
		12	Khutár	32,912	17,665	15,247	29,354	15,740	13,614
		13	Sehra Mau North	28,206	15,116	13,090	24,701	13,196	11,505
		14	Khudaganj	39,769	21,462	18,307	35,149	19,003	16,146
		15	Jaitipur	45,228	25,064	20,159	42,685	23,648	19,037
		16	Míránpur Katra	38,964	21,370	17,594	33,079	18,185	14,894
		17	Kundaria	33,308	18,512	14,796	31,108	17,304	13,804
		18	Bafiabad	38,348	21,196	17,152	36,444	20,157	16,287
		19	Mirzapur	35,394	19,395	15,999	32,745	18,040	14,705
			Total ...	918,551	495,306	423,245	787,136	427,388	359,748

Circles distributed by Religion—(*continued*).

PROVINCIAL TABLE VII.

Muhammadans.			Jains.			Christians.			Others.			Serial number of thánas.
Both sexes.	Males.	Females.	Both sexes.	Males.	Females.	Both sexes.	Males.	Females.	Both sexes.	Males.	Females.	
11	12	13	14	15	16	17	18	19	20	21	22	23
5,146	2,718	*2,428*	...	...	...	...	...	...	1	1	...	13
10,330	5,335	*4,995*	1	1	...	52	34	*18*	17	14	*3*	14
31,667	15,963	*15,704*	74	40	*34*	71	51	*20*	590	290	*300*	15
25,565	12,543	*13,022*	39	16	*23*	30	14	*16*	123	56	*67*	16
25,853	12,916	*12,937*	189	107	*82*	31	19	*12*	129	68	*61*	17
4,980	2,593	*2,387*	6	2	*4*	1	1	...	4	3	*1*	18
875	640	*235*	2	2	...	4	1	*3*	2	2	...	19
142	142	...	...	...	...	...	...	...	...	...	...	20
267,162	135,684	*131,478*	998	526	*472*	908	492	*416*	3,111	1,612	*1,499*	
35,525	17,442	*18,083*	...	...	...	691	358	*333*	433	220	*213*	1
8,267	4,380	*3,887*	...	...	...	371	220	*151*	...	...	...	2
7,155	3,941	*3,214*	...	...	...	251	137	*114*	241	118	*123*	3
8,335	4,142	*4,193*	...	...	...	96	49	*47*	5	5	...	4
6,045	3,283	*2,762*	...	...	...	155	89	*66*	82	43	*39*	5
8,476	4,505	*3,971*	...	...	...	53	31	*22*	58	34	*24*	6
16,905	8,604	*8,301*	...	...	...	141	64	*77*	14	7	*7*	7
5,003	2,555	*2,448*	...	...	...	39	16	*23*	1	1	...	8
4,258	2,319	*1,939*	4	2	*2*	...	...	...	...	...	...	9
9,245	5,051	*4,194*	194	110	*84*	244	135	*109*	75	40	*35*	10
7,603	4,054	*3,549*	31	17	*14*	72	42	*30*	127	65	*62*	11
10,106	5,447	*4,659*	...	...	...	196	101	*95*	85	45	*40*	12
4,332	2,364	*1,968*	...	...	...	16	12	*4*	34	22	*12*	13
2,703	1,432	*1,271*	...	...	...	1	1	...	...	...	...	14
6,829	3,675	*3,154*	...	...	...	206	109	*97*	8	3	*5*	15
2,126	1,164	*962*	...	...	...	30	18	*12*	1	1	...	16
2,408	1,287	*1,121*	...	...	...	6	1	*5*	148	81	*67*	17
2,968	1,632	*1,336*	...	...	...	13	10	*3*	8	5	*3*	18
148,289	77,277	*71,012*	229	129	*100*	2,581	1,393	*1,188*	1,320	690	*630*	
19,833	10,465	*9,368*	52	29	*23*	183	100	*83*	166	99	*67*	1
10,630	5,768	*4,862*	2	2	...	82	47	*35*	20	13	*7*	2
17,975	9,434	*8,541*	114	53	*61*	41	29	*12*	34	18	*16*	3
41,797	21,101	*20,696*	258	140	*118*	923	513	*410*	450	247	*203*	4
19,420	10,171	*9,249*	37	23	*14*	13	8	*5*	...	...	...	5
16,693	8,796	*7,897*	55	27	*28*	41	22	*19*	11	7	*4*	6
49,039	24,748	*24,291*	156	83	*73*	361	194	*167*	354	184	*170*	7
24,581	12,475	*12,106*	9	7	*2*	4	3	*1*	74	47	*27*	8
19,872	10,366	*9,506*	...	...	...	4	2	*2*	1	1	...	9
21,903	11,596	*10,307*	...	...	...	210	113	*97*	11	6	*5*	10
6,603	3,515	*3,088*	73	42	*31*	59	30	*29*	13	7	*6*	11
53,677	26,834	*26,843*	121	58	*63*	743	403	*340*	77	37	*40*	12
18,914	9,583	*9,331*	4	2	*2*	203	110	*93*	5	3	*2*	13
16,996	8,854	*8,142*	...	...	...	129	77	*52*	4	4	...	14
11,300	5,746	*5,554*	121	66	*55*	287	146	*141*	43	27	*16*	15
4,709	2,537	*2,172*	...	...	...	15	9	*6*	...	...	...	16
4,451	2,471	*1,980*	...	...	...	4	1	*3*	31	18	*13*	17
17,132	9,011	*8,121*	...	...	...	5	2	*3*	89	50	*39*	18
25,180	13,269	*11,911*	...	...	...	...	...	...	...	...	...	19
400,705	206,740	*193,965*	1,002	532	*470*	3,307	1,809	*1,498*	1,383	768	*615*	
33,940	16,090	*17,850*	9	4	*5*	48	26	*22*	113	46	*67*	1
3,403	1,819	*1,584*	...	...	...	20	14	*6*	181	87	*94*	2
5,162	2,837	*2,325*	...	...	...	...	...	...	4	3	*1*	3
14,462	7,262	*7,200*	6	4	*2*	871	661	*210*	213	110	*103*	4
5,654	2,955	*2,699*	...	...	...	4	1	*3*	4	2	*2*	5
13,945	7,317	*6,628*	...	...	...	46	29	*17*	56	32	*24*	6
7,841	3,858	*3,983*	...	...	...	42	29	*13*	50	28	*22*	7
1,737	1,000	*737*	...	...	...	49	30	*19*	...	...	...	8
6,665	3,585	*3,080*	...	...	...	63	32	*31*	80	48	*32*	9
5,013	2,854	*2,159*	...	...	...	23	14	*9*	...	...	...	10
4,852	2,634	*2,218*	...	...	...	...	...	...	...	...	...	11
3,557	1,924	*1,633*	...	...	...	...	...	...	1	1	...	12
3,493	1,912	*1,581*	...	...	...	4	2	*2*	8	6	*2*	13
4,546	2,417	*2,129*	...	...	...	74	42	*32*	...	...	...	14
2,484	1,384	*1,100*	...	...	...	31	18	*13*	23	14	*9*	15
5,842	3,161	*2,681*	...	...	...	26	12	*14*	17	12	*5*	16
2,120	1,162	*958*	21	12	*9*	24	14	*10*	35	20	*15*	17
1,904	1,039	*865*	...	...	...	...	...	...	...	...	...	18
2,646	1,353	*1,293*	...	...	...	3	2	*1*	...	...	...	19
129,266	66,563	*62,703*	36	20	*16*	1,328	926	*402*	785	409	*376*	

Showing the population of the Police

PROVINCIAL TABLE VII.

Serial number of district.	Name of district.	Serial number of thána.	Name of thána.	Total population. Both sexes.	Total population. Males.	Total population. Females.	Hindus. Both sexes.	Hindus. Males.	Hindus. Females.
1	2	3	4	5	6	7	8	9	10
18	Pilibhít	1	Bísalpur	102,112	54,653	47,459	89,364	47,769	41,595
		2	Barkhera	49,903	26,723	23,180	45,512	24,389	21,123
		3	Bilsanda	38,849	21,226	17,623	36,084	19,635	16,449
		4	Pilibhít	87,121	45,634	41,487	66,455	35,262	31,193
		5	Newria...	23,519	12,286	11,233	17,755	9,419	8,336
		6	Jahánabad	54,445	28,742	25,703	41,053	21,763	19,290
		7	Amaria...	34,212	18,102	16,110	20,719	11,143	9,576
		8	Puranpur	61,855	33,236	28,619	54,584	29,375	25,209
		9	Madho Tanda	33,350	17,800	15,550	30,594	16,362	14,232
			Total ...	485,366	258,402	226,964	402,120	215,117	187,003
19	Cawnpore	1	Akbarpur	62,981	33,837	29,144	57,749	31,194	26,555
		2	Gajner...	49,126	26,098	23,028	46,981	24,939	22,042
		3	Sheoli ...	53,722	28,391	25,331	51,866	27,418	24,448
		4	Sachendi	53,802	28,735	25,067	51,872	27,718	24,159
		5	Kainjri	43,008	23,081	19,927	41,133	22,111	19,022
		6	Derapur	47,936	25,650	22,286	45,166	24,183	20,983
		7	Bilhaur	66,151	35,220	30,931	59,335	31,764	27,571
		8	Kakwan	37,545	20,517	17,028	35,862	19,645	16,217
		9	Shiurájpur	50,443	26,548	23,895	48,281	25,405	22,876
		10	Bhognipur	58,267	30,772	27,495	52,099	27,644	24,455
		11	Músanagar	28,275	14,790	13,485	26,413	13,847	12,566
		12	Sikandra	49,392	26,430	22,962	46,916	25,116	21,800
		13	Mangalpur	47,992	25,641	22,351	46,041	24,630	21,411
		14	Ghátampur	61,647	31,996	29,651	58,359	30,270	28,089
		15	Sajeti ...	25,115	13,118	11,997	23,946	12,482	11,464
		16	Sárh ...	36,641	18,857	17,784	35,399	18,207	17,192
		17	Rasúlabad	45,784	25,068	20,716	43,074	23,662	19,412
		18	Narwal...	28,704	15,000	13,704	27,698	14,484	13,214
		19	Mahárájpur	44,863	23,277	21,586	42,651	22,133	20,518
		20	Bithúr ...	49,962	26,339	23,623	47,116	24,820	22,296
		21	Kotwáli	69,055	38,989	30,066	56,918	32,210	24,708
		22	Cantonment	27,903	16,880	11,023	19,797	11,780	8,017
		23	Nawábganj	9,310	4,947	4,363	8,549	4,508	4,041
		24	Kaliyánpur	29,814	15,922	13,892	28,462	15,154	13,308
		25	Bidhnu	36,440	18,925	17,515	34,812	18,109	16,703
		26	Colonelganj	36,754	20,924	15,830	27,275	15,654	11,621
		27	Fílkhána	21,731	11,711	10,020	14,935	8,123	6,812
		28	Anwarganj	37,332	20,429	16,903	25,285	13,961	11,324
			Total ...	1,209,695	648,092	561,603	1,103,990	591,171	512,819
20	Fatehpur	1	Kaliyánpur	24,201	12,536	11,665	22,814	11,845	10,969
		2	Husainganj	52,820	26,777	26,043	49,944	25,269	24,675
		3	Fatehpur	68,280	35,382	32,898	54,537	28,527	26,010
		4	Malwa ...	31,615	16,469	15,146	29,789	15,504	14,285
		5	Asothar	20,739	10,834	9,905	20,207	10,554	9,653
		6	Tharyaon	53,986	27,739	26,247	48,222	24,910	23,312
		7	Aung ...	23,101	12,142	10,959	22,290	11,700	10,590
		8	Khajuha	19,981	10,231	9,750	19,103	9,796	9,307
		9	Bindki ...	36,485	19,123	17,362	32,430	17,076	15,354
		10	Lalauli	30,311	15,758	14,553	26,566	13,871	12,695
		11	Jáfarganj	23,551	12,256	11,295	20,616	10,774	9,842
		12	Amauli	28,440	14,638	13,802	27,125	13,970	13,155
		13	Jahánabad	33,882	17,493	16,389	30,074	15,621	14,453
		14	Dhata ...	18,453	9,521	8,932	17,677	9,128	8,549
		15	Kishanpur	27,867	14,108	13,759	26,822	13,572	13,250
		16	Khakreru	41,662	21,204	20,458	32,768	16,921	15,847
		17	Gházipur	40,061	20,855	19,206	38,083	19,817	18,266
		18	Hathgaon	56,561	28,299	28,262	44,101	22,428	21,673
		19	Gaunti ...	24,859	12,432	12,427	19,526	9,874	9,652
		20	Khága ...	42,302	22,024	20,278	39,229	20,857	18,372
			Total ...	699,157	359,821	339,336	621,923	321,514	300,409
21	Bánda	1	Bánda ...	66,223	33,332	32,891	57,059	28,935	28,124
		2	Khanna	23,587	11,984	11,603	22,414	11,375	11,039
		3	Mataundh	18,208	9,144	9,064	17,486	8,775	8,711
		4	Tindwári	27,482	13,937	13,545	26,610	13,492	13,118
		5	Murwal	17,443	8,673	8,770	15,867	7,871	7,996
		6	Pailáni...	32,397	16,553	15,844	29,561	15,157	14,404
		7	Jaspura	30,214	15,676	14,538	27,806	14,441	13,365
		8	Baberu...	47,464	23,606	23,858	44,733	22,270	22,457
		9	Marka ...	18,057	9,131	8,926	17,716	8,957	8,759
		10	Oran ...	22,823	11,496	11,327	20,779	10,477	10,302
		11	Bisanda	29,254	14,489	14,765	28,171	13,965	14,206
		12	Pangara	24,470	12,149	12,321	21,521	10,804	10,717
		13	Kalinjar	30,611	15,521	15,090	28,857	14,654	14,203
		14	Khurand	15,764	7,996	7,768	15,295	7,740	7,555
		15	Girwan...	17,708	8,907	8,801	16,377	8,237	8,140

Circles distributed by Religion—(*continued*).

PROVINCIAL TABLE VII.

Muhammadans. Both sexes.	Muhammadans. Males.	Muhammadans. Females.	Jains. Both sexes	Jains. Males.	Jains. Females.	Christians. Both sexes.	Christians. Males.	Christians. Females.	Others. Both sexes.	Others. Males.	Others. Females.	Serial number of thána.
11	12	13	14	15	16	17	18	19	20	21	22	23
12,576	6,788	5,788	...	...	...	172	96	76	...	...	...	1
4,365	2,319	2,046	...	...	...	15	9	6	11	6	5	2
2,764	1,590	1,174	...	...	...	1	1	...	...	...	...	3
20,377	10,214	10,163	...	...	...	88	49	39	201	109	92	4
5,761	2,866	2,895	...	...	...	3	1	2	...	...	...	5
13,180	6,850	6,330	...	...	...	75	45	30	137	84	53	6
13,491	6,957	6,534	...	...	...	...	...	...	2	2	...	7
7,245	3,843	3,402	11	4	7	10	9	1	5	5	...	8
2,727	1,413	1,314	...	...	...	1	1	...	28	24	4	9
82,486	42,840	39,646	11	4	7	365	211	154	384	230	154	
5,095	2,561	2,534	...	...	...	11	6	5	126	76	50	1
2,144	1,158	986	...	...	...	...	...	...	1	1	...	2
1,843	967	876	...	...	...	1	1	...	12	5	7	3
1,875	998	877	...	...	...	...	...	...	55	24	31	4
1,768	917	851	...	...	...	...	...	...	107	53	54	5
2,770	1,467	1,303	...	...	...	...	...	...	...	...	...	6
6,768	3,430	3,338	...	...	...	9	6	3	39	20	19	7
1,680	869	811	...	...	...	...	...	...	3	3	...	8
2,149	1,138	1,011	...	...	...	13	5	8	...	...	...	9
6,107	3,091	3,016	4	2	2	1	1	...	56	34	22	10
1,842	933	909	...	...	...	...	...	...	20	10	10	11
2,475	1,313	1,162	...	...	...	...	...	...	1	1	...	12
1,951	1,011	940	...	...	...	...	...	...	...	...	...	13
3,288	1,726	1,562	...	...	...	...	...	...	...	...	...	14
1,168	635	533	1	1	...	...	...	...	...	...	...	15
1,242	650	592	...	...	...	...	...	...	...	...	...	16
2,708	1,404	1,304	...	...	...	...	...	...	2	2	...	17
972	500	472	...	...	...	...	...	...	34	16	18	18
2,206	1,134	1,072	...	...	...	6	5	1	...	...	...	19
2,845	1,518	1,327	...	...	...	1	1	...	...	...	...	20
11,576	6,457	5,119	354	210	144	118	61	57	89	51	38	21
6,102	3,553	2,549	22	10	12	1,952	1,515	437	30	22	8	22
738	422	316	...	...	...	1	1	...	22	16	6	23
1,349	765	584	...	...	...	...	...	...	3	3	...	24
1,628	816	812	...	...	...	...	...	...	...	...	...	25
8,791	4,892	3,899	...	...	...	649	351	298	39	27	12	26
6,551	3,458	3,093	22	15	7	170	89	81	53	26	27	27
11,910	6,394	5,516	12	7	5	104	53	51	21	14	7	28
101,541	54,177	47,364	415	245	170	3,036	2,095	941	713	404	309	
1,387	691	696	...	...	...	...	...	...	...	...	...	1
2,876	1,508	1,368	...	...	...	...	...	...	...	...	...	2
13,660	6,807	6,853	1	1	...	67	38	29	15	9	6	3
1,826	965	861	...	...	...	...	...	...	...	...	...	4
532	280	252	...	...	...	...	...	...	...	...	...	5
5,764	2,829	2,935	...	...	...	...	...	...	...	...	...	6
811	442	369	...	...	...	...	...	...	...	...	...	7
878	435	443	...	...	...	...	...	...	...	...	...	8
4,051	2,043	2,008	...	...	...	...	...	...	4	4	...	9
3,745	1,887	1,858	...	...	...	...	...	...	...	...	...	10
2,935	1,482	1,453	...	...	...	...	...	...	...	...	...	11
1,314	667	647	1	1	...	...	...	...	...	...	...	12
3,733	1,833	1,900	75	39	36	...	...	...	...	...	...	13
776	393	383	...	...	...	...	...	...	...	...	...	14
1,044	535	509	1	1	...	...	...	...	...	...	...	15
8,894	4,283	4,611	...	...	...	...	...	...	...	...	...	16
1,978	1,038	940	...	...	...	...	...	...	...	...	...	17
12,460	5,871	6,589	...	...	...	...	...	...	...	...	...	18
5,333	2,558	2,775	...	...	...	...	...	...	...	...	...	19
3,064	1,660	1,404	5	3	2	4	4	...	...	...	...	20
77,061	38,207	38,854	83	45	38	71	42	29	19	13	6	
8,854	4,238	4,616	216	102	114	55	31	24	39	26	13	1
1,147	593	554	...	...	...	...	...	...	26	16	10	2
704	359	345	...	...	...	...	...	...	18	10	8	3
866	443	423	5	1	4	...	...	...	1	1	...	4
1,574	800	774	...	...	...	...	...	...	2	2	...	5
2,834	1,394	1,440	...	...	...	...	...	...	2	2	...	6
2,408	1,235	1,173	...	...	...	...	...	...	...	...	...	7
2,730	1,329	1,401	...	...	...	...	...	...	1	1	...	8
341	174	167	...	...	...	...	...	...	...	...	...	9
2,043	1,018	1,025	...	...	...	...	...	...	1	1	...	10
1,083	524	559	...	...	...	...	...	...	...	...	...	11
2,949	1,345	1,604	...	...	...	...	...	...	...	...	...	12
1,738	858	880	6	3	3	1	1	...	9	5	4	13
469	256	213	...	...	...	...	...	...	...	...	...	14
1,381	670	661	...	...	...	...	...	...	...	...	...	15

Showing the population of the Police

PROVINCIAL TABLE VII.

Serial number of district.	Name of district.	Serial number of thána.	Name of thána.	Total population. Both sexes.	Total population. Males.	Total population. Females.	Hindus. Both sexes.	Hindus. Males.	Hindus. Females.
1	2	3	4	5	6	7	8	9	10
21	Bánda—(*concluded*).	16	Badausa	39,485	19,971	*19,514*	37,766	19,102	*18,664*
		17	Itwan	5,944	2,982	*2,962*	5,837	2,928	*2,909*
		18	Raipura	26,290	13,306	*12,984*	25,683	12,985	*12,698*
		19	Karwi	40,583	20,484	*20,099*	38,336	19,439	*18,897*
		20	Mánikpur	19,993	10,405	*9,588*	19,631	10,210	*9,421*
		21	Pahari	28,720	14,418	*14,302*	27,933	13,996	*13,937*
		22	Kamásin	36,777	18,680	*18,097*	35,559	18,023	*17,536*
		23	Rájapur	36,803	18,860	*17.943*	35,750	18,313	*17,437*
		24	Bargarh	10,996	5,614	*5,382*	10,610	5,400	*5,210*
		25	Mau	38,536	19,580	*18,956*	37,322	18,973	*18,349*
			Total ...	705,832	356,894	*348,938*	664,679	336,525	*328,154*
22	Hamírpur ...	1	Sumerpur	34,019	17,493	*16,526*	32,692	16,811	*15,881*
		2	Lálpura	13,561	7,016	*6,545*	12,798	6,628	*6,175*
		3	Hamírpur	21,656	11,370	*10,286*	19,663	10,321	*9,342*
		4	Kurara	13,357	6,896	*6,461*	12,915	6,673	*6,242*
		5	Sisolar	19,835	10,134	*9,701*	19,067	9,752	*9,315*
		6	Maudha	43,366	21,720	*21,646*	35,830	18,164	*17,666*
		7	Srinagar	24,161	12,426	*11,735*	23,388	12,025	*11,361*
		8	Kabrai	19,430	9,933	*9,497*	18,780	9,581	*9,199*
		9	Mahoba	31,506	15,937	*15,569*	28,659	14,582	*14,077*
		10	Ajnar	34,607	17,700	*16,907*	33,772	17,274	*16,498*
		11	Panwári	33,073	16,537	*16,536*	31,039	15,574	*15,465*
		12	Káshipur	13,625	6,930	*6,695*	13,089	6,645	*6,444*
		13	Kulpabar	39,387	19,931	*19,456*	36,828	18,634	*18,194*
		14	Jaria	26,191	13,179	*13,012*	25,235	12,700	*12,535*
		15	Chandaut	10,688	5,426	*5,262*	10.358	5,247	*5,111*
		16	Ráth	53,938	26,756	*27,182*	48,887	24,392	*24,495*
		17	Kharela	12,333	6,282	*6,051*	11,869	6,045	*5,824*
		18	Majhgawan	15,512	7,772	*7,740*	14,858	7,437	*7,421*
		19	Jalálpur	12,150	6,125	*6,025*	11,176	5,664	*6,512*
		20	Muskara	27,858	14,160	*13,698*	26,845	13,401	*12,944*
		21	Bewar	13,467	6,880	*6,587*	12,969	6,617	*6,352*
			Total ...	513,720	260,603	*253,117*	480,215	244,162	*236,053*
23	Allahabad ...	1	Phúlpur	73,033	36,721	*36,312*	63,244	31,925	*31,319*
		2	Sarái Inaet	74,480	36,762	*37,718*	65,698	32,564	*33,134*
		3	Handia	77,959	38,845	*39,114*	69,284	34,779	*34,505*
		4	Sikandra	46,011	22,771	*23,240*	41,144	20 475	*20,669*
		5	Baraut	32,659	16,474	*16,185*	30,312	15,328	*14,984*
		6	Sarái Mamrez	51,249	26,078	*25,171*	47,474	24,215	*23,259*
		7	Mau Aima	51,970	25,212	*26,758*	42,404	20,744	*21,660*
		8	Soran	70,281	34,298	*35,983*	63,277	31,001	*32,276*
		9	Nawábganj	59,095	28,732	*30,363*	51,651	25,268	*26,383*
		10	Kheri	24,308	12,484	*11,824*	23,757	12,199	*11,558*
		11	Moja	34,662	17,618	*17,044*	32,500	16,540	*15,960*
		12	Koraon	54,247	27,429	*26,818*	52,298	26,415	*25,883*
		13	Manda	39,363	19,715	*19,648*	36,290	18,178	*18,112*
		14	Sirsa	42,641	20,816	*21,825*	40,440	19,756	*20.684*
		15	Ghurpur	37,213	18,551	*18,662*	33,087	16,547	*16,540*
		16	Mutthiganj	15,620	8,938	*6,682*	12,441	7,155	*5,286*
		17	Karchhana	75,889	38,512	*37,377*	72,032	36,591	*35,441*
		18	Bárah	37,164	18,947	*18,217*	36,173	18,394	*17,779*
		19	Dando	22,493	11,597	*10,896*	21,953	11,302	*10,651*
		20	Sheorájpur	17,679	9,028	*8,651*	16,551	8,457	*8,094*
		21	Saini	67,409	34,007	*33,402*	54,993	28,072	*26,921*
		22	Kohkhiraj	52,798	26,249	*26,549*	44,833	22,441	*22,392*
		23	Manjhanpur	54,479	27,729	*26,750*	47,669	24,378	*23,291*
		24	Pachhim Sarira	48,097	24,722	*23,375*	45,600	23,457	*22,143*
		25	Karari	45,679	23,022	*22,657*	38,677	19,616	*19,061*
		26	Sarái Akíl	75,100	37,071	*38,029*	66,054	32,676	*33,378*
		27	Pura Mufti	50,351	24,540	*25,811*	40,030	19,902	*20,128*
		28	Pipalgaon	29,340	14,191	*15,149*	22,593	11,151	*11,442*
		29	Kotwáli	89,302	46,662	*42,640*	55,315	29,154	*26,161*
		30	Kydganj	15,026	8,011	*7,015*	11,937	6,319	*5,618*
		31	Dáráganj	14,111	7,355	*6,756*	12,131	6,362	*5,769*
		32	Colonelganj	36,767	20,135	*16,632*	26,004	14,134	*11,870*
		33	Cantonment	1,824	931	*893*	1,342	692	*650*
		34	Cannington	9,166	5,487	*3,679*	6,183	3,800	*2,383*
		35	Sadar Bazár	7,193	5,134	*2,059*	4,580	3,044	*1,536*
			*Ráníganj**	14,079	6,735	*7,344*	11,988	5,753	*6,230*
			Total ...	1,548,737	781,509	*767,228*	1,341,934	678,784	*663,150*
24	Jhánsi ...	1	Jhánsi City	37,075	19,220	*17,855*	30,273	15,699	*14,574*
		2	New Jhánsi	19,122	11,405	*7,717*	15,644	9,147	*6,497*
		3	Sadar Bazár	9,235	7,030	*2,205*	5,165	3,794	*1,371*
		4	Baragaon	18 597	9,606	*8,991*	18,250	9,417	*8,833*
		5	Barwa Ságar	14,037	7,360	*6,677*	13.634	7,130	*6,504*
		6	Baidora	13,741	7,373	*6,368*	13,589	7,282	*6,307*

* Criminal jurisdiction vested in the

PROVINCIAL TABLE VII.

Circles distributed by Religion—(*continued*).

Muhammadans.			Jains.			Christians.			Others.			Serial number of thána.
Both sexes.	Males.	Females.	Both sexes.	Males.	Females.	Both sexes.	Males.	Females.	Both sexes.	Males.	Females.	
11	12	13	14	15	16	17	18	19	20	21	22	23
1,712	863	849	5	4	1	1	1	...	1	1	...	16
107	54	53	...	...	...	...	...	...	...	...	...	17
607	321	286	...	...	...	...	...	...	...	...	...	18
2,233	1,037	1,196	2	...	2	3	2	1	9	6	3	19
345	187	158	...	...	...	12	6	6	5	2	3	20
778	415	363	...	...	...	...	...	...	9	7	2	21
1,213	653	560	...	...	...	2	2	...	3	2	1	22
1,053	547	506	...	...	...	...	...	...	...	...	...	23
341	193	148	44	20	24	...	...	...	1	1	...	24
1,202	598	604	6	4	2	...	...	...	6	5	1	25
40,662	20,104	20,558	**284**	134	160	**74**	43	31	**133**	88	45	
1,320	678	642	...	...	...	...	...	...	7	4	3	1
761	391	370	...	...	...	...	...	...	2	2	...	2
1,968	1,031	937	...	...	...	15	11	4	10	7	3	3
442	223	219	...	...	...	...	...	...	...	...	...	4
768	382	386	...	...	...	...	...	...	...	...	...	5
7,535	3,555	3,980	...	...	...	1	1	...	...	...	...	6
748	387	361	23	11	12	...	...	...	4	3	1	7
649	351	298	...	...	...	...	...	...	1	1	...	8
27,80	1,313	1,467	1	1	...	33	21	12	33	20	13	9
763	388	375	72	38	34	...	...	...	...	...	...	10
2,024	959	1,065	5	2	3	...	...	...	5	2	3	11
535	284	251	1	1	...	...	...	...	...	...	...	12
2,558	1,296	1,262	...	...	...	...	...	...	1	1	...	13
956	479	477	...	...	...	...	...	...	...	...	...	14
330	179	151	...	...	...	...	...	...	...	...	...	15
5,047	2,361	2,686	...	...	...	...	...	...	4	3	1	16
463	236	227	...	...	...	1	1	...	...	...	...	17
649	333	316	5	2	3	...	...	...	...	...	...	18
974	461	513	...	...	...	...	...	...	...	...	...	19
1,513	759	754	...	...	...	...	...	...	...	...	...	20
498	263	235	...	...	...	...	...	...	...	...	...	21
33,281	16,309	16,972	**107**	55	52	**50**	34	16	**67**	43	24	
9,789	4,796	4,993	...	...	...	...	...	...	...	...	...	1
8,782	4,198	4,584	...	...	...	...	...	...	...	...	...	2
8,675	4,066	4,609	...	...	...	...	...	...	...	...	...	3
4,859	2,294	2,565	...	...	...	8	2	6	...	...	...	4
2,347	1,146	1,201	...	...	...	...	...	...	...	...	...	5
3,775	1,863	1,912	...	...	...	...	...	...	...	...	...	6
9,566	4,468	5,098	...	...	...	...	...	...	...	...	...	7
7,004	3,297	3,707	...	...	...	...	...	...	...	...	...	8
7,444	3,464	3,980	...	...	...	...	...	...	...	...	...	9
551	285	266	...	...	...	...	...	...	...	...	...	10
2,007	1,012	995	155	66	89	...	...	...	...	...	...	11
1,949	1,014	935	...	...	...	...	...	...	...	...	...	12
3,073	1,537	1,536	...	...	...	...	...	...	...	...	...	13
2,196	1,056	1,140	...	...	...	4	3	1	1	1	...	14
4,113	1,998	2,115	...	...	...	13	6	7	...	...	...	15
2,732	1,440	1,292	4	3	...	173	70	103	270	270	...	16
3,852	1.917	1,935	1	1	...	4	3	1	...	...	...	17
990	552	438	1	1	...	...	...	...	...	...	...	18
540	295	245	...	...	...	...	...	...	...	...	...	19
1,126	570	556	2	1	1	...	...	...	...	...	...	20
12,378	5,916	6,462	37	18	19	1	1	...	...	...	...	21
7,962	3,805	4,157	...	...	...	3	3	...	...	...	...	22
6,810	3,351	3,459	...	...	...	...	...	...	...	...	...	23
2,495	1,263	1,232	2	2	...	...	...	...	...	...	...	24
6,994	3,402	3,592	8	4	4	...	...	...	...	...	...	25
8,904	4,324	4,580	138	67	71	4	4	...	...	...	...	26
10,317	4,636	5,681	3	1	2	1	1	...	...	...	...	27
6,747	3,040	3,707	...	...	...	...	...	...	...	...	...	28
32,899	16,937	15,962	216	107	109	872	464	408	...	...	...	29
2,762	1,441	1,321	...	...	...	322	247	75	5	4	1	30
1,980	993	987	...	...	...	...	...	...	...	...	...	31
9,064	5,078	3,986	...	...	...	1,548	823	725	151	100	51	32
482	239	243	...	...	...	...	...	...	...	...	...	33
1,453	955	498	1	...	1	1,507	715	792	22	16	6	34
1,140	801	339	...	...	...	1,473	1,289	184	...	...	...	35
2,096	982	1,114	...	...	...	...	...	...	...	...	...	
199,853	98,431	101,422	**568**	272	296	**5,933**	3,631	2,302	**449**	391	58	
6,400	3,280	3,120	239	136	103	25	12	13	138	93	45	1
2,570	1,738	832	31	22	9	782	428	354	95	70	25	2
2,063	1,404	659	53	33	20	1,057	932	125	897	867	30	3
339	184	155	8	5	3	...	...	...	...	...	...	4
331	191	140	72	39	33	...	...	...	...	...	...	5
76	49	27	76	42	34	...	...	...	...	...	...	6

Deputy Commissioner of Partábgarh.

Showing the population of the Police

PROVINCIAL TABLE VII.

Serial number of district.	Name of district.	Serial number of tháua.	Name of tháua.	Total population. Both sexes.	Males.	Females.	Hindus. Both sexes	Males.	Females.
1	2	3	4	5	6	7	8	9	10
24	Jhánsi—(concluded).	7	Babina	15,545	8,174	*7,371*	**14,835**	7,807	*7,028*
		8	Chirgaon	25,426	12,946	*12,481*	**24,687**	12,573	*12,114*
		9	Raksa	9,828	5,301	*4,527*	**9,648**	5,189	*4,459*
		10	Mau	46,495	23,276	*23,219*	**43,336**	21,783	*21,553*
		11	Uldán	17,006	8,683	*8,323*	**16,417**	8,369	*8,048*
		12	Sakrar	16,289	8,480	*7,809*	**15,451**	8,051	*7,400*
		13	Bonda	7,859	4,114	*3,745*	**7,611**	3,982	*3,629*
		14	Siaori	28,075	14,450	*13,625*	**27,025**	13,911	*13,114*
		15	Garotha	21,464	10,933	*10,531*	**20,352**	10,353	*9,999*
		16	Kakarbai	14,594	7,664	*6,930*	**14,104**	7,422	*6,682*
		17	Pandwaha	19,650	10,081	*9,569*	**18,777**	9,565	*9,212*
		18	Gursarai	16,530	8,399	*8,131*	**15,636**	7,950	*7,686*
		19	Moth	23,073	11,738	*11,335*	**22,260**	11,306	*10,954*
		20	Erich	18,618	9,454	*9,164*	**17,534**	8,928	*8,606*
		21	Baghera	17,160	8,842	*8,318*	**16,576**	8,529	*8,047*
		22	Lalitpur	35,669	18,560	*17,109*	**31,835**	16,363	*15,272*
		23	Jakhaun	10,869	5,603	*5,266*	**10,402**	5,349	*5,053*
		24	Birdha	11,592	6,009	*5,583*	**11,104**	5,736	*5,368*
		25	Khajuria	9,947	5,066	*4,881*	**9 388**	4,778	*4,610*
		26	Kailwara	10,282	5,377	*4 905*	**9,836**	5,151	*4,685*
		27	Jakhora	19,159	10,132	*9,027*	**17,910**	9,501	*8,409*
		28	Bánsi	10,150	5,215	*4,935*	**9,778**	5,020	*4,758*
		29	Tálbehat	23,357	12,142	*11,215*	**22,662**	11,763	*10,899*
		30	Nathi Khera	14,424	7,469	*6,955*	**14,094**	7,300	*6,794*
		31	Bar	28,340	14,605	*13,735*	**27,187**	13,998	*13,189*
		32	Dudhai	10,329	5 467	*4,862*	**9,830**	5,210	*4,620*
		33	Narhat	14,514	7,424	*7,090*	**13,569**	6,948	*6,621*
		34	Bánpur	18,644	9,484	*9,160*	**17,499**	8,928	*8,571*
		35	Mehroni	17,496	8,807	*8,689*	**16,345**	8,254	*8,091*
		36	Sojna	12,410	6,415	*5,995*	**11,908**	6,158	*5,750*
		37	Maraura	13,967	6,943	*7,024*	**12,817**	6,408	*6,409*
		38	Girar	7,106	3,676	*3,430*	**6,846**	3,551	*3,295*
		39	Madanpur	5,945	3,042	*2,903*	**5,585**	2,853	*2,732*
			Total ...	683,619	355,964	*327,655*	**639,399**	331,656	*307,743*
25	Jalaun ...	1	Orai	34,365	17,729	*16,636*	**30,678**	15,879	*14,799*
		2	Ait	15,789	8,084	*7,705*	**14,994**	7,664	*7,330*
		3	Mohana	9,547	4,822	*4,725*	**9,195**	4,647	*4,548*
		4	Ata	20,024	10,360	*9,664*	**19,060**	9,835	*9,225*
		5	Kunch	45,177	23,096	*22,081*	**41,538**	21,296	*20,242*
		6	Sayednagar	21,390	10,838	*10,552*	**19,374**	9,858	*9,516*
			Jalaun	39,596	20,128	*19,468*	**37,304**	19,001	*18 303*
		8	Kuthaund	25,679	13,306	*12,373*	**24,692**	12 780	*11,912*
		9	Hadrukh	28,199	14,527	*13,672*	**26,343**	13,613	*12,730*
		10	Churkhi	24,626	12,745	*11,881*	**23,879**	12,372	*11,507*
		11	Madhogarh	24,166	12,701	*11,465*	**23,651**	12,413	*11,238*
		12	Kálpi	33,973	17,315	*16,658*	**28,644**	14,770	*13,874*
		13	Mau	15,061	7,811	*7,250*	**14,651**	7,587	*7,064*
		14	Rendhar	24,798	12,813	*11,985*	**24,041**	12,441	*11,600*
		15	Rámpura	13,845	7,325	*6,520*	**13,090**	6,894	*6,196*
		16	Gopálpura	6,528	3,353	*3,175*	**6,273**	3,236	*3,037*
		17	Jagamanpur	13,598	7,137	*6,461*	**13,197**	6,933	*6,264*
			Total ...	396,361	204,090	*192,271*	**370,604**	191,219	*179,385*
26	Benares ...	1	Baragaon	64,550	32,383	*32,167*	**61,775**	30,975	*30,800*
		2	Sikraul	58,560	31,313	*27,247*	**51,965**	27,550	*24,415*
		3	Phúlpur	54,856	27,592	*27,264*	**52,264**	26,289	*25,975*
		4	Chaubepur	63,180	30,830	*32,350*	**61,679**	30,069	*31,610*
		5	Rohania	40,862	20,603	*20,259*	**38,035**	19,100	*18,935*
		6	Adampura	20,834	10,569	*10,265*	**13,931**	7,101	*6,830*
		7	Chetganj	29,768	15,573	*14,195*	**23,547**	12,368	*11,179*
		8	Camp	8,757	5,351	*3,406*	**6,268**	3,744	*2,524*
		9	Bhelupur	39,867	20,780	*19,087*	**33,534**	17,547	*15,987*
		10	Jaitpura	22,815	11,901	*10,914*	**11,402**	5,972	*5,430*
		11	Dasassumedh	41,539	20,856	*20,683*	**83,855**	16,916	*16,939*
		12	Kotwáli	27,658	14,735	*12,923*	**23,143**	12,318	*10,825*
		13	Kálbhairon	30,980	16,039	*14,941*	**28,810**	14,899	*13,911*
		14	Cholapur	63,662	32,058	*31,604*	**61,631**	31,022	*30,609*
		15	Mirzamurád	102,513	51,670	*50,843*	**98,934**	49,920	*49,014*
		16	Sakuldiha	43,711	21,804	*21,907*	**41,605**	20,725	*20,880*
		17	Chandauli	45,801	22,919	*22,882*	**42,720**	21,378	*21,342*
		18	Saidrája	54,710	27 155	*27,555*	**50,928**	25,355	*25,573*
		19	Balua	46,264	22,571	*23,693*	**42,258**	20,739	*21,519*
		20	Alinagar	33,569	17,189	*16,380*	**30,207**	15,439	*14,768*
		21	Rámnagar	27,487	13,562	*13,925*	**23,239**	11,609	*11,630*
			Total ...	921,943	467,453	*454,490*	**831,730**	421,035	*410,696*

PROVINCIAL TABLE VII.

Circles distributed by Religion—(*continued*).

Muhammadans.			Jains.			Christians.			Others.			Serial number of thána.
Both sexes.	Males.	Females.	Both sexes.	Males.	Females	Both sexes.	Males.	Females.	Both sexes.	Males.	Females.	
11	12	13	14	15	16	17	18	19	20	21	22	23
271	141	130	429	219	210	10	7	3	...	...	...	7
669	335	334	68	36	32	2	1	1	...	...	...	8
179	111	68	...	...	...	...	...	...	1	1	...	9
2,694	1,267	1,427	457	222	235	1	1	...	7	3	4	10
556	296	260	31	16	15	...	...	...	2	2	...	11
376	187	189	462	242	220	...	...	...	...	...	...	12
160	86	74	88	46	42	...	...	...	...	...	...	13
984	498	486	66	41	25	...	...	...	...	...	...	14
1,090	567	523	22	13	9	...	...	...	...	...	...	15
470	232	238	20	10	10	...	...	...	...	...	...	16
838	493	345	34	22	12	...	...	...	1	1	...	17
783	393	390	111	56	55	...	...	...	...	...	...	18
745	395	350	60	34	26	...	...	...	8	3	5	19
1,051	512	539	32	13	19	...	...	...	1	1	...	20
422	226	196	162	87	75	...	...	...	...	...	...	21
2,070	1,090	974	1,717	868	849	27	15	12	20	18	2	22
305	168	137	158	83	75	...	...	...	4	3	1	23
294	166	128	192	106	86	...	...	...	2	1	1	24
250	121	129	278	149	129	31	18	13	...	...	...	25
109	54	55	836	171	165	...	...	...	1	1	...	26
198	109	89	1,046	520	526	...	...	...	5	2	3	27
106	59	47	265	135	130	...	...	...	1	1	...	28
362	201	161	329	175	154	4	3	1	...	...	...	29
68	35	33	262	134	128	...	...	...	...	...	...	30
246	132	114	906	474	432	...	...	...	1	1	...	31
218	118	100	277	137	140	...	...	...	4	2	2	32
436	237	199	504	234	270	...	...	...	5	5	...	33
446	209	237	696	344	352	...	...	...	3	3	...	34
436	221	215	714	331	383	1	1	...	...	...	...	35
34	19	15	468	238	230	...	...	...	...	...	...	36
262	128	134	885	406	479	...	...	...	3	1	2	37
22	12	10	237	112	125	...	...	...	1	1	...	38
84	41	43	276	148	128	...	...	...	...	...	...	39
29,013	15,711	13,302	12,067	6,099	5,968	1,940	1,418	522	1,200	1,080	120	
3,564	1,787	1,777	57	31	26	54	29	25	12	3	9	1
770	421	349	25	14	11	...	...	...	...	...	...	2
852	175	177	...	...	...	...	...	...	...	...	...	3
964	529	435	...	...	...	...	...	...	...	...	...	4
3,628	1,795	1,833	10	4	6	...	...	...	1	1	...	5
1,993	954	1,039	23	11	12	...	...	...	...	...	...	6
2,283	1,120	1,163	8	6	2	1	1	...	...	...	...	7
987	526	461	...	...	...	...	...	...	...	...	...	8
1,856	914	942	...	...	...	...	...	...	...	...	...	9
747	373	374	...	...	...	...	...	...	...	...	...	10
511	284	227	1	1	...	...	...	...	3	3	...	11
5,275	2,513	2,762	39	18	21	11	8	3	4	2	2	12
409	223	186	1	1	...	...	...	...	...	...	...	13
756	371	385	...	...	...	...	...	...	1	1	...	14
750	426	324	4	4	...	1	1	...	...	...	...	15
255	117	138	...	...	...	...	...	...	...	...	...	16
401	204	197	...	...	...	...	...	...	...	...	...	17
25,501	12,732	12,769	168	90	78	67	39	28	21	10	11	
2,775	1,408	1,367	...	...	...	...	...	...	...	...	...	1
6,207	3,438	2,769	1	1	...	133	70	63	254	254	...	2
2,592	1,303	1,289	...	...	...	...	...	...	...	...	...	3
1,501	761	740	...	...	...	...	...	...	...	...	...	4
2,827	1,503	1,324	...	...	...	...	...	...	...	...	...	5
6,885	3,456	3,429	3	3	...	3	...	3	12	9	3	6
6,167	3,175	2,992	...	...	...	54	30	24	...	...	...	7
1,724	1,021	703	...	...	...	738	573	165	27	13	14	8
6,321	3,225	3,096	...	...	...	12	8	4	...	...	...	9
11,407	5,928	5,479	...	...	...	6	1	5	...	...	...	10
7,389	3,842	3,547	...	...	...	295	98	197	...	...	...	11
4,394	2,341	2,053	94	56	38	10	6	4	17	14	3	12
2,147	1,126	1,021	14	10	4	9	4	5	...	...	...	13
2,028	1,033	995	...	...	...	3	3	...	...	...	...	14
3,553	1,734	1,819	26	16	10	...	...	...	...	...	...	15
2,106	1,079	1,027	...	...	...	...	...	...	...	...	...	16
3,081	1,541	1,540	...	...	...	...	...	...	...	...	...	17
3,782	1,800	1,982	...	...	...	...	...	...	...	...	...	18
4,006	1,832	2,174	...	...	...	...	...	...	...	...	...	19
3,261	1,691	1,570	...	...	...	101	59	42	...	...	...	20
4,248	1,953	2,295	...	...	...	...	...	...	...	...	...	21
88,401	45,190	43,211	138	86	52	1,364	852	512	310	290	20	

Showing the population of the Police

PROVINCIAL TABLE VII.

Serial number of district.	Name of district.	Serial number of thána.	Name of thána.	Total population. Both sexes.	Total population. Males.	Total population. Females.	Hindus. Both sexes.	Hindus. Males.	Hindus. Females.
1	2	3	4	5	6	7	8	9	10
27	Mirzapur ...	1	Marihan	21,572	10,855	*10,717*	20,916	10,537	*10,379*
		2	Parari	36,839	18,301	*18,538*	35,065	17,410	*17,655*
		3	Kotwáli	116,222	57,269	*58,953*	102,669	50,421	*52,248*
		4	Bindhyachal	40,278	19,040	*21,238*	38,208	18,055	*20,153*
		5	Gaipurwa	28,959	14,043	*14,916*	26,324	12,769	*13,555*
		6	Hallia	23,454	11,859	*11,595*	22,036	11,146	*10,890*
		7	Drummondganj	13,079	6,556	*6.523*	12,478	6,240	*6,238*
		8	Lálganj	48,967	24,638	*24,329*	47,459	23,840	*23,619*
		9	Gopiganj	69,135	34,227	*34,908*	64,572	32,004	*32,568*
		10	Kachhwa	32,735	16,223	*16,512*	31,701	15,704	*15,997*
		11	Chunár	103,158	49,950	*53,208*	95.200	46,122	*49,078*
		12	Mirzapur khurd	59,597	29,553	*30,044*	55,030	27,270	*27,760*
		13	Ahraura	22,827	11,528	*11,299*	20,762	10,459	*10,303*
		14	Pannuganj	53,149	26,108	*27,041*	51,269	25,178	*26,091*
		15	Ghorawal	18,972	9,389	*9,583*	17,867	8,855	*9,012*
		16	Sháhganj	27,160	13,282	*13,878*	25,866	12,673	*13,193*
		17	Robertsganj	33,806	16,682	*17,124*	32,070	15,802	*16,268*
		18	Chopan	25,967	13,366	*12,601*	25,532	13,125	*12,407*
		19	Kone	9,078	4,441	*4,637*	8,600	4,191	*4,409*
		20	Khairwa	33,704	17,114	*16,590*	32,449	16,468	*15,981*
		21	Dúdhi	39,943	20,095	*19,848*	38,998	19,599	*19,399*
		22	Bhadohi	56,113	27,990	*28,123*	50,451	25,279	*25,172*
		23	Aurai	100,048	50,101	*49,947*	92,076	46,159	*45,917*
		24	Ujh	34,885	17,040	*17,845*	33,617	16,407	*17,210*
		25	Surianwan	40,947	20,440	*20,507*	38,605	19,290	*19,315*
		26	Chakia	70,914	36,251	*34,663*	65,412	33,411	*32,001*
			Total ...	1,161,508	576,341	*585,167*	1,085,232	538,414	*546,818*
28	Jaunpur ...	1	Kotwáli	100,401	49,778	*50,623*	75,312	37,844	*37,468*
		2.	Bakhsha	83,361	41,916	*41,445*	78,962	39,832	*39,130*
		3	Sarai Khojah	78,184	39,140	*39,044*	66,747	33,650	*33,097*
		4	Kerakat	102,623	51,755	*50,868*	95,986	48,439	*47,547*
		5	Gulzárganj	47,507	23,975	*23,532*	45,953	23,181	*22,772*
		6	Bamniaon	59,296	29,956	*29,340*	56,165	28,353	*27,812*
		7	Bádsháhpur	53,242	27,210	*26,032*	50,028	25,572	*24,456*
		8	Sujanganj	84.766	42,148	*42,618*	79,313	39,510	*39,803*
		9	Badlapur	81,661	41,433	*40,228*	76,891	39,073	*37,818*
		10	Rámpur	88,334	44,171	*44,163*	84,270	42,193	*42,077*
		11	Khutahan	61,560	30,739	*30,821*	56,093	28,047	*28,046*
		12	Sarpatha	66,259	33,908	*32,351*	59,939	30,796	*29,143*
		13	Sháhganj	62,117	30,924	*31,193*	47,308	24,026	*23,277*
		14	Chandwak	53,222	26,921	*26,301*	51,464	26,047	*25,417*
		15	Jalálpur	76,792	38,284	*38.508*	73,195	36,560	*36,635*
		16	Machhlishahr	63,404	31,636	*31,768*	55,568	28,018	*27,550*
		17	Mariahu	102,220	51,056	*51,164*	95,316	47,755	*48,561*
			Total ...	1,264,949	634,950	*629,999*	1,148,505	578,896	*569,609*
29	Gházipur ...	1	Gházipur	103,696	51,930	*51,766*	83,005	41,903	*41,102*
		2	Muhammadabad	89,531	48,779	*45,752*	79,562	39,185	*40,377*
		3	Nandganj	47,293	23.454	*23,839*	43,700	21,736	*21,964*
		4	Karanda	31,438	15,095	*16,343*	29,141	14,026	*15,115*
		5	Birno	64,449	32,728	*31,721*	61,475	31,265	*30,210*
		6	Kásimabad	91,239	46,048	*45,191*	82,890	41,768	*40,622*
		7	Mardah	45,366	23,038	*22,328*	43,299	21,983	*21,316*
		8	Shadiabad	85,715	43.466	*42,249*	81,039	41,206	*39,833*
		9	Saidpur	100,503	50,206	*50,297*	94,574	47,405	*47,169*
		10	Sadat	42,706	21,489	*21,217*	39,432	19,973	*19,459*
		11	Zamania	69,609	33,456	*36,153*	60,639	29,881	*31,258*
		12	Gahmar	58,178	27,753	*30,425*	51,536	24,818	*26,723*
		13	Dildárnagar	53,638	25,837	*27,801*	44,349	21,623	*22,726*
		14	Dhanapur	51,761	25,806	*25,955*	47,882	23,996	*23,886*
		15	Karon	44,373	21,361	*23,012*	40,457	19,610	*20,847*
		16	Narhi	25,271	12,122	*13,149*	24,238	11,648	*12,595*
		17	Korantadih	73,143	34,133	*39,010*	67,622	31,621	*36,001*
			Total ...	1,077,909	531,701	*546,208*	974,340	483,137	*491,203*
30	Ballia ...	1	Bansdih	127,574	60,804	*66,770*	121,078	57,698	[illegible]
		2	Reoti	49,053	22,479	*26,574*	46,995	21,570	[illegible]
		3	Ubhaon	56,800	27,196	*29,604*	49,199	23,779	[illegible]
		4	Sikandarpur	93,606	45,374	*48,232*	83,229	40,803	[illegible]
		5	Nagra	91,910	45,713	*46,197*	86,826	43,284	[illegible]
		6	Ballia	135,208	63,746	*71,457*	124,577	58,693	[illegible]
		7	Haldi	66,367	29,688	*36,679*	62,921	28,148	[illegible]
		8	Bairia	89,545	41,914	*47,631*	86,297	40,433	[illegible]
		9	Garwar	94,223	46,178	*48,045*	86,718	42,755	[illegible]
		10	Haldharpur	59,500	30,073	*29,427*	57,233	28,906	[illegible]
		11	Rasra	78,684	39,446	*49,238*	71,022	35,904	[illegible]
			Total ...	942,465	452,611	*489,854*	876,095	421,968	[illegible]

Circles distributed by Religion—(*continued*).

PROVINCIAL TABLE VII.

Muhammadans.			Jains.			Christians.			Others.			Serial number of thána.
Both sexes.	Males.	Females.	Both sexes.	Males.	Females.	Both sexes.	Males.	Females.	Both sexes.	Males.	Females.	
11	12	13	14	15	16	17	18	19	20	21	22	23
651	316	*335*	...	...	...	5	2	*3*	...	...	...	1
1,728	867	*861*	...	...	...	37	21	*16*	9	3	*6*	2
13,182	6,671	*6,511*	224	106	*118*	108	52	*56*	39	19	*20*	3
2,070	985	*1,085*	...	...	...	...	...	...	...	...	...	4
2,635	1,274	*1,361*	...	...	...	...	...	...	...	...	...	5
1,418	713	*705*	...	...	...	...	...	...	...	...	...	6
601	316	*285*	...	...	...	...	...	...	...	...	...	7
1,508	798	*710*	...	...	...	...	...	...	...	...	...	8
4,557	2,220	*2,337*	...	...	...	5	2	*3*	1	1	...	9
987	493	*494*	47	26	*21*	...	...	...	...	...	...	10
7,656	3,702	*3,954*	5	1	*4*	212	85	*127*	85	40	*45*	11
4,552	2,276	*2,276*	...	...	...	15	7	*8*	...	...	...	12
1,918	1,011	*907*	...	...	...	...	...	...	147	58	*89*	13
1,879	929	*950*	...	...	...	...	...	...	1	1	...	14
1,104	533	*571*	...	...	...	1	1	...	...	...	...	15
1,293	608	*685*	1	1	...	...	...	...	...	...	...	16
1,732	880	*852*	4	...	*4*	...	...	...	...	...	...	17
435	241	*194*	...	...	...	...	...	...	...	...	...	18
478	250	*228*	...	...	...	...	...	...	...	...	...	19
1,248	644	*604*	...	...	...	...	...	...	7	2	*5*	20
864	452	*412*	...	...	...	81	44	*37*	...	...	...	21
5,662	2,711	*2,951*	...	...	...	...	...	...	...	...	...	22
7,971	3,941	*4,030*	...	...	...	1	1	...	...	...	...	23
1,268	633	*635*	...	...	...	...	...	...	...	...	...	24
2,341	1,149	*1,192*	...	...	...	...	...	...	1	1	...	25
5,502	2,840	*2,662*	...	...	...	...	...	...	...	...	...	26
75,240	37,453	*37,787*	**281**	134	*147*	**465**	215	*250*	**290**	125	*165*	
25,007	11,888	*13,119*	...	...	...	82	46	*36*	...	...	...	1
4,399	2,084	*2 315*	...	...	...	...	...	...	...	...	...	2
11,429	5,485	*5,944*	...	...	...	8	5	*3*	...	...	...	3
6,636	3,315	*3,321*	...	...	...	1	1	...	...	...	...	4
1,554	794	*760*	...	...	...	...	...	...	...	...	...	5
3,131	1,603	*1,528*	...	...	...	...	...	...	...	...	...	6
3,207	1,633	*1,574*	6	4	*2*	...	...	...	1	1	...	7
5,452	2,637	*2,815*	...	...	...	1	1	...	...	...	...	8
4,770	2,360	*2,410*	...	...	...	...	...	...	...	...	...	9
4,064	1,978	*2,086*	...	...	...	...	...	...	...	...	...	10
5,467	2,692	*2,775*	...	...	...	...	...	...	...	...	...	11
6,320	3,112	*3,208*	...	...	...	...	...	...	...	...	...	12
14,813	6,897	*7,916*	...	...	...	1	1	...	...	...	...	13
1,758	874	*884*	...	...	...	...	...	...	...	...	...	14
3,597	1,724	*1,873*	...	...	...	...	...	...	...	...	...	15
7,836	3,618	*4,218*	...	...	...	...	...	...	...	...	...	16
6,904	3,301	*3,603*	...	...	...	...	...	...	...	...	...	17
116,344	55,995	*60,349*	**6**	*4*	*2*	**93**	54	*39*	**1**	1	...	
20,342	9,828	*10,514*	4	3	*1*	279	145	*134*	66	51	*15*	1
9,936	4,575	*5,361*	23	14	*9*	10	5	*5*	...	...	...	2
3,588	1,715	*1,873*	...	...	...	...	...	...	5	3	*2*	3
2,168	998	*1,170*	...	...	...	...	...	...	129	71	*58*	4
2,970	1,461	*1,509*	...	...	...	4	2	*2*	...	...	...	5
8,838	4.276	*4,562*	...	...	...	11	4	*7*	...	...	...	6
2,066	1,055	*1,011*	...	...	...	1	...	*1*	...	...	...	7
4,640	2,235	*2,405*	...	...	...	...	...	...	36	25	*11*	8
5,926	2,799	*3,127*	...	...	...	3	2	*1*	...	...	...	9
3,274	1,516	*1,758*	...	...	...	...	...	...	...	...	...	10
8,943	4,063	*4,880*	...	...	...	23	10	*13*	4	2	*2*	11
6,635	2.935	*3,700*	...	...	...	7	5	*2*	...	...	...	12
9,051	4,111	*4,940*	...	...	...	238	103	*135*	...	...	...	13
3,879	1,810	*2,069*	...	...	...	...	...	...	...	...	...	14
3,916	1,751	*2,165*	...	...	...	...	...	...	...	...	...	15
1,033	479	*554*	...	...	...	...	...	...	...	...	...	16
5,521	2,512	*3,009*	...	...	...	...	...	...	...	...	...	17
102,726	48,119	*54,607*	**27**	17	*10*	**576**	276	*300*	**240**	152	*88*	
6,496	3,111	*3,385*	...	...	...	...	...	...	...	...	...	1
2,058	909	*1,149*	...	...	...	...	...	...	...	...	...	2
7,601	3,417	*4,184*	...	...	...	...	...	...	...	...	...	3
10,377	4,571	*5,806*	...	...	...	...	...	...	...	...	...	4
5,084	2,429	*2,655*	...	...	...	...	...	...	...	...	...	5
10,609	5,040	*5,569*	...	...	...	15	11	*4*	2	2	...	6
3,446	1,540	*1,906*	...	...	...	...	...	...	...	...	...	7
3,248	1,481	*1,767*	...	...	...	...	...	...	...	...	...	8
7,505	3,423	*4,082*	...	...	...	...	...	...	...	...	...	9
2,267	1,167	*1,100*	...	...	...	...	...	...	...	...	...	10
7,662	3,542	*4,120*	...	...	...	...	...	...	...	...	...	11
66,3[illegible]	30,630	*35,723*	...	...	...	**15**	11	*4*	**2**	2	...	

Showing the population of the Police

PROVINCIAL TABLE VII.

Serial number of district.	Name of district.	Serial number of thána.	Name of thána.	Total population. Both sexes.	Total population. Males.	Total population. Females.	Hindus. Both sexes.	Hindus. Males.	Hindus. Females.
1	2	3	4	5	6	7	8	9	10
31	Gorakhpur	1	Deoria	106,516	53,103	53,413	98,199	48,914	49,285
		2	Chaura	65,839	33,163	32,676	62,773	31,610	31,163
		3	Ruddarpur	132,923	65,364	67,559	125,625	61,787	63,838
		4	Háta	124,752	62,904	61,848	114,093	57,598	56,495
		5	Tarkulwa	122,329	62,122	60,207	103,724	52,627	51,097
		6	Mansúrganj	81,739	41,377	40,362	72,731	36,836	35,895
		7	Pipraich	76,224	38,570	37,654	70,437	35,619	34,818
		8	Bánsgaon	141,215	69,851	71,364	132,692	65,624	67,068
		9	Barhalganj	101,722	49,040	52,682	94,876	45,667	49,209
		10	Rudrapur	85,331	42,772	42,559	80,331	40,327	40,004
		11	Gola	74,260	36,424	37,836	69,304	33,995	35,309
		12	Belghát	74,679	37,288	37,391	70,098	35,018	35,080
		13	Mahárájganj	88,140	44,547	43,593	76,528	38,795	37,733
		14	Rigauli	67,304	33,916	33,388	64,000	32,191	31,809
		15	Biraicha	55,471	28,239	27,232	49,205	25,067	24,138
		16	Panaira	29,681	15,323	14,358	28,007	14,421	13,586
		17	Semra	112,585	58,141	54,444	97,899	50,614	47,285
		18	Paisia	51,194	26,852	24,342	45,839	23,983	21,856
		19	Thuthibari	25,074	13,145	11,929	21,759	11,417	10,342
		20	Kothibhar	99,514	50,484	49,030	86,965	44,098	42,867
		21	Nichlaul	45,449	23,356	22,093	40,428	20,830	19,598
		22	Padrauna	102,085	51,368	50,717	86,447	43,400	43,047
		23	Ramkola	60,323	30,655	29,668	52,431	26,634	25,797
		24	Kasia	95,279	47,833	47,446	81,025	40,560	40,465
		25	Kázipur	95,519	47,096	48,423	78,932	38,905	40,027
		26	Tariya Sojan	77,278	38,044	39,234	65,028	31,939	33,089
		27	Bishanpura	51,313	25,074	26,239	44,969	21,966	23,003
		28	Barhaj	74,634	37,433	37,201	69,120	34,604	34,516
		29	Salempur	117,042	56,077	60,965	102,406	49,281	53,125
		30	Kotwáli	220,682	111,506	109,176	188,476	95,553	92,923
		31	Sahjanwa	63,564	31,418	32,146	59,972	29,629	30,343
		32	Barhi	57,377	28,545	28,832	55,679	27,686	27,993
		33	Khukhundu	88,573	43,842	44,731	83,114	41,168	41,946
		34	Ghauti	128,447	62,412	66,035	118,052	57,394	60,658
			Total	2,994,057	1,497,284	1,496,773	2,691,164	1,345,757	1,345,407
32	Basti	1	Basti	136,607	70,075	66,532	118,205	60,585	57,620
		2	Sonha	59,743	30,916	28,827	53,080	27,468	25,612
		3	Dudhara	72,354	36,306	36,048	43,537	21,948	21,589
		4	Rudhauli	62,705	32,111	30,594	54,564	27,945	26,619
		5	Bara Koni	38,378	19,219	19,159	34,476	17,268	17,208
		6	Budha	51,049	26,062	24,987	45,060	22,995	22,065
		7	Kalwari	67,177	34,239	32,938	59,566	30,379	29,187
		8	Uska	61,269	31,668	29,601	55,161	28,414	26,747
		9	Bánsi	101,886	51,581	50,305	86,186	43,739	42,447
		10	Bankata	56,737	28,463	28,274	43,799	22,044	21,755
		11	Chilhia	105,174	53,106	52,068	83,455	41,937	41,518
		12	Lotan	43,428	22,023	21,405	37,859	19,152	18,707
		13	Tilokpur	52,071	25,812	26,259	40,592	20,133	20,459
		14	Dhebarua	31,068	15,899	15,169	25,052	12,799	12,253
		15	Misraulia	47,198	23,954	23,244	33,547	17,151	16,396
		16	Chhapia	66,251	33,898	32,353	52,197	26,816	25,381
		17	Domariaganj	116,502	59,009	57,493	86,359	43,792	42,567
		18	Parasrámpur	61,275	31,142	30,133	55,638	28,293	27,345
		19	Paikaulia	69,093	35,245	33,848	62,170	31,729	30,441
		20	Chhaoni	78,458	39,757	38,701	72,919	36,962	35,957
		21	Harria	55,085	28,317	26,768	51,505	26,458	25,047
		22	Kaptanganj	71,747	36,333	35,414	66,767	33,817	32,950
		23	Khalilabad	70,678	35,747	34,931	61,787	31,311	30,476
		24	Menhdawal	84,476	43,023	41,453	70,686	35,910	34,776
		25	Dhaughata	61,303	31,070	30,233	57,412	29,084	28,328
		26	Mahuli	64,132	32,362	31,770	58,410	29,446	28,964
			Total	1,785,844	907,337	878,507	1,509,989	767,575	742,414
33	Azamgarh	1	Azamgarh (Kotwáli)	78,911	40,292	38,619	66,949	34,275	32,674
		2	Abraula	85,873	43,521	42,352	77,488	39,365	38,123
		3	Jahánaganj	52,002	26,463	25,539	48,772	24,891	23,881
		4	Sarái Mír	59,903	29,496	30,407	40,489	20,278	20,211
		5	Kandhrapur	60,106	30,320	29,786	52,324	26,552	25,772
		6	Gambhirpur	75,025	37,251	37,774	60,026	30,036	29,990
		7	Mehnagar	61,104	30,613	30,491	56,258	28,256	28,002
		8	Nizámabad	72,832	36,550	36,282	62,437	31,477	30,960
		9	Chiriákot	87,660	44,768	42,892	82,221	42,064	40,157
		10	Maunat Bhanjan	108,205	54,701	53,504	90,117	45,809	44,308
		11	Ghosi	96,286	47,852	48,434	84,758	42,367	42,391
		12	Muhammadabad	117,746	58,922	58,824	88,047	44,282	43,765
		13	Dobri	49,125	24,221	24,904	46,795	23,075	23,7[illegible]0
		14	Raunapár	49,792	24,994	24,798	44,754	22,483	22,[illegible]71
		15	Sagri	101,554	50,506	51,048	86,005	42,935	4[illegible],070
		16	Madhuban	90,776	43,955	46,821	80,475	39,124	41,351
		17	Mahárájganj	79,224	39,868	39,356	73,388	36,974	36,414

Circles distributed by Religion—(*continued*).

PROVINCIAL TABLE VII.

Muhammadans.			Jains.			Christians.			Others.			Serial number of thánas.
Both sexes.	Males.	Females.	Both sexes.	Males.	Females.	Both sexes.	Males.	Females.	Both sexes.	Males.	Females.	
11	12	13	14	15	16	17	18	19	20	21	22	23
8,316	4,188	*4,128*	...	...	...	1	1	...	...	...	...	1
3,066	1,553	*1,513*	...	...	...	...	...	...	...	...	...	2
7,298	3,577	*3,721*	...	...	...	...	...	...	...	...	...	3
10,657	5,304	*5,353*	...	...	...	1	1	...	1	1	...	4
18,604	9,494	*9,110*	...	...	...	1	1	...	...	...	...	5
9,008	4,541	*4,467*	...	...	...	...	...	...	...	...	...	6
5,785	2,950	*2,835*	...	...	...	2	1	*1*	...	...	...	7
8,523	4,227	*4,296*	...	...	...	...	...	...	...	...	...	8
6,846	3,373	*3,473*	...	...	...	...	...	...	...	...	...	9
4,999	2,444	*2,555*	...	...	...	1	1	...	...	...	...	10
4,948	2,425	*2,523*	...	...	...	8	4	*4*	...	...	...	11
4,581	2,270	*2,311*	...	...	...	...	...	...	...	...	...	12
11,612	5,752	*5,860*	...	...	...	...	...	...	...	...	...	13
3,299	1,724	*1,575*	...	...	...	5	1	*4*	...	...	...	14
6,263	3,169	*3,094*	...	...	...	3	3	...	...	...	...	15
1,674	902	*772*	...	...	...	...	...	...	...	...	...	16
14,657	7,512	*7,145*	...	...	...	29	15	*14*	...	...	...	17
5,354	2,868	*2,486*	...	...	...	...	...	...	1	1	...	18
3,311	1,727	*1,584*	...	...	...	4	1	*3*	...	...	...	19
12,549	6,386	*6,163*	...	...	...	...	...	...	...	...	...	20
5,020	2,526	*2,494*	...	...	...	1	...	*1*	...	...	...	21
15,627	7,963	*7,664*	...	...	...	11	5	*6*	...	...	...	22
7,892	4,021	*3,871*	...	...	...	...	...	...	...	...	...	23
14,252	7,271	*6,981*	...	...	...	2	2	...	...	...	...	24
16,587	8,191	*8,396*	...	...	...	...	...	...	...	...	...	25
12,234	6,093	*6,141*	...	...	...	15	11	*4*	1	1	...	26
6,341	3,106	*3,235*	...	...	...	3	2	*1*	...	...	...	27
5,508	2,825	*2,683*	...	...	...	6	4	*2*	...	...	...	28
14,635	6,795	*7,840*	...	...	...	1	1	...	...	...	...	29
31,046	15,337	*15,709*	44	26	*18*	1,076	565	*511*	40	25	*15*	30
3,592	1,789	*1,803*	...	...	...	...	...	...	...	...	...	31
1,698	859	*839*	...	...	...	...	...	...	...	...	...	32
5,459	2,674	*2,785*	...	...	...	...	...	...	...	...	...	33
10,389	5,013	*5,376*	...	...	...	6	5	*1*	...	...	...	34
301,630	150,849	*150,781*	**44**	26	*18*	**1,176**	624	*552*	**43**	28	*15*	
18,290	9,430	*8,860*	...	...	...	54	30	*24*	58	30	*28*	1
6,663	3,448	*3,215*	...	...	...	...	...	...	...	...	...	2
28,817	14,358	*14,459*	...	...	...	...	...	...	...	...	...	3
8,141	4,166	*3,975*	...	...	...	...	...	...	...	...	...	4
3,902	1,951	*1,951*	...	...	...	...	...	...	...	...	...	5
5,989	3,067	*2,922*	...	...	...	...	...	...	...	...	...	6
7,611	3,860	*3,751*	...	...	...	...	...	...	...	...	...	7
6,103	3,250	*2,853*	...	...	...	5	4	*1*	...	...	...	8
15,700	7,842	*7,858*	...	...	...	...	...	...	...	...	...	9
12,938	6,419	*6,519*	...	...	...	...	...	...	...	...	...	10
21,712	11,164	*10,548*	...	...	...	7	5	2	...	...	...	11
5,569	2,871	*2,698*	...	...	...	...	...	...	...	...	...	12
11,479	5,679	*5,800*	...	...	...	...	...	...	...	...	...	13
6,016	3,100	*2,916*	...	...	...	...	...	...	...	...	...	14
13,651	6,803	*6,848*	...	...	...	...	...	...	...	...	...	15
14,054	7,082	*6,972*	...	...	...	...	...	...	...	...	...	16
30,143	15,217	*14,926*	...	...	...	...	...	...	...	...	...	17
5,637	2,849	*2,788*	...	...	...	...	...	...	...	...	...	18
6,923	3,516	*3,407*	...	...	...	...	...	...	...	...	...	19
5,539	2,795	*2,744*	...	...	...	...	...	...	...	...	...	20
3,580	1,859	*1,721*	...	...	...	...	...	...	...	...	...	21
4,980	2,516	*2,464*	...	...	...	...	...	...	...	...	...	22
8,891	4,436	*4,455*	...	...	...	...	...	...	...	...	...	23
13,788	7,111	*6,677*	...	...	...	...	...	...	2	2	...	24
3,891	1,986	*1,905*	...	...	...	...	...	...	...	...	...	25
5,722	2,916	*2,806*	...	...	...	...	...	...	...	...	...	26
275,729	139,691	*136,038*	...	...	...	**66**	39	*27*	**60**	32	*28*	
11,902	5,984	*5,918*	...	...	...	59	32	*27*	1	1	...	1
8,382	4,153	*4,229*	...	...	...	3	3	...	...	...	...	2
3,230	1,572	*1,658*	...	...	...	...	...	...	...	...	...	3
19,414	9,218	*10,196*	...	...	...	...	...	...	...	...	...	4
7,782	3,768	*4,014*	...	...	...	...	...	...	...	...	...	5
14,999	7,215	*7,784*	...	...	...	...	...	...	...	...	...	6
4,846	2,357	*2,489*	...	...	...	...	...	...	...	...	...	7
10,395	5,073	*5,322*	...	...	...	...	...	...	...	...	...	8
5,437	2,704	*2,733*	...	...	...	2	...	*2*	...	...	...	9
18,087	8,892	*9,195*	...	...	...	1	...	*1*	...	...	...	10
11,528	5,485	*6,043*	...	...	...	...	...	...	...	...	...	11
29,699	14,640	*15,059*	...	...	...	...	...	...	...	...	...	12
2,330	1,146	*1,184*	...	...	...	...	...	...	...	...	...	13
5,038	2,511	*2,527*	...	...	...	...	...	...	...	...	...	14
15,549	7,571	*7,978*	...	...	...	...	...	...	...	...	...	15
10,297	4,829	*5,468*	...	...	...	4	2	*2*	...	...	...	16
5,831	2,892	*2,939*	...	...	...	5	2	*3*	...	...	...	17

Showing the population of the Police

PROVINCIAL TABLE VII.

Serial number of district.	Name of district.	Serial number of thána.	Name of thána.	Total population. Both sexes.	Total population. Males.	Total population. Females.	Hindus. Both sexes.	Hindus. Males.	Hindus. Females.
1	2	3	4	5	6	7	8	9	10
33	Azamgarh—(*concluded*).	18	Atraulia	90,038	46,001	44,037	83,666	42,819	40,847
		19	Barda	47,143	23,757	23,386	43,000	21,720	21,280
		20	Pawai	45,301	23,077	22,224	39,890	20,478	19,412
		21	Didárganj	85,727	42,799	42,928	69,848	35,228	34,625
		22	Tarwa...	58,244	29,456	28,788	56,006	28,330	27,676
		23	Deogaon	76,048	38,228	37,820	69,198	35,020	34,178
			Total ...	1,728,625	867,611	861,014	1,502,911	757,833	745,078
34	Lucknow ...	1	Banthara	58,912	30,539	28,373	54,258	28,200	26,058
		2	Gosainganj	55,631	28,510	27,121	51,554	26,469	25,085
		3	Lucknow	104,701	55,749	48,952	88,717	47,599	41,118
		4	Mohanlálganj	104,697	53,774	50,923	94,539	48,891	45,648
		5	Malihabad	114,984	60,125	54,859	98,626	52,026	46,600
		6	Chauk	60,160	30,440	29,720	32,902	17,281	15,621
		7	Saadatganj	31,292	15,809	15,483	19,692	10,220	9,472
		8	Daulatganj	37,619	18,803	18,816	21,158	11,048	10,110
		9	Wazírganj	39,273	20,505	18,768	19,169	10,453	8,716
		10	Hasanganj	27,184	14,456	12,728	20,078	10,832	9,246
		11	Dilkusha	23,517	16,019	7,498	15,245	10,107	5,138
		12	Itaunja	62,067	32,579	29,488	55,768	29,340	26,428
		13	Ganeshganj	54,126	29,893	24,233	33,319	18,684	14,635
			Total ...	774,163	407,201	366,962	605,025	321,150	283,875
35	Unao ...	1	Unao	113,268	59,473	53,795	104,308	54,696	49,612
		2	Safipur	110,167	57,600	52,567	95,478	50,257	45,221
		3	Ajgain	84,229	43,832	40,397	79,674	41,481	38,193
		4	Achalganj	65,367	32,126	33,241	62,589	30,740	31,849
		5	Bara	70,264	33,878	36,386	67,725	32,599	35,126
		6	Purwa	73,230	36,192	37,038	67,632	33,487	34,145
		7	Auras	80,099	42,650	37,449	72,773	38,885	33,888
		8	Bangermau	89,785	47,769	42,016	76,119	40,653	35,466
		9	Fatehpur Chaurási... ...	35,564	19,091	16,473	34,496	18,516	15,980
		10	Asoha	50,188	25,593	24,595	47,673	24,812	23,861
		11	Behar	40,672	19,310	21,362	39,570	18,724	20,846
		12	Maurawan	70,195	35,047	35,148	65,510	32,821	32,689
		13	Hasanganj	70,608	36,951	33,657	63,904	33,705	30,199
			Total ...	953,636	489,512	464,124	877,451	450,876	426,575
36	Rae Bareli ...	1	Bachhrawan	95,642	47,949	47,693	89,911	45,023	44,888
		2	Jagatpur	104,423	51,562	52,861	98,547	48,815	49,732
		3	Digbijaiganj	123,939	61,645	62,294	116,859	58,259	58,600
		4	Rao Bareli	113,229	56,757	56,472	101,743	51,005	50,738
		5	Gurbakshganj	78,688	38,946	39,742	75,285	37,286	37,999
		6	Mau	101,452	50,686	50,766	84,810	42,750	42,060
		7	Mohanganj	119,076	58,475	60,601	102,129	50,416	51,713
		8	Salon	127,596	62,766	64,830	115,504	56,984	58,520
		9	Dalmau	83,259	40,992	42,267	79,476	39,129	40,347
		10	Sareni	89,217	43,202	46,015	86,026	41,524	44,502
			Total ...	1,036,521	512,980	523,541	950,290	471,191	479,099
37	Sitapur ...	1	Sidhauli	131,915	69,357	62,558	120,198	63,288	56,910
		2	Kamalpur	58,006	30,421	27,585	53,151	27,927	25,224
		3	Sitapur	108,669	58,159	50,510	86,652	46,698	39,954
		4	Misrikh	92,299	49,269	43,030	81,547	43,685	37,862
		5	Maholi	97,304	52,241	45,063	90,461	48,547	41,914
		6	Hargam	51,002	26,931	24,071	48,437	28,011	20,426
		7	Laharpur	139,980	73,114	66,866	112,284	59,026	53,258
		8	Biswan	122,027	64,078	57,949	97,807	51,667	46,140
		9	Tambour	83,697	43,088	40,609	71,734	36,990	34,744
		10	Thangaon	62,662	33,031	29,631	55,398	29,193	26,205
		11	Mahmudabad	127,852	67,493	60,359	104,011	55,153	48,858
			Total ...	1,075,413	567,182	508,231	916,680	485,185	431,495
38	Hardoi ...	1	Hardoi	117,384	64,258	53,126	109,756	60,035	49,721
		2	Beghaoli	94,888	51,081	43,807	88,788	47,871	40,917
		3	Bilgrám	96,526	51,488	45,038	83,500	44,926	38,574
		4	Tandiawan	74,678	39,737	34,941	66,251	35,419	30,832
		5	Pihani	101,774	54,443	47,331	87,841	47,238	40,603
		6	Beniganj	51,163	27,596	23,567	48,549	26,173	22,376
		7	Shálabad	113,427	60,639	52,788	96,968	52,164	44,804
		8	Harpálpur	91,352	49,785	41,567	88,031	47,966	40,065

Circles distributed by Religion—(*continued*).

Muhammadans. Both sexes.	Muhammadans. Males.	Muhammadans. Females.	Jains. Both sexes.	Jains. Males.	Jains. Females.	Christians. Both sexes.	Christians. Males.	Christians. Females.	Others. Both sexes.	Others. Males.	Others. Females.	Serial number of thána.
11	12	13	14	15	16	17	18	19	20	21	22	23
6,372	3,182	3,190	...	...	...	...	...	...	...	...	...	18
4,143	2,037	2,106	...	...	...	...	...	...	...	...	...	19
5,411	2,599	2,812	...	...	...	...	...	...	...	...	...	20
15,879	7,576	8,303	...	...	...	...	...	...	...	...	...	21
2,238	1,126	1,112	...	...	...	...	...	...	...	...	...	22
6,850	3,208	3,642	...	...	...	...	...	...	...	...	...	23
225,639	109,738	115,901	...	...	...	74	39	35	1	1	...	
4,652	2,337	2,315	...	...	...	...	...	...	2	2	...	1
4,021	2,013	2,008	...	...	...	5	2	3	51	26	25	2
15,772	7,951	7,821	...	...	...	35	26	9	177	173	4	3
10,141	4,870	5,271	1	1	...	14	11	3	2	1	1	4
16,329	8,082	8,247	1	1	...	...	...	...	28	16	12	5
26,588	12,823	13,765	562	277	285	28	15	13	80	44	36	6
11,526	5,547	5,979	63	35	28	9	5	4	2	2	...	7
16,399	7,722	8,677	28	17	11	...	...	...	34	16	18	8
19,607	9,755	9,852	6	6	...	407	239	168	84	52	32	9
6,966	3,538	3,428	26	17	9	51	26	25	63	43	20	10
5,246	3,356	1,890	26	16	10	2,785	2,372	413	215	168	47	11
6,256	3,220	3,036	43	19	24	...	...	...	...	...	...	12
17,866	9,664	8,202	41	30	11	2,435	1,259	1,176	465	256	209	13
161,369	80,878	80,491	797	419	378	5,769	3,955	1,814	1,203	799	404	
8,847	4,718	3,129	...	...	...	79	38	41	34	21	13	1
14,678	7,338	7,340	6	2	4	4	2	2	1	1	...	2
4,511	2,327	2,184	...	...	...	3	2	1	41	22	19	3
2,723	1,360	1,363	...	...	...	...	...	...	55	26	29	4
2,521	1,269	1,252	...	...	...	...	...	...	18	10	8	5
5,590	2,701	2,889	...	...	...	8	4	4	...	...	...	6
7,326	3,765	3,561	...	...	...	...	...	...	...	...	...	7
13,664	7,114	6,550	2	2	...	...	...	...	...	...	...	8
1,068	575	493	...	...	...	...	...	...	...	...	...	9
2,515	1,281	1,234	...	...	...	...	...	...	...	...	...	10
1,102	586	516	...	...	...	...	...	...	...	...	...	11
4,684	2,225	2,459	...	...	...	...	...	...	1	1	...	12
6,691	3,238	3,453	...	...	...	12	7	5	1	1	...	13
75,920	38,497	37,423	8	4	4	106	53	53	151	82	69	
5,729	2,924	2,805	...	...	...	...	...	...	2	2	...	1
5,875	2,746	3,129	...	...	...	1	1	...	...	...	...	2
7,070	3,380	3,690	...	...	...	9	5	4	1	1	...	3
11,265	5,617	5,648	2	1	1	129	70	59	90	64	26	4
3,403	1,660	1,743	...	...	...	...	...	...	...	...	...	5
16,621	7,927	8,694	20	8	12	...	...	...	1	1	...	6
16,945	8,057	8,888	1	1	...	...	...	...	1	1	...	7
12,086	5,778	6,308	...	...	...	5	3	2	1	1	...	8
3,781	1,861	1,920	...	...	...	1	1	...	1	1	...	9
3,190	1,677	1,513	...	...	...	...	...	...	1	1	...	10
85,965	41,627	44,338	23	10	13	145	80	65	98	72	26	
11,681	6,050	5,631	9	6	3	5	3	2	22	10	12	1
4,853	2,493	2,360	...	...	...	...	...	...	2	1	1	2
21,196	10,821	10,375	23	18	5	691	553	138	107	69	38	3
10,734	5,573	5,161	...	...	...	10	7	3	8	4	4	4
6,841	3,692	3,149	...	...	...	1	1	...	1	1	...	5
7,565	3,920	3,645	...	...	...	...	...	...	...	...	...	6
27,677	14,075	13,602	13	7	6	6	6	...	...	...	...	7
24,202	12,404	11,798	17	6	11	...	...	...	1	1	...	8
11,958	6,093	5,865	4	4	...	...	...	...	1	1	...	9
7,264	3,838	3,426	...	...	...	...	...	...	...	...	...	10
23,668	12,250	11,418	168	85	83	4	4	...	1	1	...	11
157,639	81,209	76,430	234	126	108	717	574	143	143	88	55	
7,536	4,178	3,363	1	1	...	78	44	34	13	5	8	1
6,097	3,208	2,889	...	...	...	...	...	...	3	2	1	2
13,022	6,560	6,462	...	...	...	4	2	2	...	...	...	3
8,425	4,316	4,109	...	...	...	2	2	...	...	...	...	4
13,927	7,201	6,726	...	...	...	6	4	2	...	...	...	5
2,614	1,423	1,191	...	...	...	...	...	...	...	...	...	6
16,416	8,450	7,966	...	...	...	43	25	18	...	...	...	7
3,817	1,818	1,499	...	...	...	4	1	3	...	...	...	8

Showing the population of the Police

PROVINCIAL TABLE VII.

Serial number of district.	Name of district.	Serial number of thána.	Name of thána.	Total population. Both sexes.	Total population. Males.	Total population. Females.	Hindus. Both sexes.	Hindus. Males.	Hindus. Females.
1	2	3	4	5	6	7	8	9	10
38	Hardoi—(concluded).	9	Pali	64,416	35.122	29,294	60,607	33,158	27,449
		10	Malláwan	101,814	53,852	47,962	90,774	48,138	42,636
		11	Sandila	127,312	66.802	60,510	104,958	55,576	49,382
		12	Atrauli	78,477	41,694	36,783	72,219	38,336	33,883
			Total ...	1,113,211	596,497	516,714	998,339	536,997	461,342
39	Kheri ...	1	Bhira	51,966	28,335	23,631	47,174	25,635	21,539
		2	Gola	94,022	50,592	43.430	81,606	44,001	37,605
		3	Phulbehar	58,862	31,108	27,754	51,188	27,066	24,122
		4	Nimgaon	65,008	34,233	30,775	55,521	29,305	26,216
		5	Lakhimpur	143,032	75.375	67,657	118,464	62.668	55,796
		6	Nighasan	101,067	53.523	47,544	89,301	47,247	42,054
		7	Mitauli	72,366	38,695	33.671	65,910	35,249	30,661
		8	Muhamdi	80,682	43,107	37.575	69,022	37,038	31,984
		9	Pasgawan	59,060	31,797	27.263	50,217	27,145	23,072
		10	Palia	34,542	20,385	14,157	30,168	17,772	12,396
		11	Dhaurahra	73,858	38.568	35.290	64,400	33,630	30,770
		12	Ísanagar	69,150	36,317	32,833	61,884	32,460	29,424
			Total ...	903,615	482,035	421,580	784,855	419,216	365,639
40	Fyzabad ...	1	Ronahi...	118,964	58,027	60.937	104,879	51,498	53,381
		2	Milkipur	112,497	55,380	57,117	104,637	51,649	52,988
		3	Mahárájganj	109,563	54,894	54,669	101,035	50,751	50,284
		4	Bikapur	132,616	65,413	67,203	125,208	61,900	63,308
		5	Jalálpur	144,758	73,835	70,923	128,319	65,593	62,726
		6	Tanda	165,609	83,233	82,376	137,255	69,165	68,090
		7	Akbarpur	142,850	72,374	70.476	125,250	63,689	61,561
		8	Rámnagar	125,767	63.731	62 036	113.550	57,746	55,804
		9	Sadar or pura Kalandar ...	86,463	42,514	43.949	79,059	39,065	39,994
		10	Ajudhia	24,165	13.491	10,674	20,811	11,796	9,015
		11	Cantonment	6,235	4,398	1.837	3,623	2,431	1,192
		12	Kotwali	47,472	25,312	22,160	33,205	17,939	15,266
			Total ...	1,216,959	612,602	604,357	1,076,831	543,222	533,609
41	Gonda ...	1	Andhiari	75,560	39,266	36.294	68,451	35,530	32,921
		2	Itia Thok	91,690	46,176	45,514	80,661	40,519	40,142
		3	Rámapur	82,475	41,763	40,712	73,495	37,208	36,287
		4	Srinagar	57,069	29,155	27,914	48,854	24,933	23,921
		5	Gonda	133,920	68,348	65,572	118,473	60,487	57,986
		6	Colonelganj	111,047	57,033	54,014	96,911	49,941	46,970
		7	Wazírganj	59,075	30,253	28,822	54,241	27,745	26,496
		8	Nawábganj	61,825	32,499	29,326	56,813	29,714	27,099
		9	Tarabganj	114,137	57,220	56,917	108,099	54,297	53,802
		10	Paraspur	66,535	33,598	32,937	61,582	31.131	30,451
		11	Utraula	138,433	70,787	67,646	98,785	50,708	48,077
		12	Sadullanagar	80,096	40,845	39,251	60,649	31,036	29,613
		13	Birpur	56,905	29,437	27,468	52,299	27,058	25,241
		14	Balrámpur	82,098	41,750	40,348	69,027	35,096	33,931
		15	Tulsipur	109,123	56,275	52,848	89,949	46,253	43,696
		16	Lalia	78,896	41,151	37,745	71,426	37,203	34,223
		17	Pachperwa	60,345	30,847	29,498	43,799	22,408	21,391
			Total ...	1,459,229	746,403	712,826	1,253,514	641,267	612,247
42	Bahraich ...	1	Kaisarganj	116,222	60,329	55,893	90,151	47,230	42,921
		2	Fakharpur	83,471	43,684	39,787	69,646	36,497	33,149
		3	Piagpur	109,460	56,622	52,838	99,846	51,614	48,232
		4	Bahraich	127,494	67.027	60.467	97,812	51,887	45,925
		5	Sisaya	66,774	34,941	31,833	59,956	31,302	28,654
		6	Kheri Ghát	52,810	27,237	25,573	47,257	24,344	22,913
		7	Nánpára	123,839	64,663	59,176	92,399	48,211	44,188
		8	Malhipur	80,489	41,847	38,642	63,599	33,044	30,555
		9	Motipur	55,053	29,562	25,491	45,894	24,596	21,298
		10	Sujauli	17,531	10,397	7,134	15,538	9,143	6,395
		11	Ikauna	58,395	30,356	28,039	53,754	27,930	25,824
		12	Bhinga	108,894	56,902	51,992	93,849	49,012	44,837
			Total ...	1,000,432	523,567	476,865	829,701	434,810	394,891

Circles distributed by Religion—(*continued*).

PROVINCIAL TABLE VII.

Muhammadans.			Jains.			Christians.			Others.			Serial number of thánas.
Both sexes.	Males.	Females.	Both sexes.	Males.	Females.	Both sexes.	Males.	Females.	Both sexes	Males.	Females.	
11	12	13	14	15	16	17	18	19	20	21	22	23
3,809	1,964	*1,845*	...	...	...	...	...	...	...	...	...	9
11,013	5,698	*5,315*	12	7	*5*	15	9	*6*	...	...	...	10
22,339	11,220	*11,119*	...	...	...	15	6	*9*	...	...	...	11
6,258	3,358	*2,900*	...	...	...	...	...	...	...	...	...	12
114,674	35,390	*55,284*	13	8	*5*	167	93	*74*	18	9	*9*	
4,740	2,671	*2,069*	...	...	...	13	4	*9*	39	25	*14*	1
12,381	6,570	*5,811*	...	...	...	35	21	*14*	...	..	...	2
7,671	4,040	*3,631*	...	...	...	3	2	*1*	...	...	...	3
9,485	4,926	*4,559*	...	...	...	1	1	...	1	1	...	4
24,429	12,634	*11,795*	8	6	*2*	48	22	*26*	83	45	*38*	5
11,745	6,267	*5,478*	...	...	...	...	...	...	21	9	*12*	6
6,453	3,445	*3,008*	...	...	...	1	1	...	2	...	*2*	7
11,603	6,029	*5,574*	2	2	...	52	36	*16*	3	2	*1*	8
8,498	4,453	*4,045*	...	...	...	345	199	*146*	...	...	...	9
4,357	2,601	*1,756*	...	...	...	7	5	*2*	10	7	*3*	10
9,439	4,927	*4,512*	...	...	...	...	...	...	19	11	*8*	11
7,256	3,851	*3,405*	...	...	...	...	...	...	10	6	*4*	12
118,057	62,414	*55,643*	10	8	*2*	505	291	*214*	188	106	*82*	
14,075	6,522	*7,553*	1	1	...	9	6	*3*	...	...	...	1
7,860	3,731	*4,129*	...	...	...	...	...	...	...	...	...	2
8,493	4,124	*4,369*	...	...	...	35	19	*16*	...	...	...	3
7,403	3,513	*3,890*	...	...	...	5	...	*5*	...	...	...	4
16,439	8,242	*8,197*	...	...	...	...	...	...	...	...	...	5
28,347	14,064	*14,283*	...	...	...	4	1	*3*	3	3	...	6
17,582	8,675	*8,907*	11	3	*8*	7	7	...	...	...	...	7
12,217	5,985	*6,232*	...	...	...	...	...	...	...	...	...	8
7,395	3,444	*3,951*	...	...	...	9	5	*4*	...	...	...	9
3,156	1,591	*1,565*	148	72	*76*	34	20	*14*	16	12	*4*	10
1,577	1,125	*452*	...	...	...	889	715	*174*	146	127	*19*	11
13,917	7,198	*6,719*	262	131	*131*	1	1	...	87	43	*44*	12
138,461	68,214	*70,247*	161	77	*84*	1,254	904	*350*	252	185	*67*	
7,070	3,717	*3,353*	...	...	...	39	19	*20*	...	...	...	1
11,028	5,656	*5,372*	...	...	...	1	1	...	...	...	...	2
8,980	4,555	*4,425*	...	...	...	...	...	...	...	...	...	3
8,215	4,222	*3,993*	...	...	...	...	...	...	...	...	...	4
15,296	7,792	*7,504*	...	...	...	126	55	*71*	25	14	*11*	5
14,115	7,084	*7,031*	...	...	...	21	8	*13*	...	...	...	6
4,831	2,506	*2,325*	...	...	...	3	2	*1*	...	...	...	7
5,000	2,778	*2,222*	...	...	...	12	7	*5*	...	...	...	8
6,038	2,923	*3,115*	...	...	...	...	...	...	...	...	...	9
4,953	2,467	*2,486*	...	...	...	...	...	...	...	...	...	10
39,636	20,075	*19,561*	...	...	...	7	2	*5*	5	2	*3*	11
19,446	9,808	*9,638*	...	...	...	...	...	...	1	1	...	12
4,606	2,379	*2,227*	...	...	...	...	...	...	...	...	...	13
13,034	6,634	*6,400*	...	...	...	37	20	*17*	...	...	...	14
19,163	10,014	*9,149*	...	...	...	...	...	...	11	8	*3*	15
7,470	3,948	*3,522*	...	...	...	...	...	...	...	...	...	16
16,544	8,437	*8,107*	...	...	...	2	2	...	...	...	...	17
205,425	104,995	*100,430*	...	...	...	248	116	*132*	42	25	*17*	
26,045	13,084	*12,961*	1	1	...	5	4	*1*	20	10	*10*	1
13,768	7,151	*6,617*	...	...	...	3	1	*2*	54	35	*19*	2
9,614	5,008	*4,606*	...	...	...	...	...	...	...	...	...	3
29,495	15,022	*14,473*	47	32	*15*	78	44	*34*	62	42	*20*	4
6,790	3,617	*3,173*	...	...	...	...	...	...	28	22	*6*	5
5,553	2,893	*2,660*	...	...	...	...	...	...	...	...	...	6
30,881	16,146	*14,735*	...	...	...	15	10	*5*	544	296	*248*	7
16,874	8,791	*8,083*	...	...	...	...	...	...	16	12	*4*	8
9,159	4,966	*4,193*	...	...	...	...	...	...	...	...	...	9
1,984	1,249	*735*	...	...	...	6	3	*3*	3	2	*1*	10
4,620	2,415	*2,205*	...	...	...	...	...	...	21	11	*10*	11
15,015	7,873	*7,142*	...	...	...	17	11	*6*	13	6	*7*	12
169,798	88,215	*81,583*	48	33	*15*	124	73	*51*	761	436	*325*	

Showing the population of the Police

PROVINCIAL TABLE VII.

Serial number of district.	Name of district.	Serial number of thána.	Name of thána.	Total population. Both sexes.	Total population. Males.	Total population. Females.	Hindus. Both sexes.	Hindus. Males.	Hindus. Females.
1	2	3	4	5	6	7	8	9	10
43	Sultánpur ...	1	Sultánpur	114,844	55,630	59,214	89,027	43,479	45,548
		2	Piparpur	73,693	35,788	37,905	67,574	32,886	34,688
		3	Musáfirkhána	98,879	47,927	50,952	88,471	43,046	45,425
		4	Lumbhua	87,252	43,569	43,683	80,631	40,330	40,301
		5	Haliapur	67,411	32,982	34,429	59,523	29,357	30,166
		6	Jaisingpur	81,077	40,995	40,082	76,277	38,645	37,632
		7	Kurebhar	75,707	37,128	38,579	68,797	33,926	34,871
		8	Jagdispur	91,769	44,505	47,264	73,136	35,855	37,281
		9	Bazár-Sukul	34,561	16,845	17,716	27,859	13,733	14,126
		10	Gauriganj	65,084	31.855	33.229	58,854	28,783	30,071
		11	Raipur	108.574	52.608	55,966	103,578	50,157	53,421
		12	Kadipur	94,986	48,803	46.183	90,528	46,503	44,025
		13	Dostpur	82,014	41,851	40,163	74,697	38,279	36,418
			Total ...	1,075,851	530,486	545,365	958,952	474,979	483,973
44	Partábgarh ...	1	Macandrewganj	125,576	61,297	64,279	108,534	52,901	55,633
		2	Ràniganj	96,427	46,977	49,450	84,059	41,058	43,001
		3	Katka Manapur	42,700	20,614	22,086	39,635	19,153	20,482
		4	Jethwara	148,214	71,475	76,739	130,126	62,821	67,305
		5	Sangipur	112,550	54,498	58,052	106,685	51,720	54,965
		6	Kunda	130,660	63,589	67.071	114,339	56,050	58,289
		7	Sangramgarh	109,941	54,249	55,692	102,730	50,746	51,984
		8	Patti	135,345	67,721	67,624	124,802	62,468	62,334
			*Soraon**	210	112	98	210	112	98
			*Machhlishahr**	7,209	3,627	3,582	6,970	3,500	3,470
			*Sikandra**	690	323	367	465	225	240
			*Mau**	1,373	689	684	1,280	651	629
			Total ...	910,895	445,171	465,724	819,835	401,405	418,430
45	Bara Banki ...	1	Nawábganj	170,324	88,155	82,169	134,018	69,953	64,065
		2	Zaidpur	101,686	51,606	50,080	82,066	41,989	40,077
		3	Kursi	99,893	52,321	47,572	83,572	44,201	39,371
		4	Rámnagar	117,178	61.834	55,339	100,065	52,932	47,133
		5	Tikaitnagar	117,839	60,439	57,400	100,417	51,882	48,535
		6	Fatehpur	138,443	72,272	66,171	112,917	59,329	53,588
		7	Ramsanehighát	117,997	59,064	58.933	104,347	52,320	52,027
		8	Bhilsar...	141,016	68,866	72 150	110,733	54,658	56,075
		9	Haidergarh	126,535	62,558	63,977	115,605	57,291	58,314
			Total ...	1,130,906	577,115	553,791	943,740	484,555	459,185

* Criminal jurisdiction for the population shown as belonging to Thánas Soraon, Sikandra and Mau is vested in the

PROVINCIAL TABLE VII.

Circles distributed by Religion—(*concluded*).

Muhammadans. Both sexes.	Muhammadans. Males.	Muhammadans. Females.	Jains. Both sexes.	Jains. Males.	Jains. Females.	Christians. Both sexes.	Christians. Males.	Christians. Females.	Others. Both sexes.	Others. Males.	Others. Females.	Serial number of thána.
11	12	13	14	15	16	17	18	19	20	21	22	23
25,775	12,129	13,646	...	...	...	42	22	20	...	...	...	1
6,119	2,902	3,217	...	...	...	...	...	...	...	...	...	2
10,403	4,878	5,525	...	...	...	5	3	2	...	...	...	3
6,621	3,239	3,382	...	...	...	...	...	...	...	...	...	4
7,888	3,625	4,263	...	...	...	...	...	...	...	...	...	5
4,800	2,350	2,450	...	...	...	...	...	...	...	...	...	6
6,908	3,200	3,708	...	...	...	2	2	...	...	...	...	7
18,633	8,650	9,983	...	...	...	...	...	...	...	...	...	8
6,702	3,112	3,590	...	...	...	...	...	...	...	...	...	9
6,230	3,072	3,158	...	...	...	...	...	...	...	...	...	10
4,996	2,451	2,545	...	...	...	...	...	...	...	...	...	11
4,458	2,300	2,158	...	...	...	...	...	...	...	...	...	12
7,313	3,569	3,744	...	...	...	4	3	1	...	...	...	13
116,846	55,477	61,369	...	...	...	53	30	23	...	...	...	
16,848	8,299	8,549	126	62	64	57	25	32	11	10	1	1
12,360	5,914	6,446	1	1	...	7	4	3	...	...	...	2
3,065	1,461	1,604	...	...	...	...	...	...	...	...	...	3
18,087	8,653	9,434	...	...	...	1	1	...	...	...	...	4
5,865	2,778	3,087	...	...	...	...	...	...	...	...	...	5
16,311	7,535	8,776	...	...	...	10	4	6	...	...	...	6
7,205	3,499	3,706	...	...	...	2	2	...	...	...	...	7
10,540	5,250	5,290	3	3	...	...	...	...	4	2	2	8
...	...	...	...	...	...	...	...	...	...	...	...	
239	127	112	...	...	...	...	...	...	...	...	...	
225	98	127	...	...	...	...	...	...	...	...	...	
93	38	55	...	...	...	...	...	...	...	...	...	
90,838	43,652	47,186	130	66	64	77	36	41	15	12	3	
35,871	17,997	17,874	344	164	180	76	47	29	15	8	7	1
19,617	9,600	10,017	2	2	...	1	1	...	...	...	...	2
16,320	8,119	8,201	1	1	...	...	...	...	...	...	...	3
16,952	8,811	8,141	129	75	54	23	13	10	4	3	1	4
17,031	8,350	8,681	366	188	178	17	11	6	8	8	...	5
25,396	12,869	12,527	122	68	54	8	6	2	...	...	...	6
13,620	6,726	6,894	26	15	11	4	3	1	...	...	...	7
30,206	14,174	16,032	52	25	27	14	5	9	11	4	7	8
10,925	5,265	5,660	1	1	...	4	1	3	...	...	...	9
185,938	91,911	94,027	1,043	539	504	147	87	60	38	23	15	

Magistrate of Allahabad. For the population shown against Thána Machhlishahr it is vested in the Magistrate of Jaunpur.

PROVINCIAL TABLE VII. Supplement.

SUPPLE

Showing by religion the population of the pattis of the

Serial number of district.	Name of district.	Name of mortuary circle.	Serial number of patti.	Name of patti.	Total population. Both sexes.	Total population. Males.	Total population. Females.	Hindus. Both sexes.	Hindus. Males.	Hindus. Females.
1	2	3	4	5	6	7	8	9	10	11
46	Almora.	Almora rural Circle.	1	Goriphat	4,514	2,330	2,184	4,514	2,330	2,184
			2	Talla Des	6,274	3,171	3,103	6,272	3,169	3,103
			3	Dánpur Malla	5,562	2,801	2,761	5,562	2,801	2,761
			4	Dánpur Bichla	3,342	1,678	1,664	3,342	1,678	1,664
			5	Dánpur Talla	5,408	2,789	2,619	5,398	2,783	2,615
			6	Dug	4,208	2,172	2,036	4,111	2,119	1,992
			7	Katyur Malla	7,218	4,199	3,019	7,154	4,161	2,993
			8	Katyur Bichla	4,693	2,423	2,270	4,660	2,400	2,260
			9	Katyur Talla	3,999	2,062	1,937	3,965	2,036	1,929
			10	Nakuri	4,250	2,147	2,103	4,250	2,147	2,103
			11	Darun	5,588	2,935	2,653	5,588	2,935	2,653
			12	Kharain	2,164	1,149	1,015	2,164	1,149	1,015
			13	Lakhanpur Malla	5,173	2,708	2,465	5,173	2,708	2,465
			14	Lakhanpur Talla	4,592	2,195	2,397	4,592	2,195	2,397
			15	Rithagarh	3,551	1,824	1,727	3,549	1,822	1,727
			16	Rangor	7,249	3,810	3,439	7,249	3,810	3,439
			17	Salam Malla	4,649	2,280	2,369	4,649	2,280	2,369
			18	Salam Talla	4,246	2,059	2,187	4,246	2,059	2,187
			19	Bel	6,737	3,515	3,222	6,731	3,512	3,215
			20	Bherang	2,294	1,149	1,145	2,294	1,149	1,149
			21	Baraun	7,668	3,988	3,680	7,653	3,979	3,674
			22	Kamsyar	6,776	3,531	3,245	6,751	3,514	3,237
			23	Pungraun	3,679	1,846	1,833	3,679	1,846	1,833
			24	Athigaon	6,117	3,178	2,939	6,104	3,172	2,932
			25	Bisaud Malla	1,388	663	725	1,388	663	725
			26	Boraraw Palla	6,034	3,149	2,885	6,006	3,133	2,873
			27	Boraraw Walla	4,762	2,389	2,373	4,715	2,368	2,347
			28	Dwarsyun	1,068	482	586	1,065	482	583
			29	Kairarau	4,316	2,211	2,105	4,309	2,207	2,102
			30	Kaligarh	2,439	1,183	1,256	2,439	1,183	1,256
			31	Khasparja...	13,459	6,722	6,737	12,293	6,077	6,216
			32	Uchyur	3,797	1,857	1,940	3,797	1,857	1,940
			33	Ryuni	1,064	534	530	1,048	518	530
			34	Syunara Malla	5,385	2,721	2,664	5,385	2,721	2,664
			35	Syunara Talla	6,015	3,125	2,890	5,989	3,114	2,875
			36	Tikhun Malla	4,585	2,237	2,348	4,580	2,234	2,346
			37	Tikhun Talla	4,711	2,263	2,448	4,700	2,256	2,444
			38	Athaguli Palla	7,286	3,957	3,329	6,849	3,683	3,166
			39	Athaguli Walla	2,909	1,783	1,126	2,908	1,782	1,126
			40	Chaugaon	2,832	1,364	1,468	2,825	1,357	1,468
			41	Dhuraphat	1,666	828	838	1,666	828	838
			42	Kandar Khua	2,319	1,163	1,156	2,319	1,163	1,156
			43	Malli Doti...	4,894	2,812	2,082	4,883	2,803	2,080
			44	Chaukot Malla	7,931	3,897	4,034	7,928	3,895	4,033
			45	Chaukot Bichla	8,887	4,333	4,554	8,885	4,331	4,554
			46	Chaukot Talla	7,450	3,646	3,804	7,446	3,644	3,802
			47	Dora Malla	6,868	3,390	3,478	6,813	3,348	3,465
			48	Dora Bichla	5,875	2,823	3,052	5,875	2,823	3,052
			49	Dora Talla	7,629	3,789	3,840	7,628	3,788	3,840
			50	Giwar Palla	6,595	3,346	3,249	6,565	3,334	3,231
			51	Giwar Talla	7,342	3,649	3,693	7,314	3,634	3,680
			52	Giwar Walla	5,905	2,931	2,974	5,905	2,931	2,974
			53	Kaklasaun Malla	6,546	3,107	3,439	6,546	3,107	3,439
			54	Kaklasaun Talla	1,816	895	921	1,816	895	921
			55	Naya Palla	5,360	2,673	2,687	5,358	2,672	2,686
			56	Naya Walla	4,514	2,165	2,349	4,505	2,161	2,344
			57	Silaur Malla	4,591	2,206	2,385	4,541	2,183	2,358
			58	Silaur Talla	4,707	2,258	2,449	4,695	2,254	2,441
			59	Salt Malla...	7,247	3,577	3,670	7,247	3,577	3,670
			60	Salt Palla	5,348	2,624	2,724	5,345	2,622	2,723
			61	Salt Talla	7,564	3,717	3,847	7,548	3,706	3,842
			62	Salt Walla...	5,845	2,870	2,975	5,836	2,866	2,970
				Total, Almora rural Circle ...	318,900	161,278	157,622	316,610	159,954	156,656
		Champawat rural Circle.	63	Chalsi	4,648	2,297	2,351	4,648	2,297	2,351
			64	Charal Malla	448	230	218	448	230	218
			65	Charal Talla	500	272	228	481	260	221
			66	Gumdes	5,611	2,770	2,841	5,611	2,770	2,841
			67	Gungol	1,562	791	771	1,562	791	771
			68	Khilpatti Phat	1,880	913	967	1,880	913	967
			69	Palbilon Malla	994	504	490	994	504	490
			70	Palbilon Talla	4,249	2,230	2,019	4,249	2,230	2,019
			71	Pharka	16	7	9	16	7	9
			72	Regruban	5,696	2,926	2,770	5,696	2,926	2,770
			73	Sipti	645	317	328	645	317	328
			74	Sui Bisung	610	370	240	599	366	233
			75	Asi	355	162	193	355	162	193
			76	Talli Rao	1,640	798	842	1,640	798	842
			77	Talla Des	4,697	2,438	2,259	4,697	2,438	2,259
				Total Champawat rural circle ...	33,551	16,526	16,626	33,521	17,009	16,512

MENT.

Kumaun Division arranged according to mortuary circles.

PROVINCIAL TABLE VII.

Supplement.

Muhammadans.			Jains.			Christians.			Others.			
Both sexes.	Males.	Females.	Both sexes.	Males.	Females.	Both sexes.	Males.	Females.	Both sexes.	Males.	Females.	Serial number of patti.
12	13	14	15	16	17	18	19	20	21	22	23	24
...	...	...	...	...	...	...	...	...	...	...	...	1
...	...	...	...	...	...	2	2	...	...	...	...	2
...	...	...	...	...	...	...	...	...	...	...	...	3
...	...	...	...	...	...	...	...	...	...	...	...	4
8	4	4	...	...	...	2	2	...	...	...	...	5
96	52	44	...	...	...	1	1	...	...	...	...	6
44	23	21	...	...	...	20	15	5	...	...	...	7
27	21	6	...	...	...	6	2	4	...	...	...	8
34	26	8	...	...	...	...	...	...	...	...	...	9
...	...	...	...	...	...	...	...	...	...	...	...	10
...	...	...	...	...	...	...	...	...	...	...	...	11
...	...	...	...	...	...	...	...	...	...	...	...	12
...	...	...	...	...	...	...	...	...	...	...	...	13
...	...	...	...	...	...	...	...	...	...	...	...	14
2	2	...	...	...	...	...	...	...	...	...	...	15
...	...	...	...	...	...	...	...	...	...	...	...	16
...	...	...	...	...	...	...	...	...	...	...	...	17
...	...	...	...	...	...	...	...	...	...	...	...	18
6	3	3	...	...	...	...	...	...	...	...	...	19
...	...	...	...	...	...	...	...	...	...	...	...	20
10	6	4	...	...	...	5	3	2	...	...	...	21
25	17	8	...	...	...	...	...	...	...	...	...	22
...	...	...	...	...	...	...	...	...	...	...	...	23
13	6	7	...	...	...	...	...	...	...	...	...	24
...	...	...	...	...	...	...	...	...	...	...	...	25
28	16	12	...	...	...	...	...	...	...	...	...	26
47	21	26	...	...	...	...	...	...	...	...	...	27
3	...	3	...	...	...	...	...	...	...	...	...	28
7	4	3	...	...	...	...	...	...	...	...	...	29
...	...	...	...	...	...	...	...	...	...	...	...	30
900	526	374	5	4	1	247	105	142	14	10	4	31
...	...	...	...	...	...	...	...	...	...	...	...	32
16	16	...	...	...	...	...	...	...	...	...	...	33
...	...	...	...	...	...	...	...	...	...	...	...	34
18	8	10	...	...	...	8	3	5	...	...	...	35
5	3	2	...	...	...	...	...	...	...	...	...	36
...	...	...	...	...	...	11	7	4	...	...	...	37
423	266	157	...	...	...	14	8	6	...	...	...	38
1	1	...	...	...	...	...	...	...	...	...	...	39
7	7	...	...	...	...	...	...	...	...	...	...	40
...	...	...	...	...	...	...	...	...	...	...	...	41
...	...	...	...	...	...	...	...	...	...	...	...	42
11	9	2	...	...	...	...	...	...	...	...	...	43
3	2	1	...	...	...	...	...	...	...	...	...	44
2	2	...	...	...	...	...	...	...	...	...	...	45
4	2	2	...	...	...	...	...	...	...	...	...	46
3	2	1	...	...	...	52	40	12	...	...	...	47
...	...	...	...	...	...	...	...	...	...	...	...	48
1	1	...	...	...	...	...	...	...	...	...	...	49
30	12	18	...	...	...	...	...	...	...	...	...	50
24	12	12	...	...	...	4	3	1	...	...	...	51
...	...	...	...	...	...	...	...	...	...	...	...	52
...	...	...	...	...	...	...	...	...	...	...	...	53
...	...	...	...	...	...	...	...	...	...	...	...	54
2	1	1	...	...	...	...	...	...	...	...	...	55
9	4	5	...	...	...	...	...	...	...	...	...	56
44	20	24	...	...	...	6	3	3	...	...	...	57
12	4	8	...	...	...	...	...	...	...	...	...	58
...	...	...	...	...	...	...	...	...	...	...	...	59
3	2	1	...	...	...	...	...	...	...	...	...	60
16	11	5	...	...	...	...	...	...	...	...	...	61
9	4	5	...	...	...	...	...	...	...	...	...	62
1,893	1,116	777	5	4	1	378	194	184	14	10	4	
...	...	...	...	...	...	...	...	...	...	...	...	63
...	...	...	...	...	...	...	...	...	...	...	...	64
10	7	3	...	...	...	9	5	4	...	...	...	65
...	...	...	...	...	...	...	...	...	...	...	...	66
...	...	...	...	...	...	...	...	...	...	...	...	67
...	...	...	...	...	...	...	...	...	...	...	...	68
...	...	...	...	...	...	...	...	...	...	...	...	69
...	...	...	...	...	...	...	...	...	...	...	...	70
...	...	...	...	...	...	...	...	...	...	...	...	71
...	...	...	...	...	...	...	...	...	...	...	...	72
...	...	...	...	...	...	...	...	...	...	...	...	73
1	1	...	...	...	...	10	3	7	...	...	...	74
...	...	...	...	...	...	...	...	...	...	...	...	75
...	...	...	...	...	...	...	...	...	...	...	...	76
...	...	...	...	...	...	...	...	...	...	...	...	77
11	8	3	...	...	...	19	8	11	...	...	...	

SUPPLE

Showing by religion the population of the pattis of the

PROVINCIAL TABLE VII.

Supplement.

Serial number of district.	Name of district.	Name of mortuary circle.	Serial number of patti.	Name of patti.	Total population.			Hindus.		
					Both sexes.	Males.	Females.	Both sexes.	Males.	Females.
1	2	3	4	5	6	7	8	9	10	11
46	Almora—(concluded).	Sor rural Circle.	78	Byans	115	57	58	115	57	58
			79	Chaudans	1,296	602	694	1,296	602	694
			80	Darma Malla	217	111	106	217	111	106
			81	Darma Talla	885	457	428	885	457	428
			82	Athbisi Malla	1,044	518	526	1,044	518	526
			83	Athbisi Talla	1,118	577	541	1,118	577	541
			84	Barabisi	5,129	2,641	2,488	5,129	2,641	2,488
			85	Dindihat	2,902	1,490	1,412	2,902	1,490	1,412
			86	Mali	3,303	1,711	1,592	3,294	1,708	1,586
			87	Askot Malla	5,783	2,780	3,003	5,783	2,780	3,003
			88	Askot Talla	6,387	3,221	3,166	6,387	3,221	3,166
			89	Kharayat	3,087	1,617	1,470	3,078	1,612	1,466
			90	Kharkdes	1,221	638	583	1,221	638	583
			91	Mahar	4,827	2,287	2,540	4,561	2,248	2,313
			92	Nayades	3,245	1,630	1,615	3,245	1,630	1,615
			93	Rawal	3,313	1,762	1,551	3,313	1,762	1,551
			94	Seti Malla	491	245	246	491	245	246
			95	Seti Talla	3,494	1,783	1,711	3,449	1,760	1,689
			96	Saun	3,537	1,804	1,733	3,537	1,804	1,733
			97	Waldia Malla	1,567	818	749	1,567	818	749
			98	Waldia Bichla	984	483	501	984	483	501
			99	Waldia Talla	5,105	2,578	2,527	5,010	2,534	2,476
				Total, Sor rural Circle	59,050	29,810	29,240	58,626	29,696	28,930
				Total, Almora district	411,501	208,113	203,388	408,757	206,659	202,098
47	Garhwál.	Dasoli Painkhunda Circle.	1	Painkhunda Malla	2,556	1,260	1,296	2,556	1,260	1,296
			2	Painkhunda Talla	2,324	1,158	1,166	2,324	1,158	1,166
			3	Dasoli Malla	3,299	1,579	1,720	3,299	1,579	1,720
			4	Dasoli Talla	10,476	5,054	5,422	10,454	5,043	5,411
				Total, Dasoli Painkhunda Circle	18,655	9,051	9,604	18,633	9,040	9,593
		Badhan Circle.	5	Pindarwar	8,911	4,375	4,536	8,892	4,367	4,525
			6	Pindarpar	10,116	5,077	5,039	10,108	5,074	5,034
			7	Kapiri	2,770	1,369	1,401	2,770	1,369	1,401
			8	Karakot	3,387	1,650	1,737	3,387	1,650	1,737
			9	Nandak	4,464	2,200	2,264	4,462	2,199	2,263
			10	Khansar	1,084	508	576	1,084	508	576
				Total, Badhan Circle	30,732	15,179	15,553	30,703	15,167	15,536
		Nagpur Circle.	11	Bamsu	1,479	594	885	1,479	594	885
			12	Maikhanda	1,437	726	711	1,437	726	711
			13	Prakandi with Urgam villages	3,051	1,496	1,555	3,051	1,496	1,555
			14	Kaliphat Malla	4,248	2,116	2,132	4,248	2,116	2,132
			15	Kaliphat Talla	10,547	5,074	5,473	10,363	4,982	5,381
			16	Nagpur Talla	10,079	4,894	5,185	10,079	4,894	5,185
			17	Nagpur Bichla	12,922	6,288	6,634	12,885	6,273	6,612
			18	Nagpur Malla	8,068	3,898	4,170	8,065	3,896	4,169
				Total, Nagpur Circle	51,831	25,086	26,745	51,607	24,977	26,630
		Chándpur Circle.	19	Chándpur Sili	6,151	2,974	3,177	6,143	2,969	3,174
			20	Sirgur	2,508	1,210	1,298	2,508	1,210	1,298
			21	Chándpur Taili	7,049	3,292	3,757	6,917	3,227	3,690
			22	Lohba	8,100	3,905	4,195	8,006	3,855	4,151
			23	Chauthan	5,049	2,455	2,594	5,049	2,455	2,594
			24	Choprakot	9,092	4,378	4,714	9,070	4,368	4,702
			25	Dhai Jyuli	2,757	1,334	1,423	2,757	1,334	1,423
			26	Ránigadh	1,392	669	723	1,389	666	723
				Total, Chándpur Circle	42,098	20,217	21,881	41,839	20,084	21,755

MENT.

Kumaun Division arranged according to mortuary circles—(continued).

PROVINCIAL TABLE VII.

Supplement.

Muhammadans.			Jains.			Christians.			Others.			Serial number of patti.
Both sexes.	Males.	Females.	Both sexes.	Males.	Females.	Both sexes.	Males.	Females.	Both sexes.	Males.	Females.	
12	13	14	15	16	17	18	19	20	21	22	23	24
...	...	...	—	...	...	...	...	...	...	...	...	78
...	...	...	...	...	...	...	...	...	...	...	...	79
...	...	...	...	...	...	...	...	...	...	...	...	80
...	...	...	...	...	...	...	...	...	...	...	...	81
...	...	...	...	...	...	...	...	...	...	...	...	82
...		...	...	...	...	...	...	...	...	...	...	83
...	...	...	...	...	...	...	...	...	...	...	...	84
...	...	...		...	...	...	...	...	...	...	...	85
9	3	6	...	...	...	...	...	...	...	...	...	86
...	...	...	...	...	...	...	...	...	...	...	...	87
...	...	...	...	...	...	...	...	...	...	...	...	88
5	3	2	...	...	...	4	2	2	...	...	...	89
...	...	...	...	...	...	...	...	...	...	...	...	90
16	6	10	...	...	...	250	33	217	...	...	...	91
...	...	...	...	...	...	...	...	...	...	...	...	92
...	...	...	...	...	...	...	...	...	...	...	...	93
...	...	...	...	...	...	...	...	...	...	...	...	94
...	...	...	...	...	...	45	23	22	...	...	...	95
...	...	...	...	...	...	...	...	...	...	...	...	96
...	...	...	...	...	...	...	...	...	...	...	...	97
...	...	...	...	...	...	...	...	...	...	...	...	98
85	39	46	...	...	...	10	5	5	...	...	...	99
115	51	64	...	...	...	309	63	246	...	...	...	
2,019	1,175	844	5	4	1	706	265	441	14	10	4	
...	...	...	...	...	...	...	...	...	...	...	...	1
...	...	...	...	...	...	...	...	...	...	...	...	2
...	...	...	...	...	...	...	...	...	...	...	...	3
22	11	11	...	...	...	...	...	...	...	...	...	4
22	11	11	...	...	...	...	...	...	...	...	...	
14	6	8	...	...	...	5	2	3	...	...	...	5
8	3	5	...	...	...	...	...	...	...	...	...	6
...	...	...	...	...	...	...	...	...	...	...	...	7
...	...	...	...	...	...	...	...	...	...	...	...	8
2	1	1	...	...	...	...	...	...	...	...	...	9
...	...	...	...	...	...	...	...	...	...	...	...	10
24	10	14	...	...	...	5	2	3	...	...	...	
...	...	...	...	...	...	...	...	...	...	...	...	11
...	...	...	...	...	...	...	...	...	...	...	...	12
...	...	...	...	...	...	...	...	...	...	...	...	13
184	92	92	...	...	...	...	...	...	...	...	...	14
...	...	...	...	...	...	...	...	...	...	...	...	15
8	4	4	...	...	...	...	...	...	...	...	...	16
3	2	1	...	...	...	...	...	...	29	11	18	17
			...	...	...	...	...	...	...	...	...	18
195	98	97	...	...	...	...	...	...	29	11	18	
6	3	3	...	...	...	2	2	...	...	...	...	19
...	...	...	...	...	...	...	...	...	...	...	...	20
132	65	67	...	...	...	...	...	...	...	...	...	21
81	48	38	...	...	...	9	5	4	4	2	2	22
...	...	...	...	...	...	...	...	...	...	...	...	23
15	7	8	...	...	...	7	3	4	...	...	...	24
...	...	...	...	...	...	...	...	...	...	...	...	25
3	3	...	...	...	...	...	...	...	...	...	...	26
237	121	116	...	...	...	18	10	8	4	2	2	

SUPPLE

Showing by religion the population of the pattis of the

TABLE VII PROVINCIAL. Supplement.

Serial number of district.	Name of district.	Name of mortuary circle.	Serial number of patti.	Name of patti.	Total population. Both sexes.	Total population. Males.	Total population. Females.	Hindus. Both sexes.	Hindus. Males.	Hindus. Females.
1	2	3	4	5	6	7	8	9	10	11
47	Garhwál—(continued).	Dewalgarh Circle.	27	Chalan Syun	5,161	2,549	2,612	5,122	2,510	2,612
			28	Bachhan Syun	4,021	1,967	2,054	4,014	1,963	2,051
			29	Dhánpur	6,160	3,085	3,075	6,150	3,079	3,071
			30	Bidol Syun	1,707	842	865	1,643	806	837
			31	Ghurdur Syun	4,781	2,306	2,475	4,766	2,296	2,470
			32	Kandar Syun	6,673	3,205	3,468	6,617	3,172	3,445
			33	Kathul Syun	4,378	2,053	2,325	4,355	2,030	2,325
				Total, Dewalgarh Circle ...	32,881	16,007	16,874	32,667	15,856	16,811
		Barah Syun Circle.	34	Nandul Syun	3,940	2,145	1,795	3,676	2,007	1,669
			35	Gagwar Syun	4,151	2,028	2,123	4,137	2,014	2,123
			36	Paidul Syun	4,677	2,224	2,453	4,623	2,192	2,431
			37	Maniyar Syun	7,169	3,425	3,744	7,155	3,415	3,740
			38	Aswal Syun	7,139	3,285	3,854	7,121	3,272	3,849
			39	Kandwal Syun	2,157	1,050	1,107	2,143	1,036	1,107
			40	Bangarh Syun	2,356	1,164	1,192	2,356	1,164	1,192
			41	Banel Syun	5,322	2,563	2,759	5,318	2,559	2,759
			42	Patwal Syun	1,834	886	948	1,816	876	940
			43	Kaphol Syun	3,866	1,856	2,010	3,843	1,844	1,999
			44	Khat Syun	2,970	1,402	1,568	2,933	1,383	1,550
			45	Idwal Syun	4,404	2,125	2,279	4,375	2,096	2,279
			46	Siton Syun	5,186	2,545	2,641	5,167	2,526	2,641
			47	Rawat Syun	1,294	611	683	1,294	611	683
				Total, Barah Syun Circle ...	56,465	27,309	29,156	55,957	26,995	28,962
		Srinagar Circle.	48	Srinagar	2,386	1,228	1,158	2,213	1,128	1,085
				Total, Srinagar Circle ...	2,386	1,228	1,158	2,213	1,128	1,085
		Chaundkot Circle.	49	Maundar Syun	6,834	3,188	3,646	6,834	3,188	3,646
			50	Mawal Syun	5,360	2,537	2,823	5,360	2,537	2,823
			51	Ringwar Syun	1,993	921	1,072	1,993	921	1,072
			52	Jaintol Syun	2,426	1,211	1,215	2,426	1,211	1,215
			53	Kimgaddigad	3,881	1,898	1,983	3,879	1,897	1,982
			54	Pingla Kakha	1,711	844	867	1,703	840	863
			55	Gurar Syun	4,368	2,022	2,346	4,359	2,018	2,341
				Total, Chaund Kot Circle ..	26,573	12,621	13,952	26,554	12,612	13,942
		Malla Salan Circle.	56	Talain	5,330	2,540	2,790	5,328	2,539	2,789
			57	Saindhar	1,879	920	959	1,879	920	959
			58	Gujru	4,255	2,076	2,179	4,254	2,075	2,179
			59	Dhaundyal Syun	2,837	1,349	1,488	2,837	1,349	1,488
			60	Sabli	8,052	3,888	4,164	8,052	3,888	4,164
			61	Meldhar	787	375	412	787	375	412
			62	Bangar Syun	2,673	1,295	1,378	2,671	1,293	1,378
			63	Kolagad	1,945	971	974	1,945	971	974
			64	Khatli	11,502	5,586	5,916	11,502	5,586	5,916
			65	Iriakot	8,334	3,954	4,380	8,334	3,954	4,380
				Total, Malla Salan Circle ...	47,594	22,954	24,640	47,589	22,950	24,639
		Talla Salan Circle.	66	Sila Talla	1,940	988	952	1,878	957	921
			67	Sila Malla	5,774	2,843	2,931	5,681	2,786	2,895
			68	Painun	7,241	3,445	3,796	7,241	3,445	3,796
			69	Bijlot Walla	3,374	1,638	1,736	3,874	1,638	1,736
			70	Bijlot Palla	4,248	2,052	2,196	4,248	2,052	2,196
			71	Badalpur Malla	6,823	3,209	3,614	6,823	3,209	3,614
			72	Badalpur Talla	2,890	1,375	1,515	2,890	1,375	1,515
			73	Kauria Walla	2,248	1,130	1,118	2,248	1,130	1,118
			74	Kauria Palla	425	202	223	425	202	223
			75	Bungi	4,351	2,101	2,250	4,351	2,101	2,250
			76	Bhabar villages and Forests Garhwál Division.	4,285	2,597	1,688	3,842	1,720	1,622
				Total, Talla Salan Circle ...	43,599	21,580	22,019	42,501	20,615	21,886

MENT.

Kumaun Division arranged according to mortuary circles—(continued).

Muhammadans.			Jains.			Christians.			Others.			Serial number of patti.
Both sexes.	Males.	Females.	Both sexes.	Males.	Females.	Both sexes.	Males.	Females.	Both sexes.	Males.	Females.	
12	13	14	15	16	17	18	19	20	21	22	23	24
39	39	...	...	...	...	...	...	...	...	...	...	27
7	4	3	...	...	...	...	...	...	...	...	...	28
10	6	4	...	...	...	...	...	...	...	...	...	29
...	...	...	...	...	...	64	36	28	...	...	...	30
...	...	...	...	...	...	15	10	5	...	...	...	31
...	...	...	...	...	...	56	33	23	...	...	...	32
23	23	...	...	...	...	...	...	...	...	...	...	33
79	72	7	...	...	...	135	79	56	...	...	...	
47	37	10	...	...	...	215	99	116	2	2	...	34
14	14	...	...	...	...	...	...	...	...	...	...	35
9	9	...	...	...	...	45	23	22	...	...	...	36
8	8	...	...	...	...	6	2	4	...	...	...	37
18	13	5	...	...	...	...	...	...	...	...	...	38
14	14	...	...	...	...	...	...	...	...	...	...	39
...	...	...	...	...	...	...	...	...	...	...	...	40
4	4	...	...	...	...	...	...	...	...	...	...	41
18	10	8	...	...	...	...	...	...	...	...	...	42
3	3	...	...	...	...	20	9	11	...	...	...	43
...	...	...	...	...	...	37	19	18	...	...	...	44
28	28	...	...	...	...	1	1	...	...	...	...	45
19	19	...	...	...	...	...	...	...	...	...	...	46
...	...	...	...	...	...	...	...	...	...	...	...	47
182	159	23	...	...	...	324	153	171	2	2	...	
145	83	62	...	...	...	28	17	11	...	...	...	48
145	83	62	...	...	...	28	17	11	...	...	...	
...	...	...	...	...	...	...	...	...	...	...	...	49
...	...	...	...	...	...	...	...	...	...	...	...	50
...	...	...	...	...	...	...	...	...	...	...	...	51
...	...	...	...	...	...	...	...	...	...	...	...	52
...	...	...	...	...	...	2	1	1	...	...	...	53
8	4	4	...	...	...	...	...	...	...	...	...	54
...	...	...	...	...	...	9	4	5	...	...	...	55
8	4	4	...	...	...	11	5	6	...	...	...	
...	...	...	...	...	...	2	1	1	...	...	...	56
...	...	...	...	...	...	...	...	...	...	...	...	57
...	...	...	...	...	...	1	1	...	...	...	...	58
...	...	...	...	...	...	...	...	...	...	...	...	59
...	...	...	...	...	...	...	...	...	...	...	...	60
...	...	...	...	...	...	...	...	...	...	...	...	61
2	2	...	...	...	...	...	...	...	...	...	...	62
...	...	...	...	...	...	...	...	...	...	...	...	63
...	...	...	...	...	...	...	...	...	...	...	...	64
...	...	...	...	...	...	...	...	...	...	...	...	65
2	2	...	...	...	...	3	2	1	...	...	...	
61	30	31	...	...	...	1	1	...	...	...	...	66
91	55	36	...	...	...	2	2	...	...	...	...	67
...	...	...	...	...	...	...	...	...	...	...	...	68
...	...	...	...	...	...	...	...	...	...	...	...	69
...	...	...	...	...	...	...	...	...	...	...	...	70
...	...	...	...	...	...	...	...	...	...	...	...	71
...	...	...	...	...	...	...	...	...	...	...	...	72
...	...	...	...	...	...	...	...	...	...	...	...	73
...	...	...	...	...	...	...	...	...	...	...	...	74
...	...	...	...	...	...	...	...	...	...	...	...	75
937	877	60	...	...	...	6	...	6	...	...	...	76
1,089	962	127	...	...	...	9	3	6	...	...	...	

SUPPLE

Showing by religion the population of the pattis of the

PROVINCIAL TABLE VII.

Supplement.

Serial number of district.	Name of district.	Name of mortuary circle.	Serial number of patti.	Name of patti.	Total population. Both sexes.	Total population. Males.	Total population. Females.	Hindus. Both sexes.	Hindus. Males.	Hindus. Females.
1	2	3	4	5	6	7	8	9	10	11
47	Garhwál—(*concluded*).	Ganga Salan Circle.	77	Dhangu Malla	6,395	2,937	*3,458*	6,395	2,937	*3,458*
			78	Dhangu Talla	5,003	2,416	*2,587*	5,003	2,416	*2,587*
			79	Ajmir	5,942	2,838	*3,104*	5,783	2,754	*3,029*
			80	Langur	7,308	3,478	*3,830*	7,230	3,436	*3,794*
			81	Karoundu Walla	2,115	984	*1,131*	2,112	983	*1,129*
			82	Karoundu Palla	2,105	983	*1,122*	2,105	983	*1,122*
			83	Udaipur Malla	3,583	1,750	*1,833*	3,583	1,750	*1,833*
			84	Udaipur Bichla	7,029	3,320	*3,709*	7,023	3,316	*3,707*
			85	Udaipur Talla	8,030	3,968	*4,062*	8,029	3,968	*4,061*
			86	Bhábar villages and forests, Ganges Division.	5,434	4,744	*690*	4,254	3,645	*609*
				Total, Ganga Salan Circle ...	52,944	27,418	*25,526*	51,517	26,188	*25,329*
		Kotdwára Circle.	87	Kotdwára	706	492	*214*	599	412	*187*
				Total, Kotdwára Circle ...	706	492	*214*	599	412	*187*
		Lansdowne Circle.	88	Lansdowne	1,354	1,177	*177*	1,224	1,082	*142*
				Total, Lansdowne Circle ...	1,354	1,177	*177*	1,224	1,082	*142*
				Total, Garhwál district ...	407,818	200,319	*207,499*	403,603	197,106	*206,497*
48	Naini Tal.	Naini Tal rural Circle.	1	Jaspur	30,125	16,192	*13,933*	20,695	11,095	*9,600*
			2	Káshipur	43,043	22,831	*20,212*	25,933	13,770	*12,163*
			3	Bazpur	32,554	17,890	*14,664*	16,725	9,247	*7,478*
			4	Gadarpur	18,855	10,683	*8,172*	8,266	4,798	*3,468*
			5	Rudarpur	29,556	16,288	*13,268*	17,165	9,530	*7,635*
			6	Kilpuri	56,435	31,576	*24,859*	46,376	25,867	*20,509*
				Total ...	210,568	115,460	*95,108*	135,160	74,807	*60,853*
			7	Chakhata	21,895	14,920	*6,975*	19,881	13,504	*6,377*
			8	Kota Malla	1,797	981	*816*	1,765	967	*798*
			9	Kota Talla	2,167	1,127	*1,040*	2,165	1,126	*1,039*
			10	Malla Kosian	1,048	510	*538*	1,048	510	*538*
			11	Talla Kosian	1,467	747	*720*	1,467	747	*720*
			12	Dhania Kot	1,250	745	*505*	1,214	716	*498*
			13	Ucha Kot	2,309	1,166	*1,143*	2,309	1,166	*1,143*
			14	Chauthan	3,366	1,619	*1,747*	3,366	1,619	*1,747*
			15	Rámgarh Talla	16	7	*9*	16	7	*9*
			16	Rámgarh Malla	289	218	*71*	254	195	*59*
			17	Agar	245	129	*116*	245	129	*116*
			18	Kotauli Malli	1,148	583	*565*	1,148	583	*565*
			19	Kotauli Talli	736	360	*376*	736	360	*376*
			20	Bisaud Talla	152	85	*67*	152	85	*67*
			21	Bisaud Bichla	446	217	*229*	446	217	*229*
			22	Mahruri Malli	15	9	*6*	15	9	*6*
			23	Mahruri Talli	600	366	*234*	577	352	*225*
			24	Mahruri Bichli	310	176	*134*	310	176	*134*
			25	Chaubansi	202	99	*103*	202	99	*103*
			26	Chhabbis Dumoli	1,602	844	*758*	1,602	844	*758*
			27	Bisjula	1,171	571	*600*	1,171	571	*600*
			28	Malli Rao	798	386	*412*	798	386	*412*
			29	Chaugarh	3,102	1,671	*1,431*	3,102	1,671	*1,431*
			30	Bhábar Chakhata	33,202	18,777	*14 425*	30,492	16,992	*13,500*
			31	Bhábar Chaubansi	4,566	2,506	*2,060*	4,506	2,448	*2,058*
			32	Bhábar Chilkia	20,158	11,103	*9,055*	17,734	9,711	*8,023*
			33	Bhábar Kota	39,806	22,664	*17,142*	36,457	20,302	*16,155*
			34	Bhábar Talla Des	7,817	4,258	*3,559*	7,637	4,089	*3,548*
				Total, Naini Tal rural Circle ...	151,680	86,844	*64,836*	140,815	79,581	*61,234*
				Total, Naini Tal district ...	362,248	202,804	*159,944*	275,975	153,888	*122,087*

MENT.

Kumaun Division arranged according to mortuary circles—(concluded).

PROVINCIAL TABLE VII.

Supplement.

Muhammadans.			Jains.			Christians.			Others.			Serial number of patti.
Both sexes.	Males.	Females.	Both sexes.	Males.	Females.	Both sexes.	Males.	Females.	Both sexes.	Males.	Females.	
12	13	14	15	16	17	18	19	20	21	22	23	24
...	...	...	...	...	...	...	...	...	...	...	...	77
...	...	...	...	...	...	...	...	...	...	...	...	78
159	84	75	...	...	...	...	...	...	...	...	...	79
78	42	36	...	...	...	...	...	...	...	...	...	80
3	1	2	...	...	...	...	...	...	...	...	...	81
...	...	...	...	...	...	...	...	...	...	...	...	82
...	...	...	...	...	...	...	...	...	...	...	...	83
6	4	2	...	...	...	...	...	...	...	...	...	84
1	...	1	...	...	...	...	...	...	...	...	...	85
1,175	1,098	77	2	1	1	3	...	3	...	...	...	86
1,422	1,229	193	2	1	1	3	...	3	...	...	...	
99	76	23	...	...	...	8	4	4	...	...	...	87
99	76	23	...	...	...	8	4	4	...	...	...	
101	81	20	...	...	...	29	14	15	...	...	...	88
101	81	20	...	...	...	29	14	15	...	...	...	
3,605	2,908	697	2	1	1	573	289	284	35	15	20	
9,338	5,049	4,289	30	15	15	...	...	...	62	33	29	1
17,021	9,004	8,017	9	7	2	4	4	...	76	46	30	2
15,829	8,643	7,186	...	...	...	...	...	...	...	...	...	3
10,588	5,884	4,704	...	...	...	1	1	...	...	...	...	4
12,382	6,752	5,630	...	...	...	8	5	3	1	1	...	5
10,049	5,703	4,346	...	...	...	10	6	4	...	...	...	6
75,207	41,035	34,172	39	22	17	23	16	7	139	80	59	
1,479	1,136	343	...	...	...	535	280	255	...	...	...	7
...	...	...	...	...	...	32	14	18	...	...	...	8
2	1	1	...	...	...	...	...	...	...	...	...	9
...	...	...	...	...	...	...	...	...	...	...	...	10
...	...	...	...	...	...	...	...	...	...	...	...	11
27	27	...	...	...	...	9	2	7	...	...	...	12
...	...	...	...	...	...	...	...	...	...	...	...	13
...	...	...	...	...	...	...	...	...	...	...	...	14
...	...	...	...	...	...	...	...	...	...	...	...	15
20	20	...	...	...	...	7	3	4	8	...	8	16
...	...	...	...	...	...	...	...	...	...	...	...	17
...	...	...	...	...	...	...	...	...	...	...	...	18
...	...	...	...	...	...	...	...	...	...	...	...	19
...	...	...	...	...	...	...	...	...	...	...	...	20
...	...	...	...	...	...	...	...	...	...	...	...	21
...	...	...	...	...	...	...	...	...	...	...	...	22
23	14	9	...	...	...	...	...	...	...	...	...	23
...	...	...	...	...	...	...	...	...	...	...	...	24
...	...	...	...	...	...	...	...	...	...	...	...	25
...	...	...	...	...	...	...	...	...	...	...	...	26
...	...	...	...	...	...	...	...	...	...	...	...	27
...	...	...	...	...	...	...	...	...	...	...	...	28
...	...	...	...	...	...	...	...	...	...	...	...	29
2,459	1,645	814	...	...	...	251	140	111	...	...	...	30
59	57	2	...	...	...	1	1	...	...	...	...	31
2,422	1,390	1,032	...	...	...	2	2	...	...	...	...	32
3,282	2,322	960	...	...	...	55	32	23	12	8	4	33
177	167	10	...	...	...	3	2	1	...	...	...	34
9,950	6,779	3,171	...	...	...	895	476	419	20	8	12	
85,157	47,814	37,343	39	22	17	918	492	426	159	88	71	

PROVINCIAL TABLE VIII.

SHOWING THE AGES OF THE POPULATION OF TOWNS WITH ABOVE 10,000 INHABITANTS.

The ages of the population of towns

PROVINCIAL TABLE VIII.

Serial number of district.	Name of district.	Serial number of town.	Name of town.	Total population. Total.	Total population. Males.	Total population. Females.	Age: Under 1 year. Males.	Under 1 year. Females.	1 year. Males.	1 year. Females.
1	Dehra Dún ...	1	Dehra	25,684	16,019	9,665	868	861	186	156
2	Sahāranpur ...	1	Sahāranpur ...	63,194	34,266	28,928	1,317	1,205	296	305
		2	Hardwár Union ...	29,125	17,886	11,239	481	272	159	168
		3	Deoband ...	19,250	10,363	8,887	367	342	81	69
		4	Roorkee ...	17,367	10,534	6,833	271	273	108	103
		5	Gangoh ...	12,007	6,046	5,961	250	269	89	101
		6	Manglaur ...	10,037	5,188	4,849	151	202	60	50
3	Muzaffarnagar	1	Kairána ...	18,420	9,628	8,792	383	395	86	106
		2	Muzaffarnagar ...	18,166	10,997	7,169	270	260	112	78
4	Meerut ...	1	Meerut ...	119,390	68,016	51,374	2,146	2,203	880	799
		2	Hápur ...	14,977	7,891	7,086	295	279	70	79
		3	Sardhana ...	12,059	6,238	5,821	222	212	48	45
		4	Khekra ...	10,315	5,467	4,848	212	213	52	63
		5	Gháziabad ...	10,193	5,540	4,653	195	185	42	71
5	Bulandshahr ...	1	Khúrja ...	26,349	13,594	12,755	590	575	182	151
		2	Bulandshahr ...	16,931	9,392	7,539	357	333	126	121
		3	Sikandarabad ...	15,231	7,764	7,467	312	285	98	86
		4	Shikárpur ...	11,596	6,124	5,472	247	236	106	114
6	Aligarh ...	1	Koil	61,485	32,843	28,642	1,260	1,246	484	384
		2	Hathras ...	39,181	21,066	18,115	839	813	275	281
		3	Atrauli ...	15,408	7,933	7,475	381	388	101	88
		4	Sikandra Rao ...	13,024	6,866	6,158	206	225	80	72
7	Muttra ...	1	Muttra ...	61,195	33,284	27,911	1,155	1,074	305	277
		2	Brindaban ...	31,611	16,369	15,242	358	322	112	115
8	Agra ...	1	Agra	168,662	90,923	77,739	3,478	3,369	1,002	960
		2	Fírozabad ...	15,278	8,029	7,249	314	315	83	112
9	Farukhabad ...	1	Farukhabad ...	78,032	41,140	36,892	1,348	1,246	317	374
		2	Kanauj ...	17,648	8,763	8,885	328	343	111	108
10	Mainpuri ...	1	Mainpuri ...	18,551	10,146	8,405	317	323	48	74
11	Etáwah ...	1	Etáwah ...	38,793	20,337	18,456	751	792	163	177
12	Etah ...	1	Kásganj ...	16,050	8,680	7,370	338	287	79	74
		2	Jalesar ...	13,420	6,869	6,551	302	284	69	82
		3	Soron	11,265	5,848	5,417	222	205	38	36
13	Bareilly ...	1	Bareilly ...	121,039	64,435	56,604	2,672	2,623	665	652
		2	Aonla	13,559	6,967	6,592	341	334	90	78
14	Bijnor ...	1	Nagína ...	22,150	11,145	11,005	646	628	26	22
		2	Najíbabad ...	19,410	9,814	9,596	452	466	118	111
		3	Bijnor	16,236	8,630	7,606	354	389	84	97
		4	Sherkot ...	15,589	7,740	7,849	280	315	110	105
		5	Kiratpur ...	14,823	7,223	7,600	389	398	100	95
		6	Chándpur ...	12,256	5,982	6,274	258	277	91	62
		7	Nihtor ...	10,811	5,300	5,511	258	266	72	55
15	Budaun ...	1	Budaun ...	35,372	17,187	18,185	753	714	224	269
		2	Sahaswán ...	15,601	7,843	7,758	399	371	60	69
16	Moradabad ...	1	Moradabad ...	72,921	37,249	35,672	1,576	1,562	533	536
		2	Sambhal ...	37,226	18,719	18,507	882	861	258	258
		3	Amroha ...	35,230	16,782	18,448	774	728	175	190
		4	Chandausi ...	28,111	15,048	13,063	618	537	165	148
		5	Solah Sarai ...	10,304	5,140	5,164	232	247	61	64
17	Sháhjahánpur ...	1	Sháhjahánpur ...	78,522	39,169	39,353	1,689	1,675	466	533
		2	Tilhar	17,265	8,904	8,361	423	455	114	106
18	Pilibhít ...	1	Pilibhít ...	33,799	17,235	16,564	728	689	271	264
19	Cawnpore ...	1	Cawnpore ...	188,712	106,713	81,999	3,104	3,148	801	866
20	Fatehpur ...	1	Fatehpur ...	20,179	10,140	10,039	295	314	66	73
21	Bánda ...	1	Bánda	23,071	11,444	11,627	417	403	124	126
22	Hamírpur ...	1	Ráth	12,311	5,919	6,392	181	136	77	97
23	Allahabad ...	1	Allahabad ...	175,246	94,784	80,462	3,025	3,005	1,170	1,268
24	Jhánsi ...	1	Jhánsi	53,779	30,986	22,793	948	869	151	171
		2	Mau-Ránipur ...	19,675	9,629	10,046	320	324	116	120
		3	Lalitpur ...	11,348	6,002	5,346	104	94	95	113
25	Jalaun ...	1	Kúnch ...	13,408	6,911	6,497	218	205	82	94
		2	Kálpi	12,713	6,310	6,403	197	231	86	76
26	Benares ...	1	Benares ...	219,467	115,062	104,405	2,918	2,780	1,859	1,290
		2	Rámnagar ...	11,093	5,553	5,540	212	200	44	48

with above 10,000 inhabitants.

PROVINCIAL TABLE VIII.

periods.												
2 years.		3 years.		4 years.		Total (0 to 4 years).		5 to 9 years.		10 to 14 years.		Serial number of town.
Males.	Females.	Males.	Females.	Males.	Females.	Males.	Females.	Males.	Females.	Males.	Females.	
245	252	243	268	230	247	1,222	1,284	1,229	1,121	1,821	936	1
647	609	653	709	691	615	3,604	3,443	3,263	2,980	3,578	2,563	1
276	322	282	289	329	310	1,527	1,361	1,390	1,163	1,456	926	2
232	210	214	200	200	211	1,094	1,032	822	708	1,333	973	3
170	191	201	197	198	179	948	943	897	831	884	688	4
161	156	147	133	189	149	836	808	628	605	648	562	5
127	122	129	137	130	142	597	653	635	611	646	433	6
197	206	210	228	218	218	1,094	1,153	1,146	1,060	1,096	770	1
197	168	184	185	211	164	974	855	909	777	1,075	689	2
1,303	1,303	1,495	1,512	1,439	1,317	7,263	7,134	6,958	6,375	6,239	4,575	1
150	171	191	184	171	143	877	856	864	832	799	650	2
141	123	151	141	163	138	715	659	719	665	740	586	3
110	119	122	109	152	117	648	621	703	604	566	363	4
127	115	109	120	118	108	586	599	609	530	504	364	5
287	271	317	323	267	267	1.593	1,587	1,825	1,258	1,531	1,168	1
186	189	181	193	150	131	1,000	967	824	728	869	624	2
167	180	188	206	151	162	916	919	780	732	779	546	3
154	138	150	155	127	113	784	756	744	654	667	501	4
652	658	676	705	735	760	3,757	3,753	3,022	2,932	3,510	2,486	1
427	414	483	456	471	409	2,495	2,373	1,975	1,881	2,240	1,548	2
170	181	172	193	207	187	1,031	1,037	943	869	868	629	3
126	120	156	138	152	138	720	693	817	805	762	530	4
566	540	634	627	679	579	3,339	3,097	3,223	2,977	3,027	2,025	1
161	154	209	209	184	175	1,024	975	1,087	897	1,149	678	2
1,780	1,870	2,065	2,186	1,984	1,974	10,309	10,359	10,213	9,348	8,260	5,917	1
146	153	152	203	176	168	871	951	1,007	843	903	644	2
707	719	765	940	700	759	3,837	4,038	3,936	3,811	4,107	3,375	1
246	237	229	275	216	222	1,130	1,185	1,111	1,159	1,039	810	2
167	164	195	205	150	167	877	933	811	708	1,104	745	1
404	365	444	476	414	415	2,176	2,225	2,237	2,148	2,277	1,636	1
146	138	184	187	137	141	884	827	944	823	1,033	728	1
131	149	158	184	143	156	803	855	782	747	678	505	2
127	94	148	147	97	86	632	568	596	504	686	429	3
1,382	1,474	1,512	1,669	1,402	1,306	7,683	7,724	6,456	6,176	6,606	5,137	1
156	152	206	220	181	145	974	929	858	791	803	598	2
294	324	281	291	250	248	1,497	1,513	1,199	1,188	1,252	913	1
286	278	238	218	245	223	1,389	1,296	1,226	1,079	1,054	853	2
194	208	193	226	168	166	993	1,086	956	907	959	686	3
217	213	227	204	212	213	1,046	1,050	1,083	1,006	955	740	4
215	235	219	242	205	196	1,128	1,166	1,007	922	784	657	5
188	195	180	195	160	157	877	886	760	715	680	572	6
171	175	163	169	145	149	809	814	639	640	595	465	7
423	421	408	420	406	419	2,214	2,243	2,133	2,044	2,101	1,641	1
220	208	233	233	203	189	1,115	1,060	1,015	899	885	660	2
959	975	951	973	878	837	4,807	4.883	4,082	3.893	4.173	3,296	1
490	460	532	543	519	457	2,681	2.579	2,350	2,191	2,219	1,687	2
452	447	465	546	458	469	2,324	2.390	2,083	2,055	1,959	1,716	3
348	345	368	331	264	261	1,763	1,622	1,510	1,521	1,705	1,239	4
134	148	180	151	144	143	751	753	633	612	643	421	5
945	990	1,013	1,158	915	934	5,028	5,290	4,450	4,272	4,150	3,457	1
192	214	243	267	199	205	1,171	1,247	1,072	986	1,014	659	2
488	454	476	515	407	401	2,370	2,323	2,211	1,885	1,809	1,403	1
1,735	1,908	1,920	2,087	1,828	1,924	9,388	9,933	9,911	9,410	9,759	6,559	1
192	218	203	265	250	220	1,096	1,089	1,213	1,263	1,235	962	1
209	259	265	317	267	228	1,282	1,332	1,301	1,343	1,218	1,035	1
141	144	160	171	139	138	698	686	755	781	724	560	1
1,893	2,039	2,456	2,387	2,344	2,362	10,888	11,061	9,702	9,108	9,128	7,157	1
509	548	644	605	554	502	2.801	2,695	2,975	2,727	2,745	1,858	1
196	199	267	311	216	232	1,115	1,186	1,299	1,183	1,017	851	2
113	117	146	173	128	142	586	639	783	760	721	495	3
165	145	149	201	160	170	769	815	835	792	805	638	1
139	156	159	191	168	150	744	804	728	763	717	601	2
2,059	8,790	2,389	2,690	2,269	4,280	10,994	14,830	10,535	10,429	11,423	12,469	1
122	149	152	166	101	109	631	667	554	544	607	635	2

The ages of the population of towns

PROVINCIAL TABLE VIII.

Serial number of district.	Name of district.	Serial number of town.	Name of town.	Age: 15 to 19 years. Males.	15 to 19 years. Females.	20 to 24 years. Males.	20 to 24 years. Females.	25 to 29 years. Males.	25 to 29 years. Females.	30 to 34 years. Males.	30 to 34 years. Females.
1	Debra Dún ...	1	Dehra	1,498	926	2,227	1,055	2,111	950	1,851	889
2	Saháranpur ...	1	Saháranpur ...	3,148	2,462	3,359	3,099	3,178	2,658	3,515	2,699
		2	Hardwár Union ...	1,673	916	2,014	1,116	2,109	1,091	2,136	1,102
		3	Deoband ...	1,047	848	1,018	940	976	899	1,056	894
		4	Roorkee ...	916	558	1,438	672	1,272	654	1,194	647
		5	Gangoh ...	636	672	511	612	493	546	516	484
		6	Manglaur ...	459	477	403	433	399	438	441	431
3	Muzaffarnagar	1	Kairána ...	1,000	766	850	832	801	789	885	770
		2	Muzaffarnagar ...	1,151	663	1,243	737	1,288	698	1,223	676
4	Meerut ...	1	Meerut ...	5,476	4,180	8,840	6,060	7,008	4,513	6,598	4,533
		2	Hápur ...	691	581	773	698	708	585	729	608
		3	Sardhana ...	616	497	555	554	537	568	597	548
		4	Khekra ...	509	406	470	451	476	437	516	476
		5	Ghάziabad ...	482	431	651	534	528	448	555	436
5	Bulandshahr ...	1	Khúrja ...	1,182	1,048	1,469	1,464	1,273	1,234	1,351	1,216
		2	Bulandshahr ...	962	669	1,194	990	963	720	896	681
		3	Sikandarabad ...	753	717	809	881	748	655	678	714
		4	Shikárpur ...	553	494	586	545	530	497	564	505
6	Aligarh ...	1	Koil	3,229	2,670	3,332	2,866	2,928	2,479	3,143	2,718
		2	Háthras ...	1,958	1,669	2,201	1,919	1,806	1,540	2,084	1,604
		3	Atrauli ...	676	623	779	837	696	707	702	663
		4	Sikandra Rao ...	618	576	740	707	641	526	710	609
7	Muttra ...	1	Muttra ...	3,091	2,624	4,360	3,224	3,416	2,558	3,447	2,794
		2	Brindaban ...	1,376	993	1,857	1,370	1,719	1,310	1,987	1,823
8	Agra ...	1	Agra	8,537	7,201	10,577	8,517	8,348	6,820	8,949	7,183
		2	Fírozabad ...	740	649	800	758	676	636	753	699
9	Farukhabad ...	1	Farukhabad ...	3,500	3,037	4,138	3,617	3,889	3,355	4,223	3,543
		2	Kanauj ...	698	713	754	770	703	770	838	851
10	Mainpuri ...	1	Mainpuri ...	1,051	818	1,185	1,006	986	785	1,148	877
11	Etáwah ...	1	Etáwah ...	1,953	1,711	2,184	2,077	1,847	1,678	2,074	1,742
12	Etah ...	1	Kásganj ...	856	634	930	856	744	666	900	745
		2	Jalesar ...	588	572	754	780	658	642	718	629
		3	Soron	587	475	599	624	488	500	659	583
13	Bareilly ...	1	Bareilly ...	5,688	4,591	7,150	5,478	6,274	4,732	6,097	5,163
		2	Aonla	609	528	688	636	587	494	639	584
14	Bijnor ...	1	Nagína ...	1,060	922	1,011	1,162	931	906	871	901
		2	Najíbabad ...	834	834	874	918	776	725	786	864
		3	Bijnor	839	641	841	693	719	640	755	575
		4	Sherkot ...	709	615	657	721	564	597	512	559
		5	Kiratpur ...	689	662	543	703	496	620	489	580
		6	Chándpur ...	523	485	508	583	413	457	450	531
		7	Nihtor ...	507	513	456	505	391	420	358	446
15	Budaun ...	1	Budaun ...	1,589	1,594	1,529	1,786	1,826	1,530	1,402	1,647
		2	Sahaswán ...	623	565	696	786	629	694	694	713
16	Moradabad ...	1	Moradabad ...	3,696	3,237	3,749	3,652	2,991	2,975	3,196	2,976
		2	Sambhal ...	1,757	1,543	1,691	1,782	1,447	1,603	1,426	1,600
		3	Amroha ...	1,679	1,563	1,436	1,684	1,159	1,486	1,258	1,623
		4	Chandausi ...	1,331	1,093	1,476	1,399	1,364	1,147	1,513	1,169
		5	Solah Sarai ...	465	401	446	507	409	502	462	431
17	Sháhjahánpur ...	1	Sháhjahánpur ...	3,404	3,126	3,582	3,695	3,026	3,253	3,284	3,553
		2	Tilhar	748	680	849	907	714	786	887	806
18	Pilibhít ...	1	Pilibhít ...	1,560	1,349	1,636	1,648	1,489	1,442	1,646	1,524
19	Cawnpore ...	1	Cawnpore ...	8,770	6,646	12,208	8,794	11,125	7,664	12,020	7,874
20	Fatehpur ...	1	Fatehpur ...	804	786	941	977	929	993	926	911
21	Bánda ...	1	Bánda	938	857	1,108	1,040	993	992	1,120	1,107
22	Hamírpur ...	1	Ráth	450	431	533	589	463	570	623	689
23	Allahabad ...	1	Allahabad ...	7,480	6,137	9,412	7,460	8,857	6,928	9,125	7,230
24	Jhánsi ...	1	Jhánsi	2,479	1,719	3,987	2,297	3,682	2,164	3,674	2,807
		2	Mau-Ránipur ...	784	748	711	816	747	797	963	942
		3	Lalitpur ...	473	418	627	453	561	502	623	518
25	Jalaun ...	1	Kúnch ...	528	474	627	526	527	541	727	664
		2	Kálpi	481	539	548	555	519	508	618	665
26	Benares ...	1	Benares ...	9,187	7,945	9,758	9,243	11,982	7,628	13,065	6,810
		2	Rámnagar ...	453	520	748	500	543	598	451	538

with above 10,000 inhabitants.

PROVINCIAL TABLE VIII.

periods.

35 to 39 years.		40 to 44 years.		45 to 49 years.		50 to 54 years.		55 to 59 years.		60 years and over.		Serial number of town.
Males.	Females.	Males.	Females.	Males.	Females.	Males.	Females.	Males.	Females.	Males.	Females.	
1,083	444	1,134	706	697	260	797	476	204	101	745	517	1
2,249	1,473	2,775	2,249	1,046	848	1,978	1,889	485	385	2,088	2,180	1
1,110	474	1,637	925	602	324	1,161	890	184	122	887	829	2
618	441	764	669	835	270	601	637	157	136	542	540	3
707	348	806	484	358	172	544	364	120	94	455	378	4
337	278	400	391	163	154	341	360	95	100	442	489	5
314	268	395	358	177	146	306	323	75	69	341	309	6
499	450	640	675	307	252	559	547	140	142	611	585	1
714	403	825	637	372	230	606	435	196	122	421	347	2
3,858	2,323	5,052	3,892	2,200	1,405	3,597	3,032	1,028	662	3,899	3,690	1
424	353	658	597	233	215	524	464	135	97	476	550	2
313	278	500	486	221	174	317	363	95	71	313	372	3
331	287	387	362	229	210	238	253	131	97	268	281	4
357	253	407	368	216	134	317	257	76	64	252	236	5
650	549	1,096	1,116	405	342	866	804	186	163	667	807	1
486	374	742	542	286	235	585	478	133	102	452	429	2
469	394	621	585	309	265	406	486	138	104	368	469	3
289	277	501	402	166	130	344	336	81	72	315	303	4
2,195	1,708	2,596	2,082	1,164	877	1,708	1,614	633	603	1,631	1,864	1
1,152	914	1,840	1,558	759	526	1,207	1,090	349	338	1,050	1,155	2
399	365	637	541	237	225	466	435	97	115	402	429	3
351	233	550	561	209	151	345	351	75	76	328	340	4
1,654	1,182	2,993	2,720	975	695	1,819	1,927	408	321	1,532	1,767	1
959	903	1,808	2,171	662	555	1,298	1,635	308	284	1,185	1,648	2
4,692	3,425	7,257	6,282	2,972	2,036	4,873	4,548	1,176	857	4,760	5,246	1
375	269	672	611	241	182	423	423	110	76	458	504	2
2,481	1,099	3,575	3,204	1,637	1,213	2,555	2,672	789	634	2,473	2,694	1
467	450	597	666	299	269	439	511	185	147	503	584	2
526	347	870	772	364	227	639	558	161	130	424	499	1
963	805	1,714	1,501	648	499	1,006	1,086	277	194	981	1,154	1
393	278	824	676	202	158	482	478	79	56	409	445	1
301	256	590	677	167	160	375	382	78	50	382	396	2
244	189	588	585	141	114	374	456	45	48	259	342	3
3,077	2,301	5,133	4,622	1,915	1,514	3,743	3,925	931	778	3,733	4,463	1
315	274	542	497	184	180	378	412	90	174	400	495	2
561	540	796	791	345	351	655	827	155	172	812	819	1
500	431	779	744	311	262	577	622	130	131	628	837	2
472	386	649	550	273	264	485	477	158	133	581	568	3
404	397	528	567	246	270	395	486	119	164	522	677	4
362	406	485	517	212	260	426	466	111	108	541	533	5
298	305	409	474	198	241	364	425	97	101	405	499	6
260	274	342	364	161	214	345	366	95	104	347	386	7
772	754	1,273	1,612	538	515	985	1,202	276	277	1,049	1,440	1
331	293	628	645	197	159	470	582	93	87	472	615	2
1,623	1,450	2,878	2,770	1,090	922	2,069	2,452	518	476	2,292	2,690	1
811	794	1,470	1,436	482	461	1,027	1,220	214	233	1,144	1,378	2
763	883	1,247	1,490	453	515	955	1,253	242	307	1,229	1,493	3
709	499	1,351	1,180	403	275	918	886	164	114	841	919	4
225	255	371	361	137	134	227	340	68	58	303	389	5
2,016	1,740	2,918	3,108	1,411	1,152	2,276	2,602	694	547	2,935	3,558	1
408	329	739	685	271	177	493	472	90	80	448	547	2
897	710	1,362	1,369	503	411	877	1,019	214	213	861	1,268	1
6,234	3,815	9,459	6,722	3,786	2,413	6,512	5,461	1,718	1,075	5,889	5,633	1
525	513	732	778	336	338	578	647	202	192	623	590	1
630	594	951	1,045	418	389	640	791	200	167	650	935	1
337	421	533	556	210	239	289	391	84	83	220	396	1
5,709	4,325	7,206	5,873	3,927	3,056	5,592	4,916	2,285	1,823	5,473	5,333	1
1,944	1,231	2,727	1,968	1,073	681	1,421	1,274	326	309	1,152	1,563	1
508	624	880	928	365	338	553	652	153	172	525	809	2
308	304	490	498	220	172	333	242	80	57	197	287	3
396	333	687	530	254	184	318	376	86	105	332	519	1
342	336	592	498	239	196	318	382	100	89	374	477	2
6,136	4,497	9,712	7,048	5,812	3,597	6,403	7,577	2,096	2,267	8,064	10,070	1
312	332	296	388	308	164	211	277	96	176	343	406	2

The ages of the population of towns

PROVINCIAL TABLE VIII.

Serial number of district.	Name of district.	Serial number of town.	Name of town.	Total population.			Age			
							Under 1 year.		1 year.	
				Total.	Males.	Females.	Males.	Females.	Males.	Females.
27	Mirzapur ...	1	Mirzapur ...	84,130	41,921	42,209	1,313	*1,829*	499	*567*
		2	Ahraura ...	11,631	5,904	5,727	196	*195*	84	*93*
		3	Chunár ...	11,423	5,445	5,978	276	*269*	9	*13*
28	Jaunpur ...	1	Jaunpur ...	42,819	21,494	21,325	700	*772*	235	*240*
29	Gházipur ...	1	Gházipur ...	44,970	23,077	21,893	687	*787*	198	*186*
		2	Sherpur ...	12,156	5,785	6,371	150	*153*	93	*109*
		3	Gahmar ...	11,129	5,266	5,863	168	*152*	72	*92*
		4	Reotipur ...	10,961	5,198	5,763	157	*148*	106	*108*
30	Ballia ...	1	Ballia	16,372	8,478	7,894	219	*215*	146	*151*
		2	Sehtwar ...	11,519	5,311	6,208	196	*196*	83	*83*
		3	Chit Firozpur or Baragaon.	10,725	4,961	5,764	171	*161*	47	*62*
31	Gorakhpur ...	1	Gorakhpur ...	63,620	32,675	30,945	868	*959*	304	*295*
		2	Barhaj ...	11,421	6,200	5,221	112	*121*	86	*108*
32	Basti ...	1	Basti	13,630	7,957	5,673	203	*200*	80	*90*
		2	Menhdawal ...	10,991	5,736	5,255	144	*206*	92	*89*
33	Azamgarh ...	1	Azamgarh ...	19,442	10,487	8,955	269	*293*	99	*107*
		2	Mau	15,547	7,565	7,982	266	*321*	122	*152*
		3	Mubarakpur ...	14,872	7,146	7,226	275	*276*	72	*90*
34	Naini Tal ...	1	Káshipur ...	14,717	7,477	7,240	281	*283*	108	*90*
35	Lucknow ...	1	Lucknow ...	273,028	145,848	127,180	5,540	*5,427*	1,413	*1,607*
36	Unao ...	1	Unao	12,831	7,342	5,489	234	*234*	38	*56*
		2	Purwa ...	10,463	5,091	5,372	237	*216*	48	*44*
37	Rae Bareli ...	1	Rae Bareli ...	18,798	10,220	8,578	331	*311*	94	*110*
		2	Jais	11,926	5,779	6,147	222	*223*	47	*41*
38	Sitapur ...	1	Sitapur ...	21,380	12,704	8,676	395	*429*	63	*57*
		2	Khairabad ...	13,773	6,577	7,196	336	*351*	24	*39*
		3	Laharpur ...	11,452	5,708	5,744	284	*341*	71	*85*
39	Hardoi ...	1	Sháhabad ...	20,153	10,292	9,861	444	*415*	185	*202*
		2	Sandila ...	16,813	8,478	8,335	355	*409*	111	*116*
		3	Malláwan ...	11,894	5,964	5,930	343	*296*	82	*83*
		4	Bilgram ...	11,457	5,712	5,745	236	*236*	72	*77*
		5	Hardoi ...	11,152	6,733	4,419	219	*227*	47	*39*
40	Fyzabad ...	1	Fyzabad ...	78,921	43,720	35,201	1,266	*1,197*	487	*499*
		2	Tanda	19,724	9,691	10,033	395	*389*	123	*150*
41	Gonda ...	1	Gonda	17,423	9,648	7,775	318	*294*	79	*101*
		2	Balrámpur ...	14,849	7,869	6,980	286	*256*	72	*102*
42	Bahraich ...	1	Bahraich ...	24,046	12,702	11,344	492	*507*	89	*111*
43	Bara Banki ...	1	Nawábganj ...	14,432	7,816	6,616	282	*276*	41	*69*
		2	Rudauli ...	11,767	5,571	6,196	261	*235*	59	*78*

with above 10,000 inhabitants.

PROVINCIAL TABLE VIII.

periods.												
2 years.		3 years.		4 years.		Total (0 to 4 years).		5 to 9 years.		10 to 14 years.		Serial number of town.
Males.	Females.	Males.	Females.	Males.	Females.	Males.	Females.	Males.	Females.	Males.	Females.	
801	916	998	1,066	968	896	4,574	4,774	4,810	4,491	4,504	3,797	1
132	137	177	183	134	165	728	773	778	749	694	598	2
142	151	184	197	154	156	765	786	616	620	649	554	3
517	535	579	659	568	548	2,599	2,745	2,592	2,455	2,529	1,900	1
555	620	627	617	585	531	2,602	2,741	2,575	2,526	2,592	2,000	1
164	180	180	199	174	206	761	847	803	805	731	569	2
138	140	151	167	159	131	688	682	749	686	718	610	3
142	159	135	166	137	143	677	724	708	623	667	571	4
267	246	215	255	201	231	1,048	1,098	1,097	916	1,078	740	1
163	168	152	222	146	188	740	857	794	768	688	577	2
165	195	151	200	149	160	683	768	693	692	592	592	3
702	818	875	971	873	867	3,622	3,910	4,005	3,892	3,549	2,731	1
129	179	148	169	144	150	619	727	663	675	580	479	2
174	164	208	207	155	179	820	840	751	700	809	480	1
152	159	178	181	170	179	731	814	774	716	643	507	2
182	228	237	280	258	267	1,045	1,165	1,072	1,118	1,227	877	1
219	220	239	291	245	263	1,091	1,247	1,100	1,045	999	805	2
197	211	214	242	262	301	1,020	1,120	1,065	1,007	907	718	3
195	238	211	208	185	158	980	977	882	844	798	656	1
2,688	2,775	2,706	2,952	2,500	2,513	14,842	15,274	13,380	12,953	12,509	9,553	1
125	136	156	150	145	155	698	731	719	707	730	430	1
113	112	126	152	99	124	623	648	663	643	588	459	2
163	202	232	230	175	191	995	1,044	1,019	1,026	949	714	1
121	149	170	179	156	147	716	739	839	739	631	485	2
280	247	249	253	219	187	1,156	1,173	1,175	1,047	1,084	931	1
165	205	168	215	111	138	804	948	822	837	765	696	2
149	178	200	183	131	140	835	927	828	702	670	550	3
262	271	256	298	250	233	1,397	1,419	1,319	1,126	1,108	877	1
204	207	218	216	168	205	1,051	1,153	1,001	1,017	897	745	2
134	146	183	190	111	133	708	848	791	748	572	461	3
110	113	147	169	127	139	692	734	706	704	585	515	4
89	103	113	137	135	111	608	617	575	551	600	374	5
872	843	952	961	884	897	4,461	4,897	3,891	3,631	3,749	2,690	1
280	291	287	298	286	284	1,371	1,412	1,235	1,182	1,024	886	2
214	227	229	239	238	229	1,073	1,090	963	895	940	658	1
158	176	214	223	196	206	926	963	919	849	810	606	2
238	285	343	347	268	284	1,430	1,534	1,427	1,377	1,312	974	1
134	158	144	158	121	185	722	786	671	657	695	529	1
141	160	147	168	159	158	767	799	712	707	608	511	2

The ages of the population of towns

PROVINCIAL TABLE VIII.

Serial number of district.	Name of district.	Serial number of town.	Name of town.	Age: 15 to 19 years. Males.	15 to 19 years. Females.	20 to 24 years. Males.	20 to 24 years. Females.	25 to 29 years. Males.	25 to 29 years. Females.	30 to 34 years. Males.	30 to 34 years. Females.
27	Mirzapur ...	1	Mirzapur ...	3,251	*2,944*	3,756	*3,702*	3,718	*3,828*	4,014	*4,102*
		2	Ahraura ...	497	*417*	558	*548*	528	*523*	564	*543*
		3	Chunár ...	429	*438*	463	*562*	456	*492*	447	*513*
28	Jaunpur ...	1	Jaunpur ...	1,671	*1,427*	1,851	*1,947*	1,735	*1,833*	1,861	*1,840*
29	Gházipur ...	1	Gházipur ...	1,936	*1,519*	2,216	*2,049*	2,089	*1,877*	2,028	*1,877*
		2	Sherpur ...	423	*399*	472	*573*	499	*576*	549	*590*
		3	Gahmar ...	429	*415*	424	*551*	407	*554*	384	*562*
		4	Reotipur ...	419	*335*	428	*448*	406	*514*	436	*536*
30	Ballia ...	1	Ballia	785	*470*	813	*760*	740	*683*	697	*727*
		2	Sehtwar ...	380	*413*	403	*484*	387	*519*	432	*577*
		3	Chit Firozpur or Baragaon.	372	*411*	389	*504*	361	*468*	385	*510*
31	Gorakhpur ...	1	Gorakhpur ...	2,540	*2,082*	3,016	*2,908*	3,105	*2,795*	2,985	*2,722*
		2	Barhaj ...	365	*337*	594	*479*	686	*446*	683	*493*
32	Basti ...	1	Basti	608	*375*	946	*587*	848	*551*	801	*525*
		2	Menhdawal ...	464	*318*	529	*522*	538	*512*	507	*409*
33	Azamgarh ...	1	Azamgarh ...	934	*651*	1,055	*813*	925	*776*	922	*679*
		2	Mau	534	*581*	682	*831*	628	*605*	504	*608*
		3	Mubarakpur ...	463	*501*	574	*636*	508	*588*	535	*591*
34	Naini Tal ...	1	Káshipur ...	714	*677*	737	*805*	728	*612*	760	*660*
35	Lucknow ...	1	Lucknow ...	11,371	*9,450*	15,498	*11,558*	13,422	*10,418*	13,780	*11,371*
36	Unao ...	1	Unao	664	*407*	850	*529*	751	*488*	708	*503*
		2	Purwa ...	403	*365*	419	*494*	394	*486*	437	*486*
37	Rae Bareli ...	1	Rae Bareli ...	810	*618*	1,016	*826*	1,044	*839*	1,100	*782*
		2	Jais	468	*444*	418	*527*	473	*577*	530	*547*
38	Sitapur ...	1	Sitapur ...	1,027	*661*	1,682	*880*	1,402	*769*	1,312	*600*
		2	Khairabad ...	553	*576*	555	*663*	508	*613*	578	*572*
		3	Laharpur ...	464	*397*	455	*551*	462	*456*	434	*464*
39	Hardoi ...	1	Sháhabad ...	880	*722*	836	*947*	791	*924*	925	*864*
		2	Sandila ...	669	*616*	707	*844*	715	*737*	800	*692*
		3	Mallánwan ...	472	*427*	505	*559*	521	*505*	581	*555*
		4	Bilgram ...	435	*381*	490	*571*	528	*490*	528	*536*
		5	Hardoi ...	555	*339*	781	*417*	759	*869*	775	*440*
40	Fyzabad ...	1	Fyzabad ...	3,821	*2,509*	4,464	*3,107*	4,886	*3,179*	4,480	*3,263*
		2	Tanda	742	*634*	861	*986*	824	*919*	844	*882*
41	Gonda ...	1	Gonda	750	*528*	875	*704*	941	*734*	954	*702*
		2	Balrámpur ...	568	*416*	684	*577*	801	*600*	730	*571*
42	Bahraich ...	1	Bahraich ...	973	*808*	1,260	*1,138*	1,238	*1,118*	1,313	*978*
43	Bara Banki ...	1	Nawábganj ...	632	*500*	796	*653*	766	*628*	790	*674*
		2	Rudauli ...	391	*412*	382	*519*	414	*531*	462	*549*

with above 10,000 inhabitants.

PROVINCIAL TABLE VIII.

periods.												
35 to 39 years.		40 to 44 years.		45 to 49 years.		50 to 54 years.		55 to 59 years.		60 years and over.		Serial number of town.
Males.	Females.	Males.	Females.	Males.	Females.	Males.	Females.	Males.	Females.	Males.	Females.	
2,240	2,082	3,758	3,951	1,531	1,316	2,624	3,305	598	598	2,543	3,324	1
329	278	499	427	142	146	272	344	65	69	265	312	2
302	269	394	483	183	204	307	439	72	100	362	518	3
1,070	923	1,688	1,942	714	659	1,386	1,594	371	301	1,427	1,759	1
1,191	1,079	1,838	1,989	852	740	1,418	1,473	283	282	1,457	1,741	1
317	419	409	437	189	262	254	264	81	125	297	505	2
320	484	389	424	183	181	226	212	50	75	299	427	3
310	385	379	493	130	194	228	342	69	93	346	506	4
505	413	599	650	249	228	373	483	79	71	465	655	1
301	402	384	510	175	223	258	329	51	81	318	468	2
336	433	366	431	179	157	238	317	72	62	295	419	3
1,825	1,501	2,386	2,358	1,216	1,059	1,782	1,948	592	522	2,052	2,517	1
501	302	580	429	252	166	341	276	74	95	262	317	2
562	296	607	418	275	180	454	311	161	84	315	326	1
334	295	432	329	193	170	277	252	69	69	250	342	2
632	479	837	717	445	329	608	568	213	154	572	640	1
341	390	505	576	280	264	349	364	97	108	455	558	2
367	366	465	452	235	271	410	361	133	151	474	464	3
368	272	562	513	182	173	346	457	84	97	336	497	1
8,164	5,883	11,822	10,686	5,390	4,348	10,162	10,406	3,093	2,475	12,425	12,810	1
406	246	530	442	288	185	436	405	151	83	416	333	1
256	250	337	459	148	139	331	413	99	90	393	440	2
633	425	738	656	386	275	658	580	234	144	638	649	1
262	272	435	502	185	215	334	439	89	122	399	539	2
702	368	951	654	460	244	752	613	213	137	788	599	1
298	327	433	562	197	202	406	496	113	75	545	629	2
295	292	833	421	189	160	299	316	79	75	365	433	3
553	407	761	785	349	292	543	606	210	165	620	727	1
360	356	653	595	257	286	561	650	178	149	620	595	2
313	284	453	455	206	182	352	391	135	81	360	434	3
308	304	426	394	175	178	342	368	116	106	386	464	4
420	214	519	355	257	146	424	292	115	49	350	256	5
2,968	1,983	3,383	2,654	1,915	1,433	2,647	2,395	1,088	860	3,017	3,100	1
447	453	701	771	318	303	573	675	145	147	606	783	2
645	469	755	565	453	268	546	464	189	107	564	596	1
545	423	550	580	340	277	454	421	138	126	404	671	2
733	539	919	803	497	347	702	760	219	143	679	825	1
463	300	689	535	303	206	567	508	182	115	540	525	1
273	271	373	526	215	231	323	410	119	103	532	627	2